Nefesh HaTzimtzum

VOLUME 1

נפש הצמצום

Nefesh HaTzimtzum

by

AVINOAM FRAENKEL

VOLUME 1

Rabbi Chaim Volozhin's
Nefesh HaChaim
with Translation and Commentary

URIM PUBLICATIONS
Jerusalem • New York

Nefesh HaTzimtzum, Vol. 1: Rabbi Chaim Volozhin's *Nefesh HaChaim*
with Translation and Commentary
by Avinoam Fraenkel

Copyright © 2015 Avinoam Fraenkel

All rights reserved.

No part of this book may be used
or reproduced in any manner whatsoever without written permission from
the copyright owner, except in the case
of brief quotations embodied
in reviews and articles.

Typeset by Ariel Walden

Printed in Israel

First Edition

ISBN 978-965-524-165-5

Urim Publications, P.O. Box 52287
Jerusalem 9152102 Israel

www.UrimPublications.com

Library of Congress Cataloging-in-Publication Data

Volozhiner, Hayyim ben Isaac, 1749–1821, author.
Nefesh HaTzimtzum: Rabbi Chaim Volozhin's Nefesh Hachaim / with
translation and commentary by Avinoam Fraenkel.
pages cm
Hebrew text with English translation.
ISBN 978-965-524-165-5 (hardback)
1. Jewish ethics. 2. Judaism—Essence, genius, nature. I. Fraenkel,
Avinoam, translator, writer of added commentary. II. Volozhiner, Hayyim
ben Isaac, 1749–1821. Nefesh ha-hayim. Selections. III. Volozhiner, Hayyim
ben Isaac, 1749–1821. Nefesh ha-hayim. Selections. English. IV. Title.
BJ1287.H33N3213 2015
296.3—dc23   2014050128

APPROBATIONS

Letters of approbation are listed and printed
in order of receipt date.

1. RABBI MOSHE SCHATZ   6
    Kabbalist and Author

2. RABBI YITZCHOK MEIR MORGENSTERN   8
    Rosh Yeshiva of Toras Chochom, Jerusalem

3. RABBI DOVID COHEN   10
    Congregation Gvul Yaabetz, Brooklyn, New York

4. RABBI AVROHOM CHAIM FEUER   11
    Rosh Yeshiva of Mesoras Mordechai, Ramat Bet Shemesh

5. RABBI LORD JONATHAN SACKS   12
    Former Chief Rabbi, the United Hebrew Congregations
    of the Commonwealth

6. RABBI HERSHEL SCHACHTER   13
    Rosh Yeshiva of Rabbi Isaac Elchanan Theological Seminary,
    Yeshiva University

7. RABBI YITZCHOK MENACHEM WEINBERG   14
    The Tolner Rebbe of Jerusalem

8. PROFESSOR JONATHAN GARB   16
    Professor of Jewish Thought, Hebrew University, Jerusalem

Rabbi Moshe Schatz	משה ש"ץ
17a Givat Shaul St.	רחוב גבעת שאול 17 א'
Jerusalem, 9547762 Israel	ירושלים עיה"ק
Tel. 972-2-6512649	תיקון ליל שבועות הרש"ש זיע"א עטרת תפארת
Fax 972-2-6535438	כתר מלכות על ספירת העומר
Author: *Sparks of the Hidden Light*	מעין משה

בס"ד

Dec. 26, 2013   כ"ג טבת תשע"ד

Nefesh HaTzimtzum is a monumental and awe-inspiring work which for the first time in any language brings together and truly explains the teachings and the worldview of Rabbi Chaim Volozhin זצלל"ה in his *Nefesh HaChaim* and all of his related writings. The challenging style and level of difficulty of R. Chaim's writings has until now made them inaccessible to all except for the most seasoned scholar. However, *Nefesh HaTzimtzum* has overcome all of these challenges by making R. Chaim's teachings truly accessible to English speakers especially with its innovative presentation format. The work is extensive and great effort has been expended to provide THE BACKGROUND SOURCE MATERIAL for many of R. Chaim's source references so that the reader can gain a real in-depth understanding of all of R. Chaim's messages. A work of this significance MUST ALSO BE PUBLISHED IN HEBREW and hopefully, God willing, that will happen in due course.

I would like to note that *the Hebrew text in this edition* has been compared with all the editions available and any apparent typos and mistakes have been corrected. Of course it goes without saying that where it is evident that R. Chaim quoted a source version that could not be corroborated, it has been left unchanged. THEREFORE, THE HEBREW TEXT IS PROBABLY THE MOST ACCURATE AND AUTHORITATIVE VERSION ever printed.

On seeing the huge manuscript that Avinoam Fraenkel שליט"א brought me over a year and a half ago, I did not know how I would fit its review into my schedule. However, Hashgacha Elyona, Divine Providence, had it that I must get involved. I taught him fundamental concepts of the Arizal's *Etz Chaim* (*Tree of Life* of Rabbi Isaac Luria, known as "Arizal") and *Leshem Shevo VeAchlama* of Rabbi Shlomo Elyashiv (who wrote an extensive commentary on *Etz Chaim*) which became the basis of the section, "Tzimtzum – the Key to Nefesh HaChaim" in Volume 2.

My lengthy discussions and learning sessions with Avinoam about the process of Tzimtzum, etc., enabled me to see his ability to develop throughout this whole period. I observed how he grew from his previous understanding of the Tzimtzum process and debate which was based on centuries of total confusion by many of our great Rabbis. He wrote and rewrote the section on Tzimtzum several times over a period of more than a year. Towards the end of these learning sessions together new insight was gained about this topic which prompted Avinoam to rewrite it again one final time. It now PROVES ELOQUENTLY AND BEAUTIFULLY that in essence, once you understand the Arizal *properly*, the understanding of Tzimtzum is UNEQUIVOCALLY THE SAME *from the points of view of the Vilna Gaon, the Baal Tanya, the Nefesh HaChaim, and the Leshem, and their understanding is entirely drawn directly from the Arizal!* What caused the confusion with the Tzimtzum debate until today is the concept of the "Exile of the Torah" and Avinoam amazingly dispels the confusion by explaining the historical factors and providing scholarly proof!

If this clarity alone comes through to the reader from the section on Tzimtzum, then I am happy to say that I achieved my objective in helping to mold the structure and significantly contributing to the content of this part of the book and also in having contributed to other parts of it. As Avinoam points out, this understanding of the Tzimtzum process is the key to understanding the whole of Nefesh HaChaim, how to serve God and our relationship with Him when fulfilling the Mitzvot and learning Torah. These same fundamentals are in Tanya and other Chassidic works, as Avinoam writes, therefore there's no *Machloket*, dispute, between the Nefesh HaChaim and Chassidut as one will see when delving into the depth of the matter.

It is important to note that the *Nefesh HaChaim* IS ONE OF THE ESSENTIAL GATEWAYS TO THE ZOHAR AND THE KABBALAH OF THE ARIZAL. It is an excellent place for a beginner to start, but there is no shortcut to directly learning the works of the Arizal.

May *Nefesh HaTzimtzum* be instrumental in bringing all who will read it seriously, with an open heart and mind, to the conclusion that it is long overdue for true *Shalom* and to realizing that all the different aspects of Klal Yisrael branch out from the same ultimate unity. Therefore, in the end, we are all in essence a unified whole (known as "Knesset Yisrael") which reflects God's Unity. May Klal Yisrael attain this consciousness speedily in our time that we will merit the full redemption with compassion.

I sign with Honor of Torah,

RABBI MOSHE SCHATZ

Rabbi Y.M. Morgenstern Rosh hayeshiva of "Toras Chochom" Yerushalaim	יצחק מאיר מארגנשטערן רב ור"מ דק"ק "תורת חכם" לתורת הנגלה והנסתר פעיה"ק ירושלים תובב"א

בס"ד, יום רביעי בשבת, כ"ז לחודש אדר הראשון תשע"ד לפ"ק, פעיה"ק ירושת"ו

כבר יצא טבעו של הספר הקדוש נפש החיים להגה"ק המקובל האלה"י חסידא קדישא כמוהר"ר חיים מוואלאזין זיע"א, תלמיד מובהק לרבינו הגדול קה"ק הגר"א זיע"א, ומי יעיד על השמש בצהרים, והן עתה קם הרה"ג אביגדור פרענקל שליט"א, שיצק מים לבאר הספר הק' הנזכר בתרגום לשפת העגליש, בתוספת מקורות בהרחבה, ונקרא בשם 'נפש הצמצום', והביא לשון הנפה"ח בלשה"ק בהגהה מדוקדקת בתוספת ועליו חונה תרגומו בלע"ז. גם האריך להוכיח מתוך דברי רבינו הנפש החיים ומתוך דברי הלשם שבו ואחלמה, דכו"ע מודו דענין הצמצום אינו נדרש כפשוטו ממש, ולא נחלקו רבנן בשרשי הדת ח"ו, ואלו ואלו דברי אלהים חיים, וכמובא בספר חיי נפש להגר"ג קעניג (אות ד' עמוד י') "קבלה בידי מבית אבא מארי ומבית רבי [ה"ה הגה"צ מהר"א שטערנהארץ] ז"ל שאין סלע המחלוקת וכו' תלויה בעיקרי ויסודי האמונה, כי עיקרי ויסודי אמונתינו הקדושה אינם שניים במחלוקת ח"ו, וכל ישראל כולם שוים בדיעה אחת ביסוד האמונה הקדושה ביחוד הבורא ית"ש ובהשגחתו הפרטית". וזאת נודע כי הגה"צ מהר"א שטערנהארץ זצ"ל היה נכד להגה"ק מוהר"ר נתן מברסלב זיע"א והגה"ק מוהר"ן מטשערין זיע"א, וכל אורחותיו הק' וכל עיקר סמיכת קבלתו היה מפיהם, ולכן מסתבר שזאת הקבלה היתה מקובלת אצלו איש מפי עד עד רבה"ק מברסלב זיע"א, ועיין בספר הק' ליקוטי מוהר"ן ח"א סימן ס"א וסימן נ"ז בעניין הדעת של שלום שהיא הדעת דבחי' קודש הקדשים, עיי"ש ומה שהאריך הרבה בזה בספה"ק ליקוטי הלכות, והק"ש לכאן. ואך למותר להאריך בגודל התועלת בלימודי קודש אלה שיש בהם תועלת גדולה לעבודת השי"ת. ובגוף העניין יש להאריך טובא בדברים העומדים ברום רומו של עולם ומטין עד ציץ שמיא, ולא עת האסף, והמעט הארכנו בס"ד בספרי ים החכמה, ואין כאן המקום.

איברא, האמת אגיד דמאוד רחוק ממני לעלות בהסכמה על ספרים בתרגום לשפת העגליש מחמת כמה וכמה טעמים, האמנם הפעם יצאתי מגדרי מפני כבודו של גדול, ה"ה הגאון המופלא המקובל הנעלה מו"ר כמוהר"ר משה שץ שליט"א, שהמחבר הנזכר זכה ליצק מים על ידו ולקבל לקח מפיו כאשר העיד עליו בהסכמה, והוא שהכניסו לעומק רזי הקבלה וסודות הצמצום, וידיו רב לו בזה החיבור. ולכן לא נצרכה אלא לאשר ולחזק חילו לאורייתא, שיזכה עוד רבות בשנים ללמוד וללמד, יפוצו מעיינותיו חוצה, להגדיל תורה ולהאדירה, ויהי חלקו עם מזכי הרבים עדי תמלא הארץ דעה את ה' כמים לים מכסים, אכי"ר.

בברכה נאמנה

TRANSLATION OF RABBI MORGENSTERN'S APPROBATION

The nature of the book, *Nefesh HaChaim*, by the saintly, pious, holy Kabbalist, Rabbi Chaim of Volozhin, the leading disciple of the great master, the Vilna Gaon, is already widely known. What need is there for anyone to testify about the existence of the sun at noon! Now, R. AVINOAM FRAENKEL has *poured water* [i.e., studied with a master, see below] to provide an elucidation of this holy book with an English translation and with the addition of extensive source material, called "Nefesh HaTzimtzum." He includes a precision-checked Hebrew version of Nefesh HaChaim upon which his translation is based. He has also proven, at length, from the words of our master, the Nefesh HaChaim, and from the words of the Leshem Shevo VeAchlama, that everyone agrees that the concept of Tzimtzum is not to be understood literally, that the Rabbis did not argue over the principles of our faith, God forbid, and that "all their opinions are the words of the Living God." This is as brought in the book Chayei Nefesh of Rabbi Gedalia Kenig: "For I have received a tradition from the house of my father and master as well as from the house of my teacher (Rabbi Avraham Sternhartz) that the substance of the dispute [between the Chassidim and Mitnagdim] was not based on the principles of faith. These principles of faith are beyond dispute, God forbid, and all of Israel entirely agree on the same principles of faith about God's Unity and His Divine Providence." It is known that Rabbi Avraham Sternhartz was the [great-]grandson of Rabbi Natan of Breslov and [the grandson] of Rabbi Nachman of Tcherin and all of his holy ways and received traditions came from them. Therefore, it can be logically concluded that this tradition was handed down directly from our holy master [Rabbi Nachman] of Breslov. Refer to how the holy book Likutei Moharan relates to the concept of Daat of peace which is the Daat on the level of the Holy of Holies. Refer there and to the connected details which are dealt with at length in Likutei Halachot. It is therefore superfluous to provide lengthy explanations about the objective of these holy studies, as they have great purpose in serving God. However, there is much to elaborate about the substance of the concept, matters which stand at the highest point of the Universe and reach until the Heavens, but this is not the occasion to do so. A small part of this has been set out, with God's help, in my book Yam HaChochma, but this is not the place to elaborate.

In all honesty, for many reasons, it is very far from me to provide approbations for books with English translations. However, on this occasion I have made an exception out of the honor of a great person, the wondrous genius, exalted Kabbalist, *my master and teacher* RABBI MOSHE SCHATZ, who the aforementioned author merited to *pour water on his hands* [i.e., to become his student] and to receive an acquisition from his mouth as [Rabbi Schatz] testifies about him in his approbation. It is [Rabbi Schatz] who entered [the author] into the depths of the secrets of the Kabbalah and the secret of Tzimtzum, and [Rabbi Schatz] has been very involved with this work. Therefore, there is no need to do more than to endorse and support [Rabbi Schatz's] ability in Torah, that he should merit many further years of study and teaching, to disseminate his wellsprings, to raise the profile of Torah and glorify it. His portion should be among those who give merit to the public until the world is filled with God's knowledge covering it like water covers the sea. Amen and so it should be God's Will.

With faithful blessing,
Yitzchok Meir Morgenstern

Rabbi Dovid Cohen
Congregation Gvul Yaabetz
Brooklyn, New York

ביחמ"ד גבול יעבץ
ברוקלין, נוא יארק

דוד קאהן

בס"ד

מכתב ברכה

I have been asked by the author to write a haskama/michtav bracha to his monumental work concerning Rav Chaim of Volozhin's understanding of the kabbalistic doctrine of TZIMTZUM. I can undertake the second part of the author's request, since I have no mastery of kabbalistic writings.

Rav Avinoam Fraenkel is certainly deserving of a michtav bracha. The lucidity is outstanding, and even my reading of his introduction inspired me.

Rav Fraenkel's work shall certainly expand the conceptions and weltanschauung of the reader. His translation and elucidation of the Nefesh Hachaim is outstanding. I bless him that he continues in his avodas hakodesh and find hatzlocho in all his endeavors.

בב"ק קאהן
פ"ק איצטר לונדון יצ"ו

Rabbi Avrohom Chaim Feuer
Shaarei Chesed, Yerushalayim

24 Tamuz 5774   בס"ד

While he was a young American *bachur* learning in Lithuania, the Telshe Rosh Hayeshiva, Rav Mordechai Gifter, developed a very close relationship with the "*illui of Lita*," Rav Mordechai Pogromanski, who literally knew "*kol haTorah kulla*" both the *nigleh* and the *nistar*. Rav Gifter, who was my Rebbe and my father-in-law, enjoyed relating the following story to me:

"Once, I visited Rav Mordechai in his private apartment and he was studying *nistar*. He asked me to take a seat while he spent the next four hours explaining the complex opinions of the *Vilna Gaon*, the *Baal HaTanya* and the *Baal HaLeshem* on the subjects of *Tzimtzum* and *Les assar ponui minei*. At first, I protested that I was merely a young *bachur* who knew absolutely nothing about *Kabbala* so it was a waste of time to speak to me of such secrets and mysteries. But 'Reb Muttel,' as he was fondly called, would not relent. For four hours he kept me spellbound, and his power of explanation was so crystal clear that I understood every word he said, despite my total ignorance of these esoteric matters. The minute this impromptu *shiur* came to an end I promptly forgot every word he said. I could never repeat his discourse. But it didn't matter, because my mind had been stretched forever. During this one dramatic encounter, my mind had expanded to catch a glimpse of infinity and eternity. I would never be the same person I was before." With this personal recollection Rav Gifter taught me that it is worthwhile dabbling in things that are presently beyond our comprehension, because these cosmic concepts open our minds to the vast, unlimited expanses of Torah wisdom which we will pursue in the future.

Almost a half-century ago, as a young *bachur* in *Telshe Yeshiva*, I myself was introduced to the wonders of this deep masterpiece, *Nefesh Hachaim*, by *Rabbeinu Chaim of Volozhin*. Since then I have studied and taught this amazing *sefer* numerous times, yet I have never lost my youthful fascination for each and every word of this classic. Every line and every thought in this timeless work fill me with fresh excitement and awe because I feel as if *Rav Chaim* himself is taking me by the hand and standing me at the foot of *Har Sinai* where I am receiving the fundamentals of Torah and Emunah from the source, *"Me'pi Hagevura."* The concepts of *Tzimtzum* and *Les assar ponui minei* are major themes of this work, *Nefesh Hachaim*.

Therefore, when Rav Avinoam Fraenkel requested that I review this monumental work on the *Nefesh Hachaim* containing both his lucid translation and thorough analysis of this classic, I was happy to do so. I was not able to make an exhaustive investigation but I did carefully study many sections and was delighted with what I saw. I must admit that I do not understand all of the deep Kabbalistic concepts included in this work but I rely on R' Avinoam's painstaking research, sharp intellect and uncompromising integrity to rest assured that all ideas expressed herein are *al pi Daas Torah*.

I wish R' Avinoam great *Siyata D'shmaya* in publishing this magnum opus, *Nefesh HaTzimtzum*, so that the sacred teachings of the *Nefesh Hachaim* will be accessible to a wider audience. The holy *Zohar* teaches that the widespread study of *Toras Hanistar* will hasten the arrival of *Moshiach Tzidkeinu*. May this *sefer* be among those which will help us realize the fulfillment of this dream, *kein yehi ratzon!!*

PO Box 72007　　T +44 (0)20 7286 6391
London　　　　info@rabbisacks.org
NW6 6RW　　　www.rabbisacks.org

Nefesh ha-Tzimtzum

This is a truly remarkable work, bringing together key texts from the writings of Rabbi Chaim Volozhin, the most important disciple of the Vilna Gaon, thus allowing us to see the full vista of his masterly and mystical vision of God, Torah and the world. Not only does it include the most accurate available text of Nefesh ha-Chayyim, his greatest work, but also many of his related writings. The translation of these texts into English will widen their accessibility, and allow many who have heard of Rabbi Chaim's teachings to encounter them at first hand in their full subtlety and depth.

The central idea around which this work is built, that of Tzimtzum, is one of the most remarkable in the history of religious thought, and as is now clear, it was a concept held in common by both Hassidim and their opponents. May the fact that we can now see this, bring healing and unity to the Jewish world.

We owe Avinoam Fraenkel an immense debt of gratitude for a monumental labour of scholarship. Truly this is a work by which, at every level, we are enriched.

Jonathan Sacks

Rabbi Lord Jonathan Sacks
Ellul 5774 - August 2014

I have reviewed a significant part of the book of the dear *Avrech*, R. Avinoam Fraenkel. I very much enjoyed his style of writing, the revealing of the intention of the *Gaon*, Rabbi Chaim [Volozhin] in his book, Nefesh HaChaim, as well as the listing of all the sources for every expression and reference in that holy book. I am certain that the publication of this book will cause the "lips of that *Gaon* and *Tzaddik* to move in the grave" [Sanhedrin 90b], as the *Avrech* mentioned above will "expand its boundaries with students" [Berachot 16b], since many will now begin to properly study this holy book.

Tzvi (Hershel) Schachter

RABBI Yitzchok M. Weinberg
Tolner Rebby
10 David Chazan st.
Jerusalem . Israel

Tel. 02-5825543 :טלפון

ב"ה, יום של"ג גבי אשר מופלא

בס"ד הרבה ידיעות יועיל לחבר גדול וקדוש הגאון
מוהר"ר אברהם פינקל שליט"א – הלא ודברי
הישישים נפש (ס) החיים הוא דבר מופלא
וגם של את מגן פסוק נגלת ונותים כל
ולחזק ענין הנוראא אשר לען ין נדול כלו
המופלא אשר אמנת העם העם של
אומר הסק הן הענין בר בינים וחשובל ונרוש
לעריכה נם הלה אין 20/62 בינך הנילון לצלח
ואני ל- בחנה אהדות ונדו ניהן נברנים של
אני לעים אלור'ר חיים וברכות הבה בזיו של
כל הסג נעים לציה עוון הנן ודואה
ואת יה' גן לא הלו בני ברכנה ועיניה
שם סוכם מצוה העצה שמעת הרב האלקים הרב
יציע דואר ואחרון אמר אהא אהוב ותמים ציפור

הנאה בידידות מופלאה

יצחק מנחם נכד אדמו"ר גדול זצללה"ה

TRANSLATION OF RABBI WEINBERG'S APPROBATION

To the Rabbi who is involved with the depths of the concepts of how the Creator conducts Himself, R. Avinoam Fraenkel, peace and blessing.

It is a wonderful privilege to be involved with the book Nefesh HaChaim. Not everyone merits to be involved with such exalted concepts, and in particular with the comparison between [Rabbi Chaim Volozhin's] holy words and [those of] the illustrious leaders of his generation, who followed the worldview of the Baal Shem Tov and his students, headed by the Alter Rebbe, the Baal HaTanya, of righteous and holy blessed memory. Many were severely confused about the nature of the schism [between the Chassidim and Mitnagdim] such that they considered that there were fundamental differences in outlook. However, it is already well-known that "all their opinions are words of the living God," and that, on the contrary, "They all are hinged on a single principle" [Kohelet 1:6; 3:20]. You are fortunate that you have merited to delve into the depths of the matter and to demonstrate how they can all be reconciled with each other and that "through them and through you, the Supernal One will be praised" [Sotah 40a]. Therefore, I bestow my blessing, the blessing of an ordinary person, that your book should increase awareness at this time [the year] 5775, [forming the initial letters of] "May this year be one that creates awareness," and that you should see this and rejoice.

> The one who writes and signs with tremendous admiration,
> Yitzchak Menachem Weinberg
> grandson of the Tolner Rebbe

THE HEBREW UNIVERSITY OF JERUSALEM

Nefesh HaTzimtzum by Avinoam Fraenkel,

It is my great pleasure to recommend that all interested in Kabbalah and Jewish spirituality in general obtain a copy of R. Fraenkel's book. It is a blessing that in recent decades many works of Kabbalah are available in stores and in databases, yet this is all the more reason to stress the repeated and thorough study of deep classics such as R. Hayyim of Volozhin's *Nefesh ha-Hayyim* and R. Shneur Zalman of Liadi's *Tanya*. If one studies – to cite one example – the main works of the renowned R. Joseph B. Soloveitchik, one sees clearly that these were the central modern books that inspired him. R. Fraenkel has now provided us with an incredible learning tool for the study of *Nefesh Ha-Hayyim* and also for the study of the central topic of the *Tzimtzum* – that he persuasively argues is the central theme organizing the unique structure of the book (which is not apparent to superficial readers). Through doing so, the author has also provided us with crucial keys for understanding *Tanya* and other writings of the Alter Rebbe.

There are many layers and levels in the wonderful contribution of this book:

Firstly, the Hebrew reader has an excellent layout for *Nefesh Ha-Hayyim* and a compilation of all of the non-Halakhic works of R. Hayyim, together with a selection of all the key texts necessary for learning the *sugya* of the *Tzimtzum* in general. The English reader also has an excellent translation of all of these texts, many of which were not previously accessible in this language. However, this section also provides anyone with basic English another wonderful tool: very extensive annotation with referencing and cross-referencing. However, the pinnacle of the book is the clear and profound section that analyzes and discusses the topic of *Tzimtzum* in a highly innovative, truth-seeking and meticulous manner. One should add that this discussion is based on intensive dialogue with one of the great theoreticians of this generation, R. Moshe Schatz.

There are many *hiddushim* contained here and I will only enumerate a few of them:

- As academic scholarship is also beginning to realize, the difference between *Nefesh Ha-Hayyim* and *Tanya* is far smaller than previously imagined, as indeed is the difference between the protagonists in the earlier debate on *Tzimtzum* (between R. Yosef Irgas and R. Immanuel Hai Ricci). R. Fraenkel helps us to realize this by moving our attention away from terminology towards analytics. Here the question of perspective (that, as the Rashash stressed, is central for understanding the Kabbalah of the Arizal) is crucial. An accompanying move is disclosing that all of the writers on *Tzimtzum* focus on *Malkhut* as the arena of this process.
- On the historical level, R. Fraenkel has courageously corrected several errors blocking understanding of this key topic. In doing so, he has paved the way for appreciating the centrality of the Kabbalah of the Arizal for all subsequent generations, and also (despite my own initial doubts) has persuaded me that though "statistically" *Tzimtzum* is not a frequent theme in this corpus, nonetheless it informs many key discussions, as in Gate 42 of *Etz Hayyim*. Finally, the author's diachronic analysis of the non-Halakhic writings of R. Hayyim of Volozhin demonstrates that the themes of *Nefesh ha-Hayyim* developed constantly from much earlier stages in his life. So we now have the key for understanding his thought as a whole, especially as the author has cross-referenced his *Ruach Ha-Hayyim* and translated many key passages from the latter work.

I hope and pray that R. Fraenkel publish many more such books for the benefit of all who seek in-depth Jewish knowledge. As R. Yoel Kluft (mentioned in the present book) wrote in his approbation for the first book by my first teacher, R. Wolbe, *zt"l*, there is much pseudo-depth in this generation and it is a true pleasure and comfort to encounter a writer who invests maximal effort towards reaching the truth of the Torah and of wisdom.

Professor Jonathan Garb
Professor of Jewish Thought
Hebrew University
Koach (28) Tishrei 5775 / 22 October 2014

In memory of our beloved father
YOSEF FRAENKEL
ר' יוסף בן ר' אורי ז"ל
נלב"ע בעש"ק ט"ז מרחשון תשמ"ב

And in honor of our beloved mother
MALKA FRAENKEL
מרת מלכה בת ר' יצחק צבי תבלחט"א

Who will forever be exemplar role models for us in their
Respect and support of Torah – תורה
Dedication to serving God – עבודה
Commitment to helping others – גמילות חסדים

೩

Gershon and Rivka Fraenkel
Jonathan and Fay Turetsky
Avinoam and Tania Fraenkel

In memory of one of the foremost Talmidei Chachamim amongst the communal Rabbis in the United Kingdom during the twentieth century

Rabbi Dr. Moshe Turetsky

הרב משה בן הרב יהושע דוב טורצקי זצ"ל

נלב"ע כ"ז אלול תשנ"ג

As a Dayan, Semicha tutor, Halachic authority, and community leader, Rabbi Turetsky committed his life to learning and teaching Torah. He was also devoted to his beloved family. Long before my sister Fay married his eldest son Jonathan, he was known affectionately to me as "Uncle Maishie." He, his wife, my "Auntie Rochel," and their children, Sorrel, Jonathan, Geoffrey, Daniel, and Michael were like extended family. I know that he would be proud that the majority of both of our families now live in Eretz Yisrael.

Rabbi Turetsky was a kind and gentle man as well as an exceptional orator and intellectual, committed to truth, tolerance, and humility throughout his life. He was a scion of many generations of distinguished Lithuanian rabbis from whom he inherited these same traits. His great-grandfather was Rabbi Yehuda Lev Turetsky of Lenin near Pinsk who was related to Rabbi Avraham Shmuel Rabinowitz, the Amudei Eish. After being among the first students to study at the Mir Yeshiva, Rabbi Avraham Shmuel subsequently became the Rosh Yeshiva in Eishyshok where he taught the Chafetz Chaim. Rabbi Yehuda Lev was also related to Rabbi David Tebel, the Nachlat David from Minsk, who was one of the leading Talmidim of none other than Rabbi Chaim of Volozhin.

May Rabbi Turetsky's memory be forever blessed through the study of Rabbi Chaim of Volozhin's Torah.

☙

Avinoam Fraenkel

CONTENTS
VOLUME 1

APPROBATIONS	5
DEDICATIONS	18

TRANSLATOR'S INTRODUCTION — 29

1. Background and Structure of Nefesh HaTzimtzum — 29
    - *The Motivation for and Meaning of "Nefesh HaTzimtzum"* — 29
    - *Translation Challenges* — 32
    - *Presentation Approach* — 33
    - *Translation Deepens Understanding – Acknowledgments* — 35
2. The Context of Nefesh HaChaim — 39
    - *Key Dates Related to Rabbi Chaim and Nefesh HaChaim* — 39
    - *Rabbi Chaim's Relationship with the Vilna Gaon* — 41
    - *The Leader of the Mitnagdim* — 45
    - *Volozhin Yeshiva* — 47
    - *The Writing of Nefesh HaChaim* — 49
3. The Essence and Structure of Nefesh HaChaim — 51
    - *A Methodology for Serving God* — 51
    - *A Book with an Agenda* — 52
    - *The Structure* — 53

NEFESH HACHAIM

TITLE PAGE OF THE FIRST EDITION	66
THE INTRODUCTION BY RABBI YITZCHAK, RABBI CHAIM'S SON	68

FIRST GATEWAY — 106

1. Image concept is fundamentally deep, image implies some likeness — 106
2. Constant creation of physical from non-physical — 108
    - *Note 1* – Constant re-creation indiscernible, YHVH represents four elements — 110
    - *Note 2* – Elohim is a generic description, God is Elokay HaElohim — 112
3. Thought, speech, and action create or destroy worlds — 114
4. Thought, speech, and action have Supernal consequence — 118

	Note 3 – Know that what is above – is from you	126
	Note 4 – Jew and Mishkan have same Shiur Komah, thus Jew can be Mishkan	126
5.	A Jew is a hybrid being – both lowly and Supernal	132
	Note 5 – Body is a shoe for soul connecting lowest to the highest realms	138
6.	Man's actions impact image of God	142
	Note 6 – Angel sanctification is not simultaneous but follows man	152
	Note 7 – Sins of Adam/Golden Calf internalized Evil requiring death to purify	154
	Note 8 – Commitment to do good/bad brings holiness/evil within one	160
	Note 9 – Let us make man in plural implies worlds make up Shiur Komah	166
7.	Man's actions reflected in: 1. the worlds 2. God's reaction	168
8.	Man's action results in God's reaction – e.g., Cherubim, livelihood	172
	Note 10 – Service with might is for individuals and not for the majority	178
9.	Further emphasis that man's action invokes God's reaction	180
	Note 11 – Apple tree analogy that God reflects our attitude towards Him	186
10.	Man greater than angel and vice versa	188
11.	Man initiates process enabling angels to sanctify God	192
12.	*Physical Action* generates our future world experience	198
	Note 12 – Effect of good is everlasting, impact of bad ceases with punishment	204
13.	*Speech* has even greater impact than Physical Action	206
	Note 13 – Constant Yesh MiYesh and MiAyin, four world levels described	212
14.	*Thought* has even greater impact, three levels of soul and expression	218
15.	Three-level glassblower analogy, sparks of Neshama can enter body	226
16.	Connection to Neshama, desire for that connection	232
	Note 14 – Simple meaning of God, Torah, and Israel all being connected	244
17.	Perfection is the interconnection of world and soul levels	246
18.	Sin disconnects Nefesh and damages Ruach – Neshama unaffected	252
	Note 15 – Constant connection through Fear, e.g., forcing until wanting divorce	258
	Note 16 – Even souls entrenched in ultimate vice/Egypt redeemed with Keter	260
19.	Soul level interconnectivity prevents anyone being lost	262
20.	Repentance on each of three levels	274

	Note 17 – Both person and God invest Yehay Shmey with all strength	280
	Note 18 – Torah involvement reinstates Nefesh, Adam's connection to David	282
21.	Complete Torah immersion purifies, intention to rectify worlds	290
22.	Physical Mitzvah performance is key, intention adds impact	296

SECOND GATEWAY — 304

1.	Prayer with concentration to be exclusively focused on God	304
2.	*Baruch* is an *increase* in the revealed part of God	310
	Note 19 – Time only exists from the world level of Atzilut and downwards	316
3.	Absolute Hidden Essence vs. Revealed Aspects of God	318
	Note 20 – Israel created at world's inception and is purpose of God's connection	324
4.	Prayer to concentrate on *connection* of God to worlds	324
	Note 21 – Prayer focus on Unified Essence of God but not specific Sefirot	330
5.	Shiur Komah – man's structure reflects God's structure	334
	Note 22 – Analogy of God in World to soul in body is absolutely not literal	342
	Note 23 – God/man's descriptions relate to their connection with worlds	342
6.	Food and drink are to body as Torah, Mitzvot and prayer are to worlds	348
	Note 24 – World requires the four elements/winds/directions/angels	356
	Note 25 – Good deeds are described as food for man's soul	358
	Note 26 – Soul will not be sated with a small diet of Torah study and good deeds	358
	Note 27 – Man's food quality parallels absorption quality of his actions in worlds	360
7.	Bad deeds damage the worlds as bad food damages the body	362
	Note 28 – God gradually rejects evil vs. instant rejection for idol worship	368
8.	Adverse impact of sin is a natural consequence and not a punishment	372
9.	Prayer at its prescribed time is main form of sustenance of worlds	374
	Note 29 – Prayer in place of sacrifices as food for God at specific times	376
10.	Every spoken word of prayer has tremendous impact	380
11.	Prayer focus to draw Holiness; difficulties are bitter but sweet	386
	Note 30 – Two ways to approach prayer hinted to in Mishna	394

	Note 31 – Burdened head and arm, Tefillin connects God and man	396
12.	Two levels of God's pain, prayer to focus on God's pain	398
13.	Simple focus on words is proven method for purity of prayer	404
	Note 32 – Difference between prayer in Hebrew and other languages	408
14.	Service of the soul with spoken prayer to cleave to God	410
	Note 33 – Prayer and sacrifices interconnect and unify worlds with God	416
	Note 34 – Rabbeinu Yona: Focus thoughts on Creator and not the physical	424
15.	Prayer with all/part soul; Torah and Mitzvot lead to prayer focus	426
	Note 35 – Prayer with soul to be on both general and component level	430
16.	Three components of soul/words of prayer to connect to source	432
	Note 36 – Letter tags go together with letters just like the soul to a body	438
	Note 37 – Regular and repentance sequences of thought, speech, and action	440
17.	Will relate to another soul/word component after resurrection	444
	Note 38 – Knesset Yisrael is the mother, and God is the father of souls	452
18.	Methodology for advanced prayer	458
	Note 39 – Tachanun: Focus on ceasing to be after soul connection of prayer	460
	Note 40 – Detailed focus on prayer sequence to connect to Knesset Yisrael	462

THIRD GATEWAY — 466

1.	Makom's simple meaning is causing all to constantly be	466
2.	Depth of Makom – is an analogy – all is exclusively God	470
	Note 41 – Chochma causes all from Ayin, no intellect can understand this	480
	Note 42 – God called Makom as unaffected by anything within Creation	480
3.	Emphasis of a. all being exclusively God, and b. its sensitivity	482
4.	Relative to God: He fills worlds, but to us: He circumvents	488
	Note 43 – YHVH is relative to God's perspective and has not changed	496
5.	Concealment creates difference and a human perspective of God	498
6.	Halacha only relevant to Human environment/perspective	504

CONTENTS: VOLUME 1

7.	Tzimtzum and Kav – two perspectives but one single concept	510
8.	Tzimtzum awareness helps concentration but *never* to be actioned	520
9.	Prayer to focus on YHVH alone, focus on *Elokim* is idol worship	526
10.	Life force of all cascades down from Elokim – i.e., the Kav	538
11.	He and His Speech are One, YHVH is identical to *Elokim*	546
	Note 44 – Hear that which is seen and see that which is heard	554
	Note 45 – Baruch Shem not praise but God accepts it so we say it quietly	554
12.	Evil forces are creations but have no impact if focused on His Unity	558
	Note 46 – Focus on God irrespective of difficulties sweetens harsh decrees	566
13.	Patriarchs fully focused but still saw physicality unlike Moshe	566
	Note 47 – Dust and ashes like Red Heifer; and their difference is like skin and light	572
14.	Moshe's level unattainable but try to aspire to it during prayer	574
	Note 48 – Moshe/absolute/Shema, Yaakov/difference/Baruch Shem	582

CHAPTERS 584

1.	Carefully watch for pitfall of haughtiness on path to purity	584
2.	Honor those involved in Torah and Mitzvot even for wrong reasons	586
3.	Encourage any Torah study – wrong reasons lead to right reasons	592
4.	Evil Inclination disguised as noble destroys self and Torah	598
	Note 49 – Good inclination on right, bad inclination jumps from left to right	604
5.	Action is key as per First and Second Gateways	606
6.	Action is key as per Third Gateway	614
7.	No latitude to sin or change Mitzvot for the sake of Heaven	618
8.	Mitzvah performance to inspire thought purity but not vice versa	622

FOURTH GATEWAY 628

1.	Background of why importance of Torah study is to be accentuated	628
2.	For its sake not to be confused with inspirational fervor	634
3.	For its sake = for the sake of Torah	638
4.	Fear of God is to Torah as a storehouse is to produce	642
5.	The greater the Fear of Heaven the more Torah can be preserved	644
	Note 50 – Fear of Heaven is the initial wisdom given to the wise	648
6.	Preparation allows cleaving to word of God and to God	650
7.	Focus a little on Fear of God before and during Torah study	654

8.	Empty storehouse is no storehouse – Fear with no Torah is nothing	658
9.	Too much preservative/fear is theft	660
10.	Torah is the continuous life force of *all* existence	662
11.	Worlds continue to exist when Jews engaged in Torah study	672
12.	Even greater impact of new Torah insights	684
13.	God's intention in Creation completed when Torah studied	688
14.	Torah study brings enlightenment and blessing to the worlds	692
15.	One who studies Torah brings blessing and protection on himself	696
	Note 51 – Bestowal of good on those who study for, and also, not for its sake	700
16.	More Torah study leads to less need to earn living	702
17.	Torah protects from death/Gehinom/World to Come/i.e., always	706
18.	Torah *for its sake* results in control over natural order	714
19.	Torah scholars called by God's Name and all fearful of them	720
20.	Secrets revealed to and Shechina rests upon Torah Sages	724
21.	Torah Sages greater after death, and are sustained by Stored Light	728
22.	Minimal Torah exposure subjects one to worldly control	734
23.	Lack of Torah involvement prevents entry to World to Come	740
24.	Non-study of Torah leads to complete cut off from World to Come	746
25.	Universe exists all the while at least one Jew studies Torah	752
26.	High source of Torah causes study to have universal impact – unlike Mitzvot	756
27.	Torah higher than worlds as unchanged by its descent	760
28.	Torah speaks to all world levels, its essence will be revealed	764
29.	Torah vs. Mitzvot – heals entire body vs. heals specific limb	770
30.	Torah gives existence to Mitzvot but both are required	778
31.	Torah study atones for even grave sins	784
32.	Torah restores, protects, and is the only environment of life	790
	Note 52 – Torah study is the only remedy for removing the Evil Inclination	798
33.	Attach yourself to Torah to live, otherwise you are literally dead	800
34.	Torah study causes God to dwell in this world	804

ABOUT THE AUTHOR 813

CONTENTS
VOLUME 2

Approbations	5
Dedications	18
Introduction	23

ESSENTIAL CONCEPTS IN NEFESH HACHAIM 25

1.	The Limit of Understanding – The Deeper Meaning of Makom	27
2.	Tzimtzum – The Key to Nefesh HaChaim	35
	1. *The Central Theme Underpinning R. Chaim's Approach*	35
	2. *The Concept of Tzimtzum*	38
	3. *Relative Reality and Tzimtzum Terminology*	58
	4. *The Key Historical Positions*	63
	5. *The Vilna Gaon*	71
	6. *The Baal HaTanya*	91
	7. *Nefesh HaChaim*	96
	8. *R. Dessler, the Lubavitcher Rebbe and R. Kluft*	106
	9. *Confusion and Clarification*	119
	10. *Methodologies of Nefesh HaChaim and Sefer HaTanya*	125
	11. *The Real Essence and Structure of Nefesh HaChaim*	142
	12. *The Basis of the Entire Kabbalah*	145
	13. *In Conclusion*	151
	14. *Postscript – Tzimtzum, Kabbalah and Science*	152
	15. *Tzimtzum Sources*	166
3.	The World of The Malbush	343

WRITINGS ORIGINALLY PUBLISHED
WITH NEFESH HACHAIM 363

4.	Maamar BeTzeLeM by Rabbi Yitzchak, Rabbi Chaim's Son	365
5.	The Approbations Published with Nefesh HaChaim	425

WRITINGS BY RABBI CHAIM VOLOZHIN
RELATED TO NEFESH HACHAIM 445

6.	Introduction to the Vilna Gaon's Commentary on Shulchan Aruch	447
7.	Introduction to the Vilna Gaon's Commentary on Zohar	459

8.	Introduction to the Vilna Gaon's Commentary on Sifra DeTzniyuta	469
9.	Letter to Grandson	519
10.	Yeshiva Letter – Written on Opening the Volozhin Yeshiva	525
11.	Rabbi Chaim's Sermon	541
	Part One	542
	Part Two	566
	Part Three	580
	Part Four	600

WRITINGS RELATED TO NEFESH HACHAIM RECORDED BY RABBI CHAIM VOLOZHIN'S STUDENTS 603

12.	Related Extracts from Ruach Chaim	605
	Introduction	605
	Chapter One	606
	Chapter Two	616
	Chapter Three	622
	Chapter Four	628
	Chapter Five	631
	Chapter Six	634
	Ruach Chaim Indexed to Nefesh HaChaim	648
13.	Intention in Prayer – A Brief Extract Rabbi Yosef Zundel of Salant	649

RESOURCES AND INDEXES 671

14.	Sources and Resources	673
15.	Nefesh HaChaim – Detailed Outlines	677
	Outline of the First Gateway	677
	Outline of the Second Gateway	679
	Outline of the Third Gateway	684
	Outline of the Chapters Section	690
	Outline of the Fourth Gateway	693
16.	Thematic Index	701
17.	Index of People's Names	731
18.	Index of Book References	737

About the Author 759

TRANSLATOR'S INTRODUCTION

1. BACKGROUND AND STRUCTURE OF NEFESH HATZIMTZUM

The Motivation for and Meaning of "Nefesh HaTzimtzum"

Rabbi Chaim of Volozhin needs no introduction. He is famous for being the primary student of the Vilna Gaon, for having reinstated the concept of an international large scale Yeshiva, and for his magnum opus, Nefesh HaChaim.

Nefesh HaChaim is a work which has been described as nothing less than a "*Shulchan Aruch* of *Hashkafa*,"[1] a formal presentation of how a Jew is to view and philosophically interact with the world. As such it is a work of significant importance and one which needs to be very carefully studied.

Nefesh HaTzimtzum originally started out as a personal study program to attain some level of understanding of this most important work. Early on in this study, I was astonished to discover that while Nefesh HaChaim is a work which is regularly studied and accorded tremendous respect, it has nevertheless become common practice to omit the study of major parts of it. Of those Yeshivot where it is formally studied, most only focus on specific sections.[2] In addition, most of the existing commentaries and translations, of which there are surprisingly few, actively highlight in their introductions that they either partially or fully omit comment on major sections of this work.

The reason generally stated for these significant omissions is related to what is considered to be sensitive Kabbalistic subject matter which frequently appears throughout all sections of the book as R. Chaim draws richly and openly from many Kabbalistic sources and uses the framework of Kabbalistic language to express his outlook.

---

1. A description generally attributed to the Brisker Rav, R. Yitzchak Zeev Halevi Soloveichik. In a similar vein, the Rosh Yeshiva of Telshe, R. Yosef Leib Bloch used to say that he had two masters in Hashkafa, R. Moshe Chaim Luzzato and R. Chaim. See *Reb Chaim of Volozhin* (New York: ArtScroll, 1993), p. 165. (See the Volume 2 section, "Sources and Resources.") R. Chaim Pinchas Scheinberg also writes that "It is well-known that the leaders of the generations have recommended [Nefesh HaChaim] for study as it is a foundation for Hashkafa and for Torah. It contains and explains many of the basic principles of the Torah through which a person can reach a level of service of God with holiness and purity" (as per his approbation to the commentary Hakdamot U'Shearim, p. 9).
2. Usually just the Fourth Gateway and sometimes also the Second Gateway.

In persevering with the study program, it became clear to me that it is simply not possible to properly understand the philosophical objectives of this work without engaging in the Kabbalistic concepts presented.

The fact that Nefesh HaChaim is primarily a Kabbalistic exposition is highlighted by R. Avraham Abeli, the head of the Vilna Bet Din, who issued one of the original approbations for it. He goes so far as to describe the book as being a gateway through which to access the world of Kabbalistic knowledge for one who studies it genuinely out of repentance.[3]

It should be noted that R. Chaim himself chose to publish these concepts and place them in the public domain. In addition, he made these concepts central to the only formal book that he personally wrote in his lifetime and he also prioritized the urgent need for his book to be published and brought to public attention without delay on his deathbed.[4] It is therefore clearly evident that R. Chaim's intention is that his work is very specifically meant for public consumption and that every effort should be made to properly understand all the concepts he presents.

Furthermore, there is a section in the book,[5] in which R. Chaim openly deliberates the appropriateness and warns of the pitfalls of discussing one of the deepest Kabbalistic concepts, the concept of Tzimtzum, as a result of its sensitivity and the possibility for it to be taken out of context. It should be noted that at the time this concept was already very much in the public domain.[6] R. Chaim himself concludes his deliberations by stating that times had changed and that this deep concept was being taken out of context and he saw it as very important to present it in its proper balanced context.

As R. Chaim himself chose to place these concepts in the public domain for our consumption in such a high profile way, we are surely obliged to fully engage in all of them. To not do so can only compromise the very messages that he urgently wanted to convey to us.

Moreover, an attempt to partially present the ideas in his book sends out misleading false messages that (a) it may be acceptable to not attempt to understand every part of this extremely important work; (b) that it is possible for this work to be understood in its proper context without covering all of

---

3. See R. Avraham Abeli's approbation in Volume 2, Section 5.
4. Prioritized over and above the collecting of the remnants of his scattered Responsa, after most had been destroyed by fire, as per R. Chaim's son, R. Yitzchak, in his introduction to Nefesh HaChaim.
5. The first three chapters of the Third Gateway.
6. Courtesy of Chassidic literature which was already widely available at the time and studied by large numbers of people, e.g., Sefer HaTanya authored by the R. Shneor Zalman of Liadi, although R. Chaim makes no direct reference by name to the Chassidic movement or any Chassidic literature anywhere in his book.

its detail, and c) that it is possible to properly understand the later sections without first understanding the earlier sections of the work.[7]

In the close to 200 years that have elapsed since first publication, these Kabbalistic concepts are now more widespread than ever and are widely accessible to virtually anyone irrespective of their background, especially via the Internet. The potential vulnerability to their associated risks is at least as high today as it was in R. Chaim's day. However, the balanced context that R. Chaim was so urgently trying to publicize has not correspondingly been successfully disseminated especially as his work has not been made easily accessible. Furthermore, the very issues which R. Chaim was trying to address in his day are still rife today, albeit generally manifest in different ways.

Consequently, there is a sore need to bring R. Chaim's ideas to the fore and make them as accessible as possible. This was therefore the impetus to provide a comprehensive translation together with enough explanatory comment, background from sources quoted, and contextual reference from other writings of R. Chaim, to make the original Hebrew text as meaningful and understandable as possible.

During the course of the extensive research performed during compilation, a deeper understanding of Nefesh HaChaim was gained such that it can now be unequivocally stated that Nefesh HaChaim, across all of its sections, is entirely about the concept of Tzimtzum and how to adopt this concept in practice. This is demonstrated at length in the analysis of the concept of Tzimtzum, which also, most importantly, clarifies centuries of confusion and misunderstanding about the essence of what Tzimtzum is and shows that there was no historic disagreement over the principles of Tzimtzum among the key Kabbalists who described the concept. The popular name by which R. Chaim's work is known, "Nefesh HaChaim"/"The Soul of Chaim," was not assigned to it by R. Chaim, but was given posthumously by his son as this expression was used by R. Chaim as his signature in his writings and also in part to serve as a memorial for him.[8] This name, however, does not capture the essence of R. Chaim's monumental work. Therefore, taking Nefesh HaChaim together with all of R. Chaim's additional related writings, the added commentary, and the analysis of Tzimtzum, this compilation has been named "Nefesh HaTzimtzum"/"The Soul of Tzimtzum," to highlight that in reality Nefesh HaChaim truly en-

---

7. As there is a clear sequential dependency in the ideas presented as mentioned later in this Introduction.
8. The term "Nefesh HaChaim" is used in the context of "A Memorial for Chaim" in the Title Page. It is also referenced as R. Chaim's signature in both the Title Page and in R. Yitzchak's introduction.

capsulates the essence of the concept of Tzimtzum and describes how the understanding of this concept should be used as a tool for serving God.

"Nefesh HaTzimtzum" is presented in two volumes:
- Volume 1: *Rabbi Chaim Volozhin's Nefesh HaChaim with Translation and Commentary*:
    This volume contains the complete Hebrew text of Nefesh HaChaim accompanied by a comprehensive translation and commentary. It additionally provides extensive translated source material necessary to properly understand the basic text. Context is given by this Introduction which includes a historical overview.
- Volume 2: *Understanding Nefesh HaChaim through the Key Concept of Tzimtzum and Related Writings*:
    This companion volume presents a number of important concepts, including the concept of Tzitmzum, which enable access to a greater depth of understanding of Nefesh HaChaim. It also adds valuable insight by providing the full Hebrew text and translation of all of Rabbi Chaim Volozhin's published writings which are related to Nefesh HaChaim. Additional related writings are also included together with detailed outlines and a full index for both volumes.

Translation Challenges

The objective of this translation was first and foremost to make the original Hebrew text as accessible as possible. It was very tempting to translate by rephrasing the gist of each sentence into flowing English. However, while this may sound good and read well, it more often than not loses touch with and omits nuances of the original text which were felt to be too valuable to lose, so this has been avoided wherever possible.

R. Chaim's style frequently uses long-winded sentences which were typical of his times. In addition to using difficult Kabbalistic language in places, R. Chaim goes out of his way to corroborate every statement by quoting many sources including very cryptic sources. Often these sources are only partially quoted and they are also regularly just referenced, requiring further expansion and explanation in both instances. Frequently, R. Chaim explicitly requires the reader to refer to these sources at further length to truly understand the point being made.

In addition, R. Chaim uses a high-powered rabbinic language where he repeatedly peppers his text with phrases culled, very often obscurely, from the length and breadth of traditional Jewish sources. This is to the extent that, on occasion, sentences are almost completely constructed by seamlessly weaving together a string of back-to-back phrases borrowed from diverse sources.[9] In some cases, the background to these phrases adds insight into the point R. Chaim is making. In other instances, the knowledge that an otherwise extremely cryptic phrase is simply borrowed, goes a long way to help the basic understanding of the text.

Presentation Approach

In light of the above challenges, instead of providing a standard prose style translation, a radically different presentation approach has been adopted. Paragraphs and sentences have been broken down into a hierarchical bullet point structure, in both the Hebrew text and the English translation, to serve the following purposes:

1. To break long sentences down into component parts, making them easier to digest while at the same time preserving R. Chaim's original expressions as closely as possible.
2. To provide clear visibility of the difference between the main points that R. Chaim makes and the numerous quotations that he generally brings to corroborate them.

Where sentences have been broken down into component parts, they are spread over multiple bullet points. Such sentences can be identified by their punctuation in that a bullet point which ends with no punctuation represents an incomplete sentence and will be followed by the next bullet point which starts off with a lowercase letter.[10] Generally this approach has been used for longer sentences but it has also been used sometimes to emphasize points made within shorter sentences.

Extended quotations have also been provided in many places and have generally been placed in footnotes.

Square brackets are used in the following way:
- To identify additional comments added:
  - to the main body of either or both of the Hebrew and English text
  - to facilitate understanding of the additional formal notes
  - to the extended quotations.
- To add extended quotations within the main body of the text. This usage should be obvious from the context.
- To denote, on occasion, more accurate manuscript versions in the Hebrew text of Volume 2. In these instances, the Hebrew contents

---

9. E.g., in the first chapter of the Fourth Gateway.
10. Unless the first word of the next bullet point is a name or a transliterated Hebrew word in which case it will begin with a capital letter.

of the square brackets will appear in the translated English text either without brackets or with round brackets depending on the context.

Footnotes have also been provided with supporting information wherever it was thought helpful to understand the point being conveyed.

Almost all references in the English translation have been placed in the footnotes even if they were originally presented as part of the original Hebrew text.

Borrowed expressions are bounded with single quotation marks. Wherever their source has been successfully identified it has been brought in the footnotes.

Quotations are either bounded by double quotation marks or form the entirety of a bulleted paragraph. All quotations have an identifying footnote reference.

Italics have generally been used for emphasis although there has been the occasional use of bolded text. Transliterated Hebrew words begin with an uppercase letter and have not been italicized unless they are being emphasized. Transliterated Hebrew letters are generally italicized, in lowercase and have been spelled out in full.

Nefesh HaChaim in its entirety, forms the majority of the contents of Volume 1. Its chapter headings were not provided in the original Hebrew text, but they have been provided here in the form of key phrase summaries which are designed only to serve as memory triggers to aid quick review of the contents. These key phrase summaries are intentionally limited and have been restricted to one line per chapter and are collected together in the table of contents to facilitate review. They do not necessarily reflect all of a chapter's contents.

The sections of Nefesh HaChaim have been assigned individual reference codes which are referenced throughout Nefesh HaTzimtzum. The reference codes used are as follows:
- First Gateway: G1
- Second Gateway: G2
- Third Gateway: G3
- Chapters Section: GC
- Fourth Gateway: G4

Chapter references have been constructed as per the following example: Chapter 6 of the First Gateway is referenced as G1:06.

Key phrase summaries have been provided for R. Chaim's fifty-two additional formal notes, and they have also been collected together in the table of contents. These notes are presented at the end of the chapter they relate to. They are clearly identified by bolded footnotes accompanying the main English text and are also referred to directly from the Hebrew text.

These notes have also been assigned individual reference codes which are used to refer to them throughout Nefesh HaTzimtzum. They are constructed by combining the source section and chapter it belongs to with its own unique note number (from N01 to N52). An example reference for note 9 which appears in the sixth chapter of the First Gateway is: G1:06:N09.

R. Chaim's son, R. Yitzchak, appended eight notes to his introduction and eight sub-notes to his lengthy note known as Maamar BeTzeLeM (which appears in Volume 2). These notes and sub-notes have also been uniquely numbered. They have been included at the end of each related section and are referenced from the main text.

Volume 2 is divided into self-contained sections which are collected together in related groups. It is referred to as V2. The section numbers within it have been uniquely consecutively numbered. For example, the fifth section of Volume 2 is referenced as V2:05.

During the course of compiling the translation, the existence and accuracy of sources and references within the text were never taken at face value. Very close to one hundred percent of all the sources quoted and references provided have been referenced in their original source text, corroborating and in some instances correcting them. Details relating to sources and resources used are to be found in Volume 2.

Translation Deepens Understanding – Acknowledgments

The translation process involves careful comparison of concepts and phrases in different languages with the need of the final phrases selected to be optimized to convey the original concept as closely as possible. While the act of translation inevitably results in a loss of information through both obvious and subtle language differences, the attempt to find a comparative expression in another language is one which very significantly deepens the understanding of the original text and of the concepts being communicated by it.[11]

This same comparative process also applies to the study of ideas by review of a text in its original language and the comparison of the differences between that text and the text of an already existing translation. This type of study also very much deepens the resulting understanding. I would like

---

11. This touches on an idea presented in the V2:01, "The Limit of Understanding – The Deeper Meaning of Makom" which adds insight into the concept of difference and how understanding results from difference. This is closely linked to concepts presented by R. Chaim in the Third Gateway.

to suggest that this is the reason why our Sages/Chazal require us to always review Torah text together with its translation,[12] as that review process itself is one, which if done properly, will significantly deepen the reviewer's understanding of the original Torah text.

It can also be suggested that this idea explains another statement of Chazal in relation to when Moshe instructs the Jewish People with tasks to be performed after they cross over the Jordan River into Israel that they should set up large stones upon which the Torah should be written in a "well explained" manner. Chazal define the meaning of "well explained" as being in "seventy languages"[13] and they therefore clearly prioritize the benefits of a translation as being a medium of explanation over and above the provision of an explanation via explanatory comments.

I therefore thank God from the depths of my soul for affording me a remarkable opportunity to provide a translation for this most important work and to thereby allow me to increase my personal understanding of it. He has enabled me to do this, in every sense of enablement, and in a way which can only be understood fully after relating to the concepts in this book.

I would also like to thank and acknowledge the contribution of the following individuals who either directly or indirectly significantly contributed to this project, providing their wisdom, guidance and support:

R. Moshe Schatz: It has been a distinct privilege for me to have merited to learn from you. You have generously afforded me the opportunity to glimpse at the depth and breadth of your Kabbalistic knowledge and have introduced me to your original unique encompassing gestalt. In addition to providing review feedback, focusing in particular on the Kabbalistic subject matter, you have literally coached me through a necessary process of personal change required to present key concepts within Nefesh HaChaim. You have enabled me to move away from my preconceived notions of irreconcilable difference in relation to the key concept of Tzimtzum which deeply bothered me. You showed me how to look at the bigger picture where all aspects of difference and question fall away and are unified within the greater Whole, to the extent that it has become clear to me that there are no differences or questions to begin with. I am truly indebted to you for being able and willing to take responsibility to ensure concepts have been accurately presented and for having saved me from error.[14]

---

12. Berachot 8a as brought down in Halacha in Rambam, Mishneh Torah, Hilchot Tefillah 13:25 and in Shulchan Aruch Orach Chaim 285:1.
13. Sotah 32a and 36a in explaining the words from Devarim 27:8. This meaning is also brought down by Rashi on the verse.
14. See the "Author's Note" at the beginning of V2:02, "Tzimtzum – The Key to

R. Yosef Kamenetsky: I have been blessed to meet you and for you to have graciously given me the opportunity of accessing your vast Torah knowledge in general, and your exquisitely detailed understanding of Nefesh HaChaim in particular. Our email conversation over a protracted period has been the source of great joy for me and over the course of time you have kindly reviewed numerous points within my manuscript, challenging and correcting my understanding of many of them. I have come to learn that every word you write and say requires careful study and in applying this study I have been enabled to add much rich detail to this project. I cannot thank you enough for your help, not only for your feedback, but also for your advocacy of this project with all interested parties.

R. Chaim Perlmutter: Thank you for having given me the opportunity to sit at your feet and learn Torah from you in your working man's Kollel program. It is difficult to describe just how much you have given me, a small part of which includes many tools that have made this project possible. I am also grateful for the valuable feedback you provided on my manuscript.

Rebbetzin Rubin and R. Dov Eliach: Thank you for your encouragement of Torah study by providing the authoritative Hebrew texts of the popular Nefesh HaChaim Rubin edition and of R. Chaim's additional writings.[15]

R. Avishai David: Having the good fortune to have you as my Kehilla Rav, your continuous and enthusiastic support throughout the development of this project has been particularly encouraging. Thank you for taking the time to review the manuscript at various stages of completion.

R. Yehoshua Gerzi: It was your exuberant encouragement at the very start of this project that gave me the momentum to continue. It would not have happened without you!

Marc Reiss: One of the objectives of this project was to provide material we could study together in our Chavruta sessions. Thank you for always being a challenging study partner and for never taking anything at face value.

My friends, Tzvi Escott, David Guedalia, Joe Hyman, R. Moshe Lichtman, Dr. Laurence Lovat, Avi Schneider, Alan Strauss, Gershon Tokayer: Thank you for your advice and valuable review feedback generously provided throughout the various stages of this project.

Tzvi Mauer and The Team at Urim Publications: Thank you for turning a dream to make R. Chaim's Torah widely accessible, into a beautiful reality. In particular, thank you to Tzvi, for your timely and sage advice; to Batsheva Pomerantz, for your exceptional editing, investing a tremendous level of care and attention to detail; and to Ariel Walden, for overcoming a complex layout design challenge producing nothing less than a work of art.

Nefesh HaChaim."

15. See V2:14, "Sources and Resources" for more details.

My father, of blessed memory, and my mother, may she be well: If this project has been successful in any way, it is unquestionably due to my parents. As my primary role models, they blazed the trail for me to aspire to value and prioritize the pursuit of knowledge and the need to permanently be connected to the Torah. I have come to understand that the ultimate fulfillment of the command of honoring parents is to live by aspiring to attain these values. I hope and pray that this project truly fulfills the next ongoing step in my life's journey in honoring my parents, providing an Aliyat Neshama for my father and Nachat Ruach for my mother.

My wife, Tania, and daughters, Miri and Gila: Please forgive me if the time I have devoted to this project may have caused you any duress. You may not realize it but deep down you provided a significant part of the inspiration for me to take it on in the first place. I have so much to thank you for and no words to express my appreciation. I must however highlight my deep-felt gratitude, in particular, for all of your love and care during the challenges that God sent me while I was in the throes of this project.

*

It is my fervent prayer that this translation and compilation accurately represents and truly captures at least some of the essence of R. Chaim's profound work and that it will be found of real practical use to you the reader, in understanding R. Chaim's messages.

The concepts presented by R. Chaim are a basic platform to give us knowledge of the closest that is humanly achievable in relating to God and by extension, our ability to serve Him. This body of knowledge becomes increasingly important, as we draw closer to the imminent times of Mashiach. In particular, in the times of Mashiach, it is about this very knowledge that the prophet says "that the Earth will become filled with the knowledge of God just as water covers the sea bed."[16] It is therefore very fitting that R. Chaim directly refers to this in his closing prayer to this monumental work, that it should be God's Will that these concepts should universally bring us to a state where "each creation will know its Creator"[17] "and God will be One and His Name will be One."[18]

Avinoam Fraenkel
Bet Shemesh, Israel
Kislev 5775

---

16. Yishayahu 11:9.
17. From *Tefilot* on Yamim Noraim.
18. Zecharia 14:9.

2. THE CONTEXT OF NEFESH HACHAIM

Extensive works have been written which present biographical details of R. Chaim's life together with a wide range of theories related to many unknown facts about his life and the burning issues of his day. In many respects the mere study of Nefesh HaChaim provides a remarkable portal to glimpse at the sheer measure of the man that R. Chaim was, his extensive erudition, the depth and range of his knowledge and most significantly, his ability to synthesize it into an expertly woven fine tapestry presenting his immensely important worldview and messages for public consumption. The purpose of this section is to very briefly capture just a few salient background details relevant to add some insight to the context within which the ideas of Nefesh HaChaim took root.[19]

Key Dates Related to Rabbi Chaim and Nefesh HaChaim

- **5509 (1749), 7 Sivan:** R. Chaim Itzkovitz, the third of five sons, is born. His father, R. Yitzchak, was the Parnass, the lay leader, of Volozhin and he was a Torah scholar with a reputation for honesty and benevolence. His mother, Rivka, was the daughter of R. Yosef Rappaport, the head of the Piesk Bet Din. The Itzkovitz home was always open to passing Torah scholars.
- **5517–5524 (1757–1764):** R. Rephael HaCohen Hamburger who served as a rabbi in the Minsk area is R. Chaim's first teacher, teaching him from age eight until fifteen. R. Rephael later on became a major antagonist of the Haskalah movement.
- **5524 (1764):** R. Aryeh Leib Gotleib, author of the Shaagat Aryeh, is a guest in the Itzkovitz home for a number of weeks. R. Chaim, at age fifteen, together with his elder brother, R. Simcha, regularly study with the Shaagat Aryeh who deeply impacts them with his approach to Torah study throughout the period.
- **5528 (1768):** After becoming a student in Vilna, at age nineteen, through his initiative, he resolves to become a student of R. Eliyahu, the Vilna

---

19. The specific details of this chapter have been amalgamated and distilled from R. Yitzchak's Introduction to Nefesh HaChaim which is rich in its biographical detail; the ArtScroll biography; R. Dov Eliach's *Kol HaKatuv LeChaim*, 3rd Ed. (Jerusalem: Moreshet HaYeshivot, 2009); R. Dr. Norman Lamm's *Torah for Torah's Sake* (New York: Ktav Publishing House, 1989); and an anecdote from the writings of R. Chaim Dov Ber Gulevsky. More details of these sources are to be found in V2:14, "Sources and Resources."

Gaon. This commences a near thirty-year relationship which ended with the passing of the Vilna Gaon.
- **Circa 5528** (1768):[20] Marries Sarah, daughter of R. Aryeh Leib Ginsburg, one of the leaders of Vilna Jewry.
- **5534-5536** (1774-1776): At age twenty-five, together with his youngest brother, the outstanding genius, R. Shlomo Zalman, studies daily with the Vilna Gaon.
- **5536** (1776): Becomes Rabbi of Volozhin.
- **5536** (1776): Sarah runs a textile mill and the family becomes free from all financial worries.
- **5541** (1781): The second Vilna ban is released against the Chassidic movement. Signed by the Vilna Gaon and R. Shlomo Zalman. Not signed by R. Chaim.
- **5558** (1797): The Vilna Gaon passes away.
- **5563** (1802): The Volozhin Yeshiva is established with ten students, initially funded entirely by income from the textile mill. R. Chaim sends out a letter during the Aseret Yemei Teshuva on opening the Yeshiva. This letter contains a number of points related to Torah study which later appear in the Fourth Gateway of Nefesh HaChaim.
- **5563** (1803): Publishes his introduction to the Vilna Gaon's commentary on Shulchan Aruch which clearly, but briefly, presents key ideas from what later would be included in the First and Second Gateways and also the Chapters Section of Nefesh HaChaim.
- **5570** (1810): Publishes his introduction to the Vilna Gaon's commentary on Zohar which clearly, but briefly, presents further key ideas from what later would be included in the First Gateway of Nefesh HaChaim.
- **5572** (1812), 21 Elul, First day of Selichot: R. Chaim delivers his only published sermon. This sermon presents extensive details from what later would become dominant parts of the First and Second Gateways and also touches on themes which appear in the other sections.
- **5575** (1815): A major fire breaks out in Volozhin. R. Chaim's house burns down together with his manuscripts and most of his Responsa. The Volozhin Yeshiva is spared from the fire.
- **5580** (1820): Publishes his introduction to the Vilna Gaon's commentary on Sifra DeTzniyuta which contains warm anecdotes describing his sheer reverence, awe, admiration of and enrapture with the Vilna Gaon.
- **5581** (1821), 14 Sivan: R. Chaim, from his deathbed, hands over the urgent task of publishing Nefesh HaChaim to his son, R. Yitzchak. He also asks that R. Yitzchak invest all of his efforts to support the Volozhin Yeshiva. Following these final instructions, he passes away.

---

20. The precise date is unknown. This is an approximate guess.

- 5584 (1824): The First Edition of Nefesh HaChaim is published by R. Yitzchak.
- 5597 (1837): The Second Edition of Nefesh HaChaim is published by R. Yitzchak.[21]

Rabbi Chaim's Relationship with the Vilna Gaon

Although R. Chaim's earlier teachers had a tremendous impact on him, his relationship with the Vilna Gaon was profoundly intense for close to almost thirty years. This relationship commenced when he was aged nineteen and intensified for the two-year period when he turned twenty-five in his daily study sessions with the Gaon. Subsequently, on assuming rabbinic leadership of Volozhin, R. Chaim would generally visit Vilna some three or four times a year for up to a month at a time to spend time with the Gaon.

The awe and respect that the disciple R. Chaim had for his master, the Gaon, is captured in his anecdotes presented in his introduction to the Gaon's commentary on Sifra DeTzniyuta,[22] published just one year before his passing. R. Yitzchak in his introduction to Nefesh HaChaim describes that the extent of his father's veneration of the Gaon was even manifest physically, that "When he would talk in learning and mention the name of his teacher [the Gaon], his whole body would tremble and his appearance changed."

R. Chaim's efforts to absorb the Gaon's path, the "Mantle of Eliyahu" as R. Yitzchak puts it, earned him the deep respect of the Gaon's sons and his contemporary disciples of the Gaon. They all unquestionably related to him as the Gaon's primary disciple.

It was in many senses that R. Chaim revealed the Torah of the Vilna Gaon. He supervised the publication of the Gaon's writings and it was he who validated authenticity and gave approval to all comments published in his day in the name of the Gaon. The Gaon's approach to Talmud study

---

21. According to the archives of the National Library of Israel, only two other editions were published in the 19th century, both after the passing of R. Yitzchak in 1849. The third edition was published in Koenigsburg in 1860 (there is some confusion about another Koenigsburg edition in 1861 but it is really the same as the 1860 edition which records 1861 on the last page). The fourth edition was published in Vilna in 1874. It should be noted that the bibliographic list Beit Eked Sefarim compiled by Friedberg lists additional 19th century editions, but these appear to have been in error as there is no evidence of their existence in any current libraries and they do not appear on the authoritative bibliographic list of the Hebrew University published at the following Internet link: http://www.hebrew-bibliography.com/.
22. This has been translated in full in V2:08.

and to learning all of Torah was the backbone of his Yeshiva, which inspired many leaders of the subsequent generations in the Torah world, who were alumni of the Yeshiva, in the Torah of the Gaon.

The Gaon's approach to Talmud study was directly at odds with the then common approach of Pilpul where elaborate theories were developed in order to deepen the understanding of the Talmud texts. In contrast, he advocated *straight thinking*, that one should always seek the simplest, least complex, understanding of the Talmud. His focus was very much on understanding the depth of the Halacha directly and as simply as possible from the Talmud itself and that works summarizing Halachic decisions, such as the Shulchan Aruch, should never replace the Talmud as being the source for and providing the context of Halachic derivation.[23]

In addition the Gaon's approach to Torah study was comprehensive. His view was that *all* of Torah needs to be studied, including all aspects of both the revealed and hidden Kabbalistic parts of Torah. Since all of Torah comes from one single source, it is one-hundred percent consistent. There is therefore no scope for deriving practices from one part of Torah which contradict prescriptions from another part of Torah. In particular, there is no basis whatsoever to suggest that the hidden parts of Torah can advocate any practices which contradict the dictates of the revealed parts of Torah and that any such conclusion derives from a misunderstanding of Torah.[24]

This approach to Torah study is clearly manifest in and is the driving force of a major theme in Nefesh HaChaim, that one must never let the focus on inspirational fervor, often derived from an understanding, or more often than not a misunderstanding of the hidden parts of Torah, to allow any departure from Halacha.

The following anecdote beautifully captures the nature of the relationship between the Vilna Gaon and R. Chaim:[25]

> It was on one Purim and a number of the Vilna Gaon's disciples, of the Lions of Lithuania, had convened in his house. Among them was the Gaon's favorite, his beloved student R. Chaim.

---

23. This approach is clearly presented in R. Chaim's introduction to the Vilna Gaon's commentary on Shulchan Aruch which was published at around the same time as the establishment of the Volozhin Yeshiva. (See V2:06.)
24. This approach is clearly articulated in R. Chaim's introduction to the Vilna Gaon's commentary on Zohar. (See V2:07.)
25. It is sourced in the writings of R. Chaim Dov Ber Gulevsky, who heard it from his grandfather, R. Simcha Zelig Rieger, the Dayan of Brisk, who was a descendant of R. Simcha, R. Chaim's oldest brother. It is translated here from the original Hebrew.

Suddenly, the Gaon turned to R. Chaim and said: "You are a wise one! But beware that your fear should not precede your wisdom. Beware and beware!!!"[26]

R. Chaim was already tipsy but not to the extent that he didn't carefully weigh and pay attention to every word of his teacher. He understood, having properly absorbed the words. He then suddenly burst into tears. Perhaps his teacher had seen something inappropriate in him, for if this was not the case, why would he say such harsh words? He, being a sensitive soul, was unable to restrain himself and started crying.

The Gaon turned to him and asked: "You don't appear to be crying from drunkenness but rather from depression and sadness, God forbid. Isn't it Purim today?"

R. Chaim answered apologetically: "How could I not cry after hearing such terrible words from our teacher?"

The Gaon answered him:

"Why do you cry? Every person who comes to this world is bestowed with specific abilities from Heaven. Each person is born with his own skills, senses and character traits and with his own weaknesses and deficiencies. There are those created with tremendous memories or with deep analytical capabilities and there are those who lack these skills. There are those created with pleasure-seeking desire, such as the desire for honor, and there are those created with bad character traits such as anger and the like.

"But it is vital for a person to be aware that he has the ability and the will to control himself and to behave as he chooses.

"This is comparable to a person who has a good horse with a calm temperament which is easy to restrain. Another person may have a wild horse which is difficult to control. If the second person studies taming techniques, then he will be successful in controlling his horse.

"However, it is understood that much effort needs to be invested in this. This effort is even required of one created with weaknesses and corrupted character traits.

"It is vital for a person to control his character traits and to behave as per his own will in order to rectify them to the best of his ability.

"Just as this is true with character traits, it is also true of Torah study. A person is obligated to use all of his wisdom in order to maximize his study to the best of his ability."

The Gaon now turned to face R. Chaim and continued:

---

26. This seems to contradict a well-known statement of Chazal. See the next footnote which sheds light on the entire anecdote and resolves the apparent contradiction.

"You have a soul which comes from the level of Chochma of Atzilut and of Supernal Binah [i.e., a very high source]. [At those levels,] there is a greater danger that, God forbid, one can glimpse [at things beyond one] and be hurt.

"Therefore, you must invest all of your strength to study the path that I have taught you and that I have shown you that you must follow."

The Gaon suddenly stopped talking and glanced at one or two of those assembled there. It appeared that he had stopped talking as he did not want to continue his words in public.

After almost all those assembled had left, leaving just a few of his Kabbalist students, the Gaon then turned to his student again and continued:

"In this world, you are my continuation. You are the one who prepares himself to be my student.

"However, according to our roots in the supernal worlds, I am a preparation for you and it is for you that I came to this world."

He concluded his remarks with this and did not elaborate.[27]

There is therefore scope to suggest that if R. Chaim is the continuation of the Vilna Gaon in this world, then Nefesh HaChaim is an encapsulation of the Gaon's general worldview. If, on the other hand, as the Gaon suggests,

---

27. This anecdote provides profound insight into how the Vilna Gaon viewed R. Chaim's personality. It starts with the Vilna Gaon seemingly contradicting Chazal's statement that Fear of God should *precede* wisdom (see G4:04). However, in this instance the Gaon is simply using this statement to express that striving to attain Fear of God should not be *prioritized* over the attaining of wisdom. He therefore recognizes R. Chaim's tendency to want to pursue Fear of God, strongly warning him that his focus on the pursuit of Fear of God should not become his primary focus over and above his focus on the pursuit of wisdom, i.e., Torah knowledge. The Gaon then highlights that even though each person has different tendencies, everyone must overcome these tendencies and develop strategies to maximize Torah study. He finally explains that R. Chaim's unique talents, rooted in his high soul source, expose him to potentially going too far, and that with his natural tendency to over-develop his Fear of God he could end up damaging himself. This description of R. Chaim's personality is particularly insightful as we can now understand that it was specifically his super sensitivity to potentially over-develop his own levels of Fear of God which motivated and allowed him to so ably express the pitfalls of this very tendency throughout Nefesh HaChaim, as we shall see. In particular, in the Fourth Gateway, he describes the importance of placing rigid limits around the necessary act of acquiring Fear of God and inspirational fervor in preparation for subsequent Torah study. In that context, he explains strategies as to how to view the implementation of these limits such that Torah study is prioritized and maximized to the best of one's ability.

that the reality is reversed and that his reason to be in this world was to be a preparation for R. Chaim, then the Gaon is the one who prepared R. Chaim to be able to express his own worldview in Nefesh HaChaim. Either perspective attaches huge significance and relevance to Nefesh HaChaim.

The Leader of the Mitnagdim

In a letter addressed to a grandson,[28] R. Chaim emphasizes the importance of being tolerant and never being strict in one's relationship with another. He highlights that a person can only achieve his desired objectives of another with tolerance and that a policy of tolerance is far, far more effective than that which can be achieved with any aggression.

R. Chaim unquestionably took over from the Vilna Gaon after his passing to become the leader of the Mitnagdim. While the Vilna Gaon was the key signatory of three Vilna bans of the Chassidic movement,[29] in contrast, the one single fact that we have relating to R. Chaim's view of the Chassidic movement is that he was absolutely silent! He did not participate in any of the bans. Even more significantly, he does not directly mention the Chassidic movement or any of its adherents by name anywhere in any of his writings including Nefesh HaChaim.

There are many theories as to why R. Chaim was silent and was not a cosignatory of the bans. These theories range from focusing on R. Chaim's policy of tolerance to the simple fact that R. Chaim was not a Rabbi in Vilna at the time the bans were issued so it would not have been relevant for him to sign.

In addition, the nature of the Chassidic movement fundamentally changed over the years between the Vilna Gaon's day and in R. Chaim's times. In the Vilna Gaon's day, the fledgling movement had a relatively small following, whereas during R. Chaim's life, especially later on, the movement had very much become a mainstream reality, forming the majority of the Jewish population in many areas outside of Lithuania. The approach to dealing with it would therefore need to be different.

R. Chaim showed his tolerance by admitting a number of Chassidim into his Yeshiva, accepting them with warmth. He additionally displayed great restraint in connection with a member of his family who joined the Chassidim,[30] and is reported not to have forbidden his family members from marrying into Chassidic families.

---

28. See V2:09, "Letter to Grandson."
29. The first ban was in 5532 (1772), the second in 5541 (1781), and the third in 5556 (1796).
30. Instructing him to at least observe three practices: 1. to study Talmud and

While R. Chaim does not mention Chassidim directly in Nefesh HaChaim, there are indirect references to some of their practices which were contrary to the Halacha, and the Chassidim appear to be referred to under the umbrella description of those who "desire closeness to God."[31] This description of those who "desire closeness to God" is used to identify a group who are unquestionably one target group which Nefesh HaChaim is aimed at, but the beauty of it is that, as an expression, it is far more encompassing than just having to relate to the Chassidim. Even if one were to conclude that it fully relates to the Chassidim, it does so with warmth.

Against the background of the widespread success of the spread of the Chassidic movement in R. Chaim's day, there are some who speculate that this success motivated the urgent writing of Nefesh HaChaim as a defense of the Mitnagdic philosophy which was in danger of becoming drowned by the success of Chassidic philosophy. This speculation would explain R. Chaim's style in corroborating almost every statement made with many, many sources as if to justify his argument every step of the way.[32]

Even if, as some will argue, R. Chaim was partially or even fully motivated to write Nefesh HaChaim because of widespread Chassidic practices at the time, the truth is that now, almost 200 years later, the theoretical debate simply does not matter any more. Irrespective of the motivation, what really does matter today is that R. Chaim maintained his silence at the time and that he did not make direct references to the Chassidim. As a result, the messages of Nefesh HaChaim are not constrained to a specific time in Jewish History. Instead they are timeless. They are therefore just as relevant today as they always were.

Many works have been written in response to issues arising in their day which have become timeless classics. A healthy view of this is that God, through His Divine Providence, arranged the circumstances through which

---

treat its study as part of serving God; 2. to observe the laws of the Talmud; 3. to never speak badly of the Vilna Gaon. (As per *Torah for Torah's Sake*, p. 47, n. 115.)

31. An expression borrowed from Yishayahu 58:2. This is used by R. Chaim in GC:08 and in G4:01. It is also used by R. Yitzchak in his introduction.

    It should be noted that this expression is also used by R. Chaim in his introduction to the Vilna Gaon's commentary on Sifra DeTzniyuta (see translation in V2:08) in a context which cannot be construed to be referring to the Chassidim in any way. This introduction was published at a similar time to the handing over of Nefesh HaChaim for publication and it therefore would be wrong to conclude that this expression purely relates to the Chassidim.

32. A much more compelling reason for R. Chaim's extensive corroboration is explained in context at the end of V2:02, "Tzimtzum – The Key to Nefesh HaChaim," Chap. 10.

these works would be written. This has left the Jewish people with works which shine as jewels emanating light and direction for many subsequent generations.

So, irrespective of the original motivation for writing this classic work and any associated theories, Nefesh HaChaim is still nothing less than a *Shulchan Aruch* of *Hashkafa* in our times and will remain so for generations to come.

Volozhin Yeshiva

The founding of the Volozhin Yeshiva was marked by R. Chaim's distribution of a Yeshiva Letter during the Aseret Yemei Teshuva of 5563 (late in 1802).[33]

This letter identifies a sore need for those who want to learn but either did not have the physical means to do so or simply did not have a teacher to enable them to do so.

Until the establishment of the Volozhin Yeshiva, it was common for a local Rabbi to collect some ten or so students around him and to use communal facilities to teach them Torah with the support of the local community. The students would tend to live locally as there were no dormitory facilities and it was an imposition on the generally impoverished communities to expect them to host students. The local Rabbi would give classes and the students would study, sometimes sleeping in the local prayer houses. They were subject to the whim of the caretakers of those prayer houses.

As a result there were a number of provincial pockets of Torah study around the local Rabbis but this was haphazard, without any formal organization across any particular region. These students were not generally held in high esteem by the people.

This Volozhin Yeshiva marked the materialization of a dream that R. Chaim had to reintroduce the concept of an internationally recognized Torah institution, which would significantly raise the profile of global Torah study.[34] The burden of supporting the infrastructure of the Yeshiva would

---

33. See V2:10, "Yeshiva Letter Written on Opening the Volozhin Yeshiva" where this letter is translated. The precise date of the opening of the Yeshiva is not clear. The Yeshiva Letter was dated, Sunday, the 7th day of Aseret Yemei Teshuva 5563, i.e., late in 1802. This letter solicited help for the Yeshiva which had already started some time earlier, being personally funded by R. Chaim. It could have started as early as 1801. The common date given for the founding of the Yeshiva is as per the Yeshiva building's foundation stone which was laid in 1803.
34. High profile internationally recognized Torah institutions used to exist in the time of the redaction of the Talmud (e.g., Sura and Pumpedita), but over the

not fall on local communal resources, so the Yeshiva would have appeal to attract appropriate students from out of town and become a widely recognized center for learning and excellence.

R. Chaim founded the Yeshiva using his personal financial resources, funding it with income from the textile mill run by his wife. After establishing it with a nucleus of some ten students, R. Chaim then sought assistance for further resources to increase it. In his lifetime, the Yeshiva's intake grew to somewhere between fifty and one hundred students.[35]

As mentioned earlier, the Vilna Gaon's approach was the basis of Torah study in the Volozhin Yeshiva. It focused on clarifying the simplest understanding of the Halacha and was dedicated to the study of absolutely all of Torah including the hidden parts of Torah.

In his Yeshiva Letter, R. Chaim sets out some details of his motivation to set up the Yeshiva including some philosophical points which are subsequently repeated later in his Nefesh HaChaim.[36]

This letter omits mention of two points:
1. There is no mention of any instruction or initiative of the Vilna Gaon to open this Yeshiva. It is therefore understood that the opening of the Yeshiva was not on the Vilna Gaon's initiative but rather was that of R. Chaim. If this was not the case, R. Chaim would most certainly have clarified this in such a letter.
2. There is no articulation of the principle of *Torah for its sake* which is a key principle in the approach to Torah study as set out later in Nefesh HaChaim.[37]

On his deathbed, R. Chaim issued two instructions to his son R. Yitzchak. One was to publish his Nefesh HaChaim as soon as possible. The other

---

ages had ceased to be.
35. Subsequently growing to 200 students when R. Yitzchak took over as the head of the Yeshiva and ultimately to an official 250 and an unofficial 400 in the days when R. Naftali Tzvi Berlin (the Netziv) headed the Yeshiva.
36. See V2:10, "Yeshiva Letter Written on Opening the Volozhin Yeshiva" where the concepts which appear later in Nefesh HaChaim are highlighted. They all appear in the Fourth Gateway.
37. This is significant as there are other detailed points in this Yeshiva Letter which do ultimately appear in Nefesh HaChaim, in the very same section in which the principle of *Torah for its sake* is expressed. The high profile of this principle within Nefesh HaChaim would have made it very suitable for its inclusion in such a letter, so it would therefore appear that the articulation of this principle was not yet formally expressed at the time the Yeshiva was established and was only expressed at a later time.

instruction was that R. Yitzchak should invest all his efforts to support the Yeshiva.

The Volozhin Yeshiva subsequently became a template model for the many other Yeshivot which have come into existence since that time, while Nefesh HaChaim became the philosophical backbone for serving God and motivating Torah study in these Yeshivot. As such, R. Chaim is commonly referred to as Avi HaYeshivot, The Father of the Yeshivot.

There is scope to speculate that a primary motivation[38] for R. Chaim to write Nefesh HaChaim was specifically to provide his Yeshiva concept with a philosophical framework to ensure its success. Again, irrespective of the original motivation, Nefesh HaChaim is still currently of immense value and will continue to be so for generations to come.

The Writing of Nefesh HaChaim

R. Yitzchak in his introduction highlights his personal deliberations over R. Chaim's deathbed instruction to urgently prioritize the publication of Nefesh HaChaim over and above his Responsa. R. Yitzchak even mentions his consultations with other Torah scholars over this and they concluded that they should abide by R. Chaim's dying wish.

Notwithstanding R. Yitzchak's deliberations, it is very, very clear that R. Chaim considered his Nefesh HaChaim to be his seminal work which had to be urgently published.

What is not clear, however, is exactly when Nefesh HaChaim was written and over how long a period the underlying ideas within it may have developed within R. Chaim's mind.

Nefesh HaChaim itself gives us two pieces of information related to this. Firstly from R. Yitzchak, who mentions R. Chaim's deathbed instruction to urgently publish it. Secondly, from the approbation of R. Avraham Abeli, that R. Chaim wrote the book late in his life.[39]

There are very few writings of R. Chaim in existence which are dated, but significant among them are his introductions to a number of the Vilna Gaon's works.

In particular, R. Chaim's introduction to the Vilna Gaon's commentary on Shulchan Aruch[40] was written in 5563 (1803), shortly after the estab-

---

38. Either in conjunction with or separate to other possible motivations mentioned earlier.
39. See translation of approbation in V2:05.
40. See V2:06 for a full translation of the "Introduction to the Vilna Gaon's Commentary on Shulchan Aruch" and details of its connection to Nefesh HaChaim.

lishment of his Yeshiva and some eighteen years before his passing. This contains a clear, but brief, presentation of a sequence of key ideas from what later would be included in the First and Second Gateways and also of significant points uniquely made in the Chapters Section of Nefesh HaChaim. So we can conclude that these key ideas and equally importantly, the sequence of these ideas, were developing in R. Chaim's mind at the very least for eighteen years before he handed over his completed work to his son for publication. We can also conclude that the details of the Chapters Section were very much on his mind at this early stage.[41]

A few more brief ideas from the First Gateway are presented in R. Chaim's introduction to the Vilna Gaon's commentary on Zohar dated 5570 (1810),[42] some eleven years before R. Chaim's passing.

In addition, as mentioned earlier, R. Chaim's Yeshiva Letter, dated 5563 (late in 1802), articulates a number of very detailed points which are later found in the Fourth Gateway,[43] but this letter very noticeably omits the principle of *Torah for its sake*, as mentioned above.

On the first day of Selichot 5572 (1812), R. Chaim delivered his only published sermon.[44] This sermon contains extensive details from what later became dominant parts of the First and Second Gateways and also touches on themes which appeared in the other sections. Interestingly, it presents some of these details in the context of material which is not later found in Nefesh HaChaim.

Whatever may have been the motivation for R. Chaim to write Nefesh HaChaim – whether it may have been any or all of the need to articulate the Vilna Gaon's worldview, as a challenge to or defense against the danger of Halachic compromise by some trends within the Chassidic movement or as a founding philosophy for the enormously successful modern-day Yeshiva concept – it is clear that R. Chaim was not suddenly inspired with the subject matter of Nefesh HaChaim and that he developed its ideas over at least an eighteen-year period. We can therefore understand that the book was written with very great precision and this gives insight into R. Chaim's

---

41. So the contents of the Chapters Section were certainly not an afterthought as some historians have incorrectly theorized.
42. See V2:07 for a full translation of the "Introduction to the Vilna Gaon's Commentary on Zohar" and details of its connection to Nefesh HaChaim.
43. See V2:10 for a full translation of the "Yeshiva Letter Written on Opening the Volozhin Yeshiva" and details of its connection to Nefesh HaChaim.
44. See V2:11 for a full translation of "R. Chaim's Sermon" together with details of its connection to Nefesh HaChaim.

deathbed instruction to his son to be careful to "not change his words from the way in which they were written."[45]

It is therefore incumbent upon us in our study of this profound work to pay very careful attention to all of R. Chaim's messages, to take note of his exact phraseology and to appreciate the precise sequence with which he presents his ideas.

3. THE ESSENCE AND STRUCTURE OF NEFESH HACHAIM

A Methodology for Serving God

First and foremost, Nefesh HaChaim charts out what R. Chaim himself describes as a guaranteed methodology for serving God.[46]

It frames this methodology within a context of deep Kabbalistic ideas which R. Chaim very intentionally is presenting for wider public consumption. As mentioned earlier, he openly deliberates the decision to publically express the deepest of these ideas and concludes that the times dictated the need for this.[47]

The importance of this methodology cannot be overstated. It provides a clear and fully corroborated statement on the approach that a Jew must adopt in order to relate to God and to the world. It explains what a Jew is and what he is capable of doing together with providing profound insight into the immense responsibility attached to these capabilities. It provides a deep appreciation of what a Jew must do in order to achieve his life's objective and an overview of his toolset of thought, speech, and action that are at his disposal to help him achieve this objective. It sets out the way that he must apply these tools to study Torah, perform Mitzvot, and conduct himself in prayer and also to the acquisition and use of inspirational fervor.

Focus on this methodology is essential for every Jew to be intimately aware of how to maximize his ability to serve God.

Please note that while this introduction presents a basic overview and outlined structure of Nefesh HaChaim, a far deeper understanding of the structure of the book is presented at the end of the section on Tzimtzum in Volume 2. The section on Tzimtzum provides a comprehensive clarification of the concept of Tzimtzum and demonstrates how this concept underpins the entire structure and presentation of Nefesh HaChaim. It is

---

45. As per R. Yitzchak's introduction.
46. As per the beginning of GC:01.
47. See the end of G3:03.

A Book with an Agenda

Although, Nefesh HaChaim describes a methodology for serving God which is of great value in its own right, it also has a very clear and specific agenda. The presentation of the methodology is structured in a way which builds up a compelling case to balance the pursuit of inspirational fervor in serving God, against the actual performance of Mitzvot and study of Torah.

The intention is to widely publicize the pitfalls of this pursuit and to prevent it from becoming an objective in its own right with the potential consequence that one can end up being completely diverted from actual service of God.

R. Chaim emphasizes the need to present this agenda in the light of his own personal observations of incorrect practices attempting to increase inspirational fervor which were widespread in his day and which he personally thoroughly investigated.[48]

While this agenda was specifically addressed to the needs of R. Chaim's day, it is just as relevant today as it ever was and is a truly timeless agenda.

R. Chaim specifically brings a witnessed example of the practice of investing so much time in preparing oneself to pray Mincha in the optimally inspired manner that one ends up praying after nightfall, when it is no longer Halachically relevant to do so.

Many current practices can be highlighted which compromise Halacha under the guise of wanting to reach a high of inspirational fervor in serving God. For example, it is sadly true that the practice which R. Chaim documents of praying Mincha at the wrong time still exists today in some circles. In addition, acts of physical aggression against Jews are perpetrated by some extremist Jews publicly breaching basic Torah principles in their misguided effort to enforce what they define as required standards of religiosity and modesty.

R. Chaim's key message is therefore to highlight the profound psychological trap of the Evil Inclination. Compromise of even the most peripheral Halachically required practice in the pursuit of increasing inspirational fervor is unacceptable in its own right. But much worse than this, it potentially exposes a person to destroying the very Torah principles which the inspirational fervor was supposedly meant to uphold in the first place!

---

48. See the end of GC:o8.

The Structure

The book is comprised of five sections. There are four Gateways and a Chapters Section which is placed between the Third and Fourth Gateways.

In a nutshell:
- **First Gateway:** Describes the structure of the soul and forms the basis of a framework of how to relate to oneself and to God.
- **Second Gateway:** Using the understanding of the soul's structure, a methodological framework is presented as to how to relate to prayer and in particular, prayer with one's soul.
- **Third Gateway:** A key meditation is presented, the concept of *Makom*, which is to be focused on while praying with the soul and as a tool to motivate Torah study.
- **Chapters Section:** This section describes the first three Gateways as together forming the *guaranteed method for advancing in truth*. It builds the key message of the book by tying together the main points of the first three Gateways to express the importance of balancing inspirational fervor against Mitzvah performance. In the context of this key message, it also introduces the subject matter of the Fourth Gateway.
- **Fourth Gateway:** Builds on subject matter from all previous sections to publicize the importance of not focusing on inspirational fervor at the expense of Torah study.

These sections must not be viewed as standalone and self-contained in any way. There is a very definite cumulative build-up of ideas which progress sequentially through both the individual chapters and also across the sections of the book. The intended messages simply cannot be properly appreciated by either partial or non-sequential study.[49]

Throughout all the sections of the Nefesh HaChaim, R. Chaim added

---

49. As mentioned earlier, it has become commonplace in current times for Yeshivot to focus on teaching either just the contents of the Fourth Gateway, or in some cases, both the Second and Fourth Gateways. This is an unfortunate practice which misleads students into thinking that they may have formed some sort of understanding of this work and as a result they will not have the impetus to study the rest of the book and to truly absorb its important messages. Furthermore, the currently commonplace uninformed perspective with which the Fourth Gateway is related to, sees it as less Kabbalistically challenging compared with the rest of the work and therefore easier to focus on. Ironically, this is not true, as a central theme in the Fourth Gateway starting from G4:10 and continuing throughout the rest of the remaining chapters touches on Kabbalistic ideas which are arguably the most esoteric in the work.

fifty-two formal notes which have been translated in full. Although they do not form part of the main flow of the subject matter presented, they do provide important complementary insights which are necessary to understand the book and should be studied together with each related chapter.

The importance and relevance of these formal notes is highlighted by R. Chaim who, in places, directly refers the reader to these notes from the main body of his text.[50] They should therefore not be dismissed as being less relevant than the main body of the text and care should be taken in their study.

R. Chaim was the author of all the notes in Nefesh HaChaim except for the very first note on G1:01 which was authored by his son, R. Yitzchak. This first note is exceptionally long and is known as Maamar BeTzeLeM. It is accompanied by eight formal sub-notes. In the layout of the original print editions, it was integrated within the main body of the text just like R. Chaim's notes.[51] In more recent printings, however, this note was placed in

---

50. These direct references are as follows:
    - G1:12: There is a reference to a concept "as explained above" which only appears in G1:06:No8, which deals with the impression on one's source in the Supernal Realms of the thought of doing a Mitzvah.
    - G2:09: There is a reference to a Zohar in Vayechi "mentioned above" which refers to R. Chaim's note earlier in this chapter, G2:09:N29.
    - G2:14: It says "As per Zohar in Vayakhel which is mentioned in the note" referring to R. Chaim's first note of this chapter, G2:14:N33.
    - G2:16: It says in brackets "that is together with the letter tags as written in the note" referring to the first note of this chapter, G2:16:N36.
51. The authorship of Maamar BeTzeLeM (the BeTzeLeM discourse) is attributed to R. Yitzchak in a small note that was tucked away at the very end of the First Gateway in both the first (5584/1824) and second (5597/1837) print editions of Nefesh HaChaim which were both brought to print by R. Yitzchak. Curiously, no mention is made of this until then and one would have thought that R. Yitzchak would have at least alerted the reader to this by a comment in his Introduction at the beginning of the book.

    In addition, the presentation of Maamar BeTzeLeM in the initial print layout is indistinguishable from any of R. Chaim's notes, so a reader who begins at the beginning would not be aware of this at that point and would inevitably start working through Maamar BeTzeLeM as if it were authored by R. Chaim, as its location as the first note in the book coupled with its sheer length gives it great prominence.

    The question is why R. Yitzchak chose to present Maamar BeTzeLeM in this way especially as R. Chaim, after acknowledging the fundamental nature of this concept, chooses not to divert the reader's attention to the digression of its details.

    This question is strengthened by the fact that it is a pre-requisite to review

an appendix which makes it much easier to follow the main body of the text. A complete translation of this note together with all of its additional formal sub-notes has also been included here in Volume 2.

R. Chaim did not write a formal introduction to his work[52] but his son R. Yitzchak provides a posthumous introduction which mainly focuses on glowingly describing the measure of his father's qualities and deeds. It also describes the prioritized importance with which R. Chaim considered his book over and above any of his other writings[53] and the urgency with which it needed to be published. A complete translation of this introduction has been included before the commencement of the First Gateway.

---

the flow of concepts which R. Chaim presents in his book in order to understand the complex Kabbalistic ideas presented in Maamar BeTzeLeM. It is also further compounded by the comment that R. Yitzchak makes himself towards the beginning of his introduction that "the talk of my lips brings only loss." So why would R. Yitzchak highlight the presentation of Maamar BeTzeLeM in this way?

This is an open question.

It could be suggested that the key to this is found at the end of Maamar BeTzeLeM. R. Yitzchak builds up an elaborate deeply Kabbalistic presentation of the fundamental nature of the TzeLeM concept and why we should be motivated to perform Mitzvot and study Torah, but at the end of it all he highlights that "we are unable to understand the true root of the rectifications of the worlds" but that we should just appreciate that there is awesome impact of Mitzvah performance and Torah study – so this further supports R. Chaim's main thesis that one should never divert oneself from physical Mitzvah performance and Torah study in the pursuit of deeper mystical understanding and greater inspirational fervor. In the absence of any knowledge of a specific reason, one can speculate that perhaps R. Yitzchak felt it was necessary to emphasize this point, front and center, in the context of a deeply elaborate Kabbalistic discourse aimed at individuals who, at the time, would have needed this deeper context to absorb this very important point.

52. See comments related to the Chapters Section later on in the structure description.

53. R. Chaim only formally wrote one book, Nefesh HaChaim. His other writings were collections of Responsa many of which were destroyed by fire as described towards the end of R. Yitzchak's introduction. The book Ruach Chaim was not written by him and was posthumously compiled from notes recorded from R. Chaim's lectures by his students. It was only published after R. Yitzchak's passing. Refer to comments made by R. Yitzchak in his introduction to Nefesh HaChaim of his intention to compile Ruach Chaim. Also refer to V2:15, "Related Extracts from Ruach Chaim."

The First Gateway

This section builds up an architectural overview of the inner structure of a Jew's Spiritual Soul and how it interacts with the Universe.

The understanding of both the Soul's structure and the impact of its interaction provides a person with a powerful motivational framework for relating to himself and to God, together with practical tools for self-improvement.

It enables a person to deeply appreciate the impact and significance of his actions, speech, and thoughts providing a guide as to how to utilize these abilities to maximize performance of Torah study and Mitzvot and thereby optimize service of God.

While presenting this architectural overview and motivational framework, which in and of itself is highly significant, this presentation builds up to express the concluding key point, as set out in the last two chapters of this section.

This concluding key point is simply that:
- *Action* is the essential part of all Mitzvot.
- Purity of thought complements the *act* of a Mitzvah, but lack of such thought does not invalidate the Mitzvah.
- There is *no latitude whatsoever* to use the pursuit of and desire to perfect one's purity of thought as an excuse to deviate in even so much as the minutest detail of performance of any Mitzvah.
  - Even in relation to associated rabbinic statements or in respect of a Mitzvah's required time constraints.

This key point is reiterated and emphasized three times in the Chapters Section[54] where R. Chaim constructs and summarizes the primary argument of Nefesh HaChaim.

The Second Gateway

This section describes the objectives of prayer together with a methodology of how to achieve them.

It is succinctly summarized by R. Chaim in the Chapters Section as follows:[55]

- The purpose of prayer is to correct the worlds and elevate their inner essence by interconnecting one's soul components, one's Nefesh with one's Ruach and Neshama.
- The worlds are connected through the physical movement of one's

---

54. GC:02, GC:05, and GC:07.
55. GC:05.

lips during prayer, i.e., the action of speech, which is the level of Nefesh. The speech itself is the level of Ruach and the concentration of the heart while uttering the words is the level the Neshama.

This section charts out a framework consisting of two levels of prayer, one of the heart and the other of the soul, and predominantly focuses on describing what is and how to achieve the level of prayer of the soul in general and of utilizing the components of the soul for prayer, in particular.

To do this, this section builds on concepts already presented in the First Gateway including:
- The interconnectivity of soul levels.
- The Shiur Komah – the structure of man which parallel's God's Structure.
- Concepts of acceptance and repentance.

R. Chaim uses the understanding of proper prayer to highlight what constitutes inappropriate prayer as part of the construction of Nefesh HaChaim's primary argument in the Chapters Section.

Please note that R. Yosef Zundel of Salant compiled a brief extract of the ideas of this Gateway which is to be found in Volume 2.

The Third Gateway

This section is a continuation of the Second Gateway in that it provides details of a key meditation with which to focus our thoughts when engaging the prayer methodology presented in the Second Gateway.

The objective of this section is to provide a key intellectual motivational tool to help us to:
- Primarily – achieve greater heights of service of the heart and service of the soul *during prayer*
- Secondly – further motivate our:
  - Focus on Torah study
  - Avoidance of sin

It presents the concept of Makom which incorporates the meditations relevant for the prayer service in general and its key components in particular – including the Shema and Kedushah prayers.

It should be noted that with all the emphasis that R. Chaim gives to the concept of Makom and notwithstanding the fact that he devotes an entire Gateway to the subject, he still strongly emphasizes in the Chapters Section that:[56]
- This intellectual tool of Makom will enhance Mitzvah performance (e.g., of prayer) but is not a requirement of it.

---

56. GC:06.

- Not even any minute detail of Mitzvah performance should, God forbid, be omitted as a result of wanting to achieve intellectual heights using this tool – a key example being the possible delaying of performing the Mitzvah at its proper time to enable one to perfect one's thoughts in the interim.

Please refer to the Volume 2 section, "The Limit of Understanding – The Deeper Meaning of Makom," for background analysis which, it is hoped, will be found useful to help understand the concept presented in this section.

This concept of *Makom* is based on the Arizal's notion of Tzimtzum which R. Chaim explains in his own unique way in this section. An analysis of R. Chaim's perspective of Tzimtzum leads us to a precise understanding of exactly why he adopts the position that he does in relation to inspirational fervor, prayer, Torah study, and Mitzvah performance. This concept of Tzimtzum was subject to much historical confusion and misunderstanding and an in-depth highly detailed and comprehensive explanation of the concept of Tzimtzum is provided in Volume 2. This explanation very significantly and unequivocally demonstrates that R. Chaim, the Baal HaTanya,[57] and R. Chaim's master, the Vilna Gaon all totally agreed on the underlying principles relating to the concept of Tzimtzum. Engagement in the details of the concept of Tzimtzum allows for a significantly deeper understanding of R. Chaim's approach in Nefesh HaChaim which is not directly visible when simply reading the text. The section on Tzimtzum is supported by the extensive translation of many relevant source texts.

The Chapters Section

These chapters between the Third and Fourth Gateways bring together the key lessons from the first three Gateways. They apply these lessons to practical action to highlight the pitfalls of practices which were prevalent in R. Chaim's times. The message is still extremely relevant today!

They also introduce the subject matter of the Fourth Gateway.

As mentioned, R. Chaim did not provide an introduction to his work[58] and it is almost as if these chapters would have formed this introduction – except that an initial deep understanding of the issues as presented in

---

57. Rabbi Shneor Zalman of Liadi, the first Rebbe of Lubavitch. He was considered by many to be a key protagonist with whom R. Chaim is contending in presenting the ideas of Nefesh HaChaim.
58. The introduction was written posthumously by R. Chaim's son, R. Yitzchak, and it does not deal with the subject matter of the book in any detail.

the first three Gateways is required to precede these eight chapters and to enable them to effectively convey their message.

The key concluding messages of each of the three preceding Gateways[59] together with the main points presented in the subsequent Fourth Gateway[60] are therefore directly referenced in the course of these chapters as R. Chaim builds up his key messages, which in many ways should be viewed as the key messages of this book.[61]

---

59. With explicit mention within GC:05 and GC:06.
60. Explicitly referred to in GC:02.
61. It should be noted that there is a difference between the First Edition and the Second Edition in the presentation of the page numbering. The page numbering in the First Edition restarted with each section whereas in the Second Edition global page numbering was introduced in addition to the individual section page numbering. The book is referred to as "Kuntresim"/pamphlets on the Title Page and also in R. Yitzchak's introduction, which suggests that the book may have originally, in its first printing, been printed as separate sections and only later bound together in book form.

    This would explain some anomalies relating to the appearance of the Chapters Section in the First Edition. It appears that while many of the copies of the First Edition have the Chapters Section in their correct place between the Third and Fourth Gateways, there are some copies which either don't have it included or do have it included but in a different location (e.g., there is a digitized copy of the First Edition held at the Israel National Library, available for all to download from the Internet, which has the Chapters Section included between the First and Second Gateways). The omission or accidental misplacement in the binding of the Chapters Section in the First Edition would easily have been overlooked by any reader due to the lack of global page numbering which was only introduced in the Second Edition.

    This would explain why a number of academic historians erroneously refer to the Chapters Section as having been completely omitted in the First Edition and having only been introduced by R. Yitzchak in the Second Edition. This error has unfortunately been used as a basis for some to form elaborate and clearly incorrect theories as to the nature and relative importance of the ideas presented in the Chapters Section compared with the other sections. The possible occasional omission of the Chapters Section has also fuelled stories that due to it containing some of the most historically contentious points of the book it was removed on binding by those who disagreed with it.

    The only difference in the presentation of the Chapters Section between the First and Second Editions (excluding corrections of minor printing errors) is the omission of the two words "apostates" and "informers" in GC:03 from the Second Edition, most likely as a result of censorship. (This is not the only change between the First and Second Editions that appears to result from censorship. E.g., the word "nations" that appears in G1:02:No2 in the First Edition was changed to "idol worshippers" in the Second Edition.)

The key messages presented are that:
- The essence of a Mitzvah is to perform it at its correct time together with all its fine points of detail.
- Inspirational fervor should always only be applied to Mitzvah performance and never be independent of it.
- However, if inspirational fervor has not been applied to Mitzvah performance, then even if the Mitzvah has not been performed in its optimal way, it is still valid.
- There is no basis whatsoever for anyone to look down on this performance without inspirational fervor and consider it invalid in any way – either in terms of his own or of anyone else's Mitzvah performance.

As mentioned above, R. Chaim emphasizes the need to present this message in the light of his own personal observations and investigations which he describes in this section.

The early parts of Chapters Section also introduce and summarize ideas dealt with at length in the Fourth Gateway by:
- Introducing the conceptual insight of studying Torah *for its sake* which is an idea that R. Chaim extracts from comments made by the Rosh and forms the backbone of his approach to Torah study.[62]
- Emphasizing the importance of Torah study which is not *for its sake* over and above Mitzvah performance with full inspirational fervor.[63]
- Highlighting the importance of encouraging any form of Torah

---

The placement of the Chapters Section between the Third and Fourth Gateways is unquestionably correct as, apart from its placement there by R. Yitzchak in the Second Edition with global page numbering, it is definitely the most logical location in terms of the way in which it brings together the ideas from the first three Gateways in building up its argument.

Irrespective of any historic conjecture, it is beyond any doubt that the Chapters Section is an integral part of the book on an equal footing to the Gateways as can be seen from the ideas presented by R. Chaim in his introduction to the Vilna Gaon's commentary on the Shulchan Aruch. A complete translation of this introduction has been provided in V2:06 and the reader is referred to the introductory remarks to it which highlight the point being made here.

62. As per GC:02 where R. Chaim references the concept from the Rosh which he will develop in G4:03.
63. See end of GC:02. This idea is revisited in G4:30. Not that Mitzvah performance should in any way be neglected, God forbid, but rather to highlight the sheer magnitude and importance of Torah study.

study – of oneself and of others – even if it is not for its sake and even if for ulterior motives.[64]

The Fourth Gateway

R. Chaim devotes the first chapter of the Fourth Gateway to introduce and provide an overview of its subject matter. A summary of this first chapter is as follows:

- The objective is to detail the magnitude of a person's obligation to study Torah, which is now at a low ebb, as a result of
  - the burden of seeking a livelihood, and
  - those, who in an effort to draw near to God, devote all of their time to the study of ethical works.
- The ethical works were initially written to enthuse those who studied Torah in a sterile manner
  - to reinforce their Torah study
  - but not to replace it.
- In recent times many have taken up the study of ethical works to the extent that Torah study has been replaced or virtually replaced with it
  - and this serious error, causing the sin of diverting time from Torah study, *must be publicized*.
- The comments in this section initially relate to Torah study *for its sake*
  - as many in their effort to achieve this don't study Torah if not accompanied by constant inspirational fervor
  - and consider such study to be of no value.
- Subsequently, an explanation is provided of the virtue of the Torah and those who study it
  - detailing well-known statements from Chazal which will stimulate those seeking inspirational fervor to achieve a love of the Torah.

After having explained, in previous sections, the importance of not allowing the pursuit of inspirational fervor to impact on any part of the details of Mitzvah performance, R. Chaim now focuses on the key potential casualty of such a pursuit, i.e., that one's personal engagement in and general encouragement of Torah study will be adversely impacted by it.

The extent to which R. Chaim goes to in collating sources from Chazal to support the message of this section – after having already briefly presented the message in the Chapters Section – emphasizes just how deep-rooted and widespread he felt this problem was at the time and how easily a person can be lured into the trap of the pursuit of inspirational fervor at the expense of Torah study.

---

64. As per GC:03.

Nefesh HaChaim builds up its presentation cumulatively through its sections. Although some view the Fourth Gateway as a standalone section, in truth, it cannot be properly understood without a deep understanding of the previous Gateways which are directly referred to in many places.[65]

While the Fourth Gateway accentuates the tremendous significance of Torah study over and above prayer, it is important to reconcile – what at first glance may seem to be a contradiction by a statement in the Second Gateway,[66] that prayer is the principal medium for drawing additional sustenance into the world in contrast to Torah study:

- This contrast is expressed and reconciled directly in the Fourth Gateway, i.e.:[67]
  - Prayer provides additional rectification of the world, when enacted at the specific prescribed times – therefore if one misses those times there is no further opportunity to bring down the specific related additional holiness and blessing to the world.
  - Torah study impacts on the very fabric of the world's existence, preventing it from being totally destroyed. Therefore, a person is obligated to continuously engage in it to ensure the world continues to exist.

---

65. For example:
    - G4:03: Reference to G1:22, expressing the importance of physical Mitzvah performance.
    - G4:06 and G4:10: The need to deeply understand concepts of God's Speech as per G3:11. R. Chaim introduces new Kabbalistic material in G4:10 which builds on and requires a deep understanding of the concept of Tzimtzum which is developed throughout the Third Gateway.
    - G4:24: The direct reference to the First Gateway, G1:17, and the concept of Teshuva.
    - G4:27: The direct reference to the Third Gateway – relating to the relative perspective of God and of us, as per G3:04 and then in the presentation of the concepts of Tzimtzum and Kav in G3:07.
    - G4:28: The direct reference to the Second Gateway, G2:17 and the difference between Adam before and after he sinned.
    - G4:29: The direct reference to G1:06 in connection with the concept of Shiur Komah.
    - G4:32: The direct reference to G1:20, relating to the recitation of "Amen, Yehei Shmei Rabba."
66. At the beginning of G2:09.
67. G4:26.

In Conclusion

In the concluding statement of the Fourth Gateway and of the book, R. Chaim highlights that the details of the methodology that he has presented in this book will be adequate for a thinking person to understand the required path to achieve holiness.

He then articulates a clearly Messianic prayer touching on the depths of the concepts he has presented in this book.[68] This prayer is repeated here:

- May it be God's Will
  - 'that He open up our hearts with His Torah and that He should place Love and Fear of Him in our hearts'[69]
  - and thereby complete His intention in creating His Universe
  - 'that the Universe will be rectified with His Sovereignty'[70] and 'each creation [will know its Creator]'[71]
  - 'and All will accept the yoke of His Majesty'[72]
  - according to The Blessed Supernal Will
  - 'and God will be One and His Name will be One.'[73]

---

68. I.e., in that it will only be in the times of the Messiah that the world will truly recognize God's Sovereignty and relate to His Absolute Unity – concepts which are developed and presented within Nefesh HaChaim.
69. From the U'va LeZion prayer.
70. From the Aleynu prayer.
71. From the prayers of Yamim Noraim.
72. From the Aleynu prayer.
73. Zecharia 14:9 and the Aleynu prayer.

נפש החיים

Nefesh HaChaim

The Fear of God *brings* Life

Pamphlets, holy letters of the true prodigy famous for his Torah, righteousness and deeds which are publicized about him • the splendor of the generation and its wonder • pious and humble one • the honorable holy name of his splendor, our teacher Chaim, whose soul is in Eden, the Head of the Bet Din and Head of the Yeshiva of the Holy Community of Volozhin.
Which is named as per his signature in his writings •

Nefesh HaChaim

As per Chazal (Yerushalmi Shekalim 6 [Chapter 2, Halacha 5]): R. Shimon the son of R. Gamliel taught – Nefashot/Memorials are not made for the righteous as their words are their memory and the memory of a righteous person is for a blessing.

[Printed in] Vilna and Grodno

In the year 5584 [1824]

Translation of the Title Page opposite.

Title Page from the copy of the First Edition held
by The National Library of Israel.

The Introduction by Rabbi Yitzchak, Rabbi Chaim's Son

- **Formerly**,[1] it would be that an author of a work would place an introduction at the beginning of his book.
  - Some would customarily inform as to why 'the book came into being.'[2]
  - Some would inform of the objectives of the work.
  - Some would express the humility and Fear of God which preceded [the author's] wisdom [to present their attainment] in words of Torah in a self-demeaning way so as to not be boastful about their composition.
  - **But if** publication has been [posthumously] designated to [the author's] son, it is for the son to honor his father by 'expressing the tremendous deeds of his father the author, and to publicize praise'[3] of the work 'according to his ability to praise.'[4]
- **As for me**, where should I begin? I am but immature and do not know anything 'that my words should be inscribed in a book.'[5]
  - Even though it isn't within me to focus on where to start
  - if it would be to publicize praise for the words which are said in '**The Fear of God Brings Life**'[6] and their objective
  - surely, 'the talk of my lips brings only loss'[7] (Note 1)[8] [when describing] something that 'with their own eyes they will see'[9]
  - [and even without my added description,] it will be 'spoken between those who fear God'[10] who 'desire closeness to God'[11]

---

1   In the early print editions, R. Yitzchak's introduction was broken down into paragraphs whose initial words are bolded. In addition, some key words are also bolded. The paragraph structure and bolded words of the early print editions have been replicated here.
2   Tehillim 40:8.
3   An interwoven expression borrowed from Tehillim 106:2.
4   Mishlei 27:21.
5   Iyov 19:23.
6   From the Title Page, this is the primary title of the book which is taken from Mishlei 19:23 and plays on the name of R. Chaim. It associates the book with being one which leads a person to attain Fear of God. This title is referred to three times in R. Yitzchak's introduction and twice in R. Shaul Katzenellenbogen's approbation. The original printings of the book additionally included a brief introduction by R. Yitzchak's younger brother, R. Yosef, which simply endorses his elder brother's introduction and also only refers to the book by this primary title.

הקדמת ר' יצחק בן הגר"ח מוואלוזין

- מלפנים זאת. שכל מחבר חבוה. מקדים הקדמה בראש ספרו.
  - מהם נהגו להודיע מה ראו כל ככה לבוא במגילת ספר.
  - מהם מודיעים תכלית כוונת תועלת החבור.
  - מהם עקבותיהם עקב ענוה ויראת ה' הקודמת לחכמתם. להשפיל עצמו על ד"ת לבל יתרברב במחברתו.
  - ואם לבנו ייעדנה לקבעו בדפוס. הנה בן יכבד אב למלל גבורת אביו המחבר ולהשמיע תהלת החבוה. איש איש לפי מהללו:
- ואנכי במה אקדם. נער אנכי לא ידעתי דבר שיוחקו מלי בספה.
  - ואף כי לא בי הוא לכוין לב במה אחל.
  - אם כה אומר להשמיע תהלות דברים שנאמרו ביראת ה' לחיים ותכליתם.
  - הלא דבר שפתים אך למחסור (הגהה א') בדבר אשר עין בעין יראו.
  - ויהיו נדברים בין יראי ה' אשר קרבת אלהים יחפצון.

The subtitle "Nefesh HaChaim" is the primary name by which the book is known and as mentioned later on in the Introduction (and also on the Title Page) was the expression with which R. Chaim would provide his signature in his writings and letters. The three introductions of R. Chaim to the Vilna Gaon's works which are translated in Volume 2 (V2:06–08) were all signed off as being from "Nefesh HaChaim."

It is of interest to note that R. Chaim specifically chose to sign with reference to his Nefesh and not to the more refined parts of the soul, e.g., to Ruach or Neshama. R. Chaim explains in G2:16, that it is specifically written words that relate to the level of Nefesh. It therefore follows that R. Chaim would sign off his written letters by referring to his Nefesh and that his written words of Torah in this book should also be labeled this way.

7 Mishlei 14:23.
8 **R. Yitzchak adds Note 1 here.** This note is brought at the end of this Introduction and is entitled "Only if a lack is visually apparent does *talk of the lips* make good."
9 Yishayahu 52:8, i.e., that one can read for oneself.
10 An expression derived from Malachi 3:16.
11 An expression borrowed from Yishayahu 58:2 which is particularly relevant as it is used by R. Chaim in G4:01 to describe those people who focus a

- and 'all who read his book who read it in truth'[12] will say of him [the author] 'Blessed is He who has imparted His wisdom to those who Fear Him.'[13]
- **If** I [were] to state praise which is fitting to honor my prodigious, saintly, and renowned father whose soul is in Eden
  - I am naked from being able to acquire understanding to assess his ways in Torah and piety
  - and it is not with me to recognize it or make it recognizable to others.
  - The elder Sages, and prodigious leading Rabbis of our city, may their light illuminate
  - who know the power of his deeds in the revealed and hidden [parts of Torah]
  - it is appropriate for them to tell of his name and memory – for it is great – they will all write about his book.
  - **Then surely** the 'righteousness of his ways which fill the earth'[14] and of his actions will publicize him.
- **'Is there any** human who has not heard'[15] 'the sound of the whistle'[16] of praise of what he did in the world
  - the 'strength and power which was given to him'[17] 'in learning the true Torah and the good deeds and truth which he performed'[18]
  - 'established him with great authority'[19] 'to discuss as he wishes about the hosts of the God of the Heavens.'[20]
- **He** is the man who established the yoke of Torah in his time and city with the Torah of kindness
  - and he 'opened his mouth with wisdom'[21] to hundreds of students.
  - He merited in raising the profile of Torah, to teach it and to explain it.
  - 'He listened, investigated, and arranged'[22] and built his large house of study 'which stands on the three pillars of **Torah, Service and Kind Deeds.**'[23]
- **It** is not surprising that he merited and caused many to merit
  - for from his youth he bore the yoke of Torah with amazing diligence.
  - When he was [just] over fourteen years old he had fixed study sessions with his older brother, the prodigy, our teacher **Simcha, of blessed memory**, and they would study day and night.

---

disproportionate amount of their time studying ethical works at the cost of their Torah study and is a key target group to whom R. Chaim's book is aimed. Also used in GC:08 and in R. Chaim's introduction to the Vilna Gaon's commentary on Sifra DeTzniyuta (see V2:08).

12 A play on Tehillim 145:18.
13 This is the blessing recited on seeing Sages of Israel as per Berachot 58a.

- וכל קוראי ספרו אשר יקראוהו באמת. לעומתו יאמרו ברוך שחלק מחכמתו ליראיו:

• ואם אתן אומר בשבח הראוי לכבוד מר אבא הגאון צדיק המפורסם נ"ע.
  ◦ עירום אנכי מלהבין בין להעריך דרכי תורתו וצדקתו.
  ◦ ולא עמדי הוא להכיר ולהכירנו לאחרים.
  ◦ זקני ת"ח וגאוני גדולי רבני מדינתינו נ"י.
  ◦ שלהם נודע כח מעשיו בנגלה ובנסתה.
  ◦ להם נאה לספר שמו וזכרו. כי רב הוא. ועל ספרו כלם יכתבו.
  ◦ והאומנם צדק דרכיו ארץ מלאה. ומעשיו הכריזוהו:

• ומי כל בשר אשר לא שמע קל משרוקיתא. שבחא דעבד בארעא.
  ◦ וחסנא ותוקפא איתיהיבת ליה באורייתא קשוט ועובדין טבון וקשוט דעבד.
  ◦ התקנת ברבו יתירא להחויא כמצביי' בחילא דאלהא דשמיא:

• הוא הגבר שהקים עולה של תורה בזמנו במדינתא בתורת חסד.
  ◦ ופיהו פתח בחכמה למאות תלמידים.
  ◦ וזכה להגדיל תורה. לאגמורי. ולמסבר.
  ◦ אזן וחקר ותקן. ובנה לו בית תלמוד גדול עומד על שלשה עמודים. תורה ועבודה וגמילות חסדים:

• ולא נפלאת היא שזכה וזיכה את הרבים.
  ◦ כי מנעוריו נשא עולה של תורה בשקידה נפלאה.
  ◦ ובהיותו למעלה מבר ארביסר. קבע למודו עם אחיו הגדול הגאון מהו' שמחה ז"ל. והוו גרסי יממא ולילי.

---

14   A play on Tehillim 48:11.
15   An expression derived from Devarim 5:23.
16   Daniel 3:5.
17   Daniel 2:37.
18   Zohar II Vayakhel 206a – a section commonly known as Brich Shmei and recited by many just before public Torah readings.
19   Daniel 4:33.
20   Daniel 4:32, i.e., about the hidden parts of Torah.
21   Mishlei 31:26.
22   Kohelet 12:9.
23   Mishna Avot 1:2.

- ○ Our elders told us that when they could not find any candlelight that the moonlight was good for them to study by at night.
- ○ They then received the 'Path of Torah'[24] from the Rabbi of Rabbis, prodigy of prodigies, 'lion/Aryeh of the supernal house [of study],'[25] **Aryeh Leib**, whose soul is in Eden, the author of the Shaagat Aryeh. (Note 2).[26]
- **When** he was already twenty-five years old he had completed [study] of the entire Talmud, Rishonim, and Acharonim
  - ○ and he would study Torah with his brother, the prodigy and Tzaddik, who was comparable to a heavenly being, our teacher, **Rabbi Shlomo Zalman**, whose soul is in Eden, (Note 3)[27] 'and how good and pleasant it was for brothers to sit together'[28] in Torah and service.
  - ○ Both of them learned Torah together from the Rabbi who was similar to an angel of the Lord of Hosts, 'a holy angel from heaven,'[29] our teacher, the great one, the Rabbi of all the Diaspora, the prodigy, our master and teacher **Eliyahu** The Chasid, of saintly, holy and blessed memory, from the Holy Community of Vilna
  - ○ and he, of blessed memory, 'disseminated from his spirit upon them,'[30] 'the spirit of wisdom, etc.'[31]
  - ○ Happy is the eye which saw all this: those who looked, saw, and were happy, and those who heard, the sound of the ear generated a yearning of the soul.
- **More** than his learning was the greatness of his service with which he attended to his mentor, The Chasid, whose soul is in Eden.
  - ○ In the many days in which he stood before him, he lit[32] up for him pathways in the revealed Torah and amazing byways[33] in the hidden [parts of Torah]
  - ○ he is the very person 'who saw his teacher from the front' (Note 4)[34] who elucidated for him Talmudic tracts and the enlightenment of wisdom.

---

24 Mishna Avot 6:4.
25 Chullin 59b.
26 **R. Yitzchak adds Note 2 here.** This note is brought at the end of this Introduction and is entitled "Detail of interaction between Shaagat Aryeh and R. Chaim."
27 **R. Yitzchak adds Note 3 here.** This note is brought at the end of this Introduction and is entitled "Biographical reference for R. Shlomo Zalman, dates of birth and passing."
28 Tehillim 133:1.
29 Daniel 4:10.
30 Bamidbar 11:25.

- וזקנינו ספרו לנו. שכאשר לא הוה להון אור הנר מצוי. אור הלבנה הוה יפה להון לגירסא דלילא.
- וקבלו אז דרכה של תורה מרב רבנן גאון הגאונים ארי' דבי עלאה רבנא **אריה ליב** נ"ע. בעל שאגת אריה (הגהה ב'):

• וכד היה כבר עשרים וחמש. הוה גמיר בכלא תלמודא. ופוסקים ראשונים ואחרונים.

- והיה לומד תורה עם אחיו הגאון וצדיק דמי לבר אלהין מוה' **שלמה זלמן** נ"ע (הגהה ג') ומה טוב ונעים היה שבת אחים גם יחד בתורה ועבודה.
- ושניהם כאחד למדו תורה מהרב הדומה למלאך ה' צבאות עיר וקדיש מן שמיא רבינו הגדול רשכבה"ג הגאון מרנא ורבנא אליהו החסיד זצוק"ל מק"ק ווילנא.
- והוא ז"ל האציל מרוחו עליהם. רוח חכמה וכו'.
- אשרי עין ראתה כל אלה. הרואים ראו ושמחו. והשומעים למשמע אזן תאבה נפש:

• ויותר מלמודו היה גדול שמושו ששמש את רבו החסיד נ"ע.

- ובימים הרבים שעמד לפניו. אנהיר ליה שבילי דאורייתא בנגלה ונתיבות פליאות בנסתר
- הוא הוא דחזא רבי' מקמי' (הגהה ד') וגליה ליה מסכתא ונהירו דחכמתא.

---

31 Yishayahu 11:2.
32 This phrase of "enlightenment/Anhir" is taken from Eruvin 13b which talks of R. Nehorai whose name has the meaning that he enlightened the eyes of the Sages in Halacha. R. Yitzchak quotes directly from the continuation of this section of the Talmud in relation to R. Meir (who according to some was the same person as R. Nehorai) later on in this sentence and adds Note 4 with an insight on it.
33 This sentence touches on the verse from Yirmiyahu 18:15 where the word for "pathway/Shevil" uniquely appears together with the word for "byways/Netivot."
34 **R. Yitzchak adds Note 4 here.** This note is brought at the end of this Introduction and is entitled "Student grasps inner level of teacher's thought by seeing his face."

- Just as in the days in which he studied before him in awe, fear, trembling and shaking 'from the river of fire which was flowing before him'[35]
- similarly, when he was teaching and informing his sons and students of the days in which he stood before him, the awe of his teacher came over him with a wonderful respect as if he stood before him in Heaven.
- When he would talk in learning and mention the name of his teacher, his whole body would tremble and his 'appearance changed'[36] from the fire erupting in his heart when thinking of his ways of righteousness, piety, and purity of holiness
- and he acquired the light of his Torah in that he was well-enabled in the qualities through which the Torah is acquired,[37] and with the 'Mantle of **Eliyahu**'[38] he was clothed with humility and fear.

- **Great** was the humility of my honorable father, the prodigy, whose soul is in Eden, and it was manifest in all his ways and paths.
  - I will relate 'just the tip of his ways'[39] of the path of humility.
  - To [descend to] be with the despondent or to raise the despondent to be with him[40]
  - both of these, 'every precious eye would see in him'[41]
  - as throughout his life until his old age, he gave his soul to enliven lowly spirits with his wealth and his righteous distributions, and to being with the depressed
  - and when the 'poor among the people'[42] would come to him, they would revel and rejoice that he 'drew them near with his right hand'[43] to delight their hearts by reconciling things and with words of 'charm which poured from his lips.'[44]
- **Additional** [detail] from the path of true humility
  - that all aspects of the physical body were truly despised and loathed in his eyes to the extent that he would consider them to be null and void and would have no sensitivity towards [physical] *delight or affliction*[45]

---

35 Daniel 7:10.
36 Daniel 5:6.
37 As per Mishna Avot 6:5.
38 An expression from 2 Melachim 2:13 used here to refer to Eliyahu the Vilna Gaon.
39 Iyov 26:14.
40 Sotah 5a – this section of the Talmud interprets the verse "[I am] with the despondent and lowly of spirit" (Yishayahu 57:15) in two ways relating to the Shechina: 1. That the Shechina descends to be with the despondent one or 2. That the Shechina raises the despondent one up to It.
41 Iyov 28:10.

- ובימים אשר למד לפניו באימה וביראה ברתת וביע. מן נהר דינור דהוה נגיד ונפיק מן קדמוהי.
- כן כאשר לימד והודיע לבניו ותלמידיו הימים אשר עמד לפניו. אימתיה דרביה הוה עליה במורא נפלאה כאלו עומד לפניו במרום.
- וכאשר פתח בשמעתתא ודכיר שמי' דרבי'. הוי מרתע כלא גופיה וזיוהי שנין עלוהי מאש המתלקחת בלבבו בהגיגו דרכי צדקתו וחסידותו וטהרת קדושתו.
- ואור תורתו נקנית לו. באשר היה כחו יפה בהמעלות שהתורה נקנית בהם. ומאדרת אליהו התלבש ענוה ויראה:
- וגדולה ענוה של כבוד מר אבא הגאון נ"ע. ונתלבש בכל דרכי' ונתיבותי'.
  - וקצות דרכיו אספרה באשר מדרך ענוה.
  - להיות את דכא. או לרוממם את דכא אתו (סוטה ה' ע"א).
  - הן שתי אלה ראתה בו עין כל יקר.
  - שמעודו ועד שיבה נתן נפשו להחיות רוח שפלים במאדו וצדקת פזרונו. ולהיות את נדכאים.
  - וגם עדיו כי באו אביוני אדם. ששו ושמחו כי קרבם ימין. והרחיב לבבם בפיוסי דברים. ובדברי חן שהוצק בשפתותיו:
- עוד מדרך הענוה האמיתית.
  - שיהיו כל עניני הגוף נבזה ונמאס בעיניו באמת. עד שלאפם ותהו יחשבו מבלי הרגיש לא ענג ולא נגע.

---

42   Yishayahu 29:19.
43   Sotah 47a.
44   Tehillim 45:3.
45   To not have any feeling of delight or affliction of the physical body is to reach the ultimate level of relating to the physical as absolutely irrelevant. This is the key requirement to be completely self-effacing and of true humility. Sefer Yetzirah Chap. 2 Mishna 4 writes that there is nothing in good higher than *delight/Oneg* and nothing in bad lower than *affliction/Nega*. In Hebrew the words "Oneg" and "Nega" are simply a permutation of each other and are closely linked. The difference between Oneg over Nega can be very subtle and be simply dependent on the perception of a situation where by just changing one's perception a state of Nega can be transformed into one of Oneg. (This is hinted to by the fact that the difference between the two words

- and he would only 'rise up in the ways of God'[46] such that [his] heart should be receptive to Torah, service and holiness, and to only rejoice with God, to set [his] heart to be a fitting residence for God, as per the verse "the humble shall increase their joy in God."[47]
  - This is as per the expressions which are constantly on our lips when we stand in prayer [first] saying: "Let my soul be silent to those who curse me, let my soul be as dust to all," and then [only] after that [saying]: "Open my heart with your Torah and my soul will pursue your Mitzvot."[48]
- Indeed, all those who knew my honorable father, the prodigy, of blessed memory will testify and tell of his great humility
  - where if he was 'insulted he would never take offense'[49]
  - and he was 'humble of spirit before all people.'[50]
- With respect to bodily pleasures, he was 'concerned to not [even benefit] from the vaguest of minor'[51] [pleasures]
  - and he arranged his ways such that he would not be sensitive towards [physical] delight.
  - Even when he reached old age when he was afflicted with 'afflictions of love'[52] – he received them with all his strength and soul with joy and a cheerful face
  - without letting out a sigh, (as per Chazal:[53] "he received afflictions in silence"), and he was of happy disposition all the years that he suffered from afflictions.
- That Tzaddik was only troubled that he was forced to sustain his body as a result of his illness and [as a result] when secluded, his eyes would be weepy ('my eyes have seen it and not a stranger's')[54] – his heart was sickened by this.
- He rejoiced in his afflictions in that they reduced his feelings of [physical] pleasure – to the extent that he did not pay attention to [physical] *delight or affliction.*

• **All** who saw 'the sun in his strength'[55] – 'they saw and were astounded'[56]

Oneg and Nega is the position of the letter *Ayin*. The word "Oneg" starts with *Ayin*, whereas the word "Nega" ends with *Ayin*. *Ayin*, in addition to being a letter, also means "eye" and the movement of the *Ayin* from the beginning to the end of the word denotes a change in visual perspective.) The feelings of Oneg and Nega should be reserved as much as possible for spiritual pursuits, e.g., to be delightfully challenged by attending a Shiur and to not view it as a burdensome affliction. R. Yitzchak highlights this point by emphasizing the lack of R. Chaim's physical feeling of Oneg and Nega twice in this paragraph, once at its beginning and again at the end of it.

46 2 Divrei Hayamim 17:6.

- ורק בדרכי ה' יגבהו. שיהא לבם פתוח לתורה ועבודה וקדושה. ואך בה' ישמחו כי ישיתו לבם מדור נאה לו ית"ש. ככתוב (ישעי' כט.) ויספו ענוים בה' שמחה.

- וכמאמר הרגיל תמיד בפינו בעמדנו בתפלה לאמר ולמקללי נפשי תדום ונפשי כעפר לכל תהיה. ואח"כ פתח לבי בתורתך ואחרי מצותיך תרדוף נפשי.

- הן כל מכירי כבוד מר אבא הגאון ז"ל. המה יעידו ויגידו מעונתנותו הגדולה.
  - אשר אם היה נעלב לא העליב.
  - והיה שפל רוח בפני כל אדם.
- ובתענוגי הגוף אף למעוטא דמעוטא היה חושש.
  - ושם דרכיו לבלי הרגיש תענוג.
- ואף כי הגיעו ימי הזקנה שנתייסר ביסורים של אהבה במאדו ונפשו קבלם בשמחה ובצהלת פנים.
- מבלי הוציא אנחה (כמאמר חז"ל (ברכות סב ע"א) קבלה דיסורי שתיקותא) ודעתיה הוה בדיחא עליה כל שני דקביל עליה יסורים.
- ורק ע"ז היה מצטער אותו צדיק על שהוכרח לכלכל גופו לפי מחלהו. ובמסתרים היו עיניו יורדים טיף טיף. (ועיני ראו לא זר). ועם כי לבו לא היה דוי ע"ז.
- היה שמח ביסוריו הממעטים לו הרגש התענוג. עד שלא שם לבו לא לענג ולא לנגע:

• וכל רואי השמש בגבורתו. המה ראו כן תמהו.

---

47 Yishayahu 29:19.
48 Berachot 17a.
49 Gittin 36b.
50 Mishna Avot 4:10.
51 Phrase borrowed from Yevamot 119b said in connection with R. Meir.
52 A concept from Bereishit Rabba Miketz 92:1 where if one does not abandon Torah study as a result of afflictions, these afflictions are deemed "afflictions of love."
53 Berachot 62a.
54 Iyov 19:27.
55 Shoftim 5:31.
56 Tehillim 48:6.

- that with all the subjugation of his [physical] body and the lowering of his spirit towards worldly matters
- similarly, he would turn his heart towards heavenly matters, 'to clothe himself with strength and glory'[57]
- and 'until the last shovelful [of dirt was placed on his grave],'[58] he set his heart to make a fitting residence for Torah, service, and kind deeds.
- With such strength, he lifted his heart in the ways of God to fight the battle of Torah
- and every Mitzvah which began with the spirit of wisdom and fortitude was completed with a spirit of knowledge and Fear of God.
- Not one of his words returned [in dispute] and he published his good thoughts to the multitudes
- it was all with 'calm'[59] and wise words which 'with gentleness are heard.'[60]

- **The key** part of humility was to not feel his good deeds that he performed and the importance of the accomplishments that he attained
  - and all the while that his actions, accomplishments, and intellect grew, he increased his recognition of the Greatness of God
  - correspondingly, the spirit of God strengthened his feeling of deficiency and silenced the feeling of the potency of his accomplishments
  - and when he saw that he was dear in the eyes of others such that they would honor him, he would [view] his actions 'as contracted and bad'[61] (Note 5)[62] and consider his faults in order to diminish [his view of] himself without haughtiness
  - (as we find with Rav that when he saw the crowds, etc.)[63]

- **Whoever** did not see the behavior of my honorable father the prodigy, of blessed memory, with this, 'would not believe it if told.'[64] All the subterfuge and plotting which he would put into it.
  - He would frequently mention that with all the insights which he would generate, whether in Talmud, Commentaries, Tosafot, or in Responsa
  - he would imagine that his heart would be gladdened by his argumentation, and he would [therefore] suspect himself of having benefited from words of Torah
  - such that in his eyes it would almost be that the insight was not consistent with the truth of Torah.
  - As per Chazal: All who are haughty, his wisdom is removed from him[65]

---

57   Mishlei 31:25.
58   Berachot 8a.
59   Yishayahu 30:15.

○ שעם כל כניעת גופו ונמיכת רוחו למילי דעלמא.

○ כן נהפוך לבבו במילי דשמיא. ללבוש עוז והדר.

○ ועד זיבולא בתרייתא. לבו היתה שומה לעשות מדור נאה לתורה ועבודה וג"ח.

○ ומה מאוד גבה לבו בדרכי ה' ללחום מלחמתה של תורה.

○ וכל מצוה שהחל ברוח חכמה וגבורה. גמרה ברוח דעת ויראת ה'.

○ ודבר אחד מדבריו לא שב. והוציא לאור מחשבתו הטובה לפני רבבות עם.

○ והכל בשובה ודברים מחוכמים אשר בנחת היו נשמעים:

• עיקר הענוה. שלא להרגיש מעשיו הטובים שפעל. וערך מעלותיו שהשיג.

○ וכל אשר יגדלו פעולותיו ומעלותיו ושכלו ירבה להכיר גדולתו ית"ש.

○ כן רוח האלקים תוסיף תת כח הרגש חסרונו. ותדמים הרגש עצמות מעלותיו.

○ וכשרואה שמתיקר בעיני אנשים לכבדו מצטמק ורע עליו המעשה (הגהה ה') ומחשב לו חסרונותיו להקטין עצמו לבלתי רום לבבו.

○ (כמו שמצינו ברב (יומא פז א') כד הוה חזי אמבוה כו'):

• ומי שלא ראה דרכי כבוד אבא הגאון ז"ל בזה. לא יאומן כי יסופר. כל תחבולותיו ועלילותיו אשר שם שם לו בזה.

○ רגיל על לשונו היה. שכל חדושים שמחדש. הן בגפ"ת. או בשו"ת.

○ ושיערה דעתו דחדי לבי' מפלפולי'. הוא חושש לנהנה מד"ת.

○ והיה קרוב בעיניו שהחדוש אולי אינו לאמתה של תורה.

○ ממאמרם ז"ל (ר"פ אלו דברים) כל המתיהר חכמתו מסתלקת הימנו

---

60 Kohelet 9:17, i.e., the gentleness causes the words to be heard and internalized.

61 E.g., as per expression in Shabbat 37b.

62 **R. Yitzchak adds Note 5 here.** This note is brought at the end of this Introduction and is entitled "Be careful not to become haughty from accorded honor."

63 Yoma 87a. When Rav saw the crowds of people following him to accord him honor, he would recite appropriate verses to prevent himself becoming haughty.

64 Chabakuk 1:5.

65 Pesachim 66b.

- (and in a joking way, he would say that he considers this as bribery, that he would bribe himself with the 'joy [of the insight] sufficing for it [to be the limit of its reward]')[66]
- he would toil to contradict himself to repeat over and change his words and to intellectually weigh up how to establish the truth with straight logic and correct consideration
- and an observer would see and understand from the perspective of their own wisdom – how he would view his intellect as diminished and his knowledge as low
- as per Chazal:[67] "Words of Torah are only sustained in the humble."

- **He would** love reproving discipline and all of his words were fire, with 'the flame of God'[68] glowing from his lips with love, and 'flashes of fire'[69] with fear
  - and the hearts of all who heard would melt as 'wax melts'[70]
  - and they would be drawn after his 'graceful words'[71] in the Agadah that he would expound on in his lessons
  - and out of his humility it would never enter his head to rebuke anyone and he would 'honestly rebuke'[72] himself with all his words.
  - He would be like one who comes to 'teach [a subject] but [he himself would] transpire to be the teaching'[73] (Note 6)[74] with most of his admonitions relating to the reduction of haughtiness.

- **Notwithstanding** [the fact] that most of the content of his sermons[75] involved matters fundamental to the Universe and were based on the Zohar and the writings of the Arizal (as per the understanding of those capable)
  - he, of blessed memory, out of pious humility, clothed them, stripped them down and hid them so as to be unpretentious when expounding hidden concepts
  - to sweeten them as 'honey and milk under his tongue'[76] and as suppressed under his clothes
  - refraining from explicitly teaching them publicly to the masses and to the many who had not yet matured in their Talmud study and [had not yet] refined their deeds with a correct spirit in the Fear of God – so that they would not fail with the vanity of the 'cords of falsehood'[77]

---

66   Berachot 55a.
67   Taanit 7a.
68   Shir Hashirim 8:6.
69   Shir Hashirim 8:6.
70   Tehillim 68:3.
71   Gittin 7a, as per a description of R. Chisda's name.

- (ודרך בדיחותא היה אומר. שזהו נחשב אצלו לשוחה. שמשחד עצמו בחדותא דמסתיי׳).
- והיה מתיגע לסתור דברי עצמו ולחזור לשנות דבריו, ולשקול בפלס שכלו איך להעמיד על האמת בסברה ישרה. ובשקול דעת נכונה.
- והרואה יראה ויבין מחכמתו שנתקיימה לו. איך היה מקטין שכלו בעיניו ודעתו היה שפלה עליו.
- כמאמרם ז״ל (תענית ז׳ א׳) אין ד״ת מתקיימין אלא במי שדעתו שפלה עליו:
• היה אוהב תכחת מוסר. וכל דבריו היו כאש. והוה להיט מפומיה שלהבת י״ק באהבה. ורשפי אש בוראה.
- וכל אזן שמעה היה נמס לבבו כהמם דונג.
- ונמשך אחרי מיליו דחסדאין באגדתא דהוה דריש בפרקיה.
- ומענותנותי׳ לא מלאו לבו להוכיח לבריתא. והכיח במישור לעצמו בכל דבריו.
- והיה כבא ללמד ונמצא למד (הגהה ו׳) ורובי מוסריו היו להשפיל גבהות הלב:
• ועם כי רובי דבריו בדרשותיו היו עומדים ברומו של עולם. מיוסדים ע״פ זוהר וכתבי האר״י ז״ל (כאשר המבינים הבינו בדברים).
- הוא ז״ל מענות צדקתו. הלבישם והפשיטם וגנם. לבל יגדיל דבריו כדורש בנסתרות.
- להמתיקם כדבש וחלב תחת לשונו. וכבשם תחת לבושו.
- מלדורשן להדיא בהמון. ורבים שלא מלאו כריסם בתלמוד. להטהר ממעשיהם ברוח נכון ביראת ה׳. לבל יכשלו בהבלי חבלי השוא.

---

72 Yishayahu 11:4.
73 A common Talmudic expression, e.g., Pesachim 25b.
74 **R. Yitzchak adds Note 6 here.** This note is brought at the end of this Introduction and is entitled "God arouses a person to learn from reproving discipline."
75 See R. Chaim's Sermon, translated in V2:11.
76 Shir Hashirim 4:11, R. Yitzchak's Note 4 relates to this verse.
77 Yishayahu 5:18.

- and according to the needs of the times he saw fit to reveal various matters from their concealment and he would relate [the following Mishna] to himself: "the key is not the study but the action"[78]
  - (and in any case his intention is understood from the last part of this Mishna that "all who are *Marbeh* words [bring sin]" – [where *Marbeh*] is an expression of "*Rabei*/captains of the king"[79] – 'that he should speak words regarding the Supreme One'[80] to make more of them in the eyes of those listening [and thereby encourage sinful action] – Refer to Midrash Shmuel there).[81]
- **In all** of his ways, he would diminish his personal honor in order to increase the honor of Heaven with public matters and specifically in relation to matters [impacting] the Jewish People.
  - It is known that he endangered himself [by] involving himself far more than he was able to
  - even 'in his old age,'[82] 'his hands were faithful until the sun set'[83]
  - and even when he was no longer able, God should save us, 'his thoughts also came while on his sickbed'[84] 'with his eyes raised Heavenward'[85] to involve God in the troubles of [both] the Jewish People and of individuals
  - with sighing and 'groaning with a shattering of the loins,'[86] with his many groans over this, 'they would break the bodies'[87] of those hearing them.
    - (He would regularly rebuke me when he saw that I did not involve myself with the troubles of others
    - and he would constantly say to me that this is all of what man is,

---

78 Mishna Avot 1:17, i.e., that R. Chaim would restrict the sharing of esoteric material to be relevant to facilitate action and did not reveal everything he could have revealed. This point is highly relevant to the entire presentation of Nefesh HaChaim which reveals concealed matters. R. Chaim's objective in Nefesh HaChaim is precisely to encourage the action of Mitzvah performance and Torah study in their correct manner and a balanced way. He therefore hesitantly reveals deeply esoteric material for this specific purpose to meet the needs of the times, as he highlights at the end of G3:03.

79 Yirmiyahu 41:1, where Rabei is used as an expression of authority and in this context meaning to give authority to words which should not otherwise be spoken were it not for the needs of the times.

80 Daniel 7:25.

81 This is thought to refer to Midrash Shmuel 2:9 which relates to Chana being *Marbeh* in prayer as follows:
    - ... From here, all who are *Marbeh* in prayer are answered ... "and the talk of my lips bring only loss" [Mishlei 14:23, see the quotation of this state-

○ ולפי הוראת השעה שהיו נראה לו להוציא איזה דברים מבלי הצפינם. היה קורא ע"ע לא המדרש עיקר אלא המעשה

□ (וממילא נשמע כוונתו על סיפא דמשנה זו וכל המרבה דברים כו' (לשון רבי המלך) שממלל מלין לצד עלאה להגדילם בעיני השומעים (ועיין מדרש שמואל שם)):

• **בכל דרכיו.** היה ממעט כבוד עצמו להרבות כבוד שמים. הן במילי דצבורא. בפרט בעניני הכלל.

○ מודעת שהשליך נפשו מנגד ועסק הרבה יתר על כדי כחו.

○ ואף כי זקן היה. היו ידיו אמונה עד בא השמש.

○ ואף ככלות כח רח"ל גם על משכבו בחליו רעיוניו סליקו. ועיניו היו נשואות השמימה. לשתף שם שמים בצערא דהכלל והפרט.

○ בגנוחי ואנחות בשברון מתנים. ואנחותיו הרבות בזה היו שוברות כל גוף השומע.

□ (והיה רגיל להוכיח אותי על שראה שאיני משתתף בצערא דאחרינא.

□ וכה היה דברו אלי תמיד שזה כל האדם לא לעצמו נברא. רק להועיל לאחריני בכל אשר ימצא בכחו לעשות).

---

ment towards the beginning of R. Yitzchak's introduction] . . . that Chana, as a result of Rabta/*increasing/aggrandizing* her words of prayer shortened the life of [her son] Shmuel [for whom she was praying] . . .

The underlying idea here is that any time there needs to be a compromise of traditional practice because the times warrant it, as per the guidelines of our Sages following the principle of *Et Laasot* (see p. 488, fn. 61), there is always an undesired repercussion, and therefore, such a compromise should never be taken lightly. R. Chaim therefore greatly weighed the potential benefits of revealing certain esoteric ideas and chose to do so, but only after much deliberation out of concern for the undesired repercussions. It should be noted that once he took this step to make these ideas publicly available, it is not for us to decide that they should not be by omitting any of the esoteric ideas that R. Chaim presents when studying Nefesh HaChaim, as doing so prevents our possible absorption of his very important messages.

82 Bereishit 27:1.
83 Shemot 17:12, i.e., he was faithfully involved until the very end of his life.
84 Daniel 2:29.
85 Yishayahu 51:6.
86 Yechezkel 21:11.
87 This sentence is based on Ketubbot 62a.

that he was not created for himself but just to facilitate others in all that he finds himself able to do.)
- He judged and prescribed [Jewish Law], 'loved peace, pursued peace, loved people and drew them near to Torah.'[88] (Note 7)[89]

- **This was** always his way of teaching in holiness, be it of Torah or of [how to follow in] 'the straight paths of God'[90] which he would teach.
  - He would set aside his personal honor and would choose to teach that which was good for others, 'whether they would be small or great they would listen,'[91] with all of his abundant teachings which he merited and caused the public to merit.
  - He never refrained from saying over something from the weekly Torah portion to his townspeople after morning prayers each day
  - and all who entered into his study hall would exit fully laden, with each individual absorbing [information] in his own way
  - those who loved the textual explanation would absorb the depth of the textual explanation of the Scriptures, and those who would 'expound writings'[92] would 'surely expound'[93] from what they heard from his brief asides during the course of his comments.
  - All listeners rejoiced with his 'sweet speech'[94] which was as 'clearly spoken'[95] as when reading the Torah portion to children.
  - This Mitzvah was so precious in his eyes that he would drop all of his holy activities and run to the house of study while the whole community was still praying, 'with the small and the great being there'[96]
  - and he would fully rejoice from it and he would say that when it comes to completing something that requires in-depth study, not everyone is capable of [reaching] completion – [but] with this Torah all 'fish are equal'[97] in understanding, and it is good for all
  - and 'his heart would revel in this'[98] – 'the humble should learn from his ways.'[99]

- **It is known** 'that his heart saw much wisdom,'[100] that he raised [the profile of] Torah, added [to levels of] service
  - 'and from his many deeds, his wisdom was preserved'[101] even with all [of his] knowledge, to generate Torah insights which are sweeter than honey in Talmud, Commentaries, Tosafot

---

88 Mishna Avot 1:12.
89 **R. Yitzchak adds Note 7 here.** This note is brought at the end of this Introduction and is entitled "God compared to one who gives up comfort to bestow kindness."
90 Hoshea 14:10.
91 Devarim 1:17.

- ודן והורה. אוהב שלום. ורודף שלום. אוהב את הבריות וקרבן לתורה (הגהה ז׳):
- וזה היה דרך למודו בקדש מעודו. הן בתורה. והן בדרכי ה׳ הישרים שהיה מורה.
- הניח כבוד עצמו. ובחר לו ללמד באשר ייטב להם לאחריני. אשר כקטן כגדול ישמעון. בכל רובי תורותיו אשר זכה וזיכה את הרבים.
- לא הניח ידו מלהגיד לבני עירו אחר תפלת השחר פרשה מסדרא דשבוע יום יום
- וכל הנכנסין לביהמ״ד יצאו מלא דבר כאשר כ״א קלט לפי דרכו.
- אוהבי הפשט קלטו עומק פשוטו במקרא. ודורשי הרשומים. דרוש דרשו ממה שלקחה אזנם. מה שנזרקה מפיו מדי דברו בקצרה.
- וכל השומעים שמחו במתק שפתיו אשר ברור מללו כקורא הפרשה לפני תינוקות של בית רבן.
- וכ״כ היתה מצוה זו חביבה בעיניו שהניח כל דבריו בקדש והוה רהיט לבי מדרשא בעוד שכל הצבור מתפללין וקטן וגדול שם הוא
- וחדותא שלימתא הוה חדי מינה. באמרו בלאגמורי דבר הצריך תלמוד. לאו כולי עלמא גמירי. וזאת התורה כל אפין שוין באבנתא. ומטיב לכולם.
- ועליץ לבו בזה. ילמדו ענוים דרכו:
- ומודעת שלבו ראה הרבה חכמה. והגדיל תורה. והוסיף עבודה.
- וממעשיו המרובים. אף חכמתו נתקיימה לו בכל מדע. לחדש חדושי תורה בגפ״ת המתוקים מדבש

---

92 Bava Kama 82a.
93 Vayikra 10:16.
94 Mishlei 16:21.
95 Iyov 33:3.
96 Iyov 3:19.
97 Eicha Rabba Introduction 9.
98 1 Shmuel 2:1.
99 Tehillim 29:9.
100 Kohelet 1:16.
101 Mishna Avot 3:9.

- - (but very few are in writing [only] those recorded by his students, as he was uncomfortable to write his own book of topics unrelated to practical Halacha)
  - and from his youth to old age he frequently [sent] Responsa to the Great Rabbis of our region and the prodigies of our time, with all of them being established as practical Halacha
    - (and through our many sins a large number of stored Responsa were destroyed by fire sent from Above on Wednesday 14 Iyar 5575 [1815] which burned half the city, the Merciful One should save us, and he was one whose house burned down. It was only his Yeshiva which, through God's mercy while being enveloped in the fire which consumed its surroundings and extremities, it remained as 'a firebrand saved from a fire.'[102] The Torah scrolls were also saved. Blessed is He who performed a miracle in this place. However many of [the Responsa] remained with students who had copied them and many of them are scattered throughout the world. God should help to gather them together).
  - Now even though my father, of blessed memory, saw fit to gather them [his Responsa] together, he did not however command me to publish them.
  - It was only about this that he explicitly commanded me on the day of his passing with awesome words that
    - I should invest all of my efforts to support his Yeshiva so that Torah should not depart, God forbid, and
    - also in connection with these pamphlets,[103] he expressed himself to me from the depths of his heart, that I should not change his words from the way in which they were written[104] – this is how he commanded me to publish them with alacrity.
- **'Let's bring** a scroll'[105] and see his humility
  - that he diverted his attention from compiling grandiose works and restricted himself to focus on these pamphlets which are few and of a low level compared to his great ability.
  - For it is known that the *word of God* was with **Eliyahu** the Chasid, whose soul is in Eden, and the 'Hidden Recesses of Wisdom'[106] were revealed to him

---

102 Zecharia 3:2.
103 I.e., Nefesh HaChaim – also referred to as "Kuntresim"/pamphlets on the Title Page.
104 It should be noted that even though R. Yitzchak received this direct command from his father not to change anything, there were two small changes that

- (והנם בכתובים פסקי פסקי מה שכתבו תלמידיו. כי לא הוה ניחא ליה לכתוב על ספר בעצמו כל דבר שאינו הלכה למעשה)
- והרבה להשיב מנעוריו ועד שיבה לכל גדולי רבני מדינתינו וגאוני זמנינו. וכולם נקבעו הלכה למעשה.
- (ועם כי בעו"ה המון גנזי שו"ת שגנזם. נשרפו בעו"ה באש ששולח ממרום יום ד' י"ד אייר בשנת תקע"ה. ונשרפה ר"ל כחצי העיר וגם הוא היה מהם שהיו בתיו לאכול אש. ורק על בית אולפנא דידי'. רחמי ה' מתלקחת בתוך האש שאכלה סביביו וקצותיו והוא נשאר כאוד מוצל מאש. וגם הספרים נצולו. ברוך שעשה נם במקום הזה. אמנם הרבה מהם נשארו ביד התלמידים שהעתיקו להם. והרבה מבדרן בעלמא. ה' יהא עוזר לאספם ולחברם יחד).
- ועם כי חזינא לדעתיה דמר אבא ז"ל דיהיב דעתיה עליהון לקבצם יחד. אמנם על כולם לא נצטויתי מאתו להדפיסם.
- רק על דא נצטויתי מפורש יוצא מפיו יום העלותו השמימה בנוראות דברים.
- להתחזק בכל כחי לחזק בית אולפנא דידיה שלא תמוש תורה ח"ו.
- וגם על הקונטרסים הללו נתן קולו עלי מקירות לבבו. שלא אשנה מדבריו כאשר המה כתובים. ככה צוויתי להדפיסם בזרוז:

• וניתי ספר ונחזי ענותנותי'.
- שהניח דעתו מחבורים גדולים. והמעיט עצמו למיהב דעתי' על הקונטרסים הללו המעטים ונמוכים לפי ערכו הגבוה.
- כי מודעת שדבר ה' היתה אל אליהו חסידא נ"ע. ונגלו לו תעלומות חכמה.

---

he made to the main body of his father's text between the First and Second Editions (apart from typographical error corrections and minor censorship changes). These changes were most likely influenced by the polemics between the Chassidim and Mitnagdim at the time. These changes were in G4:01 and G4:02 and are highlighted on p. 632, fn. 21 and p. 636, fn. 36.

105 This is an expression meaning "Let's check the facts," sourced in Yalkut Shimoni Shemini Remez 545 where a factual issue is raised and the suggestion is made to bring a Torah scroll and check it.

106 Iyov 11:6.

- with the 'issuing light'[107] of his words already having been published and another tenfold measure still in unpublished manuscripts, as my father, the prodigy, whose soul is in Eden, details at length in his introduction to Sifra DeTzniyuta.[108]
- (I heard from my father, the prodigy, of blessed memory, that all of the unpublished writings of the master Eliyahu, of blessed memory, were written before he reached the age of forty, as from that time he received an additional dimension of understanding[109] such that he had insufficient time to allow him to record all that which was revealed to him.)

○ My father, of blessed memory, absorbed fine flour from all of the 'treasury'[110] of his master, of blessed memory, [which enabled him] to understand the depths of the ways of the Etz Chaim of the Arizal from his own knowledge of the chapter headings, and these [concepts] were 'inscribed on the notice board of his heart.'[111]

○ Out of his 'humility he bowingly entered'[112] a tiny fraction of this into these pamphlets
- and made an opening like [a hole the size of the eye of a] sewing needle – for one whose heart is open wide – [to be] like the size an entrance way to a large hall[113]
- and through the breadth of his understanding, he etched and hewed the words – weighing, substituting, and combining them [to chart out] the path of Torah and service and Fear of God
- to teach the path which we should tread and the action which we should take
- and from an early age his soul desired to merit the public with [generic teachings] that suited all people, with his soul's objective being bound up with this in 'one knot'[114] when it ascended Above.

• **Anyone** who did not see his strength and humility on the day he was taken from us has never seen strength and humility.
  ○ From the time of morning prayers until the time his soul departed heavenward, with each hour his energy renewed
  ○ one moment he would verbally express the lowliness of his [physical]

---

107 Iyov 28:11.
108 The Vilna Gaon wrote a commentary on an ancient section of Zohar known as Sifra DeTzniyuta, *The Book of the Modest*. R. Chaim wrote an introduction to this commentary in which he explains the context of Sifra DeTzniyuta as paralleling the Mishna, with the main sections of Zohar being compared to the Talmud which expands on and are entirely based on the Sifra DeTzniyuta. Subsequent generations of Kabbalists then explained more and more until

- כאשר כבר יצא אור דבריו בדפוס. ועוד עשר ידות לו בנסתרות בכתובים כמו שהאריך מר אבא הגאון נ"ע בהקדמתו לספרא דצניעותא.
- (ושמעתי ממר אבא הגאון ז"ל. שכל כתבי הקדש בנסתרות ממרן אלי' ז"ל. נכתבו קודם שהגיע לארבעים כי מאז בינה יתירה התוספת ליה שלא היה הזמן מספיק להכתב כל מה שנגלה לו).
- ומר אבא ז"ל קלט סלת מכל בית נבאות רבו ז"ל. להבין מדעתו ראשי פרקים פנימיות דרך עץ החיים להאר"י ז"ל. והיו חקוקים על לוח לבו.
- ומענותנותיה שייף ועייל מעט מזעיר בקונטרסים הללו.
- ופתח כמחט סדקית למי שלבו פתוח פתח כפתחו של אולם
- וברוחב בינתו חקק וחצב הדברים שקלן והמירן וצרפם לדרך התורה ועבודה ויראת ה'.
- להורות הדרך ילכו. והמעשה אשר יעשון.
- וכאשר מעודו נפשו אותה לזכות את הרבים בדבר השוה לכל נפש. כן היתה מגמת נפשו קשורה בזה בחד קטירא בעלותה למרום:
- ומי שלא ראה העוז והענוה דיליה ביום הלקחו מאתנו. לא ראה עוז וענוה.
- שמעת תפלת השחר עד עת צאת נשמתו למרום. כל שעה ושעה החליף כח.
- רגע היה משפיל גופו בדבריו כאשר הרגיש שישוב העפר אל הארץ כשהי', ופניו שחורות כעורב.

---

the Arizal revealed previously unrevealed explanations and arranged the information with his writings being likened to the Shulchan Aruch. R. Chaim also describes the extent of the Vilna Gaon's genius and abilities in bringing together this body of knowledge into his commentary and provides a number of very interesting anecdotes complementing this description, some of which are well-known as per biographies of the Vilna Gaon. A complete translation of R. Chaim's introduction to the Vilna Gaon's commentary on Sifra DeTzniyuta has been provided in V2:08.

109 Mishna Avot 5:21.
110 2 Melachim 20:13 as explained by Shmuel in Sanhedrin 104a.
111 Mishlei 3:3.
112 This plays on expressions from Sanhedrin 88b which refers to one who is humble and who bows on entry.
113 Expressions from Eruvin 53a.
114 E.g., Zohar Idra Zuta III, Haazinu 288a.

body when he felt the dust was about to return to its former state in the earth and 'his face would darken as a raven'[115]
- and in another moment he would strengthen himself with amazing devotion and his face would shine like the 'light of a **Chaim**/living king'[116]
  - to bind his Nefesh with his Ruach[117] – so that it should be returned to God who gave it in purity – until his Ruach and Neshama were gathered to God with a Divine Kiss – 'and they were bound with the bond of **Chaim**/life with God.'[118]
- **Before** God took him, that day he made himself small, tensed his face, and with a low voice, 'a speaking spirit'[119] of the **Chaim**/living soul, these were his words:
  - 'But my son make an effort'[120] to publish the pamphlets exceedingly quickly
  - and you my son know, that even though I did not merit to study, Heaven merited me to teach others and to make Torah study established – this is so even though I did not merit to fear God (Note 8)[121]
  - perhaps I will merit from Heaven, that my words in these pamphlets will be accepted – to set down the roots of the Fear of God, Torah [study], and refined service – in the hearts of honest people – for those who seek the ways of God.
  - These are the words which he spoke to me!
- **After** these words, surely 'tears will flow freely from the eye'[122] of all those who fear the word of God
  - when they enter these words into their heart, which come from the heart resulting from humility 'and the Fear of God brings **Chaim**/Life'[123]
  - and if for the man who is the great in Torah, his toil was with Torah and was the source of joy to his Creator all his days, it appears to him that he has no Fear of God – then what can we answer after him?
- **With that**, [the guilt lies] with me, that I did not speedily fulfill my father's words to perform his commands of me with alacrity
  - (and I was doubly punished for this with the 'fruit of my belly for the sin of my soul.'[124]
    - The first – in the next year on 14 Sivan 5582 [1822], the anniversary of the passing of my father, of blessed memory – I had a son and on entering him into the Covenant named him after *Nefesh HaChaim*.

---

115 An expression from Eruvin 22a based on Shir Hashirim 5:11 describing a person who never ceases studying Torah.
116 I.e., a Divine Light.

- וכרגע היה מתאזר עוז בדביקות נפלא ופניו היו מאירים כאור פני מלך חיים.
- לקשר נפשו ברוחו שתשוב אל האלהים אשר נתנה בטהרה, עד רוחו ונשמתו אליו ית"ש נאספו בנשיקה. והיו צרורים בצרור החיים את ה':

• וטרם לקח אותו אלהים. אותו יום אזעיר גרמיה וקמיט פניו בנמיכת קול ורוח ממללא מנשמת חיים. וכה היו דבריו ז"ל:

- אף ברי יטריח להדפים הקונטרסים חיש מהר.
- ואתה בני ידעת. שאף שללמוד לא זכיתי. זכוני מן השמים ללמד לאחריני. ולעשות קיום לת"ת כן אם שלא זכיתי ליראה את ה' (הגהה ח')
- אולי אזכה מן השמים. שיתקבלו דברי בקונטרסים הללו. להשריש יראת ה' ותורה ועבודה זכה בלב ישרי לב המבקשים דרכי ה'.
- אלה הדברים אשר דבר לי:

• ואחרי הדברים האלה. הלא דמוע תדמע עין כל הירא את דבר ה'.
- כאשר יכנים בלבו דברים הללו היוצאים מן הלב בעקב ענוה ויראת ה' לחיים.
- ואם האדם הגדול בתורה. ועמלו היה בתורה. כל ימיו עשה נ"ר ליוצרו. נדמה לו שאין בו יראת ה', אנן מה נעני אבתריה:

• ועם כי בי הוא. שלא נזדרזתי לקיים מילי דאבוהא. להזדרז לאשר ציווני.
- (ונענשתי ע"ז כפליים בפרי בטני על חטאת נפשי.
- א' שלשנה האחרת י"ד סיון תקפ"ב יום פטירת מר אבא ז"ל. נולד לי בן זכר והכנסתיו לברית. ונקרא על שם נפש החיים

---

117 See G1:14 for some details relating to levels of the soul.
118 1 Shmuel 25:29.
119 Targum Onkelos on Bereishit 2:7.
120 Iyov 37:11. This has not been translated literally but as a play on words.
121 **R. Yitzchak adds Note 8 here.** This note is brought at the end of this Introduction and is entitled "More humility feels less humble but think others are humble."
122 Yirmiyahu 13:17.
123 From the Title Page, this is the primary title of the book. See p. 68, fn. 6.
124 Michah 6:7.

- - But 'he is no more for God has taken him'[125] on the third day following the circumcision, and
  - in this year on 5 Kislev, Shabbat of the weekly portion of "And he went out"[126] – my precious, beautiful, charming, and beloved eight-year old *went* from me
    - he already knew how to analyze Talmud, [my son] Simcha Naftali Hertz.
  - 'God is righteous for I have disobeyed his utterance.'[127] 'He is merciful and will atone sin'[128] 'and He will not continue to agonize any more'.)[129]
  - However, this was not, God forbid, of my own initiative, but caused by the bad times as a result of our many sins
    - for from the day that the crown was lifted,[130] we have seen no good and I have remained in shock and broken hearted from being intertwined and tied up
    - and I have not found the time to discharge myself from the work of Heaven which was commanded of me in connection with his Yeshiva, as is known to all
    - and I assessed the will of my father, of blessed memory, according to the best of my ability, that perhaps it would not be acceptable to him to push aside the great action of public Torah study for this commandment [to publish].
- **In addition**, I envisage compiling his comments expounding on Ethics of the Fathers which he would expound each Shabbat with fragrant words
  - with the appropriate name for it being **Ruach Chaim**[131] in that they are filled with 'the Ruach/spirit of counsel, the spirit of understanding and knowledge'[132] and that 'they are **Chaim**/life to those who find them.'[133]
- **I also** [intend] to gather and arrange all the Responsa and to name them **Nishmat Chaim** as he put his Neshama and understanding into his words for those who understand, as per "Whose Neshama has gone out from you?"[134]
  - (I have called these pamphlets **Nefesh HaChaim** as per the signature of my father, of blessed memory, in his Responsa and on all of his letters).

---

125 Bereishit 5:24.
126 Bereishit 28:10.
127 Eicha 1:18.
128 Tehillim 78:38.
129 Yirmiyahu 31:11.

◦ ואיננו כי לקח אותו אלהים ביום שלישי למילה

▪ ושנה זו ה' כסליו יום ש"ק היה פרשה ויצא יצא ממני הדר כבן שמונה יפה תואר נחמד ואהוב.

◦ וכבר היה יודע לישא וליתן בגמרא כמר שמחה נפתלי הערץ.

▪ צדיק הוא ה' כי פיהו מריתי, והוא רחום יכפר עון. ולא יוסיף לדאבה עוד.)

◦ אמנם לא מלבי ח"ו ברם הורעת השעה בעו"ה היא שגרמה.

▪ כי מיום שהורם העטרה. טובה בעינינו לא ראינו, ונשארתי כאיש נדהם רצוץ לבב. מאשר השתרג. ומשתרג.

▪ ולא מצאתי לי עת לפטור עצמי ממלאכת שמים שצוויתי ממנו על בית אולפנא דידיה. כאשר מודעת לכל.

▪ ולפום שיעורא דילי שיערתי רצון מר אבא ז"ל. שאולי לא יהא ניחא ליה לדחות מעשה גדול ת"ת דרבים מפני מצוה זו:

• וגם דמיתי לחבר מילין דאגדתא דיליה לדרושיו על פרקי אבות שהיה דורש שבת בשבתו במילין בסימין

◦ ושמו נאה לו רוח חיים. באשר מלאים רוח עצה ורוח בינה ודעת וחיים הם למוצאיהם:

• וגם לקבץ כל השו"ת ולסדרם. לקרותם בשם נשמת חיים. כי בדבריו נותן נשמה ותבונה למבינים בענין ונשמת מי יצא ממך (איוב כ"ו).

▪ (וקונטרסים הללו קראתים נפש החיים כחתימתו של מר אבא ז"ל בתשובותיו וכל מכתביו.

---

130 I.e., of R. Chaim's passing.
131 Ruach Chaim was indeed published, but only in 5619 (1858) after R. Yitzchak's passing. This statement explaining R. Yitzchak's desired naming of the book as "Ruach Chaim" was quoted verbatim in its Title Page. Refer to V2:12 "Related Extracts from Ruach Chaim."
132 Yishayahu 11:2.
133 Mishlei 4:22.
134 Iyov 26:4.

- However, I don't have time to attend to this due to the volume of the obligations which fall upon me – God should increase [my time] – but as a result of this I have been delayed until now, and God should atone if I have erred.
- (I also took holy counsel from two great prodigies from the Holy Community of Vilna, God should protect it, who agreed that no delay should be made with that which my honorable father, the prodigy, whose soul is in Eden, thought to prioritize, in order to collect the Responsa which have been scattered throughout the world.)[135]

- **Now**, since I have been stimulated by Heaven to carry out the will of my righteous, honorable father, the prodigy, whose soul is in Eden
  - may it be His Will that He should carry out the will of those who fear God who desire the Living/**Chaim** Torah
  - 'and may the pleasantness of God establish the work of our hands'[136] to additionally publish further manuscripts.
  - Heaven should strengthen the eminent Rabbi who seeks the hidden treasures of the Fear of God, the honorable one, our teacher, **Rabbi Avraham Simcha**,[137] that he should live, who concerned himself and toiled in the righteous work **To Chaim**/life, in his involvement in the publication of these pamphlets
    - and God should do good for the good people who helped out of their [financial] goodness and God should raise for blessing those who bodily involved themselves
    - and may the merit of my honorable father, the prodigy, may his memory be a blessing for life in the future world, assist with all desires to carry out good will, to bring upon them good blessing.

- **You**, the House of Israel, go and see the straight path which a person should cleave to.
  - Pay attention to the words said in **"The Fear of God Brings Life"**[138] and how fitting they are to the one who said them and to whom they are addressed
  - and may it be His Will that these words of excellence will be spoken of between those who fear God

---

135 It should be noted that this intention of collecting and publishing all of R. Chaim's Responsa never materialized. Twenty-five of his Responsa were however collected and published by R. Chaim's grandson, R. Eliezer Yitzchak, together with his own Responsa and also those of his father, R. Hillel, who was R. Chaim's son-in-law. This set of Responsa was appropriately named "Chut HaMeshulash" and published in Vilna in 5642 (1882). The book Kol HaKatuv LeChaim, third edition, p. 293, records that in addition to the fire of 5575 (1815) in which most of R. Chaim's Responsa were destroyed, some

- ברם לית אתר פנוי לזה מרובי הטרדות והעבודה המוטלת עלי. ה' ירחיב. ובגין דא לדא אשתהי עד האידנא. ואם שגיתי ה' יכפה.
- (וגם חוו לי דעת קדושי' תרי הגאונים הגדולים אשר בק"ק ווילנא יע"א. שהסכמתם שלא לאחר המוקדם בדעת כבוד מר אבא הגאון נ"ע. עדי יוקבצו השו"ת דאתבדרן בעלמא):

• ועתה אחרי שמן השמים עוררוני לעשות רצון צדיק כבוד מר אבא הגאון נ"ע
- יהא רעוא להפיק רצון יראי ה' המתאויים לתורת חיים.
- ויהי נועם ה' לכונן מעשי ידינו להוציא לאור מה שהנם עוד בכתובי'.
- ומשמיא יאמצו כח ב"ד הרב המופלג מבקש מטמוני יראת ה' כש"ת מוה' **אברהם שמחה** שי' שטרח ויגע בפעולות צדיק לחיים בעסק הדפסת הקונטרסים האלו.
- והטיבה ה' לטובים שהטיבו מטובם לסייע. והמתעסקים בגופם כולם ישאו ברכה מה'.
- וזכותי' דכבוד מר אבא הגאון זלה"ה יהוי בסעדא דכל החפצים לעשות רצונו הטוב. להביא עליהם ברכת טוב ומטיב:

• ואתם בית ישראל. צאו וראו הדרך הישרה שידבק בה האדם.
- שימו לבבכם לכל הדברים שנאמרו בידאת ה' לחיים וראויין הם למי שאמרן. ולמי שנאמרו.
- ויהא רעוא דיתאמרו הני מילי מעליותא בין יראי ה'.

---

more were destroyed in another fire in 5625 (1865). It also notes that it was later discovered that the 23rd Responsum out of the 25 collected in Chut HaMeshulash was actually not written by R. Chaim but by one of his students. A further 8 Responsa are published in Kol HaKatuv LeChaim, third edition, bringing the total number of R. Chaim's published Responsa to 32.

136 Tehillim 90:17.
137 This was R. Avraham Simcha of Amshislav, R. Chaim's nephew, who prepared the final draft of Nefesh HaChaim for print as he also mentions in his introductory comments to Ruach Chaim. He is also commended in both of the original approbations (see V2:05).
138 From the Title Page, this is the primary title of the book. See p. 68, fn. 6.

- to capture the recesses of the hearts of our Brethren, the House of Israel, to [study] Torah with kindness, to perform complete service and to refine prayer
- and the action of the righteous one *to Chaim/life* who gave up his life over Torah and service, shall add strength to each person who desires life with Torah and service with all their heart and soul
- and to awaken the treasure house of good with kindness and mercy
  - for all the souls of the House of Israel, that it should live, and
  - for 'afflicted souls.'[139]

Yitzchak the son of the prodigy the author, our teacher, Rabbi **Chaim**, may his memory be a blessing for life in the future world, of Volozhin.

RABBI YITZCHAK'S NOTES ON HIS INTRODUCTION

Note 1 – Only if a lack is visually apparent does talk of the lips *make good*

- **Perhaps** it is possible that the interpretation of the verse "and the talk of my lips bring only loss"[140] is that for something about which it is visually apparent that there is something lacking, that it needs *talk of the lips* to make good. However, if there is no fault, why should many words [be necessary]?

Note 2 – Detail of interaction between Shaagat Aryeh and Rabbi Chaim

- **The prodigy**, the author of the Shaagat Aryeh, of blessed memory, was the head of the Bet Din here in this holy community for a number of years and was known to the family of my father and teacher, of blessed memory.
- When he was here, he authored his precious work, the Responsa Shaagat Aryeh, and when he journeyed from here to print it, my father, whose soul is in Eden, was young
- and when he passed by here after printing his book, as mentioned above, he lodged in the house of my grandfather, of blessed memory, for a number of weeks
- 'and he encamped before the city'[141] and finalized rulings here.
- At the time, my father and teacher, of blessed memory, was already fifteen and out of his love for him, together with his elder brother, whose soul is in Eden, he fixed a regular learning schedule with them.

Note 3 – Biographical reference for Rabbi Shlomo Zalman, dates of birth and passing

- '**Known** in Judah, his name is of a prodigy in Israel.'[142]

- לאחוז קירות לבב אחב"י לתורת חסד. ועבודה שלמה. ותפלה זכה.
- ופעולת צדיק לחיים שמסר נפשו בחייו על תורה ועבודה. תוסיף אומץ לכל האיש החפץ חיים. בתורה ועבודה בכל לבבם ונפשם.
- ולעורר אוצר הטוב בחסד ורחמין
  - נפישין על נפשות בית ישראל שי'
  - ונפש נענה:

יצחק בהגאון המחבר מוה' חיים זלה"ה מוולאזין:

הגהה א'

- ואולי יתכן פי' הכתוב ודבר שפתים אך למחסור (משלי י"ד) שלדבר שנראה בהשקפה שיש בו איזה חסרון, נצרך דבר שפתים להמתיקו, אבל באין מחסור למה זה רוב דברים:

הגהה ב'

- והגאון בעל ש"א ז"ל, היה כמה שנים אב"ד פה ק"ק, והיה מודע למשפחת אבא מארי ז"ל
- ובהיותו פה חבר חבורו היקר שו"ת ש"א, ובנסעו מפה להדפיסו, היה מר אבא נ"ע קטן בשנים
- ומדי עברו דרך פה אחרי הדפים ספרו הנ"ל, נתאכסן בבית א"ז ז"ל כמה שבועות
- ויחן את פני העיר וקבע הוראות פה.
- והיה אז אבא מארי ז"ל כבר חמיסר, ומאהבה שאהבו, ואת אחיו הגדול נ"ע, קבע להם משנתם שתהא סדורה:

הגהה ג'

- ונודע ביהודה וגאון שמו בישראל.

---

139 Yishayahu 58:10.
140 Mishlei 14:23.
141 Bereishit 33:18.
142 Tehillim 76:2.

- Some of his holy ways are recorded in the book Toldot HaAdam volumes one and two, authored by the outstanding Rabbi, the lecturer, the great, our teacher **Yechezkel Feivel**, the preacher of the straight, of the great town of Vilna, with more in volume three which is in writing, may God be with him, to [help] publish it.
- My father, of blessed memory, was seven years and nine days older than his brother, the prodigy, our teacher R. Shlomo Zalman whose soul is in Eden. He [my father] was born in **5509** [1749] in the month of Sivan on the second day of Shavuot [7 Sivan], the day Torah was given to Israel, and he ascended from us at the age of 72, on the day of his pardoning, on 14 Sivan, the Thursday of the week of "and it was when the Ark travelled,"[143] in the year **"All that is written goes to Chaim."**[144]

Note 4 – Student grasps inner level of teacher's thought by seeing his face

- **Perhaps** the concept presented in Eruvin[145]
  - [which says: Rebbi said, the reason why I am sharper than my colleagues is that I saw (R. Meir) from behind him (i.e., that he sat behind him in his lectures)] but if I saw him from his front [I would be even sharper as it is written] "and your eyes will see your mentor"
  - is like the idea, as per the verse "and you shall see My Back, but My Front you shall not see."
- This is as per the Midrash[146] – "I will be as I will be," that My Actions determine how I am referred to.
  - (and that the details of concluding actions incorporate their preceding thoughts)
  - and therefore, *thought* is called *front[/internal]* which precedes, and *action* is called *back[/external]*.
- With *thought* itself, there is [a level] of preceding thought which incorporates and this [level] is internal
  - and a [level of] following[/external] thought which reveals the internal [thought in the form of] speech or action (and this is Daat/knowledge which extends into the inner essence of the Middot)[147]
  - and this [second level of thought] is recognizable within action, or that which follows [e.g., through speech as in] the movement of one's lips which is an action.
  - However, the internal [level] of preceding thought, cannot be manifest in speech, as per "Honey and milk under your tongue"
    - (Refer to Chagiga)[148]

---

143 Bamidbar 10:35, i.e., the weekly portion of Behaalotcha.
144 From Yishayahu 4:3, i.e., the numerical value of the year 5581 (1821).

- וקצות דרכו בקדש. הנם כתובים על ספר תולדות האדם ח"א וח"ב שחבר הרב המובהק הדרשן הגדול מהו' יחזקאל פייוויל מ"מ דקרתא רבתי ווילנא, ועוד ח"ג אצלו בכתובים, יהי ה' אתו להדפיסו.
- ואבא מארי ז"ל היה גדול בשנים מאחיו הגאון מוהר"ש זלמן נ"ע ז' שנים וט' ימים, ונולד שנת תק"ט בחודש סיון יו"ט שני של חג השבועות יום שנתנה תורה לישראל, ונתעלה מאתנו בן ע"ב ביום חנינתו י"ד סיון ה' לסדר ויהי בנסע הארון שנת כל הכתוב לחיים:

הגהה ד'

- **ואולי ענין הנאמר בעירובין** (י"ג ב')
  - ואלו חזיתיה מקמיה כו' והיו עיניך ראות את מוריך.
  - הוא כענין הכתוב (שמות ל"ג) וראיתי את אחורי ופני לא יראו.
- עפ"י מדרש שמות פ"ג אקי"ק אשר אקי"ק ע"ש מעשי אני נקרא
  - (וסוף פרטי המעשים כלולים במחשבה הקדומה)
  - ולזאת נקראת המחשבה פנים שקודמת, והמעשה מאוחרת
- **ובמחשבה עצמה יש מחשבה קדומה וכוללת, והיא פנימית**
  - ומחשבה מאוחרת המתפשטת מהפנימית לדבור או למעשה. (והוא דעת המתפשט בפנימית המידות)
  - והיא היא הנכרת מתוך מעשה, או דבר המאוחר, בעקימת שפתיו דהוי מעשה.
  - אבל פנימית המחשבה הקדומה, א"א להביאה בדיבור, כענין דבש וחלב תחת לשונך
    - (עי' חגיגה י"ג א')

- and this is Supernal Knowledge as per the idea that a person does not attain the level of intellectual prowess of his teacher [until after forty years of study with him][149]
  - and a student can only grasp this [level of inner thought] by seeing his teacher's face/front, for a student who is a scholar and understands from his own knowledge[150]
  - with all this being in 'the thoughts of a person's heart.'[151]
- However, with God about whom it is written, "For My thoughts are not like your thoughts"[152]
  - no thought can in any way grasp the encompassing [nature] of His Thought – not even the supernal beings – and it is only His Thoughts which have been expressed within the existence of actions, which are recognizable from all of His deeds to each prophet according to his level
  - this is the meaning of "and you shall see, *Et*, My Back" where the [additional word] "Et" is used to refer to the [level] of thought which is manifest to sustain action, and is recognizable through the power of His action, and is referred to by the name of the action
  - [whereas] "but My Front you shall not see" – even through the power of His actions which are back [compared] to what preceded them [i.e., the level of inner thought], (as per what is taught by the grammatical form of the Hebrew word "Yerau/you shall see").

Note 5 – Be careful not to become haughty from accorded honor

- **By way of** homily it can perhaps be a second meaning of that which R. Eliezer said to his students:[153] "Be careful with your colleagues' honor," meaning that care needs to be taken that he not become haughty from the honor that his colleagues give to him.[154]

Note 6 – God arouses a person to learn from reproving discipline

- **Perhaps** this is the meaning of the verse "My Lord, God, has given me a tongue for teaching . . . He arouses *ear* to understand as students are taught"[155]
- that is that God gave him the tongue to teach reproving discipline to another and God aroused his ear such that he would learn the discipline himself just like [as if] the teaching is [directly] taught to another.[156]

---

justify that something which is sweeter than honey and milk should stay under one's tongue and not be disclosed.
149 Avodah Zarah 5b.

- והוא דעת העליון, כענין לא קאים איניש אדעתיה דרבי' (עבודת זרה ה' ע"ב)
- ואינה נתפסת להתלמיד אלא בהארת פנים של רבו, לתלמיד חכם ומבין מדעתו
- וכל זה הוא במחשבות שבלב איש

- אבל בו ית"ש אשר לא מחשבותי מחשבותיכם כתיב (ישעיה נ"ה)
- כללות מחשבתו לית מחשבה תפיסא בשום אופן, אף לעליונים, ורק מחשבתו המתפשטת לקיום מעשיו, ניכרת ממעשיו לכל נביא ונביא כפי מדרגתו
- וזהו וראית את אחורי, "את" לרבות המחשבה המתפשטת לקיום המעשה וניכרת ע"י כח מעשיו, ונקראת ע"ש המעשה
- ופני לא יֵרָאוּ אף על ידי כח מעשיו המאוחרים אל הקודם. (וכהוראת מלת יראו בציר"י):

הגהה ה'

- ודרך דרש אולי הוא כוונה שניי' במה שאמר ר"א לתלמידיו (ברכות כח ב) הזהרו בכבוד חבריכם, שצריך זהירות שלא יוגבה לבו מהכבוד שחביריו נוהגים בו:

הגהה ו'

- ואולי כן כוונת הכתוב (ישעיה נ) ה' אלהים נתן לי לשון למודים וגו' יעיר לי אזן לשמוע כלמודים
- היינו שה' ית' ית"ש נתן לו לשון למודים בתוכחת מוסר לאחריני. והוא ית"ש העיר אזנו שילמד גם הוא מוסר לעצמו. כלימודים שמלמד לאחריני:

---

150 This is also the idea underpinning the qualities of a student of deeper ideas as expressed in Chagiga 11b.
151 Mishlei 19:21.
152 Yishayahu 55:8.
153 Berachot 28b.
154 This is in addition to the basic meaning that one should be careful to properly honor one's colleagues.
155 Yishayahu 50:4.
156 This is understood from the verse as it mentions *ear* but doesn't specify whose

Note 7 – God compared to one who gives up comfort to bestow kindness

- **This is similar to what** we have become accustomed to present with King Shlomo's prayer[157] "Would God truly dwell on earth?"
  - by way of analogy, just as it is believable that a kind person who
    - although is abundantly wealthy and greatly honored by powerful people, with wisdom, strength, and wealth
    - will choose a low place of residence, to be with the depressed, in salty unfertile land, without water to drink
    - in order that he can bestow all manner of kindnesses as per his heart's desire to only do good in every possible way
  - [so too] with this entire vision, King Shlomo says there "Cause your word to be trusted . . . that *Ha'umnam/indeed* (an expression of *Emunat Omen*[158]/*steadfast faith*) God would dwell on earth"[159]
    - that Your hand should be available to bestow all kindnesses
    - which when one person sins against another you will perform kindness with strength to save the oppressed from the oppressor
    - that the person who encroaches on the land of his neighbor shall be returned to his land
    - when they thirst for water, you will give them rain, when they are hungry you will give them bread
    - to the sick and feeble, you will raise in recovery, to one with an afflicted heart, you will bandage his depression
    - and the earth will be filled with your good ways, to do good in every which way.

Note 8 – More humility feels less humble but think others are humble

- Anyone who knew that out of his [R. Chaim's] humility he still considered himself to be pompous would not be surprised that it appeared to him that he did not understand Fear of Heaven.
- This is like the concept brought down by Chazal:[160]
  - ["And now Israel, what does YHVH your God ask *of you* – just to fear Him"] . . . Is Fear of Heaven a small matter? . . . Yes, for Moshe it is a small matter. This is analogous to a person from whom it is requested to provide a large vessel which he has. This vessel appears to him like a small vessel [which is easy to acquire. If however a person is requested to provide] a small vessel and he does not have it, it appears to him like a large vessel [which he does not have].

---

ear, as it could be of the teacher or the student. The common understanding is of the teacher, but the insight here is that it is of the student.

הגהה ז'

- וכגוונא שהורגלנו להציע תפלת שהמע"ה (מלכים א' ח' כ"ז) כי האמנם ישב אלקים על הארץ
  - ד"מ שכמו שקרוב להאמין שאיש חסד
    - עם כי הוא עתיר נכסין וגדול כבודו לאדירי עם, בחכמה וגבורה ועושר
    - יבחר לו מקום לישב בשפל, ולהיות את נדכאים, ארץ מלחה, לא מקום זרע, ומים אין לשתות
    - למען יוכל גמול כל מיני חסדים טובים בחפץ לבו רק להיטיב בכל מילי דמיטב
  - בכל החזיון הזה אמר שהמע"ה שם, יאמן נא דברך כו' כי האמנם (לשון אמונת אומן) ישב אלקים על הארץ
    - שתמצא ידך לגמול כל חסדים טובים
    - אשר יחטא איש לרעהו תעשה חסד בגבורה להציל עשוק מיד עושקו
    - איש אשר יסיג גבול רעהו תשיבהו על אדמתו
    - כי יצמאו למים ונחת להם מטר, רעב כי יהיה ונתת לחם
    - לקצירי ומריעי תעלה ארוכה, לכל נגוע לבב תחבוש לעצבותו
    - ומלאה הארץ דרכי טובך להטיב בכל מיני הטבה:

הגהה ח'

- ומי שידע שמענותנותו הי' נחשב בעיניו עוד ליהיר, לא נפלאת היא מה שנדמה לו שלא הבין יראת ה'.
- כענין מאמר חז"ל (ברכות ל"ג ב')
  - אטו יראה מלתא זוטרתי היא וכו' אין לגבי משה מלתא זוטרתי היא. משל

---

157 1 Melachim 8:27.
158 Yishayahu 25:1.
159 "Ha'umnam" usually relates to a rhetorical question but it is being used here as a statement.
160 Berachot 33b quoting Devarim 10:12.

- This concept is that the more humble one is, the less they feel their humility – on the contrary they see themselves as more pompous and consider their colleagues to be humble.
- With Moshe our Teacher who was the most humble of all men, he certainly would have perceived himself to be pompous and from his perspective all of Israel were held to be humble
  - This is the meaning of "for Moshe," that he was exceptionally humble and considered Israel to be humble
  - he [therefore] said that for [Israel], Fear of God is a small matter as it [is a trait] which follows [and is connected to] humility, as per Chazal:[161]
    - That which he made wisdom . . . he made humility a sandal for the heel . . . [as it says: "the result of humility is Fear of God"]
  - and he only considered Fear [of God] to be a challenging matter compared to himself as he still considered himself to be pompous.
- Perhaps this is why the Talmud [in Berachot] brings the analogy of the second vessel with the [request for] the small vessel which the person does not have
  - in order to explain the word "of you" in the verse [i.e., that from Israel's point of view, and not Moshe's, Fear of Heaven appears daunting as we do not have it].

---

161 Midrash Mishlei 15:32 quoting Mishlei 22:4.

לאדם שמבקשים ממנו כלי גדול ויש לו דומה עליו ככלי קטן, קטן, ואין לו דומה עליו ככלי גדול.

- והענין שכל מי שהוא עניו יותר אינו מרגיש ענוותנותו ואדרבה נחשב בעיניו למתיהר ואת חביריו מחשיב לעניים.
- ומשרע"ה העניו מאד מכל האדם, ודאי הי' מחזיק עצמו למתיהר ואת כל ישראל החזיק לעניים נגדו
  ○ וזהו לגבי משה שהי' עניו ביותר והחזיק את ישראל לעניים
  ○ אמר שאצלם יראה מלתא זוטרתי, כי היא עקב ענוה, כמאמרם ז"ל
  □ מה שעשתה חכמה וכו' עשתה ענוה עקב לסוליתה
  ○ ורק לגבי דידי' נחשב לו יראה לדבר גדול, מחמת שנחשב בעיניו ליהיר עוד.
- ואולי לזאת מביא הגמרא משל השני מכלי קטן ואין לו
  ○ למען דרוש תיבת מעמך שבקרא:

FIRST GATEWAY

1. IMAGE CONCEPT IS FUNDAMENTALLY DEEP, IMAGE IMPLIES SOME LIKENESS

- It is written, "God/Elokim created man *in His Image*. In the *image of Elokim* He created him,"[1] and similarly, it is written, "For in the *image of Elokim* He made the man."[2]
- The depth of the *image* concept is one of those things which stands at the highest point of the Universe and it incorporates the majority of the hidden secrets of the Zohar. (Maamar BeTzeLeM)[3]
- But here we will be relating to the word "image" in the way of the early Scriptural Commentators,[4] of blessed memory, on the verse "Let us make man in our image, in our likeness."[5]
- The basic definition here of something being in an *image* or *likeness* [of another] is not literal
    - as the verse explicitly states: "and what *image* can be compared to Him!"[6]
    - but its meaning is that there is some form of likeness [between them], as in "I am *like* the bird of the wilderness,"[7] which does not mean a likeness in the sense of having wings and a beak or having changed to a birdlike form – but is just a likeness in the way he acts, in that he wanders about like the bird of the wilderness, a bird which is in solitude and flies from place to place.
    - This is the understanding of the early Scriptural Commentators, of blessed memory.
- Similarly, in this vein, the concept of *image* means that they [man and Elokim] are meaningfully comparable in a specific way.

---

1 Bereishit 1:27.
2 Bereishit 9:6.
3 **R. Yitzchak, R. Chaim's son, adds an extremely long note here.** It details the depth of the image concept. Due to its sheer size, the translation is to be found in V2:04, Maamar BeTzeLeM (the BeTzeLeM discourse). In the original printings of Nefesh HaChaim, this note was printed alongside the main text, just like all of R. Chaim's notes.

This note touches on many of the deep Kabbalistic themes referenced within Nefesh HaChaim and it is suggested that it may be easier to relate to this note after first having reviewed the entire contents of Nefesh HaChaim.

שער א'

שער א' - פרק א'

- כְּתִיב (בראשית א, כז) "וַיִּבְרָא אֱלֹקִים אֶת הָאָדָם בְּצַלְמוֹ בְּצֶלֶם אֱלֹקִים בָּרָא אֹתוֹ", וְכֵן כְּתִיב (שם ט, ו) "כִּי בְּצֶלֶם אֱלֹקִים עָשָׂה אֶת הָאָדָם":

- הִנֵּה עֹמֶק פְּנִימִיּוּת עִנְיַן הַצֶּלֶם, הוּא מִדְּבָרִים הָעוֹמְדִים בְּרוּמוֹ שֶׁל עוֹלָם, וְהוּא כּוֹלֵל רֹב סִתְרֵי פְּנִימִיּוּת הַזֹּהַר: (מאמר בצלם)

- אָמְנָם, כָּאן נְדַבֵּר בְּמִלַּת 'צֶלֶם', בְּדֶרֶךְ הַפַּשְׁטָנִים הָרִאשׁוֹנִים ז"ל עַל פָּסוּק "נַעֲשֶׂה אָדָם בְּצַלְמֵנוּ כִּדְמוּתֵנוּ" (שם א, כו):

- וְהוּא, כִּי מִלַּת 'צֶלֶם' וּ'דְמוּת' כָּאן, אֵינוֹ כְּמַשְׁמָעוֹ
  - כִּי כָתוּב מְפֹרָשׁ (ישעי' מ', יח) "וּמַה דְּמוּת תַּעַרְכוּ לוֹ"
  - אֶלָּא פֵּרוּשׁוֹ, דִּמְיוֹן מַה בְּאֵיזֶה דָּבָר, כְּמוֹ "דָּמִיתִי לִקְאַת מִדְבָּר" (תהלים קב, ז), כִּי לֹא נַעֲשׂוּ לוֹ כְּנָפַיִם וְחַרְטוֹם, וְלֹא נִשְׁתַּנָּה צוּרָתוֹ לְצוּרַת הַקָּאַת, רַק שֶׁנִּדְמָה אָז, בְּמִקְרֶה פְּעֻלָּתָיו שֶׁהָיָה נָע וָנָד, כְּמוֹ הַקָּאַת מִדְבָּר, שֶׁהוּא צִפּוֹר בּוֹדֵד וּמְעוֹפֵף מִמָּקוֹם לְמָקוֹם.
  - כָּךְ הוּא לְפִי הַפַּשְׁטָנִים הָרִאשׁוֹנִים זִכְרוֹנָם לִבְרָכָה:

- וְכֵן עַל דֶּרֶךְ זֶה הוּא עִנְיַן מִלַּת 'צֶלֶם', כִּי הֵמָּה דּוֹמִים בְּמַשְׁמָעָם בְּצַד מָה:

---

4 Rambam, the very beginning of Moreh HaNevuchim 1, Chap. 1, which continues to quote the example brought later in this chapter relating to the bird of the wilderness.

5 Bereishit 1:26.

6 Yishayahu 40:18.

7 Tehillim 102:7. R. Yitzchak also refers to this verse in Note 1 to his Maamar BeTzeLeM.

2. CONSTANT CREATION OF PHYSICAL FROM NON-PHYSICAL

- However, when the verse states "image of Elokim," we need to understand the connection of *image* with the specific name of God stated [that is of *Elokim*] and not [with His] other names – for the explanation of the name Elokim is known in that it indicates that God is *The All Powerful One* as explained in the Tur.[8]
- In that God is called *All Powerful*, His characteristics are not like those of flesh and blood:
  - As man: By way of an analogy, when he constructs a wooden structure, he does not create the wood with his own power but takes wood which already exists and arranges it in a structure
    - then after he has satisfactorily arranged it, if he removes his power [of arrangement] from it, the structure nevertheless continues to exist.
  - Whereas with God: Just as at the Creation of all the worlds, He created and caused them all to exist in a physical way (Yesh) from the non-physical (Ayin)[9] with His infinite power
    - similarly, since then, each day and literally at every moment
    - all the power of their continued existence and arrangement is entirely dependent on God constantly bestowing power and a renewed light upon them with His Will
    - and if He were to remove the power that He bestows even momentarily from them, they would immediately become null and void.[10]
- This is consistent with [the prayer] instituted by the Men of the Great Assembly of "He who in His Goodness *constantly* renews (Note 1)[11] His Act of Creation"[12]
  - that is literally *constantly* at each and every moment
  - and their proof is as explicitly stated, as per "to the *Maker* [present tense] of the heavenly luminaries"[13]

---

8   See Shulchan Aruch, Orach Chaim 5:1 which defines Elokim in this way, i.e., "Baal HaKochot Kulam." Part Two of Rabbi Chaim's Sermon directly quotes this from the Shulchan Aruch (see V2:11). In contrast, the same Siman in the Tur which is directly quoted in the text of the Nefesh HaChaim, while expressing this sentiment does not use this particular phrase.
9   See p. 472, fn. 18, for comments on the concept of Ayin.
10 I.e., they will cease to physically exist. This idea is extensively developed in the Third Gateway and is presented in G3:01 as the simple meaning of the reference to God as Makom.
    Note that R. Chaim uses the expression "Efes VeTohu" meaning "null and

שער א' - פרק ב'

- אָמְנָם, לְהָבִין עִנְיַן אָמְרוֹ "בְּצֶלֶם אֱלֹקִים" דַּיְקָא, וְלֹא שֵׁם אַחֵר, כִּי שֵׁם 'אֱלֹקִים' יָדוּעַ פֵּרוּשׁוֹ, שֶׁהוּא מוֹרֶה שֶׁהוּא יִתְבָּרַךְ שְׁמוֹ בַּעַל הַכֹּחוֹת כֻּלָּם, כְּמוֹ שֶׁמְּבֹאָר בְּטוּר אֹרַח חַיִּים סִימָן ה':

- וְעִנְיַן מַה שֶּׁהוּא יִתְבָּרַךְ נִקְרָא 'בַּעַל הַכֹּחוֹת', כִּי לֹא כְּמִדַּת בָּשָׂר וָדָם מִדַּת הַקָּדוֹשׁ בָּרוּךְ הוּא

  ○ כִּי הָאָדָם, כְּשֶׁבּוֹנֶה בִּנְיַן דֶּרֶךְ מָשָׁל מֵעֵץ, אֵין הַבּוֹנֶה בּוֹרֵא וּמַמְצִיא אָז מִכֹּחוֹ הָעֵץ, רַק שֶׁלּוֹקֵחַ עֵצִים שֶׁכְּבָר נִבְרְאוּ, וּמְסַדְּרָם בַּבִּנְיָן

    ▫ וְאַחַר שֶׁכְּבָר סִדְּרָם לְפִי רְצוֹנוֹ, עִם שֶׁכֹּחוֹ הוּסַר וְנִסְתַּלֵּק מֵהֶם, עִם כָּל זֶה הַבִּנְיָן קַיָּם.

  ○ אֲבָל הוּא יִתְבָּרַךְ שְׁמוֹ, כְּמוֹ בְּעֵת בְּרִיאַת הָעוֹלָמוֹת כֻּלָּם, בְּרָאָם וְהִמְצִיאָם הוּא יִתְבָּרַךְ יֵשׁ מֵאַיִן, בְּכֹחוֹ הַבִּלְתִּי תַכְלִית

    ▫ כֵּן מֵאָז, כָּל יוֹם וְכָל רֶגַע מַמָּשׁ

    ▫ כָּל כֹּחַ מְצִיאוּתָם וְסִדְרָם וְקִיּוּמָם, תָּלוּי רַק בְּמַה שֶּׁהוּא יִתְבָּרַךְ שְׁמוֹ מַשְׁפִּיעַ בָּהֶם בִּרְצוֹנוֹ יִתְבָּרַךְ כָּל רֶגַע, כֹּחַ וְשִׁפְעַת אוֹר חָדָשׁ

- וְאִלּוּ הָיָה הוּא יִתְבָּרַךְ מְסַלֵּק מֵהֶם כֹּחַ הַשְׁפָּעָתוֹ אַף רֶגַע אַחַת, כְּרֶגַע הָיוּ כֻּלָּם לְאֶפֶס וָתֹהוּ:

- וּכְמוֹ שֶׁיִּסְּדוּ אַנְשֵׁי כְּנֶסֶת הַגְּדוֹלָה "הַמְחַדֵּשׁ (הגהה א') בְּטוּבוֹ בְּכָל יוֹם תָּמִיד מַעֲשֵׂה בְרֵאשִׁית"

  ○ הַיְנוּ 'תָּמִיד' מַמָּשׁ, כָּל עֵת וָרֶגַע

  ○ וּרְאִיתָם מְפֹרֶשֶׁת כָּאָמוּר "לְעוֹשֵׂה אוֹרִים גְּדוֹלִים" (תהלים קלו, ז)

---

void" here. These words refer to different things as is explained in V2:02, Chap. 15, "Tzimtzum Sources," I1.1. In particular, when used in this context, the word "Tohu" is synonymous with "Ayin." There are a number of instances throughout Nefesh HaChaim where the expressions "Efes VeTohu" or "Efes VeAyin" or "Ayin VeEfes" are used and they all have the same meaning.

11 R. Chaim adds Note 1 here. This note is brought at the end of this chapter and is entitled "Constant re-creation indiscernible, YHVH represents four elements."

12 Blessing of Yotzer Ohr preceding Kriat Shema of the Shacharit prayer.

13 Tehillim 136:7.

- it does not say "Asah"/"the One who made" [in the past tense] but "Oseh"/"Maker" [in the present tense].
- This is the meaning of calling God [by the name] *The Elokim, The All Powerful One*
  - (Note 2)[14] that God is the All Powerful power of each individual power that exists in all of the worlds
  - Who bestows power and strength upon them every moment
  - and that they are all constantly dependent on His hand to change and arrange them as He Wishes.

Rabbi Chaim's Notes:
Note 1 – Constant re-creation indiscernible, YHVH represents four elements

- Even though [as a result of this constant re-creation process] there is nothing new which is discernable to the eye – nevertheless the four supernal elements [of fire, wind, water, dust], which are the primary roots, the fathers of all
  - as mentioned in the Zohar,[15] that they are the root of the Act of Creation and the inner essence of all
  - they are the four letters of God's Name *YHVH*
  - their continuous amalgamation and combination with their ultimate source is not perceivable at all
  - and God continuously renews them in accordance with His Will.
- The concept of their continuous amalgamation
  - is the 1,080 combinations of God's Name through changes of vowels[16]

---

14   **R. Chaim adds Note 2 here.** This note is brought at the end of this chapter and is entitled "Elohim is generic description, God is Elokay HaElohim."

15   Zohar II VaEra 23b:
  - R. Shimon said: Come and see, there are four primary components to the secret of faith, and they are the fathers of all the worlds and the secret of the Supernal Holy Merkava. They are the four elements of fire, wind, water, earth, these form the supernal secret and these are the fathers of all the worlds . . . [This source is also quoted in G2:17, G3:10 and towards the beginning of Maamar BeTzeLeM.]

16   See G2:16 and G2:16:N36 which describe a word's components, one of which is its vowels. A detailed breakdown of how there are 1,080 vowel combinations of God's Name is provided by the Shela, Shaar HaOtiyot, Ot Hey. A detailed breakdown is also provided by the Vilna Gaon among the collected writings published at the end of his commentary on Sefer Yetzirah (from the manuscript of the book Hadrat Kodesh) together with an explanation attributed to his student, R. Menachem Mendel of Shklov which in summary is as follows:

- שֶׁלֹּא אָמַר 'עָשָׂה' אֶלָּא 'עוֹשֶׂה':
- וְזֶהוּ שֶׁנִּקְרָא הוּא יִתְבָּרַךְ שְׁמוֹ, "הָאֱלֹקִים", בַּעַל הַכֹּחוֹת כֻּלָּם.
- (הגהה ב') שֶׁכָּל כֹּחַ פְּרָטֵי הַנִּמְצָא בְּכָל הָעוֹלָמוֹת, הַכֹּל, הוּא יִתְבָּרַךְ שְׁמוֹ, הַבַּעַל כֹּחַ שֶׁלָּהֶם
- שֶׁמַּשְׁפִּיעַ בָּהֶם הַכֹּחַ וּגְבוּרָה כָּל רֶגַע
- וּתְלוּיִים בְּיָדוֹ תָּמִיד לְשַׁנּוֹתָם וּלְסַדְּרָם, כִּרְצוֹנוֹ יִתְבָּרַךְ:

הגהה א'

- וְאַף שֶׁאֵין חִדּוּשׁ נִכָּר לָעַיִן. אָמְנָם הַד' יְסוֹדִין עִלָּאִין, דְּאִינוּן הָשָׁרָשִׁין קַדְמָאִין, וַאֲבָהָן דְּכֹלָּא
  - כַּנִּזְכָּר בַּזֹּהַר (וארא כ"ג ע"ב) שֶׁהֵם שֹׁרֶשׁ כָּל מַעֲשֵׂי בְרֵאשִׁית וּפְנִימִיּוּת כֻּלָּם
  - וְהֵם ד' אוֹתִיּוֹת הֲוָיָ"ה בָּרוּךְ הוּא
  - הִתְמַזְּגוּתָם וְהַרְכָּבָתָם כָּל עֵת וָרֶגַע בְּשֹׁרֶשׁ שָׁרְשָׁם, אֵינוֹ מוּשָׂג כְּלָל
  - וְהוּא יִתְבָּרַךְ שְׁמוֹ מְחַדְּשָׁם כָּל רֶגַע לְפִי רְצוֹנוֹ:
- וְעִנְיַן הִתְמַזְּגוּתָם כָּל רֶגַע
  - הֵם הַתתר"ף צֵרוּפֵי הַשֵּׁם בָּרוּךְ הוּא, עַל פִּי הִשְׁתַּנּוּת נְקֻדּוֹתֵיהֶם

- There are 5 major vowels which with the addition of the vowel, *Shva*, are as follows: אָ, אֶ, אִ, אֹ, אֻ, אְ.
- Each of these 6 vowels are applied to each of the four letters of YHVH forming 24 (i.e., 6 × 4) letter vowel combinations.
- Each of these 24 letter vowel combinations of YHVH are then paired up with the 6 forms of the letter *Aleph*, where each form has a separate vowel combination. E.g., for the first letter vowel combination for the letter *Yud* of YHVH, its pairs are as follows: יָאָ, יָאֶ, יָאִ, יָאֹ, יָאֻ, יָאְ.
- If this pairing sequence is followed for each of the 24 letter vowel combinations of YHVH paired with each of the 6 *Aleph* vowel combinations, this will result in 144 letter pair and vowel combinations (i.e., 24 × 6).
- In total these 144 letter pairs will contain 36 instances of each of the letters *Yud*, *Hey*, *Vav*, and *Hey* plus 144 instances of the letter *Aleph*. The numerical value of 36 instances of YHVH is 936 (i.e., 36 × 26). The numerical value of 144 instances of *Aleph* is 144 (i.e., 144 × 1). Therefore, the total numerical value of the 144 letter pairs is 1,080 (i.e., 936 + 144).
- Each hour of the day is therefore associated with 1,080 unique numerical value increments of the 144 letter pair vowel combinations of God's Name.
- [The specific relevance of pairing YHVH with the letter *Aleph* is that the letter *Aleph* itself also depicts the numerical value of YHVH or 26. The

- ○ [corresponding to the change of the] 1,080 specific parts of an hour[17]
- ○ and they similarly undergo further change each hour into different combinations
- ○ and in addition, the characteristic of day is not the same as the characteristic of night
- ○ and no consecutive day is similar to its previous or subsequent day at all
- ○ this being as specifically written *"Renewing.... the Act of Creation."*[18]

Note 2 – Elohim is a generic description, God is Elokay HaElohim

- Even though this name [Elohim] is generically used to describe all power wielding beings which exist in the Universe
  - ○ and all the angels of the supernal and lower realms are called *Elohim*
  - ○ as per "The gods (Elohay) of the peoples,"[19] and "For each person of the peoples will follow the name of his god (Elohav)."[20]
  - ○ Refer to the Zohar[21] in relation to the use of the expression "and god (Elohim) came" in connection with Avimelech, Lavan, and Bilam, meaning their angel, for they are appointed over them to direct them
  - ○ similarly, Earthly judges are referred to as Elohim[22]
  - ○ and in the Zohar:[23] "There is one name – from all of His Names." Refer there.

---

letter *Aleph* is constructed with a slanting line, corresponding to the letter *Vav*, with two letter *Yud*s, one above and the other below the slanting line. The numerical value of two *Yud*s and *a Vav* is 26.]

17 Midrash Sechel Tov, Shemot 12:20. See Rambam, Mishneh Torah, Hilchot Kiddush HaChodesh 6:2 where he states that this number is used to divide an hour as it is divisible by many numbers.
18 Siddur, the Shacharit prayer. Also Chagiga 12b.
19 Tehillim 96:5.
20 Michah 4:5.
21 Zohar III Vayikra 8a quoting Bereishit 20:3 and Bamidbar 22:20:
  - This "and Elohim came to Avimelech," what is the difference with the nations of the world [about whom it says] "and Elohim came," and with Israel [about whom] it does not say this? ... but we have learned that each instance like this of Elohim relates to the powers/angels appointed to govern over [the nations of the world] just like "and Elohim came to Bilaam at night," that is the power appointed over him.

  Zohar III Balak 208b quoting Bamidbar 22:20 and Bamidbar 22:12:
  - ... and because of this it says "and Elohim came to Bilaam," "and Elohim spoke to Bilaam," as sometimes angels are referred to with a supernal name....

- תתר״ף רִגְעֵי הַשָּׁעָה
- וְכֵן מִשְׁתַּנִּים עוֹד כָּל שָׁעָה לְצֵרוּפִים אֲחֵרִים
- וְגַם אֵין מִדַּת יוֹם שָׁוָה לְמִדַּת לַיְלָה
- לֹא כָּל יוֹם דּוֹמֶה לַחֲבֵרוֹ שֶׁלְּפָנָיו וְאַחֲרָיו כְּלָל
- זֶה שֶׁאָמַר 'הַמְחַדֵּשׁ' כו' 'מַעֲשֵׂה בְרֵאשִׁית' דַּיְקָא:

הגהה ב'

- וְאַף שֶׁהוּא שֵׁם מְשֻׁתָּף לְכָל בַּעַל כֹּחַ שֶׁנִּמְצָא בָּעוֹלָם
- וְכָל שָׂרֵי מַעְלָה וּמַטָּה נִקְרָאִים "אֱלֹקִים"
- כְּמוֹ שֶׁכָּתוּב (תהלים צו, ה) "אֱלֹהֵי הָעַמִּים", "כִּי כָּל הָעַמִּים יֵלְכוּ אִישׁ בְּשֵׁם אֱלֹהָיו" (מיכה ד, ה).
- וְעַיֵּ' זֹהַר (ויקרא ח' ע"א וּבְפָרָשַׁת בָּלָק ר"ח ב') בְּעִנְיַן "וַיָּבֹא אֱלֹקִים" דִּכְתִיב בַּאֲבִימֶלֶךְ וְלָבָן וּבִלְעָם, פֵּרוּשׁ, הַשַּׂר שֶׁלּוֹ, כִּי הֵם מְמֻנִּים עֲלֵיהֶם לְהַנְהִיגָם
- וְכֵן דַּיָּנֵי מַטָּה נִקְרָאִים 'אֱלֹקִים'.
- וּבְסָבָא (צ"ו א') וּשְׁמָא חַד מִכֹּל שְׁאָר שְׁמָהָן וכו' עַיֵּן שָׁם:

(The above references which are brought in the text just mention Avimelech and Bilaam. However R. Chaim also mentions Lavan. There is one place in the Zohar which mentions all three in this context and this quotation is brought here as it adds further insight. Zohar III Bechukotai 113a:
- ... and therefore Elohim is written with all of them "and Elohim came to Bilaam," "and Elohim came to Lavan," "and Elohim came to Avimelech," [Elohim] came to them, but they did not come to Him for they do not have a place prepared for Him. If you ask, but it says "Elohim" [and surely this name would not be associated with the impure]? But this name is connected with all, and even idol worship is also called "Elohim" [as in] "other Elohim/gods," and these appointees are incorporated within "other Elohim/gods," and since they are incorporated in this category they are therefore referred to in this way.)

22   E.g., Shemot 21:6, where Rashi comments that the words "will bring him to the *Elohim*" means "will bring him to the *Bet Din*."

23   Zohar II Mishpatim 96a:
- Come and see. All the names and the descriptions of the Names of God, they all disseminate in their own ways, and they are all clothed within each other, and all of them are split into known ways and paths. Except for one name which is differentiated from the other names which is inherited by the One Nation who are differentiated from the other nations, and it is

- Nevertheless, none of them have power which derives from themselves – but only from the power and control which God assigns to them to enable them to rule.[24]
  ○ Therefore, God is referred to as the "God of gods (Elokay HaElohim)."[25]
  ○ Similarly, it is written, "For God (YHVH) is greater than all the gods (Elohim)"[26] and "all gods (Elohim) will prostrate before Him"[27]
  ○ and the idol worshippers[28] also refer to God as "God of gods."[29]
- Therefore, [these angels and idols] are referred to as "other gods (Elohim)"[30]
  ○ meaning that they have no intrinsic ability of their own but only from a power higher than them – which in turn also draws from an [even] higher power – until ultimately drawing from God, the true source of all power.
- Therefore, the verse states "and God (YHVH) is the true God (Elokim)"[31]
  ○ that He is the true power of All, that All receive their power from God, this is as per "and they fell on their faces and said God is *the* Elokim."[32]

3. THOUGHT, SPEECH, AND ACTION CREATE OR DESTROY WORLDS

- God created man in this analogous way, so to speak [in the "image of Elokim"]
  ○ giving him [continuous] control over innumerable powers and worlds
  ○ handing them over to him such that he commands and directs them

---

YHVH, as per "For His people are a part of YHVH" (Devarim 32:9) and it is written "and you [Israel] who cleave to YHVH" (4:4), who literally cleave to this name more than all other names. There is one name – from all of His Names, which is one which disseminates to many ways and paths, and is called "Elokim," and this name is inherited and divided up among the lowest parts of this world, and this name is divided there into [those powers which] serve, are appointed over, and control the other peoples [of the world], as per "and Elohim came to Bilaam at night" (Bamidbar 22:20), and "and Elohim came to Avimelech in a dream at night" (Bereishit 20:3), and similarly all the appointed ones which God causes the other nations to inherit are incorporated in this name.

24 The Vilna Gaon, in Aderet Eliyahu on Bereishit 1:2, makes the following comments:
- "and the Spirit of Elokim": Be attentive and internalize that all beings above the firmament and those of them which reach us, are close to and associ-

- אָמְנָם כֻּלָּם אֵין הַכֹּחַ שֶׁלָּהֶם מֵעַצְמָם, רַק מִמַּה שֶׁקָּבַע בָּהֶם הוּא יִתְבָּרֵךְ כֹּחַ וּגְבוּרָה לִהְיוֹת מוֹשְׁלִים וְכוּ'.
  - לָכֵן נִקְרָא הוּא יִתְבָּרֵךְ שְׁמוֹ "אֱלֹקֵי הָאֱלֹהִים" (תהלים קלו, ב)
  - וְכֵן כְּתִיב (שמות יח, יא) "כִּי גָדוֹל ה' מִכָּל הָאֱלֹהִים", "הִשְׁתַּחֲווּ לוֹ כָּל אֱלֹהִים" (תהלים צז, ז)
  - וְגַם הָעוֹבְדֵי כּוֹכָבִים קוֹרְאִים אוֹתוֹ יִתְבָּרַךְ "אֱלָהָא דֶּאֱלָהִין", (דניאל ב, מז):
- וְלָכֵן נִקְרָאִים 'אֱלֹהִים אֲחֵרִים'
  - רוֹצֶה לוֹמַר שֶׁאֵין הַכֹּחַ שֶׁלָּהֶם מֵעַצְמָם, רַק מִכֹּחַ הַגָּבוֹהַּ, וְהַגָּבוֹהַּ מִמֶּנּוּ מוֹשֵׁךְ גַּם כֵּן כֹּחוֹ מֵהַכֹּחַ שֶׁעָלָיו, עַד הַבַּעַל כֹּחַ הָאֲמִתִּי שֶׁל כֻּלָּם הוּא יִתְבָּרֵךְ שְׁמוֹ:
- וְלָכֵן נֶאֱמַר (ירמיה י, י) "וַה' אֱלֹקִים אֱמֶת"
  - שֶׁהוּא הַבַּעַל כֹּחַ הָאֲמִתִּי שֶׁל כֻּלָּם, שֶׁכֻּלָּם מְקַבְּלִים כֹּחָם, מִמֶּנּוּ יִתְבָּרֵךְ שְׁמוֹ, ז"ש (מלכים א. יח, לט) "וַיִּפְּלוּ עַל פְּנֵיהֶם וַיֹּאמְרוּ ה' הוּא הָאֱלֹהִים":

שער א' - פרק ג'

- כֵּן בְּדִמְיוֹן זֶה, כִּבְיָכוֹל, בָּרָא הוּא יִתְבָּרֵךְ אֶת הָאָדָם
  - וְהִשְׁלִיטוֹ עַל רִבֵּי רִבְבָן כֹּחוֹת וְעוֹלָמוֹת אֵין מִסְפָּר
  - וּמְסָרָם בְּיָדוֹ, שֶׁיְּהֵא הוּא הַמְדַבֵּר וְהַמַּנְהִיג אוֹתָם, עַל פִּי כָּל פָּרְטֵי תְּנוּעוֹת

---

ated with the word "Elohim" as they fulfill [God's] word without being deflected from His Will . . . and similarly "the Spirit of Elokim," this is the spirit which resides above the firmament which is upon us, and this is what Chazal say (refer to Sefer Pardes Rimonim 1:5) that the soul of Israel *is a part of Eloka/God Above*, meaning that it is some small aspect of the Spirit of Elokim which resides Above.

25 Tehillim 136:2.
26 Shemot 18:11.
27 Tehillim 97:7.
28 The term "idol worshippers" appeared in the Second Edition apparently as a result of censorship replacing the word "nations" which appeared in the First Edition.
29 Daniel 2:47.
30 E.g., Shemot 20:2.
31 Yirmiyahu 10:10.
32 1 Melachim 18:39.

according to his specific actions, speech, and thoughts together with his behavior whether positive or negative, God forbid.
- For with his positive actions, speech, and thoughts
  - he maintains and provides power to many supernal holy powers and worlds
  - adding Holiness and Light to them.
  - As per "and I will place My Words in your mouth . . . to plant heavens and establish earth"[33]
  - and as per Chazal "Don't call them my sons but rather my builders,"[34] for they arrange the supernal worlds like a builder who arranges his construction and provides them with much power.
- And the opposite, God forbid, through his actions or speech and thoughts which are not positive
  - he immeasurably destroys, Heaven should save us, countless powers and holy supernal worlds
  - as per "and those that will annihilate and destroy you, will come from you"[35]
  - darkening or reducing their light and holiness, God forbid
  - and instead, increasing the corresponding power in the chambers of impurity, Heaven should save us.
- This is the meaning of "Elokim created man *in His Image*. In the *image of Elokim* [He created him]"[36] and "For in the *image of Elokim* He made man"[37]
  - that just as God is The Elokim – the One who empowers All existence in all of the worlds, arranging and controlling them all each moment as per His Will
  - similarly, God willed it that man is enabled to exert control such that he is the one who *opens and closes*[38] a myriad of powers and worlds
  - according to the detail of his behavior in all that he does at each and every moment
  - corresponding to his supernal source of his actions, speech and thoughts
  - as if he [man] were also the source of their power, so to speak.
  - As per Chazal:

---

33 Yishayahu 51:16.
34 Berachot 64a, where the sons who are the Torah Sages are referred to as "builders." (There is another reference to builders being Torah Sages in Mishna Mikvaot 9:6.)
35 Yishayahu 49:17.
36 Bereishit 1:27.

מַעֲשָׂיו, וְדִבּוּרָיו, וּמַחְשְׁבוֹתָיו, וְכָל סִדְרֵי הַנְהָגוֹתָיו, הֵן לְטוֹב אוֹ לְהֵפֶךְ חַס וְשָׁלוֹם:

- כִּי בְּמַעֲשָׂיו וְדִבּוּרָיו וּמַחְשְׁבוֹתָיו הַטּוֹבִים
  - הוּא מְקַיֵּם וְנוֹתֵן כֹּחַ בְּכַמָּה כֹחוֹת וְעוֹלָמוֹת עֶלְיוֹנִים הַקְּדוֹשִׁים
  - וּמוֹסִיף בָּהֶם קְדֻשָּׁה וָאוֹר
  - כְּמוֹ שֶׁכָּתוּב (ישעי׳ נא, טז) "וָאָשִׂים דְּבָרַי בְּפִיךָ וְגו׳ לִנְטֹעַ שָׁמַיִם וְלִיסֹד אָרֶץ"
  - וּכְמַאֲמָרָם זִכְרוֹנָם לִבְרָכָה (ברכות סד.) אַל תִּקְרָא בָּנַיִךְ אֶלָּא בּוֹנַיִךְ, כִּי הֵמָּה הַמְסַדְּרִים עוֹלָמוֹת הָעֶלְיוֹנִים, כְּבוֹנֶה הַמְסַדֵּר בִּנְיָנוֹ, וְנוֹתְנִים בָּהֶם רַב כֹּחַ:
- וּבְהִפּוּךְ חַס וְשָׁלוֹם, עַל יְדֵי מַעֲשָׂיו אוֹ דִבּוּרָיו וּמַחְשְׁבוֹתָיו אֲשֶׁר לֹא טוֹבִים
  - הוּא מְהָרֵס רַחֲמָנָא לִצְּלָן כַּמָּה כֹחוֹת, וְעוֹלָמוֹת עֶלְיוֹנִים הַקְּדוֹשִׁים, לְאֵין עֵרֶךְ וְשִׁעוּר
  - כְּמוֹ שֶׁנֶּאֱמַר (שם מט, יז) "מְהָרְסַיִךְ וּמַחֲרִיבַיִךְ מִמֵּךְ יֵצֵאוּ"
  - אוֹ מַחְשִׁיךְ, אוֹ מַקְטִין אוֹרָם וּקְדֻשָּׁתָם חַס וְשָׁלוֹם
  - וּמוֹסִיף כֹּחַ לְעֻמַּת זֶה, בַּמְדוֹרוֹת הַטֻּמְאָה ר"ל:
- זֶהוּ "וַיִּבְרָא אֱלֹקִים אֶת הָאָדָם בְּצַלְמוֹ בְּצֶלֶם אֱלֹקִים וְגו׳ (בראשית א, כז), כִּי בְּצֶלֶם אֱלֹקִים עָשָׂה" וְגו׳ (שם ט, ו)
  - שֶׁכְּמוֹ שֶׁהוּא יִתְבָּרַךְ שְׁמוֹ, הוּא הָאֱלֹקִים, בַּעַל הַכֹּחוֹת הַנִּמְצָאִים בְּכָל הָעוֹלָמוֹת כֻּלָּם, וּמְסַדְּרָם וּמַנְהִיגָם כָּל רֶגַע כִּרְצוֹנוֹ
  - כֵּן הִשְׁלִיט רְצוֹנוֹ יִתְבָּרַךְ אֶת הָאָדָם שֶׁיְּהֵא הוּא הַפּוֹתֵחַ וְהַסּוֹגֵר שֶׁל כַּמָּה אַלְפֵי רִבְבוֹת כֹּחוֹת וְעוֹלָמוֹת
  - עַל פִּי כָּל פְּרָטֵי סִדְרֵי הַנְהָגוֹתָיו בְּכָל עִנְיָנָיו בְּכָל עֵת וְרֶגַע מַמָּשׁ
  - כְּפִי שָׁרְשׁוֹ הָעֶלְיוֹן שֶׁל מַעֲשָׂיו וְדִבּוּרָיו וּמַחְשְׁבוֹתָיו
  - כְּאִלּוּ הוּא גַם כֵּן הַבַּעַל כֹּחַ שֶׁלָּהֶם כִּבְיָכוֹל.
  - וְאָמְרוּ זִכְרוֹנָם לִבְרָכָה

---

37 Bereishit 9:6.
38 The expression "opens and closes" is expanded on in G1:19 where man is described as a "key."

- R. Azarya said in the name of R. Yehuda bar Simon: At the time when Israel perform the Will of God, they add power to the strength of that which is Above, as per "*through* God (Elokim) we shall do valiantly," but when Israel do not perform the Will of God they, so to speak, diminish the great power of that which is Above, as per "the Rock that gave birth to you shall be weakened."[39]
- People's sins do damage Above[40] and similarly, vice versa as above.
- This is in line with the verse "Give strength *to* God (Elokim)."[41]
  - "It happened one day [that the angels (Bnei Elokim) came] to stand before God." When they come to stand to accuse those actions of Israel, they are certainly standing in accusation of God, as when Israel perform improper actions they, so to speak, diminish God's power, and when they perform proper actions they add impetus and power to God; it is about this that it is stated "Give strength to God (Elokim)." With what? With proper deeds.[42]

- Therefore, the verse says "*to* God (Elokim)," and similarly, "*through* God (Elokim) we shall do valiantly," as its meaning is [that He is] the Power of All things as stated above.

4. THOUGHT, SPEECH, AND ACTION HAVE SUPERNAL CONSEQUENCE

- 'It is therefore the unequivocal law of man'[43]
  - that each Jew should not, God forbid, say in his heart "What am I and what is my power such that my lowly actions should impact on any aspect of the Universe?"
  - but he should understand, know, and internalize in the thoughts of his heart that every detail of his actions, speech, and thoughts at each and every moment is never lost, God forbid
  - and how great and tremendous are his actions such that each one rises, according to its source, to impact on the highest heights in the supernal worlds and [on] the subtle shining of the [supernal] lights.[44] (Note 3)[45]

---

39 Eicha Rabba 1:33 quoting Tehillim 60:14 and Devarim 32:18.
40 In many places in the Zohar, e.g., Zohar III Vayikra 8a.
41 Tehillim 68:35.
42 Zohar II Bo 32b quoting Iyov 1:6 and Tehillim 68:35.
43 R. Chaim uses the emphatic language "VeZot Torat Haadam," borrowed from 2 Shmuel 7:19, also used at the beginning of G1:21.

בְּאֵיכָה רַבָּתִי (בפסוק וילכו בלא כח ג') רַבִּי עֲזַרְיָה בְּשֵׁם רַבִּי יְהוּדָה בֶּן סִמוֹן אוֹמֵר, בִּזְמַן שֶׁיִשְׂרָאֵל עוֹשִׂין רְצוֹנוֹ שֶׁל מָקוֹם, מוֹסִיפִין כֹּחַ בִּגְבוּרָה שֶׁל מַעְלָה, כְּמָה דְאַתְּ אָמַרְתְּ "בֵּאלֹקִים נַעֲשֶׂה חָיִל" (תהלים ס, יד), וּבִזְמַן שֶׁאֵין יִשְׂרָאֵל עוֹשִׂין רְצוֹנוֹ שֶׁל מָקוֹם, כִּבְיָכוֹל מַתִּישִׁין כֹּחַ גָּדוֹל שֶׁל מַעְלָה, דִּכְתִיב (דברים לב, יח) "צוּר יְלָדְךָ תֶּשִׁי" וְגו'.

○ וּבְכַמָּה מְקוֹמוֹת בַּזֹּהַר הַקָּדוֹשׁ, דְּחוֹבֵי בַּר נָשׁ, עַבְדִין פְּגִימוּ לְעֵילָּא כו', וְכֵן לְהֵפֶךְ כַּנַּ"ל.

○ וְזֶהוּ שֶׁאָמַר הַכָּתוּב "תְּנוּ עֹז לֵאלֹקִים" (תהלים סח, לה).

◊ וּבַזֹּהַר רֵישׁ פָּרְשַׁת בֹּא, "וַיְהִי הַיּוֹם וַיָּבֹאוּ גו' לְהִתְיַצֵּב עַל ה'" (איוב א, ו), כַּד בָּעָאן לְקַיְּמָא עַל אִינוּן עוֹבְדִין דְּיִשְׂרָאֵל, עַל ה'. וַדַּאי קַיְּמִין, דְּהָא כַּד יִשְׂרָאֵל עָבְדִין עוֹבְדִין דְּלָא כַּשְׁרָן, כִּבְיָכוֹל מַתִּישִׁין חֵילָא דְּקוּדְשָׁא בְּרִיךְ הוּא, וְכַד עָבְדִין עוֹבְדִין דְּכַשְׁרָן, יָהֲבִין תּוּקְפָא וְחֵילָא לְקוּדְשָׁא בְּרִיךְ הוּא, וְעַל דָּא כְּתִיב "תְּנוּ עֹז לֵאלֹקִים", בַּמָּה, בְּעוֹבְדִין דְּכַשְׁרָן:

• וְלָכֵן אָמַר "לֵאלֹקִים", וְכֵן "בֵּ'אלֹקִים' נַעֲשֶׂה חָיִל" (תהלים ס, יד), שֶׁפֵּרוּשׁוֹ בַּעַל הַכֹּחוֹת כֻּלָּם וְכַנַּ"ל:

שַׁעַר א' - פֶּרֶק ד'

• וְזֹאת תּוֹרַת הָאָדָם

○ כָּל אִישׁ יִשְׂרָאֵל, אַל יֹאמַר בְּלִבּוֹ חַס וְשָׁלוֹם, כִּי מָה אֲנִי וּמָה כֹּחִי לִפְעוֹל בְּמַעֲשַׂי הַשְּׁפֵלִים שׁוּם עִנְיָן בָּעוֹלָם.

○ אָמְנָם יָבִין וְיֵדַע וְיִקְבַּע בְּמַחְשְׁבוֹת לִבּוֹ, שֶׁכָּל פְּרָטֵי מַעֲשָׂיו וְדִבּוּרָיו וּמַחְשְׁבוֹתָיו כָּל עֵת וָרֶגַע, לֹא אִתְאֲבִידוּ חַס וְשָׁלוֹם

○ וּמַה רַבּוּ מַעֲשָׂיו וּמְאֹד גָּדְלוּ וְרָמוּ, שֶׁכָּל אַחַת, עוֹלָה כְּפִי שָׁרְשָׁהּ, לִפְעוֹל פְּעֻלָּתָהּ בְּגָבְהֵי מְרוֹמִים, בָּעוֹלָמוֹת וְצַחְצָחוֹת הָאוֹרוֹת הָעֶלְיוֹנִים: (הגהה ג')

---

44 The reference to the subtle shining of the supernal lights relates to a level so high and subtle that it cannot even be described by one of the standard world levels, as per G1:13:N13.

45 **R. Chaim adds Note 3 here.** This note is brought at the end of this chapter and is entitled "Know that what is above – is from you."

- In reality, for 'a wise person who truly understands this'[46]
  - his heart will tremble and shake within him when he appreciates that the destructive consequences of even minor sins, God forbid, are far greater than the destruction of Nevuchadnezar and Titus [who destroyed the First and Second Temples respectively].
  - For the actions of Nevuchadnezar and Titus did not damage or corrupt the supernal worlds at all, as they did not have a part and [soul] root in the supernal worlds such that they were capable of impacting them at all with their actions.
  - It is however our sins which diminish and weaken the power and strength of that which is Above, 'the Sanctuary of God is defiled,'[47] so to speak, the Supernal Temple
  - and as a result of this, Nevuchadnezar and Titus were enabled to destroy the lower [physical] Temple which corresponded to the Supernal Temple
  - as per Chazal referring to the grinding of flour.[48]
  - Therefore, it was our sins which destroyed the Supernal Abode, holy supernal worlds, and they only destroyed the lower [physical] abode.[49]
- This is what King David, peace be upon him, prayed for [in connection with the attack of the enemy] that "It has been regarded as bringing axes in the thicket of trees to the Above,"[50] that he wanted it to be considered

---

46 Yirmiyahu 9:11.
47 Bamidbar 19:20.
48 Eicha Rabba 1:41, end of section 4b, and also Sanhedrin 96b. Both refer to the verse "take a mill and grind flour" (Yishayahu 47:2), i.e., flour has already been ground so there is no real meaning for it to be milled again. Similarly, Jerusalem was already destroyed by our sins so there is no real meaning to the fact it was physically destroyed by Nevuchadnezar or Titus.
49 R. Chaim is highlighting the difference between Jew and non-Jew here. A Jew's soul is structured in such a way that his thoughts, speech, and actions literally have supernal consequence both for the good and the bad. This concept is developed throughout the First Gateway and the general reference to "man" in the First Gateway is really a reference to a Jew. In contrast, the structure of a non-Jew's soul is such that his actions can only impact this physical world, but only if a Jew has first impacted on the supernal worlds in such a way which enables the non-Jew's actions to take effect in this physical world. R. Chaim highlights here that this is even the case with powerful non-Jewish leaders such as Nevuchadnezar and Titus.
   The relationship of Jew to non-Jew is like that of a priest to a member of the congregation he serves, as per the Scriptural description of the Jewish

- וּבֶאֱמֶת, כִּי הָאִישׁ הֶחָכָם וְיָבֵן אֶת זֹאת לַאֲמִתּוֹ
○ לִבּוֹ יָחִיל בְּקִרְבּוֹ בְּחִיל וּרְעָדָה, בְּשׂוּמוֹ עַל לִבּוֹ עַל מַעֲשָׂיו אֲשֶׁר לֹא טוֹבִים חַס וְשָׁלוֹם, עַד הֵיכָן הֵמָּה מַגִּיעִים לְקַלְקֵל וְלַהֲרֹס בַּחֲטֹא קַל חַס וְשָׁלוֹם, הַרְבֵּה יוֹתֵר מִמַּה שֶּׁהֶחֱרִיב נְבוּכַדְנֶצַּר וְטִיטוּס.
○ כִּי הֲלֹא נְבוּכַדְנֶצַּר וְטִיטוּס לֹא עָשׂוּ בְּמַעֲשֵׂיהֶם, שׁוּם פְּגָם וְקִלְקוּל כְּלָל לְמַעְלָה, כִּי לֹא לָהֶם חֵלֶק וְשֹׁרֶשׁ בָּעוֹלָמוֹת הָעֶלְיוֹנִים, שֶׁיִּהְיוּ יְכוֹלִים לִנְגֹּעַ שָׁם כְּלָל בְּמַעֲשֵׂיהֶם.
○ רַק שֶׁבַּחֲטָאֵינוּ נִתְמַעֵט וְתָשׁ כִּבְיָכוֹל כֹּחַ גְּבוּרָה שֶׁל מַעְלָה, אֶת מִקְדַּשׁ ה' טִמְּאוּ כִּבְיָכוֹל הַמִּקְדָּשׁ הָעֶלְיוֹן
○ וְעַל יְדֵי כָּךְ הָיָה לָהֶם כֹּחַ לִנְבוּכַדְנֶצַּר וְטִיטוּס לְהַחֲרִיב הַמִּקְדָּשׁ שֶׁל מַטָּה, הַמְכֻוָּן נֶגֶד הַמִּקְדָּשׁ שֶׁל מַעְלָה
○ כְּמוֹ שֶׁאָמְרוּ רַבּוֹתֵינוּ זִכְרוֹנָם לִבְרָכָה (איכה רבתי א, מא) קִמְחָא טְחִינָא טָחִינַתְּ.
○ הֲרֵי כִּי עֲוֹנוֹתֵינוּ הֶחֱרִיבוּ "נְוֵה מַעְלָה" — עוֹלָמוֹת עֶלְיוֹנִים הַקְּדוֹשִׁים, וְהֵמָּה הֶחֱרִיבוּ רַק "נְוֵה מַטָּה":
- וְזֶהוּ שֶׁהִתְפַּלֵּל דָּוִד הַמֶּלֶךְ עָלָיו הַשָּׁלוֹם (תהלים עד, ה) "יִוָּדַע כְּמֵבִיא לְמָעְלָה

People who are "a Kingdom of Priests and a Holy Nation" (Shemot 19:6). Both positions of priest and congregant have significance and corresponding obligations. A priest is not a priest if he has no congregation, and a congregation requires a priest to provide assistance. The Jew is obliged to observe 613 Mitzvot and the non-Jew similarly has the obligation to observe the 7 Noachide laws. Both Jew and non-Jew have the ability and the free choice to generate Tikkun/rectification or Kilkul/damage through their actions; however, the Jew's obligation and responsibility is to rectify both himself and the worlds around him, whereas the non-Jew's obligation is to rectify himself. Therefore, the impact of a Jew's actions reaches further. Should any non-Jew wish to take on a greater level of obligation, he also has the free choice to convert to Judaism as long as it is done with full conviction. However, a non-Jew is able to reach meaningful spiritual heights of perfection in serving God without converting to Judaism, e.g., as the Midrash states (Eliyahu Rabba Parsha 10 or Chap. 9 in some versions):

- ... I call on the heavens and earth to bear witness that irrespective of whether one is a non-Jew, a Jew, a man, a woman, a manservant or maidservant, that the Holy Spirit/Ruach HaKodesh can be drawn upon him/herself in a way which corresponds to his/her level of action ...

50   Tehillim 74:5.

as if there was destruction in the Supernal Realms; however, in reality [the enemies'] actions had no impact there at all, as mentioned above.[51]

- Every Jewish heart will further tremble when reflecting on the fact that his structure incorporates the entirety of all of the powers and the worlds (Note 4)[52] as will be explained, with God's Will later[53] in G1:06 and G2:05
  - that they themselves are the very Supernal Holy and Temple
  - and a person's heart, the center of the body, incorporates all, corresponding to the Holy of Holies, the center of the residence, the foundation stone [of the Supernal Temple] – incorporating all roots of similar sources of holiness, as hinted to by Chazal that "One should focus one's heart to correspond to the Holy of Holies."[54]
- This is as per the Zohar:[55]
  - Come and see, when God created man in this world he established him as a distinguished reflection of [the structure of] the Supernal Realms, and gave him power and strength in the center of his body where the heart resides . . . God established the world in this way and made it as one body . . . with the heart residing at its center which is the strength of everything and everything is dependent on it . . . and the Sanctuary which [encompasses] the Holy of Holies containing the Shechina, Cherubim, and the Ark – this is the heart of each land and world and from here all parts of the world are sustained . . . Refer to this at length.
- Therefore, when a person's thoughts stray to think impure incestuous thoughts in his heart, the Merciful One should save us
  - he [literally] brings a prostitute, the 'Image of Provocation,'[56] into the awesome Supernal Holy of Holies of the holy supernal worlds, God forbid
  - and thereby increases the potency of impurity and the *Sitra Achara*[57] in the Supernal Holy of Holies in a far far greater way than that which was caused to increase the strength and powers of impurity by Titus, who brought a prostitute into the Holy of Holies of the lower [physical] Temple.
- Similarly, with each sin, every Jew enters a 'strange fire'[58] into his heart,

---

51 As per the beginning of Sanhedrin 96b and in line with Shemot Rabba Pekudei 51:5 and Midrash Tanchuma Pekudei 3.
52 **R. Chaim adds Note 4 here.** This note is brought at the end of this chapter and is entitled "Jew and Mishkan have same Shiur Komah, thus Jew can be Mishkan."

בְּסָבְכָךְ עֵץ קַרְדֻּמּוֹת", בִּקֵּשׁ שֶׁיֵּחָשֵׁב לוֹ כְּאִלּוּ לְמַעְלָה בִּשְׁמֵי מְרוֹמִים הָרַס, אֲבָל בֶּאֱמֶת לֹא נָגְעוּ שָׁם מַעֲשָׂיו כְּלָל כנ"ל:

- גַּם עַל זֹאת יֶחֱרַד לֵב הָאָדָם מֵעַם הַקֹּדֶשׁ, שֶׁהוּא כּוֹלֵל בְּתַבְנִיתוֹ כָּל הַכֹּחוֹת וְהָעוֹלָמוֹת כֻּלָּם (הגהה ד'), כְּמוֹ שֶׁיִּתְבָּאֵר אי"ה לְהַלָּן בְּפֶרֶק ו' וּבְשַׁעַר ב' פֶּרֶק ה' שֶׁהֵן הֵמָּה הַקֹּדֶשׁ וְהַמִּקְדָּשׁ הָעֶלְיוֹן

  ○ וְהַלֵּב שֶׁל הָאָדָם, אֶמְצָעִיתָא דְגוּפָא, הוּא כְּלָלִיּוּת הַכֹּל, נֶגֶד הַבֵּית קָדְשֵׁי קָדָשִׁים, אֶמְצַע הַיִּשּׁוּב, אֶבֶן שְׁתִיָּה, כּוֹלֵל כָּל שָׁרְשֵׁי מְקוֹר הַקְּדֻשּׁוֹת כָּמוֹהוּ, וְרִמְּזוּהוּ זִכְרוֹנָם לִבְרָכָה בַּמִּשְׁנָה פֶּרֶק תְּפִלַּת הַשַּׁחַר (ברכות כח, ב) יְכַוֵּן אֶת לִבּוֹ כְּנֶגֶד בֵּית קָדְשֵׁי הַקֳּדָשִׁים:

- וּבַזֹּהַר שְׁלַח (קס"א סוף ע"א)

  ○ תָּא חֲזֵי, כַּד בְּרָא קוּדְשָׁא בְּרִיךְ הוּא בַּר נָשׁ בְּעָלְמָא, אַתְקִין לֵיהּ כְּגַוְנָא עִלָּאָה יַקִּירָא, וִיהַב לֵיהּ חֵילֵיהּ וְתוּקְפֵּיהּ בְּאֶמְצָעִיתָא דְגוּפָא דְתַמָּן שָׁרְיָא לִבָּא כו', כְּגַוְנָא דָא אַתְקִין קוּדְשָׁא בְּרִיךְ הוּא עָלְמָא, וְעָבֵיד לֵיהּ חַד גּוּפָא כו', וְלִבָּא שָׁרֵי בְּאֶמְצָעִיתָא וכו' דְּהַהוּא תּוּקְפָּא דְכֹלָּא, וְכֹלָּא בֵּיהּ תַּלְיָין כו', וְהַהֵיכָל לְבֵית קָדְשֵׁי הַקֳּדָשִׁים דְתַמָּן שְׁכִינָה וְכַפֹּרֶת וּכְרוּבִים וְאָרוֹן, וְהָכָא הוּא לִבָּא דְכָל אַרְעָא וְעָלְמָא, וּמֵהָכָא אִתְּזָנוּ כו', עַיֵּן שָׁם בְּאֹרֶךְ:

- אִם כֵּן, בְּעֵת אֲשֶׁר יָתוּר הָאָדָם לַחֲשֹׁב בְּלִבּוֹ, מַחֲשָׁבָה אֲשֶׁר לֹא טְהוֹרָה בְּנִאוּף ר"ל.

  ○ הֲרֵי הוּא מַכְנִיס זוֹנָה, סֵמֶל הַקִּנְאָה, בְּבֵית קָדְשֵׁי הַקֳּדָשִׁים הָעֶלְיוֹן נוֹרָא בָּעוֹלָמוֹת הָעֶלְיוֹנִים הַקְּדוֹשִׁים חַס וְשָׁלוֹם

  ○ וּמַגְבִּיר רַחֲמָנָא לִצְלָן כֹּחוֹת הַטֻּמְאָה וְהַסִּטְרָא אָחֳרָא בְּבֵית קָדְשֵׁי הַקֳּדָשִׁים הָעֶלְיוֹן, הַרְבֵּה יוֹתֵר וְיוֹתֵר מִמַּה שֶּׁנִּגְרַם הִתְגַּבְּרוּת כֹּחַ הַטֻּמְאָה עַל יְדֵי טִיטוֹס, בְּהַצִּיעוֹ זוֹנָה בְּבֵית קָדְשֵׁי הַקֳּדָשִׁים בְּמִקְדָּשׁ מַטָּה:

- וְכֵן כָּל חֵטְא אֲשֶׁר כָּל אִישׁ יִשְׂרָאֵל מַכְנִיס בְּלִבּוֹ חַס וְשָׁלוֹם אֵשׁ זָרָה, בְּכַעַס אוֹ שְׁאָרֵי תַּאֲווֹת רָעוֹת ר"ל

---

53 Referring to the concept of Shiur Komah.
54 Berachot 28b.
55 Zohar III Shelach Lecha 161a.
56 Yechezkel 8:3 and 8:5.
57 See p. 564, fn. 280.
58 E.g., Vayikra 10:1.

God forbid, with anger or other evil lusts, the Merciful One should save us
- is it not literally, as per the verse "The Temple of our holiness and our splendor . . . has become burnt up with fire"?[59] the Merciful One should save us.

- This is [the meaning of] what God said to Yechezkel: "[this is] the place of My Throne . . . where I will dwell in the midst of the Children of Israel forever and the House of Israel will no longer defile My Holy Name . . . with their promiscuity . . . Now they will distance their promiscuity . . . and I will dwell within them forever."[60]

- With this, we can now understand the verse "God formed man out of dust . . . and He breathed the soul of life in through his nostrils, and man became a living soul."[61]
  - The simple meaning of this verse is certainly as per the Targum which says "and man became a speaking spirit."
    - Meaning, that when he was just a body – he was literally just earth without any life or movement
    - but when a living soul was breathed into him – he became a live animated person and able to speak.
    - Refer to the Ramban's commentary on the Torah.[62]
  - The verse, however, does not state [that with the soul] "it was *with* man" but rather that "it was *the* man"
    - which allows room for the interpretation as has been explained
    - that man is transformed through the soul of life within him into the living soul of an infinite number of worlds
    - and just as all the detailed behaviors of the body and its movements are empowered by the soul within him
    - similarly, "*the* man," he is the one who empowers and is the living soul of an infinite number of supernal and lower worlds whose [existence and qualities] are controlled entirely by him, as mentioned above.

---

59 Yishayahu 64:10.
60 Yechezkel 43:7–9.
61 Bereishit 2:7.
62 Ramban's comments on Bereishit 2:7:
  - And this verse indeed hints what it implies, that when it says that God formed man as "dust from the earth," he was a raw material like an inani-

- הֲלֹא הוּא מַמָּשׁ כָּעִנְיָן הַכָּתוּב (ישעיה סד, י) "בֵּית קָדְשֵׁנוּ וְתִפְאַרְתֵּנוּ אֲשֶׁר וְגוֹ' הָיָה לִשְׂרֵפַת אֵשׁ", הָרַחֲמָן יִתְבָּרַךְ שְׁמוֹ יַצִּילֵנוּ:
- וְזֶה שֶׁאָמַר הַשֵּׁם לִיחֶזְקֵאל (מג ז) "אֶת מְקוֹם כִּסְאִי גוֹ' אֲשֶׁר אֶשְׁכָּן שָׁם בְּתוֹךְ בְּנֵי יִשְׂרָאֵל לְעוֹלָם וְלֹא יְטַמְּאוּ עוֹד בֵּית יִשְׂרָאֵל שֵׁם קָדְשִׁי גוֹ' בִּזְנוּתָם גוֹ' עַתָּה יְרַחֲקוּ אֶת זְנוּתָם גוֹ' וְשָׁכַנְתִּי גוֹ' בְּתוֹכָם לְעוֹלָם":
- וּבָזֶה יוּבַן הַכָּתוּב (בראשית ב, ז) "וַיִּיצֶר ה' אֱלֹקִים אֶת הָאָדָם עָפָר גוֹ' וַיִּפַּח בְּאַפָּיו נִשְׁמַת חַיִּים, וַיְהִי הָאָדָם לְנֶפֶשׁ חַיָּה".
  - וּפְשׁוּטוֹ שֶׁל מִקְרָא וַדַּאי הוּא כְּתַרְגּוּמוֹ — "וַהֲוַת בָּאָדָם לְרוּחַ מְמַלְּלָא"
    - וְרָצָה לוֹמַר שֶׁכַּאֲשֶׁר הָיָה הַגּוּף לְבַדּוֹ, הָיָה עָדַיִן עָפָר מַמָּשׁ בְּלֹא שׁוּם חִיּוּת וּתְנוּעָה
    - וְכַאֲשֶׁר נָפַח בּוֹ נִשְׁמַת חַיִּים, אָז נַעֲשָׂה אִישׁ חַי לְהִתְנוֹעֵעַ וּלְדַבֵּר.
    - וְעַיֵּן רַמְבַּ"ן בְּפֵרוּשׁ הַתּוֹרָה.
  - אָמְנָם בַּמִּקְרָא "וַיְהִי בָּאָדָם" לֹא כְּתִיב, אֶלָּא "וַיְהִי הָאָדָם"
    - לָזֹאת יֵשׁ מָקוֹם לְפָרְשׁוֹ עַל פִּי שֶׁנִּתְבָּאֵר
    - שֶׁהָאָדָם בְּנִשְׁמַת הַחַיִּים שֶׁבְּתוֹכוֹ, הוּא נַעֲשָׂה 'נֶפֶשׁ חַיָּה' לְרִבּוּי עוֹלָמוֹת אֵין מִסְפָּר
    - שֶׁכְּמוֹ שֶׁכָּל פְּרָטֵי הַנְהָגוֹת הַגּוּף וּתְנוּעוֹתָיו, הוּא עַל יְדֵי כֹּחַ הַנֶּפֶשׁ שֶׁבְּקִרְבּוֹ
    - כֵּן הָאָדָם הוּא הַכֹּחַ וְנֶפֶשׁ הַחַיָּה שֶׁל עוֹלָמוֹת עֶלְיוֹנִים וְתַחְתּוֹנִים לְאֵין שִׁעוּר, שֶׁכֻּלָּם מִתְנַהֲגִים עַל יָדוֹ כַּנַּ"ל:

---

mate stone – "and God blew a living soul into his nostrils," and then man became an animated "living soul" like the animals and the fish . . . and after he was formed, a living soul was sensitively blown into his nostrils from the Supernal Mouth to add this soul to the previous mentioned form resulting in man becoming a totally living being, for with this soul he can think, speak, and perform actions. . . .

Rabbi Chaim's Notes:
Note 3 – Know that what is above – is from you

- 'Draw near and listen'[63] that this is also part of Chazal's intention in stating "Know what is above *is from you*"[64]
  - meaning that even though you don't physically see the awesome things which are made from your deeds
  - nevertheless you should faithfully know that all that occurs Above in the Highest Realms, it all "*is from you*"
  - according to your actions and to which direction they tend towards, 'it is according to them that they go and come.'[65]

Note 4 – Jew and Mishkan have same Shiur Komah, thus Jew can be Mishkan

- For the Mishkan and the Temple incorporated all the powers, worlds, and holy arrangements
  - in that all of its houses, storehouses, attics, rooms, and holy vessels, all reflected the supernal form, image, and structure of the Holy Supernal Realms and also of the arrangement of the parts of the Merkava.[66]
  - As David and Shmuel the Seer established: "Everything is in writing, by the Hand of God, which He gave me understanding to know all the workings of the structure."[67]
- Chazal state:[68] [Rav expounded the verse "He/(David) and Shmuel went and sat in Nayot . . . Nayot in the Rama"]. What is the connection of Noyot[69] with Rama? It is that they were sitting in Rama [i.e., Shmuel's city] and dealing with the adornment [i.e., Noy] of the world [i.e., the Temple].[70]
  - This is as per Midrash[71] that equates [the construction of the Mishkan] with the Creation of the world and details the parallels between the verses describing the Creation and the [construction of] the Mishkan.
  - Therefore, the verse states about Betzalel that "I will fill him with the spirit of God, with *wisdom, understanding, and knowledge,*"[72] as the world was created with these three things as per "God established the Earth with *wisdom*, set up the Heavens with *understanding* [and split the depths with his *knowledge*]."[73]

---

63 Kohelet 4:17.
64 Mishna Avot 2:1. This understanding of the Mishna is in addition to the standard simple meaning of the words, "Know what is above you."
65 Bamidbar 27:21.
66 The Merkava (i.e., chariot) refers to the vision describing the workings of the Heavenly Realms and the interrelationship of the worlds as depicted in

הגהה ג'

- וְקָרוֹב לִשְׁמֹעַ, שֶׁגַּם זֶה בִּכְלָל כַּוָּנָתָם זִכְרוֹנָם לִבְרָכָה בְּאָבוֹת (ב, א) "דַּע מַה לְמַעְלָה מִמְּךָ".
  - רוֹצֶה לוֹמַר, אִם כִּי אֵינְךָ רוֹאֶה בְּעֵינֶיךָ — הָעִנְיָנִים הַנּוֹרָאִים הַנַּעֲשִׂים מִמַּעֲשֶׂיךָ
  - אֲבָל תֵּדַע נֶאֱמָנָה, כִּי כָּל מַה שֶׁנַּעֲשָׂה לְמַעְלָה בָּעוֹלָמוֹת הָעֶלְיוֹנִים גְּבוֹהֵי גְבוֹהִים, הַכֹּל "מִמְּךָ" הוּא
  - עַל פִּי מַעֲשֶׂיךָ לְאָן נוֹטִים, עַל פִּיהֶם יֵצְאוּ וְיָבוֹאוּ:

הגהה ד'

- כִּי הַמִּשְׁכָּן וְהַמִּקְדָּשׁ הָיוּ כּוֹלְלִים כָּל הַכֹּחוֹת וְהָעוֹלָמוֹת, וְכָל הַסִּדְרֵי קְדֻשּׁוֹת כֻּלָּם
  - כָּל בָּתָּיו וְגִנְזָכָיו עֲלִיּוֹתָיו וַחֲדָרָיו וְכָל כְּלֵי הַקֹּדֶשׁ, כֻּלָּם הָיוּ בְּדֻגְמָא עֶלְיוֹנָה, צֶלֶם, דְּמוּת, תַּבְנִית הָעוֹלָמוֹת הַקְּדוֹשִׁים, וְסִדְרֵי פִּרְקֵי הַמֶּרְכָּבָה
  - הֵמָּה יְסָדָם דָּוִד וּשְׁמוּאֵל הָרוֹאֶה, "הַכֹּל מִיַּד ה' עָלֵיהֶם הִשְׂכִּיל כָּל מַלְאֲכוֹת הַתַּבְנִית" (דה"י א' כח, יט):

- וְאָמְרוּ זִכְרוֹנָם לִבְרָכָה בְּפֶרֶק אֵיזֶהוּ מְקוֹמָן (זבחים נ"ד ב') מַאי דִכְתִיב כוּ' וְכִי מַה עִנְיַן נָיוֹת אֵצֶל רָמָה, אֶלָּא שֶׁהָיוּ יוֹשְׁבִין בְּרָמָה, וְעוֹסְקִין בְּנוֹיוֹ שֶׁל עוֹלָם כוּ'.
  - ז"ש בְּתַנְחוּמָא (ריש פקודי) שֶׁהוּא שָׁקוּל נֶגֶד בְּרִיאַת הָעוֹלָם, וּמוֹנֶה שָׁם כְּסִדְרָן כְּלַל הָעִנְיָנִים שֶׁהָיוּ בַּבְּרִיאָה, שֶׁהֵמָּה הָיוּ כֵן גַּם בַּמִּשְׁכָּן
  - וְלָכֵן אָמַר הַכָּתוּב בִּבְצַלְאֵל "וָאֲמַלֵּא אוֹתוֹ רוּחַ אֱלֹקִים בְּחָכְמָה וּבִתְבוּנָה

Yechezkel 1. Also, see reference to the workings of the Merkava in the first two chapters of Rambam, Mishneh Torah, Hilchot Yesodei HaTorah as he comments in 2:11.

67   1 Divrei Hayamim 28:19.
68   Zevachim 54b quoting 1 Shmuel 19:18–19.
69   A play on the word "Nayot."
70   As Rashi explains that they were identifying the source for the location of the Temple from the Torah.
71   Midrash Tanchuma (Warsaw edition), Pekudei 3.
72   Shemot 31:3.
73   Mishlei 3:19–20.

- See the Zohar at length.[74]
- Therefore, Chazal state[75] that Betzalel knew how to combine the letters with which the Heavens and the Earth were created.
- Therefore, a Jew, who incorporates both the entire arrangement of Creation and of the Merkava within him
  - he also reflects the structure of the Mishkan and the Temple and all of its vessels
  - in that this structure corresponds to the interconnection between his limbs, sinews, and all of his abilities
  - therefore, the Zohar details[76] the structure and contents of the Mishkan, which are all hinted to in a 'one to one mapping'[77] sequence with the make up of man.
- Therefore, it is certain that the principal objective of Holiness, the Temple and the manifestation of [God's] Shechina is for man
  - who, if he properly sanctifies himself by performing all the Mitzvot which are also dependent on his supernal source
  - in the arrangement of the limbs of the *Shiur Komah*,[78] so to speak, of all the worlds
  - (Refer to Zohar,[79] refer there well)

---

74   Zohar II Pekudei 221a:
  - ... and when God wanted to create the world, He looked into the Torah and created it, and He looked at the Holy Name [YHVH] which includes the Torah and caused the world to exist. The world was created with three *sides*, with wisdom, understanding, and knowledge ... and with these three the Mishkan was constructed ... and everything was made corresponding to each other – for all that God created in this world, He created it as a likeness of Above, and all of it is fixed within the service of the Mishkan.

   Zohar II Pekudei 231b quoting Bereishit 1:1:
  - It is written "In the beginning, God created the heavens and the earth" and He established it, for everything is like that which the Mishkan was made from, which was made like [this] lowest world and like the supernal world, and all the actions He performed [in this world], they are like those Above – similarly the Mishkan is so, that all of His actions are like those of the supernal world. This is the secret of all of the construction of the Mishkan, actions and rectifications Above and below so that the Shechina can reside in the Universe, within the supernal residents [i.e., the Angels] and within the residents of the lowest realm [i.e., man] ...

   Zohar Chadash I Terumah 71a quoting Shemot 25:17:
  - "and you shall make the Kaporet." Come and see, in this Torah section [which deals with the construction of the Mishkan] the details of the Creation of the heavens and earth and of all the hosts which are there, are

נפש שער א' - פרק ד' החיים 129

וּבְדַעַת" (שמות לא, ג) כִּי בְּאֵלּוּ הַג' דְּבָרִים נִבְרְאוּ הָעוֹלָמוֹת, כְּמוֹ שֶׁכָּתוּב (משלי ג) "ה' בְּחָכְמָה יָסַד אָרֶץ כּוֹנֵן שָׁמַיִם בִּתְבוּנָה" וכו'

○ וְעַיֵּן זֹהַר (פקודי רכ״א א' ושם רל״א ב') וּבְזֹהַר חָדָשׁ (תרומה ע״א א') עַיֵּן שָׁם בָּאָרֶךְ.

○ וְלָכֵן אָמְרוּ זִכְרוֹנָם לִבְרָכָה (ברכות נ״ה א') יוֹדֵעַ הָיָה בְּצַלְאֵל לְצָרֵף אוֹתִיּוֹת שֶׁנִּבְרְאוּ בָּהֶם שָׁמַיִם וָאָרֶץ:

• וְלָכֵן הָאָדָם מֵעַם הַקֹּדֶשׁ, שֶׁכּוֹלֵל גַּם כֵּן כָּל סִדְרֵי בְרֵאשִׁית וְסִדְרֵי הַמֶּרְכָּבָה, כְּלָל כָּל הַבְּרִיאָה כֻּלָּהּ

○ הוּא גַם כֵּן דֻּגְמַת וְתַבְנִית הַמִּשְׁכָּן וְהַמִּקְדָּשׁ וְכָל כֵּלָיו

○ מְכֻוָּן בְּסֵדֶר הִתְקַשְּׁרוּת פִּרְקֵי אֵבָרָיו וְגִידָיו וְכָל כֹּחוֹתָיו

○ וְכֵן מְחַלֵּק בַּזֹּהַר כָּל תַּבְנִית הַמִּשְׁכָּן וְכֵלָיו, שֶׁהֵמָּה רְמוּזִים כֻּלָּם בָּאָדָם, אֶחָד בְּאֶחָד יִגַּשׁוּ כְּסֵדֶר:

• לָזֹאת, הֲרֵי כִּי וַדַּאי עִקַּר עִנְיַן הַקֹּדֶשׁ וְהַמִּקְדָּשׁ וּשְׁרִיַּת שְׁכִינָתוֹ יִתְבָּרַךְ, הוּא הָאָדָם

○ שֶׁאִם יִתְקַדֵּשׁ עַצְמוֹ כָּרָאוּי, בְּקִיּוּם הַמִּצְוֹת כֻּלָּן, שֶׁהֵם תְּלוּיִין גַּם כֵּן בְּשָׁרְשָׁן הָעֶלְיוֹן

○ בְּפִרְקֵי אֵבְרֵי הַשִּׁעוּר קוֹמָה כִּבְיָכוֹל שֶׁל כְּלָל כָּל הָעוֹלָמוֹת כֻּלָּם

○ (וְעַיֵּן זֹהַר תְּרוּמָה קס״ב ב' וְאֶת הַמִּשְׁכָּן תַּעֲשֶׂה גו', הָא הָכָא רָזָא דְיִחוּדָא כו' עַיֵּן שָׁם הֵיטֵב)

---

written. For God only commanded that the Mishkan be constructed such that it should be like the work of the Creation of the heavens and the earth, such that the dwelling place in this world would be like the supernal dwelling place, and that they would be interconnected with each other like a soul and a body so that they should all be one entity.

75 Berachot 55a.
76 In the continuation of the previously mentioned sources.
77 Iyov 41:8.
78 See G1:06 and G2:05.
79 Zohar II Terumah 162b quoting Shemot 26:1 and 26:6:
• He began and said "and for the Mishkan you shall make ten sheets." This here is the secret of the Unity [as the ten sheets correspond to the Ten Sefirot], for the rectification of the Mishkan is on many levels about which it is written "and the Mishkan shall then be One," to show that all the limbs of the body of the Mishkan, that they are all the secret of a single body. [This is as] with a person who has many supernal and worldly limbs, [the

- then he himself literally becomes the Sanctuary and God resides within him
- as per "*They are* the Sanctuary of God, the Sanctuary of God"[80]
- and as per Chazal, who state that when it says "and I will dwell *in them*," it does not say "in it" [i.e., the Mishkan] but rather "*in them*" [i.e., the people].[81]

- This is as per Chazal[82] that the acts of Tzaddikim are greater than the Creation of the Heavens and Earth
  - as with the Creation it is written "My Hand [i.e., singular] established the Earth and My Right Hand formed Heaven"[83]
  - but with reference to the acts of Tzaddikim it is written "God's Sanctuary was prepared by Your Hands."[84]
  - Chazal's proof here starts with the actions of Tzaddikim but concludes with reference to the Sanctuary, as in reality it is the Tzaddikim whose actions are desirable before God that they are literally God's Sanctuary.

- In this vein, it is also possible to explain the verse "Make a Sanctuary for Me . . . according to everything I will show you . . . and so shall you do" which Chazal explain[85] that "so shall you do" means for the generations to come.
  - Following our context this can also mean
  - don't think that My objective is to construct an external Temple [structure]
  - but know that the entire purpose of My Will in the structure of the Mishkan and all of its vessels, is only to hint to you that it is from it that you will see [how] and [to] similarly make yourselves
  - that you with your desirable actions will be like the structure of the Mishkan and its vessels, which are all holy, fitting and prepared for My Shechina to literally reside within you.

---

supernal limbs] being innermost and [the worldly limbs] being externally revealed, and they are all called one body, and he is called a single person with a single connection. Similarly, it is so with the Mishkan, all of [its] limbs are like those Above and when they are all connected together, it then writes "and the Mishkan shall then be One." The commandments of the Torah, they are all parts and limbs of the Secret of Above and when they are integrated together as one, then they all ascend Above. The secret of the Mishkan which is parts and limbs all make up the secret of man, like the commandments of the Torah . . .

80 Yirmiyahu 7:4.
81 E.g., Alshich Shemot 31:13 quoting Shemot 25:8:

- אָז הוּא עַצְמוֹ הַמִּקְדָּשׁ מַמָּשׁ, וּבְתוֹכוֹ ה' יִתְבָּרַךְ שְׁמוֹ
- כְּמוֹ שֶׁכָּתוּב (ירמיה ז') הֵיכַל ה' הֵיכַל ה' הֵמָּה
- וּכְמַאֲמָרָם זִכְרוֹנָם לִבְרָכָה (עה"כ שמות כה, ח) "וְשָׁכַנְתִּי בְּתוֹכָם", בְּתוֹכוֹ לֹא נֶאֱמַר אֶלָּא בְּתוֹכָם כו':

• וְזֶה שֶׁאָמְרוּ רַבּוֹתֵינוּ זִכְרוֹנָם לִבְרָכָה (כתובות ה, א) גְּדוֹלִים מַעֲשֵׂי צַדִּיקִים, יוֹתֵר מִמַּעֲשֵׂה שָׁמַיִם וָאָרֶץ
- דְּאִלּוּ בְּמַעֲשֵׂה שָׁמַיִם וָאָרֶץ כְּתִיב (ישעיה מח, יג) "אַף יָדִי יָסְדָה אֶרֶץ וִימִינִי טִפְּחָה שָׁמָיִם"
- וְאִלּוּ בְּמַעֲשֵׂה צַדִּיקִים כְּתִיב "מִקְּדָשׁ אֲדֹנָי כּוֹנְנוּ יָדֶיךָ" (שמות טו, יז)
- פָּתְחוּ בְּמַעֲשֵׂי צַדִּיקִים וְסִיְּמוּ רְאִיָּתָם מִמִּקְדָּשׁ, כִּי כֵן בֶּאֱמֶת שֶׁהַצַּדִּיקִים עַל יְדֵי מַעֲשֵׂיהֶם הָרְצוּיִים לְפָנָיו יִתְבָּרַךְ, הֵן הֵם מִקְדָּשׁ ה' מַמָּשׁ:

• וְיֵשׁ לְפָרֵשׁ עַל דֶּרֶךְ זֶה, הַכָּתוּב (שמות כה, ח—ט) "וְעָשׂוּ לִי מִקְדָּשׁ גו' כְּכֹל אֲשֶׁר אֲנִי מַרְאֶה אוֹתְךָ וגו' וְכֵן תַּעֲשׂוּ", וְרַבּוֹתֵינוּ זִכְרוֹנָם לִבְרָכָה דָּרְשׁוּ (סנהדרין ט"ז) וְכֵן תַּעֲשׂוּ לְדוֹרוֹת.
- וּלְדַרְכֵּנוּ יֵשׁ לוֹמַר גַּם כֵּן שֶׁרוֹצֶה לוֹמַר
- אַל תַּחְשְׁבוּ שֶׁתַּכְלִית כַּוָּנָתִי הוּא עֲשִׂיַּת הַמִּקְדָּשׁ הַחִיצוֹנִי
- אֶלָּא תֵּדְעוּ שֶׁכָּל תַּכְלִית רְצוֹנִי בְּתַבְנִית הַמִּשְׁכָּן וְכָל כֵּלָיו, רַק לְרַמֵּז לָכֶם שֶׁמִּמֶּנּוּ תִּרְאוּ וְכֵן תַּעֲשׂוּ אַתֶּם אֶת עַצְמְכֶם
- שֶׁתִּהְיוּ אַתֶּם בְּמַעֲשֵׂיכֶם הָרְצוּיִים כְּתַבְנִית הַמִּשְׁכָּן וְכֵלָיו, כֻּלָּם קְדוֹשִׁים רְאוּיִים וּמוּכָנִים לְהַשְׁרוֹת שְׁכִינָתִי בְּתוֹכְכֶם מַמָּשׁ

- ... therefore since the residence of the Shechina in the Mishkan is not from its perspective but rather from that of man, as it says "Make a Sanctuary for Me and I will dwell *in them*," it does not say *"in it"* but rather *"in them,"* as God's Sanctuary is man, and it is from him that He extends [His Presence] to the Mishkan.

See also e.g., Shela Masechet Taanit, Perek Ner Mitzvah 28, and Kli Yakar Shemot Terumah 25:3.

82 Ketubbot 5a.
83 Yishayahu 48:13.
84 Shemot 15:17, i.e., *Hands* in plural, implying the act is greater, as per Rashi.
85 Sanhedrin 16b quoting Shemot 25:8–9.

- ○ This is the specific meaning of "Make a Sanctuary for Me and I will reside in them"
- ○ that "according to everything I will show you, the structure of the Mishkan . . . ," the objective of My intention is that you shall similarly make this of yourselves.
- Similarly, God said to Shlomo on completion of the construction of the Temple: "This house which you build" – it is just "if you follow My Statutes . . . and I will dwell among My People Israel"[86] specifically.
- Therefore, when the inner essence of the Temple was corrupted within them [the People of Israel], its physical external structure could not stand and its foundations were destroyed, the Merciful One should save us.
- This is what God said to Yechezkel: "Tell the House of Israel about the Temple and let them be ashamed of their sins . . . If they become ashamed of all they have done, then make known to them the structure of the Temple and its design, its exists and entrances, and all its buildings' forms, all its laws, designs, and teachings, and write all this down before their eyes, so that they may safeguard its entire form and its rules, and perform them."[87]
  - ○ This is as explained
  - ○ and as per the Targum[88] "and if they suppress themselves [i.e., take corrective note] when they see the structure of the Temple and its design. . . ."

5. A JEW IS A HYBRID BEING – BOTH LOWLY AND SUPERNAL

- In relation to that which arose in God's Will that man of this lowest world[89] be constructed [in such a way] that the supernal worlds are controlled by him.
- For it is known from the Zohar and the writings of the Arizal[90] in relation to the sequence of the hierarchical descent and the interconnections of the worlds
  - ○ that the detail, arrangement, and behavior of every lower world is entirely dependent on the characteristics of the power of the world [immediately] above it

---

86 1 Melachim 6:12.
87 Yechezkel 43:10–11.
88 Targum Yonatan on Yechezkel 43:10–11.
89 Expression used here is "Adam HaTachton" referring to man in this physical world. It should be noted that there is another Kaballistic expression "Adam

- זֶהוּ וְעָשׂוּ לִי מִקְדָּשׁ וְשָׁכַנְתִּי בְּתוֹכָם דַּיְקָא
- שֶׁבַּכֹּל אֲשֶׁר אֲנִי מַרְאֶה אוֹתְךָ אֵת תַּבְנִית הַמִּשְׁכָּן וגו', תַּכְלִית כַּוָּנָתִי שֶׁבֶּן תַּעֲשׂוּ אֵת עַצְמְכֶם:
- וְכֵן אָמַר הוּא יִתְבָּרַךְ שְׁמוֹ לִשְׁלֹמֹה, אַחַר גְּמַר בִּנְיַן הַמִּקְדָּשׁ (מלכים א' ו') "הַבַּיִת הַזֶּה אֲשֶׁר אַתָּה בּוֹנֶה" הוּא רַק "אִם תֵּלֵךְ בְּחֻקֹּתַי גו' וְשָׁכַנְתִּי בְּתוֹךְ בְּנֵי יִשְׂרָאֵל" דַּיְקָא:
- לָזֹאת כְּשֶׁקִּלְקְלוּ פְּנִימִיּוּת הַמִּקְדָּשׁ שֶׁבְּתוֹכָם, אָז לֹא הוֹעִיל הַמִּקְדָּשׁ הַחִיצוֹנִי, וְנֶהֶרְסוּ יְסוֹדוֹתָיו רַחֲמָנָא לִיצְלָן:
- וְזֶה שֶׁאָמַר הַשֵּׁם לִיחֶזְקֵאל (מ"ג) "הַגֵּד אֶת בֵּית יִשְׂרָאֵל אֶת הַבַּיִת וְיִכָּלְמוּ מֵעֲוֹנוֹתֵיהֶם גו', וְאִם נִכְלְמוּ מִכֹּל אֲשֶׁר עָשׂוּ צוּרַת הַבַּיִת וּתְכוּנָתוֹ וּמוֹצָאָיו וּמוֹבָאָיו וְכָל צוּרוֹתָיו וְאֵת כָּל חֻקֹּתָיו וְכָל צוּרוֹתָיו וְכָל תּוֹרֹתָיו, הוֹדַע אוֹתָם וּכְתֹב לְעֵינֵיהֶם וְיִשְׁמְרוּ אֶת כָּל צוּרָתוֹ וְאֶת כָּל חֻקֹּתָיו וְעָשׂוּ אוֹתָם"
  - וְהוּא מְבֹאָר
- וּכְתַרְגּוּמוֹ וְאִם יִתְכַּנְעוּן מִכֹּל דַּעֲבָדוּ בְּמֶחֱזֵיהוֹן צוּרַת בֵּיתָא וְטִיקוּסֵיהּ כו':

שער א' - פרק ה'

- וּמַה שֶּׁעָלְתָה בִּרְצוֹנוֹ יִתְבָּרַךְ שְׁמוֹ, לְהַרְכִּיב אֶת הָאָדָם הַתַּחְתּוֹן — לְרָאשֵׁי הָעוֹלָמוֹת עֶלְיוֹנִים, שֶׁיִּתְנַהֲגוּ עַל יָדוֹ:
  - כִּי יָדוּעַ בַּזֹּהַר וְכִתְבֵי הָאֲרִיזַ"ל בְּסֵדֶר הִשְׁתַּלְשְׁלוּת וְהִתְקַשְּׁרוּת הָעוֹלָמוֹת
    - שֶׁכָּל עוֹלָם הוּא מִתְנַהֵג, בְּסִדּוּר מַצָּבוֹ וְכָל פְּרָטֵי עִנְיָנָיו, כְּפִי נְטִיַּת כֹּחַ הָעוֹלָם שֶׁעָלָיו

HaElyon" (Supernal Man) which refers to God. (See the beginning of G1:16 together with p. 233, fn. 399 and p. 235, fn. 400.) The use of these expressions reflects: 1. the word for man, "Adam," which is an expression of "Dimuy," i.e., a likeness; 2. the idea of man being in God's Image.

90 The Arizal's writings were not penned directly by the Arizal, but were all recorded by his students. The Arizal's primary student, R. Chaim Vital, was also his primary scribe and when the Arizal's writings are generally referred to, it usually is a reference to those works recorded by R. Chaim Vital. In G4:10, however, R. Chaim will introduce us to some concepts which were uniquely recorded in the writings of another of the Arizal's students, R. Yisrael Sarug.

- such that the [upper world] controls the [lower world] like a soul does a body
- and similarly, [all the world levels are connected] in this sequence of level above level until they ultimately [connect] to God, who is the Soul of all of them. As per:
  - With each world ... upper and lower – from the secret originating upper point – until the lowest of all the levels – each is the container of the next level ... each one within the next.[91]
  - With all the lights interconnected with each other and enlightening each other ... the revealed light being referred to as the container of the King and the inner light [is hidden].[92]
  - In particular, the concept is explained [by R. Chaim Vital], that the external presentation of each Partzuf and world emanates and is clothed within the Partzuf and world of the level below it, becoming its internal essence and soul.[93]
- All of the worlds are grouped into four [general] categories, as is known, which [in ascending order of level] are: Ophanim, Chayot, Kiseh Kevodo/ the Throne of Glory, Atzilut.[94]
- The soul of each [world category] is the world [category] above it.
  - As it is written "and when the Chayot were lifted ... the Ophanim were lifted corresponding to them, for the spirit of the Chayot was also in the Ophanim: when they [the Chayot] moved, they [the Ophanim also] moved, and when they [the Chayot] stopped, they [the Ophanim also] stopped."[95]
  - The behavior of the Chayot also corresponds to the world of the Throne of Glory above them, as per Chazal[96] that the Throne of Glory would carry those who carried it.
  - As per the Zohar:[97] The Chayot carry those who carry them ... the Throne of Glory carries the Chayot.

---

91 Zohar I Bereishit 19b.
92 Zohar Idra Zuta III Haazinu 291b.
93 R. Chaim quotes this from Etz Chaim Shaar 40, Shaar Pnimiyut VeChitzoniyut, Derush 2, and from Pri Etz Chaim Shaar HaShabbat, Chaps. 7, 8, and 24.

   See p. 233, fn. 399, which presents details of the Partzuf concept. Also see V2:02, Chap. 15, "Tzimtzum Sources," I1.1, which explains the difference between Partzufim and Sefirot.

   For insight into this relationship between Partzuf/world levels, see V2:02, Chap. 12. This follows the system of "Yosher," describing the interconnection between levels. (In contrast the system of "Igulim," describes the difference between levels, where each world level is analogous to a layer of an onion encompassing all layers below it as per e.g., Zohar III Vayikra 9b.)

○ שֶׁמַּנְהִיגוֹ כִּנְשָׁמָה אֶת הַגּוּף

○ וְכֵן הוֹלֵךְ עַל זֶה הַסֵּדֶר גָּבוֹהַּ מֵעַל גָּבוֹהַּ, עַד הוּא יִתְבָּרַךְ שְׁמוֹ נִשְׁמַת כֻּלָּם.

○ עַיֵּן זֹהַר (בראשית י"ט ב') וְכָל עָלְמָא כו' עֵילָא וְתַתָּא מֵרֵישׁ רָזָא דִּנְקוּדָה עִלָּאָה עַד סוֹפָא דְּכָל דַּרְגִּין, כֹּלָּא אִיהוּ, דָּא לְבוּשָׁא לְדָא וְדָא לְדָא כו' דָּא לְגוֹ מִן דָּא וְדָא לְגוֹ מִן דָּא כו'.

○ וּבְאִדְרָא (זוטא רצ"א ב') וְכֻלְּהוּ נְהוֹרִין אֲחִידָן, נְהוֹרָא דָּא בִּנְהוֹרָא דָּא וּנְהוֹרָא דָּא בִּנְהוֹרָא דָּא, וְנַהֲרִין דָּא בְּדָא כו', נְהוֹרָא דְּאִתְגַּלְיָא אִקְרֵי לְבוּשָׁא דְּמַלְכָּא, נְהוֹרָא דִּלְגוֹ לְגוֹ כו', עַיֵּן שָׁם.

○ וּפְרָטוּת הָעִנְיָן מְבֹאָר בְּעֵץ חַיִּים שַׁעַר פְּנִימִיּוּת וְחִיצוֹנִיּוּת דְּרוּשׁ ב', וּבִפְרִי עֵץ חַיִּים בְּהַקְדָּמַת שַׁעַר הַשַּׁבָּת פֶּרֶק ז' וּפֶרֶק ח', וּבְשַׁעַר הַשַּׁבָּת פֶּרֶק כ"ה, שֶׁחִיצוֹנִיּוּת שֶׁל כָּל פַּרְצוּף וְעוֹלָם, מִתְפַּשֵּׁט וּמִתְלַבֵּשׁ בְּהַפַּרְצוּף וְהָעוֹלָם שֶׁתַּחְתָּיו, וְנַעֲשֶׂה לוֹ לִפְנִימִיּוּת וּנְשָׁמָה:

• וְכָל הָעוֹלָמוֹת נִכְלָלִים וְנֶחְלָקִים לְד' כַּיָּדוּעַ, שֶׁהֵן הָאוֹפַנִּים, וְהַחַיּוֹת, וְכִסֵּא כְבוֹדוֹ, וַאֲצִילוּת קָדְשׁוֹ יִתְבָּרַךְ:

• וְנִשְׁמַת כָּל אֶחָד הוּא הָעוֹלָם שֶׁעָלָיו

○ כְּמוֹ שֶׁנֶּאֱמַר (יחזקאל א', יט) "וּבְהִנָּשֵׂא הַחַיּוֹת גו' יִנָּשְׂאוּ הָאוֹפַנִּים לְעֻמָּתָם כִּי רוּחַ הַחַיָּה בָּאוֹפַנִּים, בְּלֶכְתָּם יֵלֵכוּ וּבְעָמְדָם יַעֲמֹדוּ" וגו'

○ וְהַחַיּוֹת גַּם כֵּן מִתְנַהֲגִים עַל יְדֵי עוֹלָם הַכִּסֵּא שֶׁעֲלֵיהֶם, כְּמוֹ שֶׁאָמְרוּ רַבּוֹתֵינוּ זִכְרוֹנָם לִבְרָכָה, שֶׁהַכִּסֵּא נוֹשֵׂא אֶת נוֹשְׂאָיו.

○ וּבְזֹהַר חָדָשׁ יִתְרוֹ (בְּמַעֲשֵׂה מֶרְכָּבָה ס"ו ב') דְּחֵיוָות נָטְלִין לְדַנְטְלִין לוֹן כו' כָּרְסַיָּיא קַדִּישָׁא נָטִיל לְחֵיוָות:

---

94 These four levels of worlds are expressed using the language of Yechezkel in his description of the Merkava. Their main synonyms (in ascending levels of closeness to God) are: Ophanim–Asiyah, Chayot–Yetzirah, Kiseh Kevodo/Throne of Glory–Beriyah, Atzilut. (See G1:13:N13 for details of the four worlds.)

95 Yechezkel 1:19–21.

96 E.g., Rikanti on Shemot 32:19 quotes Sotah 35a referring to the Holy Ark carrying those who carried it and extending this concept to the Chayot and the Throne of Glory.

97 Zohar Chadash I Yitro 66b.

- The living soul of the Throne of Glory[98] is the secret of the supernal root of the collective of the souls of Israel which is far higher than the level of Throne itself. It is The Man [who sits] on the Throne as written[99] "and on the image of the Throne there is the image of a person. . . ." (Note 5)[100]
- This explains the Zohar's comment[101] on the verse "Back and front, you have restricted/bound me"[102] where *back* refers to the Act of Creation and *front* to the act of the Merkava.
  - From the perspective of [man's physical] body – it is *Back* [i.e., created last in the sequence] of the Act of Creation [and is the lowest level in the hierarchy]
  - and from the perspective of the supernal root of [man's] living soul – it is *Front* [i.e., the starting point preceding] the act of the Merkava and also of the world of the Throne [of Glory].
    - In addition [Man's] living soul is the secret of God's Breath, so to speak, as will be explained, God willing, later on in G1:15, refer there.
- Therefore, the worlds are controlled through man's actions, which according to their inclination [whether good or bad] invoke the root of his supernal soul which is above them and is the soul which enlivens them. When he moves, they move and when he stops, they stop.
- This is the meaning of what is said that when the living soul was breathed into his nostrils, that it is higher than the worlds and their inner essence; resulting in "and the man became a living soul" of the worlds.
- This is similarly written by R. Chaim Vital,[103] that man's soul is the inner essence of everything.[104]

---

98 The *Soul of the Throne of Glory* is the external presentation of the world level above the *Throne of Glory*, i.e., the external presentation of the world level of Atzilut.
99 Yechezkel 1:26.
100 **R. Chaim adds Note 5 here.** This note is brought at the end of this chapter and is entitled "Body is a shoe for soul connecting lowest to the highest realms."
101 Zohar II Yitro 70b.
102 Tehillim 139:5.
103 Sefer Shaarei Kedushah Part 3 Gate 2:
  - . . . and you should know that [God's Name] YHVH with each letter expanded completely with the letter *Aleph* [i.e., *Yud*=YUD=20; *Hey*=HA=6; *Vav*=VAV=13; *Hey*=HA=6] has the same numerical value as "man"/ADM/45, and in this way in each and every detail and all levels [of YHVH], with each of their levels being called a specific "man," which incorporates the unified

- וְנִשְׁמַת הַחַיִּים שֶׁל הַכִּסֵּא, הוּא סוֹד שֹׁרֶשׁ הָעֶלְיוֹן שֶׁל כְּלָלוּת נִשְׁמוֹת יִשְׂרָאֵל יַחַד, שֶׁהוּא יוֹתֵר גָּבוֹהַּ וּמְאֹד נַעֲלָה גַּם מֵהַכִּסֵּא, שֶׁהוּא הָאָדָם שֶׁעַל הַכִּסֵּא, כְּמוֹ שֶׁנֶּאֱמַר שָׁם "וְעַל דְּמוּת הַכִּסֵּא" וְגוֹ': (הגהה ה')

- וְזֶהוּ שֶׁאָמְרוּ בַּזֹּהַר יִתְרוֹ ע' ע"ב בְּעִנְיַן הַפָּסוּק "אָחוֹר וָקֶדֶם צַרְתָּנִי" (תהלים קלט, ה), 'אָחוֹר' — לְעוֹבְדָא דִבְרֵאשִׁית, 'וְקֶדֶם' — לְעוֹבְדָא דְמֶרְכָּבָה.

  ○ שֶׁמִּצַּד הַגּוּף — הוּא 'אָחוֹר' — לְמַעֲשֵׂי בְרֵאשִׁית

  ○ וּמִצַּד שֹׁרֶשׁ הָעֶלְיוֹן שֶׁל הַנִּשְׁמַת חַיִּים שֶׁלּוֹ — הוּא 'קֶדֶם' לְעוֹבְדָא דְמֶרְכָּבָה, גַּם מֵעוֹלָם הַכִּסֵּא.

  □ וְגַם כִּי הַנִּשְׁמַת חַיִּים הִיא סוֹד נְשִׁימַת פִּיו יִתְבָּרַךְ שְׁמוֹ כִּבְיָכוֹל, כְּמוֹ שֶׁיִּתְבָּאֵר אִי"ה לְהַלָּן פֶּרֶק ט"ז עַיֵּן שָׁם:

- לָכֵן הָעוֹלָמוֹת מִתְנַהֲגִים עַל יְדֵי מַעֲשֵׂי הָאָדָם, כִּי הֵמָּה כְּפִי נְטִיָּתָם מְעוֹרְרִים שֹׁרֶשׁ נִשְׁמָתוֹ הָעֶלְיוֹנָה שֶׁמֵּעֲלֵיהֶם, שֶׁהִיא הַ'נֶּפֶשׁ חַיָּה' שֶׁלָּהֶם, בְּהִתְנוֹעֲעוֹ יָנוּעוּ וּבְעָמְדוֹ תִּרְפֶּינָה:

- זֶהוּ שֶׁאָמְרָה, כַּאֲשֶׁר נָפַח בְּאַפָּיו הַנִּשְׁמַת חַיִּים, שֶׁהִיא גָּבוֹהַּ מֵהָעוֹלָמוֹת וּפְנִימִיּוּתָם, אָז "וַיְהִי הָאָדָם לְנֶפֶשׁ חַיָּה" — לְהָעוֹלָמוֹת:

- וְכֵן כָּתַב רַבֵּנוּ חַיִּים וִיטַאל זִכְרוֹנוֹ לִבְרָכָה בְּשַׁעַר הַקְּדֻשָּׁה חֵלֶק ג' שַׁעַר ב'. שֶׁנִּשְׁמַת הָאָדָם הִיא הַפְּנִימִי שֶׁבְּכֻלָּם:

YHVH split into four elements [see G1:02:N01 and Maamar BeTzeLeM] and Ten Sefirot ... and all the worlds together, and similarly each of the individual details were created in the image of man of the lowest world and this is the secret of "Let us make man in our image, in our likeness" (Bereishit 1:26) – understand this well ... and after this He created the Jewish Man, more refined in all of his levels than all of the other creations – in [terms of] his body and of the four levels of his souls – the inanimate, vegetable, animal, and speech – from the refined inner essence of the four elements contained within them and their form. I mean to say their souls, and that he is more refined than all the creations on earth. More than this, he also incorporates and interconnects all of the worlds and all of their details from [the lowest point of the] bottom upwards [to the highest point] ... for the light of the foundry of [man's] souls is more internal and higher than the light of the foundry of angels and therefore they [the angels] are [man's] servants. He [man] is the cause of the [angel's] light and life force extending to them from the light of the Ten Sefirot. This is the secret of "Behold their Erelim/angels cried out, outside" (Yishayahu 33:7) – for

Rabbi Chaim's Note:
Note 5 – Body is a shoe for soul connecting lowest to the highest realms

- For the essence of man is fixed in the Supernal Realms in his soul source, and as a result, his physical body is referred to as a *shoe* (refer to Tikkunim)[105] relative to the soul, and it is only *the level of the heels*[106] from the source which enters into [and is contained within] man's physical body.
- With this, Chazal's statement[107] can now be understood
  - that God did not want to instill jealousy in the creation, and that on the first day [of Creation], He created heaven and earth; on the second, the firmament; on the third, the earth sprouted, and similarly on the fourth and fifth days [resulting in an equal distribution of days between the creation of the supernal and lower realms]
  - on the sixth day, He came to create man, He said: If I create him from the Supernal Realms there will be no peace in the world [as a result of the imbalance], and [similarly] if I create him from the lower realms . . .
  - I will however create him from both the supernal and lower realms – "dust from the earth and He breathed the soul of life in through his nostrils."[108]
- It seems that surely now there would be increased jealousy compared to if He created [man] from the lower realms alone
  - as now he has a part of the Supernal Realms within him
  - but he is entirely in the lower realms together with the supernal part within him?
- However, the idea is
  - that with a properly complete man
  - his essence is fixed in the Supernal Realms in the supernal source of his soul
  - it then descends through thousands of myriads of worlds until its lower end enters into man's physical body in the lower realms

---

when the bestowal from the Ten Sefirot does not extend to the souls of Israel [as a result of their sins], which are more inner than [the angels], they [the angels] lack bestowal which is external to them. It transpires that they cried out, at the time of the desctruction [of the Temple] as a result of their being "outside" of the souls.

104 A Jew is therefore a unique hybrid being simultaneously connected to both the source and end result of all Creation – giving him the power to control even though he exists in the lowest world.

הגהה ה'

- כִּי עִקַּר הָאָדָם הוּא נָטוּעַ לְמַעְלָה בְּשֹׁרֶשׁ נִשְׁמָתוֹ, וְלָזֹאת נִקְרָא הַגּוּף 'נַעַל' (עַיֵּין בְּתִקּוּנִים) נֶגֶד הַנְּשָׁמָה. כִּי רַק בְּחִינַת עֲקֵבַיִים מֵהַשֹּׁרֶשׁ נִכְנָס לְתוֹךְ גּוּף הָאָדָם:

- וּבָזֶה יוּבַן מַאֲמָרָם זִכְרוֹנָם לִבְרָכָה בִּבְרֵאשִׁית רַבָּה פִּ"ב וּבְוַיִּקְרָא רַבָּה פּ"ט
  - שֶׁלֹּא רָצָה הַקָּדוֹשׁ בָּרוּךְ הוּא לְהַטִּיל קִנְאָה בְּמַעֲשֵׂי בְרֵאשִׁית, וּבְיוֹם א' בָּרָא שָׁמַיִם וָאָרֶץ, בַּשֵּׁנִי רָקִיעַ, בַּשְּׁלִישִׁי תַּדְשֵׁא הָאָרֶץ, וְכֵן עַל דֶּרֶךְ זֶה בַּד' וה'
  - בַּשִּׁשִּׁי בָּא לִבְרֹא אֶת הָאָדָם, אָמַר אִם אֲנִי בּוֹרֵא אוֹתוֹ מִן הָעֶלְיוֹנִים אֵין שָׁלוֹם בָּעוֹלָם, וְאִם אֲנִי בּוֹרֵא אוֹתוֹ מִן הַתַּחְתּוֹנִים כוּ'
  - אֶלָּא הֲרֵינִי בּוֹרֵא אוֹתוֹ מִן הָעֶלְיוֹנִים וּמִן הַתַּחְתּוֹנִים, "עָפָר מִן הָאֲדָמָה וַיִּפַּח בְּאַפָּיו נִשְׁמַת חַיִּים" (בראשית ב, ז):

- וְלִכְאוֹרָה, הֲלֹא עַתָּה תִּתְגַּבֵּר הַקִּנְאָה יוֹתֵר מִשֶּׁאִם הָיָה בּוֹרֵא אוֹתוֹ מִן הַתַּחְתּוֹנִים לְבַד
  - שֶׁעַתָּה יֵשׁ בּוֹ חֵלֶק מִן הָעֶלְיוֹנִים
  - וְהוּא כֻּלּוֹ לְמַטָּה עִם הַחֵלֶק הָעֶלְיוֹן שֶׁבּוֹ:

- אַךְ הָעִנְיָן הוּא
  - שֶׁהָאָדָם הַשָּׁלֵם כָּרָאוּי
  - עִקָּרוֹ הוּא נָטוּעַ לְמַעְלָה בְּשֹׁרֶשׁ נִשְׁמָתוֹ הָעֶלְיוֹנָה
  - וְעוֹבֵר דֶּרֶךְ אַלְפֵי רִבּוֹאוֹת עוֹלָמוֹת עַד שֶׁקְּצֵהוּ הַשֵּׁנִי הוּא נִכְנָס בְּגוּף הָאָדָם לְמַטָּה

---

105 E.g., Tikkunei Zohar Tikkun 13 27a quoting Shemot 3:5:
  - ... God said to [Moshe] "do not come closer, take off your shoe" – here He hinted that [Moshe] remove himelf from his [physical] body which was [like] a shoe – to be clothed by another body [instead, i.e., by a refined spiritual body which Moshe merited at the burning bush, as per Etz Chaim Shaar 49, Shaar Kelipat Nogah, Chap. 5]. ...
106 This is a Kabbalistic expression which relates to the lowest of all levels in the descent of holiness to be manifest into physicality. E.g., Zohar I Chayei Sarah 124a:
  - ... this is in this world which is [called] "Akev"/heel. ...
107 Bereishit Rabba Bereishit 12:8, and Vayikra Rabba Tzav 9:9.
108 Bereishit 2:7.

- this is the meaning of "God's people are a part of Him, Yaakov[109] is the cord of His possession"[110]
- that his essence is tied and fixed to the Supernal Realms, literally a part of God (YHVH), so to speak,[111] from which it descends like a dangling cord until it reaches a person's body (see G1:17)
- and all of his [earthly] deeds impact to arouse his source in the Supernal Realms just as when one shakes a cord at its lower end it sends a wave up the cord which also shakes its upper end.

- ('Wisdom will come easily to the understanding one'[112] that this same idea is true of the supernal source of things with the secret of *Adam HaElyon*,[113] so to speak.
  - Refer to the Zohar[114] which relates to the verse "And God Elokim formed man" and explains it in relation to Adam HaElyon concluding:
    - ... and what is all this for, in order to extract and insert within [creation] that which is ultimately hidden as is written: "and He breathed the soul of life in through his nostrils" – a soul upon which all life in the supernal and lower realms is dependent and whose existence is maintained by it – "and Man [i.e., Adam HaElyon] became a living Soul" to be impacted and enter into a state of rectification like this[115] and to bring out this Soul from level to level

---

109 Note that the name "Yaakov" incorporates the word "Akev"/heel.
110 Devarim 32:9.
111 It is of interest to highlight the expression used here by R. Chaim in the context of the verse from Devarim 32:9 where he states that a person's soul is *"literally a part of YHVH"* but he qualifies this with the comment *"so to speak."* R. Chaim does this again at the end of G1:17. (In contrast, Ruach Chaim quotes R. Chaim as referring to a person's soul being a part of *Eloka*. See V2:12, "Related Extracts from Ruach Chaim," subsection 19.)

Most references to the soul being part of God are in relation to being *"a part of Eloka/God Above,"* an expression borrowed from Iyov 31:2. For example, the Vilna Gaon expresses the same point in the standard way in Imrei Noam Berachot 58a as follows:
- [Chazal state – Berachot 58a]
  - One who sees Sages of Israel should recite the blessing "Blessed is He who has given a portion of His Wisdom to those who fear Him" but with the Sages of the Nations one should recite "Blessed is He who has given from His Wisdom to flesh and blood."
- With those who received the Torah, who are *a part of Eloka/God Above*, it is appropriate to say [that He has given] a portion – [i.e.,] that He has given a portion of Himself.

זֶהוּ "כִּי חֵלֶק ה' עַמּוֹ יַעֲקֹב חֶבֶל נַחֲלָתוֹ" (דברים לב, ט).

שֶׁעִקָּרוֹ קָשׁוּר וְנָטוּעַ לְמַעְלָה חֵלֶק הֲוָיָ"ה מַמָּשׁ כִּבְיָכוֹל, וּמִשְׁתַּלְשֵׁל כְּחֶבֶל עַד בּוֹאָה לְגוּף הָאָדָם (וְעַיֵּן לְקַמָּן פֶּרֶק י"ז).

וְכָל מַעֲשָׂיו מַגִּיעִים לְעוֹרֵר שָׁרְשׁוֹ הָעֶלְיוֹן, כְּעִנְיַן הַחֶבֶל שֶׁאִם יָנַעְנֵעַ קָצֵהוּ הַתַּחְתּוֹן, מִתְעוֹרֵר וּמִתְנוֹעֵעַ גַּם רֹאשׁ קָצֵהוּ הָעֶלְיוֹן:

• (וְדַעַת לְנָבוֹן נָקֵל, שֶׁכֵּן הוּא הָעִנְיָן גַּם בְּשֹׁרֶשׁ הַדְּבָרִים לְמַעְלָה בְּסוֹד הָאָדָם הָעֶלְיוֹן כִּבְיָכוֹל.

○ עַיֵּן אַדְּ"ר קַמָּ"א ב' בַּפָּסוּק "וַיִּיצֶר ה' אֱלֹקִים אֶת הָאָדָם" (בראשית שם) גו' עַל סוֹד הָאָדָם הָעֶלְיוֹן, וְסִיֵּם.

▫ וְכָל דָּא לָמָּה בְּגִין לְאִשְׁתַּלְפָא וּלְעַיְלָא בֵּיהּ סָתִים דְּסָתִימָא עַד סוֹפָא

- However, with the Nations, He has given something, but not of His Essence, as per "and to the children of Avraham's concubines, Avraham gave gifts" [Bereishit 25:6] and Rashi comments that he gave them names of impurity [which they could use for their benefit, but they were not a gift of things or concepts which Avraham associated with himself].
- [See comments of Magen Avraham and Mishna Berura on Shulchan Aruch Orach Chaim 224:6 that the meaning of being given a portion as per the blessing is that Israel are a part of Eloka/God and are cleaved to him.]

The concept is expressed elsewhere in a number of comments recorded from the Vilna Gaon, e.g., Aderet Eliyahu on Bereishit 1:2 which refers to a Jew's soul (Neshama) as being *a part of Eloka Above* (translated on p. 114, fn. 24.) and also refers to Sefer Pardes Rimonim 1:5 as a source which, in turn, refers to the verse in Bereishit 2:7, "He breathed a living soul into his nostrils" and states that when One blows (i.e., God in this context), He imparts part of His Essence.

It is presumed that the reference here to YHVH instead of *Eloka* is because of the reference to YHVH in the verse brought from Devarim 32:9. It could be said that the standard expression is not qualified with the statement of "so to speak" as it refers to the soul as being a part of *Elokim* which is not as sublime a level as YHVH (as per G3:09). See V2:02, p. 128, fn. 201.

112 Mishlei 14:6.
113 I.e., Supernal Man, referring to the manifestation of God within Zeer Anpin of Atzilut. See p. 233, fn. 399 and p. 235, fn. 400, for more details on the Partzuf of Zeer Anpin.
114 Zohar Idra Rabba III Naso 141b quoting Bereishit 2:7.
115 Referring to the section immediately preceding this quotation which is not brought here.

G1:05:N05

[filtering down to all levels] until the end of all levels such that this Soul is found in everything and permeates everything. Refer there.)

6. MAN'S ACTIONS IMPACT IMAGE OF GOD

- However the matter [i.e., the analogy] still requires clarification
  - (as [R. Chaim Vital,] of blessed memory, speaks in his usual concise holy way as he does in all of his holy writings of the hidden part of Torah, as he himself writes in his introduction there[116] that "he reveals one handbreadth and conceals two thousand cubits")
  - as it is not as apparently implied by his words above, that the relationship of man to the worlds is literally like that of a soul to a person's body within which it is placed and attached
  - where the action of the soul is only performed simultaneously through the medium of the action of the organs of the body
  - as this certainly cannot possibly be. (Note 6)[117]
- The key principle is that God, after He created all of the worlds, created man last in the Creation sequence
  - a wondrous creation
  - a power which 'gathers in from all of the camps'[118]
  - with all the supernal wondrous subtle shining lights,[119] worlds, and chambers which preceded him [in the Creation sequence] being incorporated within him
  - and the entire supernal glorious structure of the arrangement of the components of the Merkava (Note 7)[120]
  - and all the specific powers found in all of the supernal and lower worlds
  - they all contribute power and part of their essence to his construction and are incorporated within him among the many detailed powers within him.[121]

---

116 As R. Chaim Vital writes in his introduction to Sefer Shaarei Kedushah which was referenced at the end of the previous chapter.
117 **R. Chaim adds Note 6 here.** This note is brought at the end of this chapter and is entitled "Angel sanctification is not simultaneous but follows man."
118 Bamidbar 10:25, i.e., is connected with and a part of all levels.
119 The reference to the wondrous subtle shining lights relates to a level so high and subtle that it cannot even be described by one of the standard world levels, as per G1:13:N13.
120 **R. Chaim adds Note 7 here.** This note is brought at the end of this chapter

דְּכָל סְתִימִין, הה"ד (שם) "וַיִּפַּח בְּאַפָּיו נִשְׁמַת חַיִּים" נִשְׁמָתָא דְּכָל חַיֵּי דְעֵלָּא וְתַתָּא תַּלְיָן מֵהַהוּא נִשְׁמָתָא וּמִתְקַיְּמִין בָּהּ, "וַיְהִי הָאָדָם לְנֶפֶשׁ חַיָּה" לְאִתְרַקָּא וּלְעֵילָא בְּתִקּוּנִין כג"ד וּלְאַשְׁלָפָא לְהַהִיא נִשְׁמָתָא מִדַּרְגָּא לְדַרְגָּא עַד סוֹפָא דְּכָל דַּרְגִּין, בְּגִין דִּיהֵוֵי הַהִיא נִשְׁמָתָא מִשְׁתַּכְּחָא בְּכֹלָּא וּמִתְפַּשְׁטָ' בְּכֹלָּא כו'. עַיֵּן שָׁם):

שער א' - פרק ו'

- אָמְנָם עֲדַיִן הָעִנְיָן צָרִיךְ בֵּאוּר
  - (כִּי הוּא זִכְרוֹנוֹ לִבְרָכָה דִּבֶּר בְּקָדְשׁוֹ דֶּרֶךְ קְצָרָה כְּדַרְכּוֹ בְּכָל כִּתְבֵי קָדְשׁוֹ בַּנִּסְתָּרוֹת, כְּמוֹ שֶׁכָּתַב בְּעַצְמוֹ בְּהַקְדָּמָתוֹ שָׁם, שֶׁהוּא מְגַלֶּה טֶפַח וּמְכַסֶּה אַלְפַּיִם אַמָּה)
  - שֶׁלֹּא כְּדְמַשְׁמַע לִכְאוֹרָה מִדְּבָרָיו זִכְרוֹנוֹ לִבְרָכָה שָׁם, שֶׁהָאָדָם אֶל הָעוֹלָמוֹת הוּא נֶפֶשׁ מַמָּשׁ, כְּמוֹ הַנֶּפֶשׁ הַנִּתָּן וְדָבוּק בְּתוֹךְ גּוּף הָאָדָם
  - אֲשֶׁר אֵיזֶה דָבָר, שֶׁהַנֶּפֶשׁ עוֹשָׂה, הוּא רַק עַל יְדֵי כְּלֵי הַגּוּף, שֶׁבָּאוּתוֹ רֶגַע מַמָּשׁ גַּם הַגּוּף עוֹשֵׂהוּ
  - דָּזֶה וַדַּאי לֹא יִתָּכֵן (הגהה ו'):
- אֲבָל עִקָּרוֹ שֶׁל דָּבָר, כִּי הוּא יִתְבָּרַךְ שְׁמוֹ, אַחַר שֶׁבָּרָא כָּל הָעוֹלָמוֹת, בָּרָא אֶת הָאָדָם אָחוֹר לְמַעֲשֵׂי בְרֵאשִׁית
  - בְּרִיאָה נִפְלָאָה
  - כֹּחַ מְאַסֵּף לְכָל הַמַּחֲנוֹת
  - שֶׁכָּלַל בּוֹ כָּל צַחְצָחוֹת אוֹרוֹת הַנִּפְלָאוֹת וְהָעוֹלָמוֹת וְהֵיכָלִין הָעֶלְיוֹנִים שֶׁקָּדְמוּ לוֹ
  - וְכָל תַּבְנִית הַכָּבוֹד הָעֶלְיוֹן בְּסֵדֶר פִּרְקֵי הַמֶּרְכָּבָה (הגהה ז')
  - וְכָל הַכֹּחוֹת פְּרָטִים הַנִּמְצָאִים בְּכָל הָעוֹלָמוֹת עֶלְיוֹנִים וְתַחְתּוֹנִים
  - כֻּלָּם נָתְנוּ כֹּחַ וְחֵלֶק מֵעַצְמוּתָם בִּבְנִינֵנוּ, וְנִכְלְלוּ בּוֹ בְּמִסְפַּר פְּרָטֵי כְחוֹתָיו שֶׁבּוֹ:

and is entitled "Sins of Adam/Golden Calf internalized Evil requiring death to purify."

121 The Vilna Gaon expresses this in Aderet Eliyahu in his commentary on Bereishit 1:26 as follows:
- "God said: Let us make man in our Tzelem/image and in our form": The explanation of this is that because man was created last after all the other

- As per:
  - When God created man, He set out within him all the forms and supernal secrets of the supernal and lower realms and they are all etched in man who stands in the image of God . . . as per "and Elokim created man in His Image."[122]
  - [All that which is in this world is only for the sake of man and only exists for him . . . and] we learn that since man was created [all was corrected – all that is above and below – all is incorporated within man.][123]
  - R. Abba began and said: "Elokim created man in His Image." Come and see, [when God created man, He made him in the image of above and below – incorporating everything.][124]
  - Like the appearance of man [who incorporates all images . . . like the appearance of man which has within it the secrets of all the supernal and lower worlds – like the appearance of man who incorporates all the secrets said and established before the Creation of the world.][125]
  - The image which incorporates all images . . . [because the image of man, which is] the image of the supernal and lower realms [which is incorporated within him.][126]
  - "And Elokim said, Let us make man" [after each *artisan* completed his work, God said to them: he is one creation to be collectively made connecting each and every part of creation and I will join with them to give him a part of Me, and this is the meaning of] "let us make man in our image"[127]
  - [I, God, want all of you to join together to make *the vessel* (man), and each of you will contribute a part of what was given to you, and I will join you in *this vessel* by providing My part. They said to Him: "Why is this vessel so important to you that it should incorporate everything?" He said to them: "This vessel is man who is in the image of Supernal Man."][128]
  - The image of man – this is the image which incorporates all images . . . [Man incorporates all from one end of the heavens to the other].[129]
  - [All the secrets of the Supernal and Lower Realms are all within man . . . God etched all the images of the Supernal and Lower Realms into man so that he would be at peace with everything.][130]

---

creations, God therefore told all of the creations to contribute a part of their attributes to man's body. For strength is attributed to the lion, speed to the deer, swiftness to the eagle, cunning to the fox, and their association. Similarly, the sprouting soul which is in vegetation and the animated soul which is in the animals – all of these have a corollary in man. The word "Tzelem"

• כְּמוֹ שֶׁאָמְרוּ

○ בְּזֹהַר יִתְרוֹ ע"ה ע"ב: קוּדְשָׁא בְּרִיךְ הוּא כַּד בְּרָא לֵיהּ לְבַר נָשׁ סַדֵּר בֵּיהּ כָּל דְּיוֹקְנִין דְּרָזִין עִלָּאִין דְּעָלְמָא דִּלְעֵילָא, וְכָל דְּיוֹקְנִין דְּרָזִין תַּתָּאִין דְּעָלְמָא דִּלְתַתָּא, וְכֹלָּא מִתְחַקְּקָא בְּבַר נָשׁ דְּאִיהוּ קָאִים בְּצֶלֶם אֱלֹקִים כו', דִּכְתִיב "וַיִּבְרָא אֱלֹהִים אֶת הָאָדָם בְּצַלְמוֹ", עַיֵּן שָׁם.

○ וּבְפָרָשַׁת תַּזְרִיעַ מ"ח א' תָּאנָא כֵּיוָן דְּנִבְרָא אָדָם כו'

○ וּבְרֵישׁ פָּרָשַׁת בַּמִּדְבָּר רַבִּי אַבָּא פָּתַח וַיִּבְרָא אֱלֹקִים אֶת הָאָדָם בְּצַלְמוֹ' וְגוֹ' תָּא חֲזֵי כו'

○ וּבְאִדְרָא רַבָּא קל"ה א' "כְּמַרְאֵה אָדָם" כו'.

○ וְשָׁם בְּדַף קמ"א סוֹף ע"א דְּיוֹקְנָא דִּכְלִיל כָּל דְּיוֹקְנִין כו'.

○ וּבְרַעְיָא מְהֵימְנָא פָּרָשַׁת פִּנְחָס רל"ח ב' "וַיֹּאמֶר אֱלֹקִים נַעֲשֶׂה אָדָם" כו' עַד וְהַיְנוּ "נַעֲשֶׂה אָדָם בְּצַלְמֵנוּ" כו'.

○ וְכֵן אָמְרוּ זֶה הַלָּשׁוֹן יוֹתֵר בְּאֹרֶךְ בְּתִקּוּנֵי זֹהַר חָדָשׁ צ"ז ע"א עַיֵּן שָׁם

○ וּבְזֹהַר חָדָשׁ יִתְרוֹ בְּמַעֲשֵׂה מֶרְכָּבָה ס"ד ע"א דְּיוֹקְנָא דְּאָדָם ס"ד ע"א דְּדָא אִיהוּ דְּיוֹקְנָא דְּכָלִיל כָּל דְּיוֹקְנִין כו' וְשָׁם דַּף ס"ד רֵישׁ ע"ב

○ וְשָׁם בְּשִׁיר הַשִּׁירִים כ"ג ב' "וַיֹּאמֶר אֱלֹקִים נַעֲשֶׂה אָדָם בְּצַלְמֵנוּ" כו'

---

relates to the image of something and how it is finished, with animals being superior to vegetation in that they have an animated soul, which is their image, and with vegetation over and above the inanimate. This is the meaning of "in our Tzelem," that the image of all species are united within the specie of man so that he can control all of them [encompassing the four levels of life of] inanimate, vegetation, animate, speech, and the seventy powers of nature and the intellect; therefore, [man] rules over all. [God] contributed *a part of God/Eloka Above* so that [man] should serve God. "In our form" [means] that all that which is in the world is in man and similarly, his soul is similar to that of God in five ways (as per Berachot 10a [see G2:05 and the description of how man's structure reflects God's structure])....

122 Zohar II Yitro 75b quoting Bereishit 1:27.
123 Zohar III Tazria 48a.
124 Zohar III Bamidbar 117a.
125 Zohar Idra Rabba III Naso 135a.
126 Zohar Idra Rabba III Naso 141b.
127 Zohar Raya Mehemna III Pinchas 238b quoting Bereishit 1:26.
128 Zohar Chadash Tikkunim II 97a.
129 Zohar Chadash I Yitro 64b.
130 Zohar Chadash II Shir Hashirim 23b.

- Refer to all the above references well.[131]
- and refer to Etz Chaim,[132] Likutei Torah Ki Tisa,[133] and Haazinu.[134]
- 'This being all that man is,'[135] that each specific power within him directly corresponds to a single specific world and power from the secret of the *Shiur Komah*[136] of the collective of the powers and the worlds, which are arranged, so to speak, as per the structure of man,[137] as will be explained if God Wills it in G2:05.
- Similarly, all of the Mitzvot are bound and dependent on their supernal root source in the arrangement of the parts of the Merkava and in the Shiur Komah of all of the worlds, with each individual Mitzvah incorporating a myriad of powers and lights from the arrangement of the Shiur Komah within its root.
- As the Zohar explains:
  - All the Mitzvot of the Torah are unified with the Holy Supernal King – some of them are in the King's Head and some are in His Body, Hands or Feet.[138] This idea is further expanded in the Tikkunim.[139]
  - The Mitzvot of the Torah are all Heavenly *limbs* of the supernal secret and when they join together as one they ascend to form a unified secret.[140]

---

131 These references have been expanded in the bullets above.
132 Etz Chaim Shaar 26, Shaar HaTzelem, Chap. 1:
- It is in this same way with lower man [of this world (in contrast with Supernal Man which is God)] who incorporates all of the worlds of Atzilut, Beriyah, Yetzirah, and Asiyah [see G1:13:N13 for details of the four worlds].
133 Likutei Torah Ki Tisa (by R. Chaim Vital), in the paragraph beginning "VeAtah Hored Edyecha":
- Now with the creation of man it says "Let *us* make," in the plural, which is not used for the other [creations] – rather it states "Let there be light" and "Let there be a firmament," in the singular – The *Supernal Disseminator* [relating to God as manifest in the world of Atzilut, a world which is *next to* God and does have awareness of Him] created the [world of] Beriyah and there is nothing in the world of Beriyah which has the ability to perceive anything above its world level [i.e., the concept of Yesh MiAyin where a lower world level has no awareness of the world level above it, see p. 472, fn. 18]. The same is true of [the world of Yetzirah] and [the world of] Asiyah [that they have no awareness of the worlds above them]. But man was not made like this for He wanted it that he [man] should perceive all of the worlds and to bind all of them together. It transpires that the *Disseminator* wanted that each and every world would willingly give [man] part of itself so that they all should have mercy on him – if he would sin then he would damage the entire universe and all would request mercy for him – if he should have merit they would all rejoice and be happy with him. Therefore, He

- עַיֵּן שָׁם הֵיטֵב בְּכָל הַמְּקוֹמוֹת הַנִּזְכָּרִים.
- וְעִנְיַן בְּעֵץ חַיִּים שַׁעַר הַצֶּלֶם פ"א, וּבְלִקּוּטֵי תּוֹרָה פָּרָשַׁת תִּשָּׂא וּפָרָשַׁת הַאֲזִינוּ:

- וְזֶה כָּל הָאָדָם, שֶׁכָּל כֹּחַ פְּרָטִי שֶׁבּוֹ, מְסֻדָּר נֶגֶד עוֹלָם וְכֹחַ אֶחָד פְּרָטִי, מִסּוֹד הַ'שִּׁעוּר קוֹמָה' שֶׁל כְּלָל הַכֹּחוֹת וְהָעוֹלָמוֹת, שֶׁמְּסֻדָּרִים כִּבְיָכוֹל כְּתַבְנִית קוֹמַת אָדָם, כְּמוֹ שֶׁיִּתְבָּאֵר אי"ה בְּשַׁעַר ב' פֶּרֶק ה':

- וְכֵן הַמִּצְווֹת, כֻּלָּן קְשׁוּרִין וּתְלוּיִין, בִּמְקוֹר שָׁרְשָׁן הָעֶלְיוֹן, בְּסִדְרֵי פִּרְקֵי הַמֶּרְכָּבָה וְשִׁעוּר קוֹמָה שֶׁל הָעוֹלָמוֹת כֻּלָּם, שֶׁכָּל מִצְוָה פְּרָטִית בְּשָׁרְשָׁהּ כּוֹלֶלֶת רִבֵּי רִבְבָן כֹּחוֹת וְאוֹרוֹת מְסִדְרֵי הַשִּׁעוּר קוֹמָה:

- כְּמוֹ שֶׁאָמַר

- בַּזֹּהַר יִתְרוֹ (פ"ה ב') כָּל פִּקּוּדֵי אוֹרַיְתָא מִתְאַחֲדָן בְּמַלְכָּא קַדִּישָׁא עִלָּאָה, מִנְּהוֹן בְּרֵישָׁא דְמַלְכָּא, וּמִנְּהוֹן בְּגוּפָא, וּמִנְּהוֹן בִּידֵי מַלְכָּא, וּמִנְּהוֹן בְּרַגְלוֹי כו'. וְהָעִנְיָן יוֹתֵר מְבֹאָר בַּתִּקּוּנִים ת"ע קכ"ט ב' ק"ל א' עַיֵּן שָׁם.

- וּבַזֹּהַר תְּרוּמָה קס"ב ב' פִּקּוּדֵי אוֹרַיְתָא כֻּלְּהוּ שַׁיְפִין וְאֵבָרִין בְּרָזָא דִלְעֵילָּא. וְכַד מִתְחַבְּרָן כֻּלְּהוּ כְּחַד, כְּדֵין כֻּלְּהוּ סָלְקָן לְרָזָא חַד.

---

wanted them to give him a part of themselves ... and therefore it says "Let *us* make" in the plural, that he counseled with his entourage, the supernal and lower [worlds], that they should willingly give him a part of themselves, and so it was, and [man] acquired a part of all of them.

134 Likutei Torah Haazinu:
- However God created the four worlds of Aztilut, Beriyah, Yetzirah, and Asiyah, and He created man to bind them all together as he has part of all the worlds within him, and He said to the worlds "Let *us* make man," that the world of Beriyah should give him the part of Neshama and the [world of] Yetzirah, Ruach, which is the part of the angels, and there is no person in Israel who does not have within him a part of an angel above ... it transpires that when a person is good and walks in the path of God, he binds all the worlds together.

135 Kohelet 12:13.

136 I.e., the structure of the aspect of God which incorporates and arranges the specific sequential interconnectivity of all creative abilities and all of the worlds.

137 This refers to the physical structure of his limbs and sinews as well as the emotional and spiritual structure as referenced by R. Chaim in G2:05.

138 Zohar II Yitro 85b.

139 Tikkunei Zohar Tikkun 70 129b and 130a.

140 Zohar II Terumah 162b.

- In this Name is incorporated the 613 Mitzvot of the Torah which themselves incorporate all the secrets of the Supernal and Lower Realms. All the Mitzvot, they are all parts and limbs which reveal the secret of faith through them. One who does not look into the secrets of the Mitzvot of the Torah will not know how the limbs rectify with the supernal secret. Limbs of the body are all rectified through the secret of the Mitzvot of the Torah.[141] Refer there.
- This is similarly written by the Arizal.[142]
- So when a person performs God's Will by using a specific limb and power within him to perform a specific Mitzvah
  - the resulting rectification impacts the supernal world and power which it parallels
  - to rectify it, or raise it, or increase its level of light and holiness, from God's Desire and Will
  - according to the quality and the way in which it was performed
  - and according to the degree of refinement and purity of the holiness of his thought at the time of performing the Mitzvah, which adds to the good of the [physical] performance[143] [which is] the key element
  - and according to the quality and level of that supernal world and power
  - and from there holiness and life force is also drawn to that power of the man (Note 8)[144] who performed the Mitzvah of his Creator which corresponds to it.
- When a person has completely fulfilled all of the Mitzvot
  - in all of their details and their points of precision, principally in their [physical] action
  - and additionally attaches to them the sheer purity and holiness of [associated] thought
  - this rectifies all the worlds and their supernal arrangements
  - and with all of his powers and limbs, he thereby is totally transformed into a Merkava [i.e., a chariot] for them [meaning that he becomes a platform upon which they exist and function]
  - and is sanctified from their supernal holiness with God's Glory constantly hovering over him.
  - As per "Everyone who is called by My Name and whom I have created

---

141 Zohar II Terumah 165b.
142 Shaar HaYichudim Chap. 2:
- ... and similarly, each and every Mitzvah has its place, as is known, within a specific limb of the supernal Shiur Komah. . . .

143 This sentence borrows the language of Kiddushin 40a but uses it in a

וְשָׁם בְּדַף קס"ה ב' בְּהַאי שְׁמָא כְּלִילָן תַּרְיָ"ג פְּקוּדֵי אוֹרַיְתָא, דְּאִנּוּן כְּלָלָא דְּכָל רָזִין עֲלָאִין וְתַתָּאִין כו', וְכֻלְּהוּ פְּקוּדִין כֻּלְּהוּ שַׁיְפִין וְאֵבְרִין לְאִתְחֲזָאָה בְּהוּ רָזָא דִּמְהֵימְנוּתָא, מַאן דְּלָא יַשְׁגַּח וְלָא אִסְתַּכַּל בְּרָזִין דִּפְקוּדֵי אוֹרַיְתָא, לָא יָדַע וְלָא אִסְתַּכַּל הֵיךְ מִתְתַּקְּנָן שַׁיְפִין בְּרָזָא עֲלָאָה, שַׁיְפִין דְּגוּפָא כֻּלְּהוּ מִתְתַּקְּנָן עַל רָזָא דִּפְקוּדֵי אוֹרַיְתָא. עַיֵּן שָׁם:

- וְכֵן כָּתַב הָאֲרִיזַ"ל בְּשַׁעַר הַיִּחוּדִים פֶּרֶק ב':

- וּבַעֲשׂוֹת הָאָדָם רְצוֹן קוֹנוֹ יִתְבָּרַךְ שְׁמוֹ, וּמְקַיֵּם בְּאֵיזֶה אֵבֶר וְכֹחַ שֶׁבּוֹ, אַחַת מִמִּצְוֹת ה'

  - הַתִּקּוּן נוֹגֵעַ לְאוֹתוֹ עוֹלָם וְכֹחַ הָעֶלְיוֹן הַמַּקְבִּילוֹ

  - לְתַקְּנוֹ, אוֹ לְהַעֲלוֹתוֹ, אוֹ לְהוֹסִיף אוֹר וּקְדֻשָּׁה עַל קְדֻשָּׁתוֹ, מֵחֵפֶץ וּרְצוֹן הָעֶלְיוֹן יִתְבָּרַךְ שְׁמוֹ

  - כְּפִי עֶרֶךְ וְאֹפֶן עֲשִׂיָּתוֹ

  - וּלְפִי רֹב הִזְדַּכְּכוּת וְטָהֳרַת קְדֻשַּׁת מַחֲשַׁבְתּוֹ בְּעֵת עֲשִׂיַּת הַמִּצְוָה, הַמִּצְטָרֶפֶת לְטוֹבָה לַמַּעֲשֶׂה הָעִקָּרִית

  - וּכְפִי עֶרֶךְ מַדְרֵגַת אוֹתוֹ הָעוֹלָם וְהַכֹּחַ עֶלְיוֹן.

  - וּמִשָּׁם נִמְשָׁךְ הַקְּדֻשָּׁה וְחִיּוּת גַּם עַל אוֹתוֹ הַכֹּחַ שֶׁל הָאָדָם (הגהה ח') שֶׁבּוֹ קִיֵּם מִצְוַת בּוֹרְאוֹ הַמְכֻוֶּנֶת נֶגְדּוֹ:

- וְכַאֲשֶׁר קִיֵּם כָּל הַמִּצְוֹת בִּשְׁלֵמוּת

  - בְּכָל פְּרָטֵיהֶם וְדִקְדּוּקֵיהֶם בְּעִקַּר הַמַּעֲשֶׂה

  - וְנוֹסָף עֲלֵיהֶם הִצְטָרֵף עֹצֶם טָהֳרַת וּקְדֻשַּׁת הַמַּחֲשָׁבָה

  - הֲרֵי תִקֵּן כָּל הָעוֹלָמוֹת וְהַסְּדָרִים הָעֶלְיוֹנִים

  - וְנַעֲשָׂה כֻּלּוֹ בְּכָל כֹּחוֹתָיו וְאֵבָרָיו מֶרְכָּבָה לָהֶם

  - וּמִתְקַדְּשִׁים מִקְּדֻשָּׁתָם הָעֶלְיוֹנָה, וּכְבוֹד ה' חוֹפֵף עָלָיו תָּמִיד.

  - וְעַיֵּן זֹהַר תְּרוּמָה קנ"ה א, "כֹּל הַנִּקְרָא בִשְׁמִי וְלִכְבוֹדִי בְּרָאתִיו" כו' (ישעיה מג,

---

different context. In Kiddushin 40a, the joining of a good thought to physical performance is understood to mean that having the good thought alone is as if the physical performance was done. In contrast, the idea here is that a good thought will add good to the physical performance of a Mitzvah, but it cannot replace the physical performance which is the essential part of the Mitzvah.

144 **R. Chaim adds Note 8 here.** This note is brought at the end of this chapter and is entitled "Commitment to do good/bad brings holiness/evil within one."

from My Glory" ... we learn that this Glory ... is only rectified above from the rectifications of the people of this world, when people are meritorious and pious and know how to perform rectification.[145] Refer there at length.
- Refer well to the Zohar.[146]
- This is what Chazal[147] meant in saying that the Patriarchs are the Merkava.

- Similarly, with the converse, God forbid
  - if one damages one of his powers and limbs as a result of 'his sin which he sinned'[148]
  - this damage also reaches that supernal world and power which corresponds to [his power and limb] in the arrangement of the Shiur Komah, so to speak, according to his root
  - to break it and destroy it, God forbid, or to lower it, damage it, or darken and reduce the clarity of its light
  - to wear out, weaken, and diminish the power of the purity of its holiness, God forbid.
  - All is according to the level of the sin and the way in which it was performed
  - and according to the quality and aspect of that world and its relative level.
  - For not all the worlds are equal in terms of how they are damaged and corrupted
    - with the lowest worlds – it is a shattering and destruction, the Merciful One should save us
    - with the supernal worlds – it is a withholding of light
    - and with the more supernal worlds – it just causes a diminishing of the bestowal of light or its reduction
    - and with even higher world levels – it just causes a diminishing in the greatness of the clarity of its light and of the purity of its awesome holiness
    - and similarly there are many graduated levels [of impact].

---

145 Zohar II Terumah 155a quoting Yishayahu 43:7.
146 Zohar Raya Mehemna III Pinchas 239a:
   - Happy is he who exerts effort during the final exile to know the Shechina, to value it with [the performance] of all the Mitzvot and to endure difficulties for it, as per the reward for discomfort endured when listening to a Torah lecture [Berachot 6a – in line with "according to the level of difficulty is the reward" (Mishna Avot 5:23)]. [Then] "and he rested/YiShCaV in that place" [Bereishit 28:11] – if "there are" "22" letters of the Torah – then [the Shechina] will rest upon him. [The word "YiShCaV" is comprised of

ז). וְלִכְבוֹדִי בְּרָאתִיו דַּיְקָא, וְרָזָא דָא כו' אוֹלִיפְנָא דְּהַאי כָּבוֹד כו', כֻּלָּא אִתְתַּקַּן לְעֵלָּא מִגּוֹ תִּקּוּנָא דִּבְנֵי עָלְמָא, כַּד אִנּוּן בְּנֵי נָשָׁא זַכָּאִין וַחֲסִידִין, וְיָדְעִין לְתַקְּנָא תִּקּוּנֵי כו' עַיֵּן שָׁם בָּאֹרֶךְ.

◦ וְעַיֵּן הֵיטֵב בְּרַעְיָא מְהֵימְנָא פָּרָשַׁת פִּנְחָס רל"ט א'.

◦ וְזֶהוּ שֶׁאָמְרוּ רַבּוֹתֵינוּ זִכְרוֹנָם לִבְרָכָה (ב"ר מ"ז), הָאָבוֹת הֵן הֵן הַמֶּרְכָּבָה:

• וְכֵן לְהֶפֶךְ חַס וְשָׁלוֹם

◦ בִּפְגַם אֶחָד מִכֹּחוֹתָיו וְאֵבָרָיו, עַל יְדֵי חַטָּאתוֹ אֲשֶׁר חָטָא

◦ גַּם כֵּן הַפְּגָם מַגִּיעַ לְפִי שָׁרְשׁוֹ, לְאוֹתוֹ הָעוֹלָם וְהַכֹּחַ הָעֶלְיוֹן הַמְכֻוָּן נֶגְדּוֹ בְּסִדְרֵי הַשִּׁעוּר קוֹמָה כִּבְיָכוֹל

◦ לְהָרְסוֹ וּלְהַחֲרִיבוֹ חַס וְשָׁלוֹם, אוֹ לְהוֹרִידוֹ, אוֹ לְפָגְמוֹ, אוֹ לְהַחֲשִׁיךְ וּלְהַקְטִין צִחְצוּחַ אוֹרוֹ

◦ וּלְהַתִּישׁ וּלְהַחֲלִישׁ וּלְמַעֵט כֹּחַ טָהֳרַת קְדֻשָּׁתוֹ חַס וְשָׁלוֹם

◦ הַכֹּל כְּפִי עֵרֶךְ הַחֵטְא וְאֹפֶן עֲשִׂיָּתוֹ.

◦ וּכְפִי עֵרֶךְ וְעִנְיַן אוֹתוֹ הָעוֹלָם וְגֹבַהּ מַדְרֵגָתוֹ.

◦ כִּי לֹא כָּל הָעוֹלָמוֹת שָׁוִין בְּשִׁעוּרָן בְּעִנְיַן הַפְּגָם וְהַקִּלְקוּל

▫ שֶׁבַּתַּחְתּוֹן — הוּא הֲרִיסָה וְחֻרְבָּן ר"ל

▫ וּלְמַעְלָה — מְנִיעַת הָאוֹר

▫ וּבָעֶלְיוֹן יוֹתֵר מִמֶּנּוּ — גּוֹרֵם רַק הִתְמַעֲטוּת שִׁפְעַת אוֹרוֹ אוֹ הַקְטָנָתוֹ

▫ וּבְיוֹתֵר גָּבוֹהַּ וְנַעֲלֶה — גּוֹרֵם רַק הִתְמַעֲטוּת בְּגֹדֶל צִחְצוּחַ אוֹרוֹ וְטָהֳרַת קְדֻשָּׁתוֹ הַנִּפְלָאָה

▫ וְכָהֵנָּה רַבּוֹת בְּחִינוֹת שׁוֹנוֹת:

---

letters which form "Yesh/there are" and *Kaf Bet* which has the numerical value of "22," referring to the 22 letters of the Torah. Therefore, if a person performs all of the Mitzvot of the Torah which is comprised of 22 letters, the Shechina, the immediate presence of God, rests upon him resulting in God's Glory hovering over him.]

147 Bereishit Rabba Lech Lecha 47:6.
148 E.g., Vayikra 4:23.

- Chazal refer to this in many places – to the damage of sin, the damage of the image of The King.
  - As per: And because of this, one who transgresses the commands of the Torah is as if he damaged the Body of the King as per "and they will go out and see the corpses of the men who rebelled against me" – literally against me. Woe to those culpable who transgress the words of the Torah and don't know what they are doing.[149]
  - As per: All who transgress the commandments are as if they damaged the image of the King.[150]
- As mentioned above, [one's sinful] damage extends to and impacts on the components and the arrangement of powers and worlds within the Shiur Komah as they are all contained within him and contribute part of their essence to his construction and creation. (Note 9)[151]

Rabbi Chaim's Notes:
Note 6 – Angel sanctification is not simultaneous but follows man

- Furthermore, according to this, it would certainly be that when we say Sanctification[152] in this physical world, then it would be inevitable that at that very same moment, the angels in the Supernal Realms would simultaneously recite Sanctification together with us.
- [However,] Chazal state[153] that the angels do not say Shira/[Sanctification] in the Supernal Realms until *after* Israel has said this in the lower realms as it says "When the morning stars sang in unison"[154] which is *followed by* "and all the heavenly beings shouted."
  - The expressions "and this is followed by" and "they shouted" strongly imply that the [angels] will not begin to sanctify their Creator at all until after Israel has completed their triplication of Sanctification in the lower realms.
  - Therefore, the Men of the Great Assembly set out the blessing of Sanctification of God's Name[155] [by Israel first stating] "You are Holy" and [only] afterwards [stating that] "holy beings praise You daily."
- The language of the Zohar[156] also seems to imply that there is a literally simultaneous Sanctification on the part of the angels with us

---

149 Zohar II Yitro 85b quoting Yishayahu 66:24.
150 Tikkunei Zohar Tikkun 70 131a.
151 **R. Chaim adds Note 9 here.** This note is brought at the end of this chapter and is entitled "Let us make man in plural implies worlds make up Shiur Komah."
152 By reciting the Kedushah prayer.
153 Chullin 91b.

- וְזֶהוּ הָעִנְיָן שֶׁקָּרְאוּ רַבּוֹתֵינוּ זִכְרוֹנָם לִבְרָכָה בְּכַמָּה מְקוֹמוֹת לִפְגָם הֶעָוֹן פְּגָם אִיקוֹנִין שֶׁל מֶלֶךְ.

- וּבַזֹּהַר יִתְרוֹ פ"ה ב' וּבְגִין כָּךְ מָאן דְּפָשַׁע בְּפִקּוּדֵי אוֹרַיְתָא כְּמָאן דְּפָשַׁע בְּגוּפָא דְמַלְכָּא, כְּמָה דִכְתִיב (ישעיה סו, כד) "וְיָצְאוּ וְרָאוּ בְּפִגְרֵי הָאֲנָשִׁים הַפּוֹשְׁעִים בִּי", בִּי מַמָּשׁ, וַי לְחַיָּבַיָּא דְעָבְרִין עַל פִּתְגָּמֵי אוֹרַיְתָא וְלָא יָדְעִין מַאי קָא עָבְדִין.

- וּבַתִּקּוּנִים ת"ע קל"א וְכָל מַאן דְּפָשַׁע בְּפִקּוּדָא כְּאִלּוּ פָּשַׁע בְּדִיּוֹקְנָא דְמַלְכָּא:

- כנ"ל שֶׁהַפְּגָם נִמְשָׁךְ וְנוֹגֵעַ בְּפִרְקֵי וְסִדְרֵי הַכֹּחוֹת וְהָעוֹלָמוֹת הַשִׁעוּר קוֹמָה, מִצַּד שֶׁכֻּלָּם נִכְלְלוּ בּוֹ וְנָתְנוּ חֵלֶק מֵעַצְמוּתָם בְּבִנְיָנוֹ וּבְרִיאָתוֹ: (הגהה ט')

הגהה ו'

- וְגַם שֶׁלְּפִי זֶה יְחֻיַּב הָיָה, שֶׁבְּעֵת אֲמִירָתֵנוּ קְדֻשָּׁה לְמַטָּה, מִמֵּילָא בְּאוֹתוֹ רֶגַע מַמָּשׁ גַּם הַמַּלְאָכִים הָיוּ מַקְדִּישִׁים בַּמָּרוֹם אִתָּנוּ כְּאֶחָד:

- וְרַבּוֹתֵינוּ זִכְרוֹנָם לִבְרָכָה אָמְרוּ בְּפֶרֶק גִּיד הַנָּשֶׁה (חולין צ"א ב) אֵין מַלְאֲכֵי הַשָּׁרֵת אוֹמְרִים שִׁירָה לְמַעְלָה עַד שֶׁיֹּאמְרוּ יִשְׂרָאֵל לְמַטָּה שֶׁנֶּאֱמַר (איוב לח, ז) "בְּרָן יַחַד כּוֹכְבֵי בֹקֶר" וְהָדַר "וַיָּרִיעוּ כָּל בְּנֵי אֱלֹהִים"

- וּלְיִשָּׁנָא דְ'וְהָדַר וַיָּרִיעוּ' טְפֵי מַשְׁמַע שֶׁהֵמָּה לֹא יַתְחִילוּ כְּלָל לְהַקְדִּישׁ לְיוֹצְרָם עַד אֲשֶׁר יִגְמְרוּ יִשְׂרָאֵל שָׁלוֹשׁ קְדֻשָׁתָם לְמַטָּה

- וְכֵן סִדְּרוּ אַנְשֵׁי כְּנֶסֶת הַגְּדוֹלָה בְּבִרְכַּת קְדֻשַּׁת הַשֵּׁם "אַתָּה קָדוֹשׁ" וְכוּ' וְאַחַר כָּךְ "וּקְדוֹשִׁים בְּכָל יוֹם יְהַלְלוּךָ":

- הֲגַם דְּמִלִּישָׁנָא דְּהַזֹּהַר (פרשת תרומה קכ"ט ריש ע"ב, ושם קס"ד ריש ע"ב) לִכְאוֹרָה מַשְׁמַע שֶׁהַמַּלְאָכִים מַקְדִּישִׁים קְדֻשָּׁתָם אִתָּנוּ יַחַד כַּחֲדָא מַמָּשׁ

---

154 Iyov 38:7.
155 The third blessing of the Amidah.
156 Zohar II Terumah 129b:
- ... but the angels are holier than us and they receive more holiness, and if it were not for us taking and drawing upon ourselves these Sanctifications, we could not be *friends* with them, and God's honor would not be simultaneously complete in the Supernal and Lower Realms. ...

Zohar II Terumah 164b:
- ... at that time when Israel in the lower realms arrange their prayers and requests, and praise The Supernal King, all those who are in the supernal camps [i.e., the angels] arrange their praise and are rectified with that holy rectification. For the supernal camps are all *friends* with Israel of the lower

- however, this is only because their Sanctification is entirely dependent on and immediately follows sequentially from our [Sanctification], as if it were a unified statement.

Note 7 – Sins of Adam/Golden Calf internalized Evil requiring death to purify

- This relates to [mankind's status] before [Adam's] sin [of eating from the Tree of Knowledge of Good and Evil], at which time he was only comprised of all the worlds and powers of Holiness alone, and not of powers of Evil.
- However, after the sin, powers of impurity and Evil were also incorporated and mixed into him
  - and inevitably, as a result of this, also mixing them in with the worlds as he is a composite of and connected to all of [the worlds]
  - and they respond and change according to his actions
  - and this is the concept of the Tree of Knowledge of Good and Evil.
- The concept is, that before [Adam's] sin
  - while [man] certainly had complete free choice to do good or the opposite, God forbid, as he pleased, as this was the objective of the entirety of Creation
  - and indeed, he subsequently sinned
  - nevertheless, his free choice did not come from powers of Evil which were incorporated within him, as he was a totally *straight* person and only incorporated powers of Holiness alone
  - and everything about him was completely *straight*, holy, and refined – absolutely good
  - without any intermingling or inclination to the opposite [of Evil] at all
  - with the powers of Evil being on the side, as a separate concept being external to him.
- He had the freedom of choice to engage in the powers of Evil, God forbid, in the same way as a person has the free choice to enter into a fire.
  - Therefore, when the Sitra Achara [i.e., the other side – the forces of Evil] wanted to cause him to sin it needed the snake to come to externally entice him.
  - This is unlike the current situation [i.e., after the sin], where the Evil Inclination entices man from within himself
  - and makes out to the person that he himself is the one who desires to and is drawn after the sin
  - and not that something else external to him is enticing him.

---

realms, such that they praise God together, so that God's [resulting] ascen-

הַיְנוּ מִשּׁוּם שֶׁקִּדְּשָׁתָם תְּכוּפָה מַמָּשׁ תֵּכֶף אַחַר סִיּוּם אֲמִירָתֵנוּ, כְּחַדָא קָרֵי לֵהּ:

הגהה ז'

- וְזֶה הָיָה קֹדֶם הַחֵטְא, לֹא הָיָה כָּלוּל אָז רַק מִכָּל הָעוֹלָמוֹת וְכֹחוֹת הַקְּדֻשָּׁה לְבַד, וְלֹא מִכֹּחוֹת הָרָע:
- אֲבָל אַחַר הַחֵטְא, נִכְלְלוּ וְנִתְעָרְבוּ בּוֹ גַּם כֹּחוֹת הַטֻּמְאָה וְהָרָע
- וּמִמֵּילָא עֵרֵב אוֹתָם עַל יְדֵי זֶה גַּם בְּהָעוֹלָמוֹת, מִזֶּה הַטַּעַם שֶׁהוּא כָּלוּל וּמְשֻׁתָּף מִכֻּלָּם
- וְהֵם מִתְעוֹרְרִים וּמִשְׁתַּנִּים כְּפִי נְטִיַּת מַעֲשָׂיו
- וְהוּא עִנְיַן "עֵץ הַדַּעַת טוֹב וָרָע":

- וְהָעִנְיָן, כִּי קֹדֶם הַחֵטְא
- אִם כִּי וַדַּאי שֶׁהָיָה בַּעַל בְּחִירָה גָּמוּר, לְהַטּוֹת עַצְמוֹ לְכָל אֲשֶׁר יַחְפֹּץ, לְהֵיטִיב אוֹ לְהֵפֶךְ חַס וְשָׁלוֹם, כִּי זֶה תַּכְלִית כַּוָּנַת כְּלַל הַבְּרִיאָה
- וְגַם כִּי הֲרֵי אַחַר כָּךְ חָטָא.
- אָמְנָם לֹא שֶׁהָיָה עִנְיַן בְּחִירָתוֹ מֵחֲמַת שֶׁכֹּחוֹת הָרָע הָיוּ כְּלוּלִים בְּתוֹכוֹ, כִּי הוּא הָיָה אָדָם יָשָׁר לְגַמְרֵי, כָּלוּל רַק מִסִּדְרֵי כֹּחוֹת הַקְּדֻשָּׁה לְבַד
- וְכָל עִנְיָנָיו הָיוּ כֻּלָּם יְשָׁרִים קְדוֹשִׁים וּמְזֻכָּכִים טוֹב גָּמוּר
- בְּלִי שׁוּם עֵרוּב וּנְטִיָּה לְצַד הַהֵפֶךְ כְּלָל
- וְכֹחוֹת הָרָע הָיוּ עוֹמְדִים לְצַד, וְעִנְיָן בִּפְנֵי עַצְמָם, חוּץ מִמֶּנּוּ:
- וְהָיָה בַּעַל בְּחִירָה לִיכָּנֵס אֶל כֹּחוֹת הָרָע חַס וְשָׁלוֹם — כְּמוֹ שֶׁהָאָדָם הוּא בַּעַל בְּחִירָה לִיכָּנֵס אֶל תּוֹךְ הָאֵשׁ.
- לָכֵן כְּשֶׁרָצָה הַסמ"א לְהַחֲטִיאוֹ, הֻצְרַךְ הַנָּחָשׁ לָבֹא 'מִבַּחוּץ' לְפַתּוֹת
- לֹא כְּמוֹ שֶׁהוּא עַתָּה, שֶׁהַיֵּצֶר הַמְפַתֶּה אֶת הָאָדָם הוּא 'בְּתוֹךְ' הָאָדָם עַצְמוֹ
- וּמִתְדַּמֶּה לְהָאָדָם שֶׁהוּא עַצְמוֹ הוּא הָרוֹצֶה וְנִמְשָׁךְ לַעֲשׂוֹת הֶעָוֹן
- וְלֹא שֶׁאַחֵר חוּץ מִמֶּנּוּ מְפַתֵּהוּ:

- With [Adam's] sin after being attracted to the enticement of the Sitra Achara
  - the powers of Evil were then literally mixed up within him and similarly with the worlds.
  - This is the [meaning of the] Tree of *Knowledge* of Good and Evil which literally interconnected and mixed good and bad within him and the worlds
  - as the term "knowledge" means "connection," as is known.[157]
- This issue is explained, although very briefly, for one who understands in Etz Chaim.[158]
- Also refer well to Sefer HaGilgulim.[159]
- This is as per Chazal,[160] that when the snake came upon Chava it placed poison in her, meaning it was literally placed within her.
- From that point onwards, it caused great confusion in [man's] actions
  - that all of man's actions are mixed up and change many times
  - sometimes being Good and sometimes Evil
  - and constantly switching from Good to Evil and from Evil to Good.
- Even the Good actions are virtually impossible for most people to be absolutely holy, refined, and pure – without any remote ulterior motive.
- Similarly, with the opposite, with actions which are not Good, they also occasionally contain some imaginary thought of Good [intention].
- Even with a perfect Tzaddik who has never done any deed which isn't good
  - and has never spoken even a hint of an inappropriate word, God forbid, in his entire life
  - it is nevertheless virtually impossible that his good deeds performed all of his life are truly completely perfect, without even one of them being wanting and defective at all.
  - As per the verse "For there is no man so wholly righteous on earth that he always does good and never sins"[161]

---

157 E.g., as per the verse "and Adam *knew* Chava" (Bereishit 4:1), referring to the marital connection between Adam and Chava.

158 Etz Chaim Shaar 49, Shaar Kelipat Nogah, Chap. 2:
- . . . Samael and Lilit who enticed Adam and Chava were from the three external Kelipot . . . but the enticement was through the medium of Kelipat Nogah . . . and it was this Kelipat Nogah which became mixed within Adam and Chava making man a composite of Good and Evil.

159 Sefer HaGilgulim Chap. 1:
- On the initial creation of Adam, he incorporated within himself all souls which came from the side of good and they were dependent on him. After he sinned and mixed Good with Evil, then Good and Evil were intermixed,

- וּבְחָטְאוֹ, שֶׁנִּמְשַׁךְ אַחַר פִּתּוּי הס"א
  ○ אָז נִתְעָרְבוּ הַכֹּחוֹת הָרַע 'בְּתוֹכוֹ' מַמָּשׁ, וְכֵן בְּהָעוֹלָמוֹת
  ○ וְזֶהוּ "עֵץ הַדַּעַת טוֹב וָרָע", שֶׁנִּתְחַבְּרוּ וְנִתְעָרְבוּ בְּתוֹכוֹ וּבְהָעוֹלָמוֹת — הַטּוֹב וְהָרַע יַחַד, זֶה בְּתוֹךְ זֶה מַמָּשׁ
  ○ כִּי 'דַּעַת' פֵּרוּשׁוֹ 'הִתְחַבְּרוּת' כַּיָּדוּעַ:
- וְהָעִנְיָן מְבֹאָר לַמֵּבִין בְּעֵץ חַיִּים שַׁעַר קְלִפַּת נֹגַהּ פ"ב, אֶלָּא שֶׁקִּצֵּר שָׁם בָּעִנְיָן:
- וְעַיֵּן הֵיטֵב בְּגִלְגּוּלִים פֶּרֶק א':
- וְזֶה שֶׁאָמְרוּ רַבּוֹתֵינוּ זִכְרוֹנָם לִבְרָכָה (שבת קמו א) כְּשֶׁבָּא נָחָשׁ עַל חַוָּה הִטִּיל 'בָּהּ' זֻהֲמָא, רוֹצֶה לוֹמַר בְּתוֹכָהּ מַמָּשׁ:
- וּמֵאָז, גָּרַם עַל יְדֵי זֶה עִרְבּוּבְיָא גְדוֹלָה בְּמַעֲשָׂיו
  ○ שֶׁכָּל מַעֲשֵׂי הָאָדָם הֵמָּה בְּעִרְבּוּבְיָא וְהִשְׁתַּנּוּת רַבִּים מְאֹד
  ○ פַּעַם טוֹב וּפַעַם רַע
  ○ וּמִתְהַפֵּךְ תָּמִיד מִטּוֹב לְרַע וּמֵרַע לְטוֹב:
- וְגַם הַמַּעֲשֶׂה הַטּוֹב עַצְמָהּ, כִּמְעַט בִּלְתִּי אֶפְשָׁר לְרֹב הָעוֹלָם שֶׁתִּהְיֶה כֻּלָּהּ קֹדֶשׁ קָדָשִׁים זַכָּה וּנְקִיָּה לְגַמְרֵי, בְּלִי שׁוּם נְטִיָּה לְאֵיזֶה פְּנִיָּה וּמַחֲשָׁבָה קַלָּה לְגַרְמֵיהּ:
- וְכֵן לְהֵפֶךְ — בְּהַמַּעֲשֶׂה אֲשֶׁר לֹא טוֹבָה, גַּם כֵּן מְעָרָב בָּהּ לִפְעָמִים אֵיזֶה מַחֲשָׁבָה לְטוֹב לְפִי דִּמְיוֹנוֹ:
- וְגַם הַצַּדִּיק גָּמוּר, שֶׁמִּיָּמָיו לֹא עָשָׂה שׁוּם מַעֲשֶׂה אֲשֶׁר לֹא טוֹבָה
  ○ וְלֹא שָׂח מִיָּמָיו שׁוּם שִׂיחָה קַלָּה אֲשֶׁר לֹא טוֹבָה חַס וְשָׁלוֹם
  ○ עִם כָּל זֶה כִּמְעַט בִּלְתִּי אֶפְשָׁר כְּלָל שֶׁמַּעֲשָׂיו הַטּוֹבִים עַצְמָם, כָּל יְמֵי חַיָּיו, יִהְיוּ כֻּלָּם בִּשְׁלֵמוּת הָאֲמִתִּי לְגַמְרֵי, וְלֹא יִהְיֶה אֲפִלּוּ בְּאַחַת מֵהֵנָּה שׁוּם חִסָּרוֹן וּפְגָם כְּלָל.
  ○ וְזֶה שֶׁאָמַר הַכָּתוּב (קהלת ז' כ') "כִּי אָדָם אֵין צַדִּיק בָּאָרֶץ אֲשֶׁר יַעֲשֶׂה טּוֹב וְלֹא יֶחֱטָא"

---

and it is from that Evil part that idol worshippers were later on descended from him, but the essential part of Adam was Good which is the souls of Israel . . . and when he ate of the Tree of Knowledge of Good and Evil, he mixed the Good with the Evil, and then the good of Adam was intermixed with the Evil of the Kelipot. . . .

160 Shabbat 146a.
161 Kohelet 7:20.

- meaning that it is impossible that there shouldn't be at least some minor omission in the good deeds that he performs
  - as the term "sin" means "omission" as is known.[162]
- Therefore, when man [ultimately] stands before God in judgment
  - he requires innumerable calculations concerning the finer points of details of all his actions, speech, and thoughts
  - with all the details of his behavior and to which way they tended.
  - This is the meaning of the verse "God created man straightforward [and they seek many calculations]"[163]
  - [that man is *straight*] as mentioned above
  - but that "they" out of their sins "seek many calculations."
  - Refer to the Zohar and this is explained there according to our words.[164]
- This concept extended in this way until the time of the Giving of the Torah, when this poison ceased to be within them [the people of Israel], as per Chazal.[165]
- Therefore, after the sin of the Golden Calf, Chazal say[166] that the Satan came and *mixed up* [the world]
  - that is he came in an external way, just as with the sin of Adam, as mentioned above
  - as it had been expelled from being within them
  - but as a result of the sin of the Golden Calf that same poison was returned *and mixed up within them* as it was originally [with Adam's sin]
  - as per the verse "and they, like Adam, transgressed the Covenant."[167]
- This is as God said to Adam: "For on the day you shall eat of it, you shall die"[168]
  - not that this was a curse or a punishment as "From the mouth of God no [bad and good] will emanate"[169]
  - but it means that through your eating of it the poison of Evil will be mixed in within you
  - and you will have no other remedy to separate it from yourself so that you will be good in the end
  - other than through death and decomposition in the grave.

---

162 E.g., as per Shela, Ten Maamarot, Maamar Three and Four 130.
163 Kohelet 7:29.
164 Zohar III Emor 107a:
  - . . . and they certainly *sought many calculations*, then their hearts literally turned to that side, sometimes to Good and sometimes to Evil, sometimes to mercy and sometimes to judgment . . .
165 Shabbat 146a.

נפש שער א' - פרק ו' החיים

- רוֹצֶה לוֹמַר, שֶׁאִי אֶפְשָׁר שֶׁלֹּא יִהְיֶה עַל כָּל פָּנִים קְצָת חִסָּרוֹן בַּמַּעֲשֶׂה הַטּוֹב עַצְמָהּ שֶׁעוֹשֶׂה
- כִּי 'חֵטְא' פֵּרוּשׁוֹ חִסָּרוֹן כַּיָּדוּעַ:
- לָכֵן כְּשֶׁמַּכְנִיסִין הָאָדָם לַמִּשְׁפָּט לְפָנָיו יִתְבָּרַךְ שְׁמוֹ
- צָרִיךְ חֶשְׁבּוֹנוֹת רַבִּים לְאֵין שִׁעוּר, עַל כָּל הַפְּרָטֵי פְרָטִים שֶׁל כָּל מַעֲשָׂיו וְדִבּוּרָיו וּמַחְשְׁבוֹתָיו
- וְכָל פְּרָטֵי הַנְהָגוֹתָיו בְּאֹפְנֵי נְטִיָּתָם לְאָן הָיוּ נוֹטִים.
- וְזֶה שֶׁאָמַר הַכָּתוּב (קהלת ז, כט) "אֲשֶׁר עָשָׂה אֱלֹקִים אֶת הָאָדָם יָשָׁר" כנ"ל
- "וְהֵמָּה" — בְּחֶטְאָם, "בִּקְשׁוּ חִשְּׁבֹנוֹת רַבִּים".
- וְעַיֵּן זֹהַר (אמור ק"ז סוף ע"א) וְהוּא מְבֹאָר שָׁם עַל פִּי דְּבָרֵינוּ:

- וְנִמְשַׁךְ הָעִנְיָן כֵּן — עַד עֵת מַתַּן תּוֹרָה, שֶׁאָז פָּסְקָה אוֹתָהּ הַזֻּהֲמָא מִתּוֹכָם, כְּמוֹ שֶׁאָמְרוּ רַבּוֹתֵינוּ זִכְרוֹנָם לִבְרָכָה (שבת שם):
- וְלָכֵן אַחַר כָּךְ בְּחֵטְא הָעֵגֶל אָמְרוּ רַבּוֹתֵינוּ זִכְרוֹנָם לִבְרָכָה (שם פ"ט א') שֶׁבָּא שָׂטָן וְעֵרְבֵּב כוּ'
  - הַיְנוּ שֶׁבָּא "מִבַּחוּץ", כְּמוֹ בְּעִנְיַן חֵטְא אָדָם הָרִאשׁוֹן כנ"ל
  - כִּי "מִתּוֹכָם" נִתְגָּרֵשׁ.
- וְעַל יְדֵי חֵטְא הָעֵגֶל — חָזְרָה אוֹתָהּ הַזֻּהֲמָא, וְ"נִתְעָרְבָה בְּתוֹכָם" כְּבַתְּחִלָּה
- וְזֶה שֶׁאָמַר הַכָּתוּב (הושע ו, ז) "וְהֵמָּה כְּאָדָם עָבְרוּ בְרִית":

- וְזֶה שֶׁאָמַר הוּא יִתְבָּרַךְ לְאָדָם הָרִאשׁוֹן (בראשית ב, יז) "כִּי בְּיוֹם אֲכָלְךָ מִמֶּנּוּ מוֹת תָּמוּת"
  - לֹא שֶׁהָיָה עִנְיַן קְלָלָה וְעֹנֶשׁ, כִּי מִפִּי עֶלְיוֹן לֹא תֵצֵא כוּ' (איכה ג, לח)
  - אֶלָּא פֵּרוּשׁוֹ, שֶׁעַל יְדֵי אָכְלְךָ מִמֶּנּוּ, תִּתְעָרֵב בְּךָ הַזֻּהֲמָא שֶׁל הָרַע
  - וְלֹא יִהְיֶה תִּקּוּן אַחֵר לְהַפְרִידָהּ מִמְּךָ, כְּדֵי לְהֵטִיבְךָ בְּאַחֲרִיתֶךָ
  - אִם לֹא עַל יְדֵי הַמִּיתָה וְהָעִכּוּל בַּקֶּבֶר:

---

166 Shabbat 89a.
167 Hoshea 6:7.
168 Bereishit 2:17.
169 Eicha 3:38.

- This is also the point which God made afterwards – "Behold, man has become [like the Unique One among us, knowing good and bad,] and now, lest he put his hand forward and also take to eat from the Tree of Life and live forever"[170]
  - but surely God desires good for His creations and why should it bother Him if he lives forever?
- However this means that were he to eat of the Tree of Life and live forever
  - he would forever remain without remedy, God forbid
  - as the Evil would never separate from him forever, God forbid
  - and he would never see or experience good for all of his days.
  - Therefore, it was for his own good that he was exiled from the Garden of Eden so that he would be able to achieve a full remedy
  - when Evil separates from him through death and decomposition in the grave.
- This explains the concept of the four who died as a result of the counsel of the snake[171]
  - that even though they themselves did not have any sins of their own
  - they nevertheless needed to die as a result of the original intermixing of Evil through Adam's sin on the advice of the snake.
- This concept will remain like this until the end of days when
  - "He will eliminate death forever"[172]
  - and there also will be a further advantage that Evil will be completely eradicated from existing in the world
  - as per "and I will remove the spirit of impurity from the world."[173]

Note 8 – Commitment to do good/bad brings holiness/evil within one

- This is what [Chazal] instituted in the syntax of the blessing over Mitzvot "who has sanctified us with His Commandments," and similarly, "and Sanctified us with His Commandments"[174]
  - for when it occurs to a person to do a Mitzvah it immediately has an impact Above in its supernal source
  - and draws an *encompassing light* upon himself from there
  - and a supernal holiness hovers over and envelopes him.
- This is as per the explicit verse – "and you shall make yourselves Holy and become Holy"[175]

---

170 Bereishit 3:22.
171 Shabbat 55b, i.e., Binyamin, Amram, Yishai, and Kilav the son of David.
172 Yishayahu 25:8.

- וְזֶהוּ גַּם כֵּן הָעִנְיָן, מַה שֶּׁאָמַר הוּא יִתְבָּרַךְ אַחַר כָּךְ (שם ג, כב) "הֵן הָאָדָם הָיָה כְּאַחַד מִמֶּנּוּ לָדַעַת טוֹב וָרָע וְעַתָּה פֶּן יִשְׁלַח יָדוֹ וְלָקַח גַּם מֵעֵץ הַחַיִּים וְאָכַל וָחַי לְעוֹלָם"
  - וַהֲלֹא חֶפְצוֹ יִתְבָּרַךְ שְׁמוֹ לְהֵטִיב לִבְרוּאָיו, וּמַה אִכְפַּת לֵיהּ אִם יִחְיֶה לְעוֹלָם:
- אָמְנָם רוֹצֶה לוֹמַר, שֶׁכַּאֲשֶׁר יֹאכַל מֵעֵץ הַחַיִּים וְחַי לְעוֹלָם
  - יִשָּׁאֵר חַס וְשָׁלוֹם בְּלֹא תִּקּוּן
  - שֶׁלֹּא יִתְפָּרֵד הָרַע מִמֶּנּוּ עַד עוֹלָם חַס וְשָׁלוֹם
  - וְלֹא יִרְאֶה מְאוֹרוֹת וְטוֹבָה מִיָּמָיו
  - לָזֹאת לְטוֹבָתוֹ גֵּרְשׁוֹ מִגַּן עֵדֶן, כְּדֵי שֶׁיּוּכַל לָבֹא לִידֵי תִּקּוּן גָּמוּר
  - כְּשֶׁיִּתְפָּרֵד הָרַע מִמֶּנּוּ עַל יְדֵי הַמִּיתָה וְהָעִכּוּל בַּקֶּבֶר:
- וְזֶהוּ עִנְיָן הַד' שֶׁמֵּתוּ בְּעֶטְיוֹ שֶׁל נָחָשׁ (שבת נה:)
  - שֶׁאַף שֶׁלֹּא הָיָה לָהֶם חֵטְא עַצְמָם כְּלָל
- עִם כָּל זֶה הֻצְרְכוּ לְמִיתָה מֵחֲמַת הִתְעָרְבוּת הָרִאשׁוֹן שֶׁל הָרַע, עַל יְדֵי חֵטְא אָדָם הָרִאשׁוֹן מֵעֲצַת הַנָּחָשׁ:
- וְיִמְשֹׁךְ הָעִנְיָן כֵּן עַד אֶת קֵץ הַיָּמִין
  - "בִּלַּע הַמָּוֶת לָנֶצַח" (ישעיה כה, ח).
  - וְגַם עוֹד יִתְרוֹן, שֶׁיִּתְבַּעֵר אָז הָרַע מִן הָעוֹלָם מִמְּצִיאוּתוֹ
  - כְּמוֹ שֶׁכָּתוּב (זכריה יג, ב) "וְאֶת רוּחַ הַטֻּמְאָה אַעֲבִיר מִן הָאָרֶץ":

הגהה ח'

- וְזֶה שֶׁתִּקְּנוּ נֻסַּח בְּרָכוֹת הַמִּצְוֹת "אֲשֶׁר קִדְּשָׁנוּ בְּמִצְוֹתָיו", וְכֵן "וְקִדַּשְׁתָּנוּ בְּמִצְוֹתֶיךָ"
  - כִּי מֵעֵת שֶׁעוֹלָה עַל רַעְיוֹן הָאָדָם לַעֲשׂוֹת מִצְוָה, תֵּכֶף נַעֲשָׂה רִשּׁוּמוֹ לְמַעְלָה, בִּמְקוֹר שָׁרְשָׁהּ הָעֶלְיוֹן
  - וּמַמְשִׁיךְ מִשָּׁם עַל עַצְמוֹ "אוֹר מַקִּיף"
  - וּקְדֻשָּׁה עֶלְיוֹנָה חוֹפֶפֶת עָלָיו וְסוֹבֶבֶת אוֹתוֹ:
- וְכָתוּב מְפֹרָשׁ (ויקרא כ, ז) "וְהִתְקַדִּשְׁתֶּם וִהְיִיתֶם קְדֹשִׁים"

- - as Chazal say[176] that one who sanctifies himself in this world is sanctified from Above
  - meaning that he draws holiness upon himself from Above, from the supernal source of the Mitzvah.
- As per the Zohar:
  - One who sanctifies himself in the lower world is sanctified from Above ... for God's Holiness resides upon him ... if his deeds in the lower world are performed with holiness they arouse holiness Above which comes and resides over him and he is sanctified with it.[177] Refer there.
  - At the time when a person sees fit to perform a good deed in this world ... he extends a spirit of supernal holiness to reside upon himself ... and with this [good] deed a spirit of holiness rests upon him, a supernal spirit which he is sanctified with. One who comes to sanctify himself is sanctified, as it says "and you shall make yourselves Holy. . . ."[178]
  - He draws upon himself a spirit of supernal holiness as per "until a spirit from on High will be poured out upon us."[179] Refer there.
- Through this holiness and encompassing light, the [person], so to speak, cleaves to God even while being alive
  - as per "and you who cleave to the Lord your God," that even while still [in this world] "are alive today."[180]
- This encompassing light provides assistance to complete the Mitzvah
  - and through its completion the light intensifies and lifts its supernal head
  - and it is in this connection that Chazal say one who comes to purify himself is helped.[181]
- It also draws his heart towards the acquisition of additional Mitzvot
  - since he is now literally sitting in the Garden of Eden he is protected by the shade of the holy wings of the concealed Supernal Realms
  - and there is no possibility for the Evil Inclination to govern him and to entice him away from Mitzvah performance
  - as Chazal say[182] that performance of a Mitzvah causes performance of subsequent Mitzvot in its wake.
- When focusing his heart at the time of performing a Mitzvah

---

176 Yoma 39a.
177 Zohar III Tzav 31b.
178 Zohar III Kedoshim 86b.
179 Zohar III Naso 122a quoting Yishayahu 32:15.

- וּכְמַאֲמָרָם זִכְרוֹנָם לִבְרָכָה (יומא ל"ט א') כָּל הַמְקַדֵּשׁ עַצְמוֹ מִלְּמַטָּה מְקַדְּשִׁין אוֹתוֹ מִלְּמַעְלָה
- רוֹצֶה לוֹמַר, שֶׁמִּלְמַעְלָה נִמְשָׁךְ עָלָיו הַקְּדֻשָּׁה, מִשָּׁרְשָׁהּ הָעֶלְיוֹן שֶׁל הַמִּצְוָה:
- כְּמוֹ שֶׁכָּתוּב בַּזֹּהַר
- צַו ל"א רֵישׁ ע"ב, כְּתִיב "וְהִתְקַדִּשְׁתֶּם וִהְיִיתֶם קְדֹשִׁים" (שם) מַאן דִּמְקַדֵּשׁ גַּרְמֵיהּ מִלְּרַע מְקַדְּשִׁין לֵיהּ מִלְעֵילָּא, מְקַדְּשִׁין לֵיהּ מִלְעֵילָּא כו', דְּהָא קְדוּשָּׁה דְּמָארֵיהּ שַׁרְיָא עֲלֵיהּ כו', אִי עוֹבָדָא דִּלְתַתָּא הִיא בִּקְדוּשָּׁה, אִתְעַר קְדוּשָּׁה לְעֵילָּא וְאָתֵי וְשַׁרְיָא עֲלֵיהּ וְאִתְקַדֵּשׁ בֵּיהּ כו'. עַיֵּן שָׁם.
- וּבְפָרָשַׁת קְדוֹשִׁים פ"ו ב', בְּשַׁעְתָּא דְּבַר נָשׁ אַחֲזִי עוֹבָדָא לְתַתָּא בְּאֹרַח מֵישׁוֹר כו', נָגִיד וְנָפִיק וְשַׁרְיָא עֲלֵיהּ רוּחַ קַדִּישָׁא עִלָּאָה כו', וּבְהַהוּא עוֹבָדָא שַׁרְיָא עֲלֵיהּ רוּחַ קַדִּישָׁא רוּחַ עִלָּאָה לְאִתְקַדְּשָׁא בֵּיהּ, אָתָא לְאִתְקַדְּשָׁא מְקַדְּשִׁין לֵיהּ דִּכְתִיב "וְהִתְקַדִּשְׁתֶּם וִהְיִיתֶם קְדֹשִׁים" כו'
- וּבְפָרָשַׁת נָשֹׂא רֵישׁ דַּף קכ"ב ע"ב דְּמָשִׁיךְ עֲלֵיהּ רוּחָא קַדִּישָׁא עִלָּאָה, כְּמָה דְאַתְּ אָמַרְתְּ (ישעיה לב, טו) "עַד יֵעָרֶה עָלֵינוּ רוּחַ מִמָּרוֹם". עַיֵּן שָׁם:
- וְעַל יְדֵי זֶה הַקְּדֻשָּׁה וְהָ'אוֹר הַמַּקִּיף, הוּא דָּבוּק כִּבְיָכוֹל בּוֹ יִתְבָּרַךְ גַּם בְּחַיָּיו
- וְזֶה שֶׁאָמַר הַכָּתוּב (דברים ד, ד) "וְאַתֶּם הַדְּבֵקִים בַּה' אֱלֹהֵיכֶם" — גַּם בְּעוֹדְכֶם "חַיִּים כֻּלְּכֶם הַיּוֹם":
- וְזֶה הָאוֹר מַקִּיף, הוּא לוֹ לְעֵזֶר לִגְמֹר הַמִּצְוָה
- וְעַל יְדֵי הַגְּמָר, הָאוֹר מִתְחַזֵּק יוֹתֵר וְיָרִים רֹאשׁ עֶלְיוֹן
- וְעַל זֶה אָמְרוּ זִכְרוֹנָם לִבְרָכָה (יומא לח:) "הַבָּא לִטַּהֵר מְסַיְּעִין אוֹתוֹ":
- גַּם מוֹשֶׁכֶת וְגוֹרֶרֶת אֶת לִבּוֹ מִזֶּה לְסַגֵּל עוֹד כַּמָּה מִצְוֹת
- אַחַר שֶׁהוּא יוֹשֵׁב עַתָּה בְּגַן עֵדֶן מַמָּשׁ, חוֹסֶה בְּצֵל כַּנְפֵי הַקְּדֻשָּׁה בְּסֵתֶר עֶלְיוֹן
- אֵין מָקוֹם לְהַיֵּצֶר הָרַע לִשְׁלֹט בּוֹ וּלְהָסִיתוֹ וּלְהַדִּיחוֹ מֵעֵסֶק הַמִּצְוֹת.
- זֶה שֶׁאָמְרוּ (אבות ה, ב) שֶׁמִּצְוָה גּוֹרֶרֶת מִצְוָה:
- וְכַאֲשֶׁר יָשִׂים אֵלָיו לִבּוֹ בְּעֵת עֲשִׂיַּת הַמִּצְוָה

---

180 Devarim 4:4.
181 Yoma 38b.
182 Mishna Avot 4:2.

- he will understand and feel with his soul that he is currently surrounded in holiness 'and a correct spirit will be generated within him'[183]
- as per these are the Mitzvot "which a person shall do and live *with them*,"[184] "with them" literally meaning *within them* that he is then encompassed with the holiness of the Mitzvah and surrounded by the ambience of the Garden of Eden.

• Similarly, the opposite occurs, God forbid, when transgressing one of God's Commandments
  - that Chazal also say[185] that one who defiles himself in this lower world is defiled from above
  - also meaning that which is stated above
  - that from the source of that sin Above in the powers of impurity
  - he draws down the spirit of impurity upon himself, the Merciful One should save us, and it hovers over and encompasses him. As per:
    - If he defiles himself in this world, it arouses the spirit of impurity above which comes and resides upon him and he is defiled by it. For there is no good or evil, holiness or impurity, which has no supernal root above. It is action in this world which arouses the [corresponding re-]action in the supernal world.[186]
    - When he sees fit to perform a corrupted action in this world ... then a different spirit resides upon him.[187] Refer there.

• It is about this that the verse states "and you become defiled through them,"[188] meaning literally within them, God forbid
  - that he then becomes connected to and encompassed with a spirit of impurity
  - and the air of Gehinom encompasses him even while alive in this world
  - as per Chazal,[189] that a person who transgresses one sin in this world, it encompasses him and goes before him to the Day of Judgment, as it says "They determine [their own courses] ..."[190] ... R. Elazar says it is attached to him [like a dog]. This is as King David said, "when the transgressions that I trod upon will surround me."[191]

• With this, Chazal's statement[192] is understood

---

183 Tehillim 51:12.
184 Vayikra 18:5.
185 Yoma 39a.
186 Zohar III Tzav 31b.
187 Zohar III Kedoshim 80a.
188 Vayikra 11:43.
189 Avodah Zarah 5a.

יָבִין וְיַרְגִּישׁ בְּנַפְשׁוֹ שֶׁהוּא מְסָבָּב וּמְלֻבָּשׁ כָּעֵת בְּהַקְּדֻשָּׁה, וְרוּחַ נָכוֹן נִתְחַדֵּשׁ בְּקִרְבּוֹ.

וְזֶה שֶׁאָמַר הַכָּתוּב (ויקרא יח, ה) אֵלֶּה הַמִּצְוֹת "אֲשֶׁר יַעֲשֶׂה אוֹתָם הָאָדָם וָחַי בָּהֶם", 'בָּהֶם' הַיְנוּ בְּתוֹכָם מַמָּשׁ, שֶׁהוּא מְסָבָּב אָז בִּקְדֻשַּׁת הַמִּצְוָה, וּמֻקָּף מֵאֲוִירָא דְּגַן עֵדֶן:

• וְכֵן לְהֶפֶךְ חַס וְשָׁלוֹם, בְּעֵת עָבְרוֹ עַל אַחַת מִמִּצְוֹת ה'

◦ אָמְרוּ גַּם כֵּן בְּמַאַמְרָם זִכְרוֹנָם לִבְרָכָה הַנַּ"ל כָּל הַמְטַמֵּא עַצְמוֹ מִלְּמַטָּה מְטַמְּאִין אוֹתוֹ מִלְמַעְלָה

◦ פֵּרוּשׁ גַּם כֵּן כנ"ל

◦ שֶׁמְּשָׁרֵשׁ אוֹתוֹ הֶעָוֹן לְמַעְלָה בְּכֹחוֹת הַטֻּמְאָה

◦ הוּא מַמְשִׁיךְ רַחֲמָנָא לִצְלָן רוּחַ הַטֻּמְאָה עַל עַצְמוֹ, וְחוֹפֶפֶת עָלָיו וְסוֹבַבְתּוֹ. כְּמוֹ שֶׁכָּתוּב

▪ בְּמַאֲמַר פָּ' צַו הנ"ל וְאִי אִיהוּ אִסְתָּאַב לְתַתָּא, אִתְּעַר רוּחָא מְסַאֲבוּתָא לְעֵלָּא וְאָתֵי וְשָׁרְיָא עֲלֵיהּ, וְאִסְתָּאַב בֵּיהּ, דְּהָא לֵית לָךְ טַב וּבִישׁ, קְדוּשָּׁה וּמְסַאֲבוּתָא, דְּלֵית לָהּ עִקָּרָהּ וְשָׁרְשָׁא לְעֵילָּא, וּבְעוֹבָדָא דִּלְתַתָּא אִתְּעַר עוֹבָדָא דִּלְעֵילָּא. עי"ש.

▪ וּבְפָּ' קְדוֹשִׁים הנ"ל וּבְשַׁעְתָּא דְּאִיהוּ אַחֵזֵי עוֹבָדָא לְתַתָּא בְּאָרְחָא עֲקִימָא כו', כְּדֵין נָגִיד וְנָפִיק וְשָׁרְיָא עֲלֵיהּ רוּחַ אַחֲרָא כו' עַיֵּן שָׁם:

• וְעַל זֶה אָמַר הַכָּתוּב (ויקרא יא, מג) "וְנִטְמֵתֶם בָּם", הַיְנוּ בְּתוֹכָם מַמָּשׁ חַס וְשָׁלוֹם

◦ שֶׁהוּא קָשׁוּר וּמְסֻבָּב אָז בְּרוּחַ טֻמְאָה

◦ וַאֲוִירָא דְּגֵיהִנֹּם מְלַפְּפוֹ וּמַקִּיפוֹ גַּם בְּעוֹדֶנּוּ חַי בָּעוֹלָם

◦ כְּמוֹ שֶׁאָמְרוּ רַבּוֹתֵינוּ זִכְרוֹנָם לִבְרָכָה (ע"ז ה' א') כָּל הָעוֹבֵר עֲבֵרָה אַחַת בָּעוֹלָם הַזֶּה, מְלַפַּפְתּוֹ וְהוֹלֶכֶת לְפָנָיו לְיוֹם הַדִּין, שֶׁנֶּאֱמַר (איוב ג, יח) יִלָּפְתוּ גו', ר"א אוֹמֵר קְשׁוּרָה בּוֹ וכו'. וְזֶה שֶׁאָמַר דָּוִד הַמֶּלֶךְ עָלָיו הַשָּׁלוֹם "עֲוֹן עֲקֵבַי יְסֻבֵּנִי" (תהלים מט, ו):

• וּבָזֶה יוּבַן מַאַמְרָם זִכְרוֹנָם לִבְרָכָה בְּפֶרֶק יוֹם הַכִּפּוּרִים (פ"ו ב')

---

190 Iyov 6:18.
191 Tehillim 49:6.
192 Yoma 86b quoting Yechezkel 33:19.

- that repentance is great as it converts sins to be like Mitzvot, as per the verse "With the return of a wicked one from his wicked ways and he then acts with justice and righteousness – on them he will live."
- This proof does not initially appear compelling for it could easily be understood that "on them he will live" relates to the justice and righteousness performed after repentance?
- But as per that which I wrote above, this is an appropriate proof, for the syntax of the verse is very precise
  - for if "on them he will live" relates to the justice and righteousness it should have said, "with them he will live" as stated "and you shall live with them"[193] and as explained
  - but as it says "on them" it certainly relates to his former wickedness and sins
  - which through his repentance by leaving his former deeds and his subsequent performance of justice and righteousness, these overpower his original deeds and also convert them into merits and everlasting life.

Note 9 – Let us make man in plural implies worlds make up Shiur Komah

- This is the simple explanation of the verse "Let us make man"[194] which is expressed in the plural
  - meaning that they all [i.e., all the worlds] contribute power to and are a part of his construction such that he will be comprised from and connected to all of them.
  - This is as explained in the Zohar[195] and the writings of R. Chaim Vital.[196] Refer there.
- This is as per Chazal:
  - "God said, Let us make man." From whom did He take advice? R. Yehoshua said in the name of R. Levi, He took advice from the handiwork of the Heavens and the Earth. R. Shmuel bar Nachman said,

---

193 Vayikra 18:5.
194 Bereishit 1:26.
195 Zohar Chadash Tikkunim II 97a:
  - [This text is quoted directly in the translation of G1:06 on p. 144.]
  Zohar Raya Mehemna III Pinchas 219b:
  - God says, "I and My Shechina are partners of the soul, and his mother and father are partners of the body ... the heavens and the earth and all of their hosts also partner in [man's] formation" ...
196 Shaarei Kedushah, Part 3 Shaar 2 (the last section of this Shaar):
  - It has been explained that man is comprised of all of the worlds as per "for *this* is all of man" [Kohelet 12:13, upon which Berachot 6b comments that

נפש שער א' - פרק ו' החיים

○ גְּדוֹלָה תְּשׁוּבָה שֶׁזְּדוֹנוֹת נַעֲשׂוֹת לָהֶם כִּזְכֻיּוֹת, שֶׁנֶּאֱמַר (יחזקאל לג, יט) "וּבְשׁוּב רָשָׁע מֵרִשְׁעָתוֹ וְעָשָׂה מִשְׁפָּט וּצְדָקָה עֲלֵיהֶם הוּא יִחְיֶה".

○ וְלִכְאוֹרָה אֵין הָרְאָיָה מְכְרַחַת, דִּבְרַוְחָא טְפֵי יֵשׁ לְפָרֵשׁ 'דַעֲלֵיהֶם הוּא יִחְיֶה' קָאֵי עַל הַמִּשְׁפָּט וּצְדָקָה שֶׁעָשָׂה אַחֲרֵי שׁוּבוֹ.

○ וּלְפִי מַה שֶּׁכָּתַבְתִּי, רְאָיָתוֹ נְכוֹנָה, דִּלִישְׁנָא דִקְרָא דַּיֵק הָכִי

  ▪ דְאִי קָאֵי "עֲלֵיהֶם הוּא יִחְיֶה" עַל הַמִּשְׁפָּט וּצְדָקָה, הֲוָה לֵיהּ לוֹמַר "בָּהֶם" הוּא יִחְיֶה, כְּמוֹ שֶׁכָּתוּב (ויקרא יח, ה) "וָחַי בָּהֶם" וּכְמוֹ שֶׁנִּתְבָּאֵר.

  ▪ וּמִדְּקָאָמַר "עֲלֵיהֶם", וַדַּאי דְקָאֵי עַל רִשְׁעָתוֹ וַעֲווֹנוֹתָיו הַקּוֹדְמִין שֶׁעַל יְדֵי תְּשׁוּבָתוֹ, בַּעֲזִיבַת מַעֲשָׂיו הָרִאשׁוֹנִים וַעֲשׂוֹתוֹ אַחַר כָּךְ מִשְׁפָּט וּצְדָקָה, הֵמָּה יִתְגַּבְּרוּ עַל מַעֲשָׂיו הָרִאשׁוֹנִים, לַהֲפֹךְ גַּם אוֹתָם לִזְכֻיּוֹת וְחַיֵּי עוֹלָם:

הגהה ט'

• וְזֶהוּ פְּשָׁטוּת עִנְיַן הַכָּתוּב (בראשית א, כו) "נַעֲשֶׂה אָדָם" לְשׁוֹן רַבִּים

  ○ רָצָה לוֹמַר שֶׁכֻּלָּם יִתְּנוּ כֹּחַ וְחֵלֶק בְּבִנְיָנוֹ, שֶׁיְּהֵא כָּלוּל וּמְשֻׁתָּף מִכֻּלָּם

  ○ כְּמְבֹאָר פֵּרוּשׁוֹ בְּאֹרֶךְ בְּתִקּוּנֵי זֹהַר חָדָשׁ צ"ז א' וּבְרַעְיָא מְהֵימְנָא פִּנְחָס רִי"ט ב', וְכֵן כָּתַב רח"ו זִכְרוֹנוֹ לִבְרָכָה בְּשַׁעַר הַקְּדֻשָּׁה ח"ג שַׁעַר ב' וּבְלִקּוּטֵי תּוֹרָה פָּרָשַׁת תִּשָּׂא וּפָרָשַׁת הַאֲזִינוּ עַיֵּי"שׁ:

• וְזֶה שֶׁאָמַר

  ○ בִּבְרֵאשִׁית רַבָּה פָּרָשָׁה ח' "וַיֹּאמֶר אֱלֹקִים נַעֲשֶׂה אָדָם" (בראשית א, כו) בְּמִי

---

the entire universe was created for "*this*"]. This is the secret of "Let us make man in our image, in our likeness" [Bereishit 1:26], and this is the secret of "Let *us* make" which is stated in the plural, for all of the worlds partnered in making him and therefore he incorporates the image of man in all of the worlds for they all require his actions . . . and this is the secret of "and I have placed My words in your mouth . . . to plant heavens [and established earth and to say to Zion 'You are My People.']" [Yishayahu 51:16], for man draws life to the heavens and the earth through his actions and it is as if he planted and established them and as a result "You are My People," as Chazal state [Tikkunei Zohar Tikkun 69 106a, that you are] my partner; I am the Creator and you cause to exist.

Likutei Torah Ki Tisa and Likutei Torah Haazinu:
• [These texts are quoted on p. 146, fn. 133 and p. 147, fn. 134.]

He took advice from [the creations of] each day of creation [i.e., all creations and not just the Heavens and the Earth]. [197]
- "It has already been done." This verse does not use the singular form of "done" but rather the plural form. It is as if God together with His Bet Din govern each of your limbs establishing you as required, and if you say this implies that there is more than one God, the verse states "He (singular) made you and established you."[198] This is explained.

7. MAN'S ACTIONS REFLECTED IN: 1. THE WORLDS 2. GOD'S REACTION

- The idea mentioned above in G1:05 is now explained, that man is referred to as the soul and the life force of a myriad of worlds.
  - This does not mean a soul in the sense of a soul which is literally placed and attached within a person's body, as this cannot be the case.
  - But rather in the sense that just as all of the body's detailed movements and tendencies of its limbs are according to the movements of the life force and tendencies of the living soul within it
  - similarly, the idea that all the tendencies of the powers, the worlds, and the arrangement of the Merkava in relation to their rectification, construction, and destruction, God forbid
  - are purely activated according to the actions of man in the lowest world
  - and this is because he is constructed and composed [from the supernal and lower powers and worlds]
    - with his many detailed powers and their arrangement which are according to the sequence of the cascading down and interconnection of all the supernal and lower powers and worlds
  - and he, from the perspective of the root of his supernal soul, is the highest and innermost of all the worlds and creations, as mentioned above in G1:05.
  - Therefore, he incorporates all of them.
- The reason for this as explained in G1:05
  - is as a result of [man's] soul root which is higher and more internal than the worlds.
- The reason for this as explained in G1:06
  - is that [man] is constructed from all of the worlds.
- These [reasons] are [both] entirely one [and the same] as has been explained.

נִמְלָךְ, ר׳ יְהוֹשֻׁעַ בְּשֵׁם ר׳ לֵוִי אָמַר בִּמְלֶאכֶת הַשָּׁמַיִם וְהָאָרֶץ נִמְלָךְ, ר׳ שְׁמוּאֵל בַּ"נ אָמַר בְּמַעֲשֵׂה כָּל יוֹם וָיוֹם נִמְלָךְ

וּבְקֹהֶלֶת רַבָּה סִימָן ב׳ פָּסוּק יַ"ב "אֵת אֲשֶׁר כְּבָר עָשׂוּהוּ" (שם) אֵין כְּתִיב כָּאן 'עָשׂוּהוּ' אֶלָּא 'עָשׂוּהוּ׳, כִּבְיָכוֹל הַקָּדוֹשׁ בָּרוּךְ הוּא וּבֵית דִּינוֹ נִמְנוּ עַל כָּל אֵבֶר וְאֵבֶר מִשֶּׁלָּךְ וּמַעֲמִידְךָ עַל תִּקּוּנָךְ, וְאִם תֹּאמַר שְׁתֵּי רָשֻׁיּוֹת הֵן, וַהֲלֹא כְּבָר נֶאֱמַר (דברים לב) "הוּא עָשְׂךָ וַיְכֹנְנֶךָ", וְהוּא מְבֹאָר:

שער א׳ - פרק ז׳

• וְעַתָּה מְבֹאָר הָעִנְיָן הַנַּ"ל בְּפֶרֶק ה׳, שֶׁהָאָדָם נִקְרָא הַנֶּפֶשׁ וְנִשְׁמַת הַחַיִּים שֶׁל רִבִּי רִבְוָן עוֹלָמוֹת.

  ○ לֹא נֶפֶשׁ כְּנֶפֶשׁ הַנָּתוּן וְדָבוּק מַמָּשׁ בְּתוֹךְ גּוּף הָאָדָם, דְּזֶה לֹא יִתָּכֵן.

  ○ אָמְנָם הַיְנוּ שֶׁכְּמוֹ שֶׁכָּל פְּרָטֵי תְּנוּעוֹת וּנְטִיַּת אֶבְרֵי הַגּוּף, הֵם עַל יְדֵי הַנְּשָׁמַת חַיִּים שֶׁבּוֹ, כְּפִי תְּנוּעוֹת חִיּוּתוֹ וּנְטִיָּתוֹ

  ○ כֵּן הָעִנְיָן שֶׁכָּל נְטִיַּת הַכֹּחוֹת וְהָעוֹלָמוֹת וְסִדְרֵי הַמֶּרְכָּבָה, תִּקּוּנָם וּבִנְיָנָם וַהֲרִיסוּתָם חַס וְשָׁלוֹם

  ○ הוּא רַק כְּפִי עִנְיָן הַהִתְעוֹרְרוּת מִמַּעֲשֵׂי הָאָדָם לְמַטָּה

  ○ וּמִטַּעַם שֶׁהוּא כָּלוּל וּמְשֻׁכְלָל

    ▪ בְּמִסְפַּר פְּרָטֵי כֹּחוֹתָיו וְסִדְרֵיהֶם עַל פִּי סִדְרֵי הִשְׁתַּלְשְׁלוּת וְהִתְקַשְּׁרוּת הַכֹּחוֹת וְהָעוֹלָמוֹת עֶלְיוֹנִים וְתַחְתּוֹנִים כֻּלָּם

  ○ וְהוּא מִצַּד שֹׁרֶשׁ נִשְׁמָתוֹ הָעֶלְיוֹנָה, שֶׁהִיא הַגְּבוֹהַּ וְהַפְּנִימִית מֵהָעוֹלָמוֹת הַנִּבְרָאִים כֻּלָּם, כַּנִּזְכָּר לְעֵיל בְּפֶרֶק ה׳

  ○ לָכֵן הוּא כּוֹלֵל אֶת כֻּלָּם:

• וְהַטַּעַם שֶׁנִּתְבָּאֵר בְּפֶרֶק ה׳

  ○ מֵחֲמַת שֹׁרֶשׁ נִשְׁמָתוֹ שֶׁהִיא גְּבוֹהַּ וּפְנִימִית מֵהָעוֹלָמוֹת:

• וְהַטַּעַם שֶׁנִּתְבָּאֵר בְּפֶרֶק הֶעָבָר

  ○ מֵחֲמַת שֶׁהוּא כָּלוּל מִכָּל הָעוֹלָמוֹת:

• הַכֹּל אֶחָד כְּמוֹ שֶׁנִּתְבָּאֵר:

---

197 Bereishit Rabba Bereishit 8:3 quoting Bereishit 1:26.
198 Kohelet Rabba 2:12 quoting Devarim 32:6.

- Therefore, [man] alone has been given the choice to direct himself and the worlds in whichever way he desires.
  - Even if he has already, God forbid, caused the destruction and lowering of the worlds and the arrangement of the Merkava through his sins
  - he has the power and the ability to rectify that which he corrupted and to rebuild the destroyed
  - as he is constructed and combined from all of the [worlds and powers].
- This is expressed by King David: "God is your shadow, on your right hand"[199]
  - meaning that just as the tendency of a shadow of an item exclusively reflects the item's movements in whichever way it goes
  - similarly, according to this analogy, God, so to speak, connects to direct the worlds according to the movements and direction of man's actions in the lowest [physical] world.
- This is as per the Midrash:[200]
  - God instructed Moshe to tell Israel that his name is "I will be as I will be."[201] What is the meaning of "I will be as I will be?" That just as you [a Jew] are with Me, so too I [God] will be with you.
  - Similarly, King David said "God is your shadow, on your right hand." What is the meaning of "God is your shadow?" [He is] like your shadow. Just as with your shadow, if you play with it, it plays with you. If you cry, it cries. If you show it an angry or hopeful face, it similarly gives you the same. So too "God is your shadow" and just as you are with Him, He is with you.
- As per Zohar:[202] Come and see. The lowest world stands to continuously receive . . . and the supernal world only gives according to the way this [lowest world] stands. If it stands in an enlightened way below, it will be enlightened from above. If it stands in a depressed state, it is judged accordingly. In this vein, the verse states "Serve God with joy," for a person's joy draws upon him a separate supernal joy. Just as this lowest world is aroused, it correspondingly draws down from the supernal worlds . . .
- This is the idea of the Cherubim[203] which were "all braced firmly

---

199 Tehillim 121:5.
200 The details of this Midrash appear to have been quoted verbatim from Shela Toldot Adam, HaShaar HaGadol 306. The Shela's source for this Midrash appears to be from Sefer VeHizhir Mishpatim 43a which was first published in 1873 from an ancient manuscript.

The first part of this Midrash, relating to "I will be as I will be" only, appears in the Ramban Shemot 3:13.

- וְלָזֹאת, לוֹ לְבַדּוֹ נִתְּנָה מִשְׁפַּט הַבְּחִירָה, לְהַטּוֹת עַצְמוֹ וְאֶת הָעוֹלָמוֹת לְאֵיזֶה צַד אֲשֶׁר יַחְפֹּץ.
  - אוֹ אַף אִם כְּבָר גָּרַם וְסִבֵּב חַס וְשָׁלוֹם בַּחֲטָאָיו הֲרִיסַת הָעוֹלָמוֹת וְסִדְרֵי הַמֶּרְכָּבָה, וְחָרְבָנָם וִירִידָתָם חַס וְשָׁלוֹם
    - יֵשׁ כֹּחַ וְסִפֵּק בְּיָדוֹ לְתַקֵּן אֶת אֲשֶׁר עִוֵּת וְלִבְנוֹת הַנֶּהֱרָסוֹת
  - מִצַּד שֶׁהוּא כָּלוּל וּמְשֻׁתָּף מִכֻּלָּם:
- וְזֶה שֶׁאָמַר דָּוִד הַמֶּלֶךְ עָלָיו הַשָּׁלוֹם (תהלים קכא) "ה' צִלְּךָ עַל יַד יְמִינֶךָ".
  - הַיְנוּ שֶׁכְּמוֹ שֶׁנְּטִיַּת הַצֵּל שֶׁל אֵיזֶה דָבָר, הוּא מְכֻוָּן רַק כְּפִי תְּנוּעוֹת אוֹתוֹ הַדָּבָר לְאָן נוֹטֶה
  - כֵּן בְּדִמְיוֹן זֶה כִּבְיָכוֹל הוּא יִתְבָּרַךְ שְׁמוֹ מִתְחַבֵּר לִנְטוֹת הָעוֹלָמוֹת כְּפִי תְּנוּעוֹת וּנְטִיַּת מַעֲשֵׂי הָאָדָם לְמַטָּה:
- וְכֵן מְפֹרָשׁ בַּמִּדְרָשׁ
  - אָמַר לוֹ הַקָּדוֹשׁ בָּרוּךְ הוּא לְמֹשֶׁה לֵךְ אֱמוֹר לָהֶם לְיִשְׂרָאֵל כִּי שְׁמִי אקי"ק אֲשֶׁר אקי"ק. מַהוּ אקי"ק אֲשֶׁר אקי"ק, כְּשֵׁם שֶׁאַתָּה הֹוֶה עִמִּי, כָּךְ אֲנִי הֹוֶה עִמָּךְ.
  - וְכֵן אָמַר דָּוִד (שם) "ה' צִלְּךָ עַל יַד יְמִינֶךָ". מַהוּ ה' צִלְּךָ, כְּצִלְּךָ, מַה צִלְּךָ אִם אַתָּה מְשַׂחֵק לוֹ הוּא מְשַׂחֵק לְךָ, וְאִם אַתָּה בּוֹכֶה הוּא בּוֹכֶה כְּנֶגְדְּךָ, וְאִם אַתָּה מַרְאֶה לוֹ פָּנִים זְעוּמוֹת אוֹ מְסַבְּרוֹת אַף הוּא נוֹתֵן לְךָ כָּךְ, אַף הַקָּדוֹשׁ בָּרוּךְ הוּא "ה' צִלְּךָ", כְּשֵׁם שֶׁאַתָּה הֹוֶה עִמּוֹ הוּא הֹוֶה עִמָּךְ, עַד כָּאן:
- וּבַזֹּהַר תְּצַוֶּה קפ"ד ב'. תָּא חֲזֵי עָלְמָא תַּתָּאָה קַיְמָא לְקַבְּלָא תָּדִיר כו', וְעָלְמָא עִלָּאָה לָא יָהִיב לֵיהּ אֶלָּא כְּגַוְנָא דְּאִיהוּ קַיְמָא, אִי אִיהוּ קַיְמָא בִּנְהִירוּ דְּאַנְפִּין מִתַּתָּא, כְּדֵין הָכִי נָהֲרִין לֵיהּ מִלְּעֵילָּא, וְאִי אִיהוּ קַיְמָא בַּעֲצִיבוּ, יַהֲבִין לֵיהּ הַאי דִּינָא בְּקַבְלֵיהּ. כְּגַוְנָא דָּא "עִבְדוּ אֶת ד' בְּשִׂמְחָה" (תהלים ק, ב), חֶדְוָה דְּבַר נַשׁ מָשִׁיךְ לְגַבֵּיהּ חֶדְוָה אַחֲרָא עִלָּאָה, הָכִי נָמֵי הַאי עָלְמָא תַּתָּאָה, כְּגַוְנָא דְּאִיהוּ אִתְעַר הָכִי אַמְשִׁיךְ מִלְּעֵילָּא כו':
- וְהוּא עִנְיַן הַכְּרוּבִים שֶׁהָיוּ מְעוֹרִין כְּמַעַר אִישׁ וְלִוְיוֹת (מלכים א, ז, לו) "פְּנֵיהֶם אִישׁ

---

201 Shemot 3:14.
202 Zohar II Tetzaveh 184b quoting Tehillim 100:2.
203 The pair of golden angelic forms which sat on the Holy Ark. They had the faces of a young boy and girl. The first verse describes the configuration of the Cherubim of the Ark of Moshe. The second verse however describes the

around"[204] "in a face to face configuration."[205] But in relation to the Cherubim of Shlomo it is written that they were "with their faces to the House,"[206] as will be explained, God willing [as below].

8. MAN'S ACTION RESULTS IN GOD'S REACTION – E.G., CHERUBIM, LIVELIHOOD

- Now Chazal[207] explain the arrangement of the Cherubim
    - [that] R. Yochanan and R. Elazar [have differing views]
    - one of them saying that "they faced each other"[208]
    - and the other one saying that "they faced the house."[209]
    - According to the opinion that "they faced each other," the verse which says "they faced the house" is not problematic, as here [i.e., when facing each other] it relates to a time when Israel fulfill God's Will, and here [i.e., when facing the house] it relates to a time when Israel do not fulfill God's Will.
        - Refer to Rashbam.[210]
    - According to the opinion that "they faced the house," the verse which says "they faced each other" [teaches] that their position was partially angled, meaning partially facing the house and partially facing each other.
        - Refer to Rashbam:[211] The above answer that "when Israel perform God's Will, etc." is not applicable here. Since the Cherubim were principally made to be facing the house it was not relevant for it to be taken as a sign of when Israel do not perform God's Will.

---

configuration of the Cherubim of the Ark of Shlomo. See the continuation in G1:08.
204 1 Melachim 7:36.
205 Shemot 25:20.
206 2 Divrei Hayamim 3:13.
207 Bava Batra 99a.
208 Shemot 25:20 and 37:9.
209 2 Divrei Hayamim 3:13, i.e., eastwards towards the Holy from the Holy of Holies in which the Ark resided.
210 In the original print editions, this reference to Rashbam was recorded as a reference to Rashi. The commentary of Rashi on Bava Batra ended on page 29a. The Rashbam continued Rashi's commentary from that point onwards until the end of the Tractate. The Rashbam's comments are as follows:
- *And they faced each other*: This is written in connection with the [Cherubim] of Moshe. *And they faced the house*: This is written in connection with the

אֶל אָחִיו" (שמות כה, כ). וּבְכְרוּבֵי שְׁלֹמֹה כְּתִיב (דה"י ב' ג, יג) "וּפְנֵיהֶם לַבָּיִת" כְּמוֹ שֶׁיִּתְבָּאֵר בְּעֶזְרַת ה':

שער א' - פרק ח'

- הִנֵּה רַבּוֹתֵינוּ זִכְרוֹנָם לִבְרָכָה אָמְרוּ בְּעִנְיָן הַכְּרוּבִים (בבא בתרא צ"ט א) כֵּיצַד הֵן עוֹמְדִין
  - ר' יוֹחָנָן וְר' אֶלְעָזָר
  - חַד אָמַר פְּנֵיהֶם אִישׁ אֶל אָחִיו
  - וְחַד אָמַר פְּנֵיהֶם לַבַּיִת.
  - וּלְמַאן דְּאָמַר פְּנֵיהֶם אִישׁ אֶל אָחִיו הַכְּתִיב וּפְנֵיהֶם לַבַּיִת, לֹא קַשְׁיָא כָּאן בִּזְמַן שֶׁיִּשְׂרָאֵל עוֹשִׂין רְצוֹנוֹ שֶׁל מָקוֹם, כָּאן בִּזְמַן שֶׁאֵין יִשְׂרָאֵל עוֹשִׂין רְצוֹנוֹ שֶׁל מָקוֹם
    - וְעַיֵּן רַשְׁבָּ"ם.
  - וּלְמַאן דְּאָמַר פְּנֵיהֶם לַבַּיִת, הַכְּתִיב וּפְנֵיהֶם אִישׁ אֶל אָחִיו, דִּמְצַדְּדֵי אַצְדּוּדֵי, רוֹצֶה לוֹמַר קְצָת לַבַּיִת וּקְצָת זֶה לָזֶה
    - וְעַיֵּן רַשְׁבָּ"ם ז"ל, וְהָא לֵיכָּא לְתָרוּצֵי כִּדְלְעֵיל, כָּאן בִּזְמַן שֶׁיִּשְׂרָאֵל עוֹשִׂין

Cherubim of Shlomo in Divrei Hayamim which writes "and they are standing on their feet facing the house (the Sanctuary)," and they are not like those of Moshe which were on the Kaporet [i.e., on top of the Holy Ark], but these were on the ground and made of olive wood and covered in gold as written in Melachim. *But it writes "and they faced the house"?*: Irrespective of whether they are the Cherubim on top of the Kaporet or those on the ground, they [surely] should have been configured in the same way? *Here it relates to a time when Israel fulfill God's Will*: They face each other with the analogous affection of a male and female who love each other as a sign of God's love for Israel. They were initially made in this face to face configuration so that the Shechina should reside in Israel and that Israel should perform God's Will. But when [Israel] don't perform [God's Will] they turn their faces to the house by way of a miracle.

211 The Rashbam's commentary continues (from the previous footnote):
- *Their position was partially angled*: Partially to the house and partially to each other like a person who when speaking to his friend partially turns his head to one side. The above answer that "when Israel perform God's Will, etc." is not applicable here. Since the Cherubim were principally made to be facing the house it was not relevant for it to be taken as a sign of when Israel do not perform God's Will.

G1:08

- Tosafot similarly write there[212] that the [Cherubim] were just initially placed according to the fact that [Israel] were performing God's Will.
  - It is therefore seemingly problematic as to why the Cherubim of Shlomo were initially placed to be facing at an angle and not totally facing each other?
- The idea is as Chazal state[213]
  - Our Rabbis taught, "And you shall gather in your grain"[214] . . . is according to that which is said, "This Book of Torah shall not move from your mouth"[215] . . . I might have thought that these words are literal[216]
  - therefore the verse "And you shall gather in your grain" teaches that one should deal with them according to *the way of the world.*[217]
  - These are the words of R. Yishmael.
  - R. Shimon bar Yochai says: Is it possible a person ploughs at the time of ploughing . . . then what will become of Torah? Rather at a time when Israel perform God's Will, their work is done by others . . . and at a time that Israel does not perform God's Will, they have to do their work themselves, as it says "And you shall gather in your grain."
- Now it is seemingly strange that the verse "And you shall gather in your grain" is brought [by R. Shimon bar Yochai] to describe Israel's requirement to work when they don't fulfill God's Will, as the context of this verse is [specifically in a paragraph which clearly describes Israel fulfilling God's Will, opening with] "And it will be that when you shall surely listen to My Commandments . . . to love . . . and to serve Him with all your heart,"[218] and about this it says, "And you shall gather in your grain?"
- However the idea is that R. Yishmael certainly holds that a person has no permission to separate himself, God forbid, even momentarily from Torah involvement
  - to be involved in earning a livelihood such that at that time he will be totally uninvolved with Torah, God forbid
  - however, R. Yishmael hinted to this with his holy words "one should deal *with them* according to the way of the world" – "with them" meaning with the words of Torah

---

212 Text of the Tosafot:
- *Their position was fixed*: It is not relevant to say, "here it relates to a time when Israel fulfill God's Will" as they were just initially placed according the fact that [Israel] were performing God's Will.

213 Berachot 35b.

כו', דְּכֵיָון דְּעָקַר עֲשִׂיַּת כְּרוּבִים פְּנֵיהֶם לַבַּיִת, לֹא הָיָה לָהֶם לַעֲשׂוֹתוֹ לְסִימָן שֶׁאֵין יִשְׂרָאֵל עוֹשִׂין רְצוֹנוֹ שֶׁל מָקוֹם.

וְכֵן כָּתְבוּ תּוֹסָפוֹת שָׁם (ד"ה דמצדדי) דְּמִסְתָּמָא הֶעֱמִידוּם תְּחִלָּה לְפִי מַה שֶׁהָיוּ עוֹשִׂין רְצוֹנוֹ שֶׁל מָקוֹם.

וְלִכְאוֹרָה אַכַּתֵּי תִּקְשֵׁי לָמָּה הֶעֱמִידוּם תְּחִלָּה כְּרוּבֵי שְׁלֹמֹה פְּנֵיהֶם מְצֻדָּדִין וְלֹא אִישׁ אֶל אָחִיו מַמָּשׁ:

- וְהָעִנְיָן הוּא כְּמוֹ שֶׁאָמְרוּ פֶּרֶק כֵּיצַד מְבָרְכִין (ל"ה ב')

  - תָּנוּ רַבָּנָן וְאָסַפְתָּ דְגָנֶךָ כו', לְפִי שֶׁנֶּאֱמַר (יהושע א) "לֹא יָמוּשׁ סֵפֶר הַתּוֹרָה הַזֶּה מִפִּיךָ" גו', יָכוֹל דְּבָרִים כִּכְתָבָן

  - תַּלְמוּד לוֹמַר (דברים יא) "וְאָסַפְתָּ דְגָנֶךָ" — הַנְהֵג בָּהֶן מִנְהַג דֶּרֶךְ אֶרֶץ
  - דִּבְרֵי רַבִּי יִשְׁמָעֵאל
  - רַשְׁבִּ"י אוֹמֵר אֶפְשָׁר אָדָם חוֹרֵשׁ בִּשְׁעַת חֲרִישָׁה כו' תּוֹרָה מַה תְּהֵא עָלֶיהָ, אֶלָּא בִּזְמַן שֶׁיִּשְׂרָאֵל עוֹשִׂין רְצוֹנוֹ שֶׁל מָקוֹם מְלַאכְתָּן נַעֲשֵׂית עַל יְדֵי אֲחֵרִים וכו' וּבִזְמַן שֶׁאֵין יִשְׂרָאֵל עוֹשִׂין רְצוֹנוֹ שֶׁל מָקוֹם מְלַאכְתָּן נַעֲשֵׂית עַל יְדֵי עַצְמָן, שֶׁנֶּאֱמַר "וְאָסַפְתָּ דְגָנֶךָ":

- וְלִכְאוֹרָה תָּמוּהַּ דְּמוּקִי לִקְרָא דְוָאָסַפְתָּ דְגָנֶךָ, כְּשֶׁאֵין עוֹשִׂין רְצוֹנוֹ שֶׁל מָקוֹם, וְהָא לְעֵיל מִינֵּהּ כְּתִיב וְהָיָה אִם שָׁמוֹעַ תִּשְׁמְעוּ אֶל מִצְוֹתַי וְגו' לְאַהֲבָה וְגו' וּלְעָבְדוֹ בְּכָל לְבַבְכֶם וְגו', וְעָלָה קָאָמַר וְאָסַפְתָּ דְגָנֶךָ:

- אֲבָל הָעִנְיָן, כִּי וַדַּאי שֶׁאֵין דַּעַת רַבִּי יִשְׁמָעֵאל שֶׁיְּהֵא הָרְשׁוּת נְתוּנָה לָאָדָם לִפְרֹשׁ חַס וְשָׁלוֹם אַף זְמַן מְעַט מֵעֵסֶק הַתּוֹרָה

  - וְלַעֲסֹק בְּפַרְנָסָה, וְיִהְיֶה בָּטֵל אוֹתוֹ הָעֵת מֵעֵסֶק הַתּוֹרָה לְגַמְרֵי חַס וְשָׁלוֹם
  - אָמְנָם רְמָזוֹ רַבִּי יִשְׁמָעֵאל בִּלְשׁוֹנוֹ הַקָּדוֹשׁ, הַנְהֵג "בָּהֶן" מִנְהַג דֶּרֶךְ אֶרֶץ, רוֹצֶה לוֹמַר עִמָּהֶן עִם הַדִּבְרֵי תוֹרָה

---

214 Devarim 11:14.
215 Yehoshua 1:8.
216 That one should only be involved in Torah study and not in earning a livelihood.
217 That while one should learn Torah as much as possible, one must work for a living (which is the *way of the world*), as below.
218 Devarim 11:13.

- meaning that even while you engage in the minimum amount of work required to sustain yourself, at the very least your thoughts should exclusively be focused on words of Torah.
- Similarly, Rava told his students[219] to work and not come to the study hall during the months of Nissan and Tishrei, that for sure Rava's students were not entirely idle, God forbid, from being involved in Torah study in their homes during these [working] days.
- The Talmud [concludes] that:[220]
  - Many acted according to R. Yishmael and were successful.
  - Many acted according to R. Shimon bar Yochai and were not successful.
    - Meaning, specifically *for most people*. That it is certainly virtually unsustainable for the general public to be solely diligent all their lives in Torah study without even brief involvement in some activity of earning a livelihood at all
    - and it is about this that Chazal say,[221] "And Torah study which is not accompanied by work [will become irrelevant and will cause sin]."
    - However for an individual who has the means to constantly involve himself in Torah study and service of God
    - he is certainly obligated to not separate even momentarily from Torah study and service [in order] to involve himself in earning a livelihood, God forbid, and [should act] according to the opinion of R. Shimon bar Yochai. (Note 10)[222]
- The verse "And you shall gather in your grain" is actually separated from [its context] in the paragraph of "And it will be" which is entirely stated in the plural [except for] the verse "And you shall gather" [which] is stated in the singular. Therefore, [R. Shimon bar Yochai] concludes that even when one is minimally involved in earning a livelihood, one does not fulfill God's Will.
- It is known that with the Cherubim, one represented God while the other represented Israel, His beloved treasure
  - and the measure of Israel's closeness and attachment to God, or the converse, God forbid, was entirely evident in the arrangement of the Cherubim by way of a miracle and wonder.
  - If [Israel's] 'faces would directly look at'[223] God, then the Cherubim would also be arranged as facing each other
  - or if they angle their faces away a small amount, it would be immediately evident from the Cherubim

---

219 In the continuation of the section of the Talmud in Berachot 35b.
220 Berachot 35b.

נפש שער א' - פרק ח' החיים

○ הַיְנוּ שֶׁגַּם בְּאוֹתוֹ הָעֵת וְשָׁעָה מְעֶטֶת שֶׁאַתָּה עוֹסֵק בְּפַרְנָסָה כְּדֵי הַצֹּרֶךְ וְהֶהֶכְרֵחַ לְהַחֲיוֹת נֶפֶשׁ, עַל כָּל פָּנִים בְּרַעְיוֹנֵי מַחֲשַׁבְתְּךָ תְּהֵא מְהַרְהֵר רַק בְּדִבְרֵי תוֹרָה:

• וְכֵן רָבָא אָמַר לְתַלְמִידָיו (ברכות לה:), בְּיוֹמֵי נִיסָן וְתִשְׁרֵי לָא תִּתְחֲזוֹ קַמַּאי דַּיְקָא, שֶׁלֹּא לָבֹא לְבֵית מִדְרָשׁוֹ, אֲבָל וַדַּאי שֶׁתַּלְמִידֵי רָבָא לֹא הָיוּ בְּטֵלִים חַס וְשָׁלוֹם לְגַמְרֵי מֵעֵסֶק הַתּוֹרָה גַּם בְּבֵיתָם בְּאֵלּוּ הַיָּמִים:

• וְאָמְרוּ שָׁם

○ הַרְבֵּה עָשׂוּ כְּר' יִשְׁמָעֵאל וְעָלְתָה בְּיָדָם

○ וְהַרְבֵּה עָשׂוּ כְּרַשְׁבִּ"י וְלֹא עָלְתָה בְּיָדָם

□ הַיְנוּ רַבִּים דַּוְקָא, כִּי וַדַּאי שֶׁלִּכְלָל הֶהָמוֹן כִּמְעַט בִּלְתִּי אֶפְשָׁר שֶׁיַּתְמִידוּ כָּל יְמֵיהֶם רַק בְּעֵסֶק הַתּוֹרָה, שֶׁלֹּא לִפְנוֹת אַף שָׁעָה מְעֶטֶת לְשׁוּם עֵסֶק פַּרְנָסַת מְזוֹנוֹת כְּלָל

□ וְעַל זֶה אָמְרוּ בְּאָבוֹת[221] כָּל תּוֹרָה שֶׁאֵין עִמָּהּ מְלָאכָה וכו'

□ אֲבָל יָחִיד לְעַצְמוֹ, שֶׁאֶפְשָׁר לוֹ לִהְיוֹת אַף עָסוּק כָּל יָמָיו בְּתוֹרָתוֹ וַעֲבוֹדָתוֹ יִתְבָּרַךְ שְׁמוֹ

□ וַדַּאי שֶׁחוֹבָה מֻטֶּלֶת עָלָיו שֶׁלֹּא לִפְרֹשׁ אַף זְמַן מְעַט מִתּוֹרָה וַעֲבוֹדָה לַעֲסֹק פַּרְנָסָה חַס וְשָׁלוֹם, וּכְדַעַת רַבִּי שִׁמְעוֹן בַּר יוֹחַאי (הגהה י')[222]:

• וְהִנֵּה פָּסוּק "וְאָסַפְתָּ דְגָנֶךָ" וְגוֹ' הוּא מוּצָא מִכְּלָל פָּרָשַׁת 'וְהָיָה' שֶׁכֻּלָּהּ נֶאֶמְרָה בִּלְשׁוֹן רַבִּים, וּפָסוּק "וְאָסַפְתָּ" נֶאֱמַר בִּלְשׁוֹן יָחִיד, לָכֵן קָרֵי לֵיהּ אֵין עוֹשֶׂה רְצוֹנוֹ שֶׁל מָקוֹם כְּשֶׁמַּפְנֶה עַצְמוֹ אַף מְעַט לְעֵסֶק פַּרְנָסָה:

• וְיָדוּעַ שֶׁהַכְּרוּבִים, הָאֶחָד — רֶמֶז עָלָיו יִתְבָּרַךְ שְׁמוֹ, וְהַשֵּׁנִי — עַל יִשְׂרָאֵל סְגֻלָּתוֹ[223].

○ וּכְפִי שִׁעוּר הַתְקָרְבוּתָם וּדְבֵיקוּתָם שֶׁל יִשְׂרָאֵל אֵלָיו יִתְבָּרַךְ שְׁמוֹ, אוֹ לְהֵפֶךְ חַס וְשָׁלוֹם, הָיָה נִכָּר הַכֹּל בְּעִנְיַן עֲמִידַת הַכְּרוּבִים דֶּרֶךְ נֵס וָפֶלֶא.

○ אִם פְּנֵיהֶם יָשָׁר יֶחֱזוּ אֵלָיו יִתְבָּרַךְ שְׁמוֹ, גַּם הַכְּרוּבִים עָמְדוּ אָז פְּנֵיהֶם אִישׁ אֶל אָחִיו

○ אוֹ אִם הָפְכוּ פְּנֵיהֶם מְעַט וּמְצַדְּדֵי אִצְדוּדֵי, כֵּן הָיָה נִכָּר הָעִנְיָן תֵּכֶף בַּכְּרוּבִים

---

221 Mishna Avot 2:2.
222 **R. Chaim adds Note 10 here.** This note is brought at the end of this chapter and is entitled "Service with might is for individuals and not for the majority."
223 Tehillim 11:7.

- or if, God forbid, they would turn their back [on God], then the Cherubim would also immediately turn to completely face away from each other, God forbid.
- As per Chazal:
  - That they would roll back the curtain of the Holy of Holies – to show the people of Israel who went up to the Temple on the Foot Festivals that the Cherubim were joined together [in an embrace] and they said to them, "See that God's love for you [is like that of a male and female]."[224]
  - When is a time of mercy? At a time when the Cherubim are facing each other and looking at each other's faces, then all the color differences are rectified [and interchanged . . . with an interchanging between judgment and mercy] . . . reflecting how much Israel engage in rectifying themselves with God, where they stand, and how engaged they are. . . .[225]
  - [What is the meaning of the verse] "brothers are dwelling together" . . . for at the time when they [the Cherubim] are looking at each other it is written about them, "How good and how pleasant [that brothers are dwelling together]" . . . and when the male [Cherub representing God] looks away from the female [Cherub representing Israel], woe to the world. . . .[226]
  - Whenever Israel merited – the Cherubim cleaved to each other face to face – but when they sinned, they [the Cherubim] would look away from each other . . . therefore the Cherubim would face each other when Israel merited . . . with these secrets they would know if Israel were meritorious or not . . . It is written "Serve God with happiness," the happiness of the two Cherubim . . . when happiness rests upon them, the world is restored to a state of mercy . . .[227] Refer there at length.

Rabbi Chaim's Note:
Note 10 – Service with might *is for individuals and not for the majority*

- Therefore, it is written in the first paragraph of the Shema [that one is to serve God with] "all one's might," [whereas] the second paragraph of the Shema does not write "all one's might."
- For the first paragraph of the Shema is all stated in the singular and an individual who is able to is obligated to literally fulfill the verse "This Book of Torah shall not move from your mouth."[228]
  - Therefore, it states [that service of God must be] "with all one's might"

נפש　שער א' - פרק ח'　החיים　179

○ אוֹ אִם חַס וְשָׁלוֹם הֵפְנוּ עֹרֶף, גַּם הַכְּרוּבִים כְּרֶגַע הֵפְנוּ וְהָפְכוּ פְּנֵיהֶם אִישׁ מֵעַל אָחִיו לְגַמְרֵי חַס וְשָׁלוֹם:

• וּכְעִנְיָן שֶׁאָמְרוּ זִכְרוֹנָם לִבְרָכָה

○ בְּיוֹמָא (נ״ד א') שֶׁהָיוּ מְגַלְּלִין הַפָּרֹכֶת לְעוֹלֵי רְגָלִים, וּמַרְאִין לָהֶם הַכְּרוּבִים שֶׁהָיוּ מְעוֹרִין זֶה בָּזֶה, וְאוֹמְרִים לָהֶן, רְאוּ חִבַּתְכֶם לִפְנֵי הַמָּקוֹם כו'.

○ וּבַזֹּהַר תְּרוּמָה קנ״ב ב', אֵימָתַי אִיהִי בְּרַחֲמֵי, א״ל בְּשַׁעְתָּא דִּכְרוּבִים מְהַדְרָן כו', וּמִסְתַּכְּלָן אַנְפִּין בְּאַנְפִּין, כֵּיוָן דְּאִנּוּן כְּרוּבִים מִסְתַּכְּלָן אַנְפִּין בְּאַנְפִּין כְּדֵין כָּל גְּוָנִין מִתְתַּקְּנָן כו'. כְּמָה דִּמְסַדְּרִין יִשְׂרָאֵל תִּקּוּנַיְהוּ לְגַבֵּי קוּדְשָׁא בְּרִיךְ הוּא, הָכִי קַיְמָא כֹּלָּא וְהָכִי אִתְסַדַּר כו'.

○ וּבְפָרָשַׁת אַחֲרֵי נ״ט רֵישׁ ע״ב, שֶׁבֶת אַחִים כו', בְּשַׁעְתָּא דַּהֲווֹ חַד בְּחַד מַשְׁגִּיחִין אַנְפִּין בְּאַנְפִּין כְּתִיב, "מַה טּוֹב וּמַה נָּעִים" וְגוֹ', וְכַד מְהַדֵּר דְּכוּרָא אַנְפּוֹי מִן נוּקְבָא וַי לְעָלְמָא כו'.

○ וּבַזֹּהַר חָדָשׁ סוֹף פָּרָשַׁת תְּרוּמָה ע״ב א', בְּכָל זִמְנָא דְּיִשְׂרָאֵל הֲווֹ זַכָּאִין, כְּרוּבִים הֲווֹ דְּבִיקִין בְּדַבִּיקוּ אַפִּין בְּאַפִּין. כֵּיוָן דַּהֲווֹ סָרְחָן, הֲווֹ מְהַדְּרִין אַפַּיְהוּ דָּא מִן דָּא כו', וְעַל דָּא כְּרוּבִים בְּהַהוּא זִמְנָא דַּהֲווֹ יִשְׂרָאֵל זַכָּאִין, הֲווֹ אַנְפִּין בְּאַנְפִּין כו'. וְעַל רָזִין אִלֵּין הֲווֹ יָדְעֵי אִי יִשְׂרָאֵל זַכָּאִין אִי לָא כו'. כְּתִיב, "עִבְדוּ אֶת ה'" בְּשִׂמְחָה", חֶדְוָתָא דִּתְרֵין כְּרוּבִין כו', כֵּיוָן דְּשַׁאֲרֵי עֲלַיְהוּ, אִתְהַדַּר בְּחֶדְוָה כו', וְעָלְמָא אִתְהַדַּר בְּרַחֲמֵי כו'. וְעַיֵּן שָׁם בְּאֹרֶךְ:

הגהה י'

• וְלָכֵן בְּפָרָשָׁה רִאשׁוֹנָה שֶׁל קְרִיאַת שְׁמַע כְּתִיב "וּבְכָל מְאֹדֶךָ", וּבְפָרָשָׁה "וְהָיָה" לֹא כְּתִיב "וּבְכָל מְאֹדְכֶם":

• כִּי פָּרָשַׁת שְׁמַע כֻּלָּהּ בְּלָשׁוֹן יָחִיד נֶאֶמְרָה, וְיָחִיד שֶׁאֶפְשָׁר לוֹ הוּא צָרִיךְ לְקַיֵּם "לֹא יָמוּשׁ סֵפֶר הַתּוֹרָה הַזֶּה מִפִּיךָ" (יהושע א', ח') דְּבָרִים כִּכְתָבָן מַמָּשׁ

○ לָכֵן נֶאֱמַר "וּבְכָל מְאֹדֶךָ"

224　Yoma 54a – the Cherubim's faces were images of a boy and girl.
225　Zohar II Terumah 152b.
226　Zohar III Acharei Mot 59b quoting Tehillim 133:1.
227　Zohar Chadash I Terumah 72a quoting Tehillim 100:2.
228　Yehoshua 1:8.

- meaning with all of one's wealth[229]
- that is one should not engage in earning a livelihood at all.
- However, the second paragraph of the Shema which is stated in the plural [i.e., relating to the majority]
  - as the majority of people are virtually forced to involve themselves, even if only a little bit, to earn money to provide for life's essentials
  - therefore the statement "with all your [plural] might" is omitted.
- (Even though according to R. Shimon bar Yochai this is not the most optimum method of truly satisfying the Will of God
  - nevertheless he does not classify this, God forbid, as *not* performing God's Will when they free themselves a little bit to also be involved with earning a livelihood
  - and while they are engaged in earning a living, their hearts are engaged with wisdom and they are thinking thoughts of Torah and Fear of God.
  - [However,] according to R. Yishmael this approach is the key Will of God for the majority of people to serve Him.
  - Their argument is in what is the key way of serving God and the optimum method for the majority of people to achieve this.)[230]

9. FURTHER EMPHASIS THAT MAN'S ACTION INVOKES GOD'S REACTION

- Now, with respect to the generation [who received the Torah] in the wilderness who 'merited to eat from God's Table',[231] 'Heavenly bread on a daily basis'[232] and their 'clothing did not wear out'[233]
  - and they did not need to be involved with any worldly activity of earning a livelihood at all
  - all agree that they would only be viewed as fulfilling God's Will if they looked Heavenwards with total honesty and would devote their hearts solely to Torah study, service and Fear of God – 'day and night not moving from their mouths'[234] literally, without any side distractions at all, even for brief involvement in earning a livelihood.

---

229 Berachot 54a.
230 In his commentary, Shenot Eliyahu on the Mishna, Peah 1:1, the Vilna Gaon explains that one fulfills a separate Mitzvah with each and every single word of Torah as supported by this Mishna that Torah study corresponds to (and outweighs) all other Mitzvot. He explains that notwithstanding this, this Mishna is coming to teach us that there is no maximum or minimum limit to fulfill one's obligation of Torah study every day and night and that one can,

- פֵּרוּשׁ, בְּכָל מָמוֹנְךָ, כְּמוֹ שֶׁכָּתוּב בַּמִּשְׁנָה סוֹף בְּרָכוֹת
- רָצָה לוֹמַר שֶׁלֹּא לַעֲסֹק בְּפַרְנָסָה כְּלָל:
- אֲבָל פָּרָשָׁה "וְהָיָה" שֶׁנֶּאֶמְרָה בִּלְשׁוֹן רַבִּים
- לָרַבִּים כִּמְעַט מֻכְרָחִים לְהִתְעַסֵּק עַל כָּל פָּנִים מְעַט גַּם בְּרֶוַח מָמוֹן לְחַיֵּי נֶפֶשׁ
- לָכֵן לֹא כְּתִיב בָּהּ "וּבְכָל מְאֹדְכֶם":
- (וְהֲגַם שֶׁעֲדַיִן לֹא זוֹ הַדֶּרֶךְ וְהַמַּדְרֵגָה הַגְּבוֹהָה לְפִי אֲמִתַּת רְצוֹנוֹ יִתְבָּרַךְ שְׁמוֹ, לְדַעַת רַשְׁבִּ"י
- עִם כָּל זֶה, גַּם לְדִידֵיהּ לֹא מִקְרוּ חָס וְשָׁלוֹם בָּזֶה אֵין עוֹשִׂין רְצוֹנוֹ שֶׁל מָקוֹם כְּשֶׁמְּפַנִּין עַצְמָם מְעַט גַּם לְעֵסֶק פַּרְנָסָה
- וּבְעֵת עָסְקָם בְּפַרְנָסָה לִבָּם נוֹהֵג בְּחָכְמָה, וּמְהַרְהֲרִים בְּדִבְרֵי תוֹרָה וְיִרְאַת ה'.
- וּלְרַבִּי יִשְׁמָעֵאל זוֹ הִיא עִקַּר רְצוֹנוֹ יִתְבָּרַךְ בְּהַנְהָגַת כְּלָל הֶהָמוֹן
- וּפְלוּגְתָּתָם מַה הִיא עִקַּר רְצוֹנוֹ יִתְבָּרַךְ וְהַמַּדְרֵגָה הַיּוֹתֵר גְּבוֹהָה בְּהַנְהָגַת כְּלָל הֶהָמוֹן):

שַׁעַר א' - פֶּרֶק ט'

- וְהִנֵּה דּוֹר הַמִּדְבָּר שֶׁזָּכוּ לִהְיוֹת מֵאוֹכְלֵי שֻׁלְחַן גָּבוֹהַּ, לֶחֶם מִן הַשָּׁמַיִם דְּבַר יוֹם בְּיוֹמוֹ, וְשִׂמְלָתָם לֹא בָלְתָה מֵעֲלֵיהֶם
- וְלֹא הָיוּ צְרִיכִים לְשׁוּם עֵסֶק פַּרְנָסָה בָּעוֹלָם כְּלָל
- לָדְבָרֵי הַכֹּל לֹא מִקְרוּ עוֹשִׂין רְצוֹנוֹ שֶׁל מָקוֹם אֶלָּא אִם כֵּן הָיוּ מִסְתַּכְּלִין כְּלַפֵּי מַעֲלָה בְּיֹשֶׁר גָּמוּר, וּמְשַׁעְבְּדִין אֶת לִבָּם רַק לַתּוֹרָה וַעֲבוֹדָה, וְיִרְאָתוֹ יִתְבָּרַךְ

---

on occasion, even fulfill one's obligation with a single word of Torah. This minimum performance is however only valid in a scenario where one has a personal obligation to perform other Mitzvot apart from Torah study and that those Mitzvot cannot be performed by anyone else. In our context here, it is particularly interesting to note that the Vilna Gaon explicitly mentions that "earning a livelihood *is* also a Mitzvah" which can legitimately reduce one's permanent obligation to study Torah.

231 An expression normally used to refer to consumption of the Cohanim of sacrifices on the Altar, e.g., Beitzah 21a.
232 Shemot 16:4, referring to the Manna.
233 Devarim 8:4.
234 Yehoshua 1:8.

- ○ As Chazal say, The Torah was only given to those who ate the Manna.[235]
- ○ Therefore, the Cherubim at that time were arranged to reflect that they were performing God's Will, literally facing each other, to show that 'they were directly looking at His Face,'[236] face to face with His Holy People.
- However, in the times of Shlomo, the majority of Israel needed to minimally divert themselves aside, to involve themselves with earning a livelihood, to provide for basic necessities
  - ○ which is the key part of the truth of God's Will according to R. Yishmael's opinion who holds that it is more appropriate for the general public to act in this way
  - ○ as per Pirkei Avot[237] – "Torah study is [only] appropriate when combined with earning a livelihood . . . and any Torah study which is not accompanied with work [will become irrelevant and will cause sin]"
  - ○ and Pirkei Avot relates to how to conduct oneself with piety[238] – that even while engaged in the pursuit of their livelihoods, their hearts should be engaged with wisdom, with thoughts of words of Torah.
  - ○ Therefore, [Shlomo] initially arranged the Cherubim according to how [Israel] were fulfilling God's Will, with their faces angled a little bit aside, but notwithstanding this, they were 'joined together [in an embrace],'[239] "all braced firmly"[240] with faces of affection – to show God's affection for us, that this [approach] principally fulfills His Will, as mentioned above
  - ○ (and this is according to R. Yishmael. The opinion that even with the Cherubim of Shlomo, that they were arranged to reflect how [Israel] would be performing God's Will, as literally facing each other, holds like R. Shimon bar Yochai.)
- Why [in the times of Shlomo] was it necessary to arrange both Cherubim at an angle? Surely the Cherub which represented God should have been arranged as directly facing [whereas only the Cherub representing Israel would be arranged at an angle according to R. Yishmael]?
- However, this idea is as we have written, that God's connection, so to speak, with all of the worlds and powers

---

235 E.g., Mechilta Beshalach Introduction which brings this statement in the name of R. Shimon bar Yochai. Interestingly, although R. Chaim does not mention the statement's author, it is often quoted in the name of R. Shimon bar Yochai which is very relevant to our context.

This statement is made a number of times in the Mechilta (e.g., Beshalach 13:17) and also in other Midrashim. Although, it is generally in the name of R. Shimon bar Yochai, it is also brought in the name of R. Eliezer. (It is also

שְׁמוֹ, יוֹמָם וָלַיְלָה לֹא יָמוּשׁ מִפִּיהֶם, דְּבָרִים כִּכְתָבָן מַמָּשׁ, בְּלִי נְטוֹת אֶל הַצַּד כְּלָל, אַף שָׁעָה קַלָּה לְעֵסֶק פַּרְנָסָה.

○ וּכְמַאֲמָרָם זִכְרוֹנָם לִבְרָכָה (מכילתא בשלח י"ג) לֹא נִתְּנָה תוֹרָה אֶלָּא לְאוֹכְלֵי מָן לָכֵן הֶעֱמִידוּ אָז אֶת הַכְּרוּבִים לְפִי מַה שֶׁהָיוּ עוֹשִׂין רְצוֹנוֹ שֶׁל מָקוֹם, פְּנֵיהֶם אִישׁ אֶל אָחִיו מַמָּשׁ, לְהַרְאוֹת כִּי יָשָׁר יֶחֱזוּ פָּנֵימוֹ יִתְבָּרַךְ, פָּנִים בְּפָנִים עִם עַם קְדוֹשׁוֹ:

• אָמְנָם בִּימֵי שְׁלֹמֹה, שֶׁהָיוּ כְּלַל הֲמוֹן יִשְׂרָאֵל צְרִיכִים וּמֻכְרָחִים לִנְטוֹת מְעַט אֶל הַצַּד לְעֵסֶק הַפַּרְנָסָה, עַל כָּל פָּנִים כְּדֵי חַיֵּי נֶפֶשׁ

○ שֶׁזֶּה עִקַּר אֲמִתַּת רְצוֹנוֹ יִתְבָּרַךְ לְדַעַת רַבִּי יִשְׁמָעֵאל דְּסָבַר דְּלָרַבִּים טְפֵי אָרִיךְ לְמֶעֱבַד הָכִי

○ וּכְמוֹ שֶׁאָמְרוּ בְּאָבוֹת, 'יָפֶה תַּלְמוּד תּוֹרָה עִם דֶּרֶךְ אֶרֶץ כו', וְכָל תּוֹרָה שֶׁאֵין עִמָּהּ מְלָאכָה כו'.

○ וְכָל מִלֵּי דְּאָבוֹת מִילֵּי דַּחֲסִידוּת נִינְהוּ, רַק שֶׁגַּם בְּעֵת עָסְקָם בְּפַרְנָסָה יְהֵא לָהֶם נוֹהֵג בְּחָכְמָה בְּהִרְהוּר דִּבְרֵי תוֹרָה

○ לָכֵן הֶעֱמִידוּ אָז בִּתְחִלָּה אֶת הַכְּרוּבִים, לְפִי מַה שֶׁיִּהְיוּ עוֹשִׂין רְצוֹנוֹ שֶׁל מָקוֹם, פְּנֵיהֶם מְצֻדָּדִין מְעַט, וְעִם כָּל זֶה הָיוּ מְעֹרִים "כְּמַעַר אִישׁ וְלֹיוֹת" (מלכים א' ז, לו) בְּפָנִים שֶׁל חִבָּה, לְהַרְאוֹת חִבָּתוֹ יִתְבָּרַךְ אֶצְלֵנוּ, שֶׁזֶּה עִקַּר רְצוֹנוֹ יִתְבָּרַךְ כנ"ל.

○ (וְסוֹבֵר כְּרַבִּי יִשְׁמָעֵאל. וּמַאן דְּאָמַר שֶׁגַּם בְּכְרוּבֵי שְׁלֹמֹה, הֶעֱמִידוּם תְּחִלָּה לְפִי מַה שֶׁיִּהְיוּ עוֹשִׂין רְצוֹנוֹ שֶׁל מָקוֹם, פְּנֵיהֶם אִישׁ אֶל אָחִיו מַמָּשׁ, סוֹבֵר כְּרַשְׁבִּ"י):

• וְלִכְאוֹרָה אַכַּתִּי לָמָּה הֻצְרְכוּ לְהַעֲמִיד ב' הַכְּרוּבִים מְצֻדָּדִין, הֲלֹא הַכְּרוּב הָאֶחָד שֶׁרָמַז עָלָיו יִתְבָּרַךְ שְׁמוֹ, הָיוּ צְרִיכִים לְהַעֲמִידוֹ יָשָׁר מַמָּשׁ:

• אָמְנָם הָעִנְיָן כְּמוֹ שֶׁכָּתַבְנוּ, שֶׁהִתְחַבְּרוּתוֹ יִתְבָּרַךְ כִּבְיָכוֹל לְהָעוֹלָמוֹת וְהַכֹּחוֹת כֻּלָּם

---

brought in the name of R. Shimon ben Yehoshua but it is likely that this is an erroneous expansion of the initial letters where Yehoshua should be Yochai.)

236 Tehillim 11:7.
237 Mishna Avot 2:2.
238 As per Bava Kama 30a.
239 Yoma 54a.
240 1 Melachim 7:36.

- and all of their arrangement and interconnection
- and similarly, the process with which God conducts himself with us
- is according to the measure of the movement and arousal which reaches them from our actions in the lowest world
- and according to this measure [of action] 'a laughing and pleased face'[241] cascades down [through the world levels] and is even drawn to us in the lowest world.
- Therefore, it is for this reason that even the Cherub which represented God also needed to be slightly angled to reflect the measure of the angle of the Cherub representing us [Israel]. (Note 11)[242]

• Therefore, at the time of the splitting of the Reed Sea, God said to Moshe: "Why do you cry out to Me? Tell the Children of Israel to just go . . ."[243]
- meaning that the matter is in their hands
- so that if they will be at their peak force of faith and trust
- and will enter into and travel through the sea, without fear out of the sheer strength of their trust that it will certainly split before them
- then this will cause a supernal arousal which [will be drawn down and] will perform the miracle and split the sea before them.[244]

---

241 E.g., Midrash Tanchuma Yitro 17.
242 **R. Chaim adds Note 11 here.** This note is brought at the end of this chapter and is entitled "Apple tree analogy that God reflects our attitude towards Him."
243 Shemot 14:15.
244 It is of interest to note the Vilna Gaon's comments towards the end of his commentary on Sifra DeTzniyuta Chap. 4 on the verse quoted above from Shemot 14:15 as follows:
   • It says "*to Me*" specifically: This means that God is within [the level of] Zeer Anpin [of Atzilut] and He says "Why do you cry out *to Me*, the matter is determined by Mazal/fate/destiny."
   • It says "*just go*" specifically: This means that Israel all cried out to [God at the level of] Zeer Anpin [of Atzilut]. He said "Just go from this place." Therefore, God did not want Israel to be aroused, as Above, [the level of] the Holy Atik is not affected by the actions of those in this world . . . for the actions of those in this world and their prayer only reach the level of Zeer Anpin [of Atzilut]. Therefore, it says "God will fight for you and you will be silent."
   The Zohar II Beshalach 52b quotes the statement from the Sifra DeTzniyuta of "to Me specifically" and explains that the miracle of the splitting of the Reed Sea was "entirely dependent on the level of Atik" and seemingly not able to be influenced by the actions of man in this world as the Vilna Gaon explains. This

○ וְכָל סִדְרֵיהֶם וְהִתְקַשְּׁרוּתָם
○ וְכֵן כָּל סִדְרֵי הַנְהָגָתוֹ יִתְבָּרַךְ אִתָּנוּ
○ הוּא כְּפִי שִׁעוּר הַתְּנוּעָה וְהַהִתְעוֹרְרוּת הַמַּגִּיעַ אֲלֵיהֶם מִמַּעֲשֵׂינוּ לְמַטָּה
○ וּכְפִי זֶה הַשִּׁעוּר מִשְׁתַּלְשֵׁל וְנִמְשָׁךְ גַּם אֵלֵינוּ לְמַטָּה פָּנִים שׂוֹחֲקוֹת וּמְסְבָּרוֹת.
○ לָכֵן, גַּם הַכְּרוּב שֶׁרָמַז עָלָיו יִתְבָּרַךְ שְׁמוֹ, הָיוּ גַם כֵּן צְרִיכִים לְהַעֲמִידוֹ מִצִּדָּד מְעַט, כְּפִי שִׁעוּר הַצִּדּוּד שֶׁל הַכְּרוּב שֶׁרוֹמֵז עָלֵינוּ, מִזֶּה הַטַּעַם: (הגהה י"א)
● וְלָכֵן בְּעֵת קְרִיעַת יַם סוּף, אָמַר הוּא יִתְבָּרַךְ לְמֹשֶׁה, "מַה תִּצְעַק אֵלָי דַּבֵּר אֶל בְּנֵי יִשְׂרָאֵל וְיִסָּעוּ" (שמות יד, טו)
○ רָצָה לוֹמַר דִּבְדִידְהוּ תַּלְיָא מִלְּתָא
○ שֶׁאִם הֵמָּה יִהְיוּ בְּתֹקֶף הָאֱמוּנָה וְהַבִּטָּחוֹן
○ וְיִסְעוּ הָלוֹךְ וְנָסוֹעַ אֶל הַיָּם, סָמוּךְ לִבָּם לֹא יִירָא, מֵעֹצֶם בִּטְחוֹנָם שֶׁוַּדַּאי יִקָּרַע לִפְנֵיהֶם
○ אָז יִגְרְמוּ עַל יְדֵי זֶה הִתְעוֹרְרוּת לְמַעְלָה, שֶׁיֵּעָשֶׂה לָהֶם הַנֵּס וְיִקָּרַע לִפְנֵיהֶם:

---

seems to contradict what R. Chaim is saying here that "the matter is in their hands" and that it was up to Israel to do something to invoke their salvation?

The explanation is that under normal circumstances action and prayer impact in a natural way within the natural order. The action and prayer of Israel have an effect on the level of Zeer Anpin which results in a natural response. In contrast, for the supernatural to occur, it can only be in response to a corresponding supernatural relationship between Israel and God. To invoke the supernatural, Israel must demonstrate a supernatural level of faith which contradicts all natural rationale. Therefore, the supernatural splitting of the Reed Sea only occurred when Israel unwaveringly actively demonstrated their supernatural faith for God by stepping into the Reed Sea. It was only this action expressing their supernatural faith, being specifically a "matter which was in their hand," which could result in a corresponding supernatural bestowal from the level of the Holy Atik to cause the splitting of the Reed Sea. Therefore, God says don't call out "to Me" to get a natural response as this will not help. Instead "just go," actively reach a supernatural level of faith and this will invoke the required supernatural response.

R. Chaim is therefore very specifically bringing this extreme example to show that God modulates His reaction to the actions of Israel – to the extent that if the actions of Israel are supernatural, they will even invoke a corresponding supernatural reaction. This is consistent with R. Chaim's comments about how God is our shadow in G1:07 and about the ability of a person who is suitably connected to cause supernatural events at the end of G3:12.

- This is "With My mighty horses [who battled] with Pharaoh's riders, I revealed that you are My beloved,"[245] meaning that
  - just as with the horses of Pharaoh, where in contrast to the norm where the rider guides the horse, with Pharaoh and his army, the horse directed its rider, as per Chazal.[246]
  - Similarly, "I revealed that you are [My beloved]" and I am controlled by you My beloved literally in this way
  - that even though I am "He who Rides above the Heavens"[247]
  - nevertheless you, so to speak, guide Me through your actions
  - in that My connection, so to speak, to the worlds is only according to the tendencies of your actions
    - as per "He Who Rides across the Heavens to help you"[248]
    - and similarly, as per Chazal, "Our service fulfills the needs of the Most High."[249]

Rabbi Chaim's Note:
Note 11 – Apple tree analogy that God reflects our attitude towards Him

- According to this, Chazal's statement is understood:[250] R. Chama son of R. Chanina said: What is the meaning of the verse "Like an apple tree among the trees of the forest," why is Israel compared to an apple tree?
- Tosafot[251] query that the reference to the apple tree in this verse does not relate to Israel but rather relates to God, as per the continuation of the verse "so is my Beloved [i.e., God] among the gods [i.e., the idols of the nations]"?

---

245 Shir Hashirim 1:9.
246 Shemot Rabba Beshalach 23:14 and Shir Hashirim Rabba 1:6.
247 Tehillim 68:5.
248 Devarim 33:26.
249 E.g., Shabbat 116b, Shabbat 131b, Yevamot 5b, Menachot 64a. R. Chaim is not quoting these sources verbatim but is adding his interpretation of them as they could otherwise be understood differently in that a specific type of service is necessary to be done for God but not that He specifically needs its performance. R. Chaim is therefore explaining these sources as saying that God needs our actions and that they have an impact on God – not that they change Him in any way (as per G3:04), but that these actions are the cause of God's corresponding response to us. This expression is also used and explained further at the end of G2:04 and in G2:10. Further light is shed on the expression that R. Chaim uses here in the Shela Toldot Adam, HaShaar HaGadol 322 as follows:
  - . . . [quoting R. Bechaye . . .] and therefore Israel has the power to weaken or intensify the power of Supernal strength, according to their deeds. . . . .

- וְזֶהוּ "לְסֻסָתִי בְּרִכְבֵי פַרְעֹה דִּמִּיתִיךְ רַעְיָתִי" (שה"ש א, ט), רוֹצֶה לוֹמַר
  - כְּמוֹ בְּסוּסֵי פַרְעֹה שֶׁהָיָה הֵפֶךְ מִנְהָגוֹ שֶׁל עוֹלָם שֶׁהָרוֹכֵב מַנְהִיג לַסּוּס, וּבְפַרְעֹה וְחֵילוֹ — הַסּוּס הִנְהִיג אֶת רוֹכְבוֹ, כְּמוֹ שֶׁאָמְרוּ רַבּוֹתֵינוּ זִכְרוֹנָם לִבְרָכָה (שמו"ר כג ושהש"ר א, ו)
  - כֵּן דִּמִּיתִיךְ וְהִמְשַׁלְתִּיךְ רַעְיָתִי עַל זֶה הָאֹפֶן מַמָּשׁ
  - שֶׁאַף שֶׁאֲנִי "רוֹכֵב עֲרָבוֹת"
  - עִם כָּל זֶה כִּבְיָכוֹל אַתְּ מַנְהִיגָה אוֹתִי עַל יְדֵי מַעֲשַׂיִךְ
  - שֶׁעִנְיַן הִתְחַבְּרוּתִי כִּבְיָכוֹל לְהָעוֹלָמוֹת, הוּא רַק כְּפִי עִנְיַן הִתְעוֹרְרוּת מַעֲשַׂיִךְ לְאָן נוֹטִים
    - וְזֶהוּ שֶׁאָמַר הַכָּתוּב, (דברים לג, כו) "רוֹכֵב שָׁמַיִם בְּעֶזְרֶךָ"
    - וְכֵן מַה שֶּׁאָמְרוּ רַבּוֹתֵינוּ זִכְרוֹנָם לִבְרָכָה (עי' שבת קטז: יבמות ה: מנחות סה) "הָעֲבוֹדָה צֹרֶךְ גָּבוֹהַּ":

הַגָּהָה י"א

- וְעַל פִּי זֶה יוּבַן מַאֲמָרָם זִכְרוֹנָם לִבְרָכָה בְּפ"ט דְּשַׁבָּת (פ"ח א) אָמַר ר' חָמָא בְּרַבִּי חֲנִינָא מַאי דִּכְתִיב (שה"ש ב, ג) "כְּתַפּוּחַ בַּעֲצֵי הַיַּעַר" גו', לָמָּה נִמְשְׁלוּ יִשְׂרָאֵל לְתַפּוּחַ כו':
- וְהִקְשׁוּ תּוֹסָפוֹת שָׁם, דְּהָא בְּהַאי קְרָא לֹא יִשְׂרָאֵל נִמְשְׁלוּ לְתַפּוּחַ אֶלָּא הַקָּדוֹשׁ בָּרוּךְ הוּא, כְּדִמְסַיֵּם "כֵּן דּוֹדִי בֵּין הַבָּנִים":

[the Shela continues . . .] Your eyes which see the unanimous agreement that "Our service fulfills the needs of the Most High," for it is with this [service] that the Great Name is rectified, and the righteous one who [causes his] form to be like its Creator, consistent with the secret that man of the lowest world is made in the image and form of Supernal Man as I have explained above, therefore, when he sanctifies his internal and external limbs, then the [physical] limbs grasp [and connect with] the [spiritual] limbs, the secret of the limbs of the Supernal Merkava, adding strength to them. If, God forbid, the likeness of man changes, I mean to say, that he turns from the side of holiness and attaches himself to the side of impurity, then he damages all of the worlds and the damage also impacts Above. . . .

250 Shabbat 88a quoting Shir Hashirim 2:3.
251 Starting "Piryo Kodem L'Alav."

- This can be answered, with God's help, as I wrote above, that after Israel related to God with the analogy of an apple tree, it is certainly because Israel's actions are [also] comparable to an apple tree, and that in the same way as we appear before Him, He correspondingly comes to appear to the worlds, literally in direct proportion.
- Therefore, [R. Chama son of R. Chanina] asks – in what way are Israel's desirable actions compared and analogous to an apple tree, as it is through this that God is related to, like the idea of an apple tree.

10. MAN GREATER THAN ANGEL AND VICE VERSA

- On this basis, a difference of opinion between the greatest of the Rishonim,[252] of blessed memory, will be explained
   - as to whether a Jew is greater than an angel or an angel is greater than him.
   - With each of the two opinions bringing supporting proofs from explicit Scriptural texts.
   - On the basis of our words above, it will be explained that in truth 'both these and these are words of the Living God,'[253] but in different contexts.
- For an angel is certainly [incomparably] greater than a Jew in terms of:
   - his essence
   - the greatness of his holiness
   - the awesomeness of his perception.
   - There is no vague comparison between them at all.
   - As per Zohar:
      - [R. Keruspedai learned] The perception of the angels is very great in contrast to that which is below them ... the second level [of perception is] ... the third level of perception is at the lowest level, [dominated by] the element of earth which is the perception of man. ... .[254]
      - [R. Elazar said in the name of R. Tanchum] The angels which are close [to God] are the first to receive their ability to perceive clarity of the Above; it is from them that this perception descends to the Heavens and all the Hosts, and from them to man.[255] Refer there.
      - The angels of the Supernal Realms are holier than us.[256]

---

252 Ramban, Even Ezra, R. Saadiah Gaon, Moreh HaNevuchim.
253 Eruvin 13b; Gittin 6b.
254 Zohar Chadash I Bereishit 15b–16a.

- וּלְפִי מַה שֶּׁכָּתַבְתִּי יִתְיַשֵּׁב בְּעֶזְרַת הַשֵּׁם, כִּי אַחַר שֶׁיִּשְׂרָאֵל הִשִּׂיגוּהוּ וְהִמְשִׁילוּהוּ יִתְבָּרַךְ שְׁמוֹ בְּדִמְיוֹן הַתַּפּוּחַ, וַדַּאי הוּא מֵחֲמַת שֶׁיִּשְׂרָאֵל נִמְשָׁלִים וּמִתְדַּמִּים בְּמַעֲשֵׂיהֶם לְעִנְיַן הַתַּפּוּחַ, וּכְדֶרֶךְ שֶׁאֲנַחְנוּ מִתְרָאִים לְפָנָיו יִתְבָּרַךְ שְׁמוֹ, כָּךְ הוּא יִתְבָּרַךְ שְׁמוֹ בָּא לֵירָאוֹת אֶל הָעוֹלָמוֹת, עַל זֶה הַהַדְרָגָה וְהַשִּׁעוּר מַמָּשׁ:

- לָכֵן שׁוֹאֵל, בְּאֵיזֶה דָּבָר וְעִנְיָן נִתְדַּמּוּ וְנִמְשְׁלוּ יִשְׂרָאֵל בְּמַעֲשֵׂיהֶם הָרְצוּיִים לְתַפּוּחַ, אֲשֶׁר עַל יְדֵי זֶה הִשִּׂיגוּהוּ יִתְבָּרַךְ שְׁמוֹ, בְּעִנְיַן הַתַּפּוּחַ:

שַׁעַר א' - פֶּרֶק י'

- וְעַל פִּי זֶה יְבֹאַר פֵּשֶׁר דָּבָר, בְּעִנְיַן שִׁנּוּי דֵּעוֹת שֶׁבֵּין גְּדוֹלֵי הָרִאשׁוֹנִים זַ"ל
  ◦ אִם הָאָדָם מִיִּשְׂרָאֵל גָּדוֹל מֵהַמַּלְאָךְ, אוֹ מַלְאָךְ גָּדוֹל מִמֶּנּוּ
  ◦ וְכָל אֶחָד מִשְּׁנֵי הַדֵּעוֹת מֵבִיא רְאָיוֹת מְפֹרָשׁוֹת מִמִּקְרָאוֹת מְפֹרָשִׁים.
  ◦ וְעַל פִּי דְּבָרֵינוּ הַנַּ"ל יִתְבָּאֵר אֲשֶׁר בֶּאֱמֶת אֵלּוּ וָאֵלּוּ דִּבְרֵי אֱלֹהִים חַיִּים, רַק בִּבְחִינוֹת חֲלוּקִים:

- כִּי וַדַּאי מַלְאָךְ גָּדוֹל מֵהָאָדָם
  ◦ הֵן בְּעֶצֶם מַהוּתוֹ
  ◦ הֵן בְּגֹדֶל קְדֻשָּׁתוֹ
  ◦ וְנִפְלָאוֹת הַשָּׂגָתוֹ
  ◦ אֵין עֵרֶךְ וְדִמְיוֹן בֵּינֵיהֶם כְּלָל.
  ◦ וּכְמוֹ שֶׁכָּתוּב
    □ בַּזֹּהַר חָדָשׁ בְּרֵאשִׁית בַּמִּדְרָשׁ הַנֶּעְלָם בְּפָרָשַׁת וַיִּקְרָא אֱלֹהִים לָאוֹר יוֹם, "הַשָּׂגַת הַמַּלְאָכִים הִיא הַשָּׂגָה גְּדוֹלָה, מַה שֶּׁאֵין כֵּן לְמַטָּה מֵהֶם, הַשָּׂגָה שְׁנִיָּה כוּ', הַשָּׂגָה שְׁלִישִׁית הִיא הַשָּׂגַת הַמַּדְרֵגָה הַתַּחְתּוֹנָה אֲשֶׁר בֶּעָפָר יְסוֹדָהּ, וְהִיא הַשָּׂגַת בְּנֵי אָדָם".
    □ וְשָׁם כ"ח ב', "הַמַּלְאָכִים הַקְּרוֹבִים מְקַבְּלִים כֹּחַ שֶׁפַע אַסְפַּקְלַרְיָא שֶׁל מַעְלָה תְּחִלָּה, וּמֵהֶם יוֹרֵד לַשָּׁמַיִם וְכָל צְבָאָם, וּמֵהֶם אֶל הָאָדָם", עַיֵּן שָׁם.
    □ וּבַזֹּהַר תְּרוּמָה קכ"ט ב', "מַלְאֲכֵי עִלָּאֵי אִנּוּן קַדִּישִׁין יַתִּיר מִנָּן":

---

255 Zohar Chadash I Bereishit 28b.
256 Zohar II Terumah 129b.

- However, in one respect man has a distinct significant advantage over an angel in that he can elevate and interconnect the worlds, the powers, and the lights with each other, and that no angel is capable of doing this at all.
  - This is for the reason mentioned above that an angel is essentially a single unique power which does not incorporate all the worlds together.
    - (It is similarly written in Etz Chaim:[257] An angel is only a specific element of the specific world in which he exists, whereas the soul of man, with its three parts of Nefesh, Ruach, and Neshama, is made up of all the worlds. Refer there.)
  - Therefore, the angel has no power or ability to raise, interconnect, and unify each world with the world above it as he is not made up of or combined from [the worlds].
  - In addition the angel himself cannot raise his essence to a level which can connect to the world above him.
  - Therefore, angels are referred to as *stationary*, like that which is written "Standing Seraphim"[258] and "I have given you the ability to move among these stationary ones."[259]
  - It is only man alone who can raise, interconnect and unify the worlds and the lights with the power of his actions as he is made up of all of [the worlds]
    - and then even the angel is able to achieve an elevation and an additional holiness over and above his level of holiness, which comes from the power of man's action, as he [the angel] is also incorporated within the man. (Refer to a similar idea in Etz Chaim.)[260]
- In addition – the three levels of man's soul – Nefesh, Ruach and Neshama – are only enabled to raise and interconnect the worlds and themselves when they descend to this [physical] world of action and are manifest within man's body

---

257 Etz Chaim Shaar 40, Shaar Pnimiyut Vechiztoniyut, at the beginning of Derush 10.
258 Yishayahu 6:2.
259 Zecharia 3:7.
260 Etz Chaim Shaar 28, Shaar HaIbburim at the beginning of Chap. 4:
  - Know the secret of what Chazal say "... You may look at all of them except for R. Chiya's throne which you may not look at. What are the characteristics [of R. Chiya's throne]? All of the [other thrones] have angels which go [to assist them] as they ascend and descend – apart from R. Chiya's throne which ascends and descends by itself" (Bava Metzia 85a). The souls of the Tzaddikim are above the level of angels and this is what is written here that angels would help raise all the thrones of the souls of the Tzaddikim except

• אָמְנָם בְּדָבָר אֶחָד, יִתְרוֹן גָּדוֹל לָאָדָם מֵהַמַּלְאָכִים, וְהוּא הָעֲלָאַת וְהִתְקַשְּׁרוּת הָעוֹלָמוֹת וְהַכֹּחוֹת וְהָאוֹרוֹת אֶחָד בַּחֲבֵרוֹ, אֲשֶׁר זֶה אֵין בְּכֹחַ כְּלָל לְשׁוּם מַלְאָךְ.

○ וְהוּא מִטַּעַם הַנַּ"ל, כִּי הַמַּלְאָךְ הוּא בְּעַצֶם כֹּחַ אֶחָד פְּרָטִי לְבַד, שֶׁאֵין בּוֹ כְּלִילוּת כָּל הָעוֹלָמוֹת יַחַד.

▫ (וְכֵן כָּתוּב בְּעֵץ חַיִּים שַׁעַר פְּנִימִיּוּת וְחִיצוֹנִיּוּת רֵישׁ דְּרוּשׁ י', שֶׁהַמַּלְאָךְ אֵינוֹ רַק בְּחִינָה פְּרָטִית שֶׁל אוֹתוֹ הָעוֹלָם שֶׁעוֹמֵד בּוֹ, אֲבָל נִשְׁמַת הָאָדָם, בְּכָל ג' הַחֲלָקֵי נר"ן שֶׁלָּהּ, הִיא כְּלוּלָה מִכָּל הָעוֹלָמוֹת, עַיֵּן שָׁם)

○ לָכֵן אֵין בְּכֹחַ וִיכֹלֶת הַמַּלְאָךְ כְּלָל לְהַעֲלוֹת וּלְקַשֵּׁר וּלְיַחֵד כָּל עוֹלָם בְּהָעוֹלָם הַנָּטוּי עַל רָאשֵׁיהֶם, כֵּיוָן שֶׁאֵינוֹ כָּלוּל וּמְשֻׁתָּף מֵהֶם.

○ וְגַם עֲלִיַּת עַצְמוּתוֹ שֶׁל הַמַּלְאָךְ עַד מַדְרֵגָתוֹ, לְהִתְקַשֵּׁר בָּעוֹלָם שֶׁעָלָיו, אֵין תָּלוּי בּוֹ בְּעַצְמוֹ.

○ לָכֵן נִקְרָאִים הַמַּלְאָכִים "עוֹמְדִים", כְּמוֹ שֶׁכָּתוּב (ישעיה ו') "שְׂרָפִים עוֹמְדִים", "וְנָתַתִּי לְךָ מַהְלְכִים בֵּין הָעוֹמְדִים הָאֵלֶּה" (זכריה ג').

○ וְרַק הָאָדָם לְבַד הוּא הַמַּעֲלֶה וְהַמְקַשֵּׁר וּמְיַחֵד אֶת הָעוֹלָמוֹת וְהָאוֹרוֹת בְּכֹחַ מַעֲשָׂיו, מֵחֲמַת שֶׁהוּא כָּלוּל מִכֻּלָּם.

▫ וְאָז גַּם הַמַּלְאָךְ מַשִּׂיג עֲלִיָּה וְתוֹסֶפֶת קְדֻשָּׁה עַל קְדֻשָּׁתוֹ, אֲשֶׁר בָּא בְּכֹחַ מַעֲשֵׂה הָאָדָם, מִפְּנֵי שֶׁגַּם הוּא כָּלוּל בְּהָאָדָם. (וְעַיֵּן בְּעִנְיָן זֶה בְּעֵץ חַיִּים שַׁעַר הָעִבּוּרִים רֵישׁ פֶּרֶק ד'):

• וְגַם הַג' בְּחִינוֹת נר"ן שֶׁל הָאָדָם עַצְמוֹ, לֹא נִתַּן לָהֶם זֶה הַכֹּחַ הַהַעֲלָאָה

---

for the throne of R. Chiya as he would ascend himself. It appears that it would be a greater honor that the ascending should be with angels rather than on one's own and therefore in what way is this superior [as the Talmud is stating]? The explanation is that these angels who raise the thrones of the Tzaddikim, these are the angels which were hewn with the soul and the throne which carry them. As Chazal state, the throne carries those who carry it and "the Ark carries those who carry it" (Sotah 35a). That it appears that the angels carry the throne but (in truth) the throne carries them up until a level from which the angels can ascend no further by even a small amount. Therefore, R. Chiya's throne, which was higher than the level of the angels, would ascend on its own as the angels were unable to ascend with it, and this is the meaning of "it ascends and descends by itself" as stated above, that the level of the Tzaddikim who are involved with Torah and good deeds is higher than the angels.

- as the verse describes "He breathed a living soul into his nostrils"²⁶¹ of man's body and [only] then "and the man became a living soul" of all the worlds as per G1:04.
- This is also the idea represented by the vision of the ladder in Yaakov's dream.
  - Refer to the Zohar:²⁶² "He breathed a living soul into his nostrils" [this is the image which is above a person] about which it says "he dreamed and there was a ladder" – the ladder is certainly his living soul . . .
  - refer to it there and it is as will be explained, God willing, later on in G1:19.
  - It was through this [ladder/soul] that "and behold the angels of God were ascending and descending on it"²⁶³
    - meaning that this [ascending and descending of the angels] happens through [man's] living soul which is set towards the ground, with its lowest end being manifest within man's body.²⁶⁴

11. MAN INITIATES PROCESS ENABLING ANGELS TO SANCTIFY GOD

- This is the reason why the angels who sanctify [God] in the highest heavens
  - wait before reciting their *triplication of sanctification*²⁶⁵
  - until after we [Israel] have recited the *triplication of sanctification* in [this] lowest world (as per the note G1:06:No6 above)
  - even though their sanctification is superior to ours.
  - This is not because they accord Israel with any honor
  - but it is because they do not have any inherent ability at all to open their mouths to sanctify their Creator until the sound of Israel's sanctification rises to them from [this] lowest world.
- The recitation of the sanctification elevates and interconnects the worlds
  - each world with the world above it
  - to increase their holiness and refine their light.
  - As per Zohar:²⁶⁶ And those [angels] on the right sing praise and elevate the will above by saying "Holy . . . ," and those on the left sing praise and elevate the will above by saying "Blessed . . . ," and they join together in holiness with all those who know how to sanctify their Master in unity . . . , and they all are incorporated within each other in a single unity and bound up with each other until they all form one knot and one spirit, and they are connected to those above with all becoming one and incorporated within each other.

- וְהִתְקַשְּׁרוּת שֶׁל הָעוֹלָמוֹת וְשֶׁל עַצְמָם, עַד רִדְתָּם לְזֶה הָעוֹלָם הַמַּעֲשִׂי בְּגוּף הָאָדָם

  - וּכְמוֹ שֶׁכָּתוּב (בראשית ב. ז) "וַיִּפַּח בְּאַפָּיו נִשְׁמַת חַיִּים" בְּגוּף הָאָדָם, אָז "וַיְהִי הָאָדָם לְנֶפֶשׁ חַיָּה" שֶׁל כָּל הָעוֹלָמוֹת, כנ"ל בפ"ד:

- וְהוּא גַּם כֵּן עִנְיַן מַרְאֵה הַסֻּלָּם שֶׁל יַעֲקֹב אָבִינוּ עָלָיו הַשָּׁלוֹם.

  - עַיֵּן רַעְיָא מְהֵימְנָא נָשֹׂא קכ"ג ב' "וַיִּפַּח בְּאַפָּיו נִשְׁמַת חַיִּים כו', דְּאִתְּמַר בֵּיהּ (בראשית כח, יב) "וַיַּחֲלֹם וְהִנֵּה סֻלָּם", סֻלָּם וַדַּאי אִיהוּ נִשְׁמַת חַיִּים כו'

  - עַיֵּן שָׁם, וּכְמוֹ שֶׁיִּתְבָּאֵר אִי"ה לְהַלָּן בְּפֶרֶק י"ט

  - וְעַל יְדֵי זֶה "וְהִנֵּה מַלְאֲכֵי אֱלֹהִים עֹלִים וְיוֹרְדִים בּוֹ"

  - רוֹצֶה לוֹמַר, עַל יְדֵי הַנְּשָׁמַת חַיִּים שֶׁהוּא מַצָּב אַרְצָה, מִתְלַבֶּשֶׁת קָצֶה הַתַּחְתּוֹן שֶׁלָּהּ בְּגוּף הָאָדָם:

שער א' - פרק י"א

- וְזֶהוּ הַטַּעַם שֶׁהַמַּלְאָכִים הַמַּקְדִּישִׁים בִּשְׁמֵי מָרוֹם

  - מַמְתִּינִים מִלְּשַׁלֵּשׁ קְדֻשָּׁתָם

  - עַד אַחַר שֶׁאָנוּ מְשַׁלְּשִׁים קְדֻשָּׁה לְמַטָּה (כנ"ל פרק ו' בהגהה)

  - אַף שֶׁקְּדֻשָּׁתָם לְמַעְלָה מִקְּדֻשָּׁתֵנוּ.

  - לֹא שֶׁהֵם חוֹלְקִים כָּבוֹד לְיִשְׂרָאֵל

  - אֶלָּא שֶׁאֵין בְּכֹחָם וִיכָלְתָּם כְּלָל מִצַּד עַצְמָם לִפְתֹּחַ פִּיהֶם לְהַקְדִּישׁ לְיוֹצְרָם, עַד עֲלִיַּת קוֹל קְדֻשַּׁת יִשְׂרָאֵל אֲלֵיהֶם מִלְּמַטָּה:

- כִּי עִנְיַן אֲמִירַת הַקְּדֻשָּׁה הוּא הַעֲלָאַת הָעוֹלָמוֹת וְהִתְקַשְּׁרוּתָם

  - כָּל עוֹלָם בָּעוֹלָם שֶׁמֵּעָלָיו

  - לְהוֹסִיף קְדֻשָּׁתָם וְצַחְצוּחַ אוֹרָם.

- וְעַיֵּן בְּהֵיכָלוֹת דִּפְקוּדֵי בְּהֵיכָלָא תְּנִינָא רמ"ז סוֹף ע"ב בְּעִנְיַן קְדֻשַּׁת הַמַּלְאָכִים הַבָּא מִכֹּחַ אֲמִירַת קְדֻשָּׁתֵנוּ, ז"ל "וְאִלֵּין דִּימִינָא אָמְרֵי שִׁירָתָא, וְסַלְקֵי רְעוּתָא

---

261 Bereishit 2:7.
262 Zohar Raya Mehemna III Naso 123b, quoting Bereishit 2:7 and 28:12.
263 Bereishit 28:12.
264 See G1:05:No5.
265 As per Yishayahu 6:3, i.e., the Kedushah prayer.
266 Zohar II Pekudei 247b, describing Israel's sanctification enabling the angels.

- ○ Refer to Pri Etz Chaim,[267] which explains there that the objective of saying the sanctification is to raise and interconnect the supernal worlds, and thereby increase their holiness and level of supernal light (and perhaps this is the source of the custom to raise oneself at the time of saying the Kedushah prayer).
- This is a process which no angel or Seraph[268] is capable of initiating as stated above.
  - ○ Therefore, no [angel] can open his mouth until the breath of recitation of sanctification has ascended from Israel, the group in [this] lowest world.
- [Therefore,] if all of Israel in the entire world were quiet and did not recite the sanctification, God forbid, it would then inevitably be that they [the angels] would also be quiet from reciting their sanctification. As per:
  - ○ Zohar[269]
  - ○ "[I heard the sound of their (the angels) wings, like the sound of the great waters, like the sound of God, as they moved, the sound of a commotion, like the sound of a camp.] When they [Israel] would halt, they [the angels] would release their wings,"[270] meaning that when Israel in the lowest world stop and are silent inevitably the wings of the angels above are released [i.e., weakened]
    - ▫ as the [angel's] recitation of sanctification also involves their wings
    - ▫ as per Chazal:[271] One verse says ... Which of [the wings] were diminished? R. Chananel said in the name of Rav, those with which they sing praise ...
    - ▫ [This *weakening of wings* is also described] in the Zohar – although there the *wings* are interpreted as an expression of *gathering*.[272]
- Therefore, among the many hosts of angels there are many groups:
  - ○ One [group] says "Holy ... ," and they are the Seraphim
    - ▫ as per Heichalot HaZohar[273]

---

267 Pri Etz Chaim Chap. 3 from Shaar Chazarat HaAmidah.
268 A type of angel, as mentioned later on in this chapter.
269 Zohar III Balak 190b:
- But they [the angels] have not been handed [permission to recite] "Holy ..." except together with Israel, as they don't recite the Kedushah prayer except with Israel. If you ask, but surely there is the verse "and they [the angels] call out to each other and say [Kedushah]" (Yishayahu 6:3), when is this? At the time when Israel sanctify in the lowest world, and until Israel sanctify in this lowest world, they cannot sanctify.

270 Yechezkel 1:24–25.
271 Chagiga 13b.

לְעֵלָּא, וְאָמְרֵי קָדוֹשׁ, וְאִלֵּין דִּשְׂמָאלָא אָמְרֵי שִׁירָתָא, וְסַלְּקֵי רְעוּתָא לְעֵלָּא, וְאָמְרֵי בָּרוּךְ כו', וּמִתְחַבְּרָאן בְּקִדּוּשָׁה בְּכָל אִנּוּן דְּיָדְעֵי לְקַדָּשָׁא לְמָארִיהוֹן בְּיִחוּדָא כו', וְכֻלְּהוּ כְּלִילָן אִלֵּין בְּאִלֵּין בְּיִחוּדָא חֲדָא, וּמִתְקַשְּׁרָאן דָּא בְּדָא, עַד דְּכֻלְּהוּ אִתְעֲבִידוּ קִשּׁוּרָא חֲדָא וְרוּחָא חַד, וּמִתְקַשְּׁרָן בְּאִנּוּן דִּלְעֵלָּא לְמֶהֱוֵי כֹּלָּא חַד, לְאִתְכְּלָלָא דָּא בְּדָא".

○ וְעַיֵּן בִּפְרִי עֵץ חַיִּים בְּכָל פֶּרֶק ג' מִשַּׁעַר חֲזָרַת הָעֲמִידָה, מְבֹאָר שָׁם כַּוָּנַת עִנְיַן אֲמִירַת הַקְּדֻשָּׁה, שֶׁהוּא הָעֲלָאַת וְהִתְקַשְּׁרוּת עוֹלָמוֹת עֶלְיוֹנִים, לְהוֹסִיף בָּהֶם עַל יְדֵי זֶה תּוֹסֶפֶת קְדֻשָּׁה וְאוֹר עֶלְיוֹן. (וְאוּלַי מִזֶּה יָצָא מִנְהָגָן שֶׁל יִשְׂרָאֵל שֶׁנּוֹהֲגִים לְהַעֲלוֹת עַצְמָן בְּעֵת אֲמִירַת הַקְּדֻשָּׁה):

• וְזֶה אֵין בְּכֹחַ שׁוּם מַלְאָךְ וְשָׂרָף לַעֲשׂוֹתוֹ בְּעַצְמוֹ תְּחִלָּה כנ"ל.

○ לָזֹאת, לֹא יִפְתַּח פִּיו עַד עֲלִיַּית הֶבֶל פִּיהֶם שֶׁל קְדֻשַּׁת יִשְׂרָאֵל קְבוּצֵי מַטָּה.

• וְאִלּוּ הָיוּ כָּל יִשְׂרָאֵל, מִסּוֹף הָעוֹלָם וְעַד סוֹפוֹ, שׁוֹתְקִים חַס וְשָׁלוֹם מִלּוֹמַר קְדֻשָּׁה, מִמֵּילָא בְּהֶכְרֵחַ הָיוּ גַּם הֵמָּה נִשְׁתָּקִים מִלְּהַקְדִּישׁ קְדֻשָּׁתָם.

○ וְעַיֵּן בַּזֹּהַר בָּלָק ק"צ ע"ב.

○ וְזֶהוּ שֶׁאָמַר הַנָּבִיא (יחזקאל א' כד כה) "בְּעָמְדָם תְּרַפֶּינָה כַנְפֵיהֶן", רָצָה לוֹמַר כְּשֶׁיִּשְׂרָאֵל לְמַטָּה עוֹמְדִים שׁוֹתְקִים, מִמֵּילָא תְּרַפֶּינָה כַּנְפֵיהֶם שֶׁל הֲמוֹנֵי מַעְלָה

▫ כִּי עִנְיַן אֲמִירַת קְדֻשָּׁתָם הוּא גַּם בְּכַנְפֵיהֶם

▫ וּכְמַאֲמָרָם זִכְרוֹנָם לִבְרָכָה (חגיגה י"ג ב') כָּתוּב אֶחָד אוֹמֵר וְכוּ', הֵי מִנַּיְהוּ אַמְעֲטוּ אָמַר רַבִּי חֲנַנְאֵל אָמַר רַב אוֹתָן שֶׁאוֹמְרוֹת בָּהֶן שִׁירָה כוּ'.

○ וְעַיֵּן זֹהַר חָדָשׁ בְּרֵאשִׁית כ"א ע"ב "קוֹל הַמֻּלָּה" כו' (יחזקאל שם), אֶלָּא שֶׁשָּׁם פֵּרֵשׁ כַּנְפֵיהֶם לְשׁוֹן כְּנוּפְיָא

• וְלָזֹאת, הֲמוֹן צְבָאוֹת מַעְלָה, כִּתּוֹת כִּתּוֹת יֵשׁ.

○ אַחַת אוֹמֶרֶת "קָדוֹשׁ", וְהֵם הַשְּׂרָפִים

▫ כְּמוֹ"שׁ בְּהֵיכָלוֹת דִּבְרֵאשִׁית וּפְקוּדֵי בְּהֵיכָלָא תִּנְיָנָא שָׁם מ"ב א', וְשָׁם רמ"ז סוֹף ע"א

---

272 Zohar Chadash I Bereishit 21b, where the Hebrew words for "wings" (Kanfeihem) and "gathering" (Kenufiya) are similar and understood to have overlapping meaning.

273 Heichalot HaZohar of Bereishit and Pekudei, Heichala Tinyana, Bereishit 42a and end of Pekudei 247a: describing that there are two groups of angels

- ○ as per "The Seraphim were standing above, at His service . . . calling to each other and saying 'Holy'. . . ."[274]
- ○ The second [group], opposing [the first group] praise [God] and say "Blessed . . . ," and these are the Ophanim and Chayot
  - ▫ as per Chazal, and there is *Blessed*? Ophanim say "Blessed."[275]
- ○ As per the prayer arrangement of the Men of the Great Assembly of the sanctification of [the blessing of] Yotzer Ohr where each group of angels only sanctifies God according to their root source in the worlds.[276]
- However, Israel, the group in this [physical] world, say both [statements], i.e., "Holy . . ." and "Blessed . . ." as they are made up of all of the sources and roots together.
- This is also the concept underpinning the reciting of Perek Shira, as Chazal state: "Those who recite Perek Shira every day [are guaranteed a place in the World to Come] . . ."[277]
  - ○ that through man reciting it
  - ○ as he incorporates all the powers of everything
  - ○ he empowers the angels [which govern] all of these creations to say these songs
  - ○ and as a result they draw life and a bestowal to all of the lower worlds.
  - ○ Refer to Likutei Torah.[278]

 – Seraphim saying "Holy . . . ," and Chayot saying "Blessed . . . ." (Also see Heichala Tinyana, end of Pekudei 247b.)

274 Yishayahu 6:2–3.
275 Chullin 91b–92a.
276 See G3:06 for more details about the angels reciting the Kedushah/sanctification prayer and p. 507, fn. 123, explaining the different perspective of the two groups of angels.
277 Eliyahu Rabba 1:14. Perek Shira is a short ancient Midrashic-like text of unknown origin to which Chazal lend great importance. It describes the song of 85 components of Creation.
278 As per Likutei Torah, VaEtchanan, in Taamei HaMitzvot:
- What is the idea of the requirement to recite Perek Shira every day? Know that all the creations in the world have an angel in heaven over them, and this is the secret of "there is no blade of grass in this world which does not have a constellation *hitting* it saying to it *grow*!" [refer to this Midrash quoted in G3:10]. It is through this angel that bestowal and life force is drawn

שער א' - פרק י"א

- וכמו"ש (ישעי' ו') "שְׂרָפִים עוֹמְדִים מִמַּעַל לוֹ" וגו', "וְקָרָא זֶה אֶל זֶה וְאָמַר קָדוֹשׁ" גו'.
- וְהַשֵּׁנִית לְעֻמָּתָם מְשַׁבְּחִים וְאוֹמְרִים "בָּרוּךְ", וְהֵם הָאוֹפַנִּים וְחַיּוֹת
- כְּמוֹ שֶׁאָמְרוּ רַבּוֹתֵינוּ זִכְרוֹנָם לִבְרָכָה (חולין צא ב') רֵישׁ פֶּרֶק גִּיד הַנָּשֶׁה "וְהָאִכָּא בָּרוּךְ, בָּרוּךְ, אוֹפַנִּים הוּא דְּאָמְרֵי לֵיהּ"
- וּכְמוֹ שֶׁסִּדְּרוּ אַנְשֵׁי כְּנֶסֶת הַגְּדוֹלָה בִּקְדֻשָּׁה יוֹצֵר, שֶׁכָּל כַּת מְקַדֶּשֶׁת כְּפִי מְקוֹרָהּ וְשָׁרְשָׁהּ בָּהָעוֹלָמוֹת:

• אֲבָל יִשְׂרָאֵל קְבוּצֵי מַטָּה אוֹמְרִים שְׁנֵיהֶם "קָדוֹשׁ" וּ"בָרוּךְ", לִהְיוֹתָם כּוֹלְלִים כָּל הַמְּקוֹרוֹת וְהַשָּׁרָשִׁים יַחַד:

• וְזֶהוּ גַּם כֵּן עִנְיַן אֲמִירַת פֶּרֶק שִׁירָה שֶׁאָמְרוּ ז"ל "כָּל הָאוֹמֵר פֶּרֶק שִׁירָה בְּכָל יוֹם" כו'
  - שֶׁעַל יְדֵי אֲמִירַת הָאָדָם אוֹתוֹ
  - שֶׁהוּא כּוֹלֵל כָּל הַכֹּחוֹת כֻּלָּם
- הוּא נוֹתֵן כֹּחַ לְהַמַּלְאָכִים וְהַשָּׂרִים שֶׁל כָּל אֵלּוּ הַבְּרִיּוֹת שֶׁיֹּאמְרוּ אֵלּוּ הַשִּׁירוֹת
- וְעַל יְדֵי זֶה הֵם מוֹשְׁכִים חִיּוּתָם וְשִׁפְעָם לְהַשְׁפִּיעַ בְּכָל הַתַּחְתּוֹנִים.
  - וְעַיֵּן בָּזֶה בְּלִקּוּטֵי תּוֹרָה בְּטַעֲמֵי מִצְוֹת פָּרָשַׁת וָאֶתְחַנַּן:

---

down to it, and this angel can only impact the lower worlds when he recites his Shira/song, it is through this Shira that he [the angel] receives his life force and sustenance to be able to bestow it on the lower worlds, therefore, all of these songs are of the angels and constellations, each one according to its kind . . . but that which is written in Perek Shira that a person who recites it each day will merit many great things, the reason for this is, as you already know, that "He created man in the image of Elokim," and just as all the worlds are dependent on the Shiur Komah of God, so too all the creations in the lower worlds grasp on to the Shiur Komah of man of the lower worlds, and through him [man] all are blessed; therefore, one who recites Perek Shira and knows how to focus on how the creations are hinted to within it and recites those songs, he causes a bestowal [to be drawn] upon all the creations which are dependent on him, and his reward is large. [A similar sentiment is expressed in the book Chesed LeAvraham, Maayan 4 Nahar 3 authored by R. Avraham Azulai, the grandfather of the Chida.]

12. PHYSICAL ACTION GENERATES OUR FUTURE WORLD EXPERIENCE

- A person's Nefesh, Ruach, and Neshama are unable to interconnect with the worlds until they descend to [this] lowest world within a person's body, as mentioned above (in G1:10)
  - as they are absolutely required to be clothed within the body in the world where actions occur in order to rectify the World of Action.
  - Similarly, we find many Scriptural verses which relate to these three levels, as mentioned above.[279]
- In relation to the impact in the Supernal Realms as a result of [physical] action:
  - King David, may he rest in peace, said "He who fashions their hearts together, who understands *El* all their deeds"[280]
    - and according to the simple meaning it would have been appropriate to say "who understands all their deeds"
    - but he said "*El* all their deeds," meaning that which is impacted by their deeds
    - that is, that the Creator, knows and understands the extent to which their deeds reach and impact in the rectification of the worlds – or the contrary, God forbid.
- Similarly, Kohelet says "He will bring *Et* all the *actions of Elokim* to judgment, with every secret thing [whether it is good or whether it is bad.]"[281]
  - He does not say that Elokim brings each action to judgment, etc.
  - and this is that "Elokim" means "all powerful"
  - that when a person stands in judgment before God, he is not judged for his simple actions alone but consideration is also given to what his actions caused and their affect, whether good or whether bad, on all the powers and the worlds
  - this is the meaning of *actions of Elokim*.
- This verse uses the word "Et," relating to all the action – instead of the word "Al," which would relate to the *actual* actions performed.
  - This is in line with "For He repays man according to his deeds"[282]
  - and is as explained above (in G1:06 in the note)[283] that from the moment it enters the purity of a person's thought to perform a Mitzvah

---

279 There were two sets of three levels mentioned above. One set is the three levels of Action, Speech, and Thought. The second set is the three levels of the soul: Nefesh, Ruach, and Neshama. R. Chaim will now focus on the three levels of Action (G1:12), Speech (G1:13), and Thought (G1:14) providing Scriptural

שער א' - פרק י"ב

- וּמַה שֶּׁהַנֶּפֶשׁ רוּחַ נְשָׁמָה שֶׁל הָאָדָם אֵין בִּכְלָתָם לְקַשֵּׁר הָעוֹלָמוֹת עַד רִדְתָּם לְמַטָּה בְּגוּף הָאָדָם כַּנַּ"ל (בפ"י).
  - כִּי לְתַקֵּן "עוֹלָם הָעֲשִׂיָּה" הֻצְרְכוּ בְּהֶכְרֵחַ לְהִתְלַבֵּשׁ בַּגּוּף, בְּעוֹלָם הַמַּעֲשֶׂה.
  - וְכֵן מָצִינוּ כַּמָּה מִקְרָאוֹת הַמְדֻבָּרִים בְּאֵלּוּ הַג' בְּחִינוֹת הַנַּ"ל:
- בְּעִנְיַן הַהִתְעוֹרְרוּת שֶׁלְּמַעְלָה עַל יְדֵי בְּחִינַת "הַמַּעֲשֶׂה".
  - אָמַר דָּוִד הַמֶּלֶךְ עָלָיו הַשָּׁלוֹם (תהלים לג, טו) "הַיּוֹצֵר יַחַד לִבָּם הַמֵּבִין אֶל כָּל מַעֲשֵׂיהֶם"
    - וּלְפִי פְּשׁוּטוֹ הָיָה רָאוּי לוֹמַר 'הַמֵּבִין כָּל מַעֲשֵׂיהֶם'.
    - וְאָמַר 'אֶל' כָּל מַעֲשֵׂיהֶם, רוֹצֶה לוֹמַר הַנּוֹגֵעַ לְמַעֲשֵׂיהֶם
    - וְהַיְנוּ, שֶׁהוּא הַיּוֹצְרָם יִתְבָּרַךְ שְׁמוֹ, הַיּוֹדֵעַ וּמֵבִין עַד הֵיכָן מַעֲשֵׂיהֶם מַגִּיעִים וְנוֹגְעִים בְּתִקּוּנֵי הָעוֹלָמוֹת, אוֹ לְהֵפֶךְ חַס וְשָׁלוֹם:
- וְכֵן קֹהֶלֶת אָמַר (יב, יד) "כִּי אֶת כָּל מַעֲשֶׂה הָאֱלֹקִים יָבִא בְּמִשְׁפָּט עַל כָּל נֶעְלָם גו'
  - וְלֹא אָמַר 'כִּי הָאֱלֹקִים יָבִא בְּמִשְׁפָּט אֶת כָּל מַעֲשֶׂה' וְגוֹ'.
  - וְהַיְנוּ, כִּי "אֱלֹקִים" פֵּרוּשׁוֹ "בַּעַל הַכֹּחוֹת כֻּלָּם'
  - וּבְעֵת עֲמֹד הָאָדָם לַמִּשְׁפָּט לְפָנָיו יִתְבָּרַךְ שְׁמוֹ, לֹא יָדוּנוּ אֶת הַמַּעֲשֶׂה לְבַדָּהּ כְּפִי שֶׁהִיא, אַךְ יַחְשְׁבוּ גַּם כָּל מַה שֶּׁגָּרַם וְסִבֵּב עַל יְדֵי מַעֲשָׂיו, אִם טוֹב וְאִם רָע, בְּכָל הַכֹּחוֹת וְהָעוֹלָמוֹת
  - זֶהוּ אָמְרוֹ "מַעֲשֵׂה הָאֱלֹקִים":
- וְאָמַר 'כִּי "אֶת" כָּל מַעֲשֶׂה', וְלֹא "עַל" כָּל מַעֲשֶׂה
  - הָעִנְיָן כְּמוֹ שֶׁאָמַר (איוב לד, יא) "כִּי פֹעַל אָדָם יְשַׁלֶּם לוֹ".
  - וְהוּא כְּמוֹ שֶׁנִּתְבָּאֵר לְמַעְלָה (בפרק ו' בהגהה), שֶׁמֵּעֵת שֶׁעוֹלָה עַל טֹהַר

---

sources for each level, and then describe how they directly correspond to the three levels of the soul: Nefesh, Ruach, and Neshama (at the end of G1:14).

280 Tehillim 33:15, where the preposition "El" appears to be superfluous.
281 Kohelet 12:14.
282 Iyov 34:11.
283 This refers to R. Chaim's note G1:06:No8. Clearly, even though R. Chaim's additional notes are presented as not being central to the flow of ideas – they

– it immediately makes an impression Above, in his supernal source – to build and plant many supernal worlds and powers
- as per "and I will place My words in your mouth ... to plant the Heavens"[284]
- and, as per Chazal,[285] "Don't call them my sons but rather my builders," as mentioned above.[286]
- This [impression Above] inevitably also arouses and draws down an enveloping light upon him from the Supernal Holiness, which assists him to complete [the performance of the Mitzvah after the initial thought], and on completion of the Mitzvah this holiness and light returns to his source.
- This therefore is the concept of reward in the future world, which is a person's actual actions, which after the separation of the soul from the body, his soul ascends to enjoy and be sustained by the subtle shining of the holy lights, powers, and worlds, which have been added to and increased by his good deeds.

- This is as Chazal state "Each Jew has a portion *To* the future world"[287]
  - they do not say [that the portion is] "*In* the future world," as this would imply that the future world already existed at the time of creation as an entity in its own right and that if a person would justify [receipt of it], he would be rewarded by being given a part of it.
  - However, in reality, the future world is generated by a person's actual actions, whereby he extends, adds to, and rectifies his own portion through his own deeds.
  - Therefore, Chazal say that each individual Jew has the portion of holiness, light and subtle shining that he himself rectified and added to in the future world from his good deeds. (Note 12)[288]
- Similarly, the punishment of Gehinom is the same idea, that the sin itself is [a person's] punishment
  - as per "His own sins will trap the wicked person and he shall be firmly held by the cords of his sins"[289] and "your own wickedness will afflict you"[290]
  - this is as explained, that when a person 'performs one of God's commands that one should not do,'[291] the damage and destruction, God forbid, makes an immediate impression above in his source

---

touch on important concepts and are directly referred to on occasion from within the main body of his text.

284 Yishayahu 51:16.
285 Berachot 64a.
286 G1:03.

מַחֲשֶׁבֶת הָאָדָם לַעֲשׂוֹת מִצְוָה, תֵּכֶף נַעֲשֶׂה רִשּׁוּמוֹ לְמַעְלָה, בְּשָׁרְשׁוֹ הָעֶלְיוֹן, לִבְנוֹת וְלִנְטֹעַ כַּמָּה עוֹלָמוֹת וְכֹחוֹת עֶלְיוֹנִים.

- כְּמוֹ שֶׁכָּתוּב (ישעי' נא, טז) "וָאָשִׂים דְּבָרַי בְּפִיךָ וגו' לִנְטֹעַ שָׁמַיִם" גו'.

- וּכְמַאֲמָרָם זִכְרוֹנָם לִבְרָכָה (סוף ברכות סד, א) "אַל תִּקְרֵי בָּנַיִךְ אֶלָּא בּוֹנָיִךְ", כמש"ל (רפ"ג).

- וּמִמֵּילָא מִתְעוֹרֵר וּמַמְשִׁיךְ גַּם עָלָיו "אוֹר מַקִּיף" מֵהַקְּדֻשָּׁה הָעֶלְיוֹנָה, וְהוּא הַמַּסִּיעוֹ לְגָמְרָהּ. וְאַחַר גָּמְרוֹ הַמִּצְוָה, הַקְּדֻשָּׁה וְהָאוֹר מִסְתַּלֵּק לְשָׁרְשׁוֹ.

- וְזֶהוּ עִנְיַן שְׂכַר הָעוֹלָם הַבָּא, שֶׁהוּא מַעֲשֵׂי יְדֵי הָאָדָם עַצְמוֹ, שֶׁאַחַר פְּרִידַת נַפְשׁוֹ מֵהַגּוּף, הוּא הָעֲלִיָּה לְהִתְעַדֵּן וּלְהַשְׂבִּיעַ נַפְשׁוֹ בְּצַחְצָחוֹת הָאוֹרוֹת וְהַכֹּחוֹת וְהָעוֹלָמוֹת הַקְּדוֹשִׁים, שֶׁנִּתְוַסְּפוּ וְנִתְרַבּוּ מִמַּעֲשָׂיו הַטּוֹבִים:

• וְזֶהוּ שֶׁאָמְרוּ רַבּוֹתֵינוּ זִכְרוֹנָם לִבְרָכָה (סנהדרין צ, א) "כָּל יִשְׂרָאֵל יֵשׁ לָהֶם חֵלֶק לָעוֹלָם הַבָּא"

- וְלֹא אָמְרוּ "בָּעוֹלָם הַבָּא", שֶׁמִּשְּׁמָעוֹ הָיָה שֶׁהָעוֹלָם הַבָּא הוּא מוּכָן מֵעֵת הַבְּרִיאָה עִנְיָן וְדָבָר לְעַצְמוֹ, וְאִם יִצְדַּק הָאָדָם יִתְּנוּ לוֹ בִּשְׂכָרוֹ חֵלֶק מִמֶּנּוּ.

- אֲבָל הָאֱמֶת, שֶׁהָעוֹלָם הַבָּא הוּא מַעֲשֵׂה יְדֵי הָאָדָם עַצְמוֹ, שֶׁהִרְחִיב וְהוֹסִיף וְהִתְקִין חֵלֶק לְעַצְמוֹ בְּמַעֲשָׂיו.

- לְכָךְ אָמַר שֶׁכָּל יִשְׂרָאֵל יֵשׁ לָהֶם, לְכָל אֶחָד, חֵלֶק הַקְּדֻשָּׁה וְהָאוֹרוֹת וְהַצַּחְצָחוֹת, שֶׁהִתְקִין וְהוֹסִיף לָעוֹלָם הַבָּא מִמַּעֲשָׂיו הַטּוֹבִים: (הגהה י"ב)

• וְכֵן עֹנֶשׁ הַגֵּיהִנֹּם, עִנְיָנוֹ גַּם כֵּן, שֶׁהַחֵטְא עַצְמוֹ הוּא עָנְשׁוֹ

- כְּמוֹ שֶׁכָּתוּב (משלי ה' כב) "עֲוֹנוֹתָיו יִלְכְּדֻנוֹ אֶת הָרָשָׁע וּבְחַבְלֵי חַטָּאתוֹ יִתָּמֵךְ", "תְּיַסְּרֵךְ רָעָתֵךְ" גו' (ירמיה ב' יט).

- כְּמוֹ שֶׁנִּתְבָּאֵר, שֶׁכַּאֲשֶׁר הָאָדָם עוֹשֶׂה אַחַת מִמִּצְוֹת ה' אֲשֶׁר לֹא תֵעָשֶׂינָה, הַפְּגָם וְהַחֻרְבָּן נִרְשָׁם חַס וְשָׁלוֹם תֵּכֶף לְמַעְלָה בְּשָׁרְשׁוֹ.

---

287 Sanhedrin 90a.
288 **R. Chaim adds Note 12 here.** This note is brought at the end of this chapter and is entitled "Effect of good is everlasting, impact of bad ceases with punishment."
289 Mishlei 5:22.
290 Yirmiyahu 2:19.
291 Vayikra 4:27.

- - and correspondingly, "I will be filled with destruction"[292] – he establishes and strengthens the power and strength of impurity and the Kelipot,[293] may God save us
  - and from there he brings a spirit of impurity upon himself, which twists around him when performing the sin
  - and following his performance, the spirit of impurity departs to its place and he, while alive, is literally in Gehinom which encompasses him when he performs the sin
  - it is just that he does not yet feel it until after he passes on [from this world] that he is trapped in the net which he prepared, the powers of impurity and the beings that damage which were created from his actions.
- This is as Chazal state that – "the wicked deepen their Gehinom,"[294] meaning that they themselves deepen their own Gehinom, that they expand it and intensify it with their sins, as per "Behold, all of you ignite fire . . . go in the light of your fire and in the sparks you have lit; this has come to you from My Hand . . . ."[295]
- Therefore, when the Men of the Great Assembly [temporarily] captured the Evil Inclination,[296] [the fire of] Gehinom was automatically put out, as per:
  - In the way in which the wicked warm themselves with the fire of the Evil Inclination . . . with each and every warming . . . so burns the fire the Gehinom. It once happened that the Evil Inclination was not to be found in this world . . . at that time the fire of Gehinom was put out and did not burn at all. When the Evil Inclination was reinstated and the wicked of the world started to warm themselves with it, the fires of Gehinom started to burn [again] – for Gehinom does not burn without the power of the warmth of the Evil Inclination of the wicked.[297]
- This is in line with the verse "For He repays man according to his deeds,"[298] that the action itself, whether good or, God forbid, bad, in and of itself is his reward, as above. As per:
  - [That the actual sin itself is what pays a person back in the next world.][299]
  - "The reward of a Mitzvah is a Mitzvah and the reward of a sin is a sin."[300]

---

292 Yechezkel 26:2.
293 See G1:18.
294 Eruvin 19a.
295 Yishayahu 50:11.
296 Yoma 69b.

- וּלְעֻמַּת זֶה "אִמְלְאָה הָחֳרָבָה" (יחזקאל כו, ב), הוּא מֵקִים וּמַגְבִּיר כֹּחוֹת וְחֵילֵי הַטֻּמְאָה וְהַקְּלִפּוֹת, הָרַחֲמָן יִתְבָּרַךְ שְׁמוֹ יַצִּילֵנוּ.
- וּמִשָּׁם מַמְשִׁיךְ גַּם עַל עַצְמוֹ "רוּחַ הַטֻּמְאָה", שֶׁמְּלַפַּפְתּוֹ בְּעֵת עֲשִׂיַּת הֶעָוֹן
- וְאַחַר עֲשׂוֹתוֹ הָרוּחַ טֻמְאָה מִסְתַּלֵּק לִמְקוֹמוֹ, וְהוּא בְּחַיָּיו בְּגֵיהִנָּם מַמָּשׁ, הַמַּקִּיפוֹ בְּעֵת עֲשִׂיַּת הַחֵטְא
- רַק שֶׁאֵינוֹ מַרְגִּישׁ עֲדַיִן עַד אַחַר פְּטִירָתוֹ, שֶׁנִּלְכַּד אָז בָּרֶשֶׁת אֲשֶׁר הֵכִין, הֵן כֹּחוֹת הַטֻּמְאָה וְהַמַּזִּיקִין שֶׁנִּבְרְאוּ מִמַּעֲשָׂיו:
- וְזֶהוּ שֶׁאָמְרוּ רַבּוֹתֵינוּ זִכְרוֹנָם לִבְרָכָה (עירובין יט.) "רְשָׁעִים מַעֲמִיקִין לָהֶם גֵּיהִנָּם", רְצוֹנוֹ לוֹמַר שֶׁהֵן עַצְמָם הַמַּעֲמִיקִים לְעַצְמָם הַגֵּיהִנָּם, וּמַרְחִיבִין אוֹתוֹ וּמַבְעִירִין אוֹתוֹ בְּחֶטְאֵיהֶם, וּכְמוֹ שֶׁכָּתוּב (ישעיה נ, יא) "הֵן כֻּלְּכֶם קוֹדְחֵי אֵשׁ גוֹ', לְכוּ בְּאוּר אֶשְׁכֶם וּבְזִיקוֹת בִּעַרְתֶּם מִיָּדִי הָיְתָה זֹּאת לָכֶם" וְגוֹ':
- לָכֵן כְּשֶׁתִּפְסוּ אַנְשֵׁי כְּנֶסֶת הַגְּדוֹלָה לְהַיֵּצֶר הָרָע, נִכְבָּה אָז גַּם הַגֵּיהִנָּם מֵעַצְמוֹ כְּמוֹ שֶׁכָּתוּב בַּזֹּהַר תְּרוּמָה ק"נ רֵישׁ ע"ב
- כְּגַוְנָא דְּחַיָּבַיָּא מִתְחַמְּמָן בְּנוּרָא דְּיֵצֶר הָרָע כוּ', בְּכָל חִמּוּמָא וְחִמּוּמָא כוּ', הָכִי אִתּוֹקַד נוּרָא דְּגֵיהִנָּם. זִמְנָא חֲדָא לָא אִשְׁתַּכַּח יֵצֶר הָרָע בְּעָלְמָא כוּ', וְכָל הַהוּא זִמְנָא כָּבָה נוּרָא דְּגֵיהִנָּם וְלָא אִתּוֹקַד כְּלָל. אַהֲדַר יֵצֶר הָרָע לְאַתְרֵיהּ, שָׁרוּ חַיָּבֵי עָלְמָא לְאִתְחַמְּמָא בֵּיהּ, שָׁארֵי נוּרָא דְּגֵיהִנָּם לְאִתּוֹקְדָא, דְּהָא גֵּיהִנָּם לָא אִתּוֹקַד אֶלָּא בַּחֲמִימוּ דְּתוּקְפָּא דְּיֵצֶר הָרָע דְּחַיָּבַיָּא:
- זֶהוּ שֶׁאָמַר הַכָּתוּב (איוב לה, יא) "כִּי פֹעַל אָדָם יְשַׁלֶּם לוֹ", שֶׁהַפְּעֻלָּה עַצְמָהּ, הַטּוֹבָה הִיא אִם רָעָה חַס וְשָׁלוֹם, הִיא הִיא עַצְמָהּ הַתַּשְׁלוּמִין שֶׁלּוֹ כַּנַּ"ל
- וְעַיֵּן זֹהַר קֹרַח קע"ז א'.
- וְזֶהוּ שֶׁאָמְרוּ בְּאָבוֹת (פ"ה, מ"ב) "שְּׂכַר מִצְוָה מִצְוָה וּשְׂכַר עֲבֵרָה עֲבֵרָה"

---

297 Zohar II Terumah 150b referring to the incident in Yoma 69b when it once happened that the Men of the Great Assembly temporarily removed the Evil Inclination from the world.
298 Iyov 34:11.
299 Zohar III Korach 177a, which makes this comment on the verse from Iyov 34:11.
300 Mishna Avot 4:2.

- ○ "For [Elokim brings] all actions [to the final judgment]."[301]
- ○ Meaning that it is the action itself which stands and makes an impression as it is, as explained above.
- Therefore, Chazal state that "one who says that God overlooks sin, overlooks his life"[302] – now this appears strange, as even a merciful man is able to overlook things [so surely God who is ultimately merciful would overlook things]?
  - ○ However, it is as stated above, that it is not out of punishment or vengeance, God forbid – but rather "Evil pursues sinners"[303] – it is the very act of sin which is the punishment in and of itself.
  - ○ For since the Creation, God has established the [natural] order of behavior of the worlds, that they are dependent on the level of arousal of man's actions – whether good or bad, God forbid, that the actions of each individual automatically impact his source and root[304]
  - ○ and he is is forced to accept his fate through those powers of impurity which he strengthened with his actions according to the level and type of damage, and through this[305] the damage done to the worlds and his soul will inevitably be rectified
  - ○ or [alternatively this repair can take place] through the power of repentance, which reaches its supernal source in the *World of Repentance* – a world which is completely free and bright, and from there, there is an emanation and bestowal of additional supernal holiness and bright light – to terminate and end all impurity and to restore the worlds to their previous state, and with an additional new light from the World of Repentance which now is bestowed upon them.
- So there is no relevance for *overlooking*, as stated "and all your deeds are recorded in a book,"[306] that is all deeds are automatically inscribed and impact the Supernal Realms.

Rabbi Chaim's Note:
Note 12 – Effect of good is everlasting, impact of bad ceases with punishment

- But "The characteristic of good [is distinctly better than of punishment]"[307]
  - ○ with this distinction being very great

---

301 Kohelet 12:14.
302 Bava Kama 50a. R. Chaim also cites: Talmud Yerushalmi, Shekalim 5:1; Bereishit Rabba, Toldot 67:4; Midrash Tanchuma Ki Tisa 26; Midrash Tehillim 10:3.
303 Mishlei 13:21.
304 Therefore, there is no license to abrogate responsibility for sinning, to say that God will overlook it, as one must understand that by performing a sin a person

- זֶהוּ שֶׁכָּתוּב (קהלת יב, יד) "כִּי אֶת כָּל מַעֲשֶׂה" וְגוֹ'
- רָצָה לוֹמַר הַמַּעֲשֶׂה עַצְמָהּ, הָעוֹמֶדֶת וְנִרְשֶׁמֶת כְּמוֹת שֶׁהִיא, כְּמוֹ שֶׁנִּתְבָּאֵר לְעֵיל:

- וְלָכֵן אָמְרוּ רַבּוֹתֵינוּ זִכְרוֹנָם לִבְרָכָה (בבא קמא נ' ע"א) "כָּל הָאוֹמֵר הַקָּדוֹשׁ בָּרוּךְ הוּא וַתְּרָן הוּא, יִוָּתְרוּ חַיָּיו" כו'. וְכֵן הוּא בִּירוּשַׁלְמִי פֶּרֶק חֲמִישִׁי דִּשְׁקָלִים, וּבְרֵאשִׁית רַבָּה פָּרָשָׁה ס"ז, וּבְתַנְחוּמָא פָּרָשַׁת תִּשָּׂא, וּבְשׁוֹחֵר טוֹב תְּהִלִּים. וְלִכְאוֹרָה יִפָּלֵא, הֲלֹא אֲפִלּוּ אָדָם אִישׁ חֶסֶד מִתְנַהֵג בְּמִדַּת וַתְּרָנוּת.

- אָמְנָם הוּא כְּמוֹ שֶׁכָּתַבְנוּ לְעֵיל, שֶׁאֵינוֹ עַל דֶּרֶךְ הָעֹנֶשׁ וּנְקִימָה חַס וְשָׁלוֹם, רַק "חַטָּאִים תְּרַדֵּף רָעָה" (משלי יג כא), שֶׁהַחֵטְא עַצְמוֹ הוּא עָנְשׁוֹ.

- כִּי מֵעֵת הַבְּרִיאָה קָבַע הוּא יִתְבָּרַךְ שְׁמוֹ כָּל סִדְרֵי הַנְהָגַת הָעוֹלָמוֹת, שֶׁיִּהְיוּ תְּלוּיִים כְּפִי הִתְעוֹרְרוּת מַעֲשֵׂה הָאָדָם, הַטּוֹבִים וְאִם רָעִים חַס וְשָׁלוֹם, שֶׁכָּל מַעֲשָׂיו וְעִנְיָנָיו נִרְשָׁמִים מֵאֲלֵיהֶם, כָּל אֶחָד בִּמְקוֹרוֹ וְשָׁרְשׁוֹ.

- וְהוּא מֻכְרָח לְקַבֵּל דִּינוֹ עַל יְדֵי אוֹתָן כֹּחוֹת הַטֻּמְאָה שֶׁהִגְבִּיר בְּמַעֲשָׂיו, כְּפִי עֵרֶךְ וְעִנְיַן הַפְּגָם. וּבָזֶה מִמֵּילָא יְתַקֵּן הַפְּגָם שֶׁל הָעוֹלָמוֹת וְשֶׁל נַפְשׁוֹ.

- אוֹ עַל יְדֵי כֹּחַ הַתְּשׁוּבָה, שֶׁמַּגַּעַת עַד שָׁרְשָׁהּ הָעֶלְיוֹן, עוֹלַם הַתְּשׁוּבָה, עָלְמָא דְחִירוּ וּנְהִירוּ דְכֹלָּא, וּמִשָּׁם מִתְאַצֵּל וְנִשְׁפַּע תּוֹסֶפֶת קְדֻשָּׁה עֶלְיוֹנָה וְאוֹר מַבְהִיק, לְהָתֵם וּלְכַלּוֹת כָּל טֻמְאָה וּלְתַקֵּן הָעוֹלָמוֹת כְּמִקֹּדֶם, וּבְיִתְרוֹן אוֹר חָדָשׁ מֵעוֹלַם הַתְּשׁוּבָה הַמּוֹפִיעַ עֲלֵיהֶם:

- לָזֹאת, אֵין שַׁיָּךְ וַתְּרָנוּת בָּזֶה. וְזֶהוּ שֶׁאָמְרוּ בְּאָבוֹת (פ"ב, מ"א) "וְכָל מַעֲשֶׂיךָ בַּסֵּפֶר נִכְתָּבִים", הַיְנוּ שֶׁמֵּעַצְמָן נִכְתָּבִים וְנִרְשָׁמִים לְמַעְלָה:

הגהה י"ב

- אָמְנָם מַרְבֶּה מִדָּה טוֹבָה כו'
  - בְּהֶפְרֵשׁ וְיִתְרוֹן רַב.

---

compromises himself. Another perspective of this point is presented in G2:08, where the *punishment* of a sin is described as the natural consequence of the action performed, e.g., of becoming ill after eating bad food or being burnt when playing with fire, etc.

305 I.e., the experience of the difficulties which his sin has caused him in Gehinom.
306 Mishna Avot 2:1.
307 Yoma 76a.

- as the subtle shining and additional holiness added as a result of [a person's] good deeds are eternal and everlasting
  - with his soul enjoying everlasting benefit from them.
- Whereas, the powers of impurity and malevolent forces which were created and increased as a result of his sins
  - they die and automatically cease to be after he has received the corresponding punishment.
  - For the essence of their existence only derives from the damage of sin and the destruction he caused in the holy powers and worlds
  - as it is from this that a small bestowal of life force and sparks of light are drawn to them via lengthy twisted channels [i.e., via a backhanded route], as per the principle of "I shall be filled with her that is laid waste."[308]
  - But once he has received the resulting judgment, "He devoured wealth [i.e., bad in this context] but will expel it"[309]
  - and the life force [of the powers of impurity] will automatically cease.
  - This is why Gehinom is referred to as a leech,[310] as a leech sucks out the bad blood from which it immediately dies [as per ancient medical practices].
  - The same process happens with Gehinom, as mentioned above.

13. *SPEECH* HAS EVEN GREATER IMPACT THAN PHYSICAL ACTION

- Similarly, it is so in relation to the impact on the Supernal Realms of the medium of *speech*.
  - Amos the Prophet, peace be upon him, said "For behold, He forms (Yotzer) mountains and creates (Boreh) winds; (Note 13)[311] He recounts (U'Maggid) to a person what he spoke about"[312]
  - As the Zohar[313] says that the expression of recounting (Hagadah) relates to the secrets of speech.

---

308 Megillah 6a, where the verse from Yechezkel 26:2 is quoted in reference to Rome and Jerusalem where it states that when one is built up, the other will be fallow and vice versa – Rome is Edom which represents evil – so in this context when there is good, there is no evil and vice versa.
309 Iyov 20:15.
310 Avodah Zarah 17a, see Tosafot.
311 **R. Chaim adds Note 13 here.** This note is brought at the end of this chapter and is entitled "Constant Yesh MiYesh and MiAyin, four world levels described."

- כִּי הַצַּחְצָחוֹת וְתוֹסֶפֶת קְדֻשָּׁה שֶׁנִּתּוֹסְפוּ מִמַּעֲשָׂיו הַטּוֹבִים, הֵם נִצְחִיִּים, וְקַיָּמִים לְעוֹלָם
- וְנַפְשׁוֹ מִתְעַדֵּן בָּהֶם תַּעֲנוּג נִצְחִי:
- אֲבָל הַכֹּחוֹת הַטְּמֵאָה וְהַמַּזִּיקִין שֶׁנִּבְרְאוּ וְנִתְרַבּוּ מֵחֲטָאָיו
- אַחַר קִבּוּל כָּל הָעֹנֶשׁ הַנִּקְצָב לוֹ, הֵם מֵתִים וְכָלִים מֵאֲלֵיהֶם.
- כִּי עַצְמוּת חִיּוּתָן הוּא רַק מִפְּגַם הַחֵטְא וְהַהֲרִיסָה שֶׁגָּרַם בַּכֹּחוֹת וְהָעוֹלָמוֹת הַקְּדוֹשִׁים
- שֶׁמִּזֶּה נִמְשַׁךְ לָהֶם שֶׁפַע חִיּוּת וְנִצּוֹצֵי אוֹר מְעַט דֶּרֶךְ צִנּוֹרוֹת אֳרָחוֹת עֲקַלְקַלּוֹת, כְּעִנְיַן "אִמָּלְאָה הָחֳרָבָה" (מגילה ו ע״א)
- וְכֵיוָן שֶׁקִּבֵּל דִּינוֹ עַל יְדֵיהֶם, "חַיִל בָּלַע וַיְקִאֶנּוּ" (איוב כ, טו)
- וְנִפְסַק חִיּוּתָם מִמֵּילָא וְכָלִים מֵאֲלֵיהֶם.
- וְזֶהוּ הָעִנְיָן שֶׁהַגֵּיהִנֹּם נִקְרָא "עֲלוּקָה" (עבודה זרה יז, א) שֶׁהָעֲלוּקָה מוֹצֶצֶת הַדָּמִים הָרָעִים, וּמִזֶּה הִיא מֵתָה תֵּכֶף
- כֵּן הוּא עִנְיַן הַגֵּיהִנֹּם כַּנַּ״ל:

שער א׳ - פרק י״ג

- וְכֵן בְּעִנְיַן הַהִתְעוֹרְרוּת שֶׁלְּמַעְלָה עַל יְדֵי בְּחִינַת "הַדִּבּוּר"
- אָמַר עָמוֹס הַנָּבִיא עָלָיו הַשָּׁלוֹם (ה, יג) "כִּי הִנֵּה יוֹצֵר הָרִים וּבוֹרֵא רוּחַ (הגהה י״ג) וּמַגִּיד לְאָדָם מַה שֵּׂחוֹ".
- כִּי אָמְרוּ בַּזֹּהַר (לך לך פ״ו ב׳, ויחי רל״ד ב׳ ורמ״ט א׳, יתרו פ׳ ע״א, תזריע נ ב׳, שלח

---

312 Amos 4:13.
313 R. Chaim quotes eight references in the Zohar which are expanded below:
Zohar I Lech Lecha 86b quoting Yishayahu 45:19:
- R. Elazar said – I realized that [the Hebrew synonyms of the word "and He spoke"] Vayedaber, Vayaged, Vayomer have different meanings. "*Vayedaber*" relates to a revealed level alone and is not an inner level like those supernal levels, and this is "Who speaks/Dover righteousness." "*Vayaged*" [i.e., Hagadah] hints to an inner supernal level which controls speech, and this is "Who says/*Maggid* upright things."

Zohar I Vayechi 234b:
- ... Vaagida or Vayaged or Vayagidu ... they are the secret of wisdom. Why is this [type of] speech the secret of wisdom? ... because it has a *Gimmel*

G1:13

- This [verse] warns a person
  - that even while he is in this lowly physical world
  - and he doesn't relate to the construction or destruction, God forbid, in the supernal worlds resulting from every single one of his words
  - it may occur to him to say, God forbid – "in what way can trivial speech and talk have any impact whatsoever on the world?"
  - However, he should absolutely know that all of his trivial speech and talk – everything that his lips utter – is not lost and does not go to waste, God forbid.
- As per Chazal:
  - Even the breath of one's mouth has its place, and God does what He does with it, and even a human word and even voice – none of these are in vein and all have their place.[314]
  - Each and every word which comes out of a person's mouth ascends to the Supernal Realms and breaks through the heavens and enters a high place.[315]
  - Each word which a person utters ascends and breaks through heavens and stands in the place that it stands.[316]
- 'As everything which comes out of one's mouth'[317] impacts above and arouses supernal powers – if it is positive speech, it adds power to the powers of holiness, as per:
  - "and I will place My Words in your mouth . . . to plant heavens [and establish earth]."[318]

---

followed by a *Dalet* with no separation . . . and even though a *Yud* sometimes separates between *Gimmel* and *Dalet* this is not a separation . . .

Zohar I Vayechi 249a:
- . . . with *Hagadah* which is the secret of wisdom . . .

Zohar II Yitro 80a quoting Shemot 19:3:
- . . . "and tell/*Vataged* the Children of Israel" to see wisdom . . .

Zohar III Tazria 50b quoting Vayikra 14:35:
- . . . "and the one who owns the house should come and tell/*Vehigid* the Cohen saying – I saw a leprous looking stain on the house" . . . why does it say "Vehigid"? But in every place [this word is used] it relates to speech of wisdom . . .

Zohar III Shelach Lecha 161a:
- . . . Vayagidu – in every place [this word is used] it hints at the secret of wisdom . . .

Zohar Idra Zuta III Haazinu 293a:
- . . . Vayaged – is established as entirely being the secret of wisdom . . .

קס"א א', ובא"ז ריש דף רצ"ג, ובזוהר חדש שיר השירים י"ז ב'), שֶׁלְּשׁוֹן "הַגָּדָה" שֶׁיָּךְ עַל רָזָא דְמִלְּתָא.

○ הִזְהִיר כָּאן אֶת הָאָדָם

□ מֵחֲמַת הֱיוֹתוֹ עַתָּה בְּזֶה הָעוֹלָם הַשָּׁפֵל

□ שֶׁאֵינוֹ רוֹאֶה וּמַשִּׂיג הַבִּנְיָן אוֹ הַהֲרִיסָה, חַס וְשָׁלוֹם, הַנַּעֲשֶׂה לְמַעְלָה בָּהָעוֹלָמוֹת מִכָּל דִּבּוּר וְדִבּוּר שֶׁלּוֹ

□ וְיָכוֹל לְהַעֲלוֹת עַל דַּעְתּוֹ חַס וְשָׁלוֹם לוֹמַר, בַּמֶּה נֶחְשָׁב דִּבּוּר וְשִׂיחָה קַלָּה, שֶׁתִּתְפָּעֵל שׁוּם פְּעֻלָּה וְעִנְיָן בָּעוֹלָם

□ אֲבָל יֵדַע נֶאֱמָנָה שֶׁכָּל דִּבּוּר וְשִׂיחָה קַלָּה שֶׁלּוֹ, לְכָל אֲשֶׁר יִבַּטֵּא בִשְׂפָתָיו, לֹא אִתְאֲבִיד וְאֵינוֹ הוֹלֵךְ לְבַטָּלָה חַס וְשָׁלוֹם:

• וּכְמוֹ שֶׁכָּתוּב

○ בסבא ק' ע"ב, "אֲפִלּוּ הֶבֶל דְּפוּמָא אֲתַר וְדוּכְתָּא אִית לֵיהּ, וְקוּדְשָׁא בְּרִיךְ הוּא עָבִיד מִנֵּיהּ מַה דְּעָבִיד, וַאֲפִלּוּ מִלָּה דְּבַר נָשׁ, וַאֲפִלּוּ קָלָא, לָא הֲוֵי בְּרֵיקַנְיָא, וַאֲתַר וְדוּכְתָּא אִית לְהוּ לְכֹלָּא".

○ וּבְפָרָשַׁת מְצֹרָע נ"ה א', "כָּל מִלָּה וּמִלָּה דְּאַפִּיק בַּר נָשׁ מִפּוּמֵיהּ, סַלְקָא לְעֵלָּא וּבָקְעָא רְקִיעִין וְעָאלַת לְאֲתַר דְּעָאלַת".

○ וּבְרֵישׁ פָּרָשַׁת נָשֹׂא, "דְּהַהוּא מִלָּה דְּאַפִּיק בַּר נָשׁ מִפּוּמֵיהּ, סַלְקָא וּבָקַע רְקִיעִין וְקַיְמָא בְּאֲתַר דְּקַיְמָא":

• שֶׁבְּכָל הַיּוֹצֵא מִפִּיו יַעֲשֶׂה לְמַעְלָה, וּמְעוֹרֵר כֹּחַ עֶלְיוֹן, הֵן בְּדִבּוּר טוֹב מוֹסִיף כֹּחַ בַּכֹּחוֹת הַקְּדוֹשִׁים

○ כְּמוֹ שֶׁכָּתוּב (ישעיה נ"א טז) "וָאָשִׂים דְּבָרַי בְּפִיךָ" וְגו' "לִנְטֹעַ שָׁמַיִם" גו'.

Zohar Chadash II Shir Hashirim 17b:
• ... and here it is written "Hagidah Li," which is the secret of wisdom. ...

314 Zohar II Mishpatim 100b.
315 Zohar III Metzora 55a.
316 Zohar III Naso 121b.
317 Bamidbar 30:3.
318 Yishayahu 51:16.

- There is no word [which comes out of a person's mouth which has no voice and does not ascend upwards] ... and one who utters a holy word from his mouth – a word of Torah – makes a sound with it which ascends upwards and arouses the Holiness of the Supernal King, and it is crowned on His Head, resulting in rejoicing in the Supernal and Lower realms.[319]
- How wondrous and amazing is the concept of spoken holy words of Torah, as all worlds are enlightened with joy, and they are brought with happiness and rejoicing to the supernal holy chambers, and are crowned with holy crowns.[320]
- [A word of Torah which comes out of a mouth ... ascends upwards and much supernal holiness is attached to this word ... and a supernal light emanates and crowns the person who uttered it all day.][321]

• Similarly, it is explained in many places in the Tikkunim that from each instance of speech,[322] of the sound and breath of Torah or prayer
  - many holy angels are created
  - and in contrast, with speech which is not good, God forbid, he creates false heavens and worlds for Samael,[323] The Merciful One should save us
  - causing destruction, God forbid, of the worlds and the arrangements of the Holy Merkava which are related to the source of speech.

• Refer to the Zohar. There is no good or bad [holiness or impurity which does not have a supernal root source ... each spoken word inspires a corresponding word in the supernal worlds ...].[324]

• 'Woe to those people who see but do not know what they see,'[325] as there is no speech which does not have its place, "For the bird of the heavens will take the voice."[326] [As per:]
  - Many thousands of winged beings take hold of the sound and raise it up to the judges who judge it ... whether for good or the opposite, God forbid.[327]
  - There is no word [uttered which does not have a sound which rises upwards], and many angels of destruction connect with that sound raising it and arousing the place of the great abyss ... This impacts greatly on that person! Woe to one who utters bad speech![328]

---

319 Zohar III Emor 105a.
320 Zohar II Vayakhel 217a.
321 Zohar III Kedoshim 85a.
322 The parsing of these words is in line with R. Chaim's comment in GC:05 that speech itself is defined as breath and sound.

- וּבַזֹּהַר אֲמַר קֻדְשָׁא ב"ה א', "דְּלֵית לָךְ מִלָּה וּמִלָּה כו', וּמַאן דְּאַפִּיק מִלָּה קַדִּישָׁא מִפּוּמֵיהּ, מִלָּה דְּאוֹרַיְתָא, אִתְעֲבִיד מִנֵּיהּ קָלָא וְסָלִיק לְעֵילָּא, וְאִתְעָרוּ קַדִּישֵׁי מַלְכָּא עִלָּאָה וּמִתְעַטְּרָן בְּרֵישֵׁיהּ, וּכְדֵין אִשְׁתַּכַּח חֶדְוָתָא לְעֵילָּא וְתַתָּא".
- וְעַיֵּן בְּאֹרֶךְ בְּפָרָשַׁת וַיַּקְהֵל רִי"ז א' נוֹרָאוֹת נִפְלָאוֹת עִנְיַן הַדִּבּוּר שֶׁל מִלִּין קַדִּישִׁין דְּאוֹרַיְתָא, שֶׁכָּל עָלְמִין נְהִירִין מֵחֶדְוָתָא, וּשְׂמָחוֹת וָגִיל תָּבֹאנָה בְּהֵיכְלִין קַדִּישִׁין עִלָּאִין, וּמְעַטְּרָן לְהוּ בְּעַטְרִין קַדִּישִׁין.
- וְעַיֵּן בְּפָרָשַׁת קְדוֹשִׁים פ"ה סוֹף ע"א:
• וְכֵן מְבֹאָר בִּמְקוֹמוֹת רַבּוֹת בַּתִּקּוּנִים, שֶׁמִּכָּל דִּבּוּר וְקוֹל וְהֶבֶל דְּאוֹרַיְתָא אוֹ דִצְלוֹתָא
  - נִבְרָאִים כַּמָּה מַלְאָכִים קְדוֹשִׁים.
  - וּבְהֶפֶךְ, בְּדִבּוּר אֲשֶׁר לֹא טוֹב חַס וְשָׁלוֹם, הוּא בּוֹנֶה רְקִיעִים וְעוֹלָמוֹת שֶׁל שָׁוְא לְסָמָ"ל ר"ל
  - וְגוֹרֵם חַס וְשָׁלוֹם הֲרִיסַת וְחֻרְבַּן הָעוֹלָמוֹת סִדְרֵי הַמֶּרְכָּבָה הַקְּדוֹשָׁה הַנּוֹגְעִים לְשֹׁרֶשׁ הַדִּבּוּר:
• וְעַיֵּן זֹהַר צַו ל"א ב' "דְּהָא לֵית לָךְ טַב וּבִישׁ כו':
• וְאוֹי לָהֶם לַבְּרִיּוֹת שֶׁרוֹאוֹת וְאֵינָן יוֹדְעוֹת מַה הֵם רוֹאוֹת, כִּי אֵין לְךָ דִּבּוּר שֶׁאֵין לוֹ מָקוֹם, "כִּי עוֹף הַשָּׁמַיִם יוֹלִיךְ אֶת הַקּוֹל" (קהלת י, כ)
  - וְכַמָּה אַלְפֵי מָארֵי דְגַדְפֵי דְּאַחֲדִין לָהּ, וְסַלְּקִין לָהּ לְמָארֵי דְמָדְרִין, וְדַיְנִין לָהּ, הֵן לְטוֹב אוֹ לְהֶפֶךְ חַס וְשָׁלוֹם, כְּמוֹ שֶׁכָּתוּב בַּזֹּהַר דַּף צ"ב א'.
  - וּבְפָרָשַׁת קְדוֹשִׁים הַנַּ"ל "וְלֵית לָךְ מִלָּה וּמִלָּה וְכוּ' וְכַמָּה קַסְטוּרִין מִתְחַבְּרִין

---

323 Samael is the Angel of Death, as per e.g., Devarim Rabba VeZot HaBeracha 11:10 which describes how he attempts to take Moshe's soul. He is also the Angel of Edom (Esav), as per the sixth comment of Rashi down the page on Sotah 10b. He is also the accusing angel, as per e.g., Shemot Rabba Bo 18:5.

The Angel of Death is empowered by our negative speech as ultimately death is the mechanism by which the bad impact of this speech is extracted from the soul, as per G1:06:No7.

324 Zohar III Tzav 31b.
325 This expression is taken from Chagiga 12b.
326 Kohelet 10:20.
327 Zohar I Lech Lecha 92a.
328 Zohar III Kedoshim 85a.

- It is written "Why should God be angry with your speech and destroy the action of your hands."[329] As Chazal state:
  - The impact of speech is greater than physical action.[330]
  - One who disguises his speech is as if he practices idol worship.[331]
- This is the meaning of the verse "He recounts (U'Maggid) to a person what he spoke about,"[332] meaning that when a person will stand before God in judgment, God will tell him the secret of words, of how his speech impacted on the supernal worlds, as explained above that the expression of recounting (Hagadah) relates to the secrets of speech.

Rabbi Chaim's Note:
Note 13 – Constant Yesh MiYesh and MiAyin, four world levels described

- According to the [descending] sequence of the four world levels – Atzilut, Beriyah, Yetzirah, and Asiyah – it would have been more appropriate that this verse[333] would have first referred to creation (Beriyah) and only then to formation (Yetzirah)?
- The idea is that Yetzirah is an expression of forming one thing from another which already exists (Yesh MiYesh), whereas Beriyah is an expression of creating something new from nothing (Yesh MiAyin), as agreed by all Scriptural Commentators (and as similarly stated in the Zohar).[334]
- The meaning of this verse is that even now, after Creation, when He appears to us to just be *forming* mountains
  - [via a process of] Yesh MiYesh
  - as the novelty of creation of Yesh MiAyin already happened in the six days of Creation
  - however, in truth, just as it was then [during the six days of Creation], it is also now at each and every moment[335]
  - that [God] creates them and renews them as Yesh MiAyin, through the living spirit which he continuously bestows within them anew out of His Will.

---

329 Kohelet 5:5.
330 Arachin 15a.
331 Sanhedrin 92a. Disguising speech so that one cannot be recognized (Rashi) or that one does not keep one's word (Meiri) – the point being one who speaks in a bad way is like one who worships idols.
332 Amos 4:13.
333 I.e., from Amos 4:13 which is quoted at the beginning of G1:13 as follows: "For behold, He forms (Yotzer) mountains and creates (Boreh) winds; He recounts (U'Maggid) to a person what he spoke about."
334 Zohar Chadash I Bereishit 29b:

עָמֵיהּ דְּהַהוּא קָלָא, עַד דְּסַלְקָא וְאִתְעַר אֲתַר דִּתְהוֹם רַבָּה כוּ', וְכַמָּה מִתְעָרִין עֲלֵיהּ דְּהַהוּא בַּר נָשׁ, וַי לְמָאן דְּאַפִּיק מִלָּה בִּישָׁא מִפּוּמֵיהּ". עַיֵּן שָׁם:

- וּכְתִיב (קהלת ה' ה) "לָמָּה יִקְצֹף הָאֱלֹהִים עַל קוֹלֶךָ וְחִבֵּל אֶת מַעֲשֵׂה יָדֶיךָ".
  ○ וְאָמְרוּ (ערכין טו.) "גָּדוֹל הָאוֹמֵר בְּפִיו מִן הָעוֹשֶׂה מַעֲשֶׂה" כוּ'
  ○ וְאָמְרוּ זִכְרוֹנָם לִבְרָכָה (סנהדרין צ"ב א') "כָּל הַמַּחֲלִיף בְּדִבּוּרוֹ כְּאִלּוּ עוֹבֵד עֲבוֹדַת כּוֹכָבִים":
- זֶהוּ שֶׁכָּתוּב (עמוס ה, יג) "וּמַגִּיד לְאָדָם מַה שֵּׂחוֹ", רָצָה לוֹמַר שֶׁבְּעֵת עָמַד הָאָדָם לָתֵת דִּין וְחֶשְׁבּוֹן לְפָנָיו יִתְבָּרַךְ, אָז הוּא יִתְבָּרַךְ מַגִּיד לוֹ הַסּוֹד, רָזָא דְמִלְּתָא, מַה שֶּׁגָּרַם שִׂיחוֹ לְמַעְלָה בָּעוֹלָמוֹת הָעֶלְיוֹנִים, כְּמוֹ שֶׁנִּתְבָּאֵר לְעֵיל שֶׁלְּשׁוֹן "הַגָּדָה" פֵּרוּשׁוֹ רָזָא דְמִלְּתָא:

הגהה י"ג

- וּלְפִי סֵדֶר הַד' עוֹלָמוֹת אֲצִילוּת, בְּרִיאָה, יְצִירָה, עֲשִׂיָּה, הָיָה רָאוּי לוֹמַר תְּחִלָּה לְשׁוֹן בְּרִיאָה וְאַחַר כָּךְ יְצִירָה:
- אָמְנָם הָעִנְיָן, כִּי לְשׁוֹן "יְצִירָה" פֵּרוּשׁוֹ הִצְטַיְּרוּת דָּבָר יֵשׁ מִיֵּשׁ, וּלְשׁוֹן "בְּרִיאָה" פֵּרוּשׁוֹ דָּבָר מְחֻדָּשׁ יֵשׁ מֵאַיִן, כְּמוֹ שֶׁהִסְכִּימוּ כָּל הַפַּשְׁטָנִים (וְכֵן אָמְרוּ בְּזֹהַר חָדָשׁ בְּרֵאשִׁית כ"ט ב'):
- ז"ש אַף עַל פִּי שֶׁנִּרְאָה לָנוּ שֶׁעַתָּה אַחַר הַבְּרִיאָה הוּא רַק "יוֹצֵר" הָרִים יֵשׁ מִיֵּשׁ
  ○ כִּי הַהִתְחַדְּשׁוּת יֵשׁ מֵאַיִן כְּבָר הָיָה בְּשֵׁשֶׁת יְמֵי קֶדֶם
  ○ אֲבָל הָאֱמֶת, כְּמֵאָז כֵּן גַּם עַתָּה בְּכָל עֵת וָרֶגַע
  ○ הוּא "בּוֹרֵא" אוֹתָם וּמְחַדְּשָׁם יֵשׁ מֵאַיִן, עַל יְדֵי חִיּוּת הָרוּחַ שֶׁמַּשְׁפִּיעַ בָּהֶם מְחֻדָּשׁ בִּרְצוֹנוֹ יִתְבָּרַךְ כָּל רֶגַע

- When God created His world, He created them [the original text switches to plural] from Ayin/nothing and brought them into existence and made them tangible. Any place where you find [the expression] Boreh/creates, it relates to something created from Ayin/nothing which was brought into existence.

335   See G1:02.

- This is similarly stated by Chazal "He is the *Yotzer*, He is the *Boreh*"[336] and this is as mentioned above.[337]
- 'From the origin of the matter the inquirer will understand'[338] simply, the concept of the four world [levels] which are called Atzilut, Beriyah, Yetzirah, and Asiyah.
- For it is known that the worlds gradually cascaded down from level to level
  - and the more it cascaded and descended downwards, it became more unrefined/materialistic.
  - And the general world entities are grouped into four separate groupings which relate to their level (excluding the very refined/extremely subtle supernal shining [lights] which are too refined to even be described as being part of Atzilut).
- The first world [level grouping] of the four levels which emanated from Him which we are able to give a name to is called Atzilut.
  - Aztilut has two meanings:
    - An expression of connection, as in *Etzlo* (*next to him*)
    - and an expression of spiritual emanation, as per "and part of the spirit *Vayatzel* (*emanated*)."[339]
    - (Also like "Atzilei Yadav"[340] [meaning *armpits*], which are both permanently *connected* to the body and also the beginning of the *emanation* of the hands from the body.)
  - For the world of Atzilut is totally Divine
    - as per Zohar, "He and His Causes are One"[341]
    - as per Etz Chaim.[342]
  - It is called Ayin [i.e., non-physical],[343] as no intellect is capable of grasping the essence of Atzilut and its connection, as He and His Life Force and His Causes are One.

---

336 Mishna Avot 4:22.
337 I.e., in the same sequence as the verse quoted.
338 Based on Daniel 9:25.
339 Bamidbar 11:25, relating to the spirit of Moshe which emanated to the 70 elders.
340 Yechezkel 13:18.
341 Tikkunei Zohar Introduction 3b, where His Causes relate to His Middot within Atzilut. A lengthier quotation is found in G3:04.
342 R. Chaim quotes the following sources from Etz Chaim. Note that R. Chaim also quotes this identical set of sources from Etz Chaim in G3:04 and they have all been expanded there:
- Etz Chaim Shaar 42, Shaar Derushei Atzilut, Beriyah, Yetzirah, and Asiyah Chap. 5 (see V2:14, p. 676)

- וְכֵן אָמְרוּ בְּאָבוֹת (ה, כב) "הוּא הַיּוֹצֵר הוּא הַבּוֹרֵא", וְהוּא כַּנַּ"ל:
- וּמִמּוֹצָא דָּבָר יַשְׂכִּיל הַמֵּעַיֵּן עַל פִּי פָּשׁוּט עִנְיַן הד' עוֹלָמוֹת שֶׁנִּקְרְאוּ אֲצִילוּת, בְּרִיאָה, יְצִירָה, עֲשִׂיָּה:
- כִּי מוּדַעַת שֶׁהָעוֹלָמוֹת נִשְׁתַּלְשְׁלוּ בְּהַדְרָגָה מִמַּדְרֵגָה לְמַדְרֵגָה
- וְכָל שֶׁנִּשְׁתַּלְשֵׁל וְיָרַד יוֹתֵר לְמַטָּה נִתְעַבָּה יוֹתֵר.
- וּכְלָלוּת הָעוֹלָמוֹת הֵם נֶחְלָקִים לד' חֲלוּקוֹת שׁוֹנִים בְּעֵרֶךְ מַעֲלָתָם (לְבַד הַצַּחְצָחוֹת הָעֶלְיוֹנִים שֶׁאֵין לְכַנּוֹתָם אֲפִלּוּ בְּשֵׁם אֲצִילוּת:
- וְעוֹלָם הָרִאשׁוֹן — מֵהד' שֶׁהֶאֱצִיל הוּא יִתְבָּרַךְ שְׁמוֹ, אֲשֶׁר אָנוּ יְכוֹלִין לְכַנּוֹתוֹ בְּשֵׁם, נִקְרָא אֲצִילוּת.
- וַאֲצִילוּת פִּי שְׁנַיִם לוֹ
  - לְשׁוֹן חִבּוּר, כְּמוֹ "אֶצְלוֹ"
  - וּלְשׁוֹן הִתְפַּשְּׁטוּת רוּחָנִי, כְּמוֹ (במדבר יא, כה) "וַיָּאצֶל מִן הָרוּחַ"
  - (וּכְמוֹ (יחזקאל יג, יח) "אַצִּילֵי יָדַי", שֶׁהֵם מְחֻבָּרִים בַּגּוּף תָּמִיד וְגַם הַתְחָלַת הִתְפַּשְּׁטוּת יָדָיו.)
- כִּי עוֹלָם הָאֲצִילוּת הוּא הַכֹּל אֱלֹקוּת גָּמוּר
  - כְּמוֹ שֶׁכָּתוּב בְּהַקְדָּמַת הַתִּקּוּנִים, בָּאֲצִילוּת "אִיהוּ וְגַרְמוֹהִי חַד" כו'
  - וּבְעֵץ חַיִּים שַׁעַר דְּרוּשֵׁי אבי"ע פֶּרֶק ז', וּבְרֵישׁ שַׁעַר צִיּוּר עוֹלָמוֹת אבי"ע בְּהַקְדָּמַת הרח"ו, וּבְשַׁעַר הִשְׁתַּלְשְׁלוּת הי' סְפִירוֹת פֶּרֶק ג', וּבְשַׁעַר הַצֶּלֶם פֶּרֶק א', וּבְשַׁעַר הַשֵּׁמוֹת פֶּרֶק א', וּבְשַׁעַר סֵדֶר אבי"ע פֶּרֶק ב', וְרֵישׁ פֶּרֶק ג', עַיֵּן שָׁם.
- וְנִקְרָא "אַיִן", דְּלֵית מַחֲשָׁבָה תְּפִיסָא מַהוּת הַהִתְאַצְּלוּת וְהֶחָבוּר, דְּאִיהוּ וְחַיּוֹהִי וְגַרְמוֹהִי חַד:

- Etz Chaim Shaar 43, Shaar Tziyur Olamot Atzilut, Beriyah, Yetzirah, Asiyah in the introduction of R. Chaim Vital
- Etz Chaim Shaar 2, Shaar Hishtalshelut HaYud Sefirot Chap. 3
- Etz Chaim Shaar 26, Shaar Hatzelem Chap. 1
- Etz Chaim Shaar 44, Shaar Hashemot Chap. 1
- Etz Chaim Shaar 47, Shaar Seder Atzilut, Beriyah, Yetzirah, Asiyah Chap. 1 and the beginning of Chap. 2 (see V2:14, p. 676).

343 The concept of Ayin is developed in G3:02.

- The second world [level group]:
  - This cascades and descends down a further level from the first world [level]
  - where its own existence is perceived, albeit in a very small measure, such that it can be called Yesh [i.e., the physical]
  - and this is the Yesh MiAyin
  - therefore it is called Beriyah/Creation, and as I explained above.
- The third world [level group]:
  - This cascades down in sequence of levels from the second world [level]
  - it is less refined/more materialistic
  - its existence is more perceivable
  - it is Yesh MiYesh [i.e., something physical formed from something physical]
  - therefore it is described as Yetzirah/Formation like one who forms material [from something else that already exists], which is Yesh MiYesh.
- The fourth world [level group]:
  - This is the completion of the work of all worlds preceding it and is their ultimately good rectification
  - which God intended in terms of the entire Creation.
  - This [level] is this lowest [physical] world which is the residence of man who controls the worlds with the power of his actions.
  - As per Chazal:
    - "Elokim saw all that he made and behold, it was very good," that "it was very/Meod good" means "Man/Adam was good."[344]
    - R. Shmuel bar Ami said, from the outset of the Creation of the Universe, God desired to make a partnership with the lowest world level.[345]
    - Similarly, [R. Ami said, God desired that just like he has a dwelling place in the supernal worlds, similarly he should have a dwelling place in this lowest world].[346]
    - Similarly, [R. Shmuel bar Nachman said, When God created the Universe, He desired to have a dwelling place in the lowest world level].[347]
  - Therefore, [this world level] is called Asiyah (the World of Action)
    - which relates to the rectification of a matter

---

[344] Bereishit Rabba Bereishit 8:5 and 9:12 quoting Bereishit 1:31, where the words of *Meod* and *Adam* are made up of the same letters and considered equivalent and that it was therefore the creation of Man which was the epitome of Creation.

- וְעוֹלָם הַשֵּׁנִי
  ○ נִשְׁתַּלְשֵׁל וְיָרַד מַדְרֵגָה יוֹתֵר מֵהָרִאשׁוֹן
  ○ שֶׁמְּשַׁגֵּג עַל כָּל פָּנִים קְצָת מְצִיאוּתוֹ שֶׁיּוּכַל לְהִקָּרֵא יֵשׁ
  ○ וְהוּא הַיֵּשׁ מֵאַיִן
  ○ לָכֵן נִקְרָא בְּשֵׁם "בְּרִיאָה", וּכְמוֹ שֶׁכָּתַבְתִּי לְעֵיל:

- וְעוֹלָם הַג'
  ○ נִשְׁתַּלְשֵׁל בְּסֵדֶר הַמַּדְרֵגוֹת מֵהָעוֹלָם הַשֵּׁנִי
  ○ וְנִתְעַבָּה יוֹתֵר
  ○ שֶׁמְּצִיאוּתוֹ מֻשָּׂג יוֹתֵר
  ○ וְהוּא הַיֵּשׁ מִיֵּשׁ
  ○ וְלָכֵן מְתֹאָר בְּשֵׁם "יְצִירָה", כְּמוֹ יוֹצֵר חֶמֶר שֶׁהוּא יֵשׁ מִיֵּשׁ:

- וְעוֹלָם הַד'
  ○ הוּא גְּמַר מְלֶאכֶת כָּל הָעוֹלָמוֹת שֶׁקְּדָמוּהוּ, וְתִקּוּנָם עַל תַּכְלִית הַטּוֹב הָאֲמִתִּי
  ○ שֶׁכֵּוֵּן הוּא יִתְבָּרַךְ שְׁמוֹ בְּעִנְיַן כְּלַל הַבְּרִיאָה כֻּלָּהּ
  ○ וְהוּא זֶה הָעוֹלָם הַתַּחְתּוֹן שֶׁבּוֹ דִּירַת הָאָדָם הַמַּנְהִיג הָעוֹלָמוֹת בְּכֹחַ מַעֲשָׂיו.
  ○ וּכְמוֹ
    □ שֶׁכָּתוּב (בראשית א, לא) "וַיַּרְא אֱלֹהִים אֶת כָּל אֲשֶׁר עָשָׂה וְהִנֵּה טוֹב מְאֹד",
    וְאָמְרוּ בִּבְרֵאשִׁית רַבָּה פָּרָשָׁה ח', "וְהִנֵּה טוֹב מְאֹד" — אָדָם, וְכֵן הוּא שָׁם בְּפָרָשָׁה ט'.
    □ וּבְפָרָשָׁה ג' שָׁם, "אָמַר רשב"א מִתְּחִלַּת בְּרִיָּתוֹ שֶׁל עוֹלָם נִתְאַוָּה הַקָּדוֹשׁ בָּרוּךְ הוּא לַעֲשׂוֹת שֶׁתָּפוּס בַּתַּחְתּוֹנִים".
    □ וְכֵן הוּא בְּתַנְחוּמָא בְּפָרָשַׁת בְּחֻקֹּתַי
    □ וּפָרָשַׁת נָשֹׂא, עַיֵּן שָׁם.
  ○ לָכֵן נִקְרָא "עֲשִׂיָּה"
    □ הַמּוֹרָה עַל תִּקּוּן הַדָּבָר

---

345 Bereishit Rabba Bereishit 3:9.
346 Midrash Tanchuma (Warsaw), Bechukotai 3.
347 Midrash Tanchuma (Warsaw), Naso 16.

- as per the expression used in "and he gave it to the lad and he hurried *Laasot* it"[348] and many other similar examples.[349]
- Similarly, [R. Tanchum said], Asiyah is a rectification of something such that it becomes improved compared to its former state as in "and David *made* a name."[350]

14. *THOUGHT* HAS EVEN GREATER IMPACT, THREE LEVELS OF SOUL AND EXPRESSION

- Similarly, in connection with the impact on the Supernal Realms through the medium of *thought*. King David, peace be upon him, said "He who fashions their hearts together, who understands *El* all their deeds"[351] – the verse should have said "who understands all their deeds" – [the use of the extra word El] was explained above in G1:12 to relate to the medium of action. It is also possible to explain it as relating to the medium of thought.
- That is, it is possible for two different people to perform the same sin but their punishment will not be the same – since:
  - Either, one of them has greater intellectual abilities and perception than his fellow as a result of his soul root coming from a higher place than that of his fellow, and the resulting punishment is according to the damage caused in the Supernal Realms, with the damage of each individual reaching his soul root.
    - As per:
      - One who does damage in the lower realms, does damage in the Supernal Realms – to the place from which his soul is hewn.[352]
      - When a person sins, the sin rises to the place from which the person's soul is hewn according to his level . . . and the magnitude of his punishment is according to his level.[353]
      - As per the Arizal.[354]

---

348 Bereishit 18:7, i.e., where "Laasot" means to prepare it to make it fit for consumption/usage.

349 R. Yisrael Salanter in his Even Yisrael, Derush 3, p. 12 of the 1883 edition, says the following:
- R. Chaim Volozhin explains the verse [Bereishit 2:3, in relation to God's resting on Shabbat after creating the world] "as on that [day] He rested from His work which He created – Laasot/to make." The word "Laasot" here is not understood at all and [R. Chaim] said that the meaning of "Laasot" is "to rectify" as in "and he hurried Laasot it" . . . as from after the Creation and onwards, God handed it over to Man that he be the one who "makes,"

מִלְּשׁוֹן (בראשית יח, ז) "וַיִּתֵּן אֶל הַנַּעַר וַיְמַהֵר לַעֲשׂוֹת אוֹתוֹ", וְהַרְבֵּה כַּיּוֹצֵא.

וְכֵן אָמְרוּ בְּזֹהַר חָדָשׁ שָׁם, עֲשִׂיָּה הוּא תִּקּוּן הַדָּבָר בְּגִדּוּל וּמַעֲלָה מִכְּמוֹת שֶׁהָיָה כד"א (שמו"ב ח, יג) "וַיַּעַשׂ דָּוִד שֵׁם", ע"כ:

שער א' - פרק י"ד

וְכֵן עַל הַהִתְעוֹרְרוּת שֶׁלְּמַעְלָה עַל יְדֵי בְּחִינַת "הַמַּחֲשָׁבָה". אָמַר דָּוִד הַמֶּלֶךְ עָלָיו הַשָּׁלוֹם (תהלים לג) "הַיּוֹצֵר יַחַד לִבָּם הַמֵּבִין אֶל כָּל מַעֲשֵׂיהֶם", וְהָיָה צָרִיךְ לוֹמַר "הַמֵּבִין כָּל מַעֲשֵׂיהֶם", וּלְמַעְלָה בְּפֶרֶק י"ב פֵּרַשְׁנוּ עַל בְּחִינַת "הַמַּעֲשֶׂה". וְיֵשׁ לְפָרְשׁוּ גַּם כֵּן עַל בְּחִינַת "הַמַּחֲשָׁבָה":

וְהוּא, כִּי יִתָּכֵן כִּי שְׁנֵי אֲנָשִׁים עוֹשִׂין עֲבֵרָה אַחַת, וְעִם כָּל זֶה אֵין עָנְשָׁן שָׁוֶה:

אוֹ מִפְּנֵי שֶׁהָאֶחָד שִׂכְלוֹ וְהַשָּׂגָתוֹ יוֹתֵר גְּדוֹלָה מֵחֲבֵרוֹ, מִצַּד שֶׁשֹּׁרֶשׁ נִשְׁמָתוֹ מִמָּקוֹם גָּבוֹהַּ וְעֶלְיוֹן מִשֶּׁל חֲבֵרוֹ, וְהָעֹנֶשׁ הוּא כְּפִי עִנְיַן הַפְּגָם שֶׁגָּרַם לְמַעְלָה, וְהַפְּגָם שֶׁל כָּל אֶחָד מַגִּיעַ עַד שֹׁרֶשׁ נִשְׁמָתוֹ.

כְּמוֹ שֶׁכָּתוּב

בַּתִּקּוּנִים סוֹף תמ"ג, "מַאן דְּפָגַם לְתַתָּא, פָּגִים לְעֵלָּא, לַאֲתַר דְּאִתְגְּזַר נִשְׁמָתֵיהּ".

וְשָׁם בת"ע קכ"ד א', "וְכַד בַּר נָשׁ עָבִיד חוֹבִין, כְּפוּם הַהוּא בַּר נָשׁ הָכִי סָלִיק חוֹבֵיהּ לַאֲתַר דְּאִתְגְּזַר נִשְׁמָתֵיהּ כו', וְעוֹנְשֵׁיהּ אִיהוּ סַגִּי כְּפוּם דַּרְגֵּיהּ"

וְכֵן כָּתַב הָאֲרִיזַ"ל בְּשַׁעַר הַיִּחוּדִים רֵישׁ תִּקּוּן עֲוֹנוֹת, וּבִפְרִי עֵץ חַיִּים בְּהַקְדָּמַת שַׁעַר הַשַּׁבָּת פֶּרֶק א' וּבַגִּלְגּוּלִים.

---

and He handed over the keys of the arrangement of the worlds to him, that he should maintain or destroy them according to his actions....

350 Zohar Chadash I Bereishit 29b quoting 2 Shmuel 8:13, i.e., David became famous after his action of battle.
351 Tehillim 33:15.
352 Tikkunei Zohar Tikkun 43 82b.
353 Tikkunei Zohar Tikkun 70 124a.
354 Shaar HaYichudim at the beginning of Tikkun Avonot:
- The general concept of repentance/Teshuva is the returning of the *Hey* (Tashuv *Hey*). This idea is:
- You should know that man is made up of all of the worlds and even if he

- There is no comparison between one who soils the King's courtyard and one who soils the King's palace, and how much more so the King's throne, royal clothes, and even his crown.
- Even though when the world level is higher, sin has less ability to do damage and have an impact, nevertheless the punishment is greater.
  - For one responsible for polishing the King's crown, will nevertheless be held incomparably more culpable for leaving even a little dust on it – than one who is responsible for cleaning the King's courtyard and leaves a large pile of refuse in it.
  - Therefore, there are infinite levels of 'God's true judgment'[355] in distinguishing punishment, according to each person's level of damage to the source of his soul from whichever world it was hewn.

---

only merits that his Nefesh is from the world of Action/Asiyah, he is nevertheless enabled to receive all of them.
- But the difference [between the level of soul source] is
  - with one who merits a Nefesh from the world level of Asiyah
  - his soul is comprised from 248 limbs and 365 sinews – this being a general principle
  - and when he sins he damages the limb, of the level of Nefesh, corresponding to the 248 or the 365.
  - But when his Nefesh is from [a higher world level] of Yetzirah, Beriyah or Atzilut then
  - according to the greatness of his Nefesh, so too is the extent of the damage of his sin.
- This is in man's control according to his actions, and he similarly will need to repent [on a correspondingly higher level if his Nefesh is sourced in the higher world levels of] Atzilut or Beriyah.
- This is the meaning of "He forms the spirit of man within him" (Zecharia 12:1).
- Therefore, when Adam sinned, his damage Above was extensive reflecting the greatness of his soul which was made up of all of the worlds.
- Therefore, every righteous and pious individual has an Evil Inclination which proportionally matches his greatness, as per Chazal: "One who is greater than his fellow, his Evil Inclination is also greater" (Sukkah 52a).
- "For God has made one to correspond to the other" (Kohelet 7:14) and just as there are seven chambers in the world levels of Beriyah, Yetzirah, and Asiyah – so too they are [correspondingly] in the Kelipot . . . [the Arizal continues to say that the required level of repentance corresponds to the level of the sin as per the level of the source of the soul].

□ וְאֵינוֹ דוֹמֶה הַמְטַנֵּף חֲצַר הַמֶּלֶךְ לִמְטַנֵּף פַּלְטִין שֶׁל מֶלֶךְ, וְכָל שֶׁכֵּן הַכִּסֵּא אוֹ בִּגְדֵי תִפְאַרְתּוֹ, וְכָל שֶׁכֵּן הַכֶּתֶר.

□ וְאַף שֶׁכָּל עוֹלָם שֶׁהוּא יוֹתֵר גָּבוֹהַּ וְנַעֲלֶה, אֵין בְּכֹחַ הֶעָוֹן לִפְעוֹל בּוֹ פְּגָם וְרֹשֶׁם גָּדוֹל כָּל כָּךְ, עִם כָּל זֶה עָנְשׁוֹ גָּדוֹל יוֹתֵר.

□ כִּי מִי שֶׁהוּא מְמֻנֶּה לְטַהֵר וּלְצַחְצֵחַ כִּתְרוֹ שֶׁל מֶלֶךְ, אִם הִשְׁאִיר עָלָיו אֲפִלּוּ אָבָק מְעַט לָבָד, אֵין עֲרוֹךְ וְדִמְיוֹן לְעָנְשׁוֹ, לְעֹנֶשׁ הַמְמֻנֶּה לְנַקּוֹת חֲצַר הַמֶּלֶךְ אַף אִם הִשְׁאִיר אוֹ הִנִּיחַ בְּתוֹכוֹ הַרְבֵּה רֶפֶשׁ וְטִיט.

□ וְלָכֵן רַבּוּ מִשְׁפְּטֵי ה' אֱמֶת, בְּשִׁנּוּי חִלּוּקֵי הָעֳנָשִׁים לְאֵין קֵץ, לְכָל אֶחָד כְּפִי מַדְרֵגַת הַפְּגָם בְּשֹׁרֶשׁ נִשְׁמָתוֹ, מֵאֵיזֶה עוֹלָם חֻצְבָה:

Pri Etz Chaim in Chap. 1 of the introduction to Shaar HaShabbat:
- [The Arizal explains that the levels of a person's soul are elevated on Shabbat in such a way that an empty gap remains in place of the lowermost levels which were elevated and that therefore actions which are forbidden to be performed on Shabbat can cause serious damage by penetrating into this empty gap. This is in contrast to those same actions performed on regular weekdays] . . . however, one who performs work on Shabbat causes Kelipot to be entered into the realm of holiness, reaching the source of his soul which is suspended there, and therefore, it is fitting for him to be liable to the death penalty because he causes the entry of Kelipot to defile God's Sanctuary, God forbid . . . [See p. 288, fn. 543, which expands on this idea.]

Sefer HaGilgulim at the beginning of Chap. 2
- . . . and when the souls and the Shechina are manifest within them [i.e., the powers of impurity/Kelipot/Chitzonim] they certainly draw a great bestowal
- and therefore their entire objective is to cause Israel to sin to bring their souls, together with the Shechina, to be within them
- and it is certainly the case that the greater the level of the holiness of the soul, so too is the level of impact of the bestowal that they can draw through it
- and therefore, the greater the preciousness of the level of the soul, [the Chitzonim] correspondingly plan to cause it to sin and to enter into the depths of the Kelipot.
- Therefore, most of the Kelipot are with the Torah Sages, and therefore Chazal say that Torah Sages "are forbidden to go out alone at night" (Berachot 43b), and this is also the concept relating to "One who is greater than his fellow, his Evil Inclination is also greater" (Sukkah 52a).

355 Tehillim 19:10.

- Or – the punishment of the two people is not the same due to their different thoughts at the time of performing the sin, with the damage also impacting the worlds according to the thought at the time of its performance.
  - If one attaches more thought to the sin, then he is certainly fitting for a far greater punishment, as the damage then, God forbid, reaches higher worlds.
  - It is for this reason that one who unintentionally sins has a lighter punishment than one who sins intentionally, and therefore Chazal say: "Thoughts of sin are worse than the sin itself."[356]
  - This is as it is written: "He who fashions their hearts together" (that is He sees the thoughts of their hearts together),[357] "who understands *El* all their deeds" which means that the Supernal Creator sees and understands the thoughts of their hearts which are attached to their actions and judges each person according to the thoughts of his heart at the time the sin was performed.
  - Similarly, King Shlomo said: "For God will judge *all* [of a] deed, on *all* that is hidden . . . ,"[358] meaning that apart from the punishment for the act of the sin actually performed, God will, when passing judgment, additionally take into account *all* of the deed to additionally include, within the judgment, the hidden thoughts of how and in what way the action was done.
  - Similarly, it says "God founded the *earth* with wisdom, He established the *heavens* with understanding and through His knowledge the *depths* were cleaved."[359]
    - This [verse] generally incorporates all the worlds – *earth* relating to intermediate worlds, *heavens* relating to supernal worlds, *depths* relating to the lower worlds
    - and shortly thereafter the verse continues "My child, do not let them *stray* your *eyes*":[360]
      - The expression *eyes* [/sight] as found in many Scriptural sources relates to thought, as in "and my heart saw [much wisdom and knowledge],"[361] and "The eyes of a wise person are in his head."[362]
      - The expression *straying* is found in the Mishna and expresses

---

356 Yoma 29a.
357 As per Rosh Hashana 18a commenting on the verse Tehillim 33:15.
358 Kohelet 12:14.
359 Mishlei 3:19–20.
360 Mishlei 3:21.

◦ גַּם לֹא יִהְיֶה שָׁוֶה עֹנֶשׁ שְׁנֵי הָאֲנָשִׁים, מִטַּעַם שֶׁלֹּא הָיְתָה מַחֲשֶׁבֶת שְׁנֵיהֶם שָׁוָה בְּעֵת עֲשִׂיַּת הֶעָוֹן, וְהַפְּגָם נִמְשָׁךְ בָּעוֹלָמוֹת גַּם לְפִי עִנְיַן הַמַּחֲשָׁבָה בִּשְׁעַת הָעֲשִׂיָּה.

◦ וְאִם הָאֶחָד הִדְבִּיק יוֹתֵר מַחֲשַׁבְתּוֹ לְהָעֲבֵירָה, וַדַּאי שֶׁהוּא רָאוּי לְעֹנֶשׁ יוֹתֵר גָּדוֹל, כִּי אָז הַפְּגָם מַגִּיעַ חַס וְשָׁלוֹם לְעוֹלָמוֹת יוֹתֵר עֶלְיוֹנִים.

◦ וּמִטַּעַם זֶה הַשּׁוֹגֵג עָנְשׁוֹ יוֹתֵר קַל מֵהַמֵּזִיד. וְלָכֵן אָמְרוּ (יומא כ״ט) שֶׁהִרְהוּרֵי עֲבֵירָה קָשִׁין מֵעֲבֵירָה.

◦ זֶהוּ שֶׁכָּתוּב (תהלים שם) "הַיּוֹצֵר יַחַד לִבָּם" (הַיְנוּ שֶׁרוֹאֶה יַחַד מַחְשְׁבוֹת לִבָּם כְּמוֹ שֶׁפֵּרְשׁוּ רַבּוֹתֵינוּ זִכְרוֹנָם לִבְרָכָה בְּמַסֶּכֶת ראש הַשָּׁנָה י״ח א') "הַמֵּבִין אֶל כָּל מַעֲשֵׂיהֶם", רָצָה לוֹמַר שֶׁהַיּוֹצֵר עֶלְיוֹן יִתְבָּרַךְ שְׁמוֹ רוֹאֶה וּמֵבִין מַחְשְׁבוֹת לִבָּם הַמִּצְטָרֵף אֶל מַעֲשֵׂיהֶם, וְדָן אֶת כָּל אֶחָד כְּפִי עִנְיַן מַחֲשֶׁבֶת לִבּוֹ שֶׁהָיָה בְּעֵת עֲשִׂיַּת הֶעָוֹן.

◦ וְכֵן אָמַר שְׁלֹמֹה הַמֶּלֶךְ עָלָיו הַשָּׁלוֹם (קהלת יב, יד) "כִּי אֶת כָּל מַעֲשֶׂה הָאֱלֹהִים יָבִא בְמִשְׁפָּט עַל כָּל נֶעְלָם" גו'. רָצָה לוֹמַר שֶׁמִּלְּבַד הָעֹנֶשׁ עַל מַעֲשֵׂה הֶעָוֹן בְּפֹעַל, עוֹד יָבִיא הָאֱלֹהִים יִתְבָּרַךְ שְׁמוֹ בְּמִשְׁפָּט אֶת 'כָּל מַעֲשֶׂה', לְגַלְגֵּל עָלֶיהָ לְדוּנָהּ גַּם עַל הַמַּחֲשָׁבָה הַנֶּעְלָמָה, אֵיךְ וּבְאֵיזֶה אֹפֶן הָיְתָה בְּעֵת הָעֲשִׂיָּה.

◦ וְכֵן אָמַר (משלי ג' יט) "ה' בְּחָכְמָה יָסַד אֶרֶץ כּוֹנֵן שָׁמַיִם בִּתְבוּנָה בְּדַעְתּוֹ תְּהוֹמוֹת נִבְקָעוּ".

◦ כָּלַל כָּאן דֶּרֶךְ כְּלָל אֶת כָּל הָעוֹלָמוֹת, 'אֶרֶץ' — הוּא עוֹלָם הָאֶמְצָעִי, 'שָׁמַיִם' — הֵם כְּלַל הָעוֹלָמוֹת הָעֶלְיוֹנִים, 'וּתְהוֹמוֹת' — הֵם כְּלַל הַתַּחְתּוֹנִים.

◦ וְאָמַר אַחַר זֶה "בְּנִי אַל יָלֻזוּ מֵעֵינֶיךָ"

▽ וּלְשׁוֹן "עַיִן" מָצִינוּ כַּמָּה פְּעָמִים בַּמִּקְרָא נֶאֱמַר עַל עִנְיַן הַמַּחֲשָׁבָה, כְּמוֹ שֶׁכָּתוּב (קהלת א, טז) "וְלִבִּי רָאָה" גו'. "הֶחָכָם עֵינָיו בְּרֹאשׁוֹ" (שם ב, יד)

▽ "וְיָלֻזוּ" — מָצִינוּ בַּמִּשְׁנָה שֶׁהוּא לְשׁוֹן עַקְמוּמִית, כְּמוֹ "נָלוֹז הוּא

---

361 Kohelet 1:16.
362 Kohelet 2:14.

warped thinking, as per "he is warped and crooked with His Father in Heaven above him."[363]
- The meaning of these verses is: My child, please have mercy on the precious worlds which were created with wisdom, understanding, and knowledge, and beware not to cause them all, God forbid, to be warped and corrupted with [even] a single inappropriate thought, God forbid.

- These three levels of *action*, *speech*, and *thought*[364] directly correspond to the general inner levels of man['s soul] which are Nefesh, Ruach, and Neshama:
  - *Action* comes from the level of Nefesh, as written "and the *Nefesh* which will *do*"[365] and "the *Nefashot doing* so"[366] and many similar verses.
    - "For the blood is the *Nefesh*"[367] – the Nefesh resides and is clothed within the blood of man
    - therefore it is principally resident in the liver, which is all blood
    - and the blood is distributed throughout all the specific parts of the limbs of the body – the tools of action – it being that which gives them their movement and arousal so that they are enabled to act and perform that which is within their power.
    - If the distribution of blood is held back from reaching a particular limb, that limb will dry out, become immobile and unable to function, and it is a dead limb.
  - *Speech* comes from the level of Ruach, as it is written "*Ruach* of God speaks within me"[368] and "and with the *Ruach* of his lips."[369]
    - As Onkelos translates the verse "and the man became a *Nefesh Chaya*"[370] as "a speaking Ruach."
    - It is similarly visibly evident that each spoken word is expressed from a person's mouth via *Ruach* and the *wind* of speech.
    - The principal residence of Ruach is in the heart, as the principal part and starting point for Ruach/spirit and the wind of speech, rises from the heart.
  - *Thought* comes from the level of Neshama, as it is that which teaches a person knowledge and understanding of the Holy Torah.
    - Therefore, its principal residence is within the brain, the tool of thought.
    - It is the most superior of these [levels].

---

363 Mishna Kilayim 9:8 with reference to Shatnez.
364 As described in G1:12, 13, and 14.
365 Bamidbar 15:30.
366 Vayikra 18:29.

וּמֵלִיז אֶת אָבִיו שֶׁבַּשָּׁמַיִם עָלָיו" (סוֹף כִּלְאַיִם).

זֶהוּ שֶׁכָּתוּב, בְּנֵי חוּס נָא וַחֲמֹל עַל עוֹלָמוֹת הַיְקָרִים, שֶׁנִּבְרְאוּ בְּחָכְמָה וּבִתְבוּנָה וּבְדַעַת, וְהִזָּהֵר שֶׁלֹּא תִגְרֹם חַס וְשָׁלוֹם עָקוּם וְקִלְקוּל לְכֻלָּם בְּמַחֲשָׁבָה אַחַת אֲשֶׁר לֹא טוֹבָה חַס וְשָׁלוֹם:

- וְאֵלּוּ הַשְּׁלֹשָׁה בְּחִינוֹת מַעֲשֶׂה דִּבּוּר מַחֲשָׁבָה, הֵן כְּלַל הַבְּחִינוֹת פְּנִימִיּוֹת שֶׁל הָאָדָם, שֶׁהֵם הַשְּׁלֹשָׁה בְּחִינוֹת נֶפֶשׁ רוּחַ נְשָׁמָה:
  - כִּי הַמַּעֲשֶׂה — הוּא מִבְּחִינַת הַנֶּפֶשׁ, כְּמוֹ שֶׁכָּתוּב (במדבר טו, ל) "וְהַנֶּפֶשׁ אֲשֶׁר תַּעֲשֶׂה" "הַנְּפָשׁוֹת הָעוֹשׂוֹת" (ויקרא יח, כט), וְהַרְבֵּה כַּיּוֹצֵא.
    - "כִּי הַדָּם הוּא הַנֶּפֶשׁ" (דברים יב, כג), שֶׁהַנֶּפֶשׁ שׁוֹרָה וּמִתְלַבֶּשֶׁת בְּדַם הָאָדָם
    - וְלָכֵן עִקַּר מִשְׁכָּנָהּ בַּכָּבֵד, שֶׁהוּא כֻּלּוֹ דָם
    - וּמֵרוּצַת הַדָּם בְּכָל פְּרָטֵי חֶלְקֵי הָאֵבָרִים, כְּלֵי הַמַּעֲשֶׂה, הוּא הַנּוֹתֵן לָהֶם חִיּוּת הַתְּנוּעָה וְהַהִתְעוֹרְרוּת, שֶׁיּוּכְלוּ לִפְעֹל וְלַעֲשׂוֹת אֶת אֲשֶׁר בְּכֹחָם.
    - וְאִם יִמָּנַע מְרוּצַת הַדָּם מֵאֵבָר אֶחָד, אוֹתוֹ הָאֵבָר מִתְיַבֵּשׁ וְאֵין בּוֹ שׁוּם תְּנוּעָה לַעֲשׂוֹת שׁוּם דָּבָר, וְהוּא אֵבָר מֵת:
  - וְהַדִּבּוּר — הוּא מִבְּחִינַת הָרוּחַ, כְּמוֹ שֶׁכָּתוּב (ש"ב כ"ג ב) "רוּחַ ה' דִּבֶּר בִּי", "וּבְרוּחַ שְׂפָתָיו" (ישעיה י"א ד)
    - וּכְמוֹ שֶׁתִּרְגֵּם אוּנְקְלוֹס עַל פָּסוּק (בראשית ב' ז) "וַיְהִי הָאָדָם לְנֶפֶשׁ חַיָּה", — לְרוּחַ מְמַלְּלָא.
    - וְכֵן נִרְאֶה לָעַיִן, שֶׁבְּכָל דִּבּוּר שֶׁהָאָדָם מוֹצִיא מִפִּיו, יוֹצֵא רוּחַ וְהֶבֶל מֵהַפֶּה
    - וּמִשְׁכַּן הָרוּחַ עִקָּרוֹ הוּא בַּלֵּב, כִּי רוּחַ וְהֶבֶל הַדִּבּוּר, עִקָּרוֹ וְרֵאשִׁיתוֹ הוּא עוֹלֶה מֵהַלֵּב:
  - וּמַחֲשָׁבָה — הִיא בְּחִינַת הַנְּשָׁמָה, שֶׁהִיא הַמְלַמֶּדֶת לָאָדָם דֵּעָה וּבִינָה בַּתּוֹרָה הַקְּדוֹשָׁה
    - לָכֵן עִקַּר מִשְׁכָּנָהּ הוּא בַּמֹּחַ, כְּלִי הַמַּחֲשָׁבָה
    - וְהִיא הַבְּחִינָה הָעֶלְיוֹנָה שֶׁבָּהֶם.

---

367 Devarim 12:23.
368 2 Shmuel 23:2.
369 Yishayahu 11:4.
370 Bereishit 2:7.

- As Chazal say:[371] "There are five parts [of the soul: Nefesh, Ruach, Neshama, Yechida, Chaya]. Nefesh is the blood ...; Ruach [rises and descends] ...; Neshama is the *character* of the being ..." meaning [it is the being's] knowledge and thought as explained by the Aruch[372] and Rashi.

15. THREE-LEVEL GLASSBLOWER ANALOGY, SPARKS OF NESHAMA CAN ENTER BODY

- It is surprising – doesn't Neshama/soul mean Neshima/breath? – [However, how can this be] as a person's breathing is breath which visibly rises from the heart, ascending from a low place, and furthermore, it is 'reflected light'[373] which is not a high level?
- However this idea [that Neshama] is called Neshima – does not refer to man's breath – but rather to the breath of God's Lips, so to speak, as per "and He [God] breathed a living Neshama in through his [Man's] nostrils."[374]
- Chazal have already analogously compared the way in which a person's life force cascades down into him to the way in which glass vessels are made with reference to the way in which the resurrection occurs, as per:
  - Given that glassware which is made through the breath of man [can be fixed if broken], how much more so is this true with man who is made through the breath of God [that he can be resurrected].[375]
  - And similarly, in Midrash Tehillim. Refer to it there.[376]
- The subject of this discussion [i.e., the forming of glass vessels] is similar to a proof – in that when we analyze the breath from the mouth of a craftsman as it progresses through the glassware when making it, we have three stages:
  - Stage One: This is the breath which is still in the [glassblower's] mouth, before it has entered into the empty blowpipe – while there, it is just called Neshima/breath.
  - Stage Two: When the breath enters into the blowpipe and extends down it like a Kav/line – while there, it is called Ruach/wind.
  - Stage Three, the lowest stage: When the wind exits the blow pipe into

---

371 Bereishit Rabba Bereishit 14:9.
372 Sefer HaAruch quotes this Midrash as part of the entry for the word "Nefesh."
373 The expression "Ohr Chozer" (reflected light) is used to describe how we see the moon with reflected light of the sun, where the moon's light is incomparable to that of the sun. In this sense, here it is a reflection of the light of God's life force breathed into man which is reflected in human breath,

- וְכֵן אָמְרוּ בִּבְרֵאשִׁית רַבָּה פָּרָשָׁה י״ה, "חֲמִשָּׁה שֵׁמוֹת נִקְרְאוּ לָהּ כו׳, נֶפֶשׁ — זֶה הַדָּם כו׳, רוּחַ כו׳, נְשָׁמָה — זוֹ הָאוֹפְיָה דְבִרְיָתָא", רָצָה לוֹמַר דַּעְתּוֹ וּמַחְשַׁבְתּוֹ, כְּמוֹ שֶׁפֵּרְשׁוּ הֶעָרוּךְ וְרַשִׁ"י זִכְרוֹנָם לִבְרָכָה:

שער א׳ - פרק ט״ז

- וְכִי יִפָּלֵא, הֲלֹא "נְשָׁמָה" פֵּרוּשׁוֹ הוּא נְשִׁימָה, וַהֲרֵי נִרְאֶה לָעַיִן שֶׁנְּשִׁימַת הָאָדָם הוּא הַהֶבֶל הָעוֹלֶה מֵהַלֵּב מִמַּטָּה לְמַעְלָה. וְגַם כִּי הֲרֵי הוּא בְּחִינַת אוֹר חוֹזֵר, וְאֵינוֹ בְּחִינָה עֶלְיוֹנָה:

- אָמְנָם הָעִנְיָן שֶׁנִּקְרֵאת בִּלְשׁוֹן "נְשִׁימָה", אֵין הַכַּוָּנָה בְּחִינַת נְשִׁימַת הָאָדָם, אֶלָּא כִּבְיָכוֹל נְשִׁימַת פִּיו יִתְבָּרַךְ שְׁמוֹ, כְּמוֹ שֶׁכָּתוּב (בראשית ב, ז) "וַיִּפַּח בְּאַפָּיו נִשְׁמַת חַיִּים":

- וּכְבָר הִמְשִׁילוּ רַבּוֹתֵינוּ זִכְרוֹנָם לִבְרָכָה (סנהדרין צא. ריש פרק חלק) עִנְיַן הִשְׁתַּלְשְׁלוּת הָרוּחַ חַיִּים בָּאָדָם — לַעֲשִׂיַּת כְּלִי זְכוּכִית, לְעִנְיַן תְּחִיַּת הַמֵּתִים

- וְאָמְרוּ "קַל וָחֹמֶר מִכְּלֵי זְכוּכִית שֶׁעֲמָלָן בְּרוּחַ בָּשָׂר וָדָם כו׳, בָּשָׂר וָדָם שֶׁבְּרוּחוֹ שֶׁל הַקָּדוֹשׁ בָּרוּךְ הוּא עַל אַחַת כַּמָּה וְכַמָּה."

- וְכֵן הוּא בְּשׁוֹחֵר טוֹב תְּהִלִּים מִזְמוֹר ב׳, עַיֵּן שָׁם:

- כִּי הַנִּדּוֹן דּוֹמֶה לָרְאָיָה, שֶׁכְּשֶׁנִּתְבּוֹנֵן בִּנְשִׁימַת פִּי הָאוּמָן בִּכְלִי הַזְּכוּכִית בְּעֵת עֲשִׂיָּתוֹ, נִמְצָא בּוֹ שְׁלֹשָׁה בְּחִינוֹת.

- בְּחִינָה הָרִאשׁוֹנָה הוּא כְּשֶׁנְּשִׁימַת הַהֶבֶל הוּא עֲדַיִן תּוֹךְ פִּיו, קֹדֶם בֹּאוֹ לְתוֹךְ חֲלַל הַשְּׁפוֹפֶרֶת הַחֲלוּלָה, אֵין לִקְרוֹתָהּ אָז אֶלָּא בְּשֵׁם "נְשִׁימָה".

- וְהַבְּחִינָה הַשֵּׁנִית — כְּשֶׁיִּכָּנְסֵם הַהֶבֶל וּבָא לְתוֹךְ הַשְּׁפוֹפֶרֶת וְנִמְשֶׁכֶת כְּמוֹ קַו, אָז נִקְרָא "רוּחַ".

- וְהַבְּחִינָה הַשְּׁלִישִׁית הַתַּחְתּוֹנָה — הוּא כְּשֶׁיּוֹצֵא הָרוּחַ מֵהַשְּׁפוֹפֶרֶת לְתוֹךְ

---

which is incomparably low compared to the high level of life force breathed into man.

374 Bereishit 2:7.
375 Sanhedrin 91a.
376 Midrash Tehillim 2:11:
- Just as with a glass vessel that is made through the blowing from the wind of flesh and blood, which if broken can be fixed. How much more so with man who is made from the blowing of God as it says "and He breathed a living Neshama in through his nostrils."

the [molten] glass and fills it to fashion the vessel according to the will of the glass blower, [the glass vessel] then contains his Ruach/wind, and is then called Nefesh, an expression of stopping and resting.[377]

- Similarly, using this analogy, this is the concept of the three [soul] levels of Nefesh, Ruach, and Neshama which are bestowed, so to speak, from God's breath.
  - [Stage Three:] That the level of Nefesh is the lowest level [where God's breath has descended to] being completely within a person's body.
  - [Stage Two:] The level of Ruach which descends like a pouring flow from above, with the highest part of [Ruach] being connected above to the lowest part of the Neshama, from which it cascades down and also enters into man's body, [where the lowest part of Ruach] is connected there with the highest part of the Nefesh.
    - As is written: "until *Ruach* will be poured upon us from above"[378] and "I will pour out My *Ruach,*"[379] where [Ruach] impacts a person by being poured, as mentioned above, with the interconnection [of the parts of the soul] being further explained later on at length.[380]
  - [Stage One:] But with the level of Neshama, it is [God's] actual breath, whose essence is entirely concealed and its source is blessed, so to speak, within the breath of God's Mouth, whose essence does not enter into man's [physical] body at all.
- Before his sin,[381] Adam merited having the essence [of the level of Neshama in his body], but after and as a result of his sin, [the level of Neshama] was removed from within him and just remains as hovering around him.[382]
  - [This is true for all of mankind] except for Moshe, who merited that the essence [of Neshama] was contained within his body, and therefore he is referred to as "the man of Elokim."[383]
    - As is known that with all three world levels of Beriyah, Yetzirah, and Asiyah, from their levels of Neshama and above, [they are all] absolutely Godly.[384]

---

377 I.e., stopping at the end of the process as in "Shavat VaYinafash," (Shemot 31:17). Note that this glassblower analogy expands on a similar analogy brought down in Etz Chaim Shaar 5, Shaar Taamim Nekudot Tagim Otiyot, Chap. 5 and also in the Vilna Gaon's commentary on Sefer Yetzirah 1:9.
378 Yishayahu 32:15.
379 Yoel 3:1.
380 G1:17.
381 Of eating from the Tree of Knowledge of Good and Evil.

הַזְּכוּכִית, וּמִתְפַּשֶּׁטֶת בְּתוֹכָהּ, עַד שֶׁנַּעֲשֵׂית כְּלִי כְּפִי רְצוֹן הַמְּזַגֵּג, אָז מַכְלִיא רוּחוֹ, וְנִקְרָא אָז "נֶפֶשׁ", לְשׁוֹן שְׁבִיתָה וּמְנוּחָה:

- כֵּן בְּדִמְיוֹן זֶה, הוּא עִנְיַן הַשְּׁלֹשָׁה בְּחִינוֹת נֶר"ן, שֶׁמַּשְׁפִּיעִים כִּבְיָכוֹל מִנְּשִׁימַת פִּיו יִתְבָּרַךְ שְׁמוֹ

  ○ שֶׁבְּחִינַת הַנֶּפֶשׁ — הִיא הַבְּחִינָה הַתַּחְתּוֹנָה, שֶׁהִיא כָּלָּהּ בְּתוֹךְ גּוּף הָאָדָם.

  ○ וּבְחִינַת הָרוּחַ — הוּא בָּא דֶּרֶךְ עֲרוּי מִלְמַעְלָה, שֶׁחֶלְקוֹ וְקָצֵהוּ הָעֶלְיוֹן שֶׁלּוֹ קָשׁוּר וְנֶאֱחָז לְמַעְלָה בַּבְּחִינָה הַתַּחְתּוֹנָה שֶׁל הַנְּשָׁמָה, וּמִשְׁתַּלְשֶׁלֶת וְנִכְנֶסֶת גַּם בְּתוֹךְ גּוּף הָאָדָם, וּמִתְקַשֶּׁרֶת שָׁם בַּבְּחִינָה הָעֶלְיוֹנָה שֶׁל הַנֶּפֶשׁ

  ▪ כְּמוֹ שֶׁכָּתוּב (ישעיה לב, טו) "עַד יֵעָרֶה עָלֵינוּ רוּחַ מִמָּרוֹם", "אֶשְׁפּוֹךְ אֶת רוּחִי" וְגוֹ' (יואל ג, א), שֶׁהוּא מֻשְׁפָּע בָּאָדָם דֶּרֶךְ שְׁפִיכָה וְעֵרוּי כַּנַּ"ל, וּכְמוֹ שֶׁיִּתְבָּאֵר עוֹד לְהַלָּן אִ"ה (פי"ז) עִנְיַן הִתְקַשְּׁרוּתָם בָּאָרֶץ.

  ○ אָמְנָם בְּחִינַת הַנְּשָׁמָה — הִיא הַנְּשָׁמָה עַצְמָהּ שֶׁפְּנִימִיּוּת עַצְמוּתָהּ מִסְתַּתֶּרֶת בְּהַעֲלֵם, וּמְקוֹרָהּ בָּרוּךְ כִּבְיָכוֹל בְּתוֹךְ נְשִׁימַת פִּיו יִתְבָּרַךְ שְׁמוֹ, שֶׁאֵין עַצְמוּת מַהוּתָהּ נִכְנֶסֶת כְּלָל בְּתוֹךְ גּוּף הָאָדָם:

- וְאָדָם הָרִאשׁוֹן — קֹדֶם הַחֵטְא — זָכָה לְעַצְמוּתָהּ, וּבְסִבַּת הַחֵטְא נִסְתַּלְּקָה מִתּוֹכוֹ, וְנִשְׁאֲרָה רַק חוֹפֶפֶת עָלָיו.

  ○ לְבַד מֹשֶׁה רַבֵּנוּ עָלָיו הַשָּׁלוֹם, שֶׁזָּכָה לְעַצְמוּתָהּ תּוֹךְ גּוּפוֹ, וְלָכֵן נִקְרָא "אִישׁ הָאֱלֹקִים" (דברים לג, א)

  ▪ כַּיָּדוּעַ שֶׁבְּכָל שְׁלֹשָׁה עוֹלָמוֹת, בְּרִיאָה יְצִירָה עֲשִׂיָּה, מִבְּחִינַת הַנְּשָׁמָה דִּלְהוֹן וּלְמַעְלָה, הוּא אֱלֹקוּת גָּמוּר, כְּמוֹ שֶׁכָּתוּב בְּעֵץ חַיִּים שַׁעַר הַצֶּלֶם פֶּרֶק א', וּבְרֵישׁ שַׁעַר צִיּוּר עוֹלָמוֹת אֲצִילוּת בְּרִיאָה יְצִירָה עֲשִׂיָּה, בְּהַקְדָּמַת הָרַ"ח וִיטַאל זִכְרוֹנוֹ לִבְרָכָה, וּבְשַׁעַר הַשֵּׁמוֹת פֶּרֶק א'.

---

382 See G4:28.

383 Devarim 33:1. See also G3:13 and 14.

384 Etz Chaim Shaar 26, Shaar HaTzelem, Chap. 1 and the beginning of Shaar 43, Shaar Tziyur Olamot ABY"A in R. Chaim Vital's introduction and Shaar 44, Shaar HaShemot, Chap. 1.

  The point here is that pure Godliness is related to every world level and therefore it was possible for Moshe to be both a physical man resident in the world level of Asiyah and also to be simultaneously Godly as in *the man of Elokim*.

- [However with the rest of mankind] apart from [Moshe], no person merited this – but [they] only [merit] the clarity of sparks of light which emanate from [the level of Neshama, hovering] above the person's head of one who merits it – each one according to his level and capacity.
  - Refer to:
    - "and He breathed the soul of life in through his nostrils" – this is the image which is *above* a person.[385]
    - If [the Nefesh through Mitzvah performance and Ruach through Torah study] should merit . . . then an additional greatness will descend upon [a person] from above . . . a holiness will be roused upon him from above and rest above the person and surround him on all sides . . . and that arousal which rests above him comes from a high place, and what is its name? Neshama is its name.[386]
- It is this [emanation of sparks from the level of Neshama] that provides a person with additional understanding to intellectually relate to the inner intellect which is hidden in our Holy Torah. As written:
  - Neshama arouses a person with understanding.[387]
  - It will arouse him with Supernal Wisdom . . .[388]
  - "But not every person merits this. Know that one who has the power to do . . . then he will have a tremendous ability to remember Torah and to understand all the secrets of Torah . . . and the secrets of Torah will be properly revealed to him . . ."[389] See later in connection with a person's supernal root and understand![390]
  - "It is true that *Ruach* is in man and it is the *Neshama* of God that gives them understanding,"[391] meaning that the level of Ruach cascades down, impacts on and enters into [the body of] a person, but the Neshama is a *Neshama of God*, meaning that with the breath of God, its essence does not [directly] influence and is not revealed in man, as it resides in the heights above within God's Mouth, so to speak – but it is that which provides understanding through the sparks of light which are above [the person] – enabling him to intellectually engage in the depths of the hidden parts of the Holy Torah.
- In relation to references made by the Zohar and the Kabbalists to the level of Neshama as residing within a person's brain – their intention is to relate to the sparks of emanating light which provide inteligence to his brain and intellect – but not to the essence [of the level of Neshama] itself.

---

385 Zohar Raya Mehemna III Naso 123b quoting Bereishit 2:7.
386 Zohar Chadash II Rut 38b.

וְזוּלָתוֹ לֹא זָכָה אֵלֶיהָ שׁוּם אָדָם, רַק בְּהִירוּת נִצּוֹצֵי אוֹר מִתְנוֹצְצִים מִמֶּנָּה, עַל רֹאשׁ הָאָדָם הַזּוֹכֶה אֵלֶיהָ, כָּל אֶחָד לְפִי מַדְרֵגָתוֹ וּלְפוּם שְׁעוּרָא דִילֵיהּ.

וְעַיֵּן

○ רַעֲיָא מְהֵימְנָא נָשֹׂא קכ"ג ב', "וַיִּפַּח בְּאַפָּיו נִשְׁמַת חַיִּים, דָּא אִיהִי דִיוֹקְנָא דְעַל בַּר נָשׁ" כו'

○ וּבְזֹהַר חָדָשׁ רוּת ל"ח ע"ב, "וְאִי זָכֵי כו', כְּדֵין נָחֲתָא עָלֵיהּ רְבוּ יַתִּיר מִלְּעֵילָּא כו', אִתְּעַר עָלֵיהּ מִלְּעֵילָא אִתְּעָרוּ קַדִּישָׁא, וְשָׁרְיָא עָלֵיהּ דְּבַר נָשׁ, וְסַחֲרָא לֵיהּ מִכֹּל סִטְרִין. וְהַהוּא אִתְּעָרוּ דְשָׁרְיָא עָלֵיהּ, מֵאֲתָר עִלָּאָה הוּא, וּמַאי שְׁמֵיהּ, נִשְׁמָה שְׁמֵיהּ". עַיֵּן שָׁם:

● וְהִיא הַנּוֹתֶנֶת לְהָאָדָם בִּינָה יְתֵרָה, לְהַשְׂכִּיל הַשְּׂכָלִיּוֹת הַפְּנִימִיִּים הַגְּנוּזִים בַּתּוֹרָה הַקְּדוֹשָׁה. וּכְמוֹ שֶׁכָּתוּב.

○ בְּסֵ"ת לֶךְ לְךָ ע"ט ב', "נְשָׁמָה אִתְּעָרַת לְאֵינָשׁ בְּבִינָה".

○ וּבְזֹהַר חָדָשׁ רוּת ל"ח ב', "וְאִתְּעַר בֵּיהּ בְּחָכְמְתָא עִלָּאָה" כו'.

○ וְעַיֵּן בְּעֵץ חַיִּים (שַׁעַר מוֹחִין דְּקַטְנוּת פֶּרֶק ג') ז"ל "אָמְנָם לֹא כָל אָדָם זוֹכֶה לָזֶה. וְדַע כִּי מִי שֶׁיֵּשׁ בְּיָדוֹ כֹּחַ בְּמַעֲשָׂיו כו' אָז יִהְיֶה לוֹ זְכִירָה נִפְלָאָה בַּתּוֹרָה, וְיָבִין כָּל רָזֵי הַתּוֹרָה כו' וְיִתְגַּלּוּ לוֹ רָזֵי הַתּוֹרָה כְּתִקּוּנָן", עַד כָּאן. וְעַיֵּן לְהַלָּן (פֶּרֶק ט"ז) הָעִנְיָן בְּשָׁרְשׁוֹ הָעֶלְיוֹן, וְתָבִין.

● וְזֶהוּ שֶׁאָמַר הַכָּתוּב (אִיּוֹב ל"ב ח) "אָכֵן רוּחַ הִיא בֶאֱנוֹשׁ וְנִשְׁמַת שַׁדַּי תְּבִינֵם", רָצָה לוֹמַר, שֶׁבְּחִינַת הָרוּחַ הוּא מִשְׁתַּלְשֵׁל וּמֻשְׁפָּע וְנִכְנָס בְּתוֹךְ הָאָדָם, אֲבָל הַנְּשָׁמָה שֶׁהִיא "נִשְׁמַת שַׁדַּי", רָצָה לוֹמַר, נְשִׁימַת פִּיו יִתְבָּרַךְ, אֵין עַצְמוּתָהּ מֻשְׁפָּע וּמִתְגַּלֶּה בְּתוֹךְ הָאָדָם, כִּי הִיא מְרוֹמִים תִּשְׁכֹּן, בְּתוֹךְ פִּיו יִתְבָּרַךְ כִּבְיָכוֹל, רַק שֶׁהִיא הַנּוֹתֶנֶת לוֹ בִּינָה בְּנִצּוֹצֵי אוֹרָהּ עָלָיו, לְהַשְׂכִּילוֹ בְּעָמְקֵי מַצְפּוּנֵי הַתּוֹרָה הַקְּדוֹשָׁה:

● וּמַה שֶּׁכָּתוּב בַּזֹּהַר וְהַמְקַבְּלִים זִכְרוֹנָם לִבְרָכָה, שֶׁבְּחִינַת הַנְּשָׁמָה מִשְׁכְּנָהּ בְּמֹחַ

---

387 Zohar Sitrei Torah I Lech Lecha 79b.
388 Zohar Chadash II Rut 38b.
389 Etz Chaim Shaar 22, Shaar Mochin Dekatnut, Chap. 3.
390 G1:16.
391 Iyov 32:8.

- Their key intention, relates to the level of the *Three Heads of Ruach*,[392] the secret of the intellect, which sometimes emanate as sparks and sometimes are concealed, and they come as a *Secret of Addition*[393] to one who merits this, as is known, [and they do] not [come to a person] as the main level of Neshama.[394]
- Our great master, the prodigy, the Chasid, our teacher Eliyahu of blessed memory, similarly writes this in his commentary on the Heichalot in Heichala Tinyana.[395]

• But it is all one thing, as the lowest part of Neshama which provides sparks within [a person's] knowledge and intellect, to give him intelligence, is identical with the Three Heads of Ruach in his intellect, as will be explained, God Willing.[396]

16. CONNECTION TO NESHAMA, DESIRE FOR THAT CONNECTION

• 'The intellectuals will understand'[397] that this same concept[398] is reflected in a [person's] supernal root, where only the lowest part of the *Mother of the Children*,[399] the secret of the soul of supernal life, enters into and

---

[392] This refers to the first three Sefirot (i.e., the heads of the Ten Sefirot) of Ruach, i.e., to the levels of Chochma, Binah, and Daat which together form the intellectual part of the level of Ruach.

[393] I.e., they come to a person as an acquired level of holiness resulting from the person's actions in this world through the *Secret of Addition* – in contrast with a level which is innately within him and which *just* needs to be revealed. See the quotation of Pri Etz Chaim Shaar HaAmidah, Chap. 19 brought on p. 268, fn. 483, for an insight into the *Secret of Addition*.

[394] So these sparks relate to the way the level of Neshama is manifest in the highest part of the level of Ruach but they are not a direct part of the level of Neshama.

[395] See the quotation from Heichalot HaZohar Bereishit 41b from within the Vilna Gaon's gloss no. 17 brought on p. 256, fn. 456, which differentiates between the level of Neshama which does not enter into a person and the *Three Heads of Ruach* which are incorporated within the Neshama which does enter the body.

[396] Over the coming chapters.

[397] Daniel 12:10, an expression generally used to describe those versed in Kabbalistic knowledge. Although a common expression, its use here also appears to subtly refer to one who has merited these *intellectual* abilities of Kabbalistic mastery and engagement in the depths of the hidden parts of Torah as detailed in the last few sentences of G2:15. This is borne out by

הָאָדָם, כַּוָּנָתָם זִכְרוֹנָם לִבְרָכָה עַל הַנִּצוֹצֵי זִיו אוֹרָה הַמַּשְׁכֶּלֶת מֹחוֹ וְשִׂכְלוֹ, לֹא עַצְמוּתָהּ מַמָּשׁ.

- וְעִקַּר כַּוָּנָתָם זִכְרוֹנָם לִבְרָכָה, עַל בְּחִינַת שְׁלֹשָׁה רֵישִׁין שֶׁל הָרוּחַ סוֹד הַמֹּחִין, שֶׁהֵן פְּעָמִים מִתְנוֹצְצִים פְּעָמִים מִסְתַּלְּקִין, וּבָאִים בְּסוֹד תּוֹסֶפֶת לְמִי שֶׁזּוֹכֶה לָזֶה, כַּיָּדוּעַ, לֹא עַל בְּחִינַת הַנְּשָׁמָה הָעִקָּרִית.

- וְכֵן כָּתַב רַבֵּנוּ הַגָּדוֹל הַגָּאוֹן הֶחָסִיד מוֹהַרְ"א זִכְרוֹנוֹ לִבְרָכָה בְּבֵאוּרוֹ עַל הַהֵיכָלוֹת בְּהֵיכָלָא תִּנְיָנָא:

• וְהַכֹּל אֶחָד, שֶׁבְּחִינָה הַתַּחְתּוֹנָה שֶׁל הַנְּשָׁמָה הַמִּתְנוֹצֶצֶת בְּדַעְתּוֹ וְשִׂכְלוֹ לְהַשְׂכִּילוֹ, הִיא הִיא הַשְּׁלֹשָׁה רֵישִׁין שֶׁל הָרוּחַ בְּמוֹחִין שֶׁלּוֹ, כְּמוֹ שֶׁיִּתְבָּאֵר לְפָנֵינוּ אִי"ה:

שער א' - פרק י"ז

• וְהַמַּשְׂכִּילִים יָבִינוּ, שֶׁכֵּן הוּא הָעִנְיָן גַּם בְּשָׁרְשׁוֹ הָעֶלְיוֹן. שֶׁרַק בְּחִינָה הַתַּחְתּוֹנָה שֶׁל אִם הַבָּנִים, סוֹד נִשְׁמַת חַיִּים עִלָּאָה, הִיא נִכְנֶסֶת וּמִתְפַּשֶּׁטֶת בִּפְנִימִיּוּת הָאָדָם הָעֶלְיוֹן בְּסוֹד תּוֹסֶפֶת, אַחַר הַתִּקּוּן, עַל יְדֵי מַעֲשֵׂי הַתַּחְתּוֹנִים הָרְצוּיִים:

R. Chaim's use of different expressions to refer to those with Kabbalistic knowledge elsewhere in his work, e.g., "a man of understanding" in G1:19 and "one who is able will understand" in G1:18:N16.

398 Where the secret that the *Three Heads* influence via the *Secret of Addition* and in particular that the *Three Heads* sometimes emanate as sparks and sometimes are concealed, as presented in G1:15.

399 Some contextual background:

The simple Kabbalistic model of the Universe is that there are many worlds, each at different levels. The world levels have many levels within levels and within each level there is a set of sublevels corresponding to the Ten Sefirot starting with the three intellectual Sefirot, known as the *Three Heads*, i.e., Chochma, Binah, and Daat (also known as Mochin). These three intellectual Sefirot generate and are manifest within the Six Middot/characteristics, where the relevance of a characteristic is made meaningful by the intellectual motivation which drives it, e.g., as highlighted by the difference between a child who can bestow mercy or love on a meaningless toy and an adult who can express love for a subtle concept. These Six Middot are referred to as "VaK" – an acronym for *Vav Ketzavot*, *Six Ends*, and are referred to as the sons born of the intellectual process. These Six Middot are Chesed, Gevurah, Tiferet, Netzach, Hod, and Yesod. The final level of the Ten Sefirot is Malchut, which is the recipient of the flow from the other nine Sefirot and as such is referred to as a female, the *daughter* of the process. This lowest level of Malchut, in turn becomes the highest level of the next lower world level, referred to as

distributes within the inner essence of the *Supernal Man*,[400] through the

Keter/crown (where a crown is connected above but still abstracted from that next world level) and flows down to form the intellect of the next lower world level, i.e., the *Three Heads* of the next world level. The result is that in essence the *Three Heads*, the intellect/Mochin, of the lower world are generated from the *Six Ends*, the Middot, of the world above it (and in turn the *Three Heads* of the lower world are manifest within the presentation of the *Six Ends* in the lower world).

In addition to the simple Kabbalistic model of the world levels being comprised of a continuous recursive sequence of the Ten Sefirot which cascade down from higher world level to lower world level, the Kabbalists provide a much more sophisticated model, built on the basis of the simple model, where human personas are constructed from sets of Ten Sefirot. These individual human personas then each act as a single complex presentation to impact on the next level down in a specific way.

These presentations are known as *Partzufim* and there are 6 primary *Partzufim* with the following names: Atik Yomin, Arich Anpin, Abba, Imma, Zeer Anpin, and Nukva of Zeer Anpin.

The difference between a single Sefira and a Partzuf can be understood in terms of a Sefira being like a primary particle of matter (a sub-atomic particle), whereas a Partzuf is like a molecule made up of a complex configuration of atoms and as a result has some very specific properties which are in addition to the simple sum of its parts.

The collective of all Partzufim provides a complex model which describes the total composition of man, incorporating both his entire physical construction and also his psychological make-up.

Each of these Partzufim directly relate to specific Sefirot, but at the same time either contain or are able to contain a complete configuration of Ten Sefirot. Atik Yomin and Arich Anpin are related to Keter. (These two Partzufim of Keter are sometimes counted as one, so sometimes there are references to five instead of six primary Partzufim). Abba/Father to Chochma. Imma/Mother to Binah. Zeer Anpin is related to the Six Middot, and Nukva/the female part of Zeer Anpin is related to Malchut.

The Partzufim of Atik Yomin, Arich Anpin, Abba, and Imma each have an initially complete configuration of Ten Sefirot. On the other hand Zeer Anpin and Nukva are initially incomplete. They start off with a configuration only containing *Six Middot* and *Malchut* respectively, but they are both able to grow, to be perfected, to ultimately contain a full configuration of Ten Sefirot.

While each of the Partzufim represent human personas, it is the Partzufim of Zeer Anpin and Nukva which most closely resemble man as they start off as incomplete and ultimately become complete, tending towards perfection as they grow.

One key element of this growth directly parallels human growth in that when children are born, their intellect is not developed, but they acquire intellect as they mature.

So Zeer Anpin, while initially starting off with a configuration of just the Six Middot, can subsequently acquire intellect, i.e., the Three Heads of Mochin, as it matures.

The existence of these Partzufim/personas/presentations in the higher worlds allows the template of man to exist and become a reality of man in this lowest world.

Man, in this lowest world, is therefore a reflection of the persona/presentation of man in the highest worlds. As man perfects himself in this world, and completes his own personal set of Ten Sefirot, there is a parallel completion of the corresponding persona of Zeer Anpin in the higher worlds.

The persona of man, Zeer Anpin, in the supernal world of Atzilut is therefore referred to as Supernal Man.

The expression "Em HaBanim" (Mother of the Children) as used here is referring to the Partzuf of Imma/Mother/Binah in the supernal world of Atzilut, where its union (Daat) with the Partzuf of Abba/Father/Chochma produces (*gives birth*) to Zeer Anpin (initially starting off as just being the Six Middot) and Nukveh (initially starting off as just being Malchut). The passing of the intellect/Three Heads on to the Supernal Man/Zeer Anpin from *Em HaBanim* is dependent on the positive actions of man and is the *Secret of Addition* (as presented in G2:15).

It should be noted that there is an additional layer of complexity to the Partzuf model in that every Partzuf also contains some vestige of every other Partzuf, which means that the fabric of reality described by the Partzuf model is intrinsically and very deeply interconnected. (See the comments of the Vilna Gaon recorded by his brother in Maalot HaTorah at the end of V2:03, "The World of The Malbush.")

For deeper insight into the Partzuf model, further details are explained in V2:02, Chap. 12 and also in Chap. 15, "Tzimtzum Sources," I1.1.

400 As explained in the previous footnote, Adam HaElyon (Supernal Man) is equivalent to the Partzuf of Zeer Anpin in the supernal world of Atzilut.

In this expression, the word for man, "Adam," is used in the sense of being a *likeness* of God as in "Edameh L'Elyon" (Yishayahu 14:14). If man fulfills his principal objective in this world, he reflects the Supernal Man and completes his structure, both in this world, and in parallel, also in the supernal worlds by drawing the intellect of the *Three Heads* into it. On the other hand, if man does not fulfill his purpose and does not emulate God in this lowest world, then he disconnects from the *Three Heads* and *Adam* becomes nothing more than *Adamah*/earth from where his physical body was taken and to where it will return. (Shela – Introduction to Toldot Adam.)

The concept of Supernal Man is also explicitly connected by R. Chaim to the concept of Shiur Komah at the end of G4:29.

In addition R. Chaim quotes from the Zohar in the bracketed section at

Secret of Addition.⁴⁰¹ [This process occurs] after the rectification made by [physical man's] favorable actions.
- This is the secret of the Holy Intellect, the *Three Heads* of [Supernal Man], whose essence is the *Six Ends*⁴⁰² as is known, as is explained for one who understands in Etz Chaim.⁴⁰³

---

the end of G1:05:N05 explaining that Supernal Man is the Soul of God which filters down to all levels permeating everything. When God creates each world level, there is a part of Him which entirely fills that world giving life to it, referred to as "Memaleh Kol Almin," and there is a part of Him which circumvents and does not enter that world which is referred to as "Sovev Kol Almin." The actions of physical man directly influence the level of man's perception of God's manifestation within each world.

See R. Chaim's definition (G3:04) of "Memaleh Kol Almin" as being *God's perspective* in that there is no change in God as a result of the Act of Creation and that it is as if the Creation did not happen, whereas "Sovev Kol Almin" is defined as being solely from *our perspective* where we see God as a separate entity from this world and therefore can relate to this world as an entity in its own right.

We have the ability to modulate our experience of God's connection to this world and increase our level of perception of His presence in this world by our pursuit of Torah and Mitzvot. On reaching a level of perfection of our perception, we make this world a *dwelling place* for God, meaning that we reach a level of perceiving God as being manifest in every part of this world. This level of perfection can only truly be achieved in the times of Mashiach, but in the interim it is for us to work as hard as we can on ourselves to strive towards this level.

It is our actions, which influence the level of God's connection to this world within our own perception. This is analogous to our perfecting Zeer Anpin so that it becomes a complete set of Ten Sefirot.

Therefore, the two concepts of God's level of manifestation in this world, and Zeer Anpin are both depicted by the concept of Supernal Man.

(This is an idea which is also expressed in the Second Gateway in that the concept of *blessing* relates to God's connection with the world, i.e., His level of revelation within this world which is dependent on us, and does not relate to His absolute Essence).

401 See the quotation of Pri Etz Chaim Shaar HaAmidah, Chap. 19 brought on p. 268, fn. 483, for an insigh*t into the Secret* of Addition.

402 I.e., as explained in the previous footnotes in this chapter, Supernal Man which is Zeer Anpin starts off as an incomplete Partzuf with only the Six Middot/Six Ends and then, depending on man's actions ultimately completes its full set of the Ten Sefirot including the Three Heads/the three Sefirot forming the intellect.

• וְהוּא סוֹד הַמּוֹחִין קַדִּישִׁין, ג' רֵישִׁין דִּילֵיהּ, שֶׁעֶקָרוֹ הוּא ו"ק כַּיָּדוּעַ, כַּמְבֹאָר

403 R. Chaim provides the references below which have been expanded. They can be understood in the light of earlier footnotes in this chapter.

Etz Chaim Shaar 14, Shaar Abba VeImma, Chap. 8:
- [A description is given of the union of Chochma and Binah where at a higher level they are inseparable but they separate at a lower level and] they are manifest in the Zeer Anpin to form its *secret intellect* . . .

Etz Chaim Shaar 27, Shaar Pratei Ibbur, Yenikat Mochin:
- [This reference is to the entire Shaar which describes processes related to Mochin among other things. The short quotation which follows is taken from Chap. 4:] . . . the Six Ends of Zeer Anpin are called Elokim, and the Mochin [of Zeer Anpin] is called YHVH . . . for all of Zeer Anpin is called "Elokim" . . . [Therefore, Zeer Anpin is the external presentation of the hidden/secret Mochin – just as Elokim is the external presentation/manifestation in this world of the hidden essence of YHVH. Elokim has the numerical value of *HaTeva*/nature and represents God's manifestation within each world level – this manifestation is the way in which He fills each world level, which is precisely what Zeer Anpin is. See earlier footnotes in this chapter.]

Etz Chaim Shaar 15, Shaar HaZivugin, beginning of Chap. 4:
- Know that above, in Supernal Mother [i.e., Imma/Binah] there are three levels . . . [and aspects of the Supernal Mother] are manifest within Zeer Anpin to form its Mochin.

Etz Chaim Shaar 23, Shaar Mochin DeTzelem, Chap. 4 (see V2:14, p. 676):
- . . . the Malchut [the lowest part] of Binah [Em HaBanim] is that which enters within the inner essence of Zeer Anpin [Supernal Man] . . .

Etz Chaim Shaar 25, Shaar Derushei HaTzelem, all of Derush 1 (see V2:14, p. 676):
- [The whole chapter deals with this topic. The following is a short quotation from it which captures the point:] . . . and now, in an expanded way, Abba and Imma reunite their level of inner vessels with the lights which are there, which is called Neshama, and they give birth to the expanded Mochin of Zeer Anpin and they are a Neshama to it, and it is called the image of the soul of Zeer Anpin and these are the true Mochin which extend from the inner essence of Abba [Chochma] and Imma [Binah/Em HaBanim] . . .

Etz Chaim Shaar 25, Shaar Derushei HaTzelem, Derush 8:
- . . . and all levels of the three Mochin, they are the [seminal] drops of the Father/Abba [Chochma] in the Mother/Imma [Binah] and form in the womb of the Mother, and afterwards are manifest in and then enter into Zeer Anpin . . .

Pri Etz Chaim Shaar HaTefillin, Chap. 3:
- [This chapter explains how the elements of Mochin are expressed within and from the Father, Chochma, and Mother, Binah. It continues to explain that there is a latent element of Mochin which is] hidden within the Fa-

- This is [the meaning] of that which they said that the *Neshama* resides in the brain [i.e., the intellect],[404] as written in Etz Chaim[405] and is explained to one who carefully analyzes all of the expositions of Tzelem.[406]

---

ther and Mother like a hidden deposit, which is called the two Mochins of Chesed and Gevurah, which form a single brain, which is the Daat of Zeer Anpin.

Sefer Shaar HaYichudim, Tikkun Avonot, Chap. 5:
- ... for it is known that Father [Chochma] and Mother [Binah] are within the Zeer Anpin within its *Secret of Intellect/Mochin* ...

404 See end of G1:14.

405 R. Chaim provides the following references:

Etz Chaim Shaar 19, Shaar Orot Nitzotzim veKeilim Chap. 6:
- [This chapter describes the process of the completion of the Ten Sefirot of Zeer Anpin and of *Nukva of Zeer Anpin* – a process which is effected by man's positive actions and ultimately restores the level of Neshama into the body as before Adam's sin (as per G1:15). This process is synonymous with the restoration of the 288 sparks of holiness which fell into impurity during the part of the Creation process known as *Shevirat HaKeilim*, the result of the mystical understanding of the death of the seven kings (Bereishit 36:31). This restoration process is gradually and iteratively completed by successive generations and only fully completed at the time of the coming of Mashiach, and it is therefore at that time that the level of Neshama is fully restored into the human body. This point is explicitly made as follows:] Know, that even though we have explained that [with the rectification via the completion of the Ten Sefirot of Zeer Anpin that impurities from] all of the seven kings have been purified, it is not complete, for they will not be completely purified until Mashiach comes, as mentioned above. The concept is that they are purified as much as possible at the time of emanation, returning each time until the purification is complete ...

Etz Chaim Shaar 20, Shaar HaMochin, Chap. 7:
- ... its entire root is the *Six Ends* which are called Ruach and it now grows its *Three Heads* [i.e., the intellect] which are the level of Neshama ...

Etz Chaim Shaar 20, Shaar HaMochin, Chap. 8:
- We will now explain the concept of this *inner* vessel of Zeer Anpin [i.e., the Mochin/Intellect] which is the level of Neshama of greatness, which is the inner vessel of Mother [Binah] and within it is the inner vessel of Father [Chochma].

Etz Chaim Shaar 20, Shaar HaMochin, Chap. 12:
- ... for the *inner* vessel of Zeer Anpin [i.e., the Mochin/Intellect] which contains the Neshama ...

Etz Chaim Shaar 25, Shaar Derushei HaTzelem, Derush 1, and further elaborated on in R. Chaim Vital's note to Derush 1 (see V2:14, p. 676):

לַמֵבִין בְּעֵץ חַיִים שַׁעַר או"א פֶּרֶק ח', וּבְשַׁעַר פְּרָטֵי עי"מ, וּבְשַׁעַר הַזִּוּוּגִים רֵישׁ פֶּרֶק ד', וּבְסוֹף שַׁעַר מוֹחִין דְּצֶלֶם, וּבְשַׁעַר דְּרוּשֵׁי הַצֶּלֶם דְּרוּשׁ ב', עַיֵּן שָׁם הֵיטֵב בְּכָל הַדְּרוּשׁ, וּבִדְרוּשׁ ח' שָׁם, וּבִפְרִי עֵץ חַיִים פֶּרֶק ג' מִשַּׁעַר הַתְּפִלִּין, וּבְשַׁעַר הַיִּחוּדִים פֶּרֶק ה' מִתַּקּוּן עֲוֹנוֹת:

- וְהוּא שֶׁאָמְרוּ שֶׁהַנְּשָׁמָה שׁוֹרָה בַּמֹּחַ, כְּמוֹ שֶׁכָּתַב שָׁם בְּשַׁעַר אֲנָ"ךְ פֶּרֶק ו', וּבְשַׁעַר הַמּוֹחִין בְּכָל פֶּרֶק ז', וּבְפֶרֶק ח', וּבְפֶרֶק י"ב, וּבְשַׁעַר דְּרוּשֵׁי הַצֶּלֶם רֵישׁ

- [See the previous quotation from Etz Chaim Shaar 25, Derush 1 on p. 237, fn. 403.]

Etz Chaim Shaar 30, Shaar HaPartzufim, [towards the] beginning of Chap. 1:

- ... and when it also has the *inner* Partzuf [i.e., the *inner* presentation of Zeer Anpin which incorporates the intellect], then it also has Neshama ...

Etz Chaim Shaar 40, Shaar Penimiut VeChitzoniut, Chap. 4:

- [The levels of the soul, Chaya, Neshama, Ruach, and Nefesh, directly parallel the letters of YHVH with Ruach paralleling the *Vav*, and Chaya and Neshama paralleling the *Yud* and *Hey*. From R. Chaim's discusussion we have understood that it is the sparks of the Neshama which impact Zeer Anpin and not the actual Neshama and that the interaction of the sparks of the Neshama with Zeer Anpin is dependent on our action. With this in mind the following quotation may be understood:] ... and this is because all the *Six Ends* [i.e., the Zeer Anpin] is called *Vav* [from YHVH] and it is not separated. However, the *Three Heads* of Chochma, Binah, and Daat, which are the letters *Yud* and *Hey* [from YHVH] – they are not part of the letter *Vav*. They are not forced to stay there ... in order that they can depart at the time of the destruction and the exile, but nevertheless they do have an impact there ... and this impact is called Mochin of connection [i.e., the sparks of the Neshama] ...

Etz Chaim Shaar 40, Shaar Penimiut VeChitzoniut, Chap. 9:

- ... and the Neshama and the *Neshama of the Neshama* are in the *Three Heads* [the intellect] within it [i.e., within Zeer Anpin] ...

Etz Chaim Shaar 49, Shaar Kelipat Nogah, Chap. 1:

- ... for the brain is the vessel of Neshama, and the heart [the vessel] of Ruach, and the liver [the vessel] of Nefesh [see end of G1:14], and the Neshama disseminates throughout the body from the brain to the feet ... [An additional similar source is at the end of Etz Chaim Shaar 6, Shaar HaAkudim, Chap. 5 which says the following: ... the Neshama enlightens in a person's head, in the brain and the Ruach in the heart and the Nefesh in the liver. Know that the head itself also has the three levels except that Neshama is dominant in the brain, and Ruach in the nose and Nefesh in the mouth. ...]

406 I.e., Etz Chaim Shaar 25, Shaar Derushei HaTzelem.

- A part of [a person's Neshama from *Mother of the Children/Em HaBanim/ Imma*] hovers, surrounds, and enlightens [from] above his head in close proximity
  - this is the secret of "with the crown which his mother crowned him with"[407]
  - this is the secret of the breath which comes out of the mouth of the Mother – to become the light which surrounds him, as per Etz Chaim[408]
  - and as explained above: that the level of Neshama is the level of God's breath, but its essential part is completely hidden Above in its supernal source within [God's] Mouth and enlightens from a distance.
- With this, Chazal's intention is understood
  - in relation to the verse "For God will give wisdom (Chochma) from his mouth, knowledge (Daat), and understanding (Binah)." That they say: To what is [a Jew's desired relationship with God] compared – to a king who had a son and on his son's return from school he found a food dish in front of his father. His father took a piece of food and gave it to him . . . the son then said to him: "I only want to eat from the food which is in your mouth." What did [the king] do? He gave it to him . . .[409]
  - Meaning that the cherished son's request was to perceive and be impacted by the sparks of light of the level of Neshama whose source is hidden within the breath of God's Mouth.
  - Chazal's holy language hints further with the reference to the son specifically returning *from school* – 'faithfully telling us'[410] that there is no way in this world to perceive these sparks of light of the Neshama except through involvement, deep study, and analysis of the Holy Torah in holiness, as [the Torah and the person's Neshama] both come from the same source as is known to one who understands. (Note 14)[411]
- This is what Chazal [continue] to say there, that at the time Israel stood at Mount Sinai to receive the Torah, they sought to listen to the

---

407 Shir Hashirim 3:11, meaning that a crown is in close proximity to but not actually within the head.

408 Etz Chaim Shaar HaKlalim, end of Chap. 11:
- . . . know that the breath which completely surrounds Zeer Anpin [and the intellect which is in the head/brain] comes out of the mouth of Mother [i.e., Imma/Binah] . . .

Sefer Likutei Torah, Tehillim 53:4 "Kulo Sag":
- . . . and everything that surrounds has its root in Binah [*Imma*] . . . and this

דְּרוּשׁ ב'. וְיוֹתֵר מְבֹאָר הָעִנְיָן שָׁם בְּהַגָּהַת הרח"ו ז"ל, וּבְשַׁעַר הַפַּרְצוּפִים רֵישׁ פֶּרֶק א'. וּבְשַׁעַר פְּנִימִיּוּת וְחִיצוֹנִיּוּת דְּרוּשׁ ד' וּדְרוּשׁ ט', וּבְשַׁעַר קְלִפַּת נֹגַהּ רֵישׁ פֶּרֶק א'. וְהוּא מְבֹאָר לַמְדַקְדֵּק הֵיטֵב בְּכָל דְּרוּשֵׁי הַצֶּלֶם:

- וּקְצָתָהּ חוֹפֵף וּמַקִּיף וּמֵאִיר עַל רֹאשׁוֹ בְּקֵרוּב מָקוֹם
  - סוֹד "בָּעֲטָרָה שֶׁעִטְּרָה לּוֹ אִמּוֹ" (שה"ש ג, יא)
  - בְּסוֹד הַנְּשִׁימָה וְהַהֶבֶל הַיּוֹצֵא 'מִפֶּה' אִמָּא, לְאוֹר מַקִּיף אֵלָיו. כְּמוֹ שֶׁכָּתוּב בְּעֵץ חַיִּים שַׁעַר הַכְּלָלִים סוֹף פֶּרֶק י"א, וּבְלִקּוּטֵי תַּנָּ"ךְ בִּתְהִלִּים (נג, ד) בְּפָסוּק כְּלוֹ סָג כו'
  - כְּמוֹ שֶׁנִּתְבָּאֵר לְעֵיל, שֶׁבְּחִינַת הַנְּשָׁמָה הִיא נְשִׁימַת 'הַפֶּה הָעֶלְיוֹן', אֲבָל עִקָּרָהּ הִיא כַּלָּה לְמַעְלָה, גְּנוּזָה וְנֶעֱלָמָה בִּמְקוֹרָהּ הָעֶלְיוֹן בְּתוֹךְ הַפֶּה, וּמֵאִיר בְּרִחוּק מָקוֹם:

- וּבָזֶה יוּבַן כַּוָּנָתָם זִכְרוֹנָם לִבְרָכָה בִּשְׁמוֹת רַבָּה פָּרָשָׁה מ"א
  - עַל פָּסוּק "כִּי ה' יִתֵּן חָכְמָה מִפִּיו דַּעַת וּתְבוּנָה" (משלי ב, ו), שֶׁאָמְרוּ "לְמָה הַדָּבָר דּוֹמֶה, לְמֶלֶךְ שֶׁהָיָה לוֹ בֵּן, בָּא בְּנוֹ מִבֵּית הַסֵּפֶר מָצָא תַּמְחוּי לִפְנֵי אָבִיו, נָטַל אָבִיו חֲתִיכָה אַחַת וּנְתָנָהּ לוֹ כו', אָמַר לוֹ אֵינִי מְבַקֵּשׁ אֶלָּא מִמַּה שֶּׁבְּתוֹךְ פִּיךָ, מֶה עָשָׂה, נְתָנוֹ לוֹ" כו'.

  הַיְנוּ, שֶׁבַּקָּשַׁת הַבֵּן יַקִּיר לְהַשִּׂיג, שֶׁיִּשְׁפַּע בּוֹ מִנִּצּוֹצֵי אוֹר בְּחִינַת הַנְּשָׁמָה, אֲשֶׁר מְקוֹרָהּ נֶעֱלָמָה בִּנְשִׁימַת 'פִּיו' יִתְבָּרַךְ שְׁמוֹ.

  - וְרָמְזוּ עוֹד בִּלְשׁוֹנָם הַקָּדוֹשׁ, שֶׁהִמְשִׁילוּ לְתִינוֹק הַבָּא מִ'בֵּית הַסֵּפֶר' דַּוְקָא, הוֹדִיעוּ נֶאֱמָנָה, שֶׁאֵין מָבוֹא בָּעוֹלָם לְהַשִּׂיג בְּחִינַת נִצּוֹצֵי אוֹר הַנְּשָׁמָה, אִם לֹא עַל יְדֵי הָעֵסֶק וְהָעִיּוּן וְהִתְבּוֹנְנוּת בַּתּוֹרָה הַקְּדוֹשָׁה בִּקְדֻשָּׁה, כִּי שְׁנֵיהֶם מִמָּקוֹר אֶחָד בָּאִים, כַּיָּדוּעַ לַמֵּבִין: (הגהה י"ד)

- וְזֶהוּ שֶׁאָמְרוּ שָׁם (בשמו"ר), בְּשָׁעָה שֶׁעָמְדוּ יִשְׂרָאֵל עַל הַר סִינַי לְקַבֵּל אֶת הַתּוֹרָה,

---

hints to the surrounding *breath of light* which is from Binah, which comes out of [Binah] and surrounds the seven lower Middot, Zeer Anpin, and Nukveh of Zeer Anpin. . . .

409 Midrash Rabba Shemot 41:3 quoting Mishlei 2:6.
410 Hoshea 5:9.
411 **R. Chaim adds Note 14 here.** This note is brought at the end of this chapter and is entitled "Simple meaning of God, Torah, and Israel all being connected."

Commandments directly from God's Mouth, as per "May He kiss me with kisses of His Mouth."[412]

- That at the time of this holy gathering they all merited to have the sparks of the radiance of the level of Neshama from God's Mouth, so to speak, to hover over and enlighten them. This is the secret of the *crowns* which [Israel] merited to receive at Mount Sinai, [as in] ". . . with the happiness of the world [i.e., the crowns] on their heads. . . ."[413]

- Through this [Israel] merited to perceive the inner essence of the soul of the Holy Torah, as per:
  - The Torah has a body . . . the wise servants of the Supernal King – those that stood at Mount Sinai – they only see the [Torah's] Neshama, which absolutely is the principal part of Torah.[414]
- This is what Chazal say in many places in the Midrash that [Israel] had a weapon at Mount Sinai with God's Name etched into it[415]
  - this refers to the supernal perception of the level of Neshama and of the secrets of the Torah, the Name of God.
- As this is how it is Above at a [person's] supernal root as per G1:15
  - the secret of "with the crown which his mother crowned him with"[416] and Chazal explain [the continuation of this verse "on the day of his wedding, on the day of the rejoicing of his heart"] that:
    - "The day of his wedding" – this is [the event of receiving the Torah at] Mount Sinai.
    - "The day of the rejoicing of his heart" – these are the words of Torah.
    - This is the meaning of "with the crown . . . ." They are the crowns mentioned above that were at Mount Sinai – containing the life of The King.[417] Refer to Etz Chaim.[418]

---

412 Continuation of Midrash Rabba Shemot 41:3 quoting Shir Hashirim 1:2.
413 Yishayahu 35:10, 51:11 which is quoted in Shabbat 88a describing how the crowns which Israel received at Mount Sinai will be returned to them in the future.

   See G4:28 which describes that although Israel merited perceiving the soul of the Torah at Mount Sinai, they did not, however, perceive the soul of the soul.
414 Zohar III Behaalotcha 152a. This source also states that the fools of the world only see the body of the Torah which is the Torah narrative and are not aware of anything deeper.

הָיוּ מְבַקְשִׁים לִשְׁמֹעַ הַדִּבְּרוֹת "מִפִּי' הַקָּדוֹשׁ בָּרוּךְ הוּא, וּכְמוֹ שֶׁכָּתוּב (שה"ש א, ב) "יִשָּׁקֵנִי מִנְּשִׁיקוֹת פִּיהוּ".

שֶׁבְּעֵת הַמַּעֲמָד הַמְּקֻדָּשׁ, זָכוּ כֻּלָּם, שֶׁהָיָה חוֹפֵף וּמֵאִיר עֲלֵיהֶם, זִיו נִצּוֹצֵי זֹהַר בְּחִינַת הַנְּשָׁמָה, מִנִּשְׁמַת פִּיו יִתְבָּרֵךְ כִּבְיָכוֹל. וְהוּא סוֹד הַכְּתָרִים שֶׁזָּכוּ בְּסִינַי (שבת פח, א), "וְשִׂמְחַת עוֹלָם עַל רֹאשָׁם", (ישעיה לה, י. נא, יא):

• וְעַל יְדֵי כָךְ, זָכוּ לְהַשִּׂיג סִתְרֵי פְּנִימִיּוּת נִשְׁמַת הַתּוֹרָה הַקְּדוֹשָׁה כְּמוֹ שֶׁכָּתוּב בַּזֹּהַר בְּהַעֲלוֹתְךָ קנ"ב א'

• "אוֹרַיְתָא אִית לָהּ גוּפָא כו', חַכִּימִין עַבְדֵי דְמַלְכָּא עִלָּאָה, אִנּוּן דְּקַיְמוּ בְּטוּרָא דְסִינַי, לָא מִסְתַּכְּלֵי אֶלָּא בְּנִשְׁמָתָא, דְּאִיהוּ עִקָּרָא דְּכֹלָּא אוֹרַיְתָא מַמָּשׁ":

• וְהוּא שֶׁאָמְרוּ בְּכַמָּה מְקוֹמוֹת בְּמִדְרַשׁ רַבָּה, "זַיִן הָיָה לָהֶם בְּסִינַי וְשֵׁם הַמְפֹרָשׁ חָקוּק עָלָיו"

• שֶׁהוּא הַהַשָּׂגָה עֶלְיוֹנָה בְּנִשְׁמָתָא וְסִתְרִין דְּאוֹרַיְתָא, שְׁמָא מְפָרַשׁ.

• כִּי כֵן הָיָה הָעִנְיָן אָז לְמַעְלָה בְּשָׁרְשׁוֹ הָעֶלְיוֹן, כַּנַּ"ל בְּפֶרֶק הֶעָבַר

• סוֹד "בָּעֲטָרָה שֶׁעִטְּרָה לּוֹ אִמּוֹ" (שה"ש ג, יא), וְדָרְשׁוּ עַל זֶה בֶּחָזִית (שהש"ר)

▫ "בְּיוֹם חֲתֻנָּתוֹ" — זֶה סִינַי

▫ "וּבְיוֹם שִׂמְחַת לִבּוֹ" — אֵלּוּ דִבְרֵי תוֹרָה.

▫ וְזֶהוּ 'בָּעֲטָרָה' כו', הֵם הַכְּתָרִים הַנַּ"ל שֶׁהָיוּ בְּסִינַי, חַיֵּי הַמֶּלֶךְ. וְעַיֵּן בְּעֵץ חַיִּים שַׁעַר הַכְּלָלִים סוֹף פֶּרֶק ה':

---

415 E.g., Midrash Rabba Shir Hashirim 1:2.
416 Shir HaShirim 3:11 as expounded on in Midrash Rabba Shir HaShirim 3.
417 I.e., the level of Neshama.
418 Etz Chaim Shaar HaKlalim, at the end of Chap. 5:
  • [This cryptically refers to two crowns – one which is called *Malchut of Father* and the other *Malchut of Mother*, relating to the manifestation of God's intellect, i.e., the Torah – in the context of the verse "with the crown which his mother crowned him with, on the day of his wedding."]

Rabbi Chaim's Note:
Note 14 – Simple meaning of God, Torah, and Israel all being connected

- On this basis, one who investigates will be able to have a simple understanding of the concept mentioned in the Zohar:[419] "that God, the Torah, and Israel are all connected to each other"
  - even though this certainly relates to very deep secrets, nevertheless this concept can be explained simply on this basis.
- The concept is that God is [both] hidden and revealed.[420]
  - For the Essence of the Master of All, the Ein Sof, Blessed be He,[421] is not perceivable and no intellect can grasp it at all.
  - The miniscule part that we do perceive is only from His connection to the worlds from the time when He created them and renewed them
  - to give them life and constantly cause them to exist and to control them, as written "and You *continuously* Give life to everything."[422]
- Therefore, we praise [God] in our prayers that he is the "Life of the Worlds"
  - for it is forbidden for us to focus our hearts on anything apart from God's Infinite Unity during our prayers.
  - This does not however mean [that we focus on] His Essence alone on a level which is separated from the worlds
  - but rather from the perspective of the connection of His Sublime Will to the worlds and of His concealment within them to cause them to [appear to] exist [as if they are entities in their own right].
  - This is the root principle of all service of God and Mitzvah performance, and this alone is what we are able to perceive.[423]
  - Refer to G2:04 and G2:05 where this concept is dealt with at length.
- The life force and existence of all the worlds is entirely dependent on the Holy Torah when Israel are involved with it
  - as it is 'the light of all the worlds'[424] and the soul and life force of everything
  - and if, even momentarily, the entire world was devoid of involvement in and contemplation of the Holy Torah, the worlds would return to their [original] null and void state.

---

419 Zohar III Acharei Mot 73a.
420 Zohar III Emor 98b.
421 I.e., God's Infinite Essence. The use of this expression is clarified in V2:02 in Chap. 7 on Nefesh HaChaim.
422 Nechemia 9:6. See G3:01.

הגהה י"ד

- וְעַל פִּי זֶה יַשְׂכִּיל הַמֵּעַיֵּן, לְהָבִין עַל פִּי פְּשׁוּטוֹ, עִנְיַן הַנִּזְכָּר בַּזֹּהַר פָּרָשַׁת אַחֲרֵי ע"ג א', שֶׁקּוּדְשָׁא בְּרִיךְ הוּא וְאוֹרַיְתָא וְיִשְׂרָאֵל מִתְקַשְּׁרִין דָּא בְּדָא.
  - וַדַּאי עֹמֶק כַּוָּנָתוֹ לְסוֹדוֹת עֲמֻקִּים, עִם כָּל זֶה יֵשׁ לְהַסְבִּיר הָעִנְיָן גַּם בִּפְשִׁיטוּת עַל פִּי זֶה:

- וְהָעִנְיָן, כִּי קוּדְשָׁא בְּרִיךְ הוּא סָתִים וְגַלְיָא (זהר פ' אמור צח:)
  - כִּי עַצְמוּת אֲדוֹן כֹּל, אֵין סוֹף בָּרוּךְ הוּא — אֵינוֹ מֻשָּׂג, וְלֵית מַחְשָׁבָה תְּפִיסָא בֵּיהּ כְּלָל.
  - וּמַה שֶּׁמֻּשָּׂג לָנוּ מְעַט מִן הַמְּעַט, הוּא רַק מִצַּד הִתְחַבְּרוּתוֹ לְהָעוֹלָמוֹת — מֵעֵת שֶׁבְּרָאָם וְחִדְּשָׁם
  - לְהַחֲיוֹתָם וּלְקַיְּמָם כָּל רֶגַע וּלְהַנְהִיגָם, כְּמוֹ שֶׁכָּתוּב (נחמיה ט, ו) "וְאַתָּה מְחַיֶּה אֶת כֻּלָּם":

- וְלָכֵן נְשַׁבְּחֵהוּ יִתְבָּרַךְ בִּתְפִלָּתֵנוּ שֶׁהוּא "חֵי הָעוֹלָמִים"
  - כִּי כָּל כַּוָּנַת לִבֵּנוּ בְּכָל הַתְּפִלּוֹת וְהַבַּקָּשׁוֹת, אָסוּר לִהְיוֹת רַק לְיִחוּדוֹ שֶׁל עוֹלָם הוּא אֵין סוֹף בָּרוּךְ הוּא
  - אָמְנָם לֹא מִצַּד עַצְמוּתוֹ יִתְבָּרַךְ לְבַד, בִּבְחִינַת הֱיוֹתוֹ מֻפְרָשׁ מֵהָעוֹלָמוֹת
  - אֶלָּא מִצַּד הִתְחַבְּרוּתוֹ יִתְבָּרַךְ — בִּרְצוֹנוֹ הַפָּשׁוּט — לְהָעוֹלָמוֹת וְהִסְתָּרוֹ בָּהֶם לְהַחֲיוֹתָם.
  - וְזֶהוּ כְּלָל שֹׁרֶשׁ עִנְיַן הָעֲבוֹדָה וְהַמִּצְווֹת כֻּלָּם, וְזֶה לְבַד כָּל הַשְׁגָּחָתֵנוּ.
  - וְעַיֵּן לְקַמָּן בְּשַׁעַר ב' פֶּרֶק ד' וּפֶרֶק ה' הָעִנְיָן בְּאֹרֶךְ:

- וְכָל חִיּוּתָם וְקִיּוּמָם שֶׁל הָעוֹלָמוֹת כֻּלָּם, הוּא רַק עַל יְדֵי הַתּוֹרָה הַקְּדוֹשָׁה כְּשֶׁיִּשְׂרָאֵל עוֹסְקִים בָּהּ
  - שֶׁהִיא נְהִירוּ דְּכָל עָלְמִין וְנִשְׁמָתָא וְחִיּוּתָא דְּכֻלְּהוֹן
  - וְאִלּוּ הָיָה הָעוֹלָם, מִקְּצֵהוּ וְעַד קָצֵהוּ, פָּנוּי אַף רֶגַע אֶחָד, מֵעֵסֶק וְהִתְבּוֹנְנוּת בַּתּוֹרָה הַקְּדוֹשָׁה, הָיוּ חוֹזְרִים כָּל הָעוֹלָמוֹת לְתֹהוּ וָבֹהוּ.

---

423 I.e., that the created entities appear to exist in their own right and we relate to God's connection to the created entities when serving Him.

424 Zohar III Shelach Lecha 166b.

- As Chazal say: "[the Universe only exists] *for the sake of the Torah* [which was given to Israel]"[425]
- and as written: "You have implanted everlasting life [i.e., Torah] within us."[426]
- For the [Torah's] supernal root is higher than all the worlds; therefore, they are all dependent on it for their existence.
- Chazal also say: "[the Heavens and Earth were only created] *for the sake of Israel* . . . [who are called *Reishit*]"[427]
  - as will be explained, that through a man's involvement and intellectual thinking in the Holy Torah
  - he perceives the sparks of light from the level of Neshama within it, enabling him to understand the depths of the secrets contained within it and it is then that he referred to as *Israel*, as known in the Zohar.[428]
- "[for man shall live] *on what comes out* of the Mouth of God"[429]
  - this is the level of man's Neshama, God's breath
  - with which all the powers and worlds are also given life and exist, for it is also the highest and deepest essence of all the worlds.
  - This is the meaning of "God, the Torah, and Israel are all connected to each other" and this is the meaning of what Chazal say that "*Bereishit* means for the sake of the Torah which is called *Reishit*, and also means for the sake of Israel who are called *Reishit*."

17. PERFECTION IS THE INTERCONNECTION OF WORLD AND SOUL LEVELS

- We will [now] explain the interconnection of the three levels of Nefesh, Ruach, and Neshama with each other.
  - It is the foundation and essential part of the concept of repentance
  - 'and this shall be the fruit of the sin's removal'[430] from the soul of the sinner, and the purification from the illness of its impurity.[431]
- A person should reflect on how much he needs to watch over and think about all the specific details of his service of his Creator

---

425 Esther Rabba 7:13.
426 Masechet Sofrim 13:6. See G4:11.
427 Vayikra Rabba Bechukotai 36:4. Also see the equating of the Torah and Israel in G4:11 and G4:13 including more details and sources for Chazal referring to Torah and Israel as Reishit.
428 E.g., Zohar I Vayeshev 187a:
  - Come and see how precious are words of Torah, for each and every word of Torah contains supernal holy secrets; and it says that when God gave the

- כְּמוֹ שֶׁאָמְרוּ ז"ל "בִּשְׁבִיל הַתּוֹרָה" וְכוּ'.
- כְּמוֹ שֶׁכָּתוּב "וְחַיֵּי עוֹלָם נָטַע בְּתוֹכֵנוּ".
- כִּי מְקוֹר שָׁרְשָׁהּ הָעֶלְיוֹן, הִיא לְמַעְלָה מִכָּל הָעוֹלָמוֹת, לָכֵן בָּהּ תָּלוּי הַחִיּוּת שֶׁל כֻּלָּם:

• וְאָמְרוּ גַם כֵּן "בִּשְׁבִיל יִשְׂרָאֵל" כוּ'
- כְּמוֹ שֶׁנִּתְבָּאֵר, שֶׁעַל יְדֵי עֵסֶק הָאָדָם וְהֶגְיוֹנוֹ בַּתּוֹרָה הַקְּדוֹשָׁה
- הוּא מַשִּׂיג לְהִתְנוֹצְצוּת אוֹר בְּחִינַת הַנְּשָׁמָה בּוֹ, לְהַשְׂכִּילוֹ בְּעִמְקֵי רָזִין קַדִּישִׁין דִּילֵיהּ, שֶׁאָז מְכֻנֶּה בְּשֵׁם "יִשְׂרָאֵל", כַּיָּדוּעַ בַּזֹּהַר:

• "וְעַל כָּל מוֹצָא פִי ה'" (דברים ח, ג)
- הוּא בְּחִינַת נִשְׁמַת הָאָדָם, נִשְׁימַת פִּיו יִתְבָּרֵךְ
- יִחְיוּ וְיִתְקַיְּמוּ גַּם כֵּן כָּל הַכֹּחוֹת וְהָעוֹלָמוֹת, שֶׁהִיא גַם כֵּן הַגְּבוֹהָה וְהַפְּנִימִית מִכָּל הָעוֹלָמוֹת.
- וְזֶהוּ "קוּדְשָׁא בְּרִיךְ הוּא וְאוֹרַיְתָא וְיִשְׂרָאֵל מִתְקַשְּׁרִים דָּא בְּדָא". וְז"שׁ "בְּרֵאשִׁית" — בִּשְׁבִיל הַתּוֹרָה שֶׁנִּקְרֵאת "רֵאשִׁית", וּבִשְׁבִיל יִשְׂרָאֵל שֶׁנִּקְרְאוּ "רֵאשִׁית":

שער א' - פרק י"ז

- וּנְבָאֵר עִנְיַן הִתְקַשְּׁרוּת הַשְּׁלֹשָׁה בְּחִינוֹת נר"ן אֶחָד בַּחֲבֵרוֹ.
- וְהוּא יְסוֹד וְעִקַּר עִנְיַן הַתְּשׁוּבָה.
- וְזֶה כָּל פְּרִי הָסֵר הַחַטָּאוֹת מִנֶּפֶשׁ הַחוֹטֵאת, וּלְטַהֲרָהּ מֵחֶלְאַת טֻמְאָתָהּ:

• וְיִתְבּוֹנֵן הָאָדָם כַּמָּה הוּא צָרִיךְ לְהַשְׁגִּיחַ וּלְהִתְבּוֹנֵן עַל כָּל פְּרָטֵי עִנְיְנֵי עֲבוֹדָתוֹ לְבוֹרְאוֹ יִתְבָּרַךְ שְׁמוֹ

Torah to Israel, he gave all the hidden secrets with the Torah; and He gave all of it to Israel at the time when they received the Torah at Sinai . . .

Additionally as per Chullin 101b:
- . . . and they were not called the Children of Israel until [receiving the Torah] at Sinai. . . .

429 Devarim 8:3.
430 Yishayahu 27:9.
431 The explanation is initiated in this chapter and developed over the coming chapters.

- to ensure his service is uncomplicated, complete, holy, and pure.
- He should see to it that he is constantly scrutinizing and aware of all of his *actions*, *speech*, and *thoughts*, which are the three levels mentioned above
- that perhaps, on critical reflection, he has not yet completed God's Will according to the root of his soul.
- All of his days, he should 'strengthen himself'[432] in Torah [study] and [performance of] Mitzvot
- to perfect his Nefesh, Ruach, and Neshama to [reach] the pure [state] in which they were given
- after intellectually seeing how God, out of His great mercy, wants to do good for him and perseveres with the correction of the sinning soul such that even if it is already submerged within the depths of Evil
- nevertheless, everything will be returned to its place and its source, 'without anything being lost.'[433]

• The idea is, as is known, that in the sequence [within which life force] cascades down through the world levels, that the highest level within each world is connected with the lowest level of the world above it.
- As per the Zohar, that all the worlds are interconnected with each other just like a chain [whose links] interconnect it together [and is all one].[434]
- As known from the writings of the Arizal, that the most external element of Malchut of every world/Partzuf [i.e., presentation] forms the essence of the Keter [i.e., the highest level] of the world/Partzuf below it.[435]
- (That is, with a person's acceptance of God's Malchut to raise all of his actions, speech, and thoughts of Torah and Mitzvot to a higher level – this generates an internal desire to subjugate his brain, speech, and actions [to be solely focused] on Torah and Mitzvah performance) – this is the secret of Keter Malchut.

• The same is true of the interconnection of a person's three soul levels – Nefesh, Ruach, Neshama.

---

432 Iyov 17:9.
433 2 Shmuel 14:14.
434 Zohar III Vayikra 10b.
435 See footnotes at the beginning of G1:16. The term "Partzuf" is used here in addition to "worlds," where "Partzuf" literally means a "face," i.e., a persona or a *presentation* of a more complex configuration of Middot which, like worlds (which represent a simpler configuration), also have an interaction between higher and lower levels. As noted in the footnotes at the beginning of G1:16,

- שֶׁתְּהֵא עֲבוֹדָתוֹ תַּמָּה וּשְׁלֵמָה, קְדוֹשָׁה וּטְהוֹרָה.
- וְיִרְאֶה לְפַשְׁפֵּשׁ וּלְמַשְׁמֵשׁ תָּמִיד בְּכָל מַעֲשָׂיו וְדִבּוּרָיו וּמַחְשְׁבוֹתָיו, שֶׁהֵם הַשְּׁלֹשָׁה בְּחִינוֹת הַנַּ"ל
- אוּלַי לֹא הִשְׁלִים עֲדַיִן חֶפְצוֹ וּרְצוֹנוֹ יִתְבָּרַךְ, לְפִי שֹׁרֶשׁ נִשְׁמָתוֹ, בְּהַשָּׂגָה
- וְכָל יָמָיו יוֹסִיף אֹמֶץ בַּתּוֹרָה וּמִצְוֹת
- לְהַשְׁלִים נַפְשׁוֹ וְרוּחוֹ וְנִשְׁמָתוֹ מְטֹהָרִים כַּאֲשֶׁר נְתָנָם
- אַחַר שֶׁיִּרְאֶה בְּעֵין שִׂכְלוֹ אֵיךְ שֶׁחָפֵץ הוּא יִתְבָּרַךְ בְּחַסְדּוֹ הַגָּדוֹל לְהֵיטִיב אַחֲרִיתוֹ, וְשׁוֹקֵד עַל תַּקָּנַת הַנֶּפֶשׁ הַחוֹטֵאת, שֶׁגַּם אִם כְּבָר נִטְבְּעָה בְּעֹמֶק מְצוּלוֹת הָרָע
- עִם כָּל זֶה תַּחֲזֹר כָּל דָּבָר לִמְקוֹמוֹ וּמְקוֹרוֹ, בִּלְתִּי יִדַּח מִמֶּנּוּ נִדָּח:
• וְהָעִנְיָן, כִּי יָדוּעַ בְּסֵדֶר הִשְׁתַּלְשְׁלוּת הָעוֹלָמוֹת, שֶׁהַבְּחִינָה הָעֶלְיוֹנָה שֶׁבְּכָל עוֹלָם, מִתְקַשֵּׁר עִם הַבְּחִינָה הַתַּחְתּוֹנָה שֶׁל הָעוֹלָם שֶׁעָלָיו.
- וְעַיֵּן זֹהַר וַיִּקְרָא י' ע"ב, "דְּכֻלְּהוּ עָלְמִין מִתְקַשְּׁרָן דָּא בְּדָא וְדָא בְּדָא, כְּהַאי שַׁלְשֶׁלֶת דְּאִתְקַשַּׁר דָּא בְּדָא".
- וְכַיָּדוּעַ בְּכִתְבֵי הָאֲרִיזַ"ל שֶׁחִיצוֹנִיּוּת מַלְכוּת שֶׁל כָּל עוֹלָם וּפַרְצוּף, נַעֲשָׂה פְּנִימִיּוּת כֶּתֶר לְהָעוֹלָם אוֹ הַפַּרְצוּף שֶׁתַּחְתָּיו
- (הַיְנוּ שֶׁבְּקַבָּלַת הָאָדָם עַל מַלְכוּתוֹ יִתְבָּרַךְ, לְהַעֲלוֹת כָּל מַעֲשָׂיו וְדִבּוּרָיו וּמַחְשְׁבוֹתָיו בַּתּוֹרָה וּמִצְוֹת לְמַדְרֵגָה יוֹתֵר גְּבוֹהָה, מִזֶּה נַעֲשָׂה לוֹ רָצוֹן פְּנִימִי, לְשַׁעְבֵּד מֹחוֹ וְדִבּוּרוֹ וּמַעֲשָׂיו בַּתּוֹרָה וּמִצְוֹת), בְּסוֹד כֶּתֶר מַלְכוּת:
• וְכֵן הוּא הָעִנְיָן הַשְּׁלֹשָׁה הַבְּחִינוֹת נר"ן שֶׁל הָאָדָם.

Malchut is the recipient, the *daughter/female* of the process – it therefore relates to acceptance, i.e., acceptance of God's Kingship. Once a level of acceptance has been achieved – then this acceptance becomes the unquestioned Keter, i.e., Crown, which drives the next level of the process to ultimately achieve an even greater level of acceptance. This process is parenthetically described (in the next paragraph) as the repentance process which encapsulates the secret of Keter Malchut, the Crown of Kingship, i.e., the interaction between the acceptance of God as King and the application of this acceptance to invest authority in exercising His Commands. (See V2:02, Chap. 15, "Tzimtzum Sources," I1.1, which adds insight into the difference between the conceptual configuration of the Sefirot and of the Partzufim.)

- For each level of a holy matter is comprised of ten specific levels, which are its own set of Ten Sefirot
- and the highest level of Nefesh is bound to the lowest, the tenth level of Ruach
- and the highest level of Ruach is bound to the lowest level of Neshama
- and the [highest level of] Neshama is also interconnected with and bound to the soul root – the secret of *Knesset Yisrael* – which is the root of the collective unified soul of Israel.[436]
- Similarly, in this way, the soul root [Knesset Yisrael] is also connected all the way up from level to level until it [ultimately connects with] the *Infinite Essence of God*.[437]
- This is as Avigail said to David: "May my master's *Nefesh* be bound up with the Bond of Life, with YHVH your God,"[438] meaning that even the level of *Nefesh* should be connected, so to speak, with God.
- As per Zohar: When the Ruach ascends and is decorated ... the Nefesh is connected with the Ruach and is enlightened by it ... and the Ruach is connected with the Neshama, and the Neshama is connected through to the *end of thought* which is secret. The Nefesh is connected with the supernal Ruach, and the Ruach is connected with the supernal Neshama, and the Neshama is connected with the Ein Sof, and then it brings joy to all with all being connected above and below – all with secret of unity ... this being gratification of the Nefesh below, about which it is written: "May my master's *Nefesh* be bound up with the Bond of Life, with YHVH your God."[439]
- The Zohar also explains: We learned that it is written "May my master's *Nefesh* be bound up with the Bond of Life, with YHVH your God." This verse should have referenced the Neshama [and not the Nefesh]? But as we have said: Happy is the portion of Tzaddikim with whom all the levels are interconnected: the Nefesh with the Ruach, the Ruach with the Neshama, and the Neshama with God; it therefore transpires that the *Nefesh* is bound up with the Bond of Life.[440]
- Refer further to Zohar.[441]

---

436 See G2:17 which describes the soul root as being the level of Chaya, the connection of the soul root with the level above it of Yechida and also details of Knesset Yisrael which are further elaborated on in G2:17:N38.

437 This expression, "Atzmut Ein Sof," is an attempt to use language to describe the indescribable Absolute Essence of God.

438 1 Shmuel 25:29.

439 Zohar II Terumah 142b quoting 1 Shmuel 25:29.

440 Zohar III Acharei Mot 71b quoting 1 Shmuel 25:29.

כִּי כָל בְּחִינָה מִדָּבָר שֶׁבִּקְדֻשָּׁה, כָּלוּל מֵעֶשֶׂר בְּחִינוֹת פְּרָטִיִּים, שֶׁהֵם הָעֶשֶׂר סְפִירוֹת שֶׁלּוֹ.

וְהַבְּחִינָה הָעֶלְיוֹנָה שֶׁל הַנֶּפֶשׁ, נֶאֱחֶזֶת וּמִתְקַשֶּׁרֶת עִם הַבְּחִינָה הַתַּחְתּוֹנָה הָעֲשִׂירִית שֶׁל בְּחִינַת הָרוּחַ.

וְהַבְּחִינָה הָעֶלְיוֹנָה שֶׁל הָרוּחַ מִתְקַשֶּׁרֶת עִם בְּחִינָה הַתַּחְתּוֹנָה שֶׁל הַנְּשָׁמָה.

וְהַנְּשָׁמָה גַּם כֵּן מִתְקַשֶּׁרֶת וּמִתְדַּבֶּקֶת בִּבְחִינַת שֹׁרֶשׁ הַנְּשָׁמָה, סוֹד כְּנֶסֶת יִשְׂרָאֵל, שֶׁהִיא שֹׁרֶשׁ הַכְּנֵסִיָּה שֶׁל כָּל נִשְׁמוֹת כְּלַל יִשְׂרָאֵל יַחַד.

וְכֵן עַל זֶה הַדֶּרֶךְ גַּם בְּחִינַת שֹׁרֶשׁ הַנְּשָׁמָה גַּם כֵּן מִתְקַשֶּׁרֶת לְמַעְלָה מַעְלָה, מִמַּדְרֵגָה לְמַדְרֵגָה, עַד עַצְמוּת אֵין סוֹף בָּרוּךְ הוּא.

וְזֶהוּ שֶׁאָמְרָה אֲבִיגַיִל לְדָוִד (שמו"א כה, כט) "וְהָיְתָה נֶפֶשׁ אֲדֹנִי צְרוּרָה בִּצְרוֹר הַחַיִּים אֵת ה' אֱלֹקֶיךָ", רָצָה לוֹמַר, שֶׁגַּם בְּחִינַת 'נַפְשׁוֹ' תִּתְדַּבֵּק כִּבְיָכוֹל בּוֹ יִתְבָּרַךְ שְׁמוֹ.

וּכְמוֹ שֶׁכָּתוּב בַּזֹּהַר תְּרוּמָה קמ"ב ב', "כַּד הַהִיא רוּחַ סָלְקָא וְאִתְעַטְּרָא כו', הַהִיא נֶפֶשׁ מִתְקַשְּׁרָא בְּהַהִיא רוּחַ, וְאִתְנְהִירַת מִנֵּיהּ כו', וְרוּחַ מִתְקַשְּׁרָא גּוֹ הַהִיא נִשְׁמְתָא, וְהַהִיא נִשְׁמְתָא מִתְקַשְּׁרָא גּוֹ סוֹף מַחֲשָׁבָה דְּאִיהִי רָזָא, וְהַהִיא נֶפֶשׁ אִתְקַשְּׁרַת גּוֹ הַהוּא רוּחַ עִלָּאָה, וְהַהוּא רוּחַ אִתְקַשַּׁר גּוֹ הַהִיא נְשָׁמָה עִלָּאָה, וְהַהוּא נְשָׁמָה אִתְקַשְּׁרַת בְּאֵין סוֹף, וּכְדֵין אִיהוּ נַיְחָא דְכֹלָּא וְקִשּׁוּרָא דְכֹלָּא, עֵילָא וְתַתָּא כֹּלָּא בְּרָזָא חֲדָא כו', וּכְדֵין אִיהוּ נַיְחָא דְנֶפֶשׁ דִּלְתַתָּא, וְעַל דָּא כְּתִיב "וְהָיְתָה נֶפֶשׁ אֲדֹנִי צְרוּרָה בִּצְרוֹר הַחַיִּים אֵת ה' אֱלֹהֶיךָ".

וּבְפָרָשַׁת אַחֲרֵי ע"א ב', תָּאנָא כְּתִיב "וְהָיְתָה נֶפֶשׁ אֲדֹנִי צְרוּרָה" גו', 'נִשְׁמַת' אֲדוֹנִי מִבָּעֵי לֵיהּ, אֶלָּא כְּמָה דְּאָמְרָן דּוּכְתָּא חוּלְקֵיהוֹן דְּצַדִּיקַיָּא, דְּכֹלָּא אִתְקַשַּׁר דָּא בְּדָא, נֶפֶשׁ בְּרוּחַ, וְרוּחַ בִּנְשָׁמָה, וּנְשָׁמָה בְּקֻדְשָׁא בְּרִיךְ הוּא, אִשְׁתַּכַּח דְּנֶפֶשׁ צְרוּרָה בִּצְרוֹר הַחַיִּים" כו'.

וְעַיֵּן עוֹד בְּפָרָשַׁת וַיִּקְרָא רֵישׁ דַּף כ"ה:

---

441 Zohar III Vayikra 24b/25a:
- ... and because of this: "May my master's *Nefesh* be bound up with the Bond of Life," and we have established that the Nefesh is bound with Ruach and the Ruach with Neshama and Neshama with God. . . .

- This is the idea of the verse: "God's people are a part of Him, Yaakov is the cord of His possession,"[442] for they [the people] are like a part of God (YHVH), so to speak,[443] attached to Him – through the interconnection of the three levels, as mentioned above – like a cord which is tied up above, dangling down and descending to the lowest level.

18. SIN DISCONNECTS NEFESH AND DAMAGES RUACH – NESHAMA UNAFFECTED

- All this [i.e., God's establishment of the above interconnectivity of the three levels] is
  - out of His Great Goodness and Mercy
  - with which he desires to put us right to do good for us
  - therefore 'His counsel is wondrous'[444]
  - and he established this concept that each of these three levels interconnect with the level above it
  - so that through this, man is enabled to gradually elevate and connect from the lower [worlds] to the higher [worlds]
  - according to the amount of his involvement in God's Torah and service
  - and the purity of his heart, love, and fear [of God]
  - until he ultimately ascends to cleave to the "Bond of Life," so to speak, with "YHVH his God," according to his root and level.
- 'In addition to this however,'[445] there are many sins which a Nefesh[/person] who sins with one of them results in his liability for Karet[446] or destruction, God forbid.
- The concept of Karet is where the level of Nefesh is disconnected and cut off from its supernal root with a disconnection in the cord which previously bound and attached it through the [process of] interconnectivity, as mentioned above. As per:
  - There is a Nefesh . . . about which it is written: "and that *Nefesh* shall be cut off from *before Me*, I am the Lord." What does *before Me* mean? That Ruach will not rest upon it, and when Ruach does not rest upon it, it does not have a connection with that which is above it.[447] Refer there.
  - [If he does not merit it as a result of transgressing a sin punishable by

---

442 Devarim 32:9.
443 See comments on p. 140, fn. 111, about the soul literally being part of YHVH, so to speak.

- וְזֶהוּ עִנְיָן "כִּי חֵלֶק ה' עַמּוֹ יַעֲקֹב חֶבֶל נַחֲלָתוֹ", כִּי הֵם כְּחֵלֶק ה', מְדֻבָּקִים כִּבְיָכוֹל בּוֹ יִתְבָּרַךְ שְׁמוֹ, עַל יְדֵי הִתְקַשְּׁרוּת הַג' בְּחִינוֹת הַנַּ"ל, כְּחֶבֶל הַקָּשׁוּר לְמַעְלָה, וּמִשְׁתַּלְשֵׁל וְיוֹרֵד עַד לְמַטָּה:

שער א' - פרק י"ח

- וְכָל זֶה
  - מֵרֹב טוּבוֹ וְחַסְדּוֹ הַגָּדוֹל יִתְבָּרַךְ שְׁמוֹ
  - אֲשֶׁר חָפֵץ לְהַצְדִּיקֵנוּ לְהֵטִיב אַחֲרִיתֵנוּ
  - לָזֹאת הִפְלִיא עֵצָה
  - וּקְבָעָם בְּעִנְיָן זֶה, שֶׁכָּל בְּחִינָה מֵהַשְּׁלֹשָׁה אֵלּוּ, תִּתְקַשֵּׁר בַּבְּחִינָה שֶׁעָלֶיהָ
  - כְּדֵי שֶׁעַל יְדֵי זֶה יוּכַל הָאָדָם לַעֲלוֹת וּלְהִתְקַשֵּׁר מִמַּטָּה לְמַעְלָה, מְעַט מְעַט
  - לְפִי רֹב עִסְקוֹ בְּתוֹרָתוֹ וַעֲבוֹדָתוֹ יִתְבָּרַךְ שְׁמוֹ
  - וְטָהֳרַת לִבּוֹ וְאַהֲבָתוֹ וְיִרְאָתוֹ
  - עַד שֶׁיַּעֲלֶה וְיִתְדַּבֵּק בִּצְרוֹר הַחַיִּים כִּבְיָכוֹל אֶת ה' אֱלֹקָיו יִתְבָּרַךְ שְׁמוֹ, לְפִי שָׁרְשׁוֹ וּמַדְרֵגָתוֹ:

- זֹאת וְעוֹד אַחֶרֶת, כִּי יֵשׁ כַּמָּה עֲוֹנוֹת שֶׁהַנֶּפֶשׁ הַחוֹטֵאת בְּאַחַת מֵהֵנָּה, נִתְחַיְּבָה כָּרֵת אוֹ אֲבַדּוֹן חַס וְשָׁלוֹם:

- וְעִנְיַן הַכָּרֵת הוּא, שֶׁבְּחִינַת הַנֶּפֶשׁ נִפְסַק וְנִכְרַת מִשָּׁרְשׁוֹ הָעֶלְיוֹן, וְיִנָּתֵק הַחֶבֶל שֶׁהָיָה קָשׁוּר וּמְדֻבָּק בּוֹ עַד הֵנָּה עַל יְדֵי הִתְקַשְּׁרוּת הַנַּ"ל.
  - וּכְמוֹ שֶׁכָּתוּב בַּזֹּהַר תְּרוּמָה הַנַּ"ל, "וְאִית נַפְשָׁא כו', דִּכְתִיב בָּהּ (ויקרא כב, ג) "וְנִכְרְתָה הַנֶּפֶשׁ הַהִיא מִלְּפָנַי אֲנִי ה'". מַאי מִלְּפָנַי, דְּלָא שַׁרְיָא עֲלָהּ רוּחָא. וְכַד רוּחָא לָא שַׁרְיָא עֲלָהּ, לֵית לָהּ שׁוּתָּפוּ כְּלָל בְּמַה דִּלְעֵלָּא" כו'. וְעַיֵּן שָׁם.
  - וְעַיֵּן בְּלִקּוּטֵי תּוֹרָה פָּרָשָׁה בֹּא

---

444 Yishayahu 28:29.
445 E.g., Sanhedrin 82a and 104a.
446 *Karet* meaning to be *cut off* – a term used to describe the punishment by God for a capital crime which results in death before reaching age 50. Understood more deeply here that the performance of an action which invokes Karet, cuts off the physical connection to God and therefore directly results in a person's inevitable early death.
447 Zohar II Terumah 142b quoting Vayikra 22:3.

Karet . . . the level of Nefesh is cut off and separated from the levels of Neshama and Ruach.]448
- "Shall be cut off" does not mean [the Nefesh will be] destroyed but rather it will be disconnected.449
- This is the meaning of the verse "for your sins were a separation between you and between your God."450 This is that [the sins] literally separate one from God, as mentioned above – resulting in one being submerged into the depths of impurity and of the Kelipot,451 God should save us.
- Refer to Etz Chaim,452 Shaar HaYichudim,453 Likutei Tanach on the verse "when the spirit that envelops them is from Me,"454 Sefer HaGilgulim,455 and the holy writings of our great master, our teacher Eliyahu, of blessed memory, in his commentary on the Heichalot, on

---

448 Likutei Torah Bo.
449 Mechilta DeRabbi Yishmael Bo Masechta Depischa 8; Mechilta DeRabbi Yishmael Ki Tisa Masechta Deshabta 1; Sifri Bamidbar Behaalotcha 70; Sifri Bamidbar Shelach 112, all of these sources referencing Vayikra 22:3.
450 Yishayahu 59:2.
451 *Kelipot* – these are the forces of evil which exist as a result of God creating an illusory environment which is *apparently* devoid of His existence. A Kelipah is a husk or a shell which conceals a buried spark of Godliness within it. These Kelipot only indirectly receive life source from God in a very concealed way and as a result have the ability to sustain an errant soul who has disconnected himself from God through an act of Karet (i.e., sustaining the soul even beyond the age of 50).
452 Etz Chaim Shaar 42, Shaar Klalut/Derushei ABY"A, Chap. 4 (see V2:14, p. 676):
- [Note that this Shaar is split into two parts and the chapter numbering restarts in the second part. This reference relates to the second part of the Shaar.] Man incorporates the 4 worlds. If he only merited a Nefesh of Asiyah and afterwards sinned and damaged it, he enters it into Kelipah. They say to him: "The gnat preceded you" [Sanhedrin 38a] for the gnat cannot perform an action to enter itself into Kelipah.
453 R. Chaim quotes the following sources which are expanded here:
Shaar HaYichudim towards the end of Chap. 4:
- [This section explains why one needs to be careful when wanting to prostrate oneself over the grave of a Tzaddik which may be in the vicinity of graves of the wicked and especially that one should stay away from the graves of the wicked as there is a danger one can be adversely affected by them.] The souls of the wicked which are cut off and do not ascend upwards, as explained. The Kelipot are strongly attached to them and they are

וּבְמְכִילְתָּא פָּרָשַׁת בֹּא, וּבְסוֹף פָּרָשַׁת תִּשָּׂא, וּבְסִפְרֵי פָּרָשַׁת בְּהַעֲלוֹתְךָ וּפָרָשַׁת שְׁלַח, "וְנִכְרְתָה" אֵין הַכְרָתָה אֶלָּא הַפְסָקָה.

וְזֶה שֶׁכָּתוּב (ישעיה נ"ט ב) "כִּי אִם עֲוֹנֹתֵיכֶם הָיוּ מַבְדִּלִים בֵּינֵיכֶם לְבֵין אֱלֹקֵיכֶם", הַיְנוּ לְבֵין אֱלֹקֵיכֶם מַמָּשׁ כַּנַּ"ל, וְאָז נִטְבַּעַת בְּעִמְקֵי הַטֻּמְאָה וְהַקְּלִפּוֹת רַחֲמָנָא לִיצְּלָן.

עַיֵּן בְּעֵץ חַיִּים שַׁעַר כְּלָלוּת אבי"ע רֵישׁ פֶּרֶק א', וּבְשַׁעַר הַיִּחוּדִים סוֹף פֶּרֶק ד',

---

destructive forces. They are found at graves over the bodies of the wicked and they can impact a person there [via the secret of *Ibur* where this wicked soul attaches a part of itself to the visitor].

Shaar HaYichudim Tikkunei Avonot Chap. 1:
- [This chapter introduces the Teshuva/repentance process for different types of sin and explains that the word Teshuva is *Tashuv Hey*, meaning the process of returning of the last *Hey* of God's Name YHVH back to its source from being] Bound up with Kelipah [as a result of sin. Later on in the chapter it explains that] One who wilfully and rebelliously transgresses against his Master causes the Kelipot to take *Shefa*/bestowal where *Pesha*/sin has a rearranged combination of the letters of *Shefa*.

454 Likutei Torah Yishayahu on the verse "when the spirit that envelops them is from Me" (Yishayahu 57:16):
- From this we can understand the secret of the wicked being called dead while they are alive... This concept is that when a person sins he causes his soul to descend to Gehinom while he is alive. When he is formed, [the soul] is placed in his body and when he sins it descends via his legs into Gehinom and becomes entrenched there according to the level of his sin and of his soul. Therefore, he is called *dead* while being alive. If he is particularly wicked he causes his entire soul to be thrown down into Gehinom. However, we see that such a person remains alive? However, this concept is that....

455 Sefer HaGilgulim end of Chap. 35:
- ... The concept is clear – you should know that there is no Tzaddik at all that does not have two souls, as written in Zohar Parshat Noach in explanation of the repetition [in the Torah of the names of various Tzaddikim, e.g.,] "Noach Noach," "Moshe Moshe," "Shmuel Shmuel" [see end of G3:13]. The explanation of these words is that there are two levels: an inner soul which is within the person, and a circumventing soul which hovers over a person's head in the supernal world and it is clear that a person has a supernal root through this soul. However, when a person sins, God forbid, he causes his [inner] soul to gradually descend into the Kelipot until it has all descended [with the degree of descent being] according to the degree of sin. This results in his circumventing soul descending into the person. The result is that both of these two [soul] levels descend from their places and it

Heichala Tinyana.[456]
- 'And without anything being lost,'[457] God decreed that the ten parts of the level of Nefesh are not completely severed, God forbid
  - it is only the nine lowest levels, from its [Sefira] of Chochma and below, which are severed
  - however, the uppermost level, the secret of its *Keter* [of Nefesh] (Note 15)[458] is not severed
  - which as a result of its attachment and binding with the level of Ruach, as mentioned above, (Note 16)[459] it is treated like the level of Ruach which has no Karet, as will be explained below.
- It is from God's Supernal Mercy, that through the level of Ruach, that is through the use of speech to express heartfelt confession which is on the level of Ruach, as mentioned above,[460] the nine [disconnected] levels of the Nefesh are also raised to reconnect them with the level of Ruach as [they were] previously.
- Similarly, if one damages and corrupts his level of speech through speech

---

also results in a person only having one soul as the other one has descended into the Kelipot.

456 Heichalot HaZohar Bereishit 41b from within the Vilna Gaon's gloss no. 17:
- [This is a particularly cryptic quotation and is provided without in-depth explanation but the basic point relating to the submerging of the soul into Kelipah as a result of sin is clear.] . . . With a person's Neshama, Chaya, and Yechida, they incorporate the Neshama which is the three heads [i.e., the Chochma, Binah, and Daat known as the Mochin] of a person's Ruach. However the Neshama itself, which is the three heads themselves, does not enter within a person at all – it is Godliness. This is as written [about Moshe] "man of God" [Devarim 33:1]. When a person sins, these levels [the three heads] depart in the secret of Mochin and [they also depart from] the nine lowest levels of Nefesh [i.e., the lowest soul level, which are] from the level of Chochma and below. The three heads of Ruach ascend upwards and are not impacted by the sin, they are just removed from the person as part of the secret of "Corruption is not His – the blemish is with His children . . ." [Devarim 32:5]. However, the nine lowest levels of Nefesh descend into Kelipah and nothing remains of [Nefesh] except for its level of Keter which is [synonymous with] the level of Malchut [i.e., the lowest level] of Ruach. As is known, each level of Keter is the level of Malchut of the world preceding it. It is the *adorning of [the Sefira of] Yesod of maleness* and is therefore referred to as "an adornment" as is known. From [the level of] Chochma [of Nefesh] and below, they are all able to depart. This is why all the sins which are mentioned [in the Torah are mentioned] in relation to Nefesh as per "and when the *Nefesh* sins" [Vayikra 4:2], "and I will lose that *Nefesh* . . ." [23:30], etc. The secret of this loss to the Kelipah and also

וְשָׁם פֶּרֶק א' מְתַקְּנֵי עֲוֹנוֹת, וּבְלִקּוּטֵי תַנָ"ךְ בִּישַׁעְיָה בְּפָסוּק "כִּי רוּחַ מִלְּפָנַי יַעֲטוֹף" (נז, טז), וּבַגִּלְגּוּלִים סוֹף פֶּרֶק ל"ה. וְכֵן כָּתוּב בְּכִתְבֵי קָדְשׁוֹ שֶׁל רַבֵּינוּ הַגָּדוֹל מוֹהַרְ"א ז"ל, בְּפֵרוּשׁ עַל הַהֵיכָלוֹת בְּהֵיכָלָא תִנְיָנָא:

- וּלְבַל יִדַּח מִמֶּנּוּ נִדָּח, גָּזְרָה רְצוֹנוֹ יִתְבָּרַךְ, שֶׁלֹּא יִכָּרְתוּ חַס וְשָׁלוֹם לְגַמְרֵי כָּל הָעֲשָׂרָה חֶלְקֵי בְּחִינַת הַנֶּפֶשׁ

  ○ רַק הַתִּשְׁעָה בְּחִינוֹת הַתַּחְתּוֹנִים, מֵחָכְמָה דִּילָהּ וּלְמַטָּה הֵם הַנִּכְרָתִים
  ○ אֲבָל בְּחִינָה הָעֶלְיוֹנָה סוֹד הַכֶּתֶר דִּילָהּ (הגהה ט"ו) אֵינָהּ נִכְרֶתֶת
  ○ שֶׁמִּצַּד דְּבֵקוּתָהּ וְהִתְקַשְּׁרוּתָהּ עִם בְּחִינַת הָרוּחַ כַּנַּ"ל, (הגהה ט"ז) נְדוֹנִית בִּבְחִינַת הָרוּחַ שֶׁאֵין בּוֹ כָּרֵת, כְּמוֹ שֶׁכָּתַבְנוּ לְהַלָּן:

- וְהוּא מֵחֶסֶד הָעֶלְיוֹן בָּרוּךְ הוּא, שֶׁעַל יְדֵי בְּחִינַת הָרוּחַ הַיְנוּ עַל יְדֵי וִדּוּי דְּבָרִים מִלֵּב שֶׁהוּא בְּחִינַת רוּחַ כַּנַּ"ל, יִתְעַלּוּ גַּם הַתִּשְׁעָה בְּחִינוֹת הַנֶּפֶשׁ לְהִתְקַשֵּׁר כֻּלָּם בִּבְחִינַת הָרוּחַ כְּמִקֶּדֶם:

- וְכֵן אִם פָּגַם וְקִלְקֵל חַס וְשָׁלוֹם בְּחִינַת הַדִּבּוּר שֶׁלּוֹ עַל יְדֵי עֲוֹנוֹת הַתְּלוּיִים בַּדִּבּוּר,

---

of the Karet is that when the nine levels are removed, then "the *Nefesh* is cut off from before Me" [22:3]. This is the meaning of the verse: "One who sins against Me spoils his *Nefesh*" [Mishlei 8:36], as all sins remove a small part of the Nefesh. However, the three heads of Ruach depart in one go, and they are called the *life of man*, as is known with the secret of Mochin. Therefore, the wicked are referred to as dead while they are alive!

457 2 Shmuel 14:14.

458 **R. Chaim adds Note 15 here.** This note is brought at the end of this chapter and is entitled "Constant connection through Fear, e.g., forcing until wanting divorce."

Note that there was a printing error in all of the original print editions of Nefesh HaChaim and the sequence of G1:18:N15 and G1:18:N16 was printed in wrong order. This has been reversed in this edition. This was heard directly from R. Reuven Leuchter who heard it from his teachers R. Shlomo Wolbe and R. Yonasan David. It is entirely logical that the insertion point of the note relating to how Nefesh is never disconnected is to specifically be here. It is also logical that G1:18:N16 which relates to both Nefesh and Ruach is inserted at the point which relates to the connection between Nefesh and Ruach.

459 **R. Chaim adds Note 16 here.** This note is brought at the end of this chapter and is entitled "Even souls entrenched in ultimate vice/Egypt redeemed with Keter."

460 See end of G1:14.

related sins, with evil speech and the like, or other sins rooted in the level of Ruach, and thereby corrupts the level of Ruach
- (and even though the level of Ruach cannot be cut off at all, as we only find the concept of Karet in the Torah as referencing the level of Nefesh alone, e.g., "and that *Nefesh* shall be cut off,"[461] "and the *Nefashot* which did this shall be cut off,"[462] with many similar examples, and also as per the Arizal;[463] nevertheless, with sins rooted in the level of Ruach, one can corrupt and damage it and correspondingly strengthen the power of the Ruach/spirit of impurity, God should save us)
- but as a result of its highest level, the secret of its Keter [of Ruach] being permanently connected to the lowest level of Neshama, as mentioned above – it can be rectified by the level of Neshama through thoughts of repentance, with thoughts of the heart which are on the level of Neshama.

• However, the level of Neshama cannot ever be damaged as its root source is always protected from extrinsic impact
- and it is permanently attached to the *Root of the Neshama* [i.e., Knesset Yisrael], as is known – they are permanently inseparable friends
- and man's actions cannot impact it at all to corrupt it, God forbid.
- If man sins with improper thoughts, God forbid, he causes bad to himself alone in that the sparks of his Neshama depart and are hidden from him – but not that the [Neshama] itself is damaged, God forbid.

Rabbi Chaim's Notes:
Note 15 – Constant connection through Fear, e.g., forcing until wanting divorce

• This is the Inner Will [of God] which crowns the Nefesh of a Jew which through Fear [of God] is never separated [from Him].
• Refer to the Rambam[464] [who brings the law] in connection with a forced bill of divorce [where a court, subject to appropriate circumstances, can

---

461 Vayikra 22:3.
462 Vayikra 18:29.
463 Likutei Torah Bo [at the end of the piece entitled "and that *Nefesh* shall be cut off"]:
- . . . but if he did not merit [for his Nefesh to receive light from his Neshama and Ruach] as a result of transgressing a sin punishable by Karet, his body is cut off as his Neshama no longer resides in it; and in addition, his Nefesh is cut off and also separated from the Neshama and Ruach. This is the meaning of "and that *Nefesh* shall be cut off." However, the Neshama and Ruach are never separated and the concept of Karet is not applicable to them, for the damage [of sin] never damages them. [An identical paragraph

בִּלְשׁוֹן הָרַע וְכַיּוֹצֵא, אוֹ שְׁאָרֵי עֲוֹנוֹת הַתְּלוּיִים בְּשָׁרְשָׁם בִּבְחִינַת הָרוּחַ, וְנִתְקַלְקֵל בָּזֶה בְּחִינַת הָרוּחַ

- (וְהַגַּם שֶׁאֵין בְּחִינַת הָרוּחַ נִכְרֶתֶת כְּלָל, כִּי לֹא מָצִינוּ בַּתּוֹרָה עִנְיַן הַכָּרֵת רַק אֵצֶל בְּחִינַת הַנֶּפֶשׁ לְבַד, "וְנִכְרְתָה הַנֶּפֶשׁ הַהִיא" (ויקרא כב, ג), "וְנִכְרְתוּ הַנְּפָשׁוֹת הָעוֹשׂוֹת" (שם יח, כט) וְכַיּוֹצֵא הַרְבֵּה, וְכֵן כָּתַב בְּלִקּוּטֵי תוֹרָה פָּרָשַׁת בֹּא שָׁם, וּבְפֶרֶק ו' מֵהַגִּלְגּוּלִים וּבְסוֹפוֹ שָׁם, עִם כָּל זֶה עַל יְדֵי הָעֲוֹנוֹת הַתְּלוּיִים בְּשָׁרְשָׁם בִּבְחִינַת 'הָרוּחַ', הוּא מְקַלְקְלוֹ וּפוֹגְמוֹ, וּמַגְבִּיר לְעֻמַּת זֶה כֹּחַ 'רוּחַ' הַטֻּמְאָה רַחֲמָנָא לִיצְלָן).

- מִצַּד שֶׁהַבְּחִינָה הָעֶלְיוֹנָה, סוֹד כֶּתֶר שֶׁלּוֹ, קָשׁוּר וְדָבוּק לְעוֹלָם בַּבְּחִינָה הַתַּחְתּוֹנָה שֶׁל הַנְּשָׁמָה כַּנַּ"ל, יוּכַל הוּא לְהִתָּקֵן עַל יְדֵי בְּחִינַת הַנְּשָׁמָה, בְּהִרְהוּרֵי תְשׁוּבָה בְּמַחֲשֶׁבֶת הַלֵּב, שֶׁהוּא בְּחִינַת הַנְּשָׁמָה:

- אֲבָל בְּחִינַת הַנְּשָׁמָה אֵינָהּ נִפְגֶּמֶת כְּלָל לְעוֹלָם, כִּי מְקוֹר שָׁרְשָׁהּ הוּא מֵעוֹלָם הַמִּשְׁמָר מִמַּגַּע זָרִים

- וּדְבוּקָה לְעוֹלָם בְּשֹׁרֶשׁ הַנְּשָׁמָה כַּיָּדוּעַ, שֶׁהֵם רֵעִין דְּלָא מִתְפָּרְשִׁין לְעָלְמִין
- וְאֵין מַעֲשֵׂי הָאָדָם מַגִּיעִים עָדֶיהָ כְּלָל לְקַלְקֵל חַס וְשָׁלוֹם.
- וְאִם הָאָדָם חוֹטֵא בְּמַחֲשָׁבָה אֲשֶׁר לֹא טוֹבָה חַס וְשָׁלוֹם, הוּא גּוֹרֵם רָעָה לְעַצְמוֹ לְבַד, שֶׁיִּסְתַּלֵּק וְיִתְעַלֵּם מִמֶּנּוּ נִיצוֹצֵי אוֹר הַנְּשָׁמָה, אֲבָל לֹא שֶׁהִיא נִפְגֶּמֶת חַס וְשָׁלוֹם:

הַגָּהָה ט"ו

- הַיְנוּ רָצוֹן הַפְּנִימִי הַמֻּכְתָּר נֶפֶשׁ מִיִּשְׂרָאֵל מִצַּד הַיִּרְאָה אֵינָהּ נִפְסֶקֶת לְעוֹלָם:
- וְעַיֵּן רַמְבַּ"ם סוֹף פֶּרֶק ב' מֵהִלְכוֹת גֵּרוּשִׁין בְּדִין גֵּט מְעֻשֶּׂה, עַד שֶׁיֹּאמַר רוֹצֶה אֲנִי

---

also appears in Likutei Torah Lech Lecha at the end of the piece dealing with Karet for not having performed circumcision.]
Sefer HaGilgulim Chap. 6:
- Know that the concept of Karet only relates to the part of the Nefesh which is from the World of Action, as that is the place where the Kelipot are in force and it is [therefore] possible for it to be cut off. However, the Ruach and Neshama which are from [the worlds of] Yetzirah and Beriah have no Karet. . . .

464 Rambam, Mishneh Torah, Hilchot Gerushin 2:20:
- For one who the law prescribes that he is to be forced to divorce his wife

inflict pain on a Jew] to the point where he accedes to say "I want" [to give the bill of divorce]
- that such a divorce is valid if the law prescribes that he can be forced to divorce.
- The reason explained there is that [such a person] is not considered to be under legal duress [and the bill of divorce is still valid] since his ultimate will is to perform all the Mitzvot but it is only his Evil Inclination which prevents him from doing so
- and since he is beaten until his Evil Inclination is weakened to the point that he accedes and says "I want," he has [therefore] already divorced willingly.
- Refer to his holy language there.

Note 16 – Even souls entrenched in ultimate vice/Egypt redeemed with Keter

- That is that even if the souls (Nefashot) of Israel are entrenched in vice, may the Merciful One save us, nevertheless, [God] established His Will such that their souls (Nafsham) can be elevated with the level of His Ruach, as per:
  - "as for Me, this is My covenant with them, said God, My Ruach which is upon you . . . will not move from [you]."[465]
  - This is the concept of the Exodus from Egypt
    - and this is the meaning of "*I am* the Lord your God who has taken you out of Egypt"[466]
    - and it is known in the Zohar that the statement "*I am*" is the level of Keter.[467]
    - This is the meaning of Chazal's teaching[468] [that the word] "I am/Anochi" [forms the initial letters of] "I myself (*Nafshi*) wrote and gave [the Torah]" [and also forms the initial letters of] "A pleasant

---

and that he does not want to divorce – a Jewish court of law may at any time and any place beat him until he accedes and says "I want," and that he writes a bill of divorce and that such a bill of divorce is valid. Similarly, if non-Jews beat him so that he complies with the Jewish [court's ruling] and the Jewish [court] pressures him to divorce through the hand of the non-Jews, then this is a valid [bill of divorce]. [However,] if the non-Jews force him through their own initiative to write [the bill of divorce even] though the law prescribes he write it, this is not a valid bill of divorce. Why would this bill of divorce not be considered invalid as he was under legal duress either by the hand of the non-Jews or of the Jews? Because legal duress only relates to being pressured to do something which one is not obliged to do via a Torah obligation – for example, one who is beaten until he sells

○ שֶׁהַגֵּט כָּשֵׁר אִם הַדִּין נוֹתֵן שֶׁכּוֹפִין אוֹתוֹ לְגָרֵשׁ.

○ וּפִי' שָׁם הַטַּעַם, דְּלָא מִיקְרֵי אָנוּס, כֵּיוָן שֶׁאֲמִתַּת רְצוֹנוֹ לַעֲשׂוֹת כָּל הַמִּצְוֹת, אֶלָּא שֶׁיִּצְרוֹ הוּא שֶׁתְּקָפוֹ.

○ וְכֵיוָן שֶׁהֻכָּה עַד שֶׁתָּשַׁשׁ יִצְרוֹ וְאָמַר רוֹצֶה אֲנִי, כְּבָר גֵּרַשׁ לִרְצוֹנוֹ.

○ עַיֵּן שָׁם לְשׁוֹנוֹ הַקָּדוֹשׁ:

הגהה ט"ז

• הַיְנוּ שֶׁאַף אִם נַפְשׁוֹת יִשְׂרָאֵל מְשֻׁקָּעִים חַס וְשָׁלוֹם בְּתַאֲווֹת רָעוֹת רַחֲמָנָא לִיצְּלָן, עִם כָּל זֶה יָסַד רְצוֹנוֹ יִתְבָּרַךְ שְׁמוֹ, לְהַעֲלוֹת נַפְשָׁם עַל יְדֵי בְּחִינַת רוּחוֹ יִתְבָּרַךְ שְׁמוֹ

○ כְּעִנְיַן הַכָּתוּב (ישעיה נט, כא) "וַאֲנִי זֹאת בְּרִיתִי אוֹתָם אָמַר ה' רוּחִי אֲשֶׁר עָלֶיךָ וְגוֹ', לֹא יָמוּשׁוּ" וְגוֹ'

○ וּכְעִנְיַן יְצִיאַת מִצְרַיִם

□ וְזֶהוּ "אָנֹכִי ה' אֱלֹהֶיךָ אֲשֶׁר הוֹצֵאתִיךָ מֵאֶרֶץ מִצְרָיִם" (שמות כ, ב)

□ וְיָדוּעַ בַּזֹּהַר שֶׁאָנֹכִי הוּא בְּחִינַת כֶּתֶר

□ וְזֶהוּ דְּרָשָׁתָם זִכְרוֹנָם לִבְרָכָה (שבת ק"ה א') "אָנֹכִי אֲנָא נַפְשִׁי כְּתָבִית יְהָבִית, וַאֲמִירָה נְעִימָה" וְכוּ' וְהֵם שְׁנֵי הַבְּחִינוֹת נֶפֶשׁ וְרוּחַ, וְהַמַּשְׂכִּיל יָבִין:

---

or gives something away. However, one whose Evil Inclination prevents him from performing a Mitzvah or causes him to perform a sin, and he is beaten until he performs his obligation or stops performing his sin, this is not considered to be legal duress, but rather that he has caused himself personal duress as a result of his evil outlook. Therefore, with this person who does not want to issue a bill of divorce – since he does want to remain part of the People of Israel – he wants to perform all the Mitzvot and to distance himself from sin, and it is his Evil Inclination which prevents him from doing so, and since he has been beaten up to the point that his Evil Inclination is weakened and he accedes, saying "I want," he has [therefore] already divorced willingly.

465 Yishayahu 59:21.
466 Shemot 20:2.
467 Zohar Raya Mehemna III Pinchas 256b, where the word "I am/Anochi" is broken down into the three Hebrew letters spelling the word "Ayin" (with Aleph) and the fourth letter Kaf which represents Keter.
468 Shabbat 105a.

[spoken] statement [was written and given]." This relates to the two levels [one] of Nefesh [i.e., Nafshi] and [one of] Ruach [i.e., speech], and one who is able to, will understand.[469]

19. SOUL LEVEL INTERCONNECTIVITY PREVENTS ANYONE BEING LOST

- This [as above] is the concept [underpinning] the verse "the spirit (Ruach) of a man will nourish his illness, who (*Mi*) can raise up his depressed spirit (Ruach),"[470] meaning
  - that the illness resulting from sin on the level of Nefesh
    - (that generally most sins are from the level of Nefesh, as this is the lowest level which is closest to the *Sitra Achara*[471] as in "its feet descend into death,"[472] "*Nefesh* which sins,"[473] "these sins with their *Nefashot*"[474] and many similar examples. Refer to [Arizal].)[475]
  - can be corrected and also elevated through the level of Ruach, as mentioned above.
  - [However,] if the level of "Ruach is depressed"[476]
  - in that the level of Ruach was damaged and corrupted by sins related to the level of Ruach

---

469 The concept of Egypt is associated with ultimate vice (the ultimate prison, Maytzarim) which entrapped the nine parts of Nefesh from which *I am* redeemed Israel. *I am* represents two aspects – one of Keter of Nefesh, and the other of Malchut of Ruach, which are one and the same thing.

This is explained in V2:02, Chap. 15, "Tzimtzum Sources," I1.1, which describes that the level of *I am*/*Ani*/Malchut of a higher world is the same as the level of Ayin/Keter of the lower world where the words *Ani* and *Ayin* are a rearrangement of each other.

R. Chaim's note here is purely referring to the reconnection of the disconnected parts of Nefesh which were entrenched in vice, and therefore the reference here to Ruach is specifically to the level of Malchut of Ruach which is able to reconnect the disconnected. In contrast, R. Chaim continues to make a separate point in G1:18 that in addition to Keter of Nefesh reconnecting the disconnected parts of Nefesh, the Keter of Ruach also has the ability to repair any damage done to the level of Ruach by bad speech, etc., although this damage to the level of Ruach never causes it to become disconnected.

470 Mishlei 18:14.
471 See p. 564, fn. 280, commenting on this term.
472 Mishlei 5:5, i.e., that the lowest level, *the feet* – the Nefesh, descends into *death*, which is the Sitra Achara.
473 Vayikra 5:1.

שער א' - פרק י"ט

- וְזֶהוּ עִנְיַן הַכָּתוּב (משלי יח, יד) "רוּחַ אִישׁ יְכַלְכֵּל מַחֲלֵהוּ וְרוּחַ נְכֵאָה מִי יִשָּׂאֶנָּה", רָצָה לוֹמַר

  - הַמַּחֲלָה וְחֶלְאַת הֶעָוֹן שֶׁל בְּחִינַת הַנֶּפֶשׁ

    - (שֶׁסְּתָם רֹב הָעֲוֹנוֹת מְצוּיוֹת בִּבְחִינַת הַנֶּפֶשׁ, שֶׁהִיא הַתַּחְתּוֹנָה הַקְּרוֹבָה אֶל הַסִּטְרָא אַחֲרָא, "רַגְלֶיהָ יוֹרְדוֹת מָוֶת" (משלי ה, ה), וּכְמוֹ שֶׁכָּתוּב (ויקרא ה, א) "וְנֶפֶשׁ כִּי תֶחֱטָא". "הַחַטָּאִים הָאֵלֶּה בְּנַפְשׁוֹתָם" (במדבר יז, ג) וְהַרְבֵּה כַּיּוֹצֵא. וְעַיֵּן עֵץ חַיִּים שַׁעַר הָעֲקוּדִים סוֹף פֶּרֶק ה', וּפְרִי עֵץ חַיִּים שַׁעַר קְרִיאַת שְׁמַע שֶׁעַל הַמִּטָּה פֶּרֶק ח')

  - יְכוֹלָה הִיא לְהִתָּקֵן, וְגַם לַעֲלוֹת, עַל יְדֵי בְּחִינַת הָרוּחַ כַּנַּ"ל.

  - וְאִם הָ'רוּחַ נְכֵאָה'

    - שֶׁפְּגָמָהּ וְקִלְקְלָהּ בְּחִינַת רוּחוֹ עַל יְדֵי עֲוֹנוֹת הַתְּלוּיִים בִּבְחִינַת הָרוּחַ

---

474 Bamidbar 17:3.
475 Etz Chaim Shaar 6, Shaar HaAkudim, End of Chap. 2 (see V2:14, p. 676):
- ... when man of the physical world is at a level of the secret of Nefesh, then he cleaves to and is restrained by the Evil Inclination which is the Kelipot as per the secret of "*Nefesh* which *sins*" (Vayikra 5:1), but when [man] is at a level of the secret of Ruach he does not sin so much as per the secret of "God, create a pure *heart* for me, renew within me a just *Ruach*" (Tehillim 51:12); and when [man] is at a level of the secret of Neshama he is far from the sin but needs to be guarded from the influence of Achoraim [Indirect Evil]; and when [man] is at a level of the secret of *Neshama of the Neshama* [i.e., Chaya] then he does not sin at all ...

Pri Etz Chaim Shaar Kriat Shema She'al HaMitah, Chap. 8:
- ... after that, get up, stand and say confession for your sins, for isn't sleep one sixtieth of death? Especially now that your intention is to *elevate Mayim Nukvim* [i.e., the absolute and complete giving of yourself in every way to God], and you are like one who has passed on from this world to ascend to Above. Therefore, first say confession for your sins, with the secret of "the *Nefesh* which sins shall die" (Yechezkel 18:4), for the secret of sin is dependent on his Nefesh which is in the world of Action, and through this, it will be separated from the world of Action and you will not be affected by the *Chitzonim*/powers of impurity.

476 As per the verse above, Mishlei 18:14.

- then "*Mi* can raise it up"
- its correction is through the level of Neshama which is called *Mi*, as known in the Zohar.[477]

• 'A thinking person'[478] will understand that the general points made above in relation to the three levels of a person's [soul], Nefesh, Ruach, and Neshama
  - are also similarly reflected in the supernal source of these three levels
  - which are [the levels of] *Kudsha Brich Hu*, *Shechina*[479] and *Em HaBanim* (Mother of the Children).
  - So sins performed in the lower worlds cause the Shechina of our strength, the secret of the supernal Nefesh, to be disconnected from its [ultimate] supernal source[480] – being the secret of exile (that is when the Nefashot/souls of Israel are submerged within bad desires, God forbid).

---

477 The verse in Yishayahu 40:26 states "Lift up your eyes heavenward and see who (Mi) created these (Eileh)." In the introduction to the Zohar 1b, there is a cryptic explanation of this verse which differentiates between two levels of *Mi* and *Mah*, where *Mi* relates to an unrevealed level of God (where *Mi* implies an unknowable source – being a statement of question of *who?*), whereas *Mah* relates to a revealed level (a knowable source, the starting point for knowledge as hinted to by the word Chochma/wisdom which can be rearranged into *Koach Mah*, i.e., the potential [of knowing] what is. See the quotation from Pri Etz Chaim Shaar Olam HaAsiyah, Chap. 2 brought on p.455, fn. 429, which defines *Mah* as Malchut, which is the level of ultimate manifestation of God. Therefore, *Koach Mah* is the conceptual initiation of this manifestation.) In this sense, the verse is simply saying that when we look to the physical creations we should understand that an abstract unknowable God created them.

However, on a deeper level, it is *Mi* that creates *Eileh*, where *Mi* here refers to the singular and *Eileh* is a statement of plural. Therefore, when we look at this world which appears to us to be separate from the One God (i.e., plural) we should really appreciate that it truly is all just the One God (i.e., singular). This idea is expressed in the name Elokim which is a rearranged composite of the two words *Mi* and *Eileh*. Elokim is the aspect of God which modulates His life force which causes All to appear to exist in a natural way, i.e., to exist in a way which appears separate from Him. This is hinted to in that the numerical value of Elokim is HaTeva/nature. So in this world, the existence of God is cloaked in nature. Our task in this world is to therefore look deeper and appreciate that all around us in the natural world is really and truly just God. In contrast, those sinning with the Golden Calf [the Erev Rav] stated (Shemot 32:4): "These/*Eileh* are your gods, O Israel." They separated *Eileh* from *Mi* and stated that *plurality* is an absolute reality and denied the existence of the

- אָז "מִי יְשׁאֶנָּה"
- תִּקּוּנוֹ הוּא עַל יְדֵי בְּחִינַת הַנְּשָׁמָה שֶׁנִּקְרֵאת 'מִ"י', כַּיָּדוּעַ בַּזֹּהַר:
- וְאִישׁ תְּבוּנוֹת יָבִין, שֶׁכְּלַל הַדְּבָרִים הַנַּ"ל בְּעִנְיָן הַשְּׁלֹשָׁה בְּחִינוֹת נֵר"ן שֶׁל הָאָדָם
  - הֵם גַּם כֵּן עַל זֶה הַדֶּרֶךְ, גַּם בְּשָׁרְשָׁם הָעֶלְיוֹן שֶׁל אֵלּוּ הַשְּׁלֹשָׁה בְּחִינוֹת
  - שֶׁהֵם קוּדְשָׁא בְּרִיךְ הוּא וּשְׁכִינְתֵּיהּ וְאֵם הַבָּנִים.
  - שֶׁעֲוֹנוֹת הַתַּחְתּוֹנִים גּוֹרְמִים לִשְׁכִינַת עֻזֵּינוּ, רָזָא דְ'נֶפֶשׁ' דִּלְעֵילָּא, שֶׁנּוֹדֶדֶת

singular Unified God in their lives. This statement encapsulates the ultimate essence of idol worship whose primary motivation is to deny the unity of the world so that those practicing it can release themselves from the responsibilities and obligations of living with a Unified God. (See Shela Shaar HaOtiot Hagah, Ot *Kuf* – Kedushah.)

On an even deeper level, the Arizal states in Mevo Shearim 1:1 that:
- "Binah/understanding ... is the root of Dinim/Judgments ... and is called '*Mi*' ... Din/Judgment is exercised through the placing of appropriate boundaries ... therefore Tzimtzum is entirely Din/judgment."

The Arizal is therefore saying that Binah, which is an analytical process of understanding, is also one of differentiation, a process which creates a limit and boundary between concepts or entities (as explained in V2:01, "The Limit of Understanding – The Deeper Meaning of Makom"). It is the same as the process of Tzimtzum which creates a boundary between God and our perception of Him, enabling us to see a world which appears separate from God and an entity in its own right. Binah, as expressed with "Mi" is therefore intrinsically included in Elokim which is the aspect of God which cloaks Him within an apparently separate existence of nature. As part of his explanation of the Tzimtzum process later on, R. Chaim explains, in G3:04, that Elokim represents the aspect of God as perceived by the creations.

In that a Jew's soul structure is an analogous mirror of God (BeTzelem); a Jew's soul source, the Neshama, is part of God, the unknowable source, and is therefore referred to here as "*Mi*." More than this, the different levels of the soul map to different Sefirot (see p. 444, fn. 389), and the level of Neshama directly maps to the Sefira of Binah, which is called "Mi."

478 Mishlei 11:12.
479 The *resident one*, i.e., the manifestation of God within the lowest level corresponding to Nefesh. Note that the sequence of these three levels is different to the sequence of the Nefesh, Ruach, and Neshama, as *Shechina* maps to Nefesh, *Kudsha Brich Hu* to Ruach, and *Em HaBanim* to Neshama. This is simply because of the sequence of the common expression *Kudsha Brich Hu u'Shechinteh*.
480 I.e., from the level of *Em HaBanim* which is referred to in G1:16 above as the supernal level of Neshama.

- Refer [to the writings of the Arizal].[481]
- However, not all ten levels [of Shechina are disconnected], only the nine levels from [the level of] Chochma and below, as mentioned above in relation to man
- but the highest level, the secret of its *Keter*, which is its point of origin

---

481 Etz Chaim Shaar 36, Shaar Miut HaYareach, Chap. 2:
- [This chapter generally refers to the 4 exiles of the Jewish People and the corresponding state of descent of holiness caused by their actions. In and among this detail, it brings the Midrash explaining that Adam's sin caused a removal, a level of *exile*, of the Shechina (Bereishit Rabba Bereishit 19:7).]

Etz Chaim Shaar 47, Shaar Seder ABY"A, Chap. 6 (see V2:14, p. 676):
- [The following quotation is cryptic, but it is clear that our sins cause the Shechina to be exiled.] . . . every act of holiness has an impact in its place [i.e., its source] such that even if it is removed from there [its source], there will always be a point remaining at the top of Beriyah. However, at a time when its diminishing is through the damage of the lower worlds [i.e., by our sins], then the other 9 points [i.e., Sefirot of Chochma and below] are removed from it and do not return to Zeer Anpin, their source, from the place that they came from, but they descend with our sins to the Kelipah, as per the *secret of the Shechina in exile* . . .

Etz Chaim Shaar 48, Shaar HaKelipot, all of Chap. 3:
- [This chapter starts off by describing the 4 world levels and how they were structured before Adam's sin. It then continues to describe the impact of the damage of Adam's sin on the holy worlds and how it caused disconnection of the 9 Sefirot from holiness. It explains that the concepts of Adam's sin, of exile, and of the destruction of the Temple are all one concept.]

Pri Etz Chaim Introduction, Klalei Z"A U'Nukva:
- . . . and after [Adam] sinned then all of its 9 levels [i.e., the 9 Sefirot of Chochma and below] descended into the *Kelipot*, meaning that the inner vessels became the soul of *Beriyah*, the middle vessels became the soul of *Yetzirah*, and the outer vessels became the soul of *Asiyah*, resulting in the *Kelipot* of *Beriyah*, *Yetzirah*, and *Asiyah* being able to also draw [life force] from it – this is the exile of the Shechina as also mentioned elsewhere.

Sefer Shaar HaYichudim, Tikkunei HaAvonot, Chap. 1:
- [The Arizal explains that God's name YHVH relates to the world levels as follows – *Yud* is Aztilut; *Hey* is Beriyah; *Vav* is Yetzirah, and *Hey* is Asiyah, the world of Action] . . . Let us return to our subject matter, when a person

מֵהִתְקַשְּׁרוּתָהּ הָעֶלְיוֹן, בְּסוֹד גָּלוּת (הַיְינוּ כְּשֶׁנַּפְשׁוֹת יִשְׂרָאֵל מְשֻׁקָּעִים בְּתַאֲוֹת רָעוֹת חַס וְשָׁלוֹם).

○ וְעַיֵּן עֵץ חַיִּים שַׁעַר מִעוּט הַיָּרֵחַ פֶּרֶק ב', וּבְשַׁעַר סֵדֶר אֲבִ"עַ פֶּרֶק ב', וּבְשַׁעַר הַקְּלִפּוֹת כָּל פֶּרֶק ג', וּבְהַקְדָּמַת פְּרִי עֵץ חַיִּים בִּכְלָלֵי ז"א וְנוּק', וּבְשַׁעַר הַיִּחוּדִים פֶּרֶק א' מְתַקְּנֵי עֲוֹנוֹת.

○ אָמְנָם לֹא כָּל עֶשֶׂר בְּחִינוֹתֶיהָ, רַק הַתֵּשַׁע בְּחִינוֹתֶיהָ מֵחָכְמָה וּלְמַטָּה, כַּנַּ"ל בְּעִנְיַן הָאָדָם.

○ אֲבָל בְּחִינָה הָעֶלְיוֹנָה, סוֹד כִּתְרָהּ, שֶׁהִיא נְקֻדָּה הַשָּׁרְשִׁית דִּילָהּ

---

transgresses a negative commandment, the repentance process is suspended and Yom Kippur atones as [the sin] separates the *Hey* of Asiyah and brings it down into the Kelipot. Know that there are four types of repentance which can return the *Hey* of Asiyah which has become entangled in the Kelipot according to the [level] of sin. Know that sometimes Asiyah descends to the first three sublevels of Kelipah and with it, it is immediately rectified when he repents. For the first three sublevels of Kelipah themselves sometimes return to become holy with the secret of "the River Jordan which took from this one and gave to that one" [Bava Metzia 22a] as is known with the secret of the stones upon which God commanded that a good explanation of the Torah be written [Devarim 27:8]. This is the secret of the three cities of refuge for sometimes they are the secret of the three cities of refuge in the Land of Israel [i.e., there were three cities of refuge on the other side of the River Jordan and three inside the Land of Israel, so sometimes refuge was in one place– a holy place, and sometimes in the other – a place of impurity] – until in future times there will be an additional three cities of refuge [in the Land of Israel as per] "and you shall add three more cities" [Devarim 19:9], and know that the three cities of refuge on the other side of the River Jordan they are outside of Israel and they are the first three sublevels of Kelipah – [whereas] the three [cities of refuge] in the Land of Israel are the descent of the level of Malchut of Yetzirah into Asiyah, and in future times when all [six of the cities of refuge] will be in the Land of Israel [the exile in a city of refuge will represent the corresponding descent of all levels] with the [Malchut] of Asiyah being within the first three sublevels of Kelipah, [and the Malchut of Yetzirah in the first three sublevels of Asiya], and the Malchut of Beriyah in the first three sublevels of Yetzirah, and the [Malchut] of Atzilut in the first three sublevels of Beriyah. This is the secret of the exile of the Shechina, therefore it [the Shechina] is also exiled there, and it is also possible for a person's sin to cause the exile of the Shechina . . .

- it remains permanently bound and attached to the *Adorning of the [Sefira] of Yesod*[482] of the level of Ruach, never separating from it (and is therefore referred to as an *adornment* as it becomes the *Keter* [i.e., crown of the lower level of Shechina]).
- Refer to the Arizal,[483] and as our great master, of blessed memory, similarly wrote in his commentary on the Heichalot, on Heichala Tinyana.[484]
- (Refer to the [writings of the Arizal].)[485]
- But the supernal level of the Ruach can never be separated, God forbid, from its place by the sins [of those in] the lower worlds, however they do cause damage and corruption, God forbid, to [the way it propagates downwards through] the *Vav Ketzavot*,[486] as is known.

---

482 The adornment of the Sefira of Yesod is the Sefira of Malchut which becomes the Keter of the next level down.

483 Pri Etz Chaim Introduction, Klalei Z"A U'Nukva:
- [This quotation was brought on p. 266, fn. 481.]

Pri Etz Chaim Shaar HaAmidah, Chap. 19, in relation to the blessing relating to the non-believers:
- This is understood together with that which we have already explained, for this is the reason that the 9 points [i.e., lowest parts] of Malchut are in the format of a *Secret of Addition*, as it is revealed and known to God that people are destined to sin, and that the damage of the sins of Israel reach up above, God forbid, and if Israel were to damage that which has an existing root, their punishment would be double, therefore, all 9 [levels] within it are a *Secret of Addition*, for if Israel sin, God forbid, they will fly up and depart and the Chitzonim/powers of impurity will have no control over them. In contrast, if these [levels] were rooted in it, the Chitzonim would grasp onto it. However, the level within it which is rooted is the level of Keter within it, for, in that it is highest, the Chitzonim have no power to grasp onto it and there is no concern for it if it remains there, and in addition, in order to do damage there, a great sin is required to reach up to that [level].

484 This section of the Vilna Gaon's commentary on the Heichalot has been quoted on p. 256, fn. 456.

485 R. Chaim refers the reader to the following three sources to understand what is written in the two references to Pri Etz Chaim above (i.e., Pri Etz Chaim Introduction, Klalei Z"A U'Nukva, and Pri Etz Chaim Shaar HaAmidah Chap. 19).

Etz Chaim Shaar 11, Shaar HaMelachim, Chap. 6 (see V2:14, p. 676):
- ... it is possible that the level of damage is that he causes the removal from it of the 9 lowest parts, only leaving 1 part ... which is its Keter ... and

- הִיא קְשׁוּרָה וּדְבוּקָה לְעוֹלָם בַּעֲטֶרֶת יְסוֹד בְּחִינַת הָרוּחַ, וְאֵינָהּ נִפְרֶדֶת מִשָּׁם לְעוֹלָם (וְלָכֵן נִקְרֵאת 'עֲטָרָה' שֶׁהוּא כִּתְרָהּ).

- וְעַיֵּן בְּהַקְדָּמַת פְּרִי עֵץ חַיִּים הַנַּ"ל, וּבְשַׁעַר הָעֲמִידָה שָׁם בְּעִנְיַן בִּרְכַּת הַמִּינִים, וְכֵן כָּתַב רַבֵּינוּ הַגָּדוֹל זִכְרוֹנוֹ לִבְרָכָה בְּפֵרוּשׁ עַל הַהֵיכָלוֹת בְּהֵיכָלָא תִּנְיָנָא שָׁם.

- (וְעַיֵּן בְּעֵץ חַיִּים שַׁעַר הַמְּלָכִים פֶּרֶק ז', וּבְשַׁעַר מִעוּט הַיָּרֵחַ, וּבְשַׁעַר הַקְּלִפּוֹת, וְתָבִין בַּמַּ"שׁ בִּפְרִי עֵץ חַיִּים בְּאֵלּוּ ב' הַמְּקוֹמוֹת הַנַּ"ל, וְעַיֵּן עוֹד בִּפְרִי עֵץ חַיִּים שַׁעַר ר"ה פֶּרֶק ב' וְתָבִין כָּל הַנַּ"ל).

- אֲבָל בְּחִינַת הָ'רוּחַ' עִלָּאָה, אֵינוֹ נִפְרָד חַס וְשָׁלוֹם מִמְּקוֹמוֹ עַל יְדֵי עֲוֹנוֹת הַתַּחְתּוֹנִים אֶלָּא שֶׁגּוֹרְמִים בּוֹ פְּגָם וְקִלְקוּל חַס וְשָׁלוֹם בּוּ"קׅ שֶׁלּוֹ, כַּיָּדוּעַ.

---

the reason for this is that all which initially acts as a source root does not subsequently depart at the time of the damage . . . .

Etz Chaim Shaar 36, Shaar Miut Hayareach:
- [The whole Derush of Shaar Miut HaYareach deals with the 9 Sefirot which fell into the lower realms and as a result of which the moon's light was diminished and became a *reflected light* where the moon had no light to emanate of its own. It also deals with Adam's sin and what it caused in the 4 holy worlds of Atzilut, Beriyah, Yetzirah, and Asiyah, in terms of the presentation of these worlds. In explaining what Adam's sin did to the 4 worlds and the Kelipot, it also explains the concept of the diminishing of the moon and the concept of this bitter exile and also the concept of the destruction of both Temples and the Egyptian exile.]

Etz Chaim Shaar 48, Shaar HaKelipot, e.g., Chap. 3:
- [This source describes the impact of the damage of Adam's sin on the holy worlds and how it caused disconnection of the 9 Sefirot from holiness.]

R. Chaim also refers the reader to the following source to understand all that which has been mentioned above: Pri Etz Chaim Shaar Rosh Hashana, Chap. 2:
- . . . however [Adam's] sin was so great that it cannot completely be rectified in one go . . . with a diminishing . . . being the secret of God swearing that he will not enter the Jerusalem of the Supernal Realms etc . . . but is rectified [gradually over time] . . . until Mashiach comes when it will be entirely rectified . . . [See Taanit 5a, God says He will not come to the Jerusalem of the Supernal Realms until He has come to the Jerusalem of the lower realms. This is the concept of exile where sin causes God's presence to be disconnected in the lower realms and correspondingly in the Supernal Realms.]

486 I.e., the *Six Ends* referring to the Middot. See p. 233, fn. 399.

- However, the supernal level of Neshama, which is the secret of intellect, its *Three Heads*, as mentioned above in G1:15
- there the actions of [those in] the lower worlds do not impact in any way to corrupt or damage them, God forbid
- but their deeds can cause their [apparent] removal [from the lower worlds], God forbid
- as is known from Etz Chaim that [their influence] only comes through the *Secret of Addition*[487] alone and is dependent on the deeds of those in the lower worlds
- for they come from an emanation from the lowest level of *Em HaBanim* within it, as is known
- as per "He established the Heavens with understanding (Binah)"[488] – a world protected from external impact, as is known.

- This is represented by the vision of [Yaakov's] "ladder standing towards the ground"[489] where [the ladder] is not said to be "standing *on* the ground (BaAretz)," but rather [is said to be standing] "*towards* the ground (Artzah)"
  - meaning that the top of its essential root, is [fixed] in the Heavens Above and cascades downwards from there until it reaches the ground.
  - This is the life force [the Neshama] of a person, which emanates, so to speak, from God's breath
  - and cascades downwards from there like a ladder and a chain
  - to connect with Ruach, and then the Ruach with the Nefesh
  - until it descends all the way down to this world to be manifest in a person's physical body.
  - This is explicitly stated: "He breathed a living soul into his nostrils," [this is the image over a person] about which it says "and he dreamed and behold there was a ladder" – the ladder is certainly his living soul.[490] Refer there.
  - "Behold the angels of God were ascending and descending on it,"[491] as I wrote above at length,[492] that he [i.e., man] is the *living soul* of the supernal worlds, powers, and angels, and that their entire ascent, descent, and behavior at any moment is entirely dependent on the actions, speech, and thoughts of man's physical body at each moment
    - (and in relation to that which the verse first references "ascent" and only then "descent," this is because the principal objective of man is to first raise to each world, going from the bottom up, and only then to draw down light from above downwards), to the extent that

---

487 As per the quotation on p. 268, fn. 483, from Pri Etz Chaim Shaar HaAmidah,

○ אָמְנָם בִּבְחִינַת הַנְּשָׁמָה, שֶׁהוּא סוֹד הַמּוֹחִין, ג' רִאשׁוֹנוֹת דִּילֵיהּ, כַּנַּ"ל בְּפֶרֶק ט"ו

○ שָׁם אֵין מַעֲשֵׂה הַתַּחְתּוֹנִים מַגִּיעִים כְּלָל, לְקַלְקְלָם אוֹ לְפָגְמָם חַס וְשָׁלוֹם

○ אֶלָּא שֶׁיְּכוֹלִים לִגְרֹם בְּמַעֲשֵׂיהֶם הִסְתַּלְּקוּתָם הֵימֶנּוּ חַס וְשָׁלוֹם

○ כַּיָּדוּעַ בְּעֵץ חַיִּים, שֶׁהֵם בָּאִים בְּסוֹד תּוֹסֶפֶת לְבַד, וּתְלוּיִים בְּמַעֲשֵׂי הַתַּחְתּוֹנִים

○ כִּי הֵם בָּאִים מֵהִתְפַּשְּׁטוּת בְּחִינָה הַתַּחְתּוֹנָה שֶׁל אִם הַבָּנִים בּוֹ כַּיָּדוּעַ

○ וּכְמ"שׁ (משלי ג, יט) "כּוֹנֵן שָׁמַיִם בִּתְבוּנָה", וְהוּא עוֹלָם הַמִּשְׁמָר מִמַּגַּע זָרִים, כַּיָּדוּעַ:

• וְהוּא עִנְיַן מַרְאֵה הַסֻּלָּם מֻצָּב אַרְצָה גוֹ' (בראשית כח, יב), וְלֹא אָמַר מֻצָּב 'בָּאָרֶץ', אֶלָּא 'אַרְצָה', שֶׁפֵּרוּשׁוֹ לָאָרֶץ

○ וּמַשְׁמָעוֹ שֶׁרֹאשׁ עִקַּר שָׁרְשׁוֹ — בַּשָּׁמַיִם מִמַּעַל, וּמִשָּׁם הוּא מִשְׁתַּלְשֵׁל וְיוֹרֵד, עַד לָאָרֶץ יַגִּיעַ.

○ וְהוּא הַנִּשְׁמַת חַיִּים שֶׁל הָאָדָם, שֶׁמִּתְאַצֶּלֶת כִּבְיָכוֹל מִנְּשִׁימַת פִּיו יִתְבָּרַךְ שְׁמוֹ

○ וּמִשָּׁם מִשְׁתַּלְשֶׁלֶת כְּסֻלָּם וְשַׁלְשֶׁלֶת

○ וּמִתְקַשֶּׁרֶת עִם הָרוּחַ, וְהָרוּחַ בַּנֶּפֶשׁ

○ עַד רִדְתָּהּ לָזֶה הָעוֹלָם בְּגוּף הָאָדָם.

○ וְכֵן מְפָרֵשׁ בְּרַעְיָא מְהֵימְנָא נָשֹׂא קכ"ג ב', "וַיִּפַּח בְּאַפָּיו נִשְׁמַת חַיִּים" גוֹ' (בראשית ב, ז) דְּאִתְּמַר בֵּיהּ (שם כח, יב) "וַיַּחֲלֹם וְהִנֵּה סֻלָּם", סֻלָּם וַדַּאי אִיהִי נִשְׁמַת חַיִּים כוּ', עַיֵּן שָׁם.

○ "וְהִנֵּה מַלְאֲכֵי אֱלֹקִים עוֹלִים וְיוֹרְדִים בּוֹ", כְּמוֹ שֶׁכָּתַבְתִּי לְעֵיל בָּאֹרֶךְ, שֶׁהִיא הַנֶּפֶשׁ חַיָּה שֶׁל הָעוֹלָמוֹת וְהַכֹּחוֹת וּמַלְאֲכֵי עֶלְיוֹן, שֶׁכָּל עֲלִיָּתָם וִירִידָתָם וְכָל סִדְרֵי הַנְהָגָתָם כָּל רֶגַע, תָּלוּי רַק כְּפִי נְטִיַּת מַעֲשֵׂיהָ דִּבּוּרָהּ וּמַחֲשַׁבְתָּהּ בְּגוּף הָאָדָם כָּל רֶגַע.

▫ (וּמַ"שׁ "עוֹלִים" תְּחִלָּה, וְאַחַר כָּךְ "יוֹרְדִים", כִּי כָּל עִקַּר תּוֹרַת הָאָדָם

after [this process] "God is standing over him,"[493] as mentioned above.

- How sweet are Chazal's words: "Reish Lakish said in the name of R. Yochanan that God connected His Name to Israel. This is analogous to a king who has a small key to [his] palace and says: 'If I leave it as it is, it will be lost – so I will fix it to the end of a chain and if it is lost the chain is connected to it.' Similarly, God says, 'If I leave Israel how they are, they will be lost among the nations and therefore I am associating My Name with them.'"[494]
  - Chazal here are relating to the collective of the unique Nation.
  - However, Chazal's 'eyes see from afar,'[495] as is their way in holy things, and they are additionally referring to an individual person, and their comments require study, as they use an analogy of a key and chain, which is as I wrote above,[496] that man [is the key] which opens and closes the powers and the worlds, the upper and lower palaces, that all of them are controlled through the power of his actions at the level of Nefesh, which is the essence and root of the level of Nefesh of all the worlds.
  - The Master of All – out of his great benevolence to do good to His creations – diligently focused on our rectification and said: "If I leave it as it is without any connection between the three levels of Nefesh, Ruach, and Neshama – if one should fall, [i.e.,] the lowest level of Nefesh into the depths of evil, God forbid, then there is no other [level] that can re-establish it and it is lost there forever, God forbid, as per 'and I will destroy that *Nefesh*,'[497] so how would a sinful Nefesh be atoned?"
  - Therefore, God 'provided a wondrous solution'[498] and established that the three levels of Nefesh, Ruach, and Neshama
  - that each one of them interconnects its first and highest attribute with the lowest attribute of the level above it
  - like a chain, where the top of each of its links interconnects within the lowest end of the link above it
  - and as a result, even if the Nefesh is cut off and falls into the depths of the powers of impurity, God forbid

---

493 Bereishit 28:13, i.e., the continuation from the verse quoted above.
494 Yerushalmi Taanit 2:6.
495 An expression from Bava Kama 92b used in relation to a bird, which Rashi explains is always on the lookout for food. In the context here, it means that

— לְהַעֲלוֹת תְּחִלָּה כָּל עוֹלָם מִמַּטָּה לְמַעְלָה, וְאַחַר כָּךְ נִמְשָׁכִים אוֹרוֹת מִלְמַעְלָה לְמַטָּה) עַד שֶׁאַחַר כָּךְ וְהִנֵּה הֲוָיָ"ה בָּרוּךְ הוּא נִצָּב עָלָיו כַּנַּ"ל:

- וּמַה נָּעֲמוּ אִמְרֵי רַבּוֹתֵינוּ זִכְרוֹנָם לִבְרָכָה בִּירוּשַׁלְמִי תַּעֲנִית פֶּרֶק ב', רֵישׁ לָקִישׁ בְּשֵׁם רַבִּי יוֹחָנָן אָמַר, שֻׁתָּף הַקָּדוֹשׁ בָּרוּךְ הוּא שְׁמוֹ בְּיִשְׂרָאֵל. מָשָׁל לְמֶלֶךְ שֶׁהָיָה לוֹ מַפְתֵּחַ שֶׁל פַּלְטֵרִין קְטַנָּה, אָמַר אִם אֲנִי מַנִּיחָהּ כְּמוֹת שֶׁהִיא הֲרֵי הִיא אֲבוּדָה, אֶלָּא הֲרֵינִי קוֹבֵעַ בָּהּ שַׁלְשֶׁלֶת, שֶׁאִם אָבְדָה, תְּהֵא שַׁלְשֶׁלֶת מַנַּחַת עָלֶיהָ. כָּךְ אָמַר הַקָּדוֹשׁ בָּרוּךְ הוּא, אִם אֲנִי מַנִּיחַ אֶת יִשְׂרָאֵל כְּמוֹ שֶׁהֵן, הֵן נִבְלָעִין בְּאֻמּוֹת הָעוֹלָם, אֶלָּא הֲרֵינִי מְשַׁתֵּף אֶת שְׁמִי הַגָּדוֹל בָּהֶם״.

○ וְהֵם זִכְרוֹנָם לִבְרָכָה דִּבְּרוּ לְעִנְיָן כְּלַל הָאֻמָּה יְחִידָהּ.

○ אָמְנָם עֵינֵיהֶם זִכְרוֹנָם לִבְרָכָה מְטַיְּפָן כְּדַרְכָּם בַּקֹּדֶשׁ, וְרָמְזוּ גַּם עַל הָאָדָם יְחִידִי. וְשִׂיחָתָם זִכְרוֹנָם לִבְרָכָה צְרִיכָה תַּלְמוּד, שֶׁהִמְשִׁילוּ הָעִנְיָן לְמַפְתֵּחַ וְשַׁלְשֶׁלֶת, כְּמוֹ שֶׁכָּתַבְתִּי לְעֵיל, שֶׁהָאָדָם הוּא הַפּוֹתֵחַ וְהַסּוֹגֵר שֶׁל הַכֹּחוֹת וְהָעוֹלָמוֹת, פַּלְטֵרִין שֶׁל מַעְלָה וּפַלְטֵרִין שֶׁל מַטָּה, שֶׁכֻּלָּם מִתְנַהֲגִים עַל יְדֵי כֹּחַ מַעֲשָׂיו בִּבְחִינַת נֶפֶשׁ, שֶׁהוּא עִקָּרָא וְשָׁרְשָׁא דִּבְחִינַת נֶפֶשׁ כָּל עָלְמִין.

○ וַאֲדוֹן כָּל בָּרוּךְ הוּא, בְּטוּבוֹ הַגָּדוֹל לְהֵטִיב לִבְרוּאָיו, שָׁקַד עַל תַּקָּנָתֵנוּ וְאָמַר, אִם אֲנִי מַנִּיחָהּ כְּמוֹת שֶׁהִיא, שֶׁלֹּא יִהְיֶה הִתְקַשְּׁרוּת בֵּין הַג' בְּחִינוֹת נֶרְ"ן, "אִלּוּ הָאֶחָד שֶׁיִּפֹּל" בְּחִינַת נֶפֶשׁ הַתַּחְתּוֹנָה לְעָמְקֵי מְצוּלוֹת הָרַע חַס וְשָׁלוֹם, אֵין שֵׁנִי לַהֲקִימוֹ, וַהֲרֵי הִיא אֲבוּדָה שָׁם לְעוֹלָם חַס וְשָׁלוֹם, כְּעִנְיָן הַכָּתוּב "וְהַאֲבַדְתִּי אֶת הַנֶּפֶשׁ הַהִיא" (ויקרא כג, ל), וְנֶפֶשׁ הַחוֹטֵאת בַּמֶּה תִּתְכַּפֵּר.

○ לָזֹאת, הִפְלִיא עֵצָה יִתְבָּרַךְ שְׁמוֹ, וְקָבַע הַשַּׁלְשֶׁלֶת מַדְרֵגוֹת נֶרְ"ן

○ שֶׁכָּל אַחַת מֵהֶם תִּתְקַשֵּׁר בְּחִינָה הָרִאשׁוֹנָה שֶׁלָּהּ הָעֶלְיוֹנָה בִּבְחִינָה הַתַּחְתּוֹנָה שֶׁל הַמַּדְרֵגָה שֶׁעָלֶיהָ

○ כְּעִנְיָן הַשַּׁלְשֶׁלֶת, שֶׁכָּל טַבַּעַת מִמֶּנָּה, קָצֶה הָעֶלְיוֹן שֶׁלָּהּ נֶאֱחָז וְנִכְנֶסֶת תּוֹךְ קָצֶה הַתַּחְתּוֹן שֶׁל הַטַּבַּעַת שֶׁעָלֶיהָ

○ וְעַל יְדֵי כֵן גַּם אִם יְבֹרֶרֶת הַנֶּפֶשׁ וְתִפֹּל לְעָמְקֵי כֹּחוֹת הַטֻּמְאָה חַס וְשָׁלוֹם

Chazal are always on the lookout to teach and build multiple understandings into their statements.

496 G1:03.
497 Vayikra 23:30.
498 Yishayahu 28:29.

- it can be rectified and raised up through its connection with its higher levels, with the level of Ruach, and similarly, [in turn] with any corruption and damage done to the level of Ruach, as explained above.
- This is what is referred to there when it says "behold I will *attach* My Great *Name* to them" that with the three levels of *Nefesh, Ruach*, and *Neshama* and [the fourth level of] the *Root of the Neshama*, their source root is from the four letters of God's Name [YHVH, meaning that the Name itself incorporates all the component links of the chain which allows God to attach Himself to our souls].[499]

20. REPENTANCE ON EACH OF THREE LEVELS

- A detailed explanation of the sequence of their rectification and reconnection through repentance is [as follows]:
  - [Level of Nefesh:]
    - When a person damages the level of his Nefesh – even if he, God forbid, caused the [maximum] disconnection and cutting off of all the nine Sefirot from Chochma and below from being connected, as mentioned above, 'and astonishingly descends'[500] to the depths of the Kelipot,[501] God forbid.
      - Then through deeply heartfelt spoken confession
      - physically articulated on the level of *Nefesh of Ruach*[502]
      - the sound of one's words creates an arousal which ascends to the highest levels
      - and initially causes an emanation of an *Addition* of holiness from God to the source of the soul
      - and from there [it descends] to the level of his Neshama and [then] to his Ruach
      - and the level of Ruach then also shines the great [additional] light which was bestowed upon it – onto the part of the level of Nefesh which still has a connection between them, as mentioned above [i.e., the level of Keter of Nefesh]
      - to destroy and to stop the powers of evil and the levels of impurity
      - to release all of its levels, 'the prisoner from confinement'[503]

---

499 See p. 444, fn. 389, which describes the make up of *YHVH* in terms of the worlds and of the components of the Ten Sefirot.
500 Eicha 1:9.
501 Kelipot (lit., husks) referring to the impure realms which only exist in an indirect manner. Physical sin caused the lower parts of Nefesh to descend into Kelipah.

- יְכוֹלָה הִיא לְהִתָּקֵן וְלַעֲלוֹת עַל יְדֵי הִתְקַשְׁרוּת בְּחִינוֹת עֶלְיוֹנוֹת שֶׁלָּהּ בִּבְחִינַת הָרוּחַ, וְכֵן עַל דֶּרֶךְ זֶה בְּקִלְקוּל וּפְגַם הָרוּחַ כַּנַּ"ל.
- וְזֶהוּ שֶׁאָמַר שָׁם, אֶלָּא הֲרֵינִי מְשַׁתֵּף אֶת שְׁמִי הַגָּדוֹל בָּהֶם, שֶׁהַשְּׁלֹשָׁה דְּרָגִין נֶר"ן וְשֹׁרֶשׁ הַנְּשָׁמָה, מְקוֹר שָׁרְשָׁם הוּא מֵהָאַרְבַּע אוֹתִיּוֹת הַשֵּׁם הַגָּדוֹל יִתְבָּרַךְ שְׁמוֹ:

שער א' - פרק כ'

- וּבֵאוּר פְּרָטוּת סֵדֶר תִּקּוּנָם וְהִתְקַשְּׁרוּתָם עַל יְדֵי הַתְּשׁוּבָה
  - [בחינת נפש]

- שֶׁכַּאֲשֶׁר פָּגַם הָאָדָם בְּחִינַת "נַפְשׁוֹ", אוֹ אַף אִם גָּרַם חַס וְשָׁלוֹם שֶׁנִּפְסְקוּ וְנִכְרְתוּ כָּל הַתֵּשַׁע סְפִירוֹתֶיהָ — מֵחָכְמָה וּלְמַטָּה — מֵהִתְקַשְּׁרוּתָהּ הַנַּ"ל, וַתֵּרֵד פְּלָאִים לְעָמְקֵי מְצוּלוֹת הַקְּלִפּוֹת חַס וְשָׁלוֹם.
- אָז עַל יְדֵי וִדּוּי דְּבָרִים בֶּאֱמֶת מֵעִמְקָא דְלִבָּא
- בַּעֲקִימַת שְׂפָתָיו, בְּחִינַת נֶפֶשׁ דְּרוּחַ
- מְעוֹרֵר בְּקוֹל דְּבָרִים שֶׁלּוֹ עַד לְעֵלָּא וּלְעֵלָּא
- וְגוֹרֵם שֶׁיִּתְאַצֵּל תּוֹסֶפֶת קְדֻשָּׁה מִמֶּנּוּ יִתְבָּרַךְ שְׁמוֹ עַד "שֹׁרֶשׁ הַנְּשָׁמָה" תְּחִלָּה
- וּמִשָּׁם לְ"נִשְׁמָתוֹ וְרוּחוֹ"
- וְהָרוּחַ מַבְהִיק אוֹרוֹ הַגָּדוֹל הַנִּשְׁפָּע עָלָיו גַּם עַל בְּחִינַת הַ"נֶּפֶשׁ", מִצַּד הַהִתְקַשְּׁרוּת שֶׁנִּשְׁאָר עֲדַיִן בֵּינֵיהֶם כַּנַּ"ל
- לְכַלּוֹת וּלְהָתֵם הַכֹּחוֹת הָרַע וּמַדְרֵגוֹת הַטֻּמְאָה
- וּלְהוֹצִיא מִמַּסְגֵּר אָסִיר כָּל בְּחִינוֹתֶיהָ, וְלַחֲזֹר וּלְקַשְּׁרָם כְּבָרִאשׁוֹנָה עִם בְּחִינַת הָרוּחַ:

---

502 As stated previously the level of Ruach connects between the levels of Neshama and Nefesh. Each level in turn has multiple levels and the lowest level of Ruach, i.e., Nefesh of Ruach is the level which interconnects with the level of Nefesh. Since Ruach is associated with speech, this lowest level of Ruach is the physical articulation of speech, i.e., the physical movement of one's lips. This process enables a reconnection of Nefesh and Ruach.

503 Yishayahu 42:7.

[within the Kelipah], and restore their original connection to the level of Ruach.

- [Level of Ruach:]
  - Similarly, if he damaged and corrupted the level of Ruach, God forbid, through improper speech or through other Ruach related sins, with the [sin] of not learning Torah[504] corresponding to all of them, and correspondingly resulting in increased powers of impurity, God should save us.
  - This then also [prevents] his Nefesh from being complete as it was before [the sin], for it receives its bestowal of life force and light through the [medium] of Ruach, as is known.
    - It is through true heartfelt regret and complaint of the greatness of his sin as per "they shouted their hearts to God"[505]
    - [accompanied] with thoughts of repentance [where the realm of thought is the place] in which the sparks of the level of Neshama reside (which is the level of Malchut of Binah).[506]
    - This also creates an arousal which ascends to the supernal levels
    - which initially bestows an *Addition* of holiness and light upon the source of one's soul
    - and from there to the level of his Neshama
    - which also shines with the [additional] radiance of light which was bestowed upon it – onto the level of Ruach
    - "the sacrifices to God are a broken *Ruach* (/spirit),"[507] and breaks the power of impurity which was increased with his sin
    - and purifies the holy level of Ruach, enabling it to fully re-establish its original connection with the level of Neshama
    - and from there to automatically also bestow upon the level of his Nefesh, restoring it to its original state of completeness.
- [Level of Neshama:]
  - Similarly, if he sinned, God forbid, with impure thoughts – causing the removal of the sparks of his Neshama from upon him, which were 'shining their light over his head'[508] until this point.
    - Then through Torah study with increased analysis with the depths of his analytical skills
    - this arouses the emanation of an *Addition* of holiness over the root of his soul

---

504 Where fulfilment of the command to study Torah is only via verbal articulation.
505 Eicha 2:18.
506 See p. 444, fn. 389, which describes that Binah is related to the second letter,

◦ [בחינת רוח]

▪ וְכֵן אִם פָּגַם וְקִלְקֵל בְּחִינַת רוּחוֹ חַס וְשָׁלוֹם, בְּדִבּוּרִים אֲשֶׁר לֹא טוֹבִים, אוֹ בִּשְׁאָר עֲוֹנוֹת הַתְּלוּיִים בִּבְחִינַת הָרוּחַ, וּבִטּוּל תּוֹרָה כְּנֶגֶד כֻּלָּם, וְהִגְבִּיר לְעֻמַּת זֶה כֹּחַ רוּחַ הַטֻּמְאָה רַחֲמָנָא לִיצְלָן

▪ וְאָז גַּם נַפְשׁוֹ אֵינָהּ שְׁלֵמָה כְּמִקֹּדֶם, כִּי הִיא מְקַבֶּלֶת שֶׁפַע חִיּוּתָהּ וְאוֹרָהּ עַל יְדֵי הָרוּחַ כַּיָּדוּעַ

◦ הִנֵּה עַל יְדֵי הַחֲרָטָה אֲמִתִּית בַּלֵּב, וּמִתְמַרְמֵר עַל גֹּדֶל חֶטְאוֹ, כְּעִנְיָן "צָעַק לִבָּם אֶל ה'" (איכה ב, יח)

◦ וּמְהַרְהֵר הִרְהוּרֵי תְשׁוּבָה בְּמַחֲשָׁבָה, שֶׁהִיא מִשְׁכַּן נִצוֹצֵי אוֹר הַנְּשָׁמָה, (וְהוּא מַלְכוּת דִּתְבוּנָה)

◦ מְעוֹרֵר גַּם כֵּן עַד לְעֵלָּא

◦ לְהַשְׁפִּיעַ תְּחִלָּה תּוֹסֶפֶת קְדֻשָּׁה וָאוֹר עַל "שֹׁרֶשׁ הַנְּשָׁמָה" וּמִשָּׁם לְ"נִשְׁמָתוֹ"

◦ וְהִיא מַבְהֶקֶת זִיו אוֹרָהּ שֶׁנִּשְׁפַּע עָלֶיהָ גַּם עַל בְּחִינַת "הָרוּחַ"

◦ וְזִבְחֵי אֱלֹקִים רוּחַ נִשְׁבָּרָה (תהלים נא, יט), וְשׁוֹבֵר כֹּחַ רוּחַ הַטֻּמְאָה שֶׁהִגְבִּיר בַּעֲוֹנוֹ

◦ וּמְטַהֵר בְּחִינַת רוּחוֹ הַקָּדוֹשׁ לְהִתְקַשֵּׁר בִּבְחִינַת הַנְּשָׁמָה כְּבַתְּחִלָּה

◦ וּמִשָּׁם מִמֵּילָא יִשְׁפַּע גַּם עַל "נַפְשׁוֹ" לְהַשְׁלִימָהּ בִּשְׁלֵמוּתָהּ הָרִאשׁוֹן:

◦ [בחינת נשמה]

▪ וְכֵן אִם חָטָא חַס וְשָׁלוֹם בְּמַחֲשָׁבָה אֲשֶׁר לֹא טְהוֹרָה, וְגָרַם בָּזֶה שֶׁיִּסְתַּלְּקוּ מֵעָלָיו נִצוֹצֵי זֹהַר נִשְׁמָתוֹ, שֶׁהָיְתָה עַד הֵנָּה בְּהִלּוֹ נֵרוֹ עֲלֵי רֹאשׁוֹ

◦ אָז עַל יְדֵי עֵסֶק הַתּוֹרָה בְּבִינָה יְתֵרָה בְּעֹמֶק תְּבוּנָתוֹ

◦ מְעוֹרֵר שֶׁיִּתְאַצֵּל תּוֹסֶפֶת קְדֻשָּׁה עַל "שֹׁרֶשׁ נִשְׁמָתוֹ"

- - - and from there to his Neshama – to return [the light] to shine upon him
  - to make him wise in the Holy Torah with greater understanding of its hidden purity
  - with part of that [additional] holiness and light cascading downwards to also impact on his Ruach and his Nefesh to restore them completely.
- Therefore, Chazal say:[509] "One who invests all of his strength when answering [Kaddish] with 'Amen. Yehay Shmey Rabba Mevorach [LeOlam U'leOlmey Olmaya],'[510] has any adverse decrees upon him torn up, and is even forgiven for traces of the sin of idol worship."
  - For the principal objective of this praise is for the emanation and impact of *Additional Blessing* and bestowal of supernal light on each of the four worlds of Atzilut, Beriyah, Yetzirah, and Asiyah: (Note 17)[511]
    - ["Yehay Shmey Rabba Mevorach":]
      - This is "Yehay Shmey Rabba Mevorach," meaning that blessing and *Additional Holiness* from God should emanate and impact on the level of "LeOlam."
    - ["LeOlam":]
      - This is the world of Atzilut [the level of the Root of the Neshama], and from there [the additional blessing also extends] to the level of "LeOlmay."
    - ["LeOlmay":][512]
      - These are the two worlds of Beriyah and Yetzirah [the levels of Neshama and Ruach].
    - "Olmaya":
      - This is the world of Asiyah [the level of Nefesh].
    - These are the source of the four levels of man: [1] the Root of Neshama; [2] Neshama; [3] Ruach, and [4] Nefesh.
  - When a person focuses with the holiness of his thoughts when saying this praise
    - to arouse and bestow through it an additional holiness and blessing upon the *Root of his Neshama* and from there upon his *Neshama*, *Ruach*, and *Nefesh*
    - this causes the 'end and eradication'[513] of all intentional and unintentional sins[514] performed with each of these three [lower] levels to the extent that it is as if [the sins] were never committed

---

509 Shabbat 119b.
510 Literally meaning "Amen. May His Great Name be blessed, for ever and ever." However, in this context, the words "for ever and ever" are the same

- וּמִשָּׁם לְ"נִשְׁמָתוֹ", לְהַחֲזִירָהּ שֶׁתָּאִיר עָלָיו אוֹרָהּ
- לְהַשְׂכִּילוֹ בַּתּוֹרָה הַקְּדוֹשָׁה בְּבִינָה יְתֵרָה בְּסִתְרֵי טְהוֹרֶיהָ
- וּמֵאוֹתוֹ הַקְּדֻשָּׁה וְהָאוֹר מִשְׁתַּלְשֵׁל וְנִשְׁפָּע גַּם עַל "רוּחוֹ וְנַפְשׁוֹ" לְהַשְׁלִימָם בִּשְׁלֵמוּתָם:

- וְלָכֵן אָמְרוּ זִכְרוֹנָם לִבְרָכָה (שבת קיט, ב) "כָּל הָעוֹנֶה 'אָמֵן יְהֵא שְׁמֵיהּ רַבָּא מְבָרַךְ' בְּכָל כֹּחוֹ, קוֹרְעִים לוֹ גְּזַר דִּינוֹ, וַאֲפִלּוּ יֵשׁ בּוֹ שֶׁמֶץ שֶׁל עֲבוֹדָה זָרָה מוֹחֲלִים לוֹ".

- כִּי עִקַּר כַּוָּנַת זֶה הַשֶּׁבַח, הוּא שֶׁיִּתְאַצֵּל וְיִשְׁפַּע תּוֹסֶפֶת בְּרָכָה וְשִׁפְעַת אוֹר עֶלְיוֹן לְכָל הָאַרְבַּע עוֹלָמוֹת אבי"ע (הגהה י"ז).

- ["יהא שמיה רבא מברך"]
- וְזֶהוּ יְהֵא שְׁמֵיהּ רַבָּא מְבָרַךְ, הַיְנוּ, שֶׁיִּתְאַצֵּל בְּרָכָה וְתוֹסֶפֶת קְדֻשָּׁה מִמֶּנּוּ יִתְבָּרַךְ שְׁמוֹ, עַד "לְעָלַם"

- ["לעלם"]
- הוּא עוֹלַם הָאֲצִילוּת, וּמִשָּׁם גַּם "לְעָלְמֵי"

- ["לעלמי"]
- הֵם ב' עוֹלָמוֹת בְּרִיאָה יְצִירָה

- "עָלְמַיָּא"
- הוּא עוֹלָם הָעֲשִׂיָּה

- וְהֵם שֹׁרֶשׁ הד' דְּרָגִין שֶׁל הָאָדָם, שֹׁרֶשׁ הַנְּשָׁמָה, וְנָר"ן.

- וּכְשֶׁמְּכַוֵּן הָאָדָם בִּקְדֻשַּׁת מַחֲשַׁבְתּוֹ בַּאֲמִירַת זֶה הַשֶּׁבַח
- לְעוֹרֵר וּלְהַשְׁפִּיעַ עַל יָדוֹ תּוֹסֶפֶת קְדֻשָּׁה וּבְרָכָה עַל שֹׁרֶשׁ נִשְׁמָתוֹ, וּמִשָּׁם עַל נִשְׁמָתוֹ וְרוּחוֹ וְנַפְשׁוֹ

- גּוֹרֵם בָּזֶה לְהָתֵם וּלְכַלֵּה כָּל עָוֹן וְחֵטְא אֲשֶׁר חָטָא בְּאֵיזֶה בְּחִינָה מֵאֵלּוּ הַשְּׁלֹשָׁה, וְהָיוּ כְּלֹא הָיוּ

---

as the word "Olam" meaning "world," i.e., "LeOlam VeOlmay Olmaya" is a reference to four worlds through which the repentance process occurs.

511 **R. Chaim adds Note 17 here.** This note is brought at the end of this chapter and is entitled "Both person and God invest Yehay Shmey with all strength."
512 LeOlmey is plural – therefore relating to two worlds.
513 Daniel 9:24.
514 R. Chaim uses two terms for sin here – *Avon* and *Chet*. *Avon* is intentional

○ and this is the essence of true repentance, as mentioned above and therefore he is forgiven for all of his sins.
- This is *also* the idea expressed by Chazal that the "Ox that was sacrificed by Adam – its horns preceded its hooves"[515]
  ○ that [Adam's] intention with his sacrifice was to repair that which he distorted, to rebuild the destroyed, to draw near[516] that which he distanced and to unify that which he separated
  ○ and he elevated the purity of his thoughts and intention, to initially cause an emanation of light and holiness onto the highest levels within him – represented by "horns" – being [the levels of] the *Root of his Neshama* and his *Neshama*
  ○ and from there it was then drawn upon his *Ruach* and *Nefesh* – to purify all of his limbs from head to foot
  ○ in line with "and it will be *Ekev* [literally, heel] you will listen . . ."[517] referring to the commandments that a person *treads on with their heels* [ignores], and this refers to the hooves of the animal Nefesh.
  ○ This is as stated[518] that "Adam's heel [i.e., a reference to his deeds] darkens the sun." (Note 18)[519]

Rabbi Chaim's Notes:
Note 17 – Both person and God invest Yehay Shmey with all strength

- Chazal's expression "invests all his strength" can be explained in two ways:
  ○ Either relating to all the strength of the person who answers [the Kaddish]
  ○ or that God's Name *Yud-Hey* should be blessed[520] with all of His strength, as per "and now, may God's strength be increased."[521]
- However these two explanations are really 'one and the same'[522] as the

---

sin, and *Chet* is unintentional sin (Yoma 36b, as quoted in many sources, e.g., Mishna Berura 621:17 and Rashi on Shemot 34:7).

515 Avodah Zarah 8a. R. Chaim uses the word "also" here to highlight that this is an additional interpretation of the Talmud's statement that the horns preceded the hooves. The basic interpretation, e.g., as per Rashi, is that the Ox sacrificed was a special one in that it was created, like Adam, as a fully formed being and therefore as it was pulled out of the ground its horns existed before its hooves. Adam therefore specifically sacrificed an ox formed in the same way as himself to atone for himself. R. Chaim goes beyond this basic interpretation to demonstrate the process of repentance by reconnection of the parts of the soul from the top down. The example of Adam's repentance process is particularly relevant as he very seriously corrupted the world by

וְזֶה כָּל עִקַּר הַתְּשׁוּבָה הָאֲמִתִּית כַּנַּ"ל, לָכֵן מוֹחֲלִין לוֹ עַל כָּל עֲוֹנוֹתָיו:

- וְזֶה גַּם כֵּן עִנְיַן מַאֲמָרָם זִכְרוֹנָם לִבְרָכָה (ע"ז ח' א') "שׁוֹר שֶׁהִקְרִיב אָדָם הָרִאשׁוֹן, קַרְנוֹתָיו קוֹדְמוֹת לְפַרְסוֹתָיו הָיוּ"
  - שֶׁכִּוֵּן בְּהַקְרָבָתוֹ לְתַקֵּן אֲשֶׁר עִוֵּת, לִבְנוֹת הַנֶּהֱרָסוֹת, לְקָרֵב אֲשֶׁר הִרְחִיק וּלְיַחֵד אֲשֶׁר הִפְרִיד
  - וְהֶעֱלָה טֹהַר קְדֻשַּׁת מַחְשַׁבְתּוֹ וְכַוָּנָתוֹ, לְהַאֲצִיל תְּחִלָּה שִׁפְעַת אוֹר וּקְדֻשָּׁה עַל הַבְּחִינוֹת וּמַדְרֵגוֹת הָעֶלְיוֹנוֹת שֶׁבּוֹ, דִּמְיוֹן הַקַּרְנַיִם, הֵם שֹׁרֶשׁ נִשְׁמָתוֹ וְנִשְׁמָתוֹ
  - וּמִשָּׁם הִמְשִׁיךְ אַחַר זֶה עַל רוּחוֹ וְנַפְשׁוֹ, לְטַהֵר כָּל אֵבָרָיו מֵרֹאשׁוֹ וְעַד רַגְלָיו
  - עַל דֶּרֶךְ "וְהָיָה עֵקֶב תִּשְׁמְעוּן" וְגוֹ', מִצְוֹת שֶׁאָדָם דָּשׁ בַּעֲקֵבָיו, וְהוּא הַפַּרְסוֹת שֶׁל נֶפֶשׁ הַבַּהֲמִית.
  - וְזֶהוּ שֶׁאָמַר (בְּוַיִּקְרָא רַבָּה פָּרָשָׁה כ' וְקֹהֶלֶת ח') שֶׁתַּפּוּחַ עֲקֵבוֹ הָיָה מַכְהֶה גַּלְגַּל חַמָּה וְכוּ' (הגהה י"ח):

הגהה י"ז

- וְאָמְרָם זִכְרוֹנָם לִבְרָכָה 'בְּכָל כֹּחוּ', סוֹבֵל ב' פֵּרוּשִׁים
  - אוֹ בְּכָל כֹּחוֹ שֶׁל הָעוֹנֶה
  - אוֹ שֶׁיִּתְבָּרֵךְ הַשֵּׁם י"ה בְּכָל כֹּחוֹתָיו, כְּעִנְיַן "וְעַתָּה יִגְדַּל נָא כֹּחַ ה'" (במדבר יד, יז):

- אָמְנָם ב' הַפֵּרוּשִׁים הֵמָּה בְּחַדָּא מַחֲתָא, שֶׁשֹּׁרֶשׁ מְקוֹר שֶׁפַע קְדֻשָּׁה וְהַבְּרָכוֹת, הוּא בְּשֵׁם י"ה

---

bringing death to it with his sin (see G1:06:N07). Adam's repentance process therefore acts as a template for our repentance process all the while mankind is in a state where death still exists in the world.

516 The Hebrew words for *sacrifice* and *draw near* are almost identical indicating that one results in the other.

517 Devarim 7:12. The usual understanding of the word "Ekev" is *because*.

518 Vayikra Rabba (Vilna) Acharei Mot 20:2; Kohelet Rabba (Vilna) 8:2.

519 **R. Chaim adds Note 18 here.** This note is brought at the end of this chapter and is entitled "Torah involvement reinstates Nefesh, Adam's connection to David."

520 I.e., receive an addition or increase as per G2:02.

521 Bamidbar 14:17.

522 Literally, *in the same weave* as per Berachot 24a.

root source of all holiness and blessing comes from God's Name *Yud-Hey*:⁵²³
- From [this name, the holiness and blessing] cascades down to fill the world of Beriyah
  - which is the world of thought
  - and corresponds to the extension of the letter *Hey* of God's Name *Yud-Hey* with the letter *Yud*.⁵²⁴
- From the world of Beriyah [the holiness and blessing cascades down] to fill the world of Yetzirah
  - which is the root of the beginning of speech and the logic of the heart
  - and corresponds to the extension of the letter *Hey* with the letter *Aleph*.
- From the world of Yetzirah [the holiness and blessing cascades down] to fill the world of Asiyah
  - which is the world of action
  - and corresponds to the extension of the letter *Hey* of God's Name *Yud-Hey* with the letter *Hey*.

- These [worlds] are the root of the Nefesh, Ruach, and Neshama of a person, for they are all the strength of the person answering [the Kaddish]
  - and [at the same time] they are also all the strength of God's Name *Yud-Hey*, which is the hidden aspects of each letter.
- This is the meaning of "Yehay (*Yud-Hey-Aleph*) Shmey ('Shem *Yud-Hey*') Rabba Mevorach."⁵²⁵
- Refer to Tosafot on Berachot 3a beginning VeOnim.⁵²⁶

Note 18 – Torah involvement reinstates Nefesh, Adam's connection to David

- This is the meaning of what King David said: "God's Torah is perfect, it restores the *Nefesh*,"⁵²⁷ that through man's involvement with God's Torah such that it is perfect with him, as appropriate, it completely returns/reinstates his Nefesh to its source.⁵²⁸

---

523 As per Menachot 29b, which describes that the future world was created with *Yud* and this world with *Hey*.

524 I.e., each letter of the Hebrew alphabet has a name which can be *extended*, i.e., spelled out in full, but begins with the letter itself. Each letter depicts a deep concept where the letter itself represents the revealed part of the concept and the rest of the spelling of the letter's name represents the hidden part of the concept, as when the letter is written down this hidden part is not seen or pronounced. In the case of the letter *Hey*, there are three ways of spelling it out, each with the same pronunciation, and each way represents a different aspect of the concept. R. Chaim presents the idea here that each of these three

- וּמִמֶּנּוּ מִשְׁתַּלְשֵׁל וּמִתְמַלֵּא עוֹלָם הַבְּרִיאָה
  - הוּא עוֹלָם הַמַּחֲשָׁבָה
  - מִמִּלּוּי הֵה"י שֶׁל שֵׁם י"ה בְּ"יוּד".
- וּמֵעוֹלָם הַבְּרִיאָה מִתְמַלֵּא עוֹלָם הַיְצִירָה
  - הוּא שֹׁרֶשׁ הַתְחָלַת הַדִּבּוּר וְהִגָּיוֹן הַלֵּב
  - מִמִּלּוּי הֵה"א בְּ"אַלֶף".
- וּמֵעוֹלָם הַיְצִירָה מִתְמַלֵּא עוֹלָם הָעֲשִׂיָּה
  - הוּא עוֹלָם הַמַּעֲשֶׂה
  - מִמִּלּוּי אוֹת ה' שֶׁבַּשֵּׁם י"ה באוֹת ה':
- וְהֵן הֵמָּה שֹׁרֶשׁ הַנר"ן שֶׁל אָדָם, שֶׁהֵם כָּל כֹּחוֹתָיו שֶׁל הָעוֹנֶה
  - וְכָל כֹּחוֹתָיו שֶׁל הַשֵּׁם י"ה, הַיְנוּ כָּל מִלּוּאָיו:
- וְזֶהוּ י'—הֵ'—א' שֵׁם י'—ה' רַבָּא מְבָרַךְ וְכוּ':
- וְעַיֵּן תּוֹסָפוֹת בְּרָכוֹת ג' ע"א ד"ה וְעוֹנִין וְכוּ':

הגהה י"ח

- וְזֶהוּ שֶׁאָמַר דָּוִד הַמֶּלֶךְ עָלָיו הַשָּׁלוֹם (תהלים יט) "תּוֹרַת ה' תְּמִימָה מְשִׁיבַת נָפֶשׁ", שֶׁעַל יְדֵי עֵסֶק הָאָדָם בְּתוֹרַת ה', וְהִיא תְּמִימָה אֶצְלוֹ כָּרָאוּי, הִיא מְשִׁיבַת נֶפֶשׁ הָאָדָם לְשָׁרְשָׁהּ בִּשְׁלֵמוּתָהּ:

---

ways of extending the letter *Hey* represents the creative impact on a different world with *Hey-Yud* referring to the world of *Beriyah*.

525 Where *Yud-Hey-Aleph* depicts the three hidden extensions of the (*Shem*), God's Name, *Yud-Hey*, which is "great and blessed. . . ."

526 Which comments on the Talmud referring to when Israel enter the prayer houses and study halls and answer "Amen. Yehei Shmei HaGadol Mevorach . . ." that God lifts his head and says "Happy is the King who is praised in His house . . . ." Tosafot bring down a comment from the Rosh analyzing that "Yehei Shmei . . ." refers to a prayer that God's Name, i.e., *Shem Yud Hey*, should become great, complete and blessed, and that the statement "forever and ever" is a separate prayer. Tosafot reject the Rosh's interpretation understanding "Yehei Shmei . . ." to be a single prayer that God's "Great Name should be blessed forever. . . ."

527 Tehillim 19:8.

528 The idea that complete and proper repentance can only be performed with Torah study is expressed in G4:31.

- [King David] concludes there: "Also, when Your servant is *Nizhar*/scrupulous in them, in observing them there is great *Ekev*/reward."[529]
  - The term "Nizhar" [also] means "shining," meaning that through [King David's scrupulous] observance of all the Mitzvot, which corresponded to all the limbs of Adam
  - his Nefesh and his physical body were purified – to the extent that even his *Ekev* [which also means "heel"] had great light and *shining*, as per "Adam's heel darkens [the sun]."[530]
- The depth of the concept of "Also, when Your servant is scrupulous ... there is great *Ekev*" is that the purpose of the elevation/perfection of King David's nature in its ultimate supernal source
  - is [to reach higher] within [the level of] the *Unknown Beginning [of Atik]*,[531] which is [the level of] *Malchut of Adam Kadmon*, the Root of the Neshama of Adam.

---

[529] Tehillim 19:12, where "Ekev" literally means "heel," i.e., as the heel automatically follows the foot, there is a great reward which follows Mitzvah performance.

[530] Vayikra Rabba (Vilna) Acharei Mot 20:2. It is insightful to see the Vilna Gaon's comments (on p.13b/14a of the 1863 edition of Barak HaShachar) as follows:
- "Also, when Your servant is *Nizhar* in them . . .": The use of the word "also" is not obviously understood? The idea is that *man is purified when he reviews Torah*, as with Moshe who was so purified that he Nizhar/shined like the shining of the firmament, to the extent that he went forty days without eating, as the Torah greatly radiated and shone as the shining of a sun's ray. As per . . . "Adam's heel darkens the sun" . . . and this is the meaning of "*Also*, when Your servant is *Nizhar* in them" [where Nizhar] is *an expression of shining* which acts to "preserve a great Ekev/reward" [a play on "in observing them there is *Ekev*/great reward"], that even the Ekev/heel is of great quality [and purified].

[531] This is a term which comes from Zohar Idra Zuta III Haazinu 289a. The preceding part of this section of Zohar on 288a–b which provides background for this term has been translated as follows (it also adds insight into the concept of Makom and the quotation from Sefer Yetzirah in relation to *to and fro* as per G3:02 and G3:06):
- . . . This holy *Atik* is secret and hidden away, and concealed supernal wisdom is found in that head. It is certain that in this *Atik* there is nothing else revealed apart from the head/beginning alone – for it is the beginning of all beginnings. Supernal Wisdom, which is the beginning, is concealed within it and is called the supernal brain, the concealed brain, a calm and quiet brain, and there is nothing that can perceive it apart from itself. Three heads are etched, one within the other and one above the other. One head

- וְסִיֵּם שָׁם, "גַּם עַבְדְּךָ נִזְהָר בָּהֶם בְּשָׁמְרָם עֵקֶב רָב"
- וְנִזְהָר מִלְּשׁוֹן יַזְהִירוּ וכו', הַיְנוּ שֶׁעַל יְדֵי שֶׁשָּׁמַר כָּל הַמִּצְוֹת, הַמְכֻוָּנִים נֶגֶד כָּל אֶבְרֵי הָאָדָם
  - נִזְדַּכֵּךְ נַפְשׁוֹ וְגוּפוֹ, עַד שֶׁגַּם בַּעֲקֵבוֹ הָיָה אוֹר וְזֹהַר רַב, כְּעִנְיָן "תַּפּוּחַ עֲקֵבוֹ שֶׁל אָדָם הָרִאשׁוֹן הָיָה מַכְהֶה" וכו' (ויק"ר כ):
- וּפְנִימִיּוּת הָעִנְיָן "גַּם עַבְדְּךָ נִזְהָר וְגו' עֵקֶב רָב", כִּי תַכְלִית עֲלִיָּתָהּ שֶׁל מִדַּת דָּוִד הַמֶּלֶךְ עָלָיו הַשָּׁלוֹם בְּשֹׁרֶשׁ שָׁרְשָׁהּ הָעֶלְיוֹן
  - הוּא בְּרֵישָׁא דְלָא אִתְיְדַע, שֶׁהוּא מַלְכוּת דְּאָדָם קַדְמָאָה, שֹׁרֶשׁ נִשְׁמַת אָדָם הָרִאשׁוֹן

---

is concealed wisdom, which is covered and not open, and this concealed wisdom is the beginning of all beginnings of other wisdoms. It is the supernal beginning, the holy *Atik*, the most concealed of all concealed things, the beginning of all beginnings, the beginning which has no beginning of its own – for what is in *this beginning is not knowable* or known – for it is not connected to either wisdom or intellect, and it is about this that it says "you should flee to your Makom/place" (Bamidbar 24:11) "and the Chayot ran *to and fro*" (Yechezkel 1:14). It is because of this that that holy *Atik* is called Ayin/nothing as Ayin is dependent on it . . . [See p. 472, fn. 18, for comments on the concept of Ayin. Also see V2:02, Chap. 15, "Tzimtzum Sources," I1.1, which provide more details on Atik and Ayin.]

This term is also defined by the Vilna Gaon at the very beginning of his commentary on Sifra DeTzniyuta which references the Zohar section above. He says the following:

- [After explaining that the first 5 words of Sefer DeTzniyuta form an introduction to it with each word corresponding to one of the 5 books of the Torah and one of the 5 worlds of Adam Kadmon, Atzilut, Beriyah, Yetzirah, and Asiyah (see p. 444, fn. 389, describing the 5 worlds), the Vilna Gaon then details some aspects of these worlds and explains that in relation to Adam Kadmon] . . . the concealed thought, which is *Supernal Keter* [i.e., the level just above the world of Atzilut which is synonymous with Malchut, the lowest level of the world of Adam Kadmon] is not revealed at all – even the fact of its existence [is not revealed], and therefore it is called Ayin/nothing . . . it is the *Unknown Beginning* which is hidden from the eyes of all . . .

- This is in line with "Who am I, O God ... that You should have brought me *Halom* [this far – to become king] (where Halom is an expression of Malchut).[532] And yet *Zot*/this[533] was insufficient in Your eyes, O God, so You have also spoken of Your servant's household in the distant future, and You have considered me as befits a *Tor HaAdam HaMaaleh* (man of exalted nature), O God, Elokim"[534]
  - (and [a similar sentiment is expressed] in Shmuel [but the expression used there instead of *Tor HaAdam HaMaaleh* is] "VeZot Torat HaAdam")[535]
  - *Tor* has the numerical value equal to the sum of the hidden parts of the letters which comprise God's Name 'A-D-N-Y,' as understood by one who knows.[536]
- Therefore, Adam left David the last seventy years of his life
  - [the last seven decades corresponding to] the seven lowest levels of Malchut of Adam Kadmon.[537]
  - It was appropriate for David [who represented the Sefira of Malchut] to live a further three decades to complete its *Three Heads*[538] as per "the words of the man who was established *Al* (/on high)."[539]
  - This is also the Root of the Neshama of Mashiach, about whom it is written "he will be elevated, raised up and high – very much" and Chazal explain that [this verse identifies just how high Mashiach's level will be in comparison to other individuals, i.e., that "elevated" relates] to Avraham, ["raised up" relates to Yitzchak, and "high" relates to Yaakov ... and "raised up" relates] to Moshe,[540] and to Adam (that is after [Adam's] sin).[541]

---

532 Shabbat 113b.
533 The word "*Zot*" is synonymous with Malchut, e.g., as per Zohar I Lech Lecha 94a and Maggid Meisharim Miketz. In the first and second print editions, the word "Zot" is emphasized with a quotation mark.
534 1 Diverei Hayamim 17:16–17.
535 2 Shmuel 7:19.
536 See R. Chaim's previous note, G1:20:N17, for an explanation of how the hidden parts of each Hebrew letter identify its hidden meaning. God's name ADNY relates to Him being Master, i.e., King, and therefore the level of Malchut. The revealed level of Malchut is in the form of the revealed letters of the name ADNY. However, the hidden part of Malchut, i.e., as it is manifest in its supernal source in the highest world level of Adam Kadmon – is represented by the hidden parts of each letter of the name ADNY, and represented numerically by the word "*Tor*." It is interesting to note that in the book Kol Eliyahu which compiles comments of the Vilna Gaon, the comment is brought down on Megillat Rut from the Talmud in Berachot (7b): What is the meaning

- וּכְעִנְיָן הַכָּתוּב (ד״ה א׳ י״ז) "מִי אֲנִי ה׳ גו׳ "כִּי הֲבִיאֹתַנִי עַד הֲלֹם" (וְאֵין הֲלֹם אֶלָּא מַלְכוּת), וַתִּקְטַן זֹאת בְּעֵינֶיךָ אֱלֹקִים וַתְּדַבֵּר עַל בֵּית עַבְדְּךָ לְמֵרָחוֹק וּרְאִיתַנִי כְּתוֹר הָאָדָם הַמַּעֲלָה ה׳ אֱלֹקִים"
  - (וּבִשְׁמוּאֵל ב׳ ז׳ י״ט וְזֹאת תּוֹרַת הָאָדָם)
  - וְתוֹר הוּא גִּלּוּפִין דַּאֲ׳דְ׳נָ׳יְ׳, וְהַמַּשְׂכִּיל יָבִין:
- וְלָכֵן הִשְׁאִיר אָדָם הָרִאשׁוֹן לְדָוִד שִׁבְעִים שְׁנוֹתָיו הָאַחֲרוֹנִים
  - ז׳ תַּחְתּוֹנוֹת דְּמַלְכוּת דא״ק.
- וְרָאוּי הָיָה לִחְיוֹת עוֹד ל׳ שָׁנָה, לְהַשְׁלִים ג׳ רִאשׁוֹנוֹת דִּילֵהּ, כְּעִנְיָן "נְאֻם הַגֶּבֶר הֻקַם עָל" (שמואל ב׳ כג).
- וְהוּא גַם כֵּן שֹׁרֶשׁ נִשְׁמַת מָשִׁיחַ, שֶׁכָּתוּב עָלָיו (ישעיה נ״ב) יָרוּם וְנִשָּׂא וְגָבַהּ

---

of the name "Rut?" R. Yochanan said that she merited that David, who *sated* [a play on words on the word "Rut"] God with his praises and songs, would be descended from her. Now why should the name Rut be appropriate, surely the name Shir (i.e., song) would have been more appropriate? However, before Rut converted to Judaism, she was obliged to observe the 7 Noachide Laws, but after she converted she had an additional 606 laws, being the numerical value of *Rut*. But one may have asked, that according to this, her name may have equally been *Tor* (i.e., a different arrangement of the letters which also sum to the numerical value of 606)? So the Talmud explains that the specific reason why the combination "Rut" was chosen was that she merited a descendant that *sated*. So in that Rut, King David's ancestor, is described as being "Em (the mother of) HaMalchut" where a mother contains the hidden essence which is eventually revealed when born – therefore "Rut/Tor" represents the hidden part of the name ADNY.

537 As per Psikta Rabbati Piska 40 that Adam was destined to live for one of God's days, i.e., 1,000 years, but God only gave him 930 years and left the balance of 70 for David. So each century of Adam's life represented a Sefira with each decade representing a sub-Sefira.

538 I.e., the levels of Chochma, Binah, and Daat of Malchut of Adam Kadmon.

539 2 Shmuel 23:1, where the word "*Al*" has Hebrew letters with the numerical value of 70 and 30 referring to the years David actually lived, i.e., 70 and the additional years which he should have lived, i.e., 30.

540 Midrash Tanchuma (Warsaw), Toldot 14 quoting Yishayahu 52:13.

541 The previously quoted Midrash does not refer to Adam at all although R. Chaim appends the reference to Adam such that it looks like it is the continuation of it and that therefore the level of Mashich (who will restore the soul of Adam to its former state before he sinned) is much higher than the level of Adam after he sinned.

○ This is the meaning of "the words of the man who was established on high, the Mashiach of the God of Yaakov,"⁵⁴² as then [with the Mashiach who is the continuation of the line of King David and who will raise Malchut of God in this world to the level of the *Three Heads*, i.e., the intellect, then] the honor of the Kingship/Majesty of God will be raised up within its original root source.⁵⁴³

The following sources explain this statement in the context of Yishayahu 52:13 but neither of them are totally consistent with R. Chaim's presentation: Zohar Raya Mehemna III Pinchas 246b:
- ... "he will be elevated, raised up and high – *Meod*/very much" ... where the numerical value of *Meod* is equivalent to that of Adam and the word "Meod" is a rearrangement of the word "Adam" ... [This source is not overtly relating to Mashiach.]

Shela VaEtchanan Torah Ohr 12:
- [In connection with Mashiach and also the generation of Mashiach] ... "[Now, My servant] will succeed [he will be elevated, raised up and high – *Meod*/very much]," for the elevation will be gradual. To begin with he "*will succeed*," following which "*elevated*," then "*raised up*," then "*high*," and then "*Meod*" which are the same letters as *Adam* – for he will ultimately be like Adam before he sinned, and then all will be rectified with the end action being according to the initial thought, with this being the highest possible level. [*Meod* here is understood to relate to the level of Adam before his sin, in contrast to R. Chaim's interpretation of it relating to Adam's level after his sin.]

Also see Etz Chaim Shaar 3, Shaar Seder Atzilut BeKitur Muflag LeRav Chaim Vital, Chap. 2.

542   2 Shmuel 23:1.
543   It should be noted that in Chap. 1 of the introduction to Shaar HaShabbat of Pri Etz Chaim (which R. Chaim references in G1:14), the Arizal explains that on Shabbat all levels of all worlds from Asiyah all the way up until the level of *almost the unknowable beginning* are elevated three levels. The top three levels of each world level are elevated into the next world level above it, thereby leaving an empty gap in the space of the very lowest three levels between holiness and impurity. This gap is then exposed to become seriously defiled by impurity if a Jew, God forbid, performs any of the prohibitions of Shabbat, causing damage to his soul. On regular weekdays, however, all the world levels return to their previous state with no such gap, and therefore work which is forbidden on Shabbat is permitted on regular weekdays as it can do no harm to his soul.

In this note, R. Chaim describes the permanent elevation of three levels within the level of *the unknowable beginning* in the times of Mashiach, when correspondingly all levels below will also be consistently elevated. Given that

מְאֹד, וְדָרְשׁוּ זִכְרוֹנָם לִבְרָכָה עַל זֶה (תנחומא תולדות) מֵאַבְרָהָם וּמִמֹּשֶׁה וּמֵאָדָם הָרִאשׁוֹן (רוֹצֶה לוֹמַר אַחַר הַחֵטְא)

○ וְזֶה (שמואל ב' כג, א) "נְאֻם הַגֶּבֶר הֻקַם עַל מְשִׁיחַ אֱלֹקֵי יַעֲקֹב", שֶׁאָז תִּתְגַּדֵּל וְתִתְעַלֶּה כְּבוֹד מַלְכוּתוֹ יִתְבָּרֵךְ בִּמְקוֹם שָׁרְשָׁהּ הָרִאשׁוֹן:

---

we refer to those future times as the "day which is completely Shabbat" (as per Mishna Tamid 7:4), there will be a permanent elevation of all world levels and souls. However, this will be in a way which no longer leaves a gap as God will have permanently removed Evil from the Earth (as per Zecharia 13:2). This is consistent with the idea expressed in Berachot 57b that Shabbat is one of the three entities which resemble the future world.

Therefore, it is clear that the current set of Mitzvot that we have are linked to our current soul levels and that in future times of Mashiach/Resurrection, the nature of Mitzvot as we know them today (e.g., the Mitzvot of Shabbat as we currently know them as per this example) will change in direct proportion to the way in which our soul levels will change at that time. This idea is expressed in Niddah 61b which states that "Mitzvot will become nullified in future times." Refer to the quotation on p. 620, fn. 87, from Sefer Ha-Emunot Shaar 10 Chap. 2 which explains that in future times Mitzvot will be nullified because the nature of our existence will change and we will be *pure intellects* instead of physical beings. It must be emphasized that when Chazal talk of a Mitzvah being nullified, this means relative to the way it is currently performed. The Torah is everlasting and therefore so are the Mitzvot. This is also expressed by R. Chaim Vital in Etz HaDaat Tov, Bechukotai as follows:

- The fools and other nations think that the World to Come is entirely comprised of [physical] enjoyments [such as] eating and drinking etc., and God forbid that we should believe in this. However the true reward is according to Chazal, who say that the righteous sit with crowns on their heads and enjoy the radiance of the Shechina while God sits and expounds to them the secrets of the Torah and the [sublime] reasons of the Mitzvot. Such [details] were not explained in this world . . . This is the secret of "they will go from strength to strength" for they are study houses, one on a higher level than the other [with the righteous continuously ascending in the World to Come as they further their studies]. Not only this, but the Mitzvot are also observed there in their prescribed Halachic manner [but] *in a spritual way* . . .

(The above example of one's soul level affecting one's obligation to perform Mitzvot is time-related, and relates to the Shabbat. Another interesting example of how Mitzvot are affected by one's soul level is brought down on p. 20b of "Tuv HaAretz," 1891 edition, by R. Natan Shapira and is space related. R. Shapira explains that a person's soul level is affected by his location and therefore the obligation to observe a second day of Yom Tov outside of Israel is due to the fact that one who permanently lives outside of Israel has a lower

21. COMPLETE TORAH IMMERSION PURIFIES, INTENTION TO RECTIFY WORLDS

- 'It is therefore the unequivocal law of man'[544]
  - that when he studies Torah for its sake, to observe and keep all that is written within it
  - that it purifies his body from head to foot.[545]
- As per Chazal:[546] "Why are the words for *springs* and *tents* [used together in a particular verse]?[547] To tell us that just as [ritual immersion in] *springs* raise a person from a state of impurity to one of purity, *tents* [of Torah study] similarly elevate the person from a position of liability to one of merit."
  - This is like the concept that Chazal expound[548] in relation to the purification of the impure through ritual immersion, that [to achieve ritual purity it is required] "to completely immerse oneself in the water," water through which the entire body is elevated
  - similarly, it is with words of Torah, that the entirety of a person's body is elevated with them.
  - (Chazal defined [the minimum dimensions of a ritual bath] to be of one cubit by one cubit by three cubits [i.e., a total of three cubic cubits]. These correspond to:
    - The three worlds [i.e., Asiyah, Yetzirah, and Beriyah].
    - Nefesh, Ruach, and Neshama.
    - Action, speech, and thoughts of Torah.)
- Just as a person's entire body is elevated and purified through Torah study and Mitzvot, so too, all of the worlds, which reflect the *Shiur Komah* of a person as I wrote above in G1:06, are similarly refined, purified, and elevated.
- An honest person who truly serves [God][549]
  - will not distract his connection and thoughts when serving God
  - not even to elevate and purify his own body and soul
  - but will elevate the purity of his thoughts and focus to exclusively focus on [matters] Above

---

soul level. However, when a person lives permanently in Israel his soul is on a higher level which results in his obligation to only observe a single day of Yom Tov.)

544 R. Chaim uses the emphatic language "VeZot Torat HaAdam," a term also used at the beginning of G1:04 and borrowed from 2 Shmuel 7:19 (which R. Chaim happens to mention in G1:20:N18, of the previous chapter).

שער א' - פרק כ"א

- וְזֹאת תּוֹרַת הָאָדָם
  - שֶׁבְּעֵת עָסְקוֹ בַּתּוֹרָה לִשְׁמָהּ, לִשְׁמֹר וְלַקַיֵּם כְּכָל הַכָּתוּב בָּהּ
  - מְטַהֵר אֶת גּוּפוֹ מֵרֹאשׁוֹ וְעַד רַגְלָיו:
- כְּמִדְרָשָׁם זִכְרוֹנָם לִבְרָכָה (ברכות טז, א) "לָמָה נִסְמְכוּ אֹהָלִים לִנְחָלִים כו', מָה נְחָלִים מַעֲלִין אֶת הָאָדָם מִטֻּמְאָה לְטָהֳרָה, אַף אֹהָלִים מַעֲלִין אֶת הָאָדָם מִכַּף חוֹבָה לְכַף זְכוּת".
- וּכְעִנְיָן שֶׁדָּרְשׁוּ זִכְרוֹנָם לִבְרָכָה (עירובין ד:) גַּבֵּי טָהֳרַת הַטְּמֵאִים בַּמִּקְוֶה, "כָּל בְּשָׂרוֹ בַּמַּיִם", מַיִם שֶׁכָּל גּוּפוֹ עוֹלֶה בָּהֶם.
  - כָּךְ בְּדִבְרֵי תוֹרָה כָּל גּוּפוֹ שֶׁל אָדָם עוֹלֶה בָּהֶם.
  - (וְשִׁעֲרוּ חֲכָמִים אַמָּה עַל אַמָּה בְּרוּם שָׁלשׁ אַמּוֹת, הֵן
    - הַשְּׁלשָׁה עוֹלָמוֹת
    - וְנֵר"ן
    - מַעֲשֶׂה דִבּוּר מַחֲשָׁבָה בַּתּוֹרָה):
- וּכְשֵׁם שֶׁכָּל גּוּפוֹ שֶׁל אָדָם עוֹלֶה וּמִזְדַּכֵּךְ עַל יְדֵי עֵסֶק הַתּוֹרָה וְהַמִּצְוֹת, כָּךְ הָעוֹלָמוֹת כֻּלָּם, אֲשֶׁר הֵן הֵמָּה שִׁעוּר קוֹמַת אָדָם, כְּמוֹ שֶׁכָּתַבְתִּי לְעֵיל פֶּרֶק ו', הֵם מִזְדַּכְּכִים וּמִתְטַהֲרִים וּמִתְעַלִּים:
- וְהָאָדָם הַיָּשָׁר הָעוֹבֵד אֲמִתִּי
  - לֹא יְפַנֶּה דַעְתּוֹ וּמַחְשַׁבְתּוֹ בְּעֵת עֲבוֹדָתוֹ לוֹ יִתְבָּרַךְ שְׁמוֹ
  - אֲפִלּוּ כְּדֵי לַעֲלוֹת וּלְטַהֵר גּוּפוֹ וְנַפְשׁוֹ
  - אֶלָּא שֶׁיַּעֲלֶה טֹהַר מַחֲשַׁבְתּוֹ וְכַוָּנָתוֹ וּפָנָה לְמַעְלָה

---

545 I.e., by drawing down positive influence through thought, speech, and action as per the process laid out in the previous chapter.
546 Berachot 16a.
547 Bamidbar 24:6.
548 Eruvin 4b, Pesachim 109a–b.
549 *Service* here refers to general service of God in all things that a person does. G2:01 in contrast focuses on *Service of the Heart* which is *prayer*, and the idea here also forms one of the themes developed in the Second Gateway that the *Service* of prayer should also be focused on matters Above and not on one's personal needs (e.g., G2:12).

- on the repair and purification of the holy worlds.
* This was also the nature of the Patriarchs' service [of God] and of all the Early Righteous who performed the Torah before it was given
  - as expounded by Chazal:
    - "From the pure animals"[550] – "From here we know that Noach studied Torah."[551]
    - "Avraham observed all the Torah."[552]
    - (and similarly in the Midrash.)[553]
  - It is not that their performance was commanded by legal obligation
    - for if so, they would have never, God forbid, used their intellectual initiative
    - even though they perceived that according to the substance of the roots of their Neshamot
    - that they would need to transgress or change even just 'one of the Mitzvot of God'[554] in a minor way
    - and Yaakov would never have married two sisters
    - and Amram would never have married his aunt, God forbid.
  - However, from the perspective of their perception, out of the purity of their intellect
    - [they appreciated] the awesome rectifications that each Mitzvah performed within the supernal and lower worlds and powers
    - and the great damage and destruction, God forbid, that they would cause in them if the [Mitzvot] were not performed.
  - Similarly, Noach specifically offered sacrifices from the pure animals as he saw and perceived the supernal power and root of each animal
    - identifying which of them derived their power and root from the side of holiness, and he offered these up
    - and which of them derived their power and root from the side of

---

550 Bereishit 7:8.
551 Rashi on Bereishit 7:2 explains how Noach could have known which animals the Torah considered pure when selecting animals to offer as sacrifices after exiting from the ark (Rashi amalgamates comments from Zevachim 116a and Bereishit Rabba 26:1).
552 Yoma 28b, Kiddushin 82a.
553 Bereishit Rabba 92:4:
* ... that Yosef observed Shabbat before [the command] was given ...
Bamidbar Rabba 14:2:
* ... with Yosef who preceded and observed Shabbat before it was given ...
Midrash Tanchuma (Warsaw), Behar 1:
* ... Avraham the Patriarch observed the Torah before it was given. R.

- לְתִקּוּן וְטָהֳרַת הָעוֹלָמוֹת הַקְּדוֹשִׁים:
• וְזוֹ הָיְתָה גַּם כָּל עִנְיַן עֲבוֹדָתָם שֶׁל הָאָבוֹת, וְכָל הַצַּדִּיקִים הָרִאשׁוֹנִים, שֶׁקִּיְּמוּ אֶת הַתּוֹרָה קֹדֶם נְתִינָתָהּ.
- כְּמוֹ שֶׁדָּרְשׁוּ רַבּוֹתֵינוּ זִכְרוֹנָם לִבְרָכָה
  - עַל פָּסוּק "מִן הַבְּהֵמָה הַטְּהוֹרָה" גּוֹ' (בראשית ז, ח), וְאָמְרוּ "מִכָּאן שֶׁלָּמַד נֹחַ תּוֹרָה"
  - וְאָמְרוּ (יומא כ"ח ב') "קִיֵּם אַבְרָהָם אָבִינוּ אֶת כָּל הַתּוֹרָה"
  - (וְכֵן אִיתָא בִּבְרֵאשִׁית רַבָּה פָּרָשָׁה צ"ב, וּבְבַמִּדְבָּר רַבָּה פָּרָשָׁה י"ה, וּבְתַנְחוּמָא בְּהַר, וּבְמִדְרַשׁ תְּהִלִּים מִזְמוֹר א').
- לֹא שֶׁהָיוּ מְצֻוִּים וְעוֹשִׂים כָּךְ מִצַּד הַדִּין
  - דְּאִם כֵּן לֹא הָיוּ מַעֲמִידִים חַס וְשָׁלוֹם עַל דַּעְתָּם וְהַשָּׂגָתָם
  - אַף שֶׁהִשִּׂיגוּ שֶׁלְּפִי עִנְיַן שֹׁרֶשׁ נִשְׁמָתָם
  - הַהֶכְרֵחַ לָהֶם לַעֲבֹר וּלְשַׁנּוֹת אַף מִקְצָת מֵאַחַת מִכָּל מִצְוֹת ה'
  - וְלֹא הָיָה יַעֲקֹב אָבִינוּ עָלָיו הַשָּׁלוֹם נוֹשֵׂא שְׁתֵּי אֲחָיוֹת
  - וְלֹא הָיָה עַמְרָם נוֹשֵׂא דּוֹדָתוֹ חַס וְשָׁלוֹם.
- רַק מִצַּד הַשָּׂגָתָם בְּטֹהַר שִׂכְלָם
  - הַתִּקּוּנִים הַנּוֹרָאִים הַנַּעֲשִׂים בְּכָל מִצְוָה בְּהָעוֹלָמוֹת וְכֹחוֹת הָעֶלְיוֹנִים וְתַחְתּוֹנִים
  - וְהַפְּגָמִים הַגְּדוֹלִים וְהַחֻרְבָּן וְהַהֲרִיסָה חַס וְשָׁלוֹם שֶׁיִּגָּרְמוּ בָּהֶם אִם לֹא יְקִימוּם.
- וְכֵן נֹחַ הִקְרִיב דַּוְקָא מִן הַבְּהֵמָה הַטְּהוֹרָה, כִּי רָאָה וְהִשִּׂיג הַכֹּחַ וְהַשֹּׁרֶשׁ הָעֶלְיוֹן שֶׁל כָּל בְּהֵמָה וְחַיָּה
  - אֵיזֶה מֵהֶם כֹּחַ שָׁרְשׁוֹ מִצַּד הַקְּדֻשָּׁה, וְהִקְרִיבָהּ
  - וְאֵיזֶה מֵהֶם כֹּחַ נַפְשָׁהּ מִצַּד הַטֻּמְאָה וְהַסִּטְרָא אַחֲרָא, וְלֹא בָחַר בָּהּ לְהַקְרִיבָהּ לְפָנָיו יִתְבָּרַךְ, כִּי לֹא יֶרְצֶה:

Shmuel son of Nachman said in the name of R. Alexandrai, Avraham even observed the laws of Eruv Tavshilin! . . .
Midrash Tehillim 1:13:
- . . . R. Shmuel son of Nachmeini said in the name of R. Yonatan that Avraham even knew the laws of Eruv Tavshilin and Eruv Chatzerot. . . .

554 Vayikra 4:13.

impurity and *Sitra Achara*, and he did not choose these to offer up before God, as they would not be acceptable.
- This is the meaning of the verses:
  - "Chanoch *walked* with *Elokim*."[555]
  - "Noach *walked* with *Elokim*."[556]
  - "Ha*Elokim* before whom my fathers *walked*."[557]
  - Where the meaning of *Elokim* is *The All Powerful One*
  - that [these individuals] perceived the concepts of the powers of the supernal and lower worlds
  - the statutes of the heavens and earth and their rules
  - and the sequence of their behavior, interconnection, and composition as a result of all aspects of man's actions
  - and each one of them would conduct himself according to this sequence in all of his matters
  - according to what he saw and perceived would be the resulting supernal rectifications according to the root of his soul.
- Therefore, when Yaakov perceived
  - that accoding to the root of his soul that he could effect great rectifications in the supernal powers and worlds if he married the two sisters, Rachel and Leah
  - and that they would both build the House of Israel
  - he therefore invested much toil and service in order to get them to marry him.
- This was similarly the case with Amram who married his aunt, Yocheved – from whom would issue Moshe, Aharon, and Miriam.
- This is also one of the reasons why the Torah was not given to Noach or to the holy Patriarchs
  - as if it were given to them, Yaakov would not have been permitted to marry two sisters and neither Amram his aunt
  - even if they would have understood the appropriateness of doing so according to the root of their souls.
  - And, in truth, this [delay in the giving of the Torah enabled] the building of the entire House of Israel, the Chosen People, and the rectification of all the supernal and lower worlds.
    - As per Chazal,[558] who state that when Kayin married his sister, that "the world is built on the basis of [Chesed] kindness."[559]

---

555 Bereishit 5:24.
556 Bereishit 6:9.
557 Bereishit 48:15, as spoken by Yaakov.
558 Sanhedrin 58b.

- וְזֶהוּ
  ○ "וַיִּתְהַלֵּךְ חֲנוֹךְ אֶת הָאֱלֹקִים" (בראשית ה, כד)
  ○ "אֶת הָאֱלֹקִים הִתְהַלֶּךְ נֹחַ" (שם ו, ט)
  ○ "הָאֱלֹקִים אֲשֶׁר הִתְהַלְּכוּ אֲבוֹתַי לְפָנָיו" (שם מח, טו)
  ○ שֶׁפֵּרוּשׁ "אֱלֹקִים" — בַּעַל הַכֹּחוֹת כֻּלָּם
  ○ הַיְנוּ, שֶׁהִשִּׂיגוּ עִנְיְנֵי הַכֹּחוֹת הָעֶלְיוֹנִים וְתַחְתּוֹנִים
  ○ וְחֻקּוֹת שָׁמַיִם וָאָרֶץ וּמִשְׁטָרָם
  ○ וְסִדְרֵי הַנְהָגָתָם וְהִתְקַשְּׁרוּתָם וְהַרְכָּבָתָם עַל יְדֵי כָּל עִנְיְנֵי מַעֲשֵׂי הָאָדָם
  ○ וְעַל פִּי סֵדֶר וְעִנְיָן זֶה הָיָה כָּל אֶחָד מֵהֶם מִתְהַלֵּךְ וּמִתְנַהֵג בְּכָל עִנְיָנָיו
  ○ כְּפִי שֶׁרָאָה וְהִשִּׂיג הַתִּקּוּנִים הָעֶלְיוֹנִים לְפִי שֹׁרֶשׁ נִשְׁמָתוֹ
- לָכֵן כְּשֶׁהִשִּׂיג יַעֲקֹב אָבִינוּ עָלָיו הַשָּׁלוֹם
  ○ שֶׁלְּפִי שֹׁרֶשׁ נִשְׁמָתוֹ יִגְרֹם תִּקּוּנִים גְּדוֹלִים בְּכֹחוֹת וְעוֹלָמוֹת הָעֶלְיוֹנִים אִם יִשָּׂא הַשְּׁתֵּי אֲחָיוֹת אֵלּוּ רָחֵל וְלֵאָה
  ○ וְהֵמָּה יִבְנוּ שְׁתֵּיהֶן אֶת בֵּית יִשְׂרָאֵל
  ○ יָגַע כַּמָּה יְגִיעוֹת וַעֲבוֹדוֹת לְהַשִּׂיגָם שֶׁיִּנָּשְׂאוּ לוֹ:
- וְכֵן הָעִנְיָן בְּעַמְרָם, שֶׁנָּשָׂא יוֹכֶבֶד דּוֹדָתוֹ שֶׁיָּצְאוּ מִמֶּנָּה מֹשֶׁה, אַהֲרֹן וּמִרְיָם:
- וְזֶה גַם כֵּן אֶחָד מֵהַטְּעָמִים שֶׁלֹּא נִתְּנָה הַתּוֹרָה לְנֹחַ וְהָאָבוֹת הַקְּדוֹשִׁים
  ○ שֶׁאִם הָיְתָה נִתֶּנֶת לָהֶם, לֹא הָיָה יַעֲקֹב רַשַּׁאי לִישָּׂא שְׁתֵּי אֲחָיוֹת, וְלֹא עַמְרָם דּוֹדָתוֹ
  ○ אַף אִם הָיוּ מַשִּׂיגִים שֶׁכֵּן רָאוּי לָהֶם לְפִי שֹׁרֶשׁ נִשְׁמָתָם
  ○ וּבֶאֱמֶת זֶה הָיָה כָּל בִּנְיַן בֵּית יִשְׂרָאֵל עַם סְגֻלָּה וְתִקּוּן כָּל הָעוֹלָמוֹת עֶלְיוֹנִים וְתַחְתּוֹנִים.
    □ כְּעִנְיַן מַאֲמָרָם זִכְרוֹנָם לִבְרָכָה (סנהדרין נח, ב) וְאִם תֹּאמַר קַיִן נָשָׂא אֲחוֹתוֹ, "עוֹלָם חֶסֶד יִבָּנֶה" (תהלים פט, ג):

---

559 Tehillim 89:3. A forbidden relationship with one's sister is described as *Chesed* in Vayikra 20:17. R. Pam of Yeshiva Torah VeDaat explains that the nature of Chesed is to do kindness and that it can be applied in a good or a bad way. When Chesed is applied to other people it is considered good, however when Chesed is applied to oneself it is considered bad. The use of the word *"Chesed"* in the context of a forbidden relationship is therefore a bad application of Chesed. However before the Torah was given this was not categorized as bad and therefore it was legitimate and in this case of Kayin, necessary, for the

22. PHYSICAL MITZVAH PERFORMANCE IS KEY, INTENTION ADDS IMPACT

- When Moshe came and brought [the Torah] down to the physical world, [since then] "it is not in the Heavens"[560]
  - so a great person with a great deal of perception should not be too smart to say
    - "I see the secret and the reasons of the Mitzvot [and their impact] on the supernal powers and worlds
    - such that it is appropriate for me according to the root of my Neshama or for someone else according to his root
    - to transgress a specific Mitzvah, God forbid
    - or to push aside any minute detail of practical performance to perform [the Mitzvah] in a diminished manner
    - even in relation to one of the fine details of one of the rabbinic statements
    - or to change the time of its performance, God forbid."
- Therefore, the Torah concludes with: "And there will not be another prophet like Moshe"[561]
  - as per Chazal, who explain the verse "These are the Mitzvot," that no [subsequent] prophet has the mandate to institute anything new[562]
  - and as per[563] "all the things which I Command . . . do not add to it or detract from it," as even if "a prophet will subsequently arise," meaning to add or detract [from the Torah], God forbid – "do not listen to the words of that prophet, [but] you should follow after the Lord your God. . . ."
- [We see this] with King Chizkiyahu who did not [initially] marry, as he saw with Divine Inspiration that he was destined to have wicked descendants.[564]

---

world to be built up on the basis of this type of relationship which would later become forbidden. Avraham was the embodiment of *Chesed*. He propogated good *Chesed* to Yitzchak and bad *Chesed* to Yishmael. It is therefore the nature of Yishmael to do *Chesed* to himself by wanting to acquire everything, e.g., the Land of Israel.

(In contrast, R. Pam also explains the nature of *Gevurah*/restraint, as per Mishna Avot 4:1: "Who is a Gibor, one who controls himself," that it is a good thing if restraint is applied to oneself and a bad thing if it is applied to others. Yitzchak was the embodiment of *Gevurah*. He propogated good *Gevurah* to Yaakov and bad *Gevurah* to Esav. It is therefore the nature of Esav

שער א' - פרק כ"ב

- וּמִשֶּׁבָּא מֹשֶׁה וְהוֹרִידָהּ לָאָרֶץ, לֹא בַּשָּׁמַיִם הִיא.
  - וּלְבַל יִתְחַכֵּם הָאָדָם הַגָּדוֹל שֶׁהַשָּׂגָתוֹ מְרֻבָּה, לוֹמַר
    - אָנֹכִי הָרוֹאֶה סוֹד וְטַעֲמֵי הַמִּצְוֹת בְּכֹחוֹת וְעוֹלָמוֹת הָעֶלְיוֹנִים
    - שֶׁרָאוּי לִי לְפִי שֹׁרֶשׁ נִשְׁמָתִי, אוֹ לְמִי וָמִי לְפִי שָׁרְשׁוֹ
    - לַעֲבֹר חַס וְשָׁלוֹם עַל אֵיזֶה מִצְוָה
    - אוֹ לִדְחוֹת שׁוּם פְּרָט מִפְּרָטֵי הַמַּעֲשֶׂה, לַעֲשׂוֹתָהּ בְּמִגְרַעַת
    - אַף דִּקְדּוּק אֶחָד מִדִּבְרֵי סוֹפְרִים
    - אוֹ לְשַׁנּוֹת זְמַנָּהּ חַס וְשָׁלוֹם:
- וְלָזֶה סִיְּמָה הַתּוֹרָה (דברים לד, י) "וְלֹא קָם נָבִיא כְּמֹשֶׁה"
  - וּכְמוֹ שֶׁלְּמָדוּ זִכְרוֹנָם לִבְרָכָה "אֵלֶּה הַמִּצְוֹת" (ויקרא כז, לד), שֶׁאֵין נָבִיא רַשַּׁאי לְחַדֵּשׁ דָּבָר מֵעַתָּה (שבת קה, א)
  - וּכְמוֹ שֶׁסָּמְכָה הַתּוֹרָה (דברים יג) "אֵת כָּל הַדָּבָר אֲשֶׁר אָנֹכִי מְצַוֶּה גו' לֹא תֹסֵף עָלָיו וְלֹא תִגְרַע מִמֶּנּוּ" וגו' שֶׁגַּם "כִּי יָקוּם בְּקִרְבְּךָ נָבִיא" וגו' רָצָה לוֹמַר לְהוֹסִיף אוֹ לִגְרֹעַ חַס וְשָׁלוֹם "לֹא תִשְׁמַע אֶל דִּבְרֵי הַנָּבִיא הַהוּא. אַחֲרֵי ה' אֱלֹקֵיכֶם תֵּלֵכוּ" וגו':
- וַהֲרֵי חִזְקִיָּהוּ הַמֶּלֶךְ שֶׁרָאָה בְּרוּחַ הַקֹּדֶשׁ דְּנָפְקִין מִנֵּיהּ בְּנִין דְּלָא מַעֲלֵי, וְלָכֵן לֹא נְסִיב אִתְּתָא (ברכות י, א)

---

to apply *Gevurah* to others by wanting to control everything, e.g., via the Crusades. Therefore, the challenge of the next level of *Tiferet* is the amalgam of two opposing approaches – one of focusing on others, to apply kindness, and the other, to focus on oneself, to apply restraint. While most people are able to reach a level of kindness to others, fewer are able to reach a level of restraint and it is rare for a person to simultaneously encompass both of these approaches and reach the level of *Tiferet*. Yaakov was the embodiment of *Tiferet* and he is therefore referred to as the "Choice of the Patriarchs," as per Midrash Sechel Tov, Bereishit 37:17.)

560 Devarim 30:12.
561 Devarim 34:10.
562 Shabbat 104a quoting Vayikra 27:34.
563 Devarim 13:1 and the continuation.
564 Berachot 10a.

- While his intentions were for the sake of Heaven, as he did not want to increase the wicked people of the world
- nevertheless, Yishayahu the Prophet delivered God's rebuke to him saying to him "you are dead . . ." and that "you will not live"[565] in the future world as you did not involve yourself in fulfilling the Mitzvah of having children
- with [Chizkiyahu's] great and awesome righteousness currying no favor to bring him to the future world, as he considered it appropriate to omit the performance of just one of the Mitzvot of Moshe's Torah
- even though he saw, with the perception of his Divine Inspiration, that wicked descendants would issue from him and additionally that this was merely a case of passive inaction [in contrast to an active transgression].

• This is because the full reasons for the Mitzvot have not yet been revealed to any living person
- not even to Moshe our Teacher
- they were only [revealed] to Adam before his sin, [and these reasons were] the "wine unreleased from its grapes since the six days of Creation"[566] and "the [Primordial] light which enabled Adam to see from one end of the world to the other."[567]

• The Torah is abstracted beyond one's intellectual grasp – above all perception – so how can one use his own reasoning to change either the details of the laws [of the Mitzvot] or their required timing through his [thoughts that he has] wide knowledge or perception.
- As Yishayahu answered Chizkiyahu: "Why do you concern yourself with these hidden things of God? What you are commanded to do, you must do and what is found to be good before God, He will do."[568]

• While prophecy still existed in Israel, a prophet did have a mandate to initiate changes of Mitzvot but only for the sake of temporary need, and this [mandate] even extended to allow the transgression of one of the Mitzvot of God, as with Eliyahu who offered up a sacrifice on Mount Carmel,[569] and similar examples.
- However, this [mandate] itself is incorporated within that which Moshe's Torah commands us that "You shall listen to him,"[570] which is a command and warning to listen to the words of the prophet, even if his prophecy in God's Name requires the transgression of a specific Mitzvah at a time deemed necessary for this,[571] with the exception of idol worship.

---

565 2 Melachim 20:1.
566 Berachot 34b. The Talmud makes this statement in response to the question:

נפש - שער א' - פרק כ"ב - החיים

○ וְכַוָּנָתוֹ לְשֵׁם שָׁמַיִם שֶׁלֹּא לְהַרְבּוֹת רִשְׁעֵי עוֹלָם

○ עִם כָּל זֶה בָּא אֵלָיו יְשַׁעְיָה בִּדְבַר ה' וְאָמַר לוֹ (מלכים ב' כ, א) "כִּי מֵת אַתָּה" וְגוֹ', "וְלֹא תִחְיֶה" — לָעוֹלָם הַבָּא, מִשּׁוּם דְּלָא עָסַקְתָּ בִּפְרִיָּה וּרְבִיָּה

○ וְלֹא הוֹעִיל לוֹ כָּל עֹצֶם צִדְקוֹתָיו הַנּוֹרָאִים לַהֲבִיאוֹ לְחַיֵּי עוֹלָם הַבָּא, בִּשְׁבִיל שֶׁסָּבַר לְהִפָּטֵר מִמִּצְוָה אַחַת מִתּוֹרַת מֹשֶׁה

○ אַף שֶׁכֵּן רָאָה בְּהַשָּׂגַת רוּחַ קָדְשׁוֹ דְּיִפְּקוּן מִנֵּהּ בְּנִין דְּלָא מַעֲלֵי, וְגַם שֶׁהָיָה בְּשֵׁב וְאַל תַּעֲשֶׂה:

• כִּי טַעֲמֵי מִצְוֹת עַד תַּכְלִיתָם, לֹא נִתְגַּלּוּ עֲדַיִן לְשׁוּם אָדָם בָּעוֹלָם

○ אַף לְמֹשֶׁה רַבֵּנוּ עָלָיו הַשָּׁלוֹם

○ רַק לְאָדָם הָרִאשׁוֹן קֹדֶם הַחֵטְא, וְהוּא הַיַּיִן הַמְשֻׁמָּר בַּעֲנָבָיו מִשֵּׁשֶׁת יְמֵי בְּרֵאשִׁית (ברכות ל"ד ע"ב), וְהָאוֹר שֶׁשִּׁמֵּשׁ בְּיוֹם רִאשׁוֹן שֶׁהָיָה אָדָם הָרִאשׁוֹן צוֹפֶה וּמַבִּיט בּוֹ מִסּוֹף הָעוֹלָם (חגיגה יב, א) וְכוּ':

• כִּי הַתּוֹרָה הַקְּדוֹשָׁה אֲצוּלָה מִלְמַעְלָה רֹאשׁ, מֵעַל כָּל הַהַשָּׂגוֹת, וְאֵיךְ אֶפְשָׁר שֶׁיְּהֵא הַדָּבָר מָסוּר לְהַשָּׂגַת הָאָדָם, לְשַׁנּוֹת מֵהִלְכָתָם וְסֵדֶר זְמַנָּם עַל פִּי רֹחַב דַּעְתּוֹ וְהַשָּׂגָתוֹ

○ וּכְמוֹ שֶׁהֱשִׁיבוֹ יְשַׁעְיָה לְחִזְקִיָּה "בַּהֲדֵי כַּבְשֵׁי דְרַחֲמָנָא לָמָּה לָךְ, מַאי דְּמִפַּקְּדַתְּ אִבְעֵי לָךְ לְמֶעְבַּד, וּמַאי דְּנִיחָא קַמֵּי קוּדְשָׁא בְּרִיךְ הוּא לֶעֱבִיד":

• וַעֲדַיִן כְּשֶׁהָיְתָה נְבוּאָה בְּיִשְׂרָאֵל, הָיָה נָבִיא רַשַּׁאי לְחַדֵּשׁ דָּבָר לְהוֹרָאַת שָׁעָה לְבַד, וְאַף גַּם לַעֲבֹר עַל אַחַת מִמִּצְוֹת ה', כְּגוֹן אֵלִיָּהוּ בְּהַר הַכַּרְמֶל וְכַיּוֹצֵא

○ אָמְנָם זֶה עַצְמוֹ הוּא מֵאֲשֶׁר נִצְטַוֵּינוּ בְּתוֹרַת מֹשֶׁה "אֵלָיו תִּשְׁמָעוּן" (דברים י"ח), שֶׁהוּא צִוּוּי וְאַזְהָרָה לִשְׁמֹעַ אֶל דִּבְרֵי הַנָּבִיא, גַּם כְּשֶׁיִּתְנַבֵּא בִּשְׁמוֹ יִתְבָּרַךְ לַעֲבֹר עַל אֵיזֶה מִצְוָה, בְּשָׁעָה הַצְּרִיכָה לְכָךְ, כְּמוֹ שֶׁדָּרְשׁוּ רַבּוֹתֵינוּ זִכְרוֹנָם לִבְרָכָה (יבמות צ:) לְבַד מֵעֲבוֹדָה זָרָה.

What is the meaning of the verse "No eye has seen" (Yishayahu 64:3). See G4:21.

567 Chagiga 12a.
568 Berachot 10a.
569 At a time when it was not permitted to offer up sacrifices outside of the Sanctuary.
570 Devarim 18:16.
571 Yevamot 90b.

G1:22

- But [this is] not, God forbid, [a mandate] to initiate permanent changes
  - as [we see] with Esther, that even though she was one of the seven prophetesses,[572] when she sent her request to the Sages[573] to "inscribe me for generations," they answered her with the verse "have I not written to you three times," but [her request was granted] by the Sages as they were later able to find a way of connecting her [and therefore her requirement] to supporting text in the Torah
  - and this was similarly the case with [the rabbinic Mitzvah of] Chanukah candles, where it is certain that Chazal also found a Scriptural connection. Refer to the Midrash cited by the Ramban on Parshat Behaalotcha in the name of R. Nissim Gaon.[574]
- From the time, as a result of our sins, that prophecy ceased from within Israel
  - even if all the Sages of Israel were to be gathered together
  - to whom the [secret knowledge] of the workings of creation and of the structure of the Merkava is handed over
  - and with their perception and pure intellect delve deeply into [and identify the need] to change even a specific detail of a specific Mitzvah, or to advance or delay its time of performance, God forbid
  - we are not to allow this nor should we listen to them, and this is even if a Heavenly Echo is heard, as Chazal state: "[The Torah] is not [decided] in the Heavens."[575]
- However, the Sages of the Talmud still did have a mandate to institute rabbinic Commandments when they could find a Scriptural connection, as with Chanukah candles, etc., as mentioned above, and also to create rabbinic decrees as with "the eighteen decrees [that were made in the attic of Channaniah ben Chizkiya ben Garon]"[576] and similar examples.
- But following the completion of the Holy Talmud, it is for us to just keep and practice all the dictates of the Holy Written and Oral Torah – in all of their laws, statutes, timings, details, and punctilious points – without any deviation whatsoever
  - and when a Jew properly performs them

---

572 Megillah 14a.

573 This request and answer is recorded in Megillah 7a. Esther requested that Megillat Esther be included as one of the books of the Tanach and that the Purim holiday be permanently included in the Jewish calendar. In response, the Sages quoted the verse from Mishlei 22:20: "Have I not written to you three times," which is a reference by King Shlomo to the mention of the war against Amalak being limited to three places in Tanach. So with Esther's request to include Megillat Esther as one of the books of the Tanach, it would

- אֲבָל לֹא חָלִילָה לְחַדֵּשׁ דָּבָר לְקָבְעוֹ לְדוֹרוֹת.
- שֶׁהֲרֵי אֶסְתֵּר שֶׁהָיְתָה אַחַת מִשֶּׁבַע נְבִיאוֹת (מגילה י"ד א'), עִם כָּל זֶה כְּשֶׁשָּׁלְחָה לַחֲכָמִים כִּתְבוּנִי "לְדוֹרוֹת", הֱשִׁיבוּהָ "הֲלֹא כָתַבְתִּי לְךָ שָׁלִשִׁים", (משלי כב, כ), עַד שֶׁמָּצְאוּ לָהּ אַחַר כָּךְ סָמָךְ מִן הַמִּקְרָא (שם ז' א').
- וְכֵן נֵרוֹת חֲנֻכָּה, וַדַּאי שֶׁמָּצְאוּ לָהֶם גַּם כֵּן סָמָךְ מֵהַמִּקְרָא, וְעַיֵּן בַּמִּדְרָשׁ שֶׁהֵבִיא הָרַמְבַּ"ן זִכְרוֹנוֹ לִבְרָכָה בְּפָרָשָׁה בְּהַעֲלֹתְךָ מִשֵּׁם רַבֵּנוּ נִסִּים גָּאוֹן ז"ל:

- וּמֵעֵת שֶׁבַּעֲוֹנֵינוּ פָּסְקָה נְבוּאָה מִיִּשְׂרָאֵל
  - אַף אִם יִתְאַסְּפוּ כָּל חַכְמֵי יִשְׂרָאֵל
  - אֲשֶׁר נִמְסַר לָהֶם מַעֲשֵׂה בְרֵאשִׁית וּמַעֲשֵׂה מֶרְכָּבָה
  - וְיַעֲמִיקוּ הַשָּׂגָתָם וְטֹהַר שִׂכְלָם לְשַׁנּוֹת אַף אֵיזֶה פְּרָט מֵאֵיזֶה מִצְוָה, אוֹ לְהַקְדִּים וּלְאַחֵר זְמַנָּהּ חַס וְשָׁלוֹם
  - לֹא נֹאבֶה וְלֹא נִשְׁמַע אֲלֵיהֶם. וְאַף בְּבַת קוֹל אָמְרוּ (בבא מציעא נ"ט ב') "לֹא בַשָּׁמַיִם הִיא":

- וַעֲדַיִן בִּימֵי חַכְמֵי הַתַּלְמוּד הָיוּ רַשָּׁאִים לְחַדֵּשׁ מִצְוֹת דְּרַבָּנָן כְּשֶׁמָּצְאוּ סָמָךְ מֵהַתּוֹרָה, כְּגוֹן נֵרוֹת חֲנֻכָּה וְכַיּוֹצֵא, כַּנַּ"ל, וְכֵן לִגְזֹר גְּזֵרוֹת, כְּמוֹ י"ח דָּבָר (שבת יג:) וְכַיּוֹצֵא:

- וְכַאֲשֶׁר נֶחְתַּם הַתַּלְמוּד הַקָּדוֹשׁ, אָנוּ אֵין לָנוּ אֶלָּא לִשְׁמֹר וְלַעֲשׂוֹת כְּכָל הַכָּתוּב בַּתּוֹרָה הַקְּדוֹשָׁה שֶׁבִּכְתָב וּבְעַל פֶּה, כְּכָל מִשְׁפָּטָם וְחֻקָּתָם וּבִזְמַנָּם וּפְרָטֵיהֶם וְדִקְדּוּקֵיהֶם, בְּלִי נְטוֹת מֵהֶם נְטִיָּה כָּל דְּהוּ.
  - וּכְשֶׁיְּקַיְּמֵם אִישׁ יִשְׂרָאֵל כָּרָאוּי

---

have been a fourth mention, which would not have ordinarily been allowed were it not for the fact that the Sages were able to identify another way of connecting her request to a source in the Torah.

574 Ramban on Bamidbar 8:2 where he quotes the Megillat Setarim of R. Nissim Gaon in which he connects another Chanukah of candle lighting with the lighting of the Menorah in the Mishkan and states that this is the reason why the details of lighting the Menorah in the Mishkan is juxtaposed next to the passage detailing the Chanukah (the dedication) of the Altar.

575 Bava Metzia 59b, in response to an incident where a Heavenly Echo was used to support a Halachic position which was rejected by Chazal with this response.

576 Shabbat 13b.

- even if it is not accompanied with appropriate intention
- and even though he may not be aware of the reasons for the Mitzvot and the secrets of their objectives
- nevertheless, the Mitzvot have been validly performed
- and they will rectify and increase Holiness and light in all the worlds
- with each Mitzvah being performed according to its [proper] time, source, and way
- with [resulting] strength being given to God.
- As this is how God fixed the nature of the worlds, that they operate according to the actions of man, with the performance of each Mitzvah automatically ascending to impact in its own specific way.

• Those who God merited to intellectually grasp the secrets of our Holy Torah
  - who bequeathed blessing to us
  - those supernal holy Sages of the Talmud such as R. Shimon bar Yochai, his colleagues, and students[577]
  - and of those who drank its waters in the later generations such as the exalted holy awesome man of God, the Arizal[578]
  - who enlightened our eyes us with a small amount of the reasons and intentions of the Mitzvot
  - [all this] is purely to enable each individual to appreciate according to his intellect and perception
  - just how far-reaching are all the details of his actions, speech, thoughts, and all of his matters
  - on the supernal and lower worlds and powers
  - and he should be affected and motivated by this to perform and observe every Mitzvah
  - and that all of his service of God should be with ultimate precision, with tremendous awe, fear and love, and with the holiness and purity of [his] heart
  - and as a result of this, he will cause greater rectifications in the worlds than those that would have been if he were to perform the Mitzvah without the holiness and purity of intention.

• However, the essential parts of all Mitzvot without which they are rendered invalid, are the details of their physical performance.[579]

END OF THE FIRST GATEWAY

---

[577] Their blessing here referring to the Holy Zohar.
[578] The Arizal's blessing being the extensive body of his Kabbalistic teachings as recorded by his students – mainly R. Chaim Vital.

- אַף אִם לֹא יְכַוֵּן
- וְגַם לֹא יֵדַע כְּלָל טַעֲמֵי הַמִּצְוֹת וְסוֹדוֹת כַּוָּנָתָם
- עִם כָּל זֶה נִתְקַיְּמוּ הַמִּצְוֹת
- וִיתַקְּנוּ עַל יְדֵיהֶם הָעוֹלָמוֹת, וְיִתְרַבֶּה בָּהֶם קְדֻשָּׁה וְאוֹר
- בְּכָל מִצְוָה לְפִי שְׁעָתָהּ וּמְקוֹרָהּ וְעִנְיָנָהּ
- וְיִתֵּן עֹז לֵאלֹקִים יִתְבָּרַךְ שְׁמוֹ.
- שֶׁכֵּן קָבַע הַבּוֹרֵא יִתְבָּרַךְ שְׁמוֹ טִבְעָם שֶׁל הָעוֹלָמוֹת, שֶׁיִּתְנַהֲגוּ עַל יְדֵי מַעֲשֵׂי הָאָדָם, וְכָל מִצְוָה, הִיא הָעוֹלָה מֵעַצְמָהּ לִפְעֹל פְּעֻלָּתָהּ הַמְיֻחָד לָהּ:

• וּמִי שֶׁזִּכָּהוּ יִתְבָּרַךְ שְׁמוֹ לְהַשִּׂיג נִסְתָּרוֹת תּוֹרָתֵנוּ הַקְּדוֹשָׁה
  ○ אֲשֶׁר הִשְׁאִירוּ לָנוּ בְּרָכָה
  ○ קְדוֹשֵׁי עֶלְיוֹנִין חַכְמֵי הַתַּלְמוּד, כְּגוֹן רַבִּי שִׁמְעוֹן בֶּן יוֹחַאי וַחֲבֵרָיו וְתַלְמִידָיו
  ○ וְשׁוֹשַׁנְתִּין מֵימָיו בַּדּוֹרוֹת הָאַחֲרוֹנִים כְּמוֹ הָרַב הַקָּדוֹשׁ אִישׁ אֱלֹקִים נוֹרָא הָאֲרִיזַ"ל
  ○ אֲשֶׁר הֵאִירוּ עֵינֵינוּ בִּקְצָת טַעֲמֵי וְכַוָּנוֹת הַמִּצְוֹת
  ○ הוּא רַק כְּדֵי שֶׁיִּתְבּוֹנֵן כָּל אֶחָד לְפִי שִׂכְלוֹ וְהַשָּׂגָתוֹ
  ○ עַד הֵיכָן מַגִּיעִים כָּל פְּרָטֵי מַעֲשָׂיו וְדִבּוּרָיו וּמַחְשְׁבוֹתָיו וְכָל עִנְיָנָיו
  ○ בָּעוֹלָמוֹת וְהַכֹּחוֹת עֶלְיוֹנִים וְתַחְתּוֹנִים
  ○ וְיִתְפַּעֵל וְיִתְעוֹרֵר מִזֶּה לַעֲשׂוֹת וּלְקַיֵּם כָּל מִצְוָה
  ○ וְכָל עִנְיְנֵי עֲבוֹדָתוֹ לְבוֹרְאוֹ יִתְבָּרַךְ שְׁמוֹ, בְּתַכְלִית הַדִּקְדּוּק וּבְאֵימָה וְיִרְאָה וְאַהֲבָה עֲצוּמָה וּבִקְדֻשָּׁה וְטָהֳרַת הַלֵּב
  ○ וְעַל יְדֵי זֶה יִגְרֹם תִּקּוּנִים יוֹתֵר גְּדוֹלִים בָּעוֹלָמוֹת, מֵאִם הָיָה מְקַיֵּם הַמִּצְוָה בְּלֹא קְדֻשַּׁת וְטָהֳרַת הַכַּוָּנָה.

• אָמְנָם הָעִקָּר בְּכָל הַמִּצְוֹת לְעִכּוּבָא, הוּא פְּרָטֵי הַמַּעֲשֶׂה שֶׁבָּהֶם:

סְלִיק שַׁעַר א'

---

579 I.e., the lack of intention does not invalidate performance of the Mitzvah.

SECOND GATEWAY

1. PRAYER WITH CONCENTRATION TO BE EXCLUSIVELY FOCUSED ON GOD

- It is written[1] "to love God, your God, and to serve Him with all your heart and soul" and Chazal state:[2] "What is *Service of the Heart*? You must say that it is prayer."[3]
- This love, about which it states that it needs to be "*With all of one's heart*" – it is obviously one of those commandments which are dependent on the heart.
- Similarly, the concept of love about which it is said to be "*With all of one's soul*"
  - this means that one should even be prepared to give up one's life for God out of the sheer awesomeness of one's love for Him
  - and as stated in the first paragraph [of the Shema]: "And you shall love God, your God, with all of your heart, *soul* [and might]. . . ."[4]
- However, in this [second] paragraph [of the Shema], it innovates the idea that even service, which is prayer, needs to be performed with all of one's heart and soul.
  - (And therefore this [second] paragraph, in contrast to the first paragraph, does not state "with all your might"
    - as the first paragraph solely focuses on the command of *love*, about which it is also relevant that love should be "*with all of one's might*," which is one's financial resources

---

1 Devarim 11:13. This statement is part of the second paragraph of the Shema.
2 Taanit 2a; Sifri Devarim Ekev 41.
3 The translation of the word "Lev" is heart and is normally understood to relate to emotion and the seat of desire. It is clear that the word "Lev" is used across Scriptures and by Chazal to not only relate to pure emotion but also to relate to the heart as significantly influencing thought. In modern-day language, this meaning can be considered to be a person's intuition or even a part of the mind.

We see verses associating the word "Lev" with thought, e.g., "the thoughts of one's Lev" (Tehillim 33:11 and Mishlei 19:21). R. Chaim himself states outright "For the Lev is the level of thought as is known" (G2:16:N37). We see other verses associating Lev with knowledge, e.g., "God gave him a Lev to know and eyes to see" (Devarim 29:3). The Shulchan Aruch (Hilchot Tefillin 25:5) states that the soul is in the brain and the heart is the main source

שַׁעַר ב'

שער ב' - פרק א'

- כְּתִיב (דברים י"א, י"ג) "לְאַהֲבָה אֶת ה' אֱלֹקֵיכֶם וּלְעָבְדוֹ בְּכָל לְבַבְכֶם וּבְכָל נַפְשְׁכֶם", וְאָמְרוּ רַבּוֹתֵינוּ זִכְרוֹנָם לִבְרָכָה בְּפֶרֶק קַמָּא דְּתַעֲנִית (ב.) וּבְסִפְרִי "אֵיזוֹהִי עֲבוֹדָה שֶׁבַּלֵּב, הֱוֵי אוֹמֵר זוֹ תְּפִלָּה":

- הִנֵּה הָאַהֲבָה שֶׁאָמַר שֶׁצְּרִיכָה לִהְיוֹת "בְּכָל לֵב", הוּא פָּשׁוּט, כִּי הִיא מִמִּצְווֹת הַתְּלוּיוֹת בַּלֵּב:

- וְכֵן עִנְיַן הָאַהֲבָה "בְּכָל נֶפֶשׁ" שֶׁאָמַר
  ○ הַיְנוּ אַף גַּם לִמְסֹר נַפְשׁוֹ עָלָיו יִתְבָּרַךְ שְׁמוֹ, מֵעֹצֶם נִפְלָאַת הָאַהֲבָה לוֹ יִתְבָּרַךְ.
  ○ וּכְמוֹ שֶׁכָּתוּב בְּפָרָשָׁה רִאשׁוֹנָה "וְאָהַבְתָּ אֵת ה' אֱלֹקֶיךָ בְּכָל לְבָבְךָ וּבְכָל נַפְשְׁךָ" גו':

- אָמְנָם בְּפָרָשָׁה זוֹ חִדּוּשׁ הוּא שֶׁחִדְּשָׁה, שֶׁגַּם הָעֲבוֹדָה, הִיא הַתְּפִלָּה, צְרִיכָה לִהְיוֹת 'בְּכָל לֵב וּבְכָל נֶפֶשׁ'.

- (וּלְהָכִי נַמִי לֹא כְּתִיב "וּבְכָל מְאֹדְכֶם" בְּפָרָשָׁה זוֹ, כְּמוֹ בְּפָרָשָׁה רִאשׁוֹנָה דִּכְתִיב בָּהּ נַמִי "וּבְכָל מְאֹדֶךָ"
  □ כִּי פָּרָשָׁה רִאשׁוֹנָה מַיְירֵי מֵעִנְיַן מִצְוַת הָאַהֲבָה לְחוּד, שַׁיָּךְ לוֹמַר שֶׁתִּהְיֶה הָאַהֲבָה גַּם 'בְּכָל מְאֹד, זֶה הַמָּמוֹן

---

of desires and thoughts. In *Emet LeYaakov, VaEtchanan*, fn. 21, R. Yaakov Kamenetsky observes that, in contrast to the Mishna, there is no word for *brain* in the Scriptures and considers that the Scriptural use of the word "Lev" means the "brain."

In this translation, "Lev" has been translated as "heart" as R. Chaim does use "Lev" to refer to the heart in contrast to the word "Moach" for the brain (e.g., at the end of G1:14). However, it is particularly instructive to view the use of the word "heart" throughout the Second and Third Gateways as mind and to think of prayer as not being *Service of the Heart* but instead as really being *Service of the Mind*, i.e., an intellectual meditation. So the love, discussed in this chapter is to be understood as being intellectually inspired.

Devarim 6:5.

- as per Chazal:[5] The statement "with all of your might" relates to a person who values his money more than his body.
  - However, this [second] paragraph also refers to *service*, which is prayer, about which it is less relevant to refer to it as being "*with all of one's might*").[6]
- The statement of "*with all of your heart*" in relation to prayer is straightforward and the meaning of the verse incorporates two elements:[7]
  - Firstly: To rid one's heart of any distracting thoughts and to entirely focus the depths of one's heart on the words of prayer, as per Chazal:
    - One who prays must focus his heart on Heaven. [Abba Shaul says this is indicated] as per "Guide your heart [let your ears be attentive]."[8]
    - This is also implied there from the verses relating to Chana's prayer: "and Chana was speaking to her heart," that from here we learn that one who prays must focus his heart.[9]
    - As per King David who said: "I seek You with all my heart." All who pray before the Holy King must make their requests and pray from depths of their heart so that his heart will be found to be complete with God and he will focus his heart and his will.[10]
    - Therefore, Chazal state that [if one needs to repeat a prayer] one should wait until able to compose one's thoughts.[11]
    - This is the meaning of "*with all your heart*," that the heart be filled solely with the meaning of the words of prayer, and that if any other thoughts are raised in one's heart, then the heart's [focus] is divided across two thoughts.
  - Secondly: To use the active service of prayer to absolutely rid one's heart of any earthly desires and enjoyments and thereby purely look Heavenwards, at the Greatness of the Creator, as per Chazal:
    - "One who prays must focus [his eyes downwards and] his heart Heavenwards"[12] – to the extent that the entire potential of his

---

5 Berachot 61b.
6 See G1:08:N10 for another reason for this.
7 As hinted to by the use of the plural form of the word "*Lev*" in the second paragraph of the Shema.
8 Berachot 31a quoting Tehillim 10:17 upon which Rashi explains that if one first guides one's heart *then* one's ears will be attentive. While Chazal state that prayer is focusing the heart on Heaven, in this instance, in contrast to a similar statement below, they are saying that focus is achieved specifically by being attentive to the words of prayer themselves.
9 Continuation to Berachot 31a quoting 1 Shmuel 1:13.

- כְּמוֹ שֶׁאָמְרוּ רַבּוֹתֵינוּ זִכְרוֹנָם לִבְרָכָה (ברכות סא, ב), אִם יֵשׁ לְךָ אָדָם שֶׁמָּמוֹנוֹ חָבִיב עָלָיו מִגּוּפוֹ לְכָךְ נֶאֱמַר "וּבְכָל מְאֹדֶךָ".

- אֲבָל בְּפָרָשָׁה זוֹ דִּכְתִיב בָּהּ נַמִי עֲבוֹדָה הִיא תְּפִלָּה, לֹא שַׁיָּךְ עָלֶיהָ כָּל כָּךְ "וּבְכָל מְאֹד"):

• וְהִנֵּה מַה שֶּׁנֶּאֱמַר "בְּכָל לְבַבְכֶם" עַל עִנְיַן הַתְּפִלָּה, הוּא פָּשׁוּט וּמְבֹאָר כַּוָּנַת הַכָּתוּב לִשְׁנֵי עִנְיָנִים:

- הָא' הַיְנוּ לִפְנוֹת לִבּוֹ מִטִּרְדַּת הַמַּחֲשָׁבוֹת, וּלְהַטּוֹתָהּ אֶל הַכַּוָּנָה הַשְּׁלֵמָה לְתֵבוֹת הַתְּפִלָּה, בְּלֵבָב שָׁלֵם וּמֵעֻמְקָא דְלִבָּא, כְּמַאֲמָרָם זִכְרוֹנָם לִבְרָכָה בְּבָרַיְתָא רֵישׁ פֶּרֶק אֵין עוֹמְדִין (ברכות לא, א) "הַמִּתְפַּלֵּל צָרִיךְ שֶׁיְּכַוֵּן אֶת לִבּוֹ לַשָּׁמַיִם, שֶׁנֶּאֱמַר (תהלים י) "תָּכִין לִבָּם" גו'.

- וְכִדְמַשְׁמַע לְהוּ נַמִי הָתָם מִקְּרָאֵי דְּחַנָּה "וְחַנָּה הִיא מְדַבֶּרֶת עַל לִבָּהּ" (שמו"א א. יג) מִכָּאן לַמִּתְפַּלֵּל צָרִיךְ שֶׁיְּכַוֵּן לִבּוֹ.

- וּכְמוֹ שֶׁאָמַר דָּוִד הַמֶּלֶךְ עָלָיו הַשָּׁלוֹם (תהלים קיט י) "בְּכָל לִבִּי דְרַשְׁתִּיךָ". וּבַזֹּהַר בְּשַׁלַּח ס"ג ב', "כָּל מָאן דִּמְצַלֵּי צְלוֹתָא קַמֵּי מַלְכָּא קַדִּישָׁא, בָּעֵי לְמִבְעֵי בְּעוּתֵיהּ וּלְצַלָּאָה מֵעוּמְקָא דְלִבָּא, בְּגִין דְּיִשְׁתְּכַח לִבֵּיהּ שְׁלִים בְּקֻדְשָׁא בְּרִיךְ הוּא, וִיכַוֵּין לִבָּא וּרְעוּתָא".

- וְלָכֵן אָמְרוּ זִכְרוֹנָם לִבְרָכָה שָׁם סוֹף פֶּרֶק תְּפִלַּת הַשַּׁחַר (ברכות ל, ב) שֶׁהַמִּתְפַּלֵּל צָרִיךְ לִשְׁהוֹת וְכוּ', כְּדֵי שֶׁתִּתְחוֹנֵן דַּעְתּוֹ עָלָיו.

- וְהַיְנוּ "בְּכָל לְבַבְכֶם", שֶׁיִּתְמַלֵּא כָּל הַלֵּב רַק בְּכַוָּנַת תֵּבוֹת הַתְּפִלָּה. שֶׁאִם יַעֲלֶה בְלִבּוֹ אֵיזֶה מַחֲשָׁבָה אַחֶרֶת, הֲרֵי הַלֵּב חֲלוּקָה בִּשְׁנֵי מַחֲשָׁבוֹת:

- וְהַב' הַיְנוּ גַּם לְשָׁרֵשׁ מִלִּבּוֹ בַּעֲבוֹדַת הַתְּפִלָּה תַּעֲנוּגֵי הָעוֹלָם וַהֲנָאוֹתָיו מִכֹּל וָכֹל, וְאַךְ לְהִסְתַּכֵּל כְּלַפֵּי מַעְלָה בְּרוֹמְמוּת הַבּוֹרֵא יִתְבָּרַךְ.

- כְּמוֹ שֶׁאָמְרוּ (יבמות ק"ה ב) "הַמִּתְפַּלֵּל צָרִיךְ שֶׁיִּתֵּן לִבּוֹ לְמַעְלָה", עַד שֶׁיְּהֵא כָּל כֹּחַ לִבּוֹ מְשׁוּכָה רַק לְמַעְלָה, לְהִתְעַנֵּג עַל ה' לְבַד בְּתֵבוֹת הַתְּפִלָּה.

---

10 Zohar II Beshalach 63b quoting Tehillim 119:10.

11 Berachot 30b, i.e., in relation to repeating the Amidah as a result of having erred the first time.

12 Yevamot 105b. While Chazal state that prayer is focusing the heart on Heaven, in this instance, in contrast to a similar statement above, they are saying that focus is achieved specifically by not allowing the heart to be attracted to the physical desires of what the eyes see and to be focused on Heaven alone.

heart is purely focused Heavenwards, delighting in God alone with words of prayer.
- As with the original Chassidim who would spend a [preparatory] hour [before prayer] in order to concentrate their hearts on the Makom [on God].[13]
  - This is as per R. Yona's explanation there. Refer and pay attention to it.[14]
- As per "A person must purify his heart before prayer."[15]

- (However, the whole purpose of purifying the heart merely adds dimension to Mitzvah performance but does not invalidate it [if performed with an impure heart]. This is also true of prayer even though it is called "Service of the Heart." This was touched on above at the end of G1:22, that performance is the essence of all Mitzvot [in contrast with any associated intention]. Refer there.)

- But to understand how the statement of *"with all of your soul"* relates to prayer, we first need to explain the meaning and concept of *blessing* God, so to speak
  - as we find it referenced many times in the Scriptures:
    - "You shall bless God, your God."[16]
    - "Blessed is God forever . . . ."[17]
    - "My soul blesses God,"[18] and many similar examples.
  - And this is similarly found with the words of Chazal:
    - As He, so to speak, said to R. Yishmael: "Yishmael, My son, Bless Me."[19]
    - As per the formulation of all our prayers and blessings by the Men of the Great Assembly, which start and/or end with the word *"Blessed."*

---

13 Mishna Berachot 5:1. There are two versions of this Mishna. In one, the concentration of the hearts of the original Chassidim was on the "Makom." This is the version used in the Mishna and in the Rif 21a on Berachot 30b. In the other, their concentration of their hearts was on "Avinu ShebaShamayim" – this is the version that appears to be used in the Talmud, Berachot 30b. R. Chaim specifically quotes the version with "Makom" referring to "space" and this is the specific point he picks up on to continue into and introduce the Third Gateway. Note that R. Chaim's next reference is to R. Yona's comments on this Rif 21a which specifically comments on the version with "Makom."

14 R. Yona's comments on Rif 21a to Berachot 30b:
- In order to concentrate their hearts on the Makom: . . . this certainly means that they should concentrate their hearts completely on the service of The Makom and eradicate all thoughts of enjoyment of this world, as when they

- וּכְעִנְיָן הַחֲסִידִים הָרִאשׁוֹנִים, שֶׁהָיוּ שׁוֹהִים שָׁעָה אַחַת, כְּדֵי שֶׁיְּכַוְּנוּ אֶת לִבָּם לַמָּקוֹם
- וּכְעִנְיָן שֶׁפֵּרֵשׁ רַבֵּנוּ יוֹנָה זִכְרוֹנָם לִבְרָכָה שָׁם עִנְיָנָהּ, עַיֵּן שָׁם וּלְבַד תָּשִׁית
- וּכְמוֹ שֶׁאָמְרוּ בִּשְׁמוֹת רַבָּה פָּרָשָׁה כ"ב, "אָדָם צָרִיךְ שֶׁיְּטַהֵר לִבּוֹ קֹדֶם שֶׁיִּתְפַּלֵּל":

(אָמְנָם כָּל עִקַּר עִנְיַן טָהֳרַת הַלֵּב, הִיא רַק לְמִצְוָה וְלֹא לְעִכּוּבָא, גַּם לְעִנְיַן הַתְּפִלָּה, אַף שֶׁנִּקְרֵאת "עֲבוֹדָה שֶׁבַּלֵּב", כְּמוֹ שֶׁנִּתְבָּאֵר קְצָת לְעֵיל סוֹף שַׁעַר א', שֶׁהָעִקָּר בְּכָל הַמִּצְוֹת הִיא הַמַּעֲשֶׂה. עַיֵּן שָׁם):

- וּלְהָבִין עִנְיַן מַה שֶּׁאָמַר הַכָּתוּב "וּבְכָל נַפְשְׁכֶם" עַל עֲבוֹדַת הַתְּפִלָּה, צָרִיךְ לְבָאֵר תְּחִלָּה פֵּרוּשׁ וְעִנְיַן הַ"בְּרָכָה" כִּבְיָכוֹל לוֹ יִתְבָּרַךְ שְׁמוֹ.
  - שֶׁמָּצִינוּ כַּמָּה פְּעָמִים בַּמִּקְרָא
    - "וּבֵרַכְתָּ אֶת ה' אֱלֹקֶיךָ" (דברים ח, י)
    - "בָּרוּךְ ה' לְעוֹלָם" (תהלים פט, ו) גו'
    - "בָּרְכִי נַפְשִׁי אֶת ה'" (שם קג, א), וְהַרְבֵּה כַּיּוֹצֵא.
  - וְכֵן בְּדִבְרֵי רַבּוֹתֵינוּ זִכְרוֹנָם לִבְרָכָה מָצִינוּ
    - שֶׁאָמַר כִּבְיָכוֹל לְרַבִּי יִשְׁמָעֵאל, יִשְׁמָעֵאל בְּנִי בָּרְכֵנִי. (ברכות ז, א)
    - וְכֵן כָּל נֻסַּח מַטְבֵּעַ תְּפִלּוֹת וְהַבְּרָכוֹת כֻּלָּם, שֶׁיִּסְּדוּ אַנְשֵׁי כְּנֶסֶת הַגְּדוֹלָה, הֵם פּוֹתְחִים וּמְסַיְּמִים בְּ"בָּרוּךְ":

---

purify their hearts from vain thoughts of this world and concentrate their hearts on the Greatness of God, then their prayer is appropriate and accepted by God. . . ." [R. Yona continues to refer to some of the quotations that R. Chaim has already quoted on this point providing further details.]

15 Shemot Rabba Beshalach 22:3.
16 Devarim 8:10.
17 Tehillim 89:6.
18 Tehillim 103:1.
19 Berachot 7a.

2. *BARUCH* IS AN *INCREASE* IN THE REVEALED PART OF GOD

- This concept is that the word "Baruch" (Blessed)
  - is not, as it is commonly understood to be a form of praise
    - as when [God] asked R. Yishmael: "Yishmael, My son, Bless Me" – no praise was stated in [R. Yishmael's] blessing there, but just prayer and supplication for mercy.[20]
    - Similarly, the Talmud states[21] [that with respect to the nightly obligation to return a collateral item taken from a poor person who owes you money] the Torah states: "and he shall bless you" – but this excludes [the case where a poor person has pledged an amount to the Temple as there is no obligation for the nightly return of the item as] Hekdesh[22] does not require blessing
      - [this is true even though] this section of the Talmud continues to question that the verse states explicitly that "and you shall eat, be satisfied and *bless* God"[23] . . . [however the primary understanding is that God does not need our praise].
  - In truth, the meaning of Baruch/Blessing is an expression of *addition* and *increase*
    - as in "please take my blessing,"[24] "and He shall bless your bread,"[25] "and He will bless the fruit of your womb"[26] and many other similar Scriptural examples, which cannot otherwise be explained as an expression of praise but only in the sense of an *addition* and *increase*.
    - The Zohar makes many references to the drawing down of blessing in the context of an *addition* or *increase*, [for example:]
      - [The standard syntax of a blessing] "Blessed are you God" is as it implies – to draw down life from the source of life to the Name of God . . . and it is written "and you shall eat and be satisfied and bless God, your God," these blessings are brought down with these words . . .[27] Refer there at length.
    - As per [the Arizal in] Pri Etz Chaim that "The secret of blessing is related to all types of increases,"[28] and similarly elsewhere in Pri Etz Chaim.[29]

---

20 Berachot 7a.
21 Bava Metzia 114a quoting Devarim 24:13.
22 Hekdesh refers to the needs of the Temple and therefore of God.
23 Devarim 8:10.
24 Bereishit 33:11, where "blessing" refers to a gift which *adds* to the recipient's wealth.

שער ב' - פרק ב'

- וְהָעִנְיָן כִּי מִלַּת "בָּרוּךְ"
  - אֵינוּ לְשׁוֹן תְּהִלָּה וְשֶׁבַח, כְּמוֹ שֶׁשּׁוּמָה בְּפִי הֶהָמוֹן
    - שַׁחֲרֵי (ברכות ז, א) כְּשֶׁאָמַר לְרַבִּי יִשְׁמָעֵאל, "יִשְׁמָעֵאל בְּנִי בָּרְכֵנִי", לֹא אָמַר שָׁם שׁוּם שֶׁבַח בְּבִרְכָתוֹ, אֶלָּא תְּפִלָּה וּבַקָּשַׁת רַחֲמִים.
    - וְכֵן בְּבָבָא מְצִיעָא (קיד, א) אָמְרִינָן, "וּבֵרַכְךָ" (דברים כד) יָצָא הֶקְדֵּשׁ שֶׁאֵין צָרִיךְ בְּרָכָה.
  - וּפָרִיךְ הַשַּׁ"ס — וְלֹא, וְהָא כְּתִיב "וְאָכַלְתָּ וְשָׂבָעְתָּ וּבֵרַכְתָּ אֶת ה'" (דברים ח, י) כו'.
  - אֲבָל הָאֱמֶת, כִּי "בָּרוּךְ" פֵּרוּשׁוֹ לְשׁוֹן תּוֹסֶפֶת וְרִבּוּי
    - וּכְעִנְיָן "קַח נָא אֶת בִּרְכָתִי" (בראשית לג, יא) גו', "וּבֵרַךְ אֶת לַחְמְךָ" (שמות כג, כה) "וּבֵרַךְ פְּרִי בִטְנֶךָ" (דברים ז, יג) וְגו', וְהַרְבֵּה כַיּוֹצֵא בַמִּקְרָא, שֶׁאִי אֶפְשָׁר לְפָרְשָׁם לְשׁוֹן תְּהִלָּה וְשֶׁבַח, אֶלָּא לְשׁוֹן תּוֹסֶפֶת וְרִבּוּי.
    - וּבַזֹּהַר אָמַר בְּכַמָּה מְקוֹמוֹת לְאַמְשָׁכָא בִּרְכָאן כו'. לְאַרְקָא בִּרְכָאן, לְאוֹסוּפֵי בִּרְכָאן, תּוֹסֶפֶת רִבּוּיָא דְּבִרְכָאן כו'.
  - וְעַיֵּן בְּרַעְיָא מְהֵימְנָא (ריש פָּרָשַׁת עֵקֶב) שֶׁ"בָּרוּךְ אַתָּה הֲוָיָ"ה" פֵּרוּשׁוֹ כְּמַשְׁמָעוֹ, לְאַמְשָׁכָא וּלְאַרְקָא חַיִּין מִמְּקוֹרָא דְחַיֵּי, לִשְׁמֵיהּ דְּקֻדְשָׁא בְּרִיךְ הוּא קַדִּישָׁא כו', וּכְתִיב (שם) "וְאָכַלְתָּ וְשָׂבָעְתָּ וּבֵרַכְתָּ אֶת ה' אֱלֹהֶיךָ", וְאִנּוּן בִּרְכָאן אָרִיק בַּר נָשׁ בְּאִנּוּן מִלִּין כו', עַיֵּן שָׁם בָּאֹרֶךְ.
  - וְכֵן כָּתוּב בִּפְרִי עֵץ חַיִּים שַׁעַר הַקַּדִּישִׁים פֶּרֶק א', זֶה לְשׁוֹנוֹ "סוֹד בָּרוּךְ

---

25 Shemot 23:25, where God will *increase* our sustenance in response to us serving Him.
26 Devarim 7:13, where God will *increase* our offspring in response to us fulfilling His Commandments.
27 Zohar Raya Mehemna III Ekev 270b quoting Devarim 8:10.
28 Pri Etz Chaim Shaar HaKaddishim, Chap. 1. This is said in relation to the statement of "Barchu" which precedes the blessing of the Shema.
29 Pri Etz Chaim Shaar HaBeriyah [meaning the end of Shaar Kriat Shema as Kriat Shema is associated with Beriyah. See G2:18:N40], Chap. 29:
- ... the chamber of Beriyah is also called "Baruch/Blessed" with the *addition of blessing* ....

Pri Etz Chaim Shaar HaAmidah, end of Chap. 2:

- The Rashba writes similarly in connection with "Yishmael, my son, bless me."[30] Refer there.
• However, the concept of *Blessing* God, does not mean to relate, so to speak, to the Unified Essence of God, God forbid, as this [Essence] is abstracted from any [possibility of] *blessing*,[31] but this concept is as per the Zohar[32] which describes God, as being [both] hidden and as revealed:
  - [Hidden:]
    - The Infinite Essence of God is so obscurely hidden that no name can describe it in any way, God forbid – not even the name YHVH or even the tag of the *Yud* of [YHVH].[33]
      - (Even though the Zohar uses the term *"Ein Sof"* [i.e., No End] to describe [the Essence of] God – this is not a reference to God – but it refers to our perception of Him from the perspective of His [enabling] powers which are bestowed from Him in His connection through His Will to the worlds. Therefore, He is referred to as having *No End* rather than having *No Beginning*, as in truth from His perspective, He has no end and no beginning, it is just from our perspective that His powers are only the beginning [meaning that they are just there], but we require unending perception to relate to His powers that are bestowed.)[34]
  - [Revealed:]

• . . . and our intention is to draw down a bestowal from the world of Atzilut and to raise it and include it in Atzilut with the word Baruch/Bless – the *addition* of blessing of the blessing of the Patriarchs . . . .
Pri Etz Chaim Shaar HaAmidah, beginning of Chap. 3:
• The blessing of the Patriarchs: "Blessed" relates to the world of Beriyah which is blessed from all of the supernal emanation – by way of the supernal secret which is called "blessed" which always raises all of the world of Beriyah through it . . . and through the *addition* of blessing . . . .
Pri Etz Chaim Shaar HaShabbat, beginning of Chap. 12:
• After this when the prayer leader says "Barchu/Blessed," you should have in mind to receive an *addition* of Ruach. In this way, have we not already explained with weekday prayer that the whole concept of "Barchu" is the elavating of the level of Yetzirah to Beriyah which is blessed with an *addition* of blessing . . . .
Pri Etz Chaim Shaar Tefillat Rosh Hashana, Chap. 3:
• Now we will explain the meaning of the *blessing* . . . for now through the *addition* of blessing . . . for through this it is called "Blessed" . . .

30 Chidushei HaRashba on the Agadot of the Talmud, Berachot 7a, in particular "that the word *blessing* is an expression of *addition to* and *increase*."

בְּכָל מִינֵי רִבּוּיִין", וְכֵן הוּא שָׁם סוֹף שַׁעַר הַבְּרִיאָה, וְסוֹף פֶּרֶק ב' מִשַּׁעַר הָעֲמִידָה, וּבְרֵישׁ פֶּרֶק שְׁלִישִׁי שָׁם, וּבְשַׁעַר הַשַּׁבָּת רֵישׁ פִּ"ב, וּבְשַׁעַר תְּפִלַּת ר"ה פ"ג, ע"ש.

○ וְכֵן כָּתַב הָרַשְׁבָּ"א זִכְרוֹנוֹ לִבְרָכָה בְּעִנְיַן יִשְׁמָעֵאל בְּנֵי בָּרְכֵנִי, עַיֵּן שָׁם:

• אָמְנָם, עִנְיַן הַבְּרָכָה לוֹ יִתְבָּרֵךְ שְׁמוֹ, אֵין הַכַּוָּנָה לְעַצְמוּת אָדוֹן יָחִיד בָּרוּךְ הוּא כִּבְיָכוֹל, חָלִילָה וְחָלִילָה, כִּי הוּא מְרוֹמָם מֵעַל כָּל בְּרָכָה. אֲבָל הָעִנְיָן, כְּמוֹ שֶׁאָמְרוּ בַּזֹּהַר (אמור צח: ועוד בכ"מ), דְּקוּדְשָׁא בְּרִיךְ הוּא סָתִים וְגַלְיָא:

○ [סתים]

• כִּי עַצְמוּת "אֵין סוֹף" בָּרוּךְ הוּא — סָתִים מִכָּל סְתִימִין, וְאֵין לְכַנּוֹתוֹ חַס וְשָׁלוֹם בְּשׁוּם שֵׁם כְּלָל, אֲפִלּוּ בְּשֵׁם "הֲוָיָ"ה" בָּרוּךְ הוּא, וַאֲפִלּוּ בְּקוֹצוֹ שֶׁל יוּ"ד דְּבֵיהּ.

• (וְאַף גַּם מַה שֶּׁבַּזֹּהַר הַקָּדוֹשׁ מְכַנֵּהוּ יִתְבָּרֵךְ בְּשֵׁם "אֵין סוֹף", אֵינֶנּוּ כִּנּוּי עָלָיו יִתְבָּרֵךְ שְׁמוֹ, אֶלָּא הַכַּוָּנָה עַל הַשָּׂגָתֵנוּ אוֹתוֹ מִצַּד כֹּחוֹת הַנִּשְׁפָּעִים מֵאִתּוֹ בְּהִתְחַבְּרוּתוֹ בִּרְצוֹנוֹ לְהָעוֹלָמוֹת. וְלָזֹאת כִּנּוּהוּ "אֵין סוֹף", וְלֹא "אֵין רֵאשִׁית", כִּי בֶּאֱמֶת מִצַּד עַצְמוּתוֹ יִתְבָּרֵךְ שְׁמוֹ, אֵין לוֹ לֹא סוֹף וְלֹא רֵאשִׁית, רַק מִצַּד הַשָּׂגָתֵנוּ כֹּחוֹתָיו יִתְבָּרֵךְ, הֲלֹא כָּל הַשָּׂגָתֵנוּ הוּא רַק "רֵאשִׁית", אֲבָל "אֵין סוֹף" לְהַגִּיעַ בְּהַשָּׂגָה לְהַשִּׂיג אֶת כֹּחוֹתָיו יִתְבָּרֵךְ שְׁמוֹ הַנִּשְׁפָּעִים):

○ [גליא]

---

31 There is no meaning whatsoever of mentioning addition or increase in connection with His Essence at all, God forbid.

32 E.g., Zohar III Emor 98b among other places.

33 The tag on the letter *Yud* represents a pointing upwards which indicates God's Supernal Will which is far abstracted from that which is represented by YHVH . . . and even this highly abstracted hint does not encapsulate the Essence of God in even any minor way.

34 It should be noted that an additional reason why the Infinite Essence of God is referred to as "Ein Sof" is because the term has the same numerical value as the word "Or/light." God's Will, which is that which connects Him to the worlds, is likened to light which has the property of dissemination and connection. The word "Ratzon/Will" has the same numerical value as "*Shemo*/His Name" and therefore it is only God's Will and His connection with the worlds, that can be denoted by any form of name. This is in contrast with His Essence and the Ein Sof, about which no name is meaningful.

- That small part [of God] that we can relate to and describe using a number of descriptions, names, appellations, and characteristics, as found in the Torah and in the format of all prayers
- all of these are only from the perspective of God's connection with the worlds and powers from the point of creation onwards, establishing them, giving them life, and managing them according to His Will (and they are as referred to as "the cascading down [of His life force] through the levels of the Sefirot")
- and with all the different ways in which details of the sequence of behavior cascades down to this world, whether [to implement] justice, kindness, or mercy through the supernal powers and their combination
- these names, descriptions, and characteristics change accordingly.
- As each specific manifest behavior is associated with its own specific descriptive name
- as the meaning of all the descriptions indicate that they are from the perspective of created powers
- for example, *Merciful One, Compassionate One*, whose meaning is having mercy and compassion on the creations.
- Even with the name referring to His Unified Essence, YHVH, we do not use it to solely relate to His Essence when [describing] His Unity, but [to relate to] the way in which He connects with the worlds, as per its meaning [it describes God] that He Was, Is, and Will Be[35] and that He continuously creates everything,[36] meaning

---

35   R. Chaim does not refer to a source for this meaning of YHVH. One possible source is from the Shulchan Aruch Orach Chaim 5:1 (and also the Tur) which R. Chaim explicitly refers to in a different context when he relates to the definition of Elokim in G1:02. A more likely source is the Shela quoted in the next footnote. The primary sources for this meaning however are in Zohar Raya Mehemna III Pinchas 257b and Tikkunei Zohar Tikkun 74 122b. The first of these primary sources reads as follows:

- So it is with [the name] YHVH, all entities which exist are dependent on [this name], and [this name] and all of its entities which exist testify about the Master of the Universe, that He was before all of existence, and He is *within* all of existence, and He will be after all of existence, and this is the secret, that all entities which exist testify about Him that *He Was, Is, and Will Be.*

This meaning is that YHVH is understood to be a condensed form of *Haya Hoveh VeYiheyeh* relating to God's simultaneous manifestation in and transcendence of the past, present, and future.

It should be noted that the name YHVH also relates to God's transcendence

▪ וּמַה שֶּׁמָּשָׁג אֶצְלֵנוּ קְצָת, וְאָנוּ מְכַנִּים וּמְתָאֲרִים כַּמָּה תְּאָרִים וְשֵׁמוֹת וְכִנּוּיִים וּמִדּוֹת, כְּמוֹ שֶׁמְּצִינוּם בַּתּוֹרָה וּבְכָל מַטְבֵּעַ הַתְּפִלָּה

▪ כֻּלָּם הֵם רַק מִצַּד הִתְחַבְּרוּתוֹ יִתְבָּרַךְ אֶל הָעוֹלָמוֹת וְהַכֹּחוֹת מֵעֵת הַבְּרִיאָה, לְהַעֲמִידָם וּלְהַחֲיוֹתָם וּלְהַנְהִיגָם כִּרְצוֹנוֹ יִתְבָּרַךְ שְׁמוֹ, (וְהֵם אֲשֶׁר קְרָאוּם בְּשֵׁם "הִשְׁתַּלְשְׁלוּת הַסְּפִירוֹת").

▪ וּלְפִי כָּל שִׁנּוּיֵי פְּרָטֵי סִדְרֵי הַהַנְהָגָה, שֶׁמִּשְׁתַּלְשֵׁל וְנִמְשָׁךְ לָזֶה הָעוֹלָם, אִם לְדִין, אִם לְחֶסֶד, אִם לְרַחֲמִים, עַל יְדֵי כֹּחוֹת הָעֶלְיוֹנִים וְהִתְמַזְּגוּתָם מִשְׁתַּנִּים הַשֵּׁמוֹת וְהַכִּנּוּיִים וְהַתְּאָרִים.

▪ שֶׁלְּכָל עִנְיָן פְּרָטֵי מִסִּדְרֵי הַהַנְהָגָה — מְיֻחָד לוֹ כִּנּוּי וְשֵׁם פְּרָטִי

▪ שֶׁכֵּן מוֹרִים פֵּרוּשָׁם שֶׁל כָּל הַתְּאָרִים שֶׁהֵם מִצַּד הַכֹּחוֹת הַבְּרוּאִים

▪ כְּמוֹ "רַחוּם" וְ"חַנּוּן", פֵּרוּשָׁם, רַחְמָנוּת וַחֲנִינָה עַל הַבְּרוּאִים.

▪ וַאֲפִלּוּ הַשֵּׁם הָעֶצֶם הַמְיֻחָד הֲוָיָ"ה בָּרוּךְ הוּא, לֹא עַל עַצְמוּתוֹ יִתְבָּרַךְ לְבַד

---

of space as the sum of the squares of the numerical values of each letter of YHVH sums to the numerical value of Makom/space which is 186 (e.g., as per Emek HaMelech, Shaar 14, Chap. 152). So YHVH is a name which describes that God transcends both space and time. In addition to this, the squaring of a number in terms of the numerical value of Hebrew words relates to an intensity of the base concept, so Makom can be viewed as an intense manifestation of YHVH. See the concept of Makom as it is developed in the Third Gateway.

36 With this statement, R. Chaim is adding another meaning to God's name YHVH, which at first glance appears to be in addition to the first meaning. This meaning is that God is constantly causing everything to exist at every moment. Although it appears to be a separate meaning, this second meaning of constantly causing everything to exist can be viewed as a consequence of the first that God transcends space and time. It is implied by the Zohar quoted in the previous footnote that while YHVH transcends space and time, at the same time He is *within* all of existence and therefore causing it. The name YHVH therefore depicts God's connection with the world. It is this connection which constantly creates, and if this connection is broken, even momentarily, then the fabric of time and space and everything within it would immediately cease to be and would be as if it never existed. R. Chaim mentions this meaning once more at the end of G3:09. Another source for this meaning is the verse "You are *YHVH* alone . . . and You *continuously* Give life to everything" (Nechemia 9:6) which R. Chaim quotes in G1:16:N14, G3:01, and G3:10, explaining it to mean that God continuously creates everything.

A likely source for R. Chaim's explanation of the double faceted meaning of

that God connects with His Will to the worlds, to cause them to exist and to maintain them each moment. (Note 19)[37]
- This is as stated by the Arizal in his holy language, that all the descriptions and names [of God] are names of His Essence as it is manifest in the levels of the Sefirot. Refer there.[38]

Rabbi Chaim's Note:
Note 19 – Time only exists from the world level of Atzilut and downwards

- In relation to that which is stated in Pirkei DeRabbi Eliezer[39] that before God created the Universe, *He* and *His Name* existed alone
  - this specifically relates to before *He created*
  - meaning [before He created] the world of Beriyah [the world level of *Creation*].
  - [At that point,] *He*, relating to His Essence, and *His Name*, relating to the world of Atzilut, were alone.
- But were it not for God's emanation from Himself of the world of Atzilut[40]
  - it would not have been relevant to relate to His Essence in terms of past, present and future.[41]

YHVH together with its association to the verse from Nechemia is the Shela Shaar HaOtiot, Ot Samech, Sipuk, 3 as follows:
- . . . and one who places his trust in God, literally cleaves to God as per "and you who cleave to *YHVH*, your God" (Devarim 4:4). For he cleaves to His Great Name, *Haya Hoveh VeYiheyeh*, which *continuously creates* everything and continuously gives life to all, as written "and You continuously Give life to everything," as [Chazal] expound: "You *continuously create* everything" inevitably results in "You *give life* to all."

(Refer to p. 546, fn. 234.)

37 **R. Chaim adds Note 19 here.** This note is brought at the end of this chapter and is entitled "Time only exists from the world level of Atzilut and downwards."

38 Introduction to Pri Etz Chaim:
- [After describing that in the world level of Atzilut there is an absolute unity between its three elements of Ein Sof, Sefirot, and His Essence, it highlights that in the world level of Beriyah and below there is no absolute unity and that these world levels are separate from their associated Sefirot] . . . but in Beriyah, Yetzirah, and Asiyah there is occasional unity and [therefore] all of our prayers are [only] addressed to the Ein Sof. However, we are unable to describe the Ein Sof with any description or name and therefore we pray using the medium of the Sefira – for the descriptions and names relate to

אָנוּ מְיַחֲדִים לוֹ, אֶלָּא מִצַּד הִתְחַבְּרוּתוֹ יִתְבָּרַךְ עִם הָעוֹלָמוֹת, כְּפֵרוּשׁוֹ הָיָה וְהֹוֶה וְיִהְיֶה וּמְהַוֶּה הַכֹּל, רָצָה לוֹמַר, הוּא יִתְבָּרַךְ מִתְחַבֵּר בִּרְצוֹנוֹ לְהָעוֹלָמוֹת לְהַוּוֹתָם וּלְקַיְּמָם כָּל רֶגַע (הגהה י"ט).

וְזֶה שֶׁאָמַר הָאֲרִיזַ"ל בִּלְשׁוֹנוֹ הַקָּדוֹשׁ, הוּבָא בְּהַקְדָּמַת פְּרִי עֵץ חַיִּים (בסוף הקדמה שניה), שֶׁכָּל הַכִּנּוּיִּים וְהַשֵּׁמוֹת, הֵם שְׁמוֹת הָעַצְמוּת הַמִּתְפַּשְּׁטִים בַּסְּפִירוֹת, וְעַיֵּן שָׁם:

הגהה י"ט

- וּמַה שֶּׁאָמַר בְּפִרְקֵי רַבִּי אֱלִיעֶזֶר, שֶׁקֹּדֶם שֶׁבָּרָא הַקָּדוֹשׁ בָּרוּךְ הוּא אֶת הָעוֹלָם הָיָה הוּא וּשְׁמוֹ לְבַד.
  - קֹדֶם "שֶׁבָּרָא" דַּיְקָא
  - רוֹצֶה לוֹמַר עוֹלָם הַ'בְּרִיאָה'
  - הָיָה "הוּא" — עַצְמוּתוֹ יִתְבָּרַךְ, "וּשְׁמוֹ" — הַיְנוּ עוֹלָם אֲצִילוּת — "לְבַד":
- אֲבָל אִלּוּלֵי הֶאֱצִיל יִתְבָּרַךְ שְׁמוֹ מֵאִתּוֹ עוֹלָם הָאֲצִילוּת
  - לֹא הָיָה שַׁיָּךְ עַל עַצְמוּתוֹ יִתְבָּרַךְ "הָיָה וְהֹוֶה וְיִהְיֶה":

---

the [Sefirot] – they are the names of [God's] Essence which is manifest within each Sefira . . . [See G2:04:N21].

39 Towards the beginning of Chap. 3.

40 I.e., The world of Emanation. See G1:13:N13 for a description of the world levels.

41 God's Name which describes His Essence is YHVH which is a condensed form of *Haya/He was, Hoveh/is, VeYiheyeh/will be* referring to His transcendence over time, i.e., over the *past, present, and future*. Without the emanation of the world of Atzilut there is no meaning in the application of any form of descriptive name to God and to even talk of Him transcending time. R. Chaim subsequently explains in G2:03, e.g., in his lengthy quotation from Zohar II Bo 42b, that the ability to form an image of this name and also of God's Characteristics is only from the world level of Beriyah (creation) and downwards. In other words, while the ability to relate to time is only meaningful from the perspective of a created being, the potential to relate to time and God's transcendence of it only came into being when God emanated the world of Atzilut/Emanation.

It is insightful to see comments of the Shela Bereishit Torah Ohr 23:
- . . . and then you will understand that the innovation of [the Creation of] the world was not anything new from God's perspective such that it would reflect a new Will – it is only something new from the perspective of the

3. ABSOLUTE HIDDEN ESSENCE VS. REVEALED ASPECTS OF GOD

- The above is echoed by Chazal's comments:
  - That when Moshe, in preparing for his mission, asked God with what name He should be referred to [when telling the Jewish people in Egypt that] "the God of your fathers has sent me to you"
    - God answered Moshe: You want to know My Name? I am referred to by My Actions, sometimes I am called El Shadai, Tzvaot, Elokim, or YHVH
    - when I judge my creations – I am called Elokim
    - when I wage war against the wicked – I am called Tzvaot
    - when I hold the sins of man in the balance – I am called El Shadai
    - when I am merciful with My World – I am called YHVH
    - this is the meaning of [God's answer in the next verse] "I Will Be as I Will Be," that I am referred to according to My Actions.[42]
  - "For you did not see any image [on the day God spoke to you at Horev]" . . . "and he [Moshe] looks at the image of YHVH"
    - that even this image is not in His Place [i.e., where God's Essence resides], it is only when He descends to rule over them and be manifest over His creations – [that He appears to each of them according to their ability to visualize]
    - for before He created image and form in this world, He was Unified without form or visualization, and one who is able to perceive Him before [i.e., above] the level of Beriyah [i.e., creation], which [is a level which] is still outside of the realm of form, is forbidden to [attempt to] make this form and visualization in the world [neither with the letter *Hey* nor the letter *Yud*], not even with the Holy Name and not even with any letter or vowel/point within the world

---

creations that it *occurred* to God's Will to create them. The Great R. Eliezer (Pirkei DeRabbi Eliezer, Chap. 3) hinted to this that before God created the Universe, *He* and *His Name* existed alone. I will preface an explanation of this from the book "Ginat Egoz," which elaborates on this issue and I will summarize his thoughts. Know that the name YHVH is called the "Name of His Essence." For this name relates to the essence of the truth of His Existence before and after He created the Universe, where after He created [the name relates to] *Haya/He was, Hoveh/is, VeYiheyeh/will be* [and also to] *Melech/He rules, Malach/He ruled, Yimloch/He will rule* [i.e., the existence of and His transcendence of time. However, at the same time] "I am *YHVH*, I have not changed" (Malachi 3:6) [in any way as a result of the Creation

שער ב' - פרק ג'

• וְהוּא מַאֲמָרָם זִכְרוֹנָם לִבְרָכָה בִּשְׁמוֹת רַבָּה פָּרָשָׁה ג':

○ "אֱלֹקֵי אֲבוֹתֵיכֶם שְׁלָחַנִי אֲלֵיכֶם" (שם ג, יג) אוֹתָהּ שָׁעָה נִתְבָּרֵר מֹשֶׁה עַל עֲסָקָיו כו', בְּאוֹתָהּ שָׁעָה הָיָה מֹשֶׁה מְבַקֵּשׁ שֶׁיּוֹדִיעֵנוּ הַקָּדוֹשׁ בָּרוּךְ הוּא אֶת הַשֵּׁם הַגָּדוֹל כו'

□ אָמַר לוֹ הַקָּדוֹשׁ בָּרוּךְ הוּא לְמֹשֶׁה, שְׁמִי אַתָּה מְבַקֵּשׁ לֵידַע, לְפִי מַעֲשַׂי אֲנִי נִקְרָא, פְּעָמִים אֲנִי נִקְרָא בְּ'אֵל שַׁדַּי', בִּ'צְבָאוֹת', בֵּ'אלֹהִים' אוֹ בַּ'הֲוָיָה'.

□ כְּשֶׁאֲנִי דָּן אֶת הַבְּרִיּוֹת — אֲנִי נִקְרָא "אֱלֹקִים"

□ וּכְשֶׁאֲנִי עוֹשֶׂה מִלְחָמָה בָּרְשָׁעִים — אֲנִי נִקְרָא "צְבָאוֹת"

□ וּכְשֶׁאֲנִי תּוֹלֶה חֲטָאָיו שֶׁל אָדָם — אֲנִי נִקְרָא "אֵ—ל שַׁדַּי"

□ וּכְשֶׁאֲנִי מְרַחֵם עַל עוֹלָמִי — אֲנִי נִקְרָא "הֲוָיָה" כו'

□ הֱוֵי "אֶהְיֶ"ה אֲשֶׁר אֶהְיֶ"ה" (שמות ג, יד), אֲנִי נִקְרָא לְפִי מַעֲשַׂי:

○ וּבְרַעְיָא מְהֵימְנָא פָּרָשַׁת בֹּא דַּף מ"ב ב', "כִּי לֹא רְאִיתֶם כָּל תְּמוּנָה" (דברים ה, טו) וְגוֹ', דְּהָא כְּתִיב (במדבר יב, ח) "וּתְמוּנַת ה' יַבִּיט" וְגוֹ'

□ דְּאַפִלּוּ הַאי תְּמוּנָה לֵית לֵיהּ בְּאַתְרֵיהּ, אֶלָּא כַּד נָחִית לְאַמְלָכָא עֲלַיְיהוּ, וְיִתְפַּשֵּׁט עַל בִּרְיָין כו'

□ דְּהָא קֹדֶם דְּבָרָא דִּיּוּקְנָא בְּעָלְמָא וְצִיֵּר צוּרָה, הֲוָה הוּא יְחִידָאֵי בְּלֹא צוּרָה וְדִמְיוֹן, וּמַאן דְּאִשְׁתְּמוֹדַע לֵיהּ קֹדֶם "בְּרִיאָה", דְּאִיהוּ לְבַר מִדִּיּוּקְנָא, אָסוּר לְמֶעְבַּד לֵיהּ צוּרָה וְדִיּוּקְנָא בְּעָלְמָא וְכוּ', וַאֲפִלּוּ בִּשְׁמָא קַדִּישָׁא וְלֹא בְּשׁוּם אוֹת וּנְקֻדָּה בְּעָלְמָא

---

including the creation of time]. His other names were only newly applied to Him after He created the Universe and these are [generically referenced] as "Elokim," for it is the line of judgment. Similarly, judges are in truth called "Elohim" (Shemot 22:7), for this name relates to the central concept of what it is [i.e., how God is manifest – in terms of a judgment which controls and constrains His Essence and results in the existence of creations]. Therefore, Elokim has the numerical value of *HaTeva*/nature as written in the Zohar, for nature is an organized concept, entirely through the line of judgment [i.e., controlled, to cause creations to exist] in a fitting and proper manner . . .

(Also refer to Shela, Toldot Adam, Beit YHVH, 32 onwards.)

42 Shemot Rabba 3:5 and 3:6, quoting Shemot 3:13 and 3:14.

- this is the meaning of "For you did not see any image" [you did not see anything that had an image]
- however, after He made the form of the Merkava of Supernal Man, He descended there and that form is called YHVH – to enable perception of His image as El, Elokim, Shadai, Tzvaot, Eheyeh
- so that He can be recognized in the way He manages the world through each character trait, with mercy, judgment, etc.
- woe is to he that compares Him [i.e., His Essence] with a specific character trait . . . the comparison should only be with His control over the specific character trait and even over his creations
- and when He is separated [from His character traits or creations], He has no characteristics or comparison.[43] Refer there.

◦ He is only referred to as YHVH or with all the names when He manifests His Light upon them, but when He removes Himself from them His Essence has no name at all.[44] Refer there.

◦ After the Tikkunim[45] provides lengthy details relating to the interconnectivity of the limbs [i.e., the interaction of the elements] of the Shiur Komah, so to speak, it states that all this
- is in order to show the area of control of each limb of the body [i.e., of each element of the structure].
- To make known to man how the world works so that he should know how to call Him with each limb as appropriate
- and how His Name changes with each limb
- there is a limb which is called YHVH – mercy
- there is a limb which is called Elokim . . . etc.
- Eheyeh [i.e., the name *I Will Be*] refers to the Essence of the Ultimate Cause, which is One with all the Names and does not change with any of them, as these changes are in the names and not in Him.
- Refer there.

◦ [All His names are just descriptions and He is only referred to with these names by the creations. . . .][46]

◦ [All these names and descriptions are used by the worlds and his creations to relate to how He controls them. . . .][47]

◦ Refer to Etz Chaim,[48] and it will be understood as per our words.

---

43 Zohar II Bo 42b quoting Devarim 4:15 and Bamidbar 12:8.
44 Zohar Raya Mehemna III Pinchas 225a.
45 Tikkunei Zohar Tikkun 70 122b.
46 Zohar Raya Mehemna III Pinchas 257b.
47 Zohar Raya Mehemna III Pinchas 258a.

נפש   שער ב' - פרק ג'   החיים   321

▫ וְהַאי אִיהוּ "כִּי לֹא רְאִיתֶם כָּל תְּמוּנָה" ג'

▫ אֲבָל בָּתַר דַּעֲבִיד הָא דְיוּקְנָא דִּמְרַכַּבְתָּא דְאָדָם עִלָּאָה, נָחִית תַּמָּן וְאִתְקְרֵי בְּהַהוּא דְיוּקְנָא "הֲוָיָ"ה", בְּגִין דְּאִשְׁתְּמוֹדְעוּן לֵיהּ בִּדְמוּת דִּילֵיהּ כוּ', אֵל, אֱלֹהִים, שַׁדַּי, צְבָאוֹת, אֶהְיֶ"ה

▫ בְּגִין דְּיִשְׁתְּמוֹדְעוּן לֵיהּ בְּכָל מִדָּה וּמִדָּה, אֵיךְ יִתְנַהֵג עָלְמָא בְּחֶסֶד וּבְדִינָא כוּ'.

▫ וַי לֵיהּ לְמַאן דְּיַשְׁוֵי לֵיהּ בְּשׁוּם מִדָּה כוּ', אֶלָּא דְּמִיּוּנָא דִּילֵיהּ כְּפוּם שָׁלְטָנוּתֵיהּ עַל הַהוּא מִדָּה, וַאֲפִלּוּ עַל כָּל בְּרִיָּן כוּ'

▫ כַּד אִסְתַּלִּיק מִנָּהּ, לֵית לֵיהּ מִדָּה וְלֹא דִּמְיוֹן, עַיֵּן שָׁם:

○ וּבְפָרָשַׁת פִּנְחָס רכ"ה א', "וְאִיהוּ לָא אִתְקְרֵי הֲוָיָ"ה וּבְכָל שְׁמָהָן אֶלָּא בְּאִתְפַּשְׁטוּת נְהוֹרֵיהּ עֲלַיְהוּ, וְכַד אִסְתַּלֵּק מִנַּיְהוּ, לֵית לֵיהּ מִגַּרְמֵיהּ שֵׁם כְּלָל" כוּ' עַיֵּן שָׁם:

○ וּבְתִקּוּנִים ת"ע קכ"ב ב', הֶאֱרִיךְ בְּעִנְיָן פִּרְקֵי אֵבְרֵי הַשִּׁעוּר קוֹמָה כִּבְיָכוֹל, אָמַר אַחַר זֶה, שֶׁכָּל הָעִנְיָן הוּא

▫ לְאַחֲזָאָה בְּכָל אֵבֶר וְאֵבֶר דְּגוּפֵיהּ — שָׁלְטָנוּתֵיהּ

▫ לְאִשְׁתְּמוֹדְעָא לְבַר נַשׁ אֵיךְ אִתְנְהִיג עָלְמָא, וְיִנְדַּע לְמִקְרֵי לֵיהּ בְּכָל אֵבֶר כִּדְקָא יָאוּת

▫ וְאֵיךְ אִשְׁתְּתֵי שְׁמֵיהּ לְפוּם הַהוּא אֵבֶר

▫ וְאִית אֵבֶר דְּאִתְקְרֵי בֵּיהּ "הֲוָיָ"ה" — רַחֲמֵי

▫ וְאִית אֵבֶר דְּאִתְקְרֵי בֵּיהּ "אֱלֹקִים", וְאִית אֵבֶר דְּאִתְקְרֵי בֵּי' כוּ'

▫ "אֵקִ"ק" אַחֲזֵי עַל עִלַּת הָעִלּוֹת כוּ', דְּעִלַּת עַל כָּל הָעִלּוֹת אִיהוּ חַד בְּכָל שְׁמָהָן, וְלָא אִשְׁתְּתֵי בְּכֻלְּהוּ, דְּשִׁנּוּיִין בִּשְׁמָהָן אִנּוּן, וְלָאו בֵּיהּ כוּ'.

▫ עַיֵּן שָׁם.

○ וְעַיֵּן עוֹד בְּרַעְיָא מְהֵימְנָא פִּנְחָס רנ"ז ב'

○ וְרנ"ח א'

○ וְעַיֵּן בְּעֵץ חַיִּים רֵישׁ שַׁעַר עִגּוּלִים וְיֹשֶׁר, וְשָׁם בְּסוֹף זֶה הַשַּׁעַר רֵישׁ הַמַּהֲדוּרָא תִּנְיָנָא, וְתָבִין שָׁם עַל פִּי דְּבָרֵינוּ:

---

48 Etz Chaim Shaar 1, Shaar Derush Igulim VeYosher, beginning of Chap. 1:
   • If He didn't engage His Abilities and Powers in actual action, then He

- (Note 20)[49] This is [the limit of] our ability to, so to speak, perceive God – it is all dependent on the nature of His connection with the worlds and His manifestation within them:
  - As mentioned above:[50] That even this image is not in His Place [i.e., where the essence of God resides], it is only when He descends to rule over them and be manifest over his creations that He appears to each of them according to their ability to visualize, and this is the meaning of "and in the hand of the prophets I will be imagined."
- Therefore, the Men of the Great Assembly established the syntax of all the blessings of the Mitzvot to include reference [to God as both] a revealed presence and as being concealed.
  - Beginning with "Blessed are You" – an expression of acknowledgement of presence [addressing God directly in the second person]
  - and concluding with "Who has Sanctified us . . . and Commanded us" – an expression of concealment [addressing God in the third person].
  - As from the perspective of His Connection with the worlds through which we have a miniscule perception of Him, we speak to a revealed presence "Blessed are *You* God" – for the worlds require an increase in blessing from His Essence which connects to them, explaining [why the revealed section of a blessing concludes with] "King of the Universe," as mentioned above "it is only when He descends to rule over them and be manifest over his creations . . ."[51]
  - and the One who "Commands us and Sanctifies us" – this relates to the Absolute Infinite Essence of God alone which is the most hidden of all concealments, and they therefore established a concealed syntax of "Who has Sanctified us . . . and Commanded us."

---

would not, so to speak, be referred to as complete in His actions, names, or descriptions. His great name YHVH relates to His everlasting existence, i.e., before, during, and after Creation and if the worlds and everything in them were not created, we would not be able to see the truth of His everlasting existence in the past, present, and future, and he would not be referred to as YHVH, and similarly, His name ADNY relates to Him being the Ultimate Master, i.e., when He has servants, He is their Master, but without creations He cannot be called "Master" . . .

- (הגהה כ׳) וְזֶה כָּל הַשָּׂגָתֵנוּ כִּבְיָכוֹל אוֹתוֹ יִתְבָּרַךְ, הַכֹּל מִצַּד עִנְיַן הִתְחַבְּרוּתוֹ אֶל הָעוֹלָמוֹת וְהִתְפַּשְּׁטוּתוֹ יִתְבָּרַךְ בְּתוֹכָם.

- כְּמוֹ שֶׁכָּתוּב בְּרַעְיָא מְהֵימְנָא פ׳ בֹּא הַנִּזְכָּר לְעֵיל, דְּאֲפִילוּ הַאי תְּמוּנָה לֵית לֵיהּ בְּאַתְרֵיהּ, אֶלָּא כַּד נָחִית לְאַמְלָכָא עֲלַיְיהוּ, וְיִתְפַּשֵּׁט עַל בְּרִיָּן, יִתְחֲזֵי לְכָל חַד כְּפוּם מַרְאֵה וְחֵזוּ וְדִמְיוֹן דִּלְהוֹן, וְהַאי אִיהוּ "וּבְיַד הַנְּבִיאִים אֲדַמֶּה" (הושע יב, יא):

- וְלָכֵן קָבְעוּ אַנְשֵׁי כְּנֶסֶת הַגְּדוֹלָה, הַנּוּסָח שֶׁל כָּל בִּרְכוֹת הַמִּצְוֹת בִּלְשׁוֹן נוֹכֵחַ וְנִסְתָּר.

  ○ תְּחִלָּתָם "בָּרוּךְ אַתָּה" — הוּא לְשׁוֹן נוֹכֵחַ
  ○ וּמְסַיְּמִים "אֲשֶׁר קִדְּשָׁנוּ כו׳ וְצִוָּנוּ" — לְשׁוֹן נִסְתָּר.

- שֶׁמִּצַּד הִתְחַבְּרוּתוֹ יִתְבָּרַךְ בִּרְצוֹנוֹ אֶל הָעוֹלָמוֹת, שֶׁעַל יְדֵי זֶה יֵשׁ לָנוּ קְצָת הַשָּׂגָה כָּל דְּהוּ, אָנוּ מְדַבְּרִים לְנוֹכֵחַ — "בָּרוּךְ אַתָּה ה׳" כו׳, כִּי הָעוֹלָמוֹת הֵם הַצְּרִיכִים לְעִנְיַן הַתּוֹסֶפֶת וְרִבּוּי בְּרָכָה מֵעַצְמוּתוֹ יִתְבָּרַךְ הַמִּתְחַבֵּר אֲלֵיהֶם, וְזֶהוּ "מֶלֶךְ הָעוֹלָם", כְּמוֹ שֶׁאָמְרוּ בְּרַעְיָא מְהֵימְנָא הַנִּזְכָּר לְעֵיל "כַּד נָחִית לְאַמְלָכָא עֲלַיְיהוּ וְיִתְפַּשֵּׁט עַל בְּרִיָּן" כו׳.

- וְהַמְּצַוֶּה אוֹתָנוּ וּמְקַדְּשֵׁנוּ, הוּא עַצְמוּתוֹ יִתְבָּרַךְ אֵין סוֹף בָּרוּךְ הוּא לְבַדּוֹ, הַסָּתוּם מִכָּל סְתִימִין, לָכֵן תִּקְּנוּ נִסְתָּר בִּלְשׁוֹן "אֲשֶׁר קִדְּשָׁנוּ וְצִוָּנוּ":

Etz Chaim Shaar 1, Shaar Derush Igulim VeYosher, Chap. 2 (Second Edition):
- When it came up in His Will to emanate the emanations, to create the creations, it was for the known reason that He should be called Merciful, Compassionate, etc. However if there were no one in the world to receive His Mercy then how can He be called Merciful? And similarly for His other descriptions. . . .

49 **R. Chaim adds Note 20 here.** This note is brought at the end of this chapter and is entitled "Israel created at world's inception and is purpose of God's connection."

50 Zohar II Bo 42b as above but adding a quotation from Hoshea 12:11 which was omitted above.

51 Zohar II Bo 42b.

Rabbi Chaim's Note:
Note 20 – Israel created at world's inception and is purpose of God's connection

- With this we can understand the statement in the Midrash:[52] "My Dove, My Perfection (Tamati)." R. Yanai said [this should be read as] "My Twin (Teomati)" so to speak [i.e., that Israel is God's twin] – I am not greater than her [Israel], and she is not greater than Me.
- This appears to be a strange statement, but it is understood in the context of our words
  - that the entire perception of the little that is spoken about God is only from the perspective of His connection to the worlds
  - and the entirety of God's initial intention with the Creation of the worlds and His connection to them was purely for the sake of Israel
  - as per Chazal:[53] "In the beginning" means for the sake of Israel.
- This is the meaning of "My Twin . . . I am not greater than her . . . ," meaning in *years*. Understand this.[54]

4. PRAYER TO CONCENTRATE ON *CONNECTION* OF GOD TO WORLDS

- The reason that blessings include the two elements mentioned above [i.e., both hidden and revealed references to God] is that it is pivotal to our Holy Faith that the entire objective of our concentration of our hearts with all blessings, prayers, and requests is to be purely focused on the Unified One of the Universe, the Unified Infinite Master.
- However, when we address Him, it is not to His Essence alone, so to speak
  - as it is on a level which is totally abstracted and separated, so to speak, from the worlds [and remains unchanged] as it was before the Creation
  - as if so then how could we describe Him, God forbid, with all of our blessings and prayers with any worldly name or description at all.
- Furthermore, were it not for the fact that God revealed to us that His Will is to connect to the worlds
  - and to rule as King over His creations according to their level of serving Him
  - we would not be permitted to pray to His Essence at all
  - that It should connect to the worlds and control His creations.

---

52 Shir Hashirim Rabba 5:2.
53 Midrash Tanchuma Bereishit 3.

הגהה כ'

- וּבָזֶה יוּבַן מַאֲמָרָם זִכְרוֹנָם לִבְרָכָה, בְּחַזִית (שהש"ר) עַל פָּסוּק (שה"ש ה, ב) "יוֹנָתִי תַמָּתִי" ז"ל "רַבִּי יַנַּאי אָמַר, תְאוֹמָתִי כִּבְיָכוֹל, לֹא אֲנִי גָּדוֹל מִמֶּנָּה וְלֹא הִיא גְדוֹלָה מִמֶּנִּי":

- וְלִכְאוֹרָה נִפְלָאת הוּא. וְלִדְבָרֵינוּ הוּא מְבֹאָר

- אַחַר שֶׁכָּל הַהַשָּׂגוֹת בְּמִקְצָת שֶׁמְּדַבְּרִים בּוֹ יִתְבָּרַךְ, הוּא רַק מִצַּד הִתְחַבְּרוּתוֹ יִתְבָּרַךְ אֶל הָעוֹלָמוֹת.

- וְכָל תְּחִלַּת כַּוָּנָתוֹ יִתְבָּרַךְ בִּבְרִיאַת הָעוֹלָמוֹת וְהִתְחַבְּרוּתוֹ אֲלֵיהֶם, הָיָה רַק בִּשְׁבִיל יִשְׂרָאֵל כו'

- כְּמַאֲמָרָם ז"ל "בְּרֵאשִׁית — בִּשְׁבִיל יִשְׂרָאֵל" כו':

- זֶה שֶׁאָמַר "תְּאוֹמָתִי, לֹא אֲנִי גָּדוֹל מִמֶּנָּה וְלֹא הִיא" כו', רוֹצֶה לוֹמַר בִּשְׁנַיִם. וְהָבֵן:

שער ב' - פרק ד'

- וְטַעֲמוֹ שֶׁל דָּבָר, שֶׁנִּכְלָל בְּכָל בְּרָכָה שְׁנֵי הַבְּחִינוֹת הַנַּ"ל, כִּי יְסוֹד פִּנַּת אֱמוּנָתֵנוּ הַקְּדוֹשָׁה, שֶׁכָּל מְגַמַּת כַּוָּנַת לִבֵּנוּ בְּכָל הַבְּרָכוֹת וְהַתְּפִלּוֹת וּבַקָּשׁוֹת — אַךְ רַק לִיחוּדוֹ שֶׁל עוֹלָם, אָדוֹן יָחִיד אֵין סוֹף בָּרוּךְ הוּא:

- אָמְנָם לֹא שֶׁאָנוּ מְדַבְּרִים אֵלָיו כִּבְיָכוֹל עַל עַצְמוּתוֹ יִתְבָּרַךְ לְבַד

  - בִּבְחִינַת הֱיוֹתוֹ מֻפְשָׁט וּמֻפְרָשׁ כִּבְיָכוֹל לְגַמְרֵי מֵהָעוֹלָמוֹת, כְּעִנְיָן שֶׁהָיָה קֹדֶם הַבְּרִיאָה

  - דְּאִם כֵּן אֵיךְ נְתָאֲרֵהוּ חַס וְשָׁלוֹם בְּכָל בִּרְכוֹתֵינוּ וּתְפִלָּתֵנוּ בְּשׁוּם שֵׁם וְכִנּוּי בָּעוֹלָם כְּלָל:

- וְגַם, דְּאִם לֹא מִצַּד שֶׁהִרְאָנוּ יִתְבָּרַךְ שֶׁרְצוֹנוֹ לְהִתְחַבֵּר לְהָעוֹלָמוֹת

  - וּלְאַמְלָכָא עַל בִּרְיָן כְּפוּם עוֹבָדֵיהוֹן

  - לֹא הָיִינוּ רַשָּׁאִים כְּלָל לְהִתְפַּלֵּל לְעַצְמוּתוֹ יִתְבָּרַךְ

  - שֶׁיִּתְחַבֵּר לְהָעוֹלָמוֹת וּלְאַשְׁגְּחָא עַל בִּרְיָן:

---

54 I.e., that Israel is the same age as the worlds, and was created together with the inception of the worlds. The worlds exist as a result of God's connection to them and it is this connection which allows us to call Him by His Name. Therefore, Israel is the same age as the ability to call God by His Name.

- Therefore, we start [each blessing] saying "You God are King of the Universe"
  - meaning that since it was Your Will to cause the worlds to be and to connect to rule as King over them
  - therefore, our request is that the source of the Will be blessed, to rule as King over the worlds in this way.[55]
- Additionally, relative to God's Essence, without Its connection to the worlds, there is no scope for Torah or Mitzvot at all, as per:
  - "If you have sinned, how do you affect Him? . . . If you are righteous, what do you give Him or what does He receive from your hand?"[56]
  - "If you have become wise, you have become wise for *your* own good."[57]
- As man's actions, whether good or bad, have no impact whatsoever on God's Essence, God forbid.
  - As Chazal say[58] in reference to the verse:[59] "The Speech of God forges a connection. . . ." Rav says the Mitzvot were only given to forge [a connection with His Creations] as it doesn't bother [the Essence of] God as to whether one slaughters an animal from the front or the back of its neck.[60]
  - As per Zohar:[61] The Highest of the High – higher than all – He blesses all, but He does not need blessings from others, as there is no one that can influence Him as per "and He is above all blessing and praise." (Note 21)[62]
- All of the concentration of our hearts in all blessings and prayers must, however, be on the Infinite Essence of God, from the perspective of Its connection, as per His Will, to the worlds.
  - [This connection], from the world's perspective is in the form of the interchange of descriptions and names of God
    - which act to draw down light and bestowal of holiness from the Essence of God [into the worlds]
    - in direct proportion to the level of arousal which reaches [the worlds] from each Jew's actions

---

55 I.e., to be additionally manifest in this world.
56 Iyov 35:6–7.
57 Mishlei 9:12, i.e., wise for your own good and not for God's good as there is no impact on God's Essence as per the continuation.
58 This quotation is from Bereishit Rabba 44:1. A similar statement is made in Midrash Tanchuma Shemini 12 and also in Midrash Tehillim 18:25.
59 The identical verse appears in both 2 Shmuel 22:31 and also Tehillim 18:31. A similar phraseology is also expressed in Mishlei 30:5.
60 I.e., that the minutia of detail of the Halacha only have incredible relevance as a result of the connection of God's Essence to the worlds.

- וְלָכֵן מַקְדִּימִין אֲנַחְנוּ לוֹמַר "אַתָּה ה' מֶלֶךְ הָעוֹלָם"
- פֵּרוּשׁ, אַחַר שֶׁרְצוֹנְךָ הָיָה לִהְיוֹת הָעוֹלָמוֹת וּלְהִתְחַבֵּר אֲלֵיהֶם לְאַמְלָכָא עֲלֵיהוֹן
- לָזֹאת, בַּקָּשָׁתֵנוּ שֶׁיִּתְבָּרֵךְ מְקוֹר הָרָצוֹן לְאַמְלָכָא כֵּן לְעָלְמִין:
- וְגַם שֶׁלְּפִי בְּחִינַת עַצְמוּתוֹ יִתְבָּרֵךְ, בִּלְתִּי הִתְחַבְּרוּתוֹ אֶל הָעוֹלָמוֹת, אֵין מָקוֹם לְתוֹרָה וּמִצְוֹת כְּלָל.
- וְעַל זֶה נֶאֱמַר (איוב לה) "אִם חָטָאתָ מַה תִּפְעָל בּוֹ וְגוּ', אִם צָדַקְתָּ מַה תִּתֶּן לוֹ אוֹ מַה מִּיָּדְךָ יִקָּח"
- וְכֵן כְּתִיב (משלי ט, יב) "אִם חָכַמְתָּ חָכַמְתָּ לָּךְ":
- כִּי לְעַצְמוּת אֲדוֹן כָּל בָּרוּךְ הוּא, כָּל מַעֲשֵׂה הָאָדָם, הַטּוֹבָה הִיא אִם רָעָה, אֵינֶנָּה נוֹגַעַת לוֹ בְּעֶצֶם כְּלָל חַס וְשָׁלוֹם.
- וְהוּא מַאֲמָרָם זִכְרוֹנָם לִבְרָכָה בִּבְרֵאשִׁית רַבָּה רֵישׁ פָּרָשָׁה מ"ה, (תהלים יח, לא) "אִמְרַת ה' צְרוּפָה" ג', אָמַר רַב, לֹא נִתְּנוּ הַמִּצְוֹת אֶלָּא לְצָרֵף כוּ', וְכִי מַה אִכְפַּת לֵיהּ לְהַקָּדוֹשׁ בָּרוּךְ הוּא לְמִי שֶׁשּׁוֹחֵט מִן הַצַּוָּאר אוֹ מִי שֶׁשּׁוֹחֵט מִן הָעֹרֶף" כוּ' וְכֵן הוּא בְּתַנְחוּמָא פָּרָשַׁת שְׁמִינִי בְּפָסוּק זֹאת הַחַיָּה כוּ', וּבְמִדְרַשׁ תְּהִלִּים מִזְמוֹר י"ח, עַיֵּן שָׁם.
- וּבַתִּקּוּנִים תִּקּוּן ע' ק"לא ע"ב, "עִלַּת הָעִלּוֹת מִתְעַלֶּה עַל כֹּלָּא, אִיהוּ בְּרִיךְ לְכֹלָּא, וְלֹא צָרִיךְ אִיהוּ בִּרְכָאָן מֵאָחֳרָא, דְּלֵית עֲלֵיהּ מָאן דְּאַשְׁפַּע לֵיהּ, הֲדָא הוּא דִכְתִיב (נחמיה ט, ה) "וּמְרוֹמַם עַל כָּל בְּרָכָה וּתְהִלָּה":[61] (הגהה כ"א)
- אֶלָּא שֶׁכָּל כַּוָּנַת לִבֵּנוּ — בְּכָל הַבְּרָכוֹת וְהַתְּפִלּוֹת — צָרִיךְ שֶׁתִּהְיֶה לְעַצְמוּת אֵין סוֹף בָּרוּךְ הוּא, מִצַּד הִתְחַבְּרוּ כִּרְצוֹנוֹ יִתְבָּרַךְ אֶל הָעוֹלָמוֹת
  - שֶׁמִּצִּדָּם הֵם כָּל הַתְּאָרִים וְהַשֵּׁמוֹת מִתְחַלְּפִים
    - לִפְעֹל וּלְהַמְשִׁיךְ בָּהֶם אוֹר וְשִׁפְעַת קְדֻשָּׁה מֵעַצְמוּתוֹ יִתְבָּרַךְ
    - כְּפִי הִתְעוֹרְרוּת הַמַּגִּיעַ אֲלֵיהֶם מִמַּעֲשֵׂי הָאָדָם שֶׁל כָּל אִישׁ מֵעַם סְגֻלָּה[62]

---

61 Tikkunei Zohar Tikkun 70 131b quoting Nechemia 9:10.
62 **R. Chaim adds Note 21 here.** This note is brought at the end of this chapter and is entitled "Prayer focus on Unified Essence of God but not specific Sefirot."

- whether in kindness, justice, charity, mercy – in large or small measure
- similarly, in this way, God's connection to the powers and the worlds is in an extremely precisely weighed corresponding measure
- to change the sequence of connection [of the worlds] to draw down the bestowal of their light and all details of their behavior
  - whether it be for meting out judgment and anger, or kindness and mercy
  - and also whether the amount of the judgment and mercy is in small or large measure.

• This is the meaning of the statements of Chazal quoted above that "the Mitzvot were only given to *forge a connection* with His Creations."
  - That is, that there is a great need for them to forge and *purify* – to separate the impurities from all the created powers and worlds so that they will be forged and purified
  - and there is also the meaning that *to forge* is to *connect* and bind all the created powers and worlds to be corrected and arranged according to God's Intention and Supernal Will
  - and inevitably, the House of Israel, the Chosen People, will also be unified with God's Unifying Name [YHVH] to be His Portion and His Inheritance
  - as it is entirely and only for this purpose that the Mitzvot and Holy Service came to exist.[63]

• This is the concept of *blessing God* in all blessings and prayers, which literally means an *addition* and *increase* as above (G1:02).
  - That this is God's Will, for reasons hidden with Him, that the supernal powers and worlds should be rectified and unified through the blessings and prayers
    - that they should be prepared and made fit for the receipt of a bestowal of supernal holy light
    - and to draw and add the holy light and a multitude of blessings into them

---

63 It is of interest to see the text of Etz Chaim Shaar 49, Shaar Kelipat Nogah, Chap. 5:
   • The second [entity] is from Kelipat Nogah [i.e., a level of impurity which mediates between good and bad] which is made up of the good and bad inclinations . . . and is called the animal soul of good and bad. This real entity – which is from Kelipat Nogah – is the garment to the Nefesh, Ruach, and Neshama called the "cloak of skin" [see G3:13:N47] which incorpo-

- אִם בְּחֶסֶד, אִם בְּמִשְׁפָּט, אִם בִּצְדָקָה, אִם בְּרַחֲמִים, הַמְעַט וְאִם רַב
- כָּכָה הוּא עַל זֶה הָאֹפֶן וְהַשִּׁעוּר בְּדִקְדּוּק עָצוּם בְּמִדָּה וּבְמִשְׁקָל עִנְיַן הִתְחַבְּרוּתוֹ יִתְבָּרַךְ אֶל הַכֹּחוֹת וְהָעוֹלָמוֹת
- לְשַׁנּוֹת סֵדֶר הִתְקַשְּׁרוּתָם לְהַמְשָׁכַת שִׁפְעַת אוֹרָם, וְכָל פְּרָטֵי הַנְהָגָתָם
  ▽ אִם לְדִין וְרֹגֶז, אִם לְחֶסֶד וְרַחֲמִים
  ▽ וְגַם שִׁעוּר הַדִּין וְהַחֶסֶד הַמְעַט וְאִם רַב:
- זֶהוּ שֶׁאָמְרוּ בְּהַמַּאֲמָרִים הַנַּ"ל, "שֶׁלֹּא נִתְּנוּ הַמִּצְוֹת אֶלָּא לְצָרֵף בָּהֶן אֶת הַבְּרִיּוֹת"
- הַיְנוּ שֶׁצָּרִיךְ גָּדוֹל הֵמָּה לְצָרֵף וּלְזַקֵּק, לְהַפְרִיד הַסִּגִּים מִכָּל הַכֹּחוֹת וְהָעוֹלָמוֹת הַבְּרוּאִים יִצָּרֵף וְיִתְלַבֵּן.
- וְגַם כֵּן בְּמַשְׁמַע, "לְצָרֵף" — הַיְנוּ לְחַבֵּר וּלְקַשֵּׁר כָּל הַכֹּחוֹת וְהָעוֹלָמוֹת הַבְּרוּאִים מְתֻקָּנִים וּמְסֻדָּרִים כְּפִי הַכַּוָּנָה וְהָרָצוֹן הָעֶלְיוֹן בָּרוּךְ הוּא
- וּמִמֵּילָא גַּם בֵּית יִשְׂרָאֵל עִם סְגֻלָּה יִתְאַחֲדוּ בַּשֵּׁם הַמְיֻחָד יִתְבָּרַךְ לְחֶלְקוֹ וְנַחֲלָתוֹ
- שֶׁרַק עַל זֶה הַתַּכְלִית בָּאוּ כָּל הַמִּצְוֹת וְהָעֲבוֹדָה הַקְּדוֹשָׁה כֻּלָּהּ בִּכְלָלָהּ:
- זֶהוּ עִנְיַן הַבְּרָכָה לוֹ יִתְבָּרַךְ בְּכָל הַבְּרָכוֹת וְהַתְּפִלּוֹת, שֶׁפֵּרוּשׁוֹ הוּא, תּוֹסֶפֶת וְרִבּוּי מַמָּשׁ כְּמַשְׁמָעוֹ כַּנַּ"ל (פרק ב)
- שֶׁזֶּהוּ רְצוֹנוֹ יִתְבָּרַךְ מִטַּעַם כָּמוּס אִתּוֹ יִתְבָּרַךְ, שֶׁנִּתְתַּקֵּן וְיִתְיַחֵד עַל יְדֵי הַבְּרָכוֹת וְהַתְּפִלּוֹת הַכֹּחוֹת וְהָעוֹלָמוֹת הָעֶלְיוֹנִים
  □ שֶׁיִּהְיוּ מוּכָנִים וּרְאוּיִים לְקַבֵּל שִׁפְעַת קְדֻשַּׁת אוֹר עֶלְיוֹן
  □ וּלְהַמְשִׁיךְ וּלְהוֹסִיף בָּהֶם קְדֻשַּׁת הָאוֹר וְרֹב בְּרָכוֹת

---

rated good and bad after their intermixing through Adam's sin – requires purification. This is done through Torah and Mitzvah performance and this constitutes the entire breadth of activity of the people of Israel until the final redemption... The bad within it is called "death"... God only gave the Torah and Mitzvot to Israel in order to purify, *forge*, and remove the impurities from the silver which are within the garment of the soul. A man's positive thoughts/intentions during Torah study and Mitzvah performance remove [impurities] from the garment of the Neshama... and through [speech] of Torah study the Nogah of Yetzirah which is the garment of Ruach is purified, and the [action] of physical Mitzvah performance purifies the Nogah of Asiyah and makes it a garment for the Nefesh.

- from God's Essence which connects to them and distributes itself within them
    - and inevitably also resulting in this additional blessing and holiness impacting on the Jewish people who caused all of this honor.
- This explains the response of R. Yishmael[64] who when requested by God: "Yishmael, My son, Bless Me," [did so with] "May it be Your Will that Your Mercy should overcome Your Anger . . . and You should conduct Yourself with your children out of mercy, and go beyond the letter of the law in judging them."[65]
- Refer to the Zohar:[66] R. Nechemia began, "and You shall eat and be satisfied and bless YHVH your God" . . . and R. Yudai said the power of Grace after Meals is great, as it adds power and blessing to the Heavenly assembly
    - and therefore Chazal say that anyone who eats without saying Grace is called a thief as per "he robs from his father and his mother" . . . with his father being none other than God . . .[67]
    - as he robs and holds back from the worlds, the bestowal of blessing and holiness which he was required to impact upon them with his blessing.
- Similarly, all the verses [referring to blessing] express the same idea, for example:
    - "My soul should bless God." [68]
    - "Blessed are you God, God of Israel. . . ."[69]
- [This idea is also expressed] from the perspective of God's Will to connect with Creation about which it says: "Our service fulfills the needs of the Most High."[70]

Rabbi Chaim's Note:
Note 21 – Prayer focus on Unified Essence of God but not specific Sefirot

- In connection with that which was written in relation to intention in prayer and blessings[71]
    - to focus during each blessing on a specific intention and on a specific Sefira

---

64 See G2:02.
65 Berachot 7a.
66 Zohar Chadash II Rut 45b quoting Devarim 8:10.
67 Zohar Chadash II Rut 45b and Berachot 35b.
68 Tehillim 103:2.
69 1 Divrei Hayamim 29:10.

- מֵעַצְמוּתוֹ יִתְבָּרֵךְ הַמִּתְחַבֵּר אֲלֵיהֶם וּמִתְפַּשֵּׁט בְּתוֹכָם
- וּמִמֵּילָא יָשְׁפַּע זֶה הַתּוֹסֶפֶת בְּרָכָה וְהַקְּדֻשָּׁה גַּם עַל עַם סְגֻלָּה שֶׁגָּרְמוּ וְסִבְּבוּ לְכָל הַכָּבוֹד הַזֶּה:

- וְזֶה שֶׁאָמַר רַבִּי יִשְׁמָעֵאל, כְּשֶׁבִּקֵּשׁ הוּא יִתְבָּרֵךְ מֵאִתּוֹ, "יִשְׁמָעֵאל בְּנִי בָּרְכֵנִי", "יְהִי רָצוֹן שֶׁיִּכְבְּשׁוּ רַחֲמֶיךָ אֶת כַּעַסְךָ, וְיָגֹלּוּ רַחֲמֶיךָ כו', וְתִתְנַהֵג עִם בָּנֶיךָ בְּמִדַּת הָרַחֲמִים, וְתִכָּנֵס לָהֶם לִפְנִים מִשּׁוּרַת הַדִּין" (ברכות ז, א) :

- וְעַיֵּן זֹהַר חָדָשׁ רוּת מ"ה ב', "רַבִּי נְחֶמְיָה פָּתַח, "וְאָכַלְתָּ גו', וּבֵרַכְתָּ אֶת ה' אֱלֹהֶיךָ גו'" (דברים ח, י), וְאָמַר רַבִּי יוּדָא "גָּדוֹל כֹּחַ בִּרְכַּת הַמָּזוֹן שֶׁמּוֹסִיף כֹּחַ בְּרָכָה בְּפָמַלְיָא שֶׁל מַעְלָה".

- וְלָכֵן אָמְרוּ רַבּוֹתֵינוּ זִכְרוֹנָם לִבְרָכָה (ברכות לה: ר"פ כֵּיצַד מְבָרְכִין) וּבְזֹהַר חָדָשׁ שָׁם, "כָּל הָאוֹכֵל וְאֵינוֹ מְבָרֵךְ נִקְרָא גַּזְלָן, שֶׁנֶּאֱמַר "גּוֹזֵל אָבִיו וְאִמּוֹ" גו', וְאֵין אָבִיו אֶלָּא הַקָּדוֹשׁ בָּרוּךְ הוּא כו'

- כִּי הוּא גּוֹזֵל וּמוֹנֵעַ מֵהָעוֹלָמוֹת — שִׁפְעַת הַבְּרָכָה וְהַקְּדֻשָּׁה, שֶׁהָיָה צָרִיךְ לְהַשְׁפִּיעַ בָּהֶם עַל יְדֵי בִּרְכָתוֹ:

- וְכֵן כָּל הַמִּקְרָאוֹת
  - "בָּרְכִי נַפְשִׁי אֶת ה'" (תהלים קג)
- "בָּרוּךְ אַתָּה ה' אֱלֹהֵי יִשְׂרָאֵל" גו' (דה"י א' כט, י), וְכָל כַּיּוֹצֵא בּוֹ, הַכֹּל הוּא עַל זֶה הָעִנְיָן:

- וּמִצַּד רְצוֹנוֹ יִתְבָּרֵךְ לְהִתְחַבֵּר אֶל הַבְּרִיאָה, עַל זֶה נֶאֱמַר (עי' מנחות סד. שבת קטז:) "הָעֲבוֹדָה צֹרֶךְ גָּבוֹהַּ":

הַגָּהָה כ"א

- וּמַה שֶּׁכָּתְבוּ בְּכַוָּנוֹת הַתְּפִלָּה וְהַבְּרָכוֹת
  - לְכַוֵּן בְּכָל בְּרָכָה כַּוָּנָה מְיֻחֶדֶת לִסְפִירָה מְיֻחֶדֶת

---

70 Menachot 64a; Shabbat 116b. This expression is also used at the end of G1:09 (see p. 186, fn. 249) and G2:10.

71 This is relating to the writings of the Arizal e.g., in Pri Etz Chaim Shaar HaBerachot where descriptions are given for intentional focus on specific Sefirot during the recitation of blessings and prayer.

- ○ this does not mean the essence of the Sefira, God forbid, as this would be 'a chopping down the saplings of the orchard,'[72] God forbid.
- Just as it is with the service of an offering, about which Chazal say: Come and see what is written about the offerings, as they do not refer to *El* or *Elokim* – but just to *YHVH* – so that no excuse exists for anyone to dispute [to whom the offering was being offered].[73]
  - ○ As per the verse: "One who sacrifices to gods/*Elohim* will be excommunicated, apart from [one who sacrifices] to God/*YHVH* alone."[74] Refer to G3:09.
- Similarly, it is with the service of prayer
  - ○ That, God forbid, should one focus on any specific power or Sefira apart from the Unified Infinite Essence of the Master, who incorporates all the powers
  - ○ who connects with His Will, for reasons known only to Him, to engage a specific Sefira and its associated power which are within the sequence of the cascading down [of His Essence] that He established with His Will
  - ○ with each Sefira corresponding to a specific detail through which this detail is manifest in the worlds.
  - ○ (Refer to the She'elot U'Teshuvot HaRivash and the answer relating to this issue of the Chacham Don Yosef Ibn Shoshan to the Rivash,[75] but our explanation provides a better answer – understand this.)[76]
  - ○ Refer to the language of the Arizal mentioned above at the end of G2:02.[77]

---

72   This expression is borrowed from Chagiga 14b and 15a where it is used in relation to the sage known as "Acher" who entered into the *Pardes*, the orchard of mystical knowledge, and did damage there.
73   Menachot 110a and Sifri Bamidbar Pinchas Piska 143.
74   Shemot 22:19.
75   She'elot U'Teshuvot HaRivash Siman 157:
   - I [the Rivash] once asked him [Chacham Don Yosef Ibn Shoshan] how the Kabbalists could focus each blessing on a different Sefira? Furthermore is there Godliness in the Sefirot that [requires] a person to pray to them? He answered me that, God forbid, should prayer ever be directed to anything apart from God, the Cause of all causes, but this matter is analogous to someone involved in an argument who asks the king to adjudicate and requests of the king to command his chief justice to sit in judgment, he does not ask the king to command this of his finance minister as that would be an erroneous request, and similarly, if he asked the king for financial support he would not request that he command the judge but rather the finance minister, and similarly, if he requires wine from [the king] he requests that

- לֹא חַס וְשָׁלוֹם לְעַצְמוּת הַסְּפִירָה, כִּי הוּא קִצּוּץ נְטִיעוֹת חַס וְשָׁלוֹם:

- כִּי כְּמוֹ שֶׁבְּעִנְיַן עֲבוֹדַת הַקָּרְבָּן — אָמְרוּ רַבּוֹתֵינוּ זִכְרוֹנָם לִבְרָכָה בַּבְּרַיְתָא סוֹף מְנָחוֹת (קי.), וְהוּא מֵהַסִּפְרֵי פָּרָשַׁת פִּנְחָס, "בֹּא וּרְאֵה מַה כָּתִיב בְּפָרָשַׁת קָרְבָּנוֹת, שֶׁלֹּא נֶאֱמַר בָּהֶן לֹא "אֵ־ל", וְלֹא "אֱ־לֹקִים", אֶלָּא "הֲוָי"ה", שֶׁלֹּא לִיתֵּן פִּתְחוֹן פֶּה לְבַעַל הַדִּין לַחֲלֹק".

- וּכְמוֹ שֶׁכָּתוּב (שמות כב, יט) "זֹבֵחַ לָאֱלֹהִים יָחֳרָם בִּלְתִּי לַה' לְבַדּוֹ", וְעַיֵּן לְהַלָּן בְּשַׁעַר ג' פֶּרֶק ט':

- כֵּן בַּעֲבוֹדַת הַתְּפִלָּה

- חָלִילָה לְכַוֵּן לָשׂוּם לְשׁוּם כֹּחַ פְּרָטִי וּסְפִירָה מְיֻחֶדֶת, אֶלָּא לְעַצְמוּת אָדוֹן יָחִיד אֵין סוֹף בָּרוּךְ הוּא, כְּלַל הַכֹּחוֹת כֻּלָּם

- שֶׁמִּתְחַבֵּר בִּרְצוֹנוֹ יִתְבָּרַךְ, מִטַּעַם הַכָּמוּס אֶצְלוֹ יִתְבָּרַךְ, לִפְעֹל בְּאוֹתָהּ סְפִירָה וְאוֹתוֹ הַכֹּחַ שֶׁהֵם בְּסֵדֶר הַהִשְׁתַּלְשְׁלוּת שֶׁקָּבַע הוּא יִתְבָּרַךְ, בִּרְצוֹנוֹ

- שֶׁכָּל סְפִירָה מְיֻחֶדֶת לְעִנְיָן פְּרָטִי, שֶׁעַל יָדָהּ פּוֹעֵל עִנְיָן זֶה בָּעוֹלָמוֹת.

- (וְעַיֵּן בִּתְשׁוּבַת רִיב"ש סִימָן קנ"ז, אֲשֶׁר הֵשִׁיב הר"י ן' שׁוּשָׁן בָּזֶה לְהָרִיב"ש ז"ל, וְלִדְבָרֵינוּ אֵלֶּה יִתְיַשֵּׁב יוֹתֵר, וְהָבֵן).

- וְעַיֵּן בִּלְשׁוֹן הָאֲרִ"י זִכְרוֹנוֹ לִבְרָכָה שֶׁהִזְכַּרְנוּ בִּפְנִים לְעֵיל סוֹף פֶּרֶק ב'

[the king] command this of his butler, and if he asks for bread the instruction should be given to [the king's] baker and not the reverse. This is similarly the case in relation to prayer, which is always [to be focused on God,] the Cause of all causes, but one should focus one's thoughts on drawing down bestowal [from God] to the specific Sefira which relates to the particular matter requested, for example, in the blessing [in the Amida] of "In connection with the Righteous" one should focus on the Sefira of Chesed which is the attribute of Mercy and in the blessing of "The Apostates" one should focus on the Sefira of Gevurah which is the attribute of Judgment, and be particular about this.

76 R. Chaim's answer fuses the Sefirot together with God such that a prayer request focusing on a particular Sefira, which represents a specific way in which God connects with and is manifest within the world, is not in any way to be considered as being anything other than a direct request of God. In contrast, the answer of Chacham Don Yosef Ibn Shoshan to the Rivash, while highlighting that all prayer is only to be focused on God, nevertheless gives scope to view the Sefirot as having some dimension of differentiated existence from God. Therefore, R. Chaim's explanation is better.

77 I.e., that all names and descriptions of God refer to His Essence as it is manifest in the levels of the Sefirot.

- Also refer to the Tikkunim:[78] And He is called by all [manner of] names etc ... to show each member of Israel from which place He can be called according to their need, etc. Refer there.
- Similarly, as per Tikkunim referenced in G2:03:[79] To show each limb ... to inform man [how the world works] so that he should know how to call Him with each limb as appropriate.
- This is as written in the Zohar:[80] One can ask, why do we pray to God on multiple levels? Sometimes praying to Him with a specific Sefira and [relating to] a specific character trait; sometimes praying to the right, [as stated that one who wants to become wise should go south,[81] that is, to focus on the Menora in the Mishkan]; sometimes praying to the left, [as stated that one who wants to become rich should go north,[82] that is, to focus on the Shulchan in the Mishkan], and sometimes to the central pillar [that is, to the combination of right/left of Chesed and Gevurah together] ... Each prayer ascends to a specific level, but it certainly is that YHVH is manifest within each Sefira ... at a time when He wants to be merciful to the world it ascends to the right, etc ... Everything is for the sake of YHVH which is manifest in every place.
- As per Sifri on the verse "like God, Our God [who is close] with all who call *Him*,"[83] that is *to Him* and not to his characteristics.[84]

5. SHIUR KOMAH – MAN'S STRUCTURE REFLECTS GOD'S STRUCTURE

- However, [we need] to understand[85] the essence of
  - the *addition* and *increase* in blessing in the worlds through man's actions
  - and the essential concept of why the worlds have a need for this.
- Chazal say that the five statements of "bless my soul" were said by David relating to both God and to man's soul. (Note 22)[86] Just as God fills the entire Universe, so too does a man's soul fill his entire body, etc.[87]

---

78 Tikkunei Zohar Tikkun 22 64b.
79 Tikkunei Zohar Tikkun 70 122b.
80 Zohar Chadash Tikkunim II 80b.
81 Bava Batra 25b.
82 Bava Batra 25b.
83 Devarim 4:7.
84 This Sifri was not found anywhere in the currently available version. It appears that this comment on this section of Parshat VaEtchanan is missing and there

נֶפֶשׁ שַׁעַר ב' - פֶּרֶק ה' הַחַיִּים

- וְעַיֵּן עוֹד בְּתִקּוּנִים תכ"ב ס"ד ב', וְאִיהוּ אִתְקְרֵי בְּכָל שְׁמָהָן כו', לְאַחֲזָאָה לְכָל חַד מִיִּשְׂרָאֵל מֵאֲתָר דְּקָרְאָן לֵיהּ, לְפוּם צָרְכֵיהוֹן כו', עַיֵּן שָׁם.

- וְכֵן בת"ע הַנִּזְכָּר בִּפְנִים אָמְרוּ, לְאַחֲזָאָה בְּכָל אֵבֶר כו', לְאִשְׁתְּמוֹדְעָא לְבַר נַשׁ, וִידַע לְמִקְרֵי לֵיהּ בְּכָל אֵבֶר כִּדְקָא יָאוּת.

- וְזֶה שֶׁכָּתוּב בְּתִקּוּנֵי ז"ח דַּף פ' ע"ב, וְאִית לְמִשְׁאַל, לָמָּה מַצְלָאִין לְקוּדְשָׁא בְּרִיךְ הוּא בְּכַמָּה דַּרְגִּין, זִמְנִין מַצְלִין לֵיהּ בִּסְפִירָה יְדִיעָא וּבְמִדָּה יְדִיעָא, זִמְנִין צְלוֹתָא לִימִינָא כו', זִמְנִין לִשְׂמָאלָא כו', זִמְנִין לַעֲמוּדָא דְּאֶמְצָעִיתָא כו'. כָּל צְלוֹתָא סַלְקָא לְדַרְגָּא יְדִיעָא, אֶלָּא וַדַּאי הֲוָיָ"ה אִיהוּ בְּכָל סְפִירָה וּסְפִירָה כו', בְּזִמְנָא דְּבָעֵי לְרַחֲמָא עַל עָלְמָא סַלְקָא לִימִינָא, וּבְזִמְנָא דְּבָעֵי כו', וְכֹלָּא לְגַבֵּי הֲוָיָ"ה דְּאִיהוּ בְּכָל אֲתַר כו'.

- וְזֶה שֶׁאָמְרוּ רַבּוֹתֵינוּ זִכְרוֹנָם לִבְרָכָה בְּסִפְרֵי (דברים ה, ז) "כַּה' אֱלֹקֵינוּ בְּכָל קָרְאֵנוּ אֵלָיו", "אֵלָיו" וְלֹא לְמִדּוֹתָיו.

שַׁעַר ב' - פֶּרֶק ה'

- אָמְנָם, לְהָבִין עִקָּרוֹ שֶׁל
  - עִנְיַן הַתּוֹסֶפֶת וְרִבּוּי בְּרָכָה בְּהָעוֹלָמוֹת — עַל יְדֵי מַעֲשֵׂי הָאָדָם
  - וּמַהוּת הָעִנְיָן צֹרֶךְ הָעוֹלָמוֹת לָזֶה:

- הִנֵּה רַבּוֹתֵינוּ זִכְרוֹנָם לִבְרָכָה אָמְרוּ (ברכות י, א) "הָנֵי חֲמִשָּׁה "בָּרְכִי נַפְשִׁי", כְּנֶגֶד

---

may be another version which includes it which is not currently extant. The earliest quotation found for this Sifri is in Pardes Rimonim 32:2.

85   This understanding is explained over the coming chapters.

86   **R. Chaim adds Note 22 here.** This note is brought at the end of this chapter and is entitled "Analogy of God in World to soul in body is absolutely not literal."

87   Berachot 10a, which continues:
- Just as God sees but is not seen, so too the soul sees but is not seen. Just as God sustains the whole world, so too the soul sustains the whole body. Just as God is pure, so too the soul is pure. Just as God resides in inner chambers, so too the soul resides in inner chambers. The one who has these five things [i.e., man] should come and praise the One Who has these five things [i.e., God. These five things are referenced by the five statements of "bless my soul" by King David].

- This is as similarly stated in the Midrash[88] and Zohar.[89] Refer to Etz Chaim.[90]
- This is reflected in statements of Chazal:
  - That all images are permitted except for a human image,[91] explaining that the verse "Do not make [images of what is] *with Me*"[92] means do not make [an image] "*of Me*."
  - This is similarly stated in the Zohar.[93]
  - "For there is a man who labored with wisdom, [knowledge and skill]."[94] R. Yudan said: Great is the ability of the prophets who can describe the Creator in terms of *form*, as it says, "I heard a human voice in the middle of the Ulai."[95] R. Yehuda bar Simon said: We have a Scriptural verse which more clearly states this point as it says,[96] "and on the image of the Throne there is the image of the appearance of man."[97]
  - "Man's wisdom lights up his face."[98] R. Yudan said: Great is the ability of the prophets who can describe God in human terms.[99] Refer there.
- However this appears to contradict the concept expressed in the verse "and to whom can God be compared?"[100]

---

88 Vayikra Rabba Vayikra 4:8, Devarim Rabba VaEtchanan 2:37, Midrash Tehillim 103:4.

89 Tikkunei Zohar Tikkun 13 28a, Zohar Raya Mehemna III Pinchas 257b/258a (This Zohar is quoted in G3:02 and also referenced in G2:03).

90 Etz Chaim Shaar 40, Shaar Pnimiut VeChitzoniut, end of Derush 11:
- In each world, there is an inner essence and an external presentation . . . and know that the inner essence of each and every one of these 5 worlds [i.e., Adam Kadmon, Atzilut, Beriyah, Yetzirah, and Asiyah] is the Yechida, Chaya, Neshama, Ruach, and Nefesh of that world itself [i.e., its soul], and the external presentation of [each world] are vessels and the body in which these soul elements are manifest within . . . and within all of them is the Light of the Ein Sof [i.e., the absolute manifestation of God] . . . and this alone is within them forming their absolute inner essence.

91 Rosh Hashana 24b; Avodah Zarah 43b, reflecting the fact that the Human image mirrors God's image.

92 Shemot 20:20.

93 Zohar II Yitro 86a:
- Jews are referred to as "man" and are complete as they accepted the Torah, in contrast with Yishmael who are referred to as "wild man" (Bereishit 16:12), as they did not accept the Torah. It is written that "God's people are a part of Him, Yaakov is the cord of His possession" (Devarim 32:9). R. Yossi said that it is clear that [therefore] all images are permitted except of

מִי אֲמָרָן דָוִד, לֹא אֲמָרָן אֶלָּא כְּנֶגֶד הַקָּדוֹשׁ בָּרוּךְ הוּא וּכְנֶגֶד הַנְּשָׁמָה, (הגהה כ"ב) מַה הַקָּדוֹשׁ בָּרוּךְ הוּא מָלֵא כָּל הָעוֹלָם — אַף הַנְּשָׁמָה מְלָאָה כָּל הַגּוּף" כו':

• וְכֵן אָמְרוּ בְּוַיִּקְרָא רַבָּה פָּרָשָׁה ד', וּדְבָרִים רַבָּה סוֹף פָּרָשָׁה ב', וּבְמִדְרַשׁ תְּהִלִּים מִזְמוֹר ק"ג, וּבַתִּקּוּנִים רֵישׁ תִּקּוּן י"ג, וּכְמוֹ שֶׁבֵּאֵר בְּרַעְיָא מְהֵימְנָא פָּרָשַׁת פִּנְחָס רנ"ז ב' ורנ"ח א'. וְעַיֵּן בְּעֵץ חַיִּים שַׁעַר פְּנִימִיּוּת וְחִיצוֹנִיּוּת סוֹף דְּרוּשׁ י"א:

• וְזֶה שֶׁאָמְרוּ רַבּוֹתֵינוּ זִכְרוֹנָם לִבְרָכָה

 ○ בְּמַסֶּכֶת רֹאשׁ הַשָּׁנָה (כה, ב) וּבַעֲבוֹדָה זָרָה (מג, ב) בַּבָּרַיְתָא, כָּל הַפַּרְצוּפוֹת מֻתָּרִים חוּץ מִפַּרְצוּף אָדָם, וּמְפָרֵשׁ טַעֲמָא דִכְתִיב (שמות כ, כ) "לֹא תַעֲשׂוּן אִתִּי" — לֹא תַעֲשׂוּן אוֹתִי.

 ○ וְכֵן מָצִינוּ בַּזֹּהַר יִתְרוֹ פ"ו סוֹף ע"א, עַיֵּן שָׁם.

 ○ וּבִבְרֵאשִׁית רַבָּה רֵישׁ פָּרָשָׁה כ"ז אָמְרוּ, כְּתִיב (קהלת ב, כא) "כִּי יֵשׁ אָדָם שֶׁעֲמָלוֹ בְּחָכְמָה" ג', אָמַר רַבִּי יוּדָן גָּדוֹל כֹּחָן שֶׁל נְבִיאִים שֶׁמְּדַמִּין צוּרָה לְיוֹצְרָהּ, שֶׁנֶּאֱמַר (דניאל ח, טז) "וָאֶשְׁמַע קוֹל אָדָם בֵּין אוּלָי", אָמַר רַבִּי יְהוּדָה ב"ר סִימוֹן אִית לָן קַרְיָא אוֹחֳרָן דִּמְחַוַּר יַתִּיר מִן דֵּין, שֶׁנֶּאֱמַר (יחזקאל א, כו) "וְעַל דְּמוּת הַכִּסֵּא דְּמוּת כְּמַרְאֵה אָדָם" ג'.

 ○ וּבְבַמִּדְבַּר רַבָּה פָּרָשָׁה י"ט "חָכְמַת אָדָם תָּאִיר פָּנָיו" (קהלת ח, א), אָמַר רַבִּי יוּדָן גָּדוֹל כֹּחָן שֶׁל נְבִיאִים שֶׁמְּדַמִּין דְּמוּת גְּבוּרָה שֶׁל מַעְלָה לְצוּרַת אָדָם כוּ', עַיֵּן שָׁם. וְכֵן הוּא בְּקֹהֶלֶת רַבָּה סִימָן ח' פָּסוּק א', וּבְתַנְחוּמָא פָּרָשַׁת חֻקַּת:

• וְלִכְאוֹרָה יִפָּלֵא, כִּי "אֶל מִי תְדַמְּיוּן" (ישעיה מ, יח) וְגוֹ'.

---

man [i.e., of Jews who are a part of God and therefore their image is like an image of God].

94 Kohelet 2:21.
95 Daniel 8:16. Rashi explains that voice came from the Ulai river. The understanding is that the voice of God took on human form.
96 Yechezkel 1:26.
97 Bereishit Rabba Bereishit 27:1. This Midrash continues to provide further Scriptural sources which describe God in terms of human form and in particular in terms of wisdom, knowledge, and skill.
98 Kohelet 8:1. In the context of this chapter, "his face" can be read to simultaneously refer to both man and God.
99 Bamidbar Rabba Chukat 19:4; Kohelet Rabba 8:1; Midrash Tanchuma Chukat 6, with all of these sources continuing as per the quotation from Bereishit Rabba, i.e., quoting the verse from Yechezkel 1:26.
100 Yishayahu 40:18.

- ○ But the idea is as stated above (at the end of G2:03), that our entire perception of God, so to speak, is purely in terms of His *connection* to the worlds
- ○ and the sequential [interconnected] state of all the worlds and powers – incorporating the supernal and the lower worlds together
- ○ follows the arrangement, so to speak, in all of their detail, of the structure of man
- ○ which is reflected through the arrangement and unified interconnectivity of all of man's joints of his limbs, sinews, and all of his details[101]
- ○ as [man] incorporates all the powers and the worlds together within him, as explained above in the First Gateway.
- This is the concept of the Shiur Komah[102] which is mentioned in Chazal's statements and the Midrashim.
  - ○ Refer to Etz Chaim[103] where it is written there that this concept is hinted to in the verse[104] "and Elokim created man in His Image, in the image of Elokim. . . ." Also refer to other references in Etz Chaim.[105]
  - ○ God's Essence is distributed throughout and concealed within all of them [the entire Shiur Komah], filling them – He Is their Soul – like a soul which is distributed throughout and concealed within a person's body, so to speak

---

101 Also reflected in Chazal's statement that "man is a microcosm," as per Midrash Tanchuma Pekudei 3.
102 See G1:06.
103 The following quotations from Etz Chaim are very cryptic but convey the parallel of God's and man's similar structure.
Etz Chaim Shaar 1, Shaar Igulim VeYosher, parts 2/3/4 [a small section from part 2 is brought here]:
- Now we will explain the second level of the Ten Sefirot which is on the level of the light of *Yosher* which is analogous to the three lines which form the image of Supernal Man . . . [at all levels of manifestation from supernal to lower levels, this structure is] comprised of the Ten Sefirot in the *Secret of upright man of stature/Komah* made up of 248 limbs . . . [Yosher/upright is a property of emanation of God's light and is analogous to the structure of an upright man.]

Etz Chaim Shaar 1, Shaar Igulim VeYosher, at the end of this Shaar in the second edition (at the end of part 2):
- . . . in the middle of all of Atzilut, this *Igul* is manifest through straight lines like the light of *Igul* except that it is in *Yosher* and it has the level of [all of the Partzufim, i.e., forming a specific connected structure], and it is this level which the Torah calls "the man in His Image, in the Image of God". . . .

104 Bereishit 1:27.

נפש שער ב' - פרק ה' החיים

- אָמְנָם הָעִנְיָן כְּמוֹ שֶׁכָּתַבְתִּי לְעֵיל (סוֹף ג'), שֶׁכָּל הַשָּׁגָתֵנוּ כִּבְיָכוֹל אוֹתוֹ יִתְבָּרַךְ שְׁמוֹ, הוּא רַק מִצַּד הִתְחַבְּרוּתוֹ יִתְבָּרַךְ לְהָעוֹלָמוֹת.
- וְסֵדֶר מַצַּב הָעוֹלָמוֹת וְהַכֹּחוֹת כֻּלָּם, הָעֶלְיוֹנִים וְתַחְתּוֹנִים יַחַד בִּכְלָל מְסֻדָּרִים כִּבְיָכוֹל בְּכָל פְּרָטֵיהֶם כְּתַבְנִית קוֹמַת אָדָם
- בְּסִדּוּר כָּל פִּרְקֵי אֵבָרָיו וְגִידָיו וְכָל פְּרָטֵי הָעִנְיָנִים שֶׁבּוֹ וְהִתְאַחֲדוּתָם אֶחָד בַּחֲבֵרוֹ
- שֶׁהוּא כּוֹלְלָם יַחַד בְּתוֹכוֹ כָּל הַכֹּחוֹת וְהָעוֹלָמוֹת, כְּמוֹ שֶׁנִּתְבָּאֵר לְעֵיל בְּשַׁעַר א':
- וְהוּא עִנְיָן "הַשִּׁעוּר קוֹמָה" — הַנִּזְכָּר בְּדִבְרֵיהֶם זִכְרוֹנָם לִבְרָכָה בַּמִּדְרָשִׁים.
- וְעַיֵּן בְּעֵץ חַיִּים שַׁעַר עִגּוּלִים וְיֹשֶׁר עָנָף ב' וְג' וד' שָׁם, וְשָׁם בְּסוֹף הַשַּׁעַר בְּרֵישׁ מַהַדּוּרָא תִּנְיָנָא. וְכָתַב שָׁם שֶׁזֶּה רֶמֶז הַכָּתוּב (בראשית א, כז) "וַיִּבְרָא אֱלֹקִים אֶת הָאָדָם בְּצַלְמוֹ בְּצֶלֶם אֱלֹקִים". וְעַיֵּן עוֹד בְּרֵישׁ שַׁעַר הַצֶּלֶם, וּבְשַׁעַר צִיּוּר עוֹלָמוֹת אֲבִי"עַ שָׁם.
- וְעַצְמוּתוֹ יִתְבָּרַךְ מִתְפַּשֵּׁט וּמִסְתַּתֵּר בְּתוֹךְ כֻּלָּם, וּמְמַלְּאָם, וְהוּא נִשְׁמָתָא דִלְהוֹן, כִּבְיָכוֹל כְּעִנְיַן הַנְּשָׁמָה הַמִּתְפַּשֶּׁטֶת וּמִסְתַּתֶּרֶת בְּגוּף הָאָדָם

---

105 More cryptic sources in Etz Chaim. It is important to note that these comparisons between the structure of man and of the Universe are not just anthropomorphic analogies but that they, in a very subtle way, genuinely capture the connection between the structure of man and that of the Universe. Etz Chaim Shaar 26, Shaar HaTzelem, beginning of Chap. 1:

- The concept of *Tzelem/Image* in truth as it appears to me: Supernal Man has 5 levels of form with each one contained within the other. They are Nefesh, Ruach, Neshama, Chaya, and Yechida. They have a level of substance in which they are manifest which is called a body and vessels . . . however it is not possible for *form* to be manifest within *substance* without a medium. It transpires that there are 5 types of garments [connected via a medium with] the 5 forms, and this is the Tzelem/image of Nefesh, the Tzelem of Ruach, etc . . . and it is not possible for any *form* of these 5 forms to be manifest within the body until they have [first] been manifest within their specific *image*, and the collective of these 5 *images* is called "image of man" but it is not the essence of man, and the 5 *forms* are called the "essential soul of man," and the collective of the vessels . . . are called the body of man . . .

Etz Chaim Shaar 43, Shaar Tziyur Olamot ABY"A, Chap. 1:

- . . . and as a result this earth must be composed from the Ten [Sefirot], and it is the form of the One Man. Therefore, the earth has a mouth, ears. . . .

- ○ Therefore, [Chazal] permitted us to describe God [specifically] in this way. (Note 23)[106]
- ○ The Rambam also writes[107] that the whole world in general is called Shiur Komah, and he compares the components of the world at length – to the components of the limbs of a person and all within him – and that God is the Soul of the world in a similar way to the way that a soul relates to a person's body. Refer there.
  - ▫ His [the Rambam's] words are fitting for he who said them, as are similarly explained in the Zohar.[108] Refer there.
  - ▫ From his words, we can understand the interconnected arrangement of all the worlds.
- • We see this idea frequently reflected in statements of Chazal, that man reflects the facial image of God, for example:
  - ○ "His body should not remain [the night on the gallows] ... for a hanging person is a curse of God." R. Meir said: What can this be compared to? To twin brothers ... one is appointed as the king and the other becomes a highwayman. The king commanded that the highwayman be hanged, and all who see this say that it is the king who has been hanged.[109]
    - ▫ Rashi explains: Man is made in the image of God (Makom).
  - ○ "One who strikes a person who then dies" [What caused his death? That he did not look in the Torah where it is written that "Whoever sheds a man's blood, his blood shall be shed by man"]. This is compared to a person who beats the image of the king ... The king said ... "and anyone who damages my image will perish." Similarly, one who murders a Jew ... is as if he has ignored the image of the King.[110] The reason for this is as stated at the end of the verse "For man was made in the image of God."[111]

---

106 **R. Chaim adds Note 23 here.** This note is brought at the end of this chapter and is entitled "God/man's descriptions relate to their connection with worlds."
107 Moreh HaNevuchim I Chap. 72. The term "Shiur Komah" is not used there, but the same concept is related to.
108 Zohar I Toldot 134b:
- • Come and see. One who exerts himself with Torah, he maintains the existence of the Universe with each and every action if properly performed, and there is no limb which a person has which does not have a corresponding

לָכֵן הִרְשֵׁינוּ לְתָאֲרוֹ יִתְבָּרַךְ עַל זֶה הָאֹפֶן. (הגהה כ"ג)

וְגַם הָרַמְבַּ"ם זִכְרוֹנוֹ לִבְרָכָה כָּתַב בַּמּוֹרֶה בְּפֶרֶק ע"ב מֵחֵלֶק הא', שֶׁכָּל זֶה הָעוֹלָם בִּכְלָלוֹ נִקְרָא "שִׁעוּר קוֹמָה", וְהֶאֱרִיךְ לְהַמְשִׁיל כְּלָל חֶלְקֵי הָעוֹלָם לְחֶלְקֵי אֵבְרֵי הָאָדָם וְכָל עִנְיָנָיו שֶׁבּוֹ, וְשֶׁהוּא יִתְבָּרַךְ הוּא נִשְׁמַת הָעוֹלָם כְּעִנְיַן הַנְּשָׁמָה לְגוּף הָאָדָם עַיֵּן שָׁם

וּדְבָרָיו זִכְרוֹנוֹ לִבְרָכָה רְאוּיִים לְמִי שֶׁאֲמָרָם, שֶׁכֵּן מְבֹאָר בַּזֹּהַר (תולדות קל"ד ע"ב) עַיֵּן שָׁם.

וּמִדְּבָרָיו זִכְרוֹנוֹ לִבְרָכָה נִשְׁמַע לְדִידָן, לְעִנְיַן סֵדֶר כְּלַל הָעוֹלָמוֹת כֻּלָּם יַחַד:

וְשָׁגוּרָה בְּפִי רַבּוֹתֵינוּ זִכְרוֹנָם לִבְרָכָה שֶׁהָאָדָם הוּא אִיקוֹנִין וּדְיוֹקָן מַלְכּוּ שֶׁל עוֹלָם יִתְבָּרַךְ שְׁמוֹ, כְּמוֹ שֶׁאָמְרוּ

בְּסַנְהֶדְרִין (מו, א' וב') "לֹא תָלִין נִבְלָתוֹ גו' כִּי קִלְלַת אֱלֹהִים תָּלוּי" (דברים כא, כג) תַּנְיָא אָמַר רַבִּי מֵאִיר, מָשָׁל לְמָה הַדָּבָר דּוֹמֶה, לִשְׁנֵי אַחִים תְּאוֹמִים כו', אֶחָד מִנּוּהוּ מֶלֶךְ וְאֶחָד יָצָא לְלִסְטִיּוּת, צִוָּה הַמֶּלֶךְ וּתְלָאוּהוּ, כָּל הָרוֹאֶה אוֹתוֹ אוֹמֵר, הַמֶּלֶךְ תָּלוּי כו'

וּפֵרֵשׁ רַשִׁ"י, אַף אָדָם עָשׂוּי בִּדְיוֹקָנוֹ שֶׁל מָקוֹם.

וּבִשְׁמוֹת רַבָּה פָּרָשָׁה ל' (טז), "מַכֵּה אִישׁ וָמֵת" (שמות כא. יב) וגו', מָשָׁל לְאָדָם שֶׁקָּפַח אִיקוֹנִין שֶׁל מֶלֶךְ כו', אָמַר הַמֶּלֶךְ לֹא קְרָאתָ כו', שֶׁכָּל מִי שֶׁהוּא נוֹגֵעַ בְּאִיקוֹנִין שֶׁלִּי הוּא אָבֵד, כָּךְ אִם הָרַג אָדָם נֶפֶשׁ כו' כְּאִלּוּ הוּא מַעֲבִיר אִיקוֹנִין שֶׁל מֶלֶךְ. רוֹצֶה לוֹמַר, זֶה שֶׁסִּיֵּם בְּסֵיפֵיהּ דִּקְרָא הַטַּעַם עַל זֶה "כִּי בְּצֶלֶם אֱלֹקִים עָשָׂה אֶת הָאָדָם":

---

creation in the Universe. As much as a person is comprised of individual limbs and they exist in a multitude of layers combining together to form a single body, similarly, all the creations of the Universe form its components and combine together as one entity, and it is all like the Torah as the Torah is comprised of components which together form one entity. . . .

109 Sanhedrin 46a–b quoting Devarim 21:23.
110 Shemot Rabba Mishpatim 30:16 quoting Shemot 21:12 and Bereishit 9:6.
111 End of the verse of Bereishit 9:6.

Rabbi Chaim's Notes:
Note 22 – Analogy of God in World to soul in body is absolutely not literal

- Notwithstanding the fact that Chazal analogously compare God's connection to the worlds with the connection of a soul to a body
    - the reader of their words should not make the mistake, God forbid, of taking the comparison literally, God forbid
    - as in reality there is not even any vague comparison that can be made between them at all.
- This is as explained in many places in the Zohar and Raya Mehemna and also in explicit Scriptural verses, [for example] "and to whom can God be compared."[112]
- Furthermore, anyone with understanding will appreciate that it is impossible to extrapolate comparisons from the creations and apply them to The Creator.
- Chazal only made the comparison of the soul's essence with God's Essence in the specific detail that
    - even though the soul is an ability which is created by God
    - nevertheless, it is impossible to perceive [the soul's] essence and to describe it in any way except from the perspective of its connection to the physical body.
    - [Therefore] how much more so that God can only be perceived from the perspective of His connection with the worlds.
- [This analogy] also conveys that since it is impossible to compare Him with any creation
    - as even the level of Supernal Keter is incomparable with the highest of all levels [of God's Essence][113]
    - and any attempt of comparison cannot be equated
    - this necessitates the choice of an analogy to a spiritual creation [the soul]
    - as per the idea expressed in the verse "It [the Torah] is more precious than precious stones"[114]
        - even though there isn't even any vague comparison between the Torah and precious stones
        - and this is the reason the verse itself concludes with "all your things cannot be compared to it."

Note 23 – God/man's descriptions relate to their connection with worlds

- This is the concept underpinning all descriptions of God mentioned in the Torah
    - [for example] eye, hand, leg, etc.

הגהה כ"ב

- וְעִם כִּי רַבּוֹתֵינוּ זִכְרוֹנָם לִבְרָכָה הִמְשִׁילוּ הִתְחַבְּרוּתוֹ יִתְבָּרֵךְ לְהָעוֹלָמוֹת, לְהִתְחַבְּרוּת הַנְּשָׁמָה לְהַגּוּף.
  - אַל יִטְעֶה חַס וְשָׁלוֹם הָרוֹאֶה דְּבָרֵיהֶם, שֶׁהַנִּמְשָׁל דּוֹמֶה לַמָּשָׁל חַס וְשָׁלוֹם
  - כִּי בֶּאֱמֶת אֵין עֲרָךְ וְדִמְיוֹן בֵּינֵיהֶם בְּשׁוּם אֹפֶן:

- כַּמְבֹאָר בַּזֹּהַר וּבְרַעְיָא מְהֵימְנָא בְּהַרְבֵּה מְקוֹמוֹת, וּמִקְרָא מָלֵא דִּבֶּר הַכָּתוּב (ישעיה מ, יח) "וְאֶל מִי תְדַמְּיוּן אֵל":

- וְגַם, כָּל מִי שֶׁעֵינֵי שֵׂכֶל לוֹ, יָבִין, שֶׁאִי אֶפְשָׁר לִיקַח דִּמְיוֹן מֵהַנִּבְרָאִים — עַל הַבּוֹרֵא יִתְבָּרֵךְ שְׁמוֹ:

- וְלֹא הִמְשִׁילוּ זִכְרוֹנָם לִבְרָכָה, עַצְמוּת הַנְּשָׁמָה — לְעַצְמוּת הַבּוֹרֵא יִתְבָּרֵךְ, רַק לְדָבָר זֶה דְּמוּ.
  - שֶׁאַף שֶׁהַנְּשָׁמָה הִיא כֹּחַ נִבְרָא מֵאִתּוֹ יִתְבָּרֵךְ
  - עִם כָּל זֶה, אִי אֶפְשָׁר לְהַשִּׂיג עַצְמוּתָהּ, לְכַנּוֹת לָהּ שׁוּם תֹּאַר וּפְעֻלָּה, אִם לֹא מִצַּד הִתְחַבְּרוּתָהּ לַגּוּף.
  - מִכָּל שֶׁכֵּן הַבּוֹרֵא יִתְבָּרֵךְ — שֶׁאֵין לְהַשִּׂיגוֹ רַק מִצַּד הִתְחַבְּרוּתוֹ לְהָעוֹלָמוֹת:

- וְגַם, הִיא הַנּוֹתֶנֶת, שֶׁמֵּאַחַר שֶׁאֵין לְהַמְשִׁילוֹ לְשׁוּם נִבְרָא
  - שֶׁגַּם "כֶּתֶר עֶלְיוֹן" אוּכְמָא אִיהוּ לְגַבֵּי "עִלַּת כָּל הָעִלּוֹת"
  - וּלְכֹל דָּבָר אֲשֶׁר יְדַמּוּ, לֹא יִשְׁוֶה
  - הֻכְרְחוּ לִבְחֹר דֶּרֶךְ דִּמְיוֹן לְאֵיזֶה נִבְרָא רוּחָנִי.
  - וּבְעִנְיַן הַכָּתוּב (משלי ג, טו) "יְקָרָה הִיא מִפְּנִינִים"
    - וְאַף שֶׁאֵין דִּמְיוֹן וְעֵרֶךְ בֵּין הַתּוֹרָה הַקְּדוֹשָׁה וְהַפְּנִינִים
    - לָזֶה סִיֵּם הַכָּתוּב עַצְמוֹ, הֲרֵי "כָּל חֲפָצֶיךָ לֹא יִשְׁווּ בָהּ":

הגהה כ"ג

- וְזֶה עִנְיַן כָּל הַתְּאָרִים הַנִּזְכָּרִים בַּתּוֹרָה עָלָיו יִתְבָּרֵךְ
  - עַיִן יָד וְרֶגֶל וְכַיּוֹצֵא

---

112 Yishayahu 40:18.
113 Lit., that Supernal Keter (which is the level just above the world of Atzilut) is *black* compared to (the radiance of) the highest of the high levels of God.
114 Mishlei 3:15.

- ○ [these descriptions] all relate to the perspective of [God's] connection to the worlds
- ○ for these [worlds] are arranged according to the arrangement of all of these limbs[115]
- ○ and these names encapsulate the essence of the powers and the worlds and are not simply descriptions.
- Similarly, this is also the case with man that these names are not simply descriptions.
  - ○ In addition, they also do not just indicate and hint to supernal hidden concepts
  - ○ as with a person's name which is an indication of the form and structure which is *labeled* with this name
  - ○ however, they [the references to eye, hand, leg, etc.] also encapsulate the essence of man's [structure] as he is made up of, refined from, and arranged in the form of the image of the structure of the worlds.
- Refer to:
  - ○ Moreh HaNevuchim.[116]
  - ○ Sefer Avodat HaKodesh.[117]

---

115   I.e., of the Shiur Komah.
116   Moreh HaNevuchim Part I, beginning of Chap. 26:
  - You already know what Chazal say that incorporates many explanations connected with our subject and that is their statement that "the Torah speaks in human terms" [e.g., Midrash Sechel Tov Bereishit 30:13]. This idea is that all that man can understand and form an image of within his thought, is fitting to be applied to The Creator. Therefore, He is described with descriptions of His physical manifestation to teach about Him that He exists. For the majority of people do not initially intellectually relate to their existence except in terms of a physical body, and they do not consider something which does not have a physical body, or is not connected with a body, to exist. Therefore, anything which we regard as a state of perfection is similarly attributed to God to teach about Him that He is absolutely perfect in every respect and that there is no imperfection or deficiency in Him at all. Anything that the majority of people relate to as an imperfection or deficiency is not used to describe Him. Therefore, He is not described as eating, drinking, sleeping, as being ill, violent, or anything similar. All that which is considered by the majority of people as a state of perfection is similarly attributed to Him even though that state of perfection only applies to ourselves. However, relative to God, all that which we consider as absolute perfection is absolutely deficient. But, if people were to imagine that those attributes of human perfection were absent from God, then they would consider Him imperfect.

- הַכֹּל מִצַּד הִתְחַבְּרוּתוֹ יִתְבָּרֵךְ לְהָעוֹלָמוֹת
- שֶׁהֵם מְסֻדָּרִים עַל זֶה הַסֵּדֶר בְּכָל אֵלּוּ הָאֵבָרִים
- וְהֵם שֵׁמוֹת עַצְמִיִּים לְהַכֹּחוֹת וְהָעוֹלָמוֹת, לֹא מֻשְׁאָלִים:

• וְכֵן גַּם בָּאָדָם, אֵינָם שֵׁמוֹת מֻשְׁאָלִים
- וְגַם לֹא שֶׁהֵם בָּאָדָם רַק לְסִימָן וְרֶמֶז לְהָעִנְיָנִים הָעֶלְיוֹנִים הַנֶּעְלָמִים
- כְּעִנְיַן הַשֵּׁם שֶׁל הָאָדָם, שֶׁהוּא סִימָן לְאוֹתָהּ הַצּוּרָה וְהַתַּבְנִית שֶׁהִסְכִּים לִקְרוֹתָהּ בְּזֶה הַשֵּׁם
- אֶלָּא שֶׁגַּם בָּאָדָם הֵם עַצְמִיִּים, כֵּיוָן שֶׁהוּא כָּלוּל וּמֻשְׁכָּל וּמְסֻדָּר בְּצֶלֶם דְּמוּת תַּבְנִית הָעוֹלָמוֹת:

• וְעַיֵּן
- בְּמוֹרֵה ח"א, וּבִפְרָטוּת בְּפֶרֶק כ"ו שָׁם
- וּבְסֵפֶר עֲבוֹדַת הַקֹּדֶשׁ פֶּרֶק כ"ו מֵחֵלֶק הַתַּכְלִית, וּמַה שֶּׁהִשִּׂיג עַל הָרַמְבַּ"ם בְּפֶרֶק ס"ה מִזֶּה הַחֵלֶק

---

117 Sefer Avodat HaKodesh (authored by R. Meir ben Gabai), Section 3, the Section of Purpose, Chap. 26:

• It is known from the path of wisdom and truth that the truth of His Essence is not perceivable to anything apart from Him, and there is no comparison between Him and all of His creations in the Supernal and Lower Realms, for He has no finite boundary as He has no body or power of a body. If so, what is the meaning of the physical references relating to the Master of All which are found in the Torah – for example hand, legs, ears, eyes, and apart from this the description of events which relate to a physical body [e.g., displaying anger, etc.]? One should know and believe . . . there is no creature that is able to know and perceive the essence of this matter which is referred to as a hand, leg, eye, or ear, and if we have been made in the image and form of Elokim . . . it should therefore not enter our minds, God forbid, that it is a literal eye or hand or the form of one is the same as the other . . . but that these [descriptions] relate to ultimately deep concepts regarding the truth of the existence of the Master of All from which light and bestowal disseminate and extend to all the creations, but that the essence of [His] hand is not like a [physical] hand and neither does it have the same structure, as per the verse "and to whom can God be compared and what likeness can you attribute to Him?" (Yishayahu 40:18). The faith in all of this is that there is no comparison between us and Him in terms of essence and structure apart from the intention of the form of the limbs within us which are made in a likeness, signifying and hinting to supernal

- Sefer Shaarei Orah.[118]
- Pardes Rimonim.[119]

> hidden things which no creation can know and perceive. This likeness is not physical . . . but is like the likeness of a reference, the analogy to this is with one written as "Reuven son of Yaakov" where these letters do no reflect the form and essence of [the person] Reuven, but rather this reference that this "Reuven son of Yaakov" as written down represents the known essence and structure that is called "Reuven son of Yaakov," and because God wanted to merit us, he created many hidden and revealed limbs within man's physical body as a likeness representing the *Act of the Merkava*, and if a person merits to purify one of his limbs then that limb will be a likeness of a receptacle for that supernal inner concept that is called by this name, whether it is an eye, hand, leg, and similarly with the other limbs. We have already explained in various places in this book that the purpose of man is to rectify [His] honor and it is for this purpose that he was made in the structure of the Supernal *Merkava*, to rectify it. This purpose will not be achieved at all except through Torah involvement and Mitzvah performance, and since this is the required activity, it can only be completed with the physical limbs through which man is transformed with this construction and this structure, and the supernal honor is also rectified through the secret of the image of man within which the Supernal and Lower Realms are incorporated, and because he incorporates all, the honor is rectified through his structure.

Sefer Avodat HaKodesh, Section 3, the Section of Purpose, Chap. 65:
- [This chapter repeats the vast majority of the details translated above from Chap. 26 and closes with the following comments . . .] The Torah mentions hands, legs, ears, and eyes with reference to God in order to enthuse the hearts of man to sanctify their hands, legs, eyes, and ears in [their performance of] Mitzvot so that they should [become] comparable to [God's] counterpart [limbs] to the extent that we should merit to cleave and connect together as a single entity with no separation, and this is the cleaving about which it says "and you who cleave with YHVH your Elokeichem, you are all alive today" [Devarim 4:4]. It is the likeness of [our] limb with [His] limb [through doing Mitvot with it] which causes the cleaving, and the cleaving is the reason for being alive.

118 Sefer Shaarei Orah, Gateway 1 from the beginning of this Gateway [this is very similar to the quotation above from Sefer Avodat HaKodesh]:
- [This Gateway begins with the question of how mortal man can use the Names of God in any way. It explains that one should try as hard as possible to understand the meaning of each individual name of God and that through the process of this analysis an appreciation will be formed of how all of Torah and Mitzvot are dependent upon them. The knowledge of the meaning of each name will stimulate one to be fearful of and desirous of a deep and close connection with God. The name YHVH is then highlight-

וּבְרֵישׁ סֵפֶר שַׁעֲרֵי אוֹרָה
וּבְפַרְדֵּס שַׁעַר הַכִּנּוּיִים פֶּרֶק א'

ed as being the principal name of God upon which all other names and descriptions are based. The following statements are then made . . .] An important principle: You should know that the truth of God's Essence is not perceivable to anyone apart from Him, and there are none among the supernal multitudes who [even] know His Place and how much more so the essence of His truth. Do you not see what it says that the supernal angels say "Blessed be God's honor – from His Place" [Yechezkel 3:12], meaning in every Place He Is. If the supernal beings are like this [that they do not have knowledge of His Place], then how much more so this applies to the lower beings [to us]. If so, what is the meaning of [referring to God in human terms] with all those concepts which we read in the Torah such as [His] hand, leg, ear, eye, and anything similar? You should know and believe that with all of those concepts, even though they relate and testify as to His Greatness and Truth, nevertheless, no creature is able to know and understand the essence of the concept which is called hand, foot, ear, etc., and if we are made in [His] image and form, it should not enter our thoughts that our eye is literally the same as [His] eye or our hand, [His] hand, but that these concepts are of the innermost depth relating to the truth of the existence of God, they are the source from which bestowal comes to all that exists through God's decree, but the essence of [a physical] hand is not like the essence of [God's] hand, and their structure is not the same, as it says "and to whom should I be compared and equated" [Yishayahu 40:25]. Know and understand that there is no comparison between Him and us from the perspective of essence and structure. The intention in referring to the form of the limbs within us is that they are constructed in an analogous way signifying supernal hidden concepts which no intellect is able to fathom. It is, however, like the analogy of a reference as with when writing "Reuven son of Yaakov" where these are not the letters and not the actual form, structure, and essence [of the person] "Reuven son of Yaakov," but rather this written reference of "Reuven son of Yaakov" signifies the essence and structure that is known and referred to as "Reuven son of Yaakov."

119 Pardes Rimonim Shaar 22, Shaar Inyan HaKinuyim, Chap. 1:
- [The chapter starts as follows:] Among the surprising things in our Torah is that which is written "and beneath His *feet*," "written with the *finger* of God," "the *hand* of God," "*eyes* of God," "*ears* of God," and similar bodily expressions. This matter cannot relate to God as He has no body or power within a body . . . and if so, with these statements of bodily limitation such as "and God saw," "and God heard," "and God said," "and God spoke" . . . it is appropriate that we believe that they are a description of a deep concept and are not literally sight, hearing, and, speech. There is no doubt that [the

- Shela.[120]

6. FOOD AND DRINK ARE TO BODY AS TORAH, MITZVOT AND PRAYER ARE TO WORLDS

- Just as food and drink are required to maintain man's soul within his body
  - and without them [the soul] will be separated and removed from the body
  - similarly, it is with the connection of God's Essence to the worlds, which is the secret of The *Great Man*[121]
  - that in order that He establish and maintain [the worlds] without His Soul being repulsed by them
  - He decreed that this connection be contingent on the Torah involvement, Mitzvah performance, and the service of prayer of the Jewish people
  - and without them, He would remove His Essence from them and [the worlds] would instantly return to their [pre-creation] state of nothing and Ayin.[122]
- Therefore, Chazal say:[123] What is the meaning of the verse "for I have scattered you like the four *winds* of the heavens" . . . that just as the world cannot continue to exist without *winds*, (Note 24)[124] similarly, the world cannot continue to exist without Israel.
- This is as per Chazal:[125] "My soul should bless God." What did King David have in mind when praising God with his soul? . . . [the Midrash makes a number of comparisons between one's soul connection with the body and God's connection with the world including that] this soul does not eat within the body and God does not eat [so the soul which does not eat within the body should come and praise God who does not eat].
- In a similar vein Chazal say:[126] Just as the soul does not eat and drink, so too God does not eat and drink.

---

fact that] an eye is called "Ayin," an ear "Ozen," and the mouth "Peh," is neither accidental nor by consensus as it is in other languages, and there is no doubt that this is the language that God created when He created His world, and it is certainly the case that this language preceded this world . . . [and the chapter ends with:] and about matters like this it is written "and through my flesh I see God" [Iyov 19:26].

120 Shela, Introduction to Toldot Adam 19:
- Man who is made and created in the image of God is a sign and symbol of the existence of God – this is the secret of "and upon the image of the chair

○ וּבַשְׁלַ"ה בְּהַקְדָּמַת תּוֹלְדוֹת אָדָם:

שער ב' - פרק ו'

• וּכְמוֹ שֶׁעִנְיַן חִבּוּר וְקִיּוּם נִשְׁמַת הָאָדָם בְּגוּפוֹ, הוּא עַל יְדֵי אֲכִילָה וּשְׁתִיָּה
○ וּבִלְתָּם תִּפָּרֵד וְתִסְתַּלֵּק מֵהַגּוּף

○ כֵּן חִבּוּר עַצְמוּתוֹ יִתְבָּרֵךְ אֶל הָעוֹלָמוֹת, שֶׁהֵן סוֹד "הָאָדָם הַגָּדוֹל"
○ כְּדֵי לְהַעֲמִידָם וּלְקַיְּמָם, וְלֹא תִגְעַל נַפְשׁוֹ אוֹתָם

○ גָּזְרָה רְצוֹנוֹ יִתְבָּרֵךְ שֶׁיְּהֵא תָּלוּי בְּעֵסֶק הַתּוֹרָה וּמַעֲשֵׂי הַמִּצְוֹת וַעֲבוֹדַת הַתְּפִלָּה שֶׁל עַם סְגֻלָּה

○ וּבִלְתָּם הָיָה הוּא יִתְבָּרֵךְ מְסַלֵּק עַצְמוּתוֹ יִתְבָּרֵךְ מֵהֶם, וּכְרֶגַע הָיוּ חוֹזְרִים כֻּלָּם לְאַפְסָם וָאָיִן:

• וְלָכֵן אָמְרוּ רַבּוֹתֵינוּ זִכְרוֹנָם לִבְרָכָה (תענית ג' ע"ב) "מַאי דִכְתִיב (זכריה ב, י) "כִּי כְּאַרְבַּע רוּחוֹת הַשָּׁמַיִם פֵּרַשְׂתִּי אֶתְכֶם" כו', כְּשֵׁם שֶׁאִי אֶפְשָׁר לָעוֹלָם בְּלֹא רוּחוֹת, (הגהה כ"ד) כָּךְ אִי אֶפְשָׁר לָעוֹלָם בְּלֹא יִשְׂרָאֵל":

• וְהוּא שֶׁאָמְרוּ בְּוַיִּקְרָא רַבָּה סוֹף פָּרָשָׁה ד', "בָּרְכִי נַפְשִׁי אֶת ה'" (תהלים קד) ג', וְכִי מַה רָאָה דָוִד לִהְיוֹת מְקַלֵּס 'בְּנַפְשׁוֹ' לְהַקָּדוֹשׁ בָּרוּךְ הוּא, אֶלָּא אָמַר, הַנֶּפֶשׁ הַזּוֹ כו', הַנֶּפֶשׁ הַזֹּאת אֵינָהּ אוֹכֶלֶת בַּגּוּף, וְהַקָּדוֹשׁ בָּרוּךְ הוּא אֵין לְפָנָיו אֲכִילָה" כו':

• וְכֵן אָמְרוּ בְּסִגְנוֹן זֶה בְּמִדְרָשׁ תְּהִלִּים מִזְמוֹר ק"ג, "וּמַה הַנֶּפֶשׁ אֵינָהּ אוֹכֶלֶת וְאֵינָהּ שׁוֹתָה, כָּךְ הַקָּדוֹשׁ בָּרוּךְ הוּא אֵינוֹ אוֹכֵל וְאֵינוֹ שׁוֹתֶה":

---

is the image of the appearance of man" [Yechezkel 1:26], and it says "and through my flesh I see God" [Iyov 19:26].

121 *The Great Man* reflects the idea of Shiur Komah where the structure and interrelationship of *Physical Man* is a simile of *The Great Man*, i.e., God.

122 See p. 472, fn. 18, for comments on the concept of Ayin.

123 Taanit 3b quoting Zecharia 2:10.

124 **R. Chaim adds Note 24 here.** This note is brought at the end of this chapter and is entitled "World requires the four elements/winds/directions/angels."

125 Vayikra Rabba Vayikra 4:7–8 quoting Tehillim 104:35.

126 Midrash Tehillim 103:4.

- By mentioning eating and drinking over and above other [worldly] pleasures, Chazal are implying this idea as stated above
  - that even though the soul itself does not eat or drink, nevertheless the unified connection of body and soul for the fixed duration of a person's life is dependent on the body's consumption of food and drink.
  - Similarly, God's Unified Essence is certainly not impacted at all, God forbid, by Mitzvah performance, Torah study, and service, and He is not bothered by them in any way, as written [above], "so too God does not eat and drink," and this is as I wrote above in the statements quoted in G2:04.[127]
- However, God decreed that His connection with the worlds
  - which is structurally arranged as per man's detailed structure including the digestive organs[/processes]
  - is dependent on the good deeds of His Holy People which are the *food and drink* of the worlds
  - (Note 25),[128] (Note 26)[129] causing them to exist and be maintained and to receive additional power, holiness, and light through God's proper connection with them as per His Will.
  - All is according to the level of action of the Chosen People, which repairs and unites the worlds, enabling them to receive a bestowal of light and additional holiness from God, (Note 27)[130] just like food adds power to and refines the body.
- This is the idea expressed by Chazal
  - in explaining the verse "Go and partake of *My food*"[131] [as relating to those who study Torah]
    - that is, literally *My* food, as if to say God's food

---

127 E.g., "Man's actions, whether good or bad, have no impact whatsoever on the Essence of God," and "God is above all blessing."

128 **R. Chaim adds Note 25 here.** This note is brought at the end of this chapter and is entitled "Good deeds are described as food for man's soul."

129 **R. Chaim adds Note 26 here.** This note is brought at the end of this chapter and is entitled "Soul will not be sated with a small diet of Torah study and good deeds."

130 **R. Chaim adds Note 27 here.** This note is brought at the end of this chapter and is entitled "Man's food quality parallels absorption quality of his actions in worlds."

131 Chagiga 14a quoting Mishlei 9:5. R. Chaim also refers the reader to:
Zohar Raya Mehemna III Tzav 33b:
- ... for with it the holy sons [who study Torah] prepare food of the offerings of the King with many types of food of the bread of Torah about which it says: "Go and partake of *My food*"...

- בְּהַזְכִּירָם 'אֲכִילָה וּשְׁתִיָּה' יוֹתֵר מִשְּׁאָר הַהֲנָאוֹת, הִשְׁמִיעוּנוּ זֶה הָעִנְיָן הַנַּ"ל.
  - וְהוּא, שֶׁהֲגַם שֶׁהַנֶּפֶשׁ עַצְמָהּ לֹא אוֹכֶלֶת וְלֹא שׁוֹתָה, עִם כָּל זֶה, הֲרֵי כָּל עִקַּר חִבּוּר הַנֶּפֶשׁ עִם הַגּוּף כְּאֶחָד, וְקִיּוּמוֹ מִסְפַּר יָמָיו הַקְּצוּבִים, הוּא תָּלוּי עַל יְדֵי הַמַּאֲכָל וּשְׁתִיַּת הַגּוּף.
  - כֵּן הָעִנְיָן, עִם כִּי וַדַּאי שֶׁלְּעַצְמוּת אָדוֹן יָחִיד אֵין סוֹף בָּרוּךְ הוּא, אֵינֶנּוּ נוֹגֵעַ חַס וְשָׁלוֹם שׁוּם מַעֲשֵׂה הַמִּצְוֹת, וְתוֹרָה וַעֲבוֹדָה כְּלָל, וְלֹא אִכְפַּת לֵיהּ כְּלָל, כְּמוֹ שֶׁכָּתוּב "כָּךְ הַקָּדוֹשׁ בָּרוּךְ הוּא אֵינוֹ אוֹכֵל וְאֵינוֹ שׁוֹתֶה", וּכְמוֹ שֶׁכָּתַבְתִּי לְעֵיל בְּהַמַּאֲמָרִים הַנִּזְכָּרִים בְּפֶרֶק ד':

- אָמְנָם כָּל עִקַּר עִנְיָן הִתְחַבְּרוּתוֹ יִתְבָּרַךְ אֶל הָעוֹלָמוֹת
  - שֶׁמְּסֻדָּרִים כְּאֶחָד כְּתַבְנִית אָדָם בְּכָל הַפְּרָטִים וְאֵבְרֵי הָאֲכִילָה כֻּלָּם
  - גָּזְרָה רְצוֹנוֹ יִתְבָּרַךְ שֶׁיְּהֵא תָּלוּי בְּמַעֲשֵׂיהֶם הַטּוֹבִים שֶׁל עַם קָדוֹשׁוֹ, שֶׁהֵן הֵמָּה עִנְיַן אֲכִילָה וּשְׁתִיָּה אֶל הָעוֹלָמוֹת
  - (הגהה כ"ה) (הגהה כ"ו) לְהַעֲמִידָם וּלְקַיְּמָם וּלְהוֹסִיף כֹּחַ קְדֻשָּׁתָם וְאוֹרָם עַל יְדֵי הִתְחַבְּרוּתוֹ יִתְבָּרַךְ אֲלֵיהֶם כָּרָאוּי, כְּפִי הָרָצוֹן הָעֶלְיוֹן יִתְבָּרַךְ שְׁמוֹ
  - הַכֹּל לְפִי רֹב הַמַּעֲשֶׂה שֶׁל עַם סְגֻלָּה, שֶׁהֵמָּה הַמְתַקְּנִים וּמְאַחֲדִים הָעוֹלָמוֹת, שֶׁיִּהְיוּ רְאוּיִים לְקַבֵּל שֶׁפַע הָאוֹר וְתוֹסֶפֶת קְדֻשָּׁתוֹ יִתְבָּרַךְ, (הגהה כ"ז) כְּעִנְיַן הַמָּזוֹן שֶׁהוּא מוֹסִיף כֹּחַ בַּגּוּף וּמְעַדֵּן אוֹתוֹ:

- וְזֶהוּ
  - עִנְיַן הַכָּתוּב (משלי ט, ה) "לְכוּ לַחֲמוּ בְלַחְמִי", שֶׁפֵּרְשׁוּהוּ רַבּוֹתֵינוּ זִכְרוֹנָם לִבְרָכָה (חגיגה יד, א) וּבְרַעְיָא מְהֵימְנָא צַו ל"ג ב', וּבְפָרָשַׁת עֵקֶב רע"א ב' עַל הַתּוֹרָה, עַיֵּן שָׁם
  - הַיְנוּ "בְּלַחְמִי" מַמָּשׁ, כִּבְיָכוֹל לַחְמוֹ יִתְבָּרַךְ.

Zohar Raya Mehemna III Ekev 271b:
- ... prepare bread for your Master – for Him and for the Noble Woman [i.e., His attribute of Kingship/Malchut which is female in that it has the property to receive], from all types of delicacies – to exist with it, "This is the table [set out] before God" (Yechezkel 41:22), then everything will benefit from the bread of the King as it is written: "Go and partake of *My food* [and drink of the *wine* which I poured]" – this is the bread of the Written Torah and the wine of Oral Torah. ...

- as per "Prepare the table for your Master"[132]
- "you shall eat from it"... that *hard rock*... [for there is no benefit and longing for the Holy Spirit in this world apart from the Torah of that Tzaddik] who, so to speak, sustains [this world more effectively than all of the sacrifices of the world]... Therefore, it says "you shall eat from it," as there is no sustenance in this world apart from [this Torah Sage].[133] Refer there.
- As the Maggid told the Beit Yosef in relation to the Manna
  - that all creations require food [each one according to his level]
  - even the Sefirot which are [God's direct] emanations require food, so to speak
  - and the food of the Sefirot is the Torah studied and good deeds performed in [this] lowest world.[134]
- "Israel is Holy to God, the first of His produce"... Israel is called the big strong tree containing food for all within it. It has the Torah within it which is food for Above. It has prayer which is food for [below], even the angels do not have food if not for Israel, for if Israel were not to be involved with Torah no food would descend to them from the Torah which is compared to a tree as in "It is a tree of life [to those who grasp onto it]" and to its fruits which are the Mitzvot.[135]
- R. Moshe Cordovero hinted to this in Sefer Eilima[136] with his words being quoted in Sefer Shomer Emunim. Refer there.[137]

---

132 Zohar Raya Mehemna III Ekev 271b.
133 Zohar III Balak 202a quoting Devarim 20:19 which describes the prohibition to cut down trees on capturing a city as "man is the tree of the field" which Chazal interpret as referring to Torah sages (Taanit 7a). See a longer quotation from this section in G4:34. R. Chaim also refers the reader to:
Zohar Raya Mehemna III Behar 110a:
- ... even though sacrifices are all for God, He takes them all and divides them among those who serve Him ... and the rabbinical students whose words are like the consumption of the remnants of the Mincha sacrifices ...

Zohar Raya Mehemna III Pinchas beginning of 224b:
- ... but even though all sacrifices need to be brought before Him, He divides it up among all who serve Him: food from the sacrifices among all who are fitting for it – to the intellects, food of Torah and drink of wine and water of Torah ...

Zohar III Pinchas beginning of 225b:
- ... "Trust in God and do good, dwell in the land and nourish [yourself] in faithfulness" (Tehillim 37:3). Trust in God as appropriate and do good to repair the Holy Covenant that it should be corrected and guard it as

נפש   שער ב' - פרק ו'   החיים   353

- וּכְמוֹ שֶׁאָמְרוּ בְּפָרָשַׁת עֵקֶב שָׁם, תַּקִּין פָּתוֹרָא לְמָארָךְ כו', עַיֵּן שָׁם.

- וּבְפָרָשַׁת בָּלָק ר"ב סוֹף ע"א "כִּי מִמֶּנּוּ תֹאכֵל" (דברים כ, יט) הַהוּא טְנָרָא תַּקִּיפָא כו', דְּהַהוּא זָכָאָה כִּבְיָכוֹל, אִיהוּ מְפַרְנֵס לָהּ וְיָהֵיב לָהּ מְזוֹנָא כו', בְּגִין כָּךְ "כִּי מִמֶּנּוּ תֹאכֵל", וְלֵית מְזוֹנָא בְּהַאי עַלְמָא אֶלָּא מִמֶּנּוּ, עַיֵּן שָׁם. וְעַיֵּן עוֹד בְּרַעְיָא מְהֵימְנָא בְּהַר ק"י ע"א, וּבְפָרָשַׁת פִּנְחָס שָׁם רכ"ד רֵישׁ ע"ב, וּבַזֹּהַר שָׁם רכ"ה רֵישׁ ע"ב בָּזֶה.

- וְכֵן אָמַר הַמַּגִּיד לְהַבֵּית יוֹסֵף (בְּפָרָשַׁת בְּשַׁלַּח) בְּעִנְיַן הַמָּן

- דְּכָל הַנִּבְרָאִים צְרִיכִים מָזוֹן כו'.

- וַאֲפִלּוּ סְפִירוֹת דְּאֵינוּן נֶאֱצָלִים צְרִיכֵי כִּבְיָכוֹל מְזוֹנָא כו'

- וְהָא מְזוֹנָא דְּסַפִּירָן אִיהִי תּוֹרָה וּמַעֲשִׂים טוֹבִים דְּעַבְדִין לְתַתָּא. עַיֵּן שָׁם בְּאֹרֶךְ.

- וּבְרַעְיָא מְהֵימְנָא מִשְׁפָּטִים קכ"א א', "קֹדֶשׁ יִשְׂרָאֵל לה', רֵאשִׁית תְּבוּאָתֹה" (ירמיה ב, ג) כו', וְיִשְׂרָאֵל אִתְקְרִיאוּ אִלָּנָא רַבָּה וְתַקִּיף, וּמָזוֹן לְכֹלָּא בֵּיהּ, בֵּיהּ אוֹרַיְתָא דְּאִיהוּ מְזוֹנָא לְעֵלָּא, בֵּיהּ צְלוֹתָא דְּאִיהוּ מְזוֹנָא כו'. וַאֲפִלּוּ מַלְאָכִים לֵית לוֹן מְזוֹנָא אֶלָּא בְּיִשְׂרָאֵל, דְּאִי לָאו דְּיִשְׂרָאֵל יִתְעַסְּקוּן בְּאוֹרַיְתָא, לָא הֲוָה נָחִית לוֹן מְזוֹנָא מִסִּטְרָא דְּאוֹרַיְתָא דְּאִמְתִילָא לְעֵץ, הֲדָא הוּא דִכְתִיב "עֵץ חַיִּים הִיא" וְגוֹ' וּלְאַבָּא דְּאִיהִי מִצְוָה".

- וְהָרַמַ"ק זִכְרוֹנוֹ לִבְרָכָה רָמַז הָעִנְיָן בְּסֵפֶר אֵלִימָה, הוּבְאוּ דְּבָרָיו בָּזֶה בְּסֵפֶר שׁוֹמֵר אֱמוּנִים, עַיֵּן שָׁם

---

appropriate. If you do this, you will be here in the land and will be fed and sustained by it, from this supernal faith. . . .

134 Maggid Meisharim Beshalach commenting on the verse "Lechem Abirim Achal Ish" (Tehillim 78:25).

135 Zohar Raya Mehemna II Mishpatim 121a quoting Yirmiyahu 2:3 and Mishlei 3:18.

136 A work known as "Eilima Rabbati."

137 Sefer Shomer Emunim, authored by R. Yosef ben Immanuel Irgess, records two debates between two imaginary Torah Sages, one called Shealtiel (whose name implies *the one inquiring about God*) representing the position of the Talmudists, and one called Yehoyada (whose name implies *the one who knows God* and therefore the answers) representing the Kabbalists. The following question and answer appears in sections 74 and 75 of the second debate:

- Shealtiel: "How sweet to my palate is your word, more than honey to my mouth" [Tehillim 119:103]. You have proven that although there is a

○ [Refer to] Tolaat Yaakov and to the beginning of his book Derech Emunah.[138]

change in behavior as a result of our prayer and Mitzvah performance, these changes are only in the vessels which are the Sefirot. However, the Ein Sof will not be changed or affected at all and that we should direct the focus of our hearts to it when verbalizing every Name [of God], that it is the power which controls the specific Name or Middah. However, I still need to know who we [should] bless in all of our blessings? If you say it is the Ein Sof, this is impossible as it is beyond all blessings and praise as per Tikkunei Zohar Tikkun 70 131b, and if you say it is to the Sefirot alone and we don't focus our hearts on the Ein Sof when we mention [God's] Name in all of our blessings, then it is difficult, for if so, then the service and prayer will be to the Sefirot in part of the blessings and not to the Ein Sof, and similarly there is a difficulty with the unification and binding that we perform with the Sefirot through Mitzvah performance and prayer – for how can we prepare the focus of our hearts on the Ein Sof in these instances?

• Yehoyada: Even though we do not bless the Ein Sof as it does not need our blessing since there is nothing above it to bestow upon it, it nevertheless is to it that we direct our focus in all of our blessings, for when we [talk of] blessing the Name, the meaning is that the Name be blessed and bestowed upon by the supernal emanations which are impacted by the power of the Ein Sof upon it, and without this they would not have the power to impact on the Name, and similarly, with the drawing near of the Sefirot and their unification through Mitzvah performance and prayer, the meaning is that through the power of the [Ein Sof's] bestowal, the Sefirot are bound together and unified, and similarly with the other holy worlds in their binding to the Sefirot they unify through the truth of His Unity. All this is straightforward and known to one accustomed and expert in Sefer Kavanot and I am handing over to you one introduction through which your eyes will be opened to all the intentions of the Zohar and the other Kabbalistic works. It is written in "Sefer Eilima" and this is what it says: The Sefirot are [as] *garments* and *chairs* for the Infinite God, and when we unify the Sefirot through the performance of a Mitzvah or through prayer, and similarly with all blessings, their intention is to rectify the Sefirot and to prepare them to be a *chair* for Him, and they draw near to Him and are rectified to receive His Light and Bestowal. Now this closeness of the Sefirot and their unification, this is [a person's] service of the Ein Sof, for He is not impacted in any way from this service, it is only that His entire Desire and Will is to do good to others, for He is the good and the One who causes good, and His goodness to the world is not lacking in any way. However, the Sefirot are channels and mediums through which good is drawn down, and if we, God forbid, damage the mediums, how can this good come [to us]. For the Ein Sof only radiates to a perfect place, and therefore, it is necessary to bind

וּבְתוֹלַעַת יַעֲקֹב, וּבְרֵישׁ סֵפֶר דֶּרֶךְ אֱמוּנָה שֶׁלּוֹ.

the Sefirot and correct them so that they will be straightened out to be able to receive bestowal of the Ein Sof and His Goodness. It transpires that the one who corrects these channels and mediums and causes their preparation to be able to receive the goodness and bestowal of the Ein Sof, he is the one who serves Him and performs His Will, for he causes Him to do good to another. But one who corrupts these channels and mediums and causes that they are not prepared to be able to receive His Good and Bestowal, he is absolutely one who does not serve Him and is called one who causes anger, rage, and annoyance, due to the bad which is drawn [down] to the *servant* in the absence of good from Him as a result of the corruption of the channels and mediums, and he is like one who tore the King's clothes in a way which makes them unwearable, and one who tears the King's clothes is liable according to that which he tore or dirtied in that they are damaged from being able to be worn by the King. However, one who knows how to repair the Middot with [appropriate] intention in Mitzvah performance, Torah study, and prayer – to bind them, unify them, and to prepare them for being able to receive His Bestowal and Goodness, he is one who serves the Ein Sof. That which the Ein Sof is not impacted by our service – this is similar to food and drink consumed by the body from which the soul is not impacted, but nevertheless it is through this food and drink that it is continuously connected. Similarly, it is through service [of God] that a continuous bestowal of the Middot of Ein Sof bursts out over the lower worlds. Therefore, in all of our prayers, Torah study, and Mitzvah performance, we first express that it is "To unify God and His Shechina . . . ." This concept is that our intention in our prayer requests and Mitzvah performance is not for our personal benefit but rather for the sake of the One on High, meaning, to unify and repair the supernal Middot in order that bestowal from the Ein Sof comes upon them, and from them [in turn], the bestowal cascades down through all the world levels, and it transpires that one who serves [God] in this manner, he is one of those servants who serve their Master without requiring rewards and his merit is very great as explained in many places in the Zohar and the Tikkunei Zohar.

138 The quotations from the referenced works are brought below.
Tolaat Yaakov (authored by R. Meir ben Gabai), from towards the end of the author's introduction:

- . . . and before we begin to deal with our intended subjects, we will preface one introduction that the entire faith of Israel hinges on to be able to receive supernal holiness. And it is said that [God] is the Root of all the roots, the Cause of all the causes and the Timeless Precedent of all – the perception of His Essence is withheld, and there is no counsel or understanding that can praise and extol Him and that can restrict Him with any name or description as He is Unbounded, Infinite, and without change or

- This is the meaning of Chazal's statement that "Israel sustain their Father in Heaven."[139]

Rabbi Chaim's Notes:
Note 24 – World requires the four elements/winds/directions/angels

- Refer to Zohar[140] [in connection with] the four elements:
  - [Come and see] that Fire, Wind, Water, and Dust are the first and the root of the Supernal Realms
  - upon which basis the lower and supernal worlds exist
  - and these are the four *directions* of the world [with Fire corresponding to North, Wind to East, Water to South, and Dust to West].[141]
- Refer to Zohar[142]
  - that through the four good elements of man, the four known angels of the Merkava [Michael, Gavriel, Nuriel, and Rephael][143] control the four *directions*/winds of the world

---

multiplicity and there is no [possible] perception of Him. Therefore, he should withhold himself from praying to Him without using His Names which emanate from Him to say that He is Great, Strong, Awesome, as this obligates/restricts Him [to be confined by] descriptions and circumstances which falsify the Faith. However, it is the foundation of foundations and the pillar of wisdom to know that the purpose of [all types of] service [including prayer] is that they are focused on the Unified Master, the Root of all, and that there is no existence in all that exist apart from Him – nothing impacts Him and He has nothing lacking just as there is no impact of food and drink on the supernal soul, but nevertheless it is through food and drink that it is continuously connected, and similarly, it is through [all types of] service that there is a continuous connection bursting out over the lower worlds, and the service is necessary, but it is impossible for this service to be unlimited. However, this limit is with an infinite emanation, which are the Middot with which He manages His world as is known to the wise of heart. They are to Him and He is to them like the analogy of the soul to the body, and it is to them that one focuses all the praises, prayers, and service, and this is the key principle upon which all is dependent for it is the root of faith . . .

Derech Emunah (also authored by R. Meir ben Gabai), close to the beginning of the book within the answer to the first of a set of 10 questions which the book deals with:

- . . . and it is stated in Midrash Tehillim: "My soul should bless God" . . . and just as a soul does not eat or drink so too God does not eat or drink . . . and just as the soul does not eat, etc. so too God does not eat, etc. However, eating and drinking are mentioned above all the other [worldly] pleasures to make us aware of a tremendous concept which we very much need to know,

- וְזֶהוּ עִנְיַן מַאֲמָרָם ז"ל (זוהר ויקרא ז ריש ע"ב) "יִשְׂרָאֵל מְפַרְנְסִין לַאֲבִיהֶם שֶׁבַּשָּׁמַיִם":

הגהה כ"ד

- עַיֵּן זֹהַר וָאֵרָא כ"ג ב', דְּאַרְבַּע יְסוֹדִין
  - ארמ"ע אִינּוּן קַדְמָאֵי וְשָׁרְשִׁין דִּלְעֵלָּא
  - וְתַתָּאִין וְעִלָּאִין עֲלַיְיהוּ קַיְימִין
  - וְאִנּוּן אַרְבַּע סִטְרֵי עַלְמָא:
- וְעַיֵּן רַעְיָא מְהֵימְנָא פִּנְחָס רכ"ז ב'
  - דְּעַל אַרְבַּע יְסוֹדִין טָבִין דְּבַר נָשׁ, שַׁלְטִין אַרְבַּע מַלְאֲכֵי הַמֶּרְכָּבָה הַיְדוּעִים בְּאַרְבַּע רוּחוֹת הָעוֹלָם

---

and that is that in truth the soul does not eat or drink but it is through the eating and drinking of the body that the [body-soul] connection is maintained and they both are maintained for the duration of time that they are decreed to serve their Maker, and their existence and connection is dependent upon eating and drinking. Similarly it is through service and prayer that God is constantly attached and in love with the Chosen People and His Soul is not repulsed by us. Enough [of this point is stated] here as it is not the main point, but I wanted to incorporate this hint here to inspire you and to arouse your heart. . . .

139 Zohar III Vayikra 7b at the beginning of the page, also see Midrash Zuta Shir HaShirim 1:15.
140 Zohar II VaEra 23b.
141 While the word, "Ruchot" has the dual meaning of either "directions" or "winds," the Talmud in Taanit 3b quoted in the main text of G2:06 appears, at first sight, to initially interpret the word as used in the quoted verse as "directions" and then rejects this interpretation and relates to it as "winds," as it continues with a Halachic discussion focused on praying for wind and rain. With this quotation from Zohar, R. Chaim understands the word "Ruchot" in this section of the Talmud to mean "directions." Clearly, there is a connection between these two meanings which at face value can be simply that the *winds* emanate from the four *directions*.
142 Zohar Raya Mehemna III Pinchas 227b. R. Chaim does not directly quote this text in contrast to the vast majority of his quoted references, but paraphrases this source in the following sentences.
143 See G3:10.

- through the root of their root which comes from the four letters of YHVH
- about which the verse states "From four *Ruchot* comes the *Ruach*. . . ."[144]

Note 25 – Good deeds are described as food for man's soul

- This is also in relation to a man's soul as per
  - "There is no good in man that he should eat and drink . . . ." All references to food and drink in this Megillah [Kohelet] are in relation to Torah study and good deeds.[145]
  - "The righteous say *it will be good* as they shall *eat the fruit* of their actions"[146] [in a positive context] and similarly, in the opposite context, God forbid, as per "and they will *eat of the fruit* of their [wicked] ways."[147]
  - As food of Torah is the food of the [intellectual] Nefesh, Ruach, and Neshama [which relate to the three levels of Cohen, Levi, and Yisrael ... Cohen related to *Yud* and Chochma, Levi related to *Hey* and Binah, Yisrael related to *Vav* and Daat].[148] Refer there.
  - That the soul is sustained through words of Torah which is its bread, just like bread is to the body with physical things.[149]
  - A soul which involves itself with Torah "eats from her father's bread."[150]
  - Zohar[151] [which discusses the Show Bread].
- This is the idea of the *Table of the Righteous* in future times, as per King David "lay out the table before me,"[152] and also "Go and partake of My food."[153]

Note 26 – Soul will not be sated with a small diet of Torah study and good deeds

- Just as it is with various types of food
  - there are foods which are only able to strengthen the four elements of the body to provide basic nutrition
  - and there are foods which can add power to the four elements with greater quality.
  - All efforts of a person to increase his body's power over and above its basic health level will not suffice if he only eats the minimum (*Tzimtzum*) amount of food required (as a life line/*Kav*) to stay alive.

---

144 Yechezkel 37:9. Referring to the four *directions/winds/spirits/angels* from which the life spirit would be bestowed in Yechezkel's prophecy of the dry bones.
145 Kohelet Rabba 2:24, and similarly in Kohelet Rabba 3:12 and 8:15.
146 Yishayahu 3:10.
147 Mishlei 1:31.
148 Zohar Raya Mehemna III Tzav 29b.

- עַל יְדֵי שֹׁרֶשׁ שָׁרְשָׁן שֶׁמֵּן אַרְבַּע אוֹתִיּוֹת הֲוָיָ"ה בָּרוּךְ הוּא
- וְשֶׁעַל זֶה נֶאֱמַר הַכָּתוּב (יחזקאל לז, ט) "מֵאַרְבַּע רוּחוֹת בֹּאִי הָרוּחַ" וְגוֹ':

הגהה כ"ה

- וְגַם אֶל נִשְׁמַת הָאָדָם עַצְמוֹ כְּמוֹ שֶׁאָמְרוּ זִכְרוֹנָם לִבְרָכָה
  - בְּקֹהֶלֶת רַבָּה סִימָן ב' פָּסוּק כ"ד "אֵין טוֹב בָּאָדָם שֶׁיֹּאכַל וְשָׁתָה" וְגוֹ', כָּל אֲכִילָה וּשְׁתִיָּה שֶׁנֶּאֱמַר בִּמְגִלָּה הַזֹּאת, בַּתּוֹרָה וּבְמַעֲשִׂים טוֹבִים הַכָּתוּב מְדַבֵּר. וְכֵן הוּא שָׁם בְּסִימָן ג' פָּסוּק י"ב, וּבְסִימָן ח' פָּסוּק ט"ו
  - וּכְתִיב (ישעיה ג, י) "אִמְרוּ צַדִּיק כִּי טוֹב כִּי פְרִי מַעַלְלֵיהֶם יֹאכֵלוּ". וְכֵן בְּהֶפֶךְ חַם וְשָׁלוֹם, כְּתִיב (משלי א, לא) "וְיֹאכְלוּ מִפְּרִי דַרְכָּם"
  - וּבְרַעְיָא מְהֵימְנָא צוּ כ"ט ב', דִּמְזוֹנָא דְאוֹרַיְתָא אִיהוּ מְזוֹנָא דְנָר"ן כוּ'[149] עַיֵּן שָׁם.
  - וְשָׁם בְּפָרָשַׁת פִּנְחָס רכ"ז סוֹף ע"א, דְּנִשְׁמָתָא אִתְפַּרְנְסַת בְּמִלִּין דְּאוֹרַיְתָא, דְּאִנּוּן נַהֲמָא לָהּ, כְּעִנְיַן נַהֲמָא דְגוּפָא מִמִּלִּין דְּעָלְמָא.
  - וְשָׁם רמ"ד סוֹף ע"ב, דְּנַפְשָׁא דְּאִתְעַסְּקַת בְּאוֹרַיְתָא "מִלֶּחֶם אָבִיהָ תֹּאכֵל" (ויקרא כב, יג)[150] כוּ'.
  - וְעַיֵּן עוֹד שָׁם רנ"ב ב' בָּזֶה:[151]
- וְזֶהוּ עִנְיַן "שֻׁלְחָנָם שֶׁל צַדִּיקִים" לֶעָתִיד לָבֹא, וּכְמוֹ שֶׁאָמַר דָּוִד הַמֶּלֶךְ עָלָיו הַשָּׁלוֹם (תהלים כג, ה) "תַּעֲרֹךְ לְפָנַי שֻׁלְחָן" גוֹ',[152] וְזֶהוּ "לְכוּ לַחֲמוּ בְלַחְמִי" (משלי ט, ה):[153]

הגהה כ"ו

- וּכְמוֹ שֶׁבְּמִינֵי מַאֲכָל
  - יֵשׁ מַאֲכָלִים שֶׁכֹּחָם רַק לְחַזֵּק אַרְבַּע יְסוֹדוֹת הַגּוּף, שֶׁיִּהְיוּ בְּכֹחָם הָרִאשׁוֹן
  - וְיֵשׁ מַאֲכָלִים שֶׁבְּכֹחָם לְהוֹסִיף כֹּחַ הָאַרְבַּע יְסוֹדוֹת בְּרִבּוּי אֵיכוּת.
  - וְכָל עָמָל הָאָדָם לְהוֹסִיף לוֹ כֹּחַ גּוּפוֹ יָתֵר עַל כְּדֵי קִיּוּם בְּרִיאוּתוֹ, וְאֵינוֹ מִסְתַּפֵּק בַּאֲכִילָה מְעֻטֶּת בְּצִמְצוּם כְּדֵי קִיּוּם חִיּוּתוֹ

---

149 Paraphrased from Zohar Raya Mehemna III Pinchas 227a.
150 Zohar Raya Mehemna III Pinchas 244b quoting Vayikra 22:13.
151 Zohar Raya Mehemna III Pinchas 252b.
152 Tehillim 23:5.
153 Mishlei 9:5.

- Similarly, 'it is with the soul, which will not become full.'[154]
  - if it *eats* only a small diet of Torah study and good deeds.
  - This is all of man – to increase Torah study and Mitzvah performance – to the extent that it draws down additional holiness and blessing in the supernal and lower worlds, more than the *Kav* [the baseline measure/channel] which God established at the time of the Creation.
- (This is explained as per Etz Chaim, that all our service [of God] is to draw down a surrounding environment of great light, even more than was brought down by God at the time of the Creation through the *Kav Ohr HaYosher/the channel of direct light*, which was required to provide life and existence of the worlds.)[155]

Note 27 – Man's food quality parallels absorption quality of his actions in worlds

- Similarly, it is literally according to this property of the concept of man's food in this lowest world, in relation to its cleanliness and refinement from traces of impurity, [which directly parallels] the property of the food supplied to the worlds from [the level of refinement of] man's pure actions, whether in small or large measure.
- Therefore, before Adam's sin, his food was refined from any trace of impurity
  - as per Chazal,[156] that the angels would roast [Adam] meat and sieve wine for him.
    - (This concept of roasting and sieving – Adam's soul was so great and powerful, the secret of the First Man [whose soul incorporated all the souls of Israel], greater than all the powers of the supernal and lower worlds – to the extent that even the angels would roast him food so that the supernal flame, fire eating fire, extracting any trace of grossness as fitting for [Adam's] very high level.
    - In addition, the rejoicing of the supernal wine which was filtered from all sediment [to be made suitable] for his high level, as per "the wine kept in his grapes.")[157]
- But after [Adam's] sin, which intermingled bad with good in the food of the worlds, it is written "[the earth will sprout] thorns and thistles [for you]."[158]
- In a similar way the generation of the wilderness, before the sin of the Golden Calf, also merited to have Manna which was less gross than other foods and entirely absorbed in their limbs

---

154 Kohelet 6:7.
155 This is a general theme in the Etz Chaim so there is no specific reference that relates to it. See V2:02, p. 61, fn. 41 for further insight on this note.

- כֵּן 'גַּם הַנֶּפֶשׁ, לֹא תִּמָּלֵא'
  - בַּאֲכִילָה מֻעֶטֶת שֶׁל תּוֹרָה וּמַעֲשִׂים טוֹבִים
  - וְזֶה כָּל הָאָדָם, לְרַבּוֹת תּוֹרָה וּלְהוֹסִיף מִצְוֹת, עַד שֶׁיַּמְשִׁיךְ תּוֹסֶפֶת רִבּוּי קְדֻשָּׁה וּבְרָכָה בָּעֶלְיוֹנִים וְתַחְתּוֹנִים, יָתֵר עַל כְּדֵי מִדַּת הַ'קַו' שֶׁנָּטָה הַבּוֹרֵא יִתְבָּרַךְ שְׁמוֹ בְּעֵת הַבְּרִיאָה:
- (כַּמְבֹאָר בְּעֵץ חַיִּים, שֶׁכָּל עֲבוֹדָתֵנוּ הוּא, לְהַמְשִׁיךְ 'מַקִּיפִים' בְּהִתְרַחֲבוּת אוֹר גָּדוֹל, יָתֵר עַל כְּדֵי מִדַּת 'קַו' אוֹר הַיָּשָׁר, שֶׁהִמְשִׁיךְ הוּא יִתְבָּרַךְ בְּעֵת הַבְּרִיאָה, לְצֹרֶךְ הֶכְרֵחַ חִיּוּת וְקִיּוּם הָעוֹלָמוֹת):

הגהה כ"ז

- וְכֵן הוּא לְפִי זֶה הָעֵרֶךְ מַמָּשׁ, עִנְיַן אֲכִילַת הָאָדָם לְמַטָּה, נָקִי וְזַךְ מַסִּיג פְּסֹלֶת, כְּפִי עֵרֶךְ מְזוֹן הָעוֹלָמוֹת מִמַּעֲשָׂיו הַזַּכִּים, אִם מְעַט וְאִם הַרְבֵּה:
- וְלָכֵן, קֹדֶם חֵטְא אָדָם הָרִאשׁוֹן — הָיוּ מַאֲכָלָיו מְבֹרָרִים וּנְקִיִּים מִכָּל סִיג וּפְסֹלֶת.
  - וְאָמְרוּ (סנהדרין נט, ב), שֶׁהַמַּלְאָכִים הָיוּ צוֹלִין לוֹ בָּשָׂר וּמְסַנְּנִין לוֹ יַיִן.
  - (וְעִנְיַן זֶה הַצְּלִיָּה וְהַסִּנּוּן, שֶׁכָּל כָּךְ גָּדְלָה כֹּחַ נַפְשׁוֹ שֶׁל אָדָם הָרִאשׁוֹן, סוֹד אָדָם קַדְמָאָה, יוֹתֵר מֵעֵרֶךְ כָּל כֹּחוֹת עֶלְיוֹנֵי הָעֶלְיוֹנִים, עַד שֶׁגַּם הַמַּלְאָכִים צָלוּ לוֹ הַמַּאֲכָל שֶׁיְּהֵא נוֹרָא עִלָּאָה, אֵשׁ אוֹכְלָה אֵשׁ, מַשְׁאִיב שׁוֹאֵב כָּל שׁוּם עֲבִיּוּת הַמַּאֲכָל שֶׁלְּפִי עֶרְכּוֹ הַגָּבוֹהַּ מְאֹד
  - וְגַם שִׂמְחַת הַיַּיִן הָעֶלְיוֹן הָיָה מְסֻנָּן מִכָּל שְׁמָרִים שֶׁלְּפִי גֹּבַהּ עֶרְכּוֹ, וּכְעִנְיַן (ברכות לד:, במ"ר י"ג) "יַיִן הַמְשֻׁמָּר בַּעֲנָבָיו"):
- וְאַחַר הַחֵטְא שֶׁנִּתְעָרַב רַע בְּטוֹב בִּמְזוֹן הָעוֹלָמוֹת, כְּתִיב (בראשית ג, יח) "קוֹץ וְדַרְדַּר" גּוֹ'.
- וּמֵעֵין זֶה זָכוּ גַּם כֵּן דּוֹר הַמִּדְבָּר קֹדֶם חֵטְא הָעֵגֶל, בְּעִנְיַן הַמָּן, שֶׁהִפִיג גַּם שְׁאָר הַמַּאֲכָלִים וְנִבְלַע בְּאֵבְרֵיהֶם

---

156 Sanhedrin 59b.
157 As per Berachot 34b and Bamidbar Rabba Naso 13:2.
158 Bereishit 3:18.

- as per Chazal,[159] [after establishing that the Manna is absorbed totally, the question is asked] what is the meaning of "and you shall have a shovel in addition to your weapons"[160] [i.e., why is there a need to have shovels as these were required to dig holes to bury excrement – but surely there was no excrement due to total Manna absorption]?, this relates to the period after their sin [when the Manna was no longer totally absorbed].
- Similarly, Chazal state:[161] In future times [of Mashiach] the Land of Israel will produce [bread rolls, i.e., which are clean and free of impurities – reversing the curse placed on the land in the time of Adam of the earth sprouting thorns and thistles, as above].

7. BAD DEEDS DAMAGE THE WORLDS AS BAD FOOD DAMAGES THE BODY

- Conversely, the same applies to deeds which are not good, God forbid, whose [impact] on the worlds is similar to [a body's] consumption of bad foods, as will be explained.
- As per Chazal:
  - On the day of Rosh Hashana, Yitzchak goes out on his own and calls Esav to [bring him] cooked foods to taste from the entire world, each one [prepared] in its own way . . . and he [Yitzchak] rests on the bed of judgment and calls Esav saying: "Hunt game for me, prepare fine foods for me . . . [and bring it to me] . . . and it was as [Yaakov] went out . . . and Esav his brother returned from hunting" laden with the packages of worldly activity "and he also made fine foods," practicing to argue his case . . . and he said: "Father, get up," that [Yitzchak] should awaken his judgment and *eat* of the many bad deeds from all of the world.[162]
  - "Prepare fine foods for me as I like them" – from the positive Mitzvot . . . and those who transgress the negative commandments give sustenance to Samael,[163] and if Esav had drawn near to Yitzchak and said to him, "Father, get up and eat from his son's hunted food," then as a result, Samael would have drawn near to the left to bring God to taste of the sins of his sons which are bitter foods. . . .[164]
  - It is not the way of that heart to . . . with the ugly deeds of his people, but he takes all the purifications . . . and all of the merit and all of the good deeds. All the ugliness, soil, and dirt, which are the bad deeds are left for the liver [i.e., to be processed and filtered out, just like it processes bad foods], about which it says "Esav is a man of Sa'ir/hair

- כְּמוֹ שֶׁאָמְרוּ רַבּוֹתֵינוּ זִכְרוֹנָם לִבְרָכָה בְּפֶרֶק יוֹם הַכִּפּוּרִים (ע"ה ב') "אֶלָּא מַה אֲנִי מְקַיֵּם (דברים כג, יד), "וְיָתֵד תִּהְיֶה לָךְ" גו', לְאַחַר שֶׁסָּרְחוּ":

- וְכֵן אָמְרוּ רַבּוֹתֵינוּ זִכְרוֹנָם לִבְרָכָה (שבת ל, ב) שֶׁלֶּעָתִיד לָבֹא עֲתִידָה אֶרֶץ יִשְׂרָאֵל שֶׁתּוֹצִיא כו':

שער ב' - פרק ז'

- וְכֵן בְּהֶפֶךְ, הַמַּעֲשִׂים אֲשֶׁר לֹא טוֹבִים חַס וְשָׁלוֹם, הֵם אֶל הָעוֹלָמוֹת כְּעִנְיַן הַמַּאֲכָלִים רָעִים, אֲשֶׁר יִתְבָּאֵר עִנְיָנוֹ בְּעֶזְרַת ה':

- וּכְמוֹ שֶׁאָמְרוּ

- בְּרַעְיָא מְהֵימְנָא פָּרָשַׁת אֱמוֹר דַּף צ"ט וְדַף ק' ע"א, "בְּיוֹמָא דְרֹאשׁ הַשָּׁנָה נָפִיק יִצְחָק בִּלְחוֹדוֹי, וְקָרֵי לְעֵשָׂו לְאַטְעָמָא לֵיהּ תַּבְשִׁילִין דְּכָל עַלְמָא, כָּל חַד כְּפוּם אָרְחוֹי כו', וְשָׁכִיב עַל עַרְסֵיהּ דְּדִינָא, וְקָרֵי לְעֵשָׂו וְאָמַר (בראשית כז, ג) "וְצוּדָה לִּי צָיִד, וַעֲשֵׂה לִי מַטְעַמִּים" כו', "וַיְהִי אַךְ יָצֹא" כו' "וְעֵשָׂו אָחִיו בָּא מִצֵּדוֹ" טָעִין טַעֲנוֹת מְעוֹבָדֵי דְעַלְמָא, "וַיַּעַשׂ גַּם הוּא מַטְעַמִּים" — חָדִיד לְשׁוֹנֵיהּ לְמִטְעַן טַעֲנוֹת כו', "וַיֹּאמֶר יָקֻם אָבִי" — יִתְעַר בְּדִינוֹי "וְיֹאכַל", כַּמָּה עוֹבָדִין בִּישִׁין דְּכָל עַלְמָא" כו'.

- וּבְתִקּוּנִים תִּקּוּן כ"ד נ"ה א', "וַעֲשֵׂה לִי מַטְעַמִּים כַּאֲשֶׁר אָהַבְתִּי" מִפִּקּוּדִין דַּעֲשֵׂה כו', וּפִקּוּדִין דְּלָא תַעֲשֶׂה — פַּרְנָסָה לְסמ"מ לְמַאן דַּעֲבַר עֲלַיְיהוּ, וְאִלֵּין הֲוָה קָרִיב עֵשָׂו לְיִצְחָק וְאָמַר לֵיהּ, "יָקֻם אָבִי וְיֹאכַל מִצֵּיד בְּנוֹ", וסמ"מ בְּגִינַיְיהוּ הֲוָה קָרִיב לִשְׂמָאלָא, לְאַטְעָמָא לְקֻדְשָׁא בְּרִיךְ הוּא מֵחוֹבִין דִּבְנַיָּא, דְּאִנּוּן מַאכָלִין מְרִירָן כו'.

- בְּרַעְיָא מְהֵימְנָא פָּרָשַׁת פִּנְחָס רל"ב סוֹף ע"א, "וְהַהוּא לֵב לָאו אָרְחוֹי כו', בַּעֲכִירוּ דְעוֹבָדִין דְעַמֵּיהּ, אֶלָּא נָקִיט כָּל בְּרִירוּ כו', וְכָל זַכָּאן וְכָל עוֹבָדִין טָבִין. וְכָל הַהוּא עֲכִירוּ וְטִנּוּפִין וְלִכְלוּכָא, דְּאִנּוּן עוֹבָדִין בִּישִׁין, אֲנָא לְכָבֵד דְּאִתְּמַר

---

159 Yoma 75b.
160 Devarim 23:14.
161 Shabbat 30b.
162 Zohar Raya Mehemna III Emor 100a quoting from Bereishit 27:3 onwards.
163 Samael – the Angel of Death, and mentioned in G1:13.
164 Tikkunei Zohar Tikkun 21/20 55a quoting Bereishit 27:4.

...," as per "the Sa'ir/he-goat will carry all their sins."[165] There is more on this point at the end of the page of this source. Refer to it.[166]

- Just as with bad non-nutritious food which is not accepted by the body
  - does not nourish or satisfy the body but is converted into waste, pollutants, and excrement within it
  - and also wears out and weakens the entire body
  - it results in the soul not being properly manifest within [the body][167]
  - and it sometimes causes illness.
- Similarly, with deeds which are not good or acceptable, God forbid
  - they are converted to waste and dirt, so to speak, within the worlds
  - and are the intensification of the Evil forces and Kelipot, (Note 28)[168] God should save us, and they are referred to as "vomit and excrement."[169]
    - As per the verse "tell it to *be gone*."[170]
    - As per the Zohar quotation above, refer to it.[171]
    - And it is referred to as "filthy refuse and excrement."[172]
    - As per Tikkunim.[173]
    - As per the verse "how will I *soil* them" which is the impure Sitra Achara.[174]
    - Excrement *is* the Evil Inclination.[175]

---

165 Zohar III Pinchas 232a–b quoting Bereishit 27:11 and Vayikra 16:22.

166 ". . . From the heart, health is distributed to all limbs and this is as the heart takes that which is refined, selected and clear; the liver takes whatever it finds and what remains from the dirt and the soil and disposes of it by force to the other limbs, which are the other, idol worshiping nations, and the spleen takes from the dregs of the liver. . . ."

I.e., that the heart distributes the refined deeds, like it does with nutrients extracted and refined from food, and distributes them to the limbs of the body.

167 There are two broad categories of bad foods: 1. foods, which while not being dangerous, are intrinsically bad and the body expels them, and 2. foods which could be good, but are consumed in excess and are surplus to the requirements of the body and typically expelled by it. The process of harmful or unnecessary ingestion and conversion to waste has an impact on the body which weakens and de-optimizes its ability to perform Torah, Mitzvot, and prayer.

168 **R. Chaim adds Note 28 here.** This note is brought at the end of this chapter and is entitled "God gradually rejects evil vs. instant rejection for idol worship."

169 Yishayahu 28:8.

170 Yishayahu 30:22. This verse refers to how in the time of Mashiach we will take our idols, i.e., anything that we have in our lives that diverts our attention from God, and cast them away and "tell it to *be gone*." The expression "Be

נפש שער ב' - פרק ז' החיים

בֵּיהּ (בראשית כז, יא) "עֵשָׂו אִישׁ שָׂעִיר" כו', "וְנָשָׂא הַשָּׂעִיר עָלָיו אֵת כָּל עֲוֹנוֹתָם" (ויקרא טז, כב). וְכֵן אִיתָא עוֹד שָׁם כְּעִנְיָן זֶה בְּסוֹף הָעַמּוּד, עַיֵּן שָׁם:

- וּכְשֵׁם שֶׁמַּאֲכַל הַגּוּף, כַּאֲשֶׁר אֵינֶנּוּ טוֹב, וְאֵינוֹ מִתְקַבֵּל אֶל הַגּוּף
  - אֵינוֹ זָן וְסוֹעֵד אֶת הַגּוּף, אֶלָּא נֶהְפָּךְ בְּתוֹכוֹ לִפְסֹלֶת וְזַהֲמָא וְצוֹאָה
  - וְגַם הוּא מַתִּישׁ וּמַחֲלִישׁ אֶת כָּל הַגּוּף
  - כִּי עַל יְדֵי זֶה אֵין הַנֶּפֶשׁ מִתְפַּשֵּׁט בְּתוֹכוֹ כָּרָאוּי
  - וְלִפְעָמִים יֶחֱלֶה מִזֶּה:
- כֵּן הָעִנְיָן שֶׁהַמַּעֲשִׂים אֲשֶׁר לֹא טוֹבִים וּרְצוּיִים, חַס וְשָׁלוֹם
  - הֵמָּה נֶהְפָּכִים בְּתוֹךְ הָעוֹלָמוֹת לִפְסֹלֶת וְלִכְלוּךְ כִּבְיָכוֹל
  - וְהוּא הִתְגַּבְּרוּת כֹּחוֹת הַטֻּמְאָה וְהַקְּלִיפּוֹת, (הגהה כ"ח) הָרַחֲמָן יַצִּילֵנוּ, שֶׁנִּקְרָאִים "קִיא צוֹאָה" (עיין זוהר א' קצ: וח"ב קנב. רסה:)
    - כְּמַאֲמָרָם זִכְרוֹנָם לִבְרָכָה בַּפָּסוּק "צֵא תֹּאמַר לוֹ" (ישעיה ל, כב).
    - וְכֵן אָמַר בְּרַעְיָא מְהֵימְנָא פִּנְחָס בְּדַף רל"ב הַנַּ"ל, וְעַיֵּן שָׁם
    - וְשָׁם בְּפָרָשַׁת תֵּצֵא רפ"ב ע"א, שֶׁנִּקְרֵאת אַשְׁפָּה מְטֻנֶּפֶת וְצוֹאָה.
    - וְכֵן אִיתָא בַּתִּקּוּנִים תִּקּוּן ע' קל"א.
    - וּבַזֹּהַר חָדָשׁ בס"א פָּרָשַׁת בְּרֵאשִׁית ט' ע"א בַּפָּסוּק "אֵיכָכָה אֲטַנְּפֵם" (שה"ש ה, ג) שֶׁהוּא הס"א מְסָאֲבָא
    - וְשָׁם בְּפָרָשַׁת אַחֲרֵי פ' ע"ב, וְאֵין צוֹאָה אֶלָּא יֵצֶר הָרַע כו'.

---

gone" is "Tzeh" which is similar to the word "Tzoah," meaning "excrement" (there is also a conceptual similarity in that the excrement is ejected by the body with the sentiment of "Be gone," as completely unwanted). This is used as the basis for the Zohar to interpret this verse that in the time of Mashiach we will view these idols as "excrement." As per Zohar I Vayeshev 190b, Zohar II Pekudei 252a and 265b. Also see Shabbat 82a which interprets this verse as relating to idol worship.

171 Zohar III Pinchas 232b.
172 Zohar Raya Mehemna III Ki Tetze 282a.
173 Tikkunei Zohar Tikkun 70 130b
- ...a person has to remove it from each and every limb, i.e., all bad thoughts which soil, which are Kelipot....

174 Zohar Chadash Sitrei Otiyot I Bereishit 9a quoting Shir Hashirim 5:3.
175 Zohar Chadash I Acharei Mot 80b.

- ○ Refer to the Taamei Mitzvot of the Arizal, Yitro.[176]
- ○ Similarly, it is the place from which they suckle [from which they receive their vitality] in their supernal root. Refer to Etz Chaim.[177]
- This was also the idea underpinning the worship of Peor[178]
  - ○ and as written above "and those who transgress the negative commandments give sustenance to Samael"[179]
  - ○ and this is the idea of the verse "if God washes the excrement of the daughters of Zion"[180]
  - ○ and as stated in connection with Yeravam, when he worshipped two golden calves and caused Israel to sin, God said to the angels: all the [life force] which would have been bestowed upon them is being converted by them into waste.[181]
- [Bad deeds] thereby cause damage, illness, great corruption, and weakness, God forbid, in the worlds
  - ○ according to the nature of the action and its root level in the worlds.
  - ○ For then, in those worlds which those actions impact, God's emanation and connection to them is no [longer] truly complete as He intended, as [God's connection] no longer resides in a damaged place all the while its illness is still within it 'and [it] has not been cleansed of its excrement'[182]
  - ○ and since all the worlds in general are connected together as one, it is inevitable that all the worlds are impacted in a small way from this damage.

---

176 Taamei Mitzvot, Yitro:
- With food, all that a person eats contains supernal life force. As a person is physical, food is also physical and after it provides the body with life force, the remainder of it which contains no life force, is expelled. Therefore, those who ate the Manna did not have any excrement from it, as the Manna was entirely food without any waste, but with other foods, once the life force is extracted from it to sustain the person, the waste which has no life force is expelled.

177 Etz Chaim Shaar 32, Shaar He'arat HaMochin, Chap. 5 :
- . . . waste and food sediment goes out to the external [i.e., peripheral existence of elements which deny the existence of God] . . . which are the Kelipah and idol worship which are called excrement without space, as per "tell it – Be gone," as from there they are sustained . . . there is a form of idol worship called "Peor" which is served by excreting in front of it [with this excretion] literally providing it with sustenance and it only receives life force in this way [see next footnote].

178 Peor was an idol which was worshiped by defecating in front of it. This act placed ultimate value on body waste over and above any value on that which

- וְעַיֵּן בְּטַעֲמֵי מִצְוֹת לְהָאֲרִיזַ"ל פָּרָשַׁת יִתְרוֹ בָּזֶה.
- וְכֵן הוּא מָקוֹם יְנִיקָתָם בַּשֹּׁרֶשׁ הָעֶלְיוֹן, עַיֵּן בְּעֵץ חַיִּים שַׁעַר הֶאָרַת הַמּוֹחִין פֶּרֶק ה':

• וְזֶה הָיָה גַּם כֵּן עִנְיַן עֲבוֹדַת פְּעוֹר.
- וּכְמוֹ שֶׁכָּתוּב בְּמַאֲמָר הַתִּקּוּנִים הַנַּ"ל, וּפִקּוּדִין דְּלָא תַּעֲשֶׂה פַּרְנָסָה לְסמ"מ, לְמַאן דְּעָבַר עֲלַיְהוּ כו'.
- וְזֶהוּ עִנְיַן הַכָּתוּב (ישעיה ה, ד) "אִם רָחַץ ה' אֵת צֹאַת בְּנוֹת צִיּוֹן".
- וְזֶה שֶׁאָמְרוּ בְּזֹהַר חָדָשׁ פָּרָשַׁת אַחֲרֵי ע"ט א', בְּעִנְיַן יָרָבְעָם, כַּד עָבַד תְּרֵי עֶגְלֵי, שֶׁאָמַר הַקָּדוֹשׁ בָּרוּךְ הוּא לְהַמַּלְאָכִים, הֲרֵי כָּל שֶׁפַע דַּהֲוָה יָהִיב לְכוֹן אִתְהֲפֵךְ לְכוֹן בְּזוּהֲמָא:

• וְגוֹרֵם בָּזֶה פְּגָם וָחֳלִי וְקִלְקוּל גָּדוֹל וּתְשׁוּת כֹּחַ חַס וְשָׁלוֹם בְּהָעוֹלָמוֹת
- לְפִי עִנְיָן וְאֹפֶן הַמַּעֲשֶׂה, וּלְפִי מַדְרֵגָתוֹ בְּשָׁרְשׁוֹ בְּהָעוֹלָמוֹת.
- כִּי אָז בְּאוֹתָן הָעוֹלָמוֹת שֶׁאוֹתָן הַמַּעֲשִׂים מַגִּיעִים עֲדֵיהֶם, אֵין הַהִתְפַּשְּׁטוּת וְהִתְחַבְּרוּת עַצְמוּתוֹ יִתְבָּרֵךְ בָּהֶם עַל הַשְּׁלֵמוּת הָאֲמִתִּי כָּרָאוּי, כְּפִי כַּוָּנַת רְצוֹנוֹ יִתְבָּרֵךְ, דְּלֹא שָׁרֵי בַּאֲתַר פָּגִים כָּל עוֹד אֲשֶׁר עֲדַיִן חֶלְאָתָהּ בְּתוֹכָהּ וּמְצוֹאָתָהּ לֹא רֻחָץ.
- וּמֵאַחַר שֶׁכָּל הָעוֹלָמוֹת בִּכְלָל, הֵם מְקֻשָּׁרִים וּמְיֻחָדִים כְּאֶחָד, מִמֵּילָא גַּם כָּל הָעוֹלָמוֹת מַרְגִּישִׁים מְעַט בְּמִקְצָת מִזֶּה הַפְּגָם:

- The [worlds] do not return to their former true strength, health, and repair until these Evil forces have been extracted from them:
  - [Either] by a person's acceptance of the corresponding punishment
    - refer to the Zohar[183]
    - that as a result of this [acceptance, the Evil forces] will inevitably be expelled and immediately cease to be.
    - Refer above to the First Gateway.[184]
    - Then inevitably the damage and corruption of the worlds will be cured and purified from their illness of contamination, and [they will be] returned to their former state.
  - Or by the performance of true complete repentance which reaches all the way to its supernal source
    - known as the "World of Repentance" – a world which is free and bright and more supernal than all
    - and from there it causes an arousal which draws down holy supernal light, which is [like] the purifying waters of the Mikveh – to wash and purify all dirt of waste from the powers of impurity, and they become nullified and destroyed.
    - As per
      - "If God washes the excrement of the daughters of Zion"[185]
      - "and I threw on them waters of purification."[186]

Rabbi Chaim's Note:
Note 28 – God gradually rejects evil vs. instant rejection for idol worship

- With this we can understand Chazal's statement:[187] [R. Nachman says,] all mockery is forbidden except for mockery of idolatry which is permitted, as per "Bel is kneeling and Nevo is doubled over . . . [they have doubled over and fallen on their knees together] they could not escape being carried off."[188]
- According to this, the last verse in this section is very surprising as it

---

183 Zohar Raya Mehemna III Pinchas 234a:
- The heart is Israel, which can distinguish between good and bad, between impure blood and pure blood, and it purifies that blood, like extracting food from waste; and after the heart, which is Yaakov, has completed its purification of the blood, it leaves the liver, which is Esav, with the waste [i.e., the punishment is the equivalent of the body having to handle the impurities].

184 I.e., the end of G1:12 which explains these two methods of correction, i.e., of acceptance and repentance.

- וְאֵינָם חוֹזְרִים לְאֵיתָן בְּרִיאוּתָם וְתִקּוּנָם הָאֲמִתִּי כְּמִקֶּדֶם, עַד אֲשֶׁר יִתְרוֹקְנוּ אֵלּוּ כֹּחוֹת הַטֻּמְאָה
  ○ עַל יְדֵי קַבּוּל הָאָדָם עָנְשׁוֹ הָרָאוּי לוֹ.
  ○ וּכְמוֹ שֶׁכָּתוּב בְּרַעְיָא מְהֵימְנָא פִּנְחָס רל"ד סוֹף ע"א, וְרֵישׁ ע"ב שָׁם, עַיֵּן שָׁם
    □ שֶׁעַל יְדֵי זֶה מִמֵּילָא מִגּוֹ יְגָרְשׁוּ, וּכְרֶגַע סָפוּ תַמּוּ.
    □ וְעַיֵּן לְעֵיל בְּשַׁעַר א' (פֶּרֶק י"ב).
  ○ וְאָז מִמֵּילָא מִתְרַפֵּא הַפְּגָם וְהַקִּלְקוּל שֶׁל הָעוֹלָמוֹת, וְנִטְהָרִים מֵחֶלְאַת זֻהֲמָתָם וְחוֹזְרִים לְתִקּוּנָם הָרִאשׁוֹן.
- אוֹ עַל יְדֵי הַתְּשׁוּבָה שְׁלֵמָה אֲמִתִּית, שֶׁמַּגַּעַת עַד שָׁרְשָׁהּ הָעֶלְיוֹן הַנִּקְרָא "עוֹלָם הַתְּשׁוּבָה", עָלְמָא דְּחִירוּ וּנְהִירוּ עִלָּאָה דְּכֹלָּא
  ○ וּמִשָּׁם מִתְעוֹרֵר וְנִמְשָׁךְ אוֹר עֶלְיוֹן קָדוֹשׁ, אֲשֶׁר הוּא מֵי מִקְוֶה טָהֳרָה, לִרְחֹץ וּלְטַהֵר כָּל לִכְלוּךְ פְּסֹלֶת כֹּחוֹת הַטֻּמְאָה, וְהֵם בְּטֵלִים וְכָלִים.
  ○ וְהוּא עִנְיַן הַכָּתוּב
    ◊ "אִם רָחַץ אֲדֹנָי אֵת צֹאַת בְּנוֹת צִיּוֹן" (שָׁם)
    ◊ וְכֵן (יחזקאל לו, כה) "וְזָרַקְתִּי עֲלֵיכֶם מַיִם טְהוֹרִים" וְגוֹ':

הַגָּהָה כ"ח

- וּבָזֶה יוּבַן מַאֲמָרָם זִכְרוֹנָם לִבְרָכָה (מגילה כה, ב) "כָּל לֵיצָנוּתָא אֲסִירָא, בַּר מִלֵּיצָנוּתָא דַּעֲבוֹדָה זָרָה דְּשַׁרְיָא, דִּכְתִיב (ישעיה מו, א) "כָּרַע בֵּל קֹרֵס נְבוֹ כו' (כִּי) לֹא יָכְלוּ מַלֵּט מַשָּׂא":
- וְלִכְאוֹרָה, לְפִי זֶה יִפָּלֵא מְאֹד סֵיפֵיהּ דְּהַאי עִנְיָנָא שָׁם, שֶׁסִּיֵּם "וַאֲנִי אֶסְבֹּל וַאֲמַלֵּט", וּמְעוֹדִי נִפְלָאתִי עַל זֶה:

---

185 Yishayahu 4:4, already quoted earlier in this chapter.
186 Yechezkel 36:25.
187 Megillah 25b.
188 Yishayahu 46:1–2. Bel and Nevo are Babylonian deities upon whom Scripture is heaping ridicule. Rashi on these verses in Yishayahu understands these comments of kneeling and doubling over as with one who has a stomach ailment and passes their bowels suddenly in a squat and a splash in contrast to the normal passing of bowels.

concludes: "and I will put up with you and rescue you"[189] and I have always wondered about this?[190]

- On the basis of our words it is clear to one who understands as I wrote above[191]
  - that in all that we speak of God, we only speak of His connection with the worlds
  - which are all arranged as one as per the appearance of the image of man, so to speak, literally containing [a parallel] of all of his limbs and aspects
  - and all of a Jew's actions are to the worlds like food is to the body
  - and those actions which are not good, God forbid, are converted into dirt and filth within the [worlds] and they [become] the powers of impurity.
- This is the meaning of the verse, that idol worship cannot control itself to bear, release, and to extract the putrid load which contaminates it in a normal way
  - that "they have doubled over and fallen on their knees together."
  - It is because [the idols] have no essential or intrinsic ability to remove and rid themselves of their contamination.
- In contrast, this is not the case with God
  - 'awesome is His deed'[192] 'Whose Hand grasps judgment'[193]
  - and is in no hurry, God forbid, to instantly dispatch all the powers of judgment and the Kelipot
  - which are the dirt and filth which were made in the worlds which parallel and correspond to man's limbs which digest food
  - as to do so would destroy all the worlds [by this sudden removal].
  - Instead, He bears them and puts up with [the impurities], so to speak
  - and releases them from the worlds in a normal gradual way
  - effecting judgment in the world through afflictions which are gradually applied over an extended period
  - as per
    - "You alone did I know . . . therefore I will hold you to account for all your iniquities"[194]

---

189 Yishayahu 46:4.
190 As highlighted by Rashi this verse describes the contrast of how God bears His people and rescues them from their difficulties. The question is therefore why, with idols, there is an immediate and uncontrollable discharge of the *bowels*, i.e., the evil, but with God, He holds back and contains and controls any evil performed by His people, with the result that the evil is retained for a longer period?

- וְעַל פִּי דְבָרֵינוּ אֵלֶּה, הוּא מְבֹאָר לַמַּשְׂכִּיל, כְּמוֹ שֶׁכָּתַבְתִּי לְעֵיל
  - שֶׁכָּל מַה שֶּׁאָנוּ מְדַבְּרִים בּוֹ יִתְבָּרַךְ, הַכֹּל הוּא רַק מִצַּד הִתְחַבְּרוּתוֹ יִתְבָּרַךְ לָעוֹלָמוֹת
  - שֶׁמְּסֻדָּרִים כֻּלָּם כְּאֶחָד כְּמַרְאֵה דְמוּת אָדָם כִּבְיָכוֹל, בְּכָל הָאֵבָרִים וְהָעִנְיָנִים שֶׁבּוֹ מַמָּשׁ.
  - וְכָל מַעֲשֵׂי אִישׁ יִשְׂרָאֵל — הֵמָּה לְהָעוֹלָמוֹת כְּעִנְיַן הַמָּזוֹן לַגּוּף
  - וְהַמַּעֲשִׂים אֲשֶׁר לֹא טוֹבִים חַס וְשָׁלוֹם — הֵמָּה נֶהְפָּכִים בְּתוֹכָם לְלִכְלוּךְ וְטֻנֹּפֶת, וְהֵם כֹּחוֹת הַטֻּמְאָה:
- זֶהוּ שֶׁאָמַר הַכָּתוּב, שֶׁהָעֲבוֹדָה זָרָה אֵינָהּ יְכוֹלָה לְהִתְאַפֵּק וְלִסְבֹּל, לְמַלֵּט וּלְהוֹצִיא כַּהֹגֶן מַשָּׂא הַזֻּהֲמָא שֶׁמְּטַמְּאִים אוֹתָהּ
  - אֶלָּא "קָרְסוּ כָּרְעוּ יַחְדָּו" (שם) כו'
  - הַיְנוּ, שֶׁאֵין לָהֶם שׁוּם כֹּחַ עַצְמִיּוּת, שֶׁיּוּכְלוּ לְגָרֵשׁ וּלְהוֹצִיא מֵאִתָּם הַזֻּהֲמָא מֵעַצְמָם:
- לֹא כֵן הוּא יִתְבָּרַךְ שְׁמוֹ
  - נוֹרָא עֲלִילָה כִּי תֹאחֵז בְּמִשְׁפָּט יָדוֹ
  - וְאֵינוֹ מְמַהֵר לִשְׁלֹחַ חַס וְשָׁלוֹם בְּפַעַם אַחַת כָּל הַכֹּחוֹת הַדִּין וְהַקְּלִפּוֹת
  - שֶׁהֵן הַטֻּנֹּפֶת וְהַלִּכְלוּךְ שֶׁנַּעֲשׂוּ בְּהָעוֹלָמוֹת הַמַּקְבִּילִים וּמְכֻוָּנִים לְאֵבְרֵי מְבַשְּׁלֵי הָאֲכִילָה שֶׁבָּאָדָם
  - כִּי הָיוּ מַחֲרִיבִין חַס וְשָׁלוֹם אֶת כָּל הָעוֹלָם.
  - אֶלָּא שֶׁהוּא נוֹשְׂאָם וְסוֹבְלָם כִּבְיָכוֹל
  - וּמְמַלְּטָם מֵהָעוֹלָמוֹת כַּהֹגֶן מְעַט מְעַט
  - לִפְעֹל הַדִּין בָּעוֹלָם עַל יְדֵי יִסּוּרִין מְעַט מְעַט בְּהֶמְשֵׁךְ זְמַן
  - כְּעִנְיַן הַכָּתוּב
    - "רַק אֶתְכֶם יָדַעְתִּי גו' עַל כֵּן אֶפְקֹד עֲלֵיכֶם אֵת כָּל עֲוֹנֹתֵיכֶם" (עמוס ג, ב)

---

191 In a number of places above e.g., at the end of G2:03.
192 Tehillim 66:5.
193 Devarim 32:41.
194 Amos 3:2.

- - Chazal's comment on this[195]
  - until, over the fullness of time, the dirt and filth, which are the powers of impurity within the worlds, will have been fully extracted following the completion of man's receipt of his punishment
  - as written in the main text, that after completion of the receipt of punishment, the [impurities] automatically cease to be
  - and then the worlds return to their former state of strength, health, and repair.
- Understand this!

8. ADVERSE IMPACT OF SIN IS A NATURAL CONSEQUENCE AND NOT A PUNISHMENT

- Therefore, Chazal state that "one who says that God overlooks sin, overlooks his life."[196] This statement is strange and has partially been explained above in G1:12.[197]
- [However,] in our current context, this idea is better explained, that [God] seeks no revenge – but
  - just as it is man's nature, that if he eats food which is naturally damaging and is injurious to the body
    - then that food will injure him or also cause him to become ill
    - and if poisonous, then he will die from it and will be personally liable for his own life
  - it is similarly the case with the sins of the sinning soul, God forbid
    - as God has fixed it in His Will
    - that the nature of the arrangement and the details of the worlds is such that man's actions, whether good or bad, God forbid, are conceptually like food and sustenance for them.
    - There is no relevance [in God] overlooking this
    - and he [the sinner] is forced to empty out the dirt and impurity which has increased in the worlds as a result of his sin by one of the two previously mentioned methods.[198]
- Now you will see and surely understand the concept of the *addition* and *increase* of blessing

---

195 Avodah Zarah 4a:
- To what is this compared, to a person who lends money to two people, one that he loves and the other he hates. He takes his repayment from the one he loves gradually, and from the one he hates in one go.
- Rashi explains that so too it is with Israel that God takes repayment gradually in this world so that they can merit on the Day of Judgment.

- כַּיָּדוּעַ מַאֲמָרָם זִכְרוֹנָם לִבְרָכָה עַל זֶה (עבודה זרה דף ה, א).
- עַד שֶׁבְּרֹבוֹת הַיָּמִים יִתְרוֹקֵן לְכִלּוּךְ הַטִּנֹּפֶת, הֵם כֹּחוֹת הַטֻּמְאָה מֵהָעוֹלָמוֹת מִכֹּל וָכֹל, אַחַר שֶׁיִּגָּמֵר קִבּוּל עָנְשׁוֹ שֶׁל הָאָדָם.
- כְּמוֹ שֶׁכָּתוּב בִּפְנִים, שֶׁאַחַר גְּמַר קִבּוּל הָעֹנֶשׁ הֵם כָּלִים מֵאֲלֵיהֶם
- וְאָז יַחְזְרוּ הָעוֹלָמוֹת לְאֵיתָן בְּרִיאָתָם וְתִקּוּנָם הָרִאשׁוֹן:
- וְהֵן:

שער ב' - פרק ח'

- וְזֶהוּ מַאֲמָרָם זִכְרוֹנָם לִבְרָכָה (בבא קמא נ, א) "כָּל הָאוֹמֵר הַקָּדוֹשׁ בָּרוּךְ הוּא וַתְּרָן הוּא יַתְרוּן חַיּוֹהִי", אֲשֶׁר לִכְאוֹרָה נִפְלֵאת, וּכְבָר נִתְבָּאֵר קְצָת לְמַעְלָה בְּשַׁעַר א' פֶּרֶק י"ב:
- וְלִדְבָרֵינוּ כָּאן, הָעִנְיָן יוֹתֵר מְבֹאָר בְּטוּב טַעַם, שֶׁאֵינוֹ עַל דֶּרֶךְ הַנְּקִימָה חַס וְשָׁלוֹם, אֶלָּא
  - שֶׁכְּמוֹ שֶׁמִּטֶּבַע הָאָדָם, שֶׁאִם יֹאכַל מַאֲכָל שֶׁבְּטִבְעוֹ הוּא מְקַלְקֵל וּמַזִּיק לְגוּפוֹ
    - יַזִּיק לוֹ אוֹתוֹ הַמַּאֲכָל אוֹ גַּם יֶחֱלֶה מִמֶּנּוּ
    - וְאִם סַם הַמָּוֶת הוּא, יָמוּת מִמֶּנּוּ, וּבְעַצְמוֹ נִתְחַיֵּב בְּנַפְשׁוֹ.
  - כֵּן הוּא בְּעִנְיַן הָעֲוֹנוֹת שֶׁל הַנֶּפֶשׁ הַחוֹטֵאת חַס וְשָׁלוֹם
  - כֵּיוָן שֶׁכֵּן קָבַע הוּא יִתְבָּרַךְ בִּרְצוֹנוֹ
  - טֶבַע סִדּוּר מַצָּבָם וְעִנְיְנֵיהֶם שֶׁל הָעוֹלָמוֹת, שֶׁמַּעֲשֵׂי הָאָדָם הַטּוֹבִים אוֹ רָעִים חַס וְשָׁלוֹם הֵם כְּעִנְיַן מַאֲכָל וּמָזוֹן לָהֶם
  - אֵין שַׁיָּךְ וַתְּרָנוּת בָּזֶה
  - וְהוּא מֻכְרָח לְהָרִיק לְכִלּוּךְ הַטֻּמְאָה שֶׁהִגְבִּיר בַּעֲוֹנוֹ בָּעוֹלָמוֹת, עַל יְדֵי אֶחָד מִשְּׁנֵי הַתִּקּוּנִים הַנַּ"ל:
- וְעַתָּה תֶּחֱזֶה וּבֵין תָּבִין עִנְיַן הַתּוֹסֶפֶת וְרִבּוּי בְּרָכָה

---

196 Bava Kama 50a.
197 The question asked in G1:12 is that given that even man when merciful is able to overlook things, then surely God who is ultimately merciful would be able overlook things? The answer given there is that it is the very act of sin which is the punishment in and of itself.
198 I.e., 1. a person's acceptance of the natural consequences (the *punishment*), or 2. true repentance.

- and the tremendous requirement of our holy service in general to cause the worlds to essentially exist
- and to draw down and bestow within them a multitude of blessings and additional holiness
- through the connection of God's Essence to them as per His Supernal Will, just like the food and sustenance [analogy], as mentioned above
- and this is His Will and Honor, for reasons hidden with Him which we are unable to fathom.

• It is therefore fitting for every member of the Holy People whose heart is concerned that his actions will be acceptable before God
- to forge this thought and the appropriate purity of intention when involved with Torah study and Mitzvah performance
- to draw down and add holiness and new light to the worlds through this *food*.

9. PRAYER AT ITS PRESCRIBED TIME IS THE MAIN FORM OF SUSTENANCE OF WORLDS

• Specifically,[199] the main form of *food* for the worlds and for man's soul itself is the act of prayer[200] at its prescribed time.[201], (Note 29)[202] As per Chazal:
- His food is prayer which is equated with a sacrifice.[203]
- "And Rivka said to Yaakov" . . . that he should arouse himself with these fine foods of his, and Yaakov aroused himself, in this lower world by enwrapping himself in prayer and supplication . . . "and [Yitzchak] said, who was the one who hunted game?" with many prayers and requests "and I ate from all of it."[204]
- "And eat of the game of his son," these are the prayers that go and separate. . . .[205]
- "I ate of the honeycomb . . . ." The sequence of this verse is entirely explained as connected with the format of prayer. Refer to it.[206] The

---

199 In continuation from the previous chapter.
200 R. Chaim now accentuates the specific importance of prayer as the main form of world sustenance in contrast to Torah study and Mitzvah performance which he previously mentioned with prayer as the three methods of drawing God's sustenance into the worlds, as per G2:06.
201 R. Chaim highlights the importance of the *timing* of prayer and elaborates on this in the Chapters Section (e.g., GC:04). He also highlights in G4:26 that while prayer is capable of bringing down *additional* light into the worlds, and as per this chapter is the principal medium for doing so – nevertheless, it is eclipsed by the power of Torah study which gives existence to the worlds.

- וּמַה רַב עֹצֶם צֹרֶךְ עֲבוֹדָתֵנוּ הַקְּדוֹשָׁה בִּכְלָלָהּ אֶל עַצְמוּת קִיּוּם הַעֲמָדַת הָעוֹלָמוֹת
- וּלְהַמְשִׁיךְ וּלְהַשְׁפִּיעַ בְּתוֹכָם רֹב בְּרָכוֹת וְתוֹסֶפֶת קְדֻשָּׁה
- מִצַּד הִתְחַבְּרוּת עַצְמוּתוֹ יִתְבָּרַךְ אֲלֵיהֶם כְּפִי הָרָצוֹן הָעֶלְיוֹן יִתְבָּרַךְ שְׁמוֹ, כְּעִנְיָן הָאֲכִילָה וְהַמָּזוֹן כַּנַּ"ל
- וְזֶהוּ רְצוֹנוֹ וּכְבוֹדוֹ יִתְבָּרַךְ מִטַּעַם כָּמוּס אִתּוֹ יִתְבָּרַךְ שְׁמוֹ אֲשֶׁר אֵין בִּיכָלְתֵּנוּ לְהַשִּׂיג:
- וְרָאוּי לְכָל אִישׁ מֵעַם הַקֹּדֶשׁ, אֲשֶׁר לִבּוֹ חָרֵד שֶׁיִּהְיוּ מַעֲשָׂיו רְצוּיִים לְפָנָיו יִתְבָּרַךְ
- לְצָרֵף זֹאת הַמַּחֲשָׁבָה וְטֹהַר הַכַּוָּנָה הָרְצוּיָה, בְּעֵסֶק הַתּוֹרָה וּמַעֲשֵׂי הַמִּצְוֹת כֻּלָּם
- לְהַמְשִׁיךְ וּלְהוֹסִיף, עַל יְדֵי אוֹתוֹ הַמָּזוֹן, קְדֻשָּׁה וְאוֹר חָדָשׁ בָּעוֹלָמוֹת:

שער ב' - פרק ט'

- וּבִפְרָט בְּעֵת עָמְדוֹ לְהִתְפַּלֵּל לְפָנָיו יִתְבָּרַךְ, אֲשֶׁר בְּשַׁעֲתָהּ הַמְיֻחֶדֶת לָהּ הִיא עִקַּר הַמָּזוֹן לְהָעוֹלָמוֹת וּלְנֶפֶשׁ הָאָדָם עַצְמוֹ. (הגהה כ"ט) וּכְמוֹ שֶׁכָּתוּב
- בַּזֹּהַר בְּרֵאשִׁית כ"ד א', מְזוֹנָא דִּילֵיהּ צְלוֹתָא, דַּחֲשִׁיבָא לְקָרְבְּנָא.
- וּבְרַעְיָא מְהֵימְנָא פָּרָשַׁת אֱמוֹר (הַנַּ"ל בְּפֶרֶק ז'), "וְרִבְקָה אָמְרָה אֶל יַעֲקֹב" (בראשית כז, ו) כו', לְאִתְעָרָא אִיהוּ בְּאִנּוּן מַטְעַמִּים דִּילֵיהּ. וְיַעֲקֹב אִתְעַר מִתַּתָּא מִתְלַבֵּשׁ בִּצְלוֹתִין וּבָעוּתִין כו'. "וַיֹּאמֶר מִי אֵפוֹא הַצָּד צַיִד" (שם) בְּכַמָּה צְלוֹתִין וּבָעוּתִין "וָאוֹכַל מִכֹּל" וכו'.
- וּבְפָרָשַׁת פִּנְחָס רל"ה א' "וְיֹאכַל מִצֵּיד בְּנוֹ" אִלֵּין אִנּוּן צְלוֹתִין דְּאָזְלִין וּמִתְעָרְכִין כו'.
- וּבַזֹּהַר שָׁם רכ"ו א' וּב' בֵּאֵר כָּל סֵדֶר הַכָּתוּב "אָכַלְתִּי יַעְרִי" (שה"ש ה, א)

This is as per the quotation brought in G4:26 describing prayer as providing *transitory life* relating to the additional light that can be brought into the world by it, but only when it is performed at its specific prescribed time, whereas Torah study is described as providing *everlasting life*.

202 **R. Chaim adds Note 29 here.** This note is brought at the end of this chapter and is entitled "Prayer in place of sacrifices as food for God at specific times."
203 Zohar I Bereishit 24a.
204 Zohar Raya Mehemna III Emor 99b/100a quoting Bereishit 27:6 and 27:33.
205 Zohar Raya Mehemna III 235a quoting Bereishit 27:31.
206 Zohar III Pinchas 226a quoting Shir Hashirim 5:1.

Zohar also explains this [elsewhere] in relation to prayer but in a slightly different way. Refer to it.[207]
- R. Shimon says: This is the secret of why it is forbidden for a person to taste anything until the King of the Supernal Realms has eaten, and what [does He eat?] – prayer... until the King of the Supernal Realms has eaten, that is the first three [blessings] and last three [blessings of the Amidah], since He ate....[208] Refer to it at length.

• This is all in line with the meaning of that stated above, that it is a drawing down of additional holiness, blessing, and light to all the worlds.
- As per Zohar Vayechi mentioned above.[209] Refer to it well.
- And the true servant of God needs to focus on this.[210]

Rabbi Chaim's Note:
Note 29 – Prayer in place of sacrifices as food for God at specific times

• The service of prayer was instituted to correspond to the service of the Tamid[211] sacrifices, for they [the Tamid sacrifices] were also fixed to be at specific times and form the main staple of *food*, as mentioned above [i.e., to sustain God's connection with the worlds]. As per:
- "My offering, My food."[212]
- ("You shall make one lamb in the morning and you shall make the second lamb in the afternoon"[213] This parallels the [human] morning and evening meals which form the main food intake [for the day]).
- "For he offers up the bread of your God."[214]
- "You are my beloved (Rayati)," "Rayati" means "sustains me" as they feed me with two Tamid sacrifices.[215]
- "My offering, My food," [God commands for there to be an arousal from food in the Supernal Realms – reflecting the arousal from food in the lower realms].[216]
- "Binyamin is a predatory wolf, [in the morning he will devour prey and in the evening he will distribute spoils"... Another explanation of "predatory wolf" is that the Altar is in Binyamin's land allocation (of the Land of Israel) and the Altar is a *wolf*... because it consumes (sacrificial) meat all day, and Binyamin would sustain it (the Altar with sacrifices,) as it was in his portion – it was therefore as if he sustained this *wolf*... "he will devour prey" and will enjoy his initial connection, when will this be? In the morning, for God must first be blessed and only then others will be blessed. Therefore, a person is forbidden to bless his friend in the morning before he blesses God. This is the meaning of "in the morning he will devour his prey" and afterwards others will be blessed that "in the evening he will distribute spoils."

וְגוֹ'. גַּם עַל סֵדֶר מַטְבֵּעַ הַתְּפִלָּה כֻּלָּהּ מֵרֵאשִׁיתָהּ עַד סוֹפָהּ, עַיֵּן שָׁם. וְכֵן בְּרַעְיָא מְהֵימְנָא שָׁם רמ"ד א', פֵּרְשׁוּ גַם כֵּן עַל סֵדֶר הַתְּפִלָּה בְּאֹפֶן אַחֵר קְצָת, עַיֵּן שָׁם.

וְשָׁם רמ"א ב', אָמַר רַבִּי שִׁמְעוֹן, עַל רָזָא דָא אָסִיר לְבַר נָשׁ לְמִטְעוֹם כְּלוּם עַד דְּיֵיכוֹל מַלְכָּא עִלָּאָה, וּמַה אִיהוּ, צְלוֹתָא כו'. עַד דְּמַלְכָּא עִלָּאָה אָכִיל, וְהַיְנוּ שָׁלֹשׁ רִאשׁוֹנוֹת וְשָׁלֹשׁ אַחֲרוֹנוֹת, כֵּיוָן דְּאִיהוּ אָכִיל כו', עַיֵּן שָׁם בְּאֹרֶךְ:

• וְהַכֹּל עַל הַכַּוָּנָה הַנַּ"ל, שֶׁהוּא הַמַּמְשֶׁכֶת תּוֹסֶפֶת קְדֻשָּׁה וּבְרָכָה וּנְהִירוּ לְכָל עָלְמִין

 ○ וְכַמְפֹרָשׁ בַּזֹּהַר וַיְחִי הַנַּ"ל, עַיֵּן שָׁם הֵיטֵב.

 ○ וְצָרִיךְ הָעוֹבֵד הָאֲמִתִּי לְכַוֵּן לָזֶה:

הגהה כ"ט

• וַעֲבוֹדַת הַתְּפִלָּה נֶגֶד תְּמִידִין תִּקְּנוּהָ (ברכות כו, ב), שֶׁהָיוּ גַּם כֵּן בִּשְׁעָתָהּ הַקָּבוּעַ לָהֶם עִקַּר הַמָּזוֹן הַנַּ"ל

 ○ כְּעִנְיָן "אֶת קָרְבָּנִי לַחְמִי" (במדבר כח, ב)

 ○ ("אֶת הַכֶּבֶשׂ אֶחָד תַּעֲשֶׂה בַבֹּקֶר, וְאֵת הַכֶּבֶשׂ הַשֵּׁנִי תַּעֲשֶׂה בֵּין הָעַרְבָּיִם", כְּעִנְיָן סְעוּדַת הַבֹּקֶר וְהָעֶרֶב שֶׁהֵן עִקַּר הַמָּזוֹן.

 ○ וּכְתִיב (ויקרא כא, ח) "כִּי אֶת לֶחֶם אֱלֹהֶיךָ הוּא מַקְרִיב".

 ○ וְהוּא אָמְרָם זִכְרוֹנָם לִבְרָכָה בְּחַזִּית, "רַעְיָתִי" — אֵין רַעְיָתִי אֶלָּא פַּרְנָסָתִי הֵן שֶׁיִּרְעוּ אוֹתִי בִּשְׁנֵי תְמִידִין" כו'.

 ○ וְעַיֵּן זֹהַר וַיֵּצֵא קס"ד א', פָּתַח כו' "אֶת קָרְבָּנִי לַחְמִי" גוֹ'

 ○ וּבְפָרָשַׁת וַיְחִי רמ"ז ב', ורמ"ח א', "בִּנְיָמִין זְאֵב יִטְרָף" גוֹ'.

---

207 Zohar III Pinchas 244a (also quoting Shir Hashirim 5:1).
208 Zohar III Pinchas 241b.
209 In R. Chaim's note, G2:09:N29, earlier in this chapter.
210 That his actions, mainly of prayer but also of Torah study and Mitzvah performance, draw down additional holiness and blessing to the worlds.
211 Berachot 26b.
212 Bamidbar 28:2.
213 As the verses continue in Bamidbar 28:4.
214 Vayikra 21:8.
215 Shir Hashirim Rabba Parsha 1 9:6, i.e., play on words on Rayati/Yiruh.
216 Zohar I Bereishit Vayetze 164a quoting Bamidbar 28:2.

For the sacrifices that were (offered) first all draw near to God and the arousal rises to there, and because He is blessed, connections are formed with all the other supernal hosts and blessing is distributed to each of them as appropriate, the worlds are sweetened, and the Supernal and Lower Realms are blessed].[217]

- "My Beloved should come to His garden and *eat* [his fine fruits," What does it mean by "*eat* his fine fruits?" These are the sacrifices . . .].[218]
- Refer to all of these statements at length.
- [. . . R. Chizkiya related this verse to the sacrifices, that they are the meal of the King offered up to Him . . .][219]
- [. . . and this pleasure rests in the place where it rests when the smell of the sacrifices rises up. Come and see, when there is food in the lower realm, there is food in the Supernal Realm . . .][220]
- [. . . for there is no greater benefit and satisfaction to God in this world than from Torah study and the one who merits it sustains Him, so to speak, and provides Him with food from this world, even more than from sacrifices . . . and from the time of the destruction of the Temple and the cessation of the sacrifices, God only has these words of Torah . . .][221]
- "I ate of the honeycomb. . . ." This verse is explained in the context of the sacrifices, refer there.[222]
- Also refer to Zohar[223] which expands on this in a wonderful way.

• Similarly, [the Zohar over] there explains and details all the digestive organs of a person, which also are in [and reflect] the arrangement of the components of the Merkava, worlds and supernal powers. They are literally referred to with the same names as those organs, and are the organs which process sacrifices. Refer well to the Zohar.[224]

---

217 Zohar I Vayechi 247b and 248a quoting Bereishit 49:27.
218 Zohar II Bo 37b quoting Shir Hashirim 4:16.
219 Zohar III Vayikra 4a.
220 Zohar III Vayikra 7a–b.
221 Zohar III Balak 202a.
222 Zohar III Pinchas 241a quoting Shir Hashirim 5:1.
223 Zohar III Pinchas 252b:
  • [This source refers to the Show Bread as being God's food.]
  Zohar III Pinchas 240b:
  • [This section of Zohar explains why sacrifices come from Behemot/animals and birds, etc. In connection with Behemot, it refers to a particular Behema which consumes 1,000 mountains every day. This Behema is the numerical value of one of the expansions of the name YHVH (i.e., with a value of 52) and this *consumption*, triggered by the offering of the animal sacrifice, is

- וּבְפָרָשַׁת בֹּא ל"ז ב' "יָבֹא דוֹדִי לְגַנּוֹ וְיֹאכַל" כוּ'
- עַיֵּן שָׁם בְּכָל אֵלּוּ הַמַּאֲמָרִים בְּאֹרֶךְ.
- וּבְפָרָשַׁת וַיִּקְרָא דַף ד' ע"א
- וְשָׁם בְּדַף ז' סוֹף ע"א
- וּבְפָרָשַׁת בָּלָק ר"ב סוֹף ע"א
- וּבְפָרָשַׁת פִּנְחָס רמ"א א', דָּרְשׁוּ כָּל עִנְיַן הַכָּתוּב "אָכַלְתִּי יַעְרִי" וְגוֹ', עַל סוֹד עִנְיַן הַקָּרְבָּנוֹת, עַיֵּן שָׁם
- וְשָׁם בְּפָרָשַׁת פִּנְחָס רנ"ב ב', וְעַיֵּן שָׁם ר"מ ע"ב עִנְיָן נִפְלָא בָּזֶה:

• וְכֵן פֵּרֵט וּבֵאֵר שָׁם כָּל אֶבְרֵי כְלֵי מְבַשְּׁלֵי וּמְעַכְּלֵי הָאֲכִילָה שֶׁבָּאָדָם, שֶׁהֵמָּה גַם כֵּן בְּסִדְרֵי פִּרְקֵי הַמֶּרְכָּבָה עוֹלָמוֹת וְכֹחוֹת עֶלְיוֹנִים, מְכֻנִּים בִּשְׁמוֹת אוֹתָן הָאֵבָרִים מַמָּשׁ, שֶׁהֵן כְּלֵי מְבַשְּׁלֵי וּמְבָרְרֵי הַקָּרְבָּן, עַיֵּן שָׁם הֵיטֵב בְּדַף רכ"ד ע"ד, וְדַף רל"ה, ורל"ה, בַּזֹּהַר וּבְרַעְיָא מְהֵימְנָא שָׁם

---

as per the verse "For God, your God, is a consuming fire, a jealous God" (Devarim 4:24).]

224 Zohar III Pinchas 224a and Raya Mehemna:
- The brain, which is male [i.e., relates to the Partzuf of Zeer Anpin; see p. 233, fn. 399, for details of Partzufim], rides on and controls the heart [which is female and relates to Malchut and the Partzuf of Nukva]. The heart controls and rides on the liver. The liver is both Samael [The Angel of Death – see G1:13] and The Snake [which brought death to mankind], a unified entity comprising the diaphragm and the liver. Therefore, with a sacrifice, the diaphragm is *the snake* and the liver is the food of the male which is the secret of the Sitra Achara . . . the heart does not take from any of [the sacrifice] except from the confession which was performed with it which ascends with the smoke and prayer performed over the sacrifice, [then] the heart sacrifices to the brain, the will of the unity of the Cohanim within it and the joy of the Leviim . . .
- . . . Raya Mehemna says that sacrifices are only brought to distance the sides of impurity and to draw near the sides of holiness, and we learned from the first work [i.e., the main section of the Zohar] that there are large and small blood vessels of the liver which extend to the sides and take [sustenance] from the innards and the fats which are consumed [on the Altar] all night long, for the sacrifice is all for God [i.e., fully separating impurity from holiness].

Zohar III Pinchas 234/235 and Raya Mehemna:
- [This section of Zohar elaborates on the connection between the organs of the body and the sacrifices at length.]

- This is the secret of the four levels of sacrifice as per *"Isheh Re'ach Nichoach Lashem"*[/"a burnt offering, a fragrant fragrance to God"].[225]
  - The three levels of *Isheh*, *Re'ach* and *Nichoach* relate to the three principal digestive organs [i.e., the principal organs which ultimately absorb the food], the liver, heart, and brain.
  - *Isheh* relates to the liver, *Re'ach* relates to the heart, and *Nichoah* to the brain (this is not the place for a lengthy explanation of this concept)
  - that through these, the three levels of Nefesh, Ruach, and Neshama [are able] to reside
  - as their main place of residence is within these three organs.[226]
  - There is an additional, hidden level, the level of the *soul of the soul* which is the secret of the root of the soul which cleaves to God, so to speak. This is the level of *Lashem*.[227]
- Therefore, Chazal say:[228] In the times when the Temple existed, the Sacrificial Altar would atone, but now a man's table atones for him.

10. EVERY SPOKEN WORD OF PRAYER HAS TREMENDOUS IMPACT

- This focus is not just restricted to statements within prayer of "Blessed are You . . . ," which means an addition and increase of blessing and bestowal, but this same holy focus is also relevant to each and every word of the formulated prayer sequence.
  - For each word of prayer or of a specific blessing ascends to the highest levels, via 'winged creatures who take sounds,'[229] to impact on its supernal root which it specifically relates to, and through this [the person uttering these words] becomes a partner of the Creator, so to speak, building and establishing a multitude of worlds.
  - As per: When a person utters the breath and speech of his prayer, many winged creatures open their wings and mouths to receive them, as written "for the birds of the Heavens will take the sound and the winged ones [will tell the words]," and God will take those words and build worlds with them, as written about them: "for the new Heavens and the new Earth [which I make]," the secret of the word is "I will place My words in Your mouth [and cover you with the shadow of my hand,] to plant heavens [and to establish land] and say to Zion, "you are my people (Ami)," don't read this as "my people (Ami)" but rather as "with me (Imi)" in partnership.[230]

---

225 Vayikra 1:9.

- וּבְסוֹד אַרְבַּע דְּרָגִין דְּקָרְבָּן "אִשֶּׁה רֵיחַ נִיחֹחַ לַה'" (ויקרא א, ט).
- שָׁלֹשׁ דְּרָגִין 'אִשֶּׁה', 'רֵיחַ', 'נִיחֹחַ', כְּסִדְרָן בִּשְׁלֹשָׁה עִקְּרֵי אֵבְרֵי הָאֲכִילָה כָּבֵד לֵב מֹחַ
- אִשֶּׁה — בַּכָּבֵד, רֵיחַ — בַּלֵּב, נִיחֹחַ — בַּמֹּחַ, (וּבְבֵאוּר עִנְיָנָם אֵין כָּאן מָקוֹם לְהַאֲרִיךְ)
- שֶׁעַל יָדָם מִתְיַשְּׁבִין הַשְּׁלֹשָׁה בְּחִינוֹת נר"ן
- שֶׁעִקַּר מִשְׁכָּנָם הוּא בְּתוֹךְ אֵלּוּ שְׁלֹשָׁה אֵבָרִים.
- וְעוֹד דַּרְגָּא עִלָּאָה טְמִירָא, בְּחִינַת "נִשְׁמָתָא לְנִשְׁמָתָא", סוֹד שֹׁרֶשׁ הַנְּשָׁמָה הַדְּבוּקָה כִּבְיָכוֹל בּוֹ יִתְבָּרַךְ, וְזֶהוּ "לַה'":
- וְלָכֵן אָמְרוּ רַבּוֹתֵינוּ זִכְרוֹנָם לִבְרָכָה (ברכות נה, א) "בִּזְמַן שֶׁבֵּית הַמִּקְדָּשׁ הָיָה קַיָּם מִזְבֵּחַ מְכַפֵּר, עַכְשָׁיו שֻׁלְחָנוֹ שֶׁל אָדָם מְכַפֵּר עָלָיו":

שער ב' - פרק י'

- וְלֹא זוֹ בִּלְבַד בְּתֵיבַת "בָּרוּךְ אַתָּה", שֶׁפֵּרוּשׁוֹ הוּא תּוֹסֶפֶת רִבּוּי בְּרָכָה וְשֶׁפַע, שַׁיָּךְ זֹאת הַכַּוָּנָה, אֶלָּא שֶׁגַּם בְּכָל תֵּבָה וְתֵבָה מִכָּל נֻסַּח הַתְּפִלָּה, שַׁיָּךְ גַּם כֵּן זֹאת הַכַּוָּנָה הַקְּדוֹשָׁה.
- כִּי כָּל תֵּבָה מֵהַתְּפִלָּה, אוֹ שֶׁל אֵיזֶה בְּרָכָה, הִיא הָעוֹלָה לְמַעְלָה מַעְלָה, עַל יְדֵי מָארֵי קָלִין וְגַדְפִּין דְּנָטְלִין לָהּ, לִפְעֹל פְּעֻלָּתָהּ בְּשָׁרְשָׁהּ הָעֶלְיוֹן הַמְּיֻחָד לָהּ, וְהוּא נַעֲשָׂה בְּזֶה כִּבְיָכוֹל שֻׁתָּפוֹ שֶׁל יוֹצֵר בְּרֵאשִׁית, לִבְנוֹת וְלִנְטֹעַ כַּמָּה וְכַמָּה עוֹלָמוֹת.
- כְּמוֹ שֶׁכָּתוּב בַּתִּקּוּנִים תִּקּוּן ס"ט ק"ה ב', "וְכַד בַּר נָשׁ אָפִיק הֲבָלִים וְדִבּוּרִים

---

226 See G1:14 and the connection of Nefesh, Ruach, and Neshama with the liver, heart, and brain.

227 See G2:17.

228 Berachot 55a.

229 A very similar expression to this is used in Zohar II Mishpatim 122b where it refers to these creatures as collectively forming the "ears of God."

230 Tikkunei Zohar Tikkun 69 105b/106a quoting Kohelet 10:20, Yishayahu 66:22 and 51:16. This idea is consistent with the concept of the Shiur Komah and that just as God creates the worlds with speech, e.g., "the heavens were made with the word of God" (Tehillim 33:6), so too man creates with his speech.

- 'One who is intellectual will understand'[231] from his own knowledge that it was not for nothing that the establishment of this small supplication and short prayer [i.e., the Amidah] needed [to be precisely formulated by the combined efforts of] the 120 elders [the Men of the Great Assembly] which included a number of prophets.
  - As they were able to perceive with their Divine Inspiration and high level of prophecy
  - and the pathways of the order of Creation and the components of the Merkava were lit up for them.
  - Therefore, they established and formulated the format of the blessings and prayers with these specific words
  - as they saw and perceived the way in which light [i.e., the impact] would be manifest from each individual word
  - which was very much necessary to correct many worlds, supernal powers, and the arrangement of the Merkava.
  - As Chazal state: "Our service fulfills the needs of the Most High."[232]
- As per Chazal:
  - God desires the prayers of Tzaddikim.[233]
  - Why were the Matriarchs barren . . . R. Levi said . . . As God desires their prayer.[234]
  - Come and see, Yitzchak was married to his wife for twenty years and she did not give birth until he prayed his prayer, as God desires the prayers of Tzaddikim . . . What is the reason for this? So that there will be an increase and addition in holiness to all those who are in need, through the prayers of Tzaddikim.[235]
  - As per the explicit verse "and His Will is the prayer of the righteous."[236]
- Chazal therefore refer[237] to prayer as "*words* which stand at the highest point of the Universe," meaning that the actual *words* of prayer themselves stand at this highest point. As per:
  - A person's prayer is service of the *wind* [i.e., speech] which exists in the realm of supernal secrets [i.e., a very exalted place], and people are not

---

231 Daniel 12:10, an expression used to describe those versed in Kabbalistic knowledge.
232 Shabbat 116b and Menachot 64a. In this context, service is that of prayer and the needs of the *Most High* is understood to mean correction of the supernal worlds/powers/Merkava. This expression is also used at the end of G1:09 (see p. 186, fn. 249) and at the end of G2:04.
233 Yevamot 64a.
234 Midrash Tanchuma Toldot 9.
235 Zohar I Toldot 137a.

בִּצְלוֹתֵיהּ, כַּמָּה עוֹפִין פַּתְחִין גַּדְפַיְהוּ וּפוּמַיְהוּ לְקַבְּלָא לוֹן. הֲדָא הוּא דִכְתִיב (קהלת י, כ) "כִּי עוֹף הַשָּׁמַיִם יוֹלִיךְ אֶת הַקּוֹל וּבַעַל כְּנָפַיִם" גוֹ', וְנָטִיל קוּדְשָׁא בְּרִיךְ הוּא אִנּוּן מִלִּין וּבָנֵי בְּהוֹן עָלְמִין, דְּאִתְּמַר בְּהוֹן (ישעיה סו, כב) "כִּי כַאֲשֶׁר הַשָּׁמַיִם הַחֲדָשִׁים וְהָאָרֶץ הַחֲדָשָׁה" גוֹ', וְרָזָא דְמִלָּה "וָאָשִׂים דְּבָרַי בְּפִיךָ וְגוֹ' לִנְטֹעַ שָׁמַיִם" (שם נא, טז) וְגוֹ' "וְלֵאמֹר לְצִיּוֹן עַמִּי אָתָּה", אַל תִּקְרֵי "עַמִּי" אֶלָּא "עִמִּי", בְּשֻׁתָּפִי". וְכֵן הוּא שָׁם בְּתִקּוּן ס"ט ק"ו ב':

- וְהַמַּשְׂכִּיל יָבִין מַדַּעְתּוֹ, שֶׁלֹּא לְחִנָּם הָצְרְכוּ לְתִקּוּן תְּחִנָּה קְטַנָּה וּתְפִלָּה קְצָרָה כָּזוֹ, מֵאָה וְעֶשְׂרִים זְקֵנִים וּמֵהֶם כַּמָּה נְבִיאִים.
  - אֶלָּא שֶׁהֵמָּה הִשִּׂיגוּ בְּרוּחַ קָדְשָׁם וְהַשָּׂגַת נְבוּאָתָם הָעֶלְיוֹנָה
  - וְנִהֲרָא לְהוּ שְׁבִילִין דְּכָל סִדְרֵי בְּרֵאשִׁית וּפִרְקֵי הַמֶּרְכָּבָה
  - לָזֹאת יָסְדוּ וְתִקְּנוּ מַטְבֵּעַ בְּרָכוֹת וְהַתְּפִלּוֹת בְּאֵלּוּ הַתֵּבוֹת דַּוְקָא
  - מֵאֲשֶׁר רָאוּ וְהִשִּׂיגוּ אֵיזֶה דֶּרֶךְ יִשְׁכָּן אוֹרָהּ שֶׁל כָּל תֵּבָה פְּרָטִית מֵהֶם
  - אֲשֶׁר הִיא נִצְרֶכֶת מְאֹד לְתִקּוּן רִבּוּי עוֹלָמוֹת וְכֹחוֹת עֶלְיוֹנִים וְסִדּוּר הַמֶּרְכָּבָה.
  - וּכְמַאֲמָרָם זִכְרוֹנָם לִבְרָכָה (עי' שבת קטז: מנחות סד.) "הָעֲבוֹדָה צָרֵךְ גָּבוֹהַּ":

- וְזֶהוּ עִנְיַן מַאֲמָרָם זִכְרוֹנָם לִבְרָכָה
  - "שֶׁהַקָּדוֹשׁ בָּרוּךְ הוּא מִתְאַוֶּה לִתְפִלָּתָן שֶׁל צַדִּיקִים" (יבמות סד)
  - וּבְתַנְחוּמָא פָּרָשַׁת תּוֹלְדוֹת אָמְרוּ, "וְלָמָּה נִתְעַקְּרוּ הָאִמָּהוֹת, אָמַר רַבִּי לֵוִי שֶׁהָיָה הַקָּדוֹשׁ בָּרוּךְ הוּא מִתְאַוֶּה לִתְפִלָּתָם".
  - וּבַזֹּהַר תּוֹלְדוֹת קל"ז א', "תָּא חֲזֵי עֶשְׂרִין שְׁנִין אִשְׁתַּהֵי יִצְחָק עִם אִתְּתֵיהּ וְלָא אוֹלִידַת, עַד דְּצַלֵּי צְלוֹתֵיהּ, בְּגִין דְּקוּדְשָׁא בְּרִיךְ הוּא אִתְרְעֵי בִּצְלוֹתְהוֹן דְּצַדִּיקַיָּא כוּ', מַאי טַעְמָא, בְּגִין דְּיִתְרַבֵּי וְיִתּוֹסַף רְבוּת קוּדְשָׁא, לְכָל מַאן דְּאִצְטְרִיךְ, בִּצְלוֹתְהוֹן דְּצַדִּיקַיָּא".
  - וְכָתוּב מְפֹרָשׁ (משלי טו, ח) "וּתְפִלַּת יְשָׁרִים רְצוֹנוֹ":

- וְלָכֵן קָרְאוּ רַבּוֹתֵינוּ זִכְרוֹנָם לִבְרָכָה אֶת עִנְיַן הַתְּפִלָּה, "דְּבָרִים הָעוֹמְדִים בְּרוּמוֹ שֶׁל עוֹלָם" (ברכות ו, ב). הַיְנוּ, שֶׁהַדְּבָרִים עַצְמָם, הֵם תֵּבוֹת הַתְּפִלָּה, עוֹמְדִים בְּרוּם הָעוֹלָמוֹת.
  - וּבַזֹּהַר וַיַּקְהֵל ר"א א', "צְלוֹתָא דְּבַר נַשׁ אִיהוּ פּוּלְחָנָא דְרוּחָא, אִיהִי קַיְמָא

---

236 Mishlei 15:8.
237 Berachot 6b.

aware that a person's prayer breaks through the air and the heavens, opens up openings, and ascends upwards.[238]

- Refer to the next page there [that word which goes up, they wait for that word of prayer which ascends the air of that side, and the appointed one takes it if it is a nice word, and they all kiss that word and ascend with it . . .].[239]
- [A word of prayer is unified with the Supernal Realms.][240]
- [The prayer rises . . . and they go out, bow down to, and crown that prayer and go up with it until it reaches the sixth heaven, then many hosts come out and receive that prayer and go up with it until it reaches the seventy gates. . . .][241]

• The ascent of each and every word of prayer is an awesome and wondrous thing!

- As per: At the time of prayer, all of these words that a person utters in prayer rise upwards and break through heavens until they reach [the place that they reach] and are crowned.[242]

• [The voice of prayer] when physically articulated arouses a corresponding Supernal Voice – a *Great Voice* which is known in the Zohar[243]

- (As written in many places in the Zohar[244] that prayer ascends to draw down blessing from the depths of all, which is the

---

238 Zohar II Vayakhel 201a.
239 Zohar II Vayakhel 201b.
240 Zohar II Vayakhel 202a.
241 Zohar II Vayakhel 202b.
242 Zohar III VaEtchanan 260b.
243 Zohar II Yitro 81a:
- R. Yehuda said: There were three types of darkness [when Israel received the Torah] as is written "darkness, cloud, and thick cloud" [Devarim 4:11], and that Voice was emanating from the innermost part of all of them [the types of darkness]. R. Yossi said: [the Voice was] the innermost part of all as it says, "The unceasing Great Voice" [Devarim 5:19, referring to the Voice of God, whose words were written on the Tablets of Stone handed down when Israel received the Torah. The darkness referred to here relates to levels of concealment and therefore irrespective of the level of concealment the *Great Voice* is the real innermost part of all existence.]

Zohar III VaEtchanan 261a:
- . . . the Supernal *Hey*, [a reference to the first *Hey* of YHVH which relates to Binah] is "The unceasing Great Voice" [Devarim 5:19] whose springs of water [i.e., sustenance and maintenance of the worlds] never cease, and all those sounds which were there at the time the Torah was given to Israel, they all came from that Voice, the innermost part of all . . . [See Menachot

נפש שער ב' - פרק י' החיים

בְּרָזִין עִלָּאִין, וּבְנֵי נָשָׁא לָא יַדְעִין דְּהָא צְלוֹתָא דְּבַר נָשׁ בַּקְעַת אֲוִירִין, בַּקְעַת רְקִיעִין, פָּתְחַת פִּתְחִין וְסַלְקָא לְעֵילָּא.

○ וְעַיֵּן בַּע"ב שָׁם

○ וּבְדַף ר"ב ע"א

○ וְרֵישׁ ע"ב:

• נוֹרָאוֹת נִפְלָאוֹת עִנְיָן עֲלִיַּת כָּל מִלָּה וּמִלָּה דִּצְלוֹתָא.

○ וּבְרֵישׁ פָּרָשַׁת וָאֶתְחַנַּן ר"ס רֵישׁ ע"ב, "וּבְשַׁעֲתָא דִּצְלוֹתָא קַיְּמָא, כָּל אִנּוּן מִלִּין דְּאַפִּיק בַּר נָשׁ מִפּוּמֵיהּ בְּהַהִיא צְלוֹתָא, כֻּלְּהוּ סַלְקָן לְעֵילָּא, וּבַקְעִין רְקִיעִין, עַד דְּמָטוּ כו', וּמִתְעַטְּרֵי" כו':

• וְהוּא מְעוֹרֵר בְּקוֹלוֹ דִלְתַתָּא אֶת הַקּוֹל הָעֶלְיוֹן, "קוֹל גָּדוֹל" הַיָּדוּעַ בַּזֹּהַר (יתרו פא:, ועי' ואתחנן רסא.).

○ (וּכְמוֹ שֶׁכָּתוּב בְּכַמָּה מְקוֹמוֹת בַּזֹּהַר (ויחי רכט:, ואתחנן רסה:, בשלח סג:), דִּצְלוֹתָא סַלְקָא לְאַמְשָׁכָא בִּרְכָאָן מֵעוּמְקָא דְכֹלָּא, וְהוּא "הַקּוֹל גָּדוֹל").

29b, which describes that the future world was created with *Yud* and this world with *Hey*, referring to the Supernal *Hey*/Binah. See also Zohar Chadash I Yitro 57b which states "... and He created all with Binah but no one created Him...."]

244 Zohar I Vayechi 229b:
• When it becomes light in the morning and the arousal of the right side [of Chesed/mercy] is aroused in the world, then a person must attach himself to God's right and serve before Him in the service of prayer, this is because it is prayer which brings strength and power [to the realms] above, and draws down blessing from the supernal depths [i.e., from Binah] to all of the [supernal] worlds, and from there, blessing descends to the lower worlds, with the result that the supernal and lower worlds are blessed with the service of prayer.

Zohar II BeShalach 63b:
• Each person who sets out his request before The King must focus his thoughts and will on the root of roots – to draw blessing from the depths of the pit so that blessing should flow from the fountain of all... the depths of all, the depths of the pit from which fountains come out and extend from it to bless all...

Zohar III VaEtchanan 265b:
• One who wants to pray his prayer before the Holy King must request of the depths of all [i.e., Binah] that it should bestow blessing downwards [to the lower worlds]....

Great Voice.)[245]

- As per the verse "and the voice is the voice of Yaakov."[246] That the voice of a person's prayer correspondingly arouses the Supernal Voice.
- Therefore, Chazal comment[247] that the verse "she raised up her voice against me, therefore I hated her" relates to an unfit Prayer Leader, meaning that he just uses his voice[248] alone [to lead the community in prayer] and his voice does not cause arousal of the Supernal Voice with him. This is the meaning of "she raised up her voice" – [i.e., her voice] alone – "therefore [I hated her]."
- This is also the meaning of the verse[249] "and God placed His Voice before [the arrival of] His army."[250]
- Therefore, even though Chazal refer to prayer as "Service of the Heart," nevertheless, they learn[251] from the verses related to Chana that [to be effective,] it must be verbally articulated [with one's voice as speech].

11. PRAYER FOCUS TO DRAW HOLINESS; DIFFICULTIES ARE BITTER BUT SWEET

- The verse "before His army"[252] hints at this key principle of the concept of prayer

---

245 The following quotation from Shomer Emunim, second debate, sect. 43, sheds light on the concept of the *Great Voice* which the previous quotations from Zohar identify as being the source of blessing and existence:

- This, in my humble opinion, is the secret of Tzimtzum[/God's concealment from the perspective of this world]. It means that even though the Ein Sof[/ the Infinite One] has no limitations, He has the power to limit, for He can conceal His Unlimited Power and operate with concealed and limited power such that finite entities are able to receive it. This is in line with Chazal's statement [Shemot Rabba 5:9] on the verse "Moshe would speak and God would respond to him with a Voice" [Shemot 19:19], with a Voice that he [Moshe] was able to receive, and similarly it says "God's Voice is with power" [Tehillim 29:4], it does not say with His Power but [just] with [modulated and concealed] power.

Therefore, it is God's *Great Voice* which creates the world with His Statements of Creation by modulating and concealing His Power such that created entities are able to exist as separate entities in their own right. This is the concept of Tzimtzum. Our prayer to God, at the highest level possible which is at the level of His connection to this world, therefore draws down additional blessing to this world.

The concept of Voice is synonymous with the concept of Tzimtzum as

- וְזֶה שֶׁכָּתוּב "הַקֹּל קוֹל יַעֲקֹב". (בראשית כז, כב), שֶׁלְּקוֹל תְּפִלַּת הָאָדָם — מִתְעוֹרֵר לְעֻמָּתוֹ הַקּוֹל הָעֶלְיוֹן.

- וְלָכֵן דָּרְשׁוּ רַבּוֹתֵינוּ זִכְרוֹנָם לִבְרָכָה (תענית טז, ב) עַל פָּסוּק "נָתְנָה עָלַי בְּקוֹלָהּ עַל כֵּן שְׂנֵאתִיהָ" (ירמיה יב, ח) וְאָמְרוּ זֶה שְׁלִיחַ צִבּוּר שֶׁאֵינוֹ הָגוּן, רָצָה לוֹמַר, שֶׁאֵין נִמְצָא רַק 'קוֹלוֹ' לְבַד, וְלֹא גָרַם קוֹלוֹ לְעוֹרֵר גַּם הַ'קּוֹל הָעֶלְיוֹן' עִמּוֹ, זֶה שֶׁכָּתוּב "נָתְנָה עָלַי בְּקוֹלָהּ" לְבַד "עַל כֵּן כו'".

- וְזֶה שֶׁאָמַר הַכָּתוּב (יואל ב, יא) "וה' נָתַן קוֹלוֹ לִפְנֵי חֵילוֹ".

- וְלָזֹאת, אַף שֶׁקָּרְאוּ רַבּוֹתֵינוּ זִכְרוֹנָם לִבְרָכָה (ברכות לא, ב) אֶת עִנְיַן הַתְּפִלָּה "עֲבוֹדָה שֶׁבַּלֵּב", עִם כָּל זֶה, אַגְמְרוּ מִקְרָאֵי דְחַנָּה, שֶׁצָּרִיךְ שֶׁיַּחְתֹּךְ בִּשְׂפָתָיו:

שער ב' - פרק י"א

- וּמַה שֶּׁכָּתוּב "לִפְנֵי חֵילוֹ" (יואל שם) רָמַז זֶה הָעִקָּר הַגָּדוֹל שֶׁל עִנְיַן הַתְּפִלָּה

---

above, and also with Malchut/Kingship, e.g. as per the Arizal in Shaar Ha-Hakdamot 36a who says that "*Voice* and *Speech* are both rooted in Malchut."

See the concept of Tzimtzum as expressed in the Third Gateway, G3:05 and G3:07. Also see the concept of His Speech expressed at the beginning of G3:11. A very detailed explanation of the concept of Tzimtzum is provided in V2:02 which explains that the Tzimtzum process always and only takes place in the level of Malchut.

246 Bereishit 27:22, i.e., the repetition of the word *Kol* (voice) implies that a person's voice is echoed by God's voice.

247 Taanit 16b quoting Yirmiyahu 12:8.

248 The verse refers to a singular reference to voice which relates to an unconnected Earthly voice which the verse continues to say is hated as the Prayer Leader is focused on using his voice for personal gain, e.g., to feel good that he is leading the community in prayer or using the opportunity as a platform to show off the qualities of his voice, and not on arousing the community in effective prayer.

249 Yoel 2:11.

250 The verse continues to say "for those who carry out His Word are mighty" meaning, in our context, that our voice is only meaningful if it results in our increased capacity for carrying out the message of His Voice.

251 Berachot 31a.

252 Quoted at the end of G2:10 from Yoel 2:11.

- that one's entire focus [during prayer] is to purely be on increasing the power of holiness
- with the same [resolve] as a soldier who entirely ignores his own personal needs and willingly gives up his life solely for the honor of the king [and that his king] can be crowned as king over that land and rule as king[253]
- similarly, it is very fitting for an honest person to invest his entire focus and purity of thought during prayer to add power into the holy worlds
- by using his voice to arouse the corresponding Supernal Voice and draw down blessing and light to all from it
- to rid the Spirit of Evil from the Universe and to establish God's Kingship over the Universe
- and to not [focus his thoughts during prayer] on his own issues or personal needs at all.

• We see this
  - in the prayers of Rosh Hashana
    - which are arranged, from beginning to end, to only focus on the glory of God's Kingship
    - that it should be elevated as it was originally, before Adam's sin
  - and also in the formulation of our daily prayers
    - which even though at first glance virtually all appear to be focused on our own personal needs
    - it is certainly clear to all who understand and is inherently proven, that the Men of the Great Assembly did not intend that these words of prayer should simply fulfill the simple understanding of these words alone
    - as I wrote above in G2:10.

• Prayers were established to correspond to the Tamid sacrifices,[254] which were burnt offerings, completely offered to God with no human benefit from them at all.[255]

---

253 The commentary of Avnei Eliyahu on the Siddur Ishei Yisrael on p. 97 of the 1968 publication (with comments of either the Vilna Gaon himself or of his son Avraham as per the title page), comments as follows:
- "*U'MaAritzim*" . . . The expression of "*Arutz*" is one of absolute nullification of a person before his Master . . . The difference between a *Gibor*/mighty person and an *Arutz* is that the mighty person is the one who will withstand the throes of war and observe the rules of war, negating the enemy, rendering each part of it harmless. Whereas, the *Arutz* is the one who runs alone to the war front, giving up his life . . . and it says: "They will *HiKdishu*/sanctify the Holy One of Yaakov, and *Arutz*/revere the God

- שֶׁכְּלָל כַּוָּנָתָהּ הוּא, לְכַוֵּן רַק לְהוֹסִיף כֹּחַ בִּקְדֻשָּׁה.
- שֶׁכְּמוֹ שֶׁהָאִישׁ מֵאַנְשֵׁי הַחַיִל מַשְׁלִיךְ כָּל עִנְיָנָיו וְצָרְכֵי עַצְמוֹ מִנֶּגֶד, וּמוֹסֵר נַפְשׁוֹ בִּרְצוֹנוֹ רַק עַל כְּבוֹד הַמֶּלֶךְ, שֶׁיַּשִּׂיג הַכֶּתֶר מְלוּכָה שֶׁל אוֹתָהּ הַמְּדִינָה וְתִנָּשֵׂא מַלְכוּתוֹ.
- כֵּן רָאוּי מְאֹד לְהָאָדָם הַיָּשָׁר, לָשׂוּם כָּל כַּוָּנָתוֹ וְטֹהַר מַחֲשַׁבְתּוֹ בִּתְפִלָּתוֹ רַק לְהוֹסִיף תֵּת כֹּחַ בְּהָעוֹלָמוֹת הַקְּדוֹשִׁים
- וּלְעוֹרֵר בְּקוֹלוֹ — הַקּוֹל הָעֶלְיוֹן, לְאַמְשָׁכָא מִנֵּיהּ בִּרְכָאן וּנְהִירוּ לְכֹלָּא
- לְהַעֲבִיר רוּחַ הַטֻּמְאָה מִן הָעוֹלָם, וִיתַקֵּן עוֹלָם בְּמַלְכוּתוֹ יִתְבָּרַךְ שְׁמוֹ
- וְלֹא עַל עִנְיָנָיו וְצָרְכֵי עַצְמוֹ כְּלָל:

• וְעֵינֵינוּ הָרוֹאוֹת
- בְּנוּסָח תְּפִלַּת רֹאשׁ הַשָּׁנָה
  □ שֶׁהוּא מְסֻדָּר מֵרֹאשׁוֹ עַד סוֹפוֹ רַק עַל כְּבוֹד מַלְכוּתוֹ יִתְבָּרַךְ שְׁמוֹ
  □ שֶׁתִּתְעַלֶּה כְּבַתְּחִלָּה קֹדֶם חֵטְא אָדָם הָרִאשׁוֹן.
- וְגַם נוּסַח תְּפִלַּת כָּל הַשָּׁנָה
  □ אַף שֶׁלְּפִי פְּשׁוּטוֹ הַנִּרְאֶה רֻבּוֹ כְּכֻלּוֹ מְסֻדָּר עַל עִנְיְנֵי צָרְכֵי עַצְמֵנוּ
  □ וַדַּאי בָּרוּר לְכָל מֵבִין, וּמִמְּקוֹמוֹ הוּא מֻכְרָע, שֶׁלֹּא כִוְּנוּ אַנְשֵׁי הַכְּנֵסִיָּה הַגְּדוֹלָה עַל הַנִּרְאֶה מִפְּשׁוּטֵי פֵּרוּשׁ הַמִּלּוֹת לְבַד
  □ וּכְמוֹ שֶׁכָּתַבְתִּי לְעֵיל פֶּרֶק י':

• וּתְפִלּוֹת נֶגֶד תְּמִידִין תִּקְנוּם (ברכות כו, ב), שֶׁהָיוּ עוֹלוֹת כָּלִיל לָאִשִּׁים, כָּלָּהּ לַגָּבוֹהַּ סָלְקָא, וְלֹא הָיָה בָּהֶם חֵלֶק הֶדְיוֹט כְּלָל:

---

of Israel" (Yishayahu 29:23). For Kedusha/sanctification is not performed with one's mouth alone but one must give oneself completely over for the Holiness of His Name. This is the meaning of "They will *HiKdishu*/sanctify the Holy One of Yaakov," that it will not be with the mouth alone, but rather "and *Arutz* the God of Israel," that they will throw their lives aside to *kill themselves* over God each day. This is the meaning of what we say in the Kedushah prayer that "NaKdishach/We *sanctify* You, VeNaaritzach/ and are *Arutz* You," that we want to give over our lives for You (God) to sanctify You. . . .

254 Berachot 26b.

255 In contrast to other sacrifice types where part of the sacrifice requires human consumption.

- This is notwithstanding the law[256] that an individual is permitted to insert prayers, related to his personal needs and troubles, into the corresponding blessing [of the Amidah] according to its theme.
  - Nevertheless, his objective should also not be to focus on his personal pain, this being an inappropriate way for those with honest hearts
  - as, in truth, it would be strange, as how can it be in any way appropriate to ask and appease God to remove his pain and afflictions from him?
  - This is similar to the process of physically healing the body, where the doctor will administer bitter remedies or if the doctor is forced to, will even completely amputate a limb to prevent further spread of the poisonous effects of the illness.
  - Were the patient to beg [the doctor] to not administer the remedy or to not have the limb amputated, surely the patient himself has hired [the doctor] to do this?
  - Similarly, how can he pour out his prayer request before God to remove his afflictions, surely they are the bandage and the lifesaving remedies which atone for his sins.
  - As per Chazal:[257] "there are no afflictions without sin," and without them, how is a sinning person's soul to be atoned?
- However, the purpose of intention [in prayer] is that it needs to be solely for the sake of The Most High:
  - For matters profaning God's Name
    - for example, in relation to difficulties experienced by the Jewish People, [such as] "when it was said of them: These are the people of God"[258] [when the Jewish People were dispersed among the nations, thereby desecrating God's Name], and they are beaten and afflicted
    - [in such a case] we are obligated to seek and pour out prayer before God over the desecration of His Name, and [the prayer] will only be for the sake of His Name.[259]
  - Also for matters relating to personal difficulty
    - even if God's Name is not desecrated as a result

---

256 Avodah Zarah 8a.
257 Shabbat 55a.
258 Yechezkel 36:20.
259 In Shenot Eliyahu, the Vilna Gaon comments on the statement from the Mishna Berachot 5:1, "in order to concentrate their hearts on the Makom," as follows:
- This means that it is forbidden to concentrate prayer on one's own needs, but one should pray that all of Israel should achieve absolute perfection and

- וְאַף דְּהִלְכְתָא גְּמִירָא לָהּ בַּשַּׁ״ס (עבודה זרה ח, א) שֶׁהַיָּחִיד רַשַּׁאי לְחַדֵּשׁ דָּבָר בִּתְפִלָּתוֹ עַל צָרְכֵי עַצְמוֹ וְצַעֲרוֹ, בְּכָל בְּרָכָה לְפִי עִנְיָנָהּ.
  ○ גַּם בָּזֶה צָרִיךְ שֶׁלֹּא תְּהֵא תַּכְלִית כַּוָּנָתוֹ עַל צַעֲרוֹ, וְלֹא זוֹ הַדֶּרֶךְ הַנְּכוֹנָה לַיְשָׁרִים בְּלִבּוֹתָם.
  ○ כִּי בֶּאֱמֶת יִפָּלֵא, אֵיךְ שַׁיָּךְ לְבַקֵּשׁ לְהִתְחַנֵּן כְּלָל לְפָנָיו יִתְבָּרַךְ שְׁמוֹ, לְהָסִיר מֵעָלָיו צַעֲרוֹ וְיִסּוּרָיו.
  ○ כְּמוֹ בְּעִנְיַן רְפוּאַת הַגּוּף, הָרוֹפֵא מַשְׁקֵהוּ סַמָּנִים חֲרִיפִים, אוֹ אִם הָרוֹפֵא מֻכְרָח אַף גַּם לַחְתֹּךְ אֵבֶר אֶחָד לְגַמְרֵי, שֶׁלֹּא יִתְפַּשֵּׁט אֶרֶס הַחֹלִי יוֹתֵר.
  ○ הַאִם יִתְחַנֵּן אֵלָיו הַחוֹלֶה שֶׁלֹּא יַשְׁקֵהוּ הַסַּמָּנִים אוֹ שֶׁלֹּא יַחְתֹּךְ הָאֵבֶר, הֲלֹא הַחוֹלֶה עַצְמוֹ שׂוֹכְרוֹ לְכָךְ.
  ○ כֵּן אֵיךְ יִשְׁפֹּךְ שִׂיחַ לְפָנָיו יִתְבָּרַךְ שְׁמוֹ לְהָסִיר מֵעָלָיו הַיִּסּוּרִים, הֲלֹא הֵמָּה רְטִיָּה וְסַמָּא דְּחַיֵּי לְכַפֵּר עֲוֹנוֹתָיו
  ○ כְּמַאֲמָרָם זִכְרוֹנָם לִבְרָכָה (שבת נה, א) "אֵין יִסּוּרִין בְּלֹא עָוֹן", וְאִם לֹא, אֵפוֹא, נֶפֶשׁ הַחוֹטֵאת בַּמֶּה תִּתְכַּפֵּר:
- אָמְנָם תַּכְלִית הַכַּוָּנָה, צְרִיכָה שֶׁתִּהְיֶה רַק צֹרֶךְ גָּבוֹהַּ
  ○ כִּי בְּמָקוֹם שֶׁיֵּשׁ חִלּוּל שְׁמוֹ יִתְבָּרַךְ
    ▪ כְּגוֹן צָרַת כְּלַל יִשְׂרָאֵל, "בֶּאֱמוֹר עַם ה' אֵלֶּה" — וְהֵמָּה מַכִּים וּמְעַנִּים
    ▪ מְחֻיָּבִים לְבַקֵּשׁ וְלִשְׁפֹּךְ שִׂיחַ לְפָנָיו יִתְבָּרַךְ שְׁמוֹ עַל חִלּוּל שְׁמוֹ יִתְבָּרַךְ, וְאַף לְמַעַן שְׁמוֹ יַעֲשֶׂה.
  ○ וְגַם הַיָּחִיד עַל צַעֲרוֹ
    ▪ אַף אִם אֵין חִלּוּל הַשֵּׁם בַּדָּבָר

---

that Knesset Yisrael is perfected Above. However, one should not [pray] for one's own needs, except to pray for oneself in Elokay Netzor [i.e., the personal prayer at the very end of the Amidah], as the prayer of Elokay Netzor is for oneself.

See G2:18:N40 which describes how detailed focus on prayer sequence is to connect to Knesset Yisrael.

- there is also scope (Note 30)[260] to pray over the scale of God's *pain*, which reflects a person's pain in this world
- as Chazal say:[261] R. Meir said that when a person is in distress, what does the Shechina say? "I am burdened by my head, I am burdened by my arm." (Note 31)[262]

○ As per Chazal:
- "My perfection (Tamati)" Just as with twins, if one feels a pain in his head, the other one does so as well – so it is with God, "I am with him in his distress."[263]
- All salvation which comes to Israel is of God, as per "I am with him in his distress . . ." (meaning as per the conclusion of the chapter "and I will show him My salvation") [If You answer us,] the salvation is Yours as it says "it is for You to save us."[264]
- "My heart rejoices in Your salvation." R. Abahu said, this is one of the difficult verses as God's salvation is the salvation of Israel . . . it does not write "My salvation" but rather "Your salvation" – [David said] Your salvation is our salvation.[265]
- [He further stated: "Salvation is God's, upon Your people is Your blessing, Selah."] "Salvation is God's," [we learn that Israel is meritorious in that in each place it is exiled, the Shechina is exiled with them. This is how Israel will exit the exile, will freedom be for Israel or for God? But this is established in many verses, "Salvation is God's" for certain, when? "When Your blessing is on the people."][266]

○ This is the meaning of "I am with him in his distress"[267]
- that God joins him in his distress and then [as the verse continues] "I will release him. . . ."
- When a person does not feel his own pain from his afflictions as a result of the greatness of his bitterness over [God's] pain, so to speak – then these difficulties themselves are the very remedy of his sins, and he is atoned through them to the point that the difficulties themselves leave him (these are the holy Gevurot as is God's way to sweeten the bitter with the bitter, and this rectifies the Middot in their source).[268]

---

260 **R. Chaim adds Note 30 here.** This note is brought at the end of this chapter and is entitled "Two ways to approach prayer hinted to in Mishna."
261 Sanhedrin 46a in the Mishna.
262 **R. Chaim adds Note 31 here.** This note is brought at the end of this chapter and is entitled "Burdened head and arm, Tefillin connects God and man."
263 Shemot Rabba 2:5 and also Shir Hashirim Rabba 5:2, both quoting Shir

נפש שער ב' - פרק י"א החיים

- יֵשׁ מָקוֹם גַּם כֵּן, (הגהה ל׳) לְבַקֵּשׁ לְפָנָיו יִתְבָּרַךְ עַל גֹּדֶל הַצַּעַר שֶׁל מַעְלָה בִּזְמַן שֶׁהָאָדָם שָׁרוּי בְּצַעַר לְמַטָּה.

- כְּמַאֲמָרָם זִכְרוֹנָם לִבְרָכָה בַּמִּשְׁנָה פֶּרֶק ו' דְּסַנְהֶדְרִין (מו.) "אָמַר רַבִּי מֵאִיר, בִּזְמַן שֶׁהָאָדָם מִצְטַעֵר שְׁכִינָה מַה לָּשׁוֹן אוֹמֶרֶת, קַלַּנִי מֵרֹאשִׁי קַלַּנִי מִזְּרוֹעִי". (הגהה ל"א).

○ וְאָמְרוּ

- בִּשְׁמוֹת רַבָּה פָּרָשָׁה ב', וּבַחֲזִית בַּפָּסוּק אֲנִי יְשֵׁנָה, "תַּמָּתִי" (שה"ש ה, ב) גו' מַה הַתְּאוֹמִים הַלָּלוּ, אִם חָשַׁשׁ אֶחָד בְּרֹאשׁוֹ חֲבֵרוֹ מַרְגִּישׁ, כֵּן אָמַר הַקָּדוֹשׁ בָּרוּךְ הוּא (תהלים צא, טו) "עִמּוֹ אָנֹכִי בְצָרָה".

- וּבְתַנְחוּמָא סוֹף פָּרָשַׁת אַחֲרֵי, "כָּל יְשׁוּעָה שֶׁבָּאָה לְיִשְׂרָאֵל, הִיא שֶׁל הַקָּדוֹשׁ בָּרוּךְ הוּא, שֶׁנֶּאֱמַר "עִמּוֹ אָנֹכִי בְצָרָה" גו' (רוֹצֶה לוֹמַר וּמְסַיֵּם "וְאַרְאֵהוּ בִּישׁוּעָתִי"). הַיְשׁוּעָה שֶׁלְּךָ הִיא שֶׁנֶּאֱמַר (שם פ, ג) "וּלְכָה לִישֻׁעָתָה לָּנוּ"

- וּבְשׁוֹחֵר טוֹב תְּהִלִּים מִזְמוֹר י"ג, "יָגֵל לִבִּי בִּישׁוּעָתֶךָ" אָמַר רַב אַבָּהוּ זֶה אֶחָד מִן הַמִּקְרָאוֹת הַקָּשִׁים, שֶׁיְּשׁוּעָתוֹ שֶׁל הַקָּדוֹשׁ בָּרוּךְ הוּא הִיא יְשׁוּעָתָן שֶׁל יִשְׂרָאֵל, 'בִּישׁוּעָתֵנוּ' אֵין כְּתִיב אֶלָּא 'בִּישׁוּעָתֶךָ' כו', יְשׁוּעָתְךָ הִיא יְשׁוּעָתֵנוּ".

- וְעַיֵּן זֹהַר אֱמוֹר צ' רֵישׁ ע"ב, בְּעִנְיַן הַכָּתוּב "לַה' הַיְשׁוּעָה".

○ וְזֶהוּ "עִמּוֹ אָנֹכִי בְצָרָה" (שם צא, טו)

- הַיְנוּ, שֶׁמִּן הַמֵּצַר מְשַׁתֵּף אוֹתוֹ יִתְבָּרַךְ שְׁמוֹ, אָז "אֲחַלְּצֵהוּ" וכו'.

- וּכְשֶׁהָאָדָם אֵין מַרְגִּישׁ צַעֲרוֹ מִיִּסּוּרָיו, מִגֹּדֶל מְרִירוּתוֹ מִצַּעֲרוֹ כִּבְיָכוֹל,

---

Hashirim 5:2 and Tehillim 91:15. The word for "twins" (Teomim) is a play on words on "My Perfection" (Tamati).

264 Midrash Tanchuma Acharei Mot 18 quoting Tehillim 91:15–16, 80:3.
265 Midrash Tehillim 13:4 quoting Tehillim 13:6.
266 Zohar III Emor 90b.
267 Tehillim 91:15 as brought down in Midrash Tanchuma Acharei Mot 18.
268 As is God's way to *sweeten bitter with bitter* (e.g., Bereishit Rabba Vayishlach 77:1 among a number of other Midrashim), as with the episode of the bitter waters in Shemot 15:25, that bitterness itself becomes the cause of the resulting sweetness. The Vilna Gaon, in Imrei Noam on Berachot 5a, comments as follows:
- "Just as salt purifies [meat . . . so do afflictions remove a person's sins]": It seems that these statements are not comparable as salt *purifies* but afflictions

Rabbi Chaim's Notes:
Note 30 – Two ways to approach prayer hinted to in Mishna

- These two ways [of approaching prayer: 1. because God's Name is desecrated, and 2. because God is perceived to be *in pain*] are hinted to by the author of the Mishna [which states]:[269]
  - "When Moshe raised his hand, Israel conquered."[270] Now do the *hands* of Moshe wage war? This verse is coming to teach you [that when Israel looked Heavenwards and subjugated their hearts towards their Father in Heaven they would conquer, and if not they would fall.]
  - Similar to this is ["Make yourself a snake and place it on a pole. Then all who have been bitten will look at it and live."[271] Now does a (copper) snake determine life or death? Rather, when Israel looked Heavenwards and subjugated their hearts towards their Father in Heaven they were cured, and if not they died.]
- The first way mentioned – [to pray] because God's Name is desecrated – is hinted to by the verse relating to the war with Amalek
  - which was a desecration of God's Name as per Chazal,[272] who compare [Amalek's action of being the first nation to fight with Israel to one who is the first to jump into a boiling hot] bath [and thereby cools it down enough to allow others to also jump in. Amalek's action therefore initiated a string of attacks on Israel from other nations who would not otherwise have considered attacking]
  - similarly, Chazal comment[273] that [Amalek would] cut off the circumcised limbs [of Israel] and throw them Heavenwards [and say this is what You chose – take what You have chosen].
  - This is the meaning of "When Moshe raised his hand . . . Now do the hands of Moshe . . . ." That all the while that Israel only looked Heavenwards and did not shout out their prayer to God over their personal distress, but rather focused it solely on the desecration of the Name of their Father in Heaven, that they would also conquer, and if not [they would fall].
- It further states [in connection with the second way – to pray because God is perceived to be *in pain*] that even in a scenario where there is no desecration of God's Name, that this is Scripturally hinted to by the incident of the copper snake, being the way in which a request of and prayer to God is acceptable before Him.

---

only *remove*. However, [afflictions] initially remove, but then [a person is moved to] repent out of love as the sins are converted into merits and therefore the afflictions also result in purification.

הַמְּרוֹרוֹת הַלָּלוּ הֵן הֵן עֶצֶם מֵרוּק פְּשָׁעָיו, וּמִתְכַּפֵּר בָּזֶה עַד שֶׁיִּסּוּרֵי עַצְמוֹ בְּדָלִין הֵימֶנּוּ (וְהֵן הֵן הַגְּבוּרוֹת קְדוֹשׁוֹת, כְּדַרְכּוֹ יִתְבָּרַךְ שְׁמוֹ לְהַמְתִּיק מַר בְּמַר, וְהוּא תִּקּוּן הַמִּדּוֹת בְּשָׁרְשָׁן):

הגהה ל'

- וְאֵלּוּ שְׁנֵי הָאוֹפַנִּים, רְמָזָם הַתַּנָּא בְּמִשְׁנָא שְׁנֵיהֶם בַּמִּשְׁנָה פֶּרֶק ג' דְּרֹאשׁ הַשָּׁנָה.
  - "וְהָיָה כַּאֲשֶׁר יָרִים מֹשֶׁה יָדוֹ וְגָבַר יִשְׂרָאֵל" (שמות יז) וגו', וְכִי יָדָיו שֶׁל מֹשֶׁה עוֹשׂוֹת מִלְחָמָה כו', אֶלָּא לוֹמַר לְךָ וכו'
  - כַּיּוֹצֵא בַדָּבָר אַתָּה אוֹמֵר וכו':
- הִנֵּה הָאֹפֶן הָאֶחָד הַנִּזְכָּר, בְּמָקוֹם שֶׁיֵּשׁ חִלּוּל שְׁמוֹ יִתְבָּרַךְ, אָמַר, שֶׁרָמַז לָנוּ הַכָּתוּב בְּמִלְחֶמֶת עֲמָלֵק.
  - שֶׁהָיָה בָּזֶה חִלּוּל שְׁמוֹ יִתְבָּרַךְ, כַּיָּדוּעַ מַאֲמָרָם זִכְרוֹנָם לִבְרָכָה בִּפְסִיקְתָּא מָשָׁל לְאַמְבַּטְיָה וכו'
  - וְכֵן אָמְרוּ שָׁם שֶׁהָיָה חוֹתֵךְ מִילוֹת וְזוֹרְקָן כְּלַפֵּי מַעְלָה
  - זֶה שֶׁכָּתוּב "וְהָיָה כַּאֲשֶׁר יָרִים מֹשֶׁה" וגו', וְכִי יָדָיו שֶׁל מֹשֶׁה כו', אֶלָּא כָּל זְמַן שֶׁהָיוּ יִשְׂרָאֵל מִסְתַּכְּלִין רַק כְּלַפֵּי "מַעְלָה" לְבַד, שֶׁלֹּא הָיְתָה צַעֲקַת תְּפִלָּתָם לְפָנָיו יִתְבָּרַךְ שְׁמוֹ עַל צַעֲרָם, אֶלָּא רַק עַל חִלּוּל שֵׁם אֲבִיהֶם שֶׁבַּשָּׁמַיִם יִתְבָּרַךְ שְׁמוֹ, הָיוּ מִתְגַּבְּרִים גַּם הֵמָּה, וְאִם לָאו כו':
- וְאָמַר עוֹד, שֶׁגַּם בְּמָקוֹם שֶׁאֵין חִלּוּל הַשֵּׁם בַּדָּבָר, רָמַז לָנוּ הַכָּתוּב בְּעִנְיַן נְחַשׁ הַנְּחֹשֶׁת, אֹפֶן וְעִנְיַן הַבַּקָּשָׁה וְהַתְּפִלָּה הָרְצוּיָה לְפָנָיו יִתְבָּרַךְ שְׁמוֹ

---

269 Mishna Rosh Hashana 3:8.
270 Shemot 17:1, referring to the first war Israel had in the wilderness after coming out of Egypt which was initiated by Amalek.
271 Bamidbar 21:8, referring to the copper snake which God instructed Moshe to make to remedy the deadly effect of snakes which were sent by God among Israel in response to their complaint against God and Moshe for taking them out of Egypt.
272 Pesikta DeRav Kahana Piska 3:10.
273 In the next paragraph in the Pesikta.

- Now does a [copper] snake determine life or death? But when [Israel] would completely overlook their personal distress and solely focus their supplication and requests
  - only on the great distress they caused God when performing their sin, May the Merciful One save us
  - and the current distress that is made Above, as a result of the fact that they are currently in a state of distress from the affliction of the punishment of their sin
- then they would be healed [and if not then they would die].[274]

Note 31 – Burdened head and arm, Tefillin connects God and man

- That which the [Mishna] states "I am burdened by my head, I am burdened by my arm" relates to the Tefillin of the head and the arm
  - As Chazal state[275] that God lays Tefillin.
    - The concept of God's Tefillin is His cleaving [to us] to benefit us with everything, as this section of the Talmud continues: What is written in God's Tefillin? "and who is like Your People Israel, One nation" and "for who is the great nation, etc."[276]
    - Similarly, [the Talmud explains that] all the verses there relate only to the praises of Israel and all of them are [also] written on the Tefillin worn on the arm.
  - This is the concept of "You have designated God today to be a God for you ... and God has designated you today to be for Him as a treasured people"[277]
    - that just as our Tefillin contain praises of God, similarly, God's Tefillin, so to speak, contain our praises, and in this there is [reciprocal] cleaving[278]
    - this is as per "Israel – in you I take glory."[279] This is the secret of God's Tefillin as Tefillin are called *Pe'er* (glory), as per Chazal.[280] Refer to Zohar.[281]

---

274 See G3:12 and G3:12:N46.
275 Berachot 6a.
276 2 Shmuel 7:23, 1 Divrei Hayamim 17:21, and Devarim 4:7. The Talmud explains that these and other verses form the contents of God's Tefillin worn on the head.
277 Devarim 26:17–18, as brought down in Berachot 6a.
278 The Vilna Gaon comments (In Yahel Ohr, Raya Mehemna, Hashmatot, p. 30a of the 1882 edition) as follows:
  - With this the secret of God laying Tefillin and what is contained within them, is explained ... [the Vilna Gaon details how the parts of the Tefillin parallel the human functions of the mind and body] ... and that with the

- וְכִי נָחָשׁ מֵמִית וכו', אֶלָּא בִּזְמַן שֶׁהָיוּ מַשְׁלִיכִין צַעַר עַצְמָם מִנֶּגֶד לְגַמְרֵי, וְהָיוּ מִסְתַּכְּלִין וְשׁוֹפְכִין תְּחִנָּתָם וּבַקָּשָׁתָם
- רַק עַל גֹּדֶל הַצַּעַר שֶׁל מַעְלָה שֶׁגָּרְמוּ בְּעֵת עֲשִׂיָּתָם הֶעָוֹן, רַחֲמָנָא לִיצְלָן
- וְגַם הַצַּעַר שֶׁל עַתָּה שֶׁנַּעֲשֶׂה לְמַעְלָה מֵחֲמַת שֶׁהֵמָּה שְׁרוּיִים עַתָּה בְּצַעַר מִיִּסּוּרֵי הָעֹנֶשׁ בַּעֲוֹנָם
- אָז הָיוּ מִתְרַפְּאִין כו':

הגהה ל"א

- וּמַה שֶּׁאָמַר "קָלַנִי מֵרֹאשִׁי קָלַנִי מִזְּרוֹעִי", הָעִנְיָן הֵם תְּפִלִּין שֶׁל רֹאשׁ וּתְפִלִּין שֶׁל יָד.
- כִּי אָמְרוּ רַבּוֹתֵינוּ זִכְרוֹנָם לִבְרָכָה (ברכות ו' ע"א) שֶׁהַקָּדוֹשׁ בָּרוּךְ הוּא מַנִּיחַ תְּפִלִּין.
- וְעִנְיַן הַתְּפִלִּין שֶׁלּוֹ יִתְבָּרַךְ שְׁמוֹ, הוּא הִתְדַּבְּקוּתוֹ יִתְבָּרַךְ שְׁמוֹ — לְהֵיטִיב עִמָּנוּ בַּכֹּל, כְּמוֹ שֶׁאָמְרוּ שָׁם "תְּפִלִּין דְּמָארֵי עָלְמָא מַה כְּתִיב בְּהוּ, וּמִי כְעַמְּךָ יִשְׂרָאֵל גּוֹי אֶחָד" (שמו"ב ז, כג), "כִּי מִי גוֹי גָּדוֹל" (דברים ה, ז) וגו'.
- וְכֵן כָּל הַפְּסוּקִים דְּשָׁם הֵם רַק שִׁבְחֵי יִשְׂרָאֵל, וְכֻלְּהוּ כְּתִיבֵי בְּאִדְרָעֵיהּ.
- וְהוּא כְּעִנְיָן (דברים כו, יז) "אֶת ה' הֶאֱמַרְתָּ הַיּוֹם וה' הֶאֱמִירְךָ הַיּוֹם לִהְיוֹת לוֹ לְעַם סְגֻלָּה" גו'
- שֶׁכְּמוֹ שֶׁבַּתְּפִלִּין שֶׁלָּנוּ כְּתוּבִים שִׁבְחֵי הַקָּדוֹשׁ בָּרוּךְ הוּא, כֵּן תְּפִלִּין שֶׁלּוֹ כִּבְיָכוֹל הֵם שְׁבָחִים שֶׁלָּנוּ, שֶׁשָּׁם הוּא עִנְיַן הַהִתְדַּבְּקוּת.
- וְהוּא עִנְיַן הַכָּתוּב (ישעיה מט, ג) "יִשְׂרָאֵל אֲשֶׁר בְּךָ אֶתְפָּאָר", סוֹד הַתְּפִלִּין

---

laying of Tefillin we subjugate all [our] powers and senses for His Sake and we unify our thoughts to cleave to His Great Name . . . and it is as if God, so to speak, lays Tefillin, as we are unified with great thought. This is the meaning of the Talmud's statement "What is written in God's Tefillin? 'and who is like Your People Israel . . .' . . . you singled Me out for praise in the world and I will single you out for praise . . . ," that is I will specifically watch over you since you singled Me out to Unify Me in your thoughts.

279 Yishayahu 49:3.
280 Berachot 11a.
281 Zohar II Beshalach 62a–b:
- As we learn what is the meaning of "Israel, in you I take glory," I will certainly take glory, what does this mean? It refers to Israel in the lower realm

- Therefore, when a person is in distress, and as a result his connection with God is not properly complete, this is the concept of "I am burdened by my head, I am burdened by my arm," as these are the locations where the Tefillin are placed, for [those places] were fitting for a Holy Connection.

12. TWO LEVELS OF GOD'S PAIN, PRAYER TO FOCUS ON GOD'S PAIN

- Therefore, Chazal say:[282] "Anyone who makes God a partner in his distress – they double his livelihood for him."
- This idea [is linked to two forms of distress – a *doubling* – caused by sin]:
  - Apart from the distress caused Above when [a person] receives his punishment in the form of suffering, God should save us
  - this distress caused Above is completely incomparable with the depth of distress caused Above when performing the actual sin, God should save us.
- This is like a dear son who, in a drunken state, fell to the ground, broke his neck and body and is now in a critical condition.
  - [The son] is unaware that his life is in danger, as per "[In your drunkenness you will say] they hit me but I did not become ill, they beat me but I was unaware"[283]
  - but his father's heart is very embittered over this.
  - In response to the doctors strapping up the broken bones and applying painful treatments, the son screams out bitterly in his pain from the treatments which consume his flesh.
  - While the father is distressed by his son's current shouting and trouble, this distress is nothing compared to the father's original distress when his son broke his bones and he virtually gave up on his life.
- Similarly, this is precisely the case with sin, God should save us:
  - At the time a person performs it, he causes great and deep incomparable distress Above
  - and the person himself is not aware of this at all
  - and he does not know that he is liable with his life and is then considered to be [effectively] dead, God forbid

---

with whom God takes glory in the Supernal Realm. What is His glory? That He wears Tefillin with which He connects to their glory.

דְּמָארֵי עָלְמָא, שֶׁהַתְּפִלִּין נִקְרָאִים "פְּאֵר", כְּמוֹ שֶׁאָמְרוּ רַבּוֹתֵינוּ זִכְרוֹנָם לִבְרָכָה (ברכות יא, א) וְעַיֵּן זֹהַר בְּשַׁלַּח ס"ב רֵישׁ ע"ב:

- לָכֵן כְּשֶׁאָדָם מִצְטַעֵר, וְאָז אֵין הַהִתְקַשְּׁרוּת וְהַהִתְדַּבְּקוּת כִּבְיָכוֹל בֵּין הָאָדָם לְבֵינוֹ יִתְבָּרַךְ שְׁמוֹ בִּשְׁלֵמוּתוֹ כָּרָאוּי, הוּא עִנְיַן "קַלַּנִי מֵרֹאשִׁי קַלַּנִי מִזְּרוֹעִי", שֶׁהֵם מְקוֹמוֹת הַתְּפִלִּין, שֶׁשָּׁם הָיָה רָאוּי לִהְיוֹת הַהִתְדַּבְּקוּת הַקְּדוֹשָׁה:

שער ב' - פרק י"ב

- וְלָכֵן אָמְרוּ רַבּוֹתֵינוּ זִכְרוֹנָם לִבְרָכָה (ברכות סג, א) "כָּל הַמִּשְׁתַּתֵּף שֵׁם שָׁמַיִם בְּצַעֲרוֹ כּוֹפְלִין לוֹ פַּרְנָסָתוֹ":
- וְהָעִנְיָן
  - כִּי מִלְּבַד זֶה הַצַּעַר שֶׁנַּעֲשֶׂה לְמַעְלָה כְּשֶׁמְּקַבֵּל עָנְשׁוֹ בְּיִסּוּרִים רַחֲמָנָא לִיצְלָן
  - אֵין עֲרָךְ וְדִמְיוֹן כְּלָל זֶה הַצַּעַר שֶׁל מַעְלָה נֶגֶד עֹצֶם הַצַּעַר שֶׁגָּרַם לְמַעְלָה בְּעֵת עֲשׂוֹתוֹ הֶעָוֹן רַחֲמָנָא לִיצְלָן:
- כְּעִנְיַן הַבֵּן יַקִּיר שֶׁנִּתְפַּתְּתָה בְּיֵינוֹ וְנָפַל לָאָרֶץ וְנִשְׁבַּר מַפְרַקְתּוֹ וְגוּפוֹ וְהוּא מִסְכֵּן.
  - וְהוּא עַצְמוֹ אֵינוֹ מַרְגִּישׁ אָז כְּלָל סַכָּנַת נַפְשׁוֹ, כְּמוֹ שֶׁכָּתוּב (משלי כג, לה) "הִכּוּנִי בַל חָלִיתִי הֲלָמוּנִי בַּל יָדָעְתִּי".
  - אָמְנָם, אָבִיו לִבּוֹ מִתְמַרְמֵר מְאֹד עַל זֶה.
  - וְכַאֲשֶׁר הָרוֹפְאִים קָשְׁרוּ הַשְּׁבָרִים וְהִנִּיחוּ רְטִיָּה וְתַחְבֹּשֶׁת מְסַמָּנִים חֲרִיפִים, וְהַבֵּן מַר צוֹרֵחַ עַל הַכְּאֵב שֶׁלּוֹ מֵהַסַּמָּנִים הַחֲרִיפִים הָאוֹכְלִים בִּבְשָׂרוֹ
  - וְעִם כִּי אָבִיו מִצְטַעֵר לְצַעֲקָתוֹ וְרַבּוֹת אַנְחוֹתָיו עַתָּה, אֵין עֲרָךְ כְּלָל הַצַּעַר שֶׁל עַתָּה נֶגֶד הַצַּעַר וְהַיָּגוֹן הָרִאשׁוֹן שֶׁהָיָה לְאָבִיו בְּעֵת שֶׁנָּפַל וְשָׁבַר עַצְמוֹתָיו אֲשֶׁר כִּמְעַט נִתְיָאֵשׁ מֵחַיָּיו אָז:
- כֵּן מַמָּשׁ, עַל זֶה הָאֹפֶן, הוּא עִנְיַן הֶעָוֹן רַחֲמָנָא לִיצְלָן.
  - שֶׁבְּעֵת שֶׁהָאָדָם עוֹשֵׂהוּ, הוּא גּוֹרֵם לְמַעְלָה צַעַר גָּדוֹל וְעָצוּם לְאֵין עֲרָךְ
  - וְהָאָדָם עַצְמוֹ אֵינוֹ מַרְגִּישׁ אָז בָּזֶה כְּלָל
  - וְלֹא יֵדַע כִּי בְנַפְשׁוֹ הוּא, כִּי הוּא נֶחְשָׁב אָז כְּמֵת חַס וְשָׁלוֹם

---

282 Berachot 63a.
283 Mishlei 23:35.

- as Chazal say:²⁸⁴ "The wicked are considered dead when they are alive."²⁸⁵
- There are sins through which a person's soul is completely cut off, God forbid, from the connection to the cord of holiness
- but God, the Merciful Father, out of His pain, so to speak, and out of His great mercy and kindness, sends him sufferings which are a bandage and dressing to cleanse his sin
- then the person feels pain from his sufferings and is distressed
- and this results in a corresponding distress Above as stated earlier
- however, this distress is nothing compared to the distress caused Above at the time he actually performed the sin, God forbid.

- Therefore, when the whole purpose of a person's prayer before God to remove his own distress
  - is purely focused on the distress of the [One] Above, who joins him in his distress
  - and then he repents and has true regret for his sin which caused distress Above
  - then the sufferings are removed from him.
- More than this, but 'measure for measure,'²⁸⁶ his *livelihood is doubled*
  - corresponding to the two forms of distress that he caused Above
  - and now that he regrets both of them his sins are converted into meritorious deeds.
- This is as Chazal explain:
  - In relation to Chana, "and she was embittered and prayed to God," that she threw her words towards the [One] Above.²⁸⁷
    - Meaning that notwithstanding her own bitterness, she nevertheless disregarded her own distress and was not concerned to pray for this at all
    - but that "she threw her words" of prayer to God [to focus on] the distress of the [One] Above as a result of her current personal distress.
  - Therefore, it says there that Moshe also threw his words to the [One] Above [as per "and Moshe prayed *to* God"] – this verse should not be read as "*to*" God but rather "*about*" God.²⁸⁸
    - According to the simple understanding there would be no need

---

284 Berachot 18b.
285 See G1:06:N07 which explains the concept of death. Also see expanded references in G2:18 from Likutei Torah Yishayahu and the Vilna Gaon's commentary on Heichalot HaZohar Bereishit.
286 Mishna Sotah 1:7.

- כְּמַאֲמָרָם זִכְרוֹנָם לִבְרָכָה (בְּרֵישׁ פֶּרֶק מִי שֶׁמֵּתוֹ בְּרָכוֹת יח, ב) "רְשָׁעִים בְּחַיֵּיהֶם קְרוּיִים מֵתִים".
- וְיֵשׁ עֲווֹנוֹת שֶׁעַל יְדֵיהֶם נַפְשׁוֹ נִכְרֶתֶת חַס וְשָׁלוֹם לְגַמְרֵי מֵהִתְקַשְּׁרוּת חֶבֶל הַקְּדֻשָּׁה
- אֲבָל הוּא יִתְבָּרַךְ שְׁמוֹ, אָב הָרַחֲמָן, כִּבְיָכוֹל בְּצָרָתוֹ לוֹ צַעַר, וּמֵרֹב רַחֲמָיו וַחֲסָדָיו יִתְבָּרַךְ שְׁמוֹ, שׁוֹלֵחַ לוֹ יִסּוּרִין אֲשֶׁר הֵמָּה רְטִיָּה וְתַחְבֹּשֶׁת לְמָרֵק עֲווֹנוֹ
- וְאָז הָאָדָם מַרְגִּישׁ כְּאֵב יִסּוּרָיו וּמִצְטַעֵר
- וּבָזֶה מִתְעוֹרֵר גַּם כֵּן צַעַר לְמַעְלָה כַּנַּ"ל.
- אָמְנָם אֵין עֲרֹךְ כְּלָל זֶה הַצַּעַר נֶגֶד הַצַּעַר שֶׁגָּרַם לְמַעְלָה בְּעֵת עֲשׂוֹתוֹ הֶעָוֹן חַס וְשָׁלוֹם:

- וְלָכֵן כְּשֶׁכָּל תַּכְלִית תְּפִלַּת הָאָדָם לִפְנֵי יִתְבָּרַךְ שְׁמוֹ לְהָסִיר מֵעָלָיו צַעֲרוֹ
  - הוּא רַק עַל הַצַּעַר שֶׁל מַעְלָה הַמִּשְׁתַּתֵּף עִמּוֹ בְּצַעֲרוֹ
  - וְשָׁב וּמִתְחָרֵט בֶּאֱמֶת עַל עֲווֹנוֹ שֶׁגָּרַם עַל יָדוֹ הַצַּעַר שֶׁל מַעְלָה
  - אָז הַיִּסּוּרִין מִסְתַּלְּקִין מֵעָלָיו:

- וְלֹא עוֹד אֶלָּא שֶׁמּוֹדְדִין לוֹ כְּמִדָּתוֹ וְ"כוֹפְלִין" לוֹ פַּרְנָסָתוֹ
  - נֶגֶד הַשְּׁנֵי מִינֵי צַעַר שֶׁגָּרַם לְמַעְלָה
  - וְעַתָּה מִתְחָרֵט עַל שְׁנֵיהֶם, זְדוֹנוֹת מִתְהַפְּכִין לוֹ לִזְכֻיּוֹת:

- וְהוּא שֶׁדָּרְשׁוּ רַבּוֹתֵינוּ זִכְרוֹנָם לִבְרָכָה
  - בְּחַנָּה (בְּרָכוֹת לא, ב) "וְהִיא מָרַת נֶפֶשׁ וַתִּתְפַּלֵּל עַל ה'" (שמו"א א, י), שֶׁהֵטִיחָה דְּבָרִים כְּלַפֵּי מַעְלָה.
    - רוֹצֶה לוֹמַר, הֲגַם שֶׁהִיא עַצְמָהּ הָיְתָה מָרַת נֶפֶשׁ, עִם כָּל זֶה, הִשְׁלִיכָה צַעֲרָהּ מִמֶּנָּה, וְלֹא אִכְפַּת לָהּ לְהִתְפַּלֵּל עַל זֶה כְּלָל
    - אֶלָּא שֶׁהֵטִיחָה דִּבְרֵי תְּפִלָּתָהּ לִפְנָיו יִתְבָּרַךְ שְׁמוֹ עַל הַצַּעַר שֶׁל מַעְלָה, הַנַּעֲשָׂה מֵחֲמַת שֶׁהִיא שְׁרוּיָה עַתָּה בְּצַעַר.
- וְלָכֵן אָמְרוּ שָׁם (בְּרָכוֹת לב, א) שֶׁגַּם מֹשֶׁה הֵטִיחַ דְּבָרִים כְּלַפֵּי מַעְלָה כו', אַל תִּקְרֵי (במדבר יא, ב) "אֶל ה'" אֶלָּא "עַל ה'".
  - וּלְפִי פְּשׁוּטוֹ, מִי הִכְרִיחָם לְרַבּוֹתֵינוּ זִכְרוֹנָם לִבְרָכָה לִדְרֹשׁ אַל תִּקְרֵי, וְלוֹמַר

---

287 Berachot 30b–31b quoting 1 Shmuel 1:10.
288 Berachot 32a quoting Bamidbar 11:2.

for Chazal to interpret this verse in this way and to [just] say that he threw his words upwards [in a derisory way]. However, Chazal interpreted this to [Moshe's] credit as already explained.

- (It is for one who can understand to appreciate the continuation [of this section of the Talmud] in this same way, that Eliyahu also threw words towards [the One] Above, as per "and You have turned their hearts backwards."[289]
  - This is as per "the rock [/the one who fashions] my heart." Refer to Zohar.[290]
  - As per the verses: "and for your rebellious sins that your mother has been sent away,"[291] and "He drew back His right hand"[292] – this is the meaning of "and You have turned their hearts backwards."[293]
  - This is as explained in Pri Etz Chaim. Refer to it.)[294]

• So if in relation to a person's personal difficulties, his focus in prayer should only ever be on the needs of The Most High
  - how much more so that with the formulation of the blessings and prayer texts by the holy Men of the Great Assembly
  - that it is certainly not appropriate to have any intention [when reciting them] for one's personal needs, [in contrast] to what their simple meaning appears to be
  - but rather that they should only be for the needs of The Most High alone
  - to draw down additional blessing and holiness to the worlds from the perspective of God's connection to [the worlds], as explained above at length.

• Even though Chazal stated that it is possible to absolve [all Jews] from the obligation of prayer as in "drunk but not from wine,"[295] and what can be said now in these generations, where each person is 'like one who lies at the top of the mast and sleeps in the heart of the sea'[296] all [his] days from the burden of toiling for a living, and therefore there is no person who pays attention to rid his heart and his thoughts of the tremendous distractions of the vanities of this lowly world, to prepare himself to greet his God.
  - Notwithstanding this, each person, according to his intellectual capacity, is certainly obligated to devise methods as part of a *Commanded*

---

289 Berachot 31b quoting 1 Melachim 18:37.
290 Zohar II Terumah 128a–b quoting Tehillim 73:26, i.e., that the heart here refers to God's heart.
291 Yishayahu 50:1.
292 Eicha 2:3.

שֶׁהֵטִיחַ דְּבָרִים כְּלַפֵּי מַעְלָה. אָמְנָם לְמַעְלְיוּתָא הוּא דְּדַרְשׁוּ הָכִי, וּכְמוֹ שֶׁבִּיאַרְנוּ.

- (וְאֶת פְּנֵי מֵבִין לְהָבִין, עַל דֶּרֶךְ זֶה, מַה שֶּׁאָמְרוּ שָׁם עוֹד, שֶׁגַּם אֵלִיָּהוּ הֵטִיחַ דְּבָרִים כְּלַפֵּי מַעְלָה, שֶׁנֶּאֱמַר "וְאַתָּה הֲסִבּוֹתָ אֶת לִבָּם אֲחֹרַנִּית" (מלכים א' י״ח).
- וְהוּא כְּעִנְיָן "צוּר לְבָבִי" (תהלים עג, כו) וְגוֹ'. וְעַיֵּן זֹהַר תְּרוּמָה קכ״ח רֵישׁ ע״ב.
- וּכְמוֹ שֶׁכָּתוּב (ישעיה נ, א) "וּבְפִשְׁעֵיכֶם שֻׁלְּחָה אִמְּכֶם", "הֵשִׁיב אָחוֹר יְמִינוֹ" (איכה ב, ג) זֶהוּ "וְאַתָּה הֲסִבּוֹתָ אֶת לִבָּם אֲחֹרַנִּית".
- וְכֵן מְפֹרָשׁ בִּפְרִי עֵץ חַיִּים שַׁעַר הק"ש פֶּרֶק ח', עַיֵּן שָׁם):

• וְאִם בְּעִנְיַן תְּפִלַּת הַיָּחִיד עַל צַעֲרוֹ, צָרִיךְ שֶׁתְּהֵא כַּוָּנָתוֹ רַק צֹרֶךְ גָּבוֹהַּ לְבַד
- כָּל שֶׁכֵּן בְּמַטְבֵּעַ בִּרְכוֹת הַתְּפִלָּה הַקְּבוּעָה וּסְדוּרָה מֵאַנְשֵׁי הַכְּנֵסִיָּה הַקְּדוֹשִׁים
- וַדַּאי רָאוּי שֶׁלֹּא לְכַוֵּן בָּהֶם כְּלָל צֹרֶךְ עַצְמוֹ הַנִּרְאֶה מִפְּשׁוּטָם
- אֶלָּא צֹרֶךְ גָּבוֹהַּ לְבַד
- לְהַמְשִׁיךְ תּוֹסֶפֶת רִבּוּי בְּרָכָה וּקְדֻשָּׁה לְהָעוֹלָמוֹת, מִצַּד הִתְחַבְּרוּתוֹ יִתְבָּרַךְ שְׁמוֹ אֲלֵיהֶם, כְּמוֹ שֶׁנִּתְבָּאֵר לְעֵיל בָּאֹרֶךְ:

• וְאַף שֶׁגַּם רַבּוֹתֵינוּ זִכְרוֹנָם לִבְרָכָה אָמְרוּ (עירובין סה, א) "יְכָלְנִי לִפְטֹר אֶת כָּל הָעוֹלָם מִדִּין תְּפִלָּה שֶׁנֶּאֱמַר (ישעי' נא, כא) "שְׁכֻרַת וְלֹא מִיָּיִן", וּמַה נֹּאמַר עַתָּה בַּדּוֹרוֹת הַלָּלוּ, אֲשֶׁר כָּל אִישׁ הוּא כְּשׁוֹכֵב בְּרֹאשׁ חִבֵּל וּבְלֵב יַמִּים (מלה"כ משלי כג, לד), כָּל הַיָּמִים מֵעַל יְגִיעַת הַפַּרְנָסוֹת, וְלָזֹאת, אֵין אִישׁ שָׂם עַל לֵב לִפְנוֹת לִבּוֹ וּמַחֲשַׁבְתּוֹ, מִבִּלְבּוּלֵי טִרְדּוֹתָיו הָעֲצוּמִים בְּהַבְלֵי זֶה הָעוֹלָם הַשָּׁפֵל, לְהָכִין עַצְמוֹ לִקְרַאת אֱלֹקָיו יִתְבָּרַךְ שְׁמוֹ.

• עִם כָּל זֶה וַדַּאי שֶׂכֶל אֶחָד לְפִי שִׂכְלוֹ וְהַשָּׂגָתוֹ, מְחֻיָּב לָשִׂית עֵצוֹת בְּנַפְשׁוֹ

---

293 I.e., that Your Shechina, which is the *heart* of Israel, which when removed from Israel, resulted in them sinning.

294 Pri Etz Chaim Shaar Kriat Shema, Chap. 8:
- Therefore, there was an intensification in the Kelipot in those days and similarly in all times when Israel worshiped idols. Therefore, in the days of Achav it writes: "and You have turned their hearts backwards," for their hearts are the secret ... and therefore you caused them to fail for the power of the Kelipot increased. Therefore, they were rectified through Eliyahu's prayer.

295 Eruvin 65a quoting Yishayahu 51:21.

296 An expression taken from Mishlei 23:34 referring to being in a state of

War, to escape from the confusion of impure thoughts and 'be able to compose his thoughts'[297] in the appropriate service of prayer
- because the service of prayer currently replaces the service of the sacrifices which were entirely dependent on the thoughts of the Cohen [involved in offering them], that with the [Cohen's inappropriate] thoughts, he could invalidate the offering, and it was through the holiness of his thoughts that the offering would ascend to become a *fragrant fragrance* [to be acceptable] before God.

13. SIMPLE FOCUS ON WORDS IS PROVEN METHOD FOR PURITY OF PRAYER

- The recommended method for this[298] is as the Maggid told the Beit Yosef:[299] "To be careful to restrict one's thoughts during prayer to the words of prayer themselves, and not to think of any other thoughts – not even of Torah and Mitzvot."
- We should be very precise in understanding his words
  - as he does not say that one should focus on the intention of the words[300]
  - as we are, in truth, unable to fathom the depth of the essence of the intention of prayer
  - for even the small insight into the intention of prayer provided by our Rabbis from the supernal holy Rishonim and up until the holy, man of God, the awesome Arizal, who [expended] 'wondrous and great'[301] [effort] to [explain] the wondrous intentions
  - do not, even measure up to a drop in the ocean, to capture the depth of intention invested in the formulation of the words of prayer by the Men of the Great Assembly, comprised of 120 elders whose ranks included a number of prophets.
- Anyone who can, will understand that:
  - There is 'no one currently alive'[302] who is capable of producing such an awesome rectification, incorporating and encoding the rectifications of all the supernal and lower worlds together with the arrangements of the components of the Merkava, in a single fixed formula of prayer

---

drunkenness with sin and seasick as a result of being in a boat which is tossed around or from being on top of a mast.

297 Berachot 30b as per G2:01.
298 I.e., to devise a method to focus on prayer as per end of G2:12.
299 Maggid Meisharim Azharot 2. This is a book ascribed to R. Yosef Karo which records details of what he learned from a Heavenly sent messenger – the Maggid. (The authorship and authenticity of this book is questioned by some.

וּלְבַקֵּשׁ תַּחְבּוּלוֹת מִלְחֶמֶת מִצְוָה, לְהִמָּלֵט מִבִּלְבּוּל הַמַּחֲשָׁבוֹת אֲשֶׁר לֹא טְהוֹרִים, שֶׁתִּתְחוֹנֵן דַּעְתּוֹ עָלָיו לַעֲבוֹדַת הַתְּפִלָּה כָּרָאוּי.

כִּי עֲבוֹדַת הַתְּפִלָּה הִיא לָנוּ עַתָּה בִּמְקוֹם עֲבוֹדַת הַקָּרְבָּן, שֶׁהָיָה תָּלוּי כֻּלּוֹ בְּמַחֲשַׁבְתּוֹ שֶׁל הַכֹּהֵן, שֶׁבְּמַחֲשַׁבְתּוֹ הָיָה יָכוֹל לְפַגְּלוֹ, וְעַל יְדֵי קְדֻשַּׁת מַחֲשַׁבְתּוֹ הָיָה הַקָּרְבָּן מִתְעַלֶּה לְרֵיחַ נִיחוֹחַ לְפָנָיו, יִתְבָּרַךְ שְׁמוֹ:

שער ב' - פרק י"ג

- וְהָעֵצָה הַיְעוּצָה עַל זֶה, הוּא כְּמוֹ שֶׁאָמַר הַמַּגִּיד לְהַבֵּית יוֹסֵף בְּאַזְהָרָה הַשֵּׁנִית שֶׁבְּרֵישׁ הַסֵּפֶר מַגִּיד מֵישָׁרִים, זֶה לְשׁוֹנוֹ "לִיזָּהֵר מִלַּחֲשֹׁב בִּשְׁעַת תְּפִלָּה בְּשׁוּם מַחֲשָׁבָה, אֲפִלּוּ שֶׁל תּוֹרָה וּמִצְוֹת, כִּי אִם בְּתֵבוֹת הַתְּפִלָּה עַצְמָם":

- דַּק בִּדְבָרָיו
  - שֶׁלֹּא אָמַר לְכַוֵּן בְּ'כַוָּנַת' הַתֵּבוֹת
  - כִּי בֶּאֱמֶת בְּעֹמֶק פְּנִימִיּוּת כַּוָּנַת הַתְּפִלָּה, אֵין אִתָּנוּ יוֹדֵעַ עַד מָה
  - כִּי גַּם מַה שֶּׁנִּתְגַּלָּה לָנוּ קְצָת כַּוָּנוֹת הַתְּפִלָּה מֵרַבּוֹתֵינוּ הָרִאשׁוֹנִים זִכְרוֹנָם לִבְרָכָה קְדוֹשֵׁי עֶלְיוֹנִין, וְעַד אַחֲרוֹן הָרַב הַקָּדוֹשׁ אִישׁ אֱלֹקִים נוֹרָא הָאֲרִיזַ"ל, אֲשֶׁר הִפְלִיא הִגְדִּיל לַעֲשׂוֹת כַּוָּנוֹת נִפְלָאִים
  - אֵינָם בְּעֶרְךְ אַף כְּטִפָּה מִן הַיָּם כְּלָל נֶגֶד פְּנִימִיּוּת עֹמֶק כַּוָּנַת אַנְשֵׁי כְּנֶסֶת הַגְּדוֹלָה מְתַקְּנֵי הַתְּפִלָּה, שֶׁהָיוּ מֵאָה וְעֶשְׂרִים זְקֵנִים וּמֵהֶם כַּמָּה נְבִיאִים:

- וְכָל מֵבִין יָבִין
  - דְּלָא אִיתֵי אֱנָשׁ עַל יַבֶּשְׁתָּא שֶׁיּוּכַל לְתַקֵּן תִּקּוּן נִפְלָא וְנוֹרָא כָּזֶה, לִכְלָל וְלִגְנוֹ בְּמַטְבֵּעַ תְּפִלָּה קְבוּעָה וּסְדוּרָה בְּנֻסַּח אֶחָד, הַתִּקּוּנִים שֶׁל כָּל הָעוֹלָמוֹת, עֶלְיוֹנִים וְתַחְתּוֹנִים, וְסִדְרֵי פִּרְקֵי הַמֶּרְכָּבָה.

However, it is clear that R. Chaim considers it to be a valid source and uses it to make a pivotal point in this chapter.)

300 But just simply on the plain meaning of the words themselves.
301 Yishayahu 28:29.
302 Daniel 2:10, lit., "there is no one on dry land."

- such that with each instance of reciting this prayer formula, it causes new unique rectifications to be effected in the arrangement of the worlds and the powers, and the drawing down of new Mochin,[303] which from the time of their institution until the redemption there will never be any prayer instance which replicates any preceding or following prayer instance.
  - As the *clothes* worn in the morning are not the same as those worn in the evening, and *clothes* worn on one day are not the same as those worn on the next.[304]
  - Therefore, Chazal state that the verse "a twisted thing cannot be corrected" refers to a missed opportunity to recite the Shema or Amidah [which cannot be rectified][305]
  - as written at length in the Pri Etz Chaim, refer to it.[306]
- [This complexity of formulation was therefore] impossible if not through the medium of a high level of prophecy and divine inspiration
  - which was powerfully manifest [in the Men of the Great Assembly] when they formulated the syntax of prayer and the blessings

---

303 I.e., a bestowal from the intellect of God – Mochin relating to Chochma, Binah, and Daat, referred to as the "Three Heads" in G1:16, and from which the Middot are generated (see p.233, fn. 399 and p. 235, fn. 400).

304 Tikkunei Zohar Tikkun 22 65a. This connects to the idea R. Chaim presents in G1:02:N01 which explains that every created moment reflects a different combination of elements. Therefore, each prayer instance is a distinctly unique opportunity for rectification.

305 Chagiga 9b, Bamidbar Rabba Naso 9:6, Berachot 26a, quoting Kohelet 1:15.

306 Pri Etz Chaim Shaar HaTefillah, Chap. 7:
- You should know that there is a great difference between weekday prayer and the prayer of Rosh Chodesh, between the prayer of Yom Tov, between the prayer of Chol HaMoed, and between the prayer of Shabbat. More significantly, that even on Yom Tov itself, that the prayers of Pesach, Shavuot, and Sukkot are not similar. More significantly, that even with the weekday prayers themselves, the prayers of one day are not similar to the preceding day. Most significantly of all, that even with the prayers of each and every day, there is a great difference between them, and the morning prayers are not similar to the afternoon or evening prayers. The bottom line is that there is no [single] prayer – from the time of the Creation of the world until the ultimate future, which is similar to any other [prayer] at all. The reason for this is as we have already explained that all the prayers are in order to extract the remaining good from those seven kings which died [i.e., to ex-

- וְשֶׁבְּכָל פַּעַם שֶׁמִּתְפַּלְּלִין, יִגְרְמוּ תִּקּוּנִים חֲדָשִׁים בְּסִדּוּר הָעוֹלָמוֹת וְהַכֹּחוֹת, וְהַמְשָׁכַת מוֹחִין חֲדָשִׁים אֲחֵרִים, שֶׁמֵּעֵת שֶׁתִּקְּנוּהָ עַד בִּיאַת הַגּוֹאֵל בִּמְהֵרָה בְיָמֵינוּ, לֹא הָיָה וְלֹא יִהְיֶה שׁוּם תְּפִלָּה בִּפְרָטוּת דּוֹמָה לַחֲבֶרְתָּהּ שֶׁקָּדַם לָהּ וְאַחֲרֶיהָ כְּלָל.

- דִּלְבוּשִׁין דִּלְבִישׁ בְּצַפְרָא לֹא לָבִישׁ בְּרַמְשָׁא וּדְלָבִישׁ בְּרַמְשָׁא כוּ' כְּמוֹ שֶׁכָּתוּב בַּתִּקּוּנִים תִּקּוּן כ"ב. וְכֵן כָּל יוֹם לַחֲבֵרוֹ שֶׁלְּפָנָיו וְאַחֲרָיו.

- וְלָכֵן אָמְרוּ רַבּוֹתֵינוּ זִכְרוֹנָם לִבְרָכָה (חגיגה ט, וּבְרַבָּה בַּמִּדְבָּר פָּרָשָׁה ט') "מְעֻוָּת לֹא יוּכַל לִתְקֹן (קהלת א, טו) זֶה שֶׁבִּטֵּל קְרִיאַת שְׁמַע כוּ' אוֹ תְּפִלָּה" כוּ'.

- וּכְמוֹ שֶׁכָּתוּב בְּאֹרֶךְ בִּפְרִי עֵץ חַיִּים פֶּרֶק ז' מִשַּׁעַר הַתְּפִלָּה, עַיֵּן שָׁם:

• וְהוּא בִּלְתִּי אֶפְשָׁר אִם לֹא עַל יְדֵי הַנְּבוּאָה הָעֶלְיוֹנָה, וְרוּחַ קָדְשׁוֹ יִתְבָּרֵךְ

- אֲשֶׁר הוֹפִיעַ עֲלֵיהֶם הוֹפָעָה עֲצוּמָה, בְּעֵת תִּקּוּן נֻסַּח מַטְבֵּעַ הַתְּפִלָּה וְהַבְּרָכוֹת

---

tract the last remnants of the 288 sparks of holiness which fell into impurity as a result of the process known as Shevirat HaKeilim], and with each and every day, and with each and every prayer a new extraction of sparks is made of that which has not been previously extracted . . . and similarly this is the idea of the drawing down of lights with the recitation of Shema where the recitation of any instance of Shema is not similar to that of any other instance for the reason mentioned above, and this is the reason why we are instructed to pray three times a day and recite Shema twice a day, and if we omit any single instance it is called "a twisted thing cannot be corrected." The reason is that with each and every prayer instance and instance of reciting the Shema, new extractions of good are made, and additionally new Mochin is drawn down from Above, being unique and not [extracted or drawn down] with any other instance of prayer or Shema recitation . . . It transpires that with each and every prayer new Mochin and extraction takes place. But after prayer they return back and depart, and with this, Chazal's statement can be understood that the original Chassidim would wait for an hour before prayer, tarry for an hour after prayer and spend an hour in prayer, the reason for this being that . . . after the destruction of the Temple as a result of our sins, Mochin departed from Zeer Anpin and Nukva, and therefore, we are required to continuously pray each day to return the Mochin to its place so that there can be a union between Zeer Anpin and Nukva, as the Talmud says: "If only a person could pray all day" . . . and it appears to me, [R.] Chaim [Vital], that one who wears Tefillin all day causes the Mochin to tarry all day long . . . this was also the reason why Chazal say that the original Chassidim would not remove their Tefillin all day long. . . .

- when God placed these specific choice words with all the rectifications hidden within them – into their mouths.
- Therefore, there is no one [today] who can 'stand with the secret of God'[307] to appreciate the depths of God's intention and in what way light is manifest in each individual word [of prayer].

- Therefore, the key part of the service of prayer is that
  - when a person verbally utters each word of prayer
  - he should form a mental image of the form of the word and its letters (Note 32)[308]
  - and to focus on drawing additional power of holiness through it, which will bear fruit Above to increase their holiness and light
  - as I wrote above in G2:10: that therefore prayer is referred to by Chazal as "words which stand at the highest point of the Universe,"[309] that each word, literally in the form that it stands, is elevated to the highest realms to reach its source and root and effecting awesome rectifications.[310]
- This is a tremendous tried and tested method for those who habituate themselves with it
  - to remove all vain and troubling thoughts which prevent one from achieving purity of thought and focus
  - and all who increase their level of habituation with this, will increase their level of purity of thought in their prayer – this being [the level of] simple intentional focus.

Rabbi Chaim's Note:
Note 32 – Difference between prayer in Hebrew and other languages

- Even though it is Chazal's legal decision[311] that prayer can be uttered in any language
  - this is [a requirement] in order to fulfill the commandment of prayer
  - as was explained above (at the end of G1:22)

---

307 Yirmiyahu 23:18.
308 **R. Chaim adds Note 32 here.** This note is brought at the end of this chapter and is entitled "Difference between prayer in Hebrew and other languages."
309 Berachot 6b.
310 The following comments from the Vilna Gaon in Imrei Noam on Berachot 31 are insightful in tying together R. Chaim's opening point on prayer, that it should be exclusively focused on God (G2:01), and his statements in this chapter that focus during prayer should be on the words of prayer themselves:
- "[One who prays] should concentrate his heart on Heaven" (Berachot 31a). This means that he should concentrate on Heavenly matters and not on

- שָׁם הוּא יִתְבָּרַךְ שְׁמוֹ בְּפִיהֶם אֵלוּ הַתֵּבוֹת סְפוּרוֹת, וּגְנוּזוֹת בְּתוֹכָם כָּל הַתִּקּוּנִים.
- לָזֹאת, מִי הוּא אֲשֶׁר עָמַד בְּסוֹד ה', עַל עֹמֶק כַּוָּנָתוֹ יִתְבָּרַךְ שְׁמוֹ, אֵיזֶה דֶרֶךְ יִשְׁכָּן אוֹרָהּ שֶׁל כָּל תֵּבָה פְּרָטִית מֵהֶם:

- אֶלָּא הָעִקָּר בַּעֲבוֹדַת הַתְּפִלָּה
  - שֶׁבְּעֵת שֶׁהָאָדָם מוֹצִיא מִפִּיו כָּל תֵּבָה מֵהַתְּפִלָּה
  - יְצַיֵּר לוֹ אָז בְּמַחֲשַׁבְתּוֹ אוֹתָהּ הַתֵּבָה בְּאוֹתִיּוֹתֶיהָ כְּצוּרָתָהּ (הגהה ל"ב)
  - וִיכַוֵּן לְהוֹסִיף עַל יָדָהּ כֹּחַ הַקְּדֻשָּׁה, שֶׁיַּעֲשֶׂה פְּרִי לְמַעְלָה לְהַרְבּוֹת קְדֻשָּׁתָם וְאוֹרָם
  - כְּמוֹ שֶׁכָּתַבְתִּי לְעֵיל בְּפֶרֶק י', שֶׁלָּכֵן נִקְרֵאת הַתְּפִלָּה "דְּבָרִים הָעוֹמְדִים בְּרוּמוֹ שֶׁל עוֹלָם" (ברכות ו:), שֶׁכָּל תֵּבָה בְּצוּרָתָהּ מַמָּשׁ, הִיא הָעוֹלָה לְמַעְלָה מַעְלָה, כָּל אַחַת לִמְקוֹרָהּ וְשָׁרְשָׁהּ, לִפְעֹל פְּעֻלּוֹת וְתִקּוּנִים נִפְלָאִים:

- וְהִיא סְגֻלָּה נִפְלָאָה, בָּדוּק וּמְנֻסֶּה, לַמַּרְגִּילִים עַצְמָם בָּזֶה
  - לְבַטֵּל וּלְהָסִיר מֵעָלָיו בָּזֶה כָּל מַחֲשָׁבוֹת הַהֲבָלִים הַטּוֹרְדוֹת, וּמְנִיעוֹת טָהֳרַת הַמַּחֲשָׁבָה וְהַכַּוָּנָה
  - וְכָל אֲשֶׁר יוֹסִיף הַרְגֵּלוֹ בָּזֶה יִתּוֹסֵף לוֹ טָהֳרָה בְּמַחֲשַׁבְתּוֹ בִּתְפִלָּה, וְהִיא כַוָּנָה פְּשׁוּטָה:

הגהה ל"ב

- וְהַגַּם שֶׁהֲלָכָה פְּסוּקָה בַּשַּׁ"ס (סוטה לב. לג.) שֶׁתְּפִלָּה נֶאֱמֶרֶת בְּכָל לָשׁוֹן
  - הַיְנוּ לָצֵאת יְדֵי מִצְוַת תְּפִלָּה
  - כְּמוֹ שֶׁנִּתְבָּאֵר לְעֵיל (סוֹף שַׁעַר א)

---

other things. The meaning of "his heart" is the concentration of his heart, that is the meaning of the words. The Tanna [who authored this statement] is telling us two things: 1. that a person should concentrate on Heaven, and 2. that he should concentrate on the meaning of the words.

311 Sotah 32a in the Mishna and 33a.

- that with all the commandments
- and even with the commandment of prayer which is called "Service of the Heart"[312]
- that nevertheless, their essential element which [if absent] prevents their fulfillment – is their physical performance.
- However, to fulfill the commandment in the best way
- one certainly needs to apply purity of thought and have complete intentional focus
- and the practical fulfillment of the commandment will increase in proportion to the increased level of associated purity of intentional focus
- with this applying, in particular, to "Service of the Heart" which is with prayer.
• Notwithstanding the fact that one who prays in any language has fulfilled his obligation
  - this is incomparable to one who prays in Hebrew with these specific words which stand at the highest point of the Universe, and invests all of his energy in them.

14. SERVICE OF THE SOUL WITH SPOKEN PRAYER TO CLEAVE TO GOD

• However, the explanation of the verse mentioned above at the beginning of our words[313]
  - "to serve Him ... with all of your *soul/Nefesh*"
  - that the complete service of prayer must be with the *Nefesh*
  - is a tremendous concept for those who know and understand a little.
• The more one persists in praying at this level [with one's Nefesh], as will be explained with God's help, 'the more purity one adds to one's existing purity.'[314]
• We find many Scriptural references and statements of Chazal referring to prayer as "Nefesh":
  - For many important laws relating to the principles of prayer can be learned from the verses relating to Chana[315]
    - about whom it is written "and I will pour out my *Nefesh* before God."[316]
  - "My Nefesh should bless God."[317]

---

312 Taanit 2a.
313 R. Chaim is referring to the statement at the end of G2:01. G2:01 explains how service of God can be with one's entire heart, but then concludes that

- שֶׁבְּכָל הַמִּצְוֹת
- וַאֲפִלּוּ מִצְוַת תְּפִלָּה שֶׁנִּקְרֵאת "עֲבוֹדָה שֶׁבַּלֵּב"
- עִם כָּל זֶה עִקָּרָן לְעַכּוּבָא הוּא חֵלֶק הַמַּעֲשִׂי שֶׁבָּהֶן.
- אָמְנָם לְמִצְוָה מִן הַמֻּבְחָר
- וַדַּאי צָרִיךְ לְצָרֵף גַּם טֹהַר הַמַּחְשָׁבָה וְכַוָּנָה שְׁלֵמָה
- וּלְפִי גֹדֶל טֹהַר הַכַּוָּנָה כֵּן תִּגְדַּל מַעֲשֵׂה הַמִּצְוָה.
- וּבִפְרָט עֲבוֹדַת הַלֵּב שֶׁבַּתְּפִלָּה:

• עִם כִּי מִי שֶׁהִתְפַּלֵּל בְּכָל לָשׁוֹן יָצָא יְדֵי חוֹבָה
- אֲבָל אֵין עֲרֹךְ לְמִי שֶׁמִּתְפַּלֵּל בִּלְשׁוֹן הַקֹּדֶשׁ בְּאֵלּוּ הַתֵּבוֹת דַּוְקָא, הָעוֹמְדִים בְּרוּמוֹ שֶׁל עוֹלָם, וּמְדַבֵּק כָּל כֹּחוֹתָיו בָּהֶם:

שער ב' - פרק י"ד

• אָמְנָם בְּאוּר הַכָּתוּב הַנַ"ל בִּתְחִלַּת דְּבָרֵינוּ (פרק א)
- "וּלְעָבְדוֹ כו' וּבְכָל נַפְשְׁכֶם"
- שֶׁעֲבוֹדַת הַתְּפִלָּה הַשְּׁלֵמָה צְרִיכָה שֶׁתִּהְיֶה עִם הַנֶּפֶשׁ
- הוּא עִנְיָן גָּדוֹל לַיּוֹדְעִים וּמְבִינִים קְצָת:

• וְכַאֲשֶׁר יַתְמִיד הָאָדָם תְּפִלָּתוֹ בְּזֹאת הַמַּדְרֵגָה, שֶׁיִּתְבָּאֵר אי"ה, יִתּוֹסֵף לוֹ טָהֳרָה עַל טָהֳרָתוֹ:

• כִּי מָצִינוּ בְּכַמָּה מְקוֹמוֹת בַּמִּקְרָא וּבְדִבְרֵי רַבּוֹתֵינוּ זִכְרוֹנָם לִבְרָכָה, שֶׁהַתְּפִלָּה נִקְרָאָה בְּשֵׁם "נֶפֶשׁ"
- כִּי כַּמָּה הִלְכְתָא גַבְרְוָתָא בְּעִקְּרֵי הַתְּפִלָּה אִכָּא לְמִשְׁמַע מִקְרָאֵי דְחַנָּה
  ▪ וּכְתִיב בָּהּ (שמו"א, א, טו) "וָאֶשְׁפֹּךְ אֶת נַפְשִׁי לִפְנֵי ה'"
  ▪ וּכְתִיב (תהלים קג, א) "בָּרְכִי נַפְשִׁי אֶת ה'"

---

in order to understand what serving God means when it is with one's entire soul, that one first needs to understand the concept of "blessing." Having now explained this concept of "blessing," R. Chaim now returns to explain the meaning of service of God with one's entire soul.

314 An expression derived from Avodah Zarah 75b used in connection with the ritual immersion of vessels.
315 Berachot 31a.
316 1 Shmuel 1:15.
317 Tehillim 103:1, 103:2, 103:22, 104:1, 104:35.

- ○ "My Nefesh should praise God."[318]
- ○ Two who entered [a house of prayer] to pray and one finished first and did not wait for his colleague but just left – his prayer is tossed from before him as is written: "He who tears his *Nefesh* apart in his anger. . . ."[319]
  - □ Rashi comments on this: It is speaking to you, that you caused your Nefesh to be tossed before you, and what is the Nefesh? It is prayer, as per "and I will pour out my Nefesh before God."
- This concept is that the service of prayer replaces the service of sacrifices (Note 33)[320]
  - ○ Therefore, just as the purpose of the sacrifices was to elevate the animal's Nefesh Above, with the main atonement achieved through the sprinkling of its 'blood which is the Nefesh,'[321] and similarly, the intention of offering of the animal's innards was also on elevating the Nefesh
  - ○ similarly, the main purpose of prayer is to elevate, give over and attach one's Nefesh to God.[322]
- A person's ability to speak is called "Nefesh," as per "and the man became a *living Nefesh*"[323] which Unkelos translates as "a *speaking spirit*":
  - ○ ["*Spirit*":] It is visually evident that with each spoken word that a person utters – spirit and breath exits his mouth.
  - ○ ["*Speaking*":] Speech is the essential part of a person's Nefesh,[324] it is that which differentiates a person from an animal,[325] therefore, every word uttered is empowered by and a part of his Nefesh.
- Therefore, when standing in prayer before God, one should detach one's body from one's Nefesh: (Note 34)[326]
  - ○ That is – one should remove all fleeting thoughts which derive from the powers of the body [i.e., the physical] and which are etched into and attached to one's Nefesh – such that one's service of prayer will be solely with one's Nefesh and its elevated will.
  - ○ This necessitates [preparation] before engaging in prayer to nullify and remove from oneself all thoughts of bodily desire, earthly benefit

---

318 Tehillim 146:1.
319 Berachot 5b quoting Iyov 18:4.
320 **R. Chaim adds Note 33 here.** This note is brought at the end of this chapter and is entitled "Prayer and sacrifices interconnect and unify worlds with God."
321 Devarim 12:23.
322 The process of offering a sacrifice is one where the sacrifice is in place of the one who sinned. In a sense all the actions that are performed on the sacrificial animal needed to happen to the sinner himself, so atonement is achieved with the recognition that the sacrifice is taking his place. Therefore, intellectually

נפש　שער ב' - פרק י"ד　החיים

- "הַלְלִי נַפְשִׁי אֶת ה'" (שם קמו, א).

- וְרַבּוֹתֵינוּ זִכְרוֹנָם לִבְרָכָה בְּפֶרֶק קַמָּא דִּבְרָכוֹת (ה, ב) אָמְרוּ "שְׁנַיִם שֶׁנִּכְנְסוּ לְהִתְפַּלֵּל, וְקָדַם אֶחָד מֵהֶם לְהִתְפַּלֵּל, וְלֹא הִמְתִּין אֶת חֲבֵרוֹ וְיָצָא, טוֹרְפִין לוֹ תְּפִלָּתוֹ בְּפָנָיו, שֶׁנֶּאֱמַר (איוב יח, ד) "טוֹרֵף נַפְשׁוֹ בְּאַפּוֹ" וְגו'

  - פֵּרֵשׁ רַשִׁ"י, לְךָ אוֹמֵר, אֲשֶׁר גָּרַמְתָּ לְךָ לִטְרוֹף אֶת נַפְשְׁךָ בְּפָנֶיךָ, וּמַה הִיא הַנֶּפֶשׁ, זוֹ תְּפִלָּה, כְּמוֹ שֶׁנֶּאֱמַר "וָאֶשְׁפּוֹךְ אֶת נַפְשִׁי" (שמואל א' א, טו) כו':

- וְהָעִנְיָן, שֶׁעֲבוֹדַת הַתְּפִלָּה הִיא בִּמְקוֹם עֲבוֹדַת הַקָּרְבָּן (הגהה ל"ג).

  - וּכְמוֹ שֶׁעִנְיָן הַקָּרְבָּן הָיָה, לְהַעֲלוֹת 'נֶפֶשׁ' הַבְּהֵמָה לְמַעְלָה, וְלָכֵן עִקָּר הַכַּפָּרָה הָיָה תָּלוּי בִּזְרִיקַת הַדָּם הוּא הַ'נֶּפֶשׁ', וְכֵן הַקְטָרַת הָאֵמוּרִים עִקָּרָם הָיָה לְכַוָּנַת הַעֲלָאַת הַ'נֶּפֶשׁ'

  - כֵּן עִקַּר עִנְיַן הַתְּפִלָּה הוּא, לְהַעֲלוֹת וְלִמְסוֹר וּלְדַבֵּק 'נַפְשׁוֹ' לְמַעְלָה:

- כִּי כֹּחַ הַדִּבּוּר שֶׁל הָאָדָם נִקְרָא "נֶפֶשׁ", כְּמוֹ שֶׁכָּתוּב (בראשית ב, ז) "וַיְהִי הָאָדָם לְנֶפֶשׁ חַיָּה", וְתַרְגֵּם אוּנְקְלוּס, לְרוּחַ מְמַלְּלָא.

  - וְכֵן נִרְאֶה לָעַיִן, שֶׁבְּכָל דִּבּוּר שֶׁהָאָדָם מוֹצִיא מִפִּיו, יוֹצֵא מִפִּיו רוּחַ וְהֶבֶל הַלֵּב.

  - וְהַדִּבּוּר הוּא עִקַּר נֶפֶשׁ הָאָדָם, שֶׁזֶּה יִתְרוֹן הָאָדָם מִן הַבְּהֵמָה, אִם כֵּן, כָּל תֵּבָה הַיּוֹצֵאת מִפִּי הָאָדָם הִיא כֹּחַ וְחֵלֶק מִנַּפְשׁוֹ:

- לָזֹאת, בְּעֵת עָמְדוֹ לְהִתְפַּלֵּל לִפְנֵי קוֹנוֹ יִתְבָּרַךְ שְׁמוֹ, יַפְשִׁיט גּוּפוֹ מֵעַל נַפְשׁוֹ (הגהה ל"ד)

  - הַיְנוּ, שֶׁיָּסִיר כָּל רַעֲיוֹנֵי הַהֲבָלִים הַבָּאִים מִכֹּחוֹת הַ'גּוּף', שֶׁנִּתְחַזְּקוּ וְנִתְדַּבְּקוּ בְ'נַפְשׁוֹ', שֶׁלֹּא תִּהְיֶה עֲבוֹדַת תְּפִלָּתוֹ רַק בְּהַ'נֶּפֶשׁ' וּרְעוּתָא עִלָּאָה דִּילֵיהּ.

  - וְהוּא, שֶׁקֹּדֶם עָמְדוֹ בִּתְפִלָּה, צָרִיךְ לְבַטֵּל וּלְהָסִיר מֵעָלָיו בְּמַחֲשַׁבְתּוֹ כָּל

---

focusing on the elements of the offering and how they correspond to and are in place of oneself, is a tool which enables one to relate to the complete giving over of oneself to God during prayer.

323　Bereishit 2:7.

324　God constantly creates with His Speech. To parallel this, for us who are in His Image our Nefesh creates with our speech.

325　There are four levels of life: 1. inanimate 2. vegetation 3. animal 4. speech. Humans are differentiated from the other levels of life by their ability to speak. This ability is not simply the ability to communicate (as animals also have this ability) but to do so in an intellectually abstract manner.

326　**R. Chaim adds Note 34 here.** This note is brought at the end of this chapter and is entitled "R. Yona: Focus thoughts on Creator and not the physical."

and anything relating to it – to the extent that one is able to despise the [physical] body – becoming as if the body no longer exists and that it is only the Nefesh which speaks in prayer.[327]

- The act of verbally uttering each word, which is an expression and part of one's Nefesh, causes a great desire to literally give over and completely outpour one's Nefesh, to attach it to the supernal root of the words of prayer which stand at the highest point of the worlds.
  - As per Zohar in Vayakhel which is mentioned in the note:[328] While his mouth and lips are moving he should focus his heart, and his desire will ascend to the heights, to be completely unified with the secret of secrets, a place where all desire and thoughts are held, with the secret of the Infinite One.
  - Then he will be considered as if he is removed from this world, and one of the elevated individuals Above, such that even after prayer it will be very difficult to return his thoughts to mundane Earthly matters, and it will appear to him as if he is falling 'from a high precipice to the bottom of a deep pit.'[329]
    - This being the idea behind the original *Chassidim* who would tarry for an additional hour after prayer.[330]
      - This is in line with the reason for this that the Arizal also writes that one should tarry with the [level of] Mochin,[331] etc.
      - This is the concept underpinning Chazal's statement that "one who prays ... must focus his heart upwards."[332]
- [A person] will [thereby] so greatly increase and enthuse his love for God through the power of his Nefesh
  - to the extent that there is a true yearning and desire
  - that when he now utters holy speech of any word of the prayer formulation
  - his soul will completely leave the body, and ascend to cleave to God, so to speak.
- This is the meaning of the verse here "and you shall serve Him ... with all of your Nefesh" and similarly, also that which Chana said: "I will pour out my Nefesh before God," this is now explained.

---

327 A similar sentiment is expressed in the Shulchan Aruch's opening statement on the intention of prayer, as per Orach Chaim 98:1 (with the Rama quoting Rabbeinu Yona, as R. Chaim does in G2:14:N34).
328 Zohar II Vayakhel 213b. R. Chaim is referring to G2:14:N33, where he quotes a longer section of this Zohar.
329 Chagiga 5b.
330 Berachot 32b.

תַּעֲנוּגֵי הַגּוּף וַהֲנָאוֹתָיו וְכָל עִנְיָנָיו, עַד שֶׁיִּקָּבַע בְּמַחֲשַׁבְתּוֹ לִמְאֹם הַגּוּף, כְּאִלּוּ אֵינוֹ בַּעַל גּוּף כְּלָל, וְרַק נַפְשׁוֹ לְבַדָּהּ הִיא הַמְדַבֶּרֶת תְּפִלָּתָהּ:

- וּבְדַבְּרוֹ כָּל תֵּבָה, שֶׁהִיא כֹּחַ וְחֵלֶק מִנַּפְשׁוֹ, יַדְבִּיק בָּהּ רְעוּתֵיהּ מְאֹד, לִיתֵּן וְלִשְׁפֹּךְ בָּהּ נַפְשׁוֹ מַמָּשׁ לְגַמְרֵי, וּלְהַדְבִּיקָהּ בְּשֹׁרֶשׁ הָעֶלְיוֹן שֶׁל תֵּבוֹת הַתְּפִלָּה הָעוֹמְדִים בְּרוּמוֹ שֶׁל עוֹלָם

- וּכְמוֹ שֶׁכָּתוּב בַּזֹּהַר וַיַּקְהֵל הַנִּזְכָּר בַּהַגָּהָה — וּבְעוֹד דְּפוּמֵיהּ וְשִׂפְוָותֵיהּ מְרַחֲשָׁן, לִבֵּיהּ יְכַוֵּין רְעוּתֵיהּ יִסְתַּלֵּק לְעֵילָא לְעֵילָא, לְיַחֲדָא כֹּלָּא בְּרָזָא דְרָזִין דְּתַמָּן תְּקִיעוּ דְּכָל רְעוּתִין וּמַחֲשַׁבְתִּין בְּרָזָא דְקַיְמָא בְּאֵין סוֹף.

- וְאָז יַחְשֹׁב כְּאִלּוּ הוּא מְסֻלָּק מִזֶּה הָעוֹלָם, וְהוּא מִ"בְּנֵי עֲלִיָּה" לְמַעְלָה, עַד שֶׁגַּם אַחַר הַתְּפִלָּה יִקְשֶׁה לוֹ מְאֹד לְהִפָּנוֹת מַחֲשַׁבְתּוֹ לְעִנְיְנֵי זֶה הָעוֹלָם. וִיהֵא בְעֵינָיו כְּאִלּוּ נוֹפֵל וּמִטַּפֵּס וְיוֹרֵד מֵאִגְּרָא רָמָא לְבֵירָא עֲמִיקְתָּא.

- וּכְעִנְיָן (ברכות לב, ב) חֲסִידִים הָרִאשׁוֹנִים שֶׁהָיוּ שׁוֹהִים שָׁעָה אַחַת גַּם אַחַר הַתְּפִלָּה.

- וְהוּא שֶׁכָּתַב גַּם כֵּן הָאֲרִ"י זִכְרוֹנוֹ לִבְרָכָה הַטַּעַם עַל זֶה, כְּדֵי לְהַשְׁהוֹת עוֹד הַמּוֹחִין וְכוּ'

- וְהוּא עִנְיַן מַאַמְרָם זִכְרוֹנָם לִבְרָכָה (יבמות קה, ב) הַמִּתְפַּלֵּל צָרִיךְ שֶׁיִּתֵּן לִבּוֹ לְמַעְלָה:

- וְכָל כָּךְ תִּרְבֶּה וְתִתְלַהֵט אַהֲבָתוֹ יִתְבָּרַךְ בְּכֹחַ נַפְשׁוֹ
  - עַד שֶׁיְּהֵא חוֹשֵׁק וּמִתְאַוֶּה בֶּאֱמֶת
  - שֶׁבְּדַבְּרוֹ עַתָּה אוֹתוֹ הַדִּבּוּר הַקָּדוֹשׁ שֶׁל אֵיזֶה תֵּבָה מִנֻּסַּח הַתְּפִלָּה
  - תְּהֵא נַפְשׁוֹ יוֹצֵאת מֵהַגּוּף לְגַמְרֵי, וְתִתְעַלֶּה לְהִתְדַּבֵּק כִּבְיָכוֹל בּוֹ יִתְבָּרַךְ שְׁמוֹ:

- זֶה שֶׁכָּתוּב כָּאן "וּלְעָבְדוֹ כו', וּבְכָל נַפְשְׁכֶם", וְכֵן מַה שֶּׁאָמְרָה חַנָּה "וָאֶשְׁפֹּךְ אֶת נַפְשִׁי לִפְנֵי ה'", וְהוּא מְבֹאָר.

---

331 I.e., the intellectual connection to God using Chochma, Binah, and Daat. See the end of the quotation brought on p. 406, fn. 306, from Pri Etz Chaim Shaar HaTefillah, Chap. 7.

332 Yevamot 105b. It is explained on p. 304, fn. 3, that the use of the word "heart" really refers to what we call the "mind." It is clear that in the context here, R. Chaim is connecting "prayer from the heart" in this statement to his previous statement from the Arizal which relates to prayer as an intellectual process using the intellectual faculties/Mochin.

- Similarly, Chazal's statement can be explained: "A person's prayer is not heard unless he places his Nefesh *BeKapo*,"[333] that one should use prayer to elevate and cleave his Nefesh upwards, where "Kapo" means "his root" as in "Vechipato [i.e., his source] will not be refreshed."[334]

Rabbi Chaim's Notes:
Note 33 – Prayer and sacrifices interconnect and unify worlds with God

- That through the Temple Sacrifices [the *Korbanot*]
  - where [both the Temple and the sacrificial processes] completely reflected [the structure and processes of] the Supernal Realms
  - [including] its attics, chambers, and all the vessels used for Temple service
  - they interconnected and unified the supernal worlds, powers, and lights of the holy chambers
  - in a sequence of levels ascending all the way up to the Infinite One.
    - As per many places in the Zohar.[335] Refer well to all of these sources to appreciate the awesomeness of this point.

---

333 Taanit 8a.
334 Iyov 15:32.
335 Zohar I Bereishit 45b:
- ... the sacrifice is like this – its smoke rises and supplies each [chamber] with what it requires as is suitable for it ... entering/interconnecting one chamber with another chamber and spirit with spirit – until they are all interconnected in their place as is appropriate for them – one limb [interconnected] with another limb, with each completing each other ....

Zohar I Noach 65a:
- [In the context of offering up sacrifices ...] ... Come and see, it is all done [i.e., the sacrifices are prepared] with the secret of faith to supply this with this [i.e., all levels] and to cause that which is needed, to ascend right up until the level of the Infinite One ....

Zohar Sitrei Torah I Lech Lecha 89b:
- When a sacrifice is offered up all the worlds receive a part of it, and it disperses all of the Kelipot [the impure forces] to the sides, and unifies, and the candles give light, and it is called will and friendship in all of the worlds, and [as a result] God is appropriately found to be within the secret of Unity.

Zohar I Vayigash 206b:
- R. Chiya said: The secret of this [verse which this section of Zohar is expounding] is the rectification done by the sacrifices, for when a sacrifice is offered up and all receive their supplies [from it], each one according

וְכֵן יֵשׁ לְפָרֵשׁ מַאַמְרָם זִכְרוֹנָם לִבְרָכָה (תענית ח' ע"א) "אֵין תְּפִלָּתוֹ שֶׁל אָדָם נִשְׁמַעַת אֶלָּא אִם כֵּן מֵשִׂים נַפְשׁוֹ בְּכַפּוֹ", הַיְנוּ, לְהַעֲלוֹת וּלְדַבֵּק בִּתְפִלָּתוֹ אֶת נַפְשׁוֹ לְמַעְלָה, וְ"כַפּוֹ" פֵּרוּשׁ "שָׁרְשׁוֹ", מִלְּשׁוֹן "וְכִפָּתוֹ לֹא רַעֲנָנָה" (איוב טו, לב):

הגהה ל"ג

- שֶׁעַל יְדֵי הַקָּרְבָּנוֹת שֶׁבַּמִּקְדָּשׁ
  - שֶׁהָיָה כֻּלּוֹ בְּדֻגְמָא עֶלְיוֹנָה
  - עֲלִיּוֹתָיו וַחֲדָרָיו וְכָל כֵּלָיו אֲשֶׁר יִשְׁרְתוּ בָּהֶם
- הָיוּ מִתְקַשְּׁרִים וּמִתְיַחֲדִים עַל יְדֵיהֶם הָעוֹלָמוֹת וְהַכֹּחוֹת הָעֶלְיוֹנִים וְהַנְּהוֹרִין שֶׁל הַהֵיכָלוֹת הַקְּדוֹשִׁים
  - כֻּלָּם בְּסֵדֶר הַמַּדְרֵגוֹת לְעֵלָּא וּלְעֵלָּא עַד אֵין סוֹף בָּרוּךְ הוּא
  - כַּמְבֹאָר בִּמְקוֹמוֹת רַבּוֹת בַּזֹּהַר, בְּפָרָשַׁת בְּרֵאשִׁית מ"ה ב', נֹחַ ס"ה א',

---

to what is appropriate for it, then everything is bound up as one, with all presentations being lit up, with a single interconnected bond....

Zohar I Vayechi 244a:
- Come and see, that through the arousal in the lower worlds [through the offering of a sacrifice] there is also an arousal in the supernal worlds, and with the arousal of the supernal worlds there is also an arousal of the worlds above them, until the arousal reaches the place where it is necessary to light a candle, and it is lit. With the arousal from the [sacrificial] smoke of the lower worlds, the candle Above is lit, and when this candle is lit then all the candles are lit, and all the worlds are blessed from it. It transpires that the arousal of offering up a sacrifice is the rectification of the world and the blessing of all of the worlds.

Zohar II Pekudei 259b:
- ... and we have established in a similar way to this, that the sacrifice ascends, with its smoke, to unify the unity and to supply that which is appropriate to each and every one, that the Cohen, who is right [i.e., the Cohen involved in the offering represents Chesed which corresponds to the right side] is bound to the unity with will, and the Levi with song [i.e., the Levi involved in the general Temple service which contributes to the general atmosphere of the sacrificial offerings and represents Gevurah which corresponds to the left side], they are incorporated one with the other [i.e., the Chesed and Gevurah combine and unify], [heavenly] chamber with [heavenly] chamber, spirit with spirit, until they are all interconnected in their place, limb with limb, such that they are all comprised as one [unity] as is appropriate.

Zohar III Vayikra beginning of 5b:

- For specific details of the sequence of ascent and interconnection, refer to Pri Etz Chaim.[336]
• Therefore, it is called "*Korban*"
  - As written in Sefer HaBahir:[337]
    - Why is it called a "Korban?" – because it brings together (Mekarev) the Holy Forms [as per "Then bring them close to yourself, one to the other, like one piece of wood and they will become unified in your hand"[338]], and it says "as a *Reyach Nichoach* (a fragrant fragrance),"[339] [for there is no *Reyach* (fragrance) without the nose and "Nichoach" means "descent" . . . Therefore, a sacrifice's fragrance causes] the spirit[340] to descend and unify with those Holy Forms and draw close to them through the sacrifice. That is why it is called "Korban."
  - Refer to Zohar:
    - Zohar Vayikra.[341]

• Come and see, at the time when a person rectifies his deeds through the offering of a sacrifice, everything is beautified, and is drawn near and interconnected with each other in an absolute unity . . . .

Zohar III Vayikra Tzav 26b:

• . . . and because of this, these two [the turtledoves and young doves] are sacrificed to elevate the spirit of holiness . . . to connect the wife with her husband [i.e., the wife is the recipient level of Malchut with the husband which is the collective levels of the Zeer Anpin, the 6 Middot of Atzilut, which feed into the recipient level of Malchut] to become one entity, and everything is elevated and interconnected together above and below, and God is elevated on His own and exalted.

Zohar Chadash I Tzav 38a [This page reference was not found but the following was found in Zohar Chadash I Tzav 76b]:

• . . . and after this a refined [sacrificial] smoke rises and all the supernal [levels] including the judges gather and enter into the innermost section, until they have been gathered one within the other and one within the other, until they are all elevated, with all incorporating each other, completing each other, with each entity being interconnected.

Zohar Chadash II Shir Hashirim 51b [This page reference was not found but the following was found in Zohar Chadash II Shir Hashirim 8a]:

• . . . Fragrance – there is fragrance and there is fragrance, there are many fragrances. There is fragrance which ascends from below to above, such as sacrificial fragrance, which is a fragrance which ascends and binds everything with one another, and then interconnects everything in descent, until everything becomes one knot and one light.

336 Pri Etz Chaim Shaar HaTefillah, Chap. 5:
• . . . for it is that through the sacrifices the worlds are elevated and intercon-

בְּסִתְרֵי תוֹרָה לֶךְ לְךָ פ״ט ב׳, וַיִּגַּשׁ ר״ו ב׳, וַיְחִי רמ״ד א׳, פְּקוּדֵי רנ״ט ב׳ וַיִּקְרָא ה׳ רֵישׁ ע״ב, צַו כ״ו ב׳, זֹהַר חָדָשׁ צַו ל״ח א׳, וְשָׁם בְּשִׁיר הַשִּׁירִים נ״א ב׳, עַיֵּן שָׁם הֵיטֵב בְּכָל אֵלּוּ הַמְּקוֹמוֹת נוֹרָאוֹת הָעִנְיָן.

- וְעַיֵּן בִּפְרִי עֵץ חַיִּים פֶּרֶק ה׳, וּפֶרֶק ז׳ מִשַּׁעַר הַתְּפִלָּה, סֵדֶר הַהַעֲלָאָה וְהַהִתְקַשְּׁרוּת בִּפְרָטוּת:

• וְלָכֵן נִקְרָא "קָרְבָּן"
  ○ כְּמוֹ שֶׁכָּתוּב בַּבָּהִיר (אות קט)
  □ "אֲמַאי אִקְרֵי "קָרְבָּן", אֶלָּא עַל שֵׁם שֶׁמְּקָרֵב הַצּוּרוֹת הַקְּדוֹשׁוֹת כו׳, וְאָמְרוּ "לְרֵיחַ נִיחוֹחַ" כו׳, הָרוּחַ יוֹרֵד וּמִתְיַחֵד בַּצּוּרוֹת הַקְּדוֹשׁוֹת הַהֵם, וּמִתְקָרֵב עַל יְדֵי הַקָּרְבָּן, וְהַיְנוּ דְאִקְרֵי "קָרְבָּן". עַד כָּאן לְשׁוֹנוֹ.
  ○ וְעַיֵּן זֹהַר
  □ וַיִּקְרָא רֵישׁ דַּף ה׳, וְדַף ח׳ ע״א

---

nected and incorporated with each other up to the Infinite One – following the way mentioned above.

Pri Etz Chaim Shaar HaTefillah, Chap. 7:
• [After explaining the sequential impact of a sacrifice which elevates levels from the lowest worlds to the supernal worlds . . .] and with this you will understand . . . that it is through the sacrifices that worlds are elevated and interconnected [all the way up] until the Infinite One.

337 Sefer HaBahir Ot 109, as referenced by Shela Taanit Perek Torah Ohr 192 and also by R. Bechaye Bamidbar 6:27.
338 Yechezkel 37:17.
339 Vayikra 1:9.
340 A play on the word "Reyach."
341 Zohar III Vayikra beginning of 5a:
• R. Chizkiya was at R. Chiya's [place] and asked him: That which is called "Korban," it should have been called "Kiruv"/bringing near or "Hitkarvut"/closeness, but why is it called "Korban"? He said to him: It is known among the brotherhood that Korban is [a bringing close] of the holy crowns [which are the seven lower Sefirot] which all unify and become interconnected with each other, all becoming one in an absolute unity. This is the meaning of the verse "Korban to YHVH" [Vayikra 1:2], Korban is [the bringing close] of these holy crowns to YHVH, that is that the Holy Name will be corrected and will be properly unified such that mercy will be found in all of the worlds and the Holy Name will be crowned with its crowns and all will be beautified.

Zohar III Vayikra 8a:

- "and it is called *"Korban"* because they are drawn close through it...."[342]
  - Refer to Pri Etz Chaim.[343]
- From the time the Temple service was discontinued, through our sins, we are only left with the service of prayer in its place, which also has the quality of being able to interconnect and unify worlds all the way up to the Infinite One as explained in many places in the Zohar.
  - It is particularly detailed in the Zohar as follows:[344] When one serves his Master in prayer, his will is attached like a flaming coal – unifying these lower firmaments from the side of holiness to crown them with the One Lower Name, and from there onwards to unify these supernal inner firmaments to all become one[345] ... and while his mouth and lips are moving [in prayer] he should focus his heart, and his desire will ascend to the heights to be completely unified with the secret of secrets – a place where all will and thoughts are held, with the secret of the Infinite One.
- As explained in the Pri Etz Chaim that the principal objective of prayer in following the sequence from the beginning of the service until the end of the Amidah[346]
  - is to perform rectifications of the worlds and to raise them from lower to higher levels
  - to interconnect and include each world with the world above it
  - [with this interconnected sequence] extending upwards all the way to reach the Infinite One.
  - Refer to the general concept in Pri Etz Chaim.[347]

- ... and since [the sins of the lowest world impact Above] what is a Korban? It is what the verse says "and for your rebellious sins that your mother has been sent away" [Yishayahu 50:1] – for the sin caused separation as a result of its damage [separating the father/Zeer Anpin/the six Middot from the recipient mother/Malchut and sending the mother away], and the Korban draws near the supernal world [i.e., the Zeer Anpin] to [this] lowest world [i.e., of Malchut], and all is made one ...

342 Zohar Raya Mehemna III Pinchas 256b.
343 Pri Etz Chaim Shaar HaTefillah, Chap. 5:
- ... and therefore it is called "Korban" because it *Mekarev*/draws close all of the worlds, and it draws close the lower and elevates them to the place of the supernal.
344 Zohar II Vayakhel 213b.
345 The supernal firmaments are *inner*, i.e., more subtle, in relation to the lower firmaments, and are brought together by prayer which enables the deeper subtlety to be revealed in the lower firmaments.

שער ב' - פרק י"ד

◦ וּבְרַעְיָא מְהֵימְנָא פִּנְחָס רנ"ו ב', וְאִתְקְרִיאַת "קָרְבָּן" עַל שֵׁם דְּאִתְקְרִיבוּ בֵּהּ כו'.

◦ וְעַיֵּן פְּרִי עֵץ חַיִּים פֶּרֶק ה' מִשַּׁעַר הַתְּפִלָּה:

• וּמֵעֵת שֶׁבַּעֲוֹנוֹתֵינוּ נִפְסְקָה עֲבוֹדַת בֵּית קָדְשֵׁנוּ, לֹא נִשְׁאֲרָה רַק עֲבוֹדַת הַתְּפִלָּה בִּמְקוֹמָהּ, שֶׁגַּם הִיא סְגֻלָּתָהּ לְקַשֵּׁר וּלְיַחֵד הָעוֹלָמוֹת עַד לְעֵלָּא בְּאֵין סוֹף בָּרוּךְ הוּא, כַּמְבֹאָר בִּמְקוֹמוֹת רַבּוֹת בַּזֹּהַר.

◦ וְיוֹתֵר מְפֹרָשׁ בְּפָרָשַׁת וַיַּקְהֵל רי"ג ב', "כַּד פָּלַח לְמָארֵיהּ בִּצְלוֹתָא, אַדְּבֵק רְעוּתֵיהּ כְּנוּרָא בְּגַחַלְתָּא, לְיַחֲדָא אִנּוּן רְקִיעִין תַּתָּאִין דְּסִטְרָא דִקְדוּשָׁה, לְעַטְּרָא לוֹן בִּשְׁמָא חֲדָא תַּתָּאָה, וּמִתַּמָּן וּלְהָלְאָה לְיַחֲדָא אִנּוּן רְקִיעִין עִלָּאִין פְּנִימָאִין, לְמֶהֱוֵי כֻּלְּהוּ חַד כו', וּבְעוֹד דְּפוּמֵיהּ וְשִׂפְוָתֵיהּ מְרַחֲשָׁן, לִבֵּיהּ יְכַוֵּן רְעוּתֵיהּ יִסְתַּלַּק לְעֵלָּא לְעֵלָּא, לְיַחֲדָא כֹּלָּא בְּרָזָא דְרָזִין, דְּתַמָּן תְּקִיעוּ דְּכָל רְעוּתִין וּמַחֲשָׁבִין בְּרָזָא דְקַיְמָא בְּאֵין סוֹף":

• וְכַמְבֹאָר בִּפְרִי עֵץ חַיִּים, שֶׁכָּל עִקַּר כַּוָּנַת עִנְיַן הַתְּפִלָּה, מֵרֵאשִׁיתָהּ עַד אַחַר הָעֲמִידָה

◦ הוּא תִּקּוּן הָעוֹלָמוֹת וְהִתְעַלּוּתָם מִמַּטָּה לְמַעְלָה

◦ לְהִתְקַשֵּׁר וּלְהִתְכַּלֵּל כָּל אֶחָד בְּהָעוֹלָם שֶׁעָלָיו, לְעֵלָּא לְעֵלָּא

◦ עַד אֵין סוֹף בָּרוּךְ הוּא.

◦ וְעַיֵּן שָׁם פֶּרֶק ד', וּפֶרֶק ה', וּפֶרֶק ו', וּפֶרֶק ז' מִשַּׁעַר הַתְּפִלָּה הָעִנְיָן בִּכְלָלוּת:

---

346 Where each section of the service relates to different world levels. See G2:18:N40.

347 Pri Etz Chaim Shaar HaTefillah, Chap. 4:
• The concept of prayer and its secret, in the morning he gets up, relieves himself, and washes his hands, meaning that a person needs to rectify the four worlds with action and speech which are Asiyah and Yetzirah of the four of them [i.e., the four worlds], as brought down in the Zohar. With action, this is when he relieves himself, which corresponds to Asiyah, and he purifies his body and also focuses on purifying the world of Asiyah from Kelipot. [See p. 366, fn. 178, relating to Peor which focused on relieving oneself in a corrupt manner.] This is the aspect of Asiyah within it [i.e., Asiyah of Asiyah]. After that he should focus on rectifying the level of Asiyah of Yetzirah . . . and this is the putting on of the Tzitzit in his house before getting dressed and going out. After that he should focus on rectifying Asiyah of Beriyah by donning the Tefillin of the hand on his arm . . . After that with the Tefillin of the head he should focus on rectifying Asiyah of Atzilut, and

- Refer to Zohar[348] which explains the difference between blessings on Mitzvot and worldly benefit [on the one hand], and the blessings of prayer [on the other].
  - Blessings on Mitzvot and worldly benefit are a drawing down of the bestowal, which transfers blessing from above to below
  - whereas, blessings of prayer are the rectification of worlds themselves, and the raising of them [by] interconnecting each world with the world immediately above it.
  - Refer to Pri Etz Chaim.[349]
  - (With reference to that which is also written in Raya Mehemna Ekev in relation to drawing from above to below, this is the drawing down of a bestowal from above to below after the Amidah, and this also results from the returning and raising of the worlds with each [world being connected] to the one immediately above it, as written in Pri Etz Chaim.)[350]

---

with the large Tallit which circumvents [corresponding to above Atzilut]. This is the rectification with action. After this [is the rectification] with speech. [The recitation of the passages of the] sacrifices purifies the level of Yetzirah of Asiyah ... After that [with the recitation of the passages of] Pesukei DeZimra corresponding to [the rectification of] Yetzirah of Yetzirah, and after that [the recitation of] Kaddish, Barchu, and Shema corresponds to [the rectification of the level] Beriyah of Beriyah, with the Shema we perform unification.

Pri Etz Chaim Shaar HaTefillah, Chap. 5:
- Focus of prayer is in this way. For it has two levels: action and speech. The concept of action is first, before speech, and through the action the four worlds of Aztilut, Beriyah, Yetzirah, and Asiyah are rectified in their place ... [This chapter then goes on to describe the elements of action and speech which contribute to prayer sequence as briefly described in the preceding quotation from Chap. 4 but elaborated on much more fully in this chapter].

Pri Etz Chaim Shaar HaTefillah, Chap. 6:
- [This chapter details the specific intentions one should have relating to the four worlds in respect of the four parts of the prayer sequence which thereby effect rectification.]

Pri Etz Chaim Shaar HaTefillah, Chap. 7:
- [This chapter charts out the general principles of prayer in some detail and differentiates the prayer process between that of the weekday and that of Shabbat.]

348 Zohar Raya Mehemna III Ekev 271a.
349 Pri Etz Chaim Shaar HaBerachot, [towards the] beginning of Chap. 1:
- The general intention of all of the blessings of the Mitzvot and the blessings on worldly benefit – apart from the blessings of the Amidah – is that in all

- וְעַיֵּן בְּרַעְיָא מְהֵימְנָא רֵישׁ פָּרָשַׁת עֵקֶב (רע"א ע"א), שֶׁזֶּהוּ הַחִלּוּק בֵּין בִּרְכוֹת הַמִּצְוֹת וְהַנֶּהֱנִין לְבִרְכוֹת הַתְּפִלָּה
- שֶׁבִּרְכוֹת הַמִּצְוֹת וְהַנֶּהֱנִין — הֵם הַמְשָׁכַת הַשֶּׁפַע, לָאַרְקָא בְּרָכָאן מִלְמַעְלָה לְמַטָּה
- אֲבָל בִּרְכוֹת הַתְּפִלָּה — הֵם תִּקּוּן הָעוֹלָמוֹת עַצְמָן וְהִתְעַלּוּתָם, וְהִתְקַשְּׁרוּת כָּל עוֹלָם בָּעוֹלָם שֶׁמֵּעָלָיו.
- וְעַיֵּן בִּפְרִי עֵץ חַיִּים רֵישׁ שַׁעַר הַבְּרָכוֹת, וּבְרֵישׁ פֶּרֶק ג' שָׁם.
- (וּמַה שֶּׁכָּתוּב עוֹד שָׁם בְּרַעְיָא מְהֵימְנָא "וּמֵעֵילָּא לְתַתָּא", הַיְנוּ הַמְשָׁכַת הַשֶּׁפַע

---

of them the drawing down of bestowal is from above to below, except for the eighteen blessings of the Amidah [whose focus is] to elevate the Mayim Nukvim [i.e., complete self arousal to serve God] from below to above.

Pri Etz Chaim Shaar HaBerachot, beginning of Chap. 3:
- "Blessed are You:" Know that "Baruch/Blessed" of prayer is not like the "Blessed" of worldly benefit and Mitzvot, for "Blessed" of prayer is from below to above . . . however with the "Blessed" of worldly benefit and Mitzvot, it is from above to below. . . .

350 Pri Etz Chaim Shaar HaTefillah, at end of Chap. 5:
- . . . and after that supernal union has been made in Atzilut [i.e., after the Amidah prayer] we need to give bestowal to the worlds of Beriyah, Yetzirah, and Asiyah. Therefore, we return, once again to incorporate Beriyah in Atzilut, and Beriyah thereby receives a bestowal from [Atzilut] while it is incorporated above. This is done in the recitation of "Ashrei" until "Tefillah LeDavid" [i.e., the paragraph recited before the daily Psalm in Nusach Sefarad/HaArizal]. After this we incorporate Yetzirah with Beriyah, once again, and Yetzirah thereby receives a bestowal from Beriyah. This is done from "Tefillah LeDavid" until "Kaveh el Adonay." After this we incorporate Asiyah, once again, with Yetzirah, and Asiyah thereby receives a bestowal from Yetzirah. This is done from "Kaveh el Adonay" until "Aleynu." Following this with [the recitation of] "Aleynu," all the worlds descend [back] down with each one returning to its [initial] place. The reason for this is that on weekdays we only have power to unify the [worlds] temporarily during prayer and after this the worlds return to their place. Therefore, it is for this reason that we only perform a rectification to elevate them, as mentioned above, for the elevation is performed through our prayers, but after they have received the bestowal we do not need to bring them down for they descend by themselves during the "Aleynu Leshabeach" [prayer] . . .

Pri Etz Chaim Shaar HaKaddishim, from [the beginning of] the later edition:
- Now we have explained above in Shaar HaTefillah, that prayer is split into

Note 34 – *Rabbeinu Yona: Focus thoughts on Creator and not the physical*

- This is as R. Yona writes[351] in relation to [Chazal's statement that] "One who prays must place his eyes downwards and his heart upwards." [R. Yona's] holy comments there are:
  - That is to say, that he should contemplate in his heart as if he is standing in Heaven, and remove from his heart all pleasures of this world and all bodily enjoyments, as per the early Rabbis who when they wanted to concentrate would say [to themselves] "detach your body from your Nefesh." After he reaches this [level of] thought he should additionally contemplate that it is as if he stands in the Temple which is below [in this world], because as a result of this, his prayer will be more acceptable before God. Heard from the mouth of my teacher.
- It is known that R. Yona was a student of the holy one of God, the Ramban, and his words are the words of the Ramban as written in Acharei Mot on the verse "Carry out my laws,"[352] as the [Ramban] says there:
  - Those who leave aside all aspects of this world and do not concern themselves with them are as if they have no physical body, and all their intentions and thoughts are focused on their Creator alone, just as was the case with Chanoch and Eliyahu, who through the cleaving of their souls to the Honored Name [resulted] in their bodies and souls living forever.
- This is also that which R. Yona brought in the name of the early Rabbis "detach your body from your Nefesh"
  - meaning that the body and its related pleasures should be so 'despised in a person's eyes'[353]
  - to the extent that he has a tremendous yearning to expel his Nefesh from it

---

four sections, which are: from the beginning of "Berachot" until "Baruch She-amar," which is the world of Asiyah, and from "Baruch She-amar" until the end of "Yishtabach," which is the world of Yetzirah, and from "Yishtabach" until the "Amidah," which is the world of Beriyah, and the "Amidah" itself is Atzilut, until "Ashrei," and from "Ashrei" until "Tefillah LeDavid" it is Beriyah, and from "Tefillah LeDavid" until "Pitum HaKetoret" it is Yetzirah, and "Ketoret" itself is Asiyah.

Pri Etz Chaim Shaar HaKaddishim, [beginning of] Chap. 1:
- The concept of the Kaddishim is split into a number of parts. For I have already explained to you that from the beginning of prayer until "Baruch She-amar," it is Asiyah, and from "Baruch She-amar" until the beginning of "Yotzer," it is Yetzirah, and from there until the "Amidah," it is Beriyah, and

נפש שער ב' - פרק י"ד החיים 425

מִמַּעֲלָה לְמַטָּה אַחַר הָעֲמִידָה, וְגַם זֶה הוּא מִצַּד שֶׁחוֹזְרִים וּמַעֲלִים אֶת הָעוֹלָמוֹת, כָּל אֶחָד בְּשֶׁלְּמַעֲלָה הֵימֶנּוּ. כְּמוֹ שֶׁכָּתַב בִּפְרִי עֵץ חַיִּים בְּסוֹף פֶּרֶק ה' מִשַּׁעַר הַתְּפִלָּה, וּבְרֵישׁ שַׁעַר הַקַּדִּישִׁים בְּמַהֲדוּרָא בַּתְרָא וּבְפֶרֶק א' שָׁם):

הגהה ל"ד

- כְּמוֹ שֶׁכָּתוּב רַבֵּנוּ יוֹנָה זִכְרוֹנוֹ לִבְרָכָה בְּעִנְיַן הַמִּתְפַּלֵּל צָרִיךְ שֶׁיִּתֵּן עֵינָיו לְמַטָּה וְלִבּוֹ לְמַעֲלָה, זֶה לְשׁוֹנוֹ הַקָּדוֹשׁ שָׁם
  - כְּלוֹמַר, שֶׁיַּחְשֹׁב בְּלִבּוֹ כְּאִלּוּ עוֹמֵד בַּשָּׁמַיִם, וְיָסִיר מִלִּבּוֹ כָּל תַּעֲנוּגֵי עוֹלָם הַזֶּה וְכָל הֲנָאוֹת הַגּוּף, בְּעִנְיָן שֶׁאָמְרוּ הַקַּדְמוֹנִים, כְּשֶׁתִּרְצֶה לְכַוֵּן, פְּשֹׁט גּוּפְךָ מֵעַל נִשְׁמָתְךָ. וּלְאַחַר שֶׁיַּגִּיעַ לָזוֹ הַמַּחֲשָׁבָה, יַחְשֹׁב גַּם כֵּן כְּאִלּוּ הוּא עוֹמֵד בְּבֵית הַמִּקְדָּשׁ שֶׁהוּא לְמַטָּה, מִפְּנֵי שֶׁעַל יְדֵי זֶה תִּהְיֶה תְּפִלָּתוֹ רְצוּיָה יוֹתֵר לִפְנֵי הַמָּקוֹם, מִפִּי מוֹרִי הָרַב נֵרוֹ. עַד כָּאן לְשׁוֹן רַבֵּנוּ יוֹנָה:
- וּמוּדַעַת שֶׁהָרַבֵּנוּ יוֹנָה הָיָה תַּלְמִיד קָדוֹשׁ ה' הָרַמְבַּ"ן זִכְרוֹנוֹ לִבְרָכָה, וּדְבָרָיו הֵן הֵמָּה דִּבְרֵי הָרַמְבַּ"ן זִכְרוֹנוֹ לִבְרָכָה בְּפָרָשַׁת אַחֲרֵי (ויקרא יח, ד) בְּפָסוּק, "אֶת מִשְׁפָּטַי תַּעֲשׂוּ" וְגוֹ'. וְזֶה לְשׁוֹנוֹ שָׁם
  - וְהָעוֹזְבִים כָּל עִנְיָנֵי עוֹלָם הַזֶּה, וְאֵינָם מַשְׁגִּיחִים עָלָיו, כְּאִלּוּ אֵינָם בַּעֲלֵי גוּף, וְכָל כַּוָּנָתָם וּמַחֲשַׁבְתָּם בְּבוֹרְאָם בִּלְבַד, כַּאֲשֶׁר הָיָה הָעִנְיָן בַּחֲנוֹךְ וְאֵלִיָּהוּ, בְּהִדָּבֵק נַפְשָׁם בַּשֵּׁם הַנִּכְבָּד יִחְיוּ לָעַד בְּגוּפָם וּבְנַפְשָׁם:
- וְזֶהוּ גַּם כֵּן מַה שֶּׁהֵבִיא רַבֵּנוּ יוֹנָה בְּשֵׁם הַקַּדְמוֹנִים, "פְּשֹׁט גּוּפְךָ מֵעַל נִשְׁמָתְךָ"
  - הַיְנוּ שֶׁכָּל כָּךְ יִהְיֶה הַגּוּף וְעִנְיָנָיו וְתַעֲנוּגָיו נִבְזֶה בְּעֵינָיו נִמְאָס
  - עַד שֶׁיִּהְיֶה לוֹ תְּשׁוּקָה עֲצוּמָה לְהַשְׁלִיךְ נַפְשׁוֹ מִנֶּגֶד

---

the "Amidah" is Atzilut, and after that they descend from above to below for there is only power during the weekdays to temporarily unify them, and after that they return to their place, and from "Ashrei" to "Tefillah LeDavid" it is Beriyah, and from there until "Ein Kadosh" [i.e., the verse recited after "Kaveh"] it is Yetzirah, and from there until the end it is Asiyah. Therefore, with each change of world we recite one Kaddish.

351 R. Yona's comments are on the quotation brought in the Rif on Berachot 22b where the Rif quotes from and comments on Chazal's statement in Yevamot 105b. This statement from Yevamot 105b is quoted by R. Chaim a little later on in this chapter, G2:14. It is also quoted in G2:01 and G2:18.

352 Vayikra 18:4.

353 Tehillim 15:4.

- and that all yearning of his Nefesh should be for his Creator
- as if he does not have a body but is like one of the heavenly hosts serving on high, which are separated and abstracted from all aspects of this world.

• This is the meaning of R. Yona's comment "that he should contemplate in his heart as if he is standing in Heaven"
- meaning that he should relate to himself [in such a way] that all the feelings of the body are nullified to him as it is [just] dust from the earth
- and all of his feelings will [only] be related to matters of the Nefesh
- to connect it to its source in Heaven with great love
- to the extent that even if one of the generally attractive desires of this world would present itself before him, he would despise it with absolute disgust and hatred.
- This is the meaning of "Those who love God hate bad"[354]
- and of "Praise God from the Heavens, Praise Him in the High Places."[355]

15. PRAYER WITH ALL/PART SOUL; TORAH AND MITZVOT LEAD TO PRAYER FOCUS

• In relation to that which is written "with *all* (Kol) of your souls," there is a known debate that Chazal have in a number of Talmudic sources [as to the meaning of the word "all"].[356]
- One opinion states that "all" means "entirely" (Kulo).
- The other opinion states that "all" means "a part of" (Kol Shehu).
- This similarly applies here [with prayer] that both [of these opinions] are true.

• For there are many levels with this – related to each individual's ability to achieve purity of his heart and thought.
- As one able to achieve purity of thought and intention is able to attach his "*entire*" soul – out of the greatness of his love and desire for God.
- With each individual according to his ability, and also according to his preparation for purity of his heart at that time
  - for a person does not consistently have the same purity of thought at all times
  - but it is fitting and appropriate that one should see to it that there is acceptable concentration to cleave to God with his love and

---

354 Tehillim 97:10.

- וְשֶׁתְּהֵא כָּל תְּשׁוּקַת נַפְשׁוֹ בְּבוֹרְאוֹ יִתְבָּרַךְ שְׁמוֹ
- כְּאִלּוּ אֵינוֹ בַּעַל גּוּף, אֶלָּא כְּאֶחָד מִצְּבָא הַמָּרוֹם הַמְשַׁמְּשִׁים בַּמָּרוֹם, מְפֹרָשִׁים וּמֻבְדָּלִים מִכָּל עִנְיְנֵי עוֹלָם הַזֶּה:

• וְזֶהוּ כַּוָּנַת רַבֵּינוּ יוֹנָה זִכְרוֹנוֹ לִבְרָכָה, "שֶׁיַּחֲשׁב בְּלִבּוֹ כְּאִלּוּ עוֹמֵד בַּשָּׁמַיִם"
- הַיְנוּ, שֶׁיַּרְגִּישׁ בְּעַצְמוֹ, שֶׁנִּתְבַּטְּלוּ אֶצְלוֹ כָּל הַרְגָּשׁוֹת הַגּוּף שֶׁהוּא עָפָר מִן הָאֲדָמָה
- וְכָל הַרְגָּשׁוֹתָיו יִהְיוּ בְּעִנְיְנֵי הַנֶּפֶשׁ
- לְקָשְׁרָהּ בְּשָׁרְשָׁהּ בַּשָּׁמַיִם בְּאַהֲבָה רַבָּה
- עַד שֶׁאִם הָיוּ מַעֲמִידִים נֶגֶד עֵינָיו אֵיזֶה תַּעֲנוּג מִתַּעֲנוּגֵי עוֹלָם הַזֶּה שֶׁנַּפְשׁוֹ שֶׁל אָדָם מְחַמַּדְתָּן, הָיָה מוֹאֵס בָּהּ תַּכְלִית הַמֵּאוּס וְשׂנְאָהּ
- וְזֶהוּ (תהלים צז, י) "אוֹהֲבֵי ה' שִׂנְאוּ רָע".
- וְזֶהוּ (תהלים קמח, א) "הַלְלוּ אֶת ה' מִן הַשָּׁמַיִם הַלְלוּהוּ בַּמְּרוֹמִים":

שער ב' - פרק ט"ז

• וּמַה שֶּׁנֶּאֱמַר "וּבְכָל נַפְשְׁכֶם", יָדוּעַ פְּלוּגְתַּת רַבּוֹתֵינוּ זִכְרוֹנָם לִבְרָכָה בְּכַמָּה דוּכְתֵּי בַּשַּׁ"ס (סנהדרין עח, א)
- לְחַד מַאן דְּאָמַר תֵּבַת "כֹּל" פֵּרוּשׁוֹ כֻּלּוֹ
- וּלְחַד מַאן דְּאָמַר פֵּרוּשׁוֹ מִקְצָת וְכָל שֶׁהוּא.
- וְכֵן הוּא הָעִנְיָן כָּאן שְׁנֵיהֶם אֲמִתִּים:

• כִּי כַּמָּה בְּחִינוֹת וּמַדְרֵגוֹת יֵשׁ בָּזֶה, כָּל אָדָם לְפִי כֹּחַ טָהֳרַת לִבּוֹ וּמַחֲשַׁבְתּוֹ
- שֶׁהָאָדָם שֶׁכֹּחוֹ יָפֶה בְּטָהֳרַת הַמַּחֲשָׁבָה וְהַכַּוָּנָה, יוּכַל לְדַבֵּק אֶת "כָּל נַפְשׁוֹ", מִגֹּדֶל הָאַהֲבָה וְהַתְּשׁוּקָה לוֹ יִתְבָּרַךְ שְׁמוֹ.
- וְכָל אֶחָד לְפִי כֹּחוֹ, וְגַם לְפִי עִנְיַן הֲכָנַת טָהֳרַת לִבּוֹ אָז
  □ כִּי גַּם לֹא כָּל הָעִתִּים שָׁוִות בָּאָדָם בְּטָהֳרַת הַמַּחֲשָׁבָה
  □ רַק זֹאת רָאוּי וְנָכוֹן, שֶׁעַל כָּל פָּנִים יִרְאֶה שֶׁתְּהֵא כַּוָּנָתוֹ רְצוּיָה, לְדַבֵּק לוֹ יִתְבָּרַךְ בְּאַהֲבָתוֹ וְטָהֳרַת לִבּוֹ "מִקְצָת נַפְשׁוֹ" בְּכָל תֵּבָה:

---

355 Tehillim 148:1.
356 E.g., Sanhedrin 78a. In this source the debate relates to *soul* in the context of deriving the Halacha of exactly when a person is liable for killing another *soul*, i.e., does he have to be *entirely* responsible for the death or is he liable even if he only contributes *in part* to the death.

purity of his heart with at least "*part of*" his soul, with each word [of prayer].
- Therefore, the verse states "with all of your *souls* (in the plural form)," [where the plural form] implies there are two meanings mentioned above – related to each individual according to his ability, level, and preparation.
- The key preparation for this is according to the way [a person] conducts himself, every day and night, in the study of Torah and performance of Mitzvot.[357]
- Chana was on a level where she was [able] to outpour her "*entire*" soul in prayer before God
  - therefore, she says, "and I have poured out my Nefesh before God . . ."[358]
  - where "outpouring" means in a complete way, as is known from the Talmud.[359]
  - (That there was no residual will for her [to be attached] to any matters of this world, as "Nefesh" means "will" as per "Whatever your Nefesh should say I shall do for you,"[360] as general will is connected to the generality of the soul.)[361]
- Now, all the details mentioned above in relation to prayer which highlights its essence as being the outpouring of one's soul to attach to God with each word of prayer
  - relates to a "general" outpouring of the soul to God
  - without considering the distinction of the specific "components" within the soul.

---

[357] The Shela, on Masechet Tamid, Perek Ner Mitzvah 12, comments as follows:
- I found written in the book Derech Chaim . . . [that] "There are ten things that help intentional focus [during prayer] and their absence causes [prayer] to be ineffective. . . ." I will explain each of them. The first, which has the *most significant impact* of all of them, is Torah. Know that when a person increases his involvement in *Torah and Mitzvot*, that as a result and through this, he will draw near to God and cleave to Him and his Fear and Love of [God] will be firmly entrenched in his heart. Then when he gets up to pray, it will not be difficult at all to supplicate and focus his heart. It will be very easy indeed for him, for he will immediately find God in his thoughts, as he was prepared for this . . . However, when a person does not increase his involvement in *Torah and Mitzvot* and it goes without saying, if he were to decrease his involvement in them, or that he is not involved with them at all, and that his thoughts are not focused on God all day long but that his Evil Inclination focuses his thoughts on evil all day long – then this results in his distancing himself from God. Therefore, since God is not factored into his

- לָכֵן אָמַר הַכָּתוּב "וּבְכָל נַפְשְׁכֶם", דְּלֶהֱוֵי מִשְׁתַּמַּע לִתְרֵי אַפֵּי כְּנַ"ל, כָּל אֶחָד לְפִי כֹּחוֹ וּמַדְרֵגָתוֹ וַהֲכָנָתוֹ:

- וְעִקַּר הַהֲכָנָה לָזֶה הוּא לְפִי הַנְהָגָתוֹ כָּל הַיּוֹם וְהַלַּיְלָה בְּתַלְמוּד תּוֹרָה וּמִצְוֹת:

- וּמַדְרֵגַת חַנָּה הָיְתָה, שֶׁשָּׁפְכָה בִּתְפִלָּתָהּ לְפָנָיו יִתְבָּרַךְ שְׁמוֹ "כָּל נַפְשָׁהּ"

  ○ לָכֵן אָמְרָה "וָאֶשְׁפֹּךְ אֶת נַפְשִׁי" כו'

  ○ וְ"שְׁפִיכָה" פֵּרוּשׁוֹ לְגַמְרֵי, כַּיָּדוּעַ בַּשַּׁ"ס.

  ○ (וְהַיְנוּ שֶׁלֹּא נִשְׁאַר לָהּ שׁוּם רָצוֹן לְעִנְיְנֵי עוֹלָם הַזֶּה, כִּי "נֶפֶשׁ" פֵּרוּשׁוֹ "רָצוֹן", כְּמוֹ שֶׁכָּתוּב (שמואל א' כ) "מַה תֹּאמַר נַפְשְׁךָ וְאֶעֱשֶׂה לָּךְ", וְרָצוֹן הַכְּלָלִי קָשׁוּר בִּ'כְלַל הַנֶּפֶשׁ'):

- וְהִנֵּה, כָּל הַנַּ"ל בְּעִנְיַן הַתְּפִלָּה, שֶׁעִקָּרָהּ שְׁפִיכַת הַנֶּפֶשׁ לְדָבְקָה לוֹ יִתְבָּרַךְ בְּכָל תֵּבָה

  ○ הַיְנוּ, שְׁפִיכַת 'כְּלַל' הַנֶּפֶשׁ לוֹ יִתְבָּרַךְ

  ○ בְּלֹא כַּוָּנָה וְהַבְחָנָה בִּבְחִינַת 'הַפְּרָטִים' הַכְּלוּלִים בַּנֶּפֶשׁ:

- There is however a higher level [of prayer] which involves focusing on the specific components (Note 35)[362] within the soul
  - but it requires practice [for a person] to habituate himself to advance to higher levels [of prayer]
  - and it is only after he has habituated himself in his prayer following a period of general outpouring and general cleaving of the soul
  - that he can subsequently advance himself to focus [his prayer] on a level using the specific soul components.[363]

Rabbi Chaim's Note:
Note 35 – Prayer with soul to be on both general and component level

- It is necessary for one to know that even when he prays on the level of interconnection of the soul's components with each other, that he should not stop [praying on a level of] connecting the soul in a general way. As the general and detailed approach require each other, meaning
  - that before prayer, the main [task] is to connect his general soul and will
  - which generally encompass the details of his abilities and his will
  - so that they be incorporated within the light of God.
  - Then on [the recitation of] each and every word of prayer he should cleave the individual abilities of his Nefesh, Ruach, and Neshama
  - and according to the strength of the general level of connection, a direct Kav/line of light will be drawn down upon each [soul] component
  - such that each detail of his will should be enabled to be incorporated within the binding [to God] of the general encompassing ability.
- Refer to
  - Etz Chaim[364] and this is the concept which is explained there
    - that the Kav/line of light which extends [downwards] from the Infinite Light of God (Light of the Ein Sof) does not reach the lowest extremity of the encompassing [Light of the Ein Sof].[365]
  - And refer to Mevo Shearim[366]

---

362 **R. Chaim adds Note 35 here.** This note is brought at the end of this chapter and is entitled "Prayer with soul to be on both general and component level."
363 As detailed in the next chapter.
364 Etz Chaim Shaar 1, Derush Igulim VeYosher, Part 2 which is brought on p. 518, fn. 149. This details the Arizal's Tzimtzum in circle description.
365 As to do so would undo the Tzimtzum. The Kav can only descend to the lowest level, furthest away from the circumference, i.e., the circle center. The Kav's descent generates differentiated encompassing levels.

נפש   שער ב' - פרק ט"ו   החיים

- אָמְנָם יֵשׁ מַדְרֵגָה יוֹתֵר גְּבוֹהָה בָּזֶה, וְהוּא לְכַוֵּן בִּבְחִינַת הַפְּרָטִים (הגהה ל"ה) הַכְּלוּלִים בַּנֶּפֶשׁ.
  ○ אֶלָּא שֶׁצָּרִיךְ חִנּוּךְ לְהַרְגִּיל עַצְמוֹ מִמַּדְרֵגָה לְמַדְרֵגָה.
  ○ שֶׁאַחַר שֶׁכְּבָר הִרְגִּיל בִּתְפִלָּתוֹ אֵיזֶה זְמַן בְּעִנְיַן שְׁפִיכַת וְהִתְדַּבְּקוּת כְּלָל הַנֶּפֶשׁ
  ○ אַחַר זֶה יַעְתִּיק עַצְמוֹ לְכַוֵּן בִּבְחִינַת הַפְּרָטִים שֶׁנַּפְשׁוֹ כְּלוּלָה מֵהֶם:

הגהה ל"ה

- וְצָרִיךְ שֶׁתֵּדַע, שֶׁאַף בְּהִתְפַּלְלוֹ בְּמַדְרֵגַת הִתְקַשְּׁרוּת פְּרָטֵי הַנֶּפֶשׁ זֶה בָּזֶה, לֹא יָנִיחַ מְקוֹמוֹ מֵהִתְקַשְּׁרוּת כְּלַל הַנֶּפֶשׁ, כִּי הוּא פְּרָט הַצָּרִיךְ לַכְּלָל, וּכְלָל הַצָּרִיךְ לַפְּרָט. הַיְנוּ.
  ○ שֶׁקֹּדֶם הַתְּפִלָּה, הָעִקָּר לְקַשֵּׁר כְּלָל נַפְשׁוֹ וּרְצוֹנוֹ
  ○ הַמַּקִּיפִים כְּלָל פְּרָטֵי כֹחוֹתָיו וּרְצוֹנוֹתָיו
  ○ לְהִכָּלֵל בְּאוֹר ה'.
  ○ וְעַל כָּל תֵּבָה וְתֵבָה שֶׁמִּתְפַּלֵּל, יַדְבִּיק פְּרָטֵי כֹחוֹת נר"ן
  ○ וְעַל פִּי כֹּחַ הִתְקַשְּׁרוּת הַכְּלָלִי יַמְשִׁיךְ קַו אוֹר יָשָׁר עַל כָּל פְּרָט
  ○ שֶׁיּוּכְלוּ כָּל פְּרָטֵי רְצוֹנוֹ לְהִכָּלֵל בְּהִתְקַשְּׁרוּת כֹּחַ הַמַּקִּיף הַכְּלָלִי:

- וְעַיֵּן
  ○ עֵץ חַיִּים דְּרוּשֵׁי עִגּוּלִים וְיֹשֶׁר, וְזֶהוּ עִנְיַן הַמְבֹאָר שָׁם
  ▫ שֶׁקַּו הָאוֹר שֶׁנִּמְשַׁךְ מֵאוֹר אֵין סוֹף בָּרוּךְ הוּא לֹא הִגִּיעַ עַד קְצֵה תַּחְתִּית הַמַּקִּיף.
  ○ וְעִנְיָן בִּמְבוֹא שְׁעָרִים פֶּרֶק ב'

---

366 Mevo Shearim (a book containing the Arizal's teachings as recorded by R. Chaim Vital), Shaar 1, Part 1, Chap. 2:
- [After detailing that God created an initial space of the worlds, likened to the inside of a circle, which did not contain His Essence but was bounded on the outside of the circle by the light of His Essence, the Ein Sof, at its circumference . . .] At the time when He returned [after creating this space] to be manifest in a small way within the worlds [within the circle], it was necessary that He emanate and draw down a very fine Kav/line [of light] from the circumference of the Ein Sof, and draw it down from Above to below within the worlds like this: [see the adjacent diagram – where the line inside the circle represents the Kav/line of the Light of the Ein Sof descending into the space of

- and the concept of encompassing levels of one within another which are generated through the drawing down of the line of light will be understood
- meaning
  - that each detailed ability must be connected to the general ability according to its level
  - and the general ability is also determined by the quality of the detailed ability
  - and the beginning of the *praised Kav/line of light* is the extension of general thought to the heart, the center of the entire body, as each word extends from [and is generated] by *the breath of the heart*, as is understood to one who can understand on his own.[367]

16. THREE COMPONENTS OF SOUL/WORDS OF PRAYER TO CONNECT TO SOURCE

- For it is known that man's soul in general incorporates three specific components
  - which are Nefesh, Ruach, and Neshama
  - which are identical with the three components of action, speech, and thought[368] [respectively]
  - which is all of man.
- In addition, each word[369] also has these three specific components of action, speech, and thought – [of] Nefesh, Ruach, and Neshama – and they are the letters, vowels, and accents[370] within it.

---

the worlds]. It is through [this process] that the existence of differentiated and abstracted levels came into existence in the worlds which He created, and they are not all on the same level . . . and also within the Ten Sefirot themselves of each world level, they are differentiated in their levels from one another, for at the beginning of the line which extends into the circle from the Ein Sof, from Above to below – there at its beginning it is called "Above," which is called "Keter" [the highest level of the Sefirot], and the end of this line it is called "below," and that is "Malchut" [the lowest level of the Sefirot]. The reason for this concept is that that line which is drawn [down into the circle] does not reach [all the way to] the lower side of the circumference where the Ein Sof is and does not extend [to the bottom of the circle], and therefore, there, at the end of this Kav/line, it is called "below" for if [the line] were to reach the end and connect to the circum-

וְיוּבַן עִנְיַן הַמַּקִּיפִים זֶה תּוֹךְ זֶה, הַנַּעֲשִׂים דֶּרֶךְ הַמְשָׁכַת קַו הָאוֹר.

הַיְנוּ

שֶׁכָּל כֹּחַ פְּרָטִי לְפִי מַדְרֵגָתוֹ צָרִיךְ לְקָשְׁרוֹ בַּכְּלָל

וְגַם הַכְּלָל הוּא לְפִי עֵרֶךְ הַפְּרָט.

וְרֵאשִׁית קַו אוֹר הַמִּמְשָׁךְ, הוּא הַמְשָׁכַת מַחֲשָׁבָה הַכְּלָלִית לַלֵּב, אֶמְצָעִיתָא דְכָל גּוּפָא, שֶׁכָּל תֵּבָה נִמְשֶׁכֶת מֵהֶבֶל הַלֵּב, וְהוּא מְבָאֵר לַמֵּבִין מִדַּעְתּוֹ:

שַׁעַר ב' - פֶּרֶק ט"ז

כִּי יָדוּעַ שֶׁנֶּפֶשׁ הָאָדָם בִּכְלָלָהּ, הִיא כְּלוּלָה מִשְּׁלֹשָׁה בְּחִינוֹת פְּרָטִים

וְהֵם נר"ן

שֶׁהֵם עַצְמָם הַשְּׁלֹשָׁה בְּחִינוֹת, מַעֲשֶׂה, דִּבּוּר וּמַחֲשָׁבָה

שָׁוֶה כָּל הָאָדָם:

וְגַם בְּכָל תֵּבָה יֵשׁ שְׁלֹשָׁה בְּחִינוֹת, מַעֲשֶׂה, דִּבּוּר, מַחֲשָׁבָה, — נר"ן, וְהֵם "אוֹתִיּוֹת" וּ"נְקֻדּוֹת" וּ"טְעָמִים" שֶׁבָּהּ

---

ference of the Ein Sof [on the other side of the circle], it would then also be called "Above."

367 R. Chaim's entire note is deeply connecting prayer with the Tzimtzum process. The heart, i.e., mind, is referred to as the "center of the body," a codeword for Malchut, which is where the Tzimtzum process takes place. Each level within the person praying has its own breath/words of expression which acts as an emanation, the Kav, which generates each lower level. So the breath/words of thought from the heart/mind ultimately generate the breath/words of speech as prayer. Deeper insight is provided in V2:02, p. 133, fn. 206.

368 See G1:14.

369 Which in this context is referring to each word of prayer.

370 The word "accent" denotes cantillation. Each word of the Scriptures is assigned Masoretic notes which determine how that word is to be sung and pronounced when read from a scroll in public. R. Chaim is not referring to Scriptural text here but rather to words of prayer which do not have formally assigned Masoretic cantillation notes. He is therefore referring to the intonation used to guide the meaning of words of prayer (e.g., if intoned with a question, the word "yes" can mean "no").

371 Tikkunei Zohar Introduction 8a. R. Chaim also refers the reader to the

- As per Zohar:[371] Accents are the Neshama; Vowels are the Ruach; Letters are the Nefesh. (Note 36)[372]
- The Letters:
  - These are the level of Action.
  - For the existence of letters alone without vowels can only be at the level of Action, that is the act of writing, as they are written in a Torah scroll without vowels.
  - As with speech, it is impossible to verbally express [words] without attaching vowels to them.
  - Therefore, the letters on their own without vowels, are referred to as the level of Nefesh (that is together with the letter tags as written in the note)[373] which is the level Action as is known.
- The Vowels:
  - These are the level of Ruach of [the words], as mentioned above.
  - The vowels are associated with the letters through man's speech which is on the level of Ruach[/spirit/wind]
  - and just as the key part of man's life force is from the level of Ruach within him, and when the Ruach exits from him, he dies even though part of his Nefesh still remains within him, as is known
  - similarly, the principal existence of the animation of letters is with the vowels, and without them it is impossible to verbally express the letters
  - and as written in a number of places in the Tikkunim: What is the meaning of "wise?" These are the vowels. "Will shine"? These [vowels] illuminate the letters.[374]
- The Accents of the words:
  - These are the level of thought and concentration of the heart, which is the level of the Neshama, as is known.
  - They enable the letters and vowels to be expressed and emphasized in a specific meaningful way – a matter which is guided by thought and intellect.
  - As per Zohar:
    - "Circlets of gold" – these are the animation of the accents – [It

---

beginning of Tikkunei Zohar Tikkun 67, although this does not seem to directly relate to the point being made here. Other references were found in Tikkunei Zohar to the three separate levels of Accents, Vowels, and Letters; however, these were in the context of the levels of Keter, Chochma/Brain, and Binah/Mother respectively, e.g., as per Tikkunei Zohar Tikkun 5 20b and Tikkunei Zohar Tikkun 69 105a (see this connection on p. 438, fn. 383).

372 **R. Chaim adds Note 36 here.** This note is brought at the end of this chapter

- כְּמוֹ שֶׁכָּתוּב בְּהַקְדָּמַת הַתִּקּוּנִים ח' ע"א, "טַעֲמֵי אִנּוּן 'נִשְׁמָתִין, וְנִקּוּדִין — 'רוּחִין, וְאַתְוָן — 'נַפְשִׁין". (הגהה ל"ו) וְכֵן אִיתָא שָׁם בְּרֵישׁ תִּקּוּן ס"ז, עַיֵּן שָׁם:

- הָאוֹתִיּוֹת
  - הֵם בְּחִינַת "מַעֲשֶׂה"
  - כִּי מְצִיאוּת אוֹתִיּוֹת גְּרֵידָא, בְּלֹא נְקֻדּוֹת, אִי אֶפְשָׁר שֶׁיִּהְיוּ אֶלָּא בִּבְחִינַת מַעֲשֶׂה, הַיְנוּ מַעֲשֵׂה הַכְּתִיבָה כְּמוֹ שֶׁהֵם כְּתוּבִים בְּסֵפֶר תּוֹרָה בְּלֹא נְקֻדּוֹת.
  - כִּי בְּדִבּוּר אִי אֶפְשָׁר לְהוֹצִיאָם מֵהַפֶּה אִם לֹא עַל יְדֵי צֵרוּף הַנְּקֻדּוֹת אֲלֵיהֶם.
  - לָכֵן הָאוֹתִיּוֹת לְבַד, בְּלֹא נְקֻדּוֹת נִקְרָאִים בְּחִינַת "נֶפֶשׁ", (הַיְנוּ עִם הַתַּגִּים כְּמוֹ שֶׁכָּתוּב בְּהַגָּהָה,) שֶׁהוּא בְּחִינַת "מַעֲשֶׂה" כַּיָּדוּעַ:

- וְהַנְּקֻדּוֹת
  - הֵם בְּחִינַת "רוּחַ" שֶׁלָּהֶם כַּנַּ"ל
  - שֶׁהַנְּקֻדּוֹת בָּאִים עִם הָאוֹתִיּוֹת עַל יְדֵי הַדִּבּוּר שֶׁל הָאָדָם שֶׁהוּא בְּחִינַת "רוּחַ"
  - וּכְמוֹ שֶׁעִקַּר חִיּוּת הָאָדָם — עַל יְדֵי בְּחִינַת הָרוּחַ שֶׁבּוֹ, שֶׁבְּצֵאתָהּ מִמֶּנּוּ הָרוּחַ הוּא מֵת, אַף שֶׁחֵלֶק מִנַּפְשׁוֹ נִשְׁאָר בּוֹ עֲדַיִן כַּיָּדוּעַ
  - כֵּן עִקַּר חִיּוּת תְּנוּעוֹת הָאוֹתִיּוֹת — הֵם הַנְּקֻדּוֹת, שֶׁבִּלְתָּם אִי אֶפְשָׁר לְהוֹצִיא הָאוֹתִיּוֹת מֵהַפֶּה
  - וּכְמוֹ שֶׁכָּתוּב בְּכַמָּה מְקוֹמוֹת בַּתִּקּוּנִים "וְהַמַּשְׂכִּילִים" — אִלֵּין נְקוּדֵי, "יַזְהִירוּ" — דְּנַהֲרִין בְּאַתְוָן:

- וְהַטְּעָמִים שֶׁל הַתֵּבוֹת
  - הֵם בְּחִינַת הַמַּחֲשָׁבָה וְכַוָּנַת הַלֵּב, שֶׁהוּא בְּחִינַת "הַנְּשָׁמָה" כַּיָּדוּעַ
  - כִּי הֵם תְּנוּעוֹת וְהַנְהָגַת הַנְּקֻדּוֹת וְהָאוֹתִיּוֹת, וּנְטִיָּתָם לְאֵיזֶה צַד שֶׁהוּא, דָּבָר הַתָּלוּי בַּמַּחֲשָׁבָה, בַּשֵּׂכֶל.
  - וּבַזֹּהַר
    - חָדָשׁ שִׁיר הַשִּׁירִים כ"ב ע"א, "תּוֹרֵי זָהָב" (שיר השירים א, יא) אִינוּן תְּנוּעֵי

---

and is entitled "Letter tags go together with letters just like the soul to a body."
373 G2:16:N36.
374 E.g., Tikkunei Zohar Introduction 4b, quoting Daniel 12:3: "and the wise will shine."
375 Zohar Chadash II Shir Hashirim 22a quoting Shir Hashirim 1:11:

states "gold"] because they come from the head of the king to give knowledge and intelligence to all the letters.³⁷⁵ Refer further to this reference for details at length in relation to the three levels of accents, vowels, and letters.

- The movements of the accents which rectify and complete with knowledge and intelligence . . . all their journeys are with wisdom and intelligence . . . the movements which are the completeness of all, where are they in man, but this secret is . . . from within, it is knowledge and intelligence . . . whether static or moving . . . it is all knowledge and intelligence.³⁷⁶
- Therefore, the [accents] are called Teamim [also meaning reasons], just as the reason and explanation of any issue is the intellect hidden within that issue through which a person can understand it with his thought.

- "And letters relative to vowels are like a body relative to Ruach . . . and the container of the vowels is Nefesh. Neshama is the Keter/crown over all of them, and from it [comes] crowns which are the accents which animate the vowels and letters. [The accents] are dependent on thought, vowels are dependent on speech, and letters on action."³⁷⁷
- Therefore, one who truly wants to serve God with appropriate intention will focus his prayer on the outpouring and cleaving together of the three levels of Nefesh, Ruach, and Neshama, which make up his soul.
  - Such that at the time he verbally utters each word of prayer, which contains the three levels of Nefesh, Ruach, and Neshama – the letters, vowels, and accents
  - he will strengthen the purity of his heart with an intense passion
  - and use it to connect and cleave the lower levels with the higher levels within the sequence of levels³⁷⁸ – his Nefesh with his Ruach and his Ruach with his Neshama (Note 37) ³⁷⁹
  - and will raise them all to the root of that word in the supernal worlds.
  - This is the idea expressed by Chazal:

- "Circlets of gold," these are the animation of the accents. It states "gold" because they come from the head of the king to give knowledge and intelligence to all the letters, and because of this they all relate to the same secret. The vowels and accents are two levels and are required to correct the letters. The letters are inscribed with supernal secrets for they all come from the secret of supernal Chochma through these 32 paths which come from Chochma. All the letters are etched below . . . the letters are all inscribed in secret and are called the body of Torah through which the supernal secrets are taught and can be known. The vowels come from the secret of the brain[/Chochma] to maintain the letters, and with a single vowel a word

דְּטַעֲמֵי כו', בְּגִין דְּאִנּוּן אַתְיָן מֵרֵישָׁא דְּמַלְכָּא, לְמֵיהַב דַּעְתָּא וְסָכְלְתָנוּ לְאַתְוָן כֻּלְּהוּ. וְעַיֵּן שָׁם עוֹד בְּעִנְיַן הַשְּׁלֹשָׁה בְּחִינוֹת, ט' נ' א' בְּאֹרֶךְ.

וְשָׁם דַּף כ"ג ע"ב, תְּנוּעָה דְּטַעֲמֵי, דְּאִנּוּן תִּקּוּנָא וּשְׁלִימוּ בְּדַעְתָּא וְסוֹכְלְתָנוּ, לְמִנְדַּע יְדִיעָה כו', כֻּלְּהוּ מַטְלָנֵיהוֹן בְּחָכְמְתָא וּבְסָכְלְתָנוּ כו', תְּנוּעֵי דְּאִיהוּ שְׁלִימוּ דְּכֹלָּא, אִן אִנּוּן בְּכַר נַשׁ, אֶלָּא רָזָא דָא כו' לְגוֹ סוּכְלְתָנוּ וּמַדַּע כו' הֵן בְּזֻקְפוּ, הֵן לְמֵיזַל כו' כָּלָּא אִיהוּ מִנְדַּע וְסָכְלְתָנוּ כו'. עַיֵּן שָׁם.

וְלָכֵן נִקְרָאִים 'טְעָמִים', כְּמוֹ שֶׁהַטַּעַם וְהַפֵּרוּשׁ שֶׁל כָּל עִנְיָן, הוּא הַשֵּׂכֶל הַנִּסְתָּר שֶׁבָּעִנְיָן, שֶׁמִּתּוֹכוֹ יוּכַל הָאָדָם לְהָבִינוֹ בְּמַחֲשַׁבְתּוֹ:

וּבְתִקּוּן ס"ט ק"ח ב', וְאַתְוָן אִנּוּן נְקוּדִין כְּגוּפָא לְגַבֵּי רוּחָא כו'. וּמָאנָא דְּנָקוּדִין אִיהוּ נֶפֶשׁ, נִשְׁמָתָא אִיהִי כֶּתֶר עַל כֻּלְּהוּ, וּמִנָּהּ כִּתְרִין דְּאִנּוּן טַעֲמֵי תְּנוּעָה דְּנָקוּדִין וְאַתְוָן, וְאִיהִי תַּלְיָא בְּמַחֲשַׁבְתָּא, וּנְקוּדִין תַּלְיָן בַּאֲמִירָה, וְאַתְוָן בַּעֲשִׂיָּה:

וְלָכֵן הָעוֹבֵד הָאֲמִתִּי בְּכַוָּנָה רְצוּיָה, יְכַוֵּן לִשְׁפֹּךְ וּלְדַבֵּק בִּתְפִלָּתוֹ יַחַד כָּל הַשְּׁלֹשָׁה בְּחִינוֹת נֶפֶשׁ רוּחַ נְשָׁמָה, אֲשֶׁר נַפְשׁוֹ כְּלוּלָה בָּהֶם.

• שֶׁבַּעַת שֶׁמּוֹצִיא מִפִּיו כָּל תֵּבָה מֵהַתְּפִלָּה, שֶׁיֵּשׁ בָּהּ כָּל הַשְּׁלֹשָׁה בְּחִינוֹת נר"ן בְּאוֹתִיּוֹתֶיהָ וּנְקֻדּוֹתֶיהָ וּטְעָמֶיהָ

• יִתְעַצֵּם בְּטֹהַר לִבּוֹ, בְּעֹצֶם הַתְּשׁוּקָה

• לְקַשֵּׁר וּלְדַבֵּק עַל יָדָהּ מִמַּטָּה לְמַעְלָה בְּסֵדֶר הַמַּדְרֵגוֹת, נַפְשׁוֹ בְּרוּחוֹ וְרוּחוֹ בְּנִשְׁמָתוֹ, (הגהה ל"ז)

• וְיִתְעַלּוּ כֻּלָּם לְשָׁרֵשׁ אוֹתָהּ הַתֵּבָה בָּעוֹלָמוֹת הָעֶלְיוֹנִים.

• וְזֶהוּ הָעִנְיָן שֶׁאָמְרוּ

---

is transformed to have a different implication ... The accents are to the letters as a bridle is to a horse – to guide them straight, to the right or to the left according to the will of the accents ... Therefore, all of the letters are animated with the secret of these two – the vowels and accents together.

376 Zohar Chadash II Shir Hashirim 23b.
377 Tikkunei Zohar Tikkun 69 108a-b.
378 This interconnection of levels is described in more detail in the First Gateway, e.g., G1:17.
379 **R. Chaim adds Note 37 here.** This note is brought at the end of this chapter and is entitled "Regular and repentance sequences of thought, speech, and action."
380 Zohar Chadash Tikkunim II 66a.

- ▫ "And the wise" are those which have the wisdom to know how to pray, how to raise up ... with the letters, vowels, and accents.[380] Refer there.
- ▫ "And they have strength to stand in the Sanctuary of God," standing in prayer ... including all [components, the] accents, vowels, and letters.[381]

Rabbi Chaim's Notes:
Note 36 – Letter tags go together with letters just like the soul to a body

- Now even though in the writings of the Arizal they are split into four levels of accents, vowels, tags, and letters as is known
  ○ it is all one [concept] and they are essentially just three root levels.
- For in all [references to them] in the book of Tikkunim [Tikkunei Zohar] they are split into only three levels of accents, vowels, and letters
  ○ and there is no mention within it of the concept of the tags of all the letters
  ○ just the three tags required for each of the seven letters (*shtns gz*)[382] which are a concept in and of their own.
- The reason for this is explicitly given in Etz Chaim,[383] which is briefly stated as follows:
  ○ With this the statement[s] of the Tikkunim can also be understood
  ○ for sometimes it says that the letters are the body ... and in other places we find that the letters are the Nefesh

---

381 Zohar Chadash Tikkunim II 72a quoting Daniel 1:4.
382 Menachot 29b. The letters are *Shin Ayin Tet Nun Zayin Gimmel Tzaddi*.
383 Etz Chaim Shaar 5, Shaar Taamim Nekudot Tagim Otiyot, Chap. 5 (see V2:14, p. 676):
  • ... and with this concept the statements of the Tikkunim are understood – for sometimes it says that the letters are bodies ... and in other places that the letters are Nefesh. To understand this concept we need to be precise in their words [of the Tikkunim] when they say that "the letters compared to vowels are like a body compared to Ruach," but the Nefesh is an intermediary level between the body and the Ruach and this statement should have said that [the letters are compared to vowels] like a body compared to Nefesh? But this concept is that you should know that the accents are from [the level] of Keter, the vowels from [the level of] Chochma, the tags from the level of the three heads [the intellect] of Binah and the letters from the seven lower [Middot of Binah] ... it transpires that letters are always called body as they are the vessels [i.e., the Middot are the vessels, the attributes, through which the intellect of Binah are expressed, so e.g., kindness becomes a vessel for

- בְּתִקּוּנֵי זֹהַר חָדָשׁ ע"ו רֵישׁ ע"א "וְהַמַּשְׂכִּילִים" כו', אִנּוּן דְּאִית בְּהוֹן שֵׂכֶל לְאִשְׁתְּמוֹדַע בִּצְלוֹתָא, אֵיךְ סַלְקָא כו', בְּאַתְוָן וּנְקוּדֵי וְטַעֲמֵי" כו', עַיֵּן שָׁם.
- וְשָׁם בְּדַף ע"ב רֵישׁ ע"א, "וַאֲשֶׁר כֹּחַ בָּהֶם לַעֲמֹד בְּהֵיכַל הַמֶּלֶךְ" (דניאל א, ד) בַּעֲמִידָה דִּצְלוֹתָא כו', כְּלִילָא מִכֹּלָּא טַעֲמֵי וּנְקוּדֵי וְאַתְוָן:

הגהה ל"ו

- וְאַף שֶׁבְּכִתְבֵי הָאֲרִיזַ"ל מְחַלְּקָם לְאַרְבַּע בְּחִינוֹת, ט' נ' ת' א' כַּיָּדוּעַ
  - הַכֹּל אֶחָד, וְעִקָּרָם הֵם רַק שְׁלֹשָׁה בְּחִינוֹת שָׁרָשִׁיִּים:
- כִּי בְּכָל סֵפֶר הַתִּקּוּנִים מְחַלְּקָם רַק לִשְׁלֹשָׁה בְּחִינוֹת, ט' נ' א' לְבַד
  - וְלֹא נִזְכְּרוּ בּוֹ עִנְיַן הַתַּגִּין שֶׁל כָּל הָאוֹתִיּוֹת
  - רַק הַשְּׁלֹשָׁה זִיּוּנִין שֶׁל שַׁעַטְנֵ"ז גַּ"ץ, שֶׁהֵם עִנְיָן בִּפְנֵי עַצְמָם:
- וְהַטַּעַם בָּזֶה מְפֹרָשׁ בְּעֵץ חַיִּים (שַׁעַר ט' נ' ת' א' פֶּרֶק ו'), זֶה לְשׁוֹנוֹ שָׁם בְּקִצּוּר
  - "גַּם בָּזֶה יוּבַן עִנְיַן מַאֲמַר הַתִּקּוּנִים
- כִּי פַּעַם הוּא אוֹמֵר כִּי הָאוֹתִיּוֹת הֵם גּוּפָא כו', וּבִמְקוֹמוֹת אֲחֵרִים מָצָאנוּ כִּי הָאוֹתִיּוֹת נֶפֶשׁ כו'

one's intellect and is applied according to the level of one's intellect, so a child will apply kindness to a doll, but an adult will apply kindness to people in subtle ways] and the tags are the three heads of the Mother [i.e., the three heads of Binah, see p. 233, fn. 399] and they are the Nefesh of the letters, and just as a Nefesh never separates from a body, similarly the tags never separate from the letters of a Sefer Torah – in contrast with the vowels and the accents which do not appear in the Sefer Torah but are just [enunciated] through a person's reading of the Sefer Torah. Understand this. This is the meaning of that which was written above that this Nefesh incorporates the letters and partners the body. This concept is that the tags partner and connect with the essence of the letters which are the body, and the tags are the generality of the letters, for the three heads of the Mother incorporate the seven lower [Middot] which are the letters and the generality of the seven lower [Middot] are rooted and incorporated within the three heads which are the tags. It is for this reason that the tags are not hinted to or mentioned in the Tikkunim because they and the letters partner together. Therefore, sometimes the letters are called body for that is the reality, and sometimes they are called Nefesh, relating to their tags.

- if so the letters are called the body ... and the tags ... are the Nefesh of the letters.
- Just like the soul never separates from the body, similarly, the tags never separate from the letters of a Sefer Torah, which is not the case with the vowels and the accents ...
- for the tags partner with and are connected to the essence of the letters which are the body
- and the tags are the generality of the letters ...
- and it is for this reason that the tags are not hinted to or mentioned in the Tikkunim, because they partner together with the letters ...
- as when mentioning the body, the soul is inevitably included as they are partners, as mentioned above.
- His quoted words end here. Refer there [to this source] at length.

Note 37 – Regular and repentance sequences of thought, speech, and action

- Through this [procedure] all these three levels will be rectified
  - even if, God forbid, he damaged any of them through improper deeds, speech, or thoughts
  - and through them caused the distancing and separation of their interconnectivity, God forbid, as I wrote above in G1:18.
  - Now, through this [procedure], they will be rectified to reinstate their original interconnectivity of each level with the one above it.
  - This is the essential root of repentance as written there [G1:18–20] at length. Refer there.
- This is the concept of the verse "This people is fattening its heart, hardening its ears, and sealing its eyes – preventing it to see with its eyes, hear with its ears, and understand with its heart – so that it will return and be healed,"[384] where the end section of this verse reverses the sequence of [heart, ears, and eyes as per] the first section.
  - For the heart is the level of *thought* as is known
  - and the ears are the vehicle through which *speech* is heard
  - and the eyes are the vehicle of sight, enabling one to see physical *action*.
  - These are the three levels of Neshama, Ruach, and Nefesh.
- With the sins of man, these [levels] gradually recede away from him in [this specific] sequence
  - that as soon as the idea merely occurs to a person from the perspective of his [general] soul to perform any sin

---

384 Yishayahu 6:10 as brought in Rosh Hashana 17b by R. Yochanan who says

- אִם כֵּן הָאוֹתִיּוֹת נִקְרָאִים גּוּף כו' וְהַתָּגִין כו' הֵם הַנֶּפֶשׁ דְּהָאוֹתִיּוֹת.
- וּכְמוֹ שֶׁהַנֶּפֶשׁ אֵינָהּ נִפְרֶדֶת לְעוֹלָם מִן הַגּוּף, כָּךְ הַתָּגִין אֵינָן נִפְרָדִין מֵאוֹתִיּוֹת בְּסֵפֶר תּוֹרָה לְעוֹלָם, מַה שֶּׁאֵין כֵּן הַנְּקֻדּוֹת וּטְעָמִים כו'.
- כִּי הַתָּגִין הֵם מְשֻׁתָּפִים וּמִתְחַבְּרִין בְּעַצְמוּת הָאוֹתִיּוֹת שֶׁהֵם גּוּף
- וְהַתָּגִין הֵם כְּלָלוּת הָאוֹתִיּוֹת כו'
- וּבַעֲבוּר זֶה אֵין הַתָּגִין רְמוּזִים וְנִזְכָּרִים בַּתִּקּוּנִים, יַעַן כִּי הֵם וְהָאוֹתִיּוֹת מְשֻׁתָּפִים יַחַד כו'
- כִּי בְּהַזְכִּיר אֶת הַגּוּף, מִמֵּילָא הַנֶּפֶשׁ בִּכְלָל, כִּי הֵם מְשֻׁתָּפִים כנ"ל.
- עַד כָּאן דְּבָרָיו, וְעַיֵּן שָׁם בְּאֹרֶךְ:

הגהה ל"ז

- וְעַל יְדֵי זֶה יְתַקְּנוּ כָּל הַשְּׁלֹשָׁה בְּחִינוֹת אֵלּוּ
- אַף אִם פָּגַם חַס וְשָׁלוֹם בְּאֵיזֶה מֵהֶם, עַל יְדֵי מַעֲשָׂיו אוֹ דִּבּוּרָיו אוֹ מַחְשְׁבוֹתָיו אֲשֶׁר לֹא טוֹבִים
- וְגָרַם חַס וְשָׁלוֹם עַל יְדֵיהֶם לְרַחֵק וּלְהַפְרִיד הַהִתְקַשְּׁרוּת שֶׁבֵּינֵיהֶם, כְּמוֹ שֶׁכָּתַבְתִּי לְעֵיל בְּשַׁעַר א' פֶּרֶק י"ח
- עַתָּה עַל יְדֵי זֶה, יְתַקְּנוּ לַחֲזֹר וּלְהִתְקַשֵּׁר כָּל אֶחָד בַּחֲבֵרוֹ שֶׁעָלָיו כְּבַתְּחִלָּה
- שֶׁזֶּהוּ שֹׁרֶשׁ עִקַּר עִנְיַן הַתְּשׁוּבָה, כְּמוֹ שֶׁנִּתְבָּאֵר שָׁם בְּאֹרֶךְ, עַיֵּן שָׁם:
- וְזֶהוּ עִנְיַן הַכָּתוּב (ישעי' ו, י) "הַשְׁמֵן לֵב הָעָם הַזֶּה וְאָזְנָיו הַכְבֵּד וְעֵינָיו הָשַׁע, פֶּן יִרְאֶה בְעֵינָיו וּבְאָזְנָיו יִשְׁמָע וּלְבָבוֹ יָבִין וָשָׁב וְרָפָא לוֹ". שֶׁבְּסֵיפֵיהּ דִּקְרָא הַסֵּדֶר הָפוּךְ מִסֵּדְרֵיהּ דְּרֵישֵׁיהּ.
- כִּי הַלֵּב הוּא בְּחִינַת הַמַּחְשָׁבָה כַּיָּדוּעַ
- וְהָאָזְנַיִם הֵם כְּלֵי שְׁמִיעַת הַדִּבּוּר
- וְהָעֵינַיִם הֵם כְּלֵי הָרְאִיָּה, לִרְאוֹת עִנְיְנֵי הַמַּעֲשִׂים בְּפֹעַל
- וְהֵם הַשְּׁלֹשָׁה בְּחִינוֹת נר"ן:
- וּבְחֶטְאֵי הָאָדָם הֵמָּה מִסְתַּלְּקִים מִמֶּנּוּ מְעַט מְעַט כְּסֵדֶר.
- שְׁמִיעַת שֶׁעוֹלָה עַל רַעְיוֹן הָאָדָם לְבַד מִצַּד הַנֶּפֶשׁ, לַעֲשׂוֹת שׁוּם חֵטְא

that: Great is repentance which tears up man's judgment, as per this verse.

- then the [specific] level of Neshama immediately departs, for it is a very high level indeed [and therefore very sensitive to even the vague thought of sin].
- If, God forbid, he sins further, then the level of Ruach will also either completely depart from him or will become damaged and corrupted, God forbid – resulting in its connection with the level of Neshama no longer being properly complete.
- If, God forbid he continues to additionally sin further, then his level of Nefesh will also be damaged or completely cut-off, God forbid, from its attachment to the level of Ruach.

• When he repents, he reacquires these [levels] in a down up sequence – being a sequence reversal from the sequence in which they initially departed from him.
- First he attains the level of Nefesh
- and then Ruach will come [back] to reside over him and reconnect with him.
- Following this, sparks of the light of the Neshama will come and hover over them [the Ruach and Nefesh]
- and then each of the [levels] will properly interconnect with each other.
- With this, the verse[385] is self understood.

• Now
- Even though the explanation is given in G1:20 [which is seemingly contradictory] that
    □ if he damages or, God forbid, cuts off his level of Nefesh and lowers all nine of [the Nefesh's lower] Sefirot to be entrapped within Evil
    □ then through his repentance he causes an emanation of holy supernal light from above to first shine on his Neshama
    □ and from it, it extends onto his Ruach
    □ and then the Ruach flashes from the radiance of this great light which is bestowed upon it to also [influence] the Nefesh, and as a result [the level of Nefesh] is raised from the depths of Evil to reinstate its original connection with Ruach.
    □ Similarly, this same process occurs if the Ruach is damaged, God forbid, as written there [i.e., G1:20]
    □ and as is known from the writings of the Arizal, that to rectify any Partzuf[386] or level, it is necessary to draw down new lights and Mochin/intellect from the most supernal levels to descend via all the Partzufim and levels until it reaches the specific Partzuf and level which requires rectification and for which [the light and] intellect was drawn down.

- אָז מִסְתַּלֶּקֶת בְּחִינַת הַ"נְּשָׁמָה" תֵּכֶף, כִּי הִיא בְּחִינָה גְבוֹהַ וְנַעֲלָה מְאֹד.
- וְאִם חַס וְשָׁלוֹם חָטָא יוֹתֵר, גַּם בְּחִינַת הָ"רוּחַ" מִסְתַּלֵּק מִמֶּנּוּ לְגַמְרֵי, אוֹ נִפְגָּם וְנִתְקַלְקֵל חַס וְשָׁלוֹם, וְאָז אֵין הִתְקַשְּׁרוּתוֹ בִּבְחִינַת הַנְּשָׁמָה בִּשְׁלֵמוּת כָּרָאוּי.
- וְאִם חַס וְשָׁלוֹם הִרְבָּה וְהוֹסִיף לַחֲטֹא יוֹתֵר, אָז גַּם בְּחִינַת "נַפְשׁוֹ" נִפְגֶּמֶת אוֹ נִכְרֶתֶת חַס וְשָׁלוֹם לְגַמְרֵי מֵהִתְקַשְּׁרוּתָהּ בִּבְחִינַת הָרוּחַ:

• וּכְשֶׁהוּא חוֹזֵר בִּתְשׁוּבָה, הוּא חוֹזֵר לְהַשִּׂיג אוֹתָם כְּסֵדֶר "מִמַּטָּה לְמַעְלָה", הֶפוּךְ מִסֵּדֶר הִסְתַּלְּקוּתָם תְּחִלָּה.
  - תְּחִלָּה הוּא מַשִּׂיג לִבְחִינַת הַ"נֶּפֶשׁ"
  - וְאַחַר כָּךְ בָּא וְשׁוֹרָה עָלֶיהָ הָ"רוּחַ" וּמִתְקַשֶּׁרֶת בּוֹ
  - וְאַחַר כָּךְ בָּאִים וְחוֹפְפִים עֲלֵיהֶם נִצוֹצֵי אוֹר הַ"נְּשָׁמָה"
  - וְאָז מִתְקַשְּׁרִים כָּל אֶחָד בַּחֲבֵרוֹ כָּרָאוּי
  - וּבְזֶה מְבֹאָר הַכָּתוּב מֵאֵלָיו:

• וְאַף
  - שֶׁבַּשַּׁעַר א' פֶּרֶק כ' נִתְבָּאֵר
    - שֶׁאִם פָּגַם אוֹ הִכְרִית חַס וְשָׁלוֹם בְּחִינַת נַפְשׁוֹ, וְהוֹרִיד כָּל ט' סְפִירוֹתֶיהָ בִּמְצוּלוֹת הָרָע
    - עַל יְדֵי תְּשׁוּבָתוֹ הוּא מַאֲצִיל וּמַמְשִׁיךְ קְדֻשָּׁה וְאוֹר עֶלְיוֹן מִלְּעֵלָּא עַל בְּחִינַת 'נִשְׁמָתוֹ' תְּחִלָּה
    - וּמִמֶּנָּה נִמְשָׁךְ עַל 'רוּחוֹ'
    - וְאָז הָרוּחַ מַבְהִיק מִזִּיו הָאוֹר הַגָּדוֹל הַנִּשְׁפָּע עָלָיו גַּם עַל הַ'נֶּפֶשׁ', וְעַל יְדֵי זֶה הִיא מִתְעַלֵּית מֵעָמְקֵי הָרָע, לְהִתְקַשֵּׁר בִּבְחִינַת הָרוּחַ כְּמִקֶּדֶם.
    - וְכֵן עַל דֶּרֶךְ זֶה כַּאֲשֶׁר נִפְגַּם הָרוּחַ חַס וְשָׁלוֹם, כְּמוֹ שֶׁנִּתְבָּאֵר שָׁם
    - וְכַיָּדוּעַ בְּדִבְרֵי הָאֲרִיזַ"ל, שֶׁלְּתִקּוּן אֵיזֶה פַּרְצוּף וּבְחִינָה, צָרִיךְ לְהַמְשִׁיךְ אוֹרוֹת וּמוֹחִין חֲדָשִׁים מִלְעֵלָּא לְעֵלָּא, דֶּרֶךְ כָּל הַפַּרְצוּפִים וְהַמַּדְרֵגוֹת כֻּלָּם, עַד אוֹתוֹ הַפַּרְצוּף וְהַבְּחִינָה שֶׁצָּרִיךְ לְתַקְּנוֹ, שֶׁאֵלָיו נִמְשְׁכוּ הַמּוֹחִין.

---

385 Above from Yishayahu 6:10.
386 See p. 233, fn. 399, which describes the concept of a Partzuf.

- This process [as per G1:20] is just to raise the Nefesh from the depths of impurity in which it is submerged or to rectify its damage
  - and this requires the drawing down of holiness and supernal light from above to below
  - to expel and destroy, with its fiery fire, the powers of impurity in which it is submerged or to rectify its damage
  - and to raise it up in a purified and rectified state, so that it will be able to connect with the Ruach
  - and similarly, this same process operates on the damaged level of Ruach – to restore it to its original state.
- However
  - after it has already been rectified through repentance
  - the subsequent sequence in which they are entered[/engaged] within a person's body is from down up, as mentioned above.
  - This is the meaning of "so that it will return,"[387] meaning that once all the levels are returned to their [original] place [through the up down sequence], then "and be healed" [their process of engagement will work in the correct down up sequence].

17. WILL RELATE TO ANOTHER SOUL/WORD COMPONENT AFTER RESURRECTION

- However, 'God has more words'[388] for one who serves God with holiness [in relation to] a more specific level
  - which is the level of the Root of the Neshama – this is the Neshama of the Neshama, as mentioned in the Zohar, which is called "*Chaya*."[389]

---

387 Yishayahu 6:10.
388 Iyov 36:2.
389 In the Arizal's Kabbalah as documented by R. Chaim Vital, the worlds are split into five general categories of world levels which in descending order of level are: Adam Kadmon, Atzilut, Beriyah, Yetzirah, Asiyah. These five levels respectively correspond to the tag of the letter *Yud* (i.e., the point drawn at the top of the letter) of YHVH followed by each of the consecutive letters of YHVH which in turn respectively correspond to: (1) *The Divine Will* (or Keter – represented by the tag of the letter *Yud* which points upwards to indicate that the level of Divine Will is infinitely abstracted from Chochma). (2) *Chochma* (represented by a *Yud* which is an unexpanded point, i.e., it just exists with no analysis). (3) *Binah* (represented by a *Hey* which comprises the letter *Dalet* – numerical value 4 – around a point, i.e., around a *Yud*, and is the two-dimensional expansion in four directions, i.e., analysis of the point of Chochma). (4) *The*

נפש　　שער ב' - פרק י"ז　　החיים

- הַיְנוּ רַק כְּדֵי לְהַעֲלוֹת הַנֶּפֶשׁ מֵעָמְקֵי הַטֻּמְאָה שֶׁנִּשְׁקְעָה בְּתוֹכוֹ אוֹ לְתַקֵּן פְּגִימָתָהּ
- צָרִיךְ לְהַמְשִׁיךְ קְדֻשָּׁה וְאוֹר עֶלְיוֹן "מִלְמַעְלָה לְמַטָּה"
- לְגָרֵשׁ וּלְכַלּוֹת בְּרִשְׁפֵּי אֵשׁ הַשַּׁלְהֶבֶת הַזֶּה אֶת הַכֹּחוֹת הַטֻּמְאָה שֶׁנִּשְׁקְעָה בְּתוֹכָם, אוֹ לְמַלֹּאות פְּגִימָתָהּ
- וּלְהַעֲלוֹתָהּ מְטֹהָרָה וּמְתֻקֶּנֶת שֶׁתּוּכַל לְהִתְקַשֵּׁר עִם הָרוּחַ.
- וְכֵן עַל דֶּרֶךְ זֶה בִּבְחִינַת הָרוּחַ שֶׁנִּפְגַּם, כְּדֵי לַחֲזֹר וּלְתַקְּנוֹ כְּבַתְּחִלָּה.
- אֲבָל
- אַחַר שֶׁכְּבָר נִתְקְנוּ עַל יְדֵי הַתְּשׁוּבָה
- סֵדֶר כְּנִיסָתָם אַחַר זֶה בְּגוּף הָאָדָם הוּא "מִמַּטָּה לְמַעְלָה" כַּנַּ"ל
- וְזֶהוּ "וָיָּשָׁב", פֵּרוּשׁ כְּשֶׁהָיָה מֵשִׁיב כָּל בְּחִינָה עַל מְקוֹמָהּ, אָז הָיָה נִרְפָּא:

שער ב' - פרק י"ז

- אָמְנָם עוֹד יֵשׁ לֶאֱלוֹהַּ מִלִּין, לִפְנֵי הָעוֹבֵד אֱלֹהִים בִּקְדֻשָּׁה, בִּבְחִינָה יוֹתֵר פְּרָטִית
- וְהוּא בִּבְחִינַת "שֹׁרֶשׁ הַנְּשָׁמָה", הִיא "נִשְׁמְתָא לְנִשְׁמְתָא", הַנִּזְכָּר בַּזֹּהַר, וְנִקְרֵאת "חַיָּה":

Six Middot (represented by the *Vav* with numerical value 6. *Vav* also represents a path of descent from supernal to lower levels). (5) *Malchut* (represented by a *Hey* – numerical value 5 – relating to the five parts of the mouth which can articulate different groups of letters which in turn are represented by the five final Hebrew letters, 'MNTzPCh' (*Mem, Nun, Tzaddi, Peh, Chaf*), with these five final letters having the same numerical value as *Mem Nun=Melech, Tzaddi=Malach, Peh Chaf=Yimloch*, the ultimate expression of Kingship which spans past, present, and future – the significance of the final letters is that they are always at the end of a word and represent the final and ultimate manifestation). This structure is similarly reflected with man's soul with these five levels respectively corresponding to Yechida, Chaya, Neshama, Ruach, and Nefesh. G1:14 describes the expression of Nefesh through *action*, Ruach through *speech*, and Neshama through *thought* with thought corresponding to understanding, i.e., Binah. Understanding, Binah, is driven by a completely hidden ability of Chochma which in turn is inspired by a more subtly rooted desire/will. The level corresponding to Chaya (and of Yechida as manifest in Chaya) was completely concealed as a result of Adam's sin (the impact of Adam's sin is referred to in G1:15, G1:22, and at the end of G4:28). All of these levels are interconnected with each level being the *soul* of the level below it. Following Adam's sin, the parts of the soul we can be aware of are Nefesh,

- Adam [before his sin] was able to relate [to the level of *Chaya*], and [also] to the level of *Yechida* contained within it, the secret of the world of Adam Kadmon[390]
  - as explained to one who understands Etz Chaim that Adam merited to achieve the true and essential level of *Chaya Yechida*.[391]
  - Refer to Sefer HaGilgulim.[392]
- This was the key intention of Chazal's interpretation[393] of the verse "let the earth produce Nefesh Chaya,"[394] that this even includes the souls of Adam and Mashiach, that this level [of Chaya Yechida][395] is the secret of [the collective unified soul of Israel] – Knesset Yisrael,[396] the supernal *land of the living*.
  - (This is the root of the element of earth/dust – one of the four elements – the *primary roots* – the fathers of all the worlds, as mentioned in the Zohar.)[397]
  - Refer to the Zohar. The secret as is written: "Let the earth produce Nefesh Chaya," etc.[398]
  - and to "and all the living Nefesh," etc.[399]
  - Refer to the Zohar at the end of VaEtchanan.[400]

Ruach, and Neshama. These parts are to all intents and purposes referred to as "our soul" – so the expression of the "soul of our soul" refers to the level of Chaya.

390 See details of Adam Kadmon in previous footnote.
391 Etz Chaim Shaar 20, Shaar Mochin, end of Chap. 12.
392 Sefer HaGilgulim, Chap. 1:
- Adam, when created, contained within him all of these levels mentioned – from Nefesh of Atzilut until Yechida of Atzilut.

Sefer HaGilgulim, end of Chap. 17:
- When Adam was created, the world of Beriyah was in the place which is now the small part of Atzilut . . . but since he sinned . . . it descended from its place until it reached the current state of the lowest worlds after the destruction of the Temple.

393 Bereishit Rabba 7:5 and 8:1.
394 Bereishit 1:24.
395 As in "Nefesh Chaya," which is the source of the level of Neshama.
396 As both the souls of Adam and Mashiach are special souls which incorporate all the souls of Israel. Also see references to Knesset Yisrael in G1:16 and G1:17.
397 Zohar II VaEra 23b. This source is quoted more comprehensively in Maamar BeTzeleM. The four primary elements being Earth/Dust, Wind, Water, and Fire. See p. 539, fn. 210, for background on the four elements.
398 R. Chaim cites two identical sources for this statement, 1. Zohar II Shemot

- וְאָדָם הָרִאשׁוֹן הַשִּׁיגָהּ, וְלִבְחִינַת "הַיְחִידָה" הַנִּכְלֶלֶת בָּהּ, סוֹד עוֹלָם אָדָם קַדְמָאָה
- וְכִמְבֹאָר לְמֵבִין בְּעֵץ חַיִּים סוֹף שַׁעַר הַמּוֹחִין, שֶׁאָדָם הָרִאשׁוֹן זָכָה לִבְחִינַת "חַיָּה" "יְחִידָה" הָאֲמִתִּים בִּמְקוֹמָם הָעִקָּרִי.
- וְעַיֵּן רֵישׁ גִּלְגּוּלִים וּבְפֶרֶק י"ז שָׁם:
- וְזֶהוּ עִקַּר כַּוָּנָתָם זִכְרוֹנָם לִבְרָכָה (עַיֵּ' ב"ר ז, ה; ח, א) שֶׁדָּרְשׁוּ בַּפָּסוּק "תּוֹצֵא הָאָרֶץ נֶפֶשׁ חַיָּה" (בראשית א, כד) אֲפִלּוּ נַפְשׁוֹ שֶׁל אָדָם הָרִאשׁוֹן, אֲפִלּוּ נַפְשׁוֹ שֶׁל מָשִׁיחַ. כִּי זֹאת הַבְּחִינָה הִיא סוֹד כְּנֶסֶת יִשְׂרָאֵל, אֶרֶץ הַחַיִּים הָעֶלְיוֹנָה
- (הֵינוּ שֹׁרֶשׁ יְסוֹד הֶעָפָר מֵהַדּ' יְסוֹדִין, שָׁרָשִׁין קַדְמָאִין, אֲבָהָן דְּכֻלְּהוּ עָלְמִין, הַנִּזְכָּר בַּזֹּהַר וָאֵרָא כ"ג ע"ב, ע"ש).
- וְעַיֵּן זֹהַר שְׁמוֹת י"ב א', וּבְפָרָשַׁת שְׁלַח קע"ד ב', רָזָא דִּכְתִיב "תּוֹצֵא הָאָרֶץ נֶפֶשׁ חַיָּה" וְכוּ'
- וּבְפָרָשַׁת שְׁמִינִי ל"ט ב' "וְאֵת כָּל נֶפֶשׁ הַחַיָּה" כוּ'.
- וְעַיֵּן סוֹף פָּרָשַׁת וָאֶתְחַנַּן בְּמַתְנִיתִין.

12a, and 2. Zohar III Shelach 174b. Some additional detail from this quotation is as follows:
- ... it implies that the souls of the Tzaddikim extend from this high place ... and implies that there is a mother and father for the soul – just like there is a mother and father for the physical body, and it implies that on all sides, whether above or below, all derive from the combination of male and female, and this establishes the secret of "let the *earth* produce *Nefesh Chaya*," the "*earth*" is Knesset Yisrael [i.e., the collective soul of Israel; the *female*], "*Nefesh Chaya*" is the soul of Adam.

399 Zohar III Shemini 39b quoting Bereishit 1:21 and 1:24. A more complete quotation is as follows:
- "and all the living Nefesh," this is the Nefesh [of Adam], which comes from that supernal *earth* which is from the supernal Chaya which is [supernal] over all, as per "let the *earth* produce *Nefesh Chaya*," which is the Nefesh of Adam which extends within him.

400 Zohar III VaEtchanan 270b:
- ... It arose in [God's] Will to create mankind to rule over the lowest world. He set [a clump of] earth in this being which incorporated all ... There was one large strong tree [the Tree of Life] which connected and unified with one nice branch ... and produced a hidden Ruach and filled this clump of earth with it and [as a result Adam became alive and] stood on his feet and ruled over all of the world controlling all ... He was commanded [not to eat

- ○ Refer to Ramban on the verse "let us make man," for the spirit of God speaks within him.⁴⁰¹
- Therefore, Adam was built to be immortal, as per "The Chochma will *Techaye* (give life) to those that have it,"⁴⁰² therefore, [this level] is called "Chaya,"⁴⁰³ and this is the meaning of "let the earth produce Nefesh *Chaya*," however, with his sin, [this level] left him.⁴⁰⁴
  - ○ Refer to the writings of the Arizal.⁴⁰⁵

---

of] that tree but did not keep that command [and as a result] the King took back Adam's Ruach [resulting in Adam becoming mortal]. . . .

401 Ramban Bereishit 1:26:
- . . . In Bereishit Rabba (Bereishit 7:5), it says "let the earth produce Nefesh Chaya according to its kind." R. Elazar said "'Nefesh Chaya,' this is the Ruach of Adam" . . . it is possible that R. Elazar meant to explain that "let the earth produce" [refers to] *the earth of life* [see Zohar III Tazria 45b], which produces "Nefesh Chaya," like itself, which lives forever. . . .

402 Kohelet 7:12.

403 I.e., *Lives* forever. As per p. 444, fn. 389, that the level of Chaya is synonymous with Chochma. This idea is brought down in Sefer HaGilgulim, Chap. 1: "Chochma is called Chaya as it is the name of the source of life and the secret of 'The Chochma will give life to those that have it,' and Keter is called Yechida (*the unified one*) as the Ein Sof is called *Unified*."

404 Together with all subsequent generations, i.e., causing all people to be mortal. See G1:06:N07 for more details on the introduction of death as a result of Adam's sin.

405 Sefer HaGilgulim, Chap. 15:
- This concept has has already been explained in the previous chapter that Adam incorporated all of the Nefesh, Ruach, and Neshama of Atzilut, called the "supernal radiance," and also incorporated the components of Beriyah, Yetzirah, and Asiyah, which are called "seven thousand years," as mentioned above. When he sinned, the "supernal radiance," i.e., the Nefesh, Ruach, and Neshama of Atzilut, left and *flew away* from him . . . therefore, this part [of him] was not submerged into the Kelipot . . . With the three components of Beriyah, Yetzirah, and Asiyah, which are the seven thousand years, parts of them left and parts remained. The parts which left were those which were submerged into the Kelipot from which the majority or the entirety of each person's soul draws from, [and will continue to draw from] until the time of the Mashiach. The parts which remained from the components of Beriyah, Yetzirah, and Asiyah after he sinned, are referred to as "Chalato Shel Olam" (the bread of the world) [e.g., as per Bereishit Rabba 14:1, 17:8, and Midrash Tanchuma Noach 1].

Sefer HaGilgulim Chap. 21:
- [Towards the beginning of this chapter:] You already know that which has

נפש שער ב' - פרק י"ז   החיים   449

○ וְעַיֵּן רַמְבַּ"ן זִכְרוֹנוֹ לִבְרָכָה בַּפָּסוּק "נַעֲשֶׂה אָדָם" (בראשית א, כו), כִּי רוּחַ ה' דִּבֶּר בּוֹ:

• וְלָכֵן הָיָה אָדָם הָרִאשׁוֹן מוּכָן לִחְיוֹת לְעוֹלָם, כִּי הִיא "הַחָכְמָה תְּחַיֶּה בְעָלֶיהָ" (קהלת ז, יב), וְלָכֵן נִקְרֵאת "חַיָּה", וְזֶהוּ "תּוֹצֵא הָאָרֶץ נֶפֶשׁ חַיָּה". וּבְחֶטְאוֹ נִסְתַּלְּקָה הֵימֶנּוּ.

○ וְעַיֵּן מַה שֶּׁכָּתַב הָאֲרִ"י זִכְרוֹנוֹ לִבְרָכָה בְּפֶרֶק ט"ו, וּבְרֵישׁ פֶּרֶק כ"א, וּבְפֶרֶק ל"ה מֵהַגִּלְגּוּלִים:

---

been explained in Chap. 15 that the souls [i.e., levels of soul] that remained in Adam after his sin are called "Chalato Shel Olam" . . . this concept is further explained in Chap. 19, that the Nefesh of Atzilut was inherited by Kayin and Hevel from Adam . . . it transpires that the Nefesh of Atzilut itself was totally removed from Adam when he sinned, but the Nefesh on the level of Atzilut which is [manifest] in the three worlds of Beriyah, Yetzirah, and Asiyah was not removed and they are called "Chalato Shel Olam" . . . and this is what was left in Adam. [Then towards the end of the chapter] . . . through the sin of Adam where his sin caused death . . . and there was no way to rectify himself except with death [this idea is elaborated in G1:06:No7].

Sefer HaGilgulim, Chap. 35 (beginning of Shaar HaMalachim):
• The concept of Eliyahu, of blessed memory, and that which Chazal say that "Eliyah moves in four stages" [Berachot 4b]. What is this concept? Know that before Adam sinned, he had within him the Nefesh, Ruach, and Neshama of Beriyah, Yetzirah, and Asiyah and [also] the Nefesh, Ruach, and Neshama of Malchut, Zeer Anpin, and Binah of Atzilut [i.e., all the Sefirot of Atzilut from Binah downwards], and he incorporated all of the souls, although there were certainly a small number of souls which were not incorporated in his soul and they are the secret of the new souls. However, when he sinned, that which Chazal say is known, that Adam experienced [something similar] to that which occurred with Yiftach whose limbs were shed in multiple places as per "and he was buried in the cities [plural] of Gilad" instead of saying "in the city [singular] of Gilad" [Vayikra Rabba Bechukotai 37:4 quoting Shoftim 12:7], and the explanation is that all those parts of souls incorporated within him before he sinned, they all departed from him and were shed from him and fell into the depths of the Kelipot with 'this one in this way and this one in that way' [1 Melachim 22:20]. The Nefesh, Ruach, and Neshama of Atzilut departed from him and this is called the "supernal radiance" of Adam. But Chanoch took all the parts of it which were appropriate for him from the Nefesh, Ruach, and Neshama of Asiyah, Yetzirah, and Beriyah, and he also took a part of the Neshama

G2:17

- From that time no person merited to reach this level while being [still alive] in this world.
  - With Chanoch, when he reached this level and inherited the status of Adam
    - as per the Zohar[406] and the Arizal[407]
    - the world was not capable of tolerating him and he was forced to leave this [physical] world.[408]
  - Similarly, Eliyahu left this world[409] when he achieved a part of this level of supernal radiance[410]
    - as per the Arizal[411]

---

    of Atzilut of Adam. However a part of the Nefesh remained with Adam . . . and this Nefesh has external and internal components . . . and Eliyahu, of blessed memory, who is Pinchas, took [both the external] and internal components. . . .

406 R. Chaim refers the reader to the following references in the Zohar which are expanded as follows:
- Zohar Chadash I Terumah 71a: The light which Adam lost, and that light was hidden in the Garden of Eden – it left and ascended, but did not find its place as it was not complete from all sides [i.e., in all ways]. It was not completed in the [physical world] below due to Adam's sin. It landed [back] in the [physical world] below and was hidden in the trees of the Garden [of Eden] and spread out there to all sides of the Garden until Chanoch son of Yered was born. When he was born and came close to the Garden [of Eden, i.e., achieved this great level], this light rested upon him and radiated within him . . . until that light was completed within him.
- Zohar Chadash II Shir Hashirim 15b: . . . and enticed Adam [to sin by eating of the Tree of Knowledge of Good and Evil], his [spiritual] clothing flew from upon him and his clear and radiant supernal Neshama left him and he and his wife [Chava] were left naked of everything . . . and that radiant supernal Neshama which flew from him ascended and was stored in a storehouse which became its body until children were born and Chanoch came into the world. On Chanoch's arrival that radiant supernal holy Neshama rested upon him and Chanoch achieved greatness with that which Adam left him as per "and Chanoch walked with God" (Bereishit 5:22). . . .
- Zohar Raya Mehemna III Kedoshim 83a: Adam did not have anything of this world . . . his single body was made of greater light than all the messenger angels in the Supernal Realms . . . and he came into being into the world, when he came into being the sun and moon shone and their radiance was blocked out and darkened by the ball of his foot [i.e., Adam was on an extremely high spiritual level of existence and of such spiritual dimensions that the ball of his foot could block out the light of the sun and moon] . . . when he sinned he became dark [i.e., no longer radiated] and his bones

שער ב' - פרק י"ז

- וּמֵאָז לֹא זָכָה אֵלֶיהָ שׁוּם אָדָם בְּעוֹדוֹ בָּזֶה הָעוֹלָם.
  - וַחֲנוֹךְ כְּשֶׁהִגִּיעַ לְזֹאת הַמַּדְרֵגָה, וְיָרַשׁ מַעֲלָתוֹ שֶׁל אָדָם הָרִאשׁוֹן
    - כְּמוֹ שֶׁכָּתוּב בְּזֹהַר חָדָשׁ תְּרוּמָה ע"א ע"א, וְשָׁם בְּשִׁיר הַשִּׁירִים ט"ו ע"ב עַיֵּן שָׁם וּבְרַעְיָא מְהֵימְנָא קְדוֹשִׁים פ"ג, וּבְמַתְנִיתִין סוֹף פָּרָשַׁת וָאֶתְחַנָּן, כְּמוֹ שֶׁפֵּרְשָׁם הָאֲרִיזַ"ל בְּפָרָשַׁת בְּרֵאשִׁית בִּדְרוּשׁ אָדָם הָרִאשׁוֹן, וּבַגִּלְגּוּלִים פֶּרֶק י"ח עַיֵּן שָׁם, וּכְמוֹ שֶׁכָּתוּב שָׁם פֶּרֶק ל"ה
  - לֹא הָיָה יָכִיל עַלְמָא לְמִסְבְּלֵיהּ, וְהֻכְרַח לְהִסְתַּלֵּק מִזֶּה הָעוֹלָם.
  - וְכֵן אֵלִיָּהוּ, נִסְתַּלֵּק מִזֶּה הָעוֹלָם כְּשֶׁהִשִּׂיג קְצָת מֵאוֹתָהּ הַזִּיהֲרָא עִלָּאָה
    - כְּמוֹ שֶׁכָּתוּב בְּפֶרֶק י"ט מֵהַגִּלְגּוּלִים

---

became small requiring a different body with skin and flesh as per "and God, Elokim, made a coat of skin for Adam and his wife and clothed them" (Bereishit 3:21) ... [the original *clothes*] were not found before or after ... until Chanoch came and God took them for him from the earth ....

- Zohar III VaEtchanan 270b – the text is as brought down on p. 447, fn. 400 [although it is not obvious how this text relates to Chanoch].

407 R. Chaim refers the reader to the following Arizal related references which are expanded as follows:
- Parshat Bereishit, Derush Adam HaRishon: As per Shaar HaPesukim, Siman 2 Derush 3 starting HaKlal HaOleh: For all the souls which were included in the [soul of] Adam were on three levels ... the highest level of all, called "supernal radiance," was taken from Adam and the Kelipot did not control it at all, God forbid, but it left him as a result of the his sin, and no one merited it until Chanoch, who is [the holy angel] Matatron, came and took it.
- Sefer HaGilgulim, Chap. 18: For when Chanoch came and took the "supernal radiance" of Adam, through this he became the Angel Matatron.
- Sefer HaGilgulim, Chap. 35. See the lengthy quotation from this source on p. 449, fn. 405.

408 Without physically dying.
409 Also without physically dying.
410 This expression is defined on p. 448, fn. 405 as being the Nefesh, Ruach, and Neshama of Atzilut.
411 Sefer HaGilgulim, Chap. 19:
- Chanoch took and merited the level of Neshama of "supernal radiance," therefore, he subsequently became an angel ... and the Ruach of the level of "supernal radiance" of Atzilut was merited by Eliyahu the Prophet ... and therefore, he too is a heavenly angel like Chanoch.

- - as per the Zohar: God said to him . . . and the world cannot tolerate your being with people[412]
  - and we hope to achieve this level after the resurrection, please God, 'when He will pour Ruach over us from on High.'[413]
- This level is the root of a person's thought
  - for the level of thought is when he attaches his thought to think about a specific issue – this is the level of Neshama as per "and it is the Neshama from God that gives them understanding,"[414] and then the thought can at least be understood by the person who is thinking it
  - however, the general source generating the ability of thought is entirely concealed and even the person himself cannot grasp 'from where it comes,'[415] and this [source] is the level of the Root of the Neshama.
- This hidden level corresponds to the level of the combination of letters within each word, which is the Root of the Neshama of the letters, and of the power of their Ruach – in their supernal source.[416]
- We cannot currently relate to the true essence of these [letter] combination sequences in their supernal root
  - as we are currently unable to relate to the level of the Root of the Neshama[417]
  - but after the resurrection we will be able to have full understanding/Binah of the secret of the arrangement of the letter combinations in their holy root
  - as per: Torah . . . and in future times we will be invited to look at the Neshama of the Neshama of Torah.[418]
- This is the level of the root of all the collective souls of Israel – Malchut of Atzilut,[419] and as such is called "Knesset Yisrael." (Note 38)[420]

Rabbi Chaim's Note:
Note 38 – Knesset Yisrael is the mother, and God is the father of souls

- The Torah calls [*Knesset Yisrael*] "God, God of the spirits of all flesh"[421]

---

412 Zohar I Vayigash 209b.
413 Yishayahu 32:15.
414 Iyov 32:8.
415 R. Chaim uses the expression "MeAyin Timatzeh," as in the verse "VeHaChochma MeAyin Timatzeh," Iyov 28:12, which associates this expression with the level of Chochma (see G3:02:N41). Indeed, the level of Chaya is synonymous with Chochma and Chochma is the root of Binah, but following Adam's sin no person can directly relate to Chochma and

- וּכְמוֹ שֶׁכָּתוּב בַּזֹּהַר וַיִּגַּשׁ ר"ט רֵישׁ ע"ב, "אָמַר לֵיהּ קוּדְשָׁא בְּרִיךְ הוּא כו', וְעָלְמָא לָא יָכִיל לְמִסְבְּלָךְ עִם בְּנֵי נָשָׁא":

- וַאֲנַחְנוּ מְקַוִּים לְהַשִּׂיגָה אַחַר הַתְּחִיָּה אי"ה, שֶׁיֵּעָרֶה עָלֵינוּ 'רוּחַ' מִמָּרוֹם:

- וְהוּא בְּחִינַת שֹׁרֶשׁ הַמַּחְשָׁבָה שֶׁל אָדָם

  - כִּי בְּחִינַת "הַמַּחְשָׁבָה" הוּא — כְּשֶׁמִּדַּבֵּק מַחֲשַׁבְתּוֹ לַחְשֹׁב אֵיזֶה עִנְיָן פְּרָטִי, וְהוּא בְּחִינַת "נְשָׁמָה", כְּמוֹ שֶׁכָּתוּב "וְנִשְׁמַת שַׁדַּי תְּבִינֵם" (איוב לב, ח), וְאָז הַמַּחְשָׁבָה מְשֻׁגֶּשֶׁת עכ"פ לְהָאָדָם עַצְמוֹ הַמְחַשֵּׁב.

  - אֲבָל "שֹׁרֶשׁ" מְקוֹר מוֹצָא כְּלָלִיּוּת כֹּחַ הַמַּחְשָׁבָה — הוּא טָמִיר וְנֶעְלָם לְגַמְרֵי, שֶׁאֵינוֹ מֻשָּׂג גַּם לְהָאָדָם עַצְמוֹ מֵאַיִן תִּמָּצֵא, וְהוּא בְּחִינַת "שֹׁרֶשׁ נִשְׁמָתוֹ":

- וְזֹאת הַבְּחִינָה הַנֶּעְלָמָה, הִיא בְּחִינַת צֵרוּפֵי הָאוֹתִיּוֹת שֶׁל הַתֵּבָה, שֶׁהוּא שֹׁרֶשׁ נְשָׁמַת הָאוֹתִיּוֹת, וְכֹחַ רוּחָנִיּוּתֵיהֶם בְּשָׁרְשָׁם הָעֶלְיוֹן.

- וַאֲמִתַּת מַהוּת סִדְרֵי צֵרוּפָם בְּשָׁרְשָׁם הָעֶלְיוֹן, אֵינוֹ מֻשָּׂג לָנוּ עַתָּה

  - אַחַר שֶׁאֵין אֲנַחְנוּ מַשִּׂיגִים עַתָּה בְּחִינַת שֹׁרֶשׁ הַנְּשָׁמָה.

  - וְאַחַר הַתְּחִיָּה נִתְבּוֹנֵן בִּינָה בְּסוֹד סִדְרֵי צֵרוּפֵי הָאוֹתִיּוֹת בְּשָׁרְשָׁם קְדֻשָּׁתָם.

  - וְהוּא שֶׁאָמְרוּ בַּזֹּהַר בְּהַעֲלוֹתְךָ קנ"ב א, "אוֹרַיְתָא כו' וּלְעָלְמָא דְאָתֵי זְמִינִין לְאִסְתַּכְּלָא בְּנִשְׁמָתָא לְנִשְׁמָתָא דְאוֹרַיְתָא":

- וְהוּא בְּחִינַת שֹׁרֶשׁ נִשְׁמוֹת כְּלַל יִשְׂרָאֵל יַחַד, מַלְכוּת דַּאֲצִילוּת, לָזֹאת נִקְרֵאת "כְּנֶסֶת יִשְׂרָאֵל" (הגהה ל"ח):

הגהה ל"ח

- וְנִקְרֵאת בַּתּוֹרָה הַקְּדוֹשָׁה (במדבר טז, כב), אֵל אֱלֹהֵי הָרוּחוֹת לְכָל בָּשָׂר".

---

simultaneously exist in this world (as we see from the previous points made in respect of Chanoch and Eliyahu).
416 See end of G4:28.
417 I.e., of Chaya.
418 Zohar III Behaalotcha 152a.
419 I.e., the lowest level of the world of Atzilut – a world which corresponds to Chochma and Chaya.
420 **R. Chaim adds Note 38 here.** This note is brought at the end of this chapter and is entitled "Knesset Yisrael is the mother, and God is the father of souls."
421 Bamidbar 16:22.

- Refer to the Zohar[422] which comments on this verse: This is the place where all the souls [of the world are bound] – they ascend to there and come from there.
- Chazal expound the verses relating to mother and father, that the mother relates to Knesset Yisrael.[423]
  - Refer to Zohar
    - ["Your father and and your mother will rejoice . . .": "Your father" Above "will rejoice"; "and your mother," this is Knesset Yisrael.][424]
    - ["Listen, my child, to the discipline of your father, and do not forsake the teaching of your mother": "Listen, my child, to the discipline of your father," this is God; "and do not forsake the teaching of your mother," this is Knesset Yisrael.][425]
    - ["Honor your father and your mother": "your father," this is God; "and your mother," this is the Shechina.][426]
    - [With this feminine one, all of the lower realms are united and suckle from it.][427]
    - ["God spoke to Avram – Go for yourself, from your land, from your birthplace and from the house of your father . . .": "the house of," this is the Shechina; "your father," this is God, for he had no father except for God, and he had no mother except for Knesset Yisrael.][428]
  - Refer to Etz Chaim and Pri Etz Chaim.[429]

---

422 Zohar III Korach 176b.
423 Berachot 35b, which also highlights that God is the *Father*.
424 Zohar III Bamidbar 119a and Zohar III Pinchas 240b both quoting Mishlei 23:25.
425 Zohar III Pinchas 213a quoting Mishlei 1:8.
426 Zohar Raya Mehemna III 277b quoting Shemot 20:12. See the connection to Shechina below.
427 Zohar Idra Zuta III Haazinu 296a with "this feminine one" being a reference to Knesset Yisrael.
428 Zohar Chadash II Megillat Rut 25b quoting Bereishit 12:1. Note that the expression "house" is synonymous with "wife" (as per Mishna Yoma 1:1) and therefore the Shechina is synonymous with Knesset Yisrael.
429 Etz Chaim Shaar 11, Shaar HaMelachim beginning Chap. 6 (see V2:14, p. 676):
  - Know that the entire world is managed through Zeer Anpin and Nukva, and that just as they are called the children of Abba/Father and Imma/Mother, we [the souls of Israel] are also called children of Zeer Anpin and Nukva [where Nukva is synonymous with Knesset Yisrael and Shechina] which is

- עַיֵּן זֹהַר קֹרַח קע"ו ב' "וַיֹּאמְרוּ אֶל אֱלֹהֵי הָרוּחוֹת" כוּ', דְּאִיהוּ אֲתָר דְּנִשְׁמָתִין וְכוּ', תַּמָּן סַלְקִין וּמִתַּמָּן אַתְיָן:
- וְרַבּוֹתֵינוּ זִכְרוֹנָם לִבְרָכָה (ברכות לה, ב) דָּרְשׁוּ "אָבִיו וְאִמּוֹ" כוּ' אִמּוֹ זוֹ כְּנֶסֶת יִשְׂרָאֵל.
  - וְעַיֵּן זֹהַר
    - בַּמִּדְבָּר קי"ט א', וּבְפָרָשַׁת פִּנְחָס ר"מ ע"ב
    - וּבְרֵישׁ פָּרָשַׁת פִּנְחָס
    - וּבְרַעְיָא מְהֵימְנָא תֵּצֵא רע"ז ב'
    - וּבְסוֹף הָאִדְרָא זוּטָא רצ"ו א'
    - וּבְזֹהַר חָדָשׁ רוּת כ"ה ב'.
- וְעַיֵּן בְּעֵץ חַיִּים שַׁעַר הַמְּלָכִים רֵישׁ פֶּרֶק ז', וּבִפְרִי עֵץ חַיִּים שַׁעַר עוֹלָם הָעֲשִׂיָּה פֶּרֶק ב', וּבְשַׁעַר הַקְּרִיאַת שְׁמַע פֶּרֶק ה', וּבְשַׁעַר הָעֲמִידָה סוֹף פֶּרֶק ט"ז:

---

the secret of "you are children of YHVH, your Elokim" [Devarim 14:1] . . . [See p. 233, fn. 399, for general details about the concept of the Partzufim.]
Pri Etz Chaim Shaar Olam HaAsiyah, Chap. 2:
- [In explaining the thoughts and intentions one should have when reciting the parts of the morning prayer service which relate to the world of Asiyah, i.e., the section from Berachot until the end of the Korbanot . . .] However, the secret of the [paragraph we recite beginning with] "What/Mah are we? What/Mah is our life?" The meaning is: That the word "*Mah*/What" relates to *Malchut*/Kingship, and the meaning of the "*are we*" relates to *Israel* which derives from the characteristic of Malchut. "What/Mah is our life?" [means that] all of the souls [of Israel] relate to it [i.e., to Mah/Malchut] . . . [The Malchut referred to here is the Nukva of Zeer Anpin/Shechina/Knesset Yisrael. It is the source of all the souls of Israel. See comments on Mi and Mah on p. 264, fn. 477].

Pri Etz Chaim Shaar Kriat Shema, Chap. 5:
- Know that Zeer Anpin and Nukva are the children of Abba and Imma, and we "the children of Adam also the children of man" [Tehillim 49:3] who dwell in this world, are called "children of YHVH, your Elokim" [Devarim 14:1] which are [i.e., children of] Zeer Anpin and Nukva . . . .
- [The following is taken from a later section of this chapter which relates to a point touched on in this note:] . . . this is like that which Chazal say [Taanit 5a] that God took an oath that He will not enter into Jerusalem of the Supernal Realms until He enters into Jerusalem of the lower realms – for there are two Jerusalems – they are the secret of *Mother* and *Malchut*.

- This is the concept of the verse "[the House of Israel] who are borne [by Me] from birth."[430]
  - Refer to Pri Etz Chaim.[431]
  - Therefore, the collective of Israel together are called "limbs of the Shechina." Refer to Zohar.[432]
- This is the concept of "Go and call out in the ears of *Jerusalem* [saying, Thus says God]: I recall for you [the kindness of your youth] . . . to follow Me in the wilderness. . . ."[433]
  - This verse refers to the collective of Israel as "Jerusalem"
    - as it was the place of gathering (i.e., Kenessia) of all of Israel
    - when they went up to see the 'face of their Master, God'[434] on the Foot Festivals
    - and it is from there that the collective of Israel received a bestowal of Torah, holiness and fear
    - for each individual according to the Root of his Neshama within Knesset Yisrael.
  - Therefore, Jerusalem of the Supernal Realms is called "the love of your nuptial/Kelulotayich,"[435] meaning *incorporating all/Klilut*.[436]
- This is the concept of *Shechina*, wherever it is mentioned.
  - The simple meaning of Shechina is a fixed dwelling place
    - as per: From the day God created His Universe, He desired that He should have a dwelling place in the lower worlds [i.e., in this world][437]

Pri Etz Chaim Shaar HaAmidah, end of Chap. 16:
- . . . for we [the souls of Israel] are the children of *Malchut* [Nukva of Zeer Anpin/Shechina/Knesset Yisrael] . . . .

430 Yishayahu 46:3, i.e., that the individual souls of Israel are given birth to by their *mother*, Knesset Yisrael, and God is the father.

431 Pri Etz Chaim Shaar Rosh Chodesh, Chap. 3:
- [In explaining the sections of the Blessing of the Moon, an explanation is given for the section "and He directed the moon to renew itself as a crown of glory to those who are borne (by Him) from birth"] . . . "those who are borne [by Him] from *Baten*/birth," these are [the souls of] Israel, as they all derive from her *Baten*/womb [referring to Malchut, which is the recipient, the Nukva of Zeer Anpin]. . . .

432 Zohar III Pinchas 231b:
- . . . and then all the limbs, which are Israel . . . for they [Israel] are *the limbs of the Shechina* as it says "God's candle is man's soul" [Mishlei 20:27, meaning that man's soul is from God's candle] which is the holy Shechina . . . .

Zohar Raya Mehemna III Pinchas beginning of 238b:
- . . . [the] Raya Mehemna said "Shushan Eidut" [Tehillim 60:1], this is the

- וְהוּא עִנְיַן הַכָּתוּב (ישעיה מו, ג) "הָעֲמֻסִים מִנִּי בֶטֶן" וְגוֹ'.
  - וְעַיֵּן בִּפְרִי עֵץ חַיִּים שַׁעַר רֵ"ח פֶּרֶק ג'.
  - וְלָכֵן כְּלַל יִשְׂרָאֵל יַחַד נִקְרָאִין אֵיבָרִין דִּשְׁכִינְתָּא, עַיֵּן זֹהַר פִּנְחָס רל"א ב', וְשָׁם רל"ח רֵישׁ ע"ב, ורנ"ב סוֹף ע"ב:
- וְזֶהוּ עִנְיַן הַכָּתוּב (ירמיה ב, ב) הָלוֹךְ וְקָרָאתָ בְאָזְנֵי יְרוּשָׁלַיִם כו', זָכַרְתִּי לָךְ כו', לֶכְתֵּךְ אַחֲרַי בַּמִּדְבָּר" כו'.
  - כִּנָּה הַכָּתוּב כְּלַל יִשְׂרָאֵל בְּשֵׁם "יְרוּשָׁלַיִם".
    - כִּי הִיא הָיְתָה כְּנֶסֶת כְּלַל יִשְׂרָאֵל
    - בַּעֲלוֹתָם לֵירָאוֹת פְּנֵי הָאָדוֹן ה' בָּרֶגֶל.
    - וְשָׁם קִבְּלוּ כְּלַל יִשְׂרָאֵל שֶׁפַע תּוֹרָה קְדֻשָּׁה וְיִרְאָה
    - כָּל אֶחָד לְפִי שֹׁרֶשׁ אֲחִיזַת נִשְׁמָתוֹ מִכְּנֶסֶת יִשְׂרָאֵל.
- וְלָזֶה נִקְרֵאת "יְרוּשָׁלַיִם" שֶׁל מַעְלָה", זֶה שֶׁכָּתוּב "אַהֲבַת כְּלוּלֹתָיִךְ", רָצָה לוֹמַר כְּלִילוּת:
- וְזֶהוּ עִנְיַן "שְׁכִינָה" הַנִּזְכָּר בְּכָל מָקוֹם.
  - פִּי' הַפָּשׁוּט שֶׁל "שְׁכִינָה" הַיְנוּ קְבִיעוּת דִּירָה
    - כְּמַאֲמָרָם זִכְרוֹנָם לִבְרָכָה (בְּרֵאשִׁית רַבָּה פָּרָשָׁה ד', וּבְתַנְחוּמָא בְּחֻקֹּתַי), מִיּוֹם שֶׁבָּרָא הַקָּדוֹשׁ בָּרוּךְ הוּא עוֹלָמוֹ, נִתְאַוָּה שֶׁיְּהֵא לוֹ דִּירָה בַּתַּחְתּוֹנִים.

Eidut/testimony of the Shechina which is [called] "Shushan Eidut," for it is testimony which stands over us and testifies for us before The King and the holy supernal levels with it . . . [the] Raya Mehemna said [it is called "Shushan Eidut"] as [the Shechina] testifies for Israel that they are its limbs and it is a Neshama for them . . . .

Zohar III Pinchas end of 252b:

- . . . [the Raya Mehemna said] arise, the holy light [referring to R. Shimon bar Yochai], you and your son Elazar . . . to prepare a gift for The King and to sacrifice all the limbs, which are Israel, that they should be sacrifices to God. These are those which are called Neshama [i.e., the Neshamot of Israel], they are [sacrificed/drawn close] to the *limbs of the holy Shechina* . . . .

433 Yirmiyahu 2:2.
434 Shemot 34:23.
435 Yirmiyahu 2:2, where Kelulotayich is like Kalah/bride.
436 Where Klilut is a play on words of Kelulotayich.
437 Midrash Tanchuma (Warsaw), Bechukotai 3 and Naso 16. (The reference to Bereishit Rabba in the Hebrew text was not found.)

- and the principal fixed dwelling for God was in Jerusalem.
- It is the revelation of His uncloaked Holiness
  - as per Chazal whose statements require study:[438] As people say – When in [my own city] my name [is enough and there is no need to be cloaked in order to be honored]; when in a city not [my own, I must rely on] my clothing [for honor].

18. METHODOLOGY FOR ADVANCED PRAYER

- After [a person] has become accustomed to his prayer by interconnecting the three levels of Nefesh, Ruach, and Neshama that are within the generality of his soul
  - through [focusing on] the letters, vowels, and accents of each word as explained above in G2:16
  - he should then exert himself to focus his thoughts and intentions in purity
    - to subsequently connect the three levels of Nefesh, Ruach, and Neshama with the *soul of the soul*, as mentioned above[439]
    - which is the Root of his Neshama (Note 39) [440]
    - by [reflecting on] the letter combinations of each word as they are in their holy supernal root.
- When he is connected to this level, he is then able to consider himself as if not existing in this world at all
  - and he will inevitably become absolutely nullified in his own eyes.
- For this level is above the current attainable level of man, as I wrote above,[441] whereby he includes himself in the root of his soul which is within the supernal root of the collective of all the souls of Israel together.[442]
- Therefore, the Men of the Great Assembly instituted the recitation of the verse "*Adonay* open up my lips [to enable my mouth to say your praise]"[443] to precede the Amidah prayer
  - as for one who merits to attain this level during prayer
  - the thought of this connection can be paralyzing and [render him as] 'a dumb person who cannot open his mouth'[444]
  - were it not that God opens his lips to speak words of prayer before Him

---

438 Shabbat 145b, as per Rashi.
439 G2:17.
440 **R. Chaim adds Note 39 here.** This note is brought at the end of this chapter and is entitled "Tachanun: Focus on ceasing to be after soul connection of prayer."

- וְעִקַּר קְבִיעַת דִּירָתוֹ יִתְבָּרַךְ שְׁמוֹ הָיָה בִּירוּשָׁלַיִם
- הִתְגַּלּוּת קְדֻשָּׁתוֹ בְּלִי הִתְלַבְּשׁוּת לְבוּשִׁין
- וְהוּא שֶׁאָמְרוּ זִכְרוֹנָם לִבְרָכָה (שבת קמה, ב) "דְּאָמְרֵי אִינְשֵׁי בְּמָתָא שַׁמַּאי, בְּלָא מָתָא תּוֹתְבָאי", וְשִׂיחָתָם זִכְרוֹנָם לִבְרָכָה צְרִיכָה תַּלְמוּד:

שער ב' - פרק י"ח

- וְהִנֵּה אַחַר שֶׁכְּבָר הֻרְגַּל וְסִדּוּרָהּ לוֹ תְּפִלָּתוֹ, בְּהִתְקַשְּׁרוּת הַשְּׁלֹשָׁה בְּחִינוֹת נר"ן שֶׁבִּכְלָלוּת נַפְשׁוֹ
- עַל יְדֵי הָאוֹתִיּוֹת וּנְקֻדּוֹת וּטְעָמִים שֶׁבְּכָל תֵּבָה, כְּמוֹ שֶׁנִּתְבָּאֵר לְעֵיל פֶּרֶק ט"ז
- יִתְעַצֵּם בְּטֹהַר מַחֲשַׁבְתּוֹ וְכַוָּנָתוֹ
- לְדַבֵּק אַחַר זֶה כָּל הַשְּׁלֹשָׁה בְּחִינוֹת נר"ן, בִּבְחִינַת "נִשְׁמָתָא לְנִשְׁמָתָא" הַנַּ"ל
- שֶׁהוּא "שֹׁרֶשׁ נִשְׁמָתוֹ" (הגהה ל"ט)
- עַל יְדֵי צֵרוּפֵי הָאוֹתִיּוֹת שֶׁל הַתֵּבָה בְּשֹׁרֶשׁ קְדֻשָּׁתָם הָעֶלְיוֹן:
- וּכְשֶׁיִּתְדַּבֵּק בְּזֹאת הַמַּדְרֵגָה, אָז יוּכַל לְהַחֲשֵׁב כְּאִלּוּ אֵינוֹ בָּעוֹלָם כְּלָל
- וּמִמֵּילָא יִתְבַּטֵּל בְּעֵינָיו מִכֹּל וָכֹל:
- כִּי בְּחִינָה זֹאת הִיא נַעֲלָה מִמַּדְרֵגַת הָאָדָם עַתָּה, כְּמוֹ שֶׁכָּתַבְתִּי לְעֵיל, וְיִכְלֹל עַצְמוֹ בְּשֹׁרֶשׁ נִשְׁמָתוֹ בִּכְלַל שֹׁרֶשׁ הָעֶלְיוֹן שֶׁל כְּלַל נִשְׁמוֹת יִשְׂרָאֵל יַחַד:
- לָכֵן קָבְעוּ אַנְשֵׁי כְּנֶסֶת הַגְּדוֹלָה, לוֹמַר קֹדֶם הַתְחָלַת תְּפִלַּת הָעֲמִידָה, הַפָּסוּק "אֲדֹנָי שְׂפָתַי תִּפְתָּח"
  - כִּי מִי שֶׁזּוֹכֶה לְמַדְרֵגָה זוֹ בְּעֵת הַתְּפִלָּה
  - הֲרֵי מֵהִתְקַשְּׁרוּת הַמַּחֲשָׁבָה זוֹ יוּכַל לִהְיוֹת גּוּפוֹ כְּאֶבֶן דּוּמֵם, וּכְאִלֵּם לֹא יִפְתַּח פִּיו
  - רַק שֶׁהוּא יִתְבָּרַךְ יִפְתַּח שְׂפָתָיו לְדַבֵּר לְפָנָיו תֵּבוֹת הַתְּפִלָּה.

---

441 G2:17.

442 Although the level is currently unattainable, the mindful aspiration to connect one's Nefesh, Ruach, and Neshama to it brings us as close as possible to it and therefore to the currently highest attainable level of prayer.

443 Tehillim 51:17.

444 Tehillim 38:14.

- and therefore [this verse] specifically states [God's] name – "ADNY"
- which is the secret of Knesset Yisrael, as mentioned above.[445]
- Refer to Pri Etz Chaim[446] in relation to the recitation of this verse before prayer and about which Chazal refer to it as "a long [i.e., an extension to] prayer."[447]

• This is what Chazal refer to[448] when saying that one who prays must focus his heart upwards,[449] in line with the explanation of R. Yona there.[450]

• Similarly, the original Chassidim would spend an hour [in preparation before prayer] in order to concentrate their hearts on the "Makom"[451] [i.e., on God] as is now explained. (Note 40)[452]

Rabbi Chaim's Notes:
Note 39 – Tachanun: Focus on ceasing to be after soul connection of prayer

• Therefore, it was instituted that immediately after the Amidah, a person should [have in mind to] totally give up his Nefesh, Ruach, and Neshama [as if to put them and therefore himself] to death when reciting the verse "To you God, I raise my soul"[453]
- to raise them with the Nefesh, Ruach, and Neshama of [each of] the three worlds [Asiyah, Yetzirah, and Beriyah], and to incorporate them all together with the [level] of *Malchut of Atzilut*,[454] as per Pri Etz Chaim.[455]

• This is the main principle related to all instances of *falling on one's face* [in supplication] as mentioned in the Torah.
- As per Zohar, as mentioned above:[456] Come and see, Moshe and Aharon gave themselves up to die – for what? As it is written: "They

---

445 In G2:17, R. Chaim states that Knesset Yisrael is the source of all souls and is the Malchut of Atzilut. God's name ADNY relates to the ultimate *Master*, i.e., King, and therefore to Malchut.

A deeper insight may be gained by reviewing G1:20:N18 above and bearing in mind the additional point that the soul of Adam (and therefore David) incorporated all the souls of Israel.

446 Pri Etz Chaim Shaar Kriat Shema, Olam HaBeriyah, end of Chap. 29:
  • ... it therefore transpires that the sanctuary of holy of holies of Beriyah, which is the meaning of "Adonay open up my lips," is like an extension to prayer, because Malchut of Atzilut [also known as Knesset Yisrael as per G2:17] which is called *prayer* [i.e., the Amidah] is extended and increased by being attached to the sanctuary of holy of holies of Beriyah and transforming it all into the level of Atzilut. This is the meaning of the comparison to *a long prayer*.

○ וְלָכֵן אָמַר שֵׁם "אֲ—דֹ—נָ—י" דַּוְקָא
○ שֶׁהוּא סוֹד "כְּנֶסֶת יִשְׂרָאֵל" הַנַּ"ל.
○ וְעַיֵּן בִּפְרִי עֵץ חַיִּים סוֹף שַׁעַר הַבְּרִיאָה, בְּעִנְיַן זֶה הַפָּסוּק קֹדֶם הַתְּפִלָּה, שֶׁאָמְרוּ רַבּוֹתֵינוּ זִכְרוֹנָם לִבְרָכָה (ברכות ה, ב) עָלָיו שֶׁהוּא כִּתְפִלָּה אֲרִיכְתָּא:

• וְזֶהוּ שֶׁאָמְרוּ רַבּוֹתֵינוּ זִכְרוֹנָם לִבְרָכָה (יבמות קה, ב) "הַמִּתְפַּלֵּל צָרִיךְ שֶׁיִּתֵּן לִבּוֹ לְמַעְלָה", וּכְעִנְיָן שֶׁפֵּרֵשׁ רַבֵּנוּ יוֹנָה זִכְרוֹנוֹ לִבְרָכָה שָׁם:

• וְכֵן חֲסִידִים הָרִאשׁוֹנִים שֶׁהָיוּ שׁוֹהִים שָׁעָה אַחַת וכו', כְּדֵי שֶׁיְּכַוְּנוּ אֶת לִבָּם לַמָּקוֹם, וְהוּא מְבֹאָר: (הגהה מ')

הַגָּהָה ל"ט

• וְלָכֵן תִּקְּנוּ, שֶׁתֵּכֶף אַחַר הָעֲמִידָה, יִמְסֹר נַפְשׁוֹ וְרוּחוֹ וְנִשְׁמָתוֹ לְגַמְרֵי לְמִיתָה, בְּפָסוּק (תהלים כה, א) "אֵלֶיךָ ה' נַפְשִׁי אֶשָּׂא"

○ וּלְהַעֲלוֹתָם עִם הֹנ"ר שֶׁל שְׁלֹשָׁה הָעוֹלָמוֹת, וּלְכוֹלְלָם יַחַד בְּמַלְכוּת דַּאֲצִילוּת כְּמוֹ שֶׁכָּתוּב בִּפְרִי עֵץ חַיִּים סוֹף פֶּרֶק ז' מִשַּׁעַר הַתְּפִלָּה:

• וְהוּא עִקַּר כַּוָּנַת כָּל נְפִילַת אַפַּיִם הַנִּזְכָּר בַּתּוֹרָה

○ כְּמוֹ שֶׁכָּתוּב בַּזֹּהַר קֹרַח קע"ו ב' הַנַּ"ל בִּפְנִים, תָּא חֲזֵי מֹשֶׁה וְאַהֲרֹן מָסְרוּ

---

447 Berachot 4b.
448 Yevamot 105b.
449 I.e., to remove one's focus from this world.
450 With this statement and the following one, R. Chaim is connecting back to some of his opening statements in G2:01. In those opening statements, R. Chaim also refers the reader to R. Yona (see p. 308, fn. 14, for the details). Further related comments of R. Yona's are also brought down by R. Chaim in detail in G2:14:N34.
451 Mishna Berachot 5:1, see p. 308, fn. 13.
452 **R. Chaim adds Note 40 here.** This note is brought at the end of this chapter and is entitled "Detailed focus on prayer sequence to connect to Knesset Yisrael."
453 Tehillim 25:1. This verse, together with the entire chapter is recited as the main part of the Tachanun prayer as per the formulation of Nusach HaArizal and also of Nusach Eidot HaMizrach.
454 Which is the level of the Amidah prayer, as per p. 460, fn. 446.
455 Pri Etz Chaim Shaar HaTefillah, end of Chap. 7.
456 Zohar III Korach 176b, at the beginning of R. Chaim's previous note, G2:17:N38.

fell on their faces and said: God, God of the spirits of all flesh"⁴⁵⁷ . . . and in all places, *falling on their faces* is to that place . . . "God of the spirits" is the place of the souls of the world, and all the souls leave to go there and come from there. Therefore, one must concentrate with the heart's will to be as if one has completely passed on from this world.
- As per Zohar.⁴⁵⁸
- Also refer well to and understand Pri Etz Chaim.⁴⁵⁹
- Refer to Likutei Torah.⁴⁶⁰

Note 40 – Detailed focus on prayer sequence to connect to Knesset Yisrael

- Therefore, the general sequence of the order of the [morning] prayers is split into four, corresponding to the four levels of Nefesh, Ruach, Neshama, and the Root of the Neshama, i.e.:
  - Sacrifices correspond to the level of Nefesh and the world of the Nefesh [is] Asiyah, as [sacrifices] are brought [in response to] sins of the Nefesh as in "the *Nefesh* which sins . . . He shall bring [his guilt offering]."⁴⁶¹

---

457 Bamidbar 16:22.
458 Zohar III Bamidbar 120b–121a:
- Come and see. Once a person has prayed in this way – in action and in speech, and has tied a unifying knot, it results in the Supernal and Lower Realms being blessed through him. Then following completion of the Amidah prayer a person must view himself as if he has passed on from this world . . . for he has already confessed his sins and prayed over them, now he needs to . . . and fall [on his face] and say to Him: "To You God I raise my soul" . . . now that I have tied the unity, performed my actions and speech as appropriate and confessed my sins, I hand over my soul to You with certainty . . . For the secret of this matter is that there are sins which are not forgiven until a person has departed from this world . . . [and therefore] he gives himself up for certain death . . . as if one who has certainly passed on from this world. This rectification requires intention of the heart, and then God has mercy on him and atones his sins.

Zohar III VaEtchanan 260a:
- After he completes his prayer [the Amidah], with will, before his Master, it has been established that he must hand over his Nefesh with the will of his heart . . .

459 Pri Etz Chaim Shaar Nefilat Apayim, all of Chap. 2:
- [R. Chaim references the whole of Chap. 2 from which the following is summarized: The Arizal explains that the process of prayer is for us to initiate a bestowal from God by first elevating ourselves through the levels of prayer in order to receive this bestowal. The purpose of the Tachanun prayer and of *falling on one's face* is to descend to the lowest depths – into the Kelipot – a place of death, and as if risking death, and to attempt to utilize

גָּרְמַיְהוּ לְמִיתָה, בְּמָה, בְּגִין דִּכְתִיב "וַיִּפְּלוּ עַל פְּנֵיהֶם וַיֹּאמְרוּ אֵל אֱלֹהֵי הָרוּחוֹת" כו', וּבְכָל אֲתַר נְפִילַת אַנְפִּין לְהַהוּא אֲתַר הֲוֵי כו', "אֱלֹהֵי הָרוּחוֹת", דְּאִיהוּ אֲתַר דְּנִשְׁמָתִין דְּעָלְמָא, וְכָל נִשְׁמָתִין תַּמָּן סַלְקִין וּמִתַּמָּן אַתְיָן. וְלָכֵן צָרִיךְ לְכַוֵּן בִּרְעוּתָא דְלִבָּא כְּאִלּוּ נִפְטָר מִן הָעוֹלָם לְגַמְרֵי

○ כְּמוֹ שֶׁכָּתוּב בַּזֹּהַר סוֹף פָּרָשַׁת בַּמִּדְבָּר (ק"כ סוֹף ע"ב), וּבְרֵישׁ פָּרָשַׁת וָאֶתְחַנָּן (ר"ס סוֹף ע"א).

○ וְעַיֵּן הֵיטֵב בִּפְרִי עֵץ חַיִּים בְּכָל פֶּרֶק ב' מִשַּׁעַר נְפִילַת אַפַּיִם, וְהָבֵן. וְעַיֵּן עוֹד שָׁם בְּפֶרֶק ג' וּפֶרֶק ד'

○ וּבְלִקּוּטֵי תּוֹרָה פָּרָשַׁת שְׁלַח, עַיֵּן שָׁם:

הַגָּהָה מ'

• וְלָכֵן כְּלָל סֵדֶר הַתְּפִלָּה נֶחְלָק לְאַרְבָּעָה, שֶׁהֵן הָאַרְבָּעָה בְּחִינוֹת, נַרְ"נ וְשֹׁרֶשׁ הַנְּשָׁמָה.

○ הַקָּרְבָּנוֹת — הֵם נֶגֶד בְּחִינַת הַנֶּפֶשׁ, וְעוֹלָם הַנֶּפֶשׁ — עֲשִׂיָּה, כִּי הֵם בָּאִים

---

the additional bestowal from the prayer sequence just completed to effect a separation of residual good from the depths of the Kelipot.]

Pri Etz Chaim Shaar Nefilat Apayim, Chap. 3:
- ... for the intention of the Nefesh descending there [during the Tachanum prayer to the place of death, the Kelipot] is to grasp onto and extract a level of Mayim Nukvim which fell there in the Kelipot of all of the worlds [i.e., the self aroused inspiration to completely connect to God which by falling was prevented from connecting], and to raise them up to the level of Malchut of the world level of Atzilut [i.e., to reconnect] . . . .

Pri Etz Chaim Shaar Nefilat Apayim, Chap. 4:
- Prayer incorporates two types of handing oneself over to death. Our handing over of ourselves to sanctify God's Name in the recitation of the Shema and our handing over of ourselves into [the place of] death [during the Tachanun prayer] when *falling on our faces*, as is known.

460 Likutei Torah Shelach:
- ... with the secret of giving up one's life when we say, "To You God I raise my soul. My God . . ." when we fall on our faces [during the Tachanun prayer] . . . By the way, we will explain the secret of *falling on our faces* – for we fall to the bottom, the secret of Asiyah [after] having been at Atzilut during the Amidah . . . and when he says, "To You God I raise my soul," he binds Asiyah with Yetzirah and Yetzirah with Beriyah . . . and then afterwards with the secret of Malchut of Atzilut. . . .

461 Vayikra 5:1–6.

- Pesukei DeZimra correspond to the world of Ruach, the world of the singing angels.[462]
- Kriat Shema and its associated blessings correspond to the chambers of Beriyah, which as is known is the world of the Neshamot.[463]
* [The sequence of a person's focus through the morning prayer service is:]
  - From the recitation of the passages of the Korbanot up until [but not including] Baruch She-amar – his intention should be on elevating all of the level of the Nefashot of the world of Asiyah, which is the inner essence of the world of Asiyah,[464] so that they be incorporated in [the level] of Ruchot of Yetzirah,[465] and to also include his own Nefesh with them to be bound up with his Ruach.
  - From Baruch She-amar up until [but not including] the blessings of Kriat Shema, [his intention should be on] incorporating the levels of Nefashot of Asiyah and also of Ruchot of Yetzirah – together with his own Nefesh and Ruach, with the level of the Neshamot of Beriyah.[466]
  - From the blessings of Kriat Shema until [but not including] the Amidah, [his intention should be on] incorporating and elevating all of [the levels of] Nefesh of Asiyah, Ruach of Yetzirah, and Neshama of Beriyah – together with his own Nefesh, Ruach, and Neshama, so that they be incorporated together in [the level of] the Root of the Neshama, and the source of the collective souls of Israel.
  - Refer to a small part of all this in the Pri Etz Chaim[467] and also to what the Arizal hints there in that which he writes: ". . . and through this the Shechina [i.e., Knesset Yisrael] incorporates all."
  - This is the meaning of what the Arizal writes[468] that before prayer [a person] should accept upon himself the commandment "and you shall love your fellow [as yourself]."[469]

END OF THE SECOND GATEWAY

---

462 "Zimra" means "song." Song is expressed with breath which is Ruach.

463 R. Chaim does not specifically mention but implies that the Amidah corresponds to the level of the Root of the Neshama, i.e., to Chaya. See p. 460, fn. 446, where prayer is defined as being on the level of Malchut of Atzilut where Atzilut corresponds to Chaya.

464 I.e., reflecting physical action as in the physical offering of the sacrifices.

465 Where Ruach relates to speech as in Baruch *She-amar* (Blessed be He who *spoke*) which commences Pesukei DeZimra.

466 Where Neshama relates to intellectual thought as in the intellectual focus on God when reciting Kriat Shema.

467 Pri Etz Chaim Shaar HaTefillah, Chap. 1. The reference to Chap. 1 is a misprint. The sequence of the ascension of levels as one progresses through

עַל חֶטְאֵי בְּחִינַת הַנֶּפֶשׁ, כְּמוֹ שֶׁכָּתוּב "וְנֶפֶשׁ כִּי תֶחֱטָא כו', וְהֵבִיא כו'" (ויקרא ה, א—ו) וכו'.

○ וּפְסוּקֵי דְזִמְרָה — נֶגֶד עוֹלָם הָרוּחַ — עוֹלָם הַמַּלְאָכִים הַמְשׁוֹרְרִים.

○ וּקְרִיאַת שְׁמַע וּבִרְכוֹתֶיהָ — נֶגֶד הֵיכָלִין דִּבְרִיאָה, כַּיָּדוּעַ עוֹלָם הַנְּשָׁמוֹת:

• [סדר הכוונה בתפילה]

○ וּבַאֲמִירַת פָּרָשִׁיּוֹת הַקָּרְבָּנוֹת עַד בָּרוּךְ שֶׁאָמַר, יְכַוֵּן לְהַעֲלוֹת כָּל בְּחִינַת הַנְּפָשׁוֹת דַּעֲשִׂיָּה, שֶׁהוּא הַפְּנִימִיּוּת דַּעֲשִׂיָּה, לְכָלְלָם בְּרוּחוֹת דִּיצִירָה, וְיִכְלֹל גַּם נַפְשׁוֹ עִמָּהֶם לְקָשְׁרָם בְּרוּחוֹ.

○ וּמִבָּרוּךְ שֶׁאָמַר עַד בִּרְכוֹת קְרִיאַת שְׁמַע, יִכְלֹל כָּל הַנַּפְשִׁין דַּעֲשִׂיָּה וְהָרוּחִין דִּיצִירָה, וְגַם בְּחִינַת נַפְשׁוֹ וְרוּחוֹ בְּנִשְׁמָתִין דִּבְרִיאָה.

○ וּמִבִּרְכוֹת קְרִיאַת שְׁמַע עַד הָעֲמִידָה, יִכְלֹל וְיַעֲלֶה כָּל הַנֶּפֶשׁ רוּחַ נְשָׁמָה דִּבְרִיאָה, יְצִירָה, עֲשִׂיָּה, וְנֶפֶשׁ רוּחַ נְשָׁמָה שֶׁלּוֹ עִמָּהֶם, לְכוֹלְלָם יַחַד בְּשֹׁרֶשׁ הַנְּשָׁמָה וְשֹׁרֶשׁ הַכְּנֵסִיָּה שֶׁל כְּלַל נִשְׁמוֹת יִשְׂרָאֵל יָחַד.

○ וְעִנְיַן קְצָת מִכָּל זֶה בִּפְרִי עֵץ חַיִּים פֶּרֶק א' מִשַּׁעַר הַתְּפִלָּה. וְזֶה שֶׁרָמְזוּ שָׁם הָאֲרִיזַ"ל, בַּמֶּה שֶׁכָּתַב וְעַל יְדֵי כָּךְ נִכְלֶלֶת הַשְּׁכִינָה מִכֻּלָּם כו', עַיֵּן שָׁם.

○ וְזֶה שֶׁכָּתַב הָאֲרִיזַ"ל, לְקַבֵּל עַל עַצְמוֹ קֹדֶם תְּפִלָּה מִצְוַת וְאָהַבְתָּ לְרֵעֲךָ (ויקרא יט, יח):

סָלִיק שַׁעַר ב'

---

the sections of prayer is described in later chapters of Pri Etz Chaim Shaar HaTefillah in great detail. See the quotations from Pri Etz Chaim Shaar HaTefillah brought in the footnotes to G2:14:N33.

468 Pri Etz Chaim Shaar Olam HaAsiyah, at the end of Chap. 1:
- ... before prayer commencement at all, and principally of the morning prayer, he needs to accept upon himself the commandment of "and you shall love your fellow [Jew] as yourself" [Vayikra 19:18], and he should focus on loving each Jew as himself, as through this his prayer will ascend incorporating all of Israel, and it is enabled to ascend, be productive, and succeed. ...

469 To therefore accept that the purpose of the prayer sequence is to connect with the collective soul of Israel. R. Chaim provides us with a description of how to build up our prayer focus through the sequence of prayer such that by the time we reach the Amidah we are focused on the needs of the collective soul of Israel and not our own personal needs. It should be noted that in many prayer books there is a *Leshem Yichud* which is recited before Baruch She-amar to act as a reminder towards the beginning of the prayer sequence that the ultimate prayer focus should be for all of Israel.

THIRD GATEWAY

1. MAKOM'S SIMPLE MEANING IS CAUSING ALL TO CONSTANTLY BE

- With this reference here [to God] as "*Makom*"[/Place][1]
  - and similarly in Avot: "and when you pray, don't pray by rote, but rather by seeking mercy and supplication before the *Makom* Blessed be He"[2]
  - Chazal hint at a very great concept with this word "Makom"
  - and this concept requires explanation to understand the depth of Chazal's intention in using it and to explain the quotations which hint to it.
- Chazal have already stated in Avot that "all of [Chazal's] words are like burning coals,"[3] meaning that
  - just as with a hot coal
    - where even though only a small spark of fire is visible within it
    - if you invest effort to change it and blow on it
    - the more that you blow on it, the spark of fire flares up and spreads within it until it becomes a burning coal
    - and you can benefit from it to use its light and be warmed when near it
    - but this is only when near it and not when touching it
    - as once it becomes a burning coal, care is required that you are not burned by it.
  - Similarly, this analogy is applied to all the words of our Sages
    - where even if their words appear to be brief and simple
    - they, nevertheless, have 'explosive potential'[4]
    - that the more a person engages with them and delves into their detail
    - his eyes will be enlightened from the great light of their flame

---

1 This refers to the closing statement of the previous chapter, G2:18, where the original Chassidim would spend an hour preparing for prayer in order to concentrate their hearts on the "Makom."
2 Mishna Avot 2:13.
3 Mishna Avot 2:10, i.e., shortly before the Mishna relating to Makom.

שַׁעַר ג'

שער ג' - פרק א'

- וּמַה שֶּׁאָמְרוּ כָּאן "לַמָּקוֹם".
- וְכֵן בְּאָבוֹת (ב, יג) אָמְרוּ "וּכְשֶׁאַתָּה מִתְפַּלֵּל אַל תַּעַשׂ תְּפִלָּתְךָ קֶבַע, אֶלָּא רַחֲמִים וְתַחֲנוּנִים לִפְנֵי הַמָּקוֹם בָּרוּךְ הוּא".
- רָמְזוּ זִכְרוֹנָם לִבְרָכָה בְּתֵיבַת 'מָקוֹם' לְעִנְיָן גָּדוֹל.
- וְהָעִנְיָן צָרִיךְ בֵּאוּר, לְהָבִין עֹמֶק כַּוָּנָתָם לְבָרְכָם לִבְרָכָה בָּזֶה, וּלְמִסְבַּר קְרָאֵי הָרוֹמְזִים עַל זֶה:

- וּכְבָר אָמְרוּ זִכְרוֹנָם לִבְרָכָה בְּאָבוֹת (ב, י), שֶׁ"כָּל דִּבְרֵיהֶם כְּגַחֲלֵי אֵשׁ"
  - שֶׁכְּמוֹ הַגַּחֶלֶת
  - שֶׁאַף שֶׁלֹּא נִרְאָה בָּהּ רַק 'נִצּוֹץ' אֵשׁ
  - אִם תָּשִׂים כֹּחֲךָ בָּהּ לְהָפְכָהּ וְלַנַּפְחָהּ
  - כָּל שֶׁתִּתְנַפְּחָה יוֹתֵר, תִּתְלַהֵב וְתִתְפַּשֵּׁט בָּהּ הַנִּצּוֹץ, עַד שֶׁתֵּעָשֶׂה כֻּלָּהּ לוֹחֶשֶׁת
  - וְתוּכַל לֵיהָנוֹת מִמֶּנָּה לְהִשְׁתַּמֵּשׁ לְאוֹרָהּ וּלְהִתְחַמֵּם נֶגְדָּהּ
  - אֲבָל רַק נֶגְדָּהּ, וְלֹא לְאָחֳזָהּ
  - שֶׁכֵּיוָן שֶׁנַּעֲשֵׂית לוֹחֶשֶׁת צָרִיךְ זְהִירוּת שֶׁלֹּא תִּכְוֶה בָּהּ.
- כֵּן בְּדִמְיוֹן זֶה נִמְשְׁלוּ כָּל דִּבְרֵי חֲכָמִים
  - שֶׁאַף שֶׁנִּרְאִים דְּבָרִים קְצָרִים וּפְשׁוּטִים
  - אֲבָל הֵם כְּפַטִּישׁ יְפוֹצְצוּ
  - שֶׁכָּל שֶׁהָאָדָם מְהַפֵּךְ וּמְסַלְסֵל וּמְדַקְדֵּק בָּהֶם
  - יָאוֹרוּ עֵינָיו מְשַׁלְהֶבֶת אוֹרָם הַגָּדוֹל

---

4   This expression "KePatish Yefotzetz," "like a hammer that shatters," is borrowed from Yirmiyahu 23:29 where the entire verse expresses the sentiment that God's words are like fire and "that they are like a hammer that shatters a rock." The Mishna quoted from Pirkei Avot therefore frames Chazal's statements as an extension of God's words.

- as he will find deep concepts within them, as per Chazal, "constantly review [all of Torah] as everything is contained within it."[5]
- However, one should be very careful with their burning coals [/the words of Chazal], not to *excessively*[6] delve into areas 'beyond one's capability of understanding'[7]
- as they say there, "and one should *warm* oneself *opposite* the light of the Sages,"[8] that is, he should not avoid investigating them at all, as doing so will prevent him from deriving any benefit whatsoever
- but he should also not approach too closely, so that he should not be burned, as mentioned above
- but just be *opposite* them as the [Mishna] concludes that "one should be careful [not to be burned] by the burning coals."

- This [principle] is also [true] here with the word "Makom," that even though its simple meaning is understood, nevertheless, if one delves into it, one will find that it incorporates and hints at a further very great concept.
- The reference to God as "Makom" is explained by Chazal:
  - "And he reached the Makom(/place)," R. Huna said in the name of R. Ami: Why is God referred to and called "Makom?" Because He is the Place of the Universe, but the Universe is not His Place.[9]
  - "And God said: Behold Makom is with Me," R. Yossi bar Chanina said . . . My Place is secondary to Me, but I am not secondary to My Place.[10]
- The simple understanding of this is that
  - just as a place [i.e., space,] *tolerates* and contains any object that is placed on[/within] it
  - similarly with this analogy, The Creator and Master of All is the True Space which *tolerates* and causes all the worlds and creations to exist [within it], such that if, God forbid, He were to remove His [Constant Creative] Power from them even momentarily – then the Space of existence and life of all the worlds would cease to exist, as per "and You *continuously* Give life to everything."[11]

---

5   Mishna Avot 5:22.
6   As R. Chaim highlights at the end of G3:03 that by *excessively* delving into these areas one is at risk of making errors which result in seriously compromising the Halacha.

There are some who seem to erroneously misinterpret this chapter as a warning to avoid the concepts contained within the Third Gateway. R. Chaim is highlighting the importance of approaching these concepts in a balanced way, and would not be presenting these concepts at all if they were not meant

□ שֶׁיִּמָּצֵא בְּתוֹכָם עִנְיָנִים עֲמֻקִים, כְּאָמְרָם זִכְרוֹנָם לִבְרָכָה (אבות ה, כב) "הֲפֹךְ בָּהּ וכו' דְּכֹלָּא בָהּ".

□ אֲבָל צָרִיךְ לְהִזָּהֵר מְאֹד בְּגַחַלְתָּן, שֶׁלֹּא לִכָּנֵס לְהִתְבּוֹנֵן וְלַחֲקֹר בִּדְבָרִים שֶׁאֵין הָרְשׁוּת נְתוּנָה לְהִתְבּוֹנֵן בָּהֶם יוֹתֵר מִדַּי

□ כְּאָמְרָם שָׁם "וֶהֱוֵי מִתְחַמֵּם כְּנֶגֶד אוּרָן שֶׁל חֲכָמִים", הַיְנוּ, שֶׁלֹּא לְהִתְרַחֵק מִלְּהִתְבּוֹנֵן כְּלָל בְּדִבְרֵיהֶם, כִּי לֹא יֶהֱנֶה מֵאוֹרָם כְּלָל

□ וְגַם לֹא יִתְקָרֵב יוֹתֵר מִדַּי, שֶׁלֹּא יִכָּוֶה כַּנַּ"ל

□ רַק מִנֶּגֶד, כְּמוֹ שֶׁסִּיֵּם אַחַר זֶה "וֶהֱוֵי זָהִיר בְּגַחַלְתָּן" וכו':

• וְהִנֵּה כָּאן בְּתֵבַת 'מָקוֹם' גַּם כֵּן, הֲגַם שֶׁפְּשׁוּטוֹ מוּבָן, אֲבָל כְּשֶׁנְּדַקְדֵּק בּוֹ נִמְצָא שֶׁכָּלְלוּ וְרָמְזוּ בָּזֶה עוֹד עִנְיָן גָּדוֹל:

• כִּי עִנְיַן מַה שֶּׁהוּא יִתְבָּרֵךְ נִקְרָא 'מָקוֹם'. פֵּרְשׁוּהוּ זִכְרוֹנָם לִבְרָכָה

○ בִּבְרֵאשִׁית רַבָּה (פס"ח) עַל פָּסוּק "וַיִּפְגַּע בַּמָּקוֹם" (בראשית כח, יא) "רַב הוּנָא בְּשֵׁם רַב אַמִי אָמַר, מִפְּנֵי מַה מְּכַנִּין שְׁמוֹ שֶׁל הַקָּדוֹשׁ בָּרוּךְ הוּא וְקוֹרְאִין אוֹתוֹ 'מָקוֹם', שֶׁהוּא מְקוֹמוֹ שֶׁל עוֹלָם וְאֵין עוֹלָמוֹ מְקוֹמוֹ".

○ וּבִשְׁמוֹת רַבָּה סוֹף פָּרָשָׁה מ"ה, וּבְתַנְחוּמָא פָּרָשַׁת תִּשָּׂא "וַיֹּאמֶר ה' הִנֵּה מָקוֹם אִתִּי" (שמות לג, כא) אָמַר רַבִּי יוֹסֵי בַּ"ר חֲנִינָא וכו', אַתְרִי טָפְלָה לִי וְאֵין אֲנִי טָפֵל לְאַתְרִי. וְכֵן אִיתָא בְּשׁוֹחֵר טוֹב תְּהִלִּים מִזְמוֹר צ':

• וּלְפִי פְּשׁוּטוֹ רָצָה לוֹמַר

○ כְּמוֹ שֶׁהַמָּקוֹם, הוּא סוֹבֵל וּמַחֲזִיק אֵיזֶה דָבָר וְחֵפֶץ הַמֻּנָּח עָלָיו

○ כֵּן בְּדִמְיוֹן זֶה הַבּוֹרֵא אָדוֹן כֹּל יִתְבָּרֵךְ שְׁמוֹ, הוּא הַמָּקוֹם הָאֲמִתִּי, הַסּוֹבֵל וּמְקַיֵּם הָעוֹלָמוֹת וְהַבְּרִיּוֹת כֻּלָּם, שֶׁאִם חַס וְשָׁלוֹם יְסַלֵּק כֹּחוֹ מֵהֶם אַף רֶגַע

---

to be studied. On the contrary, as he states at the end of G3:03, the time had come that required these ideas to be published in this way.

7   R. Chaim borrows the expression here of "Hareshut Netuna," "permission is granted," from Mishna Avot 3:15, but the meaning is not that one can delve into these ideas but is not permitted to, but rather that the depth of these ideas are beyond a human's capability of understanding.

8   Mishna Avot 2:10.

9   Bereishit Rabba Vayetze 68:9 quoting the verse from Bereishit 28:11 relating to Yaakov reaching the *Place* on his way out of Israel to travel to Charan.

10 Shemot Rabba Ki Tisa 45:6; Midrash Tanchuma Ki Tisa 16; Midrash Tehillim 90:10, all quoting Shemot 33:21.

11 Nechemia 9:6, see G1:16:N14. Also see reference to this verse in the quotation

- This is the cornerstone of the Jewish Faith as described by the Rambam at the beginning of his book.[12]
- Therefore, the Zohar refers to The Master of All as "The Soul of all souls"[13]
  - just as a soul gives life to and sustains a body
    - as per "and is it possible for a piece of meat to exist for three days [without preservative and not spoil]?"[14]
  - so too God alone gives life to all the worlds
  - as is known in many places in Tikkunei Zohar and Raya Mehemna. Refer to the beginning of the second introduction to Tikkunei Zohar.[15]
- Similarly, Chazal compare the continued existence of the entire Universe through [God's] Powers to the continued existence of the body through the powers of the soul, as per "just as the soul fills and sustains the entire body, so too God fills and sustains [the Universe]."[16]
- This is the simple meaning of the concept of God being called the *Makom/Place of the Universe*.

2. DEPTH OF MAKOM – IS AN ANALOGY – ALL IS EXCLUSIVELY GOD

- However, the deeper meaning of [referring to God] as the Makom/Place of the Universe is a very great concept.
- That which God is referred to as the *Place of the Universe*
  - is in *no way comparable* whatsoever to the concept of a place which contains any object which stands upon it
  - as the essence of the creation and continued existence of the object is that it has existence in its own right
  - whereas the place just prevents it from falling and breaking[17]
  - and similarly, this is the concept of continued existence of the body as a result of the soul

---

from the Vilna Gaon in V2:02, p. 73, fn. 73, Chap. 15, "Tzimtzum Sources," F1.2.

12 Rambam, Mishneh Torah, Hilchot Yesodei HaTorah 1:1, i.e., that everything exists as a result of God and if God is absent then nothing else can exist.
13 Zohar I Bereishit 45a.
14 Sanhedrin 91b, and therefore the body has a soul which preserves it.
15 Tikkunei Zohar Introduction 17a (within the Maamar of Patach Eliyahu):
   - Eliyahu began and said: Master of the Universe, You are One . . . You are He who produces the ten rectifications and we call them the Ten Sefirot with which you conduct the hidden and the revealed worlds, and with them you are concealed from mankind . . . He is like a soul to a body, life to a body . . .

- אַחַת, אָפֵס מְקוֹם קִיּוּם וְחִיּוּת כָּל הָעוֹלָמוֹת, וּכְמוֹ שֶׁכָּתוּב (נחמיה ט, ו) "וְאַתָּה מְחַיֶּה אֶת כֻּלָּם":
- וְהוּא פִּנַּת יְסוֹד אֱמוּנַת יִשְׂרָאֵל, כְּמוֹ שֶׁכָּתַב הָרַמְבַּ"ם זִכְרוֹנוֹ לִבְרָכָה בְּרֵישׁ סִפְרוֹ:
- וְלָכֵן קוֹרֵא בַּזּוֹהַר לְאָדוֹן כֹּל יִתְבָּרַךְ שְׁמוֹ — "נִשְׁמָתָא דְּכָל נִשְׁמָתִין"
  - כְּמוֹ שֶׁהַנְּשָׁמָה מְחַיָּה וּמְקַיֶּמֶת הַגּוּף
    - וכמ"ש (סנהדרין צ"א:) וְכִי אֶפְשָׁר לַחֲתִיכַת בָּשָׂר ג' יָמִים וכו'
  - כֵּן הוּא יִתְבָּרַךְ שְׁמוֹ הוּא לְבַדּוֹ חֵי הָעוֹלָמִים כֻּלָּם
- וְכַיָּדוּעַ בִּמְקוֹמוֹת רַבּוֹת בַּתִּקּוּנִים וְרַעְיָא מְהֵימְנָא. וְעַיֵּן בְּרֵישׁ הַקְדָּמָה שְׁנִיָּה שֶׁל הַתִּקּוּנִים, בְּמַאֲמָר פָּתַח אֵלִיָּהוּ וכו':
- וְכֵן רַבּוֹתֵינוּ זִכְרוֹנָם לִבְרָכָה דִּמּוּ קִיּוּם כָּל הָעוֹלָם עַל יְדֵי כֹּחוֹ יִתְבָּרַךְ, לְקִיּוּם הַגּוּף עַל יְדֵי כֹּחוֹת הַנְּשָׁמָה, אָמְרוּ (ברכות י) "מָה הַנְּשָׁמָה מְלֵאָה וְזָנָה אֶת כָּל הַגּוּף, אַף הַקָּדוֹשׁ בָּרוּךְ הוּא מָלֵא וְזָן" כו'.
- וְזֶהוּ פַּשְׁטוּת עִנְיָן שֶׁהוּא יִתְבָּרַךְ נִקְרָא "מְקוֹמוֹ שֶׁל עוֹלָם":

שער ג' - פרק ב'

- אָמְנָם פְּנִימִיּוּת עִנְיַן "מְקוֹמוֹ שֶׁל עוֹלָם", הוּא עִנְיָן גָּדוֹל מְאֹד:
- כִּי מַה שֶּׁכִּנּוּהוּ יִתְבָּרַךְ שְׁמוֹ "מְקוֹמוֹ שֶׁל עוֹלָם"
  - אֵין עֶרֶךְ כְּלָל לְעִנְיַן מָקוֹם הַנּוֹשֵׂא כָּל חֵפֶץ הָעוֹמֵד עָלָיו
  - שֶׁעַצְמוּת הִתְהַוּוּת וְקִיּוּם הַכְּלִי יֵשׁ לָהּ מְצִיאוּת בִּפְנֵי עַצְמָהּ
  - וְהַמָּקוֹם רַק מַצֶּלֶת אוֹתָהּ שֶׁלֹּא תִּפֹּל וְתִשָּׁבֵר
  - וְכֵן עִנְיַן חִיּוּת וְקִיּוּם הַגּוּף עַל יְדֵי הַנְּשָׁמָה

---

and when You are removed from [the Sefirot] they all become like a body without a soul . . . .

16   Berachot 10a.
17   This simple understanding of space does not fit in with current day scientific understanding where every object is understood to be bounded by its dimensions and were the dimensions removed from an object then it can no longer continue to exist. This current scientific understanding lends itself to allowing us to much more easily relate to the deeper idea of Makom as R. Chaim continues to explain.

- where the body has an independent existence of its own and does not cease to exist on the departure of the soul from it.
- Whereas, with all of the worlds, the entire essence of their continued existence each moment is only as a result of God
- and if God's Will were removed from its constant creation [of these worlds] they would become absolutely nothing (Ayin).[18]

---

18 The word "Ayin" is used to express a very deep concept. It is normally translated as "nothing" but this is not an accurate translation. We talk about Ayin in the context of the creation of Yesh from Ayin (Yesh MiAyin), where, in terms of this world, Yesh is *the physical* and Ayin really means the negative of Yesh, i.e., the *non-physical*.

So Yesh MiAyin truly means the creation of something physical from something non-physical. The non-physical is not nothing, it has substance but just not physical substance. This creation process of Yesh MiAyin is so effective that the created Yesh has no awareness of what it has been created from and therefore from the point of view of the created beings, i.e., the Yesh, they appear to exist without any connection to their original source. Therefore from their point of view Ayin appears to be and can be mistaken for being *nothing*.

The concept of Ayin is, in essence, a relative concept. We say that relative to any world level, that world level itself is Yesh and the world level preceding it is Ayin. In practical terms, the classification of the general world levels can be analogously mapped to increasing levels of abstraction in human experience. So the world of Asiyah maps to physical action, Yetzirah to speech, Beriyah to analytical thought (Binah), Atzilut to initial conceptual thought (Chochma), and Adam Kadmon to will.

In this context, it is simple for us to understand that relative to a physical action, the speech or thought which causes it, is completely abstracted and is like Ayin compared to the physical action itself, the relative Yesh. Similarly, this is true all the way through the world levels, so the initial will for something stimulates the germ of the initial concept which is analyzed and then possibly discussed and finally translated into action, where all of these preceding steps are like Ayin and completely abstracted from the steps which result from them, the Yesh.

This concept of relative Ayin is expressed very clearly in V2:02, Chap. 15, "Tzimtzum Sources," I1.1. This source describes the interface between world levels which, if viewed as being the lowest level of one world level is called Malchut and is referred to as "Ani/I am," an expression of Yesh/something relative to that world. Whereas, if viewed from the world level below it, it is called "Keter" and referred to as Ayin, an expression of nothing relative to the world below it.

Ayin has the same Hebrew letters as *Ani* but in a different sequence expressing a different perspective of the same concept. (This source actually differ-

- הַגּוּף יֵשׁ לוֹ מְצִיאוּת בִּפְנֵי עַצְמוֹ, וְאֵינוֹ מִתְבַּטֵּל מִמְּצִיאוּתוֹ גַּם בְּצֵאת הַנְּשָׁמָה מִמֶּנּוּ.
- אֲבָל הָעוֹלָמוֹת כֻּלָּם, כָּל עִקַּר הִתְהַוּוּת מְצִיאוּתָם כָּל רֶגַע, הוּא רַק מֵאִתּוֹ יִתְבָּרַךְ שְׁמוֹ
- וְאִלּוּ הָיָה מְסַלֵּק רְצוֹנוֹ יִתְבָּרַךְ מִלְּהַוּוֹת אוֹתָם כָּל רֶגַע, הָיוּ לְאַיִן וָאֶפֶס מַמָּשׁ:

entiates between three relative levels of Yesh, Ayin, and a third level called "Efes." Notice that R. Chaim actually refers here to both Ayin and Efes in his Hebrew text and that these relate to two different things as explained by this source. For the moment, however, it is instructive to view Ayin and Efes as the same thing and just refer to both of these relative levels as Ayin.)

While the concept of Ayin and Yesh is a relative concept, it is relevant to understand what exactly is Ayin and Yesh relative to our position as creations which exist in the lowest world level of the world of Asiyah.

Relative to us, this concept refers to the constant re-creation of the physical world each moment where God conceals himself and is manifest in the worlds. As such, relative to our current level, there is a specific point in a very gradual manifestation process which cascades down through a myriad of levels and sublevels, where absolute Godliness is concealed and transformed into material substance – even if only in a very subtle way.

The point at which this happens is at the interface between the world levels of Adam Kadmon and Atzilut, where the lowest level of Adam Kadmon, the level of Malchut of Adam Kadmon, becomes the level of Keter, known as Supernal Keter, relative to the general world level below it of Atzilut. This level of Supernal Keter is called Ayin and is considered to be absolute Godliness without any form of even vague material form.

In contrast, with the world level of Atzilut, even though it is extremely close to Godliness (as per G1:13:N13), the fact that it contains the very subtle potential for material existence, even if indiscernible, means that it is considered to be absolute Yesh. Therefore, relative to the creations, the four world levels of Atzilut, Beriyah, Yetzirah, and Asiyah are all deemed to be the domain of Yesh, of material, non-Godly existence, i.e., where something other than and additional to the Godly appears to exist.

This framework of Ayin and Yesh relative to the creations is expressed in Zohar Raya Mehemna III Pinchas 239a and 257b which states, in a relative sense, that Chochma (referring to the world level of Atzilut) is Yesh.

In his second gloss at the very beginning of his commentary on Sifra De-Tzniyuta, the Vilna Gaon also expresses this idea very explicitly as follows:

- . . . as written in Sefer Yetzirah that He created His world with a book (*Sefer*), and a book and a story (*Sipur*) . . . the beginning of the revelation of concealed thought, which is Supernal Keter, is not revealed at all, even the fact of its existence [is not revealed], and therefore it is called Ayin.

- It is only as a result of there being no created entity, not even in the most supernal realms, that has the ability to perceive the essence of this concept
  - as to how it can be that all the worlds and all their hosts are in essence nothing (Ayin)
  - but that they are constantly being caused to exist each moment by God
  - that Chazal chose to analogously refer to God, to explain to the 'ear which hears in the midst of the wise'[19] – using the word "Makom." (Note 41)[20]
- Even though this is what God decreed in His Wisdom – to give existence to His Universe
  - in such a way that every intellect is unable to grasp how he is constantly being caused to exist by God
  - and is able to imagine, with 'eyes of flesh,'[21] that this world has a reality and existence of its own, God forbid.
  - Chazal intellectually enlightened us by analogously describing the concept of "Makom"
    - that just as an object stands on a particular place and even though the object truly has existence in its own right
    - nevertheless, if this object did not have a place to stand upon, it would be as if the object never existed
    - similarly, even though the entire Universe is felt and appears to be an existing entity in its own right

---

[Whereas the level of] Chochma [i.e., Atzilut], which is [like] a closed book [where before someone reads it,] its existence is known but its essence is unrevealed, and therefore this is called Yesh, and Binah is the second book which is revealed to the person who reads it, and Daat is the story which brings out and reveals to all. . . .

Therefore, relative to the creations, the very highest possible level of human conceptual attainment is the level of Chochma and the level of Atzilut. This is in contrast to the level of Supernal Keter which is unattainable.

However, as R. Chaim explains at the beginning of G2:17, the soul level of Chaya, which is synonymous with the level of Chochma and Atzilut, was only attainable by Adam before he sinned by eating of the fruit of the Tree of Knowledge of Good and Evil. He also comments that Adam was able to relate to the level of Yechida/Adam Kadmon but only in the way that it was manifest in level of Chaya. Before his sin, Adam was uniquely able to see from one end of this world to the other with this perspective of Chochma (see G1:22).

So, before Adam's sin, Atzilut was the highest possible level of human conceptual attainment.

- וְרַק מֵחֲמַת שֶׁאֵין בְּכֹחַ שׁוּם נִבְרָא, אַף עֶלְיוֹן שֶׁבָּעֶלְיוֹנִים, לְהַשִּׂיג מַהוּת הָעִנְיָן
  - אֵיךְ כָּל הָעוֹלָמוֹת וְכָל צְבָאָם הֵמָּה בְּעַצְמָם אַיִן
  - וְרַק כָּל רֶגַע הֵמָּה מִתְהַוִּים לִמְצִיאוּת מִמֶּנּוּ יִתְבָּרַךְ.
  - לָזֹאת בָּחֲרוּ לְהַמְשִׁילֵהוּ יִתְבָּרַךְ, וּלְהַסְבִּיר לָאֹזֶן שׁוֹמַעַת בְּקֶרֶב חֲכָמִים, בְּתֵבַת "מָקוֹם": (הגהה מ"א)

- שֶׁאַף שֶׁכָּךְ גָּזְרָה חָכְמָתוֹ יִתְבָּרַךְ, לִתֵּן מְצִיאוּת לְעוֹלָמוֹ
  - בְּאֹפֶן שֶׁיִּלְאֶה כָּל שֵׂכֶל לְהַשִּׂיג אֵיךְ הוּא הַמַּשְׁכַּת הִתְהַוְּותָם מִמֶּנּוּ יִתְבָּרַךְ שְׁמוֹ כָּל רֶגַע
  - וְיוּכַל לְהִדַּמּוֹת בְּעֵינֵי בָשָׂר שֶׁהָעוֹלָם הוּא מְצִיאוּת וְקִיּוּם בִּפְנֵי עַצְמוֹ חַס וְשָׁלוֹם.
  - הֵאִירוּ חֲז"ל עֵינֵי הַשֵּׂכֶל, בְּהַמְשִׁילָם לְעִנְיָן "מָקוֹם"
    - שֶׁכְּמוֹ שֶׁהַכְּלִי הָעוֹמֶדֶת עַל אֵיזֶה מָקוֹם, הֲגַם שֶׁהַכְּלִי הֲרֵי יֵשׁ לָהּ בֶּאֱמֶת מְצִיאוּת בִּפְנֵי עַצְמָהּ
    - עִם כָּל זֶה אִם לֹא הָיָה לְהַכְּלִי מָקוֹם שֶׁתַּעֲמֹד עָלָיו, הָיְתָה כְּלֹא הָיָה
    - כֵּן אַף שֶׁהָעוֹלָם כֻּלּוֹ מֻרְגָּשׁ וְנִדְמֶה כִּמְצִיאוּת בִּפְנֵי עַצְמוֹ

However, after Adam's sin and until the time of the resurrection (as per G4:28), no human will be able to achieve this conceptual level of relating to the Universe from the perspective of Chochma and the level of Atzilut.

Therefore, in the interim, the highest level of human conceptual attainment is restricted to the level of Binah and the level of Beriyah. (This is explained in V2:01, "The Limit of Understanding – The Deeper Meaning of Makom" which also provides deep insight into the concept of Yesh and Ayin.)

Therefore, relative to the current level of the creations in this physical world, Ayin, in our interim existence before the resurrection, is shifted down one general world level and from the human perspective the level of Atzilut is Ayin.

The fact that Atzilut is currently Ayin is explicitly stated twice by R. Chaim. Once in G4:10 and again in G1:13:N13 where he also explains that this is the case "as no intellect is capable of grasping the essence of Atzilut."

19   Mishlei 15:31.
20   **R. Chaim adds Note 41 here.** This note is brought at the end of this chapter and is entitled "Chochma causes all from Ayin, no intellect can understand this."
21   Iyov 10:4, i.e., with the filters of his physical perception.

- God is its Makom/Space
- and were it not for the Makom/Space in [God's] Will to cause the Universe to exist
- how very much more so that everything would be as if it had never previously existed. (Note 42)[22]

• This is as stated in Sefer Yetzirah:[23] "There are Ten Sefirot of *nothing*, which are beyond [the capability of] verbal expression or of the heart to think, and if your heart runs [after them] return *to Makom* as it says 'ran to and fro'[24] [and a covenant was made on this point.]"
  ○ it specifically states "*to Makom*"
  ○ that is, if the thoughts of a thinking person's heart run after trying to understand how all of their existence[25] constantly extends each moment from God
  ○ then *return to [the concept] of Makom*
  ○ to relate to this concept through the tangible analogy of the concept of "Makom"/space, as mentioned above.
  ○ Refer to the Ramban's explanation of this Mishna.[26]

• It is this meaning [of Makom] that our holy Chazal followed, to provide analogies relating to the concept of God's connection to the worlds, even though there is no vague comparison whatsoever between the comparison and that being compared, except in respect of a specific [abstracted] detail, and even in [this detail] it is also only just an analogy.
  ○ As per: One should know ... in a similar way He created the soul ... and just as God does not have a known name or a known place but His rule is over all sides, similarly, a soul does not have [a name or a known place in all of a body] but it rules over all sides and there is no limb devoid of it ... with all these names and descriptions, He is called over all the worlds ... to show that His rule is over them, similarly it is with the soul, because its rule is over all the limbs of the body, it is analogously compared to Him, but it is not that the soul is similar to Him in its essence, as He created it ... and furthermore ... and because of this the soul is similar to Him in the way that it rules over

---

22 **R. Chaim adds Note 42 here.** This note is brought at the end of this chapter and is entitled "God called Makom as unaffected by anything within Creation."

23 Chap. 1, Mishna 7. This section of Sefer Yetzirah is quoted by the Sefer HaRokeach Hilchot Chassidut Shoresh Kedushat HaYichud, in the same section from which R. Chaim's final quotation in this chapter is taken. R. Chaim requotes this section of Sefer Yetzirah in the context of Sefer HaRokeach in G3:06.

- הוּא יִתְבָּרֵךְ שְׁמוֹ הוּא מְקוֹמוֹ
- שֶׁאִלְמָלֵא הָיָה מָקוֹם בִּרְצוֹנוֹ לְהִתְהַוּוֹת הָעוֹלָמוֹת
- עַל אַחַת כַּמָּה וְכַמָּה שֶׁהָיוּ כֻּלָּם כְּלֹא הָיוּ. (הגהה מ"ב)

• וז"ש בְּסֵפֶר יְצִירָה (פֶּרֶק א' מִשְׁנָה ז') עֶשֶׂר סְפִירוֹת בְּלִימָה, בְּלֹם פִּיךְ מִלְדַבֵּר וְלִבְּךָ מִלְהַרְהֵר, וְאִם רָץ לִבְּךָ שׁוּב לַמָּקוֹם, שֶׁלְּכָךְ נֶאֱמַר "רָצוֹא וָשׁוֹב" (יחזקאל א, יד).

- אָמַר לַ"מָּקוֹם" דַּיְקָא
- הַיְנוּ, שֶׁאִם יָרוּץ מַחְשֶׁבֶת לֵב הָאָדָם לְהַשִּׂיג הַמּוּשְׂכָּל אֵיךְ נִמְשָׁךְ הִתְהַוּוּתָם כָּל רֶגַע מִמֶּנּוּ ית"ש
- "שׁוּב לַמָּקוֹם"
- לְהַשִּׂיג עֶרֶךְ הַמּוּשְׂכָּל מִדִּמְיוֹן הַמֻּרְגָּשׁ בִּבְחִינַת מָקוֹם, כַּנַּ"ל.
- וְעַיֵּן פֵּרוּשׁ רַמְבַּ"ן זִכְרוֹנוֹ לִבְרָכָה עַל מִשְׁנָה זוֹ:

• וְעַל זוֹ הַכַּוָּנָה דָרְכוּ רַבּוֹתֵינוּ זִכְרוֹנָם לִבְרָכָה הַקְּדוֹשִׁים, לְהַמְשִׁיל מְשָׁלִים בְּעִנְיָן הִתְחַבְּרוּתוֹ יִתְבָּרֵךְ לְהָעוֹלָמוֹת, אַף שֶׁאֵין עֶרֶךְ וְדִמְיוֹן כְּלָל בֵּין הַמָּשָׁל וְהַנִּמְשָׁל רַק בְּאֵיזֶה דָּבָר פְּרָטִי. וְאַף גַּם זֹאת רַק בְּדִמְיוֹן מָה.

- וּכְמוֹ שֶׁכָּתוּב בְּרַעְיָא מְהֵימְנָא פָּרָשַׁת פִּנְחָס רנ"ז ב' ורנ"ח א', "וְאִית לְמִנְדַּע

R. Chaim also relates to this concept in his note, G2:04:N21, that one is only permitted to focus on a specific Sefira if it is framed in the context of the wider connection with God, which as understood here, if one's heart is to run after these Sefirot, i.e., out of context, then one must return to Makom, i.e., the context of the wider connection with God.

Also see the quotation from Zohar Idra Zuta III Haazinu 288a–b on p. 284, fn. 531.

24 Yechezkel 1:14.
25 I.e., of the Sefirot and by extension every created entity.
26 Ramban on Sefer Yeztira Chap. 1, Mishna 7:
   • He repeats and explains why the Sefirot are called "Blimah" (i.e., nothing), as you are obligated to "Livlom" [a play on words, of "Blimah"] (i.e., to hold back) your mouth from speaking and your heart from thinking. If your heart runs after focusing thought on *what is inside*, then return to Makom, i.e., the *place* of the world, which is Chochma. Therefore, it says "ran to and fro," meaning that if your thoughts should ascend upwards then immediately return them downwards so that they should not tarry with that upper perspective of thought. For on this matter a covenant was made which gives permission to look [into this depth of thought] and then immediately return to Makom [the perspective of God] which gives honor to man for the honor of His Name.

all the limbs of the body but is not [similar] in any other way.[27] Refer to this source at length.

- Similarly, all those things which Chazal listed there[28] in respect of the comparison of God to a soul within a body, this is all only in respect of His permeation within the worlds and the way He fills and controls them, as stated above, that it is just in this respect alone that the concepts are comparable.
- This is similarly hinted to: "That His Voice and Speech are heard from The Throne – and angels, heaven, and earth to whom all is known – in the supernal and lower realms, *like a soul which controls all the body*, even a small limb, and there is no limb devoid of it."[29]
  - Be precise in [understanding] the statement "*like* a soul which controls all the body," as it is understood that even within the context of this analogy it is not a complete comparison
    - as even though Chazal say that just as a soul fills all the body, so too God fills the entire Universe
      - as per the statement in Tikkunim above "like a soul . . . and there is no limb devoid of it"
      - and as per: In each limb, it is *YHVH* . . . there is no place devoid of Him, like a soul which is found in each and every limb of the body[30]
    - the concept of God filling the Universe is not like the concept of the soul filling the body
    - as with all this the body still acts as a barrier for [complete penetration of] the soul, where even though the soul is distributed within all its inner recesses and gives it life, when the soul departs from the body, the body does not cease to exist.
    - In contrast, the Master of All Blessed be He, fills all the worlds and the creations
    - and they truly do not, God forbid, act as a barrier against Him at all
    - and there is literally absolutely nothing else apart from Him at all in all the worlds
    - from the highest of the high to the lowest depths of the depths of the earth
    - to the extent that it can be said that no creation or world exists here at all

---

27 Zohar Raya Mehemna III Pinchas 257b and 258a.
28 I.e., in the Zohar Raya Mehemna as per previous footnote.
29 Tikkunei Zohar Tikkun 38 72a.
30 Tikkunei Zohar Tikkun 70 122b.

כו', כְּגַוְונָא דָא בָּרָא נִשְׁמָתָא כו', וּמַה רִבּוֹן עָלְמִין לֵית שָׁם יְדִיעַ וְלָא אֲתַר יְדִיעַ, אֶלָּא בְּכָל סְטַר שָׁלְטָנוּתֵיהּ, אוּף הָכִי לֵית לָהּ לְנִשְׁמָתָא כו', אֶלָּא בְּכָל סְטַר שׁוּלְטָנוּתָא, לֵית אֵבָר פָּנוּי מִנָּה כו', בְּכָל אִנוּן שְׁמָהָן וְכִנּוּיִין אִתְקְרֵי עַל שֵׁם כָּל עָלְמִין כו', לְאִתְחֲזָאָה שׁוּלְטָנוּתֵיהּ עֲלַיְיהוּ, אוּף הָכִי נִשְׁמָתָא עַל שׁוּלְטָנוּתָא דְּכָל אֵבָרִים דְּגוּפָא אַמְתִּיל לָהּ לְגַבֵּיהּ, לָאו דְּאַדְמְיָא לֵיהּ אִיהִי בְּעַצְמָהּ, דְּהוּא בָּרָא לָהּ וכו', וְעוֹד כו'. וּבְגִין דָא אִיהִי אַדְמְיָא לְגַבֵּיהּ בְּשׁוּלְטָנוּתָא דִילָהּ עַל כָּל אֵבָרֵי גוּפָא, אֲבָל לָא בְּמִלָּה אַחֲרָא". וְעַיֵּן שָׁם בָּאֹרֶךְ.

◦ וְכֵן כָּל הַדְּבָרִים שֶׁמָּנוּ חַזַ"ל שָׁם בְּעִנְיַן הִתְדַּמּוּתוֹ יִתְבָּרַךְ לְהַנְּשָׁמָה בַּגּוּף, הַכֹּל הוּא רַק עַל עִנְיַן הִתְפַּשְּׁטוּתוֹ יִתְבָּרַךְ שְׁמוֹ בְּהָעוֹלָמוֹת וּמְמַלְּאָם וְשָׁלִיטָתוֹ עֲלֵיהֶם כַּנַ"ל, שֶׁרַק בְּדָבָר זֶה לְבַד מִתְדַּמִּין בְּעִנְיָנָם.

◦ וְכֵן רָמְזוּ בַּתִּקּוּנִים סוֹף תל"ח, אָמְרוּ, "דְּאִשְׁתְּמַע קָלֵיהּ וְדִבּוּרֵיהּ מִן כָּרְסַיָּא, וּמַלְאֲכַיָּא וּשְׁמַיָּא וְאַרְעָא דְּיִשְׁתְּמוֹדְעוּן לֵיהּ בְּכֹלָּא, עֵלָּא וְתַתָּא, כְּנִשְׁמָתָא דְּשָׁלְטָנוּתָהּ בְּכָל גּוּפָא, אֲפִילוּ בְּאֵבָר זְעֵירָא, וְלֵית אֵבָר פָּנוּי מִנֵּהּ".

▫ דַּיֵּק בְּאָמְרוֹ "כְּנִשְׁמָתָא דְּשָׁלְטָנוּתָהּ" וְכוּ', וּמִמֵּילָא נִשְׁמַע שֶׁגַּם בָּזֶה הָעִנְיָן עַצְמוֹ שֶׁדִּמּוּהוּ ז"ל, לֹא הִשְׁווּ בָּהּ לְגַמְרֵי

▫ כִּי אַף שֶׁאָמְרוּ "מַה הַנְּשָׁמָה מְלֵאָה אֶת כָּל הַגּוּף אַף הַקָּדוֹשׁ בָּרוּךְ הוּא מָלֵא אֶת כָּל הָעוֹלָם"

▫ וְכֵן מַ"שׁ בְּמַאֲמַר הַתִּקּוּנִים הַנַ"ל כְּנִשְׁמָתָא הַנַ"ל וְלֵית אֵבָר מִנֵּהּ

▫ וְשָׁם בַּתִּקּוּן ע' בְּכָל אֵבָר אִיהוּ הֲוָי"ה וְכוּ', לֵית אֲתַר פָּנוּי מִנֵּיהּ, כְּנִשְׁמָתָא דְּאִשְׁתַּכְּחַת בְּכָל אֵבָר וְאֵבָר דְּגוּפָא.

▫ אֵין עִנְיַן מִלּוּי הַקָּדוֹשׁ בָּרוּךְ הוּא אֶת הָעוֹלָם כְּעִנְיַן מִלּוּי הַנְּשָׁמָה אֶת הַגּוּף

▫ שֶׁעִם כָּל זֶה, גַּם הַגּוּף יֶשְׁנוֹ לְעַצְמוֹ חוּץ בִּפְנֶיהָ, רַק שֶׁמִּתְפַּשֶּׁטֶת בִּפְנִימִיּוּת כָּל פְּרָטֵי חֲלָקָיו וּמְקִימָם, שֶׁהֲרֵי גַּם בְּצֵאת הַנְּשָׁמָה מֵהַגּוּף — אֵין הַגּוּף מִתְבַּטֵּל עַל יְדֵי זֶה מִמְּצִיאוּת.

▫ אֲבָל אֲדוֹן כָּל יִתְבָּרֵךְ שְׁמוֹ, הוּא מָלֵא אֶת כָּל הָעוֹלָמוֹת וְהַנִּבְרָאִים

▫ וְאֵינָם חוֹצְצִים חֲלִילָה נֶגְדּוֹ יִתְבָּרֵךְ כְּלָל בֶּאֱמֶת

▫ וְאֵין עוֹד מִלְּבַדּוֹ יִתְבָּרֵךְ מַמָּשׁ שׁוּם דָּבָר כְּלָל בְּכָל הָעוֹלָמוֹת

▫ מֵהָעֶלְיוֹן שֶׁבָּעֶלְיוֹנִים עַד הַתְּהוֹם הַתַּחְתּוֹן שֶׁבְּתַהוֹמוֹת הָאָרֶץ

▫ עַד שֶׁתּוּכַל לוֹמַר שֶׁאֵין כָּאן שׁוּם נִבְרָא וְעוֹלָם כְּלָל

- but all is filled with His Absolute Sublime Essence, Blessed be His Name.
- Refer to Sefer Rokeach:[31] The Creator does not need a Makom/Place or residence for He was before all that is, and no walls or beams act as barriers before Him, for He would not create something which would be injurious towards Him.

Rabbi Chaim's Notes:
Note 41 – Chochma causes all from Ayin, no intellect can understand this

- This can be explained homiletically by stretching the meaning of the verses [relating to] "And The Chochma/wisdom – from where/*Ayin* can it be found."[32]
  - That The Chochma which is the greatest of all Chochma that can be perceived from God, is the wondrous Chochma which causes all of existence to exist each moment from Ayin.[33]
  - "And where is the Makom/Place of Binah/understanding?"[34] meaning that there is no existing intellect that can be described such that this intellect is the fitting place to have the understanding to understand this wondrous power.
  - These verses conclude "and He knew its Makom."[35]

Note 42 – God called Makom as unaffected by anything within Creation

- God is also analogously described as Makom/Space [to capture the fact]
  - that just as it is with *space* through which a vessel exists [within it], even though the [*space* itself] is incomparable with the vessel, and the *space* is also unaffected by its contents even if it causes many different types of vessel to exist [within it], and the *space* causes all [its contents] to exist and tolerates them in equal measure
  - similarly, it is with God who causes all the worlds to exist, even though there is not even vague comparison between Him and [the worlds]
  - as even [the level of] Supernal Keter is incomparable to Ein Sof [the Infinite One].[36]
- Even if it appears to us that many changes occur in the different levels of Creation
  - and even if powers of impurity and Sitra Achara exist at all levels [of Creation]

---

31 Sefer HaRokeach Hilchot Chassidut Shoresh Kedushat HaYichud.
32 Iyov 28:12.

▫ רַק הַכֹּל מָלֵא עַצְמוּת אַחְדוּתוֹ הַפָּשׁוּט יִתְבָּרַךְ שְׁמוֹ:

• וְעַיֵּן רוֹקֵחַ בְּסוֹף שֹׁרֶשׁ קְדֻשַּׁת הַיִּחוּד ז"ל, "הַבּוֹרֵא אֵינוֹ צָרִיךְ לְמָקוֹם וּמָכוֹן, כִּי הָיָה קֹדֶם כָּל הֱיוֹת, וְאֵין קִירוֹת וְהַקּוֹרוֹת חוֹצְצִין לְפָנָיו, כִּי לֹא הָיָה בּוֹרֵא דָבָר שֶׁהוּא מַזִּיק כְּנֶגְדוֹ":

הגהה מ"א

• וְדֶרֶךְ דְּרָשׁ נוּכַל לְהַעֲמִים בַּפְּסוּקֵי (איוב כ"ח י"ב) "וְהַחָכְמָה מֵאַיִן תִּמָּצֵא"
◦ שֶׁהַחָכְמָה הַגְּדוֹלָה עַל כָּל חָכְמָה הַמְשֻׁגֶּשֶׁת מֵאִתּוֹ יִתְבָּרַךְ, הוּא הַחָכְמָה הַנִּפְלָאָה שֶׁמֵּאַיִן תִּמָּצֵא כָּל רֶגַע מְצִיאוּת
◦ "וְאֵי זֶה מְקוֹם בִּינָה", הַיְנוּ שֶׁאֵין בַּמְצִיאוּת אֵיזֶה שֵׂכֶל, שֶׁנּוּכַל לְכַנּוֹת שֶׁהַשֵּׂכֶל הַהוּא — הוּא "מָקוֹם" מֻכְשָׁר שֶׁתָּחוּל עָלָיו בִּינָה לְהָבִין כֹּחַ הַנִּפְלָא הַזֶּה
◦ וְסַיֵּם (שם כ"ג) "וְהוּא יָדַע אֶת מְקוֹמָהּ":

הגהה מ"ב

• גַּם הִמְשִׁילוּהוּ יִתְבָּרַךְ בִּבְחִינַת "מָקוֹם"
◦ שֶׁכְּמוֹ שֶׁהַמָּקוֹם, עַל יָדוֹ מִתְקַיְּמִים הַכְּלִי, אַף אִם אֵינוֹ שָׁוֶה בְּעֵרֶךְ עִם הַכְּלִי, וְגַם הַמָּקוֹם, אַף אִם עַל יָדוֹ מִתְקַיְּמִים כַּמָּה וְכַמָּה כֵּלִים שׁוֹנִים זֶה מִזֶּה, אֵין גּוֹרְמִים עַל יְדֵי זֶה שׁוּם שִׁנּוּי בְּהַמָּקוֹם, וְהַמָּקוֹם מְקַיֵּם וְסוֹבֵל כֻּלָּם בְּהַשְׁוָאָה אַחַת.
◦ כָּךְ הוּא יִתְבָּרַךְ שְׁמוֹ מְקַיֵּם כָּל הָעוֹלָמוֹת, אַף שֶׁאֵין עֵרֶךְ כְּלָל בֵּינוֹ יִתְבָּרַךְ וּבֵינֵיהֶם
◦ דְּאַף "כֶּתֶר עֶלְיוֹן", אוּכְמָא אִיהוּ לְגַבֵּיהּ דְּ"אֵין סוֹף":

• וְגַם אִם כִּי נִרְאֶה לָנוּ שִׁנּוּיִים מְשֻׁנּוּיִים שׁוֹנִים מִצַּד הַבְּרִיאָה מַדְרֵגוֹת שׁוֹנוֹת זוֹ מִזּוֹ
◦ וְאַף כִּי נִמְצָאִים גַּם כֹּחוֹת הַטֻּמְאָה וְהַסִּטְרָא אַחֲרָא בְּכָל מַדְרֵגוֹתָם

---

33 I.e., homiletically understanding the verse as "And The Chochma – from Ayin, it[/all of existence] can be found." See p. 472, fn. 18.

34 Continuation of Iyov 28:12 and also Iyov 28:20.

35 Iyov 28:23, meaning that only God relates to this concept.

36 Lit., that Supernal Keter (which is the level just above the world of Atzilut) is *black* compared to (the radiance of) the Infinite One. A similar expression is used in G2:05:N22.

- with the existence of all purely being as a result of God alone
- nevertheless, there is no change in God, for He does not change, and from God's perspective, He causes all to exist in the imaginary environment of "Makom."
- Now even though this concept is beyond the ability of any intellect to grasp what it is, and it is wondrous
  - it is for this reason that Chazal advised[37] that "Behold Makom is *with Me*,"[38] that My place is secondary to Me
  - meaning that no intellect can grasp how He is on the level of Makom without being affected [by anything]
  - but that it is just God alone who perceives His Essence, that He perceives how He is the place of all worlds without being changed [by them]
  - as per "and He knew its Makom"[39]
  - and this is the meaning of "*with Me*," specifically, as in 'the heart does not reveal to the mouth.'[40]

3. EMPHASIS OF: A. ALL BEING EXCLUSIVELY GOD, AND B. ITS SENSITIVITY

- This[41] is the concept underpinning the verse "Do I not fill the Heavens and the Earth."[42]
  - It is even more explicitly stated in Devarim, in the verse "and you shall know this day . . . that YHVH is Elokim in the Heavens above and the Earth below. There is nothing else!"[43]
  - and similarly, "You have been shown in order to know that YHVH is Elokim – there is nothing else besides Him."[44]
  - These statements are absolutely literal
  - that there is absolutely nothing else apart from Him in any way at all and in any fine point of detail in all the supernal and lower worlds and all the creations
  - there is just God's Sublime Unified Essence alone!
- This is the deeper meaning of Chazal's statement: Another explanation of the verse "that YHVH is Elokim" . . . Yitro literally related . . . Rachav . . . Moshe even placed [God] as being the space of the Universe, as per "that YHVH [is Elokim] in the Heavens above and the Earth below. There is nothing else!" What does this verse mean by "There is nothing else!"? Not even in the space of the Universe.[45]

---

37 E.g., Bereishit Rabba Vayetze 68:9.
38 Shemot 33:21.

- וְהַקִּיּוּם שֶׁל כֻּלָּם הוּא רַק מִמֶּנּוּ יִתְבָּרַךְ לְבַד
- עִם כָּל זֶה לֵית בֵּיהּ שִׁנּוּי יִתְבָּרַךְ שְׁמוֹ, דְּאִיהוּ לֹא אִשְׁתַּנֵּי, וּמִצִּדּוֹ יִתְבָּרַךְ הוּא מְקַיְּמָם בִּדְמִיוֹן מָקוֹם:

• וְאִם כִּי דָבָר זֶה אֵין בְּשׁוּם שֵׂכֶל לְהַשִּׂיג אֵיךְ וּמָה, וְהוּא פֶּלֶא.
  - לָזֶה הִמְלִיצוּ חַזַ"ל "הִנֵּה מָקוֹם אִתִּי" (שמות לג, כא), "אַתְרָאִי טְפֵלָה לִי".
  - פֵּרוּשׁ, שֶׁלֵּית מַחֲשָׁבָה תְּפִיסָא אֵיךְ הוּא בִּבְחִינַת מָקוֹם בְּלִי שִׁנּוּי
  - רַק הוּא יִתְבָּרַךְ לְבַדּוֹ הַמַּשִּׂיג עַצְמוּתוֹ, מַשִּׂיג אֵיךְ הוּא מְקוֹמָן דְּכוּלְּהוּ עָלְמִין בְּלִי שִׁנּוּי
  - כְּעִנְיָן "וְהוּא יָדַע אֶת מְקוֹמָהּ" (איוב כח, כג)
  - וְזֶהוּ "אִתִּי" דַּיְקָא, כְּעִנְיָן "לִבָּא לְפוּמָא לֹא גַּלְיָא":

שער ג' - פרק ג'

• וְהוּא עִנְיָן הַכָּתוּב (ירמיה כ"ג כ"ד) "הֲלֹא אֶת הַשָּׁמַיִם וְאֶת הָאָרֶץ אֲנִי מָלֵא".
  - וְיוֹתֵר מְפֹרָשׁ בְּמִשְׁנֵה תוֹרָה "וְיָדַעְתָּ הַיּוֹם וְגוֹ' כִּי ה' הוּא הָאֱלֹהִים בַּשָּׁמַיִם מִמַּעַל וְעַל הָאָרֶץ מִתַּחַת אֵין עוֹד" (דברים ה, לט)
  - וְכֵן "אַתָּה הָרְאֵתָ לָדַעַת כִּי ה' הוּא הָאֱלֹהִים אֵין עוֹד מִלְבַדּוֹ" (שם ה, לה)
  - וְהוּא מַמָּשׁ כְּמַשְׁמָעוֹ
  - שֶׁאֵין עוֹד מִלְּבַדּוֹ יִתְבָּרַךְ כְּלָל, בְּשׁוּם בְּחִינָה וּנְקֻדָּה פְּרָטִית שֶׁבְּכָל הָעוֹלָמוֹת, עֶלְיוֹנִים וְתַחְתּוֹנִים וְהַבְּרִיּוֹת כֻּלָּם
  - רַק עַצְמוּת אַחְדּוּתוֹ הַפָּשׁוּט יִתְבָּרַךְ שְׁמוֹ לְבַד:

• וְהוּא פְּנִימִיּוּת אָמְרָם זִכְרוֹנָם לִבְרָכָה בִּדְבָרִים רַבָּה (פ"ב כ"ח) דָּבָר אַחֵר "כִּי ה'

---

39 Iyov 28:23. See R. Chaim's previous note, G3:02:N41.
40 Kohelet Rabba 12:10.
41 Continuing from G3:02.
42 Yirmiyahu 23:24.
43 Devarim 4:39.
44 Devarim 4:35.
45 Devarim Rabba VaEtchanan 2:28 quoting Devarim 4:35. The full text of this Midrashic statement reads as follows:
  • Another explanation of the verse "that YHVH is Elokim," our Rabbis said: Yitro literally related to other gods as per "now I know that YHVH is greater than all the other Elohim/gods" [Shemot 18:11]. Naaman partially related to the concept as per "Now I know that there is no God in the

- This is also incorporated in Chazal's statement "He is the Place of the Universe, but the Universe is not His Place"[46]
- meaning that even though all places are [humanly] perceived to exist independently, they have no independent existence apart from Him
- He is the Makom/Space of all spaces
- and that from His perspective they are all considered as if to not be in existence at all
- even now – just like before the Creation.
- However, we have already prefaced at the beginning of our words,[47] that Chazal's statements [in general] are like burning coals and one should be extremely careful not to *excessively* engage intellectually and be burned, God forbid, by concepts which are largely beyond our intellectual capacity.
  - This is similarly the case with this profound concept [of Makom].
  - This concept is only suitable for consumption by a wise person who can understand the depths of this concept from his own knowledge according to the measure of his heart alone with "to and fro"[48]
  - to use it to enthuse purity of his heart to engage in the service of prayer.
  - However, too much intellectual engagement in this concept is extremely dangerous, and it is about this that the Sefer Yetzirah stated "if your heart runs after it, return to Makom" as I wrote above in G3:02 and will write later, God willing, in G3:06.
- In truth, I would have held back from describing this concept at all as the Rishonim, of blessed memory, greatly concealed it, as we see in the words of the holy one of God, the Rokeach, which were brought above who only hinted at it, whose 'spirit is steadfast with God'[49] and they concealed the matter.

---

entire world apart from in Israel" [2 Melachim 5:15]. Rachav [related to the concept more deeply and] placed [God] in the Heavens and the Earth as per "For the Lord your God is the God of the Heavens above and the Earth below" [Yehoshua 2:11]. Moshe [related to the concept in the deepest way and] even placed [God] as being the space of the Universe as per "that YHVH is Elokim in the Heavens above and the Earth below. There is nothing else!" What does this verse mean by "There is nothing else!"? Not even in the space of the Universe.

This statement describes the different ways in which it is possible to relate to the degree of God's manifestation and Unity within the world. It explains that the ultimate way of relating to God is as Moshe related to Him, that there is absolutely nothing else in existence apart from Him. R. Chaim is emphasizing

הוּא הָאֱלֹהִים" וְגוֹ', יִתְרוֹ נָתַן מַמָּשׁ וְכוּ', רָחָב וְכוּ', מֹשֶׁה שָׁמָּהוּ אַף בַּחֲלָלוֹ שֶׁל עוֹלָם, שֶׁנֶּאֱמַר (שם) "כִּי ה' כו' בַּשָּׁמַיִם מִמַּעַל וְעַל הָאָרֶץ מִתָּחַת אֵין עוֹד", מַהוּ "אֵין עוֹד", אֲפִלּוּ בַּחֲלָלוֹ שֶׁל עוֹלָם.

○ וְזֶה גַּם כֵּן בִּכְלָל מַאֲמָרָם ז"ל שֶׁהוּא יִתְבָּרַךְ מְקוֹמוֹ שֶׁל עוֹלָם וְאֵין הָעוֹלָם מְקוֹמוֹ

○ הַיְנוּ, שֶׁאַף כָּל הַמְּקוֹמוֹת שֶׁמַּרְגִּשִׁים לַחוּשׁ בִּמְצִיאוּת, אֵין הַמְּקוֹמוֹת עַצְמָיִם, אֶלָּא הוּא יִתְבָּרַךְ שְׁמוֹ

○ הוּא הַמָּקוֹם שֶׁל כָּל הַמְּקוֹמוֹת

○ שֶׁמִּצַּדּוֹ יִתְבָּרַךְ נֶחְשָׁבִים כֻּלָּם כְּאִלּוּ אֵינָם בִּמְצִיאוּת כְּלָל

○ גַּם עַתָּה כְּקֹדֶם הַבְּרִיאָה:

• אָמְנָם כְּבָר הִקְדַּמְנוּ בִּתְחִלַּת דְּבָרֵינוּ, שֶׁהִמְשִׁילוּ דִּבְרֵיהֶם זִכְרוֹנָם לִבְרָכָה כְּ"גַחֲלֵי אֵשׁ", שֶׁיְּהֵא זָהִיר מְאֹד בְּגַחַלְתָּן שֶׁלֹּא לִיכָּנֵס לְהִתְבּוֹנֵן וְלַחֲקֹר יוֹתֵר מִדַּי, בִּדְבָרִים שֶׁאֵין הָרְשׁוּת נְתוּנָה לְהִתְבּוֹנֵן הַרְבֵּה, וְיִכְוֶה חַס וְשָׁלוֹם.

○ וְכֵן הוּא זֶה הָעִנְיָן הַנּוֹרָא.

○ אֵין הַדָּבָר אָמוּר, אֶלָּא לְחָכָם וּמֵבִין מִדַּעְתּוֹ פְּנִימִיּוּת הָעִנְיָן בְּשִׁעוּרָא דְלִבָּא לְבַד בְּרָצוֹא וָשׁוֹב

○ לְהַלְהִיב בָּזֶה טֹהַר לִבּוֹ לַעֲבוֹדַת הַתְּפִלָּה

○ אֲבָל רֹב הַהִתְבּוֹנְנוּת בָּזֶה הוּא סַכָּנָה עֲצוּמָה, וְעַל זֶה נֶאֱמַר בְּסֵפֶר יְצִירָה, "וְאִם רָץ לִבְּךָ, שׁוּב לַמָּקוֹם". כְּמוֹ שֶׁכָּתַבְתִּי לְעֵיל פֶּרֶק ב', וּכְמוֹ שֶׁאָכְתֹּב אִי"ה לְהַלָּן פֶּרֶק ו':

• וּבֶאֱמֶת הָיִיתִי מוֹנֵעַ עַצְמִי מִלְּדַבֵּר בָּעִנְיָן זֶה כְּלָל, כִּי הָרִאשׁוֹנִים זִכְרוֹנָם לִבְרָכָה הִסְתִּירוּ הָעִנְיָן מְאֹד, כְּמוֹ שֶׁתִּרְאֶה דִּבְרֵי קָדוֹשׁ ה' הָרוֹקֵחַ ז"ל, הוּבָא לְעֵיל (סוֹף ב), שֶׁלֹּא דִבֵּר בָּזֶה רַק בְּרֶמֶז, כִּי נֶאֶמְנָה אֶת אֵל רוּחָם וְכִסּוּ דָבָר.

---

the deeper meaning of Chazal's statement by only quoting the section of this Midrash which relates to Moshe's understanding.

46 Bereishit Rabba Vayetze 68:9.
47 G3:01.
48 I.e., with control, as per the quotation from Sefer Yetzirah in G3:02.
49 Tehillim 78:8.

- But I have 'relented and seen'⁵⁰ that this was appropriate in their generation
- However, now [in today's generation], when we have had an extended period without an instructor⁵¹
- and 'all of a person's ways appear just in his eyes'⁵² to follow after his intellectual leaning
- and all of a person's 'inclination of the thoughts of his heart'⁵³ is filled to only *fly his thoughts* towards the leaning of his intellect
- and above all, [he will affirm] that this is [the essence] of the Torah which applies to all of man, and he becomes a 'parable in the mouth of fools'⁵⁴
- saying, "Is not every place and every thing [just] pure Godliness?"
- and they invest their eyes and hearts in investigating this concept with all of their time
- to the extent that 'those who are easily swayed'⁵⁵ are drawn by their hearts to assign all of their actions and behaviors to this [concept] according to the way they intellectually relate to this.

• A person needs to be extremely cautious of this and greatly protect his life with multiple safeguards.
  - That if, God forbid, we were to engage this idea in practice and permit ourselves to also act and behave according to it
  - it can result, God forbid, in the destruction of many basic principles of the Holy Torah, Heaven save us.
  - He can be easily trapped by the net of the Evil Inclination to use this idea to make things permissible for himself, for example
    □ to repulsively think Torah thoughts in unfit places⁵⁶ after concluding that everything is just purely God.⁵⁷
    □ Chazal strenuously⁵⁸ objected to this by stating that one who thinks Torah thoughts in an unfit place does not merit to be part of the future world, Heaven save us, as this activity is part of the injunction "for he scorned the word of God,"⁵⁹ which also includes one who thinks Torah thoughts in unfit places, and inevitably the last part of this verse will apply that "Hikaret Tikaret," which Chazal explain⁶⁰ that "Hikaret" relates to being cut off in this world and "Tikaret" to being cut off in the next world.

---

50 Kohelet 9:11.
51 There are some who suggest that this is reference to the period following the passing of the Vilna Gaon in 5558 (1797).
52 Mishlei 21:2.
53 Bereishit 6:5.

- אֲבָל שַׁבְתִּי וְרָאִיתִי, שֶׁכָּךְ הָיָה יָפֶה לָהֶם לְפִי דּוֹרוֹתֵיהֶם.
- אֲבָל עַתָּה, הֵן יָמִים רַבִּים לְלֹא מוֹרֶה
- וְכָל דֶּרֶךְ אִישׁ יָשָׁר בְּעֵינָיו לַהֲלֹךְ אַחֲרֵי נְטִיַּת שִׂכְלוֹ
- וְכָל יֵצֶר מַחְשְׁבוֹת לֵב הָאָדָם מָלֵא רַק לָעוּף בְּמַחְשַׁבְתּוֹ אֶל כָּל אֲשֶׁר יִתְּנוּ שִׂכְלוֹ.
- וְהָעוֹלָה עַל כֻּלָּם, שֶׁזֶּה תּוֹרַת כָּל הָאָדָם, וְנַעֲשָׂה מָשָׁל גַּם בְּפִי כְּסִילִים
- לֵאמֹר, הֲלֹא, בְּכָל מָקוֹם וְכָל דָּבָר הוּא אֱלֹקוּת גָּמוּר
- וְעֵינָם וְלִבָּם כָּל הַיָּמִים לְהַעֲמִיק וּלְעַיֵּן בָּזֶה
- עַד שֶׁגַּם נְעָרִים מְנֹעָרִים מִמִּשְׁכָּא לְהוּ לְבַיְיהוּ לִקְבֹּעַ כָּל מַעֲשֵׂיהֶם וְהַנְהָגָתָם בָּזֶה לְפִי שִׂכְלָם זֶה:

• וְכַמָּה זְהִירוּת יְתֵרָה, צָרִיךְ הָאָדָם לְהִזָּהֵר בָּזֶה, וְלִשְׁמֹר אֶת נַפְשׁוֹ מְאֹד בְּמִשְׁמֶרֶת לְמִשְׁמֶרֶת.

- שֶׁאִם חַס וְשָׁלוֹם יִקָּחֵנוּ לִבֵּנוּ לִקְבֹּעַ לָנוּ מַחֲשָׁבָה זוֹ, לְהַתִּיר לְעַצְמֵנוּ לְהִתְנַהֵג גַּם בְּמַעֲשֶׂה לְפִי הַמַּחֲשָׁבָה זוֹ
- הֲלֹא יוּכַל לְהוֹלִיד מִזֶּה חַס וְשָׁלוֹם הֲרִיסַת כַּמָּה יְסוֹדוֹת הַתּוֹרָה הַקְּדוֹשָׁה ר"ל.
- וּבְנָקֵל יוּכַל לְהִלָּכֵד חַס וְשָׁלוֹם בְּרֶשֶׁת הַיֵּצֶר, שֶׁיַּרְאֶה לוֹ הֶתֵּרָא עַל פִּי מַחְשָׁבָה זוֹ דֶּרֶךְ מָשָׁל

▫ לְהַרְהֵר בְּדִבְרֵי תּוֹרָה בְּשַׁאֲטַ נֶפֶשׁ אַף בִּמְקוֹמוֹת הַמְטֻנָּפִים, אַחַר שֶׁיִּקָּבַע אֶצְלוֹ תְּחִלָּה שֶׁהַכֹּל אֱלֹקוּת גָּמוּר.

▫ וְרַזַ"ל הִפְלִיגוּ בָּזֶה מְאֹד, וּכְרָתוּהוּ בְּרוּחַ קָדְשָׁם מֵהְיוֹת לוֹ חֵלֶק לָעוֹלָם הַבָּא, רַחֲמָנָא לִיצְלָן, כְּמוֹ שֶׁכָּתוּב (ברכות כ"ד ב') שֶׁבִּכְלַל "כִּי דְבַר ה' בָּזָה"

---

54 Mishlei 26:7–9.
55 This expression is a play on Sotah 46b where the word "Ne'arim/youth" is understood to mean "Menu'arim/emptied" of Mitzvot. While youth are more easily swayed and influenced to change and are at higher risk of compromising Mitzvah performance, the more general context here is referring to anyone who may have the tendency to be swayed.
56 See G4:27.
57 And that therefore it makes no difference where one is, and one can engage in Torah study anywhere irrespective of whether the place is clean or unfit.
58 Berachot 24b.
59 Bamidbar 15:31.
60 Sanhedrin 90b.

G3:03

- ○ There are many other mistakes that one can make, God forbid, as a result of applying this concept in practice in this way!
- This has brought me to speak about this concept to warn and to distance [people] from the mistakes that can result from it, God forbid, and to explain all these concepts hinted to by Chazal in context, as all the ways of God are just and 'the time is now ripe to do so.'[61]

4. RELATIVE TO GOD: HE FILLS WORLDS, BUT TO US: HE CIRCUMVENTS

- To put this matter 'into perspective'[62] we will explain the holy statement of Chazal which is explained in Etz Chaim and taken from a number of places in Tikkunei Zohar
  - ○ that God fills all the worlds in an absolutely equally distributed way.
- Now [in contrast] we find that even in the supernal worlds, that each world is specifically differentiated from each other in various ways in relation to the way that God is connected to them
  - ○ As per: . . . that the Ten Sefirot of Atzilut are a king over them [i.e., the Ten Sefirot of Beriyah], that He [i.e., God] and His Causes [i.e., His Middot of Atzilut] are One over them, He and His life [force] are One over them, as opposed to the Ten Sefirot of Beriyah where they and He are not one. . . .[63]
  - ○ Refer to Etz Chaim which states:[64]
    - ▫ That the way in which the Infinite One, Blessed be He, is manifest and extends within the worlds
    - ▫ He only touches and cleaves to the world of Atzilut alone
    - ▫ and not to [the worlds of] Beriyah, Yetzirah, and Asiyah
    - ▫ and therefore there is a change in their essence from there [i.e., from Beriyah] and below.
  - ○ Refer to Etz Chaim which writes in explaining the statement from Tikkunei Zohar above:[65]

---

61 As per "Et Laasot LaHashem Heferu Toratecha" (Tehillim 119:126), a Halachic concept brought down in many places, e.g., Berachot 54a, which justifies developing/changing a previous practice to prevent mistakes arising from the changed circumstances of a new era.

62 The expression "Al Mechono" is uniquely used in and borrowed from Ezra 2:68.

63 Tikkunei Zohar Introduction 3b. This source is also quoted in G4:10 and a slightly longer quotation is found in G3:05.

(במדבר טו, לא) הוּא גַם הַמְהַרְהֵר דִּבְרֵי תוֹרָה בַּמְבוֹאוֹת הַמְטֻנָּפִים, וּמִמֵּילָא נִשְׁמַע סֵיפֵיהּ דְּהַאי קְרָא "הִכָּרֵת תִּכָּרֵת" וְכוּ', וּפֵירְשׁוּהוּ ז"ל בְּפֶרֶק חֵלֶק (צ' ע"ב) "הִכָּרֵת" — בָּעוֹלָם הַזֶּה, "תִּכָּרֵת" — לָעוֹלָם הַבָּא.

◦ וְעוֹד כַּמָּה טָעֻיּוֹת שֶׁיּוּכַל לָצֵאת חַס וְשָׁלוֹם, אִם הָיָה נִקְבַּע הַהַנְהָגָה בְּמַעֲשֶׂה עַל פִּי זֶה הַדֶּרֶךְ:

• וְזֶה שֶׁהֱבִיאַנִי לְהִכָּנֵס לְדַבֵּר בְּזֶה הָעִנְיָן, וּלְהַזְהִיר וּלְהַרְחִיק מִטָּעוּת שֶׁיּוּכַל לְהִוָּלֵד מִזֶּה חַס וְשָׁלוֹם, וּלְהָבִין עַל בּוּרְיוֹ כָּל מַה שֶּׁרָמְזוּ לָנוּ רַבּוֹתֵינוּ זִכְרוֹנָם לִבְרָכָה בָּזֶה, וְהֵנָם בְּכָל דַּרְכֵי ה' הַיְשָׁרִים, וְעֵת לַעֲשׂוֹת:

שער ג' - פרק ד'

• וּלְהָשֵׁב הַדָּבָר עַל מְכוֹנוֹ, נְבָאֵר מַאֲמַר קַדִּישִׁין רַזַ"ל, שֶׁמְּבֹאָר בְּעֵץ חַיִּים, לָקוּחַ מֵהַתִּקּוּנִים בְּכַמָּה מְקוֹמוֹת

◦ שֶׁהוּא יִתְבָּרַךְ שְׁמוֹ מְמַלֵּא כָּל עָלְמִין בְּהַשְׁוָאָה גְּמוּרָה:

• וַהֲרֵי מָצִינוּ שֶׁגַּם בָּעוֹלָמוֹת הָעֶלְיוֹנִים, כָּל עוֹלָם חָלוּק וּמְשֻׁנֶּה מֵחֲבֵרוֹ בִּבְחִינוֹת שׁוֹנִים, בְּעִנְיַן הִתְחַבְּרוּתוֹ יִתְבָּרַךְ אֲלֵיהֶם

◦ וְכמ"ש בְּהַקְדָּמַת הַתִּקּוּנִים (דף ג' ע"ב) דְּעֶשֶׂר סְפִירוֹת דַּאֲצִילוּת מַלְכָּא בְּהוֹן, אִיהוּ וְגַרְמֵיהּ חַד בְּהוֹן, אִינּוּן וְחַיֵּיהוֹן חַד בְּהוֹן, מַה דְּלָאו הָכִי בְּעֶשֶׂר סְפִירוֹת דִּבְרִיאָה, דְּלָאו אִינּוּן וְאִיהוּ חַד וְכוּ'.

• וְעַיֵּן בְּעֵץ חַיִּים שַׁעַר הִשְׁתַּלְשְׁלוּת הָעֲשָׂרָה סְפִירוֹת בְּרֵישׁ סֵדֶר הָאֲצִילוּת בְּקִצּוּר, כָּתַב

◦ שֶׁ"אֵין סוֹף" בָּרוּךְ הוּא, בִּבְחִינַת הִתְלַבְּשׁוּתוֹ וְהִתְפַּשְּׁטוּתוֹ בְּכָל הָעוֹלָמוֹת

◦ אֵינוֹ נוֹגֵעַ וְדָבֵק, זוּלָתִי בְּעוֹלָם אֲצִילוּת לְבַד

◦ וְלֹא בִּבְרִיאָה יְצִירָה עֲשִׂיָּה

◦ וְלָכֵן מִשָּׁם וּלְמַטָּה יִשְׁתַּנֶּה מַהוּתָם.

◦ וְשָׁם בְּשַׁעַר דְּרוּשֵׁי אבי"ע פֶּרֶק ז, בְּפֵרוּשׁ מַאֲמַר הַתִּקּוּנִים הַנַּ"ל, כָּתַב

---

64 Etz Chaim Shaar 3, Shaar Seder Atzilut Bekitzur Muflag LeRav Chaim Vital, first sentence of Chap. 1.

65 Etz Chaim Shaar 42, Shaar Derushei Atzilut Beriyah Yetzirah and Asiyah, Chap. 5 (see V2:14, p. 676):
  • ... and with this you can understand why the essence and receptacles/vessels of Atzilut are One, as is written in the introduction to Tikkunei Zohar

- That the entirety of Atzilut – even its level of Keilim[66] – is called *Absolute Divinity*
- in contrast to Beriyah, Yetzirah, and Asiyah. Refer there.
○ It similarly explains there [in Etz Chaim] the essential difference between the world of Atzilut and the other three world levels of Beriyah, Yetzirah, and Asiyah in respect of [which aspects are] Divinity.[67]
○ Similarly, many very finely detailed differences between the worlds [in respect of their relative levels] are explained throughout all of the Zohar and the words of the Arizal.

---

that His Life Force and His Causes are One over them, as His Causes are the receptacles/vessels of Atzilut and they are on a level of pure spirituality which is called the Nefesh, Ruach, and Neshama of all of the worlds, and they are only referred to as *receptacles/vessels* relative to the level of Chaya . . . and understand this well, and therefore all of Atzilut is *Absolute Divinity* for [its] receptacles/vessels are literally *Divinity* . . . Now the three world levels of Beriyah, Yetzirah, and Asiyah are all totally [comprised of] *receptacles/vessels* and are therefore not *Divinity*. . . .

66 I.e., its lowest level, the level of Malchut, *the receptacles/vessels*, which passively receive their life force from the higher levels of Atzilut.

67 See the quotation from Etz Chaim on p. 489, fn. 65. R. Chaim also refers the reader to the following additional sources:
Etz Chaim Shaar 43, Shaar Tziyur Olamot Atzilut Beriyah Yetzirah Asiyah in the introduction of R. Chaim Vital:
- . . . there is one difference between the supernal worlds and these three lowest worlds which are Beriyah, Yetzirah, and Asiyah, for the supernal worlds are all singularly holy and of *One Divinity* and there is no separation[/differentiation] within them, God forbid, but with these three worlds, their level of Neshama within them is called *Divinity*, but from [their level of] Ruach onwards, [the] Ruach, Nefesh, *body*, and *garment* [levels] of these three worlds, they are not *Divinity* but are called Seraphim, Chayot, Ophanim, and Kisey . . . .

Etz Chaim Shaar 2, Shaar Hishtalshelut HaYud Sefirot, Chap. 3:
- [This reference appears to be incorrect as it does not relate to the topic under discussion. The following was found in Etz Chaim Shaar 3, Shaar Seder HaAtzilut BeKitzur Muflag LeRav Chaim Vital, Chap. 3:] . . . But with the garments [as the world levels of Beriyah, Yetzirah, and Asiyah are classified earlier on in this chapter as being the garments of the *body of Atzilut*] the Essential Light is not revealed, therefore Beriyah, Yetzirah, and Asiyah are

- שֶׁהָאֲצִילוּת כֻּלּוֹ, גַּם בְּחִינַת הַכֵּלִים נִקְרָא אֱלֹהוּת גָּמוּר
- מַה שֶּׁאֵין כֵּן בבי"ע, עַיֵּן שָׁם.
- וְכֵן מְבֹאָר שָׁם הַחִלּוּק הָעַצְמִי שֶׁבֵּין הָאֲצִילוּת לג' עוֹלָמוֹת בי"ע בְּעִנְיָן הָאֱלֹהוּת, עַיֵּן שָׁם בְּרֵישׁ שַׁעַר צִיּוּר עוֹלָמוֹת אבי"ע, בְּהַקְדָּמַת הרח"ו, וּבְשַׁעַר הִשְׁתַּלְשְׁלוּת הי' סְפִירוֹת פֶּרֶק ג', וְשַׁעַר הַצֶּלֶם פֶּרֶק א', וְשַׁעַר הַשֵּׁמוֹת פֶּרֶק א', וְשַׁעַר סֵדֶר אבי"ע פֶּרֶק ב' וְרֵישׁ פֶּרֶק ג'
- וְכַיּוֹצֵא כַּמָּה חִלּוּקֵי בְּחִינוֹת וְעִנְיָנִים שׁוֹנִים בֵּין הָעוֹלָמוֹת, פְּרָטֵי פְּרָטִים, הַמְבֹאָר בְּכָל הַזֹּהַר וְדִבְרֵי הָאֲרִיזַ"ל.

---

not of the level of Divinity but are called "creations," "formations," and "actions"....

Etz Chaim Shaar 26, Shaar HaTzelem, Chap. 1:
- But the distinction as written elsewhere is that in Atzilut, all the lights, images, and receptacles are called "Absolute Divinity" – they are absolutely One as mentioned in the introduction to Tikkunei Zohar that He, His Causes, and His Life Force are One over them, that they are the three levels [i.e., of lights, images, and receptacles]. But with Beriyah, Yetzirah, and Asiyah, this is not the case, as up until the level of Neshama it is *Divinity* but from the level of Ruach onwards, it separates and is called "creation," "formation," "action"....

Etz Chaim Shaar 44, Shaar HaShemot, Chap. 1:
- ... but with the levels of Beriyah, Yetzirah, and Asiyah, we have already explained above that those thirty Sefirot from the *female part* of Atzilut [i.e., the lowest part of Atzilut] are distributed within them and literally form their level of Neshama, and from there onwards, meaning from the level of Neshama of Beriyah, Yetzirah, and Asiyah, from there onwards they are no longer on the level of *Divinity* but only in *secret*, and from there they split into four categories and are referred to as "separation," meaning that there is also [in addition to the category of Neshama] the category of Ruach... and also the category of Nefesh and similarly the category of the *garments*....

Etz Chaim Shaar 47, Shaar Seder Atzilut Beriyah Yetzirah Asiyah, Chap. 1 and the beginning of Chap. 2 (see V2:14, p. 676):
- ... the difference between Atzilut and the 3 worlds is that with Atzilut, the Light of the Ein Sof penetrates all the way through it without any barrier ... but with [the 10 Sefirot of] Beriyah, He and His Causes are not one over them, as the Ein Sof only passes into it via a barrier ....

- ○ Refer well to the book Four Hundred Shekels of Silver in relation to [God's] advance knowledge of man's actions where the Arizal distinguishes [this level of knowledge] between the worlds.[68]
- ○ Moreover, we find this [differentiation expressed] in many verses, which were it not written in the Scriptures it would have been impossible to make such statements, for example:
    - □ "God, the Most High."[69]
    - □ "He who dwells in the Heavens."[70]
- ○ Similarly, Chazal have also enumerated [instances of differentiation within God, for example]:
    - □ "Ten levels of holiness."[71]
    - □ The three camps of holiness one above the other.[72]
- However, [in order to appreciate] the truth of this concept, 'incline your ear . . . and apply your heart,'[73] 'and you will then go securely.'[74]
- For it is explained in many places in the Zohar that The Unified Infinite Master Blessed be He *fills all worlds* and *circumvents all worlds*, meaning that
    - ○ relative to Him, He is referred to as *filling the worlds*[75]
    - ○ but relative to us
        - □ according to the way in which we are commanded by the Holy Torah in respect of observance of Torah and Mitzvot[76]

---

68   In the book, "Four Hundred Shekels of Silver," R. Chaim Vital records comments he heard from the Arizal. On the last page of the book he records the Arizal's answer to a question asked of him by R. Avraham Monsotz related to the conundrum of God's knowledge of the outcome of man's actions while at the same time man has free choice to determine his actions. The following is stated within this answer:
   - . . . it is true that in Atzilut there is knowledge [of all that will happen], but a person has the ability to choose irrespective of that, as the verse states "Behold I have placed before you the life and the good and the death and the bad . . . and you shall choose life so that you and your descendants will live" [Devarim 30:15, 19] . . . this verse proves that there is free choice, and also according to Chazal who say, "Bad does not descend from Above" [Bereishit Rabba Vayera 51:3], for Above, in Atzilut, everying is obvious [and all is known], but this knowledge does not descend to the lowest world to force a person [to act accordingly], for there is no reward and punishment and no free will Above [in the world of Atzilut] . . . for Above in Atzilut there is knowledge and the knowledge of a person's bad actions does not descend from Above, but stays there. It is for man, who has free choice, to choose, and therefore the Torah commands its commandments [for there would not be a need to command if there was no free choice]. If man cleaves to the

- וְעַיֵּן הֵיטֵב בְּסוֹף סֵפֶר אַרְבַּע מֵאוֹת שֶׁקֶל כֶּסֶף, בְּעִנְיַן יְדִיעָתוֹ יִתְבָּרַךְ שְׁמוֹ מִקֹּדֶם בְּמַעֲשֵׂי הָאָדָם, שֶׁחָלַק הָאֲרִיזַ"ל בָּזֶה בֵּין הָעוֹלָמוֹת.
  - וְיוֹתֵר עַל כֵּן, שֶׁמָּצִינוּ כַּמָּה מִקְרָאוֹת
    - כְּמוֹ "אֵל עֶלְיוֹן" (בראשית יד, יט)
    - "יוֹשֵׁב בַּשָּׁמַיִם" (תהלים ב, ד), אֲשֶׁר אִלְמָלֵא מִקְרָא כָּתוּב אִי אֶפְשָׁר לְאָמְרָם.
  - וְכֵן מָנוּ רַבּוֹתֵינוּ זִכְרוֹנָם לִבְרָכָה
    - "עֶשֶׂר קְדֻשּׁוֹת" (כלים א, ו)
    - וְ"ג' מַחֲנוֹת" מְקֻדָּשׁוֹת זוֹ לְמַעְלָה מִזּוֹ:
- אֲבָל אֲמִתַּת הָעִנְיָן הַט אָזְנְךָ וְלִבְּךָ תָּשִׁית, וְתֵלֵךְ לָבֶטַח:
- כִּי מְבֹאָר בְּכַמָּה מְקוֹמוֹת בַּזֹּהַר, שֶׁאֲדוֹן יָחִיד אֵין סוֹף בָּרוּךְ הוּא, מְמַלֵּא כָּל עָלְמִין וְסוֹבֵב כָּל עָלְמִין, וְהַיְנוּ
  - שֶׁ"מִּצִּדּוֹ יִתְבָּרַךְ" נִקְרָא בִּבְחִינַת "מְמַלֵּא כָּל עָלְמִין"
  - וּ"מִצִּדֵּנוּ"
    - כְּפִי אֲשֶׁר נִצְטַוִּינוּ בַּתּוֹרָה הַקְּדוֹשָׁה בְּעִנְיַן הַנְהָגוֹתֵינוּ בַּתּוֹרָה וּמִצְווֹת

Torah, he draws good upon himself, for bad does not descend from Above of its own accord, but the bad only descends when man draws it upon himself. With this a section of the Zohar III Vayikra 13b [quoting Vayikra 5:1] is understood "If a soul will sin – if he accepted a demand for an oath, and he is a witness, either he saw or he knew . . ." For the soul, before its descent from Above is made to take an oath by God: "be righteous and do not be wicked." For if it is said that there is [predestined] knowledge, then [the soul] is taking a false oath as it knows it will sin and [nevertheless] takes an oath . . . and God does not want [the soul] to swear falsely in His Name . . . but these statements and many verses prove that at the time of creation [of the soul at the world level of creation/Beriyah] it does not have knowledge [of its destiny and is therefore not swearing falsely when taking this oath].

69 Bereishit 14:19.
70 Tehillim 2:4.
71 Mishna Keilim 1:6.
72 E.g., Zohar III Balak 190b.
73 Mishlei 22:17, i.e., follow the forthcoming presentation carefully.
74 Mishlei 3:23.
75 I.e., in equal distribution as stated above.
76 I.e., that the Mitzvot through which we connect with God are not equally distributed in our experience and that they are often designated to be performed at specific times and/or in specific places.

- and according to our physical perception[77]
- God is referred to as *circumventing all worlds*
- and 'God has hidden'[78] from us the level of [His] *filling the worlds* from our perspective.

• This concept is that it is certainly true from God's perspective that now, even after He created and renewed the worlds with His Will:
   ○ He fills all the worlds, places, and creations in an equally distributed manner and Absolute Unity
   ○ [with the statement of] "There is nothing else besides Him"[79] being absolutely literal
   ○ as I wrote above referring to explicit Scriptural verses[80] and in the name of the Rokeach[81]
   ○ and it is as our early Rabbis instituted to recite before prayer that "You are He who was before the Creation of the Universe and You are He [i.e., the same and unchanged] after the Creation of the Universe"[82]
   ○ meaning that even though the worlds were already created with God's Sublime Will, nevertheless, there was no change or anything new, God forbid, and no barrier resulting [from the created worlds] in the essence of His Absolute Unity.
   ○ Even now, He is exactly like He was before the Creation
   ○ when everything was entirely filled with the Infinite Essence of God, even the Makom/Space within which the worlds currently exist.

• 'Apply your heart'[83] to the words of the holy one of God, R. Shmuel, the father of the holy R. Yehuda the Pious, to the Song of Unity that he composed:[84]
   ○ "There is no limit . . . and no diagonal bisects You," refer to it.[85]
   ○ "He who circumvents all and fills all, when all exists You are in it all," refer there for more.[86]

---

77 I.e., that we do not physically see God while in this world.
78 Mishlei 25:2.
79 Devarim 4:35.
80 At the beginning of G3:03.
81 At the end of G3:02.
82 The earliest source for this statement is probably Yalkut Shimoni VaEtchanan Remez 836 with it being formulated into the Seder of R. Amram Gaon and the Machzor Vitri.
83 Mishlei 22:17, as above.
84 This is customarily recited by some following Maariv of Yom Kippur.
85 From towards the end of the Yichud of the second day. The full text of this quotation is as follows:
    • There is no limit to Your loftiness and there is no end to the depth of Your

נפש שער ג' - פרק ד' החיים

- וּכְפִי הַשָּׂגָתֵנוּ בְּחוּשׁ
- נִקְרָא יִתְבָּרַךְ שְׁמוֹ בִּבְחִינַת "סוֹבֵב כָּל עָלְמִין"
- שֶׁבְּחִינַת "מְמַלֵּא כָּל עָלְמִין" הוּא כְּבוֹד אֱלֹהִים הַסְתֵּר דָּבָר מִצִּדֵּנוּ:

• וְהָעִנְיָן כִּי וַדַּאי הָאֱמֶת, שֶׁמִּצִּדּוֹ יִתְבָּרַךְ, גַּם עַתָּה אַחַר שֶׁבָּרָא וְחִדֵּשׁ הָעוֹלָמוֹת בִּרְצוֹנוֹ

- הוּא מְמַלֵּא כָּל הָעוֹלָמוֹת וְהַמְּקוֹמוֹת וְהַבְּרִיּוֹת כֻּלָּם בְּשִׁוּוּי גָּמוּר וְאַחְדוּת פָּשׁוּט
- "וְאֵין עוֹד מִלְּבַדּוֹ" כְּמַשְׁמָעוֹ מַמָּשׁ
- וּכְמוֹ שֶׁכָּתַבְתִּי לְעֵיל מִמִּקְרָאוֹת מְפֹרָשִׁים וּבְשֵׁם הָרוֹקֵחַ ז"ל.
- וּכְמוֹ שֶׁתִּקְּנוּ לָנוּ קַדְמוֹנֵינוּ זִכְרוֹנָם לִבְרָכָה לוֹמַר קֹדֶם הַתְּפִלָּה "אַתָּה הוּא עַד שֶׁלֹּא נִבְרָא הָעוֹלָם אַתָּה הוּא מִשֶּׁנִּבְרָא הָעוֹלָם"
- רוֹצֶה לוֹמַר, אַף שֶׁכְּבָר נִבְרְאוּ הָעוֹלָמוֹת בִּרְצוֹנוֹ הַפָּשׁוּט יִתְבָּרַךְ, עִם כָּל זֶה אֵין שׁוּם שִׁנּוּי וְהִתְחַדְּשׁוּת חַס וְשָׁלוֹם, וְלֹא שׁוּם חֲצִיצָה מֵחֲמָתָם בְּעַצְמוּת אַחְדוּתוֹ הַפָּשׁוּט
- וְהוּא הוּא גַּם עַתָּה כְּקֹדֶם הַבְּרִיאָה
- שֶׁהָיָה הַכֹּל מָלֵא עַצְמוּת אֵין סוֹף בָּרוּךְ הוּא, גַּם בִּמְקוֹם שֶׁעוֹמְדִים הָעוֹלָמוֹת עַתָּה:

• וּלְבַד תָּשִׁית לְדִבְרֵי קְדוֹשׁ ה' רַבֵּנוּ שְׁמוּאֵל, אָבִיו שֶׁל הַקָּדוֹשׁ רַבִּי יְהוּדָה חֲסִיד, בְּשִׁיר הַיִּחוּד שֶׁחִבֵּר

- בְּיִחוּד יוֹם ב' "אֵין קִצָּה כו' וְאֵין תֹּךְ מַבְדִּיל בֵּינוֹתֶיךָ" כו', עַיֵּן שָׁם
- וּבְיִחוּד יוֹם ג' "סוֹבֵב אֶת הַכֹּל וּמְמַלֵּא אֶת כֹּל, וּבִהְיוֹת הַכֹּל אַתָּה בַּכֹּל" כו', עַיֵּן שָׁם עוֹד בָּזֶה:

Attributes. You have no perimeter and no edge and no living being has seen You. No side and border bound You, no width and length measure You. There is no edge to Your perimeters and no diagonal bisects You.

86 From the middle of the Yichud of the third day. Some more from this source is as follows:
  • He who circumvents all and fills all, when all exists You are in it all. Nothing is above You, nothing below You, nothing is outside You and nothing within You. There is no image or exterior to Your Oneness, nor is Your Mighty Unity tangible. Nothing is separate from Your Midst nor is the tiniest place without You.

- It is in this way that Chazal analogously compared God's connection with the worlds to the connection of a soul with a body:
  - "Just as a pure soul is within a body, so too God, is Pure, within the worlds"[87]
  - meaning that even though the soul is distributed through the entirety of all of a person's limbs, including those which are clean and those which contain dirt, filth, and pollution, and notwithstanding this, no [limb] acts as a barrier which compromises the soul's purity in any way, and the [soul] remains pure
  - so too, while God fills All, there is *no* place, whether pure and holy or impure, which acts as a barrier at all, and they do not cause any change, God forbid, in the holiness and purity of His Essence and Absolute Unity, as written:[88] "I am God, I have not changed." (Note 43)[89]
  - As per: All of Israel who received the Torah from Him, they Unify Him with it, and with all the letters and His Holy Names, and with all the supernal and lower camps which were created with them, and with all the supernal and lower creations, above them all there is Unity, and below them all and within and outside of all of them He is One . . . This is how He is within all of the worlds just as He is outside of all of the worlds, there is no change.[90]

Rabbi Chaim's Note:
Note 43 – YHVH is relative to God's perspective and has not changed

- According to what will be explained later on[91] in respect of the difference between the two names [of God] of *YHVH* and *Elokim*
  - that the meaning of the name *Elokim* is that it relates to the level of our perspective
  - and the name of His Essence, *YHVH*, relates to the level of God's perspective
  - therefore, this verse [specifically] states: "I am *YHVH*, I have not changed."[92]
- Refer to Tikkunei Zohar:[93] The four letters which are *YHVH*, they do not change in any place . . . the changes are in the vessels[94] of the body,

---

87 Vayikra Rabba Vayikra 4:8.
88 Malachi 3:6.
89 **R. Chaim adds Note 43 here.** This note is brought at the end of this chapter and is entitled "YHVH is relative to God's perspective and has not changed."
90 Zohar Chadash Tikkunim II 97a.

- וְזֶה שֶׁאָמְרוּ רַבּוֹתֵינוּ זִכְרוֹנָם לִבְרָכָה בַּדְּבָרִים שֶׁדִּמּוּ הִתְחַבְּרוּתוֹ יִתְבָּרַךְ לָעוֹלָמוֹת, לְהִתְחַבְּרוּת הַנְּשָׁמָה לְהַגּוּף
  - "מַה הַנֶּפֶשׁ טְהוֹרָה בַּגּוּף אַף הַקָּדוֹשׁ בָּרוּךְ הוּא טָהוֹר בְּעוֹלָמוֹ" (וַיִּקְרָא רַבָּה סוֹף פָּרָשָׁה ד')
  - רוֹצֶה לוֹמַר, בְּעִנְיַן הַנְּשָׁמָה, אַף שֶׁמִּתְפַּשֶּׁטֶת בְּכָל פִּרְטֵי אֵבְרֵי הָאָדָם, הַנְּקִיִּים וְגַם הַמְּלֵאִים לְכֻלּוּךְ טִנֹּפֶת וְזֻהֲמָא, וְעִם כָּל זֶה אֵינָם חוֹצְצִים כְּלָל לְעִנְיַן טָהֳרָתָהּ, וּבִקְדֻשָּׁתָהּ וְטָהֳרָתָהּ עוֹמֶדֶת.
  - כֵּן הָעִנְיָן, אִם שֶׁהוּא יִתְבָּרַךְ מְמַלֵּא אֶת כֹּל, וְכָל הַמְּקוֹמוֹת, מְקוֹמוֹת הַטְּהוֹרִים וְהַמְקֻדָּשִׁים וַאֲשֶׁר אֵינָם טְהוֹרִים, אַף עַל פִּי כֵן אֵינָם חוֹצְצִים כְּלָל, וְלֹא גוֹרְמִים שׁוּם שִׁנּוּי חָלִילָה לִקְדֻשַּׁת טָהֳרַת עַצְמוּתוֹ וְאַחְדוּתוֹ הַפָּשׁוּט יִתְבָּרַךְ. וְזֶ"שׁ (מלאכי ג, ו) "אֲנִי ה' לֹא שָׁנִיתִי". (הגהה מ"ג).
- וּכְמַ"שׁ בְּתִקּוּנֵי זֹהַר חָדָשׁ דַּף צ"ז ע"א, "וְכָל יִשְׂרָאֵל דְּקַבִּילוּ מִנֵּיהּ אוֹרַיְתָא, אִנּוּן עָבְדִין לֵיהּ אֶחָד בָּהּ, וּבְכָל אַתְוָן וּשְׁמָהָן קַדִּישִׁין דִּילֵיהּ, וּבְכָל מַשִּׁרְיָן עִלָּאִין וְתַתָּאִין דְּאִתְבְּרִיאוּ בָּהּ, וּבְכָל בְּרִיָּן עִלָּאִין וְתַתָּאִין. וּלְעֵלָּא מִכֻּלְּהוּ אֶחָד, וּלְתַתָּא מִכֻּלְּהוּ, וּמִלְּגָאו דְּכֻלְּהוּ, וּמִלְּבַר דְּכֻלְּהוּ, אִיהוּ אֶחָד כוּ', הָכִי אִיהוּ מִלְּגָאו דְּכָל עָלְמִין, כְּמוֹ מִלְּבַר דְּכָל עָלְמִין, לָא אִשְׁתַּנִּי כוּ':

הגהה מ"ג

- וּלְפִי מַה שֶּׁיִּתְבָּאֵר אִי"ה לְהַלָּן (פרק יא) עִנְיַן הַחִלּוּק שֶׁבֵּין הַב' שֵׁמוֹת הֲוָיָ"ה וֶאֱלֹקִים
  - שֶׁהַשֵּׁם "אֱלֹקִים" פֵּרוּשׁוֹ מוֹרֶה עַל הַבְּחִינָה אֲשֶׁר מִצִּדֵּנוּ
  - וְשֵׁם הָעֶצֶם "הֲוָיָ"ה" יִתְבָּרַךְ מוֹרֶה עַל הַבְּחִינָה שֶׁמִּצִּדּוֹ יִתְבָּרַךְ
  - לָזֹאת אָמַר "אֲנִי הֲוָיָ"ה לֹא שָׁנִיתִי":
- וְעִנְיַן תִּקּוּנִים תִּקּוּן ע' בְּעִנְיַן הָאוּדְנִין אָמַר, "וְאַרְבַּע אַתְוָן דְּאִנּוּן הֲוָיָ"ה אִיהוּ לָא

---

91 G3:11.
92 Malachi 3:6.
93 Tikkunei Zohar Tikkun 70 130a–b quoting Malachi 3:6, in the passage relating to the concept of *the ears*.
94 Vessels represent the level of Malchut/Kingship. Therefore all changes only occur within the level of Malchut only.

but in Him, there is no change at all, as per "I am *YHVH*, I have not changed."

5. CONCEALMENT CREATES DIFFERENCE AND A HUMAN PERSPECTIVE OF GOD

- Notwithstanding all this,[95] 'it is with God's Gevurah[96] and Awesomeness,'[97] that even so
  - He has *concealed*[98] His Glory, so to speak
  - such that it is possible for the existence of the concept of [an independent differentiated] existence of worlds, powers, and creatures – both created and regenerated – with different properties and aspects, and different types of places: places which are holy and pure, and their opposite, which are impure and filthy.
- This [concealment] is from our perspective [alone], that is, that we are unable to physically perceive anything apart from the apparent [independent] existence [of the world around us].
  - It is *on this basis* that [God] has established a framework of obligation, [the Torah,][99] that we have been commanded [to adhere to] from God's mouth as an 'immutable decree.'[100]
- It is within the context of this [concealed] setting, that Chazal compare [God's relationship with the worlds] to that of a soul inhabiting a body as written in the Zohar,[101] that God is the Soul of all the worlds

---

95 I.e., that even with the Creation of the worlds God is absolutely One and has not changed in any way.

96 The Mishna (Avot 4:1) describes Gevurah as "Who is a Gibor? One who controls himself!". So in this context, God's attribute of Gevurah is His Self-Control, His Self-Restriction, His Modulation such that He Is Manifest in this world in a way in which other things – apart from Him – appear to exist.

97 An expression from Yalkut Shimoni Nechemia Remez 1071 (and similar to Yoma 69b), which describes God's Gevurah as His Self-Control, and His Awesomeness as the cause of the Jewish People's survival among the nations.

98 The word "Tzimtzum" is often used in Rabbinic literature to mean "contraction" and indeed R. Chaim uses it in that context in G2:06:N26. However, in G3:07, R. Chaim very clearly defines the meaning of "Tzimtzum" in the context that it is brought here to mean "concealment." The word "Tzimtzum" has therefore been translated consistently as "concealment," both in the body of the main text of the Third Gateway and also in any of the translated extended references and footnotes relating to it. This Tzimtzum/concealment refers to the general Kabalistic principle stemming from the Arizal which explains why God's presence is not felt in this world. In particular, the result of Tzimtzum is

אִשְׁתַּנֵּי בְּכָל אֲתַר כו'. שִׁינוּיִין אִנּוּן בְּמָאנֵי דְגוּפָא, אֲבָל בֵּיהּ לֵית שְׁנוּיָא כְּלָל הה"ד "אֲנִי ה' לֹא שָׁנִיתִי":

שער ג' - פרק ה'

- אֲבָל עִם כָּל זֶה, הֵן הֵן גְּבוּרוֹתָיו וְנוֹרְאוֹתָיו יִתְבָּרַךְ שְׁמוֹ, שֶׁאַף עַל פִּי כֵן
  - צִמְצֵם כִּבְיָכוֹל כְּבוֹדוֹ יִתְבָּרַךְ
  - שֶׁיּוּכַל לְהִמָּצֵא עִנְיַן מְצִיאוּת עוֹלָמוֹת וְכֹחוֹת וּבְרִיּוֹת נִבְרָאִים וּמְחֻדָּשִׁים, בִּבְחִינוֹת שׁוֹנוֹת וְעִנְיָנִים מְחֻלָּקִים, וְחִלּוּקֵי מְקוֹמוֹת שׁוֹנִים, מְקוֹמוֹת קְדוֹשִׁים וּטְהוֹרִים, וּלְהֵפֶךְ טְמֵאִים וּמְטֻנָּפִים:

- וְהוּא הַבְּחִינָה אֲשֶׁר "מִצִּדֵּנוּ", הַיְנוּ, שֶׁהַשָּׂגָתֵנוּ אֵינָהּ מַשֶּׂגֶת בַּחוּשׁ רַק עִנְיַן מְצִיאוּתָם כְּמוֹ שֶׁהֵם נִרְאִים
  - שֶׁעַל פִּי זֹאת הַבְּחִינָה נִבְנוּ כָּל סִדְרֵי חִיּוּב הַנְהָגָתֵנוּ, שֶׁנִּצְטַוֵּינוּ מִפִּיו יִתְבָּרַךְ, חֹק וְלֹא יַעֲבֹר:

- וּמִצַּד זֹאת הַבְּחִינָה, הוּא שֶׁדִּמּוּהוּ רַבּוֹתֵינוּ זִכְרוֹנָם לִבְרָכָה כִּבְיָכוֹל כְּעִנְיַן הַנְּשָׁמָה אֶל הַגּוּף, וכמ"ש בַּזֹּהַר שֶׁהוּא יִתְבָּרַךְ הוּא "נִשְׁמָתָא דְכָל עָלְמִין"

---

the creation of an environment where *differences* exist, whether between world levels or between places, i.e., a difference can only exist when everything is not exclusively One. The word in Hebrew denoting a difference between things is "Bein" which also forms the word "Binah/understanding," i.e., where there is a difference between things, there can be a comparative understanding of those things; however, where there is no difference, there cannot be any understanding, so [God] creates this world in which differences between things exist and thereby generates an environment enabling comparative analysis and understanding. Our purpose in this world as the Jewish people, as highlighted by R. Chaim's quotation from Zohar Chadash at the end of G3:04, is to apply Torah and Mitzvot specifically to this *differentiated* environment and unify it in a way in which God entirely fills every aspect of our experience of this world.

See more background on the concept of differentiation in V2:01, "The Limit of Understanding – The Deeper Meaning of Makom."

A very detailed explanation of the concept of Tzimtzum is provided in V2:02.

99 "Lo BaShamayim He," i.e., the Torah does not apply to the Heavens (as per Devarim 30:12) but is only relevant to be practiced in the *differentiated* environment of this world. This is emphasized in G3:06.

100 Tehillim 148:6.

101 Zohar I Bereishit 45a which mentions the Holy of Holies in the Temple as

- that just as it is with a person, it is only the body which can be seen, whereas with the soul, even though it entirely fills the body it is concealed from physical perception[102] and only revealed intellectually
- similarly, it is according to our revealed perception that we [only physically] relate to the existence of all of the worlds and the creations, and that [God], so to speak, permeates and is concealed within the innermost part of everything to provide them with life and continued existence
- this is just like the soul which disseminates through and is concealed by the inner recesses of each specific part of the body to give it life.
• [Therefore] all the names, appellations, descriptions, and characteristics of [God] that we find [throughout] the Torah all relate to [God] from our perspective alone.
  - As does our framework of obligation [of Torah and Mitzvot] which comes from [God's] connection with the worlds, and through [performance of our obligations] we draw down all the detailed changes [to the worlds] as explained above in the Second Gateway.[103]
• This is the meaning, which is now clear, of the source quoted above which hints at the two concepts mentioned above:[104]
  - ... that the Ten Sefirot of Atzilut are a king over them [i.e., the Ten Sefirot of Beriyah]; that He [i.e., God] and His Causes [i.e., His Middot, the Sefirot of Atzilut] are One over them; He and His life [force] are One over them, as opposed to the Ten Sefirot of Beriyah where they and He are not One, they and His Causes are not One, and above all of them He descends with the Ten Sefirot of Atzilut and shines within the Ten Sefirot of Beriyah, and the ten groups of angels, and the ten spheres of the heavens, but [God] is unchanged in any place.
• Chazal also relate to these two concepts, as is clear to one who understands, as per:
  - When [God] wants to – "Do I not fill the Heavens and the Earth?" and when He wants to – He would speak with Moshe from between the two poles of the Holy Ark. R. Chanina bar Issi says: sometimes the Universe and all that fills it is just not able to contain the glory of

---

being the place of the soul of that world, where there is a corresponding site of the Holy of Holies in all world levels with the Malchut of each higher world level forming the soul of each lower world level so ultimately God is the Soul of all the worlds. The residence of this Soul in the Holy of Holies of each world level is referred to as the Shechina, see G2:17:N38. This Zohar source is also quoted in G3:01 referring to God as being the Soul of all souls.

נפש שער ג' - פרק ה' החיים 501

- שֶׁכְּמוֹ שֶׁבָּאָדָם לֹא נִרְאֶה בְּחוּשׁ רַק הַגּוּף, וְהַנְּשָׁמָה אַף שֶׁהִיא מְלֵאָה אֶת כָּל הַגּוּף הִיא בִּבְחִינַת הֶסְתֵּר לְעֵינֵי בָשָׂר, וְנִגְלֵית לְעֵינֵי שֵׂכֶל

- כֵּן כְּפִי הַשָּׂגָתֵנוּ הַנִּגְלֵית, נִרְאֶה מְצִיאוּת הָעוֹלָמוֹת וְהַבְּרִיּוֹת כֻּלָּם, וְשֶׁהוּא יִתְבָּרֵךְ שְׁמוֹ מִתְפַּשֵּׁט וּמִסְתַּתֵּר כִּבְיָכוֹל בִּפְנִימִיּוּת כֻּלָּם לְהַחֲיוֹתָם וּלְקַיְּמָם

  - כְּעִנְיַן הַנְּשָׁמָה שֶׁמִּתְפַּשֶּׁטֶת וּמִסְתַּתֶּרֶת בִּפְנִימִיּוּת כָּל פְּרָטֵי חֶלְקֵי אֶבְרֵי הַגּוּף, לְהַחֲיוֹתוֹ:

- וְכָל הַשֵּׁמוֹת וְהַכִּנּוּיִים וְהַתְּאָרִים וְהַמִּדּוֹת עָלָיו יִתְבָּרַךְ שֶׁמָּצִינוּ בַּתּוֹרָה הַקְּדוֹשָׁה, כֻּלָּם מְדַבְּרִים מִצַּד זֹאת הַבְּחִינָה — כְּפִי שֶׁהוּא "מִצִּדֵּנוּ"

  - וְסִדְרֵי חִיּוּב הַנְהָגוֹתֵינוּ, שֶׁהוּא מִצַּד הַהִתְחַבְּרוּתוֹ יִתְבָּרֵךְ אֶל הָעוֹלָמוֹת, שֶׁמִּצִּדָּם וְעַל יְדֵיהֶם נִמְשָׁךְ כָּל הַשִּׁנּוּיִים שֶׁל פְּרָטֵי סִדְרֵי הַהַנְהָגָה כֻּלָּם, כְּמוֹ שֶׁנִּתְבָּאֵר לְעֵיל בְּשַׁעַר ב' (פֶּרֶק ב'):

- וְזֶה שֶׁכָּתוּב בְּהַקְדָּמַת הַתִּקּוּנִים הַנַּ"ל

  - דְּעֶשֶׂר סְפִירוֹת דַּאֲצִילוּת מַלְכָּא בְּהוֹן, אִיהוּ וְגַרְמֵיהּ חַד בְּהוֹן, אִנּוּן וְחַיֵּיהוֹן חַד בְּהוֹן, מַה דְּלָאו הָכִי בְּעֶשֶׂר סְפִירוֹת דִּבְרִיאָה, דְּלָאו אִנּוּן וְאִיהוּ חַד, לָאו אִנּוּן וְגַרְמֵיהוֹן חַד. וְעִלַּת עַל כֹּלָּא הוּא נָחִית בְּעֶשֶׂר סְפִירָן דַּאֲצִילוּת, וְנָהִיר בְּעֶשֶׂר סְפִירוֹת דִּבְרִיאָה, וּבְעֶשֶׂר כִּתּוֹת דְּמַלְאֲכַיָּא, וּבְעֶשֶׂר גַּלְגַּלֵּי דִרְקִיעָא. וְלָא אִשְׁתַּנֵּי בְּכָל אֲתַר, רָמַז לֵב' הַבְּחִינוֹת הַנַּ"ל, כַּמְבֹאָר:

- וּבִבְרֵאשִׁית רַבָּה פָּרָשָׁה ד' אָמְרוּ

  - "כְּשֶׁהוּא רוֹצֶה 'הֲלֹא אֶת הַשָּׁמַיִם וְאֶת הָאָרֶץ אֲנִי מָלֵא'" (ירמיה כג, כד).

R. Chaim is returning to this same concept here but in the context of God's *concealment*.

102 Where *differentiation* exists, we can understand (Binah – understanding; *Bein* – difference). So as the soul permeates in equal distribution throughout the body, there is no differentiation and we cannot physically detect or discern its presence. We can only intellectually relate to it. The same is true with our restriction of physical ability to relate to God and we can only relate to Him on an intellectual level. See V2:01, "The Limit of Understanding – The Deeper Meaning of Makom."

103 G2:02.

104 Tikkunei Zohar Introduction 3b, quoted in G3:04. The same source is also quoted in G4:10. However, this is a longer quotation to emphasize that it hints at the two concepts mentioned above, of: 1. God filling the world levels as His Essence filters down to them in a concealed way, and simultaneously 2. that God circumvents the worlds and is totally unchanged by their existence.

His Divinity, and sometimes He speaks with man from between two hairs of his head.[105]

- Similarly, [When God wants to, His Glory fills the Universe, as per "Do I not fill the Heavens and the Earth says the Lord?" and when He wants to, He speaks through the storm of the heavens, as per "and God answered Iyov from the storm," and when he wants to, (He speaks to Moshe) from the burning bush.][106]

• Therefore, He is referred to in all statements of Chazal with the name of "The Holy One, Blessed be He," as this reference incorporates these two concepts together:
  - ["The Holy One":]
    - "Holy" means "abstracted and elevated"
    - and this is from His perspective
    - as He is truly separated, abstracted, and very elevated above all the differences and cyclical changes [of the Universe].
    - But all are filled [with Him] in an absolutely Unified way and with equal distribution [of His Essence].
    - He is above all blessing and praise, with there being no need for Him to be blessed, God forbid.
    - Refer to the Tikkunim.[107]
    - It is also not relevant at all, from this perspective, for there to be any concept of addition and increase in blessing [Him] as all is Absolutely One, [unchanged,] as before Creation, as per
      - "To whom can you compare Me that I should be [his] equal, says the Holy One,"[108] with this verse relating to God's Unified Essence as is known from Raya Mehemna[109] and Tikkunim.[110]
  - ["Blessed be He":]
    - Relative to our perception of the existence of the powers and the worlds
    - He is called "Blessed," so to speak
    - relating to [God's] connection to the [worlds]
    - for [the worlds] require the addition and increase in blessing and bestowal to be brought to them through the desirable actions of man as I wrote above in the Second Gateway.[111]

---

105 Bereishit Rabba Bereishit 4:4 quoting Yirmiyahu 23:24.
106 Shemot Rabba Shemot 3:6 quoting Yirmiyahu 23:24 and Iyov 40:6.
107 Tikkunei Zohar Tikkun 70 131b:
  • The Most High who is higher than all – He blesses all and is Above all blessing as per "and He is above all blessing and praise" (Nechemia 9:5), He does not need any blessing from anyone else as no one can change Him.

וּכְשֶׁהוּא רוֹצֶה, הָיָה מְדַבֵּר עִם מֹשֶׁה מִבֵּין שְׁנֵי בַדֵּי הָאָרוֹן. אָמַר רַבִּי חֲנִינָא בַּר אִיסִי, פְּעָמִים שֶׁאֵין הָעוֹלָם וּמְלֹאוֹ מַחֲזִיקִים כְּבוֹד אֱלֹהוּתוֹ, פְּעָמִים שֶׁהוּא מְדַבֵּר עִם הָאָדָם מִבֵּין שַׂעֲרוֹת רֹאשׁוֹ" כו'.

וְכֵן הוּא בִּשְׁמוֹת רַבָּה פָּרָשָׁה ג'. רָמְזוּ גַם כֵּן לְאֵלוּ בּ' הַבְּחִינוֹת, כַּמְבֹאָר לַמֵּבִין:

וְלָכֵן נִקְרָא הוּא יִתְבָּרַךְ בְּכָל דִּבְרֵי רַבּוֹתֵינוּ זִכְרוֹנָם לִבְרָכָה בְּשֵׁם "הַקָּדוֹשׁ בָּרוּךְ הוּא". כִּי כָּלְלוּ בְּזֶה הַשֵּׁם הַנִּכְבָּדָה, אֵלּוּ הַב' בְּחִינוֹת יַחַד.

[קדוש]

- כִּי 'קָדוֹשׁ' פֵּרוּשׁוֹ מֻבְדָּל וְנַעֲלֶה
- וְהוּא כְּפִי אֲשֶׁר מִצִּדּוֹ יִתְבָּרַךְ
- שֶׁהוּא בֶּאֱמֶת מֻפְרָשׁ וּמֻבְדָּל וְנַעֲלֶה מְאֹד מִכָּל עִנְיְנֵי הַחִלּוּקִים וְשִׁנּוּיִים חָלִילָה
- רַק הַכֹּל מָלֵא אַחְדוּת גָּמוּר לְבַד בְּהַשְׁוָאָה גְּמוּרָה
- וּמְרוֹמָם מֵעַל כָּל בְּרָכָה וּתְהִלָּה, וְאֵינֶנּוּ צָרִיךְ לְהִתְבָּרֵךְ חַס וְשָׁלוֹם.
- וְעִנְיַן תִּקּוּנִים תִּקּוּן ע' קַל"א ב'
- וְגַם לֹא שַׁיָּךְ כְּלָל לְפִי זֹאת הַבְּחִינָה שׁוּם עִנְיַן תּוֹסֶפֶת וְרִבּוּי בְּרָכָה, כֵּיוָן שֶׁהַכֹּל אַחְדוּת פָּשׁוּט לְבַד כְּקֹדֶם הַבְּרִיאָה
- וּכְמוֹ שֶׁכָּתוּב (ישעיה מ' כה) "וְאֶל מִי תְדַמְּיוּנִי וְאֶשְׁוֶה יֹאמַר קָדוֹשׁ", שֶׁזֶּה הַכָּתוּב נֶאֱמַר עַל עַצְמוּת אַחְדוּתוֹ יִתְבָּרַךְ, כַּיָּדוּעַ בְּרָעֲיָא מְהֵימְנָא וְתִקּוּנִים.

[ברוך הוא]

- וּמִצַּד בְּחִינַת הַשָּׂגָתֵנוּ מְצִיאוּת הַכֹּחוֹת וְהָעוֹלָמוֹת
- הוּא נִקְרָא "בָּרוּךְ" כִּבְיָכוֹל
- מִצַּד הִתְחַבְּרוּתוֹ יִתְבָּרַךְ אֲלֵיהֶם
- כִּי הֵם הַצְּרִיכִים לְעִנְיַן הַתּוֹסֶפֶת, וְרִבּוּי בְּרָכָה וְשֶׁפַע, עַל יְדֵי מַעֲשֵׂי הָאָדָם הָרְצוּיִים, כְּמוֹ שֶׁכָּתַבְתִּי לְעֵיל בְּשַׁעַר ב'.

---

108 Yishayahu 40:25.
109 E.g., Zohar Raya Mehemna III Pinchas 225a.
110 E.g., Tikkunei Zohar Introduction 6b.
111 E.g., G2:09.

- ["The Holy One, Blessed be He":]
  - This is therefore the meaning of "The Holy One, Blessed be He," that [on the one hand] from His perspective He is [called] "Holy"
  - and [on the other hand] from our perspective He, the exact same [God], is called "Blessed," so to speak
  - with them all being One thing.
- [As the Torah is established as a framework of obligation in the context of our perception of the world after God's concealment within it,] it is therefore specifically the level of our relative perspective [alone] that the many Scriptural verses [relating to God] refer to [as per the question in G2:04], for example
  - "God, the Most High."[112]
  - "He who dwells in the Heavens."[113]

6. HALACHA ONLY RELEVANT TO HUMAN ENVIRONMENT/PERSPECTIVE

- Now, all the principles of the Torah, including all the positive and negative Mitzvot follow this [human relative] perspective [alone]:
  - As it is certainly [and only] from our perspective that differentiation exists between places
    - as in places of purity, we are permitted and even obligated to speak or to think words of Torah
    - and in filthy places, we are even forbidden to think words of Torah.
  - Similarly for the entire framework of obligation which we are commanded to do by [God's] mouth as set out in the Holy Torah
    - if it would be without this [environment of human relative] perspective, there would be no scope for Torah or Mitzvot at all.[114]
- This is even though, in truth, from God's perspective where He perceives His Essence
  - He is Equally Distributed, filling All without any separation
  - and without any differentiation or change in any place at all.
  - All being a pure Absolute Unity [and unchanged], literally as before the Creation.
  - Nevertheless, we are *unable* and also *not permitted*[115] to intellectually

---

112 Bereishit 14:22.
113 Tehillim 2:4.
114 Although R. Chaim states that all aspects of the Torah are only relevant in the environment of human perception, he only highlights here that place/space is a key constraint of this perception. Clearly the other key constraint

○ [הקדוש ברוך הוא]
○ וְזֶהוּ "הַקָּדוֹשׁ בָּרוּךְ הוּא", רוֹצֶה לוֹמַר שֶׁהוּא מִצִּדּוֹ יִתְבָּרַךְ "קָדוֹשׁ"
○ וְהוּא הוּא עַצְמוֹ נִקְרָא "בָּרוּךְ" כִּבְיָכוֹל מִצַּדֵּנוּ
○ וְהַכֹּל אֶחָד:

• וְעַל זֹאת הַבְּחִינָה שֶׁמִּצַּדֵּנוּ, הוּא שֶׁנֶּאֶמְרוּ הַמִּקְרָאוֹת
○ "אֵל עֶלְיוֹן"
○ "יוֹשֵׁב בַּשָּׁמַיִם", וְהַרְבֵּה כַּיּוֹצֵא:

שער ג' - פרק ו'

• וְהִנֵּה כָּל יְסוֹדֵי תּוֹרָה הַקְּדוֹשָׁה, בְּכָל הָאַזְהָרוֹת וְהַמִּצְוֹת כֻּלָּם, עֲשֵׂה וְלֹא תַעֲשֶׂה, כֻּלָּם הוֹלְכִים עַל פִּי זֹאת הַבְּחִינָה
○ שֶׁמִּצַּד הַשָּׂגָתֵנוּ, שֶׁוַּדַּאי יֵשׁ חִלּוּק וְשִׁנּוּי מְקוֹמוֹת
□ שֶׁבַּמְּקוֹמוֹת הַטְּהוֹרִים מֻתָּרִים וְגַם חַיָּבִים אֲנַחְנוּ לְדַבֵּר אוֹ לְהַרְהֵר דִּבְרֵי תוֹרָה
□ וּבַמְּקוֹמוֹת הַמְטֻנָּפִים נֶאֱסַרְנוּ בָּהֶם אַף הַהִרְהוּר דִּבְרֵי תוֹרָה.
○ וְכֵן כָּל עִנְיְנֵי וְסִדְרֵי חִיּוּב הַנְהָגוֹתֵינוּ שֶׁנִּצְטַוֵּינוּ מִפִּיו בַּתּוֹרָה הַקְּדוֹשָׁה
○ וּבִלְתִּי זֹאת הַבְּחִינָה שֶׁמִּצַּדֵּנוּ, אֵין מָקוֹם לַתּוֹרָה וּמִצְוֹת כְּלָל:

• וְאַף שֶׁבֶּאֱמֶת שֶׁמִּצִּדּוֹ יִתְבָּרַךְ הַמַּשִּׂיג עַצְמוּתוֹ
○ הוּא מָלֵא אֶת כֹּל בְּהַשְׁוָאָה גְמוּרָה, בְּלֹא שׁוּם חֲצִיצָה
○ וְלֹא שׁוּם חִלּוּק וְשִׁנּוּי מְקוֹמוֹת כְּלָל
○ רַק הַכֹּל אַחְדוּת פָּשׁוּט כְּקֹדֶם הַבְּרִיאָה מַמָּשׁ.
○ אֲבָל אֵין אֲנַחְנוּ יְכוֹלִים, וְגַם לֹא הִרְשֵׁינוּ, לִיכָּנֵס כְּלָל לְהִתְבּוֹנֵן בִּינָה בְּזֶה הָעִנְיָן

---

of human perception is time (which although it is tightly bound up with and conceptually inseparable from space) is the other key parameter which defines many Halachic obligations which are again only relevant in the environment of human perception. R. Chaim focuses on and emphasizes the importance of time-bound obligations in GC:04, e.g., prayer at the prescribed time, the timing of Mitzvah performance such as Shofar and Lulav, etc.

115 One could ask here, if humans are *unable* to fathom this idea, why does it make sense to say that we are also *not permitted* to? As no matter how hard we try, our limitation of understanding prevents us from intellectually relating to this level of unity? Clearly, we are obligated to intellectually relate to and engage

engage in this awesome concept at all – [to attempt] to fathom how the Unified Master fills All, and all places, in a sublimely unified, and completely equal way – *God forbid*.

- As the Rokeach wrote,[116] these are his holy words:
  - "With that which is too amazing for you . . . don't investigate . . . [as you don't have any business with hidden things]"[117]
  - this is as written at the beginning of the Braita of Sefer Yetzirah, which places the Creator in perspective, that He is the Creator and He created everything [and there is nothing else apart from him]
  - and in another Braita,[118] if your heart runs [with these amazing concepts] return to "Makom" as it says "and the Chayot ran to and fro"[119] [and a covenant was made on this point]
  - meaning, that when your heart thinks about the Creator – about what He is and how He is manifest in all places and through His deeds, restrain your mouth from speaking and your heart from thinking, remove the thought from your heart
  - and if your heart runs after this thought, hurry and don't think it, and return to the Unity of the Makom of the Universe [i.e., to God] to serve and fear Him
  - and it is about this that a covenant was made, not to think about His Divinity, as none of the wise are able to know.
  - This is the end of the quotation. Refer to it at length.
- "All the Heavenly Hosts ask 'where is the *place* of His Honor?'"[120] as they are incapable of intellectually relating to the essence of this concept of His Makom/Place of the Universe, as mentioned above.
  - This is as per Chazal's comment[121] that when the angels say "Blessed is the honor of God – from His *Place*,"[122] they say this because they are unaware of His *Place*.[123]

---

in this concept as it is a pivotal thought without which we cannot perform the Mitzvah of Kriat Shema when reciting the first sentence proclaiming God's absolute Unity (as highlighted at the end of this chapter and in G3:08). What we are, however, not permitted to do is to fool ourselves to think that we can in any way attempt to fathom the depth of this concept, since if we fool ourselves in this way, we can end up incorrectly theorizing and implementing practices which are not Halachically valid (as highlighted at the end of G3:08) without regard to the space/time framework within which the Torah MUST be observed. Such practices not only do not draw us closer to the Unity of God, they also prevent us from Unifying God in our world environment which is the very purpose of our engagement in Torah and Mitzvot.

116 Sefer HaRokeach Hilchot Chassidut Shoresh Kedushat HaYichud – this is in the same section of the quotation from Sefer HaRokeach at the end of

הַנּוֹרָא, לֵידַע וּלְהַשִּׂיג אֵיךְ אָדוֹן יָחִיד בָּרוּךְ הוּא מָלֵא אֶת כֹּל, וְכָל הַמְּקוֹמוֹת, בְּאַחְדוּת פָּשׁוּט וְשִׁוּוּי גָּמוּר חָלִילָה וְחָלִילָה.

- וּכְמוֹ שֶׁכָּתַב הָרוֹקֵחַ זִכְרוֹנוֹ לִבְרָכָה בְּשֹׁרֶשׁ קְדֻשַּׁת הַיִּחוּד זֶה לְשׁוֹנוֹ הק'
  - "בַּמֻּפְלָא מִמְּךָ אַל תַּחְקֹר" כו'

- זֶה שֶׁכָּתוּב בְּרֵישׁ בְּרַיְתָא דְּסֵפֶר יְצִירָה, "הָשֵׁב הַיּוֹצֵר עַל מְכוֹנוֹ הוּא הַיּוֹצֵר כֹּל" כו'.

- וּבְבָרַיְתָא אַחֶרֶת "וְאִם רָץ לִבְּךָ, שׁוּב לַמָּקוֹם, שֶׁלְּכָךְ נֶאֱמַר (יחזקאל א, יד) "וְהַחַיּוֹת רָצוֹא וָשׁוֹב".

- פֵּרוּשׁ, כְּשֶׁתִּתְחַשֵּׁב בְּלִבְּךָ עַל בּוֹרֵא עוֹלָם מַה הוּא וְאֵיךְ חֲנִיָּתוֹ בְּכָל מָקוֹם וּמַעֲשָׂיו, "בְּלֹם פִּיךָ מִלְּדַבֵּר, וְלִבְּךָ מִלְהַרְהֵר", — הָסֵר הַמַּחֲשָׁבָה מִלִּבְּךָ

- "וְאִם רָץ לִבְּךָ" — לְמַחֲשָׁבָה זֹאת, חוּשָׁה וּמַהֵר וְאַל תְּהַרְהֲרָהּ, וְשׁוּב לְיִחוּד מְקוֹמוֹ שֶׁל עוֹלָם לַעֲבוֹדָתוֹ וּלְיִרְאָתוֹ וכו'.

- וְעַל דָּבָר זֶה נִכְרַת בְּרִית, שֶׁלֹּא לַחְשֹׁב בֶּאֱלֹקוּתוֹ, שֶׁאֵין כָּל הַחֲכָמִים יְכוֹלִין לֵידַע".

- עַד כָּאן לְשׁוֹנוֹ, וְעַיֵּן שָׁם בָּאֹרֶךְ.

- וְכָל צִבְאוֹת הַמּוֹנֵי מַעְלָה שׁוֹאֲלִין אַיֵּה מְקוֹם כְּבוֹדוֹ, שֶׁאֵין יְכוֹלִין לְהַשִּׂיג מַהוּת עִנְיַן בְּחִינַת 'מְקוֹמוֹ שֶׁל עוֹלָם' הַנַּ"ל.

- וְהוּא מַאֲמָרָם זִכְרוֹנָם לִבְרָכָה בְּפֶרֶק חֲגִיגָה אֵין דּוֹרְשִׁין (י"ג ב), "דִּמְדָאָמְרֵי "בָּרוּךְ כְּבוֹד ה' מִמְּקוֹמוֹ" (יחזקאל ג, יב) מִכְּלָל דִּמְקוֹמוֹ לֵיכָּא דְּיָדַע לֵיהּ".

G3:02 and it includes the quotation from Sefer Yetzirah which was previously separately quoted in G3:02 and referenced again in G3:03.

117 Chagiga 13a.
118 Sefer Yetzirah Chapter 1 Mishna 7.
119 Yechezkel 1:14.
120 Zohar II Mishpatim 100b.
121 Chagiga 13b.
122 Yechezkel 3:12.
123 In the Kedushah prayer there is the statement and response of the different groups of angels.

The first set state: "Holy, Holy, Holy, is God, Lord of the Hosts, who fills all the earth with His Glory" (Yishayahu 6:3). This relates to God's perspective of being equally distributed in all things.

The next set of angels states: "Blessed is the honor of God – from His Place." This relates to our perspective that God's place is unfathomable.

- Moshe earnestly sought to relate to this concept, as per "Show me Your Honor?",[124] that is the concept of the Makom/*Place* of His Honor, and this request was not granted to him.
- It is only [God] alone who can relate to His Essence. He is the [only] One who knows the essence of this awesome concealed concept, "and the hidden matters are for God alone"[125]
  - but we are only permitted to intellectually engage in that which we are allowed "and which are revealed to us,"[126] to our perception
  - and this is from our perspective
  - that God is referred to as *Circumventing all worlds*
  - that, notwithstanding all of this
  - with His Sublime Will, He has concealed His Honor
  - in such a way that the worlds, powers, and creatures both created and regenerated appear to us as entities in their own right [and separate from God].
- Therefore, we must resolutely know and immutably fix in our hearts with 'steadfast faith,'[127] that from our perspective there is certainly Halachic difference between places and other matters, as I wrote above, for this is the cornerstone of our faith[128] and the principal root of the entirety of Torah and Mitzvot.
- This is also one of the reasons why immediately after intellectually relating to the Unity of God in the first verse of Kriat Shema, that we then say "Blessed is the name of the Honor of His Majesty for ever and ever":
  - This, as will be explained in G3:11, is that the concept of Unity as expressed in the first verse with the word "*One*" is
    - to intellectually focus on the fact that The Unified Master Blessed be He is One [entity together] with all the worlds and creations
    - in an absolutely literal Unity
    - where all [other entities] are considered to be Ayin/nothing
    - and there is absolutely nothing else apart from [God] at all.
  - However, lest one should, God forbid, [attempt] to intellectually focus on the essence of how and what this concept is, therefore

---

As will be explained later in the Third Gateway, the aspect of God which is equally distributed within all things is referred to with "YHVH" whereas the aspect of God being a separate entity/ruler from this world is referred to with "Elokim." The closing statement of the Kedushah prayer is that "*YHVH* will Rule" – this refers to future times when we will all see that it is God, who is equally distributed in this world (i.e., specifically *YHVH*) who will rule (see G3:11).

נפש שער ג' - פרק ו' החיים 509

- וּמֹשֶׁה רַבֵּנוּ בְּקֵשָׁה נַפְשׁוֹ לְהַשִּׂיג הָעִנְיָן בְּאָמְרוֹ (שמות לג יח) "הַרְאֵנִי נָא אֶת כְּבוֹדֶךָ", הַיְנוּ בְּחִינַת מָקוֹם כְּבוֹדוֹ הַנַּ"ל, וְלֹא נִתַּן לוֹ:

- וְרַק הוּא לְבַדּוֹ יִתְבָּרַךְ הַמַּשִּׂיג עַצְמוּתוֹ, הוּא הַיּוֹדֵעַ עַצְמוּת מַהוּת זֶה הָעִנְיָן הַמֻּפְלָא וּמְכֻסֶּה, "וְהַנִּסְתָּרוֹת לַה' אֱלֹהֵינוּ" (דברים כט, כח)

- וַאֲנַחְנוּ אֵין רְשָׁאִין לְהִתְבּוֹנֵן אֶלָּא בְּמָה שֶׁהִרְשַׁנוּ "וְהַנִּגְלוֹת לָנוּ" — לְהַשִּׂיגֵנוּ
  - וְהוּא בְּהַבְחִינָה שֶׁ"מִּצַּדֵּנוּ"
  - שֶׁנִּקְרָא הוּא יִתְבָּרַךְ שְׁמוֹ בִּבְחִינַת "סוֹבֵב כָּל עָלְמִין".
  - מֵחֲמַת שֶׁעִם כָּל זֶה
  - צִמְצְּמָם בִּרְצוֹנוֹ הַפָּשׁוּט כְּבוֹדוֹ יִתְבָּרַךְ
  - שֶׁיִּתְרָאֶה לְעֵין הַהַשָּׂגָה מְצִיאוּת עוֹלָמוֹת וְכֹחוֹת וּבְרִיּוֹת נִבְרָאִים מְחֻדָּשִׁים:

- וְלָזֹאת, חַיָּבִים אֲנַחְנוּ לֵידַע וְלִקְבֹּעַ בְּלִבֵּנוּ אֱמוּנַת אֹמֶן בַּל תִּמּוֹט, שֶׁמִּצַּדֵּנוּ וַדַּאי שֶׁיֵּשׁ חִלּוּק מְקוֹמוֹת וְעִנְיָנִים שׁוֹנִים לְעִנְיַן דִּינָא וְהִלְכְתֵי רַבָּתֵי, כְּמוֹ שֶׁכָּתַבְתִּי לְעֵיל, כִּי הִיא פִּנַּת יְסוֹד הָאֱמוּנָה וְעִקַּר שֹׁרֶשׁ הַתּוֹרָה וְהַמִּצְוֹת כֻּלָּם:

- וְהוּא גַם כֵּן אֶחָד מֵהַטְּעָמִים, שֶׁאַחַר יִחוּד פָּסוּק רִאשׁוֹן דִּקְרִיאַת שְׁמַע, אוֹמְרִים "בָּרוּךְ שֵׁם כְּבוֹד מַלְכוּתוֹ לְעוֹלָם וָעֶד".

- וְהוּא כְּמוֹ שֶׁנִּתְבָּאֵר לְהַלָּן בְּפֶרֶק י"א, שֶׁעִנְיַן יִחוּד פָּסוּק רִאשׁוֹן בְּתֵבַת "אֶחָד", הַיְנוּ
  - לְכַוֵּן שֶׁאָדוֹן יָחִיד בָּרוּךְ הוּא, הוּא אֶחָד בְּכָל הָעוֹלָמוֹת וְהַבְּרִיּוֹת כֻּלָּם
  - אַחְדוּת פָּשׁוּט כְּמַשְׁמָעוֹ
  - וְכֻלָּם נֶחְשָׁבִים לְאַיִן
  - וְאֵין עוֹד מִלְּבַדּוֹ יִתְבָּרַךְ לְגַמְרֵי.
- וְשֶׁלֹּא נָבֹא לְהִתְבּוֹנֵן חָלִילָה עַל מַהוּת הָעִנְיָן אֵיךְ וּמַה, לָזֹאת

So the concept of Makom, together with both of its related aspects, is deeply and prominently integrated into the key parts of our prayer services.

124 Shemot 33:18.
125 Devarim 29:28.
126 Continuation of Devarim 29:28.
127 Yishayahu 25:1.
128 See the comment made in G3:01 about the cornerstone of our faith and the reference to the Rambam.

- - we immediately follow the statement [of the first line of Kriat Shema] with the statement of "Blessed is the name of the Honor of His Majesty for ever and ever"
  - which as will be explained there [in G3:11] that the intention is to relate to [the intellectual focus] from our perspective
  - which relates to the [apparent] existence of worlds and creations generated through [God's] Will, that they reqire to be blessed by Him
  - and that He Rules over them.[129]
  - This is the meaning of "Blessed is the name of the Honor of His Majesty for ever and ever."
 - (This is why the concept of the first verse of the Shema is referred to by the Zohar as "Supernal Unity" and the verse "Blessed is the name of the Honor of His Majesty for ever and ever" is referred to as "Lower Unity,"[130] and this is now explained.)

7. TZIMTZUM AND KAV – TWO PERSPECTIVES BUT ONE SINGLE CONCEPT

- These two relative perspectives mentioned above – from God's perspective and from our perspective – are the very same concepts of *Tzimtzum* and *Kav*[131] which are mentioned in the writings of the Arizal, as explained there that:
  - From the perspective of Tzimtzum, there is no justification for there being any change or differentiation of space, [no] up, down, front, or back – just true absolutely equal distribution [of God's Manifestation]
  - and the whole concept of changes and differentiation between places and the multiple names and descriptions [of God] are all only stated from the perspective of the Kav.
- Refer to the beginning of Sefer Otzrot Chaim.[132]

---

129 Where one who rules is by definition separate from the entities being ruled, so the declaration of God as a King and having Majesty is one which identifies Him as being separate from us.
130 Zohar I Bereishit 18b.
131 "Tzimtzum" here literally means "concealment." "Kav" literally means "line." These concepts are defined and explained in this chapter. See V2:02 for a detailed and extensive explanation of the concept of Tzimtzum.
132 Sefer Otzrot Chaim was written by R. Chaim Vital, the primary student of the Arizal. Its content is a partial replication and duplication of various sections of

שער ג' - פרק ז'

- אֲנַחְנוּ אוֹמְרִים אַחַר זֶה "בָּרוּךְ שֵׁם כְּבוֹד מַלְכוּתוֹ לְעוֹלָם וָעֶד"
- שֶׁיִּתְבָּאֵר שָׁם שֶׁהַכַּוָּנָה הוּא עַל הַבְּחִינָה שֶׁמִּצַּד הַשָּׂגָתֵנוּ
- שֶׁמִּתְרָאֶה מְצִיאוּת עוֹלָמוֹת וּבְרִיּוֹת מְחֻדָּשִׁים בִּרְצוֹנוֹ יִתְבָּרֵךְ הַצְּרִיכִים לְהִתְבָּרֵךְ מֵאִתּוֹ
- וְהוּא הַמּוֹלֵךְ עֲלֵיהֶם
- זֶהוּ "בָּרוּךְ שֵׁם כְּבוֹד מַלְכוּתוֹ" וְכוּ'.
- (וְזֶהוּ הָעִנְיָן שֶׁפָּסוּק רִאשׁוֹן נִקְרָא בַּזֹּהַר "יִחוּדָא עִלָּאָה", וּפָסוּק "בָּרוּךְ שֵׁם כְּבוֹד מַלְכוּתוֹ לְעוֹלָם וָעֶד" נִקְרָא "יִחוּדָא תַּתָּאָה", וְהוּא מְבֹאָר:

שער ג' - פרק ז'

- וְאֵלוּ הַב' בְּחִינוֹת הַנַּ"ל, שֶׁמִּצִּדּוֹ יִתְבָּרֵךְ וּמִצִּדֵּנוּ, הֵן הֵן עַצְמָן עִנְיַן הַצִּמְצוּם וְהַקַּו הַנִּזְכָּר בְּדִבְרֵי הָאֲרִיזַ"ל. וַאֲשֶׁר מְבֹאָר שָׁם
- שֶׁמִּצַּד הַ"צִּמְצוּם" לֹא יִצְדַּק בּוֹ שׁוּם שִׁנּוּי וְחִלּוּק מָקוֹם, מַעְלָה וּמַטָּה פָּנִים וְאָחוֹר, רַק הַשְׁוָאָה גְּמוּרָה אֲמִתִּית
- וְכָל עִנְיְנֵי הַשִּׁנּוּיִים וְחִלּוּק הַמְּקוֹמוֹת וְכָל הַשֵּׁמוֹת וְכִנּוּיִים, כֻּלָּם נֶאֱמָרִים רַק מִצַּד בְּחִינַת הַ"קַּו":
- וְעַיֵּן בְּרֵישׁ סֵפֶר אוֹצְרוֹת חַיִּים:

---

the Etz Chaim. The very beginning of it, in Shaar HaIgulim, Derush Adam Kadmon, starts as follows:
- Know that at the beginning of everything the only existence was pure light, called Ein Sof, and there was no empty space but everything was Light of the Ein Sof. When it arose in His Sublime Will to emanate the emanations, for the reason that is known, that is, to be called Merciful and Compassionate, etc., for if there is no one in the world to receive mercy from Him, how can He be called Merciful, with the same applying to all [His] descriptions. He then removed Himself from the center of His Light, at the central focal point within it, and he removed Himself there to the sides and the boundaries resulting in the formation of an empty space. This was the first removal of the Supernal Emanator. This empty space was a perfect circle which bounded the world of Atzilut and the [other] worlds, with the Light of the Ein Sof circumventing it [all] in equal distribution. Now when He removed Himself, then through one point on the edge of this circle, light extended [into the circle] via one straight fine *line* – like one pipe of light drawing from the Ein Sof into this empty space and filling

- It is known that all of the Arizal's comments relating to hidden things are analogies and the [Arizal's] intention [in expressing the] inner essence of the concepts of Tzimtzum and Kav is to relate to these two perspectives, as above, which really, in essence, are absolutely one single concept.
- The explanation of the word "Tzimtzum" *here*[133]
  - does not mean the removal [of God] from one place and transfer to another, to gather[/concentrate] and connect His Essence with His Essence, so to speak – to generate a place which is empty [of Him], God forbid
  - however, its meaning is as it is stated in the Midrashim – an expression of being *hidden* and *concealed*, as per:
    - "and she *concealed* her face, and she did not see the king"[134]
    - "and she *concealed* her face behind the pillar."[135]
  - (Refer to the [definition] of "Tzimtzem" in Sefer HaAruch.)[136]
  - Similarly *here* the word "Tzimtzum" means "hidden" and "concealed."
  - The intention is that God's Unity – at the level of His Essence which fills all the worlds in equal distribution
    - is that which we refer to with the name "Tzimtzum"
    - as God's Unity which fills all the worlds is concealed and hidden from our perception
    - as per: "Indeed, You are a God who conceals Himself."[137]
- [Kav(/*line*)]
  - and in relation to our perception

---

it. But an empty space remained between the light within this empty space and between the Light of the Ein Sof which was circumventing this space as mentioned which was removed to the sides, and [therefore] the bottom end of this *line* did not also reach the Light of the Ein Sof [i.e., this straight line was only connected at one edge inside the circle and it did not reach all the way to the other edge but ended exactly in the middle of the circle], for if it wasn't this way, the *system* would return to its former state with the light within the empty space reconnecting with the Light of the Ein Sof. Therefore this light did not disseminate and extend within the area of the empty space, it just followed the path of the single straight *line* alone as mentioned, and the emanating Light of the Ein Sof was drawn down by way of this *line* within the empty space of this circle, which is that which is emanated, and this is the only way in which the Emanator is connected with that which is emanated. Even though all of Atzilut is circular and circumvented in equal distribution by Ein Sof, nevertheless, that place[/point] which remains connected, from which the beginning of this *line* draws, that place is called the head of Atzilut and its supreme point, and all that which

- וּמוּדַעַת שֶׁכָּל דִּבְרֵי הָאֲרִיזַ"ל בַּנִּסְתָּרוֹת מָשָׁל הֵם, וּפְנִימִיּוּת עִנְיַן הַצִּמְצוּם וְהַקַּו, הַכַּוָּנָה עַל אֵלּוּ הַשְּׁנֵי בְּחִינוֹת הַנַּ"ל, שֶׁהֵן בְּעַצְמָם בְּחִינָה אַחַת וְעִנְיָן אֶחָד לְגַמְרֵי:

- כִּי בֵּאוּר מִלַּת "צִמְצוּם" כָּאן
  ○ אֵינוֹ לְשׁוֹן סִלּוּק וְהֶעְתֵּק מִמָּקוֹם לְמָקוֹם, לְהִתְכַּנֵּס וּלְהִתְחַבֵּר עַצְמוֹ אֶל עַצְמוֹ כִּבְיָכוֹל, לְהַמְצִיא מָקוֹם פָּנוּי חַס וְשָׁלוֹם
  ○ אֶלָּא כְּעִנְיָן שֶׁאָמְרוּ
    ▪ בִּבְרֵאשִׁית רַבָּה סוֹף פָּרָשָׁה מ"ה וְצִמְצְמָה פָּנֶיהָ וְלֹא רָאֲתָה הַמֶּלֶךְ.
    ▪ וּבְאֵיכָה רַבָּתִי בְּרֵישׁ א"ב דַּאֲנִי הַגֶּבֶר, הָלְכָה וְצִמְצְמָה פָּנֶיהָ אַחַר הָעַמּוּד, שֶׁפֵּרוּשׁוֹ שָׁם, לְשׁוֹן הֶסְתֵּר וְכִסּוּי
  ○ (עַיֵּן בֶּעָרוּךְ עֶרֶךְ צמצם).
  ○ כֵּן כָּאן מִלַּת "צִמְצוּם" הַיְנוּ הֶסְתֵּר וְכִסּוּי.
- וְהַכַּוָּנָה, שֶׁאַחְדּוּתוֹ יִתְבָּרֵךְ שְׁמוֹ, בִּבְחִינַת עַצְמוּתוֹ הַמְמַלֵּא כָּל עָלְמִין בְּהַשְׁוָאָה גְּמוּרָה
  ○ מְכַנִּים אֲנַחְנוּ בְּשֵׁם "צִמְצוּם"
  ○ מֵחֲמַת שֶׁאַחְדּוּתוֹ יִתְבָּרֵךְ הַמְמַלֵּא כָּל עָלְמִין הוּא מְצַמְצְמָם וּמְסַתֵּר מֵהַשָּׂגָתֵנוּ
  ○ וּכְעִנְיָן "אָכֵן אַתָּה אֵל מִסְתַּתֵּר" (ישעיה מ"ה, ט"ו):
- ["קי"]
  ○ וְהַשָּׂגָתֵנוּ

---

is drawn downwards is called the lower part of Atzilut, and as a result, there is a concept of up and down [i.e., of differentiated space] within Atzilut – for if this were not the case then there would be no up, down, head, and foot within Atzilut . . .

- . . . for the removal of the light caused the creation and existence of the *containers* [as R. Chaim mentions later on in this chapter]. . . .

133 R. Chaim is very specific in his language and is explaining the definition of "Tzimtzum" *here*, i.e., in the context of its use by the Arizal. This is in contrast to the way this word is often used in Rabbinic literature to mean "contraction" and indeed R. Chaim uses it in that context in G2:06:N26.

134 Bereishit Rabba Lech Lecha 45:10.

135 Eicha Rabba 3:1.

136 Sefer HaAruch is a word lexicon which has an entry describing "Tzimtzem" in this way with reference to the Midrash just quoted.

137 Yishayahu 45:15.

- with that which we perceive to be the existence of cascaded world levels where each higher level feeds the lower differentiated level[138]
- we refer to it with the name "*Kav*"
- as it is like a *line* which dangles down.
- This is what the Arizal writes, that:
  - From the perspective of Tzimtzum
    - which is the same as the perspective of the Unified Essence of God which fills all of the worlds
    - which, even though it is concealed and hidden from our perspective
    - nevertheless, from the perspective of His Essence there is no justification of the concept of up and down [i.e., of spatial differentiation]
  - this [the concept of spatial differentiation] is only derived from the perspective of Kav
    - which is from the perspective of our perception
    - that we, from our perspective, perceive the sequence of the worlds as they cascade [downwards] to be like an [interconnected] line
    - and this justifies our perception of the concept of up and down [i.e., of spatial differentiation].
- (Notwithstanding this, from the perspective of Tzimtzum, that is, that even though God concealed and hid the light of His Unified Essence which fills all, from our perception, nevertheless, we would not be able to justify [relating to Him in terms of] higher and lower levels even from our perspective, if we were able to relate to God's hidden state as being equally distributed in all places – like a bounding circle which has no higher or lower [point on it and also] no difference between any position [i.e., no difference between any two points on it].[139]
  - However, from the perspective of Kav, as a result of God's Will decreeing that even after His concealment, His concealment is not equally distributed in our perception in all places, we therefore are able to relate to differences between specific things, which is like the Kav/line of light cascading downwards [becoming ever-increasingly

---

[138] Or stated in another way, we relate to the concept of "difference," the differentiation between places and therefore the possibility for the conceptual difference between world levels even if we don't necessarily directly relate to multiple world levels. See V2:01, "The Limit of Understanding – The Deeper Meaning of Makom."

[139] This idea is expressed in the verse "Adon Olam" which encapsulates the Principles of Faith. It says "and He is One, and there is no other to compare with Him." This means this His Unity is so complete that there is no *difference* in His Existence, i.e., every part of Him is equally manifest everywhere – His

נפש שער ג' - פרק ז' החיים

- מַה שֶּׁאֲנַחְנוּ מַשִּׂיגִים מְצִיאוּת הִשְׁתַּלְשְׁלוּת עוֹלָמוֹת זֶה לְמַעְלָה מִזֶּה בִּבְחִינוֹת שׁוֹנִים
- מְכַנִּים אֲנַחְנוּ בְּשֵׁם "קַו"
- שֶׁהוּא כְּעֵין קַו הַמִּשְׁתַּלְשֵׁל:

• וְזֶה שֶׁכָּתַב הָאֲרִיזַ"ל
  - שֶׁמִּצַּד "הַצִּמְצוּם"
    - הַיְנוּ, מִצַּד עַצְמוּת אַחְדוּתוֹ יִתְבָּרַךְ שֶׁבְּהָעוֹלָמוֹת הַמָּלֵא אֶת כֹּל
    - אֲשֶׁר אַף שֶׁמֵּאִתָּנוּ הוּא מְצַמְצָם וּמֻסְתָּר
    - אֲבָל בִּבְחִינַת עַצְמוּתוֹ לֹא יִצְדַּק עִנְיַן מַעְלָה וּמַטָּה
  - רַק מִצַּד "הַקַּו"
    - הַיְנוּ, מִצַּד הַשָּׂגָתֵנוּ
    - שֶׁאֲנַחְנוּ מִצִּדֵּנוּ מַשִּׂיגִים סֵדֶר הָעוֹלָמוֹת דֶּרֶךְ הִשְׁתַּלְשְׁלוּת כְּעֵין קַו
    - יִצְדַּק מִצִּדֵּנוּ מַעְלָה וּמַטָּה:

• (וְאַף גַּם זֹאת, שֶׁמִּצַּד הַ"צִּמְצוּם", הַיְנוּ, אַף שֶׁהוּא יִתְבָּרַךְ שְׁמוֹ צִמְצֵם וְהִסְתִּיר מֵהַשָּׂגָתֵנוּ אוֹר עַצְמוּת אַחְדוּתוֹ הַמְּמַלֵּא כֹּל, עִם כָּל זֶה, לֹא יִצְדַּק בּוֹ מַעְלָה וּמַטָּה אַף מִצַּד הַשָּׂגָתֵנוּ, אִם הָיִינוּ מַשִּׂיגִים הַסֵּתֶר שָׁוֶה בְּהַשְׁוָאָה גְּמוּרָה בְּכָל הַמְּקוֹמוֹת, כְּעִנְיַן עִגּוּל הַמַּקִּיף שֶׁלֹּא יִצְדַּק בּוֹ עִנְיַן מַעְלָה וּמַטָּה וְחִלּוּק מָקוֹם.
- אַךְ מִצַּד הַ"קַּו", הַיְנוּ, שֶׁמֵּאַחַר שֶׁגָּזְרָה רְצוֹנוֹ יִתְבָּרַךְ, שֶׁגַּם אַחַר הַצִּמְצוּם

---

relationship with everything is like this bounding circle where each point is equally distant from the closest point of an inner circle contained within it (with the same central point). Therefore, if people were to even relate to the consistency of His concealment then we too would see no *differentiation* in anything, i.e., no difference between higher and lower levels. In this bracketed paragraph, R. Chaim is, using his own terminology, explaining the profound concept that this world is Yesh relative to our perception. It is the domain of Binah, i.e., of differentiated analysis – a place where differences exist – the word "Binah" being related to the word "Bein" denoting difference. In contrast, relative to us, Ayin, is currently the domain of Chochma (see p. 472, fn. 18, as to why this is *currently* the case), i.e., a place where there is no differentiation, with those in the domain of Binah being unable to currently perceive the abstracted domain of Chochma. The domain of God is above Chochma, and therefore, He cannot be perceived in any way at all. (See V2:01, "The Limit of Understanding – The Deeper Meaning of Makom," for more details.)

filtered], which enables us to perceive the revelation of [God's] light in differentiated worlds and powers, where each higher world and power has an increased revelation of Divine Light.

- We also relate to the revelation of His Light in this physical world in terms of also being on different levels in different places, as Chazal list[140] "ten levels of holiness"[141] and "three holy camps,"[142] each with increasing levels of holiness. Therefore, from the perspective of the Kav of Light, our perception is that it is the revelation of God's Light which justifies [the existence of] higher and lower [levels] together with differentiation between places, levels and all their details, as is explained by the Arizal.
- Similarly this is the concept underpinning the verses: "God of the Supernal Realms";[143] "God in Heaven";[144] "He who dwells in the Heavens,"[145] and many similar verses, that from the point of view of our perception it is correct to say that even we recognize a greater revelation of God's Light in a specific place, compared to another place where we perceive the revelation of God's Light to be concealed. This is like the concept expressed by Yaakov when he stood on the site of the [future] Temple as Chazal generally accepted that "This is none other than the House of Elokim,"[146] means that in that place, even man can perceive that there is only the revelation of Divine Light alone.)

• Therefore, this is the concept of "empty space" which the Arizal mentions, that the principle of Tzimtzum was invoked to reveal the containers/vessels.[147]

- Meaning that God's Will decreed, for reasons known to Himself
- to conceal the Light of His Unified Essence in this Makom/Place
- to a degree which establishes all the worlds and creations
- with a tremendous concealment
- which through this creates this wonderful concept
- that enables the apparent and perceived existence of a myriad of worlds and powers through cascaded levels
- and to enlighten them with the revelation of His refined Light

---

140 As already quoted above in G3:04.
141 Mishna Keilim 1:6–9.
142 E.g., Zohar III Balak 190b.
143 Bereishit 14:19.
144 Tehillim 115:3.
145 Tehillim 2:4.
146 Bereishit 28:17.

וְהַהֶסְתֵּר, אֵין הַהֶסְתֵּר שָׁוֶה לְהַשָּׂגָתֵנוּ בְּכָל הַמְּקוֹמוֹת בְּשָׁוֶה, וַאֲנַחְנוּ מַשִּׂיגִים הַשָּׂגוֹת שׁוֹנִים בְּחִלּוּק בְּחִינוֹת פְּרָטִיִּים, דֶּרֶךְ הִשְׁתַּלְשְׁלוּת כְּעֵין קַו אוֹר, הַמֵּאִיר הַשָּׂגָתֵנוּ לְהַשִּׂיג הִתְגַּלּוּת אוֹרוֹ יִתְבָּרֵךְ בְּעוֹלָמוֹת וְכֹחוֹת חֲלוּקִים, שֶׁכָּל עוֹלָם וְכֹחַ הַיּוֹתֵר עֶלְיוֹן, הַהִתְגַּלּוּת אוֹר הָאֱלֹקִי בּוֹ יוֹתֵר.

○ וְגַם הַשָּׂגָתֵנוּ הִתְגַּלּוּת אוֹרוֹ יִתְבָּרֵךְ בְּזֶה הָעוֹלָם, הוּא גַם כֵּן בִּבְחִינוֹת וּמַדְרֵגוֹת שׁוֹנִים בִּמְקוֹמוֹת חֲלוּקִים, כְּמוֹ שֶׁשָּׁנוּ רַבּוֹתֵינוּ זִכְרוֹנָם לִבְרָכָה (כלים א, ו) "עֶשֶׂר קְדֻשּׁוֹת" וְ"שָׁלֹשׁ מַחֲנוֹת מְקֻדָּשׁוֹת", זוֹ לְמַעְלָה מִזּוֹ בְּעֵרֶךְ קְדֻשָּׁתָם, אָז מִצַּד קַו אוֹר הַשָּׂגָתֵנוּ הִתְגַּלּוּת אוֹרוֹ יִתְבָּרֵךְ, הוּא שֶׁיִּצְדַּק בּוֹ מַעְלָה וּמַטָּה, וְכָל חִלּוּקֵי הַמְּקוֹמוֹת וְהַבְּחִינוֹת שׁוֹנִים וּפְרָטֵיהֶם, הַמְבֹאָרִים בְּדִבְרֵי הָאֲרִיזַ"ל.

○ וְכֵן עִנְיַן הַמִּקְרָאוֹת "אֵל עֶלְיוֹן" (בראשית יד, יט) וְ"אֱלֹהֵינוּ בַשָּׁמַיִם" (תהלים קטו, ג) "יוֹשֵׁב בַּשָּׁמַיִם" (תהלים ב, ד) וְהַרְבֵּה כַּיּוֹצֵא, שֶׁמִּצַּד הַשָּׂגָתֵנוּ יִצְדַּק לוֹמַר שֶׁבְּמָקוֹם זֶה נִכָּר יוֹתֵר גַּם אֶצְלֵנוּ הִתְגַּלּוּת אוֹר אֱלֹקוּתוֹ יִתְבָּרֵךְ שְׁמוֹ, מִבִּמְקוֹם אַחֵר שֶׁהִתְגַּלּוּת אוֹרוֹ יִתְבָּרֵךְ הוּא בִּבְחִינַת הֶסְתֵּר מֵהַשָּׂגָתֵנוּ, וּכְעִנְיָן שֶׁאָמַר יַעֲקֹב אָבִינוּ עָלָיו הַשָּׁלוֹם בְּעָמְדוֹ עַל מְקוֹם הַמִּקְדָּשׁ, כְּמוֹ שֶׁקִּבְּלוּ רַבּוֹתֵינוּ זִכְרוֹנָם לִבְרָכָה, "אֵין זֶה כִּי אִם בֵּית אֱלֹהִים" (בראשית כח, יז) רוֹצֶה לוֹמַר שֶׁבְּזֶה הַמָּקוֹם, מַשִּׂיג גַּם לְהַשָּׂגַת הָאָדָם, שֶׁאֵין בּוֹ רַק הִתְגַּלּוּת אוֹר אֱלֹקוּתוֹ יִתְבָּרֵךְ לְבַד):

● וְזֶהוּ עִנְיַן הַ"חָלָל וּמָקוֹם פָּנוּי" שֶׁהִזְכִּיר זַ"ל, וְשֶׁכְּלַל עִנְיַן הַצִּמְצוּם הָיָה לְהִתְגַּלּוּת הַכֵּלִים.

○ הַיְנוּ, שֶׁגָּזְרָה רְצוֹנוֹ, מִטַּעַם הַכָּמוּס אִתּוֹ יִתְבָּרֵךְ

○ לְהַסְתִּיר אוֹר אַחְדּוּת עַצְמוּתוֹ יִתְבָּרֵךְ בְּזֶה הַמָּקוֹם

○ שִׁעוּר עֲמִידַת הָעוֹלָמוֹת וְהַבְּרִיּוֹת כֻּלָּם

○ הֶסְתֵּר עָצוּם

○ לְהַמְצִיא עַל יְדֵי זֶה עִנְיָן נִפְלָא כָּזֶה

○ שֶׁיִּתְרָאֶה וְיַשִּׂיג מְצִיאוּת עוֹלָמוֹת וְכֹחוֹת אֵין מִסְפָּר דֶּרֶךְ הַדְרָגָה וְהִשְׁתַּלְשְׁלוּת

○ וּלְהָאִיר בָּהֶם הִתְגַּלּוּת אוֹרוֹ יִתְבָּרֵךְ אוֹר דַּק

---

147 I.e., meaning objects which appear to be separate from Him – these "containers/vessels" only exist in the level of Malchut/Kingship where there is a concept of separation, i.e., in the sense that a king is separate from his subjects.

- in tremendously precise measure and with an infinite number of filters
- to the extent that through these tremendous cascadings and filters – even places which are not pure are created together with the powers of impurity, Evil and the Kelipot, and the lowest of the lowest places
- such that it appears and can be imagined as if, God forbid, this space is devoid of the light of the Infinite Essence of God
- and we only perceive the merest glimmer and faintest light like a Kav/line, by way of analogy
- such that by the time it has cascaded down through all the levels and through all the many filters to become the powers of the lowest of low levels – the impure powers and the Evil – the revelation of [God's] light is [so subtle and veiled that it is] no longer recognizable to us at all.
- This is the meaning of the [Arizal] stating there that the Kav/line of [God's] Light does not reach and is not connected to the bottom end and is not attached to its base,[148] and through this [the environment is] generated where higher and lower levels exist. Refer to it there, and it is explained to one who understands.

• *Tzimtzum* and *Kav* are actually one single concept
- meaning that the place of all worlds and creations certainly only contains the Essence of God, even now, unchanged as before their creation
- but this is on a level of Tzimtzum – that is totally concealed – abstracted and concealed from our perception
- such that through this concealment all our perception of the worlds is through its cascaded levels and the drawing down of the revelation of [God's] Light into them following the defined sequence of levels alone, like with the Kav/line, by way of analogy, as stated above.

• This is the meaning of that stated[149] that the Kav of the thread of Light is not drawn and manifest all the way down, except little by little, meaning

---

148 The fact that the line descending into the circle is not reconnected at the bottom end results in there being differentiation introduced all the way down the Kav reaching its most differentiated state at its lowest disconnected point.

149 By the Arizal: Etz Chaim Shaar 1, Derush Igulim VeYosher, Part 2:
  • Know that before the emanations were emanated and the creations were created, there was a Sublime Supernal Light which filled all of existence. There was no empty space, everything was filled with that Sublime Light of the Ein Sof. There was no concept of beginning or end, all was One Sublime Light, distributed equally and this is called Light of the Ein Sof. When it arose in His Sublime Will to create the worlds and to emanate the emanations, to reveal the completeness of His Works and His Names and Descriptions, which was the reason for creating the worlds, as explained in

- בְּשִׁעוּר וְדִקְדּוּק עָצוּם וְדֶרֶךְ מְסֻכִּים אֵין קֵץ
- וְעַד שֶׁיּוּכְלוּ לְהִמָּצֵא דֶּרֶךְ הִשְׁתַּלְשְׁלוּת וּמְסֻכִּים עֲצוּמִים גַּם מְקוֹמוֹת אֲשֶׁר אֵינָם טְהוֹרִים, וְכֹחוֹת הַטֻּמְאָה וְהָרַע וְהַקְּלִפּוֹת, בְּשֵׁפֶל הַמַּדְרֵגוֹת הַתַּחְתּוֹנִים
- וְנִרְאֶה וּמִתְדַּמֶּה כְּאִלּוּ חַם וְשָׁלוֹם הוּא חָלָל פָּנוּי מֵאוֹר אַחְדוּת עַצְמוּתוֹ יִתְבָּרַךְ שְׁמוֹ
- וְאֵין אֲנַחְנוּ מַשִּׂיגִים רַק רְשִׁימָה דַּקָּה מְעַטֶּת וְאוֹר מְעַט כְּעֵין קַו דֶּרֶךְ מָשָׁל
- עַד שֶׁבְּהַגִּיעוֹ דֶּרֶךְ סֵדֶר הַהַדְרָגוֹת וְהַמְסֻכִּים הָרַבִּים אֶל הַכֹּחוֹת תַּחְתּוֹנֵי הַתַּחְתּוֹנִים כֹּחוֹת הַטֻּמְאָה וְהָרַע, אֵין הִתְגַּלּוּת אוֹרוֹ יִתְבָּרַךְ נִכָּר כְּלָל לְהַשָּׂגָתֵנוּ
- וְזֶה שֶׁאָמְרוּ שָׁם, שֶׁהַקַּו הָאוֹר לֹא הִגִּיעַ עַד קָצֶה הַתַּחְתּוֹן וְלֹא נִדְבַּק בְּתַחְתִּיתוֹ, וְעַל יְדֵי זֶה יִמָּצֵא בְּחִינוֹת מַעְלָה וּמַטָּה כו' עַיֵּן שָׁם, וְהוּא מְבֹאָר לַמֵּבִין:
• וְהַצִּמְצוּם וְהַקַּו הַכֹּל אֶחָד וְעִנְיָן אֶחָד
- וְרָצָה לוֹמַר, עִם כִּי וַדַּאי שֶׁגַּם בִּמְקוֹם כָּל הָעוֹלָמוֹת וְהַבְּרוּאִים, הַכֹּל מָלֵא גַּם עַתָּה רַק עַצְמוּתוֹ יִתְבָּרַךְ שְׁמוֹ לְבַד, כְּקֹדֶם הַבְּרִיאָה
- אָמְנָם הוּא בִּבְחִינַת צִמְצוּם, הַיְנוּ בִּבְחִינַת הֶסְתֵּר לְבַד, מֻפְלָא וּמְכֻסֶּה מֵהַשָּׂגָתֵנוּ
- כְּדֵי שֶׁעַל יְדֵי זֶה הַצִּמְצוּם וְהַהֶסְתֵּר תְּהֵא כָּל הַשָּׂגָתֵנוּ אֶת הָעוֹלָמוֹת דֶּרֶךְ הִשְׁתַּלְשְׁלוּת, וְהַמְשָׁכַת הִתְגַּלּוּת אוֹרוֹ יִתְבָּרַךְ בָּהֶם בְּסֵדֶר הַהַדְרָגָה לְבַד כְּעֵין קַו דֶּרֶךְ מָשָׁל, כַּנַּ"ל:
• וְזֶהוּ שֶׁאָמַר שָׁם בְּשַׁעַר עִגּוּלִים וְיֹשֶׁר עָנָף ב', "שֶׁהַקַּו חוּט הָאוֹר לֹא נִמְשַׁךְ

Part 1 in the first essay, He then removed Himself, [in the] Ein Sof, at the central point within it, literally at the center of its Light. He removed this Light and distanced it to the sides surrounding the central point [i.e., to form a circle around it] creating an empty space, literally from this central point [i.e., the area within the circle] like this [see the adjacent diagram]. Now, this removal was in equal distribution around the central point being empty with the space forming a perfect circle ... Now, after the removal mentioned above which resulted in the formation of empty space literally at the center of the Light of the Ein Sof, as mentioned above, there was now space within which the emanations and creations could be in. Then a single straight *line* was drawn from the Light of the Ein Sof, from its encircling Light, from up to down, and it cascaded downwards within that space, like this [see diagram on next

that it does so in a gradual diminishing way through very many levels in precise measure to enable human perception of the worlds and their levels [as separate entities in their own right].
- One who can understand will understand the entire root of the concept explained there through his own initiative, as it is impossible to detail and explain all of [the Arizal's] words there well.

8. TZIMTZUM AWARENESS HELPS CONCENTRATION BUT *NEVER* TO BE ACTIONED

- Therefore, the investigative analysis of the essence of the concept of Tzimtzum is forbidden, as written by the Arizal, as I wrote above[150]
    - that we are not at all permitted to intellectualize, to know and perceive the essence of the concept of [God] being the Makom/Place of the Universe
    - how All is filled with only His Absolute Unity, and that there is absolutely nothing else at all besides Him.
- The truth is that this concept falls within the prohibition of investigating what happened before the Creation
    - which Chazal learn from an explicit Scriptural verse: "For inquire now regarding the early days [that preceded you], from the day that God created man . . . ," and one must not inquire [what is above, below, before, and after].[151]
- The Arizal, who permitted the amazing revelation of very great and deep secrets, already explained that the deeper meaning of the [prohibition derived from the] verse "from the day that God created Adam(/man)" relates to the world of *Adam Kadmon*[152]

---

page]. The top end of the *line* drawing from the Ein Sof itself and touching it. However, the bottom end of this *line* does not touch the Light of the Ein Sof [i.e., the *line* which extends down within the circle from one side of it, does not reach all the way to the other side of the circle] and the Light of the Ein Sof is manifest downwards through this *line*. In this space, He emanated, created, formed, and made all of the worlds. This *line* is like a single fine pipe through which the waters of the supernal Light of the Ein Sof are disseminated and drawn to the worlds within this space. We will now explain a little about the Kabbalists' investigative analysis to know how there can be a beginning within the end of the Sefirot mentioned above. However, in that this *line*, whose beginning

וְנִתְפַּשֵּׁט תֵּכֶף עַד לְמַטָּה, אֶלָּא לְאַט לְאַט", רוֹצֶה לוֹמַר דֶּרֶךְ הַדְרָגוֹת רַבּוֹת מְאֹד, בְּשִׁעוּר מְדֻקְדָּק, כְּפִי הַצֹּרֶךְ לְהַשָּׂגָתֵנוּ עִנְיַן הָעוֹלָמוֹת וְסֵדֶר הַדְרָגָתָם:

- וְהַמֵּבִין יָבִין עַל פִּי זֶה מִדַּעְתּוֹ כָּל שֹׁרֶשׁ הָעִנְיָן הַמְבֹאָר שָׁם, כִּי אִי אֶפְשָׁר לְפָרֵט וּלְהַסְבִּיר הֵיטֵב כָּל דְּבָרָיו זַ"ל שָׁם:

שער ג' - פרק ח'

- וְלָכֵן נֶאֱסַר הַחֲקִירָה וְהַהִתְבּוֹנְנוּת בְּמַהוּת עִנְיַן הַצִּמְצוּם, כְּמוֹ שֶׁכָּתַב הָאֲרִיזַ"ל, כְּמוֹ שֶׁכָּתַבְתִּי לְעֵיל
  - שֶׁלֹּא הֻרְשֵׁנוּ לְהִתְבּוֹנֵן כְּלָל, לֵידַע וּלְהַשִּׂיג מַהוּת "עִנְיַן מְקוֹמוֹ שֶׁל עוֹלָם"
  - אֵיךְ שֶׁהַכֹּל מָלֵא רַק אַחְדוּתוֹ הַפָּשׁוּט יִתְבָּרַךְ, וְאֵין עוֹד מִלְּבַדּוֹ כְּלָל לְגַמְרֵי מִצִּדּוֹ יִתְבָּרַךְ:

- וְהָאֱמֶת שֶׁהוּא בִּכְלַל שְׁאֵלַת וַחֲקִירַת "מַה לְפָנִים"
  - שֶׁלְּמָדוּהוּ זִכְרוֹנָם לִבְרָכָה (חגיגה ר"פ אין דורשין) מִכָּתוּב מְפֹרָשׁ (דברים ה, לב) "כִּי שְׁאַל נָא לְיָמִים רִאשֹׁנִים לְמִן הַיּוֹם אֲשֶׁר בָּרָא אֱלֹהִים אָדָם" וכו', וְאִי אַתָּה שׁוֹאֵל וכו':

- וְהָאֲרִיזַ"ל אֲשֶׁר הֻרְשָׁה וְהִפְלִיא לְגַלּוֹת סוֹדוֹת עֲמֻקִּים וְרָמִים, כְּבָר פֵּרֵשׁ הוּא

---

touches the Light of the Ein Sof at its top end and its bottom end does not extend downwards until it reaches the location of the Light of the Ein Sof bounding underneath the worlds [i.e., at the other side of the circle] and is not connected to it [at the bottom end] – therefore, this justifies [the concept] of a beginning and end, for if both ends were to receive bestowal from the Ein Sof then both ends would be *beginnings* and the same as each other and there would be no concept of up and down [of spatial differentiation] . . . however, as the Ein Sof is only drawn down a single *line*, which is only a fine pipe, this justifies the concept of up and down, front and back . . . Now, when the Light of the Ein Sof is drawn through the straight *line* into the empty space, as mentioned above, it is not drawn and manifest all the way down, however, it is manifest little by little . . . [See the same concept from Mevo Shearim as quoted on p. 431, fn. 366.]

150 See G3:06.
151 Chagiga 11b quoting Devarim 4:32.
152 This is the highest world level as described on p. 444, fn. 389. It represents the realm of the *Divine Will* and corresponds to the soul level of Yechida.

- and in relation to Adam Kadmon, he wrote that we are also not permitted to speak of or investigate its essence but only of the *lights which emanate from it* alone [i.e., the way in which its essence is manifest]
- and of this [light], we are also only permitted to investigate from the level of the emanations of 63[153] within it and downwards
- but not [permitted to investigate its inner essence together] with the emanations of 72 within it
- so how much more so we are not permitted to, God forbid, intellectually engage in the essence of the concept of Tzimtzum from God's perspective.[154]

• The [Arizal] only provides deep explanations in relation to the concept of Kav, that is the way in which we are able to relate to the cascading down of God's Essence through the worlds
- however, he only fleetingly deals with the concept of Tzimtzum and does not speak of its essence in any detail.

• Refer to the beginning of Sefer Otzrot Chaim.[155]

• [The Arizal] only revealed the general fact that [Tzimtzum] exists for the [consumption] of a wise person who can understand it with his own initiative
- for the reason that it is certainly fitting for an honest and wise person who is permanently connected to Torah study and Mitzvah performance and 'whose spirit is steadfast with God'[156]
- to be generally aware of the existence of this awesome concept
- that the Unified Master fills All and there is nothing else besides Him
- as this will enthuse the purity of the holiness of his thoughts in *the service of prayer*
- to concentrate his heart with fear, awe, and trembling on *The Makom*,

---

153 As light emanates from the world of Adam Kadmon, it splits into Ten Sefirot which form the Sefirot of the world of *Tohu* (chaos). These Sefirot, unlike the Sefirot of the other worlds, are entirely disconnected from one another and as a result of their lack of interaction they disintegrate in a process known as Shevirat HaKeilim. As a result of its disintegration, the world of Tohu is not listed as one of the world levels. The Sefirot within each and every world level are classified in a number of different ways. One of the ways of classifying them is by their connection with different Hebrew letter combination expansions of God's Name YHVH. There are four standard expansions where the letters are spelled out in full in different ways, e.g., the letter *Hey*, when spelled out in full can be *Hey Aleph* or *Hey Hey*. The four standard expansions are separately identified by their numerical values which relate to the Sefirot as follows: 72 (Av – *Ayin Bet*) is Chochma, 63 (Sag – *Samech Gimmel*) is Binah, 45 (Mah –

זִכְרוֹנוֹ לִבְרָכָה, שֶׁפְּנִימִיּוּת כַּוָּנַת הַכָּתוּב "לְמִן הַיּוֹם אֲשֶׁר בָּרָא אֱלֹהִים אָדָם" וְכוּ', הוּא עַל עוֹלָם אָדָם קַדְמָאָה.

○ וְגַם בְּעִנְיַן אָדָם קַדְמָאָה כָּתַב, שֶׁאֵין אֲנַחְנוּ רַשָּׁאִין לְדַבֵּר וְלַחְקֹר בְּעִנְיַן עַצְמוּת פְּנִימִיּוּתוֹ, רַק בָּאוֹרוֹת הַיּוֹצְאִים מִמֶּנּוּ לְבָד

○ וְגַם זֹאת רַק מְאוֹרוֹת דס"ג שֶׁבּוֹ וְאֵילָךְ

○ וְלֹא בָּאוֹרוֹת ע"ב שֶׁבּוֹ

○ כָּל שֶׁכֵּן שֶׁלֹּא הָרְשֵׁנוּ לְהִתְבּוֹנֵן חָלִילָה בְּמַהוּת עִנְיַן הַצִּמְצוּם, כְּפִי אֲשֶׁר הוּא מִצִּדּוֹ יִתְבָּרֵךְ:

• וְרַק בְּעִנְיַן הַקַּו, הֵנוּ בְּהִשְׁתַּלְשְׁלוּת הָעוֹלָמוֹת שֶׁכְּפִי הַשָּׂגָתֵנוּ, בָּזֶה הוּא שֶׁהֶעֱמִיק הִרְחִיב הַדִּבּוּר

• אֲבָל בְּעִנְיַן הַצִּמְצוּם, דִּבֵּר בּוֹ בְּרָצוֹא וָשׁוֹב, וְלֹא דִּבֵּר בְּ'מַהוּת' עִנְיָנוֹ בִּפְרָטוּת:

• וְעַיֵּן בְּרֵישׁ סֵפֶר אוֹצְרוֹת חַיִּים דַּף ב' רֵישׁ ע"ג:

• וְלֹא גִלָּהוּ, רַק 'מְצִיאוּתוֹ' דֶּרֶךְ כְּלָל לְבַד, לְחָכָם וּמֵבִין מִדַּעְתּוֹ.

○ מִטַּעַם שֶׁוַּדַּאי רָאוּי לְהָאָדָם הַיָּשָׁר חָכָם לֵבָב, הַקָּבוּעַ כָּל הַיָּמִים בְּתַלְמוּד תּוֹרָה וּמִצְוֹת, אֲשֶׁר נֶאֶמְנָה אֶת אֵל רוּחוֹ

○ לֵידַע מְצִיאוּת זֶה הָעִנְיָן הַנּוֹרָא דֶּרֶךְ כְּלָל

○ שֶׁאֲדוֹן יָחִיד יִתְבָּרַךְ שְׁמוֹ מָלֵא אֶת כֹּל וְאֵין עוֹד מִלְּבַדּוֹ יִתְבָּרַךְ

○ לְהַלְהִיב מִזֶּה טֹהַר קְדֻשַּׁת מַחְשַׁבְתּוֹ לַעֲבוֹדַת הַתְּפִלָּה

○ לְכַוֵּן לִבּוֹ בְּאֵימָה וְיִרְאָה וְרֶתֶת לַמָּקוֹם, הוּא מְקוֹמוֹ שֶׁל עוֹלָם, ("וּמְקוֹמוֹ שֶׁל עוֹלָם" הוּא הוּא כַּוָּנַת עִנְיַן הַצִּמְצוּם, וְהוּא מְבֹאָר כַּנַּ"ל)

Mem Hey) relates to the cluster of six Sefirot of Chesed, Gevurah, Tiferet, Netzach, Hod, Yesod, and 52 (Ban – *Bet Nun*) relates to Malchut.

Even though these Sefirot of Chochma 72 and Binah 63 in the world of Tohu are not connected, nevertheless the Sefira of Chochma is on a higher level which is so sublime that we are not permitted to attempt to analytically relate to it.

154 Which relates to a higher level than the emanations of 72 from Adam Kadmon.

155 Sefer Otzrot Chaim – at the end of the first section Shaar HaIgulim Derush Adam Kadmon:
- Now, we are not permitted to involve ourselves with the depth and essence of this *Man* at all [i.e., *Man* referring in context to Adam Kadmon], but we can involve ourselves and speak of that which emanates from it.

156 Tehillim 78:8.

that [God] is the Makom/Place of the Universe (with the concept of *the Place of the Universe* being identical to the concept of *Tzimtzum* and it is now explained as above).
- As per Chazal:
  - "One who prays should concentrate his heart on Makom."[157]
  - "And when you pray, don't [pray by rote], but rather by seeking mercy and supplication before the Makom Blessed be He."[158]
  - As R. Eliezer said to his students: "Know before Whom you pray."[159]

- Similarly, this [awareness] is fitting for a true servant of God to enable him to focus the holiness of his thoughts on the Unity of God when reciting the word "One" in the first verse of Kriat Shema
  - that God, from His perspective, is literally One, even together with all His creations – an Absolute Unity [unchanged and] as before the Creation, as will be explained later, God willing
  - and also that he should be fearful and motivated from transgressing, God forbid, any of God's Commandments, as He fills all places with His Glory, as per:
    - "Can a man hide in a concealed way that I should not see him? . . . Do I not fill the heaven and the earth?"[160]
    - King David: "I have set God before me always."[161]

- This is the concept of *Chilul Hashem*[162] wherever it is mentioned, where the verse "Mechalaleha"[163] is explained by the Zohar[164] to relate to "Chalal" – an expression of "void" and "empty space."
  - Similarly here, [when a person is unconcerned over transgressing God's Commandments] he causes the appearance, God forbid, that the place in which he is, is devoid of God and he [therefore] has no hesitation to transgress God's Commandments, as Chazal say "one who transgresses a sin in secret is as if he pushes away the feet of the Shechina."[165]

- (This answers the good question which appears strange in the eyes of any wise person as to how the Arizal permitted himself to mention the

---

[157] Berachot 31a. The standard version mentions "concentrate his heart on Heaven" and not "Makom." The source for this statement is Tosefta Berachot 3:4 which only states "concentrate his heart." Clearly R. Chaim had a version which mentions "Makom." However, irrespective of the version, it still conveys the same point.
[158] Mishna Avot 2:13, as brought down at the beginning of G3:01.
[159] Berachot 28b.
[160] Yirmiyahu 23:24.
[161] Tehillim 16:8.

- כְּמַאֲמָרָם זִכְרוֹנָם לִבְרָכָה
- שֶׁהַמִּתְפַּלֵּל צָרִיךְ שֶׁיְכַוֵּן לִבּוֹ לַמָּקוֹם.
- וְכֵן אָמְרוּ (אבות ב, יג) וּכְשֶׁאַתָּה מִתְפַּלֵּל אַל תַּעַשׂ וכו', אֶלָּא רַחֲמִים וְתַחֲנוּנִים לִפְנֵי הַמָּקוֹם ב"ה.
- וּבְעִנְיָן שֶׁאָמַר רַבִּי אֱלִיעֶזֶר לְתַלְמִידָיו (ברכות כ"ח ע"ב) דְעוּ לִפְנֵי מִי אַתֶּם מִתְפַּלְּלִים:

• וְכֵן בְּיִחוּד פָּסוּק רִאשׁוֹן דִּקְרִיאַת שְׁמַע בְּתֵיבַת 'אֶחָד', רָאוּי לְהָעוֹבֵד אֲמִתִּי לְכַוֵּן בְּקַדְּשׁוֹ מַחֲשַׁבְתּוֹ

- שֶׁהוּא יִתְבָּרַךְ שְׁמוֹ מִצִּדּוֹ, הוּא "אֶחָד" כְּמַשְׁמָעוֹ, גַּם בְּכָל הַבְּרוּאִים כֻּלָּם, אַחְדוּת פָּשׁוּט לְבַד כְּקֹדֶם הַבְּרִיאָה, וּכְמוֹ שֶׁיִתְבָּאֵר אִי"ה לְהַלָּן.
- גַּם לִהְיוֹת יָרֵא וְחָרֵד מִזֶּה מִלַּעֲבֹר חַס וְשָׁלוֹם עַל אַחַת מִמִּצְוֹתָיו יִתְבָּרַךְ, כִּי מְלֹא כָל הָאָרֶץ כְּבוֹדוֹ
- כְּמוֹ שֶׁאָמַר הַכָּתוּב (ירמיה כג, כד) "אִם יִסָּתֵר אִישׁ בַּמִּסְתָּרִים וַאֲנִי לֹא אֶרְאֶנּוּ כו', הֲלֹא אֶת הַשָּׁמַיִם וְאֶת הָאָרֶץ אֲנִי מָלֵא"
- וּבְעִנְיַן שֶׁאָמַר דָּוִד הַמֶּלֶךְ עָלָיו הַשָּׁלוֹם (תהלים טז, ח) "שִׁוִּיתִי ה' לְנֶגְדִּי תָמִיד":

• וְהוּא עִנְיַן "הֶחָלוּל ה'" הַנֶּאֱמָר בְּכָל מָקוֹם. כְּעִנְיָן שֶׁפֵּרֵשׁ בַּזֹּהַר פָּסוּק "מְחַלְלֶיהָ" וכו' שֶׁהוּא לְשׁוֹן חָלָל וּפְנוּיַת מָקוֹם

- כֵּן הָעִנְיָן כָּאן, שֶׁמַּרְאֶה חַס וְשָׁלוֹם כְּאִלּוּ הַמָּקוֹם שֶׁעוֹמֵד בּוֹ הוּא חָלוּל, פָּנוּי מִמֶּנּוּ יִת', וְאֵינוֹ חוֹשֵׁשׁ מִלַּעֲבֹר עַל מִצְוֹתָיו יִתְבָּרַךְ. וּכְעִנְיָן זֶה מַאֲמָרָם זִכְרוֹנָם לִבְרָכָה (ספ"ק דְקִדּוּשִׁין לא, ע"א) "כָּל הָעוֹבֵר עֲבֵרָה בַּסֵּתֶר כְּאִלּוּ דּוֹחֵק רַגְלֵי הַשְּׁכִינָה":

• (וּבָזֶה יִתְיַשֵּׁב מַאי דְקַשְׁיָא טוּבָא וּבְעֵינַי כָּל חָכָם לֵב יִפָּלֵא, מֵאַיִן הִתִּיר הָאֲרִיזַ"ל לְעַצְמוֹ לְדַבֵּר וּלְהַזְכִּיר כְּלָל עִנְיַן הַצִּמְצוּם, כֵּיוָן שֶׁהַהִתְבּוֹנְנוּת בּוֹ אֲסוּרָה.

---

162 Desecration of God's Name by not acting in accordance with His Commandments.
163 Shemot 31:14.
164 Zohar Introduction 6a.
165 Kiddushin 31a, i.e., that he removes the ability to relate to the residence of God (the *Shechina*) causing his place to appear as if disconnected from and emptied out of God.

concept of Tzimtzum at all – given that intellectual engagement with it is forbidden?
- According to that which we have explained, the concept of Tzimtzum, in truth, relates to all places and all times, even in this world – [and is for] 'the individuals that God calls'[166] – to know of the existence of this awesome concept for the reasons mentioned above [i.e., to inspire their service of prayer, to fulfill the commandment of relating to God's Unity, and to prevent sin].
- Similarly, the Zohar Raya Mehemna, Zohar Tikkunim, and the holy one of God, R. Shmuel author of the Song of Unity mentioned above,[167] and the Rokeach mention this concept with a hint to one who understands – all for these reasons mentioned, as is explained to one who understands in the Rokeach[168] there in Shoresh Kedushat HaYichud. Refer to it.)

- However, be very careful with your life – remember and do not forget that which was explained above: this concept is only for general intellectual awareness according to individual ability, and one must not, God forbid, intellectually analyze the essence of the concept.
- One must also be very careful to never be drawn to translate this awesome concept into physical action, as this can easily result in many practices which also contradict the statutes and foundations of our Holy Torah, about which it is written: "and it will not change"[169]
  - and as written: "Know this day and instill it into *your heart*, that YHVH [is Elokim] . . . in the heavens above . . . there is nothing else,"[170] specifically emphasizing "*your heart*," meaning that it is to be just with the understanding and depth of one's heart alone – in line with Chazal's statement that to pray one must concentrate one's *heart* on Makom.

9. PRAYER TO FOCUS ON *YHVH* ALONE, FOCUS ON *ELOKIM* IS IDOL WORSHIP

- In connection with that which is written: "Know this day and instill it into your heart, that *YHVH is Elokim*,"[171] the difference between these two names of God is as follows:
  - *Elokim*: Also relates to the specific individual empowering abilities which extend from God.[172]
  - *YHVH*: Relates to the *source* of all empowering abilities which extend from God.[173]

---

166 Yoel 3:5.
167 G3:04.

◦ וּלְפִי מַה שֶּׁבֵּיאַרְנוּ עִנְיַן הַצִּמְצוּם, בֶּאֱמֶת הָעִנְיָן נוֹהֵג בְּכָל מָקוֹם וּזְמַן, גַּם בָּזֶה הָעוֹלָם, לַשְּׂרִידִים אֲשֶׁר ה' קוֹרֵא, לֵידַע מְצִיאוּת זֶה הָעִנְיָן הַנּוֹרָא מִטְּעָמִים הַנַּ"ל.

◦ וְכֵן בְּרַעְיָא מְהֵימְנָא וְתִקּוּנִים, וּקְדוֹשׁ ה' רַבֵּנוּ שְׁמוּאֵל בַּעַל שִׁיר הַיִּחוּד הַנַּ"ל, וְהָרוֹקֵחַ זִכְרוֹנוֹ לִבְרָכָה, שֶׁהִזְכִּירוּ הָעִנְיָן בְּרֶמֶז לַמֵּבִין, הַכֹּל מֵאֵלּוּ הַטְּעָמִים הַנִּזְכָּרִים, וְכַמְבֹאָר לַמֵּבִין בְּרוֹקֵחַ שָׁם בְּשֹׁרֶשׁ קְדֻשַּׁת הַיִּחוּד, ע"ש):

• אָמְנָם הִזָּהֵר מְאֹד בְּנַפְשְׁךָ, זָכֹר וְאַל תִּשְׁכַּח אֲשֶׁר נִתְבָּאֵר לְמַעְלָה, שֶׁאֵין הַדָּבָר אָמוּר אֶלָּא לָדַעַת הָעִנְיָן יְדִיעַת הַלֵּב דֶּרֶךְ כְּלָל בְּשִׁעוּרָא דְלִבָּא לְבַד, אֲבָל לֹא לַחֲקֹר וּלְהִתְבּוֹנֵן חַס וְשָׁלוֹם בְּמָהוּת הָעִנְיָן:

• וְגַם לְהִזָּהֵר מְאֹד, שֶׁלֹּא יְהֵא מִמְשָׁכָא לִבָּא לִקְבֹּעַ כָּל סֵדֶר הַהַנְהָגָה בְּמַעֲשֶׂה עַל פִּי זֶה הָעִנְיָן הַנּוֹרָא, כִּי בְּקַל יוּכַל לְהִוָּלֵד מִזֶּה לְהִתְנַהֵג בְּכַמָּה דְבָרִים גַּם נֶגֶד חֻקֵּי וִיסוֹדֵי תּוֹרָתֵנוּ הַקְּדוֹשָׁה, וְלֹא יַעֲבֹר כְּתִיב.

◦ וּכְמוֹ שֶׁאָמַר הַכָּתוּב (דברים ד, לט) "וְיָדַעְתָּ הַיּוֹם וַהֲשֵׁבֹתָ אֶל לְבָבֶךָ כִּי ה' כו'", בַּשָּׁמַיִם מִמַּעַל וכו', אֵין עוֹד", "אֶל לְבָבֶךָ" דַּוְקָא, הַיְנוּ, רַק בְּאוּבַנְתָּא דְלִבָּא וְשִׁעוּרָא דְלִבָּא לְבַד, וּכְעֵין שֶׁאָמְרוּ בִּתְפִלָּה "יְכַוֵּן 'לִבּוֹ' לַמָּקוֹם":

שער ג' - פרק ט'

• וּמַה שֶּׁכָּתוּב (דברים ד, לט) "וְיָדַעְתָּ הַיּוֹם וכו', כִּי ה' הוּא הָאֱלֹקִים", הַהֶבְדֵּל שֶׁבֵּין אֵלּוּ שְׁנֵי הַשֵּׁמוֹת הוּא

◦ שֵׁשֵׁם "אֱלֹקִים" נֶאֱמַר גַּם עַל אֵיזֶה כֹּחַ פְּרָטִי הַנִּמְשָׁךְ מִמֶּנּוּ יִתְבָּרֵךְ

◦ וְשֵׁם "הֲוָיָ"ה" נֶאֱמַר עַל מְקוֹר הַכֹּחוֹת כֻּלָּם, שֶׁנִּמְשָׁכִים מִמֶּנּוּ יִתְבָּרֵךְ שְׁמוֹ:

---

168 G3:02 and G3:06.
169 Tehillim 148:6.
170 Devarim 4:39.
171 Devarim 4:39.
172 R. Chaim uses the word "also" here as he has already defined Elokim to be *The All Powerful One* as per the beginning of G1:02. The two ways of viewing Elokim are the same as *The All Powerful One* is just the collective group of all the specific individual empowering abilities.
173 The Vilna Gaon comments on Mishlei 30:9 as follows:
  • ... The name "YHVH" relates to God's existence and is specifically reserved for Him. This name relates to Him alone and not to any minister,

- This is as per the Midrash which [identifies that] after the completion of the Creation narrative, [the Torah] "mentions the complete name (that is *YHVH* and *Elokim* together) in relation to a complete world."[174]
  - *YHVH* is the source of everything within [the world], and at the time of Creation a specific power or set of powers extended from the Source of All via each creative statement to form and create each specific thing and maintain its existence.
  - Therefore, the Creation narrative only mentions the name Elokim alone, and it is only after the completion of the drawing down of all the [relevant] powers, as God's Will decreed necessary for the world that the [Torah narrative] states: "on the day that *YHVH Elokim* Made"[175] – [using] the complete name.
- This is the meaning of "Know this day and instill it into your heart, that *YHVH* is *Elokim*," that is, one should *never* focus one's subservience and one's cleaving through any form of service [of God] on a specific empowering ability or set of specific empowering abilities "which are in the heavens above or in the earth below,"[176] but one should just channel one's entire focus to be on the name of His Unified Essence, *YHVH*, which is the all-encompassing *Source* of all-empowering abilities which are derived from it.
- This was the entire concept of idol worship of the early generations from the time of the generation of Enosh, when the concept of idol worship started in this world
  - as per "then, to call in the name of YHVH/God, became profaned"[177]
  - where they would worship the powers of the stars and constellations with each individual [focusing] on a specific star or constellation that he chose for himself
  - not that anyone thought that any particular star was a god that created all
  - for God was always related to by the nations as the "God of all gods"[178]
  - as per Chazal[179] and similarly as Malachi the Prophet said in his rebuke of Israel: "For from the rising sun to its setting . . . for My Name is great among the nations says the Lord of Hosts."[180]

Angel, or Saraf. The name "Elokim" relates to God's Ability and any entity which He gives ability to is called "Elohim."

174 Bereishit Rabba 13:3.
175 Bereishit 2:4.
176 This is the continuation of the verse from Devarim 4:39.
177 Bereishit 4:26. Rashi comments that the word "Huchal/profaned" is an expression of "Chullin/ordinary," meaning that ordinary people and objects

- וּכְמוֹ שֶׁאָמְרוּ זִכְרוֹנָם לִבְרָכָה בִּבְרֵאשִׁית רַבָּה (יג, ג), שֶׁהִזְכִּיר אַחַר גְּמַר כָּל מַעֲשֵׂי בְרֵאשִׁית "שֵׁם מָלֵא (הֲוָיָ"ה אֱלֹקִים), עַל עוֹלָם מָלֵא".
  ○ שֵׁשֵׁם הֲוָיָ"ה בָּרוּךְ הוּא, הוּא מְקוֹרָא דְכֹלָּא בֵּיהּ, וּבְעֵת הַבְּרִיאָה נִמְשָׁךְ בְּכָל מַאֲמָר, כֹּחַ אוֹ כֹחוֹת פְּרָטִיִּים מִמְּקוֹרָא דְכֹלָּא, לְהִתְהַוּוֹת וּלְהִבָּרְאוֹת אוֹתוֹ הַדָּבָר וְקִיּוּמוֹ
  ○ לָזֹאת לֹא נִזְכַּר בְּכָל מַעֲשֵׂי בְרֵאשִׁית רַק שֵׁם "אֱלֹקִים" לְבַד, וְאַחַר שֶׁנִּגְמְרוּ הַמְשָׁכַת כָּל הַכֹּחוֹת, כְּפִי שֶׁגָּזְרָה רְצוֹנוֹ יִתְבָּרַךְ לְצֹרֶךְ הָעוֹלָם, אָז נֶאֱמַר (בראשית ב, ד) "בְּיוֹם עֲשׂוֹת הֲוָיָ"ה אֱלֹקִים", שֵׁם מָלֵא:
- וְזֶהוּ "וְיָדַעְתָּ הַיּוֹם וַהֲשֵׁבֹתָ אֶל לְבָבֶךָ כִּי ה' הוּא הָאֱלֹקִים" (דברים שם) וְכוּ'. הַיְנוּ, שֶׁלֹּא לְכַוֵּן לְהִשְׁתַּעְבֵּד וּלְהִתְדַּבֵּק בְּשׁוּם עֲבוֹדָה, לְאֵיזֶה כֹּחַ אוֹ כֹּחוֹת פְּרָטִיִּים אֲשֶׁר בַּשָּׁמַיִם מִמַּעַל וַאֲשֶׁר בָּאָרֶץ מִתָּחַת, רַק לְכַוֵּן הַכֹּל לְשֵׁם הָעֶצֶם הַמְיֻחָד הֲוָיָ"ה יִתְבָּרַךְ שְׁמוֹ, מְקוֹרָא וּכְלָלָא שֶׁל כָּל הַכֹּחוֹת כֻּלָּם שֶׁנִּמְשְׁכוּ מִמֶּנּוּ:
- וְזוֹ הָיְתָה כָּל עִנְיַן הָעֲבוֹדָה זָרָה שֶׁל דּוֹרוֹת הָרִאשׁוֹנִים מִימֵי דּוֹר אֱנוֹשׁ, שֶׁאָז הִתְחִילוּ בָּעוֹלָם עִנְיַן הָעֲבוֹדָה זָרָה
  ○ כְּמוֹ שֶׁכָּתוּב (בראשית ד, כו) "אָז הוּחַל לִקְרֹא בְּשֵׁם ה'"
  ○ שֶׁהָיוּ עוֹבְדִים לְכֹחוֹת הַכּוֹכָבִים וְהַמַּזָּלוֹת, כָּל אֶחָד לְכוֹכָב וּמַזָּל מְיֻחָד שֶׁבָּחַר לְעַצְמוֹ.
  ○ לֹא שֶׁחָשַׁב כָּל אֶחָד שֶׁאוֹתוֹ הַכּוֹכָב הוּא אֱלוֹהַּ שֶׁבָּרָא אֶת כֹּל
  ○ שֶׁהֲרֵי מֵעוֹלָם הָיָה שׁוּמָה בְּפִיהֶם שֶׁל הָאֻמּוֹת לִקְרוֹתוֹ יִתְבָּרַךְ שְׁמוֹ "אֱלָהּ דֶאֱלָהִין" (דניאל ב, מז)
  ○ כְּמוֹ שֶׁאָמְרוּ רַבּוֹתֵינוּ זִכְרוֹנָם לִבְרָכָה (מנחות קי ע"א). וְכֵן אָמַר מַלְאָכִי הַנָּבִיא

---

were called godly names, treating them as gods. The Vilna Gaon in Aderet Eliyahu comments on this verse as follows:

- All the intermediaries were referred to as "Elohim," but the name YHVH was not used to refer to any entity other than The Creator, in whose power it is to bestow evil or good. But they [i.e., those who lived in the generation of Enosh] used the name YHVH to refer to the intermediaries, and this is [the definition of] Idol Worship.

178 Daniel 2:47.
179 Menachot 110a.
180 Malachi 1:11.

- However, the initial mistake of the generation of Enosh was the erroneous thought that God is too exalted to be involved with watching over the creations in this lowly world and they therefore thought that He had ceased to be involved with them and handed them over to the control of the heavenly spheres and constellations giving them the autonomy to guide the world as they saw fit.
- They therefore considered it a profanity, completely forbidden, and a great insult to pray directly to God's Honored and Awesome Name to make requests of Him for their lowly needs.
- They therefore restricted themselves to focus all aspects of their service and requests on the powers of the stars and constellations (together with the way in which they performed this idol worship, of offering sacrifices and incense to them, refer to Tikkunim).[181]
- They also knew how to engage the angels appointed over the constellations to know good and bad, and as a result to bring benefit to this world – from the abilities given to them from the Master of All.
- But there were only a few select individuals who recognized and knew the truth, that even though God is "enthroned on High," nevertheless, with all this, He also "lowers Himself to look over the heavens and the earth."[182]
- Some of them worshiped animals and birds, as is written,[183] with the intention of also attaching themselves through this to the supernal source of empowerment of the specific creation, that it should bestow upon them from its power and dominion which was appointed over it by God.

---

[181] Tikkunei Zohar Tikkun 66 97a:
- From the Tree [of Knowledge of Good and Evil] the souls of the Erev Rav descended, which are a mixture of good and evil, and many *threads* are hanging from this Tree, which are the Hosts of the Heavens that are appointed over the stars and constellations, and all of them have a mixture of good and evil, and there were branches hanging on one side putting to death and on the other side giving life, these are the demons on one side and the angels on the other. They knew all the characteristics of the branches of the Tree which were the constellations and stars, and they would gather grasses with these characteristics and would make images of the constellation which they wanted to draw down, like Aries, Taurus, Virgo, Gemini which is the form of man with a double face with a female image, Cancer, Leo, Libra, Scorpio, Sagittarius, Capricorn, Aquarius, and Pisces, and they would offer incense to them with these forms of grasses – each one according to the form that it has above. In this way they would form images of the sun, moon, and the

בְּתוֹכַחְתּוֹ לְיִשְׂרָאֵל (א, יא), "כִּי מִמִּזְרַח שֶׁמֶשׁ וְעַד מְבוֹאוֹ גָּדוֹל שְׁמִי בַּגּוֹיִם כוּ', כִּי גָדוֹל שְׁמִי בַּגּוֹיִם אָמַר ה' צְבָאוֹת".

אֶלָּא שֶׁתְּחִלַּת טָעוּת דּוֹר אֱנוֹשׁ הָיָה, שֶׁחָשְׁבוּ בְּשִׁבּוּשׁ דַּעְתָּם כִּי רָם ה' וְעַל הַשָּׁמַיִם כְּבוֹדוֹ, וְאֵין כְּבוֹדוֹ לְהַשְׁגִּיחַ עַל בְּרוּאֵי זֶה הָעוֹלָם הַשָּׁפָל, וְלָכֵן חָשְׁבוּ שֶׁהֵסִיר הוּא יִתְבָּרַךְ הַשְׁגָּחָתוֹ מֵהֶם, וּמְסָרָם לְכֹחוֹת הַגַּלְגַּלִּים וְהַמַּזָּלוֹת שֶׁהֵמָּה יַנְהִיגוּ זֶה הָעוֹלָם כִּרְצוֹנָם.

וְהָיָה נֶחְשָׁב אֶצְלָם חוּלִין וְאִסּוּר גָּמוּר וְחֻצְפָּה גְדוֹלָה נֶגְדּוֹ יִתְבָּרַךְ, לְהִתְפַּלֵּל לִשְׁמוֹ הַנִּכְבָּד וְהַנּוֹרָא, לְבַקֵּשׁ מֵאִתּוֹ צָרְכֵיהֶם הַשְּׁפָלִים לָזֹאת הִשְׁתַּעְבְּדוּ עַצְמָם, וְכִוְּנוּ כָּל עִנְיְנֵי עֲבוֹדָתָם וּבַקָּשָׁתָם לְכֹחוֹת הַכּוֹכָבִים וְהַמַּזָּלוֹת. (וְאֹפֶן עֲשִׂיָּתָם הָעֲבוֹדָה זָרָה, וְזִבּוּחָם וְקִטּוּרָם אֵלֶיהָ, עַיֵּן בְּתִקּוּן ס"ו).

וְהָיוּ יוֹדְעִים גַּם כֵּן, לְהַשְׁבִּיעַ הַמַּלְאָכִים הַמְמֻנִּים עַל הַמַּזָּלוֹת, לָדַעַת טוֹב וָרָע, וְשֶׁיַּשְׁפִּיעוּ לָהֶם עַל יְדֵי זֶה טוֹבוֹת וַהֲנָאוֹת עוֹלָם הַזֶּה, מִכֹּחָם שֶׁנִּתְמַנּוּ עָלָיו מֵאֲדוֹן כֹּל יִתְבָּרַךְ שְׁמוֹ.

וּמְעַטִּים יְחִידֵי סְגֻלָּה הָיוּ, שֶׁהִכִּירוּ וְיָדְעוּ בֶּאֱמֶת, שֶׁאַף שֶׁהוּא יִתְבָּרַךְ שְׁמוֹ "מַגְבִּיהִי לָשָׁבֶת", עִם כָּל זֶה הוּא "מַשְׁפִּילִי לִרְאוֹת בַּשָּׁמַיִם וּבָאָרֶץ" (תהלים קיג, ו).

וּמֵהֶם שֶׁהָיוּ עוֹבְדִים לְחַיּוֹת וְעוֹפוֹת, כְּמוֹ שֶׁכָּתוּב (מְלָכִים ב' יז, ל), גַּם כֵּן כַּוָּנָתָם

---

seven planets of the solar system and they would offer incense to each image [whose influence] they wanted to bring down to the world, and because of this it says about them that so says God to those who offer incense and sacrifices to the stars and constellations "to the sun or to the moon or to all of the Hosts of the Heavens, which I have not commanded" [Devarim 17:3].

182 Tehillim 113:5–6.
183 2 Melachim 17:30–31:
- "and the men of Bavel made *Sukot Benot* and the men of Kut made *Nergal* and the men of Chamat made *Asima* and the Avim made *Nivchaz* and *Tartak* and the Sefarvim burned their children in fire for *Adramelech* and *Anamelech*"

Rashi comments: *Sukot Benot* means the image of a chicken with its chicks. *Nergal* means the image of a cockerel. *Asima* means the image of a goat. *Nivchaz* means the image of a dog. *Tartak* means the image of a donkey. *Adramelech* means the image of a mule. *Anamelech* means the image of a horse.

- This is what the cursed women told Yirmiyahu: "Since we stopped to offer incense to the queen of the heavens [i.e., the Sun] and to pour her libations, we have lacked everything. . . ."[184]
- Some also worshiped an individual who was viewed to have very great control over his astrological destiny, thinking that by their subservience and worship of him they would connect with his destiny and raise their own destiny.
- For some, the focus of their service was not on benefiting from this world, but was motivated to acquire desired intellectual goals such as the mastery of Black Magic and similar concepts.
- Some also worshiped specific people in order to draw a bestowal from the Faith of Amon[185] and for divining the future.
- All of these approaches are classified as Idol Worship and fall within the command of "you shall not have other gods."[186]
  - As the Ramban writes there in his commentary.[187]
  - Refer to Likutei Torah at the end of Noach discussing the Generation of the Dispersal.[188]

---

184 Yirmiyahu 44:18.
185 Amon (or Amun) was one of the primary Egyptian gods. An Egyptian town Amon MeNo was named after this god and is referenced in Yirmiyahu 46:25 and also in Nachum 3:8. There is an interesting reference to Amon in Tzror HaMor Vayikra 13:2 which refers to Amon as the "Master of the Demons who was appointed over the wisdom of Egyptian Black Magic." The expression *Emunat Amon* appears to be a negative play on the more common positive expression of *Emunat Omen* from Yishayahu 25:1 which is used by R. Chaim in G3:06 and by R. Yitzchak in Note 7 of his Introduction.
186 Shemot 20:3.
187 The Ramban writes:
- I will now mention what Scripture teaches in relation to Idol Worship as there were three categories:
  - The first category:
    - They began to worship the intellectually abstracted angels in order to gain control over nations . . . and even though they worshiped them they knew that ultimate power rested with God.
  - The second category:
    - To worship the visible heavenly hosts including the sun, moon and constellations. All the nations knew the power of Astrology and how it affected them – thinking that if they worshiped it – they would improve their destiny . . . there were many false prophets who told the future and some had abilities in Black Magic.
    - In this category were also those who worshiped humans with great

הָיָה לְהִתְדַּבֵּק עַצְמָם עַל יְדֵי זֶה לְהַכֹּחַ וְהַמַּזָּל הָעֶלְיוֹן שֶׁל אוֹתָהּ הַבְּרִיָּה, שֶׁיַּשְׁפִּיעַ עֲלֵיהֶם מִכֹּחוֹ וּמֶמְשַׁלְתּוֹ שֶׁנִּתְמַנָּה עָלָיו מֵהַבּוֹרֵא יִתְבָּרַךְ.

- וְזֶה שֶׁאָמְרוּ הַנָּשִׁים הָאֲרוּרוֹת לְיִרְמְיָהוּ, "וּמִן אָז חָדַלְנוּ לְקַטֵּר לִמְלֶכֶת הַשָּׁמַיִם וְהַסֵּךְ לָהּ נְסָכִים חָסַרְנוּ כֹל" (ירמיה מד, יח).

- וּמֵהֶם שֶׁהָיוּ מִשְׁתַּעְבְּדִים וּמְזַבְּחִים וּמְקַטְּרִים לְאֵיזֶה אָדָם שֶׁרָאוּ שֶׁכֹּחַ מֶמְשֶׁלֶת מַזָּלוֹ גָּדוֹל מְאֹד, בְּחָשְׁבָם שֶׁעַל יְדֵי הִשְׁתַּעְבְּדָם וַעֲבוֹדָתָם אֵלָיו יַעֲלֶה מַזָּלָם עִם מַזָּלוֹ.

- וּמֵהֶם, אַף שֶׁלֹּא הָיְתָה כַּוָּנַת עֲבוֹדָתָם לְהַשְׁפָּעַת הֲנָאוֹת עוֹלָם הַזֶּה, אֲבָל כַּוָּנָתָם הָיְתָה לְהַשִּׂיג עַל יְדֵי זֶה אֵיזֶה הַשָּׂגוֹת שִׂכְלִיִּים שֶׁחָמְדוּ לָהֶם, כְּמוֹ חָכְמַת הַקְּסָמִים, וְכַיּוֹצֵא אֵיזֶה הַשָּׂגוֹת.

- וּמֵהֶם שֶׁהִתְדַּבְּקוּ לַעֲבוֹדַת אֵיזֶה אֲנָשִׁים, כְּדֵי לְהַמְשִׁיךְ הַשְׁפָּעַת אֱמוּנַת אָמוֹן וְעִנְיְנֵי עֲתִידוֹת.

- וְזֶהוּ הַכֹּל עֲבוֹדָה זָרָה גְמוּרָה, וּבִכְלַל "לֹא יִהְיֶה לְךָ אֱלֹהִים אֲחֵרִים" (שמות כ, ג).

- כְּמוֹ שֶׁכָּתַב הַכֹּל הָרַמְבַּ״ן זִכְרוֹנוֹ לִבְרָכָה בְּפֵרוּשׁוֹ עַל הַתּוֹרָה שָׁם.

- וְעַיֵּן לִקּוּטֵי תּוֹרָה סוֹף פָּרָשַׁת נֹחַ בְּעִנְיַן דּוֹר הַהַפְלָגָה:

---

power, such as Nevuchadnezar, thinking that their destiny would be raised by this worship.
- The third category:
  - Worshiped the spirits, as these were also appointed over the nations.

188 A summary of this section of Likutei Torah at the end of Noach is as follows:
- The Generation of the Dispersal
- they knew the Names of God and would use them to invoke the powers of individual angels
- they then "started to call in the Name of God" (Bereishit 4:26), i.e., using these names
- this practice only worked using the Hebrew Names of God . . . this is the meaning of "and the whole world spoke one language" (Bereishit 11:1) and "they said let us build a city and tower" (Bereishit 11:4) to reach the heavens through the use of these Names of God to draw power down to them . . . as they didn't want to be subservient to Holiness and have to refine themselves from the desires of material substance and they wanted to engage in the desires of this world . . . Idol Worship gave them the ability to draw down good using the Names of God [and still engage in the desires of this world.]
- Nimrod was the mastermind of all this . . . and this was also the objective of Nevuchadnezar

- Idol Worship even includes one's service to be subservient to and connect oneself with the Holy Spirit of a specific person, prophet, or person imbued with Holy Spirit, as with Nevuchadnezar's bowing down to Daniel, even though he did not relate to him as God who created all but, through his prostrations intended to become subservient to and attach himself to the Holy Spirit within him:
  - As per Scripture:
    - "Then King Nevuchadnezar fell on his face and prostrated himself to Daniel and with offering and incense [he wished to exalt him. The king exclaimed to Daniel and said]: In truth, I know that your God is the God of all gods, [the Lord of kings], the Revealer of secrets, since you were able to reveal this secret."[189]
    - "At last Daniel came before me . . . in whom is the spirit of the Holy God."[190]
  - As per Chazal
    - Chazal[191] state that the reason why Daniel was not present when [Chanania, Mishael, and Azariya] were commanded to bow down to the idol
      - is because Daniel said: I will go from here so that the verse "Their idolatrous statues shall you burn in fire"[192] should not be fulfilled about me
      - and Nevuchadnezar also said: Take Daniel away from here so that they should not say about me that he burned his own god in fire.
    - Similarly,[193] we find with Daniel . . . "Then King Nevuchadnezar [fell on his face] . . . offering and incense he wished to exalt him."
      - But Daniel did not accept this, why? As just as those who worship idols are punished, so too are the idols themselves.
      - Similarly, the same reason is given with Yaakov who did not want to be buried in Egypt. Chazal called this Idol Worship even though the intention was just [to attach to the] Holy Spirit of God within him.
- With this it is possible to understand the verse, "you shall not have other gods *before Me*,"[194] as meaning that one should not, God forbid, focus on any specific level or ability even if that ability comes from *"Me"*

- their entire objective was to engage in material pursuits and not Holy ones
- after their languages were confused and they were unable to speak Hebrew they were unable to put this into practice.

189 Daniel 2:46-47.
190 Daniel 4:5.

• וַאֲפִלּוּ לְהִשְׁתַּעְבֵּד וּלְהִתְדַּבֵּק בְּאֵיזֶה עֲבוֹדָה, לִבְחִינַת רוּחַ הַקֹּדֶשׁ שֶׁבְּאֵיזֶה אָדָם נָבִיא וּבַעַל רוּחַ הַקֹּדֶשׁ, גַּם זֶה נִקְרָא עֲבוֹדָה זָרָה מַמָּשׁ. כְּמוֹ שֶׁמָּצִינוּ בִּנְבוּכַדְנֶצַּר שֶׁהִשְׁתַּחֲוָה לְדָנִיֵּאל, גַּם כֵּן לֹא בַּעֲבוּר שֶׁהֶחֱזִיקוֹ לֶאֱלוֹהַּ בּוֹרֵא כֹּל, אֶלָּא שֶׁכִּוֵּן בְּהִשְׁתַּחֲוָיָתוֹ לְהִשְׁתַּעְבֵּד וּלְהִתְדַּבֵּק לְרוּחַ הַקֹּדֶשׁ שֶׁבּוֹ כְּמוֹ שֶׁכָּתוּב

  ◦ "בֵּאדַיִן מַלְכָּא נְבוּכַדְנֶצַּר נְפַל עַל אַנְפּוֹהִי וּלְדָנִיֵּאל סְגִד וּמִנְחָה וְנִיחֹחִין וְכוּ', מִן קְשֹׁט דִּי אֱלָהֲכוֹן הוּא אֱלָהּ אֱלָהִין כוּ', וְגָלֵה רָזִין, דִּי יְכֵלְתָּ לְמִגְלֵא רָזָה דְנָה". (דניאל ב, מו)

  ◦ וְשָׁם (ה, ה) "וְעַד אָחֳרֵין עַל קָדָמַי דָּנִיֵּאל כוּ', וְדִי רוּחַ אֱלָהִין קַדִּישִׁין בֵּהּ" וְכוּ'.

  ◦ וְרַבּוֹתֵינוּ זִכְרוֹנָם לִבְרָכָה אָמְרוּ (סנהדרין צ״ג)

  ◦ הַטַּעַם שֶׁלֹּא הָיָה דָּנִיֵּאל בְּעֵת צִוּוּי הַהִשְׁתַּחֲוָיָה לַצֶּלֶם

  ◦ שֶׁאָמַר דָּנִיֵּאל, אֵיזִיל מֵהָכָא, דְּלָא לִקַיֵּים בִּי "פְּסִילֵי אֱלֹהֵיהֶם תִּשְׂרְפוּן"

  ◦ וּנְבוּכַדְנֶצַּר אָמַר גַּם כֵּן, יֵזִיל דָּנִיֵּאל מֵהָכָא דְּלָא לֵימְרוּ קַלְיֵהּ לֶאֱלָהֵיהּ בְּנוּרָא. וְעַיֵּן זֹהַר חָדָשׁ רוּת כ״ח ע״ב.

  ◦ וּבִבְרֵאשִׁית רַבָּה פָּרָשָׁה צ״ו, וּבְתַנְחוּמָא רֵישׁ פָּרָשַׁת וַיְחִי. וְכֵן אַתָּה מוֹצֵא בְּדָנִיֵּאל וְכוּ' (שם), מַה כְּתִיב "בֵּאדַיִן מַלְכָּא נְבוּכַדְנֶצַּר וְכוּ', וּמִנְחָה וְנִיחֹחִין אָמַר לְנַסָּכָה לֵהּ"

  ◦ אֲבָל דָּנִיֵּאל לֹא קִבֵּל, לָמָּה, שֶׁכְּשֵׁם שֶׁנִּפְרָעִין מֵעוֹבְדֵי עֲבוֹדָה זָרָה כָּךְ נִפְרָעִין מֵהָעֲבוֹדָה זָרָה עַצְמָהּ.

  ◦ וְכֵן אָמְרוּ שָׁם זֶה הַטַּעַם, גַּם עַל יַעֲקֹב אָבִינוּ עָלָיו הַשָּׁלוֹם, שֶׁלֹּא רָצָה לִקָּבֵר בְּמִצְרַיִם, הֲרֵי שֶׁקָּרְאוּ זִכְרוֹנָם לִבְרָכָה עִנְיָן זֶה "עֲבוֹדָה זָרָה", אַף שֶׁהַכַּוָּנָה הָיְתָה לְרוּחַ אֱלָהִין קַדִּישִׁין דְּבֵיהּ:

• וְיֵשׁ לְפָרֵשׁ עַל פִּי זֶה הַכָּתוּב (שמות כ, ג) "לֹא יִהְיֶה לְךָ אֱלֹהִים אֲחֵרִים עַל פָּנָי",

---

191 Sanhedrin 93a. R. Chaim also provides an additional similar reference to this: Zohar Chadash II Rut 28b.
192 Ekev 7:25.
193 Bereishit Rabba Vayechi 96:6, Midrash Tanchuma Vayechi 3.
194 Shemot 20:3.

- that is even if it is a specific detail of Holy Spirit which resides in a specific individual, or
- a specific detail of Holiness related to a power in the highest of the worlds
  - as per Chazal on the verse "Do not make Me" that one should not even form an image of My servants who serve Me on High, for example the Ophanim, Seraphim, Holy Chayot, [and the administering angels].[195]

• Now even though Scripture forbids four specific practices of Idol Worship[196]
  - nevertheless, now that the service of prayer with its subservient concentration of the heart, replaces the service of the sacrifices
  - it is certainly also subject to this forbidden command.

• This is in line with the verse, "one who sacrifices to *Elokim* shall be excommunicated, except for [one who sacrifices to] *YHVH* alone"[197]
  - that is, one should not, God forbid, focus oneself on any form of service to any specific power implemented by God
  - (for the name *Elokim* incorporates All specific powers as is known and as mentioned above)[198]
  - but one should solely focus on the name of His Unified Essence [*YHVH*] alone, whose meaning is *Causes All to be*,[199] being the source for all of the powers, as mentioned above[200]
    - (This is the meaning of "Hear Israel – *YHVH* which is *Elokeinu* – *YHVH* is One,"[201] meaning that all the specific empowering abilities, which come from *YHVH*, are unified and gathered together in God's Power, the all-incorporating source of His Unity)
  - and this is from the perspective of His connection with the worlds.[202]

• Therefore, all places in the Torah which command us in relation to sacrifices always specifically relate to [God's Name] *YHVH*

---

195 Rosh Hashana 24b quoting Shemot 20:20.
196 Yoma 24a: "Rav says there are four practices [involved in offering sacrifices] which if implemented by a non-priest incurs the death penalty: throwing, burning, pouring water, pouring wine."
197 Shemot 22:19.
198 See end of G1:02 and R. Chaim's note there, G1:02:No2.

רָצָה לוֹמַר שֶׁלֹּא לְכַוֵּן חַס וְשָׁלוֹם בְּשׁוּם דָּבָר לְאֵיזֶה בְּחִינָה וְכֹחַ פְּרָטִי, אֲפִילוּ אִם יִהְיֶה אוֹתוֹ הַכֹּחַ בְּחִינַת "פָּנֵי"

○ הַיְנוּ, אֲפִילוּ לִפְרָט רוּחַ הַקֹּדֶשׁ שֶׁבְּאֵיזֶה אָדָם, אוֹ

○ פְּרָט בְּחִינַת הַקְּדֻשָּׁה שֶׁבְּאֵיזֶה כֹּחַ עֶלְיוֹן שֶׁבָּעֶלְיוֹנִים

▪ וּכְעִנְיָן מַאֲמָרָם זִכְרוֹנָם לִבְרָכָה (ר"ה כה, ב) עַל "לֹא תַעֲשׂוּן אִתִּי" (שמות כ, כ) אֲפִילוּ דְּמוּת שַׁמָּשַׁי הַמְּשַׁמְּשִׁין לְפָנַי בַּמָּרוֹם, כְּגוֹן אוֹפַנִּים וּשְׂרָפִים וְחַיּוֹת הַקֹּדֶשׁ:

• וְעִם כִּי עִקַּר אַזְהָרַת הַכָּתוּב עַל כָּל הָעֲבוֹדָה זָרָה הַנַּ"ל, הַיְנוּ בְּאַרְבַּע עֲבוֹדוֹת דַּוְקָא

○ אָמְנָם עַתָּה שֶׁעֲבוֹדַת הַתְּפִלָּה בְּהִשְׁתַּעַבְּדוּת כַּוָּנַת הַלֵּב הוּא בִּמְקוֹם עֲבוֹדַת הַקָּרְבָּן

○ וַדַּאי גַּם עַל זֶה שַׁיָּךְ הָאַזְהָרָה:

• וְזֶהוּ שֶׁאָמַר הַכָּתוּב (שמות כב, יט) "זוֹבֵחַ לָאֱלֹהִים יָחֳרָם בִּלְתִּי לַה' לְבַדּוֹ"

○ הַיְנוּ שֶׁלֹּא לְכַוֵּן חַס וְשָׁלוֹם בְּשׁוּם עֲבוֹדָה וְעִנְיָן לְאֵיזֶה כֹּחַ פְּרָטִי מִכֹּחוֹת שֶׁקָּבַע הַבּוֹרֵא יִתְבָּרַךְ

○ (כִּי שֵׁם אֱלֹקִים מְשֻׁתָּף לְכָל בַּעַל כֹּחַ פְּרָטִי שֶׁיִּהְיֶה כַּיָּדוּעַ, וּכְמוֹ שֶׁנִּתְבָּאֵר לְעֵיל)

○ רַק לְכַוֵּן לְשֵׁם הָעֶצֶם הַמְיֻחָד לוֹ יִתְבָּרַךְ לְבַד, שֶׁפֵּרוּשׁוֹ מְהַוֶּה הַכֹּל, הַיְנוּ כְּלָלָא וּמְקוֹרָא דְּכָל הַכֹּחוֹת כֻּלָּם כַּנַּ"ל

▪ (וְזֶהוּ "שְׁמַע יִשְׂרָאֵל ה' אֱלֹקֵינוּ ה' אֶחָד", רָצָה לוֹמַר שֶׁכָּל הַכֹּחוֹת פְּרָטִיִּים שֶׁנִּמְשָׁכִים מֵהֲוָי"ה בָּרוּךְ הוּא, הֵמָּה מְאֻחָדִים וְנִקְבָּצִים בְּכֹחוֹ יִתְבָּרַךְ שְׁמוֹ, כְּלָל מְקוֹר אַחְדוּתוֹ)

○ וְהוּא מִצַּד הִתְחַבְּרוּתוֹ יִתְבָּרַךְ עִם הָעוֹלָמוֹת:

• וְלָזֹאת, בְּכָל מָקוֹם שֶׁצִּוְּתָה הַתּוֹרָה עַל עִנְיַן הַקָּרְבָּנוֹת, בָּאֲרָה בְּפֵירוּשׁ לַ"הֲוָיָ"ה דַּוְקָא

---

199 This definition of "YHVH" also appears in G2:02. See p. 315, fn. 36.
200 At the beginning of this chapter.
201 Devarim 6:4.
202 E.g., as per G2:04.
203 Menachot 110a.

- as Chazal say:[203] Come and see what is written about the offerings, as there is no reference to *El* or *Elokim*, but just to *YHVH*, so that no excuse exists for anyone to dispute [to whom the offering was being offered].[204]
- Refer to the Zohar where this concept is explained in more detail.[205]

10. LIFE FORCE OF ALL CASCADES DOWN FROM ELOKIM – I.E., THE KAV

- Following our development of the concept of the two relative perspectives, of God and of man, as mentioned above,[206] a further distinction between the two names of God, *YHVH* and *Elokim*, will now be explained.[207]
- *Elokim* means *The All Powerful One* as explained a little in the First Gateway.[208]
- With a more detailed explanation now, *All Powerful* means
  - that each empowered ability from the very lowest to the very highest level draws its continued existence and life force from the level immediately above it
  - which is its soul that permeates its inner essence.
  - As known from the words of the Arizal, that the light and inner essence, the soul of each power and world, is in itself, the external presentation of the power and world immediately above it
  - with this sequence extending all the way up to very highest levels and incorporating all empowered abilities.[209]
- All created entities and powers in this lowest world derive [their empowered abilities] from an amalgam of the four elements[210]

---

204 See G2:04:N21.
205 Zohar Chadash I Bereishit 6b and 7a as follows:
- R. Abahu says come and see how concerned God is with the honor of His Name. You should know that in the time when the Temple existed, anyone who would offer up his sacrifice to the name *Elokim* would be liable to death, as it says "one who sacrifices to *Elokim* shall be destroyed, except for [one who sacrifices to] *YHVH* alone" (Shemot 22:19). This teaches that one should only mention the name *YHVH* alone. Therefore, so that people don't err, we are commanded in the section of the sacrifices: "A person who offers up from you, an offering to *YHVH*" (Vayikra 1:2); "and when you offer up an offering to *YHVH*" (Vayikra 22:29); "and when you offer up a peace offering to *YHVH*" (Vayikra 19:5); "and a soul who offers up a Mincha offering to *YHVH*" (Vayikra 2:1) – all of these state *YHVH* and not *Elokim*. What is the reason for this? R. Abahu says, this name is used in multiple

- וּכְאָמְרָם זִכְרוֹנָם לִבְרָכָה (מנחות קי.) "בֹּא וּרְאֵה מַה כְּתִיב בְּפָרָשַׁת קָרְבָּנוֹת, שֶׁלֹּא נֶאֱמַר בָּהֶם לֹא "אֵל" וְלֹא "אֱלֹהִים" אֶלָּא לַה', שֶׁלֹּא לִתֵּן פִּתְחוֹן פֶּה לְבַעַל הַדִּין לַחֲלֹק".

- וְעַיֵּן זֹהַר חָדָשׁ בְּרֵאשִׁית ו' ע"ב, וז' ע"א, הָעִנְיָן יוֹתֵר מְבֹאָר:

שער ג' - פרק י'

- וּלְפִי דַרְכֵּנוּ בְּעִנְיָן הַשְּׁנֵי בְחִינוֹת הַנַּ"ל, שֶׁמִּצַּדּוֹ יִתְבָּרַךְ, וּמִצִּדֵּנוּ. שֶׁנִּתְבָּאֵר, יְבֹאַר עוֹד הֶפְרֵשׁ וְחִלּוּק שֶׁבֵּין הַשְּׁנֵי שֵׁמוֹת הֲוָיָ"ה וֶאֱלֹקִים:

- כִּי שֵׁם "אֱלֹקִים" פֵּרוּשׁוֹ, בַּעַל הַכֹּחוֹת כֻּלָּם, וּקְצָת בֵּאוּר עִנְיָנוֹ עַיֵּן בְּרֵישׁ שַׁעַר א':

- וּבְיוֹתֵר בֵּאוּר עִנְיַן "בַּעַל הַכֹּחוֹת":

- כִּי כָּל כֹּחַ, מֵהַתַּחְתּוֹן שֶׁבַּתַּחְתּוֹנִים עַד הָעֶלְיוֹן שֶׁבָּעֶלְיוֹנִים, הַמְשָׁכַת קִיּוּמוֹ וְחִיּוּתוֹ הוּא עַל יְדֵי הַכֹּחַ שֶׁלְּמַעְלָה הֵימֶנּוּ

- שֶׁהוּא נִשְׁמָתוֹ, הַמִּתְפַּשֵּׁט בִּפְנִימִיּוּתוֹ.

- וְכַיָּדוּעַ בְּדִבְרֵי הָאֲרִיזַ"ל, שֶׁהָאוֹר וּפְנִימִיּוּת נִשְׁמַת כָּל כֹּחַ וְעוֹלָם, הוּא עַצְמוֹ הַחִיצוֹנִיּוּת שֶׁל הַכֹּחַ וְהָעוֹלָם שֶׁעָלָיו

- וְכֵן הוֹלֵךְ עַל זֶה הַסֵּדֶר גָּבוֹהַּ מֵעַל גָּבוֹהַּ, בֵּין בִּכְלָלוּת הַכֹּחוֹת:

- כִּי כְּלָלֵי כָּל הַבְּרוּאִים וְכֹחוֹת הַתַּחְתּוֹנִים, הֵם מֵהִתְמַזְּגוּת הָאַרְבַּע יְסוֹדוֹת

---

instances: angels are called *Elokim*, men are called *Elokim*, judges are called *Elokim*, and we don't know to which of these the sacrifice is being made. Therefore, [when sacrificing] one should only mention *YHVH* alone. . . R. Abahu says [one who curses using the name *Elokim*] is not liable to the death penalty but is liable to excommunication . . . but one who curses using *YHVH* is liable to the death penalty.

206 In the build up to and in G3:07.
207 The rest of this chapter and half of next chapter focus on further explaining Elokim. The explanation for YHVH starts in the middle of G3:11.
208 Starting from G1:02.
209 This is the concept of Kav, the line connecting upper with lower, as defined by the Arizal. See G3:07.
210 The four elements are Earth/Dust, Wind, Water, and Fire. The concept of the four elements is very ancient in all Jewish sources and was also historically pervasive in many ancient world philosophies with the first non-Jewish references to it dating back to at least 600 years before the time of the compilation of the Talmud and Zohar. For many generations, these

- and the root of the four elements are from the four angels who are called the *Four Camps of the Shechina* – symbolized by *ARGMN*, *Aleph Resh Gimmel Mem Nun*.[211]
- The root of these four angels is from the four animals of the Merkava,[212] which collectively contain the root of all created beings in the lowest world
  - for the root of the soul of all the myriads of animals cascades down from the face of the lion in the Merkava
  - and the soul of all beasts cascades down from the face of the ox
  - and of all birds from the face of the eagle
  - as brought down in the Zohar: The secret of the sacrifices . . . the face of the ox extends Ruach to the beasts . . .[213] Refer there.
  - Therefore, the species whose form and name is like the form and name of the face on the Merkava is the king over [each category of animal], as per Chazal:
    - [The king of the animals is the lion, the king of the beasts is the

---

classical elements were "scientifically" understood to be the simplest essential components of all physical things. In essence, and in contemporary terms, it is possible to relate to these elements as states of matter, i.e., solid (earth), liquid (water), gas (wind), and energy (fire). As explained by various commentators, these elements are understood to be the components of the original Creation as per Bereishit 1:2, "VeHaaretz (Earth) hayta Tohu VaVohu VeChoshech (understood to be fire) al Penei Tehom VeRuach (Wind) Elokim Merachefet al Pnei HaMayim (Water)," e.g., R. Bechaye, Seforno, Malbim. A possible source for this commentary is Zohar Chadash I Bereishit 11b.

The Rambam focuses on these elements in Mishneh Torah, Sefer HaMada Hilchot Yesodei HaTorah Chap. 4. Kabbalistic literature (e.g., Sefer Yetzirah and Zohar) references and deeply connects to the essential nature of these elements and, among other things, ascribes human characteristics to be derived from an association with specific elements, e.g., anger and haughtiness derives from Fire, lust and desire from Water, merrymaking and mindless pursuits from Wind, laziness and depression from Earth/Dust. The "Maamar BeTzeLeM" (see V2:04) focuses on the four elements as a basis of its analysis of the concept of *Tzelem* and explains that the three elements of fire, water, and wind are active elements which all actively operate in a myriad of combinations on the passive fourth element of earth to produce all the different entities that exist.

211 "ARGMN" literally means "purple" and this word is used to describe the purple cloth used in the construction of the fabrics of the Mishkan. In the context used here, it refers to five angels of which two are a variant of one:

Aleph = Uriel (Earth)

- וְשֹׁרֶשׁ הָאַרְבַּע יְסוֹדוֹת הֵם מֵהָאַרְבָּעָה מַלְאָכִים הַנִּקְרָאִים אַרְבַּע מַחֲנוֹת שְׁכִינָה שֶׁסִּימָנָם א'ר'ג'מ'ן'.

- וְהָאַרְבָּעָה מַלְאָכִים אֵלּוּ שָׁרְשָׁם מֵאַרְבַּע חַיּוֹת הַמֶּרְכָּבָה, שֶׁהֵם כְּלָלֵי כָּל שָׁרְשֵׁי נַפְשׁוֹת כָּל הַבְּרוּאִים הַתַּחְתּוֹנִים.

- שֶׁכָּל הָאֲלָפֵי רִבּוֹאֵי מִינֵי הַחַיּוֹת, שֹׁרֶשׁ נַפְשׁוֹתָם מִשְׁתַּלְשֵׁל מִן פְּנֵי 'אַרְיֵה' שֶׁבַּמֶּרְכָּבָה

- וְנַפְשׁוֹת כָּל מִינֵי הַבְּהֵמוֹת מִשְׁתַּלְשְׁלִים מִפְּנֵי 'שׁוֹר'

- וְשֶׁל כָּל מִינֵי הָעוֹפוֹת מִפְּנֵי 'נֶשֶׁר'

- וּכְמוֹ שֶׁכָּתוּב בַּזֹּהַר פִּנְחָס ר"מ ע"ב, רָזָא דְקָרְבָּנִין כוּ', פְּנֵי שׁוֹר אִתְפַּשֵּׁט לִבְעִירֵי רוּחָא מְנֵי' וְכוּ', ע"ש.

- וְלָכֵן בְּכָל אֶחָד מוֹלֵךְ עֲלֵיהֶם אוֹתוֹ הַמִּין שֶׁצּוּרָתוֹ וּשְׁמוֹ הוּא כְּצוּרַת וְשֵׁם הַפָּנִים שֶׁבַּמֶּרְכָּבָה

- כְּמוֹ שֶׁאָמְרוּ זִכְרוֹנָם לִבְרָכָה (חגיגה י"ג ב')

Resh = Rephael (Wind)
Gimmel = Gavriel (Fire)
Mem = Michael (Water)
Nun = Nuriel (Dust)

Uriel and Nuriel are connected with their name difference being in their first letter being either *Aleph* or *Nun*. (Some sources assign the element of Wind to Uriel/Nuriel and Earth/Dust to Rephael.) Sefer HaPliah notes that the numerical value of the names of the first four angels (with no *Yud* in Michael)=896=the numerical value of *Eish* (Fire) + *Mayim* (Water) + *Ruach* (Wind) + *Aretz* (Earth). It also notes that if the *Aleph* of Uriel is switched to a *Nun* to form Nuriel, then the numerical value of the last four angels names=the numerical value of *Eish* (Fire) + *Mayim* (Water) + *Ruach* (Wind) + *Afar* (Dust).

See Shela Masechet Pesachim Matzah Ashira, Derush Shlishi 344 for an overview of the interconnection between the four elements, the four angels, and the four animals of the Merkava.

See G2:06:N24.

212 The Merkava contains four faces representing animals which contain the soul root for created beings in this physical world: lion (related to Animals), ox (related to Beasts), eagle (related to Birds), man. Each of these four faces represents the *king* of its type. The other three types are rooted in the face of man.

213 Zohar III Pinchas 240b.

214 Chagiga 13b.

ox, the king of the birds is the eagle and man exalts himself over them, and God exalts Himself over all of them and the entire world.]²¹⁴
- The lion is the king over the animals.²¹⁵

☐ The soul of man is from the *face of Man*, therefore man is exalted over all of them, for the *face of Man* is the essence of and includes all of the four faces of the Merkava.
- As per "and within it there was the image of the four Chayot [i.e., the four faces], this was their appearance, they had the image of man."²¹⁶
- As per Zohar: Man incorporates all [and all is incorporated within him as written "and on the image of the Throne there is the image and appearance of man upon it from above."]²¹⁷
- As per Zohar: "and the image of their faces, [the face of man"... the face of man incorporates all of them... and all of them are incorporated within him.]²¹⁸

☐ (and the root of the root of man is from the *Man on the Throne*, as above in G1:06)

☐ and the source and life force of the four Chayot is from the world above them and so on up until the highest of the high.

☐ As per the Zohar:
- We learned the supernal secret, there are four inner Chayot – inside [the Sanctuary of Holiness], and they are the first ancient/hidden ones of all the Holy ancient/hidden ones... We learned that just as they are in the Supernal Realms, so they are in the levels below them, and this is similarly so in all the worlds – they are all an [interconnected] unity with each level connected one to the other.²¹⁹
- There are Chayot that encircle the throne of the world of Beriyah... and there are Chayot of Yetzirah... and there are the four Chayot of the four elements....²²⁰

☐ Refer to Etz Chaim.²²¹

---

215 Midrash Rabba Shemot 23:13 as follows:
- R. Avin says: There are four exalted species which were created in the world – the exalted over creatures is man, the exalted of birds is the eagle, the exalted of beasts is the ox, and the exalted of animals is the lion; each took kingship and were given greatness, and they are fixed under the Merkava of God as it says "and the facing images are the face of man and the face of the lion... the face of the ox... and the face of the eagle" (Yechezkel 1:10), and

- וּבִשְׁמוֹת רַבָּה (פכ"ג), אַרְיֵה מֶלֶךְ בַּחַיּוֹת, וכו'.

- וְנֶפֶשׁ הָאָדָם הוּא מ"פְּנֵי אָדָם", לָכֵן הָאָדָם מִתְגָּאֶה עַל כֻּלָּם, כִּי כֵן עִקְּרָם וּכְלָלָם שֶׁל כָּל הָאַרְבַּע פְּנֵי הַמֶּרְכָּבָה הוּא פְּנֵי אָדָם

- כְּמוֹ שֶׁכָּתוּב (יחזקאל א, ה) "וּמִתּוֹכָהּ דְּמוּת אַרְבַּע חַיּוֹת וְזֶה מַרְאֵיהֶן דְּמוּת אָדָם לָהֵנָּה".

- וְעַיֵּן בָּזֶה בַּזֹּהַר יִתְרוֹ פ' ע"ב, אָדָם כָּלִיל כּוּלְּהוּ וכו'.

- וּבְפָרָשַׁת תַּזְרִיעַ מ"ח סוֹף ע"א כְּתִיב "וּדְמוּת פְּנֵיהֶם" וכו', וּבְפָרָשַׁת בְּמִדְבָּר קי"ח ב' "וּדְמוּת פְּנֵיהֶם" וכו', וְעַיֵּן זֹהַר חָדָשׁ יִתְרוֹ בְּמַעֲשֵׂה מֶרְכָּבָה ס"ד ע"ב

- (וְשֹׁרֶשׁ שָׁרְשׁוֹ שֶׁל הָאָדָם הוּא מֵאָדָם שֶׁעַל הַכִּסֵּא כנ"ל בְּשַׁעַר א' פ"ו)

- וְשָׁרְשָׁם וְחִיּוּתָם שֶׁל הָאַרְבַּע חַיּוֹת הוּא מֵהָעוֹלָם שֶׁעֲלֵיהֶם, וְכֵן עַד לְעֵלָּא וּלְעֵלָּא.

- וְעַיֵּן זֹהַר

- יִתְרוֹ פ"ב ב', תָּאנָא בְּרָזָא עִלָּאָה, אַרְבַּע חֵיוָן אִית דְּאִינוּן לְגוֹ וכו', וְאִנּוּן קַדְמָאֵי עַתִּיקִין דְּעַתִּיקָא קַדִּישָׁא כו', תָּאנָא כְּגַוְונָא דִּלְעֵילָּא אִית לְתַתָּא מִנַּיְהוּ, וְכֵן בְּכֻלְּהוּ עָלְמִין כֻּלְּהוּ אֲחִידָן דָּא בְּדָא וְדָא בְּדָא.

- וּבְרַעְיָא מְהֵימְנָא, וְאִית חֵיוָן דְּסָחֲרָן לְכוּרְסַיָּא דִּבְרִיאָה כו', וְאִית חֵיוָן דִּיצִירָה כו', וְאִית אַרְבַּע חֵיוָן דְּאַרְבַּע יְסוֹדוֹת וכו'.

- וְעַיֵּן עֵץ חַיִּים קִצּוּר שַׁעַר אבי"ע ספ"ח, וְשָׁם בְּסוֹף הַשַּׁעַר בְּעִנְיַן כֹּחוֹת נֶפֶשׁ הָאָדָם ע"ש:

---

what was all this for? So that they should not become proud in the world and know that the Heavenly Kingdom rules over them...

216 Yechezkel 1:5.
217 Zohar II Yitro 80b quoting Yechezkel 1:26.
218 Zohar III Tazria 48a and Zohar III Bamidbar 118b and Zohar Chadash I Yitro 64b (all of these sources use close to the identical phrases to express the same point).
219 Zohar II Yitro 82b.
220 R. Chaim brings this quotation from Zohar Raya Mehemna. The precise source was unsuccessfully searched for.
221 Etz Chaim Shaar 50, Shaar Kitzur ABY"A:
Chap. 8:
- Know that in each world there are four animals corresponding to the four

- The ultimate source of these [elements] is the four letters of the name *YHVH* – these are the primary sources – the *secret of faith* – the *father of all worlds*, as per Zohar.²²²
- Similarly it is with all the details of the powers and species – each one has a source, and its source has a source going up to the highest height
  - as Chazal say: There is no blade of grass which does not have a Mazal/constellation in Heaven *hitting* it, saying to it "grow!", as per "Do you know the laws of Heaven." ²²³
  - Refer to the Zohar for more detail.²²⁴
  - That star and Mazal forms the inner soul and life force and source of the plant from which the plant receives the power which enables it to grow, which is its soul, as is known.
  - The source and soul of this star and Mazal is the angel appointed over it from which the star receives the growing power with which it causes the plant to grow
    - as per Zohar, as mentioned above: "and over that star there is an appointed one [who serves before God]"²²⁵
  - and the soul source of the angel is from the world immediately above it.
  - Therefore, the angels are *sworn [to act]* with their names,²²⁶ as their name is the soul, life force, and light of that angel in the world and is the power from [the level] above it which enlightens it and causes it to exist.
    - Refer to the Zohar: All these holy angels above do not exist and cannot be made to exist without the supernal light, which enlightens and sustains them. If this supernal light were to cease, they would not continue to exist.²²⁷

---

letters of *YHVH* which incorporate the Ten Sefirot of that world, and understand this. In each world they are called lion, ox, eagle, man, and [also] the four angels whose initial letters are *ARGM"N Aleph Resh Gimmel Mem Nun* . . . .

Chap. 10 (at the end of the Shaar):
- Now we will explain the concept of the abilities of the soul of man which has the four elements within it . . . .

222 Zohar II VaEra 23b as follows:
- R. Shimon said: Come and see, the four primary [sources, i.e., *YHVH*] are the secret of faith, and they are the father of all worlds, the secret of the Holy Supernal Merkava, and they are the four elements fire, water, wind, dust. . . . [This source is brought at the beginning of Maamar BeTzeLeM and G1:02:N01.]

- וְשֹׁרֶשׁ כָּל הַשָּׁרָשִׁים דִּלְהוֹן הוּא מֵאַרְבַּע אוֹתִיּוֹת שֵׁם הֲוָיָ"ה בָּרוּךְ הוּא, וְהֵן הַשָּׁרָשִׁין קַדְמָאִין, רָזָא דִּמְהֵימְנוּתָא, אֲבָהָן דְּכֻלְּהוּ עָלְמִין הַנִּזְכָּר בַּזֹּהַר וָאֵרָא כ"ג סוֹף ע"ב:

- וְכֵן פְּרָטֵי הַכֹּחוֹת וְהַמִּינִים כֻּלָּם, לְכָל אֶחָד יֵשׁ שֹׁרֶשׁ, וְשֹׁרֶשׁ לִשְׁרֹשׁ לְמַעְלָה מַעְלָה.

  ○ כְּמַאֲמָרָם ז"ל (בראשית רבה פ"י), "אֵין לְךָ כָּל עֵשֶׂב וְעֵשֶׂב שֶׁאֵין לוֹ מַזָּל בָּרָקִיעַ שֶׁמַּכֶּה אוֹתוֹ וְאוֹמֵר לוֹ גְּדַל" שֶׁנֶּאֱמַר (איוב לח לג) "הֲיָדַעְתָּ חֻקּוֹת שָׁמָיִם", וְכוּ'.

  ○ וְעַיֵּן זֹהַר תְּרוּמָה קע"א ב', וּבְפָרָשַׁת קְדוֹשִׁים פ"ו א', הָעִנְיָן בְּאֹרֶךְ קְצָת.

  ○ כִּי אוֹתוֹ הַכּוֹכָב וְהַמַּזָּל הוּא פְּנִימִיּוּת נַפְשׁוֹ וְחִיּוּתוֹ וְשָׁרְשׁוֹ שֶׁל אוֹתוֹ הַצֶּמַח, שֶׁמִּמֶּנּוּ מְקַבֵּל כֹּחַ הַצְּמִיחָה שֶׁהִיא נַפְשׁוֹ, כַּיָּדוּעַ.

  ○ וְשֹׁרֶשׁ וְנֶפֶשׁ אוֹתוֹ הַכּוֹכָב וְהַמַּזָּל הוּא הַמַּלְאָךְ הַמְמֻנֶּה עָלָיו, שֶׁמִּמֶּנּוּ מְקַבֵּל הַכּוֹכָב כֹּחַ הַצְּמִיחָה לְהַצְמִיחָהּ וּלְגַדֵּל אוֹתוֹ הַצֶּמַח

    □ כְּמוֹ שֶׁכָּתוּב בַּזֹּהַר תְּרוּמָה הַנַּ"ל, וְעַל הַהוּא כּוֹכָבָא מְמַנָּא חַד וְכוּ'.

  ○ וְשֹׁרֶשׁ וְנֶפֶשׁ הַמַּלְאָךְ הוּא מֵהַכֹּחַ וְהָעוֹלָם שֶׁעָלָיו.

  ○ וְלָכֵן מַשְׁבִּיעִין אֶת הַמַּלְאָכִים בִּשְׁמוֹת, כִּי אוֹתוֹ הַשֵּׁם הוּא נַפְשׁוֹ וְחִיּוּתוֹ וּנְהוֹרָא דִילֵיהּ שֶׁל אוֹתוֹ הַמַּלְאָךְ בְּהָעוֹלָם וְהַכֹּחַ שֶׁעָלָיו שֶׁמֵּאִירוֹ וּמְקַיְּמוֹ.

    □ וְעַיֵּן זֹהַר בָּלָק ר"ח א', כָּל אִלֵּין מַלְאָכִין קַדִּישִׁין דִּלְעֵילָּא, לָא קַיְּמִין וְלָא

---

223 Bereishit Rabba Bereishit 10:6 quoting Iyov 38:33.
224 Zohar II Terumah 171b:
  - There is no small blade of grass in the entire world which does not have a star and Mazal in the heavens controlling it, and over that star there is an appointed one who serves before God....
  Zohar III Kedoshim 86a:
  - Come and see, when God created the world ... he appointed angels [i.e., controlling powers] over it, and there is no small blade of grass without its angel above, and all that it does is only under the instruction of that supernal angel appointed over it....
225 See Zohar Terumah quoted in previous footnote.
226 See Rashi on Bereishit 32:30 where he explains that an angel's function is determined by his name and its name is changed with each separate function it is required to perform. This idea is brought down in Bereishit Rabba Vayishlach 78:4.
227 Zohar III Balak 208a.

- ▫ Refer to Etz Chaim: That the angels are receptacles, and the names are their essence and the inner part of their soul therefore [the name] operates within him and guides him to whichever way it inclines, just like a soul guides the body, and this is a similar process for all [interconnected] levels up to the highest level.[228]
- The same is true for all souls in the entire Universe, that each soul is rooted in and receives life force from the soul of the world level above it, which becomes its soul of the soul, and so on, etc.
- God Is The *Elokim* – the *All Powerful One*, and Is The Soul, Life Force, and the Ultimate Root of all powers, as in "and You give life to all,"[229] literally continuously,[230] therefore, He is called "The Soul of souls"[231] and "The Root of all the worlds."[232]

11. HE AND HIS SPEECH ARE ONE, *YHVH* IS IDENTICAL TO *ELOKIM*

- This concept,[233] as known from the Zohar,[234] is that He and His Speech are One.

---

228 Etz Chaim Shaar 43, Shaar Tziyur Olamot ABY"A, Introduction:
- Be mindful of this principle and understand that any place where one encounters angels in the chambers of Beriyah, Yetzirah, and Asiyah, that they are the limbs of the body or the clothing of that chamber.

Etz Chaim Shaar 43, Shaar Tziyur Olamot ABY"A, Chap. 1:
- There are *essence* and *receptacles*. *Essence*: are the specific names which they have in their space. *Receptacles*: are the angels.

Etz Chaim Shaar 44, Shaar HaShemot, Chap. 2 (see V2:14, p. 676):
- ... but the chambers themselves, the Ophanim, and the angels – are all on the level of the ten *receptacles*. ...

229 Nechemia 9:6.
230 The verse just quoted states "Mechayeh (give life)" which is in the present tense, meaning continuously.
231 Zohar I Bereishit 45a.
232 Zohar Introduction 11b.
233 Referring to the cascaded levels of life force to each component of creation deriving from the *All Powerful One*, i.e., *Elokim*, as per previous chapter.
234 Having closed the previous chapter with the reference to God's continuous re-creation of everything and quoting the verse "[You are YHVH alone] . . . and Atah/*You* give life to all" (Nechemia 9:6), R. Chaim now refers to Zohar I Bereishit 15b which quotes this verse.

This Zohar explains that the word "ATaH" from this verse is comprised of the letters *Aleph*, *Tav*, and *Hey*, where *Aleph* and *Tav* represent all the twen-

יָכְלִין לְמֵיקַם, בַּר בִּנְהוֹרָא עִלָּאָה, דְּנָהַר לוֹן וְקַיֵּם לוֹן. וְאִי פָּסַק מִנַּיְיהוּ נְהוֹרָא דִּלְעֵילָא, לָא יָכְלִין לְמֵיקַם.

וְעַיֵּן עֵץ חַיִּים שַׁעַר צִיּוּר עוֹלָמוֹת אבי"ע, בְּהַקְדָּמַת הרח"ו, וְשָׁם סוֹף פֶּרֶק א', וּבְשַׁעַר הַשֵּׁמוֹת פֶּרֶק ז', שֶׁהַמַּלְאָכִים הֵם בְּחִינַת "כֵּלִים", וְהַנְּשָׁמוֹת הֵם "הָעֲצָמוּת" שֶׁלָּהֶם וּפְנִימִיּוּת נִשְׁמָתָם, וְלָכֵן הוּא פּוֹעֵל בּוֹ וּמַנְהִיגוֹ לְכָל אֲשֶׁר יַחְפּוֹץ, כִּנְשָׁמָה שֶׁמַּנְהֶגֶת הַגּוּף, וְכֵן עַל זֶה הַדֶּרֶךְ עַד לְעֵילָא לְעֵילָא:

• וְכֵן בְּעִנְיַן הַנְּשָׁמוֹת שֶׁבְּכָל עוֹלָם, כָּל נְשָׁמָה שָׁרְשָׁהּ וּמְקוֹר חִיּוּתָהּ הוּא מִבְּחִינַת הַנְּשָׁמָה שֶׁל הָעוֹלָם שֶׁעָלֶיהָ, שֶׁהִיא נַעֲשֵׂית וְנִקְרֵאת אֶצְלָהּ "נְשָׁמָה לִנְשָׁמָה", וְכֵן כֻּלָּם:

• וְהוּא יִתְבָּרַךְ שְׁמוֹ, הוּא הָאֱלֹקִים — "בַּעַל הַכֹּחוֹת כֻּלָּם" — שֶׁהוּא נִשְׁמַת וְחִיּוּת וְשֹׁרֶשׁ הַשָּׁרָשִׁים שֶׁל הַכֹּחוֹת כֻּלָּם, כְּמוֹ שֶׁכָּתוּב (נחמיה ט, ו) "וְאַתָּה מְחַיֶּה אֶת כֻּלָּם", כָּל רֶגַע מַמָּשׁ, וְלָכֵן נִקְרָא הוּא יִתְבָּרַךְ, נִשְׁמָתָא דְּכָל נִשְׁמָתִין, וְעִקָּרָא וְשָׁרְשָׁא דְּכָל עָלְמִין:

שער ג' - פרק י"א

• וְהָעִנְיָן כַּיָּדוּעַ בַּזֹּהַר, שֶׁהוּא יִתְבָּרַךְ וְדִבּוּרוֹ חַד

---

ty-two letters from *Aleph* to *Tav* and the letter *Hey* connects the twenty-two letters together. From the combination of these letters from *Aleph* to *Tav* together with the binding *Hey* within the single word "ATaH," referring to God, the Zohar understands and states that this represents the fact that the letters and God/YHVH are all one, and that it is that "ATaH," both the letters and YHVH, are continuously (present tense) giving life (i.e., creating) all. The Vilna Gaon, in his commentary on Sefer Yetzirah 1:3, quotes this Zohar and explains how the letters and the word "ATaH" are connected to the name YHVH as follows:

- . . . and the concept is that "ATaH" is called Malchut/Kingship. For *Aleph* and *Tav* represent the twenty-two letters from Aleph to *Tav*
- as written in Zohar I Bereishit 15b:
  ○ "*Aleph* and *Tav*: When you take all of the letters, the general set of letters from the beginning to the end. Afterwards add the letter *Hey* to connect the twenty-two letters with the *Hey*. Then it is called 'ATaH' and this is the meaning of the verse 'and Atah/*You* give life to all' . . . ."
- This means [that the twenty-two letters] are connected with the *Hey*/five [final form] letters of "MNTzPCh" [*Mem, Nun, Tzaddi, Peh, Chaf*] . . .
- This is the secret of YHVH: YHV is Zeer Anpin and has the numerical value of 21, and together with the tag of the *Yud* adds up to 22 [parallel-

- That each of God's Statements of Creation, that "He spoke and it was,"[235] is the soul and life force of each creation that was created with it – including all the many myriads of species within it – together with the constellations appointed over them, and the angels appointed over those constellations, together with the source and the source of the source [etc.] extending upwards to the highest level of each world.[236]
- From the point [of Creation] onwards for the duration of existence of the Universe, 'His Speech stands'[237] within each [created entity] to enlighten them, and causing them to continuously exist together with all their details, changes, and arrangements.

• Therefore, in all the Ten Statements of Creation[238] only the name *Elokim* is used, as each statement itself
  - is the power[239] of the entity and [of] all the species within it which were created with it, and
  - is the soul which disseminates through the inner essence of the detail of all of their parts
  - however, now [once created], 'our physical eyes are incapable of perceiving'[240] how and in what way His Speech permeates through them.

• In future times, however, the verse writes that "together, all flesh will see that it is the mouth of *YHVH* that Speaks"[241]
  - meaning that our perception will be refined to the point that we will merit to perceive and to also physically see the concept of God's Speech permeating through every entity in the Universe

---

ing the twenty-two letters of the alphabet]. The *Hey* (i.e., the last letter of YHVH) is Nukva [of Zeer Anpin and corresponds to ultimate manifestation of Kingship/Malchut] and represents the five letters of "MNTzPCh" . . .

The five final form letters "MNTzPCh" relate to five corresponding parts of the mouth which articulate different groups of letters. Between them all twenty-two letters of the alphabet are articulated as speech. The final form letters of "MNTzPCh" have the same numerical value as *Mem Nun=Melech, Tzaddi=Malach, Peh Chaf=Yimloch*, the ultimate expression of Kingship which spans past, present, and future. Being final letters they are always at the end of a word and represent the final and ultimate manifestation, the end recipient of the bestowal, the place where Kingship is manifest, the articulation of God's Speech which constantly creates All. They represent the ultimate manifestation of YHVH who is *Haya Hoveh VeYiheyeh*, who *Was, Is, and Will Be*, transcending time – being manifest in a form which is the constant re-creation of all existence.

In that the Torah is referred to as God's Speech and is comprised of the letters from *Aleph* to *Tav* and that He and the Torah are One, therefore, He and His Speech are also One. In particular God's Ten Statements of Creation

נפש שער ג' - פרק י"א החיים 549

- וְכָל דִבּוּר וּמַאֲמָר שֶׁל הַקָּדוֹשׁ בָּרוּךְ הוּא בְּמַעֲשֵׂה בְרֵאשִׁית, שֶׁאָמַר וַיְהִי, הוּא הַנֶּפֶשׁ וְחִיּוּת אוֹתוֹ הַדָּבָר שֶׁנִּבְרָא בּוֹ, וְכָל רִבֵּי רִבְבוֹת הַמִּינִים שֶׁבּוֹ, עִם הַמַּזָּלוֹת הַמְמֻנִּים עֲלֵיהֶם, וְהַמַּלְאָכִים הַמְמֻנִּים עַל אוֹתָם הַמַּזָּלוֹת, וְשָׁרְשָׁם וְשֹׁרֶשׁ שָׁרְשָׁם לְמַעְלָה מַעְלָה שֶׁבְּכָל עוֹלָם.

- וּמֵאָז וָהָלְאָה, עוֹד כָּל יְמֵי עוֹלָם, דְּבָרוֹ יִתְבָּרַךְ נִצָּב בָּהֶם לְהָאִירָם וּלְקַיְּמָם כָּל רֶגַע, בְּכָל פְּרָטֵי עִנְיָנֵיהֶם וְשִׁנּוּיֵיהֶם וְסִדּוּר מַצָּבָם:

• לָכֵן בְּכָל הָעֶשֶׂר מַאֲמָרוֹת לֹא נִזְכַּר רַק שֵׁם "אֱלֹקִים", שֶׁאוֹתוֹ הַמַּאֲמָר

- הוּא בַּעַל הַכֹּחוֹת שֶׁל אוֹתוֹ הַדָּבָר, וְכָל הַמִּינִים שֶׁבּוֹ שֶׁנִּבְרְאוּ בוֹ

- שֶׁהוּא נַפְשָׁם הַמִּתְפַּשֵּׁט בִּפְנִימִיּוּת כָּל פְּרָטֵי חֶלְקֵיהֶם.

- רַק שֶׁעַתָּה טָח עֵינֵינוּ מֵרְאוֹת בְּעֵינֵי הַבָּשָׂר — אֵיךְ וּבְאֵיזֶה אֹפֶן דִּבּוּרוֹ יִתְבָּרַךְ מִתְפַּשֵּׁט בָּהֶם:

• וּלְעָתִיד לָבֹא כְּתִיב (ישעיה מ, ה) "וְרָאוּ כָל בָּשָׂר יַחְדָּו כִּי פִּי הֲוָי"ה דִּבֵּר"

- הַיְנוּ שֶׁיְּזַכֵּךְ הַשָּׂגָתֵנוּ עַד שֶׁנִּזְכֶּה לְהַשִּׂיג וְלִרְאוֹת גַּם — בְּעֵין הַ'בָּשָׂר' — עִנְיַן הִתְפַּשְּׁטוּת דִּבּוּרוֹ יִתְבָּרַךְ בְּכָל דָּבָר בָּעוֹלָם

---

are specifically those which continuously re-create all things as R. Chaim will now explain.

See the quotation from Shomer Emunim relating to the *Great Voice* on p. 386, fn. 245.

R. Chaim revisits and expands this concept in G4:10 where he explains that the origin of the Torah and of God's Speech is from the World of The Malbush. This is based on teachings from the Arizal which were only mentioned by his student R. Yisrael Sarug and are not included in the writings of his principal student, R. Chaim Vital.

235 Tehillim 33:9.
236 As described in G3:10.
237 This is a reference to the verse "Continuously God, Your Speech is Standing in the Heavens" (Tehillim 119:89). The Midrash Tehillim on this verse states that God's Speech is continuously *standing* within the creations that each creative statement created – causing them to continuously be.
238 Mishna Avot 5:1.
239 As in the *All Powerful One*.
240 Yishayahu 44:18.
241 Yishayahu 40:5.

- similar to the perception that existed at the time of the Receiving of the Torah as it says:[242] "and all the people *saw* the sounds." (Note 44)[243]
- This idea is also incorporated in Chazal's statement[244] that we should understand that this world is not like the future world, as
  - this world is written as *Yud Hey* and pronounced *Aleph Dalet*
  - but the future world is written as *Yud Hey* and pronounced *Yud Hey*.[245]
- This is also the same idea portrayed by the verse[246] "and your Mentor shall no longer be concealed,[247] and your eyes will see your Mentor."
- Refer to the Zohar, "Wings – they are covers to secretly conceal the Names." Refer well to the whole concept there.[248]

• Therefore, God began the Ten Commandments with "I am *YHVH* who is your *Elokim*,"[249] for this is the basis of our faith, that each individual Jew must instill within his heart that it is only God who truly wields any power, and that He is his Soul, Life Force, and Essence, and [also the Soul, Life Force, and Essence] of all the creations, powers, and worlds.

• This is the concept and explanation of how *Elokim* is the *All Powerful One*.

• But nevertheless, the implication of this explanation and the concept of this name, [*Elokim*]
  - is that the worlds and powers which are renewed from God's Sublime Will – really exist
  - and that God concealed Himself to form a Makom/Space, so to speak, for the existence of powers and worlds
  - but that God is the Soul and the Ultimate Source of the power and life force which they receive from Him, which is distributed and concealed within them, so to speak
  - just like a soul is distributed within a person's body – for even though

---

242 Shemot 20:15.
243 **R. Chaim adds Note 44 here.** This note is brought at the end of this chapter and is entitled "Hear that which is seen and see that which is heard."
244 Pesachim 50a.
245 I.e., that the Essence of God, hinted to by the letters *Yud Hey* (a part of the fuller name describing His Essence YHVH) is concealed in this world through its expression through speech and it is only pronounced as the letters *Aleph Dalet* (a part of the fuller name ADoNaY which relates to Him as our Master), i.e., as a separate entity to ourselves. In the future world, however, His name will not be concealed through its expression through speech, this will parallel our understanding that we will *see* His Speech, i.e., see Him directly in everything and that everything is One.

○ כְּמוֹ שֶׁכְּבָר הָיְתָה הַהַשָּׂגָה מֵעֵין זֶה בְּעֵת מַתַּן תּוֹרָה דִּכְתִיב (שמות כ, טו) "וְכָל הָעָם רוֹאִים אֶת הַקּוֹלוֹת". (הגהה מ"ד).

○ וְהוּא גַּם כֵּן בִּכְלַל מַאֲמָרָם זִכְרוֹנָם לִבְרָכָה סוֹף פֶּרֶק אֵלּוּ עוֹבְרִין (פסחים), לֹא כְּהָעוֹלָם הַזֶּה הָעוֹלָם הַבָּא

▫ הָעוֹלָם הַזֶּה נִכְתָּב בִּי"ה וְנִקְרָא בא"ד

▫ אֲבָל הָעוֹלָם הַבָּא נִכְתָּב בִּי"ה וְנִקְרָא בִּי"ה, וְהָבֵן.

○ וְהוּא עִנְיַן הַכָּתוּב (ישעיה ל, כ) "וְלֹא יִכָּנֵף עוֹד מוֹרֶיךָ וְהָיוּ עֵינֶיךָ רוֹאוֹת אֶת מוֹרֶיךָ".

○ וְעַיֵּן זֹהַר חָדָשׁ יִתְרוֹ ס"ח ע"א, כְּנָפַיִם כִּסּוּיִין לְאִתְכַּסְּאָה שְׁמָהָן וְכוּ', עַיֵּן שָׁם הֵיטֵב כָּל הָעִנְיָן:

• וְלָכֵן פָּתַח יִתְבָּרֵךְ שְׁמוֹ רֵאשִׁית עֲשֶׂרֶת הַדִּבְּרוֹת "אָנֹכִי הֲוָיָ"ה אֱלֹהֶיךָ", כִּי זֶה כָּל עִקַּר יְסוֹד הָאֱמוּנָה, שֶׁצָּרִיךְ כָּל אִישׁ יִשְׂרָאֵל לִקְבֹּעַ בְּלִבּוֹ, שֶׁרַק הוּא יִתְבָּרֵךְ שְׁמוֹ הוּא הַבַּעַל כֹּחַ הָאֲמִתִּי, וְנִשְׁמַת וְחִיּוּת וְשֹׁרֶשׁ הָעִקָּר שֶׁלּוֹ, וְשֶׁל כָּל הַבְּרוּאִים וְהַכֹּחוֹת וְהָעוֹלָמוֹת כֻּלָּם:

▫ זֶהוּ עִנְיָן וּפֵרוּשׁ שֶׁל שֵׁם "אֱלֹקִים" — בַּעַל הַכֹּחוֹת כֻּלָּם:

• אֲבָל עִם כָּל זֶה, לְפִי פֵּרוּשׁוֹ וְעִנְיָנוֹ שֶׁל זֶה הַשֵּׁם, מַשְׁמַע

○ שֶׁיֵּשׁ בִּמְצִיאוּת גָּמוּר גַּם עוֹלָמוֹת וְכֹחוֹת מְחֻדָּשִׁים מֵרְצוֹנוֹ הַפָּשׁוּט יִתְבָּרַךְ

○ שֶׁצִּמְצֵם כְּבוֹדוֹ וְהִנִּיחַ מָקוֹם כִּבְיָכוֹל לִמְצִיאוּת כֹּחוֹת וְעוֹלָמוֹת

○ אֶלָּא שֶׁהוּא יִתְבָּרַךְ, הוּא נִשְׁמָתָם וּמְקוֹר שֹׁרֶשׁ כֹּחַ חִיּוּתָם שֶׁמְּקַבְּלִים מֵאִתּוֹ יִתְבָּרַךְ, שֶׁמִּתְפַּשֵּׁט וּמִסְתַּתֵּר בְּתוֹכָם כִּבְיָכוֹל.

○ כְּעִנְיַן הִתְפַּשְּׁטוּת הַנְּשָׁמָה בְּגוּף הָאָדָם, שֶׁאַף שֶׁהִיא מִתְפַּשֶּׁטֶת בְּכָל חֵלֶק

---

246 Yishayahu 30:20.
247 Rashi on this verse interprets the word "Yikanef" as "concealed," as in covered by the corner of one's garment.
248 Zohar Chadash I Yitro 68a:
  • Wings – they are covers to secretly conceal the Names, and in future times the secret of the Holy Name will no longer be concealed and all righteous people of the truth will know [God's name, i.e., YHVH] in a revealed way, and not through descriptions – this is the secret of the verse "and your Mentor shall no longer be concealed, and your eyes will see your Mentor." [The word "Kanaf" has a dual meaning of "wing" and "corner," and in this context relating to concealment.]
249 Shemot 20:2.

it is distributed within each specific part of him, it nevertheless cannot be said that the body is nullified to it in a way that it appears to not exist at all
- similarly, with each higher power and world which is manifest as the essence of the power and world beneath it, notwithstanding this, the power and world beneath it nevertheless does have its own existence
- and this is from our perspective and our perception, as mentioned above.[250]

• However, the name relating to God's Essence, *YHVH*, relates to the concept from God's perspective, as explained above
- (even though the name *YHVH* also relates to God's connection, through His Will, to the worlds, as the essence of the Unified Infinite Master is totally abstracted from the worlds and no name can even vaguely capture this [concept] at all, nevertheless, the existence of the worlds is totally nullified relative to Him from the perspective of this name, and [this name comes closest] to resemble the level which relates to God's perspective)
- and therefore this name of the Essence is referred to as the "Unified Name."

• This is the meaning of the verse "that *YHVH* is *Elokim*,"[251] meaning [that irrespective of the difference in perception,] that from our perspective, He is referred to as *Elokim* and from His perspective He is referred to as *YHVH*[252] – nevertheless, they are truly one and the same thing, and *YHVH* is identical to *Elokim*, as explained above in G3:07 that Tzimtzum and Kav are one and the same concept.[253]

• This is also the general principle of the expression of [God's] Unity of the first verse of Kriat Shema "*YHVH* which is *Elokeinu* – *YHVH* is One,"[254] (Note 45)[255]
- which means that one must intellectually focus on the fact that He is

---

250 As per G3:05.
251 Devarim 4:39.
252 The Vilna Gaon comments (in Aderet Eliyahu on Devarim 1:6) as follows:
- "YHVH, our Elokim, spoke to us . . .": . . . The reason why [Moshe] opened [his lengthy soliloquy in the book of Devarim] with these two Names of God is because they incorporate the entirety of the Torah and all of the Names, for God is hidden from the perspective of His Essence and revealed from the perspective of His Actions. Therefore, we state [within the formal syntax of] each blessing [an expression of both] revelation and concealment. The Name YHVH relates to the perspective of God's Essence, and Elokim relates to His Providence over His creations, and that is why it is only the

שער ג' - פרק י"א

וּנְקֻדָּה פְּרָטִית שֶׁבּוֹ, עִם כָּל זֶה לֹא נוּכַל לוֹמַר שֶׁהַגּוּף מִתְבַּטֵּל נֶגְדָּהּ כְּאִלּוּ אֵינוֹ בִּמְצִיאוּת כְּלָל.

• וְכֵן בְּכֹחַ כֹּחַ וְעוֹלָם עֶלְיוֹן, שֶׁמִּתְפַּשֵּׁט בְּכָל עַצְמוּת הַכֹּחַ וְהָעוֹלָם שֶׁתַּחְתָּיו, עִם כָּל זֶה, גַּם הַכֹּחַ וְהָעוֹלָם הַתַּחְתּוֹן יֶשְׁנוֹ בִּמְצִיאוּת.

• וְהוּא כְּפִי אֲשֶׁר מִצִּדֵּנוּ בְּעִנְיָן הַשָּׂגָתֵנוּ כְּמוֹ שֶׁנִּתְבָּאֵר לְמַעְלָה:

• אֲבָל שֵׁם הָעֶצֶם "הֲוָיָ"ה" בָּרוּךְ הוּא מוֹרֶה עַל הַבְּחִינָה וְהָעִנְיָן כְּפִי אֲשֶׁר הוּא מִצִּדּוֹ יִתְבָּרַךְ שֶׁנִּתְבָּאֵר לְמַעְלָה.

• (וְאַף שֶׁגַּם שֵׁם "הֲוָיָ"ה" בָּרוּךְ הוּא — נִקְרָא גַּם כֵּן מִצַּד הִתְחַבְּרוּתוֹ יִתְבָּרַךְ בִּרְצוֹנוֹ לְהָעוֹלָמוֹת, כִּי עַצְמוּת אָדוֹן יָחִיד אֵין סוֹף בָּרוּךְ הוּא, בִּבְחִינַת הֱיוֹתוֹ מִפְשָׁט מֵהָעוֹלָמוֹת, לֹא אִתְרְמִיז בְּשׁוּם שֵׁם כְּלָל, אַף עַל פִּי כֵן, הָעוֹלָמוֹת הֵמָּה בְּטֵלִים וּמְבֻטָּלִים בִּמְצִיאוּת נֶגְדּוֹ יִתְבָּרַךְ מִצַּד זֶה הַשֵּׁם הַנִּכְבָּד וְהוּא מֵעֵין הַבְּחִינָה כְּפִי אֲשֶׁר מִצִּדּוֹ יִתְבָּרַךְ)

• וְלָכֵן נִקְרָא שֵׁם הָעֶצֶם "שֵׁם הַמְיֻחָד" בָּרוּךְ הוּא:

• וְזֶהוּ שֶׁאָמַר הַכָּתוּב (דברים ה, לט) "כִּי הֲוָיָ"ה הוּא הָאֱלֹקִים" כו', רָצָה לוֹמַר, עִם כִּי מִצַּד הַשָּׂגָתֵנוּ הוּא נִקְרָא בְּשֵׁם "אֱלֹקִים", וּמִצִּדּוֹ יִתְבָּרַךְ נִקְרָא בִּבְחִינַת שֵׁם "הֲוָיָ"ה" בָּרוּךְ הוּא, בֶּאֱמֶת הַכֹּל אֶחָד "וַהֲוָיָ"ה הוּא הָאֱלֹקִים" כו', כְּמוֹ שֶׁנִּתְבָּאֵר לְעֵיל פֶּרֶק ז' עִנְיָן הַצִּמְצוּם וְהַכּוּ דְכֻלָּא חֲדָא:

• וְזֶהוּ גַּם כֵּן בִּכְלַל עִנְיַן יִחוּד פָּסוּק רִאשׁוֹן דִּקְרִיאַת שְׁמַע "ה' אֱלֹקֵינוּ ה' אֶחָד", (הגהה מ"ה)

• רָצָה לוֹמַר, לְכַוֵּן שֶׁהוּא יִתְבָּרַךְ הוּא אֱלֹקֵינוּ בַּעַל הַכֹּחוֹת, וּמְקוֹר שֹׁרֶשׁ נִשְׁמָתֵנוּ וְחִיּוּתֵנוּ, וְשֶׁל כָּל הַבְּרוּאִים וְהָעוֹלָמוֹת.

---

name Elokim which is recorded throughout the entire Creation chapter. [See details of blessings being both hidden and revealed in G2:03.]

253 The Vilna Gaon comments (in Aderet Eliyahu on Bereishit 1:1) as follows:
  • For there are two aspects in every act [of creation]. [The created entity's] essence and its life. Its essence is made with the name Elokim and its life is with the name YHVH which "continuously gives life to all" [Nechemia 9:6].

254 Devarim 6:4.

255 **R. Chaim adds Note 45 here.** This note is brought at the end of this chapter and is entitled "Baruch Shem not praise, but God accepts it so we say it quietly."

Elokeinu, the *All Powerful One* – the source and root of our souls, our life force, and of all the creations and the worlds
- and even though He Created and Causes the existence of the powers, worlds, and creations, nevertheless He, from His perspective, is on the level of *YHVH* and is One, that there is, God forbid, no separation whatsoever [which divides] His Absolute Unity which fills everything, and even now[256] He is called "*YHVH*" and "One."

Rabbi Chaim's Notes:
Note 44 – Hear that which is seen and see that which is heard

- On this basis, we can understand Chazal's statement on this verse[257] that [at the receiving of the Torah, the people] were able to hear that which is seen and see that which is heard.
- This means
  - that their physical abilities had become so nullified [compared to their spiritual level], and their perception so [spiritually] refined
  - to the extent that the whole existence of their physical senses, where they initially would see things physically, now became nullified [and meaningless] to see and understand [in a physical way] at all
  - to the point that, by way of analogy
  - if someone wanted to make them understand the nature of the physical senses, they would [only be able] to describe their existence to them 'to make them understand with the hearing of the ear'[258]
  - [whereas] with spiritual concepts, while they were initially required to be made to understand them by [the indirect] *hearing of the ear* [in order to relate to them], now [as a result of their heightened spiritual perception] they could see them [directly with their new-found] sense of [spiritual] sight and with amazing perception.

Note 45 – Baruch Shem, not praise but God accepts it so we say it quietly

- With this, we can understand Chazal's statement[259] in relation to the praise "Blessed is the name of the Honor of His Majesty for ever and ever" [which is said together with the declaration of] Unity of Kriat Shema
  - that they instituted it to be said quietly
  - and gave the analogy of a princess who smelled the aroma of a spicy stew [and developed a craving for it. If she expresses her desire for it, she suffers disgrace as it is beneath her royal dignity to display a personal craving. If she does not express herself, then she suffers pain.] Her servants then started to bring it to her *quietly*.

- וְאַף שֶׁבָּרָא וְהִמְצִיא מְצִיאוּת כֹּחוֹת וְעוֹלָמוֹת וּבְרִיּוֹת, עִם כָּל זֶה הוּא בִּבְחִינַת הֲוָי״ה וְאֶחָד מִצִּדּוֹ יִתְבָּרֵךְ, שֶׁאֵין הַבְּרוּאִים כֻּלָּם חוֹצְצִים חַס וְשָׁלוֹם כְּלָל נֶגֶד אַחְדוּתוֹ הַפָּשׁוּט יִתְבָּרֵךְ הַמְמַלֵּא כֹּל, וְנִקְרָא גַּם עַתָּה הֲוָי״ה וְאֶחָד:

הגהה מ״ד

- וְיֵשׁ לְפָרֵשׁ עַל פִּי זֶה מַאֲמָרָם זִכְרוֹנָם לִבְרָכָה עַל זֶה הַכָּתוּב (מְכִילְתָּא לְגִרְסַת רַשִׁ״י בַּחֻמָּשׁ), שֶׁהָיוּ שׁוֹמְעִים אֶת הַנִּרְאֶה וְרוֹאִים אֶת הַנִּשְׁמָע:
- וְרוֹצֶה לוֹמַר
  - שֶׁכָּל כָּךְ נִתְבַּטְּלוּ מֵהֶם אָז כָּל כֹּחוֹת הַגַּשְׁמִיּוּת, וְנִזְדַּכֵּךְ הַשָּׂגָתָם מְאֹד
  - עַד שֶׁכָּל מְצִיאוּת עִנְיְנֵי הַמּוּחָשִׁים הַגַּשְׁמִיִּים, שֶׁהָיוּ תְּחִלָּה רוֹאִים אוֹתָם רְאִיָּה חוּשִׁית, עַתָּה נִתְבַּטְּלוּ אֶצְלָם מַרְאוֹתָם בְּחוּשׁ רְאוֹתָם וְהִתְבּוֹנְנוּ בָּהֶם כְּלָל עַד שֶׁדֶּרֶךְ מָשָׁל
  - אִם הָיָה רוֹצֶה מִי לְהָבִינָם עִנְיְנֵי הַמּוּחָשִׁים הַגַּשְׁמִיִּים, הָיָה צָרִיךְ לְסַפֵּר לָהֶם, לְהַשְׁמִיעָם לִשְׁמֹעַ אֹזֶן שֶׁיֶּשְׁנָם בִּמְצִיאוּת
  - וְהָעִנְיָנִים הָרוּחָנִיִּים שֶׁתְּחִלָּה הָיָה צָרִיךְ לְהָבִינָם עִנְיָנָם לִשְׁמֹעַ אֹזֶן, עַתָּה רָאוּם בְּחוּשׁ רְאוּתָם וְנִפְלָאוֹת הַשָּׂגָתָם:

הגהה מ״ה

- וּבָזֶה יוּבַן מַאֲמָרָם זִכְרוֹנָם לִבְרָכָה (פסחים נו, א) בְּעִנְיַן הַשֶּׁבַח ״בָּרוּךְ שֵׁם כְּבוֹד מַלְכוּתוֹ לְעוֹלָם וָעֶד״ בְּיִחוּד קְרִיאַת שְׁמַע
  - שֶׁהִתְקִינוּ שֶׁיֹּאמְרוּהוּ בַּחֲשַׁאי
  - מָשָׁל לְבַת מֶלֶךְ שֶׁהֵרִיחָה צִיקֵי קְדֵרָה וְכוּ׳, הִתְחִילוּ עֲבָדֶיהָ לְהָבִיא לָהּ בַּחֲשַׁאי.

---

256 I.e., even after the Creation where, from our perspective, things appear separate to Him.

257 Mechilta DeRabbi Yishmael, Yitro Masechta DeBechodesh, Parsha 9 on the verse "and all the people *saw* the sounds" from Shemot 20:14.

258 Tehillim 18:45, as their perception was so refined that they no longer directly related to the physical senses, e.g., of physical sight.

259 Pesachim 56a.

- ○ Now this analogy is seemingly strange as surely the statement [of Blessing] is a great praise [of God – so why should Chazal compare its statement to the satisfaction of an embarrassing personal craving]?
- One can simply say
  - ○ that in truth this is not a statement of praise at all
  - ○ as would one consider it a praise of a human king to say that he rules over many myriads of ants and fleas and that they willingly accept the yoke of his majesty over them?
  - ○ So how very much more so and in a totally incomparably abstracted way, it is that God's Holiness and the Essence of His Absolute Unity is totally abstracted from all the worlds to the extent that they are of no consequence before Him
  - ○ it is therefore certain that in truth it is no praise at all of God, to say that His Honored Majesty over all the worlds and creations is blessed and glorified, as they are all lowly and of no consequence relative to Him at all!
  - ○ However, God, who in His Greatness has great humility,[260] His Will decreed it that He should accept this as a praise from us.
  - ○ Therefore, Chazal made the analogy to the spicy stew and instituted that [this praise] should at least only be said quietly.
- According to our words mentioned above, Chazal's deeper meaning is that:
  - ○ After we express [God's] Unity with the first verse of the Shema
  - ○ that He is just One, an Absolute Unity, and that there is absolutely nothing else apart from Him at all
  - ○ and that it is as if all the worlds do not exist at all
  - ○ how can we follow such a statement by saying that He is Blessed in the Honor of His Majesty over the worlds, that the worlds do also exist[261] and that God Rules over them, as this cannot be considered praise relative to the expression of God's sheer Unity expressed by the first verse of the Shema?
  - ○ However, God's Will decreed it that nevertheless we should praise Him with this praise, as this concept is true from our perspective and our behavior, and that the foundation and statutes of the Holy Torah are entirely built on this principle, as I wrote above
  - ○ therefore, we should say [this praise] quietly.
- (Now this can be questioned on the basis of what R. Yirmiya said to R. Chiya bar Abba[262] [that when R. Yirmiya was sitting before R. Chiya bar Abba he saw R. Chiya bar Abba] prolong his [articulation of the] word "One" [from the Shema]. [R. Chiya bar Abba] said to him: After [intellectually] acknowledging God's Kingship, above, below, and in the

- וְלִכְאוֹרָה יַפְלֵא מְשַׁלָּם זִכְרוֹנָם לִבְרָכָה, הֲלֹא שֶׁבַח גָּדוֹל הוּא:

• וְעַל פִּי פָּשׁוּט יֵשׁ לוֹמַר
  ◦ דִּלְפִי הָאֱמֶת אֵינוֹ שֶׁבַח כְּלָל
  ◦ כְּמוֹ הָאָם יֵחָשֵׁב לְשַׁבֵּחַ לְמֶלֶךְ בָּשָׂר וָדָם לוֹמַר עָלָיו שֶׁהוּא מוֹלֵךְ עַל רִבֵּי רְבָבוֹת נְמָלִים וְיַתּוּשִׁים, וְהֵמָּה מְקַבְּלִים עֲלֵיהֶם עַל מַלְכוּתוֹ בְּרָצוֹן.
  ◦ כָּל שֶׁכֵּן וְקַל וָחֹמֶר אֵין עֲרֹךְ כְּלָל, שֶׁהוּא יִתְבָּרֵךְ אֲשֶׁר אֵין עֲרֹךְ לִקְדֻשָּׁתוֹ וְעֹצֶם אַחְדוּתוֹ הַפָּשׁוּט, וְכָל הָעוֹלָמוֹת כְּלָא חֲשִׁיבִין קַמֵּיהּ
  ◦ וַדַּאי בֶּאֱמֶת אֵינוֹ שֶׁבַח כְּלָל שֶׁנְּשַׁבְּחֵהוּ יִתְבָּרֵךְ, שֶׁהוּא בָּרוּךְ וּמְפֹאָר בִּכְבוֹד מַלְכוּתוֹ עַל עוֹלָמוֹת נִבְרָאִים, שֶׁכֻּלָּם שְׁפָלִים וְלֹא חֲשִׁיבִין קַמֵּיהּ כְּלָל.
  ◦ רַק שֶׁהוּא יִתְבָּרֵךְ — בִּמְקוֹם גְּדֻלָּתוֹ תִּמְצָא עַנְוְתָנוּתוֹ, שֶׁגָּזְרָה רְצוֹנוֹ לְקַבְּלוֹ מֵאִתָּנוּ לְשֶׁבַח
  ◦ לָזֹאת הִמְשִׁילוּהוּ זִכְרוֹנָם לִבְרָכָה לְצִיקֵי קְדֵרָה, וְהִתְקִינוּ שֶׁעַל כָּל פָּנִים לֹא נֶאֶמְרֵהוּ אֶלָּא "בַּחֲשַׁאי":

• וּלְפִי דְּהַנַ"ל, יֵשׁ לְפָרֵשׁ פְּנִימִיּוּת כַּוָּנָתָם זִכְרוֹנָם לִבְרָכָה.
  ◦ הַיְנוּ, שֶׁאַחַר שֶׁיִּחֲדְנוּהוּ בְּפָסוּק "שְׁמַע"
  ◦ שֶׁהוּא רַק אֶחָד, אַחְדוּת פָּשׁוּט, וְאֵין עוֹד מִלְּבַדּוֹ כְּלָל
  ◦ וְכָל הָעוֹלָמוֹת הֵם כְּאִלּוּ אֵינָם בִּמְצִיאוּת כְּלָל
  ◦ אֵיךְ נְשַׁבְּחֵהוּ אַחַר זֶה שֶׁהוּא מְבֹרָךְ בִּכְבוֹד מַלְכוּתוֹ עַל עוֹלָמוֹת, שֶׁגַּם הָעוֹלָמוֹת יֶשְׁנָם בִּמְצִיאוּת וְהוּא יִתְבָּרֵךְ הַמּוֹלֵךְ עֲלֵיהֶם, וְאֵינוֹ נֶחְשָׁב לְשֶׁבַח נֶגֶד עֹצֶם יִחוּד פָּסוּק "שְׁמַע".
  ◦ אֶלָּא שֶׁגָּזְרָה רְצוֹנוֹ יִתְבָּרֵךְ, שֶׁאַף עַל פִּי כֵן נְשַׁבְּחֵהוּ בָּזֶה הַשֶּׁבַח, מֵחֲמַת שֶׁכֵּן הוּא הָעִנְיָן מִצַּד הַשָּׂגָתֵנוּ וְהַנְהָגָתֵנוּ, עַל פִּי יְסוֹדוֹת וְחֻקֵּי תּוֹרָה הַקְּדוֹשָׁה, שֶׁנִּבְנוּ כֻלָּם עַל פִּי זֶה הַבְּחִינָה, כְּמוֹ שֶׁכָּתַבְתִּי לְעֵיל
  ◦ לָזֹאת נֶאֶמְרֵהוּ בַּחֲשַׁאי:

• (וְלִכְאוֹרָה יִקְשֶׁה מִמַּאי דְּאָמַר לֵיהּ רַבִּי יִרְמְיָה לְרַבִּי חִיָּיא בַּר אַבָּא, (ברכות יג, ב) דְּהָוָה מַאֲרִיךְ טוּבָא בְּתֵיבַת "אֶחָד", וְאָמַר לֵיהּ כֵּיוָן דְּאַמְלִיכְתֵיהּ לְמַעְלָה וּלְמַטָּה וּלְאַרְבַּע רוּחוֹת הַשָּׁמַיִם תּוּ לֹא צְרִיכַת.

---

260 Yalkut Shimoni Ekev Remez 856.
261 See G3:14:N48.
262 Berachot 13b.

four directions, there is no further need [for intellectual acknowledgment in the subsequent recitation of the remainder of the Shema].
- Now, according to his words, this is somewhat problematic as there is an association of the concept of "Kingship" with the word "One"?[263]
- But this is also not a contradiction, as is known to those who know from the words of the Arizal that the entirety of God's initial thought in connection with the Creation was within the secret of Malchut/Kingship of the Ein Sof. Understand this!)[264]

12. EVIL FORCES ARE CREATIONS BUT HAVE NO IMPACT IF FOCUSED ON HIS UNITY

- This is the same concept that Chazal expounded on the verse "that *YHVH* is *Elokim*, there is nothing besides Him,"[265] R. Chanina says not even Witchcraft.[266]
  - The whole concept of acts of Witchcraft is derived from the powers of impurity of the impure Merkava
  - and this is the concept of the *Wisdom of Witchcraft* which the members of the Sanhedrin were required to know[267]
  - that is the wisdom of the impure names and knowledge of the concepts of the powers of the impure Merkava inherent in their names
  - which practitioners of Witchcraft would use in order to perform various activities
  - by invoking the powers of impurity through the element of good contained within them
  - which would provide the life force to perform wonders which contradict the natural order and the constellations.
  - Refer to [the Arizal's comments in] Etz Chaim.[268]

---

263 Where *One* by definition is absolute and there is no two, whereas *Kingship* by definition requires at least two as the people are a separate entity from the king, so the concept of kingship should not be associated with the first verse of the Shema, and here we see that there is an association.

264 As explained in detail in V2:02, the very beginning of the Creation process, referred to here as God's initial thought of Creation, was the very first Tzimtzum which occurred in the level of Malchut of the Ein Sof. This is the initial point of God's engagement with and connection to all of the worlds. R. Chaim has already explained that when we address God, we are only able to do so in relation to His connection to the worlds (e.g., G2:04). The highest point of God's connection to this world is the point at which the Tzimtzum process started within the level of Malchut of the Ein Sof. This point of connection

- וּלְפִי דְבָרָיו קָשֶׁה קְצָת לִישְׁנָא דְ"אַמְלִיכְתֵּיהּ" עַל תֵּבַת "אֶחָד".
- אָמְנָם גַּם הָא לֹא תַּבְרָה, כַּיָּדוּעַ לַיּוֹדְעִים בְּדִבְרֵי הָאֲרִ"י זִכְרוֹנוֹ לִבְרָכָה, שֶׁכָּל תְּחִלַּת רֵאשִׁית מַחֲשַׁבְתּוֹ יִתְבָּרַךְ בְּעִנְיַן הַבְּרִיאָה, הָיְתָה בְּסוֹד מַלְכוּת דְּאֵין סוֹף, וְהָבֵן):

שער ג' - פרק י"ב

- וְזֶהוּ הָעִנְיָן שֶׁדָּרְשׁוּ זִכְרוֹנָם לִבְרָכָה (חולין ז, ב) עַל פָּסוּק "כִּי ה' הוּא הָאֱלֹקִים אֵין עוֹד מִלְבַדּוֹ" (דברים ד, לה), אָמַר רַבִּי חֲנִינָא, אֲפִלּוּ כְּשָׁפִים.
- כִּי כָּל עִנְיְנֵי פְּעֻלּוֹת הַכְּשָׁפִים, נִמְשָׁךְ מֵהַכֹּחוֹת הַטֻּמְאָה שֶׁל הַמֶּרְכָּבָה טְמֵאָה
- וְהוּא עִנְיַן חָכְמַת הַכִּשּׁוּף שֶׁהָיוּ הַסַּנְהֶדְרִין צְרִיכִין לֵידַע
- הַיְנוּ, חָכְמַת שֵׁמוֹת הַטֻּמְאָה, וִידִיעַת עִנְיְנֵי כֹּחוֹת הַמֶּרְכָּבָה טְמֵאָה בִּשְׁמוֹתֵיהֶם
- שֶׁעַל יָדָם יִפְעֲלוּ בַּעֲלֵי הַכִּשּׁוּפִים פְּעֻלּוֹת וְעִנְיָנִים מְשֻׁנִּים
- כְּשֶׁמַּשְׁבִּיעִין כֹּחוֹת הַטֻּמְאָה בִּבְחִינַת הַטּוֹב שֶׁבּוֹ
- שֶׁיַּשְׁפִּיעַ בְּתוֹכוֹ חִיּוּת לַעֲשׂוֹת נִפְלָאוֹת, הֵפֶךְ סֵדֶר כֹּחוֹת הַטְּבָעִים וְהַמַּזָּלוֹת.
- וְעַיֵּן עֵץ חַיִּים שַׁעַר קְלִפַּת נֹגַהּ רֵישׁ פֶּרֶק ד'.

---

is therefore the ultimate and most sublime reference point about God that we can talk of in any way at all, and it is in relation to that point that the most subtle thoughts of God's Unity can be made. When R. Chiya bar Abba was focused on fulfilling the commandment of contemplating God's Unity through the recitation of the first line of the Shema, he therefore reflected on the initial point of God's connection to the worlds, i.e., the level of Malchut of the Ein Sof.

265 Devarim 4:35.
266 Chullin 7b and Sanhedrin 67b.
267 Sanhedrin 17a.
268 Etz Chaim Shaar 49, Shaar Kelipat Nogah, beginning of Chap. 4:
- Know that all of the three types of Witchcraft which contradict the Supernal assembly are there, for the good, which is within them, impacts on their external presentation, which is their bad, enabling them to perform wonders. Understand this. Therefore, the Sanhedrin were obligated to know the details of Witchcraft as mentioned in the Tikkunei Zohar. This is the secret of the Holy Name which was placed in the mouth of Nevuchadnezar's idol, the secret of *his kingship being over all rulers*. For when he invoked the connection of the good with the bad, [the bad] was brought to life, and therefore it would say: "I am the lord your god" through pure Witchcraft as mentioned in Tikkunei Zohar....

- For the Creator, Master of All, established the concept of the powers [of Evil] to be above the natural powers which derive from the stars and constellations
- and as a result they would be empowered to perform actions which would even be against the natural order of the stars and constellations which was established in them at the time of the Creation
- as is known, that God invested the ability for each power and world to control the power and world below it, "towards wherever there was the spirit to go. . . ."[269]

• That which Chazal say [that Witchcraft] "goes against the Heavenly assembly"[270] means that God's establishment of the powers of impurity is such that they are only enabled to overpower the arrangement of powers within the assembly of stars and constellations.
- However, [Witchcraft] has no power, God forbid, to change the arrangement of holy activity of the powers of the Holy Merkava
- and, on the contrary, when invoking those names of the powers of holiness, they inevitably immediately and completely dispel the effect of the [Witchcraft].
- As per the Zohar:[271] Those knowledgeable in the Kelipot [i.e., the bad presentation which contains an internal kernel of good], invoke the Names of God over those Kelipot and thereby nullify the decree [invoked by those Kelipot]. Refer to the Arizal in the chapter mentioned above.[272]
- Since they have no inherent power of their own, God forbid, for there is nothing else besides God, the *All Powerful One*
- and also, in truth, All is only filled with the Essence of God's Absolute Unity
- and there is nothing else besides Him that has any existence or power at all
- there are no powers of impurity and there are no powers of any world or creation at all
- this is the meaning of [Chazal's statement] that "there is nothing besides Him" – not even Witchraft.[273]

---

269 Yechezkel 1:12, i.e., following the natural order.
270 In the continuation of the passage quoted from Chullin 7b and Sanhedrin 67b and quoted below.
271 Tikkunei Zohar Tikkun 69 109a.

- מֵחֲמַת שֶׁכֵּן קָבַע הַבּוֹרֵא, אֲדוֹן כֹּל יִתְבָּרֵךְ, עִנְיְנֵי כֹּחוֹתֵיהֶם לְמַעְלָה לְמַעְלָה מִכֹּחוֹת הַטְּבָעִים הַנִּמְשָׁכִים מֵהַכּוֹכָבִים וְהַמַּזָּלוֹת.
- שֶׁעַל יְדֵי זֶה יְהֵא בְּכֹחָם לַעֲשׂוֹת פְּעֻלּוֹת, גַּם הֵפֶךְ טִבְעֵי כֹּחוֹת הַכּוֹכָבִים וּמַזָּלוֹת שֶׁהִקְבַּע בָּהֶם בְּעֵת הַבְּרִיאָה.
- כַּיָּדוּעַ שֶׁכָּל כֹּחַ וְעוֹלָם, קָבַע בּוֹ הַבּוֹרֵא יִתְבָּרַךְ כֹּחַ וִיכֹלֶת, לְהַנְהִיג וּלְהַטּוֹת אֶת הַכֹּחַ וְהָעוֹלָם שֶׁתַּחְתָּיו, לְכָל אֲשֶׁר יִהְיֶה שָׁמָּה הָרוּחַ וְכוּ':
- וּמַה שֶּׁאָמְרוּ שָׁם "שֶׁמַּכְחִישִׁין פָּמַלְיָא שֶׁל מַעְלָה" רָצָה לוֹמַר, שֶׁרַק סִדּוּר כֹּחוֹת הַפָּמַלְיָא שֶׁל "הַכּוֹכָבִים וְהַמַּזָּלוֹת" קָבַע הַבּוֹרֵא יִתְבָּרַךְ כֹּחַ בְּכֹחוֹת הַטֻּמְאָה שֶׁיְּהוּ יְכוֹלִין לְהַפְּכָם.
- אֲבָל לֹא שֶׁיְּהֵא בְּכֹחָם לְשַׁנּוֹת חַס וְשָׁלוֹם מִסֵּדֶר הַפְּעֻלּוֹת הַקְּדוֹשִׁים שֶׁל כֹּחוֹת "הַמֶּרְכָּבָה קְדוֹשָׁה".
- וְאַדְּרַבָּה, כְּשֶׁמַּשְׁבִּיעִין אוֹתָם בְּשֵׁמוֹת שֶׁל כֹּחוֹת הַקְּדֻשָּׁה, מִמֵּילָא כְּרֶגַע מִתְבַּטֵּל כָּל עִנְיְנֵי פְּעֻלָּתָם לְגַמְרֵי.
- וּכְמוֹ שֶׁכָּתוּב בְּתִקּוּן ס"ט, אִלֵּין דְּיָדְעִין בְּקִלְפִין, עָבְדִין אוּמָאָה בִּשְׁמָהָן וּבַהֲוָיוֹת דְּקוּדְשָׁא בְּרִיךְ הוּא לְאִלֵּין קִלְפִין, וּבָטְלִין גְּזֵרָה. וְעֵץ חַיִּים בַּפֶּרֶק הַנַּ"ל עַיֵּי"שׁ
- כֵּיוָן שֶׁאֵין הַכֹּחַ שֶׁלָּהֶם מֵעַצְמָם חַס וְשָׁלוֹם, כִּי אֵין עוֹד מִלְּבַדּוֹ יִתְבָּרֵךְ בַּעַל הַכֹּחוֹת כֻּלָּם.
- וְגַם שֶׁבֶּאֱמֶת הֲלֹא הַכֹּל מָלֵא רַק עַצְמוּת אַחְדוּתוֹ הַפָּשׁוּט יִתְבָּרֵךְ
- וְאֵין עוֹד מִלְּבַדּוֹ שׁוּם מְצִיאוּת כֹּחַ כְּלָל
- לֹא כֹּחוֹת הַטֻּמְאָה, וְלֹא שׁוּם כֹּחַ וְשׁוּם עוֹלָם וְנִבְרָא כְּלָל
- זֶהוּ שֶׁאָמְרוּ "אֵין עוֹד מִלְּבַדּוֹ", אֲפִלּוּ כְּשָׁפִים:

---

272 I.e., Etz Chaim Shaar 49, Shaar Kelipat Nogah, beginning of Chap. 4, as per p. 559, fn. 268.

273 See the reference to Likutei Torah brought down in G2:09 in relation to the Generation of the Dispersal.

- This is the meaning of what Chazal bring there: There was a woman who sought to take dust [secretly] from beneath R. Chanina's feet [with the intention of killing him through Witchcraft]. He said to her: Take out the dust as your procedure will not succeed, as per the verse "there is nothing besides Him." But R. Yochanan said: Why are the [powers of impurity] referred to as Witchcraft, as they contradict the Supernal assembly?[274] However, R. Chanina was different for he had a great degree of merit.[275]
  - R. Chanina certainly did not consider himself to have such merit from his Torah study and plentiful good deeds to the extent that he could rely on them that the acts of Witchcraft would not affect him
  - but the concept is as I wrote above, that since, in truth, the powers of impurity have no inherent powers of their own, God forbid, but that God established their powers to be above the powers of the natural order of stars and constellations, thereby enabling them to even be physically effective in changing the arrangement of the natural order of the constellations
  - however, without God they would be nothing and void.
  - Therefore, even though R. Chanina was not confident in the merit of his holy Torah study and many good deeds, he, however, knew and was able to assess that this faith was truly fixed in his heart, that there is no power and nothing else apart from God at all
  - and he cleaved himself, through the holiness of his thought, to the All Powerful One, to the Unified Master who fills all the worlds, and that there is no ability on the part of any other power to exert control or existence
  - therefore, 'he was certain in his heart'[276] with this that acts of Witchcraft which derive their power from the impure Merkava could not exert any control over him
  - this is encapsulated in what he said: Your procedure will not work, as per the verse "there is nothing else besides him."
- In truth, it is a propitious and wonderful concept
  - to remove and nullify from oneself all [harsh] judgments and intentions of others
  - to render them powerless over oneself and unable to have any impact at all
  - that when a person
    - fixes it in his heart saying
      - surely *YHVH* is the true *Elokim*

- וְזֶהוּ שֶׁמֵּבִיא שָׁם הַשַּׁ"ס עַל זֶה, עוּבְדָא דְּהַהִיא אִתְּתָא, דַּהֲוַת קָא מְהַדְּרָא לְמִשְׁקַל עַפְרָא מִתּוּתָא כַּרְעֵיהּ דְּרַבִּי חֲנִינָא, אָמַר לָהּ, שְׁקוֹלִי, לָא מִסְתַּיְּעָא מִילְתִיךְ, "אֵין עוֹד מִלְבַדּוֹ" כְּתִיב, וּפָרֵיךְ, וְהָאָמַר רַבִּי יוֹחָנָן, לָמָה נִקְרָא שְׁמָן "כְּשָׁפִים", שֶׁמַּכְחִישִׁין פָּמַלְיָא שֶׁל מַעְלָה, שָׁאנֵי רַבִּי חֲנִינָא דְּנָפִישׁ זְכוּתֵיהּ.

- וַדַּאי שֶׁלֹּא הָיָה מַחֲזִיק עַצְמוֹ רַבִּי חֲנִינָא דְּנָפִישׁ זְכוּתֵיהּ כָּל כָּךְ מִתּוֹרָתוֹ וּמַעֲשָׂיו הַטּוֹבִים הַמְרֻבִּים, עַד שֶׁבַּעֲבוּרָם הָיָה סָמוּךְ לִבּוֹ שֶׁלֹּא יִשְׁלֹט בּוֹ פְּעֻלַּת הַכְּשָׁפִים.

- אֲבָל הָעִנְיָן כְּמוֹ שֶׁכָּתַבְתִּי לְעֵיל, כֵּיוָן שֶׁבֶּאֱמֶת אֵין בְּכֹחוֹת הַמֶּרְכָּבָה טְמֵאָה שׁוּם כֹּחַ מֵעַצְמָם חָלִילָה, אֶלָּא שֶׁהוּא יִתְבָּרַךְ קָבַע כֹּחָם לְמַעְלָה מִכֹּחוֹת טִבְעֵי הַכּוֹכָבִים וּמַזָּלוֹת, כְּדֵי שֶׁעַל יְדֵי זֶה יְהֵא בִּיכָלְתָּם לַעֲשׂוֹת פְּעֻלּוֹת, אַף גַּם לְשַׁנּוֹת סִדְרֵי טִבְעֵי הַמַּזָּלוֹת

- וּבִלְתּוֹ יִתְבָּרַךְ הֵם אֶפֶס וָתֹהוּ.

- וְלָכֵן גַּם רַבִּי חֲנִינָא, לֹא שֶׁבָּטַח עַל זְכוּת קְדֻשַּׁת תּוֹרָתוֹ וּמַעֲשָׂיו הַמְרֻבִּים, רַק שֶׁיָּדַע וְשִׁעֵר בְּנַפְשׁוֹ, שֶׁזֹּאת הָאֱמוּנָה קְבוּעָה בְּלִבּוֹ לַאֲמִתָּהּ, שֶׁאֵין עוֹד מִלְבַדּוֹ יִתְבָּרַךְ שׁוּם כֹּחַ כְּלָל

- וְהִדְבִּיק עַצְמוֹ בִּקְדֻשַּׁת מַחֲשַׁבְתּוֹ לְבַעַל הַכֹּחוֹת כֻּלָּם, אָדוֹן יָחִיד הַמָּלֵא כָּל עָלְמִין, וְאֵין כָּאן שׁוּם שְׁלִיטָה וּמְצִיאוּת כֹּחַ אַחֵר כְּלָל

- לָכֵן הָיָה נָכוֹן לִבּוֹ בָּטוּחַ בָּזֶה, שֶׁלֹּא יִשְׁלְטוּ עָלָיו פְּעֻלּוֹת הַכְּשָׁפִים הַנִּמְשָׁכִים מִכֹּחוֹת הַמֶּרְכָּבָה טְמֵאָה

- זֶה שֶׁאָמַר, לֹא מִסְתַּיְּעָא מִילְתִיךְ, "אֵין עוֹד מִלְבַדּוֹ" כְּתִיב:

- וּבֶאֱמֶת הוּא עִנְיָן גָּדוֹל וּסְגֻלָּה נִפְלָאָה
  - לְהָסֵר וּלְבַטֵּל מֵעָלָיו כָּל דִּינִין וּרְצוֹנוֹת אֲחֵרִים
  - שֶׁלֹּא יוּכְלוּ לִשְׁלֹט בּוֹ וְלֹא יַעֲשׂוּ שׁוּם רֹשֶׁם כְּלָל
  - כְּשֶׁהָאָדָם
    - קוֹבֵעַ בְּלִבּוֹ לֵאמֹר
      - הֲלֹא ה' הוּא הָאֱלֹקִים הָאֲמִתִּי

---

274 This is a play on the similarity between the Hebrew words "*Keshafim*/witchcraft" and "*Machechishim*/contradict." The question therefore asserts that Witchcraft is seemingly empowered as explained above.

275 Chullin 7b and Sanhedrin 67b.

276 Tehillim 112:7.

- - - and there is nothing else and there are no powers besides Him in this world or all the worlds at all
    - and everything is exclusively filled with His Absolute Unity
  - and completely nullifies [himself to God] in his heart
  - [such that] he is not concerned at all about [the potential malevolent impact] of any power or intention in this world
  - and he subjugates himself and cleaves the purity of his thought to be focused exclusively on the Unified Master
  - then God will enable it that
    - all of the [malevolent] powers and intentions in the world will inevitably become nullified from being upon him
    - such that they will be rendered incapable of impacting him in any way whatsoever. (Note 46)[277]
- This concept is also reflected in the Zohar,[278] understand it: The Fourth Commandment is to know that *YHVH* is *Elokim*, as per "and you shall know this day . . . that *YHVH* is *Elokim*" and that the name *Elokim* is incorporated within the name *YHVH* . . . when a person knows that all is One and that there is no separation,[279] then even the *Sitra Achara*[280] will be removed from the world.[281]
- In addition, 'one will make decrees and they will be established'[282]
  - such that one will be able to perform miraculous wonders which are against the natural order
  - that once one subjugates and truly cleaves the purity and faith of one's heart to be unwaveringly focused on God alone
  - and that with Him all [possibilities] are equal – [that] each moment – He can act either according to or contrary to the natural order.
  - As we find with R. Chanina ben Dosa who decreed, and actions were as per his will at all times, [even] against the natural order of things as in "He who said that oil should burn should also say that vinegar should burn,"[283] meaning that relative to God, all [possibilities] are equal, as mentioned above, and accordingly God granted this to him

---

277 **R. Chaim adds Note 46 here.** This note is brought at the end of this chapter and is entitled "Focus on God irrespective of difficulties sweetens harsh decrees."

278 Zohar Introduction 12a.

279 See more background on the concept of differentiation/separation in V2:01, "The Limit of Understanding – The Deeper Meaning of Makom."

280 "Sitra Achara" literally means "the other side" and refers to the domain of evil. Evil is the domain of that which is perceived to not be God even though in reality all is God. When in this world, if we can perceive any part of our

- וְאֵין עוֹד מִלְּבַדּוֹ יִתְבָּרֵךְ שׁוּם כֹּחַ בָּעוֹלָם וְכָל הָעוֹלָמוֹת כְּלָל
- וְהַכֹּל מָלֵא רַק אַחְדוּתוֹ הַפָּשׁוּט יִתְבָּרֵךְ שְׁמוֹ
  □ וּמְבַטֵּל בְּלִבּוֹ בִּטּוּל גָּמוּר
  □ וְאֵינוֹ מַשְׁגִּיחַ כְּלָל עַל שׁוּם כֹּחַ וְרָצוֹן בָּעוֹלָם
  □ וּמְשַׁעְבֵּד וּמְדַבֵּק טֹהַר מַחְשַׁבְתּוֹ רַק לְאָדוֹן יָחִיד בָּרוּךְ הוּא
- כֵּן יַסְפִּיק הוּא יִתְבָּרֵךְ בְּיָדוֹ
  □ שֶׁמִּמֵּילָא יִתְבַּטְּלוּ מֵעָלָיו כָּל הַכֹּחוֹת וְהָרְצוֹנוֹת שֶׁבָּעוֹלָם
  □ שֶׁלֹּא יוּכְלוּ לִפְעוֹל לוֹ שׁוּם דָּבָר כְּלָל: (הגהה מ״ו)

• וְזֶה הָעִנְיָן הוּא גַּם כֵּן בִּכְלַל כַּוָּנַת הַזֹּהַר (בהקדמה דף י״ב סוף ע״א), פְּקוּדָא רְבִיעָאָה, לְמִנְדַּע דַּהֲוָיָ״ה הוּא הָאֱלֹקִים, כד״א "וְיָדַעְתָּ הַיּוֹם וְגוֹ׳ כִּי הֲוָיָ״ה הוּא הָאֱלֹקִים", וּלְאִתְכְּלָלָא שְׁמָא דֶּאֱלֹקִים בִּשְׁמָא דַּהֲוָיָ״ה. וְכַד יָנְדַע בַּר נַשׁ דְּכֹלָּא חַד, וְלָא יְשַׁוֵּי פֵּרוּדָא, אֲפִילוּ הַהוּא ס״א יִסְתַּלֵּק מֵעַל עָלְמָא כו׳, וְהָבֵן:

• וְגַם יִגְזוֹר אֹמֶר וְיָקָם לוֹ
  ○ לִפְעוֹל עִנְיָנִים וְנִסִּים נִפְלָאִים הֶפּוּךְ סִדּוּר כֹּחוֹת הַטִּבְעִיִּים
  ○ כֵּיוָן שֶׁמְּשַׁעְבֵּד וּמְדַבֵּק טֹהַר אֱמוּנַת לְבָבוֹ בֶּאֱמֶת בַּל תִּמּוֹט רַק לוֹ יִתְבָּרֵךְ לְבַד
  ○ וְאֶצְלוֹ יִתְבָּרֵךְ הַכֹּל שָׁוֶה, כָּל רֶגַע, לִפְעוֹל בְּסִדּוּר הַטֶּבַע שֶׁקָּבַע אוֹ הֶפּוּךְ סִדּוּר הַטֶּבַע.
  ○ כְּמוֹ שֶׁשָּׁמַעְנוּ בְּרַבִּי חֲנִינָא בֶּן דּוֹסָא, שֶׁהָיָה גּוֹזֵר אֹמֶר, וּפוֹעֵל כְּפִי רְצוֹנוֹ כָּל עֵת, הֶפּוּךְ סִדּוּר הַטֶּבַע, כְּאָמְרוֹ (תענית כה, א) "מִי שֶׁאָמַר לַשֶּׁמֶן וְיִדְלַק יֹאמַר לַחֹמֶץ וְיִדְלַק", רוֹצֶה לוֹמַר, הֲלֹא אֶצְלוֹ יִתְבָּרֵךְ שָׁוֶה זֶה כְּמוֹ זֶה, כַּנַּ״ל, וְכֵן הִסְפִּיק הַבּוֹרֵא בָּרוּךְ הוּא בְּיָדוֹ.

---

existence as being something other than God, then we are dwelling in the domain of the Sitra Achara. In contrast, our mindful engagement on the fact that All is God rids this world of the Sitra Achara and anything that acts as a barrier to *separate* from God.

281 It should be noted that, as per the Sefer HaChinuch (end of Iggeret HaMechaber at the beginning of the book), which is also quoted by the Biur Halacha (Orach Chaim 1:1), one of the six Mitzvot that a Jew is continuously obliged to perform is that of the intellectual focus on the Unity of God. An inevitable by-product of performing this Mitzvah is the protection from Evil forces as described here.

282 Iyov 22:28.

283 Taanit 25a.

- and there are many other wondrous examples brought down in the Talmud.

Rabbi Chaim's Note:
Note 46 – Focus on God irrespective of difficulties sweetens harsh decrees

- This is the concept of Chazal's statement in the Mishna:[284]
  - "Make for yourself a serpent . . . ." Now does a serpent have the power to kill or give life? [No, this means] that when Israel look Heavenward and subjugate their hearts to their Father in Heaven [that they will live].
- This means that when they looked Heavenwards to the copper serpent, and they understood its Evil power, and notwithstanding this, still nullified and ignored its awesome power in their hearts, and that they exclusively truly subjugated their hearts to focus on their Father in Heaven alone, then they would be healed.
- This is the truth of the concept of the *sweetening* of the [harsh] decrees, in their source, and is understood to one who understands.[285]

13. PATRIARCHS FULLY FOCUSED BUT STILL SAW PHYSICALITY UNLIKE MOSHE

- This[286] was the level on which the Patriarchs served God throughout their lives
  - for they would, out of their awesome piety and the purity of the holiness of their hearts, constantly focus their thoughts on fulfilling His Will all of their lives, without even a momentary lapse
  - and they used their will to nullify all the powers in the world such that they were considered null and void relative to them
  - and therefore they also merited wondrous miracles in their military campaigns, as mentioned above
  - and therefore God Unified His Name with them to be called the "God of Avraham," the "God of Yitzchak" [and the "God of Yaakov"], as He Says of Himself ". . . The God of your Patriarchs . . ."[287]
  - therefore Chazal state: "The Patriarchs are the *Merkava*""[288]
- However, Moshe was on an even higher level as the Torah testifies "and there has been no other prophet [in Israel like Moshe]."[289]
  - The essential difference between his level and the [Patriarchs'] level

---

284 Rosh Hashana 29a quoting Bamidbar 21:8. Also see G2:11:N30.
285 I.e., one who is familiar with Kabbalistic concepts. The concept of "sweetening"

○ וְכָהֲנָה רַבּוֹת אִתּוֹ, כַּמּוּבָא בַּשַּׁ"ס מֻפְלָאוֹת עִנְיָנָיו:

הגהה מ"ו

● וְזֶהוּ עִנְיַן מַאֲמָרָם זִכְרוֹנָם לִבְרָכָה בַּמִּשְׁנָה ר"ה (כ"ט א')
○ "עֲשֵׂה לְךָ שָׂרָף" (במדבר כא) וְכוּ', וְכִי נָחָשׁ מֵמִית אוֹ נָחָשׁ מְחַיֶּה, אֶלָּא בִּזְמַן שֶׁיִּשְׂרָאֵל מִסְתַּכְּלִין כְּלַפֵּי מַעְלָה וּמְשַׁעְבְּדִין אֶת לִבָּם לַאֲבִיהֶם שֶׁבַּשָּׁמַיִם וְכוּ':
● רָצָה לוֹמַר כְּשֶׁהִסְתַּכְּלוּ כְּלַפֵּי מַעְלָה לְהַנָּחָשׁ הַשָּׂרָף, וְהִתְבּוֹנְנוּ בְּכֹחוֹ הָרַע, וְעִם כָּל זֶה בִּטְּלוּהוּ מִלִּבָּם וְלֹא הִשְׁגִּיחוּ עַל כֹּחוֹ הַנּוֹרָא, וְשִׁעְבְּדוּ אֶת לִבָּם בֶּאֱמֶת רַק לַאֲבִיהֶם שֶׁבַּשָּׁמַיִם לְבַד, הָיוּ מִתְרַפְּאִין:
● וְהוּא אֲמִתַּת עִנְיָן הַמְתָּקַת כֹּחוֹת הַדִּינִים בְּשָׁרְשָׁם, וְהוּא מְבֹאָר לַמֵּבִין:

שער ג' - פרק י"ג

● וְזֶה הָיָה עִנְיַן עֲבוֹדַת הָאָבוֹת כָּל יְמֵיהֶם.
○ כִּי הֵמָּה בְּנוֹרָאוֹת צִדְקָתָם וְטָהֳרַת קְדֻשַּׁת לִבָּם, הָיוּ מְדֻבָּקִים מַחְשַׁבְתָּם לִרְצוֹנוֹ יִתְבָּרַךְ, כָּל יְמֵיהֶם בְּלִי הֶפְסֵק רֶגַע
○ וּבִטְּלוּ בִּרְצוֹנָם כָּל הַכֹּחוֹת שֶׁבָּעוֹלָם, וּלְאֶפֶס וָתֹהוּ נֶחְשְׁבוּ אֶצְלָם.
○ וְלָכֵן זָכוּ גַּם לְנִסִּים נִפְלָאִים בְּשִׁדּוּד הַמַּעֲרָכוֹת וְצִבְאֵיהֶם כַּנַּ"ל.
○ וְלָכֵן נִתְיַחֵד שְׁמוֹ יִתְבָּרַךְ עֲלֵיהֶם לְהִקָּרֵא "אֱלֹהֵי אַבְרָהָם", "אֱלֹהֵי יִצְחָק" וְכוּ', וּכְאָמְרוֹ יִתְבָּרַךְ בְּעַצְמוֹ (שמות ג, ג) "אֱלֹהֵי אֲבוֹתֵיכֶם"
● וְלָזֶה אָמְרוּ זִכְרוֹנָם לִבְרָכָה (ב"ר מז) "הָאָבוֹת הֵן הֵן הַמֶּרְכָּבָה":
● אָמְנָם מַדְרֵגַת מֹשֶׁה רַבֵּנוּ עָלָיו הַשָּׁלוֹם הָיְתָה עוֹד יוֹתֵר גְּבוֹהַּ, כְּמוֹ שֶׁהֵעִידָה הַתּוֹרָה (דברים לה, י) "וְלֹא קָם נָבִיא" וְגוֹ'.
○ וְעֶצֶם חִלּוּק מַדְרֵגָתוֹ מִמַּדְרֵגָתָם בֵּאֵר הוּא יִתְבָּרַךְ בְּעַצְמוֹ, וְאָמַר "אֲנִי

is explained by God Himself who says [to Moshe]: "I am *YHVH* and I appeared to Avraham . . . with *El Shadai* but I did not make my name *YHVH* known to them."[290]

- This concept is exactly the same as the difference that has been explained above between the name *Elokim* and *YHVH*.
  - In general, we find the use of the name *Elokim* in relation to the perception of the Patriarchs, e.g.:
    - "The *Elokim* before Whom my Fathers walked."[291]
    - "The *Elokim* who shepherded me forever until this day."[292]
  - Similarly, we call God: *Elokei* Avraham, etc.
  - It is as I wrote above in relation to the holiness of their level, that they did not pay attention to any power or concept in this world at all
  - but their perception of prophecy was not to the extent that [worldly] powers were nullified in such a way that they completely did not appear to exist
  - this is what the verse means "and I appeared to Avraham . . . with *El Shadai*"
    - where the concept of [*El Shadai*] is also like the concept of *Elokim*
    - meaning that I am the *All Powerful One*
    - and it is My Will that each moment I rearrange the framework of all the powers which I established at the time of the creation
    - this is the meaning of *El Shadai*.[293]
  - However, in relation to the concept of "my name *YHVH*"
    - (whose concept is explained above in G3:11)
    - "I did not make known to them" [on the level] of their perception in prophecy.
- However, Moshe's perception of prophecy was on the level of the Name of God's Unified Essence – *YHVH*.
  - Therefore, no [worldly] power could act as a barrier to filter out the light of his prophetic perception.
  - Therefore, everyone could see how the [worldly] powers were completely nullified by all of God's Miracles which were performed through [Moshe], and that there is literally absolutely nothing else apart from Him, as per "You have been shown in order to know that *YHVH* is *Elokim* [there is nothing else besides Him]"[294]

---

290 Shemot 6:2-3.
291 Bereishit 48:15.
292 Bereishit 48:15, continuation.
293 As previously explained the name *Elokim* is associated with God's Gevurah, i.e., self-restraint. This concept is also seen in the name *Shadai* as per Midrash

הֲוָי"ה וָאֵרָא אֶל אַבְרָהָם וכו' בְּאֵל שַׁדַּי וּשְׁמִי הֲוָי"ה לֹא נוֹדַעְתִּי לָהֶם".
(שמות ו, ב—ג):

- וְהָעִנְיָן, הוּא הוּא עֶצֶם הַחִלּוּק שֶׁנִּתְבָּאֵר לְמַעְלָה בֵּין הַשֵּׁם "אֱלֹהִים" לְשֵׁם "הֲוָי"ה" בָּרוּךְ הוּא.
  - כִּי עַל הָרֹב, בְּעִנְיָן הַשָּׂגַת הָאָבוֹת, מָצִינוּ נֶאֱמַר הַשֵּׁם "אֱלֹקִים",
    - "הָאֱלֹקִים אֲשֶׁר הִתְהַלְּכוּ אֲבוֹתַי לְפָנָיו" (בראשית מח, טו)
    - "הָאֱלֹקִים הָרוֹעֶה אוֹתִי מֵעוֹדִי" (שם)
  - וְכֵן אֲנַחְנוּ קוֹרְאִים אוֹתוֹ יִתְבָּרַךְ "אֱלֹהֵי אַבְרָהָם" וכו'.
  - כְּמוֹ שֶׁכָּתַבְתִּי לְעֵיל בְּעִנְיַן קְדֻשַּׁת מַדְרֵגָתָם, שֶׁלֹּא הִשְׁגִּיחוּ עַל שׁוּם כֹּחַ וְעִנְיָן בָּעוֹלָם כְּלָל.
  - אָמְנָם, הַשָּׂגַת נְבוּאָתָם לֹא הָיְתָה בְּבִטּוּל הַכֹּחוֹת מִמְּצִיאוּתָם לְגַמְרֵי
  - וְזֶהוּ שֶׁאָמַר הַכָּתוּב "וָאֵרָא אֶל אַבְרָהָם וכו', בְּאֵל שַׁדַּי"
    - שֶׁעִנְיָנוּ גַּם כֵּן כְּעִנְיַן הַשֵּׁם אֱלֹהִים
    - וְרוֹצֶה לוֹמַר שֶׁאֲנִי בַּעַל הַכֹּחוֹת כֻּלָּם
    - וּבִרְצוֹתִי, כָּל רֶגַע, אֲנִי מְשַׁדֵּד מַעֲרֶכֶת כָּל הַכֹּחוֹת מֵאֲשֶׁר קָבַעְתִּי בָּהֶם בְּעֵת הַבְּרִיאָה
    - זֶהוּ "אֵל שַׁדַּי".
  - אֲבָל בִּבְחִינַת עִנְיָן "שְׁמִי הֲוָי"ה"
    - (כְּמוֹ שֶׁנִּתְבָּאֵר פֵּרוּשׁ עִנְיָנוּ לְעֵיל פֶּרֶק י"א)
    - "לֹא נוֹדַעְתִּי לָהֶם" בְּהַשָּׂגַת נְבוּאָתָם:
- אֲבָל מֹשֶׁה רַבֵּנוּ עָלָיו הַשָּׁלוֹם, הָיְתָה הַשָּׂגַת נְבוּאָתוֹ, בְּעִנְיָן בְּחִינַת הַשֵּׁם הָעֶצֶם הַמְיֻחָד, הֲוָי"ה בָּרוּךְ הוּא
  - וְלָכֵן לֹא הָיָה שׁוּם כֹּחַ חוֹצֵץ בִּפְנֵי אוֹר הַשָּׂגַת נְבוּאָתוֹ.
  - וְכֵן עַל יְדֵי כָּל נִסֵּי ה' שֶׁנַּעֲשׂוּ עַל יָדוֹ, רָאוּ כֻלָּם בִּטּוּל מְצִיאוּת כָּל הַכֹּחוֹת

Tanchuma Lech Lecha 19 which states "I am El Sha*dai*" means "I am the One Who told the world – *Dai*/Enough!", i.e., that the Creation process is one which goes up to this point and no further, therefore the name *Shadai* is also one of self-restraint and as R. Chaim states is the same concept as *Elokim*.

294 Devarim 4:35.

- ○ this is the concept and explanation of the Unified Name, *YHVH*, as mentioned above.
- This is the meaning of the verse "and *Elokim* Spoke to Moshe and He Said to him – I am *YHVH*"[295]
  - ○ it informs us of [Moshe's] level of prophetic perception
  - ○ that even the name *Elokim* relative to him was on same level of *YHVH*, as per "*YHVH* is *Elokim* – there is nothing else besides Him"
  - ○ and from that point onwards [all subsequent communication between God and Moshe is only recorded by the Torah in terms of *YHVH* alone, i.e.,] "and *YHVH* Spoke" or "and *YHVH* Said."
  - ○ This is the meaning of the verse "and no further prophet [in Israel will rise, like Moshe,] with a face to face knowledge of *YHVH*"[296]
  - ○ and as per the Zohar:[297] [with Moshe it says "remove your shoes from your feet" . . . as he did not need any barrier to see the Shechina] . . . but the Patriarchs were only able to see with [this filter] of shoes . . . but with respect to Moshe, he did not need a covering [/filter] at all . . . this is the secret of "I appeared to Avraham, [to Yitzchak and to Yaakov with *El Shadai* but I did not make my name *YHVH* known to them"].
- This is the concept that Chazal also express:[298] That which is said about Moshe and Aharon is greater than that said about Avraham, as with Avraham it says, "and I am but *dust and ashes*,"[299] but with Moshe and Aharon it says "and we are *Mah*"[300]
  - ○ For *dust and ashes* [although lowly] at least appear to exist as dust (Note 47)[301]
  - ○ However, Moshe said "and we are *Mah/What!*" as if there is no [separate] existence in the world at all
  - ○ (now even though Aharon was included in this statement to be on this level, as indicated by Chazal's statement relating to Moshe *and Aharon*, this was because Israel's complaints were against both of them and therefore [Moshe] answered them in plural, nevertheless, the essence of this awesome level related to [Moshe] alone.)
- This is as per the Midrash, which is explained to one who understands:[302] Yitzchak said to Moshe "I am greater than you as I stretched out my neck [on the Altar] and saw the face of the Shechina." Moshe said to him: "I am greater than you as when you saw the face of the Shechina your vision was dimmed . . . but I would speak face to face with the Shechina and my vision was not dimmed."

---

295 Shemot 3:2.
296 Devarim 34:10.

לְגַמְרֵי, וְאֵין עוֹד מִלְבַדּוֹ יִתְבָּרֵךְ לְגַמְרֵי כְּמַשְׁמָעוֹ, כְּמוֹ שֶׁאָמַר הַכָּתוּב "אַתָּה הָרְאֵתָ לָדַעַת כִּי הֲוָיָ"ה הוּא הָאֱלֹקִים" וכו'

◦ וְהוּא עִנְיָן וּפֵרוּשׁ הַשֵּׁם הַמְיֻחָד הֲוָיָ"ה בָּרוּךְ הוּא כַּנַ"ל:

• זֶהוּ שֶׁכָּתוּב "וַיְדַבֵּר אֱלֹקִים אֶל מֹשֶׁה וַיֹּאמֶר אֵלָיו אֲנִי הֲוָיָ"ה

◦ הוֹדִיעוֹ עֶצֶם בְּחִינַת הַשָּׂגַת נְבוּאָתוֹ

◦ שֶׁגַּם הַשֵּׁם "אֱלֹקִים" אֶצְלוֹ הַכֹּל בְּחִינַת "הֲוָיָ"ה" כְּעִנְיַן הַכָּתוּב "כִּי הֲוָיָ"ה הוּא הָאֱלֹהִים אֵין עוֹד מִלְבַדּוֹ"

◦ וּמֵאָז וָאֵילָךְ לֹא נִזְכַּר אֶצְלוֹ אֶלָּא "וַיְדַבֵּר ה'" "וַיֹּאמֶר ה'".

◦ וְזֶהוּ (דברים לה, י) "וְלֹא קָם נָבִיא וכו' אֲשֶׁר יְדָעוֹ הֲוָיָ"ה פָּנִים אֶל פָּנִים".

◦ וְזֶה שֶׁכָּתוּב בְּתִקּוּן כ"ו, וּלְגַבֵּי אֲבָהָן לָא אִתְחֲזִיָּא אֶלָּא בִּמְנָעָלִים כוּ', אֲבָל לְגַבֵּי מֹשֶׁה בְּלָא כִּסּוּיָא כְּלָל, וְרָזָא דְמִלָּה "וָאֵרָא אֶל אַבְרָהָם" וכו', עַכַ"ל:

• וְהוּא גַּם כֵּן עִנְיָן מַאֲמָרָם זִכְרוֹנָם לִבְרָכָה בְּסוֹף פֶּרֶק כִּסּוּי הַדָּם (חולין פט.), "גָּדוֹל שֶׁנֶּאֱמַר בְּמֹשֶׁה וְאַהֲרֹן יוֹתֵר מִמַּה שֶּׁנֶּאֱמַר בְּאַבְרָהָם, דְּאִלּוּ בְּאַבְרָהָם כְּתִיב (בראשית יח, כז) "וְאָנֹכִי עָפָר וָאֵפֶר", וְאִלּוּ בְּמֹשֶׁה וְאַהֲרֹן כְּתִיב (שמות טז, ז) "וְנַחְנוּ מָה".

◦ כִּי "עָפָר וָאֵפֶר" עַל כָּל פָּנִים מִתְרָאֶה עֲדַיִן לִמְצִיאוּת עָפָר, (הגהה מ"ז)

◦ אֲבָל מֹשֶׁה רַבֵּנוּ עָלָיו הַשָּׁלוֹם אָמַר "וְנַחְנוּ מָה", כְּאִלּוּ אֵין שׁוּם מְצִיאוּת בָּעוֹלָם כְּלָל לְגַמְרֵי

◦ (וְעִם כִּי גַּם אֶת אַהֲרֹן כָּלַל אִתּוֹ בְּזֹאת הַבְּחִינָה וּכְמַאֲמָרָם גָּדוֹל שֶׁנֶּאֱמַר בְּמֹשֶׁה וְאַהֲרֹן, לְפִי שֶׁתְּלוּנַת יִשְׂרָאֵל הָיְתָה עַל שְׁנֵיהֶם, הֱשִׁיבָם בִּלְשׁוֹן רַבִּים, אֲבָל הָעִקָּר בְּזֹאת הַמַּדְרֵגָה הַנּוֹרָאָה הָיָה הוּא לְבַד):

• וְזֶה שֶׁכָּתוּב בִּדְבָרִים רַבָּה פָּרָשָׁה י"א, "יִצְחָק אָמַר לְמֹשֶׁה אֲנִי גָּדוֹל מִמְּךָ

---

297 Tikkunei Zohar Tikkun 26 72a quoting Shemot 3:5, 6:3.
298 Chullin 89a.
299 Bereishit 18:27.
300 Shemot 16:7. See p. 264, fn. 477, in relation to Mi.
301 **R. Chaim adds Note 47 here.** This note is brought at the end of this chapter and is entitled "Dust and ashes like Red Heifer, and their difference is like skin and light."
302 Devarim Rabba VeZot HaBeracha 11:3.

- Refer to what is written in the Sefer HaGilgulim by R. Chaim Vital[303] in his explanation of Chazal's comment[304] [that when God called out to] "Avraham | Avraham," "Yaakov | Yaakov," and "Moshe Moshe,"[305] there is a separator between the two Avrahams and Yaakovs but not between the two Moshes[306] – that this reflects the subtle separation and barrier caused by their physical bodies [in contrast to Moshe where due to his level, his body did not even constitute a subtle separation].

Rabbi Chaim's Note:
Note 47 – Dust and ashes like Red Heifer, and their difference is like skin and light

- The concept of dust and ashes is consistent with the objective of the [service] of the Red Heifer[307] which incorporates the 280 strict judgments whose source is in [the letter] Aleph, which is the ultimate power [underpinning] all the letters.[308]

---

303 Sefer HaGilgulim, in the Likutim after Chap. 35 from within the paragraph beginning "Hinei Sod HaNevuah":
- [In this section a detailed explanation of the possible sources of the Heavenly sent voice of prophecy is given. This Heavenly voice needs to be manifest within the physical voice of the prophet when he is engaged in Torah study and prayer so that the prophet can relate to its message. There are a number of great differences between this Heavenly voice and the prophet's voice, e.g., this Heavenly voice can be channeled through other Tzaddikim, or it can be manifest in the different levels of the prophet's speech, i.e., the voice, spoken words, or breath] . . . Now Moshe was on a higher level than all the [other prophets] for the Heavenly voice that he received was his own [i.e., it was direct and not channeled through other Tzaddikim] and it was manifest in his current voice [i.e., the highest level of voice, speech, and breath] . . . (. . . now I understand that which is stated in the Zohar [I Vayera 120a–b] that [when the Torah writes] "Avraham | Avraham" and similarly, "Yaakov | Yaakov" it does so with a separator, as the former is not complete and the latter is complete, whereas with "Moshe Moshe" there is no separator as the former and the latter are complete. This concept, as it appears to me, is that when prophecy would come to a prophet, it would do so in a double voice to show that there are two [separate] voices, one of then [i.e., the Heavenly voice] and one of now [i.e., the prophet's voice], but with all of them there is a separator to show that the Heavenly voice is not his [i.e., was not received directly] but came from other Tzaddikim, for his own [receipt of Heavenly voice] was not appropriate for prophecy; this is what [the Zohar] means that *the former is not complete*, etc. However, with Moshe, there is no separator for they are all his [i.e., both of the voices] and there was no need for others

נפש שער ג' - פרק י"ג החיים 573

שֶׁפָּשַׁטְתִּי צַוָּארִי כו', וְרָאִיתִי אֶת פְּנֵי הַשְּׁכִינָה, אָמַר לוֹ מֹשֶׁה אֲנִי נִתְעַלֵּיתִי יוֹתֵר מִמְּךָ, שֶׁאַתָּה רָאִיתָ פְּנֵי הַשְּׁכִינָה וְכָהוּ עֵינֶיךָ כו', אֲבָל אֲנִי הָיִיתִי מְדַבֵּר עִם הַשְּׁכִינָה פָּנִים בְּפָנִים וְלֹא כָהוּ עֵינַי". וּמְבֹאָר לַמֵּבִין:

• וְעִיֵּן מַה שֶׁכָּתַב הרח"ו זִכְרוֹנוֹ לִבְרָכָה בְּסֵפֶר הַגִּלְגּוּלִים, בְּפֵרוּשׁ מַאֲמָרָם זִכְרוֹנָם לִבְרָכָה (שמו"ר ב) "אַבְרָהָם אַבְרָהָם, יַעֲקֹב יַעֲקֹב, פָּסִיק טַעֲמָא, וּמֹשֶׁה לֹא פָּסִיק טַעֲמָא", שֶׁהוּא עַל עִנְיַן הֶפְסֵק וַחֲצִיצָה מְעַטָּה מֵעִנְיַן הַגּוּף, עַיֵּן שָׁם:

הגהה מ"ז

• וְעִנְיַן "עָפָר וָאֵפֶר" הוּא כְּעִנְיַן כַּוָּנַת פָּרָה אֲדֻמָּה, שֶׁיִּכְלְלוּ הפ"ר דִּינִין בִּמְקוֹר שָׁרְשָׁם בָּאָלֶ"ף, שֶׁהוּא כֹּ"ח הַפָּשׁוּט שֶׁל כָּל הָאוֹתִיּוֹת:

---

as his Heavenly voice [that was received directly by him] was suitable for prophecy, and this is what [the Zohar] writes that the former and the latter are complete . . .)

304 Shemot Rabba Shemot 2:6.
305 By doubling their name when calling them out of an expression of love for them.
306 There is a vertical line written in the Torah separating the double names of "Avraham Avraham" and "Yaakov Yaakov."
307 The Red Heifer was burnt into *ashes* in order to be able to be used as a medium for cleansing ritual impurity.
308 Note that the Hebrew for "dust/APhaR," "ashes/AiPheR" and "heifer/PaRaH" all have the letters *Peh Resh* in common which have the numerical value of 280. See Malbim on Shemot Ramzey Chatzar HaMishkan VehaMizbeach where he explains the allegorical hints in the dimensions of the Mishkan and that the hanging curtains of the Mishkan (which represent the outer periphery of the worlds, i.e., the world of Action) spanned for a length of 280 cubits which together with the One Who Incorporates all of them, i.e., the source *Aleph*, forms the numerical value of 281 = ashes/AiPheR, to teach that man is just *dust and ashes*, and that the angel Sandalphon controls the world of Action and the numerical value of Sandalphon is 280 to correspond with the 280 strict judgments of the five final letters "MNTzPCh," *Mem, Nun, Tzaddi, Peh, Chaf* (which also have the numerical value of 280) which control the world of Action. Some light may be shed on these comments of the Malbim from details on p. 444, fn. 389, which explains that the *second Hey* of YHVH corresponds to Malchut/Kingship and that *the Hey* (numerical value of 5) relating to the 5 letters of "MNTzPCh" splits into an ultimate expression of God's Kingship which spans all of time with *Mem Nun* being numerically equal to Malach/He

- The concept underpinning the differentiation between dust (spelled *Ayin, Peh, Resh*) and ashes (spelled *Aleph, Peh, Resh*) is like the concept underpinning the difference between the *Cloaks of Skin* (spelled *Ayin, Vav, Resh*) and *Cloaks of Light* (spelled *Aleph, Vav, Resh*).[309]

14. MOSHE'S LEVEL UNATTAINABLE BUT TRY TO ASPIRE TO IT DURING PRAYER

- Therefore, Moshe was always available for prophecy at any time
  - as per "[and Moshe said to them] Wait, and I will hear [what God commands you]"[310]

Ruled (past tense); *Tzaddi* being numerically equal to Melech/He Rules (present tense) and *Peh Chaf* being numerically equal to Yimloch/He Will Rule (future tense). The *second Hey* of YHVH also relates to this world of Action where we see God as a separate entity to ourselves, i.e., as a King who is separate from his people so the number 280 is a numerical allegory to the ultimate expression of God's Kingship over this world where as a result of God's Gevurah/Self Restraint/Strict Judgments this world appears to be an entity in its own right. The letters *Peh Resh* form a key part of words for separation, e.g., LiPhRosh, LehaPhRid. They also can denote separation when forming part of a word, e.g., EiPheR/ashes are what is left after the other three primary elements of fire, wind, and water have been separated from it. The heifer/PaRaH incorporates the 280 plus the *Hey*, i.e., the *second Hey* of YHVH and is used as a tool to return things to their source, to change impurity into purity, to connect the separate divisions of this world, i.e., the *Peh Resh*, with their unified source, the *Aleph*, the Unity of God, by using the ashes/AiPheR.

309 The sources for the concept of "Cloaks of Light" as being a variation of "Cloaks of Skin" are identically brought down in Bereishit Rabba Bereishit 20:12 and also in Yalkut Shimoni Bereishit Remez 34 and based on the verse in Bereishit 3:21 where R. Meir's version of the Torah read "Cloaks of Light" instead of the usual reading of "Cloaks of Skin." The Shela touches on the difference between Light and Skin in a number of places. A couple of these are brought here to explain this concept.
Shela Asarah Maamarot, Maamar Sheni 58:
  - ... for man was first made with clothes of light for a clean body and afterwards was dressed with a despicable body made from gross material. He has three aspects: 1. a soul; 2. within a clean body, and 3. clothed within a despicable body. As Rashi explains, the creation of Adam from Adama/earth, that his body was collected from the earth of the Altar, or alternatively from the earth from the four corners of the globe. Both of these explanations are true: the clean body was formed from earth taken from the Altar, and the

- וְעִנְיַן הַחִלּוּק בֵּין עָפָר לְאֵפֶר כְּעִנְיַן הַחִלּוּק בֵּין כָּתְנוֹת עוֹר לְאוֹר:

שער ג' - פרק י"ד

- וְלָזֹאת, הָיָה מֹשֶׁה רַבֵּנוּ עָלָיו הַשָּׁלוֹם מוּכָן כָּל רֶגַע לִנְבוּאָה
  ○ כְּמוֹ שֶׁאָמַר (במדבר ט, ח) "עִמְדוּ וְאֶשְׁמְעָה מַה יְצַוֶּה ה' לָכֶם" וכו'

despicable body from the earth from the all the places in the world. Just as earth grows good and bad things ... similarly, the body can be refined just like having a "Cloak of Light" and it can also be materially gross and despicable just like a "Cloak of Skin." Even though now [after Adam's sin] the body is a "Cloak of Skin" – one who wants to, can purify and refine his body ... the "Cloak of Light" is never nullified, it is just absorbed within the container [of the "Cloak of Skin"] ... At the time of the receiving of the Torah ... the souls were clothed with "Cloaks of Light" ... similarly, when in the Plains of Moav [and about to enter into the Land of Israel], even though they were clothed with "Cloaks of Skin," nevertheless their pure body was aroused as per "and you who cleave with YHVH your Elokeichem, you are all alive today" [Devarim 4:4]. This is the pure and refined body which extends from generation to generation for anyone who wishes to arouse it.

Shela Masechet Taanit, Perek Torah Ohr 133:
- ... Chazal say [Pesachim 87b]: Why did God distribute/exile Israel throughout the world? To increase their numbers with converts. For God wants to provide merit for all of his handiwork ... the descendants of Sisera learned Torah in Jerusalem ... the descendants of Haman taught Torah in Bnei Berak ... and behold, from Niron Ceasar was descended R. Meir, who was known as R. Nehorai [lit., enlightenment], who enlightened the eyes of the Sages. In his Torah, it was written "Cloaks of Light" instead of "Cloaks of Skin" ... for he converted it to light.

So although there is a principle that the guttural letters can be interchanged, e.g., the letters *Ayin* and *Aleph*, nevertheless the *Ayin* represents a grosser material whereas the *Aleph* a refined and purified material. So *Clothes of Light*, with the *Aleph*, are refined and what we should aspire to in the purification of our bodies from the gross *Clothes of Skin* with the *Ayin*. Similarly, dust, with the letter *Ayin*, is used for testing the gross actions of the Sotah whereas, ashes with the letter *Aleph*, are used to purify and remove impurity from the world. (See Sotah 17a and Chullin 88b, where Rava says that in reward for Avraham saying that he is dust and ashes, his descendants merited two commandments, the ashes of the Red Heifer and the dust of the Sotah. Also see V2:02, pp. 161-162.)

310 Bamidbar 9:8.

- and as per Chazal.³¹¹ (Note 48)³¹²
- Similarly, he was able to perceive his prophecy in all places, wherever he happened to be, in an equally consistent and undifferentiated way
  - as per Chazal: Why did God speak with Moshe from within the bush . . . to teach you that there is no place in the world which is devoid of the Shechina and that He could even speak to him from within a bush³¹³
  - and this was because of his awesome level.
- He was only [denied] his plea to "Please show me Your Honor"³¹⁴
  - to understand the essence of this awesome concept
  - to see how God Fills All with His Honor and that there is no place devoid of Him
  - this was not granted to him as God answered Moshe: "You cannot see [My Face] as no man can see me [and live]."³¹⁵
- [Moshe] continuously grew in stature until he achieved this level which he merited just before his removal from this world
  - the ultimate level of perfection that is possible for man to merit while he is still in this world
  - as we find in the second paragraph of the Shema³¹⁶ which starts with [Moshe referring to God in the third person] "to love the Lord Your God," and then immediately switches in the next verse to the first person "and I will provide rain for your land"
  - indicating that he, [Moshe] is the provider and the one performing
  - as he had become entirely nullified from his own perspective and it was the Shechina alone which spoke, therefore, he said "I will provide."
  - This is as Chazal say: "The Shechina speaks from Moshe's throat"³¹⁷ as in "mouth to mouth I speak *within* him,"³¹⁸ it does not write "*to*" him but "*within*" him – literally from within him.
- From the time of Adam's sin, no one apart from [Moshe], has yet merited in achieving this level of perfection

---

311 Sifri Bamidbar Behaalotcha 68 and Yalkut Shimoni Torah Behaalotcha Remez 721: "Happy is the one born of woman who could be so sure that he could speak with [God] any time he wishes."

312 **R. Chaim adds Note 48 here.** This note is brought at the end of this chapter and is entitled "Moshe/absolute/Shema, Yaakov/difference/Baruch Shem."

313 Shemot Rabba Shemot 2:5; Bamidbar Rabba Naso 12:4; Shir Hashirim Rabba 3:10.

314 Shemot 33:18.

315 Shemot 33:20.

316 From Devarim 11:13 onwards.

317 Zohar Raya Mehemna III Pinchas 232a.

- וּכְמוֹ שֶׁאָמְרוּ רַבּוֹתֵינוּ זִכְרוֹנָם לִבְרָכָה (הגהה מ"ח):

• וְכֵן הָיָה מַשִּׂיג נְבוּאָתוֹ בְּכָל הַמְּקוֹמוֹת, בְּאֵיזֶה מָקוֹם שֶׁיִּהְיֶה, בְּהַשָּׁוָאָה גְּמוּרָה בְּלֹא שׁוּם חִלּוּק כְּלָל

- כְּמַאֲמָרָם זִכְרוֹנָם לִבְרָכָה בִּשְׁמוֹת רַבָּה פ"ב, וּבַבְּמִדְבָּר רַבָּה פָּרָשָׁה י"ב, וּבְחַזִּית סִימָן ג' בַּפָּסוּק (שה"ש) "עַמּוּדָיו עָשָׂה כֶסֶף" זֶה לְשׁוֹנָם, "לָמָּה דִּבֵּר הַקָּדוֹשׁ בָּרוּךְ הוּא עִם מֹשֶׁה מִתּוֹךְ הַסְּנֶה וכו', לְלַמֶּדְךָ שֶׁאֵין מָקוֹם פָּנוּי בָּאָרֶץ פָּנוּי מֵהַשְּׁכִינָה, שֶׁאֲפִלּוּ בְּתוֹךְ הַסְּנֶה הָיָה מְדַבֵּר עִמּוֹ". עַד כָּאן לְשׁוֹנָם.

- וְהוּא כְּפִי בְּחִינַת מַדְרֵגָתוֹ הַנּוֹרָאָה:

• וְרַק אֲשֶׁר בִּקְשָׁה נַפְשׁוֹ "הַרְאֵנִי נָא אֶת כְּבֹדֶךָ" (שמות לג, יח)

- לַעֲמֹד עַל מַהוּת זֶה הֶעָנָן הַנּוֹרָא

- וְלִרְאוֹת אֵיךְ הוּא יִתְבָּרַךְ שְׁמוֹ מָלֵא כָל הָאָרֶץ כְּבוֹדוֹ, וְלֵית אֲתַר פָּנוּי מִנֵּיהּ

- זֶה לֹא נִתַּן לוֹ, וְהֵשִׁיבוֹ הוּא יִתְבָּרַךְ "לֹא תוּכַל לִרְאוֹת וכו', כִּי לֹא יִרְאַנִי" וכו':

• וְהָיָה הוֹלֵךְ וְגָדוֹל בְּזֹאת הַמַּדְרֵגָה כָּל עֵת, עַד שֶׁעָלָה בְּיָדוֹ, וְזָכָה אֵלֶיהָ קֹדֶם סִלּוּקוֹ מִן הָעוֹלָם

- בִּשְׁלֵמוּת הַיּוֹתֵר אֶפְשָׁרִי בְּכֹחַ הָאָדָם לִזְכּוֹת בְּעוֹדוֹ בָּזֶה הָעוֹלָם.

- כְּמוֹ שֶׁשָּׁנִינוּ בְּמִשְׁנֵה תוֹרָה בְּפָרָשַׁת וְהָיָה אִם שָׁמֹעַ, (דברים יא) שֶׁתְּחִלָּה אָמַר "לְאַהֲבָה אֶת ה' אֱלֹהֵיכֶם" וגו', וְתֵכֶף לוֹ בַּפָּסוּק שֶׁאַחֲרָיו אָמַר בְּלָשׁוֹן מְדַבֵּר בַּעֲדוֹ "וְנָתַתִּי מְטַר אַרְצְכֶם" כו'

- שֶׁהוּא הַנּוֹתֵן וְהַפּוֹעֵל

- כִּי הִתְבַּטֵּל בְּעֵינֵי עַצְמוֹ מִמְּצִיאוּת כְּלָל, וְרַק הַשְּׁכִינָה לְבַד הַמְדַבֶּרֶת, לָכֵן אָמַר "וְנָתַתִּי".

- וְזֶה שֶׁאָמְרוּ זִכְרוֹנָם לִבְרָכָה (זוהר פנחס רלב) "שְׁכִינָה מְדַבֶּרֶת מִתּוֹךְ גְּרוֹנוֹ שֶׁל מֹשֶׁה", וּכְמוֹ שֶׁאָמַר הַכָּתוּב (במדבר יב, ח) "פֶּה אֶל פֶּה אֲדַבֵּר בּוֹ", וְלֹא כְּתִיב "אֵלָיו", אֶלָּא "בּוֹ", בְּתוֹכוֹ מַמָּשׁ:

• וְלָזֹאת הַמַּדְרֵגָה בִּשְׁלֵמוּת, עֲדַיִן לֹא זָכָה אֵלֶיהָ שׁוּם אָדָם זוּלָתוֹ, מֵעֵת חֵטְא אָדָם הָרִאשׁוֹן

318 Bamidbar 12:8.

- and 'no living person'[319] will merit this until the redemption – may it come speedily in our days
- as the Holy Torah testifies[320] "and there has been no other prophet in Israel like Moshe . . ."
  - (and even though this verse is stated in the past tense, the Torah is everlasting and it also relates to all future generations – such that after each generation passes it will be correct to [retrospectively] say that in this generation no prophet arose like Moshe on this level.)
- Therefore Chazal[321] say: "A person is obligated to say, when will my deeds reach the level of the deeds of my forefathers Avraham, Yitzchak, and Yaakov" and they do not mention the level of the deeds of Moshe.

• Notwithstanding this, it is nevertheless appropriate for one who truly fears God
  - to *at the very least* during times of prayer
  - to focus his heart to the best of his ability and perception to nullify all the powers in the world together with his own powers/abilities
  - to the extent that it is as if they have no existence in this world at all
  - and that his heart is solely attached to Him, the Blessed One, The Unified Master, Blessed be He.

• At the very least, [one should aspire to reach this level of focus] periodically
  - as in truth, not all times are equally propitious to achieve purity of the heart
  - and in particular, in these generations, it is virtually impossible to always [be able to] pray on this high level
  - as R. Elazar ben Azarya has already said: I can exempt the world from the obligation of prayer[322]
  - nevertheless, the pure servant of God who is constantly scrupulous with the purity of his heart in all his activities, with the grace of the Master of All, will at least be able to reach this level of prayer periodically.

• So now the intention of Chazal's statements is explained
  - "that one who prays must concentrate his heart on the Makom"[323]

---

319 Daniel 2:10, lit. "there is no one on dry land."
320 Devarim 34:10.
321 Eliyahu Rabba 23.
322 Eruvin 65a, this exemption being as a result of the Jewish People's trials and tribulations following the destruction of the Temple which prevented them from being properly focused during prayer, as if they were considered *drunk*

○ וְגַם לֹא יִזְכֶּה אֵלֶיהָ שׁוּם אֱנָשׁ עַל יַבֶּשְׁתָּא, עַד בִּיאַת הַגּוֹאֵל בִּמְהֵרָה בְּיָמֵינוּ

○ כְּמוֹ שֶׁהֶעִידָה הַתּוֹרָה הַקְּדוֹשָׁה (דברים לד, י) "וְלֹא קָם נָבִיא עוֹד בְּיִשְׂרָאֵל כְּמֹשֶׁה" כו'.

▫ (וְאַף שֶׁנֶּאֱמַר בִּלְשׁוֹן עָבָר, הַתּוֹרָה הִיא נִצְחִית, וְקָאֵי גַּם עַל זְמַן דּוֹרוֹת הַבָּאִים, שֶׁאַחַר עָבַר כָּל דּוֹר מֵהָעוֹלָם, נוּכַל לוֹמַר שֶׁלֹּא קָם בְּזֶה הַדּוֹר נָבִיא כְּמֹשֶׁה בְּזֹאת הַמַּדְרֵגָה).

○ וְלָכֵן אָמְרוּ בְּתַנָּא דְבֵי אֵלִיָּהוּ (פרק כ"ג), "חַיָּב אָדָם לוֹמַר מָתַי יַגִּיעוּ מַעֲשַׂי לְמַעֲשֵׂי אֲבוֹתַי אַבְרָהָם יִצְחָק וְיַעֲקֹב", וְלֹא אָמְרוּ לְמַעֲשֵׂי מֹשֶׁה רַבֵּנוּ עָלָיו הַשָּׁלוֹם:

• אָמְנָם, עִם כָּל זֶה, רָאוּי לְכָל יְרֵא ה' אֲמִתִּי
  ○ שֶׁעַל כָּל פָּנִים בְּעֵת עָמְדוֹ לְהִתְפַּלֵּל
  ○ יְבַטֵּל בְּטֹהַר לִבָּבוֹ כְּפִי יְכָלְתּוֹ וְהַשָּׂגָתוֹ כָּל הַכֹּחוֹת שֶׁבָּעוֹלָם וְכָל כֹּחוֹתָיו
  ○ כְּאִלּוּ אֵין שׁוּם מְצִיאוּת בָּעוֹלָם כְּלָל
  ○ וּלְהִתְדַּבֵּק בְּלִבּוֹ רַק בּוֹ יִתְבָּרַךְ אָדוֹן יָחִיד בָּרוּךְ הוּא:

• וְעַל כָּל פָּנִים, לִפְרָקִים
  ○ כִּי בֶּאֱמֶת לֹא כָּל הָעִתִּים שָׁווֹת בְּעִנְיַן טָהֳרַת הַלֵּב
  ○ וּבִפְרָט בַּדּוֹרוֹת הַלָּלוּ כִּמְעַט בִּלְתִּי אֶפְשָׁר לְהִתְפַּלֵּל בִּתְמִידוּת בְּזֹאת הַמַּדְרֵגָה הַגְּבוֹהָה.
  ○ וּכְבָר אָמַר רַב שֵׁשֶׁת בְּשֵׁם רַב אֶלְעָזָר בֶּן עֲזַרְיָה (עירובין רפ"ג סה, א), "יְכַלְנִי לִפְטֹר כָּל הָעוֹלָם מִדִּין תְּפִלָּה".
  ○ אַף עַל פִּי כֵן, הָעוֹבֵד הַטָּהוֹר הָרוֹאֶה וּמִסְתַּכֵּל תָּמִיד בְּטָהֳרַת לְבָבוֹ עַל כָּל עִנְיָנָיו, שֶׁיִּהְיוּ לְרָצוֹן לִפְנֵי כֹּל יִתְבָּרַךְ אָדוֹן שְׁמוֹ, יוּכַל לְהַגִּיעַ שֶׁיִּתְפַּלֵּל עַל כָּל פָּנִים לִפְרָקִים, בְּזֹאת הַמַּדְרֵגָה:

• וְעַתָּה מְבֹאָר כַּוָּנָתָם זִכְרוֹנָם לִבְרָכָה בְּמַאֲמָרָם
  ○ שֶׁהַמִּתְפַּלֵּל צָרִיךְ שֶׁיְּכַוֵּן אֶת לִבּוֹ לַ"מָּקוֹם" (ברכות לא:)

---

during the exile and therefore exempt from true prayer. This section of the Talmud was previously quoted in G2:12.

323 Berachot 31a.

- ○ "and when you pray, don't [pray by rote], but rather by seeking mercy and supplication before the Makom Blessed be He."[324]
- [In summary] this [concept of Makom] means
  - ○ that one should be extremely careful
  - ○ to never concentrate and focus his heart, God forbid, during prayer on any Sefira even if it is one of the Ne'etzalim[325]
  - ○ and not only to not focus on any single Sefira or supernal power alone, as this is not service of the true God and is a 'chopping down of the saplings',[326] God forbid
  - ○ but it is also appropriate and fitting that with his will he should completely nullify all the powers of the supernal and lower worlds, and also his own powers/abilities, to the extent that it appears [to him] that they do not exist
    - ▫ (and that this does not only apply to prayer alone, but additionally, in order that one's Torah study should be appropriately sustained, it also needs to be conducted on this level, as per Chazal[327] who say: "Words of Torah are only sustained with one who considers himself to not exist")
  - ○ and that he should concentrate his heart during prayer only on the Makom of the Universe alone, that He is the Unified One of the Universe, the Infinite One, Who fills All of this world and all of the worlds, and that there is no place devoid of Him.
- Refer to the words of the Rokeach,[328] and understand:
  - ○ When one says "*Blessed are you YHVH*" – do not think of God's Honor as it would be represented in the heart of prophets or of its representation on the Divine Throne, but rather that *YHVH* is *Elokim* in the Heavens and the Earth, in the sky and the sea and the entire Universe, that He is the God of the Patriarchs.

---

324 Mishna Avot 2:13.
325 The language of Sefira used here is only meaningful when viewing the world from our perspective of Kav in that God is manifest in specific differentiated ways. Emphasis is given here that we should not even focus on those Sefirot of God which are Ne'etzalim, i.e., even on a level which is very close to their Absolute Source, and that even focusing on levels so close to God still nevertheless cannot be considered as serving God.
326 This expression is borrowed from the actions of Acher, R. Elisha ben Avuya, who is recorded in Chagiga 14b–15a as being one of the four who entered the *Orchard* of Divine Knowledge and that he *Chopped down the Saplings*. In our

- וְכֵן מַאֲמָרָם זִכְרוֹנָם לִבְרָכָה בְּאָבוֹת, "וּכְשֶׁאַתָּה מִתְפַּלֵּל אַל תַּעַשׂ וְכוּ', אֶלָּא רַחֲמִים וְתַחֲנוּנִים לִפְנֵי הַ'מָקוֹם' בָּרוּךְ הוּא":

- רָצָה לוֹמַר
  - שֶׁצָּרִיךְ לִיזָּהֵר בְּנַפְשׁוֹ מְאֹד
  - שֶׁלֹּא לְכַוֵּן וְלָשׂוּם מְגַמַּת לִבּוֹ בִּתְפִלָּתוֹ חַס וְשָׁלוֹם לְשׁוּם סְפִירָה, אֲפִלּוּ מֵהַנֶּאֱצָלִים.
  - וְלֹא זוֹ בִּלְבַד שֶׁלֹּא לְכַוֵּן לְשׁוּם סְפִירָה וְכֹחַ עֶלְיוֹן לְכָךְ, כִּי הוּא עֲבוֹדָה לְלֹא אֱלֹקֵי אֱמֶת וְקִצּוּץ נְטִיעוֹת חַס וְשָׁלוֹם
  - אֶלָּא שֶׁגַּם רָאוּי וְנָכוֹן, שֶׁיְבַטֵּל בִּרְצוֹנוֹ בִּטּוּל גָּמוּר כָּל הַכֹּחוֹת עֶלְיוֹנִים וְתַחְתּוֹנִים, וְגַם כָּל כֹּחוֹתָיו, כְּאִלּוּ אֵינָם בִּמְצִיאוּת
  - (וְלֹא זוֹ בִּלְבַד בְּעִנְיַן הַתְּפִלָּה, אֶלָּא שֶׁגַּם הָעֶסֶק בַּתּוֹרָה שֶׁיִּתְעַסֵּק אֶצְלוֹ כָּרָאוּי, גַּם כֵּן צְרִיכָה שֶׁתִּהְיֶה עַל פִּי זֹאת הַמַּדְרֵגָה, כְּעִנְיַן מַאֲמָרָם זִכְרוֹנָם לִבְרָכָה (סוטה כ"א ע"ב), "אֵין דִּבְרֵי תוֹרָה מִתְקַיְּמִין אֶלָּא בְּמִי שֶׁמְּשִׂימִים עַצְמוֹ כְּמִי שֶׁאֵינוֹ")
  - וּלְכַוֵּן וּלְהַדְבִּיק טָהֳרַת לִבּוֹ בִּתְפִלָּתוֹ רַק לִמְקוֹמוֹ שֶׁל עוֹלָם, הוּא יְחִידוֹ שֶׁל עוֹלָם, אֵין סוֹף בָּרוּךְ הוּא, הַמְמַלֵּא כָּל הָעוֹלָם וְהָעוֹלָמוֹת כֻּלָּם, וְלֵית אֲתַר פָּנוּי מִנֵּיהּ:

- וְעַיֵּן רוֹקֵחַ זִכְרוֹנוֹ לִבְרָכָה, סוֹף שֹׁרֶשׁ זְכִירַת הַשֵּׁם ז"ל
  - "וּכְשֶׁיֹּאמַר "בָּרוּךְ אַתָּה ה'", אַל יַחְשֹׁב עַל הַכָּבוֹד הַנִּרְאָה בְּלֵב הַנְּבִיאִים,

---

context this expression is used to emphasize that an unbalanced perspective of God by not always viewing the Unity of the Sefirot will only result in doing damage.

327 Sotah 21b.

328 At the end of the section Sefer Rokeach Hilchot Chasidut Shoresh Zechirat Hashem.

329 Pesachim 56a. Chazal identify the difference in perceptual ability between Moshe and the Patriarchs as the reason why Moshe only said the first verse of the Shema and that Yaakov immediately followed his recitation of the first verse of the Shema with the statement of "Blessed is the name. . . ." Chazal ask

Rabbi Chaim's Note:
Note 48 – Moshe/absolute/Shema, Yaakov/difference/Baruch Shem

- This is also one of the reasons why Yaakov said: "Blessed is the name of the Honor of His Majesty for ever and ever" whereas Moshe did not say it, as per Chazal.[329]
- For the praise "Blessed is the name of the Honor of His Majesty for ever and ever" conceptually indicates that there is also [separate] existence of powers and worlds, as I wrote above in G3:11, refer to it,[330] and therefore Yaakov said this as it reflected his level as stated above.
- In contrast, Moshe's level and perception, as we explained, also reflected the essence of absolute unity as expressed by the word "One" of the first verse of the Shema, as is explained there, and therefore he did not say "Blessed is the name of the Honor of His Majesty for ever and ever" when he was expressing God's Unity.

END OF THE THIRD GATEWAY

---

if we should also say this statement and answers that as Moshe did not say it and Yaakov did – therefore we should defer to both of them and say it quietly.

330 See G3:11:N45.

וּמַרְאֶה עַל הַכִּסֵּא, כִּי אִם עַל ה' הוּא הָאֱלֹקִים בַּשָּׁמַיִם וּבָאָרֶץ בָּאֲוִיר וּבַיָּם וּבְכָל הָעוֹלָם, שֶׁהוּא אֱלֹהֵי הָאָבוֹת". עַד כָּאן לְשׁוֹנוֹ. וְהָבֵן:

הגהה מ"ח

- וְהוּא גַם כֵּן אֶחָד מֵהַטְּעָמִים, מַה שֶּׁיַּעֲקֹב אָבִינוּ עָלָיו הַשָּׁלוֹם אָמַר "בָּרוּךְ שֵׁם כְּבוֹד מַלְכוּתוֹ לְעוֹלָם וָעֶד", וּמֹשֶׁה רַבֵּנוּ עָלָיו הַשָּׁלוֹם לֹא אֲמָרוֹ, כְּמַאֲמָרָם זִכְרוֹנָם לִבְרָכָה (פסחים נו, א):

- כִּי עִנְיַן שֶׁבַח "בָּרוּךְ שֵׁם כְּבוֹד מַלְכוּתוֹ לְעוֹלָם וָעֶד" מַשְׁמַע שֶׁיֵּשׁ גַּם כֵּן מְצִיאוּת כֹּחוֹת וְעוֹלָמוֹת, וּכְמוֹ שֶׁכָּתַבְתִּי לְעֵיל פֶּרֶק י"א, עַיֵּן שָׁם, וְלָכֵן אָמְרוֹ יַעֲקֹב אָבִינוּ עָלָיו הַשָּׁלוֹם, שֶׁהוּא כְּפִי מַדְרֵגָתוֹ כַּנַּ"ל:

- אָמְנָם מַדְרֵגַת וְהַשָּׂגַת מֹשֶׁה רַבֵּנוּ עָלָיו הַשָּׁלוֹם כְּפִי שֶׁבֵּאַרְנוּ, הוּא גַם כֵּן עֶצֶם עִנְיַן הַיִּחוּד דְּתֵבַת "אֶחָד" דִּקְרִיאַת שְׁמַע, כְּפִי שֶׁנִּתְבָּאֵר שָׁם, לָכֵן הוּא לֹא אָמַר בָּרוּךְ שֵׁם כְּבוֹד מַלְכוּתוֹ לְעוֹלָם וָעֶד בְּיִחוּדוֹ יִתְבָּרַךְ שְׁמוֹ:

סָלִיק שַׁעַר ג'

CHAPTERS

1. CAREFULLY WATCH FOR PITFALL OF HAUGHTINESS ON PATH TO PURITY

- Dear Reader, I have instructed you with God's help in the paths of truth[1]
  - teaching you the guaranteed method by which you can gradually educate yourself to advance through the sequence of levels as set out above
  - according to the purity of your heart and your intellectual ability
  - and through which you can achieve more than has been laid out before you here
  - especially if assisted with repeated practice.
- You yourself will see that the more you practice these methods mentioned above, the more you will purify your heart in Torah study, Mitzvah performance, and Fear and Love of God.
- However, be extremely cautious to ensure that your focus on serving God through purity of thought, does not result in any arrogance and haughtiness.
  - At first glance, you will not initially be aware of this haughtiness, but you need to very carefully search for it within yourself
  - as explicitly written "Those who are haughty are an abomination to God"[2]
  - as even if it just resides within your thoughts and others cannot detect it within you, it is still absolutely repugnant to God
  - as is known, that [haughtiness] is the root and the 'leaven in the dough'[3] of all bad character traits.
- Chazal highlight that one who is haughty
  - is as if he built an altar for idol worship[4]
  - and the Shechina laments over him[5]
  - and is as if he pushes God aside, Who complains about him saying that "I and He cannot reside together"[6]
  - 'for the mat will be too short for stretching out'[7]

---

1 Over the course of the preceding three Gateways.
2 Mishlei 16:5.
3 An expression which appears in various Midrashim, e.g., Midrash Tanchuma Noach 4, used to denote the catalyst of bad.
4 Sotah 4b.
5 Sotah 5b.

פְּרָקִים

פרקים - פרק א'

- אַתָּה הַקּוֹרֵא נָעִים, הִנֵּה הִדְרַכְתִּיךָ בְּעֶזְרַת ה' בִּנְתִיבוֹת הָאֱמֶת
  - לְהוֹרוֹת לְפָנֶיךָ הַדֶּרֶךְ תֵּלֶךְ בָּהּ לְבֶטַח, וְתוּכַל לְחַנֵּךְ עַצְמְךָ לְאַט בְּסֵדֶר הַמַּדְרֵגוֹת הַנַּ"ל
  - לְפִי טֹהַר לְבָבְךָ, וּלְפִי הַשָּׂגָתְךָ
  - יוֹתֵר מִמַּה שֶּׁעָרוּךְ לְפָנֶיךָ כָּאן
  - וְגַם לְפִי רֹב הַהֶרְגֵּל:

- וּבְעֵינֶיךָ תִּרְאֶה, שֶׁכָּל אֲשֶׁר תַּרְגִּיל עַצְמְךָ יוֹתֵר בְּכָל מַדְרֵגָה מֵאֵלּוּ הַנַּ"ל, יִתּוֹסֵף בְּלִבְּךָ טָהֳרָה עַל טָהֳרָתְךָ, הֵן בְּעֵסֶק הַתּוֹרָה, וְהֵן בְּקִיּוּם הַמִּצְוֹת, וְיִרְאָתוֹ וְאַהֲבָתוֹ יִתְבָּרַךְ:

- אָמְנָם הִשָּׁמֵר וְהִזָּהֵר מְאֹד, שֶׁלֹּא תָּזוּחַ דַּעְתְּךָ עָלֶיךָ וְתִתְנַשֵּׂא לְבָבְךָ, מֵאֲשֶׁר אַתָּה עוֹבֵד אֶת בּוֹרַאֲךָ בְּטָהֳרַת הַמַּחֲשָׁבָה.

- וּבְהַשְׁקָפָה רִאשׁוֹנָה לֹא תַּרְגִּישׁ כָּל כָּךְ בְּהִתְנַשְּׂאוּת לְבָּךְ מִזֶּה, וְצָרִיךְ אַתָּה לְפַשְׁפֵּשׁ וּלְמַשְׁמֵשׁ בָּזֶה מְאֹד

- וְכָתוּב מְפֹרָשׁ "תּוֹעֲבַת ה' כָּל גְּבַהּ לֵב" (משלי ט"ז)

- שֶׁאַף אִם לֹא יִתְרָאֶה הַהִתְנַשְּׂאוּת לְעֵינֵי בְּנֵי אָדָם, רַק בְּמַחְשֶׁבֶת הַלֵּב לְבַד בְּעֵינֵי עַצְמוֹ, הִיא תּוֹעֵבָה מַמָּשׁ לְפָנָיו יִתְבָּרַךְ

- כַּיָּדוּעַ שֶׁהִיא הַשֹּׁרֶשׁ וְהַשְּׂאוֹר שֶׁבָּעִסָּה לְכָל הַמִּדּוֹת רָעוֹת:

- וְאָמְרוּ (סוטה דף ד':) שֶׁכָּל הַמִּתְיַהֵר
  - כְּאִלּוּ בָּנָה בָּמָה
  - וּשְׁכִינָה מְיַלֶּלֶת עָלָיו
  - וּכְאִלּוּ דּוֹחֵק רַגְלָיו יִתְבָּרַךְ שְׁמוֹ, שֶׁקּוֹבֵל עָלָיו וְאוֹמֵר, אֵין אֲנִי וְהוּא יְכוֹלִין לָדוּר כְּאֶחָד (שם ה')
  - וְקָצַר הַמַּצָּע מֵהִשְׂתָּרֵעַ

---

6 Sotah 5b.
7 An expression borrowed from Yishayahu 28:20 meaning here that haughtiness

- and woe is to the son who forcefully evicts his father from his father's palace.
- Chazal greatly debated over this until they concluded there[8] that [the haughty] are as if
  - they worship idols
  - renounce their faith
  - and have involved themselves with all manner of incestuous relationships.
- Chazal add that "With one who is haughty – if he is wise, then his wisdom departs from him."[9]
- For anyone whose heart is touched by Fear of Heaven
  - the hair on his head 'will stand on end'[10]
  - and 'tears will flow from his eye'[11]
  - when he brings to mind who Chazal learned this from
  - from Hillel the Elder, who is well-known in Chazal's statements[12] for his tremendous humility and awesome lowliness
  - nevertheless, when he was once involved in something where it appeared that he showed a vestige of haughtiness relative to the level of his lowliness of spirit
  - he was immediately punished by forgetting a law.[13]
  - Therefore what can we say – how much more so we need to constantly examine ourselves for this trait at all times.

2. HONOR THOSE INVOLVED IN TORAH AND MITZVOT EVEN FOR WRONG REASONS

- Haughtiness can also cause one who is engaged in the service of God out of purity of heart, to look down on others, God forbid, who
  - are seen to be serving God without pure intentions
  - and observe all that which is in the Torah but without motivational fervor.
- Even more so, when observing a person who is involved with Torah [study] but considers that his involvement is not *for its sake* – this [haughtiness] will result in that person being very much despised in his eyes, God forbid – 'a criminal offense,'[14] may God save us!
- For, in truth, the whole purpose of purity of one's heart in the service of

---

blows one's self perception so out of proportion that the resources of the Universe are not enough to service both the haughty and God.

8   Sotah 4b.
9   Pesachim 66b.

- וְאוֹי לוֹ לַבֵּן הַמְגָרֵשׁ אֶת אָבִיו בִּזְרוֹעַ מִבֵּית פַּלְטִין שֶׁל אָבִיו:
- וְהִפְלִיגוּ בָּהּ זִכְרוֹנָם לִבְרָכָה מְאֹד, עַד שֶׁאָמְרוּ שָׁם, שֶׁהוּא כְּאִלּוּ
  - עוֹבֵד עֲבוֹדָה זָרָה
  - וְכָפַר בָּעִקָּר
  - וּכְאִלּוּ בָּא עַל כָּל הָעֲרָיוֹת:
- וְאָמְרוּ (פסחים ס"ו ע"ב) "כָּל הַמִּתְיַהֵר, אִם חָכָם הוּא חָכְמָתוֹ מִסְתַּלֶּקֶת הֵימֶנּוּ":
- וְכָל אֲשֶׁר יִרְאַת ה' נָגַע בְּלִבּוֹ
  - תְּסַמֵּר שַׂעֲרוֹת רֹאשׁוֹ
  - וְתִדְמַע עֵינוֹ
  - בְּהַעֲלוֹתוֹ עַל לִבּוֹ מִמִּי לְמָדוּהוּ רַבּוֹתֵינוּ זִכְרוֹנָם לִבְרָכָה זֹאת
- מֵהִלֵּל הַזָּקֵן, אֲשֶׁר יָדוּעַ וּמְפֻרְסָם בְּדִבְרֵיהֶם זִכְרוֹנָם לִבְרָכָה (עי' שבת לא, א) הַפְלָגַת עַנְוְתָנוּתוֹ וְשִׁפְלוּתוֹ הַנּוֹרָאָה
  - עִם כָּל זֶה, כַּאֲשֶׁר נִזְדַּמֵּן לְיָדוֹ פַּעַם אַחַת, קְצָת עִנְיָן, שֶׁהָיָה נִרְאֶה בְּהַשְׁקָפָה כְּהִתְנַשְּׂאוּת, לְפִי מַדְרֵגַת גֹּדֶל נְמִיכַת רוּחוֹ
  - תֵּכֶף נֶעֱנַשׁ עַל זֶה שֶׁנִּתְעַלְּמָה הֵימֶנּוּ הֲלָכָה (פסחים ס"ו ע"ב)
  - מַה נֹּאמַר וּנְדַבֵּר אֲנַחְנוּ, אֵיךְ אָנוּ צְרִיכִים לְפַשְׁפֵּשׁ וּלְמַשְׁמֵשׁ עַל זֶה בְּכָל עֵת:

פרקים - פרק ב'

- גַּם תּוּכַל לִגְרֹם לְאָדָם הַהִתְנַשְּׂאוּת בַּלֵּב, מֵאֲשֶׁר הוּא עוֹבֵד אוֹתוֹ יִתְבָּרַךְ בְּטָהֳרַת הַלֵּב, שֶׁיֵּקַל בְּעֵינָיו חַס וְשָׁלוֹם אִם יִרְאֶה מִי וָמִי
  - שֶׁאֵין עִנְיְנֵי עֲבוֹדָתוֹ לוֹ יִתְבָּרַךְ בְּמַחֲשָׁבָה טְהוֹרָה
  - וּמְקַיְּמִים כְּכָל הַכָּתוּב בְּתוֹרַת ה' בְּלֹא דְּבֵקוּת:
- וְכָל שֶׁכֵּן כְּשֶׁיִּרְאֶה אֵיזֶה אִישׁ עוֹסֵק בְּתוֹרַת ה', וְיִתְבּוֹנֵן עָלָיו שֶׁהוּא 'שֶׁלֹּא לִשְׁמָהּ', יִתְבַּזֶּה בְּעֵינָיו מְאֹד חַס וְשָׁלוֹם, וְהוּא עָוֹן פְּלִילִי, הָרַחֲמָן יַצִּילֵנוּ:
- כִּי בֶּאֱמֶת כָּל עִנְיַן הַטָּהֳרַת הַלֵּב בַּעֲבוֹדָתוֹ יִתְבָּרַךְ, הוּא לְמִצְוָה, וְלֹא לְעִכּוּבָא

---

10 Iyov 4:15.
11 An expression borrowed from Yirmiyahu 13:17 which is brought there in the context of haughtiness.
12 E.g., Shabbat 31a which highlights Hillel's tremendous patience.
13 Pesachim 66b.
14 Iyov 31:28.

[God] is to add impetus to Mitzvah performance, but its absence does not detract from the performance
- as I wrote above at the end of the First Gateway[15] and will explain later if God Wills it
- and anyone who performs any Mitzvah, whether from the Written or Oral Law, even without this motivational fervor is also called a "Servant of God" and is beloved before Him.

• Similarly, with one who is involved in Torah even if not *for its sake*, even though he is certainly not on a truly high level, nevertheless, he should never, God forbid, be even so much as thought of as despised, on the contrary, every Jew is obligated to honor such a person
- as per Chazal[16] who interpret that "with the left there are riches and honor" means that even those who serve Him in a weaker[17] way [deserve honor].
- As per the Zohar:[18] "God's Torah is perfect . . . ." How much effort should a person invest in Torah study? As it is life itself to one who invests in Torah study . . . and even one who improperly invests himself in Torah study not *for its sake* merits reward in this world and is not judged in the next world, and come and see that which is written "With the right there is length of days, with the left there are riches and honor," he has good reward and tranquility in this world.
- Therefore, even a person who is improperly involved in Torah study not *for its sake* and for some personal gain
  - as long as [the personal intention] is not to taunt in which case Chazal say that:
    - "It would have been better if this person's afterbirth were turned on him."[19]
    - "[The Torah studies] becomes like a poison to him,"[20] God forbid
  - is assigned reward by God, and is deserving of riches, honor, and tranquility in this world, and is also not judged in the next world for that thought of personal intention.
- How much more so if this person does not have intention of personal gain even if his intention is not specifically *for its sake*, that is *for the sake of Torah*
  - as I will write later on in G4:03 in the name of the Rosh
  - but that the essence of this person's involvement is just casual

---

15 G1:22.
16 Shabbat 63a quoting Mishlei 3:16.
17 As denoted by the *left* in comparison to the stronger *right*.

○ כְּמוֹ שֶׁכָּתַבְתִּי לְעֵיל סוֹף שַׁעַר א', וְיִתְבָּאֵר עוֹד לְהַלָּן אי"ה.

○ וְכָל הַמְקַיֵּם מִצְוַת ה', כְּכָל אֲשֶׁר צִוָּנוּ בַּתּוֹרָה הַקְּדוֹשָׁה שֶׁבִּכְתָב וּבְעַל פֶּה, אַף בְּלֹא דְבֵקוּת, נִקְרָא גַם כֵּן עוֹבֵד אֱלֹהִים, וְאָהוּב לְפָנָיו יִתְבָּרַךְ:

● וְכֵן הָאָדָם הָעוֹסֵק בְּתוֹרַת ה' אֲפִלּוּ שֶׁלֹּא לִשְׁמָהּ, אִם כִּי וַדַּאי שֶׁעֲדַיִן אֵינוֹ בְּמַדְרֵגָה הַגְּבוֹהָה הָאֲמִתִּית, אָמְנָם חָלִילָה וְחָלִילָה לְבַזּוֹתוֹ אֲפִלּוּ בַּלֵּב. וְאַדְּרַבָּה, כָּל אִישׁ יִשְׂרָאֵל מְחֻיָּב גַּם לִנְהֹג בּוֹ כָּבוֹד.

○ כְּמוֹ שֶׁכָּתוּב (משלי ג, טז) "בִּשְׂמֹאלָהּ עֹשֶׁר וְכָבוֹד" וְדָרְשׁוּ רַבּוֹתֵינוּ זִכְרוֹנָם לִבְרָכָה (שבת ס"ג) לַמַּשְׂמְאִילִים בָּהּ כו'.

○ וּבַזֹּהַר וַיֵּשֶׁב קפ"ד ב', "תּוֹרַת ה' תְּמִימָה" כו', כַּמָּה אִית לוֹן לִבְנֵי נָשָׁא לְאִשְׁתַּדָּלָא בְּאוֹרַיְתָא, דְּכָל מַאן דְּאִשְׁתַּדַּל בְּאוֹרַיְתָא לֶהֱוֵי לֵיהּ חַיִּים כו', וַאֲפִילוּ מַאן דְּאִשְׁתַּדַּל בְּאוֹרַיְתָא וְלָא אִשְׁתַּדַּל בָּהּ לִשְׁמָהּ כְּדַקָּא יָאוֹת, זָכֵי לַאֲגַר טַב בְּעָלְמָא דֵין וְלָא דַיְינִין לֵיהּ בְּהַהוּא עָלְמָא. וְתָא חֲזֵי, כְּתִיב "אֹרֶךְ יָמִים בִּימִינָהּ בִּשְׂמֹאלָהּ עֹשֶׁר וְכָבוֹד" כו' "בִּשְׂמֹאלָהּ עֹשֶׁר וְכָבוֹד", אֲגַר טַב וְשַׁלְוָה אִית לֵיהּ בְּהַאי עָלְמָא.

○ הֲרֵי שֶׁאֲפִלּוּ הָאָדָם אֲשֶׁר עָסְקוֹ בְּתוֹרָתוֹ יִתְבָּרַךְ שֶׁלֹּא לִשְׁמָהּ כָּרָאוּי, אֶלָּא בִּשְׁבִיל אֵיזֶה פְּנִיָּה לְגַרְמֵיהּ.

◇ רַק אִם אֵינוֹ לְקַנְטוּר חַס וְשָׁלוֹם אֲשֶׁר עָלָיו אָמְרוּ רַבּוֹתֵינוּ זִכְרוֹנָם לִבְרָכָה
  ▽ "נוֹחַ לוֹ שֶׁתֵּהָפֵךְ שִׁלְיָתוֹ עַל פָּנָיו" (ירושלמי ברכות א, ב)
  ▽ וְכֵן אָמְרוּ (שבת פ"ח:) שֶׁנַּעֲשֵׂית לוֹ סַם הַמָּוֶת חַס וְשָׁלוֹם

■ הַקָּדוֹשׁ בָּרוּךְ הוּא קוֹבֵעַ לוֹ שָׂכָר טוֹב, שֶׁמַּגִּיעַ לוֹ עֹשֶׁר וְכָבוֹד וְשַׁלְוָה בְּהַאי עָלְמָא, וְגַם לֹא דַיְינִין לֵיהּ בְּהַהוּא עָלְמָא עַל אוֹתָהּ הַמַּחֲשָׁבָה וְהַפְּנִיָּה שֶׁכִּוֵּן בָּהּ.

○ וְכָל שֶׁכֵּן אִם אֵינוֹ מְכַוֵּן כְּלָל לְשׁוּם פְּנִיָּה לְגַרְמֵיהּ, הֲגַם שֶׁאֵין כַּוָּנָתוֹ לִשְׁמָהּ דַּוְקָא, הַיְנוּ לְשֵׁם הַתּוֹרָה
  ○ כְּמוֹ שֶׁאֶכְתֹּב לְקַמָּן בְּפֶרֶק ג' מִשַּׁעַר ד' בְּשֵׁם הָרֹא"שׁ זִכְרוֹנוֹ לִבְרָכָה
  ○ אֶלָּא עִקַּר עָסְקוֹ בָּהּ בִּסְתָמָא

---

18 Zohar I VaYeshev 184b quoting Tehillim 19:8.

19 I.e., that it would be better that he were not born – Yerushalmi Berachot Chap. 1 Halacha 2.

20 Shabbat 88b and Yoma 72b (both quoting a statement of Rava with slightly different versions but the same meaning).

- and is similar to being *for its sake*
- then this [person's] involvement in Torah study is very precious in God's eyes – more so than the performance of all Mitzvot for their sake and accompanied by the fitting holiness and purity of thought.
- This point is proven categorically by Chazal: It was asked of R. Yehuda the son of R. Shimon [the son of Pazi]:[21] Which is preferable, rebuke given for the sake of Heaven or humility expressed without being for the sake of Heaven? He answered: Who doesn't agree that humility for the sake of Heaven is greater, as Rav said "humility is greater than all" and humility expressed without being for the sake of Heaven is also preferable, as R. Yehuda said in the name of Rav: "One should always involve oneself with Torah study and Mitzvah performance even if not for their sake, as from this performance not for their sake one will come to the performance for their sake."[22]
  - This similarly implies that with Torah study too. Who doesn't agree that Torah study *for its sake* is preferable over Mitzvot performed for their sake, as this is expressly stated "and Torah study corresponds to all [Mitzvot]."[23]
- Similarly, Chazal[24] differentiate the relative levels of Torah study and Mitzvah performance.
  - For the merit and light of Mitzvot whether at a time of involvement with them or not – only provide protection from afflictions but do not save a person from coming to sin.
  - However, with the light of Torah study, even according to the conclusion of this debate there, at the very least does protect one from sin when one is involved in it.
- Chazal[25] highlight that all of the Mitzvot do not amount to even one part of the Torah as will be explained later on, with God's Will, in the Fourth Gateway.[26]
- Therefore, even Torah study which is not *for its sake* is also preferable to Mitzvah performance for their sake, for this same reason, as [initial study] which is not *for its sake* will lead to [study] *for its sake*.

---

21 R. Chaim's reference to this section of Talmud includes "the son of Pazi" which does not appear in the standard version. It seems that it is an alternative version which does also appear in the writings of some others who quote this section of Talmud.
22 Arachin 16b.

- אֲשֶׁר כִּ׳לִשְׁמָהּ׳ דָּמִי

- הֲרֵי עֵסֶק תּוֹרָתוֹ יָקָר מְאֹד בְּעֵינָיו יִתְבָּרַךְ, יוֹתֵר מִכָּל הַמִּצְוֹת לִשְׁמָהּ בִּקְדֻשַּׁת וְטָהֳרַת הַמַּחֲשָׁבָה כָּרָאוּי.

- כַּמְבֹאָר וּמוּכָח לְהֶדְיָא מִגְּמָרָא דַּעֲרָכִין (ט״ז ע״ב), "בְּעָא מִינֵיהּ רַב יְהוּדָה בְּרֵיהּ דְּרַב שִׁמְעוֹן בֶּן פָּזִי, תּוֹכֵחָה לִשְׁמָהּ וַעֲנָוָה שֶׁלֹּא לִשְׁמָהּ, הֵי מִנַּיְיהוּ עֲדִיפָא, וְאָמַר לֵיהּ, מִי לֹא מוֹדֵית דַּעֲנָוָה לִשְׁמָהּ עֲדִיפָא, דְּאָמַר מַר, עֲנָוָה גְּדוֹלָה מִכֻּלָּן, שֶׁלֹּא לִשְׁמָהּ נָמֵי עֲדִיפָא, דְּאָמַר רַב יְהוּדָה אָמַר רַב, לְעוֹלָם יַעֲסֹק אָדָם בַּתּוֹרָה וּבַמִּצְוֹת אֲפִלּוּ שֶׁלֹּא לִשְׁמָהּ, שֶׁמִּתּוֹךְ שֶׁלֹּא לִשְׁמָהּ בָּא לִשְׁמָהּ."

- וּמִמֵּילָא נִשְׁמַע, דִּכְוָתָהּ נָמֵי בְּעֵסֶק הַתּוֹרָה, מִי לֹא מוֹדֵית דְּתוֹרָה לִשְׁמָהּ וַדַּאי דַּעֲדִיפָא מִמִּצְוֹת לִשְׁמָהּ, שֶׁהֲרֵי מִשְׁנָה שְׁלֵמָה שָׁנִינוּ (פאה א׳) "וְתַלְמוּד תּוֹרָה כְּנֶגֶד כֻּלָּם".

- וְכֵן חִלְּקוּ רַבּוֹתֵינוּ זִכְרוֹנָם לִבְרָכָה (סוטה כ״א) בְּיִתְרוֹן עֵרֶךְ מַעֲלַת הַתּוֹרָה עַל הַמִּצְוֹת

- שֶׁזְּכוּת וְאוֹר הַמִּצְוֹת בֵּין בְּעִדָּנָא דְעָסִיק בָּהּ וּבֵין בְּעִדָּנָא דְלֹא עָסִיק בָּהּ, הִיא רַק מַגְנָה מִן הַיִּסּוּרִין וְאֵינָהּ מַצֶּלֶת אֶת הָאָדָם שֶׁלֹּא יָבֹא לִידֵי חֵטְא

- אֲבָל אוֹר הַתּוֹרָה, גַּם לְפִי הַמַּסְקָנָא שָׁם, עַל כָּל פָּנִים בְּעִדָּנָא דְעָסִיק בָּהּ גַּם הִיא מַצֶּלֶת אוֹתוֹ מֵחֵטְא.

- וְאָמְרוּ בִּירוּשַׁלְמִי פֶּרֶק א׳ דְּפֵאָה שֶׁכָּל הַמִּצְוֹת אֵינָן שָׁוִין לְדָבָר אֶחָד מִן הַתּוֹרָה, וּכְמוֹ שֶׁיִּתְבָּאֵר לְהַלָּן אי״ה בְּשַׁעַר ד׳ בְּזֶה.

- אִם כֵּן, גַּם עֵסֶק הַתּוֹרָה שֶׁלֹּא לִשְׁמָהּ נָמֵי עֲדִיפָא מִמִּצְוֹת לִשְׁמָהּ, מִזֶּה הַטַּעַם עַצְמוֹ, שֶׁמִּתּוֹךְ שֶׁלֹּא לִשְׁמָהּ בָּא לִשְׁמָהּ:

---

23 Mishna Peah 1:1.
24 Sotah 21a.
25 Yerushalmi Peah Chap. 1 Halacha 1.
26 See G4:30.

3. ENCOURAGE ANY TORAH STUDY – WRONG REASONS LEAD TO RIGHT REASONS

- In addition, when initially setting one's study schedule, it is true that it is virtually impossible to immediately reach the appropriate level of [Torah study] *for its sake*
    - as studying Torah which is not *for its sake* is a pre-requisite level which enables the level of *for its sake* to be reached
    - and therefore [this Torah study which is not *for its sake*], is also beloved before God
    - just as it is impossible to ascend from the floor to the attic without ascending the rungs of a ladder.
- This is why Chazal say "a person should *always* involve himself with Torah and Mitzvot even if not for their sake."[27] "Always" here means "regularly," as when one begins to study one is only obligated to regularly study each day and every night.
- Even if at times [during Torah study and Mitzvah performance], one will certainly have self-serving thoughts of haughtiness and [of seeking] honor and the like
    - nevertheless, one should not set one's heart to separate from or weaken [one's study effort] because of this, God forbid
    - on the contrary, one should greatly strengthen one's Torah study involvement with the confidence that through this, one will certainly reach the level of [Torah study] *for its sake*.
    - This approach is also similarly the case with Mitzvah performance.
- One who sees fit to despise and to denigrate an individual involved in Torah study and Mitzvah performance which are not *for their sake*, God forbid
    - 'will not be cleansed of evil'[28]
    - and will in the future [world] be judged unfavorably for this, God forbid
    - and not only this but is counted by Chazal among those who have no portion in the World to Come at all, God forbid, and those for whom the experience of Gehinom does not cease [as they are included in the category] of apostates, informers, and non-believers.[29]
    - Similarly, Chazal list non-believers within the category of those who do not have a portion in the future world.[30]

---

27   Pesachim 50b.
28   Mishlei 11:21.
29   R. Chaim directly quotes from Rosh Hashana 17a. See also Sanhedrin 99b.

פרקים - פרק ג׳

- וְגַם כִּי בֶּאֱמֶת כִּמְעַט בִּלְתִּי אֶפְשָׁר לָבֹא תֵּכֶף בִּתְחִלַּת קְבִיעַת לִמּוּדוֹ לְמַדְרֵגַת לִשְׁמָהּ כָּרָאוּי
  - כִּי הָעֶסֶק בַּתּוֹרָה שֶׁלֹּא לִשְׁמָהּ, הוּא לְמַדְרֵגָה שֶׁמִּתּוֹךְ כָּךְ יוּכַל לָבֹא לְמַדְרֵגַת לִשְׁמָהּ
  - וְלָכֵן גַּם הוּא אָהוּב לְפָנָיו יִתְבָּרֵךְ
  - כְּמוֹ שֶׁבִּלְתִּי אֶפְשָׁר לַעֲלוֹת מֵהָאָרֶץ לַעֲלִיָּה אִם לֹא דֶּרֶךְ מַדְרֵגוֹת הַסֻּלָּם:
- וְלָזֶה אָמְרוּ (פסחים נ׳ ע״ב) "לְעוֹלָם יַעֲסֹק אָדָם בַּתּוֹרָה וּבַמִּצְוֹת אֲפִלּוּ שֶׁלֹּא לִשְׁמָהּ". אָמְרָם "לְעוֹלָם" רוֹצֶה לוֹמַר, בִּקְבִיעוּת, הַיְנוּ שֶׁבִּתְחִלַּת לִמּוּדוֹ אֵינוֹ מְחֻיָּב רַק שֶׁיִּלְמַד בִּקְבִיעוּת תָּמִיד יוֹמָם וָלַיְלָה.
- וְאַף אִם לִפְעָמִים וַדַּאי יִפֹּל בְּמַחֲשַׁבְתּוֹ אֵיזֶה פְּנִיָּה לְגַרְמֵיהּ, לָשׂוּם גֵּאוּת וְכָבוֹד וְכַיּוֹצֵא
  - עִם כָּל זֶה אַל יָשִׂים לֵב לִפְרֹשׁ אוֹ לְהִתְרַפּוֹת מִמֶּנָּה בַּעֲבוּר זֶה חַס וְשָׁלוֹם
  - אֶלָּא אַדְּרַבָּה, יִתְחַזֵּק מְאֹד בְּעֵסֶק הַתּוֹרָה, וִיהֵא נָכוֹן לִבּוֹ בָּטוּחַ שֶׁוַּדַּאי יָבֹא מִתּוֹךְ כָּךְ לְמַדְרֵגַת לִשְׁמָהּ.
  - וְכֵן הוּא גַּם כֵּן בְּעִנְיַן הַמִּצְוֹת עַל דֶּרֶךְ זֶה:
- וּמִי שֶׁיִּמָּלְאוֹ לִבּוֹ לָבוּז וּלְהַשְׁפִּיל חַס וְשָׁלוֹם אֶת הָעוֹסֵק בַּתּוֹרָה וּמִצְוֹת אַף שֶׁלֹּא לִשְׁמָהּ
  - לֹא יִנָּקֶה רַע
  - וְעָתִיד לִתֵּן אֶת הַדִּין חַס וְשָׁלוֹם.
- וְלֹא עוֹד אֶלָּא שֶׁנִּמְנָה בְּדִבְרֵי רַבּוֹתֵינוּ זִכְרוֹנָם לִבְרָכָה (בברייתא ראש השנה י״ז, א) בֵּין אוֹתָם שֶׁאֵין לָהֶם חֵלֶק לָעוֹלָם הַבָּא לְגַמְרֵי חַס וְשָׁלוֹם, וְגֵיהִנָּם כָּלָה וְהֵם אֵינָם כָּלִין, וְהֵם הַמִּינִין וְהַמְּסוֹרוֹת וְהָאֶפִּיקוֹרְסִין.
  - וְכֵן בַּמִּשְׁנָה רֵישׁ פֶּרֶק חֵלֶק מָנוּ אֶת הָאֶפִּיקוֹרְסִים בִּכְלַל אוֹתָן שֶׁאֵין לָהֶם חֵלֶק לָעוֹלָם הַבָּא

It should be noted that the words "apostates" and "informers" (which are included in the text of Rosh Hashana 17a) only appear in the First Edition. These two words were removed in the Second Edition most likely due to censorship.

30 Sanhedrin 90a, in the Mishna.

○ This is followed by the comments: Rav and R. Chanina both say that this relates to one who despises a Torah Sage, R. Yochanan and R. Yehoshua ben Levi both say that even one who despises his colleague in the presence of a Torah Sage is also [considered to be] a non-believer ... and even one who says "what use are the Rabbis to us as they study Scripture for their benefit and they study the Oral Law for their benefit" is also included in the category of non-believers who despise the Torah Sages and also the category of one who acts insolently towards Torah God forbid.[31]
  ○ Such [a person] loses his portion in the World to Come, Heaven save us.
○ Similarly, R. Yona[32] lists the sequence of levels of severity of punishment
  ○ and lists the last level as the group about which Chazal say that they do not have a portion in the World to Come
  ○ and he also includes there one who despises a Torah Sage in this group.
○ Similarly, R. Chaim Vital also lists [such a person] as being a member of this group.[33]

---

31 Sanhedrin 99b.
32 Sefer Shaarei Teshuva Shaar 3:147 as follows:
  • That which Chazal say "One who despises a Torah Sage, he despises the word of God and has no portion in the World to Come" (Sanhedrin 99b) has a logical reason which will now be explained: Shlomo said "The wise inherit honor and fools generate disgrace" (Mishlei 3:35). The idea of "disgrace," means a "person of disgrace." Similarly, "and I am prayer" (Tehillim 109:4), means a "person of prayer." "Sit among deviousness," means "among devious people." Meaning: A lowly person raises the profile of fools, honors, and praises them, for there is great purpose in the praise of the wise and the straight and great pitfalls in the honor of fools and the wicked. For when praising the wise and raising their profile, these words are heard, all the people will join and copy in their counsel. Secondly, when people see all of their honor, they will take a lesson from this to try to acquire this honor, and knowledge will thereby increase, as Chazal say "a person should *always* involve himself with Torah and Mitzvot even if not for their sake as involvement which is not for their sake will lead to involvement for their sake" (Pesachim 50b). Thirdly, many who are asleep/disengaged, will wake up when they see the honor given to Torah and will recognize its value, they will be instilled with a desire for it and they will involve themselves to raise its profile and serve God wholeheartedly.
  Sefer Shaarei Teshuva Shaar 3:148 as follows:
  • These are notable reasons which are 'as strong as a cast mirror' (expression

נפש פרקים - פרק ג' החיים

- וְאָמְרִינָן בַּגְּמָרָא שָׁם (צ"ט ב'), "רַב וְרַבִּי חֲנִינָא דְּאָמְרֵי תַּרְוַיְיהוּ זֶה הַמְבַזֶּה תַּלְמִיד חָכָם, רַבִּי יוֹחָנָן וריב"ל אָמְרֵי שֶׁאֲפִילוּ הַמְבַזֶּה חֲבֵרוֹ בִּפְנֵי תַּלְמִיד חָכָם נָמֵי אֶפִּיקוֹרוֹס הֲוֵי", וְאַף אִם אוֹמֵר, "מַאי אַהֲנִי לָן רַבָּנָן, לְדִידְהוּ קָרוּ, לְדִידְהוּ תָּנוּ", הֲרֵי זֶה בִּכְלַל אֶפִּיקוֹרוֹס מְבַזֶּה תַּלְמִידֵי חֲכָמִים, וְגַם מְגַלֶּה פָּנִים בַּתּוֹרָה נָמֵי מִקְּרֵי חַס וְשָׁלוֹם

- וַהֲרֵי זֶה אִבֵּד חֶלְקוֹ בְּחַיֵּי עוֹלָם, הָרַחֲמָן יַצִּילֵנוּ.

- וְכֵן הָרַבֵּינוּ יוֹנָה זִכְרוֹנוֹ לִבְרָכָה בְּשַׁעַר הַתְּשׁוּבָה, שֶׁמָּנָה סֵדֶר מַדְרֵגוֹת חֹמֶר הָעֳנָשִׁים

- וּמַדְרֵגָה הָאַחֲרוֹנָה מָנָה אֶת הַכַּת שֶׁאָמְרוּ רַבּוֹתֵינוּ זִכְרוֹנָם לִבְרָכָה עֲלֵיהֶם שֶׁאֵין לָהֶם חֵלֶק לָעוֹלָם הַבָּא

- וּמָנָה גַם כֵּן שָׁם הַמְבַזֶּה תַּלְמִיד חָכָם בִּכְלַל זֹאת הַכַּת.

- וְכֵן מָנָה אוֹתוֹ הרח"ו זִכְרוֹנוֹ לִבְרָכָה בְּשַׁעַר הַקְּדֻשָּׁה בִּכְלַל אוֹתָהּ הַכַּת.

---

borrowed from Iyov 37:18). There is another reason which is even more notable than all of them and it was hinted to at the beginning of our words in respect of the evil groups mentioned. For, as is known, it is the way of sanctifying God with all speech, hinting, and action that the purpose of man is to serve God and to fear Him and His Torah, as written "this is all of man" (Kohelet 12:13). This gives honor to God. Those who despise a Torah Sage and his fear of Him, nullify this idea and demonstrate the opposite with their actions and is as if they are saying that this service is not key, and the root of the matter is not found in the service of God and they profane the Torah. Therefore, they are to be lost from the midst of the community and destroyed with their words – for they serve God without involvement in Torah.

33 R. Chaim Vital in Sefer Shaarei Kedushah Part Two Gate Eight:
- Above this are those who have no part in the future world at all. Where Gehinom ceases [for others] but will not for them – even though they have the merit of Torah study and good deeds – if they died without repenting like Doeg HaEdomi the *chief shepherd* [i.e., the Head of the Bet Din]. These are they . . . and the Non-believer – this is one who despises a Torah Sage in front of him and similarly, a student who sits in front of his teacher and states if something is forbidden or permitted without framing it as a question and similarly, one who mocks his teacher when told an exaggeration which he does not believe. Similarly, one who despises a Torah Sage when not in front of him like those who disparagingly say "those Rabbis . . ." or like those who say what use are the Rabbis to us as they study Scripture for their benefit and they study the Oral Law for their benefit . . .

- The severity of this awesome punishment is because this [person] degrades the light of the value of the Holy Torah and profanes it,[34] God forbid, as R. Yona details this at length there, refer to his holy words there.
  - (He writes there that the main punishment of all those listed in that group is also just because of the profaning of the honor of the Holy Torah, Heaven save us.)
- Since [this person] denigrates and despises the one who studies Torah but not *for its sake*
  - he causes [the one involved] to weaken his Torah study
  - preventing him from ever achieving the level of *for its sake* and becoming a fully-fledged Torah Sage.
  - [Such a person] is certainly called one who despises a Torah Sage and there is no greater desecration of God's Name and His Holy Torah.
  - [This person] has already dragged down the preciousness of the Holy Torah to the ground reaching to the dust, and also destroyed all of the associated service of God, God forbid
  - for God's service will not be properly maintained in the Community of Israel without the Torah Sages who are involved day and night in Torah study
  - for the eyes of all of Israel are focused on them to know what should be done in Israel, to teach them the way forward and what actions should be done.
  - Therefore, the person who causes that there are no Torah Sages to be found in Israel has already also completely destroyed His service
  - for the Community of Israel will be left without Torah and without a teacher and they will not be aware of how they may fall, God forbid.
  - R. Yona also wrote along these lines there, refer there.[35]
- Therefore, on the contrary, you must be careful to honor and to use all your strength to raise the profile of all who involve themselves with and support God's Torah – even if not *for its sake* – so that 'the righteous should stick to his path'[36] without veering from it, God forbid – enabling him to reach to a level of *for its sake*.
- Even if it appears that through the entirety of a person's life
  - from his youth until old age that his Torah study was never *for its sake*

---

34 "Chilela," lit. "empties it," i.e., empties the presence of God from this world in respect of it as per G3:08.

35 See quotations from Shaarei Teshuva on p. 594, fn. 32.

○ וְכָל חֹמֶר עָנְשׁוֹ הַנּוֹרָא הַזֶּה, הוּא מִטַּעַם עַל שֶׁהוּא בְּמוֹרִידֵי אוֹר מַעֲלַת הַתּוֹרָה הַקְּדוֹשָׁה, וְחָלִילָה חַס וְשָׁלוֹם, כְּמוֹ שֶׁהֶאֱרִיךְ בָּזֶה הָרַבֵּנוּ יוֹנָה זִכְרוֹנוֹ לִבְרָכָה שָׁם, עַיֵּן שָׁם דִּבְרֵי קָדוֹשׁ ה'

□ (וְכָתַב הוּא ז"ל שָׁם, שֶׁגַּם עִקַּר הָעֹנֶשׁ שֶׁל כָּל הַמְּנוּיִים שָׁם בְּאוֹתָהּ הַכַּת, הוּא גַם כֵּן רַק מִפְּנֵי חִלּוּל כְּבוֹד הַתּוֹרָה הַקְּדוֹשָׁה רַחֲמָנָא לִיצְלָן).

○ כִּי כֵּיוָן שֶׁהוּא מַשְׁפִּיל וּמְבַזֶּה אֶת הָעוֹסֵק בַּתּוֹרָה שֶׁלֹּא לִשְׁמָהּ

□ הֲרֵי הוּא מְרַפֶּה אֶת יָדָיו מֵעֵסֶק הַתּוֹרָה

□ וְלֹא יוּכַל לָבֹא לְעוֹלָם לְמַדְרֵגַת לִשְׁמָהּ לִהְיוֹת תַּלְמִיד חָכָם גָּמוּר

□ וַהֲרֵי וַדַּאי מִקְרֵי בָּזֶה מְבַזֶּה תַּלְמִיד חָכָם, וְאֵין לְךָ חִלּוּל שְׁמוֹ יִתְבָּרַךְ וְתוֹרָתוֹ הַקְּדוֹשָׁה יוֹתֵר מִזֶּה.

□ וּכְבָר הִשְׁפִּיל וְהוֹרִיד אֶת יְקַר תִּפְאַרְתָּהּ שֶׁל הַתּוֹרָה הַקְּדוֹשָׁה לָאָרֶץ יַגִּיעֶנָּה עַד עָפָר, וְהָרַס גַּם אֶת כָּל הָעֲבוֹדָה בִּכְלָלָהּ חַס וְשָׁלוֹם

□ כִּי אֵין עֲבוֹדָתוֹ יִתְבָּרַךְ מִתְקַיֶּמֶת כָּרָאוּי בַּעֲדַת יִשְׂרָאֵל בִּלְתִּי עַל יְדֵי הַתַּלְמִידֵי חֲכָמִים עוֹסְקֵי הַתּוֹרָה הַקְּדוֹשָׁה יוֹמָם וָלַיְלָה

□ כִּי עֵינֵי כָּל יִשְׂרָאֵל עֲלֵיהֶם לָדַעַת מַה יַּעֲשֶׂה בְּיִשְׂרָאֵל, לְהוֹרוֹת לָהֶם הַדֶּרֶךְ יֵלְכוּ בָהּ, וְאֶת הַמַּעֲשֶׂה אֲשֶׁר יַעֲשׂוּן.

□ אִם כֵּן, הָאִישׁ אֲשֶׁר יָבֹא לִגְרֹם שֶׁלֹּא יִהְיוּ תַּלְמִידֵי חֲכָמִים מְצוּיִים בְּיִשְׂרָאֵל, הֲרֵי כְּבָר הָרַס גַּם כְּלַל עֲבוֹדָתוֹ יִתְבָּרַךְ לְגַמְרֵי

□ כִּי יִשָּׁאֲרוּ עֲדַת יִשְׂרָאֵל חַס וְשָׁלוֹם לְלֹא תוֹרָה וּלְלֹא מוֹרֶה, וְלֹא יֵדְעוּ בַּמֶּה יִכָּשְׁלוּ חַס וְשָׁלוֹם.

○ וּכְעִנְיָן זֶה כָּתַב גַּם כֵּן רַבֵּנוּ יוֹנָה זִכְרוֹנוֹ לִבְרָכָה שָׁם, עַיֵּן שָׁם:

● לָזֹאת, אַתָּה צָרִיךְ לִיזָּהֵר אַדְּרַבָּה, לְכַבֵּד וּלְהַגְבִּיהַּ בְּכָל אֲשֶׁר בְּכֹחֲךָ אֶת כָּל הָעוֹסֵק וּמַחֲזִיק בְּתוֹרַת ה', אֲפִלּוּ שֶׁלֹּא לִשְׁמָהּ, כְּדֵי שֶׁיֹּאחֵז צַדִּיק דַּרְכּוֹ בַּל יִתְרַפֶּה מִמֶּנָּה חַס וְשָׁלוֹם, כְּדֵי שֶׁיּוּכַל לָבֹא מִמֶּנָּה לְמַדְרֵגַת לִשְׁמָהּ:

● וְגַם אִם נִרְאֶה, שֶׁכָּל יְמֵי חַיָּיו

○ מִנְּעוּרָיו וְעַד זִקְנָה וְשֵׂיבָה הָיָה עִסְקוֹ בָּהּ שֶׁלֹּא לִשְׁמָהּ

---

36 Iyov 17:9.

- you are still obligated to give him respect and how much more so not to despise him, God forbid
- as since he was continuously studying God's Torah, there is no doubt that on many occasions his intentions were *for its sake*
- as Chazal promise that "involvement which is not *for its sake* will lead to involvement *for its sake*"[37]
- this does not mean that one reaches a level of *for its sake* and thereafter always maintains this level of *for its sake* for the rest of his days
- but rather that each time he studies Torah continuously for a number of hours at fixed times
- even though his intention may not have generally been *for its sake* [throughout the duration of the study]
- nevertheless, it is virtually impossible for there not to have been at the very least momentary periods of correct intention *for its sake*
- and with this, all that he had learned so far which was not *for its sake* will be sanctified and purified through that momentary period where the intention was *for its sake*.

4. EVIL INCLINATION DISGUISED AS NOBLE DESTROYS SELF AND TORAH

- One must be particularly vigilant with these issues[38] and those similar to them
  - as Chazal state: "One who is greater than his colleague also has a greater Evil Inclination than him"[39]
  - as one's Evil Inclination deviously pitches itself against each person according to who he is, his level of Torah involvement and service of God.
  - For if [the Evil Inclination] sees, that according to the high level of a person
    - if it counsels that [the person] should leave his place and level to perform a severe or minor intentional or unintentional sin[40] – [the person] will not consent
    - [therefore] it disguises itself to present itself to the person as the Good Inclination
    - to blind his intellect, to inject poison
    - and to specifically use the very way and level that the person cleaves to, to cause him to err

---

37 Pesachim 50b.
38 I.e., in one's evaluation of the motivation of others.

○ גַּם כֵּן אַתָּה חַיָּב לִנְהֹג בּוֹ כָּבוֹד, וְכָל שֶׁכֵּן שֶׁלֹּא לְבַזּוֹתוֹ חַס וְשָׁלוֹם

○ שֶׁכֵּיוָן שֶׁעָסַק בְּתוֹרַת ה' בִּתְמִידוּת, בִּלְתִּי סָפֵק שֶׁהָיָה כַּוָּנָתוֹ פְּעָמִים רַבּוֹת גַּם לִשְׁמָהּ

○ כְּמוֹ שֶׁהִבְטִיחוּ רַבּוֹתֵינוּ זִכְרוֹנָם לִבְרָכָה (פסחים נ:) שֶׁמִּתּוֹךְ שֶׁלֹּא לִשְׁמָהּ בָּא לִשְׁמָהּ

○ כִּי אֵין הַפֵּרוּשׁ דַּוְקָא שֶׁיָּבֹא מִזֶּה לִשְׁמָהּ, עַד שֶׁאַחַר כָּךְ יַעֲסֹק בָּהּ תָּמִיד כָּל יָמָיו רַק לִשְׁמָהּ.

○ אֶלָּא הַיְנוּ, שֶׁבְּכָל פַּעַם שֶׁהוּא לוֹמֵד בִּקְבִיעוּת זְמַן כַּמָּה שָׁעוֹת רְצוּפִים

○ אַף שֶׁדֶּרֶךְ כְּלָל הָיְתָה כַּוָּנָתוֹ שֶׁלֹּא לִשְׁמָהּ

○ עִם כָּל זֶה, בִּלְתִּי אֶפְשָׁר כְּלָל שֶׁלֹּא יִכָּנֵס בְּלִבּוֹ בְּאֶמְצַע הַלִּמּוּד עַל כָּל פָּנִים זְמַן מְעַט כַּוָּנָה רְצוּיָה לִשְׁמָהּ

○ וּמֵעַתָּה כָּל מַה שֶּׁלָּמַד עַד הֵנָּה שֶׁלֹּא לִשְׁמָהּ, נִתְקַדֵּשׁ וְנִטְהַר עַל יְדֵי אוֹתוֹ הָעֵת קָטָן שֶׁכִּוֵּן בּוֹ לִשְׁמָהּ:

פרקים - פרק ד'

• וְכַמָּה זְהִירוּת יְתֵרוֹת צָרִיךְ הָאָדָם לְהִזָּהֵר בְּעִנְיָנִים כָּאֵלּוּ וְשֶׁכַּיּוֹצֵא בָּהֶם.

○ וּכְבָר אָמְרוּ רַבּוֹתֵינוּ זִכְרוֹנָם לִבְרָכָה (סוכה נ"ב א'), "כָּל הַגָּדוֹל מֵחֲבֵרוֹ יִצְרוֹ גָּדוֹל הֵימֶנּוּ"

○ כִּי הַיֵּצֶר מִתְהַפֵּךְ בְּתַחְבּוּלוֹתָיו לְכָל אָדָם, כְּפִי עִנְיָנוֹ וּמַדְרֵגָתוֹ בַּתּוֹרָה וַעֲבוֹדָה.

○ שֶׁאִם הוּא רוֹאֶה, שֶׁכְּפִי גֹבַהּ מַדְרֵגָתוֹ שֶׁל הָאָדָם

□ אִם יְשִׁיאֵהוּ שֶׁיַּנִּיחַ מְקוֹמוֹ וּמַדְרֵגָתוֹ לַעֲשׂוֹת בְּפֹעַל אֵיזֶה עָוֹן וְחֵטְא חָמוּר אוֹ קַל, שֶׁלֹּא יֹאבֶה לוֹ

□ הוּא מִתְחַפֵּשׂ לְהִתְדַּמּוֹת אֶל הָאָדָם כְּיֵצֶר טוֹב

□ לְסַמּוֹת שִׂכְלוֹ, לְהָטִיל אֶרֶס

□ וּלְהַטְעוֹתוֹ בְּאוֹתוֹ הָאֹפֶן וְהַמַּדְרֵגָה עַצְמָהּ שֶׁהָאָדָם דָּבוּק בָּהּ

---

39 Sukkah 52a.

40 R. Chaim uses two terms for sin here – "Avon" and "Chet." "Avon" is intentional sin and "Chet" is unintentional sin (Yoma 36b, as quoted in many sources, e.g., Mishna Berura 621:17 and Rashi on Shemot 34:7).

- in that it presents a path that at first glance appears to the person as the advice of the Good Inclination which is instructing him to reach a higher level (Note 49)[41]
- in the way it presents itself with signs of purity
- and the person falls in its net 'like a bird hurrying to the trap'[42] without much thought 'unaware that its life will be lost'[43] and 'her feet lead to death'[44] God forbid.

- Therefore, you must be extremely careful with your life to never be misguided by the Evil Inclination to think that your primary objective is to solely be involved all of your days with the proper purification of your thoughts
  - that your thoughts should cleave to your Creator continuously and unwaveringly
  - and you will not allow anything to steer you away from the purity of your thoughts at any time at all
  - and that everything must be for the sake of Heaven
  - when it says to you that the primary objective of Torah study and Mitzvah performance is specifically when performed with a tremendous fervor and true attachment
  - and that all the while that a person's heart is not entirely performing them with holy concentration and with a cleaving and purity of thought
  - then it is not considered to be the fulfillment of the Mitzvah or service [of God] at all
  - as already taught by the 'old and foolish king'[45] to blind one's eyes
  - and to bring proofs from Scripture, Mishna, Talmud, Midrashim, and Zohar – for example, the concept of "God wants the focus of one's heart,"[46] and many similar examples of such proofs.
- So if you merit a wise outlook according to a Torah perspective, you will understand and find that the whole objective [of the Evil Inclination]
  - is to show a person that its 'hooves have signs of purity'[47]
  - and that its way is one of holiness
  - [resulting in] 'his feet leading to death,'[48] Heaven save us.

---

41 **R. Chaim adds Note 49 here.** This note is brought at the end of this chapter and is entitled "Good Inclination on right, Evil Inclination jumps from left to right."
42 Mishlei 7:23.
43 Continuation of Mishlei 7:23.
44 Mishlei 5:5.
45 Kohelet 4:13. Rashi explains this phrase to refer to the Evil Inclination which

□ שֶׁמַּרְאֶה לוֹ בָּהּ אֵיזֶה דֶּרֶךְ, הַנִּרְאֶה לְהָאָדָם בְּהַשְׁקָפָה רִאשׁוֹנָה שֶׁהוּא עֲצַת יִצְרוֹ הַטּוֹב, לְהַדְרִיכוֹ בְּדֶרֶךְ יוֹתֵר גָּבוֹהַּ, (הגהה מ"ט)

□ כְּפִי שֶׁמַּרְאֶה לוֹ בָּהּ פָּנִים וְסִימָנֵי טָהֳרָה

□ וְהָאָדָם נוֹפֵל בְּרִשְׁתּוֹ כְּמַהֵר צִפּוֹר אֶל פָּח בְּלִי הִתְבּוֹנְנוּת רַב, וְלֹא יֵדַע כִּי בְנַפְשׁוֹ הוּא וְרַגְלֶיהָ יוֹרְדוֹת מָוֶת חַס וְשָׁלוֹם:

• לָזֹאת, הִזָּהֵר בְּנַפְשְׁךָ מְאֹד, שְׁאַל יָשִׂיאֲךָ יִצְרְךָ לֵאמֹר, שֶׁעִקַּר הַכֹּל תִּרְאֶה שֶׁתְּהֵא אַךְ עָסוּק כָּל יָמֶיךָ לְטַהֵר מַחְשַׁבְתְּךָ כָּרָאוּי

○ שֶׁתְּהֵא דְבֵקוּת מַחְשַׁבְתְּךָ בְּבוֹרְאֲךָ בִּתְמִידוּת בַּל תִּמּוֹט

○ וְלֹא תָשׁוּב מִפְּנֵי כֹל לְהַנִּיחַ טֹהַר מַחְשַׁבְתְּךָ בְּשׁוּם עֵת כְּלָל

○ וְהַכֹּל לְשֵׁם שָׁמַיִם

○ בְּאָמְרָם לְךָ שֶׁכָּל עִקַּר תּוֹרָה וּמִצְוֹת הֵמָּה דַּוְקָא כְּשֶׁהֵם בְּכַוָּנָה עֲצוּמָה וּבִדְבֵקוּת אֲמִתִּי

○ וְכָל זְמַן שֶׁאֵין לֵב הָאָדָם מָלֵא לַעֲשׂוֹתָם בְּכַוָּנָה קְדוֹשָׁה וּבִדְבֵקוּת וְטָהֳרַת הַמַּחְשָׁבָה

○ אֵינָהּ נֶחְשֶׁבֶת לְמִצְוָה וַעֲבוֹדָה כְּלָל

○ כַּאֲשֶׁר כְּבָר לָמַד הַמֶּלֶךְ זָקֵן וּכְסִיל, לְסַמּוֹת עֵינַיִם

○ וּלְהָבִיא רְאָיוֹתָיו מִמִּקְרָא וּמִשְׁנָה וְתַלְמוּד וּמִדְרָשִׁים וְסֵפֶר הַזֹּהַר, כְּעִנְיָן "רַחֲמָנָא לִבָּא בָּעֵי" (סנהדרין קו:) וְכָהֵנָּה רַבּוֹת עִמּוֹ חֲבִילוֹת רְאָיוֹת:

• אָמְנָם אִם תִּזְכֶּה לְהַבְחִין בְּעֵינֵי שֵׂכֶל עַל פִּי הַתּוֹרָה, תָּבִין וְתִמְצָא, שֶׁזֶּה כָּל עִנְיָנוֹ

○ לְהַרְאוֹת לְהָאָדָם טְלָפָיו בְּסִימָנֵי טָהֳרָה

○ שֶׁדַּרְכּוֹ בַּקֹּדֶשׁ

○ וְרַגְלָיו יוֹרְדוֹת מָוֶת רַחֲמָנָא לִצְלָן:

---

has been with a person from birth as opposed to the Good Inclination which joins a person from Bar/Bat Mitzvah, and therefore it is old.

46 Sanhedrin 106b.

47 This is a reference to the pig which is the only non-kosher animal which has split hooves but does not chew the cud (whereas all other non-kosher animals do not have split hooves). A pig is therefore the only animal which is not externally visibly non-kosher and tends to stretch its hooves as if to say "look at me, I am kosher." Chazal therefore use the pig as the analogy of one masquerading piety, e.g., Midrash Tehillim 80:6.

48 As above, an expression based on Mishlei 5:5.

- Now, see its ways and also be wise of it
  - how [the Evil Inclination] is wise to do bad in a way which looks like it is good.
  - Today it says to you that all Torah study and Mitzvah performance without cleaving [to God] is of no value at all
  - and therefore you must prepare the heart and raise the level of your thoughts before the performance of any Mitzvah or prayer to be the purest of pure
  - to the extent that you are so involved in the preparation of the Mitzvah that the time frame within which the Mitzvah or prayer is obliged to be performed, passes by
  - and it convinces you that each prayer or Mitzvah that is done with tremendous fervor in holiness and purity – even if not at its correct time – is more precious than the performance of the Mitzvah at its correct time without associated fervor.
  - Once your Evil Inclination makes you accustomed to set your heart to not be concerned with changing the time of [correct] performance of a Mitzvah or prayer
    - initially as a result of the fixation of your thoughts on the purification and refinement of the heart
    - then over the course of time, it will gradually direct you with the 'glibness of its lips'[49] from level to level without you noticing at all
    - to the extent that inevitably the missing of the correct time for Mitzvah performance and prayer becomes something which you view as permitted
    - and even to the extent that you turn your heart to idleness and mindless things, and are pushed aside from everything, and you will be left with neither the act of Mitzvah performance in its proper time nor the [appropriate associated] good thoughts.
- This [process] will also result in the destruction of all of Torah in general, the Merciful One should save us – if, God forbid, we permit it to sway the ear with the glibness of its tongue in this way. Check yourself, for example:
  - If one invests so much focus in thinking appropriate thoughts about eating the olive quantity of Matzah on Seder Night, that it should be eaten with the appropriate holiness, purity, and attachment, such that this preparation extends through the whole course of the night until it reaches to after dawn or sunrise, then the whole act of thought purity becomes 'rejected – it shall not be accepted'![50]
  - [In contrast] one who eats the olive quantity of Matzah at the proper

- וְעַתָּה רְאֵה דְרָכָיו וַחֲכַם גַּם בָּזֶה
  - אֵיךְ שֶׁהוּא חָכָם לְהָרַע מֵעֵין טוֹב
  - הַיּוֹם יֹאמַר לְךָ, שֶׁכָּל תּוֹרָה וּמִצְוָה שֶׁבְּלֹא דְבֵקוּת אֵינֶנָּה כְּלוּם
  - וְצָרִיךְ אַתָּה לְהָכִין לֵב, וּלְהַגְבִּיהַּ עוֹף מַחֲשַׁבְתְּךָ, קֹדֶם עֲשִׂיַּת כָּל מִצְוָה אוֹ תְּפִלָּה, לְמַחֲשָׁבָה טְהוֹרָה שֶׁבַּטְּהוֹרוֹת.
  - וּכְמוֹ כֵן תְּהֵא מַחֲשַׁבְתְּךָ טְרוּדָה בַּהֲכָנַת הַמִּצְוָה טֶרֶם עֲשׂוֹתָהּ עַד שֶׁיַּעֲבֹר זְמַן הַמִּצְוָה אוֹ הַתְּפִלָּה.
  - וְיֵרָאֶה לְךָ פָּנִים, שֶׁכָּל תְּפִלָּה אוֹ מִצְוָה שֶׁנַּעֲשֵׂית בְּכַוָּנָה עֲצוּמָה בִּקְדֻשָּׁה וּבְטָהֳרָה אַף שֶׁלֹּא בִּזְמַנָּהּ, הֲרֵי הִיא יְקָרָה מִקִּיּוּם הַמִּצְוָה בִּזְמַנָּהּ וְשֶׁלֹּא בְּכַוָּנָה.
  - וּכְשֶׁרְגִילְךָ יִצְרְךָ שֶׁיִּקְבַּע בִּלְבַדְךָ שֶׁלֹּא לָחוּשׁ כָּל כָּךְ לְשִׁנּוּי קְבִיעוּת זְמַן שֶׁל אֵיזֶה מִצְוָה אוֹ תְּפִלָּה
    - מֵחֲמַת קְבִיעוּת מַחֲשַׁבְתְּךָ לְהִטָּהֵר וּלְפַנּוֹת הַלֵּב תְּחִלָּה
    - בְּהֶמְשֵׁךְ הַזְּמַן יַדְרִיכְךָ לְאַט לְאַט, בְּחֵלֶק שְׂפָתָיו, מִמַּדְרֵגָה לְמַדְרֵגָה, וְלֹא תַרְגִּישׁ כְּלָל
    - עַד שֶׁמִּמֵּילָא יְהֵא לְךָ כְּהֶתֵּר לְהַעֲבִיר מוֹעֵד הַתְּפִלָּה אוֹ הַמִּצְוֹת
    - אַף גַּם שֶׁתִּפָּנֶה לְבַדְּךָ לְבַטָּלָה בִּדְבָרִים בְּטֵלִים, וְיָדֶיךָ מִכֹּל, וְלֹא יִשָּׁאֵר לְךָ, לֹא מַעֲשֵׂה מִצְוָה בִּזְמַנָּהּ וְלֹא מַחֲשָׁבָה טוֹבָה:
- וְגַם, הֲרֵי הוּא הֲרִיסַת כָּל הַתּוֹרָה בִּכְלָלָהּ רַחֲמָנָא לִצְלָן, אִם חַס וְשָׁלוֹם נֹאבֶה לוֹ לְהַטּוֹת אֹזֶן לְחֵלֶק שְׂפָתָיו בְּדַרְכּוֹ זֶה. וְהַגַּע עַצְמְךָ, כְּגוֹן
  - אִם יַטְרִיד אָדָם עַצְמוֹ לַיְלָה הָרִאשׁוֹנָה שֶׁל פֶּסַח בְּכַוָּנַת אֲכִילַת כְּזַיִת מַצָּה, שֶׁתְּהֵא הָאֲכִילָה בִּקְדֻשָּׁה וְטָהֳרָה וּדְבֵקוּת, וְיַמְשִׁיךְ הַהֲכָנָה כָּל הַלַּיְלָה, עַד שֶׁיִּמָּשֵׁךְ זְמַן הָאֲכִילָה עַד לְאַחַר שֶׁעָלָה הַשַּׁחַר, אוֹ לְאַחַר נֵץ הַחַמָּה, הֲרֵי כָּל טָהֳרַת מַחֲשַׁבְתּוֹ פִּגּוּל הוּא לֹא יֵרָצֶה.
  - וּמִי שֶׁאָכַל הַכְּזַיִת מַצָּה בִּזְמַנָּהּ אַף בְּלֹא קְדֻשָּׁה וְטָהֳרָה יְתֵרָה, הֲרֵי קִיֵּם מִצְוַת עֲשֵׂה הַכְּתוּבָה בַּתּוֹרָה, וְתָבֹא עָלָיו בְּרָכָה.

---

49 Mishlei 7:21.
50 Vayikra 19:7.

time, even without the additional holiness and purity, has fulfilled the positive Mitzvah as written in the Torah and he will be blessed.
- There are many similar examples which if we do not focus our hearts to be sensitive to perform them at their proper time
  - then what difference is there between one who blows Shofar with tremendous fervor on Seder Night instead of performing the Mitzvah of eating the olive quantity of Matzah
  - and one who eats the olive quantity of Matzah on Rosh Hashana, and fasts on the eve of Yom Kippur, and takes a Lulav on Yom Kippur instead of performing the Mitzvah of affliction[51]
  - where then is the place for the Torah!
- Even if [the Evil Inclination] does not succeed in making you stumble by missing the performance time [for a Mitzvah]
  - it will [still] incline you to refine and purify your heart
  - such that it brings you to not have enough time
    - to be particular about the performance of the Mitzvah in the correct way according to the law and with all of its detail
    - and to be careful not to transgress any explicit laws of the Talmud and the Great Rabbis.
- Do not be taken in by the Evil Inclination
  - as it cannot be that one's heavy involvement in purity of thought causes the details of Mitzvah performance to be ignored.
  - You should know that all the while that your heart is drawn towards the [Evil Inclination's] view
  - saying that the essence of the Torah of Man is that all Mitzvah performance and Torah study which is not free of any trace of residue, like fine flour, 'must not be seen or found'[52]
  - the [Evil Inclination] is bribing you and blinding your eyes so that you will not be able to be particular about the performance of the details of the laws and will transgress them, God forbid, and will not be sensitive to them at all.

Rabbi Chaim's Note:
Note 49 – Good Inclination on right, Evil Inclination jumps from left to right

- Perhaps Chazal also hint to this when they say "The Evil Inclination is comparable to a fly and sits between the two gateways of the heart."[53]
- It is known that the place of residence of the Good Inclination is in the right ventricle of the heart and the place of residence of the Evil Inclination in the left ventricle

- וְכַהֲנָה רַבּוֹת, אֲשֶׁר אִם לֹא נָכוֹן לִבֵּנוּ לָחוּשׁ לַעֲשׂוֹת כָּל הַמִּצְוֹת בְּמוֹעֲדָם וּבִזְמַנָּם
  - וְכִי מַאי נַפְקוּתָא בֵּין זֶה לְמִי שֶׁהָיָה תּוֹקֵעַ שׁוֹפָר בְּכַוָּנָה עֲצוּמָה בְּלֵיל רִאשׁוֹן שֶׁל פֶּסַח, בִּמְקוֹם מִצְוַת אֲכִילַת כְּזַיִת מַצָּה
  - וְאוֹכֵל הַכְּזַיִת מַצָּה בְּרֹאשׁ הַשָּׁנָה, וּמִתְעַנֶּה בְּעֶרֶב יוֹם הַכִּפּוּרִים, וּבְיוֹם הַכִּפּוּרִים נוֹטֵל לוּלָב בִּמְקוֹם מִצְוַת עִנּוּי
  - וְאַיֵּה מָקוֹם לַתּוֹרָה:
- וְאַף גַּם זֹאת, אִם לֹא יַכְשִׁילְךָ בְּהַעֲבָרַת הַזְּמַן
  - יָפֶה לִבְּךָ לִפְנוֹתָהּ וּלְטַהֲרָהּ
  - עַד שֶׁיְּבִיאֲךָ שֶׁלֹּא יְהֵא לְךָ פְּנַאי
  - לְדַקְדֵּק שֶׁתְּהֵא עֲשִׂיַּת הַמִּצְוָה בְּאָפְנֶיהָ כַּדִּין בְּכָל פְּרָטֶיהָ
  - וְלִיזָּהֵר מִלַּעֲבֹר עַל דִּינִים מְפֹרָשִׁים בַּתַּלְמוּד וְרַבּוֹתֵינוּ הַגְּדוֹלִים זִכְרוֹנָם לִבְרָכָה:
- וְאַל יַבְטִיחֲךָ יִצְרְךָ
  - שֶׁלֹּא יוּכַל לִהְיוֹת שֶׁמִּצַּד עֵסֶק טָהֳרַת הַמַּחֲשָׁבָה יִגָּרֵם בִּטּוּל פְּרָטֵי הַמַּעֲשֶׂה
  - כִּי תֵּדַע, שֶׁכָּל זְמַן שֶׁלִּבְּךָ יְהֵא מָשׁוּךְ לְדַעְתּוֹ
  - לֵאמֹר, שֶׁכָּל עִקַּר תּוֹרַת הָאָדָם הוּא, שֶׁכָּל מִצְוָה אוֹ לִמּוּד שֶׁאֵינָהּ נְקִיָּה מִכָּל סִיג וּפְסֹלֶת כְּסֹלֶת נְקִיָּה, הֲרֵי הִיא בְּבַל יֵרָאֶה וּבַל יִמָּצֵא
  - הֲרֵי הוּא מְשַׁחֲדֶךָ בָּזֶה וּמְעַוֵּר עֵינֶיךָ, שֶׁלֹּא תּוּכַל לְהַשְׁגִּיחַ עַל כָּל הַפְּרָטֵי מַעֲשִׂים וַהֲלָכוֹת וְדִינִים, שֶׁתִּתְעַבֵּר עֲלֵיהֶם חַס וְשָׁלוֹם וְלֹא תַּרְגִּישׁ בָּהֶם כְּלָל:

הגהה מ"ט

- וְאוּלַי גַּם לָזֶה רָמְזוּ רַבּוֹתֵינוּ זִכְרוֹנָם לִבְרָכָה בְּאָמְרָם (פֶּרֶק הָרוֹאֶה ס"א א') "יֵצֶר הָרָע דּוֹמֶה לִזְבוּב וְיוֹשֵׁב בֵּין שְׁנֵי מִפְתְּחֵי הַלֵּב":
- כִּי יָדוּעַ שֶׁמִּשְׁכַּן הַיֵּצֶר טוֹב בֶּחָלָל הַיְמִינִי שֶׁל הַלֵּב, וּמִשְׁכַּן הַיֵּצֶר הָרָע בֶּחָלָל הַשְּׂמָאלִי

---

51 We are commanded to observe five afflictions on Yom Kippur: No eating, drinking, anointing, marital relations, and wearing leather shoes.
52 Mishna Pesachim 3:3.
53 Berachot 61a.

- as per "the heart of the wise is to his right and the heart of the fool is to his left."[54]
- This is what [Chazal] are saying that the Good Inclination always stays in and recognizes its place on the right as it only ever advises a person out of goodness and truth alone
  - however, the Evil Inclination does not stay in its designated place in the left ventricle to entice open sin and transgression
  - it sometimes also jumps from its place to the right ventricle to appear to the person in the guise of the Good Inclination [as if] to direct him in ways of increased holiness
  - and [the person] is not aware that Evil and bitterness are hidden within it, God forbid.[55]

5. ACTION IS KEY AS PER FIRST AND SECOND GATEWAYS

- It is clear that the [above] approach 'is fire and consumes until destruction,'[56] God forbid, destroying many principles of the Holy Torah and words of Chazal.
- We have already mentioned above, at the end of the First Gateway
  - that *action* is the essential part of all Mitzvot
  - and that purity of thought only complements the *act* of the Mitzvah but [lack of such thought] does not invalidate [the Mitzvah].
  - Refer there.
- Similarly:
  - It is clear to any thinking person 'who walks with honesty'[57] that we have a principle relating to sacrifices that if they are offered up without any specific intention that they are considered to be as if offered for the correct express intention.[58]

---

54 Kohelet 10:2.
55 The Vilna Gaon, in his commentary on Rut on p. 3a of the 1931 Vilna edition, comments as follows:
  - "When [Naomi] saw that [Rut] was determined to go with her, [Naomi] stopped arguing with [Rut]" [Rut 1:18]: The idea here is that "The Evil Inclination is comparable to a fly and sits between the two gateways of the heart" [Berachot 61a]. This means that the Good Inclination only gives advice to perform Mitzvot. However, the Evil Inclination persuades a person to perform sins, but if it sees that it is not successful, then it tempts him to perform a Mitzvah which is cloaked in many sins . . . and if a person wants to test if at the time a Mitzvah opportunity comes before him, if it comes

- כְּמוֹ שֶׁכָּתוּב (קהלת י׳) "לֵב חָכָם לִימִינוֹ וְלֵב כְּסִיל לִשְׂמֹאלוֹ":
- וְזֶה אָמְרָם שֶׁהַיֵּצֶר טוֹב שׁוֹמֵר וּמַכִּיר אֶת מְקוֹמוֹ לְיָמִין תָּמִיד, שֶׁאֵינוֹ מְיָעֵץ לָאָדָם לְעוֹלָם רַק לְטוֹב אֲמִתִּי לְבַד
- אֲבָל הַיֵּצֶר הָרָע, אֵינוֹ שׁוֹמֵר אֶת מְקוֹמוֹ הַמְיֻחָד לוֹ בֶּחָלָל הַשְּׂמָאלִי, לְהָסִית לְעָוֹן וְחֵטְא נִגְלֶה
- אֶלָּא הוּא מְדַלֵּג מִמְּקוֹמוֹ לִפְעָמִים גַּם לֶחָלָל הַיָּמִין, לְהִתְדַּמּוֹת לְהָאָדָם כְּיֵצֶר טוֹב לְהַנְהִיגוֹ בְּתוֹסֶפֶת קְדֻשָּׁה
- וְאֵינוֹ מַרְגִּישׁ שֶׁתּוֹכָהּ טָמוּן עִנְיַן רַע וָמַר חַס וְשָׁלוֹם:

פרקים - פרק ה׳

- וְהִנֵּה גָּלוּי וּמְבֹאָר, שֶׁזֹּאת הַדֶּרֶךְ, אֵשׁ הִיא עַד אֲבַדּוֹן תֹּאכֵל חַס וְשָׁלוֹם, וְהוֹרֶסֶת כַּמָּה יְסוֹדוֹת הַתּוֹרָה הַקְּדוֹשָׁה וְדִבְרֵי רַבּוֹתֵינוּ זִכְרוֹנָם לִבְרָכָה:
- וּכְבָר הִזְכַּרְנוּ לְעֵיל סוֹף שַׁעַר א׳
  ○ שֶׁהָעִקָּר בְּכָל הַמִּצְוֹת הוּא חֵלֶק הַמַּעֲשֶׂה
  ○ וְטָהֳרַת הַמַּחֲשָׁבָה אֵינָהּ אֶלָּא מִצְטָרֶפֶת לַמַּעֲשֶׂה, וּלְמִצְוָה וְלֹא לְעִכּוּבָא
  ○ עַיֵּן שָׁם:
- וְכֵן
  ○ מְבֹאָר לְכָל מַשְׂכִּיל יָשָׁר הוֹלֵךְ, שֶׁהֲרֵי קַיְמָא לָן (זבחים ב:) בְּעִנְיַן הַקְרָבַת הַקָּרְבָּנוֹת דִּסְתָמָן כְּלִשְׁמָן דָּמֵי

---

from the Evil Inclination or not – he should check at the time of performing the Mitzvah to see if his limbs are moving with alacrity to perform the Mitzvah, and if so, it is to be assumed that it is from the Evil Inclination. For how can it be that the heavy physical limbs of the body which derive from the element of earth, and which naturally follow after physical desire which descends to the depths as is the nature of earth, will be filled with desire [to do good]. It can only be the advice of the Evil Inclination who will subsequently trap him in its net.

56 Iyov 31:12.
57 Michah 2:7.
58 Zevachim 2b.

- ○ Chazal specifically state[59] that if one eats the Pesach sacrifice for the sake of gluttony, that while not having performed the Mitzvah in the best way, one has at least performed the Mitzvah of eating the Pesach sacrifice.
  - ▫ But if a person thinks awesome deep and ultimately purified great thoughts of the concept of Pesach at the time when obligated to sacrifice and eat the Pesach and 'refrained from making the Pesach sacrifice then that soul will be cut off.'[60]
  - ▫ This principle is similarly true for [the performance of] all Mitzvot.
- It is not only the case that the key part of Mitzvot is their active performance, it is also true for the Mitzvah of prayer which is called "Service of the Heart"
  - ○ which Chazal learned from the verse "and to serve Him will all your heart."[61]
  - ○ Nevertheless, the key part of it is that a person is required to specifically use his lips to physically articulate each word of the prayer formulation
  - ○ as Chazal stated with reference to the Scriptural verses related to Chana: "Only her lips moved," it is from here that we learn that one who prays is required to verbally articulate with his lips.[62]
  - ○ It is similarly brought down: I might have thought that one can just think [words of prayer] in one's heart, [the verse] therefore comes to teach us that "only her lips moved" How is this done? By whispering with one's lips.[63]
  - ○ It is clear that this is not coming to teach us about the desired way of performing the general Mitzvah, but that it will also prevent performance if it was accidentally omitted as
  - ○ if one only thought the words of prayer in one's heart, he has not fulfilled his prayer obligation at all
  - ○ and if the time for prayer has not yet passed, he is obligated to pray again and to articulate each word
  - ○ and if the time for prayer has passed, he is obligated to pray the next prayer twice, as per the Halacha of one who entirely missed a prayer instance
  - ○ as commented on by the Magen Avraham with clear and correct proofs which are suitably convincing that he has not fulfilled his obligation with prayer by thought alone.[64]
- It is known from the Zohar and the writings of the Arizal that

---

59 Nazir 23a.
60 Bamidbar 9:13.

○ וְכֵן אָמְרוּ לְהֶדְיָא (נזיר כ"ג) בְּאוֹכֵל אֶת הַפֶּסַח לְשֵׁם אֲכִילָה גַסָּה, נְהִי דְּלֹא קָא עָבִיד מִצְוָה מִן הַמֻּבְחָר, פֶּסַח מִיהוּ קָעָבִיד.

▫ וְאִם יַחֲשֹׁב הָאָדָם בְּעֵת חִיּוּב הַקְרָבַת הַפֶּסַח וְעֵת חִיּוּב אֲכִילָתוֹ, כַּוָּנוֹת נוֹרָאוֹת שֶׁל עִנְיַן הַפֶּסַח בְּמַחֲשָׁבָה גְּבוֹהָּ שֶׁבַּגְּבוֹהוֹת וּטְהוֹרָה שֶׁבַּטְּהוֹרוֹת, וְחָדַל מֵעֲשׂוֹת הַפֶּסַח, וְנִכְרְתָה הַנֶּפֶשׁ הַהִיא

▫ וְכֵן הוּא בְּכָל הַמִּצְוֹת:

• וְלֹא זוֹ בִּלְבַד שֶׁבְּמִצְוֹת מַעֲשִׂיּוֹת הָעִקָּר בָּהֶם הוּא חֵלֶק הַמַּעֲשֶׂה, אֶלָּא שֶׁגַּם בְּמִצְוַת הַתְּפִלָּה שֶׁנִּקְרֵאת עֲבוֹדָה שֶׁבַּלֵּב

○ וְלִמְּדוּהוּ זִכְרוֹנָם לִבְרָכָה בְּרֵישׁ פֶּרֶק קַמָּא דְּתַעֲנִית מִכָּתוּב "וּלְעָבְדוֹ בְּכָל לְבַבְכֶם" (דברים יא, יג)

○ עִם כָּל זֶה, הָעִקָּר, שֶׁצָּרִיךְ הָאָדָם לַחְתֹּךְ בִּשְׂפָתָיו דַּוְקָא כָּל תֵּבָה מִמַּטְבֵּעַ הַתְּפִלָּה

○ כְּמוֹ שֶׁאָמְרוּ רַבּוֹתֵינוּ זִכְרוֹנָם לִבְרָכָה (ברכות לא) בְּרֵישׁ פֶּרֶק אֵין עוֹמְדִין, מִקְרָאֵי דְחַנָּה, דִּכְתִיב בָּהּ (שמו"א א, יג) "רַק שְׂפָתֶיהָ נָּעוֹת", מִכָּאן לַמִּתְפַּלֵּל צָרִיךְ שֶׁיַּחְתֹּךְ בִּשְׂפָתָיו.

○ וְכֵן אִיתָא בְּשׁוֹחֵר טוֹב שְׁמוּאֵל פֶּרֶק ב', "יָכוֹל יְהֵא מְהַרְהֵר בַּלֵּב תַּלְמוּד לוֹמַר רַק שְׂפָתֶיהָ נָּעוֹת כוּ' הָא כֵּיצַד מַרְחִישׁ בִּשְׂפָתָיו".

○ וּבָרוּר הוּא, דְּלָאו לְעִנְיָן לְכַתְּחִלָּה וּלְמִצְוָה בְּעָלְמָא הוּא דַּאֲמָרוּהוּ, אֶלָּא גַם לְעִכּוּבָא דִּיעֲבַד

○ שֶׁאִם הִרְהֵר תֵּבוֹת הַתְּפִלָּה בַּלֵּב לְבַד, לֹא יָצָא יְדֵי חוֹבַת תְּפִלָּה כְּלָל

○ וְאִם עֲדַיִן לֹא עָבַר הַזְּמַן, צָרִיךְ לְהִתְפַּלֵּל פַּעַם אַחֶרֶת בְּחִתּוּךְ שְׂפָתַיִם כָּל תֵּבָה

○ וְאִם עָבְרָה זְמַנָּהּ, צָרִיךְ לְהִתְפַּלֵּל שְׁתַּיִם תְּפִלָּה שֶׁאַחֲרֶיהָ, כְּדִין מִי שֶׁלֹּא הִתְפַּלֵּל כָּל עִקָּר

○ כְּמוֹ שֶׁהֵעִיר עַל זֶה הַמָּגֵן אַבְרָהָם בְּסִי' ק"א ס"ק ב' בִּרְאָיוֹת נְכוֹנוֹת, שֶׁהֵמָּה כְּדַאי לְהַכְרִיעַ בְּצֶדֶק, דִּבְהִרְהוּר הַתְּפִלָּה לְבַד לֹא יָצָא יְדֵי חוֹבָה:

• וְיָדוּעַ בַּזֹּהַר וְכִתְבֵי הָאֲרִיזַ"ל

---

61 Taanit 2a quoting Devarim 11:13.
62 Berachot 31a quoting 1 Shmuel 1:13.
63 Midrash Shmuel 2:10.
64 Magen Avraham Orach Chaim 101:2.

- the concept of prayer is about the correction of the worlds and the elevation of their inner essence
- [that is] all the levels of Nefesh, Ruach, and Neshama contained within them from the lowest to the highest levels.
- This is done by interconnecting a person's Nefesh with his Ruach and his Ruach with his Neshama[65]
- as explained, with God's help, at the end of the Second Gateway, refer to it there.
- [The worlds] are connected through
  - the physical movement of one's lips of the words of prayer
    - which is the level of physical action of speech, as per Chazal:
      - The movement of one's lips is an action.[66]
      - From where do we know that speech is like action, as it says ["with the word of God, the Heavens were *made*"].[67]
    - This is the level of Nefesh of speech.
  - The breath and the sound, which is the speech itself, is the level of Ruach within it
  - and the concentration of the heart while uttering the words is the level the Neshama of the speech.

• Therefore, one cannot fulfill one's obligation of prayer only through thought [in general] and contemplation of the words [in particular] in one's heart alone
  - for how is it possible to achieve interconnection with the level of Neshama if not following the sequence of levels from the bottom up
  - to [first] connect the Nefesh of speech which is the physical lip movements with the Ruach of speech which is the breath and the sound
  - and [only] after that to connect both of them to the Neshama which is [by having] the thought and the concentration of the heart.
  - If one were to only pray with thought alone then the prayer is not effective and does not rectify anything.
  - Whereas, if one only prays by vocally articulating the letters of speech, even if he has not attached thought and concentration of the heart to it
    - then while it is certainly not complete or on the appropriate level
    - and it is not able to ascend to the world of thought, the world of the Neshama, as it lacks the level of a person's thought
    - nevertheless, it is not in vain, God forbid, and one has fulfilled his obligation

---

65 Nefesh=action, Ruach=speech, Neshama=thought (G1:14). There are also

- שֶׁעִנְיַן הַתְּפִלָּה הוּא תִּקּוּן הָעוֹלָמוֹת, וְהִתְעַלּוּת פְּנִימִיּוּתָם
- כָּל בְּחִינוֹת נֶפֶשׁ רוּחַ נְשָׁמָה שֶׁבָּהֶם, מִמַּטָּה לְמַעְלָה
- וְהוּא עַל יְדֵי הִתְדַּבְּקוּת וְהִתְקַשְּׁרוּת נֶפֶשׁ הָאָדָם בְּרוּחוֹ וְרוּחוֹ בְּנִשְׁמָתוֹ
- כְּמוֹ שֶׁהִתְבָּאֵר בע"ה לְעֵיל שַׁעַר ב', עַיֵּן שָׁם
- וְהֵם נִקְשָׁרִים עַל יְדֵי
  - עֲקִימַת וּתְנוּעַת שְׂפָתָיו בְּחִתּוּךְ תֵּבוֹת הַתְּפִלָּה
- שֶׁהוּא בְּחִינַת הַמַּעֲשֶׂה שֶׁבַּדִּבּוּר, כְּמוֹ שֶׁאָמְרוּ רַבּוֹתֵינוּ זִכְרוֹנָם לִבְרָכָה
  - "עֲקִימַת שְׂפָתָיו הֲוֵי מַעֲשֶׂה" (סנהדרין סה).
  - וּבְפֶרֶק כָּל כִּתְבֵי (שבת קיט, ב) אָמְרוּ, "מִנַּיִן שֶׁהַדִּבּוּר כְּמַעֲשֶׂה שֶׁנֶּאֱמַר" כו'
- וְהוּא בְּחִינַת הַנֶּפֶשׁ שֶׁבַּדִּבּוּר.
- וְהַהֶבֶל וְהַקּוֹל שֶׁהוּא הַדִּבּוּר עַצְמוֹ, הוּא בְּחִינַת רוּחַ שֶׁבָּהּ.
- וְכַוָּנַת הַלֵּב בְּהַתֵּבוֹת בְּעֵת אֲמִירָתָם, הוּא בְּחִינַת הַנְּשָׁמָה שֶׁבַּדִּבּוּר:
- לָזֹאת, לֹא יָצָא יְדֵי חוֹבַת עִנְיַן הַתְּפִלָּה בְּמַחֲשָׁבָה וְהִרְהוּר הַתֵּבוֹת בַּלֵּב לְבַד
  - כִּי אֵיךְ אֶפְשָׁר לְהַגִּיעַ לְהִתְקַשֵּׁר בִּבְחִינַת הַנְּשָׁמָה, אִם לֹא יֵלֵךְ בְּסֵדֶר הַמַּדְרֵגוֹת מִמַּטָּה לְמַעְלָה
  - שֶׁיִּתְקַשֵּׁר הַנֶּפֶשׁ שֶׁל הַדִּבּוּר שֶׁהוּא תְּנוּעַת הַשְּׂפָתַיִם, בָּרוּחַ שֶׁל הַדִּבּוּר שֶׁהוּא הַהֶבֶל וְהַקּוֹל
  - וְאַחַר כָּךְ יִתְקַשְּׁרוּ גַם שְׁנֵיהֶם בַּנְּשָׁמָה, שֶׁהִיא הַמַּחֲשָׁבָה וְהַכַּוָּנָה שֶׁבַּלֵּב.
  - וּכְשֶׁהִתְפַּלֵּל רַק בְּמַחֲשָׁבָה לְבַד, לֹא הוֹעִילָה תְּפִלָּתוֹ וְלֹא תִּקֵּן כְּלוּם.
  - אָמְנָם כְּשֶׁהִתְפַּלֵּל בְּקוֹל וְחִתּוּךְ אוֹתִיּוֹת הַדִּבּוּר לְבַד, אַף עַל פִּי שֶׁלֹּא צֵרֵף הַמַּחֲשָׁבָה וְכַוָּנַת הַלֵּב אֵלֶיהָ
    - הֲגַם שֶׁוַּדַּאי אֵינָהּ בְּמַדְרֵגָה שְׁלֵמָה וּגְבוֹהָּ כָּרָאוּי
    - וְאֵינָהּ יְכוֹלָה לַעֲלוֹת לְעוֹלַם הַמַּחֲשָׁבָה עוֹלַם הַנְּשָׁמָה, כֵּיוָן שֶׁחָסֵר מִמֶּנָּה בְּחִינַת מַחֲשֶׁבֶת הָאָדָם
    - עִם כָּל זֶה אֵינָהּ לָרִיק חַס וְשָׁלוֹם, וְיוֹצֵא בָּהּ יְדֵי חוֹבָתוֹ

---

levels within levels e.g., the action within speech and the speech within thought, etc.

66 Sanhedrin 65a.
67 Shabbat 119b quoting Tehillim 33:6.

- as at least one's Nefesh has been raised and connected with one's Ruach and the world of Nefesh with the world of Ruach.
  - As per Zohar:
    - That prayer is required to be from thought, will of the heart, voice, and speech of the lips – in order to completely connect and unify above just as it is above ... in order to connect the connection as appropriate ... thought, will, voice, and speech are the four [components] which connect connections and after they have all connected together they form a single platform upon which the Shechina resides ... the audible sound ascends to connect connections from the bottom up. ....[68] Refer there well.
    - It generally states that: [Even though prayer is dependent on words and speech of the mouth,] the essential part of prayer is dependent on its initial action to be specifically followed by speech of the mouth.[69] Refer to the presentation there.
    - All that which a person thinks and all that which he looks upon with his heart does not do anything until it is articulated with his lips ... and because of this all prayer and requests ... need to be verbally articulated for if not articulated, then the prayer is no prayer and the request is no request. When the words are produced they break through the air and ascend ... and they are taken by whoever takes them and they are unified into the Holy Crown on the King's Head.[70]
    - It is generally stated that
      - one who says that action isn't required for anything or it is not necessary to vocally articulate words – is a fool,[71] the Merciful One should save us
      - and Chazal only required concentration as necessary for the blessing of Avot[72] alone.
    - One whose heart is troubled and wants to pray his prayer or is in pain, and is unable to present his praise of his Master as appropriate, what should he do? Tell him that even though he cannot concentrate his heart and will, why should he miss out by not presenting his praise of his Master? He should present his praise of his Master even though he cannot concentrate. ....[73]

---

68 Zohar II Pekudei 162b.
69 Zohar III Bamidbar 120b.
70 Zohar Idra Zuta III Haazinu 294b.

נפש · פרקים - פרק ה' · החיים · 613

- כִּי עַל כָּל פָּנִים הֲרֵי הֶעֱלָה וְקִשֵּׁר נַפְשׁוֹ בְּרוּחוֹ, וְעוֹלַם הַנֶּפֶשׁ בְּעוֹלַם הָרוּחַ.
- וְעַיֵּן בַּזֹּהַר

- פְּקוּדֵי רס"ב ע"ב דְּאִצְטְרִיךְ צְלוֹתָא מִגּוֹ מַחֲשָׁבָה וּרְעוּתָא דְּלִבָּא, וְקָלָא, וּמִלָּה דְּשִׂפְוָון, לְמֶעֱבַד שְׁלִימוּ וְקִשּׁוּרָא וְיִחוּדָא לְעֵילָא כְּגַוְונָא דִּאִיהוּ לְעֵילָא כו', לְקַשְּׁרָא קִשְׁרִין כְּדְקָא יָאוּת כו', מַחֲשָׁבָה וּרְעוּתָא קָלָא וּמִלָּה אִלֵּין ד' מְקַשְּׁרָן קִשְׁרִין, לְבָתַר דְּקְשִׁירוּ קִשְׁרִין כֻּלָּא כַּחֲדָא, אִתְעֲבִידוּ כֻּלְּהוּ רְתִיכָא חֲדָא, לְאַשְׁרָאָה עֲלַיְיהוּ שְׁכִינְתָּא כו', קָלָא דְּאִשְׁתְּמַע, סָלִיק לְקַשְּׁרָא קִשְׁרִין מִתַּתָּא לְעֵילָא כו', עַיֵּן שָׁם הֵיטֵב.

- וּבְפָרָשַׁת בַּמִּדְבָּר ק"כ ע"ב, אָמְרוּ דֶרֶךְ כְּלָל דְּעִקָּרָא דִּצְלוֹתָא תַּלְיָא בְּעוּבְדָא בְּקַדְמִיתָא, וּלְבָתַר בְּמִלּוּלָא דְּפוּמָא דּוּקָא, עַיֵּן שָׁם סִדְרָן.

- וּבְאִדְרָא זוּטָא רצ"ד ב', כָּל מַה דְּחָשִׁיב בַּר נַשׁ, וְכָל מַה דְּיִסְתַּכַּל בְּלִבֵּיהּ, לָא עָבִיד מִלָּה עַד דְּאָפִיק לֵיהּ בְּשִׂפְוָותֵיהּ כו', וּבְגִין כַּךְ כָּל צְלוֹתָא וּבָעוּתָא כו', בָּעֵי לְאַפָּקָא מִלִּין בְּשִׂפְוָותֵיהּ, דְּאִי לָא אָפִיק לוֹן, לָאו צְלוֹתֵיהּ צְלוֹתָא וְלָאו בָּעוּתֵיהּ בָּעוּתָא. וְכֵיוָן דְּמִלִּין נַפְקִין מִתְבַּקְּעִין בַּאֲוִירָא וְסַלְקִין כו', וְנָטִיל לוֹן מַאן דְּנָטִיל וְאָחִיד לוֹן לְכִתְרָא קַדִּישָׁא כו'.

- וְדֶרֶךְ כְּלָל אָמְרוּ

- בַּזֹּהַר אֱמוֹר ק"ה א', מַאן דְּאָמַר דְּלָא בָּעֲיָא עוּבְדָא בְּכוֹלָא, אוֹ מִלֵּי לַאֲפָקָא לוֹן וּלְמֶעֱבַד קָלָא בְּהוּ, תְּפַח רוּחֵיהּ רַחֲמָנָא לִיצְלָן.

- וְלֹא הִצְרִיכוּ רַבּוֹתֵינוּ זִכְרוֹנָם לִבְרָכָה עִנְיַן הַכַּוָּנָה לְעִכּוּבָא אֶלָּא בְּבִרְכַּת אָבוֹת לְבַד.

- וּבְפָרָשַׁת וַיְחִי רמ"ג סוֹף ע"ב, מַאן דְּלִבֵּיהּ טָרִיד וּבָעֵי לְצַלָּאָה צְלוֹתֵיהּ, וְאִיהוּ בְּעָקוּ וְלָא יָכִיל לְסַדְּרָא שְׁבָחָא דְּמָארֵיהּ כְּדְקָא יָאוּת מַאי הוּא, אָמַר לֵיהּ אַף עַל גַּב דְּלָא יָכִיל לְכַוְּונָא לִבָּא וּרְעוּתָא, סִדּוּרָא וְשִׁבְחָא דְּמָארֵיהּ אַמַּאי גָרַע, אֶלָּא לָא יְסַדֵּר שִׁבְחָא דְּמָארֵיהּ אַף עַל גַּב דְּלָא יָכִיל לְכַוְּונָא כו':

---

71 Zohar III Emor 105a.
72 I.e., the first blessing of the Amidah.
73 Zohar I Vayechi 143b.

6. ACTION IS KEY AS PER THIRD GATEWAY

- While it is certain that a person's thought is that which ascends to the highest heights of the highest worlds
  - and if a person also attaches purity of thought and intention when performing Mitzvot
  - his actions will enact even greater rectifications in even higher worlds
  - however, the thought is not key to us, as explained.
  - Refer to the Zohar:[74]
    - If he should have the opportunity to perform an action and can have associated thought, he has merit.
    - Even if he does not have associated thought, he [still] has merit as he is performing the command of his Master
    - but he is not considered like one who performs His Will for its sake with the intention of desiring [to look at the honor of his Master]
    - like one who doesn't know [how to understand a reason]
    - as [the concept of *for its sake*] is dependent on desire
    - [and action performed *for its sake* in this lower world causes the action of the supernal world to be raised and rectifies it; similarly, with this desire, the action of the body rectifies the action of the soul – for God wants the heart and desire of a person]
    - but, nevertheless, even if there is no desire of the heart, [which is the key to all], it is about this that David prayed that "and the action of our hands should be established for us" ... what does *established for us* mean? That it should be *established* and appropriately rectify rectifications in the supernal worlds, *for us*, even though we don't know how to place our desire and [just perform] the action on its own – our actions [will nevertheless] be established. Where? To that [high] level that needs to be rectified. ...
- Similarly, with the concept explained above in the Third Gateway relating to prayer
  - that one must focus it on [God being] the Makom/space of the Universe,[75] as per the explanation there of the concept of "Space of the Universe." Refer there.[76]
  - Similarly, the concept of the focus on the word "One" in the first verse of the Shema, as explained in G3:11. Refer there well.
  - That this [dimension of focus] is just to enhance Mitzvah performance but is not a requirement of it.
  - As even someone who is not aware of this [concept] at all
    - [whether] as a result of

פרקים - פרק ו'

- וְהֲגַם שֶׁוַּדַּאי שֶׁמַּחְשֶׁבֶת הָאָדָם הִיא הָעוֹלָה לְמַעְלָה לְרֹאשׁ בִּשְׁמֵי רוּם בָּעוֹלָמוֹת הָעֶלְיוֹנִים
  - וְאִם יְצָרֵף הָאָדָם גַּם טֹהַר הַמַּחְשָׁבָה וְהַכַּוָּנָה בְּעֵת עֲשִׂיַּת הַמִּצְוֹת
  - יַגִּיעוּ מַעֲשָׂיו לִפְעֹל תִּקּוּנִים יוֹתֵר גְּדוֹלִים בָּעוֹלָמוֹת הַיּוֹתֵר עֶלְיוֹנִים
  - אָמְנָם לֹא הַמַּחְשָׁבָה הִיא הָעִקָּר אֶצְלֵנוּ, כְּמוֹ שֶׁנִּתְבָּאֵר.
  - וְעַיֵּן בַּזֹּהַר יִתְרוֹ צ"ג רֵישׁ ע"ב
    - וְאִי אַזְדְּמַן לֵיהּ עוֹבָדָא וִיכַוֵּין בֵּיהּ, זַכָּאָה אִיהוּ.
    - וְאַף עַל גַּב דְּלָא מְכַוֵּין בֵּיהּ, זַכָּאָה אִיהוּ, דְּעָבִיד פִּקּוּדָא דְּמָארֵיהּ
    - אֲבָל לֹא אִתְחַשֵּׁב מַאן דְּעָבִיד רְעוּתָא לִשְׁמָהּ וִיכַוֵּין בָּהּ בִּרְעוּתָא כוּ'
    - כְּמַאן דְּלָא יָדַע כוּ'
    - דְּהָא בִּרְעוּתָא תַּלְיָא
    - כוּ'
    - וַאֲפִלּוּ הָכִי, אִי לָאו תַּמָּן רְעוּתָא דְלִבָּא כוּ', עַל דָּא צַלִּי דָוִד וְאָמַר "וּמַעֲשֵׂה יָדֵינוּ כּוֹנְנָה עָלֵינוּ" כוּ', מַאי "כּוֹנְנָה עָלֵינוּ", "כּוֹנְנָה" וְאַתְקִין תִּקּוּנִין לְעֵילָא כִּדְקָא יָאוּת, "עָלֵינוּ", אַף עַל גַּב דְּלֵית אֲנַן יָדְעִין לְשַׁוָּאָה רְעוּתָא, אֶלָּא עוֹבָדָא בִּלְחוֹדוֹי, "מַעֲשֵׂה יָדֵינוּ כּוֹנְנֵהוּ", לְמַאן, לְהַהוּא דַרְגָּא דְאִצְטְרִיךְ לְאַתְקָנָא כוּ', עַיֵּן שָׁם:
- וְכֵן בְּעִנְיָן שֶׁנִּתְבָּאֵר לְמַעְלָה בְּשַׁעַר ג' בְּעִנְיַן הַתְּפִלָּה
  - לְכַוֵּן אוֹתָהּ לִמְקוֹמוֹ שֶׁל עוֹלָם יִתְבָּרַךְ שְׁמוֹ, כְּפִי שֶׁנִּתְבָּאֵר שָׁם עִנְיַן "מְקוֹמוֹ שֶׁל עוֹלָם", עַיֵּן שָׁם.
  - וְכֵן עִנְיַן כַּוָּנַת "אֶחָד" דְּפָסוּק רִאשׁוֹן דִּקְרִיאַת שְׁמַע שֶׁנִּתְבָּאֵר שָׁם בְּפֶרֶק י"א, עַיֵּן שָׁם הֵיטֵב
  - הַכֹּל הוּא רַק לְמִצְוָה וְלֹא לְעִכּוּבָא.
  - שֶׁגַּם מִי שֶׁלֹּא יָדַע בָּזֶה כְּלָל
    - כִּי

---

74 Zohar II Yitro 93b quoting Tehillim 90:17.
75 G3:08.
76 G3:03.

- a lack of familiarity, or
- does not relate to it intellectually as he has not adequately researched into the depth of it, or
- out of fear for his life that this focus will result in a destruction, God forbid, of many principles of the Torah which can result from this, God forbid, for one who is not appropriately knowledgeable of this
  - as is written there, refer to it[77]
- but serves God
  - and fulfills all of the Written and Oral Torah together with the rabbinic enactments
  - and believes in and has general focus when reciting the first verse of the Shema, that He is "One," even if not aware of the concept of His Unity
  - and focuses his prayer in a general way to God without deep analysis
- such a person is still called a "Servant of God."
- (This is as per Pardes in relation to faith in the existence of the Sefirot, refer to it.)[78]
- These [ideas] are all only presented for one who is appropriately knowledgeable, and how much more so 'for those who fear God and give thought to His name'[79] who have the ability to engage in them.

• Therefore we should never, God forbid, omit any minute detail, even a single point of precision of the rabbinic practices, in our physical implementation [of Mitzvot], and how much more so to not deviate their performance from their proper time as a result of inadequate purity of thought, and the more scrupulous one is in the detail of his actions, it is praiseworthy.

---

77 G3:03.
78 Sefer Pardes Rimonim Gate 1 Chap. 9:
  • After dealing with the existence of the Sefirot and their number in earlier chapters, it is appropriate to know if one who denies the existence of the Sefirot is to be called a blasphemer or not? . . . With one who doesn't know anything about them at all – not that if he were aware of them he would deny, but that he is unfamiliar. This person is certainly fitting to not be called a blasphemer or denier . . . even though this mistake is because of unfamiliarity with Godliness and of pursuing the simple explanations of Scripture and Midrashim without delving into their depth to understand their real content . . . Similarly, it is said in relation to the Sefirot that certainly someone who does not know about them but believes in the Absolute One God is not fitting to be called a blasphemer, God forbid . . . on the

- לֹא הֻרְגַּל בָּזֶה אוֹ
- שֶׁמּוֹחֵיהּ לֹא סָבִיל דָּא שֶׁלֹּא יָרַד לְעָמְקוֹ, אוֹ
- שֶׁיָּרֵא לְנַפְשׁוֹ שֶׁלֹּא יִסְתַּכֵּן חַס וְשָׁלוֹם בַּהֲרִיסַת כַּמָּה יְסוֹדֵי הַתּוֹרָה, שֶׁיָּכוֹל לָבֹא מִזֶּה חַס וְשָׁלוֹם לְמִי שֶׁאֵין דַּעְתּוֹ יָפָה בָזֶה כָּרָאוּי
  ◦ כְּמוֹ שֶׁכָּתוּב שָׁם, עַיֵּן שָׁם
- אֶלָּא שֶׁהוּא עוֹבֵד אוֹתוֹ יִתְבָּרַךְ
- וּמְקַיֵּם בְּכָל הַכָּתוּב בְּתוֹרַת ה' שֶׁבִּכְתָב וּבְעַל פֶּה וְרַבּוֹתֵינוּ הַגְּדוֹלִים
- וּמַאֲמִין וּמְכַוֵּן דֶּרֶךְ כְּלָל בְּפָסוּק רִאשׁוֹן דִּקְרִיאַת שְׁמַע, שֶׁהוּא יִתְבָּרַךְ הוּא אֶחָד, גַּם שֶׁאֵינוֹ יוֹדֵעַ עִנְיַן אַחְדוּתוֹ יִתְבָּרַךְ
- וּמְכַוֵּן תְּפִלָּתוֹ דֶּרֶךְ כְּלָל לוֹ יִתְבָּרַךְ בְּלֹא חֲקִירָה
- גַּם כֵּן נִקְרָא "עוֹבֵד ה'"
- (כְּעִנְיָן מַ"שׁ בְּפַרְדֵּס שַׁעַר א' פֶּרֶק ט' בְּעִנְיַן הָאֱמוּנָה בִּמְצִיאוּת הַסְּפִירוֹת, עַיֵּן שָׁם)
- כִּי אֵין כָּל הַדְּבָרִים הָאֵלּוּ אֲמוּרִים אֶלָּא לְמִי שֶׁדַּעְתּוֹ יָפָה, וְכָל שֶׁכֵּן לְיִרְאֵי ה' וְחוֹשְׁבֵי שְׁמוֹ, אֲשֶׁר לָהֶם כֹּחַ לַעֲמֹד בָּזֶה:
* לָזֹאת, חָלִילָה וְחָלִילָה לָנוּ לִדְחוֹת שׁוּם פְּרָט מִפְּרָטֵי הַמַּעֲשֶׂה, אַף דְּקְדּוּק אֶחָד מִדִּבְרֵי סוֹפְרִים, וְכָל שֶׁכֵּן לְשַׁנּוֹת זְמַנָּה חַס וְשָׁלוֹם, בִּשְׁבִיל מְנִיעַת טָהֳרַת הַמַּחֲשָׁבָה, וְכָל הַמַּרְבֶּה לְדַקְדֵּק בְּמַעֲשָׂיו הֲרֵי זֶה מְשֻׁבָּח:

---

contrary it is fitting to conceal [these ideas] and only hand them over to the modest . . . but it is justified to say about such a person that he has not merited to see light in all of his days and he has not tasted of the sweetness of Torah . . . and he will die without wisdom and without seeing good!

79 Malachi 3:16. Note that the meaning of this verse is accentuated in the light of the Third Gateway and the deep thoughts about God's names, e.g., of YHVH and Elokim.

7. NO LATITUDE TO SIN OR TO CHANGE MITZVOT FOR THE SAKE OF HEAVEN

- A further way in which the Evil Inclination can disguise itself, when telling you that the entire essence of service is that all action should only be for the sake of Heaven, is that even an intentional or unintentional sin would be considered a Mitzvah if performed for the *sake of Heaven* to rectify a specific issue – bringing many [so called] proofs including:
    - "God wants the focus of one's heart."[80]
    - "A sin for the sake of Heaven is greater [than a Mitzvah not for the sake of Heaven"].[81]
- It will also suggest that you are obligated to follow in the footsteps of the Patriarchs and the pre-Torah era righteous
    - whose key approach to serving God was that all their actions, speech, and thoughts together with their interaction with this world, were entirely with inspirational fervor and purity of thought for the sake of Heaven
    - and all focused Heavenward to rectify, raise, and unify the worlds and the supernal powers by the performance of a particular action in a particular way at a particular time
    - and not by the performance of actions and commandments which are fixed and set out such that they are by 'immutable decree'[82]
    - like with Yaakov's [use of] sticks with Lavan's sheep[83]
    - and as the Maggid said to the Beit Yosef in relation to Chanoch who would sew shoes and each time he would pull the needle through the shoe he would praise God. Refer to Maggid Meisharim.[84]
- Now, even though Chazal state[85] that "the Patriarchs observed all of the Torah" and that "Noach learned Torah"
    - it is not that they were performing it as a result of being commanded to do so and that they had a defined Halacha and specific laws
    - but as I wrote above at the end of the First Gateway[86]
    - that they kept the Torah as a result of their awesome ability to perceive how each and every Mitzvah would rectify the worlds and the arrangement of the supernal powers
    - however, they also had the latitude to serve Him with actions and in

---

80 Sanhedrin 106b.
81 Nazir 23b and Horayot 10b.
82 Tehillim 148:6.
83 Bereishit 30:37.
84 Maggid Meisharim Mahadura Batra Miketz. This quotation goes on to equate

פרקים - פרק ז'

- עוֹד זֹאת יוּכַל יִצְרְךָ לְהִתְחַפֵּשׂ, בֶּאֱמוֹר לְךָ שֶׁכָּל עִקַּר הָעֲבוֹדָה הוּא שֶׁיִּהְיֶה רַק לְשֵׁם שָׁמַיִם, וְגַם עָוֹן וְחֵטְא לְמִצְוָה יֵחָשֵׁב אִם הוּא לְשֵׁם שָׁמַיִם לְתִקּוּן אֵיזֶה עִנְיָן
    - "וְרַחֲמָנָא לִבָּא בָּעֵי" (סנהדרין קו:)
    - וּ"גְדוֹלָה עֲבֵרָה לִשְׁמָהּ" (נזיר כג: הוריות י:), וְכַהֵנָּה רַבּוֹת רְאָיוֹת:
- גַּם יַרְאֶה לְךָ פָּנִים לֵאמֹר, כִּי כֵן צִוִּיתָ, לֵילֵךְ בְּעִקְבֵי אֲבוֹתֶיךָ הַקְּדוֹשִׁים וְכָל הַצַּדִּיקִים הָרִאשׁוֹנִים שֶׁהָיוּ קֹדֶם שֶׁנִּתְּנָה הַתּוֹרָה
    - שֶׁעִיקָּר דֶּרֶךְ עֲבוֹדָתָם לוֹ יִתְבָּרַךְ הָיְתָה, שֶׁכָּל מַעֲשֵׂיהֶם וְדִבּוּרָם וּמַחְשְׁבוֹתָם וְכָל עִנְיְנֵיהֶם בָּעוֹלָם הָיָה הַכֹּל בִּדְבֵקוּת וְטָהֳרַת מַחְשְׁבוֹתָם לְשֵׁם שָׁמַיִם
    - וּפָנוּ לְמַעְלָה לְתִקּוּן וְהַעֲלָאַת וְיִחוּד הָעוֹלָמוֹת וְכֹחוֹת הָעֶלְיוֹנִים, בְּאֵיזֶה מַעֲשֶׂה שֶׁתִּהְיֶה וּבְאֵיזֶה אֹפֶן וּבְאֵיזֶה זְמַן שֶׁיִּהְיֶה
    - וְלֹא בְּמַעֲשִׂים וּמִצְווֹת קְבוּעִים וּסְדוּרִים שֶׁיִּהְיוּ חֹק וְלֹא יַעֲבֹר
    - כְּמוֹ יַעֲקֹב אָבִינוּ עָלָיו הַשָּׁלוֹם בְּעִנְיַן צֹאן לָבָן וְהַמַּקְלוֹת
    - וְכֵן אָמַר הַמַּגִּיד לְהַבֵּית בְּעִנְיַן יוֹסֵף חָנוּךְ שֶׁהָיָה תּוֹפֵר מִנְעָלִים וּבְכָל זְמַנָּא דְּמָעֵיל מַחְטָא בְּסַנְדְּלָא הֲוָה מְשַׁבַּח לְקוּדְשָׁא בְּרִיךְ הוּא, עַיֵּן מַגִּיד מֵישָׁרִים פָּרָשַׁת מִקֵּץ:
- וְאַף שֶׁאָמְרוּ רַבּוֹתֵינוּ זִכְרוֹנָם לִבְרָכָה "הָאָבוֹת קִיְּמוּ כָּל הַתּוֹרָה", וְכֵן אָמְרוּ בְּוַיִּקְרָא רַבָּה פ"ב, "מְלַמֵּד שֶׁלָּמַד נֹחַ תּוֹרָה"
    - לֹא שֶׁהָיוּ מְצֻוִּים וְעוֹשִׂים וְהָיָה לָהֶם הַהֲלָכָה וְהַדִּין כָּךְ
    - אֶלָּא כְּמוֹ שֶׁכָּתַבְתִּי לְעֵיל סוֹף שַׁעַר א' (פֶּרֶק כ"א)
    - שֶׁהֵמָּה קִיְּמוּ אֶת הַתּוֹרָה מֵחֲמַת שֶׁהִשִּׂיגוּ בְּנִפְלְאוֹת הַשָּׂגָתָם תִּקּוּנֵי הָעוֹלָמוֹת, וְסִדְרֵי הַכֹּחוֹת הָעֶלְיוֹנִים אֲשֶׁר יְתַקְּנוּ בְּכָל מִצְוָה וּמִצְוָה
    - אֲבָל הָיָה גַּם כֵּן הָרְשׁוּת נְתוּנָה לָהֶם לְעָבְדוֹ גַּם בְּמַעֲשִׂים וְעִנְיָנִים אֲחֵרִים, לְבַד הַמִּצְוֹת, וְאַף גַּם לַעֲבֹר עַל אֵיזֶה מִצְוָה שֶׁלֹּא כַּתּוֹרָה

Chanoch with the angel Matatron. See the expanded quotations from the Zohar and the Arizal in the footnotes of G2:17 which throw further light on the incredibly high level which Chanoch reached.

85 Vayikra Rabba Vayikra 2:10, Mishna Kiddushin 4:14, Bereishit Rabba Toldot 64:4.
86 G1:21.

ways which did not conform to the Mitzvot, and even to transgress by performing an action which did not conform with a Mitzvah of the Torah
- according to the way they saw and related to it that this specific action was necessary to rectify the worlds.
- (Refer to this [idea] brought down at the end of Sefer HaEmunot of R. Shem Tov, and similarly it is brought there in the name of R. Chushiel Gaon, except that in the way of all the Rishonim, the matter was dealt with very briefly and the ideas were very much hidden.)[87]

• 'You will see'[88] logically that there is not even a vague proof here, not even a 'bruised reed'[89] to lean on for the truth is clear, as explained above at the end of the First Gateway
- that service of God in this manner was only valid before the Torah was given
- but from the point that Moshe came and brought [the Torah] down to the Earth, 'it is no longer in the Heavens'[90]
- and we proved there, with God's help, from the idea presented with Chizkiyahu and Yishayahu, that it is forbidden for us to change any one of God's Mitzvot, God forbid, even if the intention is for the sake of Heaven
- and even if one sees that keeping a Mitzvah required of him will result in some terrible consequences
- and even if it is a case of 'sitting and [only!] not fulfilling [a positive command]'[91]
- nevertheless, a person still does not have the latitude to refrain [from performing the Mitzvah], God forbid, as the reasons for the Mitzvot have not been revealed. Refer there at length.

---

87 Sefer HaEmunot Shaar 10 Chap. 2:
   • ... How was Yaakov permitted to marry two sisters and Amram his aunt? Therefore, he said it is Chesed and relates to the actions of the early ones [i.e., pre-Torah times] that they were prophets and they were permitted to perform [actions] out of Chesed, and I saw some amazing comments from R. Chushiel the Ashkenazi, the great Gaon and Mystic, on these ideas – for [according to] the secret of the Merkavot and their roots according to the levels of the worlds, they and others were permitted to perform forbidden actions ... in general all the early ones knew the secret of the Name as a received tradition and they observed the roots of the Mitzvot ... and that which Chazal say that in future times all sacrifices will be abolished apart from the Thanksgiving Offering is along these lines, for in the future times, after the resurrection, there will no longer be sinners on the earth "for God

○ כְּפִי שֶׁרָאוּ וְהִשִּׂיגוּ, שֶׁזֶּה הָעִנְיָן וְהַמַּעֲשֶׂה הַפְּרָטִית הוּא נִצְרָךְ אָז לְתִקּוּן הָעוֹלָמוֹת.

○ (וְעִיֵּן מִזֶּה בְּסוֹף סֵפֶר הָאֱמוּנוֹת לְרַבִּי שֵׁם טוֹב, וְכֵן הֵבִיא שָׁם כֵּן בְּשֵׁם רַבֵּינוּ חוּשִׁיאֵל גָּאוֹן זִכְרוֹנוֹ לִבְרָכָה, רַק שֶׁקִּצֵּר מְאֹד בָּעִנְיָן, כְּדַרְכָּם בַּקֹּדֶשׁ שֶׁל כָּל הָרִאשׁוֹנִים זִכְרוֹנָם לִבְרָכָה, שֶׁהֶעֱלִימוּ וְהִסְתִּירוּ מְאֹד כָּל הָעִנְיָנִים):

• וְאַתָּה תֶּחֱזֶה אִם עֵינֵי שֵׂכֶל לָךְ, שֶׁאֵין כָּאן לֹא רְאָיָה וְלֹא סֶמֶךְ כְּלָל, אַף לֹא מִשְׁעֶנֶת קָנֶה רָצוּץ, כִּי הָאֱמֶת הַבָּרוּר כְּמוֹ שֶׁנִּתְבָּאֵר לְעֵיל סוֹף שַׁעַר א'.

○ שֶׁהָעֲבוֹדָה עַל זֶה הַדֶּרֶךְ לֹא הָיְתָה נוֹהֶגֶת אֶלָּא קֹדֶם מַתַּן תּוֹרָה לְבַד

○ אֲבָל מֵעֵת שֶׁבָּא מֹשֶׁה וְהוֹרִידָהּ לָאָרֶץ — לֹא בַשָּׁמַיִם הִיא.

○ וְהוֹכַחְנוּ שָׁם בְּעֶזְרַת הַשֵּׁם מֵעִנְיַן חִזְקִיָּהוּ עִם יְשַׁעְיָהוּ, שֶׁאָסוּר לָנוּ לְשַׁנּוֹת חַם וְשָׁלוֹם מִשּׁוּם אַחַת מֵהֵנָּה מִמִּצְוֹת ה', אַף אִם תִּהְיֶה הַכַּוָּנָה לְשֵׁם שָׁמַיִם

○ וְאַף אִם יַשִּׂיג הָאָדָם שֶׁאִם יְקַיֵּם מִצְוָתוֹ הַמֻּטֶּלֶת עָלָיו, יוּכַל לְמֵיפַּק מִנֵּיהּ חוּרְבָּא בְּאֵיזֶה עִנְיָן

○ וְאַף גַּם בְּשֵׁב וְאַל תַּעֲשֶׂה

○ עִם כָּל זֶה אֵין הַדָּבָר מָסוּר בְּיַד הָאָדָם לְהִמָּנַע מִמֶּנָּה חַס וְשָׁלוֹם, כִּי טַעֲמֵי מִצְוֹת לֹא נִתְגַּלּוּ, וְעִיֵּן שָׁם בְּאָרְכּוֹ:

---

will remove the spirit of impurity from the earth" [Zecharia 13:2], and "the heart of stone will be removed from our flesh" [Yechezkel 36:26] as the prophet testifies and the Evil Inclination will become nullified and people will cleave to His Name and therefore have no need for sacrifices except for the Thanksgiving Offering which is brought for the Chesed which He performs with man. Similarly, the statement of Chazal that "Mitzvot will become nullified in future times" [Niddah 61b], for out of the great cleaving to His Name they will be like *pure intellects* and will not need to perform physical Mitzvot . . .

[Refer to p. 288, fn. 543.]

88 Shemot 18:21.
89 Yishayahu 42:3.
90 Devarim 30:12.
91 E.g., as per Berachot 20a.

8. MITZVAH PERFORMANCE TO INSPIRE THOUGHT PURITY BUT NOT VICE VERSA

- Another way in which [the Evil Inclination] can seduce a person with its [attempted] 'bundles of proofs'[92] is that
  - the purpose of a person's service of God is only to perceive *Fear of His Exaltedness*,[93] and that one's eyes and heart should be solely focused on this all of one's days
  - and that *fear of punishment and embarrassment of other people*[94] is the worst of the worst of traits and is fitting to be uprooted from your heart
  - and your Evil Inclination will cause you to [focus on] increasing your level of *Fear of His Exaltedness*
  - until it is fixed in your heart that *fear of punishment and embarrassment of other people* is a sin, and that one should flee from it like one flees from a sin
  - to the extent that you can be caught up in its net such that you will not avoid sin all the while you have not appropriately acquired *Fear of His Exaltedness*.
  - All [other] matters will become less serious for you in that [the Evil Inclination] will show you an alternative way of approaching it
  - with the possible result that if a person rebukes you and shows you that you are transgressing a specific law, your heart will persuade you not to separate from it all the while that you are still fearful of the one rebuking you, by saying that you are not [motivated] by *Fear of Heaven* in this but only by *Fear of Man* and a [superficially] external fear.
- [However,] Chazal have already taught
  - with the blessing of R. Yochanan ben Zakkai to his students that "the Fear of Heaven upon you should be like the fear of other people"[95]
  - and who do we have who is greater and more pious than R. Amram the Pious,[96] who notwithstanding all of this, when once faced with a trial to suddenly sin,[97] Heaven save us

---

92   A Rabbinic expression most notably found in the Rama's introduction to the Shulchan Aruch.
93   Yirat HaRommemut, a very refined level of Fear of God, as described in Mesilat Yesharim Chaps. 19 and 24.
94   The most basic form of fearing God, by avoiding sin because of the prospective punishment, and relating to fearing God in the same way as one relates to fearing man.
95   Berachot 28b. This was R. Yochanan ben Zakkai's parting blessing to his

פרקים - פרק ח'

- עוֹד אַחַת יוּכַל לְפָתוֹתְךָ בַּחֲבִילוֹת רְאָיוֹת
  - שֶׁתַּכְלִית עֲבוֹדַת הָאָדָם הוּא רַק לְהַשִּׂיג יִרְאַת הָרוֹמְמוּת, וְרַק עַל זֶה יִהְיוּ עֵינָיו וְלִבּוֹ כָּל הַיָּמִים
  - וְשֶׁיִּרְאַת הָעֹנֶשׁ וּבוּשָׁה מִבְּנֵי אָדָם, הִיא מִדָּה גְרוּעָה שֶׁבַּגְּרוּעוֹת, וְהָרָאוּי לְשָׁרֵשׁ אוֹתָהּ מִלְּבַד
  - וְיַנִּיחַ לְךָ יִצְרְךָ לְהוֹסִיף יִרְאָה עַל יִרְאָה בְּיִרְאַת הָרוֹמְמוּת
  - עַד שֶׁיִּקָּבַע בְּלִבְּךָ שֶׁיִּרְאַת הָעֹנֶשׁ וְהַבּוּשָׁה מִבְּנֵי אָדָם — הִיא עֲבֵרָה, וְתִהְיֶה בּוֹרֵחַ מִמֶּנָּה כְּבוֹרֵחַ מִן הָעֲבֵרָה
  - עַד שֶׁיּוּכַל לִהְיוֹת שֶׁתִּתְלַכֵּד בְּרַשְׁתּוֹ שֶׁלֹּא לְאַפְרוּשֵׁי מֵאִסּוּרָא, בִּזְמַן שֶׁאֵין לְךָ יִרְאַת הָרוֹמְמוּת כָּרָאוּי.
  - וְיָקֵל לְךָ כָּל דָּבָר, בַּאֲשֶׁר יַרְאֶה לְךָ פָּנִים מִפָּנִים שׁוֹנִים בָּזֶה.
  - וְיוּכַל לְהוֹלֵד מִזֶּה, שֶׁאִם יוֹכִיחֲךָ אָדָם, וְיֵרָאֶה לְךָ שֶׁאַתָּה עוֹבֵר עַל אֵיזֶה דִּין, יַשִּׂיאֲךָ לְבַד שֶׁלֹּא לְאַפְרוּשֵׁי מִזֶּה כָּל זְמַן שֶׁיִּרְאַת הַמּוֹכִיחַ עַל פָּנֶיךָ, בְּאָמְרְךָ, שֶׁרַק אֵין יִרְאַת אֱלֹהִים בָּזֶה רַק יִרְאַת אָדָם, וְיִרְאָה חִיצוֹנִית:
- וּכְבָר הוֹרוּנוּ חֲכָמֵינוּ זִכְרוֹנָם לִבְרָכָה
  - בְּבִרְכַּת רַבִּי יוֹחָנָן בֶּן זַכַּאי לְתַלְמִידָיו (ברכות כח), "שֶׁתְּהֵא מוֹרָא שָׁמַיִם עֲלֵיכֶם כְּמוֹרָא בָּשָׂר וָדָם" וְכוּ'.
  - וּמִי לָנוּ גָּדוֹל וְחָסִיד מֵרַב עַמְרָם חֲסִידָא, וְעִם כָּל זֶה כְּשֶׁנִּזְדַּמֵּן לְיָדוֹ פַּעַם אַחַת דְּבַר עֲבֵרָה פָּתְאֹם רַחֲמָנָא לִיצְלָן כַּמּוּבָא שִׁלְהֵי קִדּוּשִׁין (פ"א ע"א)

---

students on his deathbed, i.e., that they should be able to reach this level of Fear of God by relating to Him as a person. His students protested that surely this was not such a great blessing as they did not relate to this as a high level; he then affirmed that it is.

96 As brought down in Kiddushin 81a.

97 Who when attracted to and in the midst of exerting great physical effort to reach a beautiful woman, managed to call out to his colleagues to come to him and their presence enabled him to overcome his temptation. The Vilna Gaon comments, in Imrei Noam on R. Yochanan ben Zakkai's statement on Berachot 28b as follows:

- Before a person sins he can separate himself from it even just with Fear of God [alone]. However once he starts to perform the sin, then he will not be

- battled with deviousness to save himself from the trap of his Evil Inclination even though he was embarrassed by the presence of other people
- as long as he did not, God forbid, transgress the commandments of his Creator
- and it appears that while God has pity on the honor of Tzaddikim, nevertheless, this example was set out in the Talmud to teach us the correct ways of [serving] God.

• Now, I have shown you some of the devious methods of the Evil Inclination which
  - as Chazal teach:[98] R. Yitzchak said the Evil Inclination renews itself every day as it says "it is just bad *each day*"
  - that it is not good enough that a person overcame its deviousness yesterday and the day before yesterday, as it completely renews itself each day
  - and it is as if it has not previously incited one to do evil at all
  - on the contrary, it [tries to] show a person that all the Torah that he has learned and the Mitzvot he has performed until now were of no positive consequence and that he is just "bad each day"
  - and in this way it overpowers the person as Chazal state about the verse "the Wicked One watches the righteous and seeks to kill him . . ."[99]
  - this is the Evil Inclination, it is the 'Angel of Death which is full of eyes'[100] – it watches to see what develops and in what way it can cause [the person] to stumble (for *watching* relates to a future outcome)
  - to the extent that the person is no longer aware to be careful of it.

• Now, you the reader, do not think that I invented these things
  - as I have evaluated and tested all this when I set my heart to investigate and to search
  - and saw many with my own eyes who 'desired closeness to God'[101] and have stumbled on these things mentioned above, who directly told me what was on their hearts.
  - With my own eyes, I saw some people in one place that had become so accustomed to this for a very long time to the extent that they have virtually forgotten the defined time that Chazal set for praying Mincha
  - on the contrary, the practice has become fixed in their hearts, like judgment and Halacha, that the key time for the Mincha prayer is after nightfall, and when a person says to his colleague "let us pray the Mincha prayer" he receives the answer "let us see if we can already

- נִלְחָם בְּתַחְבּוּלוֹת לְהִנָּצֵל מֵרֶשֶׁת יִצְרוֹ אַף מֵחֲמַת הַבּוּשָׁה מֵהַבְּרִיּוֹת
- רַק שֶׁלֹּא לַעֲבֹר חַם וְשָׁלוֹם עַל מִצְוֹת בּוֹרְאוֹ יִתְבָּרַךְ שְׁמוֹ.
- וְנִרְאָה הֲגַם שֶׁהַקָּדוֹשׁ בָּרוּךְ הוּא חָס עַל כְּבוֹדָן שֶׁל צַדִּיקִים, עִם כָּל זֶה קְבָעוּהָ לְהַאי עוּבְדָּא בַּתַּלְמוּד, לְהוֹרוֹת לָנוּ דַּרְכֵי ה' הַיְשָׁרִים:
- וְעַתָּה הֶרְאֵיתִיךָ קְצוֹת דַּרְכֵי הַיֵּצֶר הַמִּתְחַפֵּשׂ בְּכָל מִינֵי תַּחְבּוּלוֹת
- כְּמוֹ שֶׁאָמְרוּ רַבּוֹתֵינוּ זִכְרוֹנָם לִבְרָכָה (קדושין ל:), "אָמַר רַבִּי יִצְחָק יִצְרוֹ שֶׁל אָדָם מִתְחַדֵּשׁ עָלָיו בְּכָל יוֹם, שֶׁנֶּאֱמַר (בראשית ו, ה) "רַק רַע כָּל הַיּוֹם".
- שֶׁלֹּא דַי לוֹ שֶׁמִּתְגַּבֵּר בְּתַחְבּוּלוֹתָיו שֶׁהִתְנַכֵּל עַל הָאָדָם מִתְּמוֹל שִׁלְשׁוֹם, אֶלָּא שֶׁעוֹד מִתְחַדֵּשׁ כָּל יוֹם בַּחֲדָשׁוֹת
- וּכְאִלּוּ אֵינוֹ מֵסִיתוֹ לָרַע כְּלָל
- וְאַדְּרַבָּה, מַרְאֶה לָאָדָם שֶׁכָּל מַה שֶּׁלָּמַד תּוֹרָה אוֹ פָּעַל מִצְוֹת, עֲדֶן לֹא הָיָה בָּהֶם שׁוּם טוֹב, וְהוּא רַק רַע כָּל הַיּוֹם.
- וּבָזֶה הוּא מִתְגַּבֵּר עַל הָאָדָם, כְּמוֹ שֶׁאָמְרוּ זִכְרוֹנָם לִבְרָכָה (סוכה נב, ב) עַל פָּסוּק "צוֹפֶה רָשָׁע לַצַּדִּיק וּמְבַקֵּשׁ לַהֲמִיתוֹ" וכו' (תהלים לז, לב)
- וְהוּא הַיֵּצֶר הָרָע, הוּא הַמַּלְאָךְ הַמָּוֶת מָלֵא עֵינַיִם, וְצוֹפֶה לִרְאוֹת הַנּוֹלָד בַּמֶּה לְהַכְשִׁיל (כִּי עִנְיַן "צְפִיָּה" הוּא עַל דָּבָר שֶׁעָתִיד לִהְיוֹת אַחַר כָּךְ)
- עַד אֲשֶׁר הָאָדָם לֹא יֵדַע לְהִזָּהֵר עוֹד:
- וְאַתָּה הַקּוֹרֵא, אַל תְּדַמֶּה שֶׁמִּלִּבִּי הוֹצֵאתִי הַדְּבָרִים
- כִּי אֶת כָּל זֹאת בָּחַנְתִּי וְנִסִּיתִי, כַּאֲשֶׁר נָתַתִּי לִבִּי לִדְרשׁ וְלָתוּר
- וְעֵינַי רָאוּ רַבִּים אֲשֶׁר יַחְפְּצוּ קִרְבַת אֱלֹקִים, וְנִכְשָׁלִים בְּמוֹ אֵלֶּה הַדְּבָרִים הַנַּ"ל, אֲשֶׁר מִפִּיהֶם אֵלַי נֶאֶמְרוּ מִלְּבָּם.
- וּבְעֵינַי רָאִיתִי בְּמָקוֹם אֶחָד אֵיזֶה אֲנָשִׁים, שֶׁהִרְגִּילוּ בְּזֶה זְמַן כַּבִּיר עַד שֶׁכִּמְעַט נִשְׁכַּח מֵהֶם זְמַן תְּפִלַּת הַמִּנְחָה שֶׁקָּבְעוּ לָנוּ רַבּוֹתֵינוּ זִכְרוֹנָם לִבְרָכָה.
- וְאַדְּרַבָּה, נִקְבַּע בְּלִבָּם מֵרֹב הַהֶרְגֵּל, כְּמוֹ דִין וַהֲלָכָה, שֶׁתְּפִלַּת הַמִּנְחָה, עִקָּרָהּ אַחַר צֵאת הַכּוֹכָבִים. וּכְשֶׁאָדָם אוֹמֵר לַחֲבֵרוֹ נִתְפַּלֵּל תְּפִלַּת מִנְחָה, הוּא

---

able to leave it [by only utilizing] Fear of God – it is only out of fear of man that [he will be able] to leave it.

98 Kiddushin 30b quoting Bereishit 6:5.
99 Sukkah 52b quoting Tehillim 37:32.
100 Avodah Zarah 20b.
101 Yishayahu 58:2.

see the stars in the sky" – God should forgive them 'and atone for the unwitting and ignorant.'[102]
- But 'you should place your heart to know the view of the Sages'[103] possessors of Torah who have already taught us
  - that the essence is to perform a Mitzvah at its correct time and with all of its detail and precision as *an immutable decree*
  - and that purity of good thought should be attached to the performance
  - then 'you will then go securely'[104] and both [the performance and the purity of thought] will be fulfilled in your hands.
  - As the explicit Mishna[105] taught that all for whom their actions are greater than their wisdom, then even their wisdom will be preserved in holiness, purity, and inspirational fervor
  - and the comparison that Chazal make about this cannot be trivialized, that all whose actions are greater than their wisdom are like a tree whose leaves are few and their roots are many, that all the winds in the world cannot move it from its place[106]
  - and 'the one who hears will internalize.'[107]

---

102 Yechezkel 45:20.
103 Mishlei 22:17.
104 Mishlei 3:23.
105 Mishna Avot 3:9.
106 Mishna Avot 3:17.
107 Yechezkel 3:27.

מְשִׁיבוֹ, נִרְאֶה וְנִגְעֵן אִם כְּבָר נִרְאוּ הַכּוֹכָבִים בָּרָקִיעַ, וה' יִסְלַח לָהֶם, וִיכַפֵּר לְשׁוֹגֵג וּפֶתִי:

- אֲבָל לְבַד תָּשִׁית לָדַעַת חֲכָמִים בַּעֲלֵי תוֹרָה, אֲשֶׁר כְּבָר הוֹרוּנוּ חז"ל
  - שֶׁהָעִקָּר הוּא עֲשִׂיַּת הַמִּצְוָה בִּזְמַנָּהּ בְּכָל פְּרָטֶיהָ וְדִקְדּוּקֶיהָ חֹק וְלֹא יַעֲבֹר
  - וְטָהֳרַת הַמַּחֲשָׁבָה טוֹבָה תִּצָּרֵף לְמַעֲשֶׂה
  - אָז תֵּלֵךְ לָבֶטַח, וְזֶה וְזֶה יִתְקַיְּמוּ בְּיָדֶיךָ.
- וּמִשְׁנָה מְפֹרֶשֶׁת שָׁנוּ (אבות ג, ט) כֹּל שֶׁמַּעֲשָׂיו מְרֻבִּין מֵחָכְמָתוֹ, אַף גַּם חָכְמָתוֹ מִתְקַיֶּמֶת בִּקְדֻשָּׁה וְטָהֳרָה וּדְבֵקוּת.
- וּמִי זוּטָר הוּא מַה שֶׁהִמְשִׁילוּ חֲכָמֵינוּ זִכְרוֹנָם לִבְרָכָה (שם, יז) כֹּל שֶׁמַּעֲשָׂיו מְרֻבִּין מֵחָכְמָתוֹ לְאִילָן שֶׁעֲנָפָיו מֻעָטִין וְשָׁרָשָׁיו מְרֻבִּין, שֶׁכָּל הָרוּחוֹת שֶׁבָּעוֹלָם אֵין מְזִיזִין אוֹתוֹ מִמְּקוֹמוֹ.
  - וְהַשּׁוֹמֵעַ יִשְׁמַע:

FOURTH GATEWAY

1. BACKGROUND OF WHY IMPORTANCE OF TORAH STUDY IS TO BE ACCENTUATED

- I additionally want to 'enshrine in writing'[1] details of the magnitude of every Jewish man's obligation to be involved in Torah study, day and night
  - and to expand a little 'with language which describes the greatness'[2]
    - of the 'precious beauty'[3] and superior nature of Torah
    - and of the honest person who is occupied with it and reviews it 'with the Torah of kindness on his tongue'[4] who brings joy to his Creator
    - and of the 'man of knowledge who grows stronger'[5] who supports it and 'resolves its difficulties.'[6]
  - Since there has been a long period in Israel
    - following many generations of progressive decline in Torah study
    - and that now in recent generations, as a result of our great sins, it has declined very greatly and is now placed at the lowest hidden level, God should save us
    - as we see now with the majority of our people, due to the burden of seeking a livelihood, God should have mercy.
- In addition, many of those who 'desire closeness to God'[7]
  - have chosen for themselves to allocate their main study efforts to works inspiring Fear of God and ethical works all of their days
  - without assigning their principal involvement with the Holy Torah to the study of Scriptures and the many Halachot
  - and they have not yet seen light in their days or been touched by the light of Torah
  - God should forgive them as their intention is for the sake of Heaven.
  - However, this is not the way in which the light of the Torah will dwell within them.
- In truth, the works inspiring fear of God are all 'virtuous ways of God'[8]
  - for the early generations were entirely entrenched in the study and

---

1 Tehillim 40:8.
2 Tehillim 12:4.
3 Esther 1:4.
4 Mishlei 31:26.
5 Mishlei 24:5.

שַׁעַר ד'

שער ד' - פרק א'

- עוֹד זֹאת אָמַרְתִּי, לָבֹא בִּמְגִלַּת סֵפֶר כָּתוּב, בְּגֹדֶל הַחִיּוּב שֶׁל עֵסֶק הַתּוֹרָה, עַל כָּל אִישׁ יִשְׂרָאֵל יוֹם וָלָיְלָה
  - וּלְהַרְחִיב מְעַט הַדִּבּוּר, בְּלָשׁוֹן מְדַבֶּרֶת גְּדוֹלוֹת,
    - יְקַר תִּפְאַרְתָּהּ וּמַעֲלָתָהּ שֶׁל הַתּוֹרָה
    - וְהָאָדָם הַיָּשָׁר הָעוֹסֵק וְהוֹגֶה בָּהּ בְּתוֹרַת חֶסֶד עַל לְשׁוֹנוֹ, לַעֲשׂוֹת נַחַת רוּחַ לְיוֹצְרוֹ וּבוֹרְאוֹ יִתְבָּרַךְ שְׁמוֹ
    - וְאִישׁ דַּעַת הַמְאַמֵּץ כֹּחַ, לְתָמְכָהּ וּלְסַעֲדָהּ וּלְהַחֲזִיק בְּדָקֶיהָ.
  - אַחֲרֵי אֲשֶׁר זֶה יָמִים רַבִּים לְיִשְׂרָאֵל
    - שֶׁהֻשְׁפַּל עֵסֶק תּוֹרָה הַקְּדוֹשָׁה בְּכָל דּוֹר וָדוֹר
  - וְהֵן עַתָּה בַּדּוֹרוֹת הַלָּלוּ בַּעֲוֹנוֹתֵינוּ הָרַבִּים, נָפְלָה מְאֹד מְאֹד, נְתוּנָה בְּסֵתֶר הַמַּדְרֵגָה הַתַּחְתּוֹנָה רַחֲמָנָא לִצְלָן
    - כַּאֲשֶׁר עֵינֵינוּ הָרוֹאוֹת עַתָּה בְּרֹבַּת בְּנֵי עַמֵּנוּ, מִגֹּדֶל סֵבֶל מַשָּׂא עַל הַפַּרְנָסָה ה' יְרַחֵם:

- וְגַם כַּמָּה מֵאוֹתָן אֲשֶׁר קִרְבַת אֱלֹקִים יֶחְפָּצוּן
  - הֵמָּה בָּחֲרוּ לְעַצְמָם לִקְבֹּעַ כָּל עִקָּר לִמּוּדָם בְּסִפְרֵי יִרְאָה וּמוּסָר כָּל הַיָּמִים
  - בְּלֹא קְבִיעוּת עִקָּר הָעֵסֶק בְּתוֹרָתֵנוּ הַקְּדוֹשָׁה, בְּמִקְרָאוֹת וַהֲלָכוֹת מְרֻבּוֹת
  - וַעֲדַיִן לֹא רָאוּ מְאוֹרוֹת מִימֵיהֶם, וְלֹא נָגַהּ עֲלֵיהֶם אוֹר הַתּוֹרָה
  - ה' יִסְלַח לָהֶם, כִּי כַוָּנָתָם לַשָּׁמַיִם
  - אֲבָל לֹא זוֹ הַדֶּרֶךְ יִשְׁכָּן בָּם אוֹר הַתּוֹרָה:

- וֶאֱמֶת, כִּי סִפְרֵי יִרְאָה, הִנָּם כְּכָל דַּרְכֵי ה' הַיְשָׁרִים
  - כִּי דּוֹרוֹת הָרִאשׁוֹנִים הָיוּ קְבוּעִים כָּל יְמֵיהֶם בְּעֵסֶק וְהִגָּיוֹן תּוֹרָתֵנוּ הַקְּדוֹשָׁה, תְּקוּעִים בְּאָהֳלֵי הַמִּדְרָשׁוֹת בְּגפ"ת

---

6 An expression from 2 Melachim 12:6 lit. meaning "fixing the cracks."
7 Yishayahu 58:2.
8 Hoshea 14:10.

- the analysis of our Holy Torah pitched in the tents of study of the main body of Torah[9]
  - and their hearts were ablaze with the flame of the love of our Holy Torah fuelled by pure Love and Fear of God
  - with their entire desire to raise the profile of its honor and 'to expand its reach with the establishment of many fitting students'[10] in order to 'fill the world with knowledge'.[11]
- Over the course of time, as has always been the way of the Evil Inclination to be jealous of 'these people of God'[12] when they are correctly following the way of God, injecting poison into them
  - resulting in many students entirely focusing themselves on the technical analysis of Torah alone with no other [focus] at all [thereby causing Torah study to be sterile]
  - as we have learned in our Mishna that "if there is no fear then there is no Torah,"[13] and also many other statements of Chazal in this vein such as will be brought later on in G4:04.
- Therefore, many leaders 'the eyes of the community'[14]
  - whose way in holiness is to persevere with the general correction of our brothers, the House of Israel
  - 'straightening out the twisted paths'[15] and 'fencing in their breaches'[16] to remove the stumbling block from being in the way of the people of God
  - aroused themselves with the initiative[17] of presenting a rebuke of ethics and character traits by authoring works of Fear of God to straighten the heart of the people
  - so that they can be involved in Torah study and service of God out of pure Fear of God.
- But every 'man of understanding'[18] whose intellect 'walks with uprightness'[19] will understand from his own knowledge
  - that [the Torah Sages] did not, God forbid, intend for [the people] to neglect involvement in the main body of Torah study
  - and to entirely dedicate all of their time to the study of their ethical works
  - but their desired objective was that the main allocation of study by the Holy People would be just of the Holy Torah – of the Scripture, Oral Law, and the many Halachot which together form the Body of Torah
  - [but to] also [allocate some study] of the pure Fear of God.

---

9   The abbreviation GP"T *Gimmel, Peh, Tav* is used here, meaning Gemara/Talmud, Perushim/Commentaries, and Tosafot.
10 E.g., as per Berachot 16b.

- וְשַׁלְהֶבֶת אַהֲבַת תּוֹרָתֵנוּ הַקְּדוֹשָׁה הָיָה בּוֹעֵר בְּלִבָּם כְּאֵשׁ בּוֹעֶרֶת, בְּאַהֲבַת וְיִרְאַת ה' טְהוֹרָה
- וְכָל חֶפְצָם לְהַגְדִּיל כְּבוֹדָהּ וּלְהַאֲדִירָהּ, וְהִרְחִיבוּ גְבוּלָם בְּתַלְמִידִים רַבִּים הֲגוּנִים, לְמַעַן תִּמָּלֵא הָאָרֶץ דֵּעָה:

• וְכַאֲשֶׁר אָרְכוּ הַיָּמִים, הִנֵּה כֵן דַּרְכּוֹ שֶׁל הַיֵּצֶר מֵעוֹלָם, לְהִתְקַנֵּא בְּעַם ה' אֵלֶּה כַּאֲשֶׁר הֵמָּה דּוֹרְכִים בְּדֶרֶךְ ה' כָּרָאוּי, לְהָטִיל בָּהֶם אֶרֶס
- עַד שֶׁכַּמָּה מֵהַתַּלְמִידִים שָׁמוּ כָּל קְבִיעוּתָם וְעִסְקָם רַק בְּפִלְפּוּלָהּ שֶׁל תּוֹרָה לְבַד, וְלֹא זוּלַת כְּלָל.
- וְשָׁנִינוּ בְּמִשְׁנָתֵנוּ (אבות ג, יז) "אִם אֵין יִרְאָה אֵין חָכְמָה", וְעוֹד הַרְבֵּה מַאַמְרֵי רַבּוֹתֵינוּ זִכְרוֹנָם לִבְרָכָה מִזֶּה, כְּמוֹ שֶׁיּוּבָא לְהַלָּן פֶּרֶק ד' אִם יִרְצֶה ה':

• לָזֹאת, הִתְעוֹרְרוּ עַצְמָם כַּמָּה מִגְּדוֹלֵיהֶם עֵינֵי הָעֵדָה
- אֲשֶׁר דַּרְכָּם בַּקֹּדֶשׁ לִשְׁקֹד עַל תַּקָּנַת כְּלָל אַחֵינוּ בֵּית יִשְׂרָאֵל
- לְיַשֵּׁר הַהֲדוּרִים וְלִגְדֹּר פִּרְצוֹתָם, לְהָרִים הַמִּכְשׁוֹל מִדֶּרֶךְ עַם ה'
- וּמִלְאוּ אֶת יָדָם לָבוֹא בְּתוֹכָחוֹת בְּמוּסָרִים וּמִדּוֹת וְחִבְּרוּ סִפְרֵי יִרְאָה לְהַיְשִׁיר לֵב הָעָם
- לִהְיוֹתָם עוֹסְקִים בַּתּוֹרָה הַקְּדוֹשָׁה וּבָעֲבוֹדָה בְּיִרְאַת ה' טְהוֹרָה:

• אָמְנָם כָּל אִישׁ תְּבוּנוֹת, אֲשֶׁר שִׂכְלוֹ יָשָׁר הוֹלֵךְ, יָבִין מַדַּעְתּוֹ
- כִּי לֹא כִוְּנוּ בָּהֶם לְהַזְנִיחַ חַס וְשָׁלוֹם הָעֵסֶק בְּגוּפֵי הַתּוֹרָה
- וְלִהְיוֹת אַךְ עָסוּק כָּל הַיָּמִים בְּסִפְרֵי מוּסָרִים
- אֶלָּא כַּוָּנָתָם רְצוּיָה הָיְתָה, שֶׁכָּל עִקַּר קְבִיעַת לִמּוּד עִם הַקֹּדֶשׁ, יִהְיֶה רַק בַּתּוֹרָה הַקְּדוֹשָׁה שֶׁבִּכְתָב וּבְעַל פֶּה, וַהֲלָכוֹת מְרֻבּוֹת, הֵן הֵן גּוּפֵי תוֹרָה וְגַם בְּיִרְאַת ה' טְהוֹרָה:

---

11 Chabakuk 2:14.
12 Yechezkel 36:20.
13 Mishna Avot 3:17.
14 An expression borrowed from Bamidbar 15:24 referring to the leading Torah Sages.
15 Yishayahu 45:2.
16 Yishayahu 58:12.
17 Milu et Yadam lit. means to inaugurate, as per Shemot 29:9.
18 Mishlei 11:12.
19 Michah 2:7.

- But now, in these [recent] generations, as a result of our many sins, this [objective] 'has been overturned'[20] and the 'exalted has been degraded'[21]
  - as so many have [misplaced] their study focus to solely be on the works of Fear of God and of ethics
  - saying that constant involvement in them is man's entire [purpose] in this world
  - that they inspire the hearts such that 'then their hearts will be humbled'[22] to subdue and break the Evil Inclination from its desires and to become upright with good character traits
  - and the 'Crown of Torah is placed in a corner.'[23]
- With my own eyes, I saw that this [phenomenon] was so widespread in one district
  - to the extent that in most of its study halls, they only had mainly ethical works and did not even have one complete Talmud
  - and 'their eyes are just incapable of seeing and their hearts from understanding'[24] that this is not the way which God has chosen – for it is not acceptable
  - and it is just a matter of time before they could be, God forbid, 'without a teacher to instruct them,'[25] and then what will become of the Torah!
- Therefore, 'who can restrain their words'[26] 'from faithfully making it known among the Tribes of Israel'[27] 'to those who fear God and rate His Name'[28] 'the way in which they should go in the light'[29] of Torah
  - 'woe to us from the Day of Judgment, woe to us from the Day of Rebuke'[30] over the sin of neglecting Torah study, for God is jealous for it to claim for its insult.
- I will initially set out my comments to relate to Torah study *for its sake* – to explain what is meant by *for its sake*
  - as this is also 'fruit of sin'[31]
  - as many hold themselves back from studying the Holy Torah
  - by thinking that the meaning of *for its sake* is with uninterrupted great inspirational fervor

---

20   Esther 9:1.
21   Yechezkel 21:31. This is the expression that appears in the Second Edition. It should be noted that in the First Edition a slightly longer phrase was taken from this verse stating "the degraded has been exalted and the exalted has been degraded." It appears that this longer expression may have been considered particularly sensitive at the time of printing in the face of the dispute between the Chassidim and Mitnagdim. After the printing of the First Edition, a little sticker was placed over the extra words "the degraded has been exalted" in all

- וְהֵן עַתָּה בַּדּוֹרוֹת הַלָּלוּ בַּעֲוֹנוֹתֵינוּ הָרַבִּים, נֶהְפּוֹךְ הוּא, הַגָּבוֹהַּ הֻשְׁפַּל
  - שֶׁכַּמָּה וְכַמָּה שָׁמוּ כָּל עִקַּר קְבִיעַת לִמּוּדָם רֹב הַיָּמִים רַק בְּסִפְרֵי יִרְאָה וּמוּסָר
  - בְּאָמְרָם כִּי זֶה כָּל הָאָדָם בְּעוֹלָמוֹ לַעֲסֹק בָּהֶם תָּמִיד.
  - כִּי הֵמָּה מַלְהִיבִים הַלְּבָבוֹת, אֲשֶׁר אָז יִכָּנַע לִבָּבוֹ לְהַכְנִיעַ וּלְשַׁבֵּר הַיֵּצֶר מִתַּאֲוֹתָיו, וּלְהִתְיַשֵּׁר בְּמִדּוֹת טוֹבוֹת.
  - וְכֶתֶר תּוֹרָה מֻנָּח בְּקֶרֶן זָוִית:
- וּבְעֵינַי רָאִיתִי בְּפֶלֶךְ אֶחָד, שֶׁכָּל כָּךְ הִתְפַּשֵּׁט אֶצְלָם זֹאת
  - עַד שֶׁבְּרֹב בָּתֵּי מִדְרָשָׁם אֵין בָּהֶם רַק סִפְרֵי מוּסָר לָרֹב, וַאֲפִלּוּ שַׁ״ס אֶחָד שָׁלֵם אֵין בּוֹ
  - וְתָח עֵינֵיהֶם מֵרְאוֹת מֵהָבִין וְהַשְׂכֵּל לִבּוֹתָם, אֲשֶׁר לֹא זוֹ הַדֶּרֶךְ בָּחַר בּוֹ ה׳, כִּי לֹא יִרְצֶה
  - וְעוֹד מְעַט בְּהִמָּשֵׁךְ הַזְּמַן יוּכְלוּ לִהְיוֹת חַס וְשָׁלוֹם לְלֹא כֹּהֵן מוֹרֶה, וְתוֹרָה מַה תְּהֵא עָלֶיהָ:
- הֵן לָזֹאת, עֲצֹר בְּמִלִּין מִי יוּכַל, מִלְּהוֹדִיעַ בְּשִׁבְטֵי יִשְׂרָאֵל נֶאֱמָנָה, לְיִרְאֵי ה׳ וְחוֹשְׁבֵי שְׁמוֹ, אֶת הַדֶּרֶךְ יֵלְכוּ בָהּ לְאוֹרָהּ שֶׁל תּוֹרָה.
  - אוֹי לָנוּ מִיּוֹם הַדִּין, אוֹי לָנוּ מִיּוֹם הַתּוֹכֵחָה עַל עֲוֹן בִּטּוּלָהּ שֶׁל תּוֹרָה, כַּאֲשֶׁר הוּא יִתְבָּרַךְ שְׁמוֹ יְקַנֵּא לָהּ לִתְבֹּעַ עֶלְבּוֹנָהּ:
- וְתִחִלָּה אָשִׂים דְּבָרַי בְּעִנְיַן עֵסֶק הַתּוֹרָה לִשְׁמָהּ, מַהוּ עִנְיַן ״לִשְׁמָהּ״.
  - כִּי גַם זֶה פְּרִי חֲטָאת
  - לְכַמָּה הַמּוֹנְעִים עַצְמָן מֵעֵסֶק הַתּוֹרָה הַקְּדוֹשָׁה
  - בְּחָשְׁבָם כִּי עִנְיַן לִשְׁמָהּ פֵּרוּשׁוֹ, בִּדְבֵקוּת גָּדוֹל בְּלִי הֶפְסֵק.

---

or most of the copies printed, and as a result, these words are somewhat faded in those copies of the First Edition which had the sticker removed.
22 Vayikra 26:41.
23 A Rabbinic expression, e.g., R. Bechaye, Devarim 33:4.
24 Yishayahu 44:18.
25 2 Divrei Hayamim 15:3.
26 Iyov 4:2.
27 Hoshea 5:9.
28 Malachi 3:16.
29 An expression most likely borrowed from Nechemia 9:12.
30 Bereishit Rabba Vayigash 93:10.
31 Michah 6:7.

- and much worse than this, they consider that Torah study without inspirational fervor is nothing and of no purpose, God forbid.
- Therefore, when they see that their hearts do not reach this level that their studies are with constant fervor – they don't even begin to study at all – 'therefore Torah is weakened,'[32] God forbid.

- In the course of setting out the details, an explanation will, God willing, be provided of the virtue of the Holy Torah and of the person who studies it properly.
  - Therefore, there is a need to set out a few statements from Chazal
    - from the Talmud, Midrash, and Zohar
    - which describe the awesome qualities of the Holy Torah and of the one who studies it
    - and the associated rewards [for its study] and punishments [for neglect], God forbid.
    - Even though all of these statements are well-known and publicized, I have nevertheless gathered them together
    - to enthuse the hearts of those desiring inspirational fervor with love of God's Torah and to rest in its awesome supernal shade.

2. FOR ITS SAKE NOT TO BE CONFUSED WITH INSPIRATIONAL FERVOR

- It is truly clear that the concept of Torah study *for its sake* is not, as is generally now thought, that *for its sake* means with inspirational fervor.
- As Chazal[33] state that David sought that God include those who involve themselves with his Tehillim/Psalms to be considered as if they had involved themselves with [and received the same merit for] the study of the laws of ritual plagues and shelters[34]
  - therefore [from the very fact that David sought this, we see that] the in-depth study of and expending of effort on the laws of the Talmud is more significant and beloved before God than the recitation of Tehillim.
  - If we assert that *for its sake* specifically means with inspirational fervor
    - and that this is the only requirement of the whole concept of Torah study
    - then surely there can be no greater inspirational fervor than that achieved by the constant proper recitation of Tehillim!
  - Furthermore, we do not know if God agreed [to David's request], for Chazal do not record what God answered to this request (as we find

---

32 Chabakuk 1:4.

- וְגַם רָעָה חוֹלָה יוֹתֵר מִזֶּה, שֶׁסּוֹבְרִים בְּדַעְתָּם שֶׁעֵסֶק הַתּוֹרָה בְּלֹא דְבֵיקוּת אֵין כְּלוּם, וּלְלֹא שׁוּם תּוֹעֶלֶת חַס וְשָׁלוֹם.
- לָזֹאת, כְּשֶׁרוֹאִין עַצְמָן שֶׁאֵין לָכֶם הוֹלֵךְ לָזֹאת הַמַּדְרֵגָה — שֶׁיְּהֵא לִמּוּדָם בִּדְבֵיקוּת תְּמִידִי, לֹא יַתְחִילוּ כְּלָל לִלְמֹד, וְעַל כֵּן תָּפוּג תּוֹרָה חַס וְשָׁלוֹם:
- וּמֵהֶמְשֵׁךְ הָעִנְיָנִים יִתְבָּאֵר אִם יִרְצֶה ה' מִמֵּילָא מַעֲלָתָהּ שֶׁל הַתּוֹרָה הַקְּדוֹשָׁה וְהָאָדָם הָעוֹסֵק בָּהּ כָּרָאוּי.
  - לָזֹאת, הֻכְרַח לְהָבִיא קְצָת מַאַמְרֵי רַבּוֹתֵינוּ זִכְרוֹנָם לִבְרָכָה בַּשַּׁ"ס וּמִדְרָשִׁים וְזֹהַר
  - אֲשֶׁר בָּם יְדַבֵּר נִפְלָאוֹת מַעֲלַת הַתּוֹרָה הַקְּדוֹשָׁה, וְהָעוֹסֵק בָּהּ וְגֹדֶל שְׂכָרָהּ וְעָנְשָׁהּ ר"ל.
  - הֲגַם שֶׁכָּל אֵלּוּ הַמַּאֲמָרִים יְדוּעִים וּמְפֻרְסָמִים, עִם כָּל זֶה קִבַּצְתִּים
  - לְהַלְהִיב לִבּוֹת הַחֲפֵצִים לְהִתְדַּבֵּק בְּאַהֲבַת תּוֹרָתוֹ יִתְבָּרַךְ, וּלְהִתְלוֹנֵן בְּצֵל הָעֶלְיוֹן נוֹרָא:

שער ד' - פרק ב'

- עִנְיַן עֵסֶק הַתּוֹרָה לִשְׁמָהּ, הָאֱמֶת הַבָּרוּר, כִּי "לִשְׁמָהּ" אֵין פֵּרוּשׁוֹ דְּבֵיקוּת, כְּמוֹ שֶׁסּוֹבְרִים עַתָּה רֹב הָעוֹלָם:
- שֶׁהֲרֵי אָמְרוּ רַבּוֹתֵינוּ זִכְרוֹנָם לִבְרָכָה בַּמִּדְרָשׁ (שוח"ט תהלים א, ח) שֶׁבִּקֵּשׁ דָּוִד הַמֶּלֶךְ עָלָיו הַשָּׁלוֹם מִלְּפָנָיו יִתְבָּרַךְ, שֶׁהָעוֹסֵק בִּתְהִלִּים יֵחָשֵׁב אֶצְלוֹ יִתְבָּרַךְ כְּאִלּוּ הָיָה עוֹסֵק בִּנְגָעִים וְאֹהָלוֹת.
- הֲרֵי שֶׁהָעוֹסֵק בְּהִלְכוֹת הַשַּׁ"ס בְּעִיּוּן וִיגִיעָה, הוּא עִנְיָן נַעֲלֶה יוֹתֵר וְאָהוּב לְפָנָיו יִתְבָּרַךְ מֵאֲמִירַת תְּהִלִּים.
  - וְאִם נֶאֱמַר שֶׁ"לִּשְׁמָהּ" פֵּרוּשׁוֹ דְּבֵיקוּת דַּוְקָא
  - וְרַק בָּזֶה תָּלוּי כָּל עִקַּר עִנְיַן עֵסֶק הַתּוֹרָה
  - הֲלֹא אֵין דְּבֵיקוּת יוֹתֵר נִפְלָא מֵאֲמִירַת תְּהִלִּים כָּרָאוּי כָּל הַיּוֹם.
- וְגַם מִי יוֹדֵעַ אִם הִסְכִּים הַקָּדוֹשׁ בָּרוּךְ הוּא עַל יָדוֹ בָּזֶה, כִּי לֹא מָצִינוּ בְּדִבְרֵיהֶם

---

33 Midrash Tehillim 1:8.
34 The laws of ritual plagues and shelters are considered to be the most complex to master, as commented by Rashi on Chagiga 14a. Also see Pesachim 50a which describes these laws as difficult to understand in this world in contrast to being relatively easy to understand in the future world.

in the Talmud, "and as to the other opinion [which, in another context, interprets a verse where David] requests mercy [as also not having been answered]"35).36

- Furthermore, if inspirational fervor [was the objective,] then it would surely suffice to focus one's lifetime of study on just a single tractate, chapter, or Mishna! We do not find any source consistent with this in Chazal!
  - As stated about R. Yochanan ben Zakkai,37 that he not even momentarily desisted from the study of Scripture, Mishna, Halachot, Agadot, etc., that is, he would constantly be aware that he had not yet fulfilled his obligation of Torah study *for its sake* with whatever he had previously studied and therefore continuously 'increased his learning'38 from day to day and from hour to hour.
  - And in the Midrash:39 R. Yishmael said: Come and see how difficult is Judgment Day, as in the future God will judge the entire world . . . One who has Scripture [study] in his hand but not Mishna will come and God will turn his face from him and the torture of Gehinom will be increased . . . and they take him and throw him in Gehinom. One who has [the study of] two or three tractates in his hand will come and God will say to him: My son, why did you not learn all the Halachot? . . . One who has [studied] Halachot will come, [God] will say: My son, why did you not learn the laws concerning Priests? . . . One who has [studied] the laws of Priests will come, God will say to him: My son, why did you not learn the five Books of the Torah which have within them details of Shema, Tefillin and Mezuza? One who has [the study of] the five Books of the Torah in his hand, God will say to him: Why did you not learn Agadah? . . . One who has [studied] Agadah will come, God will say to him: Why did you not study Talmud? One who has [the study of] Talmud in his hand will come, God will say to him: My son, since you studied Talmud did you look at the Merkava? . . . to see how My Throne of Glory is structured? . . . and how the Chashmal40 stands . . . and in how many ways it transforms [in one hour]? . . . Refer there at length.

---

35 Bava Batra 17a, where David is not initially listed among the seven people who did not experience decay of their corpse, as the scriptural source for this possible inclusion was a prayer that this should be the case, i.e., that according to the other opinion referenced here there is no scriptural evidence that David merited this and that his prayer request was actually granted.

36 The contents of this parenthesis did not appear in the First Edition and were only introduced, seemingly by R. Yitzchak, in the Second Edition. This

זִכְרוֹנָם לִבְרָכָה מַה תְּשׁוּבָה הֵשִׁיבוּ הוּא יִתְבָּרַךְ עַל שְׁאֵלָתוֹ (כְּמוֹ שֶׁמָּצִינוּ בָּבָא בַּתְרָא י"ז א', וְאִידָךְ, הַהוּא רַחֲמֵי הוּא דְקָא בָּעֵי) :

• וְגַם כִּי הָיָה דַי לְעִנְיַן הַדְּבֵקוּת, בְּמַסֶּכֶת אַחַת, אוֹ פֶּרֶק, אוֹ מִשְׁנָה אַחַת, שֶׁיַּעֲסֹק בָּהּ כָּל יָמָיו בִּדְבֵקוּת. וְלֹא כֵן מָצִינוּ לְרַבּוֹתֵינוּ זִכְרוֹנָם לִבְרָכָה

○ שֶׁאָמְרוּ עַל רַבִּי יוֹחָנָן בֶּן זַכַּאי (סוכה כח, א) שֶׁלֹּא הִנִּיחַ מִקְרָא מִשְׁנָה הֲלָכוֹת וְאַגָּדוֹת כו', וְהַיְנוּ כִּי מֵהַעֲלוֹתוֹ עַל לִבּוֹ תָּמִיד, כִּי עֶרֶן לֹא יָצָא יְדֵי חוֹבַת עֵסֶק הַתּוֹרָה לְשָׁמָהּ בְּמַה שֶּׁלָּמַד עַד עַתָּה, לָזֹאת הָיָה שׁוֹקֵד כָּל יָמָיו לְהוֹסִיף לֶקַח תָּמִיד, מִיּוֹם לְיוֹם וּמִשָּׁעָה לְשָׁעָה.

○ וּבְמִשְׁלֵי רַבָּתָא פ"י, "אָמַר רַבִּי יִשְׁמָעֵאל בֹּא וּרְאֵה כַּמָּה קָשֶׁה יוֹם הַדִּין, שֶׁעָתִיד הַקָּדוֹשׁ בָּרוּךְ הוּא לָדוּן אֶת כָּל הָעוֹלָם כֻּלּוֹ כו', בָּא מִי שֶׁיֵּשׁ בְּיָדוֹ מִקְרָא וְאֵין בְּיָדוֹ מִשְׁנָה, הַקָּדוֹשׁ בָּרוּךְ הוּא הוֹפֵךְ אֶת פָּנָיו מִמֶּנּוּ וּמְצִירֵי גֵּיהִנָּם מִתְגַּבְּרִין בּוֹ כו', וְהֵם נוֹטְלִין אוֹתוֹ וּמַשְׁלִיכִין אוֹתוֹ לְגֵיהִנָּם. בָּא מִי שֶׁיֵּשׁ בְּיָדוֹ שְׁנֵי סְדָרִים אוֹ שְׁלֹשָׁה, הַקָּדוֹשׁ בָּרוּךְ הוּא אוֹמֵר לוֹ בְּנִי כָּל הַהֲלָכוֹת לָמָּה לֹא שָׁנִיתָ אוֹתָם כו'. בָּא מִי שֶׁיֵּשׁ בְּיָדוֹ הֲלָכוֹת, א"ל בְּנִי תּוֹרַת כֹּהֲנִים לָמָּה לֹא שָׁנִיתָ בּוֹ כו'. בָּא מִי שֶׁיֵּשׁ בְּיָדוֹ תּוֹרַת כֹּהֲנִים, הַקָּדוֹשׁ בָּרוּךְ הוּא אוֹמֵר לוֹ בְּנִי חֲמִשָּׁה חֻמְשֵׁי תוֹרָה לָמָּה לֹא שָׁנִיתָ בָּהֶם קְרִיאַת שְׁמַע תְּפִלִּין וּמְזוּזָה. בָּא מִי שֶׁיֵּשׁ בְּיָדוֹ חֲמִשָּׁה חֻמְשֵׁי תוֹרָה, אוֹמֵר לוֹ הַקָּדוֹשׁ בָּרוּךְ הוּא לָמָּה לֹא לָמַדְתָּ הַגָּדָה כו'. בָּא מִי שֶׁיֵּשׁ בְּיָדוֹ הַגָּדָה, הַקָּדוֹשׁ בָּרוּךְ הוּא אוֹמֵר לוֹ תַּלְמוּד לָמָּה לֹא לָמַדְתָּ. בָּא מִי שֶׁיֵּשׁ בְּיָדוֹ תַּלְמוּד הַקָּדוֹשׁ בָּרוּךְ הוּא אוֹמֵר לוֹ בְּנִי הוֹאִיל וְנִתְעַסַּקְתָּ בְּתַלְמוּד צָפִית בַּמֶּרְכָּבָה כו', כִּסֵּא כְּבוֹדִי הֵאֵיךְ הוּא עוֹמֵד כו', חַשְׁמַל הֵאֵיךְ הוּא עוֹמֵד, וּבְכַמָּה פָּנִים הוּא מִתְהַפֵּךְ" כו' עַיֵּן שָׁם בְּאָרְךָ:

---

point that the recitation of Tehillim was not on the same level as Torah study was a contentious point at the time and debated between the Chassidic and Mitnagdic camps. It seems that, as a result of this debate, R. Yitzchak felt it was necessary to add this parenthetic proof to back up R. Chaim's statement.

37 Sukkah 28a.
38 Mishlei 1:5.
39 Midrash Mishlei Parsha 10.
40 Yechezkel 1:4 and 1:27.

- It is also logical that when a person is involved with the many detailed and complex cases of Halachot in the Talmud
  - he has to intellectually apply himself to their practical application
  - such as
    - 'the laws of Bird Offerings, and [laws of] Mensturation, these are [examples] of the main body of Halacha'[41]
    - or the details of Talmudic discussions
    - and the principles of Migo of [those who wish to obtain things] by deceit that a swindler is able to claim
  - and that it is virtually impossible to simultaneously do this at the same time as achieving properly complete inspirational fervor.

3. FOR ITS SAKE = FOR THE SAKE OF TORAH

- In truth, this concept of *for its sake* means *for the sake of Torah*.
- This concept is as per the Rosh's explanation of the statement of R. Elazar son of R. Tzadok
  - [The words of the Rosh:][42] "*Fulfill* the words [of Torah] for the sake of the One who made them": For the sake of God 'who made everything for His sake.'[43] "and *speak* them for their sake": That all of your speech and analysis of Torah study should be *for the sake of Torah*. For example, to know it, understand it, analyze it, but not to mock it or use it to bolster self-pride.
  - [The Rosh] was being particular to explain the change in the language of R. Elazar son of R. Tzadok
    - that in connection with *fulfillment* [i.e., Mitzvah performance], he states that it should be "for the sake of the One who made them"
    - whereas with *speech* [i.e., the words of Torah study], he states that it should be "for their sake."
    - Therefore, in connection with [Mitzvah] performance, he explains, "For the sake of God who made everything for His sake"
    - and in connection with [Torah] study he explains it to mean "for the sake of Torah," etc.
  - and [the Rosh's] meaning is that
    - Mitzvah performance should certainly be done in the best possible way
    - with the maximum inspirational fervor and purity of thought according to one's intellect and perception
    - in order that 'the One Above should be praised'[44]

---

41 Mishna Avot 3:18.

נפש שער ד' - פרק ג' החיים 639

- וּמִסְתַּבְּרָא נָמֵי הָכִי, שֶׁהֲרֵי כַּמָּה הֲלָכוֹת מְרֻבּוֹת יֵשׁ בַּשַּׁ"ס, שֶׁבְּעֵת אֲשֶׁר הָאָדָם עוֹסֵק בָּהֶם
  - הוּא צָרִיךְ לְעַיֵּן וּלְהַעֲמִיק מַחְשַׁבְתּוֹ וְשִׂכְלוֹ בְּעִנְיְנֵי הַגַּשְׁמִיּוּת שֶׁבָּהֶם
  - כְּגוֹן
    - קִנְיָן וּפִתְחֵי נִדָּה שֶׁהֵן הֵן גּוּפֵי הֲלָכוֹת
    - אוֹ הַמַּשָּׂא וּמַתָּן בַּשַּׁ"ס
    - וּכְלָלֵי דִּינֵי מִגּוֹ שֶׁל רַמָּאוּת שֶׁהָיָה הָרַמַּאי יָכוֹל לִטְעֹן
  - וְכִמְעַט בִּלְתִּי אֶפְשָׁר שֶׁיְּהֵא אֶצְלוֹ אָז גַּם הַדְּבֵקוּת בִּשְׁלֵמוּת כָּרָאוּי:

שער ד' - פרק ג'

- אֲבָל הָאֱמֶת כִּי עִנְיַן "לִשְׁמָהּ" פֵּרוּשׁ, לְשֵׁם הַתּוֹרָה:
- וְהָעִנְיָן כְּמוֹ שֶׁפֵּרֵשׁ הָרֹא"שׁ ז"ל עַל מַאֲמַר רַבִּי אֶלְעָזָר בְּרַבִּי צָדוֹק (נדרים ס"ב)
  - "עֲשֵׂה דְבָרִים לְשֵׁם פָּעֳלָן" לִשְׁמוֹ שֶׁל הַקָּדוֹשׁ בָּרוּךְ הוּא שֶׁפָּעַל הַכֹּל לְמַעֲנֵהוּ, "וְדַבֵּר בָּהֶן לִשְׁמָן", כָּל דִּבּוּרְךָ וּמַשָּׂאֲךָ בְּדִבְרֵי תוֹרָה יִהְיֶה לְשֵׁם הַתּוֹרָה, כְּגוֹן לֵידַע וּלְהָבִין, וּלְהוֹסִיף לֶקַח וּפִלְפּוּל, וְלֹא לְקַנְטֵר וּלְהִתְגָּאוֹת". עכ"ל.
  - דְּקָדַק לְבָאֵר שִׁנּוּי לְשׁוֹנוֹ דְּרַבִּי אֶלְעָזָר בְּרַבִּי צָדוֹק
    - שֶׁבַּעֲשִׂיָּה אָמַר "לְשֵׁם פָּעֳלָן"
    - וּבַדִּבּוּר אָמַר "לִשְׁמָן"
  - לָכֵן, בְּעִנְיַן הָעֲשִׂיָּה פֵּרֵשׁ לִשְׁמוֹ שֶׁל הַקָּדוֹשׁ בָּרוּךְ הוּא שֶׁפָּעַל הַכֹּל לְמַעֲנֵהוּ
  - וּבְעִנְיַן הַלִּמּוּד פֵּרֵשׁ, לְשֵׁם הַתּוֹרָה כוּ'.
  - וְכַוָּנָתוֹ זִכְרוֹנוֹ לִבְרָכָה מְבֹאָר, הַיְנוּ
    - כִּי עֲשִׂיַּת הַמִּצְוָה וַדַּאי שֶׁצְּרִיכָה לִהְיוֹת לְמִצְוָה מִן הַמֻּבְחָר
    - בִּדְבֵקוּת וּמַחֲשָׁבָה טְהוֹרָה שֶׁבַּטְּהוֹרוֹת כְּפִי שִׂכְלוֹ וְהַשָּׂגָתוֹ
    - כְּדֵי שֶׁיִּתְקַלֵּם עֲלָאָה

---

42 Rosh on Nedarim 62a commenting on the quotations from the Talmud page. (The Rosh on Nedarim is to be found on the Talmud page and not as usually the case at the end of the Tractate.)

43 Mishlei 16:4, the verse reads "Everything God made is for His Sake, even the wicked for the day of retribution."

44 Sotah 40a.

- to cause rectifications of the worlds, powers, and the arrangement of the Supernal Realms
- This is the meaning of "for the sake of the One who made them" – for "Everything God made is for His sake"[45] which Chazal explain[46] [to mean] *for His praise*.
  - This is notwithstanding the fact that the essential part of Mitzvot, without which they cannot be fulfilled, is their physical performance
    - and [the lack of] additional associated intention and purity of thought does not prevent fulfillment at all
    - as explained in context above at the end of the First Gateway[47]
    - nevertheless, holiness and purity of thought adds to the essence of Mitzvah performance in practice, to arouse and effect even greater rectifications in the worlds compared to Mitzvah performance without inspirational fervor and holiness of thought.
  - However, with respect to a person's behavior when studying Torah, the laws and details of the Mitzvot, he says "speak of them," meaning that speech of Mitzvah details should be "for their sake," meaning for the sake of the words of Torah, that is to know, understand, and more deeply analyze.
  - (Rashi has a different version:[48] "and speak of them for the sake of Heaven." Therefore, he explains that all of one's intentions should be for the sake of Heaven.
    - However [in keeping with] the concept and explanation of *for its sake* that Chazal state in all places, it would certainly be that Rashi would have the same explanation as the Rosh here according to the [Rosh's] version.
    - In addition, Rashi's intention [in his comment] here does not refer to inspirational fervor, but rather to exclude that one's study should not be for the sake of mocking and self-pride, as per the Rosh, and as proven from the closing words of R. Elazar son of R. Tzadok "[that the words of Torah] should not be made into a crown for self-aggrandizement.")
- This is how the Talmud concludes in relation to R. Yochanan ben Zakkai[49] who did not desist [even momentarily from Torah study]
  - to fulfill the verse "to inherit to my beloved ones *Yesh* . . ."[50]
  - where this concept is explained there throughout that entire section, which itself is a statement of the Holy Torah

---

45 Mishlei 16:4.
46 Midrash Tehillim 19:1.
47 G1:22.

- לִגְרֹם תִּקּוּנֵי הָעוֹלָמוֹת וְכֹחוֹת וּסְדָרִים הָעֶלְיוֹנִים.
- זֶהוּ "לְשֵׁם פָּעֳלוֹ", כִּי "כֹּל פָּעַל ה' לַמַּעֲנֵהוּ" (משלי טז, ד), וְאָמְרוּ רַבּוֹתֵינוּ זִכְרוֹנָם לִבְרָכָה — לְקִלּוּסוֹ.
- וְאִם כִּי וַדַּאי שֶׁגַּם בַּמִּצְוֹת, הָעִקָּר בָּהֶם לְעִכּוּבָא הוּא הָעֲשִׂיָּה בְּפֹעַל
- וְהַכַּוָּנָה הַיְתֵרָה וְטֹהַר הַמַּחֲשָׁבָה אֵינָהּ מְעַכֶּבֶת כְּלָל
- כְּמוֹ שֶׁנִּתְבָּאֵר לְעֵיל סוֹף שַׁעַר א' עַל נָכוֹן בעז"ה
- עִם כָּל זֶה, מִצְטָרֵף קְדֻשַּׁת וְטֹהַר מַחֲשַׁבְתּוֹ לְעִקָּר הָעֲשִׂיָּה בְּפֹעַל, לְעוֹרֵר וְלִפְעֹל תִּקּוּנִים יוֹתֵר גְּדוֹלִים בָּעוֹלָמוֹת, מִשֶּׁאִם הָיְתָה הַמִּצְוָה נַעֲשֵׂית בְּלֹא דְבֵקוּת וּקְדֻשַּׁת הַמַּחֲשָׁבָה.
- אֲבָל עַל הַנְהָגַת הָאָדָם בִּשְׁעַת עֵסֶק הַתּוֹרָה בְּדִינֵי הַמִּצְוֹת וְהִלְכוֹתֵיהֶן, אָמַר "וְדִבַּרְתָּ בָּם", רָצָה לוֹמַר הַדִּבּוּר בְּעִנְיְנֵי הַמִּצְוֹת וְהִלְכוֹתֵיהֶן, יִהְיֶה "לִשְׁמָן", פֵּרוּשׁ, לְשֵׁם הַדִּבְרֵי תוֹרָה, הַיְנוּ לֵידַע וּלְהָבִין וּלְהוֹסִיף לֶקַח וּפִלְפּוּל.
- (וְרַשִׁ"י ז"ל גִּירְסָא אַחֶרֶת הָיְתָה לוֹ שָׁם, "וְדִבֶּר בָּהֶן לְשֵׁם שָׁמַיִם", לָכֵן פֵּרַשׁ שֶׁתְּהֵא כָּל כַּוָּנָתְךָ לַשָּׁמַיִם.
- אָמְנָם עִנְיַן וּפֵרוּשׁ "לִשְׁמָהּ" שֶׁאָמְרוּ רַבּוֹתֵינוּ זִכְרוֹנָם לִבְרָכָה בְּכָל מָקוֹם, וַדַּאי שֶׁגַּם רַשִׁ"י ז"ל יְפָרֵשׁ כְּפֵרוּשׁ הָרֹא"שׁ ז"ל כָּאן לְפִי גִּרְסָתוֹ
- וְגַם רַשִׁ"י ז"ל כָּאן אֵין כַּוָּנָתוֹ דְּבֵקוּת, אֶלָּא דְּאָתֵי לְאַפּוּקֵי, שֶׁלֹּא יְהֵא לִמּוּדוֹ לְשֵׁם קַנְטוּר וּגֵאוּת, כְּמוֹ שֶׁכָּתַב הָרֹא"שׁ ז"ל, כִּדְסָמוּךְ מְסַיֵּם מִדִּבְרֵי רַבִּי אֶלְעָזָר בְּרַבִּי צָדוֹק, "אַל תַּעֲשֵׂם עֲטָרָה לְהִתְגַּדֵּל בָּהֶם" כו'):
- וְזֶה שֶׁמְּסַיֵּם הַשַּׁ"ס גַּבֵּי רַבָּן יוֹחָנָן בֶּן זַכַּאי, שֶׁלֹּא הִנִּיחַ כו'
- לְקַיֵּם מַה שֶּׁנֶּאֱמַר (משלי ח, כא) "לְהַנְחִיל אֹהֲבַי יֵשׁ" כו'
- שֶׁמְּבֹאָר הָעִנְיָן שָׁם בְּכָל אוֹתָהּ הַפָּרָשָׁה, שֶׁהוּא מַאֲמַר הַתּוֹרָה הַקְּדוֹשָׁה עַצְמָהּ

---

48 Of R. Elazar son of R. Tzadok's comment.
49 As per Sukkah 28a. See quotation in previous chapter.
50 Mishlei 8:21. Also see quotation in Mishna Uktzin 3:12 where Yesh is understood to be referring to 310 worlds (Yesh has the numerical value of 310) which are inherited by Tzaddikim, i.e., true Torah scholars, in the future.

- which 'sings outside,'[51] that God provides inheritance and a goodly reward to all who review and study [Torah] out of an absolute love for it
- that is to deepen their analysis of it.
- This is [the meaning] of *"my beloved ones."*

4. FEAR OF GOD IS TO TORAH AS A STOREHOUSE IS TO PRODUCE

- Nevertheless, one certainly cannot say Torah involvement does not require any purity of thought and Fear of God whatsoever, God forbid, as Chazal state:
  - In an explicit Mishna: If there is no fear, then there is no wisdom.[52]
  - What is the meaning of that which is written, "Why is there money in the hand of a fool to purchase wisdom, though he has no heart"? Woe is to those Torah scholars involved in Torah study but without Fear of Heaven.[53]
  - Anyone who knows [Torah] but has no fear of sin has nothing, as Torah is bound up with fear of sin.[54]
  - R. Shimon bar Yochai said: Fear is the gateway through which to enter faith. It is upon this Mitzvah that the world exists. It is the essence and basis of all the other Mitzvot of the Torah. One who observes fear, observes all, and one who does not observe fear does not observe the Mitzvot of the Torah![55] Refer there.
  - What is the yoke of Heavenly Kingship? It is like that ox . . . similarly, a person must first accept the yoke upon himself and then serve Him in every required way, and if he does not first accept this upon himself he will not be able to serve, as per the verse "Serve God with fear." What does "with fear" mean? It is as per the verse "the beginning of wisdom is Fear of God" . . . therefore this is the beginning of all . . . as with this he enters into the rest of holiness, but if it is not found in him, then supernal holiness does not reside within him.[56]

---

51 Mishlei 1:20, i.e., that this fact is clear.
52 Mishna Avot 3:17.
53 Yoma 72b quoting Mishlei 17:16. This section of the Talmud actually refers to the "enemies of Torah scholars" and not "Torah scholars." However, because a negative expression of woe is being used, the Talmud uses the term "enemies of Torah scholars" as a euphemism for "Torah scholars." R. Chaim simply quotes the meaning instead of the confusing euphemism.
54 Shemot Rabba Ki Tisa 40:1.

- אֲשֶׁר בַּחוּץ תָּרֹנָּה, שֶׁיֵּשׁ לְאֵל יָדָהּ לְהַנְחִיל וְלָתֵת שָׂכָר טוֹב, לְכָל הַהוֹגֶה וְעוֹסֵק בָּהּ מֵחֲמַת אַהֲבָתָהּ עַצְמָהּ מַמָּשׁ
- הַיְנוּ לְהוֹסִיף בָּהּ לֶקַח וּפִלְפּוּל
- וְזֶהוּ "אוֹהֲבַי":

שער ד' - פרק ד'

- אָמְנָם וַדַּאי דְּאִי אֶפְשָׁר לוֹמַר שֶׁאֵין צָרִיךְ לְעִנְיַן עֵסֶק הַתּוֹרָה שׁוּם טֹהַר הַמַּחְשָׁבָה וְיִרְאַת ה' חָלִילָה
- שֶׁהֲרֵי מִשְׁנָה שְׁלֵמָה שָׁנִינוּ (אבות ג, יז) "אִם אֵין יִרְאָה אֵין חָכְמָה"
- וְאָמְרוּ (יומא עב, ב), מַאי דִּכְתִיב (משלי יז, טז) "לָמָּה זֶּה מְחִיר בְּיַד כְּסִיל לִקְנוֹת חָכְמָה וְלֶב אָיִן", אוֹי לָהֶם לְתַלְמִידֵי חֲכָמִים שֶׁעוֹסְקִים בַּתּוֹרָה וְאֵין בָּהֶם יִרְאַת שָׁמַיִם" כו'.
- וּבִשְׁמוֹת רַבָּה פ"מ "כָּל מִי שֶׁהוּא יוֹדֵעַ וְאֵין בְּיָדוֹ יִרְאַת חֵטְא, אֵין בְּיָדוֹ כְּלוּם, שֶׁקַּפְלִיּוֹת שֶׁל תּוֹרָה בְּיִרְאַת חֵטְא".
- וּבְהַקְדָּמַת הַזֹּהַר י"א ב' אָמַר רַבִּי שִׁמְעוֹן בֶּן יוֹחָאי, שֶׁהַיִּרְאָה אִיהִי תַּרְעָא לְאַעֲלָא לְגוֹ מְהֵימְנוּתָא, וְעַל פְּקוּדָא דָא אִתְקַיַּם כָּל עַלְמָא כו', וְדָא עִקְּרָא וִיסוֹדָא לְכָל שְׁאָר פִּקּוּדִין דְּאוֹרַיְתָא, מַאן דְּנָטִיר יִרְאָה נָטִיר כּוּלָּא, לָא נָטִיר יִרְאָה לָא נָטִיר פִּקּוּדֵי אוֹרַיְתָא כו', עַיֵּן שָׁם.
- וּבְפָרָשַׁת בְּהַר ק"ח א', מַאי עַל מַלְכוּת שָׁמַיִם אֶלָּא כְּהַאי תּוֹרָא כו', הָכִי נָמֵי אִצְטְרִיךְ לֵיהּ לְבַר נָשׁ לְקַבְּלָא עֲלֵיהּ עוֹל בְּקַדְמֵיתָא, וּלְבָתַר דִּיפְלַח לֵיהּ בְּכֹל מַה דְּאִצְטְרִיךְ, וְאִי לָא קַבִּיל עֲלֵיהּ הַאי בְּקַדְמֵיתָא, לָא יָכוֹל לְמִפְלַח. הֲדָא הוּא דִּכְתִיב "עִבְדוּ אֶת ה' בְּיִרְאָה", מַהוּ בְּיִרְאָה, כְּד"א "רֵאשִׁית חָכְמָה יִרְאַת ה'" כו', וְעַל דָּא הַאי בְּקַדְמֵיתָא הוּא דְכֹלָּא כו', בְּגִין דִּבְהַאי עָיִל לִשְׁאָר קְדוּשָׁה, וְאִי הַאי לָא אִשְׁתְּכַח לְגַבֵּיהּ, לָא שַׁרְיָא בֵּיהּ קְדוּשָׁה דִּלְעֵלָּא כו':

---

55 Zohar Introduction 11b.
56 Zohar III Behar 108a quoting Tehillim 2:11 and Tehillim 111:10.

- Chazal further say that "All whose fear of sin precedes their wisdom, their wisdom will last"[57] as Fear of God is an essential precedent for the preservation of the wisdom of the Torah.
- It is as Chazal say:[58] Reish Lakish asked what is the meaning of the verse "The *faith* of your *time* [and *strength* of *salvation* is *wisdom* and *knowledge*, but the Fear of God is his storehouse]"[59] and [explains that each of the six key words of this verse correspond to each of the six orders of the Oral Torah,] i.e., "faith" corresponds to the order of Zeraim, ["time" to the order of Moed . . . etc.,] with this verse encapsulating all of the Oral Torah; however, the verse concludes that nevertheless "the Fear of God is his storehouse."
  - This verse compares the Torah to abundant produce, and Fear of God to a storehouse which can contain and protect a large quantity of produce.
    - Fear of God is the storehouse for the wisdom of the Holy Torah, through which [the wisdom] is preserved within a person
    - and if the person does not first prepare the storehouse of Fear of God for himself, then the abundant produce of Torah is as if laid out in the open field exposed to the treading down of oxen and donkeys,[60] God forbid, which will not be preserved within him at all.
  - Similarly, Chazal say about this verse:[61] You can find a person who studies Midrash, Halachot, and Agadah, but if he has no fear of sin then he has nothing. This is analogous to a person [who when he tells his colleague] that he has a thousand units of produce [a thousand units of oil and a thousand of wine], his colleague says to him, "do you have a storehouse to place them into?" [If you do, then these are all yours, but if not, then you have nothing in your hand. Similarly, with a person who studies all, they say to him, "if you have fear of sin then it is all yours"] as the verse says "The *faith* of your *time* and [. . . but the Fear of God is his storehouse"]. Refer there.

5. THE GREATER THE FEAR OF HEAVEN, THE MORE TORAH CAN BE PRESERVED

- The capacity of the storehouse of Fear of God which a person prepares for himself, determines the amount of produce of Torah [knowledge] which can be preserved and sustained within it.

---

57 Mishna Avot 3:9.
58 Shabbat 31a.

- וְאָמְרוּ עוֹד (אבות ג, ט) "כָּל שֶׁיִּרְאַת חֶטְאוֹ קוֹדֶמֶת לְחָכְמָתוֹ חָכְמָתוֹ מִתְקַיֶּמֶת", כִּי יִרְאַת ה' תְּחִלָּה, הִיא עִקַּר הַקִּיּוּם שֶׁל חָכְמַת הַתּוֹרָה:

- וּכְמוֹ שֶׁאָמְרוּ רַבּוֹתֵינוּ זִכְרוֹנָם לִבְרָכָה (שבת לא, א), "אָמַר רֵישׁ לָקִישׁ, מַאי דִכְתִיב (ישעיה לג, ו) 'וְהָיָה אֱמוּנַת עִתֶּיךָ' כו', 'אֱמוּנַת, זֶה סֵדֶר זְרָעִים' כו', חָשִׁיב שָׁם בָּזֶה הַפָּסוּק כָּל הַשַּׁ"ס, וּמְסַיֵּם וַאֲפִלּוּ הָכִי 'יִרְאַת ה' הִיא אוֹצָרוֹ'"

  ○ דִּמָּה הַכָּתוּב אֶת הַ"תּוֹרָה" — לְרֹב תְּבוּאוֹת, וְהַ"יִּרְאָה" — לְאוֹצָר הַמַּחְזִיק בּוֹ הֲמוֹן תְּבוּאוֹת וּמִשְׁתַּמְּרִים בְּתוֹכוֹ

  ▫ שֶׁיִּרְאַת ה' הִיא הָאוֹצָר לְחָכְמַת הַתּוֹרָה הַקְּדוֹשָׁה, שֶׁעַל יָדָהּ תִּתְקַיֵּם אֵצֶל הָאָדָם

  ▫ וְאִם לֹא הֵכִין לוֹ הָאָדָם תְּחִלָּה אוֹצַר הַיִּרְאָה, הֲרֵי רֹב תְּבוּאוֹת הַתּוֹרָה כְּמֻנָּח עַל פְּנֵי הַשָּׂדֶה לְמִרְמָס רֶגֶל הַשּׁוֹר וְהַחֲמוֹר חַס וְשָׁלוֹם, שֶׁאֵינָהּ מִתְקַיֶּמֶת אֶצְלוֹ כְּלָל.

  ○ וְכֵן אָמְרוּ עַל זֶה הַכָּתוּב (בשמות רבה פ"ל) "אַתָּה מוֹצֵא אָדָם שׁוֹנֶה מִדְרָשׁ הֲלָכוֹת וְאַגָּדוֹת, וְאִם אֵין בּוֹ יִרְאַת חֵטְא אֵין בְּיָדוֹ כְּלוּם, מָשָׁל לְאָדָם כו', יֵשׁ לִי אֶלֶף מִדּוֹת שֶׁל תְּבוּאָה, א"ל יֵשׁ לְךָ אֲפּוֹתִיקָאוֹת לִתֵּן אוֹתָם בָּהֶם כו', שֶׁנֶּאֱמַר 'וְהָיָה אֱמוּנַת עִתֶּךָ'", עַיֵּן שָׁם:

שַׁעַר ד' - פֶּרֶק ה'

- וּלְפִי עֵרֶךְ גֹּדֶל אוֹצַר הַיִּרְאָה אֲשֶׁר הֵכִין לוֹ הָאָדָם, כֵּן עַל זֶה הָעֵרֶךְ, יוּכַל לִיכָּנֵס וּלְהִשְׁתַּמֵּר וּלְהִתְקַיֵּם בְּתוֹכוֹ תְּבוּאוֹת הַתּוֹרָה, כְּפִי אֲשֶׁר יַחְזִיק אוֹצָרוֹ.

---

59 Yishayahu 33:6.
60 The reference to *oxen and donkeys* is very specific and refers to inclinations for good and for bad as per Avodah Zarah 5b. The Vilna Gaon specifically refers to them as two forms of Evil Inclination (e.g., as per the Vilna Gaon's commentary on Tikkunei Zohar Tikkun 12). They are correspondingly represented by Esav and Yishmael (e.g., as per the Vilna Gaon's commentary on Sifra DeTzniyuta Chap. 4) in contrast to a representation by Yosef (the ox, Devarim 33:17), and Yissachar (the donkey, Bereishit 49:14) on the side of Holiness.

See also Part Three of R. Chaim's Sermon (in V2:11) which quotes some of the source text from Avodah Zarah 5b.
61 Shemot Rabba Mishpatim 30:14.

- For when a father distributes produce to his children
  - he distributes a quantity of produce to each one depending on the capacity of the child's previously prepared storehouse
  - and even if the father wants to give [a child] a large amount with an open hand
  - however, since the child is unable to receive more, as a result of the limited capacity of his storehouse
  - it is impossible for the father to give him any more at this time
  - and if the child does not even prepare a small storage area, then the father cannot give him anything at all as he has no storage place to keep it.
- Similarly, it is with God – His Hand is open, so to speak, to constantly bestow all members of His Chosen People with a great deal of additional wisdom and understanding that will be preserved with them and bound upon 'the notice board of their hearts,'[62] so that He will be able to be entertained by them when they come to the next world with their Torah study in their hands.[63]
- However, this matter is dependent on the storehouse of Fear of God which a person prepares in advance. If a person prepares a large storehouse of pure Fear of God for himself, then God gives him wisdom and understanding in abundance according to the capacity of his storehouse (Note 50)[64] – it is all according to the size of his storehouse.
- If a person did not even prepare a small storehouse, and he does not even have a small amount of Fear of God within him, God forbid, then God will correspondingly not bestow any wisdom at all as it will not be preserved with him as 'his Torah is despised,'[65] God forbid, as Chazal state.

- It is about this that the verse states: "The beginning of wisdom is Fear of God"[66]
  - The Zohar explains: R. Chiya began – "The beginning of wisdom is Fear of God" – this verse should refer to the "end" of wisdom[67] . . . – however [Fear of God] is the beginning [i.e., a prerequisite] to enable entry to the level of supernal wisdom . . . the first gateway to supernal wisdom is the Fear of God.[68] Refer there.

---

62 Mishlei 3:3 or Yirmiyahu 17:1.
63 "Happy is he who comes here with his Torah study in his hand," Pesachim 50a; Moed Katan 28a; Ketubbot 77b; Bava Batra 10b.
64 **R. Chaim adds Note 50 here.** This note is brought at the end of this chapter and is entitled "Fear of Heaven is the initial wisdom given to the wise."
65 An expression from Chagiga 15b where the Torah of a Torah Sage is said to

- כִּי הָאָב הַמְחַלֵּק תְּבוּאָה לְבָנָיו
- הוּא מְחַלֵּק וְנוֹתֵן לְכָל אֶחָד מִדַּת הַתְּבוּאָה, כְּפִי אֲשֶׁר יַחֲזִיק אוֹצָרוֹ שֶׁל הַבֵּן אֲשֶׁר הֵכִין עַל זֶה מִקֹּדֶם.
- שֶׁאַף אִם יִרְצֶה הָאָב, וְיָדוֹ פְּתוּחָה לִתֵּן לוֹ הַרְבֵּה
- אָמְנָם כֵּיוָן שֶׁהַבֵּן אֵינוֹ יָכוֹל לְקַבֵּל יוֹתֵר, מֵחֲמַת שֶׁאֵין אוֹצָרוֹ גָּדוֹל כָּל כָּךְ, שֶׁיּוּכַל לְהַחֲזִיק יוֹתֵר
- גַּם הָאָב אִי אֶפְשָׁר לוֹ לִתֵּן לוֹ עַתָּה יוֹתֵר.
- וְאִם לֹא הֵכִין לוֹ הַבֵּן אַף אוֹצָר קָטָן, גַּם הָאָב לֹא יִתֵּן לוֹ כְּלָל, כֵּיוָן שֶׁאֵין לוֹ מָקוֹם מִשְׁמָר שֶׁיִּתְקַיֵּם אֶצְלוֹ.

- כֵּן הוּא יִתְבָּרַךְ שְׁמוֹ, יָדוֹ פְּתוּחָה כִּבְיָכוֹל לְהַשְׁפִּיעַ תָּמִיד, לְכָל אִישׁ מֵעַם סְגֻלָּתוֹ, רֹב חָכְמָה וּבִינָה יְתֵירָה, וְשֶׁיִּתְקַיֵּם אֶצְלָם, וְיִקְשְׁרֵם עַל לוּחַ לִבָּם, לְהִשְׁתַּעֲשֵׁעַ אִתָּם בְּבוֹאָם לְעוֹלָם הַמְּנוּחָה וְתַלְמוּדָם בְּיָדָם.
- אָמְנָם הַדָּבָר תָּלוּי לְפִי אוֹצַר הַיִּרְאָה שֶׁיִּתְקַדֵּם אֶל הָאָדָם, שֶׁאִם הֵכִין לוֹ הָאָדָם אוֹצָר גָּדוֹל שֶׁל יִרְאַת ה' טְהוֹרָה, כֵּן ה' יִתֵּן לוֹ חָכְמָה וּתְבוּנָה בְּרֹב שֶׁפַע כְּפִי שֶׁתַּחֲזִיק אוֹצָרוֹ, (הגהה נ') הַכֹּל לְפִי גֹדֶל אוֹצָרוֹ.
- וְאִם לֹא הֵכִין הָאָדָם אַף אוֹצָר קָטָן, שֶׁאֵין בּוֹ יִרְאָתוֹ יִתְבָּרַךְ כְּלָל חַס וְשָׁלוֹם, גַּם הוּא יִתְבָּרַךְ לֹא יַשְׁפִּיעַ לוֹ שׁוּם חָכְמָה כְּלָל, אַחַר שֶׁלֹּא תִּתְקַיֵּם אֶצְלוֹ, כִּי תּוֹרָתוֹ נִמְאֶסֶת חַס וְשָׁלוֹם, כְּמוֹ שֶׁאָמְרוּ רַבּוֹתֵינוּ זִכְרוֹנָם לִבְרָכָה:

• וְעַל זֶה אָמַר הַכָּתוּב (תהלים קי"א), "רֵאשִׁית חָכְמָה יִרְאַת ה'"
- וְכַמְבֹאָר בְּהַקְדָּמַת הַזֹּהַר ז' ב', "ר"ח פָּתַח "רֵאשִׁית חָכְמָה יִרְאַת ה'" כו', הַאי קְרָא הָכִי מִבָּעֵי לֵיהּ, סוֹף חָכְמָה כו', אֶלָּא אִיהִי רֵאשִׁית, לְאַעֲלָא לְגוֹ דַּרְגָּא דְחָכְמְתָא עִלָּאָה כו', תַּרְעָא קַדְמָאָה לְחָכְמְתָא עִלָּאָה יִרְאַת ה' אִיהִי כו', עַיֵּן שָׁם:

---

never "be despised," whereas in contrast, here the person cannot be a Torah Sage as they have no storehouse within which to hold the Torah and it is therefore despised.

66 Tehillim 111:10.
67 I.e., that surely Fear of Heaven would be the result of wisdom and cannot precede it.
68 Zohar Introduction 7b.

- It is clear that even though Fear of God is only one Mitzvah, and the Yerushalmi[69] states that all of the Mitzvot do not even compare to [the study of] one part of Torah – nevertheless, the Mitzvah of acquiring Fear of Heaven is very great indeed in that it is essential to enable the existence and preservation of the Holy Torah, and without it [Torah] is despised, God forbid, in the people's eyes. Therefore, it must precede a person's involvement in Torah study.

Rabbi Chaim's Note:
Note 50 – Fear of Heaven is the initial wisdom given to the wise

- With this, Chazal's comment is explained:[70] God only gives Chochma/wisdom to one who already has Chochma/wisdom as per:
  - "I have given wisdom to the heart of all those who are wise of heart."[71]
  - "He gives wisdom to the wise."[72]
- This is seemingly strange as if so, a person's initial Chochma/wisdom – 'from where can it be found?'[73]
- This concept is that Fear of God is also explicitly called wisdom as per "and He said to man, behold Fear of God is wisdom,"[74] this is for the reason stated above [in this chapter] that it is 'his storehouse of goodness'[75] of the wisdom, which is preserved and stored within it.
- This is what Chazal say that God only gives and bestows the Supernal Wisdom of the Torah
  - in order that it should be preserved [with a person] and that his learning should be in his hand
  - to one who already has wisdom within him, meaning a storehouse of Fear of God, which is a necessary precedent for a person, as mentioned above.
- (A 'man of understanding'[76] will understand the inner depth of Chazal's statement following our approach
  - on the basis of the secrets of the Zohar and the writings of the Arizal
  - which say that the Supernal Wisdom is only revealed through the characteristic of God's Malchut
  - that is, the acceptance of the yoke of God's Kingship, as mentioned above.)[77]

---

69 Yerushalmi Peah Chap. 1 Halacha 1.
70 Berachot 55a.
71 Shemot 31:6.
72 Daniel 2:21.
73 Iyov 28:12. See G3:02:N41 for further comment on this verse.

- הֲרֵי מְבֹאָר, הֲגַם שֶׁהַיִּרְאָה הִיא מִצְוָה אַחַת, וְאָמְרוּ בִּירוּשַׁלְמִי (ריש פֵּאָה) שֶׁכָּל הַמִּצְוֹת אֵינָן שָׁווֹת לְדָבָר אֶחָד מִן הַתּוֹרָה, אָמְנָם מִצְוַת קְנִיַּת הַיִּרְאָה מִמֶּנּוּ יִתְבָּרַךְ, רַבָּה הִיא מְאֹד, מִצַּד שֶׁהִיא מֻכְרַחַת לְעִקַּר הַקִּיּוּם וְשָׁמוּר הַתּוֹרָה הַקְּדוֹשָׁה, וּבִלְתָּהּ גַּם נִמְאֶסֶת חַס וְשָׁלוֹם בְּעֵינֵי הַבְּרִיּוֹת, לָכֵן צְרִיכָה שֶׁתִּקְדַּם אֵצֶל הָאָדָם קֹדֶם עֵסֶק הַתּוֹרָה:

הגהה נ'

- וּבָזֶה יְבֹאַר מַאֲמָרָם זִכְרוֹנָם לִבְרָכָה (בְּרָכוֹת נה ע"א) "אֵין הַקָּדוֹשׁ בָּרוּךְ הוּא נוֹתֵן חָכְמָה אֶלָּא לְמִי שֶׁיֵּשׁ בּוֹ חָכְמָה, שֶׁנֶּאֱמַר
  - "וּבְלֵב כָּל חֲכַם לֵב נָתַתִּי חָכְמָה" (שמות לא, ו)
  - "יָהֵב חָכְמְתָא לְחַכִּימִין" (דניאל ב, כא):
- וְלִכְאוֹרָה יִפָּלֵא, דְּאִם כֵּן, חָכְמָה הָרִאשׁוֹנָה מֵאַיִן תִּמָּצֵא אֵצֶל הָאָדָם:
- אָמְנָם הָעִנְיָן, כִּי כָּתוּב מְפֹרָשׁ שֶׁגַּם הַיִּרְאָה נִקְרֵאת חָכְמָה, כְּמוֹ שֶׁכָּתוּב (איוב כח, כח) "וַיֹּאמֶר לָאָדָם הֵן יִרְאַת ה' הִיא חָכְמָה". וְהוּא מִטַּעַם הַנַּ"ל, שֶׁהִיא אוֹצְרוּ הַטּוֹב שֶׁל הַחָכְמָה שֶׁתִּשְׁתַּמֵּר וְתִתְקַיֵּם בָּהּ:
- זֶהוּ שֶׁאָמְרוּ שֶׁאֵין הַקָּדוֹשׁ בָּרוּךְ הוּא נוֹתֵן וּמַשְׁפִּיעַ חָכְמָה הָעֶלְיוֹנָה שֶׁל הַתּוֹרָה שֶׁתִּתְקַיֵּם אֶצְלוֹ, וִיהֵא תַלְמוּדוֹ בְּיָדוֹ
- אֶלָּא לְמִי שֶׁיֵּשׁ בּוֹ חָכְמָה, הַיְנוּ אוֹצַר הַיִּרְאָה, שֶׁהִיא מֻכְרַחַת שֶׁתִּקְדַּם אֵצֶל הָאָדָם כַּנַּ"ל:
- (וְאִישׁ תְּבוּנוֹת יָבִין פְּנִימִיּוּת מַאֲמָרָם זִכְרוֹנָם לִבְרָכָה זֶה לְדַרְכֵּנוּ
  - עַל פִּי סִתְרֵי הַזֹּהַר וְכִתְבֵי הָאֲרִיזַ"ל
- אֲשֶׁר אָמְרוּ שֶׁהַחָכְמָה הָעֶלְיוֹנָה מִתְגַּלֵּית רַק עַל יְדֵי מִדַּת מַלְכוּתוֹ יִתְבָּרַךְ
  - הַיְנוּ קַבָּלַת עֹל מַלְכוּת שָׁמַיִם כַּנַּ"ל):

---

74 Iyov 28:28.
75 Devarim 28:12.
76 Mishlei 11:12, referring to one versed in Kabbalistic knowledge.
77 I.e., Kingship/Malchut is a concept of separation between the King and the people and it is only in this world that the manifestation of God's Kingship is revealed, that we perceive ourselves as separate entities to God, our King. Therefore, we who are limited to the boundaries and separateness of this world must first act as a receptacle to connect with our source by building up

- This also explains the [two] statements of Chazal that [on the one hand] "God is only present within His world within the four cubits of Halacha [i.e., the wisdom of Torah] alone,"[78] and [on the other hand] "God only has in his archive a storehouse of Fear of God alone"[79]
  - and according to our words, this is in truth all one thing and therefore [Chazal] said it is a storehouse of Fear of Heaven.

6. PREPARATION ALLOWS CLEAVING TO WORD OF GOD AND TO GOD

- This is the truth, the true way which God has chosen
  - that whenever a person prepares himself for study, it is appropriate for him to sit before he begins, at least for a short period
  - [to focus] on the purity of [his] Fear of God with a purity of heart
  - confessing his sins from the depths of his heart
  - so that his Torah study will be holy and pure
  - and he should focus on connecting through his Torah study
    - with Torah
    - [and thereby] with God.
  - That is, to cleave with all his strength to the 'word of God which is the Halacha'[80]
  - and thereby he literally directly cleaves to Him, so to speak
  - as He and His Will are One, as per the Zohar[81]
  - and all the laws and details of Halacha of the Holy Torah are His Will
  - as this is what His Will decreed should be the law, whether fit or unfit, impure or pure, forbidden or permitted, guilty or innocent.
- Even if he studies the Torah narrative which has no Halachic ramifications, even so, he still cleaves to the word of God

---

our Fear of God in order to be able to reveal/receive the Supernal Wisdom – the Torah – in a meaningful and lasting way into this world. See G3:11:N45, V2:01 and details of the Tzimtzum process being concealment which is a revelation specifically in Malchut as per V2:02.

78 Berachot 8a.
79 Berachot 33b. See R. Chaim's deeply insightful comments on this in V2:03, p. 359, fn. 43.
80 Shabbat 138b and Kritut 13b.
81 The precise source in Zohar was not found, but this is a common theme in Kabbalistic literature, e.g., R. Menachem Azarya of Fano mentions this in Pelach HaRimon Gateway 4, Chap. 3 where he explains that "Shemo"/"His Name" and "Retzono"/"His Will" have the same numerical value and that

- וּבָזֶה יוּבַן גַּם כֵּן, שֶׁמָּצִינוּ לְרַבּוֹתֵינוּ זִכְרוֹנָם לִבְרָכָה שֶׁאָמְרוּ, אֵין לוֹ לְהַקָּדוֹשׁ בָּרוּךְ הוּא בְּעוֹלָמוֹ אֶלָּא ד' אַמּוֹת שֶׁל הֲלָכָה בִּלְבַד (ברכות ח, א), וּבְפֶרֶק אֵין עוֹמְדִין (לג, ב) אָמְרוּ, אֵין לוֹ לְהַקָּדוֹשׁ בָּרוּךְ הוּא בְּבֵית גְּנָזָיו אֶלָּא אוֹצָר שֶׁל יִרְאַת שָׁמַיִם בִּלְבַד

- וְלִדְבָרֵינוּ בֶּאֱמֶת הַכֹּל אֶחָד, וְלָכֵן אָמְרוּ "אוֹצָר" שֶׁל יִרְאַת שָׁמַיִם, עַד כָּאן:

שַׁעַר ד' - פֶּרֶק ו'

- לְזֹאת הָאֱמֶת שֶׁזּוֹ הִיא הַדֶּרֶךְ הָאֲמִתִּי, אֲשֶׁר בָּזֶה בָּחַר הוּא יִתְבָּרַךְ שְׁמוֹ
  - שֶׁבְּכָל עֵת שֶׁיָּכִין הָאָדָם עַצְמוֹ לִלְמֹד, רָאוּי לוֹ לְהִתְיַשֵּׁב קֹדֶם שֶׁיַּתְחִיל, עַל כָּל פָּנִים זְמַן מְעַט
  - בְּיִרְאַת ה' טְהוֹרָה בְּטָהֳרַת הַלֵּב
  - לְהִתְוַדּוֹת עַל חֲטָאתוֹ מֵעִמְקָא דְלִבָּא
  - כְּדֵי שֶׁתְּהֵא תּוֹרָתוֹ קְדוֹשָׁה וּטְהוֹרָה.
  - וִיכַוֵּן לְהִתְדַּבֵּק בְּלִמּוּדוֹ
    - בּוֹ בַּתּוֹרָה
    - בּוֹ בְּהַקָּדוֹשׁ בָּרוּךְ הוּא
  - הַיְנוּ לְהִתְדַּבֵּק בְּכָל כֹּחוֹתָיו לִ"דְבַר ה'" — זוֹ הֲלָכָה"
  - וּבָזֶה הוּא דָּבוּק בּוֹ יִתְבָּרַךְ מַמָּשׁ כִּבְיָכוֹל
  - כִּי הוּא יִתְבָּרַךְ וּרְצוֹנוֹ חַד, כְּמוֹ שֶׁכָּתוּב בַּזֹּהַר
  - וְכָל דִּין וַהֲלָכָה מִתּוֹרָה הַקְּדוֹשָׁה, הוּא רְצוֹנוֹ יִתְבָּרַךְ
  - שֶׁכֵּן גָּזְרָה רְצוֹנוֹ שֶׁיְּהֵא כָּךְ הַדִּין, כָּשֵׁר אוֹ פָּסוּל, טָמֵא וְטָהוֹר, אָסוּר וּמוּתָּר, חַיָּב וְזַכַּאי:

- וְגַם אִם הוּא עוֹסֵק בְּדִבְרֵי אַגָּדָה, שֶׁאֵין בָּהֶם נַפְקוּתָא לְשׁוּם דִּין, גַּם כֵּן הוּא דָּבוּק בְּדִבּוּרוֹ שֶׁל הַקָּדוֹשׁ בָּרוּךְ הוּא.

"He and His Name are One" (e.g., as per G2:02:N19) is the equivalent of "He and His Will are One."

- for the entire Torah, with its generality, details, and points of precision, including any future question that a young student will ask of his teacher,[82] all of it was given over from God's Mouth to Moshe at Sinai, as per Chazal:
  - [This teaches us that God showed Moshe the precise points of Torah and the precise points of the Torah Sages and all future concepts which the Torah Sages will innovate.][83]
  - [This teaches us that they were all given to Moshe at Sinai.][84]
  - [... and that which an advanced student will teach – already was, and was given as Halacha to Moshe at Sinai. ...][85]
  - [... and even that which an advanced student will say before his teacher – all of it was given as Halacha to Moshe at Sinai. ...][86]
  - [... even that which an advanced student will expand on before his teacher was already said over to Moshe at Sinai. ...][87]
  - "You shall write these things." At the time when God revealed Himself at Sinai to give the Torah to Israel, He told [it over] to Moshe according to the sequence of Scripture, Mishna, Halachot, and Agadot, as per "and God spoke all of these things," even [including] that which a student will ask before his teacher.[88]
- Not only this but all the while one articulates words of Torah study in this world, each word uttered is, so to speak, simultaneously literally being spoken by God
  - as per Chazal[89] in connection with the Concubine of Givah that "his concubine deserted him,"[90] R. Evyatar said he found a fly [in his plate of food that caused him to become angry with her], and R. Yonatan said he found a hair. R. Evyatar met Eliyahu [the Prophet] and asked him "What is God doing?". [Eliyahu] said to him, He is studying the case of the Concubine of Givah. [R. Evyatar] asked, "and what is He saying?" [Eliyahu] replied, "Evyatar, my son, is saying this and Yonatan, my son, is saying that"
  - that is – because R. Evyatar and R. Yonatan were both involved with the case of the Concubine of Givah, therefore, at that same time – God was literally also studying their words.

---

82 R. Chaim refers here to a *young student* asking questions of his teacher. In contrast, he references sources which mention advanced students and not young students. Some insight into his choice of language can be gained from the Rambam's comments in his Mishneh Torah, Hilchot Talmud Torah 5:13:
- Students add to their teacher's wisdom and expand his mind. As Chazal say that "I learned much wisdom from my teachers, more from my colleagues, and more than all of them from my students" [e.g., Taanit 7a]. Just like a small piece of wood can be used to set fire to a large piece of wood, similarly,

כִּי הַתּוֹרָה כֻּלָּהּ, בִּכְלָלֶיהָ וּפְרָטֶיהָ וְדִקְדּוּקֶיהָ, וַאֲפִלּוּ מַה שֶׁהַתַּלְמִיד קָטָן שׁוֹאֵל מֵרַבּוֹ, הַכֹּל יָצָא מִפִּיו יִתְבָּרַךְ לְמֹשֶׁה בְּסִינַי, כְּמוֹ שֶׁאָמְרוּ רַבּוֹתֵינוּ זִכְרוֹנָם לִבְרָכָה

- סוֹף פֶּרֶק ב' דִּמְגִלָּה
- וּבְפֶרֶק קַמָּא דִבְרָכוֹת ה' א'
- וּבְקֹהֶלֶת רַבָּה ס"א פ"י
- וְשָׁם בְּסִימָן ה' פֶּרֶק ח'
- וּבִירוּשַׁלְמִי פֶּרֶק ב' דְּפֵאָה וּבְוַיִּקְרָא רַבָּה פכ"ב, עַיֵּן שָׁם.
- וּבִשְׁמוֹת רַבָּה פ' מ"ז "כְּתָב לְךָ אֶת הַדְּבָרִים הָאֵלֶּה" (שמות לה, כז), בְּשָׁעָה שֶׁנִּגְלָה הַקָּדוֹשׁ בָּרוּךְ הוּא בְּסִינַי לִתֵּן תּוֹרָה לְיִשְׂרָאֵל, אָמַר לְמֹשֶׁה עַל הַסֵּדֶר מִקְרָא וּמִשְׁנָה הֲלָכוֹת וְאַגָּדוֹת, שֶׁנֶּאֱמַר (שמות כ, א) "וַיְדַבֵּר אֱלֹהִים אֵת כָּל הַדְּבָרִים הָאֵלֶּה", אֲפִלּוּ מַה שֶׁהַתַּלְמִיד שׁוֹאֵל לָרַב, עַד כָּאן:

• וְלֹא עוֹד, אֶלָּא כִּי גַם בָּאוֹתוֹ הָעֵת שֶׁהָאָדָם עוֹסֵק בַּתּוֹרָה לְמַטָּה, כָּל תֵּבָה שֶׁמּוֹצִיא מִפִּיו, הֵן הֵן הַדְּבָרִים יוֹצְאִים כִּבְיָכוֹל גַּם מִפִּיו יִתְבָּרַךְ בְּאוֹתוֹ הָעֵת מַמָּשׁ

- כְּדְאַשְׁכְּחָן בְּפֶרֶק קַמָּא דְגִטִּין (ו, ב), גַּבֵּי פִּלֶגֶשׁ בַּגִּבְעָה "וַתִּזְנֶה עָלָיו פִּלַגְשׁוֹ", רַבִּי אֶבְיָתָר אָמַר זְבוּב מָצָא לָהּ, רַבִּי יוֹנָתָן אָמַר נִימָא כו', וְאַשְׁכְּחֵיהּ רַבִּי אֶבְיָתָר לְאֵלִיָּהוּ, אָמַר לֵיהּ, מַאי קָעָבִיד קוּדְשָׁא בְּרִיךְ הוּא, אָמַר לֵיהּ עָסִיק בְּפִלֶגֶשׁ בַּגִּבְעָה, וּמַאי קָאָמַר, אֶבְיָתָר בְּנִי כָּךְ הוּא אוֹמֵר, יוֹנָתָן בְּנִי כָּךְ הוּא אוֹמֵר.

- וְהַיְנוּ, מִפְּנֵי שֶׁרַבִּי אֶבְיָתָר וְרַבִּי יוֹנָתָן עָסְקוּ בֵּינֵיהֶם בְּעִנְיַן פִּלֶגֶשׁ בַּגִּבְעָה, אָז בְּאוֹתוֹ עֵת, גַּם הוּא יִתְבָּרַךְ שָׁנָה דִּבְרֵיהֶם מַמָּשׁ:

---

    a *young student* sharpens his teacher with his questions to the point that he achieves a rich level of wisdom.
    A similar statement is made by the Tur Shulchan Aruch, Yoreh Deah 242.

83 Megillah 19b.
84 Berachot 5a.
85 Kohelet Rabba 1:10.
86 Kohelet Rabba 5:8.
87 Talmud Yerushalmi Peah Chap. 2 Halacha 4; Vayikra Rabba Acharei Mot 22:1.
88 Shemot Rabba Ki Tisa 47:1 quoting Shemot 34:27, 20:1.
89 Gittin 6b.
90 Shoftim 19:2.

- God and His Speech are One,⁹¹ as the Torah states: "to love the Lord Your God [to listen to His Voice and to cleave to Him]"⁹² which is explained by Chazal⁹³ as relating to Torah study [which results,] at the end of the verse, in "cleaving to Him." Refer there.
- Therefore, King David says: "The Torah of *Your Mouth* is better for me [than thousands in gold and silver]."⁹⁴
  - He said: My heart rejoices in my toil in Torah with all my strength, when I bring to mind that it is the Torah of *Your Mouth*, that with each and every word of Torah that I currently study, it all emanated from and is currently emanating from Your Mouth.
- Therefore, the entirety of Torah is all equally Holy without any distinction or difference at all, God forbid, as it is all literally God's Speech, and with the omission of even a single letter from the verse "Prince of Timna"⁹⁵ [a Torah scroll] is just as invalid as when a single letter is omitted from the Ten Commandments or from the first verse of the Shema, as per the Rambam⁹⁶ and Tanna Devei Eliyahu.⁹⁷

7. FOCUS A LITTLE ON FEAR OF GOD BEFORE AND DURING TORAH STUDY

- Therefore, it is appropriate for a person to always prepare before Torah study
  - to focus a little on God with purity of heart in Fear of Heaven
  - and to purify himself from sin with thoughts of repentance
  - in order to connect and cleave to His Speech and His Will when studying the Holy Torah
  - and to also accept upon himself to carry out and uphold all of the Written and Oral Torah
  - and to see and understand his path [in life] and how he should behave from the Holy Torah

---

91 See G3:11 which adds necessary depth and detail of perspective to the point being developed here.
92 Devarim 30:20.
93 Nedarim 62a:
- That one should not say I will study Torah to be called wise, or to be called a teacher or that I should be treated as an elder, but rather that one should study Torah out of love, and honor will automatically follow.
94 Tehillim 119:72.
95 Bereishit 36:40.
96 Rambam's commentary on Mishna Sanhedrin 10:1:

- וְהוּא יִתְבָּרֵךְ שְׁמוֹ וְדִבּוּרוֹ חַד, וְכַמְפֹרָשׁ בַּתּוֹרָה הַקְּדוֹשָׁה בְּמִשְׁנֵה תּוֹרָה "לְאַהֲבָה אֶת ה' אֱלֹהֶיךָ" כו' (דברים ל, כ), וּפֵרְשׁוּהוּ רַבּוֹתֵינוּ זִכְרוֹנָם לִבְרָכָה בִּנְדָרִים בַּבָּרַיְתָא (ס"ב א'), דְּקָאֵי עַל עֵסֶק הַתּוֹרָה, עַיֵּן שָׁם, וְסֵיפֵיהּ דִּקְרָא "וּלְדָבְקָה בוֹ":

- וְלָכֵן אָמַר דָּוִד הַמֶּלֶךְ עָלָיו הַשָּׁלוֹם (תהלים קיט, עב) "טוֹב לִי תוֹרַת פִּיךָ" וכו'
  ○ אָמַר כִּי לִבִּי שָׂמֵחַ בַּעֲמָלִי בַּתּוֹרָה הַקְּדוֹשָׁה בְּרָב עֹז, בְּהַעֲלוֹתִי עַל לִבִּי שֶׁהִיא תוֹרַת "פִּיךָ", שֶׁכָּל תֵּבָה מַמָּשׁ מֵהַתּוֹרָה שֶׁאֲנִי עוֹסֵק בָּהּ כָּעֵת, הַכֹּל יָצָא וְגַם עַתָּה הִיא יוֹצֵאת מִפִּיךָ יִתְבָּרֵךְ:

- וְלָכֵן, כָּל הַתּוֹרָה, קְדֻשָּׁתָהּ שָׁוָה בְּלִי שׁוּם חִלּוּק וְשִׁנּוּי כְּלָל חַס וְשָׁלוֹם, כִּי הַכֹּל דִּבּוּר פִּיו יִתְבָּרֵךְ שְׁמוֹ מַמָּשׁ, וְאִם חָסֵר בְּסֵפֶר תּוֹרָה אוֹת אַחַת מִפָּסוּק "אַלּוּף תִּמְנָע" (בראשית לו, מ), הִיא נִפְסֶלֶת כְּמוֹ אִם הָיָה נֶחְסַר אוֹת אֶחָד מֵעֲשֶׂרֶת הַדִּבְּרוֹת, אוֹ מִפָּסוּק שְׁמַע יִשְׂרָאֵל, וּכְמוֹ שֶׁכָּתַב גַּם הָרַמְבַּ"ם זִכְרוֹנוֹ לִבְרָכָה, וְהוּא מַתְנָא דְּבֵי אֵלִיָּהוּ סָא"ז סוֹף פֶּרֶק ב':

שער ד' - פרק ז'

- וְלָזֹאת, רָאוּי לְהָאָדָם לְהָכִין עַצְמוֹ כָּל עֵת, קֹדֶם שֶׁיַּתְחִיל לִלְמֹד
  ○ לְהִתְחַשֵּׁב מְעַט עִם קוֹנוֹ יִתְבָּרֵךְ שְׁמוֹ בְּטָהֳרַת הַלֵּב בְּיִרְאַת ה'
  ○ וּלְהִטָּהֵר מֵעֲוֹנוֹתָיו בְּהִרְהוּרֵי תְּשׁוּבָה
  ○ כְּדֵי שֶׁיּוּכַל לְהִתְקַשֵּׁר וּלְהִתְדַּבֵּק בְּעֵת עָסְקוֹ בַּתּוֹרָה הַקְּדוֹשָׁה, בְּדִבּוּרוֹ וּרְצוֹנוֹ יִתְבָּרֵךְ שְׁמוֹ.
  ○ וְגַם יְקַבֵּל עַל עַצְמוֹ, לַעֲשׂוֹת וּלְקַיֵּם כְּכָל הַכָּתוּב בַּתּוֹרָה שֶׁבִּכְתָב וּבְעַל פֶּה
  ○ וַאֲשֶׁר יִרְאֶה וְיָבִין דַּרְכּוֹ וְהַנְהָגָתוֹ מִתּוֹרָתוֹ הַקְּדוֹשָׁה.

- The eighth principle is that Torah is from Heaven: That is that we believe that all of this Torah that we have in our hands today, is the Torah which was given to Moshe, and that it is entirely from the *Mouth of God* . . . and there is no difference between the verses "and the children of Cham, Kush, and Mitzraim . . ." (Bereishit 10:6), "the name of his wife is Meheitavel daughter of . . ." (Bereishit 36:39), "I am the Lord Your God" (Shemot 20:2), "Hear O' Israel, God is our Elokim, God is One" (Devarim 6:4) – it is all from the Mouth of God and it is all God's perfect pure holy true Torah.

97 Eliyahu Zuta (at end of) Parsha 2:

- From here they say that even if a person does not even have Scripture or Mishna in his hand, but he sits all day and reads the verse "and Lotan's sister is Timna" (Bereishit 36:22), even so he has the reward of Torah in his hand.

- and similarly when evaluating the Halacha it is fitting to [first] pray that God cause him to merit 'studying Torah according to the Halacha'[98] to be able to focus on the truth of Torah.

- Similarly, in the middle of a Torah study session, a person is permitted to break off for a short period
  - before his Fear of God inspired by the initial study preparation has worn off
  - to reinvigorate his focus a little with Fear of God.
  - As Chazal further state: "The analogy is to a person who says to his agent, 'Bring me up a large amount of wheat to store in the attic.' [After the agent did this,] the person asks 'Did you mix a small amount of preservative in with it?' The agent replied that he did not. So the person says that it would be better if the wheat were not stored in the attic."[99]
    - This relates to [when a person is in] the middle of studying *the produce* of Torah Wisdom, that it is also fitting to mix within it an amount of Fear of God to preserve his Torah [study] in his hand.
    - Therefore, immediately following this statement Chazal continue
      - "It was taught in the Yeshiva of R. Yishmael that one is permitted to mix a small amount of preservative in a large amount of produce and should not worry."
      - This is a law related to the laws of theft and price fraud whose rightful place is in the Tractate of Damages so why is it brought here?
      - However, [Chazal] teach us that just as with business transactions where even though this appears to be theft and price fraud, nevertheless, since the small Kav measure of preservative preserves the large Kur volume[100] of produce, there is no need to worry that this is theft.
      - Similarly, a person is permitted to break off from his Torah study for a short period to focus a little on Fear of God
      - without any concern that this can be considered part of the sin of wasting time from Torah study
      - as this action is the cause for his Torah Wisdom to be preserved.[101]

---

98 Yoma 26a.
99 Shabbat 31a, this is the continuation of the quotation in G4:04.
100 The use of the word "Kav" here is as a measurement and does not relate to the Kabbalistic concept referred to earlier. When used as a measurement a Kav is a 180th part of a Kur. See V2:12, "Related Extracts from Ruach Chaim," subsection 5, for further comment.

○ וְכֵן כְּשֶׁרוֹצֶה לְעַיֵּן בְּדָבָר הֲלָכָה, רָאוּי לְהִתְפַּלֵּל שֶׁיְּזַכֵּהוּ יִתְבָּרַךְ לַאֲסוֹקֵי שְׁמַעְתָּא אַלִּיבָּא דְּהִלְכְתָא, לְכַוֵּן לַאֲמִתָּהּ שֶׁל תּוֹרָה:

• וְכֵן בְּאֶמְצַע הַלִּמּוּד, הָרְשׁוּת נְתוּנָה לְהָאָדָם לְהַפְסִיק זְמַן מְעַט

○ טֶרֶם יְכַבֶּה מִלִּבּוֹ יִרְאָתוֹ יִתְבָּרַךְ שְׁמוֹ, שֶׁקִּבֵּל עָלָיו קֹדֶם הַתְחָלַת הַלִּמּוּד

○ לְהִתְבּוֹנֵן מֵחָדָשׁ עוֹד מְעַט בְּיִרְאַת ה'.

○ כְּמוֹ שֶׁאָמְרוּ רַבּוֹתֵינוּ זִכְרוֹנָם לִבְרָכָה עוֹד (שבת לא, א) "מָשָׁל לְאָדָם שֶׁאָמַר לִשְׁלוּחוֹ הַעֲלֵה לִי כֹּר שֶׁל חִטִּים לַעֲלִיָּה כו', אָמַר לוֹ עֵרַבְתָּ לִי בָּהֶן קַב חוּמְטִין, אָמַר לוֹ לֹא, אָמַר לוֹ מוּטָב שֶׁלֹּא הֶעֱלֵיתָ"

• וְקָאֵי עַל אֶמְצַע הָעֵסֶק בִּתְבוּאוֹת חָכְמַת הַתּוֹרָה, שֶׁרָאוּי גַּם כֵּן לְעָרֵב בְּתוֹכוֹ יִרְאָתוֹ יִתְבָּרַךְ, כְּדֵי שֶׁיִּתְקַיֵּם תַּלְמוּדוֹ בְּיָדוֹ.

□ וְלָכֵן סָמַךְ אֶצְלוֹ הַבְּרַיְתָא

○ "תָּנֵי דְּבֵי ר"י, מְעָרֵב אָדָם קַב חוּמְטִין בְּכוֹר שֶׁל תְּבוּאָה וְאֵינוֹ חוֹשֵׁשׁ"

○ וְהוּא דִין מִדִּינֵי גֶּזֶל וְאוֹנָאָה, אֲשֶׁר מְקוֹמוֹ בְּסֵדֶר נְזִיקִין, וּמַאי שַׁיְטֵיהּ הָכָא.

○ אָמְנָם הוֹרוּנוּ בָּזֶה, שֶׁכְּמוֹ בְּמַשָּׂא וּמַתָּן, הֲגַם שֶׁנִּרְאָה כְּגֵזֶל וְאוֹנָאָה, אָמְנָם כֵּיוָן שֶׁהַקַּב עָפָר הוּא הַשִּׁמּוּר וְהַקִּיּוּם שֶׁל כָּל הַכּוֹר תְּבוּאָה, אֵינוֹ חוֹשֵׁשׁ מִשּׁוּם גֵּזֶל

○ כֵּן רַשַּׁאי הָאָדָם לְהַפְסִיק וּלְבַטֵּל זְמָן מְעַט מֵהַלִּמּוּד, לְהִתְבּוֹנֵן מְעַט בְּיִרְאַת ה'

• וְאֵינוֹ חוֹשֵׁשׁ בָּזֶה מִשּׁוּם בִּטּוּל תּוֹרָה

• כֵּיוָן שֶׁהוּא הַגּוֹרֵם שֶׁיִּתְקַיֵּם אֶצְלוֹ חָכְמַת הַתּוֹרָה:

---

101 This insight echoes a teaching of the Vilna Gaon recorded in "Chidushei Halachot Al Masechet Shabbat," p. 40, published in Vilna 5686 (1926) on Shabbat 31a as follows:

• "Did you mix a small amount of preservative in with it? . . . A person is permitted to mix . . . ." This hints that a person is required to study a small amount from the Ethical Works every day, as without ethics the 'people will pay' [Mishlei 29:18]. However, just in case one would say that he should spend all of his time studying Ethical Works, it therefore says: "A person is permitted to mix a small amount of preservative with a large amount of produce," that there should be a small proportion [of preservative]; similarly, [one should study] a small quantity of ethics every day.

8. EMPTY STOREHOUSE IS NO STOREHOUSE – FEAR WITH NO TORAH IS NOTHING

- However, we can also learn from these two analogies[102] of Chazal in relation to Torah study and Fear of God the *opposite* of that which many of our people err by devoting their entire involvement in Torah study to works of Fear of God and ethical works alone.
- With [the analogy of the existence of] the storehouse as being a [necessary] precedent for being able to store produce within it:
  - Would it ever enter a person's mind, that since the storehouse enables the preservation of the produce, that one should invest all or most of one's time in building it without ever bringing any produce into it?
  - Similarly, how can it enter a person's mind to say
    - that the purpose of a Jew is to invest the entirety of his study time in the construction of the storehouse of Fear of God
    - an empty storehouse which therefore
    - for all of the efforts expended will only fulfill the requirements of the single Mitzvah of "You shall fear the Lord your God"[103]
    - and additionally cannot be called a storehouse at all.
- When Chazal stated: "God only has a storehouse of Fear of God alone"[104] this only applies to that Fear of God into which a large volume of produce is [actually] stored, of Scriptures, Mishna, Halachot, and all the other aspects of Torah
  - as the Fear of God is their 'storehouse of goodness'[105] which will preserve his Torah knowledge
  - organizing it and allowing it to be readily retrievable and etched into 'the notice board of his heart,'[106] as proven by Chazal's further statement that "God's presence in this world is only within the four cubits of Halacha."[107]
  - (The root of this matter is as known
    - of how these two levels of Torah and Fear of God [are presented] in the Supernal Middot
    - that the level of Fear of God has nothing of its own, it 'comes clean'[108]

---

102 I.e., 1. the analogy of the storehouse (Fear of God) and produce (Torah) contained within it, which is the subject of this chapter, and 2. the analogy of the large quantity of grain (Torah) with a small amount of preservative (Fear of God) mixed into it, the subject of G4:09.
103 Devarim 6:13.
104 Berachot 33b, as R. Chaim quotes in G4:05:N50. This note provides significant

שער ד' - פרק ח'

- אָמְנָם דּוּן מִינָהּ נַמִי, מֵעִנְיָן שְׁנֵי הַמְּשָׁלִים שֶׁהִמְשִׁילוּ זִכְרוֹנָם לִבְרָכָה בְּעִנְיָן הַתּוֹרָה וְהַיִּרְאָה, הֵיפֶךְ מֵאֲשֶׁר שָׂגוּ בָזֶה כַּמָּה מֵרַבַּת בְּנֵי עַמֵּנוּ, שֶׁשְּׁקוּעִים כָּל עֵסֶק לִמּוּדָם בְּסִפְרֵי יִרְאָה וּמוּסָר לְבַד:

- שֶׁכַּמּוּ בְעִנְיָן קְדִימַת הָאוֹצָר לְהַתְּבוּאָה שֶׁבְּתוֹכוֹ

  ○ וְכִי יַעֲלֶה כְּלָל עַל לֵב אָדָם, כֵּיוָן שֶׁכָּל קִיּוּם וְשִׁמּוּר הַתְּבוּאָה הוּא הָאוֹצָר, יַעֲסֹק כָּל זְמַנּוֹ אוֹ רֻבּוֹ בְּבִנְיַן הָאוֹצָר לְבַד, וְלֹא יַכְנִיס בּוֹ תְּבוּאָה מֵעוֹלָם

  ○ כֵּן אֵיךְ יַעֲלֶה עַל לֵב אִישׁ לוֹמַר

    □ שֶׁזֶּה תַּכְלִית הָאָדָם מִיִּשְׂרָאֵל, שֶׁיָּשִׂים כָּל קְבִיעוּת לִמּוּדוֹ בְּבִנְיַן הָאוֹצָר שֶׁל יִרְאַת שָׁמַיִם לְבַד

    □ וְהוּא אוֹצָר רֵיק

    □ וְלֹא עָלְתָה בְיָדוֹ מִכָּל עֲמָלוֹ רַק מִצְוָה אַחַת שֶׁל "ה' אֱלֹהֶיךָ תִּירָא" (דברים ו, ג)

    □ וְגַם אֵין עָלֶיהָ שֵׁם אוֹצָר כְּלָל:

- וְלֹא כִּוְּנוּ רַבּוֹתֵינוּ זִכְרוֹנָם לִבְרָכָה בְּמַאֲמָרָם הַנַּ"ל "אֵין לוֹ לְהַקָּדוֹשׁ בָּרוּךְ הוּא כו', אֶלָּא אוֹצָר שֶׁל יִרְאַת שָׁמַיִם בִּלְבַד", אֶלָּא עַל אוֹתָהּ הַיִּרְאָה, שֶׁבְּתוֹכָהּ מֻנָּחִים הֲמוֹן תְּבוּאוֹת, מִקְרָא מִשְׁנָה וַהֲלָכוֹת וּשְׁאָרֵי עִנְיָנֵי הַתּוֹרָה

  ○ שֶׁהַיִּרְאָה הִיא אוֹצָרָם הַטּוֹב, וּמִשְׁמֶרֶת שֶׁיִּתְקַיְּמוּ אֶצְלוֹ

  ○ עֲרוּכִים וּשְׁנוּנִים בְּפִיו, וַחֲרוּתִים עַל לוּחַ לִבּוֹ, כְּמוֹ שֶׁמּוּכָח וּמְכֻרָּח מִמַּה שֶּׁאָמְרוּ עוֹד (ברכות ח, א) אֵין לוֹ לְהַקָּדוֹשׁ בָּרוּךְ אֶלָּא ד' אַמּוֹת שֶׁל הֲלָכָה בִּלְבַד.

  ○ (וְכַיָּדוּעַ בְּשֹׁרֶשׁ דָּבָר

    □ עִנְיַן שְׁנֵי הַבְּחִינוֹת שֶׁל תּוֹרָה וְיִרְאַת ה' בַּמִּדּוֹת הָעֶלְיוֹנִים

    □ שֶׁבְּחִינַת הַיִּרְאָה לֵית לָהּ מִגַּרְמָהּ כְּלוּם, כִּי הִיא נְקֵיָה בָּאָה

---

added insight for the remaining points made in this chapter – including the bracketed subsection.

105 Devarim 28:12.
106 Mishlei 3:3.
107 Berachot 8a. See G4:05:N50.
108 This expression is from Niddah 31b. It is taken from the longer expression

- but is purely a storage container for supernal bestowal from the level of Torah
- as per "But God is in His Holy Sanctuary . . ."[109]
- refer to Tikkunim.)[110]
- This is as per the verse "Better a little gained through Fear of God than a storehouse with empty turmoil within it."[111]

9. TOO MUCH PRESERVATIVE/FEAR IS THEFT

- Similarly with Chazal's analogy of the small Kav measure of preservative required for the large Kur volume of produce which licenses the periodic breaking off from Torah study to additionally reflect a little on Fear of God
  - we can also learn that just as when mixing more than a Kav of preservative into the Kur volume of produce results in no additional ability to preserve, and would therefore be considered as theft and price fraud
  - so too with Fear of God, if a person invests more time in it than the amount necessary to preserve the large *produce* of the Torah studied, then this additional time is theft of Torah study that would have otherwise been studied at that time
  - as one is only permitted to involve oneself with the acquisition of Fear of God, in accordance with one's assessment of one's nature
  - that at this time it is necessary and a requirement to involve oneself with acquiring Fear of God and ethics
  - for the purpose of preserving and maintaining the *produce* of Torah study.
- In truth, a person who habitually studies Torah *for its sake*, as we have explained the concept of *for its sake* in G4:03, does not need to expend great effort, toil, and time in the study of works of the Fear of God to establish Fear of God in his heart as does a person who does not habitually study Torah.

---

the "female has nothing of its own, female comes clean" – the idea here is that *female* denotes one who receives (i.e., input from the male) and as such has nothing of its own. The concept of Malchut is therefore associated with the *female* and in this context so is the storehouse of *Fear of God* which while empty of any input of Torah knowledge, indeed has nothing of its own. Further comments are made on this in G4:05:N50.

109 Chabakuk 2:20, where God is YHVH which relates to the level of Torah as per Berachot 21a on the verse "Ki Shem YHVH Ekra" in relation to the blessing on the Torah, and Sanctuary (Heichal) is HYCL which has the numerical

- רַק שֶׁהִיא אוֹצָר בֵּית קִבּוּל הַשֶּׁפַע עֶלְיוֹן מִבְּחִינַת הַתּוֹרָה
- וּכְמוֹ שֶׁכָּתוּב (חבקוק ב, כ) "וה' בְּהֵיכַל קָדְשׁוֹ"
- וְעַיֵּן בַּתִּקּוּנִים תִּקּוּן ב' וג').
- וְזֶהוּ שֶׁאָמַר הַכָּתוּב (משלי טו, טז) "טוֹב מְעַט בְּיִרְאַת ה' מֵאוֹצָר רַב וּמְהוּמָה בוֹ":

שער ד' - פרק ט'

- וְכֵן בְּעִנְיַן הַהֶתֵּר לְהַפְסִיק בְּאֶמְצַע הַתַּלְמוּד, לְהִתְבּוֹנֵן עוֹד מְעַט בְּיִרְאַת ה', שֶׁהִמְשִׁילוּהוּ זִכְרוֹנָם לִבְרָכָה, לְהֶתֵּר עֵרוּב הַקַּב חוּמְטִין בְּכוֹר תְּבוּאָה
- מִינָהּ נָמֵי שֶׁכְּמוֹ שֶׁאִם שֵׁעֵרַב בְּכוֹר תְּבוּאָה יוֹתֵר מִקַּב חוּמְטִין, אֲשֶׁר אֵינֶנּוּ צָרִיךְ לְקִיּוּם הַתְּבוּאָה, הֲרֵי הוּא גֶּזֶל וְאוֹנָאָה.
- כֵּן בְּעִנְיַן הַיִּרְאָה, אִם יַאֲרִיךְ בָּהּ הָאָדָם, זְמַן יָתֵר מִכְּדֵי מִדָּתָהּ הַנִּצְרָךְ לְקִיּוּם וְשִׁמּוּר רַב תְּבוּאוֹת הַתּוֹרָה, הֲרֵי הוּא גּוֹזֵל אוֹתוֹ הַזְּמַן הָעוֹדֵף, מֵהַתּוֹרָה שֶׁהָיָה צָרִיךְ לִלְמֹד בְּאוֹתוֹ הָעֵת
- כִּי לֹא הִרְשָׁה לַעֲסֹק בְּהִתְבּוֹנְנוּת וּקְנִיַּת הַיִּרְאָה, אֶלָּא כְּפִי אֲשֶׁר יִשְׁקֹל בְּשִׂכְלוֹ לְפִי טִבְעוֹ וְעִנְיָנוֹ
- שֶׁזֶּה הָעֵת הוּא צָרֶךְ וְהֶכְרֵחִי לוֹ לַעֲסֹק בִּקְנִיַּת הַיִּרְאָה וּמוּסָר לְצֹרֶךְ הַשִּׁמּוּר וְהַקִּיּוּם שֶׁל תְּבוּאַת הַתּוֹרָה:
- וּבֶאֱמֶת, כִּי הָאָדָם הַקָּבוּעַ בְּעֵסֶק הַתּוֹרָה לִשְׁמָהּ, כְּמוֹ שֶׁפֵּרַשְׁנוּ בְּפֶרֶק ג' עִנְיַן

---

value of ADNY which is the Name of God relating to fear. (See additional comments added to G1:20:N18 which link the concepts of Malchut and ADNY.)

110 Tikkunei Zohar Third Tikkun 18b:
- How essential it is that "if there is no Fear of God, then there is no Torah Wisdom" (Mishna Avot 3:17), as Fear of God is the storehouse of Torah Wisdom. It is its archive, its hiding place, it is the house of the King [i.e., the concept of Malchut and being a receptacle which receives and has nothing of its own] . . . the secret of this matter is as per "But God is in His Holy Sanctuary . . . ." [See previous footnote.]

111 Mishlei 15:16. The straightforward meaning of this verse is "Better a little gained through Fear of God than a great treasure accompanied by turmoil," but it has a dual meaning and has been translated here within the current context.

- As [study of] the Holy Torah itself, clothes a person with a visually evident Fear of God with the investment of a small amount of time and effort – for this is the way and the precious quality of the of Holy Torah. As per:
  - One who involves himself in Torah study *for its sake* ... will be clothed with humility and Fear of God.[112]
  - "The foolish scorn wisdom and ethics" – if one has ethics why does one need wisdom and if one has wisdom [why does one need ethics?] However, if a person studied Torah and sits and involves himself with it according to his need of it, then he will have both wisdom and ethics, and if not [then wisdom and ethics will be scorned and he will be called a fool].[113]
  - "And along the stream will grow every species of fruit bearing tree . . . ." What are the trees which will grow along this stream? These are the Torah Sages who have Scriptures, Mishna, Halachot, Agadot, good deeds, and have served the Torah Sages ... The analogy is given, to what is this compared? ... Similarly, it is with Torah Sages in this world with words of Torah that since they have read Scriptures and studied ... and the words of Torah are sweet to them – God has mercy on them and gives them wisdom, understanding, knowledge, and analytical abilities to perform good deeds and study Torah, and all is prepared before them. . . .[114]

10. TORAH IS THE CONTINUOUS LIFE FORCE OF *ALL* EXISTENCE

- However during one's actual involvement in Torah study and its analysis, there is certainly no need for any inspirational fervor at all!
  - As mentioned above, that it is through the study and analysis [of Torah] alone that one cleaves to God's Will and Speech, and He, His Will, and Speech are One.[115]
- [That God and His Torah are One] is as per Chazal:
  - When a person buys an item, he does not acquire the original owner together with it; however, when God gave Israel the Torah, He said to them, "It is as if you are taking Me with it."[116]
  - This concept is written in many places in the Zohar, that God and the Torah are One, and most significantly:

---

112 Mishna Avot 6:1.
113 Midrash Mishlei 1:7 quoting Mishlei 1:7.
114 Eliyahu Rabba 18 quoting Yechezkel 47:12.

לְשָׁמָהּ, אֵינֶנּוּ צָרִיךְ לְרֹב עָמָל וִיגִיעָה וְאֹרֶךְ זְמַן הָעֵסֶק בְּסִפְרֵי יִרְאָה עַד שֶׁיִּקָּבַע בְּלִבּוֹ יִרְאָתוֹ יִתְבָּרַךְ, כְּאוֹתוֹ הָאָדָם אֲשֶׁר אֵינֶנּוּ קָבוּעַ בְּעֵסֶק הַתּוֹרָה.

- כִּי הַתּוֹרָה הַקְּדוֹשָׁה מֵעַצְמָהּ תַּלְבִּישֵׁהוּ יִרְאַת ה' עַל פָּנָיו, בִּמְעַט זְמַן וִיגִיעָה מְעֻטָּה עַל זֶה, כִּי כָּךְ דַּרְכָּהּ וּסְגֻלָּתָהּ שֶׁל הַתּוֹרָה הַקְּדוֹשָׁה, כְּמוֹ שֶׁאָמְרוּ

  □ "כָּל הָעוֹסֵק בַּתּוֹרָה לִשְׁמָהּ וּמַלְבַּשְׁתּוֹ עֲנָוָה וְיִרְאָה" (אבות ו', א).

- וּבְמִשְׁלֵי רַבָּתָא פָּרָשָׁה א', חָכְמָה וּמוּסָר אֱוִילִים בָּזוּ (משלי א, ז), אִם מוּסָר לָמָּה חָכְמָה, וְאִם חָכְמָה וְכוּ', אֶלָּא אִם לָמַד אָדָם תּוֹרָה וְיוֹשֵׁב וּמִתְעַסֵּק בָּהּ כְּדֵי צָרְכּוֹ הֲרֵי בְּיָדוֹ חָכְמָה וּמוּסָר, וְאִם לָאו כוּ'.

- וּבְתַנָּא דְּבֵי אֵלִיָּהוּ סֵדֶר אֵלִיָּהוּ רַבָּא (ריש פרק יח) "וְעַל הַנַּחַל יַעֲלֶה עַל שְׂפָתוֹ, מִזֶּה וּמִזֶּה כָּל עֵץ מַאֲכָל" כוּ' (יחזקאל מז, יב), וּמַהוּ הָעֵץ אֲשֶׁר יַעֲלֶה בַּנַּחַל זֶה, אֵלּוּ תַּלְמִידֵי חֲכָמִים, שֶׁיֵּשׁ בָּהֶם תּוֹרָה מִקְרָא וּמִשְׁנָה הֲלָכוֹת וְאַגָּדוֹת וּמַעֲשִׂים טוֹבִים וְשִׁמּוּשׁ תַּלְמִידֵי חֲכָמִים, כוּ'. מָשְׁלוּ מָשָׁל, לְמָה הַדָּבָר דּוֹמֶה כוּ', כָּךְ תַּלְמִידֵי חֲכָמִים בָּעוֹלָם הַזֶּה בְּדִבְרֵי תוֹרָה, כֵּיוָן שֶׁקָּרְאוּ אֶת הַמִּקְרָא וְשָׁנוּ כוּ', וְדִבְרֵי תוֹרָה מָתוֹק עֲלֵיהֶם, הַקָּדוֹשׁ בָּרוּךְ הוּא מְרַחֵם עֲלֵיהֶם, וְנוֹתֵן בָּהֶם חָכְמָה וּבִינָה וְדֵעָה וְהַשְׂכֵּל לַעֲשׂוֹת מַעֲשִׂים טוֹבִים וְתַלְמוּד תּוֹרָה וְהַכֹּל מְתֻקָּן לִפְנֵיהֶם כוּ':

שער ד' - פרק י'

• וּבִשְׁעַת הָעֵסֶק וְהָעִיּוּן בַּתּוֹרָה, וַדַּאי שֶׁאֵין צָרִיךְ אָז לְעִנְיַן הַדְּבֵקוּת כְּלָל

  ○ כַּנַ"ל (פ"ו) שֶׁבְּהָעֵסֶק וְעִיּוּן לְבַד, הוּא דָבוּק בִּרְצוֹנוֹ וְדִבּוּרוֹ יִתְבָּרַךְ, וְהוּא יִתְבָּרַךְ וּרְצוֹנוֹ וְדִבּוּרוֹ חַד:

• וְהוּא עִנְיַן מַאַמְרָם זִכְרוֹנָם לִבְרָכָה

  ○ בִּשְׁמוֹת רַבָּה פָּרָשָׁה ל"ג, אָדָם לוֹקֵחַ חֵפֶץ, שֶׁמָּא יָכוֹל לִקְנוֹת בְּעָלָיו, אֲבָל הַקָּדוֹשׁ בָּרוּךְ הוּא נָתַן תּוֹרָה לְיִשְׂרָאֵל, וְאוֹמֵר לָהֶם, כִּבְיָכוֹל לִי אַתֶּם לוֹקְחִים כוּ'.

  ○ וְזֶה שֶׁכָּתוּב בְּכַמָּה מְקוֹמוֹת בַּזֹּהַר דְּקוּדְשָׁא בְּרִיךְ הוּא וְאוֹרַיְתָא חַד. וּגְדוֹלָה מִזּוֹ

---

115 See G4:06. This concept is introduced in G3:11 and is expanded on significantly in this chapter.

116 Shemot Rabba Terumah 33:6.

- ... and we learn that God is called Torah ... and there is no Torah apart from God.[117]
- In addition, the supernal source of the Holy Torah is from the highest of the supernal worlds – called the *Worlds of the Ein Sof*,[118] which is the secret of the *Hidden Malbush/Garment*[119] which is mentioned in the secrets of the 'wonders of Chochma'[120] in the teachings of our teacher, the Arizal, which is the original secret [source] of the letters of the Holy Torah,[121] as per the verse "God made me [i.e., the Torah] at the beginning of His Way, before His subsequent actions [i.e., of creating the worlds]"[122]
  - and that which Chazal say [that Torah] preceded the Creation of the Universe,[123] means that it also [preceded the Creation] of all of the worlds, even the creation of the Throne of Glory[124]
  - and the truth is, [that the Torah,] so to speak, even preceded the world of Aztilut, as written above, but Atzilut is called *Ayin*,[125] and it is only from the [world level of the] secret of the Throne [of Glory, of Beriyah and below] that the secret of *Shiur Komah*[126] starts, so to speak, therefore, Chazal say that Torah preceded the Throne of Glory.[127]
- Therefore, it is within [the Torah from The World of The Malbush]

---

117 Zohar II Beshalach 60a.

118 R. Chaim introduces the concept of *The World of The Malbush/Garment* at this point. This concept becomes a central theme and is referred to along the course of the remaining chapters of the Fourth Gateway.

The World of The Malbush is the first and most subtle world of all of the worlds of the Ein Sof which are described in the Arizal's Kabbalah as disseminated by his student R. Yisrael Sarug(/Saruk). As it is the first world from which all other worlds cascaded, it is the most concealed. It is in this World of The Malbush that the Hebrew alphabet was formed and it contains both the alphabet and also the 231 matrix presentations of letter pairs which R. Chaim refers to later on in this chapter as 231 gates. These 231 gates form the *Primordial Torah* and are the basis for the derivation of all of the words of the Torah.

Extensive notes and quotations are to be found on this topic in V2:03, "The World of The Malbush." In particular, quotations have been provided to aid the understanding of the connection between the concept of *The World of The Malbush* and the statements made later on, both in this chapter and in later chapters.

119 This is a reference to *The World of The Malbush/Garment*. See V2:03, "The World of The Malbush."

120 This expression is borrowed from the opening line of the Sefer Yetzirah Chap. 1 Mishna 1 which mentions "32 Netivot/paths of *wonders of Chochma* which God engraved . . . ." The next Mishna explains the composition of the 32 paths being of the Ten Sefirot and the 22 letters of the alphabet, i.e., the secret

נפש שער ד' - פרק י' החיים

◦ בְּפָרָשַׁת בְּשַׁלַּח ס' ע"א, וְאוֹלִיפְנָא דְקוּדְשָׁא בְּרִיךְ הוּא תּוֹרָה אִיקְרֵי כו', וְאֵין תּוֹרָה אֶלָּא קוּדְשָׁא בְּרִיךְ הוּא:

• וְגַם כִּי שָׁרָשָׁהּ הָעֶלְיוֹן שֶׁל הַתּוֹרָה הַקְּדוֹשָׁה, הוּא בָּעֶלְיוֹן שֶׁבְּהָעוֹלָמוֹת הַנִּקְרָאִים עוֹלָמוֹת הָ"אֵין סוֹף", סוֹד הַמַּלְבּוּשׁ הַנֶּעְלָם, הַנִּזְכָּר בְּסִתְרֵי פְּלִיאוֹת חָכְמָה מִתּוֹרַת רַבֵּנוּ הָאֲרִיזַ"ל, שֶׁהוּא רֵאשִׁית סוֹד אוֹתִיּוֹת הַתּוֹרָה הַקְּדוֹשָׁה, וּכְמוֹ שֶׁכָּתוּב (משלי ח, כב) "ה' קָנָנִי רֵאשִׁית דַּרְכּוֹ קֶדֶם מִפְעָלָיו מֵאָז".

◦ וְזֶה שֶׁאָמְרוּ זִכְרוֹנָם לִבְרָכָה (ב"ר א, ד) שֶׁקָּדְמָה לָעוֹלָם, הַיְנוּ גַם מִכָּל הָעוֹלָמוֹת כֻּלָּם, שֶׁהֲרֵי אָמְרוּ בִּבְרֵאשִׁית רַבָּה פָּרָשָׁה א' שֶׁקָּדְמָה לְכִסֵּא הַכָּבוֹד.

◦ וְהָאֱמֶת שֶׁקָּדְמָה כִּבְיָכוֹל גַּם לְעוֹלָם הָאֲצִילוּת יִתְבָּרַךְ כַּנַּ"ל, אֶלָּא שֶׁהָאֲצִילוּת נִקְרָא "אַיִן", וּמִסּוֹד הַכִּסֵּא מַתְחִיל סוֹד הַשִּׁעוּר קוֹמָה כִּבְיָכוֹל, לָכֵן אָמְרוּ שֶׁקָּדְמָה לְכִסֵּא הַכָּבוֹד:

• וְלָכֵן בָּהּ נֶאֱצְלוּ וְנִבְרְאוּ כָּל הָעוֹלָמוֹת עֶלְיוֹנִים וְתַחְתּוֹנִים

---

source letters of the Torah. See the idea expressed in V2:03, "The World of The Malbush" related to the word "Netiv/path," which has a numerical value of 462 – being twice 231.

121 The letters of the Torah originate from within the World of The Malbush. See V2:03, "The World of The Malbush."

122 Mishlei 8:22. The Vilna Gaon comments on this verse that the word "Reishit/beginning" here relates to the 32 Netivot/paths which are incorporated in "Bereishit" at the beginning of creation.

123 Bereishit Rabba Bereishit 1:4. This Midrash uses the verse just quoted to identify that the creation of Torah preceded the Creation of the world; it also goes on to say that the creation of the Throne of Glory also preceded the Creation of the world but that the creation of the Torah preceded the creation of the Throne of Glory. See the details of the *Primordial Torah* which preceded the Creation of the world by two thousand years in V2:03, "The World of The Malbush."

124 The *Throne of Glory* is also referred to as the world level of Beriyah which is the world level below Atzilut. See G1:05.

125 See G3:02 and p. 472, fn. 18, which discuss Ayin in detail.

126 See G1:06 and G2:05. The Shiur Komah is the structure of the aspect of God which incorporates all creative abilities and all of the worlds. This structure is only formed from the world level of Beriyah and lower; however, its inception was together with the formation of the Torah. See V2:03, "The World of The Malbush."

127 I.e., even if it did not immediately precede the level of the Throne of Glory (as the level of Atzilut does).

that all the supernal and lower worlds were emanated[128] and created as Chazal say
- about the verse "and I was then his *Amon*," don't read the word as *Amon*, but rather as *Uman*[129]
- "With all forms of wisdom did she build her house," this is the Torah which built all the worlds.[130]

• This concept is that the Holy Torah *is* God's Speech, and that through His utterances of Creation all the worlds were created
- through the arrangement of letter combinations through the *231 Gates, forwards, and reverse*[131] which are contained within the first Statement of Creation [of the Heavens and the Earth]
- from which all the levels and multitudes of the most supernal worlds emanated and were created with all their specific arrangement, detail, and content
- and similarly, with all the other statements [of Creation] through which all the various details of the species related to each respective statement were created.

• This is as per the Zohar, which says:[132]
- When God created the Universe, He looked into the Torah and then created the Universe
- it was with the Torah that the Universe was created
- as we have established, as per the verse "and I was then his *Amon*"[133] – the Torah cries out that "and I was then his Amon" that with me God created the Universe.
- The Torah preceded the Creation of the Universe and when God wanted to create the Universe, He looked into it – into each individual word of the Torah and correspondingly *crafted* the Universe.
- Because every single detail of the worlds is in the Torah
- when the Torah writes: "In the beginning He created [the Heavens] . . . ," God looked at these words and created the Heavens

---

128 As everything including all of the worlds emanated from the letters and the letter pairs which formed the *Primordial Torah* of The World of The Malbush. See V2:03, "The World of The Malbush."

129 Midrash Tanchuma Parshat Bereishit 1 quoting Mishlei 8:30. This is explained by the quotation from Zohar Terumah later in the chapter, i.e., "Uman" referring to craftsmanship and that through the Torah, God crafted the Universe. See V2:03, "The World of The Malbush" where quotations related to this verse have been brought.

130 Midrash Mishlei Parsha 9 quoting Mishlei 9:1. This *wisdom* of the Torah is referred to in the quotations brought in V2:03, "The World of The Malbush."

- כְּמוֹ שֶׁכָּתוּב (משלי ח, ל) "וָאֶהְיֶה אֶצְלוֹ אָמוֹן", וְאָמְרוּ זִכְרוֹנָם לִבְרָכָה (תנחומא בראשית א) אַל תִּקְרֵי אָמוֹן אֶלָּא אוּמָן וכו'.

- וּבְמִשְׁלֵי רַבָּתָא רֵישׁ פָּרָשָׁה ט', חָכְמוֹת בָּנְתָה בֵיתָהּ (משלי ט, א), זוֹ הַתּוֹרָה שֶׁבָּנְתָה כָּל הָעוֹלָמוֹת:

• וְהָעִנְיָן, כִּי הַתּוֹרָה הַקְּדוֹשָׁה הִיא דִּבּוּרוֹ יִתְבָּרַךְ, וּבְמַאֲמַר פִּיו יִתְבָּרַךְ בְּמַעֲשֵׂי בְרֵאשִׁית נִבְרְאוּ הָעוֹלָמוֹת כֻּלָּם.

- שֶׁעַל יְדֵי סִדּוּר גִּלְגּוּל צֵרוּפֵי הָאוֹתִיּוֹת עַל פִּי סֵדֶר הרל"א שְׁעָרִים פָּנִים וְאָחוֹר שֶׁבַּמַּאֲמָר "בְּרֵאשִׁית בָּרָא" וכו'

- נֶאֶצְלוּ וְנִבְרְאוּ הָעוֹלָמוֹת, עֶלְיוֹנֵי עֶלְיוֹנִים רִבֵּי רִבְבָן, בְּכָל סֵדֶר מַצָּבָם וּפְרָטֵי עִנְיָנֵיהֶם וְכָל הַנִּכְלָל בָּהֶם

- וְכֵן בְּכָל מַאֲמָר וּמַאֲמָר שֶׁבּוֹ עַל דֶּרֶךְ הַנַּ"ל נִבְרְאוּ כָּל פְּרָטֵי הַמִּינִים וְהָעִנְיָנִים שֶׁבְּאוֹתוֹ הַסּוּג, שֶׁעָלָיו נֶאֱמַר אוֹתוֹ הַמַּאֲמָר:

• כְּמוֹ שֶׁכָּתוּב בַּזֹּהַר תְּרוּמָה קס"א א'

- דְּכַד בָּרָא קוּדְשָׁא בְּרִיךְ הוּא עָלְמָא, אִסְתַּכֵּל בָּהּ בְּאוֹרַיְתָא וּבָרָא עָלְמָא וּבְאוֹרַיְתָא אִתְבְּרֵי עָלְמָא

- כְּמָה דְּאוּקְמוּהָ, דִּכְתִיב "וָאֶהְיֶה אֶצְלוֹ אָמוֹן" כו', אוֹרַיְתָא צַוָוחַת וְאֶהְיֶה אֶצְלוֹ אָמוֹן, בִּי בָּרָא קוּדְשָׁא בְּרִיךְ הוּא עָלְמָא

- דְּעַד לָא אִתְבְּרֵי עָלְמָא אַקְדִּימַת אוֹרַיְתָא כו', וְכַד בָּעָא קוּדְשָׁא בְּרִיךְ הוּא לְמִבְרֵי עָלְמָא, הֲוָה מִסְתַּכֵּל בָּהּ בְּאוֹרַיְתָא בְּכָל מִלָּה וּמִלָּה, וְעָבִיד לְקִבְלָהּ אוּמָנוּתָא דְעָלְמָא

- בְּגִין דְּכָל מִלִּין וְעוֹבָדִין דְּכָל עָלְמִין בְּאוֹרַיְתָא אִנּוּן כו'.

- בְּאוֹרַיְתָא כְּתִיב בָּהּ "בְּרֵאשִׁית בָּרָא" וכו', אִסְתַּכֵּל בְּהַאי מִלָּה וּבָרָא אֶת הַשָּׁמַיִם.

---

131 See the extensive quotations related to this topic in V2:03, "The World of The Malbush."

132 Zohar II Terumah 161a.

133 Mishlei 8:30, as already quoted earlier in this chapter where "Amon" is understood to mean craftsmanship.

- when the Torah writes: "and God said Let there be Light," God looked at the words and created light
- and similarly with each word in the Torah, God looked at it and it was the word that *made*
- therefore, the verse "and I was then his *Amon*," that in this way the Universe was created.
• Therefore, the entire Torah in general together with all the details, arrangements, and aspects of all the worlds are incorporated within and hinted to by the Ten Statements of the Act of Creation[134]
- and as written by our teacher, the great one, the genius, the pious one, the Vilna Gaon[135]
- and refer to the Zohar in relation to this.[136]
• Therefore, the Zohar says that the Torah is the light of all worlds – it is the life, existence and root of all.[137]
• This concept is reflected in the interconnected way in which the life force gradually cascades down from a higher world level to a lower one, where each higher world level becomes the entire soul, life force, existence, and light of the lower world immediately beneath it.[138]
- However, the distinguishing quality of the world of Atzilut compared with the three world levels of Beriyah, Yetzirah, and Asiyah which extend from it and are enlightened [/enlivened] by it

---

134 I.e., in the first chapter of Bereishit.
135 From the Vilna Gaon's commentary on Sifra DeTzniyuta Chap. 5:
• The general principle is that all that is, was and ever will be, is all encapsulated within the Torah from [its first word of] "Bereishit" until [its last words of] "before the eyes of Israel." This does not just relate to the generality [of Creation] alone but even to the specific details of each species and of each person in particular, and of everything that will happen to [each person] from his birth until his end, all of his involvements, details, and details of details. This is similarly the case with each species of animal or living creature in the world and each blade of grass, plant, and inanimate object, with all of their details and their details of the details of each individual specie, and of whatever happened to them and their source. Similarly, all that which is written about the Patriarchs, Moshe, and the People of Israel, all [these details] apply to each and every generation as the sparks of their souls are reincarnated in each and every generation as is known, and similarly of their actions, [as detailed] from Adam until the end of the Torah relates to each generation as is known to one who understands. It is similarly the case with each and every individual as the Midrash HaNeelam began to explain via a hint. All of this is more generally encapsulated within the section of Torah from Bereishit up until Noach as will be explained here

נפש שער ד' - פרק י' החיים 669

○ כְּתִיב בָּהּ (בראשית א, ג) "וַיֹּאמֶר אֱלֹהִים יְהִי אוֹר", אִסְתַּכֵּל בְּהַאי מִלָּה וּבָרָא אֶת הָאוֹר.

○ וְכֵן בְּכָל מִלָּה וּמִלָּה דִכְתִיב בָּהּ בְּאוֹרַיְתָא, אִסְתַּכֵּל קוּדְשָׁא בְּרִיךְ הוּא, וַעֲבִיד הַהוּא מִלָּה.

○ וְעַל דָּא כְּתִיב "וָאֶהְיֶה אֶצְלוֹ אָמוֹן", כְּגַוְנָא דָא כָּל עָלְמָא אִתְבְּרִי, ע"כ:

• וְלָכֵן כָּל הַתּוֹרָה בִּכְלָל וְכָל הָעוֹלָמוֹת בִּכְלָלֵיהֶם וּפְרָטֵיהֶם וְסִדּוּרָם וְכָל עִנְיְנֵיהֶם, כֻּלָּם כְּלוּלִים וּרְמוּזִים בְּעֶשֶׂר הַמַּאֲמָרוֹת דְּמַעֲשֵׂה בְרֵאשִׁית.

• וּכְמוֹ שֶׁכָּתַב רַבֵּינוּ הַגָּדוֹל הַגָּאוֹן הֶחָסִיד מוֹהר"א זצוק"ל בְּפֵרוּשׁוֹ עַל הַסִּפְרָא דִצְנִיעוּתָא בְּפֶרֶק ה'

○ וְעַיֵּן בָּזֶה בַּזֹּהַר בְּרֵאשִׁית מ"ז א':

• וְלָכֵן אָמְרוּ בַּזֹּהַר, דְּאוֹרַיְתָא הִיא נְהִירוּ דְכָל עָלְמִין, וְחִיּוּתָא וְקִיּוּמָא וְשָׁרְשָׁא דִלְהוֹן:

• וְהָעִנְיָן, כִּי הָעוֹלָמוֹת הוֹלְכִים עַל סֵדֶר הַהִשְׁתַּלְשְׁלוּת וְהַהַדְרָגָה, שֶׁכָּל עוֹלָם הַיּוֹתֵר עֶלְיוֹן וְגָבוֹהַּ, הוּא נִשְׁמָתוֹ וְחִיּוּתוֹ וְקִיּוּמוֹ וְאוֹרוֹ שֶׁל הָעוֹלָם שֶׁתַּחְתָּיו לְבַד.

• אָמְנָם יִתְרוֹן עוֹלָם הָאֲצִילוּת עַל הַג' עוֹלָמוֹת בְּרִיאָה יְצִירָה עֲשִׂיָּה, שֶׁהוּא מִתְפַּשֵּׁט וּמֵאִיר לְכָל הַג' עוֹלָמוֹת בְּרִיאָה יְצִירָה עֲשִׂיָּה שֶׁתַּחְתָּיו.

---

with God's help. It is [also] even more generally encapsulated within the first chapter of Bereishit up until "which God created to make" [Bereishit 2:3], as mentioned above, and is most generally encapsulated in the first chapter, in the first seven words which reflect the seven *thousand-year periods* as written in Chap. 1 [an alternative reference being Zohar Sifra DeTzniyuta II Terumah 176b] that "the first six thousand years are dependent on the first six [words] . . .". . . .

136 Zohar I Bereishit 47a:
- "God saw all that He made and it was very good" [Bereishit 1:31]. But God saw everything [before and after Creation]! There is an opinion that says that when [the verse says "God saw] all," that this comes to include every new event in the world in each and every future generation, and that [when the verse says] "He made," that this refers to the entirety of creation, as with the Act of Creation the foundation and root of everything that would subsequently be generated was laid, and therefore, God saw before it was, and placed everything within the Act of Creation.

137 Zohar III Shelach Lecha 166b.
138 As per G1:05.

- [is that Atzilut] is pure Divinity, as per the Arizal.[139]
- As the Zohar states:[140] ... that the Ten Sefirot of Atzilut are a king over them [i.e., the Ten Sefirot of Beriyah], that He [i.e., God] and His Causes [i.e., His Middot of Atzilut] are One over them, He and His life [force] are One over them, as opposed to the Ten Sefirot of Beriyah where they and He are not one, and He and their essence are not one ...
- Therefore, the Holy Torah which is rooted in the hidden supernal realms [in The World of The Malbush] – is far abstracted from

---

[139] The first source below describes the interrelationship of the world levels and levels within levels. The subsequent sources describe the unique distinction of Atzilut compared to the other world levels.

Etz Chaim Shaar 40, Shaar Pnimiut VeChitzoniut, Derush 2:
- It transpires that all the three levels of external vessels are names of sparks of Elokim as mentioned elsewhere, but their Nefesh, Ruach, and Neshama, their existence and light, are internal; therefore, the first [i.e., the external] vessels become the [actual] containers, and the innermost vessel is called the soul relative to the external vessels ...
- ... Know that with all of the external vessels above, when they descend from their place, they totally become the inner vessels. The converse is also the case that when the innermost vessels below ascend, they become the external vessels [of the higher level] ...
- ... it transpires that the four [general levels of] worlds – Atzilut, Beriyah, Yetzirah, and Asiyah, and similarly, the five Partzufim in each of these four world [levels], each have an external presentation and internal essence ...
- ... for the external presentation of each and every world is on the level of Asiyah of that world as is known, as each of the four world levels of Atzilut, Beriyah, Yetzirah, and Asiyah are comprised of all parts/subcomponents of Atzilut, Beriyah, Yetzirah, and Asiyah, and not only that, but there is no Sefira which does not have the four subcomponents of Atzilut, Beriyah, Yetzirah and Asiyah, and in particular, the external presentation of any Sefira is its subcomponent of Asiyah.

Etz Chaim Shaar 40, Shaar Pnimiut VeChitzoniut, Derush 8:
- ... however, that which we said only applies to Atzilut alone, from there downwards the vessels of Atzilut form the Neshama of Beriyah, Yetzirah, and Asiyah. Understand this great secret as it is for this reason that Beriyah, Yetzirah, and Asiyah are not refered to as *complete Divinity* as their Neshama is just from the vessels of Atzilut and not from the light [of Aztilut]. ...

Etz Chaim Shaar 40, Shaar Pnimiut VeChitzoniut, Derush 10:
- ... and the reason is that the three vessels correspond to the three worlds of Beriyah, Yetzirah, and Asiyah and they [the vessels] themselves are the

◦ עַיֵן בְּעֵץ חַיִים שַׁעַר פְּנִימִיוּת וְחִיצוֹנִיוּת דְּרוּשׁ ב', וְשָׁם רֵישׁ דְּרוּשׁ ח' וְרֵישׁ דְּרוּשׁ י', וּבְשַׁעַר דְּרוּשֵׁי אבי"ע פֶּרֶק ז', וּבְשַׁעַר הַשֵּׁמוֹת פֶּרֶק א', וּבְשַׁעַר קְלִפַּת נֹגַהּ פֶּרֶק א' — שֶׁכֻּלוֹ אֱלֹקוּת גָּמוּר.

◦ כְּמוֹ שֶׁכָּתוּב בְּהַקְדָּמַת הַתִּקוּנִים, דְּעֶשֶׂר סְפִירוֹת דַּאֲצִילוּת מַלְכָּא בְּהוֹן, אִיהוּ וְגַרְמֵיהּ חַד בְּהוֹן, אִיהוּ וְחַיוֹהִי חַד בְּהוֹן, מַה דְּלָאו הָכִי בְּעֶשֶׂר סְפִירוֹת דִּבְרִיאָה, דְּלָאו אִנוּן וְאִיהוּ חַד, לָאו אִנוּן וְגַרְמֵיהוֹן חַד.

◦ וְלָכֵן, הַתּוֹרָה הַקְּדוֹשָׁה, שֶׁשָּׁרְשָׁהּ הָעֶלְיוֹן הַנֶּעְלָם הוּא לְמַעְלָה מַעְלָה גַּם מֵאֲצִילוּת קָדְשׁוֹ יִתְבָּרַךְ כנ"ל, וְקֻדְשָׁא בְּרִיךְ הוּא וְאוֹרַיְתָא, כֹּלָּא חַד.

Nefesh, Ruach, and Neshama within them [the three worlds]. However, corresponding to Chaya and Yechida, which [themselves] correspond to Atzilut, there are no further vessels, as there there is no Kelipah, and it is known that there are no Kelipot except within the three vessels . . . [Kelipot represents a departure from Divinity which is only manifest in the world levels of Beriyah, Yetzirah, and Asiyah. Therefore, as Atzilut has no Kelipot, it is pure Divinity.]

Etz Chaim Shaar 42, Shaar Derushei Atzilut Beriyah, Yetzirah, and Asiyah, Chap. 5 (see V2:14, p. 676):

• . . . and therefore all of Atzilut is pure Divinity . . .

Etz Chaim Shaar 44, Shaar HaShemot, Chap. 1:

• . . . however with respect to the levels of Beriyah, Yetzirah, and Asiyah, we have already explained above that the thirty Sefirot of Nukva of Atzilut are divided among them and literally form their Neshama, and from there onwards, meaning from the level of Neshama which is in Beriyah, Yetzirah, and Asiyah onwards, they are not on the level of Divinity but are in secret, and from there it splits into four channels and is referred to as *separation* . . . [Divinity is associated with absolute Unity. Any form of *separation* is a *differentiation* and therefore a compromise in Unity. By definition, from the world of Beriyah (i.e., the world of Creation) downwards there is the creation of entities which are *separate* to and *differentiated* from Unified Divinity. As explained elsewhere (e.g., see p. 444, fn. 389), Atzilut is referred to as the world of Chochma, referring to undifferentiated unity, whereas Beriyah is referred to as the world of Binah, where the existence of difference allows differentiated analysis to occur.]

Etz Chaim Shaar 49, Shaar Kelipat Nogah, Chap. 1:

• . . . however, with Atzilut, Evil is separated outside of it. . . . [I.e., there is no Evil and therefore no separation within Atzilut itself, which is therefore Unified Divinity.]

140 Tikkunei Zohar Introduction 3b. This source is also quoted in G3:04 and a slightly longer quotation in G3:05.

even the Holy level of Atzilut, as mentioned above, and God and the Torah are One.
   - [Therefore, the Torah] is the soul, life force, light, and source of all the worlds.
- Just as at the time of Creation, everything emanated within and was created from [the Torah within the World of The Malbush]
  - similarly, since then, [Torah continues] to be the soul, life force, and existence of their arrangement, and without its continuous bestowal of light within them each moment, literally – to give them light, life force, and existence – they would all literally return to be absolutely null and void.

11. WORLDS CONTINUE TO EXIST WHEN JEWS ENGAGED IN TORAH STUDY

- Therefore, the essential life force, light, and maintained existence of all the worlds are only appropriately engaged when we study [Torah] properly
  - for God, the Torah, and Israel are all One[141]

---

141 This expression appears to come from the Ramchal's commentary on Idra Rabba, Adir BaMarom, (p. 110 of the 5755/1995 Jerusalem edition). The Ramchal uses this expression when quoting the Zohar III Acharei Mot 73a (which is quoted in G1:16:N14). In quoting this Zohar, the Ramchal makes a subtle change and is therefore providing an interpretation of the Zohar. The original Zohar states "that God, the Torah, and Israel are all connected to each other" and the Ramchal's interpretation is that they are all One. It is also possible that this expression is derived from the Arizal's writings from the Shmoneh Shearim. Although the Shmoneh Shearim was not directly available to R. Chaim when he wrote Nefesh HaChaim, it is possible that sections of it filtered through to him. The following statements from the Shmoneh Shearim, Shaar Ruach HaKodesh 38b (also seen in another edition on 39b with the alternative reference of Derush 3, Introduction 3) are particularly enlightening:
  - Know that the Torah is the quarry of the souls of Israel which are hewn from it. Therefore, it is that the Torah is One, Israel is a nation that is One, and God is One. This is the secret of the six Sefirot, Chesed, Gevurah, Tiferet, Netzach, Hod, and Yesod with which the written Torah is rooted ... they are [as Moshe said] "the 600,000 people [that I am within]" [Bamidbar 11:21, i.e., the number of souls of Israel which were incorporated in Moshe's soul] ... and they are the secret of the 600,000 soul roots ... following this there are 600,000 interpretations of the written Torah for each

▫ הִיא הַנֶּפֶשׁ וְהַחִיּוּת וּנְהִירוּ וְשָׁרְשָׁא דְעָלְמִין כֻּלְּהוּ:
• שֶׁכְּמוֹ שֶׁבְּעֵת הַבְּרִיאָה, בָּהּ נֶאֶצְלוּ וְנִבְרְאוּ כֻלָּם
○ כֵּן מֵאָז, הִיא נִשְׁמָתָם וְחִיּוּתָם וְקִיּוּמָם עַל סֵדֶר מַצָּבָם, וּבִלְתִּי שִׁפְעַת אוֹרָהּ בָּהֶם, כָּל רֶגַע מַמָּשׁ לְהָאִירָם לְהַחֲיוֹתָם וּלְקַיְּמָם, הָיוּ חוֹזְרִים כֻּלָּם לְתֹהוּ וָבֹהוּ מַמָּשׁ:

שער ד' - פרק י"א

• וְלָזֹאת, עִקַּר חִיּוּתָם וְאוֹרָם וְקִיּוּמָם שֶׁל הָעוֹלָמוֹת כֻּלָּם עַל נָכוֹן, הוּא רַק כְּשֶׁאֲנַחְנוּ עוֹסְקִים בָּהּ כָּרָאוּי
○ כִּי קוּדְשָׁא בְּרִיךְ הוּא וְאוֹרַיְתָא וְיִשְׂרָאֵל כֻּלָּא חַד (עי' זהר פ' אחרי עג.).

verse ... it transpires that each and every soul of the 600,000 souls of Israel has its own approach to the entire Torah according to the level of his soul root which is attached to the Torah. Therefore each Jewish person is able to [uniquely] generate Torah insights according to his part [within Torah] that his colleague cannot generate. However, there are people who incorporate a number of sparks from different souls and they are able to generate Torah explanations according to the number of soul sparks. Therefore, Moshe's [soul] which incorporated all of Israel's [souls] knew those future insights which [even] the most seasoned scholar would be able to generate. This is the secret of that which Chazal say that Moshe was considered equal to all of Israel [e.g., as per Yalkut Shimoni Beshalach Remez 241].
The comments by R. Shalom Sharabi, the "Rashash," in his introduction to his commentary Rechovot HaNahar on the Arizal's Nahar Shalom, p. 9b, express the unity of God and Torah even more clearly:
• For the Torah is the root and source of the essence of light of [each level] of Nefesh, Ruach, Neshama, Chaya, Yechida which disseminate within every Partzuf. It is the Ohr Ein Sof/Light of the Ein Sof ....
[The Ohr Ein Sof is the highest level that is humanly possible to talk of when referring to God. As the Rashash highlights it is one and the same as the Torah. It is the level from which all of creation stems. Therefore all of creation comes from the Torah, just as it comes from the Ohr Ein Sof.]

- that the root of each Jew's supernal soul is connected and attached to one letter of the Torah[142] and is absolutely one with it.[143]
- Therefore, the Midrash states[144] that the thought of the existence of Israel preceded all [of Creation]
  - and this does not contradict the statement that Torah preceded everything
  - as they are both one and the same in their source.
  - When this [Midrash] refers to the *thought* [of the existence] of Israel
  - this is as Chazal say: "Israel came up in thought"[145]
  - this means the beginning of [God's] thought, the secret of [His] Supernal Will
  - as per the Zohar which states: "Israel arose in God's Will before the creation of the Universe."[146]
  - This Will is the beginning of All – it is absolute Divinity, so to speak – from *The Worlds of the Ein Sof*[147]
    - as per the Zohar. Refer there well:[148] R. Shimon said I lift up [my hands in prayer to above] while the Supernal Will [exists on High, and this Will is not known or grasped in the worlds at all . . . it is the beginning of that which comes out] . . . and all these lights [which come out] from the secret of supernal and lower thought are all called *Ein Sof*
    - and in the note of R. Chaim Vital there[149]
    - and in the Etz Chaim.[150]

---

142 The Vilna Gaon in his commentary on Tikkunei Zohar Tikkun 11 of the Last Tikkunim, comments as follows:
  - . . . and each [soul] has a root in [the Torah], as is written: "There are 600,000 letters of the Torah and of Israel," and each [soul] has its root, either in a letter or a Kotz [a specific form of letter tag] or a vowel or a letter tag, according to the greatness of his soul, as is known.

The precise original source for the Vilna Gaon's statement that "there are 600,000 letters of the Torah and of Israel" is not known, but this statement appears in many places, and in some places it is expressed that the name YiSRAeL/Israel forms the initial letters of the statement – Yesh Shishim Ribo Otiot LaTorah, there are 600,000 letters in the Torah (e.g., Megaleh Amukot VaEtchanan Ofen 186).

(In the very last section of Emet LeYaakov, R. Yaakov Kamenetsky provides a calculation which demonstrates how the letters of the Torah when broken down into their individual subcompnents sum to approximately 600,000 [given that there are actually 304,805 letters in the Torah]).

143 I.e., in The World of The Malbush. See V2:03, "The World of The Malbush."
144 Bereishit Rabba Bereishit 1:4.

שֶׁכָּל אֶחָד מִיִּשְׂרָאֵל, שֹׁרֶשׁ נִשְׁמָתוֹ הָעֶלְיוֹנָה מְדֻבָּק וְנֶאֱחָז בְּאוֹת אַחַת מֵהַתּוֹרָה, וְהָיוּ לַאֲחָדִים מַמָּשׁ:

- וּלְכָךְ אָמְרוּ בִּבְרֵאשִׁית רַבָּה פ"א, שֶׁמַּחְשַׁבְתָּן שֶׁל יִשְׂרָאֵל קָדְמָה לְכָל דָּבָר
- וְלֹא בָא לַחֲלֹק עַל מַה שֶּׁאָמְרוּ שֶׁהַתּוֹרָה קָדְמָה לְכָל דָּבָר
- כִּי הַכֹּל אֶחָד בְּשָׁרְשָׁן, וְהִיא הִיא.
- וז"ש 'מַחְשַׁבְתָּן' שֶׁל יִשְׂרָאֵל.
- וּכְמוֹ שֶׁאָמְרוּ "יִשְׂרָאֵל עָלָה בְּמַחְשָׁבָה"
- רוֹצֶה לוֹמַר, רֵאשִׁית הַמַּחְשָׁבָה, סוֹד הָרְעוּתָא עִלָּאָה
- כְּמוֹ שֶׁכָּתוּב בַּזֹּהַר וַיֵּרָא קי"ח ב', דְּהָא יִשְׂרָאֵל סָלִיק בִּרְעוּתָא דְקוּדְשָׁא בְּרִיךְ הוּא עַד לָא יִבְרָא עָלְמָא.
- וְהָרְעוּתָא הִיא רֵאשִׁית הַכֹּל, אֱלֹהוּת גָּמוּר כִּבְיָכוֹל, מֵעוֹלָמוֹת אֵין סוֹף
- כַּנִּזְכָּר שָׁם בְּפָרָשַׁת נֹחַ ס"ה א', וּפִקּוּדֵי רס"ח ב', אָמַר רַבִּי שִׁמְעוֹן אֲרֵימִית כו', דְּכַד רְעוּתָא עִלָּאָה כו', וְכָל אִנּוּן נְהוֹרִין מֵרָזָא דְמַחְשָׁבָה עִלָּאָה וּלְתַתָּא, כֻּלְּהוּ אִקְרוּן אֵין סוֹף. עַיֵּן שָׁם הֵיטֵב
- וּבְהַגָּהַת הרח"ו זִכְרוֹנוֹ לִבְרָכָה שָׁם
- וּבְעֵץ חַיִּים שַׁעַר עִגּוּלִים וְיֹשֶׁר רֵישׁ עָנָף ד', וּבְשַׁעַר הִשְׁתַּלְשְׁלוּת הִי' סְפִירוֹת רֵישׁ עָנָף ב'.

---

145 This statement frequently appears in Zohar, e.g., Zohar I Bereishit 24a where *Machashava*/thought is analyzed as *Chashav Mah* (see p. 264, fn. 477, which relates to *Mi* and *Mah* at the beginning of G1:19).
146 Zohar I Vayera 118b.
147 See V2:03, "The World of The Malbush."
148 Zohar I Noach 65a and Zohar II Pekudei 268b.
149 This source was unsuccessfully searched for.
150 Etz Chaim Shaar 1, Derush HaIgulim VeYosher, beginning of sect. 4:
- [This quotes the Zohar from Noach and Pekudei above and mentions that there are an infinite number of levels which precede what are called the Ten Sefirot of Atzilut.]

Etz Chaim Shaar 2, Shaar Hishtalshelut HaYud Sefirot, beginning of sect. 2:
- [This also refers to the two sections from Zohar and the infinite number of levels preceding the Ten Sefirot of Atzilut.]

- Therefore, Chazal state that *Bereishit*[151] means for the sake of Torah[152] which is called *Reishit* and it is also for sake of Israel[153] which is called *Reishit*.[154]
- (Therefore Chazal say: "One who is with a person at the time his soul leaves him is obligated to tear his garments – this is compared to one's required action on seeing a burnt Torah scroll,"[155] as the holiness of every Jew's soul is literally the same as the holiness of a Torah scroll.)

- Therefore, from the time of the Creation, when the Torah was still stored in its source which was hidden from all the supernal worlds [in The World of The Malbush]
  - but only emanating life force to and maintaining existence of the worlds from a distance
  - and its essence had not descended down for the inhabitants of this world to be involved with it
  - the worlds were still in a state of disarray and had not yet settled into their correct state; Chazal referred to this period as "two thousand years of emptiness."[156]
  - The status of the worlds were held in the balance waiting for the time of the Giving of the Torah, as per Chazal:
    - That God set a condition on creation of the Universe that if Israel would accept [the Torah, it would continue to exist] and if not [then all would be returned to emptiness].[157]
    - "I revealed that you are My beloved." The Rabbis say, "My beloved of My world," that they should accept my Torah, that if they do not accept it I will return my world to emptiness, as R. Chanina says in the name of R. Acha, the verse states: "The earth [and its inhabitants] have melted – I have firmly established its pillars," if not for Israel who stood on Mount Sinai [and said, "We will do and

---

151 Referring to the first word of the Torah, meaning *With Reishit* the heavens and earth were created, where *Reishit* is understood to be either Torah or Israel as they are one and the same. *Reishit* also means *beginning* and in this context is a reference to the beginning, i.e., the first created world, The World of The Malbush, which is the blueprint of all the other worlds. See V2:03, "The World of The Malbush."
152 Bereishit Rabba Bereishit 1:4.
153 Vayikra Rabba Bechukotai 36:4.
154 It is particularly insightful to see the words of the Shela on Parshat Kedoshim Torah Ohr:
  - Bereishit – this is for the sake of the Torah and of Israel, the holy of Israel. *Shal*/310 worlds were created for each righteous person with the 231 gates

○ וְלָכֵן אָמְרוּ "בְּרֵאשִׁית" — בִּשְׁבִיל הַתּוֹרָה שֶׁנִּקְרֵאת "רֵאשִׁית", וּבִשְׁבִיל יִשְׂרָאֵל שֶׁנִּקְרְאוּ "רֵאשִׁית".

○ (וְלָכֵן אָמְרוּ זִכְרוֹנָם לִבְרָכָה (מו"ק כה, א) "הָעוֹמֵד עַל הַמֵּת בִּשְׁעַת יְצִיאַת נְשָׁמָה חַיָּב לִקְרֹעַ, הָא לָמָּה הַדָּבָר דּוֹמֶה, לְרוֹאֶה סֵפֶר תּוֹרָה שֶׁנִּשְׂרָף", שֶׁקְּדֻשַּׁת נִשְׁמַת כָּל אֶחָד מִיִּשְׂרָאֵל הִיא הִיא קְדֻשַּׁת סֵפֶר תּוֹרָה מַמָּשׁ):

• וְלָכֵן, מֵעֵת הַבְּרִיאָה, שֶׁהָיְתָה הַתּוֹרָה גְנוּזָה עֲדַיִן בִּמְקוֹר שָׁרְשָׁהּ הַנֶּעֱלָם מִכָּל הָעוֹלָמוֹת עֶלְיוֹנִים

○ וּמֵרָחוֹק לְבַד הֵאִירָה לְכָל הָעוֹלָמוֹת לְהַחֲיוֹתָם וּלְקַיְּמָם

○ וְלֹא נִשְׁתַּלְשְׁלָה עַצְמוּתָהּ מַמָּשׁ לְמַטָּה לְזֶה הָעוֹלָם שֶׁיַּעַסְקוּ בָּהּ קְבוּצֵי מַטָּה

○ עֲדַיִן הָיוּ הָעוֹלָמוֹת רוֹפְפִים וְרוֹתְתִים, וְלֹא הָיוּ עַל מְכוֹנָם הָאֲמִתִּי, וּקְרָאוּם רַבּוֹתֵינוּ זִכְרוֹנָם לִבְרָכָה (ע"ז ט, א) "שְׁנֵי אֲלָפִים תֹּהוּ".

○ וְהָיוּ תְלוּיִים וְעוֹמְדִים עַד עֵת מַתַּן תּוֹרָה, כַּיָּדוּעַ מַאֲמָרָם זִכְרוֹנָם לִבְרָכָה

▫ שֶׁהִתְנָה הַקָּדוֹשׁ בָּרוּךְ הוּא עִם מַעֲשֵׂי בְרֵאשִׁית, אִם מְקַבְּלִין יִשְׂרָאֵל וְכוּ', וְאִם לָאו וְכוּ' (שבת פח, א). וְכֵן הוּא בִּשְׁמוֹת רַבָּה פמ"ז, וּדְבָרִים רַבָּה סוֹף פָּרָשָׁה ח', וּבְרֵישׁ הַתַּנְחוּמָא.

▫ וּבְרַבָּה שִׁיר הַשִּׁירִים (א, ט) "דְּמִיתִיךְ רַעְיָתִי", רַבָּנָן אָמְרֵי, רַעְיָתִי דְּעוֹלָמִי,

---

which are mentioned in Sefer Yetzirah. Therefore the first point of God's revelation is the spiritual *Hyle* which is called *Yesh*/physical from *Ayin*/non-physical, as per "and the *wisdom* is from Ayin" [Iyov 28:20] which explains "You made all with wisdom" [Tehillim 104:24]. This point is called YiSRAeL/Israel because of *Shin Yud*/310 and *Resh Lamed Aleph*/231 [which combine together to form the name YiSRAeL] where *ShaI* [has the same letters as] *Yesh*/physical. This is what it [Zohar I Vayera 118b] means that "Israel arose in God's Will before the creation of the Universe". [This quotation from the Shela can be fully understood by reviewing V2:03, "The World of The Malbush," as Israel's root, and the Primordial Torah of The World of The Malbush with the matrix presentations of multiple alphabets are one and the same thing. Hyle is a Greek word and is a philosophical concept that all physical entities are derived from a single substance which today we would call matter, energy or even the fabric of Spacetime.]

155 Moed Katan 25a.
156 Avodah Zarah 9a.
157 Shabbat 88a; Shemot Rabba 47:4; Devarim Rabba 8:5; Midrash Tanchuma Bereishit 1.

listen to all of that which God speaks" the world would melt and return to emptiness], and who established the world, I [established its pillars] in the merit of "I am YHVH your God" "I established its pillars."[158]

- From the time when [the Torah] cascaded downwards, so to speak, from its hidden source [in The World of The Malbush] to this world
  - as Chazal[159] say that Moshe came and brought it down to the Earth
  - all the life force and existence of all the worlds is now purely contingent on our verbal study and analysis of [Torah].
- The unequivocal truth is, that were the entire world to be even literally momentarily devoid of our study of and contemplation in Torah, God forbid
  - then all the supernal and lower worlds would immediately be destroyed and return to nothingness, God forbid
  - and similarly the bestowal of light or its diminishing, God forbid, is all purely according to our level of [Torah] involvement.
- Therefore, we make the blessing [on Torah] saying: "You have implanted everlasting life within us"[160]
  - referring to a fruit bearing planting process which increases good[161]
  - similarly, if we support the Holy Torah as we should with all of our strength, we will inherit everlasting life and will draw down additional holiness, blessing, and great light into all the worlds from its hidden source which is above all the worlds
  - as per the Midrash: "More than you guard anything, safeguard your heart . . ." that you should not flee from words of Torah. Why? ". . . for the sources of life come from it" which teaches you that life comes to the world from words of Torah.[162]
- [Torah involvement] is also necessary to rebuild with great rectification that which has been destroyed to bind, unify, and complete the supernal worlds with the lower worlds [resulting] in all the worlds being weighed together and enlightened as one [entity], as per Chazal:
  - R. Alexandrai said: All who study Torah *for its sake* are as if they make peace between the supernal and lower assemblies as it says, "If [Israel] would grasp my stronghold then he would make peace with Me. . . ." Rav said: It is as if he built the supernal and lower palaces as it says, "and I shall place My Word in your mouth [and cover you with the shadow of My Hand] to plant heavens and establish the earth. . . ."[163]

---

158 Shir Hashirim Rabba 1:9 quoting Shir Hashirim 1:9; Tehillim 75:4; Shemot 24:7; Shemot 20:2.
159 Bereishit Rabba 19:7.

שֶׁקִּבְּלוּ תּוֹרָתִי, שֶׁאִלּוּ לֹא קִבְּלוּ הָיִיתִי מַחֲזִיר אֶת עוֹלָמִי לְתֹהוּ וָבֹהוּ, דְּאָמַר ר"ח בְּשֵׁם ר"א, כְּתִיב (תהלים עה, ד) "נְמֹגִים אֶרֶץ" כו', "אָנֹכִי תִכַּנְתִּי עַמּוּדֶיהָ סֶּלָה", אִלּוּלֵי יִשְׂרָאֵל שֶׁעָמְדוּ עַל הַר סִינַי כו', וּמִי בְּסַם הָעוֹלָם, "אָנֹכִי" כו', בִּזְכוּת אָנֹכִי ה' אֱלֹהֶיךָ "תִּכַּנְתִּי עַמּוּדֶיהָ סֶּלָה":

- וּמֵאָז שֶׁנִּשְׁתַּלְשְׁלָה וְיָרְדָה כִּבְיָכוֹל מִמְּקוֹר שָׁרְשָׁהּ הַנֶּעֱלָם לְזֶה הָעוֹלָם
  - כְּמַאֲמָרָם זִכְרוֹנָם לִבְרָכָה (בראשית רבה יט), בָּא מֹשֶׁה וְהוֹרִידָהּ לָאָרֶץ
  - כָּל חִיּוּתָם וְקִיּוּמָם שֶׁל כָּל הָעוֹלָמוֹת, הוּא רַק עַל יְדֵי הֶבֶל פִּינוּ וַהֲגִיוֹנֵינוּ בָּהּ:
- וְהָאֱמֶת בִּלְתִּי שׁוּם סָפֵק כְּלָל, שֶׁאִם הָיָה הָעוֹלָם כֻּלּוֹ, מִקָּצֶה עַד קָצֵהוּ, פָּנוּי חַס וְשָׁלוֹם אַף רֶגַע אֶחָד מַמָּשׁ, מֵהָעֵסֶק וְהִתְבּוֹנְנוּת שֶׁלָּנוּ בַּתּוֹרָה
  - כְּרֶגַע הָיוּ נֶחֱרָבִים כָּל הָעוֹלָמוֹת, עֶלְיוֹנִים וְתַחְתּוֹנִים, וְהָיוּ לְאֶפֶס וְתֹהוּ חַס וְשָׁלוֹם.
  - וְכֵן שִׁפְעַת אוֹרָם אוֹ מִעוּטוֹ חַס וְשָׁלוֹם, הַכֹּל רַק כְּפִי עִנְיַן וְרֹב עִסְקֵנוּ בָּהּ:
- לָכֵן אָנוּ מְבָרְכִים עָלֶיהָ "וְחַיֵּי עוֹלָם נָטַע בְּתוֹכֵנוּ".
  - כְּעִנְיַן הַנְּטִיעָה, שֶׁנְּטִיעָתָהּ כְּדֵי לַעֲשׂוֹת פְּרִי — לְהַרְבּוֹת טוֹבָה
  - כֵּן אִם אָנוּ מַחֲזִיקִים בַּתּוֹרָה הַקְּדוֹשָׁה בְּכָל כֹּחֵנוּ כָּרָאוּי, אָנוּ מַנְחִילִין חַיֵּי עַד, וּמַמְשִׁיכִים מִשָּׁרְשָׁהּ הַנֶּעֱלָם לְמַעְלָה מִכָּל הָעוֹלָמוֹת, תּוֹסָפוֹת קְדֻשָּׁה וּבְרָכָה וְאוֹר גָּדוֹל בְּכָל הָעוֹלָמוֹת.
  - זֶה שֶׁאָמְרוּ בְּמִשְׁלֵי רַבָּתָא פָּרָשָׁה ד' "מִכָּל מִשְׁמָר נְצֹר לִבֶּךָ", שֶׁלֹּא תִּבְרַח מִדִּבְרֵי תוֹרָה, לָמָּה, "כִּי מִמֶּנּוּ תּוֹצְאוֹת חַיִּים", לְלַמֶּדְךָ שֶׁמִּדִּבְרֵי תוֹרָה יוֹצְאִין חַיִּים לָעוֹלָם:
- וְגַם לִבְנוֹת הַנֶּהֱרָסוֹת בְּתִקּוּנִים גְּדוֹלִים, לְקַשֵּׁר וּלְיַחֵד וּלְהַשְׁלִים הָעֶלְיוֹנִים עִם הַתַּחְתּוֹנִים, וְכָל הָעָלְמִין שְׁקִילִין וּנְהִירִין כַּחֲדָא. כְּמַאֲמָרָם זִכְרוֹנָם לִבְרָכָה
  - בְּפֶרֶק חֵלֶק (צט, ב), "אָמַר רַבִּי אֲלֶכְּסַנְדְּרִי, כָּל הָעוֹסֵק בַּתּוֹרָה לִשְׁמָהּ, כְּאִלּוּ

---

160 Masechet Sofrim 13:6.
161 Where the seed is hidden in the ground and if nurtured correctly grows and openly reveals its fruits.
162 Midrash Mishlei 4:23 which splits the verse from Mishlei 4:23 into two to explain it. R. Chaim's version states "you should not flee" whereas the standard version states "you should not be afraid." However, this does not change the point he is making about Torah giving life.
163 Sanhedrin 99b quoting Yishayahu 27:5 and 51:16.

- "The pillars are marble" – these are the Torah Sages. Why are they compared to pillars? For they are the pillars of the world, as per "If not for [the continued study of] My Covenant [i.e., the Torah] day and night, [then I would not have put into place the rules of the Heavens and Earth]."[164]
- "She built her house with all forms of wisdom." God said, if a person merited and studied Torah and wisdom, he is considered before Me as if he created the heavens and as if he established the entire universe.[165]
- God says to Israel: My children, be involved with Torah day and night and I will consider it as if you are establishing the entire universe.[166]
- All who involve themselves with Torah each day, will merit to have a portion in the future world and it will be considered as if they built worlds as the entirety of the Universe was created and improved with the Torah. This is as per "God established the earth with wisdom . . ." and "and I was then his *Amon*," and all who involve themselves with it improve the worlds and maintain their existence. Come and see, that with Ruach, God made the Universe, and with Ruach, he maintains its existence – this is the Ruach [i.e., the speech] of those who study the Torah.[167]
- In another section of the Zohar, after initially describing at length the great advantages of a person who involves himself in Torah in both this and the next world, and his great punishment in both worlds when he weakens his [involvement], God forbid – the section concludes by saying:
  - It is because of this that All exists as a result of keeping the Torah. The Universe only exists with Torah which is the very existence of the supernal and lower worlds as is written: "If not for My Covenant day and night, [then I would not have put into place the rules of the Heavens and Earth]."[168]

---

164 Bamidbar Rabba Naso 10:1 quoting Shir Hashirim 5:15 and Yirmiyahu 33:25. The original text from this source is as follows:
- "The pillars are marble" . . . Why are *words of Torah* compared to pillars? For they are the pillars of the world, as per "if not for [the continued study of] My Covenant [i.e., the Torah], I would not have put into place the rules of the heavens and earth."

It would appear that R. Chaim either had a slightly different version or interpreted this text in a way which effectively has the same meaning.

165 Midrash Mishlei 9:1.
166 Midrash Mishlei 31:30.
167 Zohar I Bereishit 47a quoting Mishlei 3:19 and Mishlei 8:30 (where Amon,

עוֹשֶׂה שָׁלוֹם בִּפָמַלְיָא שֶׁל מַעְלָה וּבִפָמַלְיָא שֶׁל מַטָּה, שֶׁנֶּאֱמַר (ישעיה כז, ה) "אוֹ יַחֲזֵק בְּמָעֻזִּי יַעֲשֶׂה שָׁלוֹם לִי" כו', רַב אָמַר כְּאִלּוּ בָּנָה פַּלְטֵרִין שֶׁל מַעְלָה וּפַלְטֵרִין שֶׁל מַטָּה, שֶׁנֶּאֱמַר (ישעיה נא, טז) "וָאָשִׂים דְּבָרַי בְּפִיךָ וכו', לִנְטֹעַ שָׁמַיִם וְלִיסֹד אָרֶץ".

◦ וּבְחָזִית, "שׁוֹקָיו עַמּוּדֵי שֵׁשׁ" (שה"ש ה, טו) אֵלּוּ תַּלְמִידֵי חֲכָמִים, לָמָּה נִמְשְׁלוּ לְעַמּוּדִים, שֶׁהֵם עַמּוּדֵי עוֹלָם, שֶׁנֶּאֱמַר (ירמיה לג, כה) "אִם לֹא בְרִיתִי יוֹמָם וָלָיְלָה" כו'.

◦ וּבְמִשְׁלֵי רַבָּתָא (ט, א) "חָכְמוֹת בָּנְתָה בֵיתָהּ" כו', אָמַר הַקָּדוֹשׁ בָּרוּךְ הוּא, אִם זָכָה אָדָם וְלָמַד תּוֹרָה וְחָכְמָה, חָשׁוּב לְפָנַי כְּמוֹ שֶׁבָּרָא שָׁמַיִם, וּכְאִלּוּ הֶעֱמִיד כָּל הָעוֹלָם כֻּלּוֹ.

◦ וְשָׁם (לא) בְּפֶרֶק אֵשֶׁת חַיִל אָמְרוּ, "אָמַר הַקָּדוֹשׁ בָּרוּךְ הוּא לְיִשְׂרָאֵל, בָּנַי הֱיוּ מִתְעַסְּקִין בַּתּוֹרָה בַּיּוֹם וּבַלַּיְלָה, וּמַעֲלֶה אֲנִי עֲלֵיכֶם כְּאִלּוּ אַתֶּם מַעֲמִידִים אֶת כָּל הָעוֹלָם".

◦ וּבַזֹּהַר בְּרֵאשִׁית מ"ז א', כָּל מַאן דְּאִשְׁתַּדַּל בְּאוֹרַיְתָא בְּכָל יוֹמָא, יִזְכֵּי לְמֶהֱוֵי לֵיהּ חוּלָקָא בְּעָלְמָא דְאָתֵי, וְיִתְחַשֵּׁיב לֵיהּ כְּאִלּוּ בָּאנֵי עָלְמִין, דְּהָא בְּאוֹרַיְתָא אִתְבְּנֵי עָלְמָא וְאִשְׁתַּכְלַל, הֲדָא הוּא דִכְתִיב בְּחָכְמָה יָסַד אֶרֶץ וְגוֹ', וּכְתִיב וָאֶהְיֶה אֶצְלוֹ אָמוֹן כו', וְכָל דְּאִשְׁתַּדַּל בָּהּ שַׁכְלֵל עָלְמִין וְקַיָּם לֵיהּ. וְתָא חֲזֵי, בְּרוּחָא עָבִיד קוּדְשָׁא בְּרִיךְ הוּא עָלְמָא, וּבְרוּחָא מִתְקַיְּמָא, דָּא רוּחָא דְּאִנּוּן דְּלָעָאן בְּאוֹרַיְתָא כו'.

◦ וְשָׁם בְּפָרָשַׁת וַיֵּשֶׁב, אַחַר שֶׁהֶאֱרִיךְ תְּחִלָּה בְּמַעֲלָתוֹ הַנּוֹרָאָה שֶׁל הָאָדָם הָעוֹסֵק בַּתּוֹרָה בָּעוֹלָם הַזֶּה וּבָעוֹלָם הַבָּא, וְעָנְשׁוֹ הַגָּדוֹל בִּשְׁנֵי הָעוֹלָמִים כְּשֶׁמִּתְרַפֶּה מִמֶּנָּה חַס וְשָׁלוֹם, סִיֵּם וְאָמַר

▫ "בְּגִין כָּךְ כֹּלָּא קַיְמָא עַל קִיּוּמָא דְּאוֹרַיְתָא, וְעָלְמָא לֹא אִתְקַיַּם בְּקִיּוּמֵיהּ אֶלָּא בְּאוֹרַיְתָא, דְּאִיהוּ קִיּוּמָא דְעָלְמִין עִלָּא וְתַתָּא, דִּכְתִיב "אִם לֹא בְרִיתִי יוֹמָם וָלַיְלָה" כו'.

---

as previously explained, in G4:10 is *Uman* referring to craftsmanship and that through the Torah, God crafted the Universe).

168 Zohar I Vayeshev 185a quoting Yirmiyahu 33:25.

- In a further section of Zohar,[169] after describing at length how the Torah was used to create all the worlds,[170] it then says:
  - Following the creation of the Universe, each and every word [of Torah] would not exist until it came up in God's Will to create man who would be involved with Torah, and the Universe is maintained for him.
  - Now, anyone who looks into Torah and involves himself with it, it is as if he is maintaining the Universe, so to speak.
  - God looked into the Torah and created the world; Man looks into the Torah and sustains the world.
  - It transpires that Torah is the very existence and maintenance of the entire Universe, and as a result happy is the one who is involved with Torah as he maintains the existence of the Universe.
- Since the Universe was only created for the Torah, and all the while that Israel are involved with the Torah, the Universe exists, and all the while that Israel desist from being involved with Torah, what is it that is written? "If not for My Covenant day and night [then I would not have put into place the rules of the Heavens and Earth]."[171]
• Therefore, the Mishna states[172] that one who is involved with Torah study *for its sake* is called a "friend"
  - as he becomes a partner, so to speak, with the Creator since he is currently the one sustaining all the worlds with his Torah involvement
  - and without this [the worlds] would all return to null and void
  - as written in the Midrash above: "I revealed that you are My beloved." My beloved of My world, that they should accept my Torah.[173]

---

169 Zohar II Terumah 161a.
170 I.e., the section which was quoted in G4:10 above.
171 Zohar III Vayikra 11b quoting Yirmiyahu 33:25.
172 Mishna Avot 6:1.
173 Shir Hashirim Rabba 1:9 quoting Shir Hashirim 1:9. R. Chaim highlights that a person is called a "friend/Reah" and "My Beloved/Rayati" specifically when he is involved with Torah and partners with God in sustaining the worlds. It should be noted that the words "Reah" and "Rayati" have the same spelling as or contain the word "Rah/evil." These words in which the letter sequence *Resh Ayin* are an intrinsic part of them denote separation where a friend or one's beloved is a separate entity and evil is the environment of this world which is separate to God (being the meaning of the term "Sitra Achara," the other side, as mentioned on p. 564, fn. 280). Therefore, just as God creates this world which from our perspective appears separate to Him via the Tzimtzum process, we partner in sustaining this separate world through Torah study.

- וּבְפָרָשַׁת תְּרוּמָה קס"א א', אַחַר שֶׁהֶאֱרִיךְ בָּעִנְיָן, לְבָאֵר אֵיךְ שֶׁבַּהַתּוֹרָה נִבְרְאוּ כָּל הָעוֹלָמוֹת, אָמַר אַחַר זֶה

- "כֵּיוָן דְּאִתְבְּרֵי עָלְמָא, כָּל מִלָּה וּמִלָּה לָא הֲוָה מִתְקַיֵּם, עַד דְּסָלִיק בִּרְעוּתָא לְמִבְרֵי אָדָם דִּיהֵוֵי מִשְׁתַּדֵּל בְּאוֹרַיְתָא, וּבְגִינֵיהּ אִתְקַיַּם עָלְמָא.

- הַשְׁתָּא כָּל מַאן דְּאִסְתַּכַּל בָּהּ בְּאוֹרַיְתָא וְאִשְׁתַּדֵּל בָּהּ, כִּבְיָכוֹל הוּא מְקַיֵּם כָּל עָלְמָא.

- קוּדְשָׁא בְּרִיךְ הוּא אִסְתַּכַּל בְּאוֹרַיְתָא וּבָרָא עָלְמָא וּבַר נָשׁ אִסְתַּכַּל בְּאוֹרַיְתָא וּמְקַיֵּם עָלְמָא

- אִשְׁתַּכַּח דְּעוֹבָדָא וְקִיּוּמָא דְּכָל עָלְמָא אוֹרַיְתָא אִיהִי. בְּגִין כָּךְ זַכָּאָה אִיהוּ בַּר נָשׁ דְּאִשְׁתַּדֵּל בְּאוֹרַיְתָא, דְּהַאי אִיהוּ מְקַיֵּם עָלְמָא".

- וּבְפָרָשַׁת וַיִּקְרָא י"א סוֹף ע"ב, "בְּגִין דְּעָלְמָא לָא אִתְבְּרֵי אֶלָּא בְּגִין אוֹרַיְתָא, וְכָל זִמְנָא דְיִשְׂרָאֵל מִתְעַסְּקֵי בְּאוֹרַיְתָא עָלְמָא מִתְקַיְּמָא. וְכָל זִמְנָא דְיִשְׂרָאֵל מִתְבַּטְּלֵי מֵאוֹרַיְתָא מַה כְּתִיב, "אִם לֹא בְרִיתִי יוֹמָם וָלָיְלָה" כוּ':

• וְלָכֵן אָמְרוּ בְּפֶרֶק מַעֲלוֹת הַתּוֹרָה (אבות ו, א), שֶׁכָּל הָעוֹסֵק בַּתּוֹרָה לִשְׁמָהּ נִקְרָא "רֵעַ"

- כִּי כִּבְיָכוֹל נַעֲשָׂה שֻׁתָּף לְיוֹצֵר בְּרֵאשִׁית יִתְבָּרַךְ שְׁמוֹ, כֵּיוָן שֶׁהוּא הַמְקַיֵּם עַתָּה אֶת כָּל הָעוֹלָמוֹת בְּעֵסֶק תּוֹרָתוֹ

- וּבִלְתִּי זֶה הָיוּ חוֹזְרִים כֻּלָּם לְתֹהוּ וָבֹהוּ

- וּכְמוֹ שֶׁכָּתוּב בַּמִּדְרָשׁ הַנַּ"ל "דְּמִיתִיךְ רַעְיָתִי", רַעְיָתִי דְעָלְמִי, שֶׁקִּבְּלוּ תּוֹרָתִי כוּ':

Therefore, when we are engaged in this process, we are specifically referred to as a "Reah/friend." We see this same concept and the *Resh Ayin* letter sequence in the word "Teruah" which is the Torah's terminology for the broken sound of the Shofar on Rosh Hashana (e.g., Bamidbar 29:1). The broken nature of the "Teruah" sound as a string of separate short sounds denotes separation. This is hinted to in the verse "Elokim ascends with the Teruah, YHVH with the sound of the Shofar" (Tehillim 47:6). This verse specifically associates God's Name Elokim with the concept of separation, the Teruah. In contrast it also associates God's Name YHVH with the simple unbroken/unified Shofar sound, the Tekiah. On Rosh Hashana, each Shofar sounding sequence contains a broken sound, which is preceded and also followed by an unbroken sound. The broken sound represents Gevurah/separation/judgment, whereas the wrapper of unbroken sound represents mercy which

12. EVEN GREATER IMPACT OF NEW TORAH INSIGHTS

- [In addition to tremendous impact of just studying Torah,] how much greater is the incredibly great, awesome, and wondrous impact Above of a person developing truly new Torah insights
  - as God *Kisses and Crowns* each individual word of a person's new [Torah] insight
  - and uses it to build a new and separate world – these are referenced by Scripture as the "the new heavens and the new earth."[174]
- This is as per the Zohar:[175]
  - R. Shimon taught: "and I will place My Words in your mouth"[176]
  - this emphasizes just how much a person should invest in Torah study, day and night
  - as God listens to the voice of all those studying Torah and with each word uttered by the one toiling in Torah which expresses a new Torah insight, He makes a firmament.
  - We learn that at the time when a person expresses this new Torah insight, that word ascends and gives testimony before God and He takes it and *Kisses* it and *Crowns* it with seventy developed and hewn crowns.
  - The word of wisdom, the insight, ascends to sit on [/crown] the head . . . and then flies up from there through seventy thousand worlds and ascends to Atik Yomin.[177]
  - This hidden word of wisdom which was revealed here [i.e., in this physical world,] when it ascends it attaches itself to aspects of the level of Atik Yomin; it then ascends and descends with these attached aspects and enters into the eighteen hidden worlds which "no eye has seen. . . ."[178]

---

overcomes the judgment of the broken sound. (See Tolaat Yaakov, Sod HaTeshuva.) The Torah command to sound the Shofar on Rosh Hashana is therefore underpinned by the concept of recognizing God's absolute Unity in this world that appears separate to him. It acknowledges that even with the different perspectives of God, from God's perspective of YHVH/absolute Unity and from our perspective of Elokim/separation, that they are truly one and the same thing (as per G3:11, the Shofar sounding sequence is therefore directly analogous to the statement made in the first line of the Shema that "YHVH Elokeinu YHVH" is One).

174 This verse is from Yishayahu 66:22. With the entire opening statement of this chapter, R. Chaim is summarizing the key points of a lengthy piece of Zohar which he now quotes in its entirety – putting great emphasis on the importance of studying Torah in a way which generates one's own unique Torah insights. This does not mean that one's Torah insights are unique to this world, as we

שער ד' - פרק י"ב

- וְכָל שֶׁכֵּן חִדּוּשִׁין אֲמִתִּים דְּאוֹרַיְתָא הַמִּתְחַדְּשִׁין עַל יְדֵי הָאָדָם, אֵין עֲרֹךְ לְגֹדֶל נוֹרָאוֹת נִפְלָאוֹת עִנְיָנָם וּפְעֻלָּתָם לְמָעְלָה.
  ○ שֶׁכָּל מִלָּה וּמִלָּה פְּרָטִית הַמִּתְחַדֶּשֶׁת מִפִּי הָאָדָם, קוּדְשָׁא בְּרִיךְ הוּא נָשִׁיק לָהּ וּמְעַטֵּר לָהּ.
  ○ וְנִבְנֶה מִמֶּנָּה עוֹלָם חָדָשׁ בִּפְנֵי עַצְמוֹ, וְהֵן הֵן "הַשָּׁמַיִם הַחֲדָשִׁים וְהָאָרֶץ הַחֲדָשָׁה" שֶׁאָמַר הַכָּתוּב (ישעי' סו, כב):
- כְּמוֹ שֶׁכָּתוּב בְּהַקְדָּמַת הַזֹּהַר דַּף ד' ע"ב
  ○ רַבִּי שִׁמְעוֹן פָּתַח "וָאָשִׂים דְּבָרַי בְּפִיךָ" (ישעיה נא, טז)
  ○ כַּמָּה אִית לֵיהּ לְבַר נָשׁ לְאִשְׁתַּדְּלָא בְּאוֹרַיְתָא יְמָמָא וְלֵילְיָא
  ○ בְּגִין דְּקוּדְשָׁא בְּרִיךְ הוּא צַיִּת לְקָלֵיהוֹן דְּאִנּוּן דְּמִתְעַסְּקֵי בְּאוֹרַיְתָא, וּבְכָל מִלָּה דְּאִתְחַדַּשׁ בְּאוֹרַיְתָא — עַל יְדָא דְּהַהוּא דְּאִשְׁתַּדַּל בְּאוֹרַיְתָא — עָבִיד רְקִיעָא חֲדָא.
  ○ תָּנָן בְּהַהוּא שַׁעֲתָא דְּמִלָּה דְּאוֹרַיְתָא אִתְחַדַּשׁ מִפּוּמֵיהּ דְּבַר נָשׁ, הַהִיא מִלָּה סַלְקָא וְאִתְעַתְּדַת קַמֵּיהּ דְּקוּדְשָׁא בְּרִיךְ הוּא, וְקוּדְשָׁא בְּרִיךְ הוּא נָטִיל לְהַהוּא מִלָּה, וְנָשִׁיק לָהּ, וְעָטַר לָהּ בְּשִׁבְעִין עַטְרִין גְּלִיפִין וּמְחַקְּקָן.
  ○ וּמִלָּה דְּחָכְמְתָא דְּאִתְחַדְּשָׁא סַלְקָא וְיָתְבָא עַל רֵישָׁא כוּ', וְטָסָא מִתַּמָּן וְשָׁטָאַת בְּשִׁבְעִין אֶלֶף עָלְמִין, וְסַלְּקַת לְגַבֵּי עַתִּיק יוֹמִין כוּ'
  ○ וְהַהִיא מִלָּה סְתִימָא דְּחָכְמְתָא דְּאִתְחַדְּשַׁת הָכָא, כַּד סַלְקָא, אִתְחַבְּרַת בְּאִנּוּן

---

learn that all of Torah, including any future Torah insight, was handed to Moshe when the Torah was given. However, it means that on a personal level one should be motivated to study in such a way that one is always pushing the boundaries of one's own understanding – such that it becomes a regular occurrence to have insights in new ways of understanding and expressing the details of Torah. (See V2:02, Chap. 15, "Tzimtzum Sources," A4.5 for deeper insight.)

175 Zohar Introduction 4b.
176 Yishayahu 51:16.
177 I.e., a very high place.
178 Yishayahu 64:3.

- This word of wisdom then exits and returns, full and complete, before the level of Atik Yomin, at which point Atik Yomin smells the word's fragrance and is very gratified with it; it takes this word and crowns it with three hundred and seventy thousand crowns.
- This word then goes on to form a single firmament.
- Similarly, each and every word of wisdom makes a completely permanent firmament before Atik Yomin called "New Heavens" – the hidden secrets of Supernal Wisdom.
- All the other words of new Torah insights exist before God – they ascend and form "lands of life," and then descend and are crowned ... They are then renewed and each form a new land from that new Torah insight.
- About this it is written: "For just as the new Heavens and Earth which I *make* ..."[179] – this does not say "made" but rather [continuously] "make," and these are the insights and secrets of the Torah.
- About this it is written: "And I will place My Word in your mouth, [and will cover you with the shade of My hand], to place the Heavens and establish the Earth, [saying to Zion, you are My People]."[180]
- R. Elazar asks what does it mean by "will cover you with the shade of My hand"? They said to him ... and now that this word ascends and is crowned before God, He covers that person [who uttered it] with it ... until that word becomes a new heaven and land – "saying to Zion, you are My People"; do not read this as "My People (Ami)," but rather as "with Me (Imi)" – to be My Partner with Me
- that just as I Make the Heavens and the Earth with My Speech, so do you – happy are those that toil in Torah.

• The Zohar[181] also writes [in relation to the verse "and with the children of Yissachar who had understanding of times"[182] that they reveal many new Torah insights]:
  - It is written: "The Dudaim flowers provided fragrance ... ," these are those which Reuven found ...
  - [the children of Yissachar are referred to as "all our entrances have new and old precious fruits, for you my beloved I have stored them for you"][183]
  - "all our entrances have new and old precious fruits," [the children of Yissachar] brought "new and old" Torah insights to the entrances of the study halls. How many new and old Torah insights are revealed by them ...

---

179 Yishayahu 66:22.
180 Yishayahu 51:16.

נפש   שער ד' - פרק י"ב   החיים

- מִלִּין דְּעַתִּיק יוֹמִין, וְסָלְקָא וְנַחְתָּא בַּהֲדַיְהוּ, וְעָאלַת בְּתַמְנֵיסַר עָלְמִין גְּנִיזִין דְּעַיִן לָא רָאֲתָה כו'
- נָפְקִין מֵתַּמָּן שָׁאטָן וְאַתְיָן מַלְיָאן וּשְׁלִימָן, וְאִתְעַתְּדוּ קַמֵּיהּ עַתִּיק יוֹמִין. בְּהַהִיא שַׁעְתָּא אָרַח עַתִּיק יוֹמִין בְּהַהִיא מִלָּה, וְנִיחָא קָמֵיהּ מִכֹּלָא. נָטִיל לְהַהִיא מִלָּה וְאַעֲטַר לָהּ בש"ע אֶלֶף עַטְרִין.
- הַהִיא מִלָּה טָסַת וְסַלְקָא וְנַחְתָּא, וְאִתְעֲבִידַת רְקִיעָא חֲדָא.
- וְכֵן כָּל מִלָּה וּמִלָּה דְּחָכְמְתָא, אִתְעַבְדִין רְקִיעִין קַיָּמִין בְּקִיּוּמָא שְׁלִים קַמֵּי עַתִּיק יוֹמִין, וְהוּא קָרֵי לוֹן "שָׁמַיִם חֲדָשִׁים" כו', סְתִימִין דְּרָזִין דְּחָכְמְתָא עִלָּאָה.
- וְכָל אִלֵּין שְׁאָר מִלִּין דְּאוֹרַיְתָא דְּמִתְחַדְּשִׁין, קַיְמִין קָמֵי קוּדְשָׁא בְּרִיךְ הוּא, וְסַלְקִין וְאִתְעֲבִידוּ "אַרְצוֹת הַחַיִּים", וְנַחֲתִין וּמִתְעַטְּרִין כו', וְאִתְחַדֵּשׁ וְאִתְעֲבִיד כֹּלָּא "אֶרֶץ חֲדָשָׁה" מֵהַהִיא מִלָּה דְּאִתְחַדֵּשׁ בְּאוֹרַיְתָא.
- וְעַל דָּא כְּתִיב "כִּי כַאֲשֶׁר הַשָּׁמַיִם הַחֲדָשִׁים וְהָאָרֶץ הַחֲדָשָׁה כו' אֲשֶׁר אֲנִי עוֹשֶׂה" כו' (ישעי' סו, כב). "עָשִׂיתִי" לָא כְּתִיב, אֶלָּא "עוֹשֶׂה", דְּעָבִיד תָּדִיר, וְאִנּוּן חִדּוּשִׁין וְרָזִין דְּאוֹרַיְתָא.
- וְעַל דָּא כְּתִיב "וָאָשִׂים דְּבָרַי בְּפִיךָ כו' לִנְטֹעַ שָׁמַיִם וְלִיסֹד אָרֶץ" כו'.
- אָמַר ר"א מַהוּ "בְּצֵל יָדִי כִּסִּיתִיךָ", אָמַר לֵיהּ כו', וְהַשְׁתָּא דְּהַאי מִלָּה סַלְקָא וְאִתְעַטְּרָא וְקָיְמָא קָמֵי קוּדְשָׁא בְּרִיךְ הוּא, אִיהוּ חָפֵי עַל הַהִיא מִלָּה, וְכַסֵּי עַל הַהוּא בַּר נָשׁ כו', עַד דְּאִתְעֲבִיד מֵהַהִיא מִלָּה שָׁמַיִם חֲדָשִׁים וְאֶרֶץ חֲדָשָׁה כו'. "וְלֵאמֹר לְצִיּוֹן עַמִּי אָתָּה" כו', אַל תִּקְרָא "עַמִּי" אֶלָּא "עִמִּי" לְמֶהֱוֵי שׁוּתָּפָא עִמִּי
- מַה אֲנָא בְּמִלּוּלָא דִּילִי עַבְדִית שָׁמַיִם וָאָרֶץ כו', אוּף הָכִי אַתְּ, זַכָּאִין אִנּוּן דְּמִשְׁתַּדְּלִין בְּאוֹרַיְתָא:

• וּבְפָרָשַׁת וַיְחִי רמ"ג רֵישׁ ע"א, כְּתִיב (שה"ש ז, יד)
  ○ "הַדּוּדָאִים נָתְנוּ רֵיחַ" כו', אִלֵּין אִנּוּן דְּאַשְׁכַּח רְאוּבֵן
  ○ כו'
  ○ "וְעַל פְּתָחֵינוּ כָּל מְגָדִים", אִנּוּן גָּרְמוּ לְמֶהֱוֵי עַל פִּתְחֵי בָתֵּי כְנֵסִיּוֹת וּבָתֵּי

---

181 Zohar I Vayechi 243a.
182 1 Divrei Hayamim 12:33, i.e., the children of Yissachar who were very knowledgeable in Torah.
183 Shir Hashirim 7:14.

- "for you my beloved I have stored them for you," from here we learn that all who involve themselves in the right way with words of Torah and know how to make them enjoyable and express fitting insights, that these words ascend to the Throne of the King and the Collective of Israel opens the gates for them and stores them.
- At the time when God enters Gan Eden to enjoy being with the Tzaddikim, these words are taken out before Him and God looks at them and rejoices; then God crowns Himself with Supernal Crowns and rejoices ... and at that time these words are recorded before Him ...
- happy is he whose portion is to be properly involved in Torah – he is happy in this world and in the future world!
- The Midrash[184] explains the entire verse "And along the stream will grow every species of fruit-bearing tree [... every month it will yield new fruit]" to relate to words of Torah, and it says there:
  - What does the verse "every month[185] it will yield new fruit" mean?
  - That those generating new Torah insights every day are like a firstborn son to his parents with whom all are happy
  - his father has renewed joy each day ...
  - and that in every place that the Torah insights are generated, whether in the prayer house or the house of study, God rejoices anew, continuously each day.
  - Refer there.

13. GOD'S INTENTION IN CREATION COMPLETED WHEN TORAH STUDIED

- It is through study of the Holy Torah that God's intention in the Creation [of the Universe] is completed
  - as [the Universe was created] specifically for the Torah which Israel will study
  - as per Chazal who say that *BeReishit* – [the Universe was created] for the sake of [three entities referred to as *Reishit*]:
    - Torah[186]
    - Israel[187]

---

184 Eliyahu Rabba Parsha 18 quoting Yechezkel 47:12. Part of this Midrash is also quoted at the end of G4:09.
185 The word "month" has the same root as the word "insight."
186 Bereishit Rabba Bereishit 1:4.
187 Vayikra Rabba 36:4.

מִדְרָשׁוֹת כָּל מְגָדִים, "חֲדָשִׁים גַּם יְשָׁנִים", כַּמָּה מִלֵּי חַדְתָּאן וְעַתִּיקִין דְּאוֹרַיְתָא דְּאִתְגַּלְיָא עַל יְדֵיהוּ כוּ'

○ "דּוֹדִי צָפַנְתִּי לָךְ" מֵהָכָא אוֹלִיפְנָא, כָּל מַאן דְּאִשְׁתַּדַּל בְּאוֹרַיְתָא כְּדְקָא יָאוֹת, וְיָדַע לְמֶחֱדֵי מִלִּין וּלְחַדְתּוּתֵי מִלִּין כְּדְקָא יָאוֹת, אִנּוּן מִלִּין סַלְּקִין עַד כָּרְסַיָּא דְּמַלְכָּא, וּכְנֶסֶת יִשְׂרָאֵל פָּתַח לוֹן תַּרְעִין וְגָנִיז לוֹן

○ וּבְשַׁעֲתָא דְּעָאל קוּדְשָׁא בְּרִיךְ הוּא, לְאִשְׁתַּעְשְׁעָא עִם צַדִּיקַיָּא בְּגִנְּתָא דְּעֵדֶן, אֲפִיקַת לוֹן קַמֵּי, וּמִסְתַּכַּל בְּהוֹ וְחָדֵי. כְּדֵין קוּדְשָׁא בְּרִיךְ הוּא מִתְעַטֵּר בְּעִטְרִין עִלָּאִין וְחָדֵי כוּ', וּמֵהַהִיא שַׁעֲתָא מִלּוֹי כְּתִיבִין בְּסִפְרָא כוּ'

○ זַכָּאָה חוּלְקֵיהּ מַאן דְּאִשְׁתַּדַּל בְּאוֹרַיְתָא כְּדְקָא יָאוֹת. זַכָּאָה הוּא בְּהַאי עָלְמָא, וְזַכָּאָה הוּא בְּעָלְמָא דְּאָתֵי:

● וּבְתַנָּא דְבֵי אֵלִיָּהוּ סֵדֶר אֵלִיָּהוּ רַבָּא פֶּרֶק י"ח, "וְעַל הַנַּחַל יַעֲלֶה עַל שְׂפָתוֹ מִזֶּה וּמִזֶּה כָּל עֵץ מַאֲכָל" (יחזקאל מז, יב), וּפֵרֵשׁ שָׁם כָּל זֶה הַכָּתוּב עַל דִּבְרֵי תּוֹרָה, וְאוֹמֵר שָׁם

○ מַהוּ "לֶחֳדָשָׁיו יְבַכֵּר"

○ לִמְחַדְּשֵׁי תּוֹרָה שֶׁמְּחַדְּשִׁין אֶת הַתּוֹרָה בְּכָל יוֹם תָּמִיד. לְבֵן שֶׁהוּא בְּכוֹר לְאָבִיו וּלְאִמּוֹ, שֶׁמְּחַדֵּשׁ דִּבְרֵי תוֹרָה שֶׁהַכֹּל שְׂמֵחִין בּוֹ כוּ'

○ שִׂמְחָה מִתְחַדֵּשׁ לוֹ לְאָבִיו בְּכָל יוֹם כוּ'.

○ וּבְכָל מָקוֹם שֶׁמְּחַדְּשִׁין תּוֹרָה שֶׁבִּישִׁיבַת בֵּית הַכְּנֶסֶת וּבִישִׁיבַת בֵּית הַמִּדְרָשׁ, שִׂמְחָה מִתְחַדֵּשׁ לְהַקָּדוֹשׁ בָּרוּךְ הוּא בְּכָל יוֹם תָּמִיד כוּ'

○ עַיֵּן שָׁם.

שער ד' - פרק י"ג

● וְעַל יְדֵי עֵסֶק הַתּוֹרָה הַקְּדוֹשָׁה, נִשְׁלָם כַּוָּנָתוֹ יִתְבָּרַךְ בַּבְּרִיאָה

○ שֶׁהָיָה רַק בִּשְׁבִיל הַתּוֹרָה שֶׁיַּעַסְקוּ בָּהּ יִשְׂרָאֵל

○ כְּמַאַמְרָם זִכְרוֹנָם לִבְרָכָה, "בְּרֵאשִׁית", בִּשְׁבִיל

▫ הַתּוֹרָה כוּ'

▫ וּבִשְׁבִיל יִשְׂרָאֵל כוּ'

- ○ Moshe,[188] who was the broker [when Israel] received the Torah.
- ○ God is, so to speak, happy with His handiwork, Universe, and creations, which give Him pleasure, just as at the time of the original Creation, as God had hoped of Himself, so to speak.
- As per the Midrash: A king built a palace and on seeing it was very pleased and said, "Palace, palace, if only you will always be able to give me pleasure [like you do now]." Similarly, God says to His Universe: "My Universe, My Universe, if only you will always give Me pleasure as you do now."[189]
  - ○ This is as it says in connection with praise of the Torah: "A beloved hind inspiring favor."[190]
- As per the Zohar:[191]
  - ○ R. Elazar began and said: "and I will place My Words in your mouth" ... We learn that all the while that a person is involved with and speaks words of Torah [God hovers over him and the Shechina spreads its wings over him]
  - ○ but more than this, he causes the world to exist and God rejoices with him
  - ○ as if the heavens and earth were planted at that time, as per the verse "to plant the heavens and establish earth."
- As per the Zohar:[192]
  - ○ R. Chiya began and said: "It is a time to act for God; they have nullified your Torah"[193]
  - ○ all the while that the Torah exists in the world and people are involved with it, God, so to speak, rejoices with His handiwork and rejoices with the whole world, and the heavens and the earth are maintained in existence
  - ○ more than this, God gathers together His entire assembly and says to them: "See this Holy people that I have on Earth, that the Torah is crowned because of them"
  - ○ and when [the Hosts] see the joy of their Master in His People they immediately say: "Who is like Your people Israel, a unique people in the world."[194]
- As per the Zohar:[195]

---

188 Bereishit Rabba Bereishit 1:4 and Vayikra Rabba 36:4.
189 Bereishit Rabba Bereishit 9:4.
190 Mishlei 5:19.
191 Zohar III Tzav 35a quoting Yishayahu 51:16.
192 Zohar II Terumah 155b.
193 Tehillim 119:126.

- וּבִשְׁבִיל מֹשֶׁה כו', שֶׁהוּא הַסַּרְסוּר בְּקַבָּלַת הַתּוֹרָה

- וְכִבְיָכוֹל הוּא יִתְבָּרֵךְ שָׂמֵחַ בְּמַעֲשָׂיו בְּעוֹלָמוֹ וּבְרִיּוֹתָיו, שֶׁמַּעֲלִים חֵן לְפָנָיו יִתְבָּרֵךְ כְּשָׁעָה רִאשׁוֹנָה בְּעֵת הַבְּרִיאָה, כְּמוֹ שֶׁקִּוָּה הוּא יִתְבָּרֵךְ בְּעַצְמוֹ כִּבְיָכוֹל:

• כְּמוֹ שֶׁכָּתוּב בְּרַבָּה בְּרֵאשִׁית פ"ט, לְמֶלֶךְ שֶׁבָּנָה פַּלְטְרִין, רָאָה אוֹתָהּ וְעָרְבָה לוֹ, אָמַר, פַּלְטִין פַּלְטִין, הַלְוַאי תְּהֵא מַעֲלָה חֵן כו'. כָּךְ אָמַר הַקָּדוֹשׁ בָּרוּךְ הוּא לְעוֹלָמוֹ, עוֹלָמִי עוֹלָמִי, הַלְוַאי תְּהֵא מַעֲלַת חֵן לְפָנַי בְּכָל עֵת, כְּשֵׁם שֶׁהֶעֱלֵית חֵן לְפָנַי בְּשָׁעָה זוֹ.

- וְכֵן נֶאֱמַר (משלי ה, יט) בְּשֶׁבַח הַתּוֹרָה "אַיֶּלֶת אֲהָבִים וְיַעֲלַת חֵן":

• וּבַזֹּהַר צַו ל"ה א'

- פָּתַח רַבִּי אֶלְעָזָר וְאָמַר "וָאָשִׂים דְּבָרַי בְּפִיךָ" (ישעיה נא, טז), תָּנִינָן, כָּל בַּר נָשׁ דְּאִשְׁתַּדֵּל בְּמִלֵּי דְאוֹרַיְתָא, וְשִׂפְוָתֵיהּ מְרַחֲשָׁן אוֹרַיְתָא כו'

- וְלֹא עוֹד אֶלָּא דְהוּא מְקַיֵּם עָלְמָא, וְקוּדְשָׁא בְּרִיךְ הוּא חַדֵּי עַמֵּיהּ

- כְּאִלּוּ הַהוּא יוֹמָא נָטַע שְׁמַיָּא וְאַרְעָא, הֲדָא הוּא דִכְתִיב (שם) "לִנְטֹעַ שָׁמַיִם וְלִיסֹד אָרֶץ":

• וּבְפָרָשַׁת תְּרוּמָה קנ"ה ב'

- פָּתַח רַבִּי חִיָּא וְאָמַר "עֵת לַעֲשׂוֹת לַה' הֵפֵרוּ תּוֹרָתֶךָ" (תהלים קיט, קכו)

- בְּכָל זִמְנָא דְאוֹרַיְתָא מִתְקַיְּמָא בְּעָלְמָא, וּבְנֵי נָשָׁא מִשְׁתַּדְּלִין בָּהּ, כִּבְיָכוֹל קוּדְשָׁא בְּרִיךְ הוּא חַד הוּא בְּעוֹבָדוֹי יְדוֹי, וְחַדֵּי בְּעָלְמִין כֻּלְּהוֹן, וּשְׁמַיָּא וְאַרְעָא קַיְמֵי בְּקִיּוּמֵיהּ

- וְלֹא עוֹד, אֶלָּא קוּדְשָׁא בְּרִיךְ הוּא כָּנִישׁ כָּל פָּמַלְיָא דִּילֵיהּ, וְאָמַר לוֹן, חֲמוּ עַמָּא קַדִּישָׁא דְּאִית לִי בְּאַרְעָא, דְּאוֹרַיְתָא מִתְעַטְּרָא בְּגִינֵיהוֹן כו'

- וְאִנּוּן כַּד חָמוּ חֶדְוָה דְּמָארֵיהוֹן בְּעַמֵּיהּ, מִיָּד פָּתְחֵי וְאָמְרֵי, "וּמִי כְעַמְּךָ יִשְׂרָאֵל גּוֹי אֶחָד בָּאָרֶץ" (שמו"ב ז, כג):

• וּבְרֵישׁ פָּרָשַׁת שְׁמִינִי (לה:)

---

194 2 Shmuel 7:23.
195 Zohar III Shemini 35b.

- Happy is Israel that God gave them the Holy Torah, which is the joy of All, it is the joy of God and the place where He chooses to be, as per "and I was then His Delight each day."[196]

14. TORAH STUDY BRINGS ENLIGHTENMENT AND BLESSING TO THE WORLDS

- [When Israel are involved in Torah study] all the worlds and creations also have additional rejoicing, and are enlightened by the supernal light which emanates upon them from the supernal source of Torah.[197] As per:
  - It gladdens God and the Creations.[198]
  - And I was then His Delight each day.[199]
  - The Zohar:[200]
    - He began and said: "Then those who fear God spoke [Nidberu] to each other";[201] the verse should have used [the active verb] "Dibru", for speech, why is [the passive verb], "Nidberu" used?
    - It is because the words of speech are "Nidberu" [passively spoken,] in the supernal realms, by all these holy chariots and all these holy hosts, because these holy words ascend and some of them are initially taken up and brought before the Holy King and crowned with many crowns of these supernal lights
    - and all of these words are all spoken before the Supernal King.
    - Who saw such joy and praise ascending all of the firmaments before the Holy King?
    - and the Holy King looks into the words and crowns Himself with them; they then ascend and form a crown on His Head, and then descend and sit securely in His Lap, and then ascend to His Head
    - in connection with this the Torah says: "*VaEheyeh* [and I will be] His Delight each day,"[202] it does not say "*VeHayiti*" [and I was once] but rather "*VaEheyeh*," meaning each time this lofty speech ascends before Him.
- Every time a person properly involves and attaches himself to [Torah], the words of Torah cause a level of joy like that experienced when they were given at Sinai.
  - As per the Zohar:[203] R. Yossi began, "and this Torah [which Moshe placed] . . ." . . . Come and see, the Words of Torah are Holy, They are superlative, They are sweet, as per "they are more desirable than gold [and great treasure and sweeter than honey] . . . ." One who is

---

196 Mishlei 8:30.
197 From The World of The Malbush. See V2:03, "The World of The Malbush."

- זַכָּאִין אִנּוּן יִשְׂרָאֵל, דְּקוּדְשָׁא בְּרִיךְ הוּא יָהַב לוֹן אוֹרַיְתָא קַדִּישָׁא, חֶדְוָתָא דְּכֹלָּא, חֶדְוָתָא דְקוּדְשָׁא בְּרִיךְ הוּא, וַאֲטַיְלוּתָא דִּילֵיהּ, דִּכְתִיב (משלי ח, ל) "וָאֶהְיֶה שַׁעֲשׁוּעִים יוֹם יוֹם" כו':

שער ד' - פרק י"ד

- וְגַם הָעוֹלָמוֹת וְהַבְּרִיּוֹת כֻּלָּם הֵם אָז בְּחֶדְוָתָא יְתֵרְתָא, וּנְהִירִין מִזִּיו הָאוֹר הָעֶלְיוֹן, הַשּׁוֹפֵעַ עֲלֵיהֶם מִמְּקוֹם שֹׁרֶשׁ עֶלְיוֹן שֶׁל הַתּוֹרָה, כְּמוֹ שֶׁאָמְרוּ
  - בְּפֶרֶק מַעֲלוֹת הַתּוֹרָה (אבות ו, א), מְשַׂמֵּחַ אֶת הַמָּקוֹם מְשַׂמֵּחַ אֶת הַבְּרִיּוֹת.
  - וְכֵן אָמְרָה הַתּוֹרָה (משלי ח, ל) "וָאֶהְיֶה שַׁעֲשׁוּעִים יוֹם יוֹם".
  - וּבַזֹּהַר וַיַּקְהֵל רי"ז א'
    - פָּתַח וְאָמַר "אָז נִדְבְּרוּ יִרְאֵי ה'" (מלאכי ג, טז) כו', "אָז דִּבְּרוּ" מִבָּעֵי לֵיהּ, מַאי "נִדְבְּרוּ"
    - אֶלָּא נִדְבְּרוּ לְעֵלָּא מִכָּל אִינּוּן רְתִיכִין קַדִּישִׁין, וְכָל אִנּוּן חַיָּלִין קַדִּישִׁין, בְּגִין דְּאִנּוּן מִלִּין קַדִּישִׁין סַלְקִין לְעֵלָּא, וְכַמָּה אִנּוּן דִּמְקַדְּמֵי וְנַטְלֵי לוֹן קָמֵי מַלְכָּא קַדִּישָׁא, וּמִתְעַטְּרִין בְּכַמָּה עִטְרִין בְּאִנּוּן נְהוֹרִין עִלָּאִין
    - וְכֻלְּהוּ נִדְבְּרוּ מִקַּמֵּי מַלְכָּא עִלָּאָה
    - מַאן חֲמֵי חֶדְוָן, מַאן חֲמִי תּוּשְׁבְּחָן דְּסַלְקִין בְּכָל אִנּוּן רְקִיעִין קָמֵי מַלְכָּא קַדִּישָׁא
    - וּמַלְכָּא קַדִּישָׁא מִסְתַּכֵּל בְּהוּ וְאִתְעַטַּר בְּהוֹ, וְאִנּוּן סַלְקִין עַל רֵישֵׁיהּ וַהֲווֹ עִטְרָא וְנָחֲתִין וְיָתְבִין לְגוֹ חֵיקֵיהּ עַל בְּתוּקְפֵיהּ וּמִתַּמָּן סַלְקִין עַל רֵישֵׁיהּ
    - וְעַל דָּא אָמְרָה אוֹרַיְתָא "וָאֶהְיֶה שַׁעֲשׁוּעִים יוֹם יוֹם", "וְהָיִיתִי" לֹא כְּתִיב, אֶלָּא "וָאֶהְיֶה", בְּכָל זְמַן וּבְכָל עִידָן דְּמִלִּין עִלָּאִין סַלְקִין קַמֵּיהּ, ע"כ:

- וּבְכָל עֵת שֶׁהָאָדָם עוֹסֵק וּמִתְדַּבֵּק בָּהּ כָּרָאוּי, הַדְּבָרִים שְׂמֵחִים כִּנְתִינָתָן מִסִּינַי
  - כְּמוֹ שֶׁכָּתוּב בַּזֹּהַר רֵישׁ פָּרָשַׁת חֻקַּת, ר"י פָּתַח "זֹאת הַתּוֹרָה" כו', תָּא חֲזֵי,

---

198 Mishna Avot 6:1.
199 Mishlei 8:30.
200 Zohar II Vayakhel 217a.
201 Malachi 3:16.
202 Mishlei 8:30.
203 Zohar III Chukat 179b quoting Devarim 4:44, Tehillim 19:11 and Devarim 27:9.

involved in Torah is as if he stands each day at Mount Sinai to receive the Torah; this is the meaning of "This day [i.e., today, in the present continuous], you became a people."

- As per the Zohar:[204] For we learned, one who listens to words of Torah is as happy in this world as if he received the Torah at Sinai; one must even listen to words of Torah from any person, and whoever tilts his ear to receive them gives honor to the Holy King and the Torah. It is about such a person that it is written: "This day, you became a people."

* The reason for this is that just as when we received the Torah we became attached, so to speak, to His Speech
  - similarly, now as well, absolutely any time a person studies and analyzes [Torah], he is literally attached through it to God's Speech, as All is speech from the Mouth of God [spoken] to Moshe at Sinai, and this even includes that which a young student questions his teacher, as per G4:06 above.
  - So now when a person studies [Torah], each word becomes a torch of fire from God's Mouth, so to speak, as written there, and it is considered as if it is currently being received at Sinai, directly from God's Mouth.
  - Therefore, Chazal say a number of times, "and the words cause joy – just as if they were given at Sinai."[205]

* Therefore [with Torah study], there is a cascading downwards of a bestowal of enlightenment and blessing on all of the worlds from its supernal source [in The World of The Malbush]. This world is also enlightened from its honor and is blessed, and it brings much good and blessing to the world.
  - As per the Midrash:[206] When a person studies the Torah, it brings goodness to the world – enabling him to seek mercy and pray before God, penetrating the firmament and bringing rain to the world . . .
  - This Midrash continues to say: All the while Israel is involved with Torah and performing God's Will, God personally attends to them to bestow blessing, as per "[When] Truth [i.e., Torah] sprouts from the ground [i.e., by those who study Torah], righteousness looks down from the Heavens,"[207] and there is no such "looking down" except for blessing, as per the verse "Look down . . . and bless Your People."[208]

---

204 Zohar III Acharei Mot 69a quoting Devarim 27:9.
205 E.g., Shir Hashirim Rabba Parsha 1:2, Rut Rabba Parsha 6:7.
206 Eliyahu Rabba Parsha 18.
207 Tehillim 85:12.
208 Devarim 26:15.

מִלִּין דְּאוֹרַיְתָא קַדִּישִׁין אִנּוּן, עִלָּאִין אִנּוּן, מְתִיקִין אִנּוּן, כְּמָה דִּכְתִיב "הַנֶּחֱמָדִים מִזָּהָב" כו'. מַאן דְּאִשְׁתַּדַּל בְּאוֹרַיְתָא, כְּאִלּוּ קָאִים כָּל יוֹמָא עַל טוּרָא דְסִינַי לְקַבֵּל אוֹרַיְתָא, הה"ד (דברים כז, ט) "הַיּוֹם הַזֶּה נִהְיֵיתָ לְעָם".

וּבְפָרָשַׁת אַחֲרֵי ס"ט א' דְּתָאנָא כָּל מַאן דְּאָצִית לְמַלּוֹי דְּאוֹרַיְתָא, זַכָּאָה הוּא בְּהַאי עָלְמָא, וּכְאִלּוּ קַבִּיל תּוֹרָה מִסִּינַי. וַאֲפִילּוּ מִכָּל בַּר נָשׁ נַמֵי בָּעֵי לְמִשְׁמַע מִלּוֹי דְּאוֹרַיְתָא, וּמַאן דְּאָרְכִין אוּדְנֵיהּ לְקַבְּלֵיהּ, יָהִיב יְקָרָא לְמַלְכָּא קַדִּישָׁא, וְיָהִיב יְקָרָא לְאוֹרַיְתָא, עָלֵיהּ כְּתִיב "הַיּוֹם הַזֶּה נִהְיֵיתָ לְעָם" כו':

• וְהַטַּעַם, שֶׁכְּמוֹ שֶׁבְּעֵת הַמַּעֲמָד הַמְּקֻדָּשׁ נִתְדַּבְּקוּ כִּבְיָכוֹל בְּדִבּוּרוֹ יִתְבָּרַךְ

○ כֵּן גַּם עַתָּה, בְּכָל עֵת מַמָּשׁ שֶׁהָאָדָם עוֹסֵק וְהוֹגֶה בָּהּ, הוּא דָּבוּק עַל יְדֵי דִבּוּרוֹ יִתְבָּרַךְ מַמָּשׁ, מֵחֲמַת שֶׁהַכֹּל מַאֲמַר פִּיו יִתְבָּרַךְ לְמֹשֶׁה בְּסִינַי, וַאֲפִילּוּ מַה שֶּׁתַּלְמִיד קָטָן שׁוֹאֵל מֵרַבּוֹ, כַּנַ"ל פֶּרֶק ו'.

○ וְגַם עַתָּה בְּעֵת שֶׁהָאָדָם עוֹסֵק בָּהּ, בְּכָל תֵּבָה, אוֹתָהּ הַתֵּבָה מַמָּשׁ נֶחֱצֶבֶת אָז לַהֶבֶת אֵשׁ מִפִּיו יִתְבָּרַךְ כִּבְיָכוֹל כמש"ש. וְנֶחְשָׁב כְּאִלּוּ עַתָּה מְקַבְּלָהּ בְּסִינַי מִפִּיו יִתְבָּרַךְ שְׁמוֹ

○ לָכֵן אָמְרוּ רַבּוֹתֵינוּ זִכְרוֹנָם לִבְרָכָה כַּמָּה פְּעָמִים "וְהָיוּ הַדְּבָרִים שְׂמֵחִים כִּנְתִינָתָן מִסִּינַי":

• וְאָז מִשְׁתַּלְשֵׁל וְנִמְשָׁךְ שִׁפְעַת אוֹר וּבְרָכָה, מִמְּקוֹר שָׁרְשָׁהּ הָעֶלְיוֹן, עַל כָּל הָעוֹלָמוֹת, וְגַם הָאָרֶץ הָאִירָה מִכְּבוֹדָהּ וּמִתְבָּרֶכֶת, וּמֵבִיא הַרְבֵּה טוֹבָה וְשִׁפְעַת בְּרָכָה לָעוֹלָם.

○ וּבְתַנָּא דְּבֵי אֵלִיָּהוּ סֵדֶר אֵלִיָּהוּ רַבָּא פֶּרֶק י"ח אָמַר, כֵּיוָן שֶׁלּוֹמֵד אֶת הַתּוֹרָה, הֲרֵי זֶה מֵבִיא טוֹבָה לָעוֹלָם, וְיָכוֹל הוּא לְבַקֵּשׁ רַחֲמִים וּלְהִתְפַּלֵּל לִפְנֵי הַקָּדוֹשׁ בָּרוּךְ הוּא, וִיפַקְפֵּק אֶת הָרָקִיעַ, וְיָבִיא מָטָר לָעוֹלָם כו'.

○ וְאָמַר שָׁם עוֹד, כָּל זְמַן שֶׁיִּשְׂרָאֵל עוֹסְקִין בַּתּוֹרָה וְעוֹשִׂין רְצוֹן אֲבִיהֶם שֶׁבַּשָּׁמַיִם, הַקָּדוֹשׁ בָּרוּךְ הוּא בְּעַצְמוֹ נִפְנָה אֲלֵיהֶם לִבְרָכָה, שֶׁנֶּאֱמַר (תהלים פה, יב) "אֱמֶת מֵאֶרֶץ תִּצְמָח וְצֶדֶק מִשָּׁמַיִם נִשְׁקָף", וְאֵין "הַשְׁקָפָה" אֶלָּא לִבְרָכָה, שֶׁנֶּאֱמַר (דברים כו, טו) "הַשְׁקִיפָה כו' וּבָרֵךְ אֶת עַמְּךָ" כו':

15. ONE WHO STUDIES TORAH BRINGS BLESSING AND PROTECTION ON HIMSELF

- Now, 'the one who blesses is blessed,'[209] and therefore one who properly and truly involves himself in Torah study and causes blessing to be brought to the worlds, will himself be blessed, and
  - the honor of God will be constantly 'hovering over him at all times'[210]
  - and he will acquire a noble soul from a holy place according to his level of involvement and attachment to [Torah]
  - as Chazal state:[211] A person who sanctifies himself in this world is sanctified from Above; a small effort [in sanctification] is reflected in great [sanctification] from Above.
- The Zohar states:[212]
  - The fifth command[213] ... contains three commands ... and one is to involve oneself with Torah and toil in it every day to rectify one's Nefesh and Ruach
  - as when one is involved with Torah one corrects another holy soul, as it is written: "the soul of the Chaya will swarm"[214] – the soul of that Holy Chaya ...
  - when one is involved with Torah, with one's whisper of speech of Torah one merits this soul of Chaya to become like the holy angels ...
  - this is the Torah which is called *water* – it *swarms* to generate the whisper of the *soul of the Chaya* which is drawn downwards from the place of that *Chaya*, as we have learned.
  - It is about this that David said:[215] "God create a pure heart for me" to be able to study Torah and then there will "renew within me a just Ruach."
- One [involved as such in Torah] rules over and controls all. All bad decrees are removed from him and have no power over him, God forbid, even while he is in this world. As per Chazal:
  - Reish Lakish says: Troubles are removed from all those who are involved in Torah study.[216]

---

209 An expression borrowed from e.g., Sotah 38b.
210 Devarim 33:12.
211 Yoma 39a.
212 Zohar Introduction 12b.
213 I.e., "Let the *waters swarm* with *living creatures*" (Bereishit 1:20). This section of the Zohar plays on the meaning of the italicized words.
214 The expression *Nefesh Chaya* can be understood, as it is generally, to be plural. However, it is stated in the singular and is understood here to relate to a

שער ד' - פרק ט"ו

- וְהִנֵּה, הַמְבֹרָךְ מִתְבָּרֵךְ, וּמִבִּרְכָתָם שֶׁל הָעוֹלָמוֹת יְבֹרַךְ גַּם הָאָדָם, הָעוֹסֵק בָּהּ כָּרָאוּי לַאֲמִתָּהּ, הַגּוֹרֵם לְכָל זֶה
  - וּכְבוֹד ה' חוֹפֵף עָלָיו כָּל הַיּוֹם
  - וּמַשִּׂיג לְנִשְׁמָה אֲצוּלָה מִמָּקוֹם קָדוֹשׁ, לְפִי עֵרֶךְ גֹּדֶל עִסְקוֹ וְדִבּוּקוֹ בָּהּ
  - כְּמוֹ שֶׁאָמְרוּ (יומא לט) "אָדָם מְקַדֵּשׁ עַצְמוֹ מִלְּמַטָּה, מְקַדְּשִׁין אוֹתוֹ מִלְמַעְלָה, מְעַט, מְקַדְּשִׁין אוֹתוֹ הַרְבֵּה":

- וּבְהַקְדָּמַת הַזֹּהַר י"ב ב'
  - פְּקוּדָא חֲמִישָׁאָה כו', בְּהַאי קְרָא אִית תְּלַת פִּקּוּדִין וכו', וְחַד לְמִלְעֵי בְּאוֹרַיְתָא, לְאִשְׁתַּדְּלָא בָּהּ, וּלְאַפָּשָׁא לָהּ בְּכָל יוֹמָא, לְתַקָּנָא נַפְשֵׁיהּ וְרוּחֵיהּ
  - דְּכֵיוָן דְּבַר נַשׁ אִתְעֲסַק בְּאוֹרַיְתָא, אִתְתַּקַּן בְּנִשְׁמָתָא אָחֳרָא קַדִּישָׁא, דִּכְתִיב "שֶׁרֶץ נֶפֶשׁ חַיָּה", נֶפֶשׁ דְּהַהִיא חַיָּה קַדִּישָׁא כו'
  - וְכַד אִשְׁתַּדַּל בְּאוֹרַיְתָא, בְּהַהוּא רְחִישׁוּ דְּרָחִישׁ בָּהּ זָכֵי לְהַהִיא נֶפֶשׁ חַיָּה, וּלְמֶהֱדַר כְּמַלְאָכִין קַדִּישִׁין כו'
  - דָּא אוֹרַיְתָא דְּאִקְרֵי מַיִם, יִשְׁרְצוּן, וְיִפְּקוּן רִיחֲשָׁא דְּנֶפֶשׁ חַיָּה מֵאֲתַר דְּהַהִיא חַיָּה, וּמַשְׁכִין לָהּ לְתַתָּא, כְּמָא דְאִתְּמַר
  - וְעַל דָּא אָמַר דָּוִד (תהלים נא, יב) "לֵב טָהוֹר בְּרָא לִי אֱלֹקִים", לְמִלְעֵי בְּאוֹרַיְתָא, וּכְדֵין "וְרוּחַ נָכוֹן חַדֵּשׁ בְּקִרְבִּי":

- וְהוּא הָרוֹדֶה וּמוֹשֵׁל בַּכֹּל. וְכָל הַדִּינִין בִּישִׁין מִסְתַּלְּקִין מֵעָלָיו, וְאֵין לָהֶם עָלָיו שׁוּם שְׁלִיטָה חַס וְשָׁלוֹם, בֵּין בְּעוֹדוֹ בָּזֶה הָעוֹלָם, כְּמוֹ שֶׁכָּתוּב
  - בְּפֶרֶק קַמָּא דִּבְרָכוֹת (ה, א) "אָמַר רַבִּי שִׁמְעוֹן בֶּן לָקִישׁ כָּל הָעוֹסֵק בַּתּוֹרָה יִסּוּרִין בְּדֵלִין הֵימֶנּוּ".

---

specific angelic being, the Chaya, which is impacted by one's Torah study and in turn results in the drawing down of blessing on to oneself.

215 Tehillim 51:12.
216 Berachot 5a.

- If one has a pain in one's head, throat, stomach . . . or in all of one's body, one should involve oneself in Torah as it says, "and healing for all his flesh."[217]
    - A similar sentiment is expressed in a number of other sources. Refer to them.[218]
- "Lift me up from the depths of poverty,"[219] a person who transgressed many sins and is liable to death . . . who returns and repents and studies Torah, Prophets, Writings, Mishna, Midrash, Halachot, and Agadot and serves the Sages – then even if a hundred bad decrees have been placed upon him, God will remove them from him . . .[220]
- "The King has brought me into his chambers,"[221] just as God has inner chambers within His Torah, so too, the Torah Sages also each have inner chambers within His Torah, and if you see that troubles are coming over you, run to the chambers of Torah, and these troubles will immediately flee from you as per "go my people to your chambers . . . ."[222] Therefore, it says: "The King has brought me into his chambers to rejoice and be happy with you," in that we have raised the profile and attached to ourselves the great crown of words of Torah, [connecting] one end of the world to the other.[223]
- "As they were travelling and speaking. . . ."[224] "Speaking" refers to speech of Torah, and when an angel was sent [to Eliyahu and Elisha to cut them down], he found them involved with Torah and was unable to control them. From here they said that when two people are journeying and involved in Torah, no bad thing can affect them. . . .[225] Refer there.
- As per the Zohar:[226]
    - "Yissachar is a strong-boned donkey [he rests *between the boundaries*]."[227] He began and said "To David, God is my light. . . ."[228]

---

217 Eruvin 54a quoting Mishlei 4:22.
218 R. Chaim quotes the following sources:
Vayikra Rabba Shemini 12:3:
- Words of Torah . . . are absorbed by a person's 248 limbs as it says: "and healing for all his flesh."
Midrash Tanchuma Ekev 5:
- "and healing for all his flesh," all who find words of Torah, have found life.
Midrash Tehillim 19:15:
- How do we know that [Torah] is absorbed by a person's 248 limbs? As it says: "and healing for all his flesh."
219 Tehillim 113:7.
220 Eliyahu Rabba Parsha 5.
221 Shir Hashirim 1:4.

וּבְפֶרֶק כֵּיצַד מְעַבְּרִין (עירובין נד, א) "חָשׁ בְּרֹאשׁוֹ יַעֲסֹק בַּתּוֹרָה שֶׁנֶּאֱמַר כו', חָשׁ בִּגְרוֹנוֹ יַעֲסֹק בַּתּוֹרָה שֶׁנֶּאֱמַר כו', חָשׁ בְּמֵעָיו כו', חָשׁ בְּכָל גּוּפוֹ יַעֲסֹק בַּתּוֹרָה, שֶׁנֶּאֱמַר (משלי ה, כב) "וּלְכָל בְּשָׂרוֹ מַרְפֵּא".

וּכְעֵין סִגְנוֹן זֶה אָמְרוּ בְּוַיִּקְרָא רַבָּה פָּרָשָׁה י"ב, וּבְתַנְחוּמָא פָּרָשַׁת עֵקֶב, וּבְמִדְרַשׁ תְּהִלִּים מִזְמוֹר י"ט, עַיֵּן שָׁם.

וּבְתַנָּא דְּבֵי אֵלִיָּהוּ סֵדֶר רַבָּא רֵישׁ פֶּרֶק ה', "מְקִימִי מֵעָפָר דָּל" כו' (תהלים קיג, ז), אָדָם שֶׁעָבַר עֲבֵרוֹת הַרְבֵּה, וְקָנְסוּ עָלָיו מִיתָה כו', וְחָזַר וְעָשָׂה תְּשׁוּבָה, וְקוֹרֵא תּוֹרָה נְבִיאִים וּכְתוּבִים, וְשָׁנָה מִשְׁנָה מִדְרָשׁ הֲלָכוֹת וְהַגָּדוֹת, וְשִׁמֵּשׁ חֲכָמִים, אֲפִלּוּ נִגְזְרוּ עָלָיו מֵאָה גְּזֵרוֹת, הַקָּדוֹשׁ בָּרוּךְ הוּא מַעֲבִירָן מִמֶּנּוּ כו'.

וְשָׁם רֵישׁ פֶּרֶק ז' "הֱבִיאַנִי הַמֶּלֶךְ חֲדָרָיו" (שה"ש א, ד) כְּשֵׁם שֶׁיֵּשׁ לְהַקָּדוֹשׁ בָּרוּךְ הוּא חַדְרֵי חֲדָרִים בְּתוֹרָתוֹ, כָּךְ יֵשׁ לָהֶם לְתַלְמִידֵי חֲכָמִים לְכָל אֶחָד וְאֶחָד חַדְרֵי חֲדָרִים בְּתוֹרָתוֹ, וְאִם רָאִיתָ שֶׁהַיִּסּוּרִין מְמַשְׁמְשִׁין וּבָאִין עָלֶיךָ, רוּץ לְחַדְרֵי תּוֹרָה, וּמִיָּד הַיִּסּוּרִין בּוֹרְחִין מִמְּךָ, שֶׁנֶּאֱמַר (ישעיה כו, כ) "לֵךְ עַמִּי בֹּא בַחֲדָרֶיךָ" וְגו', לְכָךְ נֶאֱמַר "הֱבִיאַנִי הַמֶּלֶךְ חֲדָרָיו נָגִילָה וְנִשְׂמְחָה בָּךְ", בַּמֶּה שֶׁגִּדַּלְתָּנוּ וְרוֹמַמְתָּנוּ, וְקָשַׁרְתָּ לָנוּ כֶּתֶר גָּדוֹל בְּדִבְרֵי תוֹרָה מִסּוֹף הָעוֹלָם וְעַד סוֹפוֹ.

וְשָׁם בְּפֶרֶק ה' "וַיְהִי הֵמָּה הוֹלְכִים הָלוֹךְ וְדַבֵּר" (מלכים ב. ב, יא) וְאֵין "דַּבֵּר" אֶלָּא דִּבְרֵי תוֹרָה כו', וּכְשֶׁנִּשְׁתַּלַּח מַלְאָךְ כו', וּבָא וּמְצָאָן שֶׁהָיוּ עוֹסְקִין בְּדִבְרֵי תוֹרָה, וְלֹא הָיָה יָכוֹל לִשְׁלֹט בָּהֶם כו', מִכָּאן אָמְרוּ שְׁנֵי בְּנֵי אָדָם שֶׁהוֹלְכִין בַּדֶּרֶךְ וְעוֹסְקִין בַּתּוֹרָה, אֵין דָּבָר רַע יָכוֹל לִשְׁלֹט בָּהֶן כו', עַיֵּן שָׁם.

וּבַזֹּהַר וַיְחִי רמ"ב סוֹף ע"א

"יִשָּׂשכָר חֲמוֹר גָּרֶם" כו', פָּתַח וְאָמַר "לְדָוִד ה' אוֹרִי" (תהלים כז, א) כו'

---

222 Yishayahu 26:20.
223 Eliyahu Rabba Parsha 7.
224 2 Melachim 2:11.
225 Eliyahu Rabba Parsha 5.
226 Zohar I Vayechi 242a.
227 Bereishit 49:14.
228 Tehillim 27:1.

- How beloved are words of Torah – how beloved before God are those who involve themselves in Torah
- as all those involved in Torah do not fear from the damaging forces of the world, they are protected above and below
- not only this but they also suppress all the destructive forces of this world and make them descend to the depths.
- Come and see that at nighttime . . . when the north wind wakens and splits the night, an awakening of holiness is aroused in the world . . . happy is the portion of that person who rises at that time and involves himself in Torah.
- When he starts studying Torah all these destructive forces are entered into the depths . . . because of this Yissachar [i.e., the Torah Sage] who is involved in Torah who has suppressed the donkey [i.e., the damaging forces] and brought them down . . . as they otherwise would have risen to damage the world and he places them *between the boundaries*.[229]

• Similarly, Chazal state that the Torah protects from troubles – at all times and not just when one is studying it.[230] Refer there.

• For [the Torah] "Bestows (only) goodness upon him, never evil, all the days of her life,"[231] that is even when one is not studying, all the while that one is still attached to it and has not separated from its everlasting life, God forbid, and one's focus of attention is constantly on it to return to it and review it. (Note 51)[232]

Rabbi Chaim's Note:
Note 51 – Bestowal of good on those who study for, and also, not for its sake

• That which is written "Gemalathu[/Bestows goodness upon him] . . ."
  ○ *Gemul* means payment of a reward [by a person] to one who was previously benevolent to him
  ○ so that which is written that the Torah pays a reward to a person who does good with it, this means one who is involved with it *for its sake*
  ○ but also if one is not involved with it *for its sake*, but for ulterior motives, and who does not do good with it, by rights the Torah should reward this person with evil, God forbid
  ○ nevertheless, it does not reward the person with evil, God forbid

---

229 The understanding of the opening verse is therefore that Yissachar is the archetypal Torah scholar who when involved in Torah study causes the damaging forces to be fully controlled.
230 Sotah 21a.

- כַּמָּה חֲבִיבִין אִנּוּן מִלִּין דְּאוֹרַיְתָא, כַּמָּה חֲבִיבִין אִנּוּן דְּמִשְׁתַּדְּלֵי בְּאוֹרַיְתָא, קָמֵי קוּדְשָׁא בְּרִיךְ הוּא

- וְכָל מַאן דְּאִשְׁתַּדַּל בְּאוֹרַיְתָא לֹא דָּחִיל מִפִּגְעֵי עַלְמָא, נָטִיר הוּא לְעֵלָּא, נָטִיר הוּא לְתַתָּא

- וְלֹא עוֹד אֶלָּא כָּפֵי כָּפֵי לְכָל פִּגְעֵי דְעַלְמָא, וְאָחִית לוֹן לְעוֹמְקָא דִתְהוֹם רַבָּה.

- תָּא חֲזֵי, בְּשַׁעֲתָא דְּעָאל לֵילְיָא כו', כַּד אִתְעַר רוּחַ צָפוֹן וְאִתְפְּלִיג לֵילְיָא, אִתְעֲרוּתָא קַדִּישָׁא אִתְעַר בְּעַלְמָא כו', זַכָּאָה חוּלְקֵיהּ דְּהַהוּא בַּר נָשׁ, דְּאִיהוּ קָאִים בְּהַהִיא שַׁעֲתָא וְאִשְׁתַּדַּל בְּאוֹרַיְתָא

- כֵּיוָן דְּאִיהוּ פָּתַח בְּאוֹרַיְתָא, כָּל אִנּוּן זִינִין בִּישִׁין, אָעִיל לוֹן בְּנוּקְבָא דִתְהוֹם רַבָּא כו'. בְּגִין כָּךְ יִשָּׂשכָר דְּאִשְׁתַּדְּלוּתֵיהּ בְּאוֹרַיְתָא, כָּפִית לֵיהּ לַחֲמוֹר וְנָחִית לֵיהּ כו', דְּאִיהוּ סָלִיק לְנַוְקָא עַלְמָא, וְשַׁוִּי מְדוֹרֵיהּ "בֵּין הַמִּשְׁפְּתָיִם" כו':

- וְכֵן אָמְרוּ זִכְרוֹנָם לִבְרָכָה בְּפֶרֶק ג' דְּסוֹטָה (כא, א) דְהַתּוֹרָה אֲגוּנֵי מַגְּנֵי מִן הַיִּסּוּרִין בֵּין בְּעִדָּנָא דְעָסִיק בָּהּ בֵּין בְּעִדָּנָא דְלֹא עָסִיק בָּהּ, ע"ש:

- כִּי הִיא "גְּמָלַתְהוּ (רק) טוֹב וְלֹא רָע כֹּל יְמֵי חַיֶּיהָ"[231] (משלי לא, יב), הַיְנוּ אֲפִלּוּ בְּעִדָּנָא דְלֹא עָסִיק בָּהּ, כָּל זְמַן שֶׁהוּא דָּבוּק וְלֹא פֵּרֵשׁ חַס וְשָׁלוֹם מֵחַיֵּי עוֹלָם שֶׁלָּהּ, וְדַעְתּוֹ עָלֶיהָ תָּמִיד לַחֲזוֹר וְלַהֲגוֹת בָּהּ (הגהה נ"א)[232]:

הגהה נ"א

- וּמַה שֶּׁכָּתַב גְּמָלַתְהוּ וְכוּ'

  - כִּי "גָּמוּל" פֵּרוּשׁ תַּשְׁלוּם גְּמוּל לְמִי שֶׁהֵיטִיב אִתּוֹ מִקֹּדֶם
  - זֶהוּ שֶׁאָמַר שֶׁהַתּוֹרָה מְשַׁלֶּמֶת גְּמוּל טוֹב לְהָאָדָם שֶׁעוֹשֶׂה טוֹבָה עִמָּהּ, הַיְנוּ כְּשֶׁעוֹסֵק בָּהּ לִשְׁמָהּ
  - וְגַם אִם עָסְקוּ בָּהּ שֶׁלֹּא לִשְׁמָהּ, לְגַרְמֵיהּ, וְלֹא לְהֵיטִיב אִתָּהּ, שֶׁמֵּהָרָאוּי הָיָה שֶׁהַתּוֹרָה תִּגְמְלֵנוּ רָעָה חַס וְשָׁלוֹם
  - עִם כָּל זֶה אֵינָהּ גּוֹמֶלֶת לוֹ רָעָה חַס וְשָׁלוֹם

---

231 Mishlei 31:12.
232 **R. Chaim adds Note 51 here.** This note is brought at the end of this chapter and is entitled "Bestowal of good on those who study for, and also, not for its sake."

- on the contrary, even "with the left," that is those who treat it as being *on the left* and *not for its sake*, it gives them "riches and honor" in this world.[233]

16. MORE TORAH STUDY LEADS TO LESS NEED TO EARN LIVING

- [One who is involved with Torah] will also be relieved of all difficulties of earning a livelihood, together will all other worldly distractions which divert one's constant focus from the study of the Holy Torah. As per Chazal:
  - One who accepts upon himself the yoke of Torah is relieved of the yoke of Government and the yoke of earning a livelihood.[234]
  - That for this reason the Torah was given in a wilderness: just as a wilderness is neither sown nor worked, so too one who accepts upon himself the yoke of Torah is divested of the yoke [of exile and the yoke of earning a livelihood], and just as one is not liable to taxation in a wilderness, so too Torah students are free [in this world].[235]
  - One who knows how to study Torah but does not do so is liable with his life, and not only this but the burden of having to earn a livelihood is placed upon him together with enslavement to bad things,[236] as the verse states in connection with Yissachar: "and he leaned his shoulder to take the strain," one who orients himself not to take the strain of the yoke of Torah will immediately "be subservient to tax"[237]
    - and similarly the converse [is true].
  - Similarly the Halacha is specified in the Talmud that Torah Sages are exempt from taxes as per:
    - A Torah scholar is permitted to say, I will not pay taxes, as per the verse "None shall have the authority to impose upon them: Minda [land tax], Belo [head tax], and Halach [king's travel tax]."[238]
    - R. Huna bar R. Chisda once imposed taxes on the Rabbis. R. Nachman bar Yitzchak said to him: "You have transgressed the Torah, Prophets, and Writings . . ." . . . the Rabbis do not need [human] protection [which was the service provided by these taxes].[239]
  - Any Torah scholar who is involved in Torah study continuously every

---

233 Shabbat 63a quoting Mishlei 3:16, which describes those whose engagement with Torah is weak as being on the left where the left is considered weaker than the right. See GC:02 and G4:17.
234 Mishna Avot 3:5.
235 Bamidbar Rabba Chukat 19:26; Midrash Tanchuma Chukat 21.

וְאַדְּרַבָּה גַּם "בִּשְׂמֹאלָהּ" הַיְנוּ לַמַּשְׂמְאִילִים בָּהּ שֶׁלֹּא לִשְׁמָהּ, הִיא נוֹתֶנֶת לוֹ "עֹשֶׁר וְכָבוֹד" בָּעוֹלָם הַזֶּה, עַד כָּאן:

שער ד' - פרק ט"ז

- וְגַם מַעֲבִירִין וּמְסַלְּקִין מֵעָלָיו כָּל הַטְּרָדוֹת וְהָעִנְיָנִים מֵעַל דֶּרֶךְ אֶרֶץ וכו', וְכָל שְׁאָר עִנְיְנֵי זֶה הָעוֹלָם הַמּוֹנְעוֹת תְּמִידוּת הָעֵסֶק בַּתּוֹרָה הַקְּדוֹשָׁה, כְּמוֹ שֶׁאָמְרוּ

  - "כָּל הַמְקַבֵּל עָלָיו עֹל תּוֹרָה, מַעֲבִירִין מִמֶּנּוּ עֹל מַלְכוּת וְעֹל דֶּרֶךְ אֶרֶץ" (אבות ג, ה).

- וְאָמְרוּ בְּבַמִּדְבַּר רַבָּה, וּבְתַנְחוּמָא פָּרָשַׁת חֻקַּת (אות כא), שֶׁמִּזֶּה הַטַּעַם נִתְּנָה הַתּוֹרָה בַּמִּדְבָּר, כְּשֵׁם שֶׁמִּדְבָּר אֵינוֹ נִזְרָע וְאֵינוֹ נֶעֱבָד, כָּךְ הַמְקַבֵּל עָלָיו עֹל תּוֹרָה, פּוֹרְקִין מִמֶּנּוּ עֹל וכו', וּכְשֵׁם שֶׁמִּדְבָּר אֵינוֹ מַעֲלֶה אַרְנוֹן (רָצָה לוֹמַר מַס), כָּךְ בְּנֵי תּוֹרָה בְּנֵי חוֹרִין כו'.

- וּבְזֹהַר וַיְחִי רמ"ב ב', דְּכָל מַאן דְּיָדַע לְאִשְׁתַּדְּלָא בְּאוֹרַיְתָא וְלָא אִשְׁתַּדַּל, אִתְחַיַּב בְּנַפְשֵׁיהּ. וְלֹא עוֹד, אֶלָּא דְּיָהֲבִין עֲלֵיהּ עוֹלָא דְאַרְעָא וְשִׁעְבּוּדָא בִּישָׁא, דִּכְתִיב בְּיִשָּׂשכָר "וַיֵּט שִׁכְמוֹ לִסְבֹּל" (בראשית מט, טו) כו', מַאן דְּסָטָא אָרְחֵיהּ וְגָרִים לֵיהּ דְּלָא לְמִסְבַּל עוֹלָא דְאוֹרַיְתָא, מִיָּד, "וַיְהִי לְמַס עֹבֵד".

  - וְכֵן לְהֵפֶךְ כו'.

- וְכָךְ הַדִּין הֲלָכָה פְּסוּקָה בַּשַּׁ"ס, שֶׁתַּלְמִידֵי חֲכָמִים פְּטוּרִין מִמִּסִּים

  - כְּמוֹ שֶׁאָמְרוּ (נדרים ס"ב ב' ב"ב ח' ע"א) שָׁאֲרֵי לֵיהּ לְצוּרְבָּא מֵרַבָּנָן לְמֵימַר לָא יָהִיבְנָא כַּרְגָּא, דִּכְתִיב (עזרא ז, כד) מִנְדָּה בְלוֹ וַהֲלָךְ לָא שַׁלִּיט לְמִרְמֵא עֲלֵיהֹם.

  - וְשָׁם, רַב הוּנָא בַּר רַב חִסְדָּא שָׁדָא כַּרְגָּא אַרַבָּנָן, אָמַר לֵיהּ רַב נַחְמָן בַּר יִצְחָק עָבַרְתְּ אַדְּאוֹרַיְתָא, אַדִּנְבִיאִים, אַדִּכְתוּבִים, דִּכְתִיב כו', כְּמוֹ שֶׁאָמְרוּ שָׁם, דְּרַבָּנָן לָא צְרִיכֵי נְטִירוּתָא.

- וּבְתָנָא דְּבֵי אֵלִיָּהוּ סֵדֶר אֵלִיָּהוּ רַבָּא פֶּרֶק ד', כָּל תַּלְמִיד חָכָם שֶׁעוֹסֵק בַּתּוֹרָה

---

236 I.e., to non-Torah distractions.
237 Zohar I Veyechi 242b which quotes the verse relating to Yissachar in Bereishit 49:15.
238 Nedarim 62b and Bava Batra 8a quoting Ezra 7:24.
239 Bava Batra 8a The standard version of this text refers to "R. Nachman bar R. Chisda" and not "R. Huna bar R. Chisda."

day, for the sake of increasing Heaven's honor, will not need any sword or spear or anything to act as a guard, as God will personally guard him. . . .[240]

- If a person conducts himself properly but only studies Torah Scripture alone, then he is given one angel to protect him . . . If he studies all parts of Tanach then he is given two angels to protect him as per "For your angels [plural] are commanded to watch over you. . . ." But for one who studies Tanach, Mishna, Midrash, Halachot, Agadot, and serves Torah Sages, God personally guards him as per "God shall watch over you."[241]

• According to one's level of true acceptance upon himself of the yoke of Torah with all of his strength, there will be a corresponding removal of the tribulations of this world, and a personal supernal protection hovers over him.
- It is like with a son who perfects his relationship with his father resulting in his father doing and satisfying everything he wants.
- As per Chazal:
  - God satisfies every want of all who study Torah.[242]
  - It is written in the Torah, and repeated in both the Prophets and Writings that the physical assets of those who study Torah thrive.[243]
  - "and elicits favor from God," God, at a time of favor, satisfies the will of one who publicly disseminates Torah.[244]
  - [One who studies Torah has] all of his needs constantly prepared for him without any toil or minor effort over them as per:
    - All the while a Torah Sage is involved in Torah study . . . and not only this but God provides his daily needs, as per the verse "and gives food to her household."[245]
  - Blessed is the Makom. Blessed be He Who has chosen Torah Sages and their students . . . Just as they sit in the prayer and study houses, and at every available opportunity read and review for the sake of Heaven and with Fear of God in their hearts, and uphold words of Torah on their lips and fulfill the verse "It is good for a man when he takes up the yoke in his youth," similarly, even if they were to request for all of the world at one time, He immediately gives it to them. . . .[246]

---

240 Eliyahu Rabba Parsha 4.
241 Eliyahu Rabba Parsha 18 quoting Tehillim 91:11 and Tehillim 121:5.
242 Avodah Zarah 19a; Midrash Tehillim 1:17.
243 Avodah Zarah 19b.
244 Midrash Mishlei 8:35.

בְּכָל יוֹם תָּמִיד, בִּשְׁבִיל לְהַרְבּוֹת כְּבוֹד שָׁמַיִם, אֵינוֹ צָרִיךְ לֹא חֶרֶב וְלֹא חֲנִית וְלֹא כָּל דָּבָר שֶׁיִּהְיֶה לוֹ שׁוֹמֵר, אֶלָּא הַקָּדוֹשׁ בָּרוּךְ הוּא מְשַׁמְּרוֹ בְּעַצְמוֹ כו'.

וְשָׁם בְּפֶרֶק י"ח, אִם יֵשׁ בּוֹ בָּאָדָם דֶּרֶךְ אֶרֶץ וּמִקְרָא לְבַד, מוֹסְרִין לוֹ מַלְאָךְ אֶחָד לְשָׁמְרוֹ, שֶׁנֶּאֱמַר כו'. קָרָא אָדָם תּוֹרָה נְבִיאִים וּכְתוּבִים, מוֹסְרִים לוֹ שְׁנֵי מַלְאָכִים, שֶׁנֶּאֱמַר כִּי מַלְאָכָיו יְצַוֶּה לָךְ לִשְׁמָרְךָ כו'. אֲבָל קָרָא אָדָם תּוֹרָה נְבִיאִים וּכְתוּבִים, וְשָׁנָה מִשְׁנָה וּמִדְרָשׁ הֲלָכוֹת וְאַגָּדוֹת, וְשִׁמֵּשׁ תַּלְמִידֵי חֲכָמִים, הַקָּדוֹשׁ בָּרוּךְ הוּא מְשַׁמְּרוֹ בְּעַצְמוֹ כו', שֶׁנֶּאֱמַר (תהלים קכ"א) "ה' שׁוֹמְרֶךָ" כו':

● וּכְפִי עֵרֶךְ הַקַּבּוּל אֲשֶׁר יְקַבֵּל עָלָיו עַל הַתּוֹרָה בֶּאֱמֶת וּבְכָל כֹּחוֹ, כֵּן לְפִי זֶה הָעֵרֶךְ יָסִירוּ וְיַעֲבִירוּ מִמֶּנּוּ טִרְדוֹת עִנְיְנֵי זֶה הָעוֹלָם, וְהַשְּׁמִירָה עֶלְיוֹנָה חוֹפֶפֶת עָלָיו
● וְהוּא כְּבֵן הַמִּתְחַטֵּא עַל אָבִיו, וְאָבִיו עוֹשֶׂה לוֹ רְצוֹנוֹ וּמַשְׁלִים לוֹ כָּל חֶפְצוֹ כְּמוֹ שֶׁאָמְרוּ רַבּוֹתֵינוּ זִכְרוֹנָם לִבְרָכָה
● "כָּל הָעוֹסֵק בַּתּוֹרָה, הַקָּדוֹשׁ בָּרוּךְ הוּא עוֹשֶׂה לוֹ חֶפְצוֹ" (ע"ז י"ט, א). וְכֵן אִיתָא בְּמִדְרַשׁ תְּהִלִּים מִזְמוֹר א'.
● וְאָמְרוּ עוֹד שָׁם, שֶׁכָּתוּב בַּתּוֹרָה וְשָׁנוּי בַּנְּבִיאִים וּמְשֻׁלָּשׁ בַּכְּתוּבִים, שֶׁכָּל הָעוֹסֵק בַּתּוֹרָה נְכָסָיו מַצְלִיחִין.
● וּבְמִשְׁלֵי רַבָּתָא סוֹף פָּרָשָׁה ח' "וְיָפֵק רָצוֹן מֵה'", כָּל מִי שֶׁהוּא מֵפִיק בְּדִבְרֵי תּוֹרָה וּמְלַמְּדוֹ בָּרַבִּים, אַף אֲנִי בְּעֵת רָצוֹן מֵפִיק לוֹ רָצוֹן כו'.
● וּמְזוֹנוֹתָיו מוּכָנִים לוֹ תָּמִיד, בְּלֹא שׁוּם עָמָל וִיגִיעָה מְעַטֶּת עֲלֵיהֶם. כְּמוֹ שֶׁאָמְרוּ שָׁם בְּפֶרֶק אֵשֶׁת חַיִל
● כָּל זְמַן שֶׁהַתַּלְמִיד חָכָם יוֹשֵׁב וְעוֹסֵק בַּתּוֹרָה כו', וְלֹא עוֹד אֶלָּא שֶׁהַקָּדוֹשׁ בָּרוּךְ הוּא מַמְצִיא לוֹ מְזוֹנוֹתָיו בְּכָל יוֹם וָיוֹם, שֶׁנֶּאֱמַר "וַתִּתֵּן טֶרֶף לְבֵיתָהּ".
● וּבְתָנָא דְּבֵי אֵלִיָּהוּ סֵדֶר אֵלִיָּהוּ רַבָּא פֶּרֶק י"ח, בָּרוּךְ הַמָּקוֹם בָּרוּךְ הוּא שֶׁבָּחַר בַּחֲכָמִים וּבְתַלְמִידֵיהֶם כו', כְּשֵׁם שֶׁהֵם יוֹשְׁבִין בְּבָתֵּי כְנֵסִיּוֹת וּבְבָתֵּי מִדְרָשׁוֹת, וּבְכָל מָקוֹם שֶׁהוּא פָּנוּי לָהֶם, וְקוֹרִין וְשׁוֹנִין לְשֵׁם שָׁמַיִם, וְיִרְאָה בִּלְבָבָם, וּמַחֲזִיקִים דִּבְרֵי תוֹרָה בְּפִיהֶם, וּמְקַיְּמִין עֲלֵיהֶם הַפָּסוּק "טוֹב לַגֶּבֶר

---

245 Midrash Mishlei 31:15.
246 Eliyahu Rabba Parsha 18 quoting Eicha 3:27.

- Even more than this but while [a person who accepts upon himself the yoke of Torah, he] will certainly flee from honor and high position, as without this it is impossible to be able to study Torah *for its sake* and [such study] will not remain with him at all
  - as per Chazal: "Don't seek greatness for yourself and don't desire honor,"[247] as these are [traits which are] forbidden for a person to pursue at all
  - however, great is God's counsel, which gives him happiness and greatness against his will
  - as per: Blessed is the Makom, Blessed be He, Who has chosen Torah Sages and their students . . . Just as they sit in the prayer and study houses all day, and read and review for the sake of Heaven, have Fear of Heaven in their hearts, support words of Torah on their lips, and happily accept the yoke of Heaven upon themselves, so too God correspondingly gives joy, so to speak, to the Tzaddikim even if against their will and [what they perceive as] not in their interest.[248]
  - This is as per the verse "Only goodness and kindness pursue me all the days of my life,"[249] meaning that even if I flee from them, they will pursue me against my will.

17. TORAH PROTECTS FROM DEATH/GEHINOM/WORLD TO COME/I.E., ALWAYS

- [Torah study also impacts a person] after his passing on from this world. As per Chazal:
  - The fire of Gehinom does not have any control over Torah Sages.[250]
  - A Torah scholar – even if he sours – his Torah does not become repulsive.[251]
  - "To understand the parable and the Melitzah/comment" This is the Torah itself, so why is it called "Melitzah"? As it saves[252] one who studies it from the judgment of Gehinom.[253]
  - "My child, if you accept My words [(i.e., Torah) and *Titzpon*/treasure My commandments with you]"[254]
    - God says to Israel at Sinai: If you merit to accept, *internalize*,[255] and perform My Torah, then I will save you from three punishments

---

247 Mishna Avot 6:4.
248 Eliyahu Rabba Parsha 18.
249 Tehillim 23:6.
250 Chagiga 27a.
251 Chagiga 15b.

כִּי יָשָׂא עַל בְּנְעוּרָיו" (איכה ג, כז) כָּךְ כִּבְיָכוֹל אֲפִלּוּ הֵם יִשְׁאֲלוּ אֶת כָּל הָעוֹלָם כֻּלּוֹ בְּשָׁעָה אַחַת, הוּא נוֹתֵן לָהֶם מִיָּד כוּ':

- וְיָתֵר עַל כֵּן, אֶלָּא הֲגַם שֶׁהוּא עַצְמוֹ וַדַּאי בּוֹרֵחַ מֵהַכָּבוֹד וּגְדֻלָּה, כִּי בְּלֹא זֶה בִּלְתִּי אֶפְשָׁר בָּעוֹלָם כְּלָל לִהְיוֹת עוֹסֵק בַּתּוֹרָה לִשְׁמָהּ, וְלֹא תִתְקַיֵּם אֶצְלוֹ כְּלָל

  ○ כְּמוֹ שֶׁאָמְרוּ זִכְרוֹנָם לִבְרָכָה בְּפֶרֶק מַעֲלוֹת הַתּוֹרָה (אבות ו, ד), "אַל תְּבַקֵּשׁ גְּדֻלָּה לְעַצְמְךָ, וְאַל תַּחְמֹד כָּבוֹד", כִּי הָאָדָם אָסוּר לוֹ לִפְנוֹת דַּעְתּוֹ לָזֶה כְּלָל.

  ○ אָמְנָם גְּדוֹל הָעֵצָה יִתְבָּרֵךְ שְׁמוֹ, נוֹתֵן לוֹ שִׂמְחָה וּגְדֻלָּה בְּעַל כָּרְחוֹ

  ○ כְּמוֹ שֶׁכָּתוּב בְּתַנָּא דְּבֵי אֵלִיָּהוּ שָׁם, בָּרוּךְ הַמָּקוֹם בָּרוּךְ הוּא, שֶׁבָּחַר בַּחֲכָמִים וּבְתַלְמִידֵיהֶם כוּ', כְּמוֹ שֶׁהֵם יוֹשְׁבִין בְּבָתֵּי כְנֵסִיּוֹת וּבְבָתֵּי מִדְרָשׁוֹת בְּכָל יוֹם, וְקוֹרִין וְשׁוֹנִין לְשֵׁם שָׁמַיִם, וְיִרְאַת שָׁמַיִם בְּלִבָּם, וּמַחֲזִיקִים דִּבְרֵי תוֹרָה עַל פִּיהֶם, וּמְקַבְּלִין עֲלֵיהֶם בְּשִׂמְחָה עֹל מַלְכוּת שָׁמַיִם, כָּךְ כִּבְיָכוֹל הַקָּדוֹשׁ בָּרוּךְ הוּא נוֹתֵן לָהֶם שִׂמְחָה לַצַּדִּיקִים בְּעַל כָּרְחָם שֶׁלֹּא בְּטוֹבָתָם כוּ', עַד כָּאן.

  ○ וּכְמַאֲמַר הַכָּתוּב (תהלים כג, ו) "אַךְ טוֹב וָחֶסֶד יִרְדְּפוּנִי כָּל יְמֵי חַיָּי", רוֹצֶה לוֹמַר, הֲגַם שֶׁאֲנִי בּוֹרֵחַ מֵהֶם, הֵמָּה רוֹדְפִים אַחֲרַי בְּעַל כָּרְחִי:

שער ד' - פרק י"ז

- בֵּין אַחַר פְּטִירָתוֹ מִזֶּה הָעוֹלָם, אָמְרוּ רַבּוֹתֵינוּ זִכְרוֹנָם לִבְרָכָה

  ○ תַּלְמִידֵי חֲכָמִים אֵין אוּר שֶׁל גֵּיהִנָּם שׁוֹלֵט בָּהֶם כוּ' (חגיגה כז, א):

  ○ וְכֵן אָמְרוּ שָׁם (טו, ב) תַּלְמִיד חָכָם שֶׁסָּרַח אֵין תּוֹרָתוֹ נִמְאֶסֶת:

  ○ וּבְמִשְׁלֵי רַבָּתָא בַּפָּסוּק "לְהָבִין מָשָׁל וּמְלִיצָה" כוּ' (משלי א), זוֹ הַתּוֹרָה עַצְמָהּ, וְלָמָּה נִקְרֵאת שְׁמָהּ מְלִיצָה, שֶׁהִיא מַצֶּלֶת עוֹסְקֶיהָ מְדִינָה שֶׁל גֵּיהִנָּם:

  ○ וְשָׁם רֵישׁ פָּרָשָׁה ב' "בְּנִי אִם תִּקַּח אֲמָרָי" כוּ'

  □ אָמַר הַקָּדוֹשׁ בָּרוּךְ הוּא לְיִשְׂרָאֵל עַל הַר סִינַי, אִם זְכִיתֶם לְהַצְפִּין וּלְקַבֵּל תּוֹרָתִי וְלַעֲשׂוֹתָהּ, אֲנִי מַצִּיל אֶתְכֶם מִשָּׁלֹשׁ פֻּרְעָנִיּוֹת

---

252 This is a play on words between "Melitzah" and "Matzil."
253 Midrash Mishlei 1:6.
254 Mishlei 2:1, with the following bullets quoted from Midrash Mishlei on this verse.
255 There is a play on words in this verse between "Titzpon" (to treasure), "Yatzpin" (to internalize) and "Tzafun" (hidden away). There is however

- the war of Gog and Magog
- the birth pangs of Mashiach
- and the judgment of Gehinom.

- "and *Titzpon*/treasure My commandments with you," if you merit to *internalize* My Torah, I will sustain you with the good which is *Tzafun/hidden away* for you in the time to come, as per the verse "How great is Your good which You have hidden [for those who fear You]."[256]

- R. Chanina ben Dosa says: The only charity which saves a person from the judgment of Gehinom is Torah alone ... It has the power to save a person from the Day of Judgment even if the person is liable through sin, it can save him from the Day of Judgment ... From here we learn that a Torah scholar who sins is saved by [his Torah study].[257]

- "Its circuit ... and there is nothing to hide its heat"[258] ... R. Yanai and Reish Lakish both say: there will be no Gehinom in the time to come, just this sun which will beat down on the wicked as per "Behold the day comes, which burns like an oven, and all who transgress ... and will beat down on them"[259] But in the time to come who will be shielded from its heat? Those who occupy themselves with Torah ... and what is written after this ... "God's Torah is perfect"[260] ... and similarly "There is no darkness and no shadow of death to conceal those who do sin there."[261] Who are concealed? Those who occupy themselves with Torah.[262]

- How much more so is the case than with Elisha [ben Avuya, known as] Acher, about whom Chazal say: "We cannot execute a judgment against him because he engaged in Torah study [and this protects him from Gehinom]"[263] ... as per Chazal[264] on the verse "and the end of the matter is good"[265] that the 'book cover was saved with the book,'[266] so Elisha was saved [from Gehinom] through the merit of his Torah.

- R. Yitzchak says: Why was the Torah given with fire and darkness ... Because all who are involved with Torah are saved from a different fire of Gehinom and from the darkness with which the other nations darken Israel.[267] Refer there.

---

similar meaning in that a concept which is treasure is indeed internalized and hidden away within oneself.

256 Tehillim 31:20.
257 Midrash Mishlei 11:4.
258 Tehillim 19:7.
259 Malachi 3:19.
260 Tehillim 19:8.

- מִמִּלְחֶמֶת גּוֹג וּמָגוֹג
- מֵחֶבְלוֹ שֶׁל מָשִׁיחַ
- מִדִּינָהּ שֶׁל גֵּיהִנָּם.

"וּמְצוּתִי תִּצְפֹּן אִתָּךְ", אִם זְכִיתֶם לְהַצְפִּין תּוֹרָתִי, אֲנִי מַשְׁבִּיעַ אֶתְכֶם מִטּוּב הַצָּפוּן לֶעָתִיד לָבֹא, שֶׁנֶּאֱמַר (תהלים לא, כ) "מָה רַב טוּבְךָ אֲשֶׁר צָפַנְתָּ" כו':

וְשָׁם בְּפָרָשָׁה י"א, אָמַר רַבִּי חֲנִינָא בֶּן דּוֹסָא, אֵין לְךָ צְדָקָה שֶׁמַּצֶּלֶת אֶת הָאָדָם מִדִּינָהּ שֶׁל גֵּיהִנָּם אֶלָּא תּוֹרָה בִּלְבַד כו', שֶׁיֵּשׁ בָּהּ כֹּחַ לְהַצִּיל אוֹתוֹ מִיּוֹם הַדִּין, וַאֲפִלּוּ נִתְחַיֵּב אָדָם בִּדְבַר עֲבֵרָה, יְכוֹלָה לְהַצִּיל אוֹתוֹ מִיּוֹם הַדִּין כו', הֲרֵי מִכָּאן לְתַלְמִיד חָכָם שֶׁעָבַר בִּדְבַר עֲבֵרָה שֶׁהִיא מַצֶּלֶת אוֹתוֹ:

וּבְמִדְרָשׁ תְּהִלִּים מִזְמוֹר י"ט "וּתְקוּפָתוֹ כו', וְאֵין נִסְתָּר מֵחַמָּתוֹ" כו', רַבִּי יַנַּאי וְרַבִּי שִׁמְעוֹן בֶּן לָקִישׁ אָמְרֵי תַרְוַיְהוּ, אֵין גֵּיהִנָּם לֶעָתִיד לָבֹא, אֶלָּא הַשֶּׁמֶשׁ הַזּוֹ הִיא מְלַהֶטֶת אֶת הָרְשָׁעִים, שֶׁנֶּאֱמַר (מלאכי ג, יט) "הִנֵּה הַיּוֹם בָּא בֹּעֵר כַּתַּנּוּר וְהָיוּ כָל זֵדִים כו', וְלִהַט אוֹתָם" כו', אֲבָל לֶעָתִיד לָבֹא, מִי נִסְתָּר מֵחַמָּתוֹ, מִי שֶׁהוּא עוֹסֵק בַּתּוֹרָה, מַה כְּתִיב אַחֲרָיו "תּוֹרַת ה' תְּמִימָה" כו', וְכֵן הוּא אוֹמֵר "אֵין חֹשֶׁךְ וְאֵין צַלְמָוֶת לְהִסָּתֵר שָׁם פֹּעֲלֵי אָוֶן" (איוב לד, כב) וּמִי נִסְתָּרָה, מִי שֶׁהוּא עוֹסֵק בַּתּוֹרָה כו', עַיֵּן שָׁם:

וְקַל וָחֹמֶר מֵאֱלִישָׁע אַחֵר, שֶׁאָמְרוּ (חגיגה טו, ב) "לָא מֵידַן נְדַיְנֵיהּ מִשּׁוּם דְּגָמִיר אוֹרַיְתָא". וְכֵן אָמְרוּ בִּירוּשַׁלְמִי שָׁם, וּבְקֹהֶלֶת רַבָּה סִימָן ז', בַּפָּסוּק "טוֹב אַחֲרִית דָּבָר" כו', וְלֹא כֵן תַּנִינָן, מַצִּילִין תִּיק הַסֵּפֶר עִם הַסֵּפֶר כו', מַצִּילִין לֶאֱלִישָׁע בִּזְכוּת תּוֹרָתוֹ:

וּבַזֹּהַר יִתְרוֹ פ"ג ב', אָמַר רַבִּי יִצְחָק אֲמַאי אִתְיְהִיב אוֹרַיְתָא בְּאֶשָּׁא וַחֲשׁוֹכָא

---

261 Iyov 34:22.
262 Midrash Tehillim 19:13.
263 Chagiga 15b, how much more so with one who does not forsake the path of Torah and also engages in its study.
264 Yerushalmi Chagiga Chapter 2 Halacha 1; Kohelet Rabba 7:8.
265 Kohelet 7:8.
266 An expression from Mishna Shabbat 16:1 which describes that if there is a fire on Shabbat, one is permitted to save a book cover, together with and in addition to the book itself.
267 Zohar II Yitro 83b.

- It is a commandment to study Torah every day as it is the secret of supernal faith, in order to know the ways of God, as all who involve themselves in Torah merit in this world and the next, and are saved from prosecution, because the Torah is the secret of faith and he who is involved with it is involved with supernal faith and [God] will have His Shechina reside in him permanently.[268]
- On the verse "Length of days is at its right, [at its left are riches and honor]"[269] – to those who believe in it –[270] it is length of days and how much more so it is riches and honor. This relates to two worlds: riches and honor in this world, and length of days in the next world.[271]
  - Where the principal meaning of *length of days* is for the future world which is long, as Chazal state in many places, e.g., as per Zohar.[272] Refer there.
- R. Elazar says: "Open my eyes and I will see the wonders of Your Torah." How foolish are those people who do not know how to and do not [interest themselves to] look to involve themselves with Torah, as Torah is all of life, all of freedom and all of good in this and the next world, and through it one merits complete days in this world and length of days in the next. For they are complete life, a life of freedom and without sadness, a real life, freedom in this world, freedom from all, for the nations of the world can have no control over one who is involved with Torah ... therefore, all who are involved with Torah have freedom from all, in this world from subservience to the nations of the world and in the next world from being subject to any judgment.[273] Refer there.
- [In the continuation of] the Midrash explaining the verse "And along the stream will grow every species of fruit bearing tree,"[274] it asks: What is meant by "and does not see when the heat comes"?[275] It tells you that all who involve themselves with Torah will not see punishment, either in this world, the times of Mashiach, or in the World to Come.[276]
  - Similarly, "When you go out it will guide you," in this world; "when

---

268 Zohar Raya Mehemna II Terumah 134b.
269 Mishlei 3:16.
270 *Those who believe in it* (i.e., "Mayminim") is a play on the word *On its right* (i.e., "Biyemina"). Those who believe are the Torah scholars.
271 Shabbat 63a.
272 Zohar I Vayeshev 190a.
273 Zohar I Chayei Sarah 131b quoting Tehillim 119:18.
274 Yechezkel 47:12.

כו', דְּכָל מַאן דְּיִשְׁתַּדֵּל בְּאוֹרַיְיתָא, אִשְׁתְּזִיב מֵאִשָּׁא אָחֳרָא בְּגֵיהִנָּם, וּמֵחֲשׁוֹכָא דִּמְחַשְּׁכִין כָּל שְׁאָר עַמִּין לְיִשְׂרָאֵל כו', עַיֵּין שָׁם:

○ וּבְרַעְיָא מְהֵימְנָא תְּרוּמָה קל"ד ב', פִּקּוּדָא לִלְמוֹד תּוֹרָה בְּכָל יוֹמָא, דְּאִיהוּ רָזָא דִּמְהֵימְנוּתָא עִלָּאָה, לְמִנְדַּע אוֹרְחֵיהּ דְּקוּדְשָׁא בְּרִיךְ הוּא, דְּכָל מַאן דְּאִשְׁתַּדֵּל בְּאוֹרַיְיתָא, זָכֵי בְּהַאי עָלְמָא וְזָכֵי בְּעָלְמָא דְּאָתֵי, וְאִשְׁתְּזִיב מִכָּל קַטְרוּגִין בִּישִׁין, בְּגִין דְּאוֹרַיְיתָא רָזָא דִּמְהֵימְנוּתָא אִיהִי, דְּמַאן דְּיִתְעֲסַק בָּהּ אִתְעֲסַק בִּמְהֵימְנוּתָא עִלָּאָה, אַשְׁרֵי שְׁכִינְתָּא בְּגַוֵּיהּ דְּלָא תַּעֲדֵי מִינֵיהּ כו':

○ וּכְמַאֲמָרָם זִכְרוֹנָם לִבְרָכָה (שבת סג, א) עַל פָּסוּק "אֹרֶךְ יָמִים בִּימִינָהּ" כו' (משלי ג, טז) לַמַּיְמִינִים בָּהּ אֹרֶךְ יָמִים, וְכָל שֶׁכֵּן עֹשֶׁר וְכָבוֹד, וְהוּא בִּשְׁנֵי הָעוֹלָמִים, "עֹשֶׁר וְכָבוֹד" בָּעוֹלָם הַזֶּה, "וְאֹרֶךְ יָמִים" לָעוֹלָם הַבָּא

○ שֶׁעִקָּר הָאֹרֶךְ יָמִים, הַכַּוָּנָה לָעוֹלָם שֶׁכֻּלּוֹ אָרֹךְ, כְּמוֹ שֶׁאָמְרוּ רַבּוֹתֵינוּ זִכְרוֹנָם לִבְרָכָה בְּכַמָּה דּוּכְתֵּי, וּבַזֹּהַר וַיֵּשֶׁב קצ"ב רֵישׁ ע"א, עַיֵּין שָׁם:

○ וְשָׁם בְּפָרָשַׁת חַיֵּי קל"א ב', רַבִּי אֶלְעָזָר פָּתַח וְאָמַר "גַּל עֵינַי וְאַבִּיטָה נִפְלָאוֹת מִתּוֹרָתֶךָ" (תהלים קיט, יח), כַּמָּה אִינּוּן בְּנֵי נָשָׁא טִפְּשִׁין, דְּלָא יַדְעִין וְלָא מִסְתַּכְּלִין לְאִשְׁתַּדְּלָא בְּאוֹרַיְיתָא, בְּגִין דְּאוֹרַיְיתָא כָּל חַיִּין, וְכָל טוֹב, בְּעָלְמָא דֵּין וּבְעָלְמָא דְּאָתֵי, אִיהוּ חֵירוּ דְּעָלְמָא דֵין וּדְעָלְמָא דְּאָתֵי אִיהִי, חַיִּין אִינּוּן בְּעָלְמָא דֵין, דְּיִזְכּוּן לְיוֹמִין שְׁלֵמִין בְּהַאי עָלְמָא, כד"א כו', וּלְיוֹמִין אֲרִיכִין בְּעָלְמָא דְּאָתֵי, בְּגִין דְּאִנּוּן חַיִּין שְׁלֵמִין אִנּוּן, חַיִּין דְּחֶדְוָה, חַיִּין בְּלָא עֲצִיבוּ, חַיִּין דְּאִנּוּן חַיִּין, חֵירוּ בְּעָלְמָא דֵין חֵירוּ דְּכֹלָּא, דְּכָל מַאן דְּאִשְׁתַּדֵּל בְּאוֹרַיְיתָא, לָא יָכְלִין לְשַׁלְטָאָה עֲלוֹי כָּל עַמִּין דְּעָלְמָא כו', וְעַל דָּא, כָּל מַאן דְּיִשְׁתַּדֵּל בְּאוֹרַיְיתָא, חֵירוּ אִית לֵיהּ מִכֹּלָּא, בְּעָלְמָא דֵין — מִשִּׁעְבּוּדָא דִּשְׁאָר עַמִּין, חֵירוּ בְּעָלְמָא דְּאָתֵי — בְּגִין דְּלָא יִתְבְּעוּן מִנֵּיהּ דִּינָא בְּהַהוּא עָלְמָא כְּלָל כו', עַיֵּין שָׁם:

○ וּבְתַנָּא דְּבֵי אֵלִיָּהוּ סֵדֶר רַבָּא פֶּרֶק י"ח, בַּפָּסוּק (יחזקאל מז, יב) "וְעַל הַנַּחַל יַעֲלֶה עַל שְׂפָתוֹ מִזֶּה וּמִזֶּה כָּל עֵץ מַאֲכָל" וכו', מַאי "וְלֹא יִרְאֶה כִּי יָבֹא חֹם", לוֹמַר לְךָ, כָּל הָעוֹסֵק בַּתּוֹרָה אֵינוֹ רוֹאֶה מִדַּת פּוּרְעָנִיּוֹת, בֵּין בָּעוֹלָם הַזֶּה בֵּין לִימוֹת בֶּן דָּוִד וּבֵין לָעוֹלָם הַבָּא.

○ וּכְמוֹ שֶׁפֵּרְשׁוּ זִכְרוֹנָם לִבְרָכָה (סוטה כא, א) "בְּהִתְהַלֶּכְךָ תַּנְחֶה אוֹתָךְ"

---

275 Yirmiyahu 17:8.
276 Eliyahu Rabba Parsha 18.

you rest, it will watch over you," in the grave; "when you awaken it will speak with you," in the World to Come.[277]

- R. Yehuda began and said: "God's Torah is perfect"[278] ... How much should people involve themselves in Torah! As one who involves himself with Torah will have life in this world and in the World to Come, and he will have merit in two worlds; even one who is involved with Torah but not properly *for its sake* will merit a good reward in this world and will not be judged in the world of truth. Come and see, it is written: "Length of days is at its right [at its left are riches and honor]."[279] "Length of days" relates to one involved with Torah *for its sake*, that he will have length of days in that world in which there is length of days [i.e., in the future world]; "at its left are riches and honor" relates to the good reward and tranquility they will have in this world. All who involve themselves with Torah *for its sake*, then at the time they pass on from this world, the Torah goes before them and announces them and protects them from prosecutors. When the body rests in the grave, the Torah protects it. When the soul returns to its origin, the Torah goes before the soul and many gates are broken by the Torah until the soul reaches its origin. It then stays with the person until the time of the resurrection and acts in their defense, as is written: "When you go out it will guide you"[280] which is as already stated, "when you rest, it will watch over you" which is at the time when the body rests in the grave as at that time the body is judged and the Torah protects it; "when you awaken, it will speak with you" which is as already stated that at the time of the resurrection it will speak to act in your defense.[281]

- "A soul which works, its work is for it." The person works [on Torah] in this place [i.e., this world] and the Torah works for him in another place [i.e., in the World to Come].[282]

- "The wise among women, builds her house ... ," meaning that one who acquires wisdom [i.e., Torah] in this world can be sure that it will build a residence for him in the World to Come, "... but the foolish one, tears it down," meaning that one who did not acquire wisdom for himself can be sure that he has acquired Gehinom for himself in the World to Come."[283]

---

277 Sotah 21a explaining the verse from Mishlei 6:22.
278 Tehillim 19:8.
279 Mishlei 3:16.
280 Mishlei 6:22.
281 Zohar I Vayeshev 184b/185a.

(משלי ו, כב) — בָּעוֹלָם הַזֶּה, "בְּשָׁכְבְּךָ תִּשְׁמֹר עָלֶיךָ" — בַּקֶּבֶר, "וַהֲקִיצוֹתָ הִיא תְשִׂיחֶךָ" — לָעוֹלָם הַבָּא:

◦ וּבַזֹּהַר פָּרָשַׁת וַיֵּשֶׁב קפ"ד ב', וקפ"ה א', רַבִּי יְהוּדָה פָּתַח וְאָמַר "תּוֹרַת ה' תְּמִימָה" (תהלים יט) כו', כַּמָּה אִית לוֹן לִבְנֵי נָשָׁא לְאִשְׁתַּדְּלָא בְּאוֹרָיְיתָא, דְּכָל מַאן דְּאִשְׁתַּדֵּל בְּאוֹרָיְיתָא, לֶהֱוֵי לֵיהּ חַיִּים בְּעָלְמָא דֵּין וּבְעָלְמָא דְּאָתֵי, וְזָכֵי בִּתְרֵין עָלְמִין. וַאֲפִילוּ מַאן דְּאִשְׁתַּדֵּל בְּאוֹרָיְיתָא, וְלָא אִשְׁתַּדֵּל בָּהּ לִשְׁמָהּ כְּדְקָא יָאוֹת, זָכֵי לַאֲגַר טַב בְּעָלְמָא דֵּין, וְלָא דַיְינִין לֵיהּ בְּהַהוּא עָלְמָא. וְתָא חֲזֵי כְּתִיב "אֹרֶךְ יָמִים בִּימִינָהּ" כו', "אֹרֶךְ יָמִים" בְּהַהוּא דְּאִשְׁתַּדֵּל בְּאוֹרָיְיתָא לִשְׁמָהּ, דְּאִית לֵיהּ "אֹרֶךְ יָמִים" בְּהַהוּא עָלְמָא דְּבֵיהּ אוּרְכָא דְּיוֹמִין כו', "בִּשְׂמֹאלָהּ עֹשֶׁר וְכָבוֹד", אֲגַר טוֹב וְשַׁלְוָה אִית לֵיהּ בְּהַאי עָלְמָא. וְכָל מַאן דְּיִשְׁתַּדֵּל בְּאוֹרָיְיתָא לִשְׁמָהּ, כַּד נָפִיק מֵהַאי עָלְמָא, אוֹרָיְיתָא אָזְלָא קָמֵיהּ, וְאַכְרְזַת קָמֵיהּ, וַאֲגִינַת עֲלֵיהּ, דְּלָא יִקְרְבוּן בַּהֲדֵיהּ מָארֵיהוֹן דְּדִינָא, כַּד שָׁכֵיב גּוּפָא בְּקִבְרָא הִיא נָטְרַת לֵיהּ, כַּד נִשְׁמָתָא אָזְלָת לְאִסְתַּלְּקָא לְמֵיתַב לְאַתְרָהּ, אִיהִי אָזְלָת קַמָּהּ דְּהַהִיא נִשְׁמָתָא, וְכַמָּה תַּרְעִין אִתְבְּרוּ מִקַּמָּהּ דְּאוֹרָיְיתָא עַד דְּעָאלַת לְדוּכְתָא, וְקַיְימָא עֲלֵיהּ דְּבַר נָשׁ, עַד דְּיִתְעָר בְּזִמְנָא דִּיקוּמוּן מֵתַיָּא דְּעָלְמָא, וְאִיהִי סָנֵיגוֹרָא עֲלֵיהּ, הֲדָא הוּא דִּכְתִיב "בְּהִתְהַלֶּכְךָ תַּנְחֶה אוֹתָךְ בְּשָׁכְבְּךָ תִּשְׁמֹר עָלֶיךָ" כו', "בְּהִתְהַלֶּכְךָ תַּנְחֶה אוֹתָךְ" — כְּמָה דְאִתְּמַר, "בְּשָׁכְבְּךָ תִּשְׁמֹר עָלֶיךָ" — בְּשַׁעְתָּא דְּשָׁכֵיב גּוּפָא בְּקִבְרָא, דְּהָא כְּדֵין בְּהַהוּא זִמְנָא אַתְדָּן גּוּפָא בְּקִבְרָא, וּכְדֵין אוֹרָיְיתָא אֲגִינַת עֲלֵיהּ, "וַהֲקִיצוֹתָ הִיא תְשִׂיחֶךָ" — כְּמָה דְאִתְּמַר, בְּזִמְנָא דְּיִתְעָרוּן מֵתֵי עָלְמָא מִן עַפְרָא, "הִיא תְשִׂיחֶךָ" — לְמֶהֱוֵי סָנֵיגוֹרָא עֲלָךְ כו':

◦ וְכֵן אָמְרוּ רַבּוֹתֵינוּ זִכְרוֹנָם לִבְרָכָה בְּפֶרֶק חֵלֶק (משלי טז, כו) בַּפָּסוּק (צט, ב) "נֶפֶשׁ עָמֵל עָמְלָה לּוֹ" כו', הוּא עָמֵל בְּמָקוֹם זֶה וְהַתּוֹרָה עוֹמֶלֶת לוֹ בְּמָקוֹם אַחֵר:

◦ וּבְמִשְׁלֵי רַבָּתָא פָּרָשָׁה י"ד "חַכְמוֹת נָשִׁים בָּנְתָה בֵיתָהּ" (משלי יד, א), כָּל מִי שֶׁקָּנָה לוֹ חָכְמָה בָּעוֹלָם הַזֶּה, יְהֵא מֻבְטָח שֶׁהִיא בָּנְתָה לוֹ בַּיִת לָעוֹלָם הַבָּא, "וְאִוֶּלֶת בְּיָדֶיהָ תֶּהֶרְסֶנּוּ" (שם) כָּל מִי שֶׁלֹּא קָנָה לוֹ חָכְמָה, יְהֵא מֻבְטָח שֶׁקָּנָה לוֹ גֵיהִנָּם לֶעָתִיד לָבֹא:

---

282 Sanhedrin 99b quoting Mishlei 16:26.
283 Midrash Mishlei 14:1.

- "Do not fear Avram, I will protect you – your reward is very great indeed,"[284] meaning I will protect you from all the evil in Gehinom; your reward is great as one who involves himself with Torah in this world, merits an inheritance in the World to Come.[285] Refer there.
- When a person studies Torah, God stands there . . . and he is saved from three judgments: from judgment in this world, from judgment of the Angel of Death which has no power over him, and from the judgment of Gehinom.[286]
- ["Charut/Inscribed on the Tablets,"][287] do not read this as "Charut" but rather as "Cherut," i.e., freedom, as only one who is involved with Torah study is free[288]
  - and Chazal explained that this freedom is from the Angel of Death, as similarly stated that "words of Torah save one from the Angel of Death."[289]
- Freedom in this world is freedom from all . . . freedom from the Angel of Death who has no ability to control over him. Similarly, it is certain that a person who attaches himself to the Tree of Life, the Torah, will not be the cause of his own death or that of the world. Therefore, when God gave the Torah to Israel, what was written in it? "*Charut* on the Tablets." God said: "I said – you are *Elokim* . . . ,"[290] so the evil snake who brings darkness to the world [i.e., the Angel of Death] cannot control one involved in Torah.[291]

18. TORAH *FOR ITS SAKE* RESULTS IN CONTROL OVER NATURAL ORDER

- Therefore, one who truly accepts upon himself the yoke of Torah *for its sake*, as per the explanation above of *for its sake*,[292] is above all matters of this world
  - and God looks out for him in a specifically personal way

---

284 Bereishit 15:1.
285 Zohar Sitrei Torah I Lech Lecha 88a.
286 Zohar II Vayakhel 200a.
287 Shemot 32:16.
288 Mishna Avot 6:2; Bamidbar Rabba 16:24; Shir Hashirim Rabba 8:6; Midrash Tanchuma (Warsaw), Ekev 8.
289 Makkot 10a.
290 Tehillim 82:6.
291 Zohar I Chayei Sarah 131b. The meaning here that one who attaches himself to *Elokim*, i.e., the Torah, is free of the Angel of Death.

וּבְסִתְרֵי תוֹרָה לֶךְ לְךָ (זוה"ק בראשית פח, א), "אַחַר הַדְּבָרִים הָאֵלֶּה", דָּא פִּתְגָּמֵי אוֹרַיְתָא כו', הֲדָא הוּא דִכְתִיב (בראשית טו, א) "אַל תִּירָא אַבְרָם אָנֹכִי מָגֵן לָךְ", מִכָּל זַיְנֵי בִּישִׁין דְּגֵיהִנָּם, "שְׂכָרְךָ הַרְבֵּה מְאֹד", בְּגִין דְּכָל מַאן דְּאִשְׁתַּדַּל בְּאוֹרַיְתָא בְּהַאי עָלְמָא, זָכֵי וְאַחֲסִין יְרוּתַת אַחֲסַנְתֵּיהּ לְעָלְמָא דְאָתֵי כו', עַיֵּן שָׁם:

וּבַזֹּהַר וַיַּקְהֵל ר' ע"א, בְּגִין דְּכַד בַּר נָשׁ עָסִיק בְּאוֹרַיְתָא, קוּדְשָׁא בְּרִיךְ הוּא קָאִים תַּמָּן כו', וְאִשְׁתְּזִיב בַּר נָשׁ מִתְּלַת דִּינִין, מִדִּינָא דְּהַאי עָלְמָא, וּמִדִּינָא דְמַלְאַךְ הַמָּוֶת דְּלָא יָכִיל לְשַׁלְטָאָה עֲלֵיהּ, וּמִדִּינָא דְּגֵיהִנָּם:

וּכְמוֹ שֶׁאָמְרוּ רַבּוֹתֵינוּ זִכְרוֹנָם לִבְרָכָה בְּפֶרֶק מַעֲלַת הַתּוֹרָה (אבות ו, ב), וּבְבַמִּדְבַּר רַבָּה פָּרָשָׁה ט"ז, וּבְחַזִּית בְּפָסוּק מִי זֹאת עוֹלָה כו'. וּבְתַנְחוּמָא פָּרָשַׁת עֵקֶב, אַל תִּקְרֵי "חָרוּת" אֶלָּא חֵרוּת, שֶׁאֵין לְךָ בֶּן חוֹרִין אֶלָּא מִי שֶׁעוֹסֵק בְּתַלְמוּד תּוֹרָה

וּפֵרְשׁוּ זִכְרוֹנָם לִבְרָכָה, חֵרוּת, מִמַּלְאַךְ הַמָּוֶת. וְכֵן אָמְרוּ בְּפֶרֶק ב' דְּמַכּוֹת (י' ע"א) שֶׁדִּבְרֵי תוֹרָה קוֹלְטִין מִמַּלְאַךְ הַמָּוֶת:

וּבַזֹּהַר פָּרָשַׁת חַיֵּי שָׂרָה בַּדַּף הַנַּ"ל (קנא, ב), חֵירוּ בְּעָלְמָא דֵין, חֵירוּ דְכֹלָּא כו', חֵירוּ דְמַלְאַךְ הַמָּוֶת, דְּלָא יָכוֹל לְשַׁלְטָאָה עֲלוֹי, וְהָכִי הוּא וַדַּאי, דְּאִי אָדָם הֲוָה אִתְדְּבִיק בְּאִילָנָא דְחַיֵּי, דְּאִיהוּ אוֹרַיְתָא, לָא גָרִים מוֹתָא לֵיהּ וּלְכָל עָלְמָא, וּבְגִין כָּךְ, כַּד יָהִיב קוּדְשָׁא בְּרִיךְ הוּא אוֹרַיְתָא לְיִשְׂרָאֵל, מַה כְּתִיב בָּהּ (שמות לב, טז), "חָרוּת עַל הַלֻּחוֹת" כו', וְקוּדְשָׁא בְּרִיךְ הוּא אָמַר (תהלים פב, ו) "אֲנִי אָמַרְתִּי אֱלֹקִים אַתֶּם" כו'. וְעַל דָּא, כָּל מַאן דְּאִשְׁתַּדַּל בְּאוֹרַיְתָא, לֹא יָכִיל לְשַׁלְטָאָה עֲלוֹי הַהוּא חִוְיָא בִּישָׁא דְּאַחְשִׁיךְ עָלְמָא:

שער ד' - פרק י"ח

וְלָזֹאת, הָאָדָם הַמְּקַבֵּל עַל עַצְמוֹ עוֹל הַתּוֹרָה הַקְּדוֹשָׁה לִשְׁמָהּ לַאֲמִתָּהּ, כְּמוֹ שֶׁהִתְבָּאֵר לְעֵיל (פ"ג) פֵּרוּשׁ "לִשְׁמָהּ" — הוּא נַעֲלָה מֵעַל כָּל עִנְיְנֵי זֶה הָעוֹלָם

וּמַשְׁגִּיחַ מֵאִתּוֹ יִתְבָּרַךְ הַשְׁגָּחָה פְּרָטִית

---

292 In G4:03, where *for its sake* is defined as being *for the sake of Torah*, i.e., for the sake of knowing, understanding, and analyzing the details of the Torah.

- overriding natural and cosmological order
- as he is, so to speak, literally attached to Torah and to God
- and he is sanctified with supernal holiness of the Holy Torah which is infinitely supernal compared to all the worlds
- and it is that which exclusively gives life and existence to everything and to all the natural powers
- therefore a person who is involved with [Torah] gives life to all and causes all to continue to exist and is higher than all[293]
- and [therefore] how can it be that God's dealing with him will be according to the natural order of things!

• As Chazal state:[294] On the one hand, the verse says, "Your kindness is up until the Heavens,"[295] but it also says, "Your kindness is above the Heavens."[296] This is no contradiction as the second verse relates to those involved with Torah *for its sake*, and the first verse relates to those involved with Torah which is not *for its sake*.
  - That is, even though one involved with Torah but not *for its sake* is certainly acceptable to God
    - notwithstanding any personal objectives as long as it is not to mock, God forbid, and how much more so if it is without any personal objectives but is just involvement out of rote
    - as this acts as a stepping stone to reach the level of *for its sake* as is known from Chazal's statement[297]
    - nevertheless, he has not yet sanctified or raised himself to [merit] the level of God's guidance in all that he does to be over and above the natural order
    - therefore, the verse refers to him as only [meriting kindness] "up to the Heavens," that is within the natural order which is fixed in the Heavens, but not higher than them.
  - Whereas with one involved with Torah *for its sake*
    - it says [he merits kindness] "above the Heavens," meaning that he receives God's guidance in a way which is exclusively above the natural order.

• As Chazal state: Come and see. Before the giving of the Torah, all creations were dependent on their preordained destiny . . . but after the giving of the Torah to Israel, they [i.e., Israel] were removed from the destiny of the stars and constellations . . . so as a result one who is involved in Torah is unaffected by the destiny of the stars and constellations, provided one studies in order to fulfill its Mitzvot. However, one who does not do this is as if he is not involved in Torah and is not removed from the influence of the destiny of the stars and constellations.[298]

- לְמַעְלָה מֵהוֹרָאַת כֹּחוֹת הַטְּבָעִים וְהַמַּזָּלוֹת כֻּלָּם.
- כֵּיוָן שֶׁהוּא דָּבוּק בַּתּוֹרָה וּבְהַקָּדוֹשׁ בָּרוּךְ הוּא מַמָּשׁ כִּבְיָכוֹל
- וּמִתְקַדֵּשׁ בִּקְדֻשָּׁה הָעֶלְיוֹנָה שֶׁל הַתּוֹרָה הַקְּדוֹשָׁה, שֶׁהִיא לְמַעְלָה לְאֵין עֲרֹךְ מִכָּל הָעוֹלָמוֹת
- וְהִיא הַנּוֹתֶנֶת הַחִיּוּת וְהַקִּיּוּם לְכֻלָּם וּלְכָל הַכֹּחוֹת הַטִּבְעִיִּים
- הֲרֵי הָאָדָם הָעוֹסֵק בָּהּ — מְחַיֶּה וּמְקַיֵּם אֶת כֻּלָּם וּלְמַעְלָה מִכֻּלָּם
- וְאֵיךְ אֶפְשָׁר שֶׁתִּהְיֶה הַנְהָגָתוֹ מֵאִתּוֹ יִתְבָּרַךְ עַל יְדֵי הַכֹּחוֹת הַטִּבְעִיִּים:

• וְזֶה שֶׁאָמְרוּ רַבּוֹתֵינוּ זִכְרוֹנָם לִבְרָכָה, כְּתִיב "עַד שָׁמַיִם חַסְדֶּךָ" וּכְתִיב "מֵעַל שָׁמַיִם חַסְדֶּךָ", לֹא קַשְׁיָא, כָּאן בְּעוֹסְקִים לִשְׁמָהּ, כָּאן בְּעוֹסְקִים שֶׁלֹּא לִשְׁמָהּ (פסחים נ' ע"ב).

- הַיְנוּ, שֶׁהָעוֹסֵק בַּתּוֹרָה שֶׁלֹּא לִשְׁמָהּ אִם כִּי וַדַּאי שֶׁגַּם הוּא מְרֻצֶּה לְפָנָיו יִתְבָּרַךְ
  □ אַף אִם כַּוָּנָתוֹ לְשֵׁם אֵיזֶה פְּנִיָּה שֶׁתִּהְיֶה רַק אִם אֵינוֹ לְקַנְטוּר חַס וְשָׁלוֹם וְכָל שֶׁכֵּן אִם אֵינוֹ מְכֻוָּן לְשׁוּם פְּנִיָּה, רַק לְפִי שֶׁהֻרְגַּל בְּכָךְ
  □ כִּי מִתּוֹךְ כָּךְ יָבֹא לְמַדְרֵגָה לִשְׁמָהּ כַּיָּדוּעַ מִמַּאֲמָרָם זִכְרוֹנָם לִבְרָכָה
  □ עִם כָּל זֶה, עֲדַיִן לֹא נִתְקַדֵּשׁ וְנִתְעַלָּה, שֶׁיִּהְיֶה הַנְהָגָתוֹ יִתְבָּרַךְ אִתּוֹ בְּכָל עִנְיָנָיו לְמַעְלָה מִכֹּחוֹת הַטִּבְעִיִּים
  □ לָכֵן כְּתִיב בֵּיהּ רַק "עַד שָׁמַיִם", הַיְנוּ עַד הַכֹּחוֹת הַטִּבְעִיִּים הַקְּבוּעִים בַּשָּׁמַיִם, וְלֹא לְמַעְלָה מֵהֶם.
- אֲבָל עַל הָעוֹסֵק בָּהּ לִשְׁמָהּ
  □ אָמַר "מֵעַל שָׁמַיִם", רוֹצֶה לוֹמַר, שֶׁכָּל הַנְהָגוֹתָיו יִתְבָּרַךְ עִמּוֹ רַק לְמַעְלָה מֵהוֹרָאַת כֹּחוֹת הַטִּבְעִיִּים:

• וְזֶה שֶׁכָּתוּב בְּרַעְיָא מְהֵימְנָא פִּנְחָס רט"ז ב', תָּא חֲזֵי, כָּל בְּרִיָּן דְּעַלְמָא, קֹדֶם

---

293 This ties back to the ideas presented in the First Gateway which describe how one's actions have supernal consequences of creation or destruction (e.g., G1:04).
294 Pesachim 50b.
295 Tehillim 57:11.
296 Tehillim 108:5.
297 Pesachim 50b and Sotah 22b: One should always be involved with Torah and Mitzvot even if not *for its sake* as through this involvement one will come to perform them *for its sake*.
298 Zohar Raya Mehemna III Pinchas 216b.

- Much more than this [one who studies Torah *for its sake*]
  - is given control over the natural order such that he can pass a decree over them and they will yield to all of his wishes
  - and fear of him is placed on all, as per Chazal:[299] "and he is given majesty and dominion"
  - for the 'Crown of God,'[300] the light of Torah, radiates from his head, and he is protected, so to speak, by the shadow of the Wings of the Shechina.
  - As per the Zohar:
    - R. Elazar began and said, "and I will place my words in your mouth and cover you with the shade of my hand." This verse means that one who is involved with words of Torah and whose lips articulate Torah, God protects him and spreads the Wings of the Shechina over him.[301]
    - Come and see how strong the power of Torah is and how it is superior over everything else, as all who are involved with Torah do not fear from the supernal or lower realms and do not fear from bad events in this world, because he holds on to the Tree of Life and eats from it daily, as the Torah teaches a person to walk in the path of truth and teaches him counsel. . . .[302]
    - R. Yossi began and said . . . How beloved is the Torah to God, as one who involves himself with Torah is loved in the supernal and lower worlds, and God listens to his words and does not forsake him either in this world or the future world.[303] Refer there.
    - . . . and when one invests effort in serving his Master and involves himself with Torah, how many guards are assigned to watch over him, and the Shechina resides over him, and all announce before him and say, "give honor to the image of the King." He is protected in this world, and happy is his lot in the next world.[304]

---

299 Mishna Avot 6:1.
300 Bamidbar 6:7.
301 Zohar III Tzav 35a quoting Yishayahu 51:16.
302 Zohar Introduction 11a; Zohar III VaEtchanan 260a.
303 Zohar II Beshalach 46a.
304 Zohar III Metzorah 52b.

דְּאִתְיְהִיבַת אוֹרַיְתָא לְיִשְׂרָאֵל הֲווֹ תַּלְיָן בְּמַזָּלָא כו', אֲבָל בָּתַר דְּאִתְיְהִיבַת אוֹרַיְתָא לְיִשְׂרָאֵל, אַפִּיק לוֹן מֵחִיּוּבָא דְּכֹכְבֵי וּמַזָּלֵי כו', וּבְגִין דָּא, כָּל הַמִּשְׁתַּדֵּל בָּאוֹרַיְתָא, בָּטִיל מִנֵּיהּ חִיּוּבָא דְּכָכְבַיָּא וּמַזָּלֵי, אִי אוֹלִיף לָהּ כְּדֵי לְקַיְּמָא פְּקוּדָהָא. וְאִי לָאו, כְּאִלּוּ לָא אִשְׁתַּדֵּל בָּהּ, וְלָא בָּטִיל מִנֵּיהּ חִיּוּבָא דְּכָכְבַיָּא וּמַזָּלֵי:

- **וְאַדְרַבָּה**
- הַכֹּחוֹת הַטִּבְעִיִּים מְסוּרִים אֵלָיו כַּאֲשֶׁר יִגְזוֹר אֹמֶר עֲלֵיהֶם, וּלְכָל אֲשֶׁר יַחְפֹּץ יִטֵּם
- וְאֵימָתוֹ מֻטֶּלֶת עַל כֻּלָּם, כְּמוֹ שֶׁאָמְרוּ בְּפֶרֶק הַתּוֹרָה (אבות ו, א) "וְנוֹתֶנֶת לוֹ מַלְכוּת וּמֶמְשָׁלָה".
- כִּי נֵר אֱלֹקָיו, אוֹר הַתּוֹרָה, מְאִירָה וּמַבְהֶקֶת עַל רֹאשׁוֹ, וְחוֹסֶה כִּבְיָכוֹל בְּצֵל כַּנְפֵי הַשְּׁכִינָה.
- כְּמוֹ שֶׁאָמְרוּ בַּזֹּהַר

- צַו ל"ה א', פָּתַח רַבִּי אֶלְעָזָר וְאָמַר "וָאָשִׂים דְּבָרַי בְּפִיךָ וּבְצֵל יָדִי כִּסִּיתִיךָ" (ישעיה נא, טז) כו', תָּנִינָן, כָּל בַּר נָשׁ דְּאִשְׁתַּדֵּל בְּמִלֵּי דְּאוֹרַיְתָא, וְשִׂפְוָתֵיהּ מְרַחֲשָׁן אוֹרַיְתָא, קוּדְשָׁא בְּרִיךְ הוּא חָפֵי עֲלֵיהּ, וּשְׁכִינְתָּא פָּרְשָׂא עֲלֵיהּ גַּדְפָּהָא, הֲדָא הוּא דִּכְתִיב "וָאָשִׂים דְּבָרַי בְּפִיךָ וּבְצֵל יָדִי כִּסִּיתִיךָ" כו'.

- וּבְהַקְדָּמַת הַזֹּהַר י"א א', וְכֵן הוּא בְּאוֹתוֹ הַלָּשׁוֹן בְּפָרָשַׁת וָאֶתְחַנַּן ר"ס ע"א, תָּא חֲזֵי, כַּמָּה הוּא חֵילָא תַּקִּיפָא דְּאוֹרַיְתָא, וְכַמָּה הוּא עִלָּאָה עַל כֹּלָּא, דְּכָל מַאן דְּאִשְׁתַּדֵּל בְּאוֹרַיְתָא, לָא דָּחִיל מֵעִלָּאֵי וְתַתָּאֵי, וְלָא דָּחִיל מֵעַרְעוּרִין בִּישִׁין דְּעָלְמָא, בְּגִין דְּאִיהוּ אָחִיד בְּאִילָנָא דְחַיֵּי, וְאָכִיל מִנֵּיהּ בְּכָל יוֹמָא, דְּהָא אוֹרַיְתָא אוֹלִיף לֵיהּ לְבַר נָשׁ בְּאֹרַח קְשׁוֹט, אוֹלִיף לֵיהּ עֵיטָא כו'.

- וּבְפָרָשַׁת בְּשַׁלַּח מ"ו א', ר"ִי פָּתַח כו', כַּמָּה חֲבִיבָא אוֹרַיְתָא קָמֵיהּ דְּקוּדְשָׁא בְּרִיךְ הוּא, דְּכָל מַאן דְּיִשְׁתַּדֵּל בְּאוֹרַיְתָא, רָחִים הוּא לְעֵילָּא, רָחִים הוּא לְתַתָּא, קוּדְשָׁא בְּרִיךְ הוּא אָצִית לֵיהּ לְמִלּוּלֵי, לָא שָׁבִיק לֵיהּ בְּהַאי עָלְמָא, וְלָא שָׁבִיק לֵיהּ בְּעָלְמָא דְּאָתֵי כו', עַיֵּן שָׁם.

- וּבְפָרָשַׁת מְצֹרָע נ"ב ב', וְכַד אִיהוּ אִשְׁתַּדֵּל בְּפוּלְחָנָא דְּמָארֵיהּ, וְלָעֵי בְּאוֹרַיְתָא, כַּמָּה נְטוֹרִין זְמִינִין לְקַבְּלֵיהּ לְנַטְּרָא לֵיהּ, וּשְׁכִינְתָּא שַׁרְיָא עֲלֵיהּ, וְכֹלָּא מַכְרְזֵי קָמֵיהּ וְאָמְרֵי, הָבוּ יְקָרָא לְדִיּוּקְנָא דְּמַלְכָּא, אִתְנְטִיר הוּא בְּעָלְמָא דֵין, וּבְעָלְמָא דְּאָתֵי, זַכָּאָה חוּלָקֵיהּ:

19. TORAH SCHOLARS CALLED BY GOD'S NAME AND ALL FEARFUL OF THEM

- [One involved with Torah] 'is called by the Name of God,'[305] as the Torah is entirely comprised of names of God,[306] as per Chazal:
  - From where do we know that the blessing recited before the reading of the Torah is a biblical requirement? From the verse "for I will call out the *Name of God*."[307]
  - The Shechina rests with one involved in Torah study, as per the verse "In every place where My *Name* is mentioned I will come to you and bless you."[308]
  - How beloved is the Torah to God, as in each place that words of Torah are heard, God together with all His Hosts listen, and God comes to reside with [the one reciting them] as per "In every place where My *Name* is mentioned [I will come to you and Bless you]."[309]
  - One who observes the ways of Torah and involves himself with it, is as if he involves himself with *The Holy Name*, as we have learned that the Torah is entirely the Name of God, and one who involves himself with it, is like one who involves himself with the Name of God, as the entire Torah is one Holy Name, a Supernal Name, a Name which incorporates all names, and one who removes one letter from it is as if he has damaged the Holy Name.[310]
  - R. Abba began: "All this came upon us, but we have not forgotten you ...," that we have not forgotten your words of Torah. From here we learn that one who forgets words of Torah and does not want to be involved in its study is as if he has forgotten God, as the entire Torah is the *Name of God*.[311]
  - For with the Torah, one who involves himself with it crowns himself with the crowns of the Name of God, for the Torah is the *Name of God*, and one who is involved with it is impacted and crowned with the Name of God, and as a result he knows the hidden pathways and the deep secrets.[312]
  - [Happy is Israel that God gave them the Holy Torah, which is the joy of All; it is the joy of God and the place where He chooses to be, as per "and I was then His Delight each day." The entire Torah is a

---

305 Devarim 28:10.
306 God's Name is entirely associated and equivalent with what is described as the Primordial Torah forming the matrix presentation of letter pairs in The World of The Malbush. For more details, see V2:03, "The World of The Malbush."
307 Berachot 21a quoting Devarim 32:3.

שער ד' - פרק י"ט

- וְשֵׁם ה' נִקְרָא עָלָיו, כִּי הַתּוֹרָה כֻּלָּהּ שְׁמוֹתָיו שֶׁל הַקָּדוֹשׁ בָּרוּךְ הוּא, כְּמַאַמְרָם זִכְרוֹנָם לִבְרָכָה

- "מִנַּיִן לְבִרְכַּת הַתּוֹרָה לְפָנֶיהָ מִן הַתּוֹרָה, שֶׁנֶּאֱמַר (דברים לב, ג) "כִּי שֵׁם ה' אֶקְרָא" וְגוֹ' (ברכות כא, א).

- וְכֵן לָמְדוּ (שם ו, א), שֶׁהָעוֹסֵק בַּתּוֹרָה שְׁכִינָה שְׁרוּיָה עִמּוֹ, דִּכְתִיב (שמות כ, כא) "בְּכָל הַמָּקוֹם אֲשֶׁר אַזְכִּיר אֶת שְׁמִי אָבוֹא אֵלֶיךָ וּבֵרַכְתִּיךָ" כוּ'.

- וּבַזֹּהַר בַּמִּדְבָּר קי"ח א', כַּמָּה חֲבִיבָא אוֹרַיְתָא קַמֵּיהּ קוּדְשָׁא בְּרִיךְ הוּא, דְּהָא בְּכָל אֲתַר דְּמִלֵּי דְאוֹרַיְתָא אִשְׁתְּמָעוּ, קוּדְשָׁא בְּרִיךְ הוּא וְכָל חַיָּילִין דִּילֵיהּ כֻּלְּהוּ צַיְּתִין לְמִלּוּלֵיהּ, וְקוּדְשָׁא בְּרִיךְ הוּא אָתֵי לְדַיָּירָא עִמֵּיהּ, הֲדָא הוּא דִכְתִיב "בְּכָל הַמָּקוֹם אֲשֶׁר אַזְכִּיר אֶת שְׁמִי" וְגוֹ'.

- וּבְפָרָשַׁת מִשְׁפָּטִים קכ"ד א', דְּכָל מַאן דְּנָטַר אָרְחֵי דְאוֹרַיְתָא וְאִשְׁתַּדַּל בָּהּ, כְּמַאן דְּאִשְׁתַּדַּל בִּשְׁמָא קַדִּישָׁא, דְּתָנֵינָן, אוֹרַיְתָא כֻּלָּהּ שְׁמָא דְקוּדְשָׁא בְּרִיךְ הוּא, וּמַאן דְּמִשְׁתַּדַּל בָּהּ כְּמַאן דְּמִשְׁתַּדַּל בִּשְׁמָא קַדִּישָׁא, בְּגִין דְּאוֹרַיְתָא כֻּלָּהּ שְׁמָא חַד קַדִּישָׁא אִיהִי, שְׁמָא עִלָּאָה, שְׁמָא דִכְלִיל כָּל שְׁמָהָן, וּמַאן דְּגָרַע אֶת חַד מִנָּהּ, כְּאִלּוּ עָבִיד פְּגִימוּתָא בִּשְׁמָא קַדִּישָׁא.

- וּבְפָרָשַׁת וַיִּקְרָא י"ג ב', רַבִּי אַבָּא פָּתַח, "כָּל זֹאת בָּאַתְנוּ וְלֹא שְׁכַחֲנוּךָ" כוּ' (תהלים מד, יח), וְלָא אַנְשִׁינַן מִלּוּלֵי אוֹרַיְתָךְ, מִכָּאן אוּלִיפְנָא, כָּל מַאן דְּאַנְשֵׁי מִלּוּלֵי אוֹרַיְתָא וְלָא בָעֵי לְמִלְעֵי בָהּ, כְּאִלּוּ אַנְשֵׁי לְקוּדְשָׁא בְּרִיךְ הוּא, דְּהָא אוֹרַיְתָא כֻּלָּהּ שְׁמָא דְקוּדְשָׁא בְּרִיךְ הוּא הֲוֵי.

- וְשָׁם דַּף י"ט סוֹף ע"א, דְּהָא אוֹרַיְתָא, מַאן דְּיִשְׁתַּדַּל בָּהּ מִתְעַטֵּר בְּעִטְרוֹי דִשְׁמָא קַדִּישָׁא, דְּהָא אוֹרַיְתָא שְׁמָא קַדִּישָׁא הוּא, וּמַאן דְּיִשְׁתַּדַּל בָּהּ, אִתְרְשִׁים וְאִתְעַטַּר בִּשְׁמָא קַדִּישָׁא, וּכְדֵין יָדַע אָרְחִין סְתִימִין וְרָזִין עֲמִיקִין כוּ'.

- וְכֵן אִיתָא בְּרֵישׁ פָּרָשַׁת שְׁמִינִי

---

308 Berachot 6a quoting Shemot 20:21.
309 Zohar III Bamidbar 118a quoting Shemot 20:21.
310 Zohar II Mishpatim 124a.
311 Zohar III Vayikra 13b quoting Tehillim 44:18.
312 Zohar III Vayikra 19a.

single Holy *Name of God* as per "and I was then his *Amon*" don't read the word as *Amon*, but rather as *Uman*. . . .][313]
- [. . . and the Torah, which is the Holy *Name of God*, is concealed and revealed. . . .][314]
- [. . . and there is no word in the Torah which does not have the Supernal Holy *Name of God* written within it. . . .][315]
- [. . . for the Torah is all one *Name of God* and each letter of the Torah is bound to the Holy Name. . . .][316]
- [. . . the Torah which is the Holy *Name of God* is also concealed and revealed. . . .][317]
- [. . . for the Torah is all the *Name of God*. . . .][318]
- [. . . and anyone involved with the Torah is involved with the Holy *Name of God*. . . .][319]

- Therefore, this is an additional reason why Chazal state that God and the Torah are One, as He and His Name are One, as per:
  - The entire Torah is One single name, the actual Holy Name of God, happy is the portion of the one who merits it, as one who merits in Torah merits in the actual Holy Name of God. R. Yossi says, he directly merits in God as He and His Name are One.[320]
  - Therefore, one who fights with a Torah Sage is as if he fights with the One Who Spoke and brought the world into being, as per "they are Datan and Aviram . . . in their fight with God"[321]
- Therefore, when a person 'comes in the Name of God'[322] [i.e., a Torah Sage], all are fearful of and shaken by him, as per:
  - Then all the peoples of the world will see that the Name of God is proclaimed over you and they will revere you.[323]
  - "For he has yearned for Me and I will deliver him, I will elevate him because he knows My Name."[324] For he has absolutely yearned for God, so to speak, as mentioned above.
  - Come and see how beloved those involved with Torah are to God, that even at a time when judgment hangs over the world and permission is

---

313 Zohar III Shemini 35b quoting Mishlei 8:30. (See how this verse relates to The World of The Malbush in G4:10 and V2:03.)
314 Zohar III Acharei Mot 71b.
315 Zohar III Acharei Mot 72a.
316 Zohar III Acharei Mot 73a.
317 Zohar III Acharei Mot 75a.
318 Zohar III Emor 89b.
319 Zohar III Korach 176a.

- וּבְפָרָשַׁת אַחֲרֵי ע"א
- וְע"ב סוֹף ע"א
- וְע"ג א'
- וְע"ה א'
- וּבְפָרָשַׁת אֱמוֹר פ"ט ב'
- וּבְרֵישׁ פָּרָשַׁת קֹרַח, עַיֵּין שָׁם:

• וְלָכֵן, גַּם מִזֶּה הַטַּעַם אָמְרוּ, דְ"קוּדְשָׁא בְּרִיךְ הוּא וְאוֹרַיְתָא חַד", כִּי הוּא וּשְׁמֵיהּ חַד הוּא, וּכְמוֹ שֶׁאָמְרוּ

- בַּזֹּהַר יִתְרוֹ צ' ע"ב, וְאוֹרַיְתָא כֹּלָּא שְׁמָא חַד הֲוֵי, שְׁמָא קַדִּישָׁא דְקוּדְשָׁא בְּרִיךְ הוּא מַמָּשׁ, זַכָּאָה חוּלְקֵיהּ דְּמַאן דְּזָכֵי בָּהּ, מַאן דְּזָכֵי בְּאוֹרַיְתָא זָכֵי בִּשְׁמָא קַדִּישָׁא דְקוּדְשָׁא בְּרִיךְ הוּא מַמָּשׁ. רַבִּי יוֹסֵי אוֹמֵר בְּקוּדְשָׁא בְּרִיךְ הוּא מַמָּשׁ זָכֵי, דְּהָא הוּא וּשְׁמֵיהּ חַד הוּא.

- וְלָכֵן אָמַר בְּתַנָּא דְּבֵי אֵלִיָּהוּ, (רבה, פי"ח ד"ה ד"א לא תלך) שֶׁכָּל מִי שֶׁעוֹשֶׂה מְרִיבָה עַל תַּלְמִיד חָכָם, כְּאִלּוּ עוֹשֶׂה מְרִיבָה עַל מִי שֶׁאָמַר וְהָיָה עוֹלָם, שֶׁנֶּאֱמַר, (במדבר כו, ט) "הוּא דָתָן וַאֲבִירָם כו' בְּהַצֹּתָם עַל ה'":

• לָכֵן, כַּאֲשֶׁר הָאָדָם בָּא בְּשֵׁם ה', הַכֹּל יְרֵאִים וּמִזְדַּעְזְעִים מִמֶּנּוּ

- כְּמוֹ שֶׁכָּתוּב (דברים כח, י) "וְרָאוּ כָּל עַמֵּי הָאָרֶץ כִּי שֵׁם ה' נִקְרָא עָלֶיךָ וְיָרְאוּ מִמֶּךָּ"
- וּכְמוֹ שֶׁכָּתוּב (תהלים צא, יד) "כִּי בִי חָשַׁק וַאֲפַלְּטֵהוּ אֲשַׂגְּבֵהוּ כִּי יָדַע שְׁמִי". כִּי "בִי" חָשַׁק, בּוֹ יִתְבָּרַךְ מַמָּשׁ כִּבְיָכוֹל, כַּנַּ"ל.
- וּבְפָרָשַׁת בָּלָק ר"ב א', תָּא חֲזֵי כַּמָּה חֲבִיבִין אִינּוּן דְּמִשְׁתַּדְּלֵי בְּאוֹרַיְתָא קָמֵי קוּדְשָׁא בְּרִיךְ הוּא, דַּאֲפִלּוּ בְּזִמְנָא דְּדִינָא תַּלְיָא בְּעַלְמָא, וְאִתְיְהִיב

---

320 Zohar II Yitro 90b.
321 Eliyahu Rabba 18 quoting Bamidbar 26:9. Datan and Aviram fought with Moshe and Aharon and are considered as if they directly fought with God.
322 1 Shmuel 17:45.
323 Devarim 28:10.
324 Tehillim 91:14.

given to the Destroyer to destroy, that with respect to those involved with Torah, God commands [the Destroyer], saying to him: "When you siege a city" as a result of its many sins, I will command you in relation to the members of My Household: "Do not destroy its trees," this is the Torah scholar in the city who is its Tree of Life which bears fruit. "Its trees," these are those who gave counsel[325] to the people of the city ... and taught them the path that they should follow, and therefore, "do not destroy its trees by swinging an axe against them," that is by not including him [the Torah scholar] in the judgment and to not wield the blazing sword over him, "for the man is the tree of the field," this one [the Torah Sage] is called "man" who is known above and below ... and God commands all this for those who involve themselves with Torah.[326] Refer there at length.

20. SECRETS REVEALED TO AND SHECHINA RESTS UPON TORAH SAGES

- [The Torah scholar] is the precious son, one of the members of the King's Palace, one of the members of the King's Temple
    - who is given sole permission to search the stores of the Holy King at any time
    - and all the supernal gates are open to him.
    - As Chazal state:[327] One who involves himself with Torah out of difficulty ... R. Acha bar Chanina says, not even the Pargod is locked before him as per "and your Mentor shall no longer be concealed. . . ."[328]
    - He enters into the gates of the Holy Torah, to perceive and look with its inner light at the depths of its supernal secrets, as per:
        - And the secrets of Torah are revealed to him.[329]
        - And not only this, but matters which are hidden from mankind are revealed to him.[330]
        - R. Shmuel [bar Abba] said: I am familiar with the streets of Heaven (and in the Talmud the version is: the streets of Heaven are lit up for me).[331] Now, did Shmuel [acquire this knowledge] by going up

---

325 Play on words: "Eitzah" literally meaning "its trees" but also meaning "counsel."
326 Zohar III Balak 202a commenting on Devarim 20:19.
327 Sotah 49a and Yalkut Shimoni Yishayahu Remez 436 (sect. 30).
328 Yishayahu 30:20. Rashi on this verse interprets the word "Yikanef" as

רְשׁוּ לִמְחַבְּלָא לְחַבָּלָא, קוּדְשָׁא בְּרִיךְ הוּא פָּקִיד לֵיהּ עֲלַוְיְהוּ עַל אִנּוּן דְּקָא מִשְׁתַּדְּלֵי בְּאוֹרַיְתָא, וְהָכִי אָמַר לֵיהּ קוּדְשָׁא בְּרִיךְ הוּא "כִּי תָצוּר אֶל עִיר" (דברים כ, יט) בְּגִין חוֹבֵיהוֹן סַגִּיאִין כו', תָּא וְאַפְקִיד לָךְ עַל בְּנֵי בֵּיתִי, "לֹא תַשְׁחִית אֶת עֵצָהּ", דָּא תַּלְמִיד חָכָם דְּאִיהוּ בְּמָתָא, דְּאִיהוּ אִלָּנָא דְחַיֵּי, אִילָנָא דְיָהִיב אִבִּין. "אֶת עֵצָהּ", הַהוּא דְיָהִיב עֵיטָא לְמָתָא כו', וְאוֹלִיף לוֹן אוֹרְחָא דְיִתְכּוּן בָּהּ, וְעַל דָּא "לֹא תַשְׁחִית אֶת עֵצָהּ לִנְדֹּחַ עָלָיו גַּרְזֶן", לְנַדְחָא עֲלֵיהּ דִּינָא, וְלָא לְאוֹשָׁטָא עֲלֵיהּ חַרְבָּא מְלַהֲטָא כו', "כִּי הָאָדָם עֵץ הַשָּׂדֶה", דָּא אִקְרֵי אָדָם, דְּאִשְׁתְּמוֹדַע עֵילָּא וְתַתָּא כו', וְכָל דָּא, פָּקִיד קוּדְשָׁא בְּרִיךְ הוּא עַל אִנּוּן דְּמִשְׁתַּדְּלֵי בְּאוֹרַיְתָא כו'. עַיֵּין שָׁם בָּאֹרֶךְ:

שער ד' - פרק כ'

- וְהוּא הַבֵּן יַקִּיר, מִבְּנֵי פַּלְטְרִין דְּמַלְכָּא, מִבְּנֵי הֵיכָלָא דְּמַלְכָּא
  - אֲשֶׁר לוֹ לְבַדּוֹ הָרְשׁוּת נְתוּנָה, בְּכָל עֵת, לַחֲפֵשׂ בְּגִנְזֵי דְּמַלְכָּא קַדִּישָׁא
  - וְכָל הַשְּׁעָרִים עֶלְיוֹנִים פְּתוּחִים לְפָנָיו
- כְּמַאֲמָרָם זִכְרוֹנָם לִבְרָכָה (סוטה מ"ט א'), "כָּל הָעוֹסֵק בַּתּוֹרָה מִתּוֹךְ הַדְּחַק כו', רַבִּי אַחָא בַּר חֲנִינָא אוֹמֵר, אַף אֵין הַפַּרְגּוֹד נִנְעָל בְּפָנָיו, שֶׁנֶּאֱמַר (ישעיה ל, כ) "וְלֹא יִכָּנֵף עוֹד מוֹרֶיךָ".
- וְנִכְנָס בְּשַׁעֲרֵי הַתּוֹרָה הַקְּדוֹשָׁה, לְהַשִּׂיג וּלְהִסְתַּכֵּל בָּאוֹר הַפְּנִימִי, בְּעוּמְקֵי רָזִין עִלָּאִין דִּילָהּ, וּכְמוֹ שֶׁאָמְרוּ
  - בְּפֶרֶק הַתּוֹרָה (אבות ו, א) "וּמְגַלִּין לוֹ רָזֵי תּוֹרָה".
  - וְכֵן אָמְרוּ (ע"ז ל"ה ב') "וְלֹא עוֹד אֶלָּא שֶׁדְּבָרִים הַמְּכֻסִּין מִבְּנֵי אָדָם מִתְגַּלִּין לוֹ".
  - וּבְמִדְרַשׁ תְּהִלִּים (מזמור יט) אָמְרוּ עַל שְׁמוּאֵל, שֶׁאָמַר, מַכִּיר אֲנִי חוּצוֹת

"concealed," as in covered by the corner of one's garment. This verse is also referenced in G3:11. The Pargod relates to the veil over physicality which conceals our ability to directly perceive God.

329 Mishna Avot 6:1.
330 Avodah Zarah 35b.
331 Berachot 58b.

to Heaven? [No,] he acquired it by toiling in the wisdom of the Torah and learned from it what there is in the Heavens.[332]
- "The opening of my straight lips." Words which open up access to the inner chambers of Heaven.[333]
- Blessed is God who chose the words of the Sages and their students . . . just as they sit in the prayer and study halls and with any available time they study for the sake of Heaven with fear in their hearts and maintain words of Torah in their mouths, so too it is with God who correspondingly reveals to them the secrets of Torah in their mouths and hearts.[334]

- The spirit [of God also] permanently 'dwells securely with him,'[335] as per:
  - Torah Sages are preferable to prophets in every way, as the Holy Spirit only periodically rests on prophets; however, the Holy Spirit does not even momentarily leave Torah Sages and they know what is above and what is below and they have no desire to reveal it.[336]
  - When one has read Tanach, Mishna, Midrash, Halachot, Agadot, Talmud, and studied and analyzed them *for their sake* – the Divine Spirit immediately rests upon him as per "the Spirit of God Speaks within me . . . ."[337]
  - In general terms this is stated:
    - One who is involved with Torah study is raised . . .[338]
    - "If you have been abused – in raising yourself," meaning that one who abuses himself [by investing all his effort] with words of Torah is [ultimately] raised.[339]
  - To the extent that Chazal say that their level will be higher than the level of prophets as stated: "A Torah scholar is greater than a prophet"[340] as per the Zohar mentioned above and as explained in further detail:
    - Come and see the difference between those who study Torah and the faithful prophets, as those involved with Torah are always more important than the prophets; the reason for this is that they are on a higher level than the prophets, for those involved with

---

332 Midrash Tehillim 19:4.
333 Midrash Mishlei 8:6.
334 There are a number of similar quotations to this one in Eliyahu Rabba (including Parsha 3, 2 instances in Parsha 18, Parsha 25). The closest one to it appears to be in Parsha 18 however even this quotation does not close with the point that God correspondingly reveals secrets of Torah to Torah students. It is presumed that R. Chaim had a different edition.
335 Devarim 33:12.

הָרָקִיעַ כו', (וּבַשַׁ"ס (ברכות נח, ב) הַגַּרְסָא נְהִירִין לִי שְׁבִילֵי דִּרְקִיעָא כו'), וְכִי שְׁמוּאֵל עָלָה לָרָקִיעַ, אֶלָּא עַל יְדֵי שֶׁיָּגַע בְּחָכְמָתָהּ שֶׁל תּוֹרָה, לָמַד מִתּוֹכָהּ מַה שֶּׁיֵּשׁ בַּשְּׁחָקִים.

▫ וּבְמִשְׁלֵי רַבָּתָא (פָּרָשָׁה ח'), "וּמִפְתַּח שְׂפָתַי מֵישָׁרִים" (משלי ח, ו) דְּבָרִים שֶׁהֵם פּוֹתְחִין לָכֶם חַדְרֵי חֲדָרִים שֶׁבַּמָּרוֹם.

▫ וּבְתַנָּא דְּבֵי אֵלִיָּהוּ (סֵדֶר אֵלִיָּהוּ רַבָּא פֶּרֶק כה), בָּרוּךְ הַמָּקוֹם שֶׁבָּחַר בְּדִבְרֵי חֲכָמִים וּבְתַלְמִידֵיהֶם כו', כְּשֵׁם שֶׁהֵם יוֹשְׁבִים בְּבָתֵּי כְּנֵסִיּוֹת וּבְבָתֵּי מִדְרָשׁוֹת וּבְכָל מָקוֹם שֶׁפָּנוּי לָהֶם, וְקוֹרִין וְשׁוֹנִין לְשֵׁם שָׁמַיִם, וְיִרְאָה בְלִבָבָם, וּמַחֲזִיקִין דִּבְרֵי תוֹרָה עַל פִּיהֶם, כְּמוֹ כֵן הַקָּדוֹשׁ בָּרוּךְ הוּא יוֹשֵׁב כְּנֶגְדָּם, וּמְגַלֶּה לָהֶם סוֹדוֹת הַתּוֹרָה בְּפִיהֶם וּבְלִבָּבָם כו':

• וְרוּחַ קָדְשׁוֹ יִתְבָּרַךְ יִשְׁכֹּן לָבֶטַח עָלָיו תָּמִיד, כְּמוֹ שֶׁכָּתוּב

▫ בַּזֹּהַר שְׁמוֹת ו' ב', חַכִּימֵי עֲדִיפֵי מִנְּבִיאֵי בְּכֹלָּא, דְּהָא לִנְבִיאֵי — לְזִמְנִין שָׁרַת עֲלַיְהוֹן רוּחַ קוּדְשָׁא, וּלְזִמְנִין לָא, וְחַכִּימִין — לָא אַעֲדֵי מִנְּהוֹן רוּחַ קוּדְשָׁא אֲפִילּוּ רִגְעָא חֲדָא זְעֵיר, דְּיָדְעִין מַה דִּי לְעֵלָּא וְתַתָּא, וְלָא בָעוּ לְגַלָּאָה.

▫ וּבְתַנָּא דְּבֵי אֵלִיָּהוּ (סֵדֶר אֵלִיָּהוּ זוּטָא פֶּרֶק א), וְכֵיוָן שֶׁקָּרָא אָדָם תּוֹרָה נְבִיאִים וּכְתוּבִים, וְשָׁנָה מִשְׁנָה מִדְרָשׁ הֲלָכוֹת וְהַגָּדוֹת, וְשָׁנָה הַגְּמָרָא, וְשָׁנָה הַפִּלְפּוּל לִשְׁמָהּ, מִיָּד רוּחַ הַקֹּדֶשׁ שׁוֹרָה עָלָיו, שֶׁנֶּאֱמַר (שמואל ב, כג, ב) "רוּחַ ה' דִּבֶּר בִּי" כו'.

• וְדֶרֶךְ כְּלָל אָמְרוּ

▫ בְּפֶרֶק הַתּוֹרָה (אבות ו, ב), שֶׁכָּל הָעוֹסֵק בְּתַלְמוּד תּוֹרָה הֲרֵי זֶה מִתְעַלֶּה כו'.

▫ וְכֵן אִיתָא (בְּסוֹף פֶּרֶק הָרוֹאֶה ברכות סג, ב), "אִם נָבַלְתָּ בְּהִתְנַשֵּׂא" (משלי ל, לב), כָּל הַמְנַבֵּל עַצְמוֹ עַל דִּבְרֵי תוֹרָה מִתְנַשֵּׂא.

עַד שֶׁאָמְרוּ זִכְרוֹנָם לִבְרָכָה, שֶׁמַּדְרֵגָתָם לְמַעְלָה מִמַּדְרֵגַת הַנְּבִיאִים, כְּמוֹ שֶׁכָּתוּב (בבא בתרא יב, א) חָכָם עָדִיף מִנָּבִיא. וּכְמוֹ שֶׁכָּתוּב בַּזֹּהַר שְׁמוֹת הַנַּ"ל. וְיוֹתֵר מְבֹאָר הָעִנְיָן בְּפָרָשַׁת צַו ל"ה א'

▫ תָּא חֲזֵי, מַה בֵּין אִינּוּן דְּמִשְׁתַּדְּלֵי בְּאוֹרַיְיתָא לִנְבִיאֵי מְהֵימְנֵי, דְּאִינּוּן דְּמִשְׁתַּדְּלֵי

---

336 Zohar II Shemot 6b.
337 Eliyahu Zuta 1 quoting 2 Shmuel 23:2.
338 Mishna Avot 6:2.
339 Berachot 63b quoting Mishlei 30:32.
340 Bava Batra 12a.

Torah stand above in the place which is called "Torah," which is the source of existence of all of faith, but the prophets stand below in the place called "Netzach and Hod"; therefore, those involved with Torah are considered more important than prophets as they are higher than them as these stand above and these stand below . . . therefore, happy are those who are involved with Torah as they are on a higher level than all others.[341]

21. TORAH SAGES GREATER AFTER DEATH, AND ARE SUSTAINED BY STORED LIGHT

- Notwithstanding the tremendously awesome level of those who toil in Torah while still in this dark world, who use their holy spirit to perceive and look at the Supernal Light, nevertheless, Tzaddikim are incomparably greater after their death than during their lifetime[342]
   - since their pure soul 'is fully sated'[343] on Torah and Mitzvot and it 'returns to the house of its Father'[344] in the original holy and pure state in which it was given
   - and with the additional light of the Holy Torah and with 'his learning in his hand,'[345] all the gates [of Heaven] are opened before him and [the soul] 'rises and breaks through the firmaments . . .'[346] 'to be bound up with the bond of life with YHVH his God.'[347]
   - As per Chazal:[348] Lest one should say that since Moshe passed on to the next world that the crown of his radiant face has diminished in any way, the verse states: "and no further prophet in Israel will rise, like Moshe, with a fa*ce to face k*nowledge of God";[349] so just as the Supernal Facial Radiance is everlasting, so too is Moshe's facial radiance which entered with him into the next world . . . This does not only apply to Moshe, but to every Torah Sage who involved himself with Torah from his youth to old age and then died; in reality he did not die, but he has everlasting life as per "and the soul of my master is bound up with the bond of life with YHVH his God."[350] This equates the Torah Sage, the Tzaddik with God. Just as with God, His Name is Great and Blessed and has everlasting life, so too a Torah Sage who was involved with Torah throughout his life and died, is still alive and has everlasting life, and where is his soul? Under the Throne of Glory.

---

341 Zohar III Tzav 35a.
342 Chullin 7b.
343 Tehillim 123:4.

בְּאוֹרָיְתָא עֲדִיפֵי מִנְבִיאֵי בְּכָל זִמְנָא, מַאי טַעֲמָא, דְּאִנּוּן קַיְמֵי בְּדַרְגָּא עִלָּאָה יַתִּיר מִנְּבִיאֵי, אִנּוּן דְּמִשְׁתַּדְּלֵי בְּאוֹרָיְתָא קַיְמֵי לְעֵילָּא — בְּאַתְרָא דְּאִקְרֵי "תּוֹרָה", דְּהוּא קִיּוּמָא דְּכָל מְהֵימְנוּתָא, וּנְבִיאֵי קַיְמֵי לְתַתָּא — בַּאֲתָר דְּאִקְרֵי "נֶצַח וָהוֹד", עַל דָּא אִנּוּן דְּמִשְׁתַּדְּלֵי בְּאוֹרָיְתָא עֲדִיפֵי מִנְבִיאֵי, וְעִלָּאִין מִנְּהוֹן יַתִּיר, דְּאִלֵּין קַיְמִין לְעֵילָּא, וְאִלֵּין קַיְמִין לְתַתָּא כו', וְעַל דָּא זַכָּאִין אִנּוּן דְּמִשְׁתַּדְּלֵי בְּאוֹרָיְתָא, דְּאִנּוּן בְּדַרְגָּא עִלָּאָה יַתִּיר עַל כּוֹלָּא כו':

שער ד' - פרק כ"א

- וְאִם כָּל כָּךְ נִפְלָאָה מַדְרֵגָתָם שֶׁל עוֹמְלֵי תוֹרָה, גַּם בְּעוֹדָם בְּזֶה הָעוֹלָם הֶחָשׁוּךְ, לְהַשִּׂיג וּלְהִסְתַּכֵּל בְּרוּחַ קָדְשָׁם בָּאוֹר הָעֶלְיוֹן, גְּדוֹלִים צַדִּיקִים בְּמִיתָתָן יוֹתֵר מִבְּחַיֵּיהֶם (חולין ז, ב) לְאֵין עֲרֹךְ.

◦ אַחַר אֲשֶׁר נִשְׁמָתוֹ הַטְּהוֹרָה רַבַּת שֶׁבְעָה לָהּ תּוֹרָה וּמִצְוֹת, וְהִיא שָׁבָה אֶל בֵּית אָבִיהָ מְקֻדֶּשֶׁת וּמְטֹהָרָה כַּאֲשֶׁר נִתָּנָה

◦ וּבִיתְרוֹן אוֹר הַתּוֹרָה הַקְּדוֹשָׁה תַּלְמוּדוֹ בְּיָדוֹ, כָּל הַשְּׁעָרִים נִפְתָּחִים לְפָנָיו, וְסָלִיק וּבָקַע רְקִיעִין כו', וְצָרוּר בִּצְרוֹר הַחַיִּים אֶת ה' אֱלֹהָיו יִתְבָּרֵךְ שְׁמוֹ.

◦ וּבְתַנָּא דְּבֵי אֵלִיָּהוּ (סֵדֶר אֵלִיָּהוּ רַבָּא פֶּרֶק ד) אָמַר, וְשֶׁמָּא תֹּאמַר הוֹאִיל וְנִכְנַס מֹשֶׁה לְבֵית עוֹלָמוֹ, שֶׁמָּא בָּטֵל מִמֶּנּוּ אוֹתוֹ הַכֶּתֶר שֶׁל מְאוֹר פָּנִים, תַּלְמוּד לוֹמַר (דברים לד, י) "וְלֹא קָם נָבִיא עוֹד בְּיִשְׂרָאֵל כְּמֹשֶׁה אֲשֶׁר יְדָעוֹ ה', פָּנִים אֶל פָּנִים", מַה אוֹר פָּנִים שֶׁלְּמַעְלָה קַיָּם לְעוֹלָם וּלְעוֹלְמֵי עוֹלָמִים, כָּךְ מְאוֹר פָּנָיו שֶׁל מֹשֶׁה נִכְנַס עִמּוֹ לְבֵית עוֹלָמוֹ כו'. וְלֹא מֹשֶׁה בִּלְבַד, אֶלָּא כָּל תַּלְמִיד חָכָם שֶׁעוֹסֵק בַּתּוֹרָה מִקַּטְנוּתוֹ וְעַד זִקְנוּתוֹ, וּמֵת, בֶּאֱמֶת לֹא מֵת, אֶלָּא הוּא עֲדַיִן בַּחַיִּים לְעוֹלָם וּלְעוֹלְמֵי עוֹלָמִים, שֶׁנֶּאֱמַר (שמו"א כה, כט) "וְהָיְתָה נֶפֶשׁ אֲדֹנִי צְרוּרָה בִּצְרוֹר הַחַיִּים אֶת ה' אֱלֹהֶיךָ", מַקִּישׁ הַתַּלְמִיד חָכָם הַצַּדִּיק אֶל אֱלֹקִים, מָה אֱלֹקִים, יְהֵא שְׁמוֹ הַגָּדוֹל מְבֹרָךְ — חַי וְקַיָּם כו', כָּךְ תַּלְמִיד

---

344 Vayikra 22:13.
345 As per Pesachim 50a, Moed Katan 28a, Ketubbot 77b, Bava Batra 10b.
346 Zohar II Terumah 146b.
347 1 Shmuel 25:29.
348 Eliyahu Rabba Parsha 4.
349 Devarim 34:10.
350 1 Shmuel 25:29.

- [After passing on from this world, the Torah Sage's] 'soul is sustained by the sparks'[351] of the hidden supernal subtle shining of light,[352] as per Chazal:
  - Every Torah scholar who involves himself with Torah out of difficulty . . . R. Avahu says he is even sustained by the radiance of the Shechina, as per the verse "and your eyes will see your Mentor."[353]
  - What is the meaning of "upon awakening I will be sated by Your Image" . . . these are Torah Sages who deprive themselves of sleep in this world and God sustains them with the radiance of the Shechina in the World to Come.[354]
  - R. Yehuda son of R. Simon expounded: One who blackens his face over Torah study in this world, God shines His Radiance upon him in the World to Come.[355]
- All this corresponds to the great level of the [Torah Sage's] involvement and tremendous attachment to the Holy Torah, as per Chazal:[356]
  - In respect of Tzaddikim, it says that "and his beloved ones are like the sun going out in its strength"[357]
  - this is in contrast to Angels of Service who don't have this quality [as their level is static and cannot change].
  - How beautiful is the ability of the Master of the House, [God], who beautifies His servants' crowns like His Own.
  - If you should say that one who has read and reviewed much and one who has read and reviewed little should have equal radiance in the future world, this is not so.
  - Blessed is the Makom, Blessed be He, before whom there is no favoritism, etc.
  - As it says elsewhere "a righteous one has an advantage over his fellow,"[358] etc.
  - that each individual [attains a level] according to his own way.
- This is the secret of the light which was created on the first day of Creation, which God stored away for Tzaddikim, as per Chazal:
  - R. Elazar said: "How great is the good which You stored [for those who fear You] . . . ."[359] Come and see, God created man in the world in such a way that he can perfect his service and his ways in order to merit the Supernal Light which God stored away for the Tzaddikim as per, "no eye [except Yours, O God,] has seen that which He will do

---

351 Yishayahu 58:11.
352 The reference to the subtle shining of light relates to a level so high and subtle that it cannot even be described by one of the standard world levels, as per G1:13:N13.

חָכָם שֶׁעָסַק בַּתּוֹרָה כָּל יָמָיו, וּמֵת, הֲרֵי הוּא בַּחַיִּים, וַעֲדַיִן לֹא מֵת, וְהוּא חַי לְעוֹלָם כו', וְהֵיכָן הוּא נִשְׁמָתוֹ, תַּחַת כִּסֵּא הַכָּבוֹד, עַד כָּאן:

- וְנַפְשׁוֹ תִּשְׂבַּע בְּצַחְצָחוֹת הָאוֹר עֶלְיוֹן הַגָּנוּז, כְּמַאֲמָרָם זִכְרוֹנָם לִבְרָכָה
  - "כָּל תַּלְמִיד חָכָם הָעוֹסֵק בַּתּוֹרָה מִתּוֹךְ הַדְּחַק כו', רַבִּי אַבָּהוּ אוֹמֵר, אַף מַשְׁבִּיעִין אוֹתוֹ מִזִּיו שְׁכִינָה, שֶׁנֶּאֱמַר (ישעיה ל, כ) "וְהָיוּ עֵינֶיךָ רוֹאוֹת אֶת מוֹרֶיךָ" (סוטה מט, א).
  - וּבְפֶרֶק קַמָּא דְּבָבָא בַּתְרָא (י, א) מַאי "אֶשְׂבְּעָה בְהָקִיץ תְּמוּנָתֶךָ" (תהלים יז, טו), אֵלּוּ תַּלְמִידֵי חֲכָמִים שֶׁמְּנַדְּדִין שֵׁנָה מֵעֵינֵיהֶם בָּעוֹלָם הַזֶּה, הַקָּדוֹשׁ בָּרוּךְ הוּא מַשְׂבִּיעָן מִזִּיו הַשְּׁכִינָה לָעוֹלָם הַבָּא.
  - וּבְפֶרֶק חֵלֶק (ק, א), דָּרִישׁ רַבִּי יְהוּדָה בְּרַבִּי סִימוֹן, כָּל הַמַּשְׁחִיר פָּנָיו עַל דִּבְרֵי תוֹרָה בָּעוֹלָם הַזֶּה, הַקָּדוֹשׁ בָּרוּךְ הוּא מַבְהִיק זִיווֹ לָעוֹלָם הַבָּא:
- וְהַכֹּל לְפִי עֵרֶךְ רֹב עִסְקוֹ וְנִפְלָאוֹת דְּבֵקוּתוֹ בַּתּוֹרָה הַקְּדוֹשָׁה, כְּמוֹ שֶׁכָּתוּב בְּתַנָּא דְּבֵי אֵלִיָּהוּ (סדר אליהו זוטא פרק יב)
  - אֵצֶל הַצַּדִּיקִים מַה נֶּאֱמַר בָּהֶם "וְאוֹהֲבָיו כְּצֵאת הַשֶּׁמֶשׁ בִּגְבֻרָתוֹ" (שופטים ה, לא)
  - מַה שֶּׁאֵין כֵּן בְּמַלְאֲכֵי הַשָּׁרֵת
  - מַה יָּפָה כֹּחוֹ שֶׁל בַּעַל הַבַּיִת, שֶׁהוּא מְיַפֶּה כֶּתֶר עֲבָדָיו כְּמוֹ כִּתְרוֹ.
  - וְאִם תֹּאמַר, מִי שֶׁקָּרָא הַרְבֵּה וְשָׁנָה הַרְבֵּה, וּמִי שֶׁקָּרָא וְשָׁנָה קִמְעָא, יִהְיֶה מְאוֹר פְּנֵיהֶם שָׁוִין כְּאֶחָד בִּמְאוֹר פָּנִים לָעוֹלָם הַבָּא, אֵינוֹ כֵּן
  - בָּרוּךְ הַמָּקוֹם בָּרוּךְ הוּא, שֶׁאֵין לְפָנָיו מַשּׂוֹא פָּנִים כו'
  - נֶאֱמַר בְּמָקוֹם אַחֵר (משלי יב, כו), "יָתֵר מֵרֵעֵהוּ צַדִּיק" כו'
  - אֶלָּא כָּל אֶחָד וְאֶחָד לְפִי דַּרְכּוֹ כו':
- וְהוּא הוּא סוֹד הָאוֹר שֶׁנִּבְרָא בְּיוֹם רִאשׁוֹן, שֶׁגְּנָזוֹ הַקָּדוֹשׁ בָּרוּךְ הוּא לַצַּדִּיקִים. וְכֵן אִיתָא
  - בַּזֹּהַר בְּרֵאשִׁית מ"ז א', רַבִּי אֶלְעָזָר פָּתַח, "מָה רַב טוּבְךָ אֲשֶׁר צָפַנְתָּ" כו'

---

353 Sotah 49a quoting Yishayahu 30:20. (This verse is also quoted in G3:11.)
354 Bava Batra 10a quoting Tehillim 17:15.
355 Sanhedrin 100a.
356 Eliyahu Zuta Parsha 12.
357 Shoftim 5:31.
358 Mishlei 12:26.
359 Tehillim 31:20.

for those who wait for Him,"[360] and how can a person merit this light? With the Torah.[361]

- "Who were cut down before their time whose foundation was swept away by a river" These are Torah scholars who "cut down" sleep from their eyes in this world; God reveals secrets to them in the World to Come as per "whose foundation was swept away by a river."[362]
  - These [secrets] are the hidden reasons for the Mitzvot which is the Supernal Light that has been hidden away.
- Therefore it [generally] states:[363] "All who involve themselves in Torah study *for its sake* merit many things"
  - but it does not specify what these things are!
  - It cannot be those things listed immediately following this statement as just after this it says "and not only this . . . ," implying that this is a separate statement in its own right
  - but it hints to the refinement and polishing of the soul with the hidden light, which angels on High, the Chayot and Holy Seraphim, prophets, and seers have all also never perceived the essence of
  - as per Chazal:[364] The prophecy of all the prophets only applies [to the days of Mashiach]; however, in relation to Torah Sages themselves "no eye [except Yours, O God,] has seen [that which He will do for those who wait for Him]."[365] This relates to the [future experience of] Eden and the matured wine about which the Talmud explains is the meaning of "no eye has seen . . ."
  - the hidden secret reasons of the Torah are one and the same as these things that have not yet been revealed, which the Mishna generally refers to as "many things," as it is not something that is capable of being perceived or explained.
- Chazal say:[366] Happy is the person who has words of Torah
  - and he sits and reads and reviews them in a modest and quiet way.
  - Where should this person reside? With God, as per "He dwells in the supernal hidden places, residing in the shadow of God."[367]
  - Just as they make themselves unique lone individuals in this world with no stranger with them, so too in the World to Come they reside with God alone.

---

360 Yishayahu 64:3.
361 Zohar I Bereishit 47a.
362 Chagiga 14a quoting Iyov 22:16.
363 Mishna Avot 6:1.
364 Berachot 34b.
365 Yishayahu 64:3.

(תהלים לא, כ). תָּא חֲזֵי, קוּדְשָׁא בְּרִיךְ הוּא בָּרָא לְבַר נָשׁ בְּעָלְמָא, וְאַתְקִין לֵיהּ לְמֶהֱוֵי שָׁלִים בְּפוּלְחָנָא, וּלְאַתְקָנָא אָרְחוֹי, בְּגִין דְּיִזְכֵּי לִנְהוֹרָא עִלָּאָה דְּגָנִיז קוּדְשָׁא בְּרִיךְ הוּא לְצַדִּיקַיָּא, כד"א (ישעיה סד, ג) "עַיִן לֹא רָאָתָה כו' יַעֲשֶׂה לִמְחַכֵּה לוֹ". וּבַמֶּה זָכָה בַּר נָשׁ לְהַהוּא נְהוֹרָא? בְּאוֹרַיְתָא כו'.

וְאָמְרוּ רַבּוֹתֵינוּ זִכְרוֹנָם לִבְרָכָה (חגיגה יד, א) "אֲשֶׁר קֻמְּטוּ וְלֹא עֵת נָהָר יוּצַק יְסוֹדָם" (איוב כב, טז), אֵלּוּ תַּלְמִידֵי חֲכָמִים, שֶׁמְּקַמְּטִין שֵׁנָה מֵעֵינֵיהֶם בָּעוֹלָם הַזֶּה, הַקָּדוֹשׁ בָּרוּךְ הוּא מְגַלֶּה לָהֶם סוֹד לָעוֹלָם הַבָּא, שֶׁנֶּאֱמַר "נָהָר יוּצַק יְסוֹדָם".

▪ וְהֵם הַטְּעָמֵי תּוֹרָה הַגְּנוּזִים, שֶׁהֵם הָאוֹר הָעֶלְיוֹן הַגָּנוּז:

• וְלָכֵן אָמַר בְּפֶרֶק הַתּוֹרָה (אבות ו, א) "כָּל הָעוֹסֵק בַּתּוֹרָה לִשְׁמָהּ, זוֹכֶה לִדְבָרִים הַרְבֵּה"

◦ סָתַם וְלֹא פֵּרֵשׁ מַה הֵם אוֹתָן הַדְּבָרִים.

◦ וְאִי אֶפְשָׁר לוֹמַר שֶׁהֵם הַדְּבָרִים שֶׁפֵּרֵט שָׁם אַחַר זֶה, שֶׁהֲרֵי אָמַר אַחַר זֶה "וְלֹא עוֹד" כו', מַשְׁמַע שֶׁהוּא מִלְּתָא בְּאַפֵּי נַפְשָׁא.

◦ אָמְנָם רָמַז לְהָעֵדוֹן וְצִחְצוּחַ הַנֶּפֶשׁ בָּאוֹר הַגָּנוּז, אֲשֶׁר גַּם כָּל מַלְאֲכֵי מַעְלָה וְחַיּוֹת וְשַׂרְפֵי קֹדֶשׁ וְשׁוּם נָבִיא וְחוֹזֶה — לֹא הִשִּׂיגוּהוּ כְּלָל עֶצֶם עִנְיָנוֹ.

◦ וּכְמַאֲמָרָם ז"ל (ברכות לד, ב) "כָּל הַנְּבִיאִים כֻּלָּן לֹא נִתְנַבְּאוּ אֶלָּא כו', אֲבָל תַּלְמִידֵי חֲכָמִים עַצְמָן "עַיִן לֹא רָאָתָה" כו', וְהוּא הָ"עֵדֶן" וְהַ"יַּיִן הַמְשֻׁמָּר בַּעֲנָבָיו", שֶׁאָמְרוּ שָׁם מַאי "עַיִן לֹא רָאָתָה" וכו'

◦ וְהַכֹּל אֶחָד, סוֹד הַטְּעָמֵי תּוֹרָה הַגְּנוּזִים שֶׁלֹּא נִתְגַּלּוּ עֲדַיִן, לָכֵן אָמַר סָתַם "לִדְבָרִים הַרְבֵּה", שֶׁאֵינוֹ דָּבָר הַמֻּשָּׂג לְאָמְרוֹ וּלְבָאֲרוֹ:

• וּבְתָנָא דְּבֵי אֵלִיָּהוּ (סדר אליהו רבה פרק כה) אָמַר, אַשְׁרֵי אָדָם שֶׁיֵּשׁ בּוֹ דִּבְרֵי תּוֹרָה וְהוּא יוֹשֵׁב וְקוֹרֵא וְשׁוֹנֶה בְּמָקוֹם צָנוּעַ וְסֵתֶר

◦ אֵצֶל מִי מְלִינִין אוֹתוֹ, הֱוֵי אוֹמֵר אֵצֶל הַקָּדוֹשׁ בָּרוּךְ הוּא, שֶׁנֶּאֱמַר (תהלים צא, א) "יֹשֵׁב בְּסֵתֶר עֶלְיוֹן בְּצֵל שַׁדַּי יִתְלוֹנָן"

◦ כְּשֵׁם שֶׁהֵם מְשִׂימִין עַצְמָן יְחִידִים בָּעוֹלָם הַזֶּה וְאֵין עִמָּהֶם זֶה, כְּמוֹ כֵן הֵם בָּעוֹלָם הַבָּא, הֵם יוֹשְׁבִין אֵצֶל הַקָּדוֹשׁ בָּרוּךְ הוּא לְבַדּוֹ כו':

---

366 Eliyahu Rabba Parsha 25.
367 Tehillim 91:1.

22. MINIMAL TORAH EXPOSURE SUBJECTS ONE TO WORLDLY CONTROL

- If, God forbid, our involvement with Torah study were to be weak, then we will, so to speak, minimize the Supernal Light which is brought down to all the worlds,[368] according to each person's level, and God's 'Soul will cry in hidden places'[369] so to speak, as per Chazal:
  - There are three over whom God cries: one of them being a person who is able to involve himself in Torah but does not do so.[370]
  - Why are these three tears shed? . . . Some say that one of them is shed over the avoidance of Torah study.[371]
- Woe is to the child who causes his father to *cry* every day. This concept of *crying* is one of the strengthening of judgment,[372] by reducing the Supernal Light which is the great mercy in the hidden worlds.[373]
- A person who has not yet seen the light of Torah in his days and never studied it cannot merit that Supernal Holiness will be manifest upon him or that he should have a purified soul.
  - As per the Zohar:[374] The fifth command . . . contains three commands . . . and one is to involve oneself with Torah . . . as when a person is not involved in Torah, he does not have a holy soul – the Supernal Holiness does not reside upon him.
  - Such a person is also 'sent away and abandoned,'[375] God forbid, to the powers of the 'Sitra Achara'[376] which are able to control him
    - as Chazal say:[377] Anyone who was able to study Torah but did not do so, God brings upon him ugly difficulties which disturb him as per "I was silent from good, though my pain was intense."[378]
  - He loses out on great good – for himself and for all of the world – for he has, God forbid, 'tipped the balance to the side of guilt.'[379]

---

368 See G1:03, where our actions modulate the level of God's light which is brought into this world. The presentation in the First Gateway of man's actions impacting on this world is relevant to understanding this chapter.
369 Yirmiyahu 13:17.
370 Chagiga 5b.
371 Chagiga 5b, from a few lines earlier in the same section as the previous quotation.
372 I.e., the increasing of Gevurah.
373 See G3:05, where Gevurah is explained to be that which restricts the ability to see God's manifestation in the worlds. The similarity to crying is that when one cries the tears restrict one's vision.
374 Zohar Introduction 12b, as already quoted in G4:15.
375 Yishayahu 27:10.

שער ד' - פרק כ"ב

- וְאִם חַס וְשָׁלוֹם אֲנַחְנוּ עוֹסְקִים בָּהּ בְּרִפְיוֹן, כִּבְיָכוֹל מִתְמַעֵט שֶׁפַע הָאוֹר עֶלְיוֹן בְּכָל הָעוֹלָמוֹת, כָּל אֶחָד לְפִי עֶרְכּוֹ. וּבַמִּסְתָּרִים תִּבְכֶּה נַפְשׁוֹ יִתְבָּרַךְ כִּבְיָכוֹל, כְּמוֹ שֶׁאָמְרוּ רַבּוֹתֵינוּ זִכְרוֹנָם לִבְרָכָה
  - שְׁלֹשָׁה הַקָּדוֹשׁ בָּרוּךְ הוּא בּוֹכֶה עֲלֵיהֶם, וְחָשִׁיב חַד מִנְּהוֹן עַל מִי שֶׁאֶפְשָׁר לוֹ לַעֲסֹק בַּתּוֹרָה וְאֵינוֹ עוֹסֵק (חגיגה ה' ב').
  - וְכֵן אָמְרוּ שָׁם שְׁלֹשָׁה דְּמָעוֹת הַלָּלוּ לָמָּה כוּ', וְאִיכָּא דְּאָמְרֵי אַחַת עַל בִּטּוּל תּוֹרָה:

- וְאוֹי לוֹ לַבֵּן הַמּוֹרִיד דִּמְעוֹת אָבִיו בְּכָל יוֹם. וְעִנְיַן זֹאת הַבְּכִיָּה, הוּא הִתְגַּבְּרוּת הַדִּין, בְּהִתְמַעֲטוּת הָאוֹר עֶלְיוֹן — שֶׁהֵם הָרַחֲמִים הַגְּדוֹלִים בָּעוֹלָמוֹת הַנִּסְתָּרִים:

- וְהָאָדָם אֲשֶׁר עֲדַיִן לֹא רָאָה אוֹר הַתּוֹרָה מִיָּמָיו, וְלֹא עָסַק בָּהּ מֵעוֹלָם, אֵינוֹ זוֹכֶה כְּלָל שֶׁתִּשְׁרֶה עָלָיו קְדֻשָּׁה הָעֶלְיוֹנָה, וְאֵינוֹ זוֹכֶה לְנֶפֶשׁ טְהוֹרָה.
  - כְּמוֹ שֶׁכָּתוּב בְּהַקְדָּמַת הַזֹּהַר י"ב ב', פְּקוּדָא חֲמִישָׁאָה כו', בְּהַאי קְרָא אִית בֵּיהּ תְּלַת פְּקוּדִין, חַד לְמִלְעֵי בְּאוֹרַיְתָא כו', דְּכַד בַּר נָשׁ לָא אִתְעַסַּק בְּאוֹרַיְתָא, לֵית לֵיהּ נַפְשָׁא קַדִּישָׁא, קְדֻשָּׁה דִּלְעֵילָא לָא שַׁרְיָא עֲלוֹי. כו'.
  - וְגַם הוּא מְשֻׁלָּח וְנֶעֱזָב חַס וְשָׁלוֹם לְכֹחוֹת הַדִּין שֶׁל הַסִּטְרָא אָחֳרָא שֶׁיִּהְיוּ יְכוֹלִין לִשְׁלֹט עָלָיו.
  - כְּמוֹ שֶׁאָמְרוּ רַבּוֹתֵינוּ זִכְרוֹנָם לִבְרָכָה בְּפֶרֶק קַמָּא דִּבְרָכוֹת (ה, א) שֶׁכָּל מִי שֶׁאֶפְשָׁר לוֹ לַעֲסֹק בַּתּוֹרָה וְאֵינוֹ עוֹסֵק, הַקָּדוֹשׁ בָּרוּךְ הוּא מֵבִיא עָלָיו יִסּוּרִין מְכֹעָרִין וְעוֹכְרִין אוֹתוֹ, שֶׁנֶּאֱמַר (תהלים לט, ג) "הֶחֱשֵׁיתִי מִטּוֹב וּכְאֵבִי נֶעְכָּר".
  - וּמְאַבֵּד טוֹבָה הַרְבֵּה, מִמֶּנּוּ וּמִכָּל הָעוֹלָם, כִּי הִכְרִיעַ חַס וְשָׁלוֹם אֶת עַצְמוֹ וְאֶת כָּל הָעוֹלָם לְכַף חוֹב

---

376 See p. 564, fn. 280 which comments on this term.
377 Berachot 5a.
378 Tehillim 39:3. "Good" here refers to Torah, so being silent from Torah results in intense pain, the *pain* relating to the whims of this physical world being in control.
379 An expression from Kiddushin 40b.

- As Chazal say:[380] "Listen [and be attentive]. Do not raise yourself in haughtiness"[381] – "Listen" to the words of Torah … "Do not raise yourself in haughtiness," do not raise the good from being able to be brought [i.e., descend] to the world.
- Similarly:[382] Punishment only comes to this world because of those illiterate in Torah.
- Therefore, if, God forbid, punishment comes to a particular person, a province, or even to a remote part of the world, 'it is caused by his [lack of Torah activity],'[383] God forbid – God should save us.

• One who was previously involved with Torah but has now, God forbid, ceased his involvement
  - he weakens the powers in the Supernal assembly, God forbid
  - and corrupts and confuses the arrangement of the worlds and of 'Holy Merkava'
  - and causes the hand of the Sitra Achara to strengthen, God should save us
  - and weakens and darkens, so to speak, the power of the supernal holiness of the presence of the Shechina of our strength, the Faith of Israel,[384] which permanently resides among us through proper Torah study.
  - As per the Zohar:[385] R. Chiya began and said: "It is a time to act for God; they have nullified your Torah";[386] all the while that Torah exists in the world and people are involved with it, God is happy, so to speak, with His Handiwork and all of the worlds, and the Heavens and Earth continue to exist … but when Israel desist from their Torah involvement, His Strength is weakened, so to speak, and therefore "It is a time to act for God" for those Tzaddikim who remain have to redouble their strength by doing good deeds so that God can strengthen them … The reason for this is that "they have nullified the Torah" by the general population not involving themselves with it as they should … Similarly, when Israel are involved with Torah, the faith is corrected and adorned with appropriate perfection, but when Israel are not involved with Torah, it is not properly manifest, is incomplete, and without light. This is what is written: "It is a time to act." What does "to act" mean? … similarly, here it is a "time to act" [otherwise] it remains uncorrected and incomplete. What is the reason? Because "they have nullified your Torah" that Israel desisted from words of Torah in this world [Israel's involvement in Torah will determine if] at that "time" there is an increase or decrease [in the manifestation of faith and Shechina] for Israel.

נפש שער ד' - פרק כ"ב החיים

- כְּמַאֲמָרָם זִכְרוֹנָם לִבְרָכָה בִּדְבָרִים רַבָּה רֵישׁ פָּרָשָׁה ב': "שִׁמְעוּ וְאַל תִּגְבָּהוּ" (ירמיה יג, טו) שִׁמְעוּ לְדִבְרֵי תוֹרָה כו', "וְאַל תִּגְבָּהוּ", אַל תַּגְבִּיהוּ אֶת הַטּוֹבָה מִלָּבא לָעוֹלָם.

- וְכֵן אָמְרוּ בְּפֶרֶק קַמָּא דְּבָתְרָא (ח' ע"א) שֶׁאֵין פּוּרְעָנוּת בָּאָה לָעוֹלָם אֶלָּא בִּשְׁבִיל עַמֵּי הָאָרֶץ.

- וְאִם חַס וְשָׁלוֹם יָבֹא פּוּרְעָנוּת עַל אֵיזֶה אָדָם אוֹ מְדִינָה, אֲפִלּוּ בִּקְצֵה הָעוֹלָם, דִּין גַּרְמָא דִּילֵיהּ חַס וְשָׁלוֹם. הָרַחֲמָן יִתְבָּרַךְ שְׁמוֹ יַצִּילֵנוּ:

- וְאִם כְּבָר עָסַק בָּהּ וּפֵרֵשׁ הֵימֶנָּה חַס וְשָׁלוֹם
  - הוּא מַתִּישׁ חַס וְשָׁלוֹם כֹּחַ פָּמַלְיָא שֶׁל מַעְלָה
  - וּמִתְקַלְקְלִים וּמִתְבַּלְבְּלִים סִדְרֵי הָעוֹלָמוֹת וְהַמֶּרְכָּבָה הַקְּדוֹשָׁה
  - וְגָבְרָה יַד הַסִּטְרָא אָחֳרָא רַחְמָנָא לִיצְלָן
  - וּכְבִיָכוֹל מַחֲלִישׁ וּמַחְשִׁיךְ כֹּחַ הַקְּדֻשָּׁה הָעֶלְיוֹנָה שְׁכִינַת עֻזּוֹ אֱמוּנַת יִשְׂרָאֵל, הַשּׁוֹכֶנֶת בְּתוֹכֵנוּ תָּמִיד עַל יְדֵי עֵסֶק הַתּוֹרָה כָּרָאוּי:

- כְּמוֹ שֶׁכָּתוּב בַּזֹּהַר תְּרוּמָה קנ"ה ב', פָּתַח רַבִּי חִיָּא וְאָמַר "עֵת לַעֲשׂוֹת לַה' הֵפֵרוּ תּוֹרָתֶךָ" (תהלים קיט), בְּכָל זִמְנָא דְּאוֹרַיְתָא מִתְקַיְּמָא בְּעָלְמָא, וּבְנֵי נָשָׁא מִשְׁתַּדְּלִין בָּהּ, כִּבְיָכוֹל קוּדְשָׁא בְּרִיךְ הוּא חֲדִי בְּעוֹבָדֵי יְדוֹי, וַחֲדִי בְּעָלְמִין כֻּלְּהוּ, וּשְׁמַיָּא וְאַרְעָא קַיְמֵי בְּקִיּוּמַיְהוּ כו', וּבְשַׁעְתָּא דְיִשְׂרָאֵל מִתְבַּטְּלִין מֵאוֹרַיְתָא, כִּבְיָכוֹל תָּשַׁשׁ חֵילֵיהּ, וּכְדֵין "עֵת לַעֲשׂוֹת לַה'", אִנּוּן בְּנֵי עָלְמָא

---

380 Devarim Rabba Re'eh 4:2, playing on the word "haughty" (Tigbehu) and interpreting it as "raised" (Tagbihu).
381 Yirmiyahu 13:15.
382 Bava Batra 8a.
383 The word "Garma" means "bone." This expression is from Berachot 5b where R. Yochanan is reported to have carried around a bone (or a tooth) of his tenth child who died. According to Rashi it acted as a permanent reminder of his bereavement and difficulty. Here too, if one were to be aware of the great tragedies one may have caused, that awareness would act as a permanent reminder.

This expression is used in a different context in V2:08, p. 471, fn. 11.
384 The perception of the Shechina's residence is not directly or intellectually tangible but inherently exists via a Jew's soul which is a part of God (as per G1:05:No5). It is therefore called the "Faith of Israel."
385 Zohar II Terumah 155b.
386 Tehillim 119:126.

- Such a person distances himself, so to speak, from God as per the Zohar:[387] "When a person distances himself from Torah, he is distant from God," as God and Torah are One, as mentioned above.
- Divine protection of holiness is removed from him; he is then known and recognizable to the powers of [adverse] judgments which he brings upon himself enabling them to control him both during his lifetime [(and also after his lifetime as per G4:23)], as per:
  - [Anyone who was able to study Torah but did not do so, God brings upon him ugly difficulties which disturb him as per "I was silent from good, though my pain was intense."][388]
  - R. Tovi said in the name of R. Oshiya: One who weakens himself from words of Torah cannot stand on a day of difficulty as per "If you were weak in your day of difficulty, your strength will be restricted."[389]
  - The soul of one who protects the Torah is protected and the soul of one who does not protect it [is not protected].[390]
  - God says to Israel: If you keep the Torah, I will keep you as per "If you keep, you will be kept. . . ."[391]
  - At the time when the voice of Yaakov is heard in the prayer and study halls, the hand of Esav has no power over them, but when the voice of Yaakov is weak, the hand of Esav takes control – God should save us.[392]
  - The sword and the book are given wrapped together . . . God says if you keep what is written in the Book [i.e., the Torah] you are saved from the sword, and if not [you will be killed by the sword].[393]

---

387 Zohar III Vayikra 21a.
388 Berachot 5a quoting Tehillim 39:3, as quoted earlier in this chapter.
389 Midrash Mishlei 24:10 and Berachot 63a quoting Mishlei 24:10.
390 Menachot 99b.
391 Midrash Tehillim 17:8 quoting Devarim 11:22.
392 Bereishit Rabba 65:20.
393 Vayikra Rabba Bechukotai 35:6 and Devarim Rabba Re'eh 4:2.

צַדִּיקַיָּא דְּאִשְׁתָּאֲרוּן, אִית לוֹן לְחַגְרָא חַרְצִין וּלְמֶעֱבַד עוֹבָדִין דְּכַשְׁרָאן, בְּגִין דְּקוּדְשָׁא בְּרִיךְ הוּא יִתְתְּקַף בְּהוּ בְּצַדִּיקַיָּא כוּ', מַאי טַעְמָא, בְּגִין דְּ"הֵפֵרוּ תוֹרָתֶךָ", וְלָא מִשְׁתַּדְלֵי בָּהּ בְּנֵי עָלְמָא כְּדְקָא יָאוֹת כוּ', וְהָכִי בְּזִמְנָא דְּיִשְׂרָאֵל מִשְׁתַּדְּלָן בְּאוֹרַיְתָא, הַהוּא עֵת, רָזָא מְהֵימְנוּתָא קַדִּישָׁא מִתְתַּקְּנָא בְּתִקּוּנְהָא, וּמִתְקַשְּׁטָא בִּשְׁלֵימוּתָא כְּדְקָא יָאוֹת, וּבְזִמְנָא דְּיִשְׂרָאֵל מִתְבַּטְּלֵי מֵאוֹרַיְתָא, הַהוּא עֵת לָאו אִיהִי בְּתִקּוּנְהָא, וְלָא אִשְׁתְּכַח בִּשְׁלִימוּ וְלָא בִּנְהוֹרָא, הָא דִכְתִיב "עֵת לַעֲשׂוֹת לַה'" מַאי "לַעֲשׂוֹת" כוּ', אוֹף הָכִי "עֵת לַעֲשׂוֹת", אִשְׁתְּאַר בְּלָא תִּקּוּנָא וּבְלָא שְׁלִימוּ, מַאי טַעְמָא, מִשּׁוּם דְּ"הֵפֵרוּ תוֹרָתֶךָ", בְּגִין דְּאִתְבַּטְּלוּ יִשְׂרָאֵל לְתַתָּא מִפִּתְגָּמֵי אוֹרַיְתָא, בְּגִין דְּהַהוּא עֵת הָכִי קַיְּמָא, אוֹ סָלְקָא אוֹ נַחֲתָא בְּגִינְהוֹן דְּיִשְׂרָאֵל:

∘ וְכִבְיָכוֹל הוּא מִתְרַחֵק מִמֶּנּוּ יִתְבָּרַךְ, כְּמוֹ שֶׁכָּתוּב בַּזֹּהַר וַיִּקְרָא כ"א א', כַּד בַּר נַשׁ אִתְרְחִיק מֵאוֹרַיְתָא, רָחִיק הוּא מִקּוּדְשָׁא בְּרִיךְ הוּא, כִּי קוּדְשָׁא בְּרִיךְ הוּא וְאוֹרַיְתָא חַד, כַּנַּ"ל:

∘ וְהַשְּׁמִירָה הָעֶלְיוֹנָה שֶׁל הַקְּדֻשָּׁה סָר מֵעָלָיו, וְאִשְׁתְּמוֹדַע וְנִכָּר לְכֹחוֹת הַדִּין אֲשֶׁר הִגְבִּיר בְּעַצְמוֹ, שֶׁיּוּכְלוּ לִשְׁלֹט עָלָיו, בֵּין בְּחַיָּיו, כְּמוֹ שֶׁאָמְרוּ רַבּוֹתֵינוּ זִכְרוֹנָם לִבְרָכָה

▫ בְּפֶרֶק קַמָּא דִּבְרָכוֹת (ה, א) הַמּוּבָא לְעֵיל

▫ וְכֵן אִיתָא שָׁם (סג, א), וּבְמִשְׁלֵי רַבָּתָא רֵישׁ פָּרָשָׁה כ"ה, אָמַר רַבִּי טוֹבִי ב"ר אַשְׁיָה, כָּל הַמְרַפֶּה עַצְמוֹ מִדִּבְרֵי תוֹרָה אֵינוֹ יָכוֹל לַעֲמֹד בְּיוֹם צָרָה, שֶׁנֶּאֱמַר "הִתְרַפִּיתָ בְּיוֹם צָרָה צַר כֹּחֶכָה" (משלי כד, י).

▫ וּבְפֶרֶק שְׁתֵּי הַלֶּחֶם (מנחות צט, ב) כָּל הַמְשַׁמֵּר אֶת הַתּוֹרָה נִשְׁמָתוֹ מִשְׁתַּמֶּרֶת, וְכָל שֶׁאֵינוֹ מְשַׁמֵּר אֶת הַתּוֹרָה כוּ'.

▫ וְאָמְרוּ בְּמִדְרַשׁ תְּהִלִּים מִזְמוֹר י"ז, "אָמַר הַקָּדוֹשׁ בָּרוּךְ הוּא לְיִשְׂרָאֵל, אִם שְׁמַרְתָּ אֶת הַתּוֹרָה אֲנִי אֶשְׁמֹר אוֹתְךָ, שֶׁנֶּאֱמַר (דברים יא, כב) "אִם שָׁמֹר תִּשְׁמְרוּן" כוּ'.

▫ וְכַיָּדוּעַ גַּם כֵּן מַאֲמָרָם זִכְרוֹנָם לִבְרָכָה בִּבְרֵאשִׁית רַבָּה פָּרָשָׁה ס"ה, בִּזְמַן שֶׁהַקּוֹל קוֹל יַעֲקֹב בְּבָתֵּי כְנֵסִיּוֹת וּבְבָתֵּי מִדְרָשׁוֹת אֵין יְדֵי עֵשָׂו שׁוֹלְטוֹת, הֵקַל קוֹל יַעֲקֹב, אָז יָדָיו שׁוֹלְטוֹת רַחֲמָנָא לִצְלָן.

▫ וְאָמְרוּ בְּוַיִּקְרָא רַבָּה פָּרָשָׁה ל"ה, וּדְבָרִים רַבָּה רֵישׁ פָּרָשָׁה ב', הַסַּיִף וְהַסֵּפֶר

- When is a government able to decree a successful decree [against Israel]? When Israel throw words of Torah to the ground. This is what is written "*Tzava*/A time will be set to [discontinue] the Tamid sacrifice *BePesha*/because of sin";[394] *Tzava* relates to governments . . . *BePesha* is the sin of neglect of Torah. All the while that Israel throw words of Torah to the ground, the government will place successful decrees as [the verse continues] "and *truth* will be thrown to the ground," where *truth* is Torah; if you throw words of Torah to the ground, then immediately the government will succeed as [the verse continues] "and it will achieve and prosper."[395]
- We find that God overlooks the sins of idol worship, illicit relationships, and murder, but does not overlook the despising of Torah, as it says: "Why was the land destroyed?" It does not mention idol worship, illicit relationships, and murder but says "God said because they forsook my Torah."[396]
- Come and see how great is the power of sin of the neglect of Torah as Jerusalem and the Temple were only destroyed as a result of the sin of the neglect of the Torah.[397]
- It is impossible for Israel to live if they are not involved with Torah study, and it is because Israel separates themselves from Torah that their enemies therefore come upon them . . . Similarly, you will find that enemies only come when desisting from Torah study.[398] Refer there.

23. LACK OF TORAH INVOLVEMENT PREVENTS ENTRY TO WORLD TO COME

- Similarly after passing on from this world, Chazal say:
  - All who weaken their commitment to words of Torah fall into Gehinom.[399]
  - All who separate themselves from Torah study and involve themselves in mundane talk are consumed by fire.[400]

---

394 Daniel 8:12, referring to a government decree to discontinue the Tamid sacrifice.
395 Eicha Rabba Introduction 2, Eliyahu Rabba Parsha 18.
396 Continuation to Eicha Rabba Introduction 2 quoting Yirmiyahu 9:11 and 9:12.
397 Eliyahu Rabba Parsha 18.
398 Midrash Tanchuma Beshalach 25.
399 Bava Batra 79a. The standard version of this text reads: "All who separate themselves from words of Torah fall in Gehinom."

נִתְּנוּ מְבָרְכִין כו', אָמַר הַקָּדוֹשׁ בָּרוּךְ הוּא, אִם שְׁמַרְתֶּם מַה שֶּׁכָּתוּב בַּסֵּפֶר, אַתֶּם נִצּוֹלִים מִן הַסַּיִף, וְאִם לָאו כו'.

▫ וּבִפְתִיחְתָּא אֵיכָה (אוֹת ב), וּבְתַנָּא דְבֵי אֵלִיָּהוּ (סֵדֶר אֵלִיָּהוּ רַבָּא פֶּרֶק יח), אֵימָתַי הַמַּלְכוּת גּוֹזֶרֶת גְּזֵירָה וּגְזֵרָתָהּ מַצְלַחַת, בְּשָׁעָה שֶׁיִּשְׂרָאֵל מַשְׁלִיכִין דִּבְרֵי תוֹרָה לָאָרֶץ, הֲדָא הוּא דִכְתִיב (דָּנִיֵּאל ח, יב) "וְצָבָא תִּנָּתֵן עַל הַתָּמִיד בְּפָשַׁע", אֵין "צָבָא", אֶלָּא מַלְכֻיּוֹת כו', "בְּפָשַׁע", בְּפִשְׁעָהּ שֶׁל תּוֹרָה, כָּל זְמַן שֶׁיִּשְׂרָאֵל מַשְׁלִיכִין דִּבְרֵי תוֹרָה לָאָרֶץ, הַמַּלְכוּת הִיא גּוֹזֶרֶת וּמַצְלַחַת, שֶׁנֶּאֱמַר (שָׁם) "וְתַשְׁלֵךְ אֱמֶת אַרְצָה וְעָשְׂתָה וְהִצְלִיחָה" וְגו', אֵין "אֱמֶת" אֶלָּא תוֹרָה כו', אִם הִשְׁלַכְתְּ דִּבְרֵי תוֹרָה לָאָרֶץ מִיָּד הִצְלִיחָה הַמַּלְכוּת הֲדָא הוּא דִכְתִיב (שָׁם) "וְעָשְׂתָה וְהִצְלִיחָה".

▫ וְאָמְרוּ שָׁם (בִּפְתִיחְתָּא אֵיכָה) עוֹד, מָצִינוּ שֶׁוִּתֵּר הַקָּדוֹשׁ בָּרוּךְ הוּא עַל עֲבוֹדָה זָרָה וְגִלּוּי עֲרָיוֹת וּשְׁפִיכוּת דָּמִים, וְלֹא וִתֵּר עַל מַאֲסָהּ שֶׁל תּוֹרָה, שֶׁנֶּאֱמַר (יִרְמְיָה ט, יא) "עַל מָה אָבְדָה הָאָרֶץ", "עַל עֲבוֹדַת כּוֹכָבִים וְגִלּוּי עֲרָיוֹת וּשְׁפִיכוּת דָּמִים" אֵין כְּתִיב כָּאן, אֶלָּא "וַיֹּאמֶר ה' עַל עָזְבָם אֶת תּוֹרָתִי".

▫ וּבְתַנָּא דְבֵי אֵלִיָּהוּ שָׁם, בֹּא וּרְאֵה כַּמָּה גָדוֹל כֹּחַ פִּשְׁעָהּ שֶׁל תּוֹרָה, שֶׁלֹּא חָרְבָה יְרוּשָׁלַיִם וְלֹא חָרַב בֵּית הַמִּקְדָּשׁ אֶלָּא בְּפִשְׁעָהּ שֶׁל תּוֹרָה, שֶׁנֶּאֱמַר כו'.

▫ וּבְתַנְחוּמָא בְּשַׁלַּח (אוֹת כה), כְּשֵׁם שֶׁאִי אֶפְשָׁר וְכו', כָּךְ אִי אֶפְשָׁר לְיִשְׂרָאֵל לִחְיוֹת אֶלָּא אִם כֵּן מִתְעַסְּקִין בְּדִבְרֵי תוֹרָה, וּלְפִי שֶׁפֵּרְשׁוּ יִשְׂרָאֵל מִדִּבְרֵי תוֹרָה לְפִיכָךְ הַשּׂוֹנֵא בָּא עֲלֵיהֶם כו', וְכֵן אַתְּ מוֹצֵא, שֶׁאֵין הַשּׂוֹנֵא בָּא אֶלָּא עַל יְדֵי רִפְיוֹן יָדַיִם מִן הַתּוֹרָה כו', עַיֵּן שָׁם:

שַׁעַר ד' - פֶּרֶק כ"ג

• וְכֵן אַחַר פְּטִירָתוֹ מִזֶּה הָעוֹלָם, אָמְרוּ,
  ○ כָּל הַמְרַפֶּה עַצְמוֹ מִדִּבְרֵי תוֹרָה נוֹפֵל בְּגֵיהִנָּם כו' (בָּבָא בַתְרָא עט, א).
  ○ וְאָמְרוּ שָׁם עוֹד, כָּל הַפּוֹרֵשׁ עַצְמוֹ מִדִּבְרֵי תוֹרָה, וְעוֹסֵק בְּדִבְרֵי שִׂיחָה, אֵשׁ אוֹכַלְתּוֹ כו'.

---

400 Bava Batra 79a. The standard version of this text reads "All who separate from words of Torah will be consumed by fire."

- "One who abandons reproof *Mat'eh*/goes astray." R. Alexandrai says: Any Torah scholar who forsakes words of Torah is as if he *Metaateah*/misleads the One Who spoke and brought the world into being, but not only this but since he forsook words of Torah in this world, God forsakes him in the World to Come.[401]
- R. Shimon said: Happy are those with a soul who have Torah who serve the Holy King; Woe to those wicked who did not merit to attach themselves with their Master and did not merit to have Torah, as one who did not merit in Torah, did not merit the levels of Ruach or Neshama[402] and his attachment is to the side of the evil blasphemers and he has no part in Holiness. Woe to him when he leaves this world as he is known to the evil blasphemers whose brazenness is as hard as of a dog, the messengers of the fire of Gehinom, who have no mercy on him.[403]
- In another section of Zohar[404] after describing at length the praise and greatness of one involved with Torah, both in this world and the next, it continues as follows:
  - Come and see that one who did not merit to involve himself with Torah in this world and he walks in darkness, when he departs from this world, they take him and enter him into the lower recesses of Gehinom where they will not have mercy on him, a place called the "pit of the raging waters of the slimy mud" as per "He raised me from the pit of the raging waters, from the slimy mud."[405] Therefore, it says about one who did not invest effort in Torah in this world and indulged in the filth of this world that "and they took him and threw him into the pit,"[406] this is Gehinom, a place where those that did not involve themselves with Torah are judged, "and the pit was empty," like he was empty, why was this? Because "there was no water in it."[407] Come and see how great is the punishment of Torah as Israel were only exiled from the Holy Land because they left and forsook the Torah. This is the meaning of "Who is the wise person who understands this; [that God Speaks to him and explains] why was the Land lost. And God said, because they forsook my Torah. . . ."[408]
- Not only this but when a person is brought before God [after leaving this

---

401 Midrash Mishlei 10:1 quoting Mishlei 10:17.
402 See First Gateway for details on the components of the soul including Ruach and Neshama.
403 Zohar III Vayikra 25b.
404 Zohar I Vayeshev 185a.

וּבְמִשְׁלֵי רַבָּתִי פָּרָשָׁה י' "וְעוֹזֵב תּוֹכַחַת מַתְעֶה" (משלי י, יז), אָמַר ר"א, כָּל תַּלְמִיד חָכָם שֶׁהוּא עוֹזֵב דִּבְרֵי תוֹרָה, מַעֲלִין עָלָיו כְּאִלּוּ מְתַעְתֵּעַ בְּמִי שֶׁאָמַר וְהָיָה הָעוֹלָם, וְלֹא עוֹד, אֶלָּא כֵּיוָן שֶׁעָזַב דִּבְרֵי תוֹרָה בָּעוֹלָם הַזֶּה, הַקָּדוֹשׁ בָּרוּךְ הוּא עוֹזְבוֹ לָעוֹלָם הַבָּא כו'.

וּבַזֹּהַר וַיִּקְרָא כ"ה ב', אָמַר רַבִּי שִׁמְעוֹן, זַכָּאִין אִנּוּן מָארֵי דְנִשְׁמָתָא, מָארֵי דְאוֹרָיְתָא, בְּנֵי פוּלְחָנָא דְמַלְכָּא קַדִּישָׁא, וַי לְאִנּוּן חַיָּבִין דְּלָא זַכָּאן לְאִתְדַּבְּקָא בְּמָארֵיהוֹן, וְלָא זַכָּאן בְּאוֹרָיְתָא, דְּכָל מַאן דְּלָא זָכֵי בְּאוֹרָיְתָא, לָא זָכֵי לֹא בְּרוּחַ וְלֹא בִּנְשָׁמָה, וְאִתְדַּבְּקוּתָא דִּדְהוֹן בְּהַהוּא סִטְרָא דְזַיְינִין בִּישִׁין, וְהַאי לֵית לֵיה חוּלְקָא דִקְדֻשָׁה, וַי לֵיה כַּד יִפּוֹק מֵהַאי עָלְמָא, דְהָא אִשְׁתְּמוֹדַע הוּא לְגַבֵּי אִנּוּן זַיְינִין בִּישִׁין, מָארֵי חֲצִיפוּתָא, תַּקִּיפֵי כְּכַלְבֵּי, שְׁלוּחֵי דְנוּרָא דְגֵיהִנָּם, דְּלָא מְרַחֲמָא עֲלַיְיהוּ כו'.

וּבְפָּרָשַׁת וַיֵּשֶׁב קפ"ה א', אַחַר שֶׁהֶאֱרִיךְ שָׁם בְּגֹדֶל שִׁבְחוֹ וּמַדְרֵגָתוֹ שֶׁל הָעוֹסֵק בַּתּוֹרָה, בָּעוֹלָם הַזֶּה וְעוֹלָם הַבָּא, אָמַר אַחַר זֶה

תָּא חֲזֵי, הַהוּא בַּר נָשׁ דְּלָא זָכֵי לְאִשְׁתַּדְלָא בְּהַאי עָלְמָא בְּאוֹרָיְתָא, וְאִיהוּ אָזֵיל בַּחֲשׁוּכָא, כַּד נָפַק מֵהַאי עָלְמָא, נַטְלִין לֵיהּ, וְאַעֲלִין לֵיהּ לְגֵיהִנָּם, אֲתַר תַּתָּאָה, דְּלָא יְהֵא מְרַחֵם עֲלֵיהּ, דְּאִקְרֵי "בּוֹר שָׁאוֹן טִיט הַיָּוֵן" כד"א (תהלים מ, ג) "וַיַּעֲלֵנִי מִבּוֹר שָׁאוֹן מִטִּיט הַיָּוֵן" כו'. וּבְגִין כָּךְ, הַהוּא דְלָא אִשְׁתַּדַּל בְּאוֹרָיְתָא בְּהַאי עָלְמָא וְאִתְמְנַע בְּטוּנוּפֵי עָלְמָא, מָה כְּתִיב (בראשית לז, כד) "וַיִּקָּחֻהוּ וַיַּשְׁלִכוּ אוֹתוֹ הַבּוֹרָה", דָּא הוּא גֵיהִנָּם, אֲתַר דְּדַיְינִין לְהוֹ לְאִנּוּן דְּלָא אִשְׁתַּדְּלוּ בְּאוֹרָיְתָא, "וְהַבּוֹר רֵיק", כְּמָה דְּאִיהוּ הֲוָה רֵיק, מַאי טַעְמָא, בְּגִין דְּלָא הֲוָה בֵּיהּ מַיִם, וְתָא חֲזֵי כַּמָּה הוּא עוֹנְשָׁא דְאוֹרָיְתָא, דְּהָא לָא אִתְגְּלוּ יִשְׂרָאֵל מֵאַרְעָא קַדִּישָׁא אֶלָּא בְּגִין דְּאִסְתַּלְקוּ מֵאוֹרָיְתָא וְאִשְׁתַּבְּקוּ מִנָּהּ, הֲדָא הוּא דִכְתִיב (ירמיה ט, יא) "מִי הָאִישׁ הֶחָכָם וְיָבֵן כו' עַל מָה אָבְדָה הָאָרֶץ וַיֹּאמֶר ה' עַל עָזְבָם אֶת תּוֹרָתִי, כו':

וְלֹא עוֹד, אֶלָּא שֶׁתְּחִלַּת דִּינוֹ שֶׁל אָדָם, בְּבֹאוֹ לַמִּשְׁפָּט לְפָנָיו יִתְבָּרַךְ, הוּא עַל דִּבְרֵי תוֹרָה כְּמוֹ שֶׁכָּתוּב בְּסוֹף פֶּרֶק קַמָּא דְקִדּוּשִׁין (מ, ב), וּבְפֶרֶק קַמָּא דְסַנְהֶדְרִין (ו' א')

---

405 Tehillim 40:3.
406 Bereishit 37:24.
407 Water is a reference to Torah as per: Bava Kama 17a; Bava Kama 82b; Avodah Zarah 5b.
408 Yirmiyahu 9:11, 12.

world] his judgment starts with [his level of involvement with] words of Torah as per Chazal:[409]
- R. Hamnuna says, the beginning of a person's judgment is only in relation to Torah study as it says: "The beginning of *judgment* is like releasing *water*. . . ."[410]

• Chazal say: Every day, a Heavenly Echo emanates from Mount Sinai and declares: [Woe to people from the insult to Torah]. For all those who are not involved with Torah are called despised.[411]
- As a person's judgment [after his passing] is sustained by the 'fruit of his actions'[412]
- since he did not wish to choose true life and good for himself, the creations, and all the worlds, and to cleave himself to God
- and he reduced the bestowal of light of the worlds
- damaging and corrupting the arrangement of the Holy Merkava
- bringing darkness to them and causing bad to himself
- that he divested himself of the clothes of holiness and instead donned filthy garments constructed from his involvement with the desires and pleasures of this world
- and he is contaminated and defiled from them
- for sure he will not be allowed to enter [Heaven]
- and all the holy forces who guard him will distance themselves from him as they cannot come into contact with his filthy garments
- and he [i.e., his soul] will return to *surf*[413] this world, 'impure, impure he will be called'[414]
- as he is attached to his kind, the impure forces of the powers of impurity, which he brought upon himself.
- As per the Zohar[415]
  - R. Abba began . . . How much should people take care of their way and to fear God so that they do not steer from the correct path, transgress the words of the Torah or move away from it.
  - For one who is not involved with Torah and does not invest his efforts in it is despised by God
  - he is far from Him and the Shechina does not reside over him.
  - Those guardians which accompany him, leave him

---

409 Kiddushin 40b and Sanhedrin 7a.
410 Mishlei 17:14.
411 Mishna Avot 6:2.
412 Michah 7:13.
413 A reference to the soul being tortured by being slung from one end of the Earth to the other, without finding its place after not having been admitted

○ אָמַר רַב הַמְנוּנָא, אֵין תְּחִלַּת דִּינוֹ שֶׁל אָדָם, אֶלָּא עַל דִּבְרֵי תּוֹרָה, שֶׁנֶּאֱמַר (משלי יז, יד) "פּוֹטֵר מַיִם רֵאשִׁית מָדוֹן" כו':

• וְאָמְרוּ (אבות ו, ב) "בְּכָל יוֹם וָיוֹם, בַּת קוֹל יוֹצֵאת מֵהַר חוֹרֵב, וּמַכְרֶזֶת כו', שֶׁכָּל מִי שֶׁאֵינוֹ עוֹסֵק בַּתּוֹרָה נִקְרָא נָזוּף" כו'.

○ כִּי כֵן מִשְׁפָּטוֹ, מִפְּרִי מַעֲלָלָיו יַשְׂבִּיעוּהוּ.

○ כֵּיוָן שֶׁלֹּא רָצָה לִבְחוֹר בַּחַיִּים וּבַטּוֹב הָאֲמִתִּי, לוֹ וּלְכָל הַבְּרִיּוֹת וְהָעוֹלָמוֹת כֻּלָּם, וּלְהִתְדַּבֵּק עַצְמוֹ בּוֹ יִתְבָּרֵךְ

○ וְהִמְעִיט שִׁפְעַת אוֹרָם שֶׁל הָעוֹלָמוֹת

○ וְקִלְקֵל וּבִלְבֵּל סִדְרֵי הַמֶּרְכָּבָה הַקְּדוֹשָׁה

○ וְהֶחְשִׁיכָם, וְגָרַם רָעָה לְעַצְמוֹ

○ שֶׁפָּשַׁט בִּגְדֵי הַקֹּדֶשׁ, וְלָבַשׁ תַּחְתָּם בְּגָדִים צוֹאִים וּמְטֻנָּפִים, הַנַּעֲשִׂים מֵעִסְקֵי תַאֲוֹת זֶה הָעוֹלָם וְתַעֲנוּגוֹת עִנְיָנָיו

○ וְהוּא מְטַמֵּא וּמְטַנֵּף מֵהֶם

○ וַדַּאי שֶׁלֹּא יַנִּיחוּהוּ וְלֹא יוּכַל לִכָּנֵס

○ וְכָל הַחֲיָלִין קַדִּישִׁין הַשּׁוֹמְרִים אוֹתוֹ, מִתְרַחֲקִים מֵאִתּוֹ, בְּלֹא יוּכְלוּ יִגְּעוּ בִּלְבוּשָׁיו הַמְטֻנָּפִים

○ וְאָזִיל וּמְשׁוֹטֵט בָּעוֹלָם, וְ"טָמֵא טָמֵא" יִקְרָא

○ שֶׁמִּתְדַּבֵּק בְּמִינוֹ, בַּחֲיָלִין טְמֵאִים שֶׁל כֹּחוֹת הַטֻּמְאָה אֲשֶׁר הִגְבִּירָם עַל עַצְמוֹ.

○ כְּמוֹ שֶׁכָּתוּב בַּזֹּהַר רֵישׁ פָּרָשַׁת מְצֹרָע (נב, ב)

□ רַבִּי אַבָּא פָּתַח כו', כַּמָּה אִית לוֹן לִבְנֵי נָשָׁא לְאִסְתַּמְּרָא אָרְחַיְהוּ, וּלְדַחֲלָא מִקַּמֵּי קוּדְשָׁא בְּרִיךְ הוּא, דְּלָא יִסְטֵי מֵאָרְחָא דְכַשְׁרָא, וְלָא יַעֲבוֹר עַל פִּתְגָּמֵי אוֹרַיְתָא, וְלָא יִתְנְשֵׁי מִנָּהּ.

□ דְּכָל מַאן דְּלָא לָעֵי בְּאוֹרַיְתָא, וְלָא יִשְׁתַּדֵּל בַּהּ, נְזִיפָא אִיהוּ מִקֻּדְשָׁא בְּרִיךְ הוּא

□ רְחִיקָא הוּא מִנֵּיהּ, לָא שַׁרְיָא שְׁכִינְתָּא עִמֵּיהּ

□ וְאִנּוּן נְטוֹרִין דְּאַזְלִין עִמֵּיהּ אִסְתַּלְּקוּ מִנֵּיהּ

---

to Heaven – a state known as Kaf HaKela (see Shabbat 152b quoting 1 Shmuel 25:29) – hinted to at the end of this chapter with the use of the word "Lehitkalea" (to be slung).

414 Vayikra 13:45.
415 Zohar III Metzora 52b.

- furthermore they announce to those around him "depart from being in the vicinity of this person as he is not concerned with the honor of his Master."
- Woe is he that is forsaken by the supernal and lower worlds, he has no part in the path of life.
- However, if he involves himself with Torah, then many guardians are prepared to meet and guard him
- and the Shechina resides over him and all announce before him "give honor to the image of the King, give honor to the prince"
- he is guarded in this world and in the World to Come, happy is his portion.

- Chazal state:[416] "A twisted thing cannot be corrected." R. Shimon bar Yochai says the term "twisted" only relates to something which was originally intact and then became twisted. What does this refer to? A Torah Sage who separated himself from Torah.
  - Woe is to people who see and do not know what they see, woe to us for the insult to Torah.
- How much should a person constantly focus on this, to place his awareness and 'to sharpen his counsel'[417] without walking in the dark, God forbid, all the days of his futile existence for the number of his days which have been allotted out of God's mercy and kindness, with the desire of his soul to be 'freely sent'[418] from the Torah – 'unaware that his life is lost.'[419]
  - For when he reaches his time 'and returns the dust to the earth but his spirit does not return to God'[420] to be bound with the bond of everlasting supernal life – for 'his portion is cursed'[421] to be *slung*[422] and to never rest, 'for it is called *discarded*,'[423] 'despised above and below,'[424] woe to it for that shame. Merciful God, save us!

24. NON-STUDY OF TORAH LEADS TO COMPLETE CUT OFF FROM WORLD TO COME

- Chazal vigorously debated the severity of a person's punishment – for one who was able to study Torah and did not, or for one who did study

---

416 Chagiga 9a quoting Kohelet 1:15.
417 An expression from Tehillim 73:21 where the word used for "counsel" is the "kidneys" as Chazal state that the kidneys are the seat of advice (e.g., Berachot 61a; Shabbat 33b).
418 Shemot 21:26.

- וְלָא עוֹד, אֶלָּא דְמַכְרְזֵי קַמֵּיהּ וְאָמְרֵי, אִסְתַּלְּקוּ מִסּוּחֲרָנֵיהּ דִפְלָנְיָא דְלָא חָשׁ עַל יְקָרָא דְמָארֵיהּ
- וַי לֵיהּ, דְהָא שְׁבָקוּהוּ עֶלָּאִין וְתַתָּאִין, לֵית לֵיהּ חוּלָקָא בְּאָרְחָא דְחַיֵּי.
- וְכַד אִיהוּ אִשְׁתַּדַּל כו', וְלָעֵי בְּאוֹרַיְתָא, כַּמָּה נְטוֹרִין זְמִינִין לְקַבְּלֵיהּ, לְנַטְרָא לֵיהּ
- וּשְׁכִינְתָּא שַׁרְיָא עֲלֵיהּ, וְכוּלְּהוּ מַכְרְזֵי קַמֵּיהּ וְאָמְרֵי, הָבוּ יְקָרָא לְדִיוּקְנָא דְמַלְכָּא, הָבוּ יְקָרָא לִבְרֵיהּ דְמַלְכָּא
- אִתְנְטִיר הוּא בְּעָלְמָא דֵין, וּבְעָלְמָא דְאָתֵי, זַכָּאָה חוּלָקֵיהּ:

• וְאָמְרוּ בַּמִּשְׁנָה פֶּרֶק קַמָּא דְּחַגִיגָה (ט' א'), "מְעֻוָּת לֹא יוּכַל לִתְקֹן" (קהלת א, טו), רַבִּי שִׁמְעוֹן בֶּן יוֹחַאי אוֹמֵר, אֵין קוֹרִין "מְעֻוָּת" אֶלָּא לְמִי שֶׁהָיָה מְתֻקָּן בַּתְּחִלָּה וְנִתְעַוֵּת, וְאֵי זֶה, זֶה תַּלְמִיד חָכָם הַפּוֹרֵשׁ מִן הַתּוֹרָה".

○ וְאוֹי לָהֶם לַבְּרִיּוֹת שֶׁרוֹאוֹת וְאֵינָן יוֹדְעוֹת מָה רוֹאוֹת, אוֹי לָנוּ מֵעֶלְבּוֹנָהּ שֶׁל תּוֹרָה:

• וְכַמָּה צָרִיךְ הָאָדָם לְהִתְבּוֹנֵן עַל זֶה תָּמִיד, וְלָשִׁית דַּעְתּוֹ וְכִלְיוֹתָיו יְשַׁתּוּנּוּ, בַּל יֵלֵךְ חֹשֶׁךְ חַס וְשָׁלוֹם כָּל יְמֵי הֶבְלוֹ, מִסְפַּר יָמָיו אֲשֶׁר נִקְצְבוּ לוֹ בְּרַחֲמָיו וַחֲסָדָיו יִתְבָּרַךְ שְׁמוֹ, בְּאַוַּת נַפְשׁוֹ מְשַׁלֵּחַ חָפְשִׁי מִן הַתּוֹרָה, כִּי בְנַפְשׁוֹ הוּא.

○ כִּי יַגִּיעַ עֵת פְּקֻדָּתוֹ, וְיָשׁוּב הֶעָפָר עַל הָאָרֶץ, וְהָרוּחַ לֹא תָשׁוּב אֶל הָאֱלֹקִים לְהִצָּרֵר בִּצְרוֹר הַחַיִּים הָעֶלְיוֹנִים, כִּי תְקַלֵּל חֶלְקָתוֹ לְהִתְקַלֵּעַ, וְלֹא תַרְגִּיעַ, כִּי נִדְחָה קָרְאוּ לָהּ, נָזִיף לְעֵלָּא נָזִיף לְתַתָּא, אוֹי לָהּ לְאוֹתָהּ בּוּשָׁה כו'. הָרַחֲמָן יִתְבָּרַךְ שְׁמוֹ יַצִּילֵנוּ:

שער ד' - פרק כ"ד

• וְכָל כָּךְ הִפְלִיגוּ רַבּוֹתֵינוּ זִכְרוֹנָם לִבְרָכָה, בְּחֹמֶר עָנְשׁוֹ שֶׁל הָאָדָם שֶׁאֶפְשָׁר לוֹ לַעֲסֹק בַּתּוֹרָה וְאֵינוֹ עוֹסֵק, אוֹ שָׁנָה וּפֵרֵשׁ חַס וְשָׁלוֹם, עַד שֶׁכִּנּוּהוּ בְּרוּחַ קָדְשָׁם מֵעוֹלָם הַבָּא לְגַמְרֵי, רַחֲמָנָא לִיצְלָן.

---

419 Mishlei 7:23.
420 Kohelet 12:7.
421 Iyov 24:18.
422 See p. 744, fn. 413, which relates to Kaf HaKela.
423 Yirmiyahu 30:17.
424 Zohar III Emor 101a.

but stopped doing so, God forbid, to the extent that they, in their Divine Inspiration, concluded that such people are *completely* cut off from the World to Come, God should save us!

- Chazal explain:[425] "For he scorned the word of God" . . . R. Natan says this relates to one who is not careful over his studies; R. Nehorai says this relates to one capable of involving himself with Torah but does not do so.
  - The double expression [of cutting off] at the end of this verse, "that soul shall surely be cut off," is explained as meaning cut off in both this world and in the World to Come.
- This verse emphasizes the severity of this *cutting off*
  - that it is unlike other instances of *cutting off* which the Torah describes in relation to other sins
  - where even if one's judgment is clearly defined as being *cut off*, God forbid, it does not however result in [a complete] loss of one's portion in the World to Come
  - as it is only the specific small spark of the soul which performed the sin which is actually cut off from its connection and cleaving, 'the broken cord,'[426] which until now was connected with and cleaved to the Root of his Neshama with God, as explained at length in the First Gateway above.[427]
  - Here, however, the double expression of *cutting off* is used, meaning that the entirety of the soul level of Nefesh has completely lost its portion in everlasting life, God forbid, and that it has no portion in the World to Come at all!
- [The interpretation of this verse in respect of neglect of Torah study] is similarly stated as Halacha by both the Rambam[428] and the Beit Yosef in the Shulchan Aruch.[429]
- Similarly, Rabbeinu Yona describes ten levels of severity of sin with the most severe level relating to the group of those about whom Chazal say that they do not have a portion in the World to Come; also listing among this group those who were able to involve themselves in Torah study but did not do so.[430]
- Similarly, R. Chaim Vital also describes[431] this sin as excluding one from the World to Come, 'weaving it in the same weave'[432] there, equating it with the cases that Chazal state for whom "Gehinom will end but for them it will not come to an end!,"[433] the Merciful One should save us.

---

425 Sanhedrin 99a quoting Bamidbar 15:31.
426 This expression comes from Michah 2:10 and is translated here according to

כְּמוֹ שֶׁכָּתוּב בְּפֶרֶק חֵלֶק (צט, א), "כִּי דְבַר ה' בָּזָה" כו' (במדבר טו, לא), רַבִּי נָתָן אוֹמֵר כָּל שֶׁאֵינוֹ מַשְׁגִּיחַ עַל הַמִּשְׁנָה, רַבִּי נְהוֹרַאי אוֹמֵר כָּל שֶׁאֶפְשָׁר לוֹ לַעֲסֹק בַּתּוֹרָה וְאֵינוֹ עוֹסֵק.

וְסֵיפֵיהּ דְּהַאי קְרָא "הִכָּרֵת תִּכָּרֵת הַנֶּפֶשׁ הַהִיא", וּפֵרְשׁוּ זִכְרוֹנָם לִבְרָכָה שָׁם לְעֵיל מִינֵהּ "הִכָּרֵת" — בָּעוֹלָם הַזֶּה "תִּכָּרֵת" — לָעוֹלָם הַבָּא.

הִשְׁמִיעָנוּ הַכָּתוּב חֹמֶר זֶה הַכָּרֵת

שֶׁאֵינוֹ כִּשְׁאָר הַכְּרִיתוֹת הָאֲמוּרוֹת בַּתּוֹרָה עַל שְׁאָר עֲוֹנוֹת

אֲשֶׁר אַף אִם דִּינוֹ חָרוּץ שֶׁהוּא נִכְרָת חַס וְשָׁלוֹם, עִם כָּל זֶה לֹא אִבֵּד חֶלְקוֹ בְּחַיֵּי עוֹלָם הַבָּא

שֶׁרַק אוֹתוֹ הַנִּצּוֹץ הַקָּטָן שֶׁל הַנֶּפֶשׁ, שֶׁעָשָׂה בּוֹ אֶת הֶעָוֹן, הוּא הַנִּכְרָת מִקִּשּׁוּר וְדִבּוּק הַחֶבֶל הַנִּמְרָץ, שֶׁהָיָה מְקֻשָּׁר וְדָבוּק עַד עַתָּה עַד שֹׁרֶשׁ נִשְׁמָתוֹ בְּקֻדְשָׁא בְּרִיךְ הוּא, כְּמוֹ שֶׁנִּתְבָּאֵר לְעֵיל בְּשַׁעַר א' בְּאָרְךְ.

אָמְנָם כָּאן אָמַר "הִכָּרֵת תִּכָּרֵת", הַיְנוּ, שֶׁכָּל חֵלֶק 'בְּחִינַת נַפְשׁוֹ' אָבְדָה חֶלְקָהּ בְּחַיֵּי עוֹלָם לְגַמְרֵי חַס וְשָׁלוֹם, וְאֵין לָהּ חֵלֶק לָעוֹלָם הַבָּא כְּלָל.

וְכֵן פָּסַק הָרַמְבַּ"ם זִכְרוֹנוֹ לִבְרָכָה לַהֲלָכָה, בְּהִלְכוֹת תַּלְמוּד תּוֹרָה (פרק ג' הֲלָכָה י"ג), וְקָבַע כֵּן הַבֵּית יוֹסֵף בְּשֻׁלְחָן עָרוּךְ שָׁם (סִי' רמ"ו סָעִיף כ"ה) לַהֲלָכָה.

וְכֵן הָרַבֵּינוּ יוֹנָה זִכְרוֹנוֹ לִבְרָכָה בְּשַׁעַר הַתְּשׁוּבָה (שַׁעַר הַשְּׁלִישִׁי), מָנָה עֶשֶׂר מַדְרֵגוֹת בְּחֹמֶר עַנְשֵׁי הָעֲוֹנוֹת, וְהַמַּדְרֵגָה הָאַחֲרוֹנָה מוֹנֶה אוֹתָם הַכַּת, שֶׁאָמְרוּ רַבּוֹתֵינוּ זִכְרוֹנָם לִבְרָכָה עֲלֵיהֶם שֶׁאֵין לָהֶם חֵלֶק לָעוֹלָם הַבָּא, וּמָנָה שָׁם (ש"ג, קנג) בִּכְלָל זֶה גַּם מִי שֶׁאֶפְשָׁר לוֹ לַעֲסֹק בַּתּוֹרָה וְאֵינוֹ עוֹסֵק.

וְכֵן הרח"ו זִכְרוֹנוֹ לִבְרָכָה בְּשַׁעֲרֵי קְדֻשָּׁה חֵלֶק ב' שַׁעַר ח', מָנָה אוֹתוֹ גַּם כֵּן

---

the understanding as presented in Bamidbar Rabba Naso 9:7 where "Chevel" relates to an unbroken chain of lineage and "Nimratz" relates to the breaking of that chain. In our context this refers to the cord of soul connection which is broken by sin.

427 From G1:17 onwards explaining the concept of repentance.
428 Mishneh Torah, Sefer HaMada Hilchot Talmud Torah 3:13.
429 Yoreh Deah Hilchot Talmud Torah 246:25.
430 Shaarei Teshuva 3:121, 3:153, 3:177 (also 3:14).
431 Shaarei Kedushah Part 2 Gate 8.
432 Berachot 24a.
433 Rosh Hashana 17a.

- The Rambam and Beit Yosef in the above references [also determine the Halacha] of one who did study and review but then stopped doing so and instead engaged in the emptiness of this world, neglecting his studies, as having the same judgment as one who was able to study Torah and did not.
- Similarly, in [his] judgment, that his actions which were not good distance him, 'and his sin withholds the good from him'[434]
  - as he was able to involve himself with and engage in Torah study, and 'out of intentional sin'[435] and 'contempt of the soul'[436] chose 'and took a bad purchase for himself,'[437] others, and all the worlds
  - despising the everlasting life of the Holy Torah – the life and light of all the worlds – through which he was attached, so to speak, with God, Who gives life to all
  - but stretched out his hand to destroy the palace of the King – diminishing, darkening, and extinguishing the bestowal of light in the worlds and also of his own soul.
  - Why should he have true life?
  - as he prevented himself from seeing the light of everlasting life and he cannot tolerate the greatness of the intensity of the Supernal Light as he has not experienced it while being in this world
  - and he is exiled and automatically cut off from Eden, God's Garden
  - preventing himself from 'being bound with the bond of life with YHVH his God,'[438] 'going from bad to worse',[439] God forbid.
  - Woe for that shame!
- Similarly, Chazal determined his fate, 'that his hope is decreed as lost'[440] forever, God forbid, that he also 'will everlastingly not see light'[441] that he will not 'live again forever'[442] at the end of days when 'those sleeping in the dust of the ground will awaken for everlasting life.'[443]
  - As per Chazal: "For Your dew is like the dew that [revives through] light."[444] Anyone who engages in the light of Torah, the Torah revives him, but for anyone who does not engage in the light of Torah, the Torah does not revive him.

---

434 Yirmiyahu 5:25.
435 E.g., from Yirmiyahu 49:16.
436 Yechezkel 36:5.
437 An expression from Sotah 10b and Sanhedrin 109b.
438 1 Shmuel 25:29.
439 Yirmiyahu 9:2.
440 Yechezkel 37:11.
441 Tehillim 49:20.

בִּכְלָל אוֹתָם שֶׁאֵין לָהֶם חֵלֶק לָעוֹלָם הַבָּא, וּבַחֲדָא מַחְתָּא מַחְתִּינְהוּ שָׁם, שֶׁדִּינוֹ שָׁוֶה עִם אוֹתָן שֶׁאָמְרוּ זִכְרוֹנָם לִבְרָכָה עֲלֵיהֶם בְּפֶרֶק קַמָּא דְרֹאשׁ הַשָּׁנָה (יז, א), שֶׁגֵּיהִנָּם כָּלָה וְהֵם אֵינָם כָּלִים, רַחֲמָנָא לִיצְלָן.

וְכָתַב הָרַמְבַּ"ם זִכְרוֹנוֹ לִבְרָכָה, וְהַבֵּית יוֹסֵף זִכְרוֹנוֹ לִבְרָכָה שָׁם, שֶׁמִּי שֶׁקָּרָא וְשָׁנָה, וּפֵרַשׁ לְהַבְלֵי עוֹלָם, וְהִנִּיחַ תַּלְמוּדוֹ וְנָח, גַּם כֵּן דִּינוֹ עִם מִי שֶׁאֶפְשָׁר לוֹ לַעֲסֹק בַּתּוֹרָה וְאֵינוֹ עוֹסֵק:

• וְכֵן בַּדִּין, מַעֲשָׂיו אֲשֶׁר לֹא טוֹבִים הֵמָּה יְרַחֲקוּהוּ, וְחַטָּאתוֹ מָנְעוּ הַטּוֹב מֵאִתּוֹ

• אַחַר שֶׁהָיָה אֶפְשָׁר לוֹ וְסִפֵּק בְּיָדוֹ לַעֲסֹק בַּתּוֹרָה, וּבִזְדוֹן לֵב וּשְׁאָט נֶפֶשׁ, בָּחַר וְלָקַח מִקַּח רַע לְעַצְמוֹ וְלַאֲחֵרִים וְהָעוֹלָמוֹת כֻּלָּם

• וּמָאַס בְּחַיֵּי עוֹלָם שֶׁל הַתּוֹרָה הַקְּדוֹשָׁה, חִיּוּתָא וּנְהִירוּ דְכָל עָלְמִין, אֲשֶׁר עַל יָדָהּ הָיָה מִתְדַּבֵּק כִּבְיָכוֹל בְּקוּדְשָׁא בְּרִיךְ הוּא יִתְבָּרַךְ שְׁמוֹ, הַמְחַיֶּה אֶת כֻּלָּם

• וְשָׁלַח יָדוֹ לַהֲרֹס פַּלְטִין שֶׁל מֶלֶךְ, וְהִמְעִיט וְהֶחֱשִׁיךְ וְכִבָּה שִׁפְעַת אוֹרָם שֶׁל הָעוֹלָמוֹת, וְגַם שֶׁל נַפְשׁוֹ

• לָמָּה לוֹ חַיִּים אֲמִתִּים

• כִּי הֲלֹא תֶחְשַׁכְנָה עֵינָיו מֵרְאוֹת וְהַבֵּט בְּאוֹר הַחַיִּים הַנִּצְחִיִּים, וְלֹא יוּכַל לִסְבּוֹל גֹּדֶל עֹצֶם הָאוֹר עֶלְיוֹן, כִּי לֹא נִסָּה בָזֶה מֵעוֹדוֹ בָּזֶה הָעוֹלָם

• וְהוּא מְגֹרָשׁ וְנִכְרָת מֵאֵלָיו מֵעֵדֶן גַּן אֱלֹקִים יִתְבָּרַךְ שְׁמוֹ

• מִלְּהִצָּרֵר בִּצְרוֹר הַחַיִּים אֶת ה' אֱלֹקָיו יִתְבָּרַךְ שְׁמוֹ, וּמֵרָעָה אֶל רָעָה הוּא יוֹצֵא חַס וְשָׁלוֹם

• אוֹי לְאוֹתָהּ בּוּשָׁה כו':

• וְכֵן פָּסְקוּ וְחָתְכוּ זִכְרוֹנָם לִבְרָכָה דִּינוֹ, שֶׁנִּגְזְרָה אֲבֵדָה תִּקְוָתוֹ לְדוֹר דּוֹרִים חַס וְשָׁלוֹם, שֶׁגַּם עַד נֵצַח לֹא יִרְאֶה אוֹר, בַּל יְחִי עוֹד לָנֶצַח בְּעֵת קֵץ הַיָּמִין, אֲשֶׁר יְשֵׁנֵי אַדְמַת עָפָר יָקִיצוּ לְחַיֵּי עוֹלָם

• כְּמַאֲמָרָם זִכְרוֹנָם לִבְרָכָה (בְּסוֹף כְּתוּבוֹת קי"א, ב), "כִּי טַל אוֹרֹת טַלֶּךָ" (יְשַׁעְיָה כו, יט) "כָּל הַמִּשְׁתַּמֵּשׁ בְּאוֹר תּוֹרָה אוֹר תּוֹרָה מְחַיֵּהוּ, וְכָל שֶׁאֵין מִשְׁתַּמֵּשׁ בְּאוֹר תּוֹרָה אֵין אוֹר תּוֹרָה מְחַיֵּהוּ".

---

442 Tehillim 49:10.
443 Daniel 12:2.
444 Yishayahu 26:19.

- With the only recourse Chazal found there, to enable the resurrection of those illiterate of Torah, by at least their strengthening and supporting the Tree of Life, supporting the Torah by benefiting Torah scholars with their assets. As the Talmud continues: My teacher! I have found a remedy for them from the Torah: "And you who cleave to YHVH your God, you are all alive today."[445] Is it possible to cleave to the Shechina ... but this means that one who marries his daughter to a Torah Sage and does business with a Torah Sage or allows the Torah Sage to benefit from his possessions is considered as if he cleaves to the Shechina.[446]
- "Wake up and be refreshed those who dwell in the dust." From here King David said: May my portion be with those who *kill* themselves over words of Torah ... "Wake up and be refreshed those who dwell in the dust" – from here they said, one who makes himself a *neighbor of dust* during his life, then *his dust* will be resurrected, but one who does not make himself a *neighbor of dust* during his life, then *his dust* will not be resurrected. For these people who nullify themselves to learn Torah, God brings upon them the "dew of the lights" of Torah ... and brings them to the World to Come ... as per [the continuation of the verse]: "For Your dew is like the dew that [revives through] light."[447]

• Therefore, Chazal refer[448] to a Torah Sage who separates himself from Torah as "a twisted thing cannot be corrected,"[449] that, God forbid, he has no possibility for remedy. May God save us from this and anything similar!

25. UNIVERSE EXISTS ALL THE WHILE AT LEAST ONE JEW STUDIES TORAH

• All of this occurs while Jews exist who cleave to God and His Torah, deeply analyzing it with great diligence and toil *for its sake*, wanting nothing but God's Torah all their days.
• Then, those who out of their poor choice are totally uninvolved with Torah
  - 'descend to the abyss while alive'[450] 'and have driven themselves away from attaching to the heritage of the servants of God'[451] who cleave to God and His Torah and 'are cut off from the land of life,'[452] God forbid
  - [this is] at the very least in this world, if not also in all of the worlds,

---

445 Devarim 4:4.
446 Ketubbot 111b.
447 Eliyahu Rabba Parsha 5 quoting Yishayahu 26:19.

וְלֹא מָצְאוּ שָׁם רַבּוֹתֵינוּ זִכְרוֹנָם לִבְרָכָה תַּקָּנָה לְעַמֵּי הָאָרֶץ — שֶׁיָּקוּמוּ לְעֵת הַתְּחִיָּה, אֶלָּא בְּהַחֲזִיקָם וְתוֹמְכִים עַל כָּל פָּנִים בְּעֵץ הַחַיִּים, תָּמְכֵי דְּאוֹרַיְתָא, לֶהֱנוֹת תַּלְמִידֵי חֲכָמִים מִנִּכְסֵיהֶם. כְּמוֹ שֶׁאָמְרוּ (שָׁם), אָמַר לוֹ, רַבִּי מָצָאתִי לָהֶם תְּרוּפָה מִן הַתּוֹרָה "וְאַתֶּם הַדְּבֵקִים בַּה' אֱלֹהֵיכֶם חַיִּים כֻּלְּכֶם הַיּוֹם" (דברים ד, ד) וְכִי אֶפְשָׁר לְדָבְקִי בַּשְּׁכִינָה כו', אֶלָּא כָּל הַמַּשִּׂיא בִּתּוֹ לְתַלְמִיד חָכָם, וְהָעוֹשֶׂה פְּרַקְמַטְיָא לְתַלְמִיד חָכָם, וְהַמְּהַנֶּה תַּלְמִיד חָכָם מִנְּכָסָיו, מַעֲלֶה עָלָיו הַכָּתוּב כְּאִלּוּ מְדַבֵּק בַּשְּׁכִינָה.

וּכְתַנָּא דְּבֵי אֵלִיָּהוּ (סֵדֶר אֵלִיָּהוּ רַבָּה פֶּרֶק ה), "הָקִיצוּ וְרַנְּנוּ שֹׁכְנֵי עָפָר" (ישעיהו שם) מִכָּאן אָמַר דָּוִד הַמֶּלֶךְ עָלָיו הַשָּׁלוֹם, יְהֵא חֶלְקִי עִם אֵלּוּ שֶׁהֵם מְמִיתִין אֶת עַצְמָן עַל דִּבְרֵי תוֹרָה כו', "הָקִיצוּ וְרַנְּנוּ שֹׁכְנֵי עָפָר", מִכָּאן אָמְרוּ, כָּל הַנַּעֲשֶׂה שָׁכֵן לְעָפָר בְּחַיָּיו עֲפָרוֹ נִנְעָר לִתְחִיַּת הַמֵּתִים, וְכָל שֶׁאֵין נַעֲשָׂה שָׁכֵן לְעָפָר בְּחַיָּיו, אֵין עֲפָרוֹ נִנְעָר לִתְחִיַּת הַמֵּתִים כו', אֵלּוּ בְּנֵי אָדָם שֶׁמַּשְׁכִּינִים עַצְמָם עַל הֶעָפָר לִלְמֹד תּוֹרָה, הַקָּדוֹשׁ בָּרוּךְ הוּא מֵבִיא עֲלֵיהֶם טַל אוֹרוֹת שֶׁל תּוֹרָה כו', וּמְבִיאָן לְחַיֵּי עוֹלָם הַבָּא, שֶׁנֶּאֱמַר (ישעיה כו, יט) "כִּי טַל אוֹרוֹת טַלֶּךָ":

וְלָזֹאת קָרְאוּ רַבּוֹתֵינוּ זִכְרוֹנָם לִבְרָכָה הַמִּקְרָא "מְעֻוָּת לֹא יוּכַל לִתְקֹן" (קהלת א, טו), עַל תַּלְמִיד חָכָם הַפּוֹרֵשׁ מִן הַתּוֹרָה (משנה חגיגה ט, א), שֶׁחָס וְשָׁלוֹם אֵין לוֹ תַּקָּנָה עוֹלָמִית. הָרַחֲמָן יִתְבָּרַךְ שְׁמוֹ יַצִּילֵנוּ מִזֶּה וְכָל כַּיּוֹצֵא בּוֹ:

שַׁעַר ד' - פֶּרֶק כ"ה

- וְכָל זֶה, כְּשֶׁעֲדַיִן יֵשׁ אֲנָשִׁים מִיִּשְׂרָאֵל, שֶׁדְּבֵקִים בּוֹ יִתְבָּרַךְ וּבְתוֹרָתוֹ בְּעִיּוּן וּשְׁקִידָה וִיגִיעָה גְדוֹלָה לִשְׁמָהּ, וְרַק בְּתוֹרַת יְיָ חֶפְצָם כָּל הַיָּמִים:

- וְאָז הָאֲנָשִׁים שֶׁבְּטֵלִים לְגַמְרֵי מֵעֵסֶק הַתּוֹרָה מֵרַע בְּחִירָתָם:

  - הֵמָּה יֵרְדוּ שְׁאוֹל חַיִּים, וּמְגֹרָשִׁים מֵהִסְתַּפֵּחַ בְּנַחֲלַת עַבְדֵי ה' הַדְּבֵקִים בּוֹ יִתְבָּרַךְ וּבְתוֹרָתוֹ, וּמֵאֶרֶץ חַיִּים יִכָּרֵתוּ חַס וְשָׁלוֹם.

  - וְעַל כָּל פָּנִים, הָעוֹלָם, גַּם כָּל הָעוֹלָמוֹת, הֲגַם כִּי נִתְמַעֲטוּ וְיָרְדוּ מִקְּדֻשָּׁתָם וְאוֹרָם, בְּסִבַּת הַחֲטָאִים הָאֵלֶּה בְּנַפְשׁוֹתָם

---

448 Chagiga 9a.
449 Kohelet 1:15.
450 Tehillim 55:16.
451 1 Shmuel 26:19.
452 Yirmiyahu 11:19.

whose holiness and light have also been diminished and lowered as a result of these sins for which they are culpable with their lives
- and 'almost turn their feet'[453] to destruction, God forbid, as per Chazal:
  - All the while that people disassociate themselves with the Torah, God seeks to destroy the world.[454]
  - "for the pillars of the world are God's and upon them He set the world" – *pillars* refers to Torah Sages ... Every day Angels of Destruction are sent by God to totally destroy the world and if it weren't for the prayer and study halls where Torah Sages sit and involve themselves with words of Torah, they would immediately destroy the entire world.[455] Refer there.

- With all this, [the worlds] are still able to exist through [the efforts of] 'the survivors who God calls'[456] who involve themselves in the Holy Torah day and night such that they do not totally return to a state of null and void, God forbid.
- However, if the world were, God forbid, completely void, even literally for one moment, of involvement and analysis of the Chosen People with the Holy Torah
  - then all the worlds would immediately be destroyed and totally cease to be, God forbid.
- Notwithstanding, even a single talented Jew alone has the ability to cause the establishment and continuation of all the worlds and the Creation in its entirety
  - by his involvement with and analysis of the Holy Torah *for its sake*, as per Chazal:
    - Whoever is involved with Torah *for its sake* ... R. Yochanan says he even protects the entire world.[457]
    - Whoever is involved with Torah *for its sake* ... and not only this but the entire world is fitting [to exist] for him.[458]
- So how can a person's heart not be enthused, when contemplating the gravity of this tremendous issue
  - to be filled with fear and dread
  - to not weaken his continuous involvement with the Holy Torah, God forbid
  - with the thought in his heart that perhaps, at this moment, God forbid, the entire world is completely devoid of anyone involved in Holy Torah study
  - and that if it weren't for his current involvement with Torah study and the analysis of his heart

---

453 Tehillim 73:2.

- וְכִמְעַט שֶׁנָּטְיוּ רַגְלָם לֵיחָרֵב חַס וְשָׁלוֹם, כְּמוֹ שֶׁכָּתוּב

- בְּתַנָּא דְּבֵי אֵלִיָּהוּ (סֵדֶר אֵלִיָּהוּ רַבָּה פֶּרֶק ב), אָמְרוּ חֲכָמִים, כָּל זְמַן שֶׁבְּנֵי אָדָם מְבַטְּלִין מִן הַתּוֹרָה מְבַקֵּשׁ הַקָּדוֹשׁ בָּרוּךְ הוּא לְהַחֲרִיב אֶת הָעוֹלָם כו'.

- וְשָׁם בְּסֵדֶר אֵלִיָּהוּ זוּטָא (פֶּרֶק ה) "כִּי לַה' מְצֻקֵי אֶרֶץ וַיָּשֶׁת עֲלֵיהֶם תֵּבֵל" (שמו"א ב, ח), וְאֵין מְצוּקִים אֶלָּא תַּלְמִידֵי חֲכָמִים כו'. בְּכָל יוֹם יוֹצְאִים מַלְאֲכֵי חַבָּלָה מִלִּפְנֵי הַקָּדוֹשׁ בָּרוּךְ הוּא לְחַבֵּל אֶת כָּל הָעוֹלָם כֻּלּוֹ, וְאִלְמָלֵא בָּתֵּי כְנֵסִיּוֹת וּבָתֵּי מִדְרָשׁוֹת, שֶׁתַּלְמִידֵי חֲכָמִים יוֹשְׁבִין בָּהֶם וְעוֹסְקִים בְּדִבְרֵי תוֹרָה, הָיוּ מְחַבְּלִין אֶת כָּל הָעוֹלָם כֻּלּוֹ מִיָּד כו', עַיֵּן שָׁם:

- עִם כָּל זֶה, עֲדַיִן יוּכְלוּ לְהִתְקַיֵּם עַל יְדֵי הַשְּׂרִידִים אֲשֶׁר ה' קֹרֵא, הָעוֹסְקִים בַּתּוֹרָה הַקְּדוֹשָׁה יוֹמָם וָלַיְלָה, שֶׁלֹּא יִתְבַּטְּלוּ לְגַמְרֵי לַחֲזֹר לְתֹהוּ וָבֹהוּ חַס וְשָׁלוֹם:

- אֲבָל אִם הָיָה חַס וְשָׁלוֹם הָעוֹלָם פָּנוּי לְגַמְרֵי, אֲפִלּוּ רֶגַע אֶחָד מַמָּשׁ, מֵעֵסֶק וְהִתְבּוֹנְנוּת עִם סְגֻלָּה בַּתּוֹרָה הַקְּדוֹשָׁה

- תֵּכֶף כְּרֶגַע הָיוּ כָּל הָעוֹלָמוֹת נֶחֱרָבִים וּנְבְטָלִים מִמְּצִיאוּת לְגַמְרֵי חַס וְשָׁלוֹם.

- וְאַף גַּם אִישׁ אֶחָד מִיִּשְׂרָאֵל לְבַד, רַב כֹּחוֹ, שֶׁבְּיָדוֹ לְהַעֲמִיד וּלְקַיֵּם אֶת כָּל הָעוֹלָמוֹת וְהַבְּרִיאָה בִּכְלָלָהּ

- עַל יְדֵי עָסְקוֹ וְהִתְבּוֹנְנוּתוֹ בַּתּוֹרָה הַקְּדוֹשָׁה לִשְׁמָהּ. כְּמוֹ שֶׁכָּתוּב

- בְּחֵלֶק (צט, ב), "כָּל הָעוֹסֵק בַּתּוֹרָה לִשְׁמָהּ כו', רַבִּי יוֹחָנָן אוֹמֵר אַף מֵגִין עַל כָּל הָעוֹלָם כֻּלּוֹ".

- וְכֵן אִיתָא בְּפֶרֶק הַתּוֹרָה (אבות ו, א), "כָּל הָעוֹסֵק בַּתּוֹרָה לִשְׁמָהּ כו', וְלֹא עוֹד אֶלָּא שֶׁכָּל הָעוֹלָם כֻּלּוֹ כְּדַאי הוּא לוֹ":

- וְאֵיךְ לֹא יִתְלַהֵב לֵב הָאָדָם, בְּהַעֲלוֹתוֹ עַל לִבּוֹ וּמִתְבּוֹנֵן בְּזֶה הָעִנְיָן הַנּוֹרָא

- וְתִפֹּל עָלָיו אֵימָתָה וָפָחַד

- לְבַל יִתְרַפֶּה חַס וְשָׁלוֹם מֵעֵסֶק הַתּוֹרָה הַקְּדוֹשָׁה תָּמִיד

- כַּאֲשֶׁר יַחְשֹׁב בִּלְבָבוֹ, אוּלַי חַס וְשָׁלוֹם לְעֵת כָּזֹאת, הָעוֹלָם כֻּלּוֹ מִקָּצֶה וְעַד קָצֵהוּ, פָּנוּי לְגַמְרֵי מֵעֵסֶק הַתּוֹרָה הַקְּדוֹשָׁה

- וּבִלְתִּי עָסְקוֹ וְהֶגְיוֹן לִבּוֹ עַתָּה בְּזֶה הָעֵת בַּתּוֹרָה

---

454 Eliyahu Rabba Parsha 2.
455 Eliyahu Zuta Parsha 5 quoting 1 Shmuel 2:8.
456 Yoel 3:5.
457 Sanhedrin 99b.
458 Mishna Avot 6:1.

- all the worlds would be destroyed and 'instantly cease to exist,'[459] God forbid.
- 'This is Torah and this is its great and incomparable reward'[460]
- that he is one who takes the reward of all, given that he, with his great abilities, causes all the worlds to exist and be established at this time.
- It is about this scenario that Chazal say: Every Jew is obligated to say that "The Universe was created specifically for me."[461]

• So even though other sins performed in this low world do not impact or damage many myriads of supernal holy worlds, God forbid
- and there is always 'might and joy in their place'[462] of honor and it is said about them that "no evil stays with you"[463]
- nevertheless, the sin of desisting from Torah study is far worse than all of them as it impacts on the very existence of all the worlds.

26. HIGH SOURCE OF TORAH CAUSES STUDY TO HAVE UNIVERSAL IMPACT – UNLIKE MITZVOT

• The reason for this [i.e., that desisting from Torah study has universal consequence], is as explained above,[464] that the supernal hidden source of the Holy Torah is far higher than all of the worlds – it is the starting point and root of God's holy emanation [of the worlds] – the secret of the *Supernal Malbush/Garment*, as explained by our master, the holy awesome man of God, the Arizal.

• However, [the Torah] cascaded all way down, so to speak, until it reached this world which 'shines in its glory'[465]
- and God has handed it over and implanted it within us so that we are able to uphold and support the Tree of Life.

• Therefore, from [the time of the Giving of the Torah], the entire life force and existence of all the worlds is dependent solely on our level of involvement and intellectual engagement with it.
- If we support it as appropriate without any compromise at all, we arouse the supernal source, the source of holiness and blessing to draw down additional blessing, everlasting life, and awesome holiness upon all of the worlds – each world according to its level of holiness which it is able to receive and tolerate.
- If however our involvement with it is weak, God forbid, then the holiness and supernal light of Torah is compacted and reduced from all the worlds

---

459 Tehillim 73:19.
460 Expression based on Berachot 61b.

- הָיוּ נֶחֱרָבִים כָּל הָעוֹלָמוֹת, וּכְרֶגַע סָפוּ תַמּוּ חַס וְשָׁלוֹם.
- זוֹ תוֹרָה וְזוֹ שְׂכָרָהּ מְרֻבָּה מְאֹד אֵין לְהַעֲרִיךְ
- שֶׁהוּא הַנּוֹטֵל שְׂכַר כֻּלָּם, אַחַר שֶׁהוּא אֲשֶׁר קַיָּם וְהֶעֱמִיד בְּרֹב כֹּחוֹ אֶת כָּל הָעוֹלָמוֹת עַתָּה.
- וְעַל כְּגוֹן זֶה אָמְרוּ רַבּוֹתֵינוּ זִכְרוֹנָם לִבְרָכָה בַּמִּשְׁנָה (סנהדרין לו, א) שֶׁכָּל אֶחָד מִיִּשְׂרָאֵל חַיָּב לוֹמַר בִּשְׁבִילִי נִבְרָא הָעוֹלָם:

- וְאַף שֶׁבַּשְּׁאָר עֲווֹנוֹת, יֵשׁ אַלְפֵי רִבְבָאוֹת עוֹלָמוֹת קְדוֹשִׁים עֶלְיוֹנִים, שֶׁאֵין שׁוּם חֵטְא וַעֲווֹן הַתַּחְתּוֹנִים מַגִּיעַ עֲדֵיהֶם כְּלָל, לְפָגְמָם חַס וְשָׁלוֹם
  - וְתָמִיד עֹז וְחֶדְוָה בִּמְקוֹם כְּבוֹדָם, וַעֲלֵיהֶם נֶאֱמַר (תהלים ה, ה) "לֹא יְגֻרְךָ רָע"
  - אָמְנָם עֲווֹן בִּטּוּל תּוֹרָה, הִיא הָעוֹלָה עַל כֻּלָּם, שֶׁהוּא נוֹגֵעַ לְקִיּוּם כָּל הָעוֹלָמוֹת:

שער ד' - פרק כ"ו

- וְטַעֲמוֹ שֶׁל דָּבָר, כְּמוֹ שֶׁנִּתְבָּאֵר לְעֵיל (פרק י), שֶׁמְּקוֹר שָׁרְשָׁהּ הָעֶלְיוֹן הַנֶּעֱלָם שֶׁל הַתּוֹרָה הַקְּדוֹשָׁה, מְאֹד נַעֲלָה מֵעַל כָּל הָעוֹלָמוֹת, רֵאשִׁית וְשֹׁרֶשׁ אֲצִילוּת קָדְשׁוֹ יִתְבָּרַךְ, סוֹד הַמַּלְבּוּשׁ הָעֶלְיוֹן, כְּמוֹ שֶׁכָּתַב רַבֵּנוּ אִישׁ הָאֱלֹקִים נוֹרָא הָאֲרִ"י ז"ל:
- רַק שֶׁנִּשְׁתַּלְשְׁלָה וְיָרְדָה כִּבְיָכוֹל, עַד לָאָרֶץ אֲשֶׁר הֵאִירָה מִכְּבוֹדָהּ
  - וּמִסָּרָה וּנְטָעָהּ הוּא יִתְבָּרַךְ בְּתוֹכֵנוּ, שֶׁנִּהְיֶה אֲנַחְנוּ הַמַּחֲזִיקִים וְתוֹמְכִים בְּעֵץ הַחַיִּים:

- לָזֹאת, מֵאָז, כָּל חִיּוּתָם וְקִיּוּמָם שֶׁל הָעוֹלָמוֹת כֻּלָּם, תָּלוּי וְעוֹמֵד רַק כְּפִי עִנְיַן וְרֹב עֵסְקֵנוּ וְהֶגְיוֹנֵנוּ בָּהּ.
  - שֶׁאִם אֲנַחְנוּ עוֹסְקִים בָּהּ וּמַחֲזִיקִים וְתוֹמְכִים אוֹתָהּ כָּרָאוּי, בְּלִי רִפְיוֹן כְּלָל, אָנוּ מְעוֹרְרִים מְקוֹר שָׁרְשָׁהּ הָעֶלְיוֹן, מְקוֹר הַקְּדֻשּׁוֹת וְהַבְּרָכוֹת, לְהַמְשִׁיךְ וּלְהָרִיק תּוֹסֶפֶת בְּרָכָה, וְחַיֵּי עוֹלָם, וּקְדֻשָּׁה נוֹרָאָה עַל כָּל הָעוֹלָמוֹת, כָּל עוֹלָם לְפִי עֶרֶךְ קְדֻשָּׁתוֹ, שֶׁיּוּכַל לְקַבֵּל וְלִסְבֹּל.
  - וְאִם חַס וְשָׁלוֹם עָסַקְנוּ בָּהּ בְּרִפְיוֹן, מִתְקַמֵּט וּמִתְמַעֵט הַקְּדֻשָּׁה וְאוֹר הָעֶלְיוֹן שֶׁל הַתּוֹרָה מִכָּל הָעוֹלָמוֹת

---

461 Sanhedrin 37a.
462 1 Divrei Hayamim 16:27.
463 Tehillim 5:5.
464 See G4:10. In particular, see V2:03, "The World of The Malbush."
465 Berachot 60b.

- with each individual causing depletion, destabilization and weakening, God forbid, according to his level
- and if we were to all completely desist from involvement with it, God forbid, then all of the worlds would also immediately completely become nullified, God forbid.
- In contrast, with all the [other] commandments, and even the commandment of prayer
  - where, even if all of Israel were to desist from praying to God, God forbid, the worlds would not be returned to their original state of null and void because of this.
  - Therefore, prayer is referred to by Chazal as "transitory life" whereas Torah is referred to as "everlasting life," as they said:[466] Rabba saw R. Hamnuna prolonging his prayer and said: "Is one to forsake eternal life and involve oneself with transitory life?"
  - The concept of prayer is [to provide] additional rectification of the worlds, with the addition of holiness and blessing at the specific times fixed for them.
  - Therefore, if one misses those times there is no further opportunity to bring down the addition of holiness and blessing to the worlds [for that specific prayer instance].
  - However, the concept of study of the Holy Torah is that it touches the very essence of the life force and existence of the worlds, preventing them from being totally destroyed
    - therefore, a person is obligated to continuously involve himself and intellectually engage it to continuously establish and cause existence of the worlds.
- Not only this, but the whole essence of prayer is solely dependent on one's study of the Holy Torah without which it is not heard, God forbid, as per:
  - One who turns his ear from hearing Torah, his prayer is also considered an abomination.[467]
  - One who involves himself with Torah out of difficulty, his prayer is heard . . . and the Pargod [i.e., the veil of God] is not locked in front of him.[468]
  - ". . . but desire attained is a tree of life." We learn, one who wants God to accept his prayer should involve himself with Torah which is the Tree of Life.[469]

---

466 Shabbat 10a.
467 Mishlei 28:9 and as also quoted in Shabbat 10a and in Midrash Mishlei 28:9.
468 Sotah 49a.

כָּל אֶחָד לְפִי עֶרְכּוֹ הוֹלֵךְ וְחָסֵר, רוֹתְתִים וּרְפוּיִים חַס וְשָׁלוֹם.

וְאִם חַס וְשָׁלוֹם הָיִינוּ כֻּלָּנוּ מַנִּיחִים וּמַזְנִיחִים אוֹתָהּ מִלְּהִתְעַסֵּק בָּהּ מִכֹּל וָכֹל, גַּם הָעוֹלָמוֹת כֻּלָּם כְּרֶגַע הָיוּ מִתְבַּטְּלִים מִכֹּל וָכֹל חַס וְשָׁלוֹם:

מַה שֶּׁאֵין כֵּן בְּכָל הַמִּצְווֹת, וַאֲפִלּוּ מִצְוַת הַתְּפִלָּה

שֶׁגַּם אִם הָיוּ חַס וְשָׁלוֹם כָּל יִשְׂרָאֵל מַנִּיחִים וְעוֹזְבִים מִלְּהִתְפַּלֵּל לוֹ יִתְבָּרַךְ, לֹא הָיוּ חוֹזְרִים הָעוֹלָמוֹת עֲבוּר זֶה לְתֹהוּ וָבֹהוּ.

וְלָכֵן הַתְּפִלָּה נִקְרֵאת בְּדִבְרֵי רַבּוֹתֵינוּ זִכְרוֹנָם לִבְרָכָה "חַיֵּי שָׁעָה", וְהַתּוֹרָה נִקְרֵאת "חַיֵּי עוֹלָם", כְּמַאֲמָרָם זִכְרוֹנָם לִבְרָכָה בְּפֶרֶק קַמָּא דְשַׁבָּת (י, א) "רָבָא חֲזֵיהּ לְרַב הַמְנוּנָא דְּקָא מַאֲרִיךְ בִּצְלוֹתָא, אָמַר, מַנִּיחִין חַיֵּי עוֹלָם וְעוֹסְקִין בְּחַיֵּי שָׁעָה".

שֶׁעִנְיַן הַתְּפִלָּה הוּא, 'הוֹסָפוֹת' תִּקּוּן בְּהָעוֹלָמוֹת, בְּתוֹסֶפֶת קְדֻשָּׁה וּבְרָכָה, בְּאוֹתוֹ עֵת הַקָּבוּעַ לָהֶם

וְלָכֵן, אִם עָבְרָה הַשָּׁעָה, שׁוּב לֹא תּוֹעִיל כְּלָל לְהוֹסִיף עֵת בְּהָעוֹלָמוֹת הַתּוֹסֶפֶת קְדֻשָּׁה וּבְרָכָה.

אָמְנָם עִנְיַן הָעֵסֶק בַּתּוֹרָה הַקְּדוֹשָׁה, הוּא נוֹגֵעַ לְ'עֶצֶם הַחִיּוּת' וְקִיּוּם עֲמִידַת הָעוֹלָמוֹת בַּל יֵהָרְסוּ לְגַמְרֵי

לָכֵן, הָאָדָם חַיָּב לַעֲסֹק וְלַהֲגוֹת בָּהּ בְּכָל עֵת תָּמִיד, כְּדֵי לְהַעֲמִיד וּלְקַיֵּם כָּל הָעוֹלָמוֹת כָּל רֶגַע:

וְלֹא עוֹד, אֶלָּא שֶׁגַּם כָּל עִקַּר עִנְיַן הַתְּפִלָּה, אֵינָהּ תְּלוּיָה רַק בְּעֵסֶק הַתּוֹרָה הַקְּדוֹשָׁה, וּבִלְתָּהּ אֵינָהּ נִשְׁמַעַת חַס וְשָׁלוֹם

כְּמוֹ שֶׁאָמַר הַכָּתוּב (משלי כח, ט) "מֵסִיר אָזְנוֹ מִשְּׁמֹעַ תּוֹרָה גַּם תְּפִלָּתוֹ תּוֹעֵבָה", וּכְמוֹ שֶׁאָמְרוּ רַבּוֹתֵינוּ זִכְרוֹנָם לִבְרָכָה בְּשַׁבָּת שָׁם, וּבְמִשְׁלֵי רַבָּתָא פָּרָשָׁה כ"ח.

וְאָמְרוּ (בְּסוֹף סוֹטָה מט, א) "כָּל הָעוֹסֵק בַּתּוֹרָה מִתּוֹךְ הַדְּחָק, תְּפִלָּתוֹ נִשְׁמַעַת, וְאֵין הַפַּרְגּוֹד נִנְעָל בְּפָנָיו".

וּבַזֹּהַר מִקֵּץ ר"ב ב' "וְעֵץ חַיִּים תַּאֲוָה בָאָה" (משלי יג, יב), תָּנִינָן, מַאן דְּבָעֵי דְקוּדְשָׁא בְּרִיךְ הוּא יְקַבֵּל צְלוֹתֵיהּ, יִשְׁתַּדֵּל בְּאוֹרַיְתָא, דְּאִיהִי עֵץ חַיִּים.

---

469 Zohar I Miketz 202b quoting Mishlei 13:12.

- Therefore, the Halacha states that it is permitted to use a House of Prayer as a place of Torah study,[470] because [Torah study] has greater holiness and only [Torah study] bestows life force, holiness, and light to all the worlds as it is on a higher level than all of [the worlds].

27. TORAH HIGHER THAN WORLDS AS UNCHANGED BY ITS DESCENT

- In addition [to the fact that the Torah comes from The World of the Malbush, the first and highest of all of the worlds], its awesome holiness is significantly superior to the worlds
  - as with the Supernal [Realms], even though their holiness is very great, however, as they cascade and descend through all [the world] levels in a tremendously filtered way, even though each [lower] world contains the blueprint within it of the entire [connected] sequence of [higher] worlds above it, and absolutely replicates their image and form as is known[471]
    - as per the Zohar:[472] We learned, just as things are above, so they are below; so too it is with all the worlds, they are all interconnected with each other
    - and as written in Etz Chaim in connection with the four [levels of] worlds Atzilut, Beriyah, Yetzirah, and Asiyah.[473]
    - Nevertheless, the level of holiness and light in a particular world cannot even vaguely be compared to that of the world above it – to the extent that ultimately through all the levels of cascaded filtering of the holiness and light, it becomes so material that this physical world becomes mundane and we treat it in a mundane way.
  - However, with the Holy Torah – even though it also cascades down through infinite levels from its high holy source and from world to world and from level to level – nevertheless, its original holiness is preserved intact, just as it is in its source, at the beginning of its way in holiness where even in this physical world, it is totally holy and it is forbidden to treat it in a mundane way, God forbid, such that it is even forbidden to think words of Torah in unclean places.

---

470 Megillah 27a.
471 See G1:05; G1:17; the concept of Kav in G3:07 and G3:10; G4:10.
472 Zohar II Yitro 82b (this section of Zohar is also quoted in G3:10).
473 Etz Chaim Shaar 42, Shaar Derushei ABY"A, Chap. 13 (see V2:14, p. 676):
  - It is straightforward, just as Atzilut is divided into these 4 levels [of Atzilut, Beriyah, Yetzirah, and Asiyah] so too are all of these general world levels.

לָכֵן הַדִּין פָּסוּק בַּשַּׁ"ס (מגילה כז, א) "בֵּית הַכְּנֶסֶת מוּתָּר לַעֲשׂוֹתוֹ בֵּית הַמִּדְרָשׁ", מִשּׁוּם דְּעִלּוּיֵי קָא מַעֲלֵי לֵיהּ לִקְדֻשָּׁה יוֹתֵר חֲמוּרָה, שֶׁרַק הִיא הַנּוֹתֶנֶת הַשֶּׁפַע חִיּוּת וּקְדֻשָּׁה וְאוֹר לְכָל הָעוֹלָמוֹת, מִטַּעַם שֶׁהִיא לְמַעְלָה מִכֻּלָּם:

שער ד' - פרק כ"ז

וְעוֹד זֹאת, יִתְרָה עֶרֶךְ וְיִתְרוֹן קְדֻשָּׁתָהּ הַנּוֹרָאָה מֵהָעוֹלָמוֹת

כִּי הָעֶלְיוֹנִים, אַף שֶׁקְּדֻשָּׁתָם רַבָּה מְאֹד, אָמְנָם כַּאֲשֶׁר נִשְׁתַּלְשְׁלוּ וְיָרְדוּ דֶּרֶךְ הִשְׁתַּלְשְׁלוּת וְהַדְרָגוֹת עֲצוּמוֹת, הֲגַם שֶׁבְּכָל עוֹלָם נִצְטַיֵּר וְנֶחְתַּם בּוֹ כָּל סִדְרֵי הָעוֹלָם שֶׁמֵּעָלָיו, בִּדְמוּתוֹ כְּצַלְמוֹ מַמָּשׁ כַּיָּדוּעַ

וּכְמוֹ שֶׁכָּתוּב בַּזֹּהַר יִתְרוֹ פ"ב ב', תָּאנָא, כְּגַוְנָא דִלְעֵלָּא אִית לְתַתָּא מִינַיְיהוּ, וְכֵן בְּכֻלְּהוּ עָלְמִין, כֻּלְּהוּ אֲחִידָן, דָּא בְּדָא, וְדָא בְּדָא.

וּכְמוֹ שֶׁכָּתוּב בְּעֵץ חַיִּים בְּעִנְיַן הָאַרְבַּע עוֹלָמוֹת אֲבִי"ע, עַיֵּן שָׁם בְּשַׁעַר דְּרוּשֵׁי אֲבִי"ע פֶּרֶק א', וּבְפֶרֶק ד' שָׁם, וּבְשַׁעַר הַשֵּׁמוֹת רֵישׁ פֶּרֶק א'

עִם כָּל זֶה אֵינוֹ שָׁוֶה וְדוֹמֶה כְּלָל, עֶרֶךְ קְדֻשָּׁתוֹ וְאוֹרוֹ לְהָעוֹלָם שֶׁמֵּעָלָיו, עַד שֶׁבְּכָל כָּךְ נִתְעַבּוּ, וְנִתְמַעֲטוּ מִקְּדֻשָּׁתָם וְאוֹרָם דֶּרֶךְ הִשְׁתַּלְשְׁלוּת וְהַדְרָגוֹת עֲצוּמוֹת, עַד שֶׁבְּזֶה הָעוֹלָם נַעֲשׂוּ חֻלִּין, שֶׁאָנוּ נוֹהֲגִין בָּהֶן מִנְהַג חֹל.

אָמְנָם הַתּוֹרָה הַקְּדוֹשָׁה, אַף שֶׁגַּם הִיא נִשְׁתַּלְשְׁלָה וְיָרְדָה מִמְּקוֹר שָׁרְשָׁהּ הָעֶלְיוֹן בַּקֹּדֶשׁ, מַדְרֵגוֹת אֵין שִׁעוּר, מֵעוֹלָם לְעוֹלָם, וּמִמַּדְרֵגָה לְמַדְרֵגָה, עִם כָּל זֶה, קְדֻשָּׁתָהּ הָרִאשׁוֹנָה, כְּמוֹ שֶׁהוּא בִּמְקוֹר שָׁרְשָׁהּ, רֵאשִׁית דַּרְכָּהּ בַּקֹּדֶשׁ, כִּדְקָאֵי קָאֵי גַּם בְּזֶה הָעוֹלָם, שֶׁכֻּלָּהּ קֹדֶשׁ, וְאָסוּר לִנְהֹג בָּהּ מִנְהַג חֹל חַס וְשָׁלוֹם, שֶׁגַּם הַהִרְהוּר בְּדִבְרֵי תוֹרָה אָסוּר בִּמְקוֹמוֹת הַמְטֻנָּפִים.

Etz Chaim Shaar 42, Shaar Derushei ABY"A Chap. 2 (see V2:14, p. 676):
- All the emanations[/worlds] are of the same format, incorporating all of the 4 elements, which are the 4 letters of YHVH and the 4 worlds of Atzilut, Beriyah, Yetzirah, and Asiyah.

Etz Chaim Shaar 44, Shaar HaShemot beginning of Chap. 1:
- [In essence the explanation is given in the bracketed section of this chapter, that each component of each world is analogous to a part of the body, with each part of the body containing the blueprint, i.e., the DNA, of the whole body, and therefore each Sefira and world similarly contains the blueprint of all of the Sefirot and worlds, except that although each Sefira contains all of the Sefirot, nevertheless one of them is dominant.]

- Therefore, Chazal were very strict when they debated the punishment [for these forbidden thoughts] saying that these thoughts are also included in the admonition "for he scorned the word of God,"[474] with the later part of this verse being "he shall surely be cut off" which is interpreted as both in this world and the World to Come.[475]
- Chazal state that one who holds a Sefer Torah with his bare hands is buried 'without that Mitzvah.'[476]
- Chazal also forbade [a Sefer Torah] to be transferred from place to place and even from one house of prayer to another,[477] as the Torah always has its original level of holiness.
- (Similarly, even though the source of man's soul is very much higher than the supernal worlds, and he adopts appropriate intellectual methods with which to refine his character, he is still permitted to engage in these thoughts in unclean places. However, Torah thoughts of [even abstract laws which do not currently apply, such as] laws of Negaim and Ohalot, or of other laws and of any words of Torah at all, are forbidden in unclean places.)[478]

* This concept relates to Chazal's statement[479] that God and the Torah are One:
  - That even though the worlds gradually diminish in their level of holiness through their cascading down and many changes [between world levels], this is only from [man's] perspective.
  - However, from [God's] perspective there is no distinction or difference in any place at all whatsoever, God forbid, as per the verse "I am God, I have not changed,"[480] and there is no change [or any concept of levels of] holiness.
  - This point has been explained at length above in the Third Gateway. Refer there.[481]

---

474 Bamidbar 15:31.
475 Sanhedrin 99a (see G3:03 and G4:24).
476 Shabbat 14a and also Megillah 32a: Meaning that the specific Mitzvah, i.e., reading from the Torah, that was performed while compromising the Holiness of the Torah by holding it with one's bare hands, is removed from a person.
477 Zohar III Acharei Mot 71b.
478 With this parenthetic statement, R. Chaim highlights that even though thoughts of character refinement are on a very high level and can encourage one to be more focused in his Torah study, nevertheless, these thoughts are simply incomparable in their level with actual Torah study to the extent that the former are permitted in unclean places. This statement can be related to

שער ד' - פרק כ"ז

וְלָזֹאת, הֶחֱמִירוּ וְהִפְלִיגוּ רַבּוֹתֵינוּ זִכְרוֹנָם לִבְרָכָה בְּעָנְשׁוֹ, וְאָמְרוּ (בפרק חלק צ"ט ע"א) שֶׁגַּם הוּא בִּכְלָל "כִּי דְבַר ה' בָּזָה" (במדבר טו,). וְסֵיפֵיהּ דְּהַאי קְרָא "הִכָּרֵת תִּכָּרֵת", וּפֵרְשׁוּ רַבּוֹתֵינוּ זִכְרוֹנָם לִבְרָכָה "הִכָּרֵת" — בָּעוֹלָם הַזֶּה, "תִּכָּרֵת" — לָעוֹלָם הַבָּא.

וְאָמְרוּ (מגילה לב, א) הָאוֹחֵז סֵפֶר תּוֹרָה עָרוֹם, נִקְבָּר עָרוּם מֵאוֹתָהּ מִצְוָה.

גַּם אָסְרוּ לְטַלְטְלָהּ מִמָּקוֹם לְמָקוֹם, וְאַף מִבֵּי כְּנִישְׁתָּא לְבֵי כְּנִישְׁתָּא אָסְרוּ בַּזֹּהַר פָּרָשַׁת אַחֲרֵי (ע"א ב) לְטַלְטְלָהּ, עַיֵּן שָׁם, מִטַּעַם שֶׁהִיא לְעוֹלָם בִּקְדֻשָּׁתָהּ הָרִאשׁוֹנָה עוֹמֶדֶת.

(וְכֵן אֲפִלּוּ הָאָדָם, שֶׁשֹּׁרֶשׁ נִשְׁמָתוֹ הִיא מֵעוֹלָם עֶלְיוֹן וְגָבוֹהַּ מְאֹד, מֵהָעוֹלָמוֹת הָעֶלְיוֹנִים, וְיִקַּח לוֹ בְּשִׂכְלוֹ מַחֲשָׁבָה נְכוֹנָה, לְהִתְדַּבֵּק לְטָהֳרַת אֵיזֶה מִדָּה נְכוֹנָה, הוּא רַשַּׁאי לֵילֵךְ בְּזֹאת הַמַּחֲשָׁבָה גַּם בִּמְקוֹמוֹת הַמְטֻנָּפִים, וַאֲפִלּוּ הִרְהוּר דִּבְרֵי תּוֹרָה בְּדִינֵי נְגָעִים וְאֹהָלוֹת, אוֹ שְׁאָרֵי דִינִים וְאֵיזֶה דִּבְרֵי תוֹרָה שֶׁתִּהְיֶה, אָסוּר בִּמְקוֹמוֹת הַמְטֻנָּפִים):

• וְהוּא גַּם כֵּן עִנְיַן מַאֲמָרָם זִכְרוֹנָם לִבְרָכָה בַּזֹּהַר, דְּקֻדְשָׁא בְּרִיךְ הוּא וְאוֹרַיְתָא חַד.
  ○ וְהוּא, שֶׁאַף עַל פִּי שֶׁהָעוֹלָמוֹת הוֹלְכִים כֻּלָּם דֶּרֶךְ הַדְרָגָה וְהִשְׁתַּלְשְׁלוּת וְשִׁנּוּיִים רַבִּים בְּעֶרֶךְ קְדֻשָּׁתָם, כָּל זֶה הוּא רַק מִצִּדֵּנוּ
  ○ אֲבָל מִצִּדּוֹ יִתְבָּרֵךְ — אֵין שׁוּם חִלּוּק וְשִׁנּוּי מְקוֹמוֹת כְּלָל חַס וְשָׁלוֹם, וּכְמוֹ שֶׁכָּתוּב (מלאכי ג, ו): "אֲנִי ה' לֹא שָׁנִיתִי", וְלֹא נִשְׁתַּנָּה הַקְּדֻשָּׁה
  ○ כְּמוֹ שֶׁכָּתוּב בְּאֹרֶךְ לְמַעְלָה בְּשַׁעַר ג' (פ"ג וכו'), עַיֵּן שָׁם:

R. Chaim's earlier comments in the Fourth Gateway from G4:04 onwards that for example, cultivation of one's character traits to inspire Fear of God is the storehouse or preservative for Torah study but that in and of itself it is of no value without Torah study. (The following comment is made by the Mishna Berura 85:5: . . . and it is obvious that a person, while in the restroom, is permitted to contemplate on the extent of his lowliness and that his end will be that he will completely return to dust and the worm and that haughtiness is [therefore] not fitting for him.)

479 E.g., Zohar II Beshalach 60a.
480 Malachi 3:6.
481 The idea is expressed throughout the Third Gateway from G3:03 onwards with the difference in God's and man's perspectives being highlighted in G3:04 and then building up to explain the concept of Tzimtzum and Kav in G3:07.

- This is similarly the case with the Holy Torah. Even with the tremendous descent of Torah through many levels, it has nevertheless remained entirely unchanged and is intact in its original state of holiness – even in this physical world – 'just as it was reared with Him'[482] [with] God in its root source – unaffected by any change of Makom/Place at all.
  - However, even though, from God's perspective all places are equal and there is no differentiation between them at all – for unclean places do not act as barriers [to separate from] God's Unity and tremendous Holiness. Similarly, this is the case with the tremendous holiness of the Holy Torah
  - but notwithstanding this, we are forbidden to speak or even to think [about Torah] in unclean places, as from our perspective there very definitely is differentiation between places as has been explained there at length.[483]
- However, the essence of the Torah has not changed in its supernal holiness and light as a result of its descent; it is just that 'our physical eyes are incapable of perceiving'[484] [the Torah's] tremendous inner holiness and light.
  - Therefore, King David said: "Open my eyes and I will see the wonders of Your Torah"[485]
  - as in truth the holiness and light of the Holy Torah which are internally hidden, are openly revealed and shine in the holiness of Its supernal light as it actually is – it is just that our physical perception is unable to tolerate [the Torah's] tremendous holiness and light as it actually is.

28. TORAH SPEAKS TO ALL WORLD LEVELS, ITS ESSENCE WILL BE REVEALED

- Therefore, [the Torah] also conceals itself [via a Tzimtzum process] as it cascades down from level to level and from world to world, to be manifest in a way which speaks to the issues of each world
  - according to the specific issues and relative level of that world such that it is able to tolerate its holiness and light
  - until it ultimately descends to this physical world where it is manifest in such a way that it speaks to the relative context and issues within this world – containing narrative which is about this world – so that this world is capable of tolerating its holiness and light.[486]

---

482 Esther 2:20.
483 In the Third Gateway.

כֵּן הַתּוֹרָה הַקְּדוֹשָׁה, אַף כִּי יָרְדָה וְנִשְׁתַּלְשְׁלָה דֶּרֶךְ הַדְּרָגוֹת רַבּוֹת עֲצוּמוֹת, עִם כָּל זֶה, הִיא לֹא נִשְׁתַּנְּתָה מִקְּדֻשָּׁתָהּ כְּלָל, וּבִקְדֻשָּׁתָהּ הָרִאשׁוֹנָה עוֹמֶדֶת גַּם בְּזֶה הָעוֹלָם הַתַּחְתּוֹן, כַּאֲשֶׁר הָיְתָה בְּאָמְנָה אִתּוֹ יִתְבָּרַךְ בִּמְקוֹר שָׁרְשָׁהּ, בְּלֹא שׁוּם חִלּוּק וְשִׁנּוּי מָקוֹם כְּלָל.

○ אָמְנָם, אַף עַל פִּי שֶׁמִּצְדּוֹ יִתְבָּרַךְ — כָּל הַמְּקוֹמוֹת שָׁוִים, בְּלִי שׁוּם שִׁנּוּי כְּלָל, שֶׁאֵין מְקוֹמוֹת הַמְטֻנָּפִים חוֹצְצִים לְאַחְדוּתוֹ וְעֶצֶם קְדֻשָּׁתוֹ יִתְבָּרַךְ, וְכֵן הוּא בְּעִנְיַן עֶצֶם קְדֻשַּׁת הַתּוֹרָה הַקְּדוֹשָׁה

○ עִם כָּל זֶה, אֲנַחְנוּ נֶאֱסַרְנוּ לְדַבֵּר, גַּם לְהַרְהֵר בָּהּ, בַּמְּבוֹאוֹת הַמְטֻנָּפוֹת, כִּי מִצִּדֵּנוּ וַדַּאי יֵשׁ חִלּוּק וְשִׁנּוּי מְקוֹמוֹת, כְּמוֹ שֶׁנִּתְבָּאֵר שָׁם בְּאָרְכּוֹ:

• אֲבָל הַתּוֹרָה הַקְּדוֹשָׁה בְּעַצְמוּתָהּ, לֹא נִשְׁתַּנְּתָה בְּסִבַּת יְרִידָתָהּ מִקְּדֻשָּׁתָהּ וְאוֹרָהּ הָעֶלְיוֹן, רַק שֶׁפָּתַח עֵינֵינוּ מֵרְאוֹת בְּעֶצֶם קְדֻשָּׁתָהּ וְאוֹרָהּ הַפְּנִימִי.

○ וְלָכֵן אָמַר דָּוִד הַמֶּלֶךְ עָלָיו הַשָּׁלוֹם "גַּל עֵינַי וְאַבִּיטָה נִפְלָאוֹת מִתּוֹרָתֶךָ" (תהלים קיט, יח)

○ כִּי בֶּאֱמֶת קְדֻשַּׁת וְאוֹר הַתּוֹרָה הַקְּדוֹשָׁה, הֵם פְּנִימִיּוּת סְתָרֶיהָ, הֵמָּה מְפָרְשִׁים וְנִגְלִים, וּמְאִירִים בִּקְדֻשַּׁת אוֹרָם הָעֶלְיוֹן כַּאֲשֶׁר הוּא, רַק שֶׁעֵינֵינוּ אֵין יְכוֹלוֹת לִסְבֹּל עֶצֶם קְדֻשָּׁתָהּ וְאוֹרָהּ כַּאֲשֶׁר הוּא:

שער ד' - פרק כ"ח

• וְלָזֹאת אַף הִיא, דֶּרֶךְ יְרִידָתָהּ וְהִשְׁתַּלְשְׁלוּתָהּ מִמַּדְרֵגָה לְמַדְרֵגָה וּמֵעוֹלָם לְעוֹלָם, צִמְצְמָה עַצְמָהּ, לְהִתְלַבֵּשׁ בְּכָל עוֹלָם לְדַבֵּר בְּעִנְיְנֵי אוֹתוֹ הָעוֹלָם

○ כְּפִי עִנְיַן וְעֵרֶךְ אוֹתוֹ הָעוֹלָם, כְּדֵי שֶׁיּוּכַל לִסְבֹּל קְדֻשָּׁתָהּ וְאוֹרָהּ

○ עַד שֶׁבִּרְדִתָּהּ לָבֹא לְזֶה הָעוֹלָם, נִתְלַבְּשָׁה גַּם כֵּן לְדַבֵּר בְּעֶרְכֵּי וְעִנְיְנֵי זֶה הָעוֹלָם, וְסִפּוּרִין דְּהַאי עָלְמָא, כְּדֵי שֶׁיּוּכַל זֶה הָעוֹלָם לִסְבֹּל קְדֻשַּׁת אוֹרָהּ.

---

484 Yishayahu 44:18.
485 Tehillim 119:18.
486 For more insight on this and the ideas presented in this chapter see the quotation from Kol Eliyahu in the name of the Vilna Gaon which is brought down on V2:03, p. 355.

- However, while it speaks to the lower worlds, [its expression within each world] nevertheless hints at the core of Torah, and at its infinite levels upon levels of abstracted innermost depth. As per:
  - R. Shimon says: [Woe to the person who says that the Torah tells ordinary stories and contains ordinary words ... However, all words of the Torah are words from On High and Secrets Most High.]487
  - R. Yossi says: It is certain that all that God does in this world is with the secret of His Wisdom [i.e., His Torah].488
  - He further began and said ... How many good things [i.e., secret things] are the ways and paths of the Torah.489
  - R. Abba began ... How much should one investigate the expressions of Torah.490
  - The Torah contains all the hidden secrets of the supernal worlds.491
- These [hints] containing the details of all the myriads of worlds and levels within which the Torah is manifest in its descent [to this physical world].
- Therefore the Zohar frequently refers to the Torah as being both hidden and revealed492 which is clear to all who understand that its meaning is
  - that it is the hidden path from the Holy Torah which is not explicitly written and explained within it, but that these concepts are concealed and hidden within its words through hints
  - whereas the revealed path of [Torah] is the straightforward textual meaning which is clearly and explicitly written in it.
  - (This is *not* as per [an idea] I saw written in a book by one who researched into this issue – [asking]
    - why do we refer to the wisdom of Kabbalah with the name "hidden"? Surely to one who understands them they are "revealed," and to those people who don't know or understand, they also don't know how to explain the simple meaning of the Scriptural texts, and even the simple meaning of the Scriptural texts is "hidden" from them?
    - and he answers there whatever he answers.)
  - As per, how beloved are words of Torah, that each and every word contains supernal secrets. Refer there.493

---

487 Zohar III Behaalotcha 152a.
488 Zohar I Toldot 145b.
489 Zohar III Balak 202a.
490 Zohar II Beshalach 55b.
491 Zohar I Toldot 134b.

- אָמְנָם, אִם שֶׁהִיא מְדַבֶּרֶת בַּתַּחְתּוֹנִים, רוֹמֶזֶת הִיא בָּהֶם גּוּפֵי תוֹרָה, וְעִנְיָנִים פְּנִימִיִּים, וּפְנִימִיִּים לִפְנִימִיִּים, גָּבוֹהַּ מֵעַל גָּבוֹהַּ עַד אֵין תַּכְלִית. וְעַיֵּן
- בַּזֹּהַר בְּהַעֲלוֹתְךָ קנ"ב א', רַבִּי שִׁמְעוֹן אוֹמֵר כו'
- וּבְפָרָשַׁת תּוֹלְדוֹת קמ"ה ב', אָמַר רַבִּי יוֹסֵי, וַדַּאי כָּל מַה דְּעָבִיד קוּדְשָׁא בְּרִיךְ הוּא בְּאַרְעָא, כֹּלָּא הֲוָה בְּרָזָא דְחָכְמְתָא, וכו'.
- וּבְפָרָשַׁת בָּלָק ר"ב א' תּוּ פָּתַח וְאָמַר כו' כַּמָּה טָבִין אִנּוּן אָרְחִין וּשְׁבִילִין דְּאוֹרַיְתָא, וכו'.
- וּבְפָרָשַׁת בְּשַׁלַּח נ"ה סוֹף ע"ב, רַבִּי אַבָּא פָּתַח כו', כַּמָּה אִית לָן לְאִסְתַּכְּלָא בְּפִתְגָמֵי אוֹרַיְתָא, וכו'.
- וּבְפָרָשַׁת תּוֹלְדוֹת קל"ד סוֹף ע"ב, בְּאוֹרַיְתָא אִנּוּן כָּל רָזִין עִלָּאִין חֲתִימִין, וכו'.
- וְהֵם פְּרָטוּת עִנְיְנֵי כָּל הָרִבֵּי רְבָבוֹת הָעוֹלָמוֹת וְהַמַּדְרֵגוֹת, שֶׁנִּתְלַבְּשָׁה בָּהֶם דֶּרֶךְ יְרִידָתָהּ:
- וְלָכֵן שֶׁגּוּרָה בְּפִי הַזֹּהַר, דְּאוֹרַיְתָא כֻּלָּהּ אִיהִי "סָתִים וְגַלְיָא", שֶׁהוּא מְבֹאָר לְכָל מֵבִין שֶׁפֵּרוּשׁוֹ הוּא
- שֶׁהוּא הַדֶּרֶךְ הַ"נִּסְתָּר" מֵהַתּוֹרָה הַקְּדוֹשָׁה, שֶׁאֵינוֹ כָּתוּב מְפֹרָשׁ וּמְבֹאָר בָּהּ, אֶלָּא שֶׁנִּסְתָּר וְנִטְמַן הָעִנְיָנִים אֵלּוּ בְּרֶמֶז בִּדְבָרֶיהָ
- וְדֶרֶךְ הַ"נִּגְלֶה" שֶׁבָּהּ הוּא הַפְּשׁוּטוֹ שֶׁל מִקְרָא, שֶׁהוּא כָּתוּב מְפֹרָשׁ וּמְבֹאָר בָּהּ.
- (וְלֹא כְּמוֹ שֶׁרָאִיתִי בְּסֵפֶר כָּתוּב, מֵאֶחָד שֶׁחָקַר עַל הָעִנְיָן
- מִפְּנֵי מָה קוֹרְאִים לְחָכְמַת הַקַּבָּלָה בְּשֵׁם "נִסְתָּר", הֲלֹא מִי שֶׁמֵּבִין בָּהֶם אֶצְלוֹ הֵם נִגְלִים, וְלַאֲנָשִׁים שֶׁאֵינָם יוֹדְעִים וּמְבִינִים הֲלֹא יֵשׁ שֶׁגַּם פְּשׁוּטוֹ שֶׁל מִקְרָא אֵינָם יוֹדְעִים לְפָרֵשׁ, וְאֶצְלָם גַּם הַפְּשׁוּטוֹ שֶׁל מִקְרָא דַּרְכּוֹ נִסְתָּרָה מֵהֶם
- וְתֵרֵץ שָׁם מַה שֶּׁתֵּרֵץ).
- וְעַיֵּן זֹהַר בְּהַעֲלוֹתְךָ קמ"ט א' וּב', כַּמָּה חֲבִיבִין מִלֵּי דְּאוֹרַיְתָא, דְּבְכָל מִלָּה וּמִלָּה אִית רָזִין עִלָּאִין, כו', עַיֵּן שָׁם.

---

492 E.g., Zohar III Acharei Mot 71b.
493 Zohar III Behaalotcha 149a, which continues on 149b to state "One who says that the Torah narrative shows that it is an ordinary story – is a fool!"

- Each individual is able to delve into the depths of these concepts according to the level of his wisdom, the refinement of his intellect, the holiness and purity of his heart, and his level of study and analysis of it.
* However, the essential meaning of the Torah,[494] the secret of the soul of its soul, the hidden part of its hidden part
  - these concepts are concealed by *Atik Yomin*,[495] which is put out of the way[496] of God's creations
  - and no person has yet known this level
  - except for our first father [Adam] who was able to perceive his soul of his soul[497]
  - and with it he was able to see the supernal radiance, the soul of the soul of the Holy Torah
  - and the ultimate supernal source of Supernal Wisdom was revealed to him.
  - But from the time that [Adam] sinned and the supernal radiance departed from him
  - and the arrangement of the supernal worlds was confused and corrupted
  - the supernal pathways to the Wisdom of Torah were also blocked – the secret of the soul of its soul.
* On the holy occasion of receiving the Holy Torah, even though there was a purification of the world – to the extent that Chazal say: "The filth was removed from Israel when they stood at Mount Sinai";[498] nevertheless, [Israel] only merited in perceiving the depth of the inner soul of Torah,[499] but not the level of soul of the soul.
* It will only be when 'He pours Spirit from above,'[500] and God pours His Spirit over all flesh [in the time to come], that the springs of wisdom will be revealed, the pathways of the amazing supernal wisdom, the soul of its soul.
  - As per the Zohar:[501] The Torah has a body . . . The fools of this world only relate to its garment . . . Those that know more do not relate to its garment but rather to its body which is under its garment. The Sages, the Servants of the Supernal King, those that stood at Mount Sinai, only relate to the soul which is literally the essence of the whole Torah, and in the World to Come they will see the soul of the soul of the Torah.

---

494 R. Chaim uses the expression "HaTaamei Torah" where "Taam" means both "meaning" and "accent." See G2:16 where the meaning/accent of a word is related to its soul.

- וְכָל אֶחָד מִסְתַּכֵּל בְּסִתְרֵי עֹמֶק פְּנִימִיּוּתָם, כְּפִי רֹב חָכְמָתוֹ וְזֹךְ שִׂכְלוֹ, וּקְדֻשַּׁת טָהֳרַת לְבָבוֹ, וְרֹב עִסְקוֹ וְהִגְיוֹנוֹ בָּהּ:

• אָמְנָם, עִקַּר הַטְּעָמֵי תוֹרָה, סוֹד נִשְׁמָתָא לְנִשְׁמָתָא דִילָהּ, סִתְרֵי סִתְרֵיהָ

- הֵמָּה דְבָרִים שֶׁכִּסָּה עַתִּיק יוֹמִין, וְהֶעְתִּיקָן מִבְּרִיּוֹתָיו
- וְאִישׁ לֹא יְדָעָם עֲדַיִן
- רַק אָבִינוּ הָרִאשׁוֹן, הוּא אֲשֶׁר הִשִּׂיג בְּחִינַת נִשְׁמָתָא דִילֵיהּ
- שֶׁבָּהּ הָיָה מִסְתַּכֵּל בְּזִיהֲרָא עִלָּאָה, נִשְׁמָתָא לְנִשְׁמָתָא שֶׁל הַתּוֹרָה הַקְּדוֹשָׁה
- וְהַחָכְמוֹת הָעֶלְיוֹנוֹת הָיוּ גְלוּיוֹת לְפָנָיו בְּשֹׁרֶשׁ שָׁרְשָׁם הָעֶלְיוֹן.
- וּמֵעֵת אֲשֶׁר חָטָא, וְאִסְתַּלֵּק מִנֵּיהּ הַזִּיהֲרָא עִלָּאָה
- וְנִתְבַּלְבְּלוּ וְנִתְעָרְבוּ הַסְּדָרִים הָעֶלְיוֹנִים
- נִסְתְּמוּ גַּם הַנְּתִיבוֹת וּשְׁבִילִין עֶלְיוֹנִים דְּחָכְמְתָא דְּאוֹרַיְתָא, סוֹד הַנִּשְׁמָתָא לְנִשְׁמָתָא דִילָהּ:

• וְגַם בְּמַעֲמָד הַקָּדוֹשׁ בְּעֵת קַבָּלַת הַתּוֹרָה הַקְּדוֹשָׁה, אַף דְּאִתְבַּסֵּם עָלְמָא, עַד שֶׁאָמְרוּ זִכְרוֹנָם לִבְרָכָה (שבת קמו, א) "יִשְׂרָאֵל שֶׁעָמְדוּ עַל הַר סִינַי פָּסְקָה זֻהֲמָתָן", עִם כָּל זֶה, לֹא זָכוּ לְהַשִּׂיג רַק עֹמֶק פְּנִימִיּוּת הַנִּשְׁמָתָא דְּאוֹרַיְתָא, אֲבָל לֹא בְּחִינַת הַנִּשְׁמָתָא לְנִשְׁמָתָא:

• עַד אֲשֶׁר יֵעָרֶה רוּחַ מִמָּרוֹם, וְיִשְׁפֹּךְ הוּא יִתְבָּרַךְ אֶת רוּחוֹ עַל כָּל בָּשָׂר, אָז יִתְגַּלּוּ מַבּוּעִין דְּחָכְמְתָא, נְתִיבוֹת פְּלִיאוֹת הַחָכְמָה הָעֶלְיוֹנָה, נִשְׁמָתָא לְנִשְׁמָתָא דִילָהּ.

- כְּמוֹ שֶׁכָּתוּב בַּזֹּהַר בְּהַעֲלוֹתְךָ קנ"ב א', אוֹרַיְתָא אִית לָהּ גּוּפָא כו', טִפְּשִׁין דְּעָלְמָא לָא מִסְתַּכְּלֵי אֶלָּא בְּהַהוּא לְבוּשָׁא כו'. אִנּוּן דְּיַדְעִין יַתִּיר — לָא מִסְתַּכְּלָן בִּלְבוּשָׁא אֶלָּא בְּגוּפָא, דְּאִיהוּ תְּחוֹת הַהוּא לְבוּשָׁא. חַכִּימִין עַבְדֵי דְּמַלְכָּא עִלָּאָה, אִנּוּן דְּקַיְמוּ בְּטוּרָא דְסִינַי — לָא אִסְתַּכְּלֵי אֶלָּא בְּנִשְׁמָתָא,

---

495 Referring to a very high place.
496 The language of "put out of the way," i.e., "veHe'etikan," is related to the word "Atik." "Atik" is normally understood to mean "ancient"; however, in the context of the term "Atik Yomin" it means that this is such a high place that it is out of the reach of all creations.
497 See G1:15, G1:22, G2:17, G3:14.
498 Shabbat 146a.
499 See G1:16 which describes more about this.
500 Yishayahu 32:15.
501 Zohar III Behaalotcha 152a.

- This is as per the verse "and your Mentor shall no longer be concealed, and your eyes will see your Mentor."[502]
- This is the concept of the light of the first day of Creation which was stored away for the Righteous in the time to come;[503] as Chazal say: "In the time to come, God will take the sun out of its shield . . . ."[504] This is the secret of *Eden* as is known,[505] which is the level of the soul of the soul.[506]

- Adam, before his sin, lived in the *Garden*, and from there was able to peer into this *Eden*, as mentioned above. But when he sinned, this supernal level departed from him and he was therefore expelled from the Garden of Eden, and this is the secret of the combination of the letters of [Torah], as they are written in the supernal realms, as explained above at the end of the Second Gateway.[507]
  - Chazal say on this: "No one knows its value"[508] . . . the paragraphs of the Torah were not given in the correct sequence, for if they were given in sequence, then anyone who reads them would immediately be able to create a universe and resurrect the dead. . . .[509]
- We will now return to explain a little about the difference between and the advantage of the light of the Holy Torah over the Commandments.

29. TORAH VS. MITZVOT – HEALS ENTIRE BODY VS. HEALS SPECIFIC LIMB

- Chazal state:[510] R. Menachem son of Yossi expounded the verse "For a Commandment is a candle, but the Torah is light"[511] as follows:
  - This verse associates a Commandment with a candle and the Torah with light to tell you that
  - just as a candle only gives light temporarily, similarly the performance of a Commandment only provides temporary protection

---

502 Yishayahu 30:20.
503 Chagiga 12a.
504 Nedarim 8b and also Avodah Zarah 3b.
505 E.g., Shela, Toldot Adam, Beit Hashem Beit David, 288.
506 The Vilna Gaon, in his commentary on Sefer Yetzirah 1:9, comments as follows:
- "and this is the Holy Breath/Spirit": It is the medium between the Creator and the creations; it is the light which was stored away which enables visibility from one end of the world to the other, and it was stored away for the Righteous, for with the Holy Breath/Spirit, it is possible to perceive from one end of the world to the other. . . .

דְּאִיהִי עִקְרָא דְּכָלָּא אוֹרַיְתָא מַמָּשׁ. וּלְעָלְמָא דְּאָתֵי — זְמִינִין לְאִסְתַּכְּלָא בְּנִשְׁמָתָא דְּנִשְׁמָתָא דְּאוֹרַיְתָא.

○ וּכְמוֹ שֶׁכָּתוּב (ישעיה ל, כ) "וְהָיוּ עֵינֶיךָ רוֹאוֹת אֶת מוֹרֶיךָ וְלֹא יִכָּנֵף עוֹד מוֹרֶיךָ".

○ וְהוּא עִנְיַן הָאוֹר שֶׁל יוֹם רִאשׁוֹן, שֶׁגְּנָזוֹ לַצַּדִּיקִים לֶעָתִיד לָבֹא (חגיגה יב, א). וְזֶהוּ שֶׁאָמְרוּ רַבּוֹתֵינוּ זִכְרוֹנָם לִבְרָכָה (נדרים ח, ב) "לֶעָתִיד לָבֹא, הַקָּדוֹשׁ בָּרוּךְ הוּא מוֹצִיא חַמָּה מִנַּרְתִּיקָהּ" כו', וְהוּא סוֹד הָ"עֵדֶן" כַּיָּדוּעַ, שֶׁהוּא הַבְּחִינַת נִשְׁמָתָא דְּנִשְׁמָתָא:

• וְאָדָם הָרִאשׁוֹן קֹדֶם חָטְאוֹ הָיָה דָּר בַּ"גַּן", וּמִתּוֹכוֹ הָיָה מִסְתַּכֵּל בָּ"עֵדֶן" הַנַּ"ל, וּבְחֶטְאוֹ אֲשֶׁר מֵאָז נִסְתַּלְּקָה מִמֶּנּוּ זֹאת הַבְּחִינָה הָעֶלְיוֹנָה, לָכֵן גֹּרַשׁ אָז מִגַּן עֵדֶן. וְהוּא סוֹד הַצֵּרוּפֵי אוֹתִיּוֹת דִּילָהּ, כַּאֲשֶׁר הִיא כְּתוּבָה בַּמָּרוֹם, כְּמוֹ שֶׁנִּתְבָּאֵר לְעֵיל סוֹף שַׁעַר ב' (סוף פרק יז).

• וְעַל זֶה אָמְרוּ בְּמִדְרַשׁ תְּהִלִּים רֵישׁ מִזְמוֹר ג', "לֹא יָדַע אֱנוֹשׁ עֶרְכָּהּ" כו' (איוב כח, יג), לֹא נִתְּנוּ פָּרָשִׁיּוֹתֶיהָ שֶׁל תּוֹרָה עַל הַסֵּדֶר, שֶׁאִלְמָלֵא נִתְּנוּ עַל הַסֵּדֶר, כָּל מִי שֶׁהוּא קוֹרֵא בָּהֶן, מִיָּד הָיָה יָכוֹל לִבְרֹאת עוֹלָם וּלְהַחֲיוֹת מֵתִים כו':

• וְנָשׁוּב לְבָאֵר קְצָת עִנְיַן הַהֶפְרֵשׁ וְיִתְרוֹן אוֹר קְדֻשַּׁת הַתּוֹרָה הַקְּדוֹשָׁה עַל הַמִּצְוֹת:

שער ד' - פרק כ"ט

• הִנֵּה רַבּוֹתֵינוּ זִכְרוֹנָם לִבְרָכָה אָמְרוּ (סוטה כ"א א') דָּרַשׁ רַבִּי מְנַחֵם בַּר יוֹסֵי "כִּי נֵר מִצְוָה וְתוֹרָה אוֹר" (משלי ו, כג).

○ תָּלָה הַכָּתוּב אֶת הַמִּצְוָה — בְּנֵר, וְאֶת הַתּוֹרָה — בָּאוֹר, לוֹמַר לְךָ

○ מַה נֵּר אֵינוֹ מֵאִיר אֶלָּא לְפִי שָׁעָה, אַף מִצְוָה אֵינָהּ מְגִנָּה אֶלָּא לְפִי שָׁעָה

The Holy Breath/Spirit is the medium between Voice and Speech (which are also referred to earlier in Sefer Yetzirah 1:9). The Voice is the potential within God to create the Universe (e.g., G2:10), whereas His Speech is the articulation of this Voice which is the constant creation of all existence (e.g., G3:11). The ability to perceive the Holy Breath/Spirit, the level of the soul of the soul, is therefore the ability to see how God is directly manifest in all of creation.

507 End of G2:17.
508 Iyov 28:13.
509 Midrash Tehillim 3:2.
510 Sotah 21a.
511 Mishlei 6:23.

- and just as light is everlasting, similarly, Torah [study] provides everlasting protection.
- This statement concludes:
  - That all the while one studies Torah it both protects and saves,[512] but while one does not study it, it still protects but does not save.
  - With the performance of Commandments [on the other hand], protection is provided both at the point of performance and at other times; however, their performance does not save a person.
- In this same section, Chazal also state that a sin can extinguish the positive impact of performance of a Commandment, but a sin can never extinguish the positive impact of Torah [study].

• Similarly, as known from the Zohar, the 613 Commandments correspond to the 613 limbs and sinews in a person's body[513]
  - so when a person properly performs one of God's positive commandments he thereby sanctifies and gives life to the corresponding limb
  - and if he has the opportunity to sin with 'one of the commands of God which should not be done'[514] and he abstains and separates himself from performing it, about which Chazal say: "When a person sits and does not perform a sin he is rewarded as if he performed a positive commandment,"[515] the corresponding sinew is also purified, sanctified and given life
  - as per the verse which says that these are the commandments "which a person should do, and live by them,"[516] as only [when he does them] is he considered to be alive.

• However, when a person studies Torah:
  - The verse writes "it heals all of his flesh."[517]
  - Chazal state:[518] One who has a pain in his head should study Torah as it says "for they are a gracious accompaniment to your head." One who has pain in his throat should study Torah as it says ... One who has pain in his stomach should study Torah ... One who has pain in his entire body should study Torah as its says "it heals all of his flesh."
  - Torah involvement is the medium through which the limbs, sinews and abilities are all sanctified and refined.[519]

---

512 "Protects" – from afflictions. "Saves" – from the Evil Inclination so that one will not stumble with sin. (This is as per both Rashi and Tosafot commenting on the page of Sotah 21a.)

513 This idea is already referenced in relation to the Shiur Komah as described in G1:06 and in particular in G2:05. R. Chaim refers to it at the end of this chapter.

- וּמַה אוֹר מֵאִיר לְעוֹלָם, אַף תּוֹרָה מְגִינָה לְעוֹלָם
- וּמַסִּיק
  - דְּתוֹרָה, בְּעִידָנָא דְּעָסִיק בָּהּ מְגִינָה וּמַצְּלָה, בְּעִדָנָא דְּלָא עָסִיק בָּהּ אַגּוּנֵי מַגְּנֵי, אַצּוּלֵי לָא מַצְּלָה
  - מִצְוָה, בֵּין בְּעִדָנָא דְעָסִיק בָּהּ בֵּין בְּעִדָנָא דְלָא עָסִיק בַּהּ, אַגּוּנֵי מַגְנֵי, אַצּוּלֵי לָא מַצְּלָה.
  - וְכֵן אָמְרוּ שָׁם, עֲבֵרָה מְכַבָּה מִצְוָה, וְאֵין עֲבֵרָה מְכַבָּה תוֹרָה:
- וְכֵן יָדוּעַ בַּזֹּהַר, שֶׁהַתַּרְיַ"ג מִצְוֹות הֵם מְכֻוָּנִים נֶגֶד הַתַּרְיַ"ג אֵיבָרִים וְגִידִים שֶׁבָּאָדָם
  - וּבַעֲשׂוֹת הָאָדָם אַחַת מִמִּצְוֹת ה' כָּרָאוּי, מִתְקַדֵּשׁ עַל יָדָהּ אוֹתוֹ הָאֵבֶר הַמְכֻוָּן נֶגְדָּהּ, וּמְחַיֶּה אוֹתוֹ.
  - אוֹ אִם בָּא וְנִזְדַּמֵּן לְיָדוֹ אַחַת מִמִּצְוֹת ה' אֲשֶׁר לֹא תֵעָשֶׂינָה וְנִמְנַע וּפֵרַשׁ וְלֹא עָשָׂאָהּ, אֲשֶׁר עָלָיו אָמְרוּ רַבּוֹתֵינוּ זִכְרוֹנָם לִבְרָכָה (קִדּוּשִׁין לט, ב), "יָשַׁב אָדָם וְלֹא עָבַר עֲבֵירָה, נוֹתְנִין לוֹ שָׂכָר כְּעוֹשֵׂה מִצְוָה", נִטְהַר וְנִתְקַדֵּשׁ גַּם כֵּן אוֹתוֹ הַגִּיד הַפְּרָטִי הַמְכֻוָּן נֶגְדָּהּ, וּמְחַיֶּה אוֹתוֹ
  - כְּמוֹ שֶׁאָמַר הַכָּתוּב (ויקרא יח, ה) אֵלֶּה הַמִּצְוֹת "אֲשֶׁר יַעֲשֶׂה אוֹתָם הָאָדָם, וָחַי בָּהֶם" שֶׁאָז הוּא נִקְרָא "אִישׁ חַי":
- אָמְנָם כְּשֶׁהָאָדָם עוֹסֵק בַּתּוֹרָה
  - כְּתִיב בָּהּ "וּלְכָל בְּשָׂרוֹ מַרְפֵּא" (משלי ה, כב)
  - וּכְמוֹ שֶׁאָמְרוּ (עירובין נ"ד א'), "חָשׁ בְּרֹאשׁוֹ יַעֲסֹק בַּתּוֹרָה, שֶׁנֶּאֱמַר "כִּי לִוְיַת חֵן הֵם לְרֹאשֶׁךָ", חָשׁ בִּגְרוֹנוֹ יַעֲסֹק בַּתּוֹרָה, שֶׁנֶּאֱמַר כו', חָשׁ בִּבְנֵי מֵעָיו יַעֲסֹק בַּתּוֹרָה כו', חָשׁ בְּכָל גּוּפוֹ יַעֲסֹק בַּתּוֹרָה שֶׁנֶּאֱמַר "וּלְכָל בְּשָׂרוֹ מַרְפֵּא".
  - וְכֵן הוּא בְּוַיִּקְרָא רַבָּה פָּרָשָׁה י"ב, וּבְתַנְחוּמָא יִתְרוֹ, וּבְמִדְרַשׁ תְּהִלִּים מִזְמוֹר י"ט, שֶׁעַל יְדֵי עֵסֶק הַתּוֹרָה, מִתְקַדְּשִׁים וּמִזְדַּכְּכִים כָּל אֵבָרָיו וְגִידָיו וְכוֹחוֹתָיו כֻּלָּם.

---

514 Vayikra 4:27.
515 Kiddushin 39b.
516 Vayikra 18:5; Yechezkel 20:11, 20:21.
517 Mishlei 4:22.
518 Eruvin 54a quoting Mishlei 1:9, 4:22.
519 Midrash Tehillim 19:15; Midrash Tanchuma (Warsaw), Yitro 8; Vayikra Rabba Shemini 12:3.

- Therefore, Chazal say "and Torah study is equated with all the Commandments."[520]
* Similarly, with the converse scenario, God forbid, the sin of neglecting Torah study – it also is equated with all [the sins]:
  - When [a person] transgresses a single Commandment of God, he just damages the corresponding limb or sinew, causing the life force from holiness and the supernal light, the secret of the name YHVH which resides upon each limb,[521] to be removed from it, God forbid, and the *death of the Sitra Achara*[522] resides within it, and the person becomes defective as he is now missing that limb.
  - Whereas with the sin of neglecting Torah study, God forbid, he damages all of his limbs, sinews and abilities, and the holy life force of the entire body departs and he immediately becomes as if absolutely dead, as he has no life, God forbid, as per "for it is your life. . . ."[523]
  - As per Chazal:
    - "You have made man like the fish of the sea." Why is man compared to the fish of the sea? To tell you that just as when fish are removed from water, they immediately die, so too, when people are removed from the Torah, they immediately die.[524]
    - Just as fish of the sea only live in water, similarly Torah Sages who possess learning only live with Torah and if they separate from it they will immediately die.[525]
* This is what Chazal state:[526] If a person sees troubles coming upon him, he should inspect his deeds; if after inspection he did not find the cause, then he should ascribe the cause to the sin of neglecting Torah study.
  - At first sight, this is strange, for if one has the sin of neglecting Torah study, God forbid, surely there is no greater cause for trouble than this – so how can Chazal say that the person initially did not find a cause?
  - However, as Rashi warns there:[527] if one did not find a sin of adequate severity to cause this trouble.

---

520 Mishna Peah 1:1.
521 See the quotation from Tikkunei Zohar Tikkun 70 122b in G3:02.
522 See p. 564, fn. 280 for details about the concept of Sitra Achara, the Other Side, i.e., a place where the perception of God is cloaked, which is the place where death exists. Or in other words, as soon as the direct perception of the presence of God leaves (where direct perception of God is specifically denoted by the name YHVH), there is immediate death. In a wider context, not directly relevant to the point being made here, this world is Sitra Achara in that we don't directly relate to God from within it, and therefore it is a place where

וְלָכֵן אָמְרוּ (פאה, א) "וְתַלְמוּד תּוֹרָה כְּנֶגֶד כֻּלָּם":

וְכֵן לְהִפּוּךְ חַס וְשָׁלוֹם, עֲוֹן בִּטּוּל תּוֹרָה הוּא גַם כֵּן כְּנֶגֶד כֻּלָּם

כִּי בְּעָבְרוֹ עַל אַחַת מִמִּצְוֹת ה', נִפְגָּם רַק אוֹתוֹ הָאֵבֶר אוֹ הִגִּיד לְבַד הַמְכֻוָּן נֶגְדָּהּ, שֶׁהַחִיּוּת שֶׁל הַקְּדֻשָּׁה וְאוֹר הָעֶלְיוֹן, סוֹד שֵׁם הֲוָיָ"ה יִתְבָּרַךְ הַשּׁוֹרָה עַל כָּל אֵבֶר, מִסְתַּלֶּקֶת הֵימֶנּוּ חַס וְשָׁלוֹם, וּמוֹתָא דְסִטְרָא אָחֳרָא שַׁרְיָא בֵּיהּ רַחֲמָנָא לִיצְלָן, וְנַעֲשָׂה בַּעַל מוּם, חָסֵר מֵאוֹתוֹ אֵבֶר.

אֲבָל בַּעֲוֹן בִּטּוּל תּוֹרָה חַס וְשָׁלוֹם, הוּא פוֹגֵם אֶת כָּל אֵבָרָיו וְגִידָיו, וְכָל כֹּחוֹתָיו כֻּלָּם, וְחִיּוּת הַקְּדֻשָּׁה שֶׁל כָּל גּוּפוֹ מִסְתַּלֶּקֶת, וְהוּא נַעֲשָׂה תֵּכֶף כְּמֵת מַמָּשׁ, שֶׁאֵין לוֹ שׁוּם חִיּוּת חַס וְשָׁלוֹם, כְּמוֹ שֶׁכָּתוּב (דברים ל, כ) "כִּי הוּא חַיֶּיךָ" וכו'.

וּכְמוֹ שֶׁאָמְרוּ

רַבּוֹתֵינוּ זִכְרוֹנָם לִבְרָכָה (ע"ז ג, ב), "מַאי דִכְתִיב (חבקוק א, יד), "וַתַּעֲשֶׂה אָדָם כִּדְגֵי הַיָּם", לָמָּה נִמְשְׁלוּ בְּנֵי אָדָם לִדְגֵי הַיָּם, לוֹמַר לְךָ, מַה דָּגִים שֶׁבַּיָּם כֵּיוָן שֶׁפּוֹרְשִׁין מִן הַמַּיִם מִיָּד מֵתִים, כָּךְ בְּנֵי אָדָם כֵּיוָן שֶׁפּוֹרְשִׁין מִן הַתּוֹרָה מִיָּד מֵתִים. (כָּךְ הִיא גִּרְסַת הַיַּלְקוּט חֲבַקּוּק רֶמֶז תקס"ב עַל פָּסוּק הַנַּ"ל).

וּבְרַעְיָא מְהֵימְנָא סוֹף פָּרָשַׁת שְׁמִינִי, מַה נוּנֵי יַמָּא חֲיוּתָן בְּמַיָּא, אוּף תַּלְמִידֵי חֲכָמִים מָארֵי מַתְנִיתִין חִיּוּתַיְהוּ בְּאוֹרַיְתָא, וְאִי אִתְפָּרְשׁוּ מִנַּהּ מִיָּד מֵתִים:

וְזֶהוּ שֶׁאָמְרוּ רַבּוֹתֵינוּ זִכְרוֹנָם לִבְרָכָה (ברכות ה, א), "אִם רוֹאֶה אָדָם שֶׁיִּסּוּרִים בָּאִים עָלָיו יְפַשְׁפֵּשׁ בְּמַעֲשָׂיו, פִּשְׁפֵּשׁ וְלֹא מָצָא יִתְלֶה בְּבִטּוּל תּוֹרָה".

וְלִכְאוֹרָה יִפָּלֵא, כֵּיוָן שֶׁיֵּשׁ בְּיָדוֹ עֲוֹן בִּטּוּל תּוֹרָה חַס וְשָׁלוֹם, הֲלֹא אֵין לְךָ "מָצָא" יוֹתֵר מִזֶּה, וְאֵיךְ אָמַר "וְלֹא מָצָא".

אָמְנָם כְּבָר נִזְהַר רַשִׁ"י זִכְרוֹנוֹ לִבְרָכָה מִזֶּה, בְּמַה שֶּׁפֵּרֵשׁ שָׁם, שֶׁלֹּא מָצָא עָוֹן שֶׁיִּהְיוּ רְאוּיִין הַיִּסּוּרִין הַלָּלוּ לָבֹא עָלָיו:

- This is the characteristic of God, for the 'actions of man shall be repaid'[528] measure for measure
  - that it is upon the specific limb itself which was corrupted and damaged with [a person's] sin, that troubles are brought
  - the purpose of God's intention with this being that through these troubles a person should understand which sin caused this
  - and will 'take it to his heart'[529] to acknowledge [the sin] and depart from it, 'and repent and he shall be healed.'[530]
- This is what Chazal refer to, [as above]
  - that if a person sees troubles coming upon him, he should inspect his deeds, and understand the path he is required to take from the troubles.
  - But if after inspection he did not find a specific sin which would be fitting measure for measure to result in that limb's specific affliction
  - then he should ascribe it to the sin of neglecting Torah study
  - as with the sin of neglecting Torah study, the concept of measure for measure does not apply, since its neglect, God forbid, impacts on the whole body and can manifest in any limb, as mentioned above.
- The reason for this is as I wrote above in G1:06
  - that the supernal source of all the Commandments is dependent on and is bound to the secret of the *Shiur Komah*, the components of the Merkava and the secret of Supernal Man,[531] so to speak
  - that the supernal source of each specific Commandment is bound to and takes hold in the world through a specific ability of the *Shiur Komah*.
  - Similarly, this is all of man, that he is also structured such that his limbs, sinews, joints, and specific abilities mirror the structure of the Merkava and the *Shiur Komah*.
  - Therefore, each Commandment corresponds to a person's specific limb or sinew.
  - However, the Holy Torah incorporates all of the worlds, as mentioned above and is therefore equated with all the Commandments; therefore, it also "heals all of his flesh."

---

528 Iyov 34:11.
529 Yishayahu 44:19.
530 Yishayahu 6:10.
531 See G1:06 and G2:05.

- וְהוּא, כִּי מִדָּתוֹ יִתְבָּרַךְ, שֶׁ"פֹּעַל אָדָם יְשַׁלֶּם" מִדָּה כְּנֶגֶד מִדָּה
  - שֶׁאוֹתוֹ הָאֵבֶר שֶׁקִּלְקֵל וּפָגַם בְּחֶטְאוֹ, עַל אוֹתוֹ הָאֵבֶר מֵבִיא עָלָיו יִסּוּרִין
  - וְתַכְלִית כַּוָּנָתוֹ יִתְבָּרַךְ בָּזֶה, כְּדֵי שֶׁמִּתּוֹךְ הַיִּסּוּרִין יָבִין הָאָדָם וְיֵדַע עַל אֵיזֶה חֵטְא בָּאוּ
  - וְיָשִׁיב אֶל לִבּוֹ לִהְיוֹת מוֹדֶה וְעוֹזֵב, וְשָׁב וְרָפָא לוֹ:
- זֶהוּ שֶׁאָמְרוּ
  - שֶׁאִם רוֹאֶה אָדָם שֶׁיִּסּוּרִין בָּאִים עָלָיו יְפַשְׁפֵּשׁ בְּמַעֲשָׂיו, וְיָבִין דַּרְכּוֹ מִתּוֹךְ הַיִּסּוּרִין.
  - וְאִם פִּשְׁפֵּשׁ, וְלֹא מָצָא עָוֹן בְּיָדוֹ אֲשֶׁר חָטָא, בְּאוֹתוֹ אֵבֶר וּבְאוֹתוֹ אֹפֶן, שֶׁיִּהְיוּ רְאוּיִין הַיִּסּוּרִין הַלָּלוּ דַּוְקָא לָבֹא עָלָיו מִדָּה כְּנֶגֶד מִדָּה
  - יִתְלֶה בְּבִטּוּל תּוֹרָה
  - כִּי בַּעֲוֹן בִּטּוּל תּוֹרָה לֹא שַׁיָּךְ מִדָּה כְּנֶגֶד מִדָּה, כִּי בְּטוּלָהּ חַס וְשָׁלוֹם הוּא נוֹגֵעַ לְכָל גּוּפוֹ, אֵיזֶה מָקוֹם וְאֵיזֶה אֵבֶר שֶׁיִּהְיֶה, כַּנַּ"ל:
- וְטַעְמוֹ שֶׁל דָּבָר, הוּא כְּמוֹ שֶׁכָּתַבְתִּי לְעֵיל בְּשַׁעַר א' פֶּרֶק ו'
  - שֶׁמְּקוֹר שָׁרְשָׁם הָעֶלְיוֹן שֶׁל הַמִּצְוֹת, תְּלוּיוֹת וּקְשׁוּרוֹת בְּסוֹד הַשִּׁעוּר קוֹמָה, וּפִרְקֵי הַמֶּרְכָּבָה סוֹד הָאָדָם הָעֶלְיוֹן כִּבְיָכוֹל
  - שֶׁכָּל מִצְוָה פְּרָטִית, שָׁרְשָׁהּ הָעֶלְיוֹן קָשׁוּר וְנֶאֱחָז בָּעוֹלָם וְכֹחַ אֶחָד מֵהַשִּׁעוּר קוֹמָה.
  - וְכֵן זֶה כָּל הָאָדָם, שֶׁהוּא גַּם כֵּן מְתֻקָּן וּמְסֻדָּר, בְּכָל אֲבָרָיו וְגִידָיו וּפְרָקָיו וְכָל פְּרָטֵי כְּחוּתָיו, בְּתַבְנִית דְּמוּת הַמֶּרְכָּבָה וְשִׁעוּר קוֹמָה.
  - וְלָזֹאת, כָּל מִצְוָה מְכֻוֶּנֶת נֶגֶד אֵבֶר אוֹ גִיד אֶחָד פְּרָטֵי שֶׁבָּאָדָם
  - אָמְנָם הַתּוֹרָה הַקְּדוֹשָׁה הִיא כּוֹלֶלֶת הָעוֹלָמוֹת כֻּלָּן כַּנַּ"ל, לָכֵן הִיא שְׁקוּלָה נֶגֶד כָּל הַמִּצְוֹת, וְלָכֵן הִיא גַּם כֵּן "לְכָל בְּשָׂרוֹ מַרְפֵּא":

30. TORAH GIVES EXISTENCE TO MITZVOT BUT BOTH ARE REQUIRED

- There is further advantage in [study] of the Holy Torah – in terms of additional light and increased holiness – over and above [the performance of] all of the Mitzvot put together
  - in that even if a person performs all of the 613 Mitzvot in a truly complete and proper manner, with all of their associated finer points of detail, intention, purity, and holiness
  - which then enables a person, together with all of his limbs, joints, and abilities to completely become a Merkava [a platform] upon which supernal holiness of all the Mitzvot can reside[532]
  - nevertheless, the holiness and light of the Mitzvot is incomparable in any way to the greatness of the tremendous holiness and light of the Holy Torah whose 'light shines upon'[533] the person who properly studies and reviews it.
  - For [Torah's point of origin at the] beginning of its way in holiness is that it is raised very greatly over and above the level of the source of holiness and the supernal light of all of the Mitzvot together, as mentioned above, as per Chazal
    - who say [about Torah that] "it raises him over all the deeds,"[534] that is over the performance of all of the Mitzvot
    - and similarly, "All of the Mitzvot together are not comparable to even one statement of Torah."[535]
- Additionally, [a further advantage of Torah study over Mitzvah performance,]
  - is that the holiness and light of a Mitzvah which resides in a physical item used to perform a Mitzvah, only resides in it temporarily while the Mitzvah is being performed with it, but following performance of the Mitzvah, it immediately ascends and is removed from [this item,] with [the item] remaining unchanged.
  - In contrast, with [study of] the Holy Torah, any place upon which its light and holiness have shined [even] once, it is permanently sanctified and always remains in this holy state, as Chazal teach[536] that items used for Mitzvah performance can be discarded after use, but items used as sacred accessories must be stored away; therefore, they included items used for Tefillin and Mezuzot within the category of holy utensils [which require special handling] as a result of even only once having contained paragraphs of Torah within them.

שער ד' - פרק ל'

- וְעוֹד זֹאת יְתֵרָה הַתּוֹרָה הַקְּדוֹשָׁה, בְּיִתְרוֹן אוֹר וְתוֹסֶפֶת קְדֻשָּׁה, גַּם עַל כָּל הַמִּצְוֹת כֻּלָּן בְּיַחַד

  - שֶׁגַּם אִם קִיֵּם הָאָדָם כָּל הַתַּרְיַ"ג מִצְוֹת כֻּלָּן, בִּשְׁלֵמוּת הָאֲמִתִּי כָּרָאוּי, בְּכָל פְּרָטֵיהֶם וְדִקְדּוּקֵיהֶם, וּבְכַוָּנָה וְטָהֳרָה וּקְדֻשָּׁה
  - אֲשֶׁר אָז נַעֲשָׂה הָאָדָם כֻּלּוֹ, בְּכָל אֵבָרָיו וּפְרָקָיו וְכָל כֹּחוֹתָיו, "מֶרְכָּבָה גְּמוּרָה", שֶׁתִּשְׁרֶה עֲלֵיהֶם הַקְּדֻשָּׁה הָעֶלְיוֹנָה שֶׁל הַמִּצְוֹת כֻּלָּן
  - עִם כָּל זֶה, אֵין עֲרֹךְ וְדִמְיוֹן כְּלָל קְדֻשַּׁת וְאוֹר הַמִּצְוֹת, לְגֹדֶל עֶצֶם קְדֻשַּׁת וְאוֹר הַתּוֹרָה הַקְּדוֹשָׁה, אֲשֶׁר תּוֹפִיעַ נְהָרָה עַל הָאָדָם הָעוֹסֵק וְהוֹגֶה בָּהּ כָּרָאוּי.
  - כִּי רֵאשִׁית דַּרְכָּהּ בַּקֹּדֶשׁ, הוּא הַגְבֵּהַּ לְמַעְלָה מַעְלָה מִשֹּׁרֶשׁ הַקְּדֻשָּׁה וְאוֹר הָעֶלְיוֹן שֶׁל הַמִּצְוֹת כֻּלָּן יַחַד כַּנַּ"ל. וְזֶהוּ שֶׁאָמְרוּ

    - בְּפֶרֶק הַתּוֹרָה (אבות ו, א) "וּמְגַדַּלְתּוֹ וּמְרוֹמַמְתּוֹ עַל כָּל הַמַּעֲשִׂים", הַיְנוּ עַל כָּל מַעֲשֵׂי הַמִּצְוֹת כֻּלָּן
    - וְכֵן אָמְרוּ בִּירוּשַׁלְמִי פֶּרֶק א' דְּפֵאָה, שֶׁכָּל הַמִּצְוֹת כֻּלָּן אֵינָן שָׁווֹת לְדָבָר אֶחָד מִן הַתּוֹרָה:

- וְגַם

  - כִּי קְדֻשַּׁת וְאוֹר הַמִּצְוָה, אֲשֶׁר תַּשְׁכִּין אוֹרָהּ עַל אוֹתוֹ הַדָּבָר וְהַחֵפֶץ, אֲשֶׁר בּוֹ וְעַל יָדוֹ תֵּעָשֶׂה הַמִּצְוָה, אֵינוֹ שׁוֹרֶה עֲלֵיהֶם רַק לְפִי שַׁעְתּוֹ, בְּעֵת שֶׁהַמִּצְוָה נַעֲשֵׂית בָּהֶם, אֲבָל אַחַר שֶׁנַּעֲשָׂה בָּהֶן מִצְוָתָן, הַקְּדֻשָּׁה וְהָאוֹר מִתְעַלֶּה וּמִסְתַּלֵּק מֵהֶם תֵּכֶף, וְנִשְׁאָר כְּבְרִאשׁוֹנָה.
  - אֲבָל הַתּוֹרָה הַקְּדוֹשָׁה, כָּל מָקוֹם שֶׁתַּזְרִיחַ וְתוֹפִיעַ אוֹרָהּ וּקְדֻשָּׁתָהּ פַּעַם אַחַת, קְדֻשַּׁת עוֹלָם תִּהְיֶה לוֹ, וְנִשְׁאָר תָּמִיד בִּקְדֻשָּׁתוֹ, כְּמוֹ שֶׁשָּׁנִינוּ בַּבָּרַיְתָא (מגילה כ"ו ב') שֶׁתַּשְׁמִישֵׁי מִצְוָה נִזְרָקִין לְאַחַר שֶׁנַּעֲשָׂה מִצְוָתָן, וְתַשְׁמִישֵׁי קְדֻשָּׁה נִגְנָזִין.

---

532 See G1:06.
533 Iyov 3:4 (or 3:3 in some versions).
534 Mishna Avot 6:1.
535 Yerushalmi Peah Chap. 1 Halacha 1.
536 Megillah 26b.

- There is nothing in all of Chazal's statements which is not hinted to in the Scriptures, and one can understand the verse "For a Commandment is a *candle*, but the Torah is *light*"[537] in an additional way to the meaning already mentioned above[538]
    - [which was] that just as a *candle* only temporarily radiates but that *light* is everlasting and Chazal used this analogy to differentiate between the protection and saving of a person
    - it is also possible to additionally explain that this verse is hinting at the [incomparable] difference between [the study of] the Holy Torah and [performance] of the Mitzvot as highlighted above.[539]
- Not only this [but an additional advantage of Torah study over Mitzvah performance]
    - is that the very holiness, life force, and light of Mitzvot which sanctify and provide life to the person who performs them
    - is solely taken and derived from the holiness and light of the Holy Torah
    - as, in and of itself, a Mitzvah has no life force, holiness, or light at all
    - and is only vested with holiness as a result of the letters of the Torah which describe its detail.
    - This point can also be understood from the verse "For a Commandment is a candle, but the Torah is light" – in the sense that the candle does not have any light of its own at all, but just has light [added to it and which is separate from it and] which shines from it [whereas the Torah itself is the very light itself].
- [On the other hand,] Torah study alone which is unaccompanied by any Mitzvah performance, God forbid, is certainly also of no consequence. As per Chazal:
    - One who says that he only has Torah, does not even have Torah.[540]
    - A favorite comment that Rava would frequently say: The purpose of wisdom [i.e., Torah knowledge] is repentance and good deeds, so a person should not learn and review [Torah] and then kick his father, [mother,] and teacher . . . [as it says "The beginning of wisdom is Fear of God, good understanding *to those who perform them.*"][541] This does not say "to those who study them" but it says "to those who *perform* them."
    - One who knows Torah but does not perform [Mitzvot], it would have been better for him to have not been born and smothered by his placenta.[542]

---

537 Mishlei 6:23.
538 At the beginning of G4:29 with the quotation from Sotah 21a.

וְלָכֵן מָנוּ שָׁם תַּשְׁמִישֵׁי תְּפִלִּין וּמְזוּזוֹת בִּכְלַל תַּשְׁמִישֵׁי קְדֻשָּׁה, מֵחֲמַת פַּרְשִׁיּוֹת הַתּוֹרָה שֶׁהָיוּ מֻנָּחִים בְּתוֹכָם פַּעַם אַחַת:

- וְלֵית לָךְ מִידֵי בְּדִבְרֵיהֶם לְבִרְכָה זִכְרוֹנָם דְּלָא רְמִיזָא בִּקְרָא, וְיֵשׁ לְכַוֵּן הַכָּתוּב (משלי ו, כג) "כִּי נֵר מִצְוָה וְתוֹרָה אוֹר" גַּם עַל זֶה הָעִנְיָן הַנִּזְכָּר, עַל פִּי פֵּרוּשָׁם זִכְרוֹנָם לִבְרָכָה הַנַּ"ל בְּסוֹטָה שָׁם (כא, א)
  - מַה "נֵר" אֵינוֹ מֵאִיר אֶלָּא לְפִי שָׁעָה, וּמַה "אוֹר" מֵאִיר לְעוֹלָם. וְהֵם זִכְרוֹנָם לִבְרָכָה עָשׂוּ הַהֶפְרֵשׁ בֵּינֵיהֶם לְעִנְיַן הַהֲגָנָה וְהַהַצָּלָה לְהָאָדָם.
  - וְאֶפְשָׁר לְפָרְשׁוֹ גַּם כֵּן, שֶׁיִּרְמֹז הַכָּתוּב גַּם לְעִנְיַן הַהֶפְרֵשׁ וְהַהֶבְדֵּל, בֵּין הַתּוֹרָה הַקְּדוֹשָׁה וְהַמִּצְוֹת, הַמְבֹאָר בַּבָּרַיְתָא דִּמְגִלָּה הַנַּ"ל:

- וְלֹא עוֹד
  - אֶלָּא שֶׁגַּם אוֹתָהּ הַקְּדֻשָּׁה, וְחִיּוּתָן וְאוֹרָן שֶׁל הַמִּצְוֹת, שֶׁמְקַדְּשִׁים וּמְחַיִּים לְהָאָדָם הַמְקַיְּמָם
  - הוּא נִלְקָח וְנִשְׁפָּע רַק מִקְּדֻשָּׁתָהּ וְאוֹרָהּ שֶׁל הַתּוֹרָה הַקְּדוֹשָׁה
  - כִּי הַמִּצְוָה לֵית לָהּ מִגַּרְמָהּ שׁוּם חִיּוּת וּקְדֻשָּׁה וְאוֹר כְּלָל
  - רַק מִצַּד קְדֻשַּׁת אוֹתִיּוֹת הַתּוֹרָה הַכְּתוּבוֹת בְּעִנְיַן אוֹתָהּ הַמִּצְוָה.
  - וְיֵשׁ לְכַוֵּן גַּם זֶה הָעִנְיָן בַּכָּתוּב "כִּי נֵר מִצְוָה וְתוֹרָה אוֹר", כְּעִנְיַן הַנֵּר שֶׁאֵין לָהּ בְּעַצְמָהּ שׁוּם אוֹר כְּלָל, רַק מֵהָאוֹר הַמֵּאִיר בָּהּ:

- וַדַּאי שֶׁגַּם הָעֵסֶק בַּתּוֹרָה לְבַד, בְּלִי קִיּוּם הַמִּצְוֹת כְּלָל חַס וְשָׁלוֹם, גַּם כֵּן אֵין כְּלוּם, כְּמוֹ שֶׁאָמְרוּ רַבּוֹתֵינוּ זִכְרוֹנָם לִבְרָכָה
  - "כָּל הָאוֹמֵר אֵין לוֹ אֶלָּא תּוֹרָה, אַף תּוֹרָה אֵין לוֹ" (יבמות קט).
  - וּבְפֶרֶק ב' דִּבְרָכוֹת (י"ז א') מַרְגְּלָא בְּפוּמֵיהּ דְּרָבָא, תַּכְלִית חָכְמָה, תְּשׁוּבָה וּמַעֲשִׂים טוֹבִים, שֶׁלֹּא יְהֵא אָדָם קוֹרֵא וְשׁוֹנֶה, וּבוֹעֵט בְּאָבִיו וּבְרַבּוֹ כוּ', "לְלוֹמְדֵיהֶם" לֹא נֶאֱמַר, אֶלָּא "לְעוֹשֵׂיהֶם".
  - וּבִשְׁמוֹת רַבָּה פָּרָשָׁה מ', כָּל מִי שֶׁהוּא יוֹדֵעַ תּוֹרָה וְאֵינוֹ עוֹשֶׂה, מוּטָב לוֹ שֶׁלֹּא

---

539 In this chapter in the quotation from Megillah 26b.
540 Yevamot 109b.
541 Berachot 17a quoting Tehillim 111:10.
542 Shemot Rabba Ki Tisa 40:1; Vayikra Rabba Bechukotai 35:7; Midrash Tanchuma (Warsaw), Ekev 6.

- R. Yehuda said: One who involves himself with Torah in this world and acquires good deeds will inherit a complete world, but one who involves himself with Torah in this world but does not do good deeds will not inherit this [world] or that [world, the future world] ... R. Yitzchak said we only learn this about one who has absolutely no good deeds at all.[543]
- This is to the extent that Chazal say: "One who just involves himself with Torah is compared to one who has no God."[544]
- For without Mitzvah performance, God forbid, there is no substance for the light of Torah to grasp on to and bind to – to allow it to reside over and remain with [a person] – analogous to a light without a wick.

- However, a Mitzvah receives the essence of its light from the letters of the Torah which describe it.
  - This is what Chazal refer to "Torah is great as it gives life to those who *perform* it."[545]
    - [This Mishna] does not say to those who study or are involved in it, but rather "to those who *perform* it"
    - meaning that it is the Torah which provides everlasting life and holiness – even to those who perform the Mitzvot written in it.
    - Therefore, Chazal say that even if [a person] is righteous, he has nothing if he does not study Torah, God forbid.[546]
- The reason for this is also as explained above[547]
  - that Mitzvot are rooted in, bound up with, and dependent on the arrangement of the components of the Merkava [being the platform] of the worlds and the supernal abilities
  - whereas the supernal source of the Holy Torah is far abstracted from this – far above all of the worlds and abilities[548]
    - and it is that which permeates the internal essence of everything
    - and everything receives their essential existence and bestowal of holiness from it
    - therefore, it is [the Torah] which provides and bestows existence, holiness, and light to all of the Mitzvot.

---

543 Zohar II Shemot 5b.
544 Avodah Zarah 17b.
545 Mishna Avot 6:7.
546 Midrash Tanchuma Bechukotai 5.
547 As per the end of G4:29 which refers to the concept of Shiur Komah (as per G1:06 and G2:05).
548 Its source is The World of The Malbush. See V2:03, "The World of The Malbush."

יָצָא לָעוֹלָם, אֶלָּא נֶהְפְּכָה הַשַּׁלְיָא עַל פָּנָיו. וְכֵן הוּא בְּוַיִּקְרָא רַבָּה פָּרָשָׁה ל"ה, וּבְתַנְחוּמָא פָּרָשַׁת עֵקֶב.

וּבַזֹּהַר שְׁמוֹת ה' רֵישׁ ע"ב, דְּאָמַר רַבִּי יְהוּדָה, כָּל מַאן דְּאִשְׁתַּדַּל בְּאוֹרַיְתָא בְּהַאי עָלְמָא, וּמְסַגֵּל עוֹבָדִין טָבִין, יָרִית עָלְמָא שְׁלֵימָא, וְכָל מַאן דְּאִשְׁתַּדַּל בְּאוֹרַיְתָא בְּהַאי עָלְמָא, וְלָא עָבִיד עוֹבָדִין טָבִין, לָא יָרִית לָא הַאי וְלָא הַאי כוּ', אָמַר רַבִּי יִצְחָק, לָא תֵּימָא אֶלָּא מַאן דְּלֵית לֵיהּ עוֹבָדִין טָבִין כְּלָל.

עַד שֶׁאָמְרוּ בְּפֶרֶק קַמָּא דַעֲבוֹדָה זָרָה (י"ז, ב), "כָּל הָעוֹסֵק בַּתּוֹרָה לְבַד, דּוֹמֶה כְּמִי שֶׁאֵין לוֹ אֱלוֹהַּ"

כִּי בִּלְתִּי קִיּוּם הַמִּצְוֹת חַס וְשָׁלוֹם, אֵין דָּבָר בַּמֶּה לְהִתְאַחֵז וּלְהִתְקַשֵּׁר בּוֹ אוֹר הַתּוֹרָה, לִשְׁרוֹת עָלָיו וּלְהִתְקַיֵּם בּוֹ, כְּדִמְיוֹן הָאוֹר בְּלֹא פְּתִילָה:

- אָמְנָם, עַצְמוּת הָאוֹר מְקַבֶּלֶת הַמִּצְוָה מֵאוֹתִיּוֹת הַתּוֹרָה הַכְּתוּבוֹת בְּעִנְיָנָהּ.

וְזֶהוּ שֶׁאָמְרוּ בְּפֶרֶק הַתּוֹרָה (אבות ו, ז) "גְּדוֹלָה תּוֹרָה שֶׁהִיא נוֹתֶנֶת חַיִּים לְעוֹשֶׂיהָ"

  □ וְלֹא אָמַר לְלוֹמְדֶיהָ אוֹ לְעוֹסְקֶיהָ, אֶלָּא "לְעוֹשֶׂיהָ"

  □ וְרוֹצֶה לוֹמַר, שֶׁהַתּוֹרָה הִיא הַנּוֹתֶנֶת חַיֵּי עַד וּקְדֻשָּׁה, גַּם לְעוֹשֵׂי הַמִּצְוֹת הַכְּתוּבוֹת בְּתוֹכָהּ.

  □ וְלָכֵן אָמְרוּ בְּתַנְחוּמָא בְּחֻקֹּתַי (אות ה), שֶׁאַף אִם הוּא צַדִּיק, וְאֵינוֹ עוֹסֵק בַּתּוֹרָה, אֵין בְּיָדוֹ כְּלוּם חַס וְשָׁלוֹם:

- וְהַטַּעַם בָּזֶה, גַּם כֵּן כְּמוֹ שֶׁנִּתְבָּאֵר לְעֵיל

  ○ שֶׁהַמִּצְוֹת בִּמְקוֹם שָׁרְשָׁן, קְשׁוּרוֹת וּתְלוּיוֹת בְּסִדּוּר פִּרְקֵי הַמֶּרְכָּבָה הָעוֹלָמוֹת וְכֹחוֹת הָעֶלְיוֹנִים

  ○ וּמְקוֹר שֹׁרֶשׁ הָעֶלְיוֹן שֶׁל הַתּוֹרָה הַקְּדוֹשָׁה הִיא מְאֹד נַעֲלָה, מֵעַל כָּל הָעוֹלָמוֹת וְהַכֹּחוֹת כֻּלָּם

    □ וְהִיא הַמִּתְפַּשֶּׁטֶת בִּפְנִימִיּוּת כֻּלָּם

    □ וּמְקַבְּלִים מִמֶּנָּה עֶצֶם חִיּוּתָם וְשִׁפְעַת קְדֻשָּׁתָם

    □ לָכֵן הִיא הַנּוֹתֶנֶת וּמַשְׁפַּעַת הַחִיּוּת וְהַקְּדֻשָּׁה וְהָאוֹר לַמִּצְוֹת כֻּלָּן:

31. TORAH STUDY ATONES FOR EVEN GRAVE SINS

- It is also for this same reason [that the Torah descends from the far abstracted World of The Malbush], that Torah study atones for all the sins of a 'soul that sinned,'[549] as per Chazal:
  - What is the meaning of the verse "This is the Torah of the Burnt Offering, Flour Offering, and Sin Offering . . ." – concluding that all who study Torah do not need Burnt, Flour, Sin, and Guilt Offerings [to atone for their sins].[550]
  - "Take with you *words* and return to God." For Israel say . . . we are paupers and cannot bring sacrifices. God says to them: "I seek *words*" . . . and I will atone for all your sins – "words" only refer to words of Torah [as it says "These are the *words* which Moshe spoke"].[551]
  - In connection with the Holy Ark, that it bears the sins of Israel, [meaning] that the Torah contained within it, bears the sins of Israel.[552]
  - A person who transgressed many sins and is judged to die . . . if he then repents, reads Torah, Prophets, and Writings, and reviews Mishna, Midrash, Halachot, and Agadot, and serves the Torah Sages, then God will even revoke one hundred decrees from upon him.[553]
  - R. Yehuda began . . . How much should people look to serve God, how much should they look to [say] words of Torah, as one who studies Torah is as if he has offered up all the sacrifices in the world to God, not only this, but God atones for all of his sins and repairs many chairs for him in the World to Come.[554]
- Torah study even atones for those severe sins which sacrifices do not atone for. As per Chazal:
  - In connection with the sons of Eli, [Rava said] the sacrifices do not atone, it is the Torah that atones.[555]

---

549 Yechezkel 18:4 and 18:20.
550 Menachot 110a quoting Vayikra 7:37.
551 Midrash Rabba Tetzaveh 38:4 quoting Hoshea 14:3 and Devarim 1:1. R. Chaim also references Midrash Tanchuma (Warsaw), Tzav 8. However, while this source expresses a similar sentiment, its text is different as follows:
   - . . . see how God forgives the sins of Israel and what would they offer to God . . . God said one who has a bull should bring the bull, one who has a ram should bring the ram, one who has a sheep should bring the sheep, one who has a dove should bring the dove, and one who has none of these should bring fine flour, and one who has nothing and not even fine flour should bring *words* as per "Take with you *words* and return to God."
552 Midrash Tanchuma Vayakhel 7.
553 Eliyahu Rabba Parsha 5.

שער ד' - פרק ל"א

- וּמִזֶּה הַטַּעַם גַּם כֵּן, עֵסֶק הַתּוֹרָה הִיא מְכַפֶּרֶת עַל כָּל הָעֲווֹנוֹת שֶׁל הַנֶּפֶשׁ הַחוֹטֵאת, כְּמַאַמְרָם זִכְרוֹנָם לִבְרָכָה

  ○ מַאי דִּכְתִיב (ויקרא ז, לז) "זֹאת הַתּוֹרָה לָעוֹלָה לַמִּנְחָה וְלַחַטָּאת" כו', וּמַסִּיק, שֶׁכָּל הָעוֹסֵק בַּתּוֹרָה, אֵין צָרִיךְ לֹא עוֹלָה וְלֹא מִנְחָה וְלֹא חַטָּאת וְלֹא אָשָׁם (סוף מנחות דף קי).

  ○ וְכֵן הוּא בְּתַנְחוּמָא פָּרָשַׁת צַו, וּבִשְׁמוֹת רַבָּה פָּרָשָׁה ל"ח, "קְחוּ עִמָּכֶם דְּבָרִים וְשׁוּבוּ אֶל ה'", לְפִי שֶׁיִּשְׂרָאֵל אוֹמְרִים כו', עֲנִיִּים אָנוּ וְאֵין לָנוּ לְהָבִיא קָרְבָּנוֹת, אָמַר לָהֶם הַקָּדוֹשׁ בָּרוּךְ הוּא, דְּבָרִים אֲנִי מְבַקֵּשׁ כו', וַאֲנִי מוֹחֵל לָכֶם עַל כָּל עֲווֹנוֹתֵיכֶם, וְאֵין "דְּבָרִים" אֶלָּא דִּבְרֵי תוֹרָה כו'.

  ○ וּבְתַנְחוּמָא וַיַּקְהֵל (אות ז) בְּעִנְיַן הָאָרוֹן אָמְרוּ, שֶׁהוּא נוֹשֵׂא עֲווֹנוֹתֵיהֶם שֶׁל יִשְׂרָאֵל, שֶׁהַתּוֹרָה שֶׁבּוֹ נוֹשֵׂא עֲווֹנוֹתֵיהֶם שֶׁל יִשְׂרָאֵל.

  ○ וּבְתַנָּא דְּבֵי אֵלִיָּהוּ סֵדֶר אֵלִיָּהוּ רַבָּה פֶּרֶק ה', אָדָם שֶׁעָבַר עֲבֵרוֹת הַרְבֵּה וְקָנְסוּ עָלָיו מִיתָה כו', וְחָזַר וְעָשָׂה תְּשׁוּבָה, וְקוֹרֵא תּוֹרָה נְבִיאִים וּכְתוּבִים, וְשָׁנָה מִשְׁנָה מִדְרָשׁ הֲלָכוֹת וְהַגָּדוֹת, וְשִׁמֵּשׁ חֲכָמִים, אֲפִלּוּ נִגְזְרוּ עָלָיו מֵאָה גְּזֵרוֹת, הַקָּדוֹשׁ בָּרוּךְ הוּא מַעֲבִירָן מִמֶּנּוּ כו'.

  ○ וּבַזֹּהַר שְׁלַח קנ"ט א', רַבִּי יְהוּדָה פָּתַח כו', כַּמָּה אִית לְהוּ לִבְנֵי נָשָׁא לְאִסְתַּכְּלָא בְּפוּלְחָנָא דְּקוּדְשָׁא בְּרִיךְ הוּא, כַּמָּה אִית לְהוּ לְאִסְתַּכְּלָא בְּמִלֵּי דְּאוֹרַיְתָא, דְּכָל מַאן דְּאִשְׁתַּדַּל בְּאוֹרַיְתָא, כְּאִלּוּ מַקְרִיב כָּל קוּרְבָּנִין דְּעָלְמָא לְקַמֵּיהּ דְּקוּדְשָׁא בְּרִיךְ הוּא, וְלֹא עוֹד, אֶלָּא דְּקוּדְשָׁא בְּרִיךְ הוּא מְכַפֵּר לֵיהּ עַל כָּל חוֹבוֹי, וּמְתַקְּנִין לֵיהּ כַּמָּה כּוּרְסִין לְעָלְמָא דְּאָתֵי:

- וְגַם עַל אוֹתָן הָעֲווֹנוֹת חֲמוּרִים, שֶׁאֵין הַקָּרְבָּנוֹת מְכַפְּרִים, עֵסֶק הַתּוֹרָה מְכַפֶּרֶת, כְּמוֹ שֶׁאָמְרוּ רַבּוֹתֵינוּ זִכְרוֹנָם לִבְרָכָה

  ○ בִּבְנֵי עֵלִי (ר"ה יח, א), "בְּזֶבַח וּבְמִנְחָה הוּא דְּאֵינוֹ מִתְכַּפֵּר, אֲבָל מִתְכַּפֵּר הוּא בְּדִבְרֵי תוֹרָה".

---

554 Zohar III Shelach Lecha 159a.
555 Rosh Hashana 18a.

- Torah study is greater than offering the daily sacrifices.[556]
- Come and see ... therefore one who studies Torah does not need sacrifices as the Torah is preferable to all of them; it is the connection of faith of all, and therefore it is written that "Its ways are ways of pleasantness, all of them ways of peace" and "Abundant peace is to those who love Torah and there is no stumbling block for them."[557]
- Offerings [do not atone] but one is atoned through words of Torah. Why? Because words of Torah rise up higher than any sacrifices in the world as established from the verse "This is the Torah of the Burnt Offering, Flour Offering, and Sin Offering ..." which equates Torah together with all of the world's sacrifices. He said that it is certain that one who studies Torah, even if he has a punishment decreed upon him from above, [the Torah study] is more effective for him than all of the sacrifices, and that punishment is revoked. Come and see, a person is only ever purified with words of Torah ... The Torah is called Holy as per "For I God am Holy" – this is the Torah which is the Holy Name; therefore, one who involves himself with it is purified and is subsequently sanctified. We learn that the Holiness of Torah is the ultimate Holiness, above all other forms of Holiness.[558] Refer there.
- The sacrifices were abandoned, but Torah was not abandoned. One who does not involve himself with sacrifices should study Torah as this will provide greater benefit. As R. Yochanan explains ... He said to him they should study Torah and I will atone them through it far more than with all the sacrifices of the world, as it says "This is the Torah of the Burnt Offering, [Flour Offering, and Sin Offering ...],ʺ meaning this Torah study is in order to impact as would a Burnt[/Flour/Sin Offering], etc. R. Keruspedai says: One who verbally articulates the details of sacrifices in the prayer and study halls ... a covenant is struck such that those angels which would mention his bad deeds to bring him down are no longer able to do so – they can only say good things.[559]
- Why are the chapters dealing with tents and brooks juxtaposed in the Torah, as per "They stretched out like brooks ... God planted them like tents ..." to tell you that just as *brooks* purify a person from a state of impurity, so too the *tents* [of Torah study] bring a person from a position of culpability to one of merit.[560]

---

556 Megillah 3b.
557 Zohar III Tzav 35a quoting Mishlei 3:17 and Tehillim 119:165.
558 Zohar III Kedoshim 80b quoting Vayikra 7:37 and Vayikra 19:2.
559 Midrash HaNeelam I Veyera 100a quoting Vayikra 7:37.

וְכֵן אָמְרוּ (מגילה ג' ע"ב), "גָּדוֹל תַּלְמוּד תּוֹרָה יוֹתֵר מֵהַקְרָבַת תְּמִידִין".

וּבַזֹּהַר צַו ל"ה א', תָּא חֲזִי כוּ', וְעַל דָּא, מַאן דְּלָעֵי בְּאוֹרַיְתָא, לָא אִצְטְרִיךְ לָא לְקָרְבָּנִין וְלָא לְעָלָוָן, דְּהָא אוֹרַיְתָא עָדִיף מִכֹּלָּא, וְקִשּׁוּרָא דִּמְהֵימְנוּתָא דְּכֹלָּא, וְעַל דָּא כְּתִיב (משלי ג, יז) "דְּרָכֶיהָ דַּרְכֵי נֹעַם וְכָל נְתִיבוֹתֶיהָ שָׁלוֹם" וְכוּ', וּכְתִיב (תהלים קיט, קסה) "שָׁלוֹם רָב לְאֹהֲבֵי תוֹרָתֶךָ וְאֵין לָמוֹ מִכְשׁוֹל".

וּבְפָרָשַׁת קְדוֹשִׁים פ' ע"ב, "בְּזֶבַח וּבְמִנְחָה" כוּ', אֲבָל מִתְכַּפֵּר הוּא בְּדִבְרֵי תוֹרָה, אֲמַאי, בְּגִין דְּדִבְרֵי תוֹרָה סַלְקִין עַל כָּל קָרְבָּנִין דְּעָלְמָא, כְּמָה דְּאוֹקְמוּהָ, דִּכְתִיב "זֹאת הַתּוֹרָה לָעוֹלָה לַמִּנְחָה וְלַחַטָּאת" כוּ', שָׁקִיל אוֹרַיְתָא לָקֳבֵיל כָּל קָרְבָּנִין דְּעָלְמָא. אָמַר לֵיהּ הָכִי הוּא וַדַּאי, דְּכָל מַאן דְּאִשְׁתַּדַּל בְּאוֹרַיְתָא, אַף עַל גַּב דְּאִתְגְּזַר עֲלֵיהּ עוּנְשָׁא מִלְעֵילָּא, נִיחָא לֵיהּ מִכָּל קָרְבָּנִין וַעֲלָוָן, וְהַהוּא עוּנְשָׁא אִתְקְרַע. וְתָא חֲזֵי, לָא אִתְדְּכֵי בַּר נָשׁ לְעָלְמִין אֶלָּא בְּמִלִּין דְּאוֹרַיְתָא כוּ'. וְאוֹרַיְתָא קְדוּשָּׁה אִתְקְרֵי, דִּכְתִיב (ויקרא יט, ב) "כִּי קָדוֹשׁ אֲנִי ה'", וְדָא אוֹרַיְתָא, דְּהִיא שְׁמָא קַדִּישָׁא עִלָּאָה, וְעַל דָּא, מַאן דְּאִשְׁתַּדַּל בָּהּ אִתְדְּכֵי, וּלְבָתַר אִתְקַדַּשׁ כוּ', תָּאנָא, קְדוּשָּׁה דְּאוֹרַיְתָא, קְדוּשָּׁה דְּסַלְּקָת עַל כָּל קִדּוּשִׁין כוּ', עַיֵּן שָׁם.

וּבְמִדְרַשׁ הַנֶּעֱלָם וַיֵּרָא ק' ע"א אָמְרוּ, בָּטְלוּ הַקָּרְבָּנוֹת לֹא בָּטְלָה הַתּוֹרָה. הַאי דְּלָא אִיעֲסַק בְּקָרְבָּנוֹת לִיעֲסֵק בַּתּוֹרָה, וְיִתְהֲנֵי לֵיהּ יַתִּיר, דְּאָמַר רַבִּי יוֹחָנָן כוּ', אָמַר לֵיהּ, יַעַסְקוּ בַּתּוֹרָה, וַאֲנִי מוֹחֵל לָהֶם בִּשְׁבִילָהּ יוֹתֵר מִכָּל הַקָּרְבָּנוֹת שֶׁבָּעוֹלָם, שֶׁנֶּאֱמַר (ויקרא ז, לז) "זֹאת הַתּוֹרָה לָעוֹלָה לַמִּנְחָה" כוּ', זֹאת הַתּוֹרָה בִּשְׁבִיל עוֹלָה, בִּשְׁבִיל מִנְחָה כוּ'. אָמַר רַבִּי כְּרוּסְפְּדַאי, הַאי מַאן דְּמַדְכַּר בְּפוּמֵיהּ בְּבָתֵּי כְּנֵסִיּוֹת וּבְבָתֵּי מִדְרָשׁוֹת עִנְיָנָא דְּקָרְבָּנַיָּא כוּ', בְּרִית כְּרוּתָה הוּא, דְּאִנּוּן מַלְאֲכַיָּא דְּמַדְכְּרָן חוֹבֵיהּ לְאַבְאָשָׁא לֵיהּ, דְּלָא יָכְלִין לְמֶעְבַּד לֵיהּ אֶלָּא טִיבוּ.

וְאָמְרוּ עוֹד בְּפֶרֶק שְׁנֵי דִּבְרָכוֹת (טז, א), וּבְתַנָּא דְּבֵי אֵלִיָּהוּ סֵדֶר אֵלִיָּה רַבָּה פֶּרֶק י"ט, לָמָּה נִסְמְכוּ אֹהָלִים לִנְחָלִים, דִּכְתִיב (במדבר כד, ו) "כִּנְחָלִים נִטָּיוּ וְכוּ' כַּאֲהָלִים נָטַע ה'" כוּ', לוֹמַר לְךָ, מַה נְּחָלִים מַעֲלִין אֶת הָאָדָם מִטֻּמְאָה לְטָהֳרָה, אַף אֹהָלִים מַעֲלִים אֶת הָאָדָם מִכַּף חוֹבָה לְכַף זְכוּת.

---

560 Berachot 15b and 16a quoting Bamidbar 24:6. Also Eliyahu Rabba Parsha 19, although the text is different but expresses a similar sentiment (this may be Parsha 21 in some editions).

- ○ "Pour out your heart like water" ... Just as this water is a Mikveh which purifies Israel and all creations ... similarly words of Torah are a Mikveh which purifies all of Israel wherever they may dwell. Come and see how great is the power of Torah, as it purifies the sinners of Israel even when they repent from Idol Worship, as per "Then I will sprinkle pure water upon you and you will become pure."[561] Refer there.
- The essential part of true and complete repentance which is from love can only be accomplished through proper Torah study. As per Chazal:
  - ○ [One who studies Torah for its sake merits many things ...] he loves God.[562]
  - ○ Return us, Our Father, to Your Torah ... and then bring us back in complete repentance before You.[563]
  - ○ When a person is far from Torah, he is far from God, and when he is close to Torah, God draws him close to be with Him.[564]
- For "all sins are covered by love"[565] of the Torah:
  - ○ ["*Love* covers over all sins," there is no love except for Torah.][566]
  - ○ ["And they left Me and did not keep My Torah," if only they would have left Me and kept My Torah, as if they were studying it,] the light within it would have returned them to good ways.[567]
  - ○ If this disgraceful one [the Evil Inclination] bothers you, drag him to the study hall; if he is made of stone, he will melt. . . .[568]
  - ○ If your Evil Inclination comes to wear you down, make it happy with words of Torah.[569]
  - ○ ["If your enemy is hungry, feed him bread" . . .] if your Evil Inclination is standing over you, feed him the bread of Torah. . . .[570]
  - ○ R. Yossi said that when a person sees that bad thoughts are coming to him, he should study Torah and then they will be removed from him; R. Elazar said that when the Evil Inclination comes to tempt a person, he should draw it to Torah and it will leave him.[571]

---

561 Eliyahu Rabba Parsha 18 quoting Eicha 2:19 and Yechezkel 36:25.
562 Mishna Avot 6:1.
563 From the Amidah, meaning that one must first be attached to Torah study and only after that can repentance follow.
564 Zohar III Vayikra 21a.
565 Mishlei 10:12.
566 Eliyahu Rabba Parsha 3 quoting Mishlei 10:12.
567 Eicha Rabba Introductions 2 quoting Yirmiyahu 16:11.
568 Sukkah 52b and Kiddushin 30b. R. Chaim also refers the reader to look up a similar sentiment expressed in Midrash Tanchuma (Warsaw), Haazinu 3:
  - ... This is as Chazal say, if it is stone, it will melt, and if it is iron, it will

וּבְפֶרֶק י"ח שָׁם "שִׁפְכִי כַמַּיִם לִבֵּךְ" כו', מַה מַּיִם הַלָּלוּ מִקְוֵה טָהֳרָה הֵן לְיִשְׂרָאֵל, וּלְכָל אֲשֶׁר נִבְרָא בָּעוֹלָם כו', כָּךְ דִּבְרֵי תוֹרָה, מִקְוֵה טָהֳרָה הֵן לְיִשְׂרָאֵל בְּכָל מְקוֹמוֹת מוֹשְׁבוֹתֵיהֶם. בֹּא וּרְאֵה כַּמָּה גְּדוֹלָה כֹחָהּ שֶׁל תּוֹרָה, שֶׁמְּטַהֶרֶת אֶת פּוֹשְׁעֵי יִשְׂרָאֵל, בִּזְמַן שֶׁעוֹשִׂין תְּשׁוּבָה, אֲפִלּוּ מֵעֲבוֹדָה זָרָה שֶׁבְּיָדָם, שֶׁנֶּאֱמַר (יחזקאל לו, כה) "וְזָרַקְתִּי עֲלֵיכֶם מַיִם טְהוֹרִים וּטְהַרְתֶּם" כו', עַיֵּן שָׁם:

- כִּי עִקַּר הַתְּשׁוּבָה שְׁלֵמָה הָאֲמִתִּית שֶׁהִיא מֵאַהֲבָה, הוּא רַק עַל יְדֵי עֵסֶק הַתּוֹרָה כָּרָאוּי, כְּמוֹ שֶׁכָּתוּב

  ○ בְּמַעֲלוֹת הַתּוֹרָה (אבות ו, א) "אוֹהֵב אֶת הַמָּקוֹם"

  ○ וּכְמוֹ שֶׁכָּתוּב "הֲשִׁיבֵנוּ אָבִינוּ לְתוֹרָתֶךָ" כו' "וְהַחֲזִירֵנוּ בִּתְשׁוּבָה שְׁלֵמָה לְפָנֶיךָ".

  ○ וּבַזֹּהַר וַיִּקְרָא כ"א א', כַּד בַּר נָשׁ אִתְרְחִיק מֵאוֹרַיְתָא, רָחִיק הוּא מִקּוּדְשָׁא בְּרִיךְ הוּא, וּמַאן דְּקָרִיב לְאוֹרַיְתָא, קָרִיב לֵיהּ קוּדְשָׁא בְּרִיךְ הוּא בַּהֲדֵיהּ:

- כִּי עַל כָּל פְּשָׁעִים תְּכַסֶּה אַהֲבַת הַתּוֹרָה

  ○ כְּמוֹ שֶׁכָּתוּב בְּתַנָּא דְבֵי אֵלִיָּהוּ (סדר אליהו רבה פרק ג) עַל זֶה הַפָּסוּק (משלי י, יב)

  ○ וְכֵן אָמְרוּ (פתיחתא איכה), "הַמָּאוֹר שֶׁבָּהּ מַחֲזִירוֹ לְמוּטָב"

  ○ וּבְפֶרֶק הֶחָלִיל (סוכה נ"ב ב') "אִם פָּגַע בְּךָ מְנֻוָּל זֶה מָשְׁכֵהוּ לְבֵית הַמִּדְרָשׁ, אִם אֶבֶן הוּא נִמּוֹחַ" וְכוּ'. וּכְעִנְיָן זֶה אָמְרוּ בְּתַנְחוּמָא פָּרָשַׁת הַאֲזִינוּ, עַיֵּן שָׁם.

  ○ וּבִבְרֵאשִׁית רַבָּה פָּרָשָׁה כ"ב "אִם בָּא יִצְרְךָ לְהַשְׂחִיקְךָ, שַׂמְּחֵהוּ בְּדִבְרֵי תוֹרָה"

  ○ וּבְמִדְרַשׁ תְּהִלִּים סוֹף מִזְמוֹר ל"ד "אִם עָמַד עָלֶיךָ יֵצֶר הָרַע, הַאֲכִילֵהוּ לַחְמָהּ שֶׁל תּוֹרָה" כו'.

  ○ וּבַזֹּהַר וַיֵּשֶׁב ק"צ ע"א, אָמַר רַבִּי יוֹסֵי, כַּד חָמֵי בַּר נָשׁ דְּהִרְהוּרִין בִּישִׁין אַתְיָן לְגַבֵּיהּ יִתְעַסֵּק בְּאוֹרַיְתָא, וּכְדֵין יִתְעַבְּרוּן מִנֵּיהּ. אָמַר רַבִּי אֶלְעָזָר, כַּד הַהוּא סִטְרָא בִישָׁא אָתֵי לְמִפְתֵּי לֵיהּ לְבַר נָשׁ, יְהֵא מָשִׁיךְ לֵיהּ לְגַבֵּי אוֹרַיְתָא, וְיִתְפְּרַשׁ מִנֵּיהּ:

---

explode; therefore, there is no good for a person except to *kill* himself over words of Torah and study it day and night. . . .

569 Bereishit Rabba 22:6.
570 Midrash Tehillim 34:2 quoting Mishlei 25:21.
571 Zohar I Vayeshev 190a.

- This is as written "and he will become a spring of ever-increasing strength,"[572] and there is scope to also explain this in line with the idea mentioned above
  - that just as a spring flows and penetrates, even though at times it can be blocked up with much slime and silt, nevertheless it still flows and penetrates, and gets gradually stronger as it goes along until, in the fullness of time, it becomes so strong that it becomes completely revealed and flows as it did formerly
  - similarly, with one who is involved with Torah study *for its sake* – even if he was initially soiled with great sins, and greatly sunken in the slime and silt of the trappings of Evil, God forbid, nevertheless, with Torah study, 'his heart will be confidently secure'[573] that "the light within it will certainly return him to good ways,"[574] and that the good will gradually overcome the bad within him until in the end the good completely prevails and completely fills him and he has sanctified himself from his impurities, and purity has disseminated through all of him.
- Similarly, it also says there that "and he will be prepared to become righteous and a Chasid"[575]
  - this is an expression of preparation, purification and cleansing from the contamination of bad which was initially within him, as per "are My Words not like fire?"[576] [that the words of Torah] cleanse him and prepare him.
  - As per Chazal, that the Torah purifies the hearts and kidneys of Torah Sages.[577]

32. TORAH RESTORES, PROTECTS, AND IS THE ONLY ENVIRONMENT OF LIFE

- All of this is for the reason mentioned above that the supernal source of the Torah transcends all of the worlds.[578]
- This concept is as I wrote above (in G1:20) and is the reason underpinning Chazal's statement[579] that one who answers "Amen, Yehey Shemey Rabba . . ." with all of his strength is forgiven all of his sins. Refer there.[580] This concept is that through a person's proper Torah study

---

572 Mishna Avot 6:1.
573 Tehillim 112:7.
574 Eicha Rabba Introductions 2. Even though he doesn't expressly mention it, R. Chaim is directly quoting Chazal with this statement as can be seen from the

- וְזֶה שֶׁכָּתוּב בְּפֶרֶק הַתּוֹרָה (אבות ו, א) "וְנַעֲשָׂה כְּמַעְיָן הַמִּתְגַּבֵּר וְהוֹלֵךְ". וְיֵשׁ מָקוֹם לְפָרְשׁוֹ גַּם עַל זֶה הָעִנְיָן הַנַּ"ל

  ○ שֶׁכְּמוֹ הַמַּעְיָן הַנּוֹבֵעַ וּבוֹקֵעַ, אַף שֶׁלִּפְעָמִים נִרְפָּשׁ וְנִשְׁחָת בְּהַרְבֵּה רֶפֶשׁ וָטִיט, עִם כָּל זֶה, הוּא נוֹבֵעַ וּבוֹקֵעַ, וּמִתְגַּבֵּר וְהוֹלֵךְ מְעַט מְעַט, עַד שֶׁבְּרֹבוֹת הַיָּמִים יִתְגַּבֵּר וְיִתְגַּלֶּה לְגַמְרֵי, וְיִתְפַּשֵּׁט כְּמֵאָז

  ○ כֵּן הָעוֹסֵק בַּתּוֹרָה לִשְׁמָהּ, אַף אִם נִתְלַכְלֵךְ תְּחִלָּה בַּעֲווֹנוֹת וַחֲטָאִים עֲצוּמִים, וְנִטְבַּע מְאֹד בְּרֶפֶשׁ וָטִיט מְצוּלוֹת הָרַע חַס וְשָׁלוֹם, עִם כָּל זֶה, עַל יְדֵי עֵסֶק הַתּוֹרָה, יְהֵא נָכוֹן לִבּוֹ בָּטוּחַ, שֶׁוַּדַּאי הַמָּאוֹר שֶׁבָּהּ יַחֲזִירוֹ לְמוּטָב, וְהַטּוֹב מִתְגַּבֵּר וְהוֹלֵךְ עַל הָרַע שֶׁבּוֹ מְעַט מְעַט, עַד שֶׁלְּבַסּוֹף בְּהֶכְרֵחַ יִתְגַּבֵּר הַטּוֹב, וְיִתְפַּשֵּׁט בְּכֻלּוֹ לְגַמְרֵי, וְהוּא מִתְקַדֵּשׁ מִטֻּמְאָתוֹ, וּפָרְחָה טָהֳרָה בְּכֻלּוֹ:

- וְכֵן אָמַר שָׁם "וּמַכְשַׁרְתּוֹ לִהְיוֹת צַדִּיק חָסִיד" כו'

  ○ לְשׁוֹן הֶכְשֵׁר וְהַגְעָלָה וְלִבּוּן מִפִּגּוּל גִּעוּלֵי הָרַע שֶׁהָיָה בּוֹ תְּחִלָּה, וּכְמוֹ שֶׁכָּתוּב (ירמיה כ"ג כט) "הֲלֹא כֹה דְבָרִי כָּאֵשׁ" וכו', שֶׁהִיא מְלַבֶּנְתּוֹ וּמַכְשַׁרְתּוֹ כו'

  ○ וְכֵן אִיתָא בְּתַנְחוּמָא וַיַּקְהֵל, שֶׁהַתּוֹרָה מְטַהֶרֶת לִבָּן וְכִלְיוֹתָן שֶׁל תַּלְמִידֵי חֲכָמִים:

שער ד' - פרק ל"ב

- וְהַכֹּל מִטַּעַם הַנַּ"ל, שֶׁשָּׁרְשָׁהּ הָעֶלְיוֹן שֶׁל הַתּוֹרָה הַקְּדוֹשָׁה הִיא מֵעַל כָּל הָעוֹלָמוֹת כֻּלָּם:

- וְהָעִנְיָן הוּא, כְּמוֹ שֶׁכָּתַבְתִּי לְעֵיל (בְּשַׁעַר א' פֶּרֶק כ'), טַעַם מַאֲמָרָם זִכְרוֹנָם לִבְרָכָה

- he arouses its supernal source, which emanates and bestows supernal light and holiness over all the worlds, 'its flashes being flashes of fire, the fire of'[581] awesomeness to banish and destroy all the impurities and filth which he caused with his deeds in all of the worlds
- to sanctify and additionally enlighten with the supernal holiness, to reconnect [the worlds] with each other, to complete all defects, correct all damage, and rebuild all that is destroyed with increased happiness, joy, and the supernal light in all of the worlds.

• Furthermore, as is known, all things can only be corrected in their supernal source with the supernal source of the soul of each Jew being one letter of the Holy Torah;[582] therefore, all damage done by 'the soul which sins'[583] can be rectified in their source in the Holy Torah, through its proper study.
  - This is as per the verse "God's Torah is perfect, it restores the Nefesh"[584]
    - that even if, God forbid, the Nefesh has already been disconnected from its source, God forbid, and has 'astonishingly descended'[585] into the depths of the abyss of Evil, God forbid
    - the Holy Torah which a person studies, raises and extracts [the Nefesh] from its trappings and restores it to its original connected state – together with additional light of the Holy Torah.
    - As per Chazal
      - R. Benaah says: One who occupies himself with Torah *for its sake*, his Torah becomes a *lifesaving potion*, as per "It is a tree of life [to those who grasp hold of it]" and "for one who finds me [i.e., the Torah] finds life."[586]
      - What do we learn from "For I am God who Heals you"? God said to Moshe: Tell Israel that the Torah that I have given to you is a remedy for you, it is life for you, as per "for they are life to he who finds them."[587]
  - Therefore, the Rishonim instituted the format of the Confession prayer to follow the sequence of the twenty-two letters of the Aleph-Bet – in order to arouse the supernal source of one's soul which is connected and grasps on to the Holy Torah, to purify and sanctify it.[588]

---

581 Shir Hashirim 8:6.
582 See G4:11.
583 Yechezkel 18:4.
584 Tehillim 19:8.
585 Eicha 1:9.

(שבת קיט, ב) שֶׁכָּל הָעוֹנֶה אָמֵן יְהֵא שְׁמֵיהּ רַבָּא — בְּכָל כֹּחוֹ, מוֹחֲלִין לוֹ עַל כָּל עֲוֹנוֹתָיו, עַיֵּן שָׁם. כֵּן הָעִנְיָן, שֶׁעַל יְדֵי עֵסֶק הַתּוֹרָה כָּרָאוּי

- הוּא מְעוֹרֵר שָׁרְשָׁהּ הָעֶלְיוֹן, לְהַאֲצִיל וּלְהַשְׁפִּיעַ שִׁפְעַת אוֹר עֶלְיוֹן וּקְדֻשָּׁה עַל הָעוֹלָמוֹת כֻּלָּם, וּרְשָׁפֶיהָ רִשְׁפֵּי אֵשׁ שַׁלְהֶבֶת נוֹרָא, לְגָרֵשׁ וּלְכַלּוֹת כָּל הַטֻּמְאוֹת וְהַזֻּהֲמוֹת שֶׁגָּרַם בְּמַעֲשָׂיו בְּכָל הָעוֹלָמוֹת

- לְהִתְקַדֵּשׁ וּלְהָאִיר בִּקְדֻשָּׁה עוֹד בִּקְדֻשָּׁה הָעֶלְיוֹנָה, לְהִתְקַשֵּׁר לְהִתְקַשֵּׁר יַחַד אֶחָד בַּחֲבֵרוֹ, וְכָל הַפְּגָמִים מִתְמַלְּאִים, וְכָל הַקִּלְקוּלִים נִתְקָנִים, וְכָל הַהֲרִיסוֹת מִתְבַּנִּים, וְהַשִּׂמְחָה וְחֶדְוָתָא יְתֵרָתָא וְאוֹר הָעֶלְיוֹן מִתְרַבֶּה בְּכָל הָעוֹלָמוֹת:

• וְגַם כִּי יָדוּעַ שֶׁכָּל דָּבָר אֵינוֹ נִתְקָן אֶלָּא בְּשָׁרְשׁוֹ הָעֶלְיוֹן, וְכָל אֶחָד מִיִּשְׂרָאֵל שֹׁרֶשׁ הָעֶלְיוֹן שֶׁל נִשְׁמָתוֹ הוּא מֵאוֹת אַחַת מֵהַתּוֹרָה הַקְּדוֹשָׁה, לָכֵן, כָּל פִּגְמֵי הַנֶּפֶשׁ הַחוֹטֵאת, נִתְקָנִים וְנִמְתָּקִים בְּשָׁרְשָׁם בַּתּוֹרָה הַקְּדוֹשָׁה, עַל יְדֵי הָעֵסֶק בָּהּ כָּרָאוּי.

- וּכְמוֹ שֶׁאָמַר הַכָּתוּב (תהלים יט, ח) "תּוֹרַת ה' תְּמִימָה מְשִׁיבַת נָפֶשׁ"

□ שֶׁאַף אִם כְּבָר נִכְרְתָה הַנֶּפֶשׁ מִשָּׁרְשָׁהּ חַם וְשָׁלוֹם, וַתֵּרֶד פְּלָאִים בְּעִמְקֵי מְצוּלוֹת הָרַע חַם וְשָׁלוֹם

□ הַתּוֹרָה הַקְּדוֹשָׁה שֶׁעוֹסֵק בָּהּ הִיא מְקִימָה וּמוֹצִיאָהּ מִמַּסְגֵּרִים, וּמְשִׁיבָה אוֹתָהּ לְהִתְקַשֵּׁר כְּבַתְּחִלָּה, וּבְיִתְרוֹן אוֹר הַתּוֹרָה הַקְּדוֹשָׁה.

□ וְזֶהוּ שֶׁאָמְרוּ

• בְּפֶרֶק קַמָּא דְּתַעֲנִית (ז, א), "תַּנְיָא רַבִּי בִּנְאָה אוֹמֵר, כָּל הָעוֹסֵק בַּתּוֹרָה לִשְׁמָהּ, תּוֹרָתוֹ נַעֲשֵׂית לוֹ סַם חַיִּים, שֶׁנֶּאֱמַר (משלי ג, יח) "עֵץ חַיִּים הִיא" כו', וְאוֹמֵר (שם ח, לה) "כִּי מוֹצְאַי מָצָא חַיִּים" כו'.

• וְאָמְרוּ בִּמְכִילְתָּא, "מַה תַּלְמוּד לוֹמַר "כִּי אֲנִי ה' רֹפְאֶךָ" (שמות טו, כו) אָמַר לוֹ הַקָּדוֹשׁ בָּרוּךְ הוּא לְמֹשֶׁה, אֱמוֹר לָהֶם לְיִשְׂרָאֵל, תּוֹרָה שֶׁנָּתַתִּי לָכֶם, רְפוּאָה הִיא לָכֶם, חַיִּים הִיא לָכֶם, שֶׁנֶּאֱמַר (שם ה, כב) "כִּי חַיִּים הֵם לְמוֹצְאֵיהֶם".

• וְלָכֵן תִּקְּנוּ הָרִאשׁוֹנִים זִכְרוֹנָם לִבְרָכָה נֻסַּח הַוִּדּוּי עַל פִּי סֵדֶר הַכ"ב אוֹתִיּוֹת,

---

586 Taanit 7a quoting Mishlei 3:18 and 8:35.

587 Mechilta DeRabbi Yishmael, Masechta Devayisa Parsha, 1 quoting Shemot 15:26 and Mishlei 4:22.

588 As each soul is directly connected with a particular letter or combination of letters in The World of the Malbush. See V2:03, "The World of The Malbush."

- All the while a person is connected and cleaves to God's Torah, and with his love for it continuously flourishes, it will enlighten him and will guard him in all of his endeavors from falling into the net of his Evil Inclination, God forbid.[589]
  - As per Chazal:
    - "I have stored Your Word in my heart so that I will not sin against you." The Evil Inclination cannot exert control when next to the Torah; the Evil Inclination has no control over one who has Torah in his heart and cannot affect him.[590]
    - R. Shimon son of Yochai said: One who places words of Torah on his heart will have the challenge of ten difficult things removed from him: sinful thoughts, concern for war, concern for government, foolish thoughts, thoughts inspired by the Evil Inclination, lustful thoughts, thoughts of a bad woman, idolatrous thoughts, thoughts of physical commitments, thoughts about mindless things.[591]
  - "He will be clothed with humility and have the Fear"[592] of God upon his face and [will have] all appropriate character traits.
  - He will not be afraid of the temptation of the Evil Inclination to benefit from this world and its delights, as he fully controls his Evil Inclination and 'it bends to all of his wishes';[593] and he will be guided with [the Torah's] counsel – he will be 'established in its shining light'[594] and the light of Torah will touch him in all of his ways to the extent that he has a positive [perception] in an appropriately measured context of all his earthly matters.
  - As per Chazal:[595]
    - "And you shall *Samtem*/place [My Words on your heart]"[596] – a *Sam Tam*/pure elixir – the Torah is compared to an elixir of life.
    - This is analogous to a person who gives his son a large beating and then places a bandage on the wound; he then says to him: My son, all the while the bandage is on the wound, eat and drink whatever you want without fear, but if you remove the bandage then it will result in boils surfacing on the wound.
    - Similarly, God says: My children, I have created the Evil Inclination and I have created its cure, the Torah (Note 52).[597] If you study

---

589 Shemot Rabba 36:3. This Midrash refers to the verse "For a Commandment is a candle, but the Torah is light" explaining that the light of the Torah prevents one from stumbling over the Evil Inclination.
590 Midrash Tehillim 119:11.
591 Eliyahu Zuta Parsha 16; Masechtot Ketanot Avot DeRabbi Natan Nusach 1 Chap. 20.

כְּדֵי לְעוֹרֵר שֹׁרֶשׁ הָעֶלְיוֹן שֶׁל נַפְשׁוֹ, אֲשֶׁר הִיא מְקֻשֶּׁרֶת וְנֶאֱחֶזֶת בַּתּוֹרָה הַקְּדוֹשָׁה, לְטָהֳרָה וּלְקַדְּשָׁה:

- וְכָל עוֹד שֶׁהָאָדָם קָשׁוּר וְדָבוּק בְּתוֹרָתוֹ יִתְבָּרַךְ, וּבְאַהֲבָתָהּ יִשְׁגֶּה תָּמִיד, אַף הִיא תָּאִיר אֵלָיו, וּמְשַׁמַּרְתּוֹ בְּכָל דְּרָכָיו וְעִנְיָנָיו, שֶׁלֹּא יִפֹּל בְּרֶשֶׁת הַיֵּצֶר חַס וְשָׁלוֹם, כְּמוֹ שֶׁכָּתוּב בִּשְׁמוֹת רַבָּה פָּרָשָׁה ל"ו, עַיֵּן שָׁם.

  - וּבְמִדְרָשׁ

    - תְּהִלִּים בְּמִזְמוֹר תְּמַנְיָא אַפֵּי (קי"ט, יא) "בְּלִבִּי צָפַנְתִּי אִמְרָתֶךָ לְמַעַן לֹא אֶחֱטָא לָךְ", אֵין יֵצֶר הָרַע שׁוֹלֵט אֵצֶל הַתּוֹרָה, וּמִי שֶׁהַתּוֹרָה בְּלִבּוֹ אֵין יֵצֶר הָרַע שׁוֹלֵט בּוֹ, וְלֹא נוֹגֵעַ בּוֹ.

    - וּבְתַנָּא דְּבֵי אֵלִיָּהוּ סֵדֶר אֵלִיָּהוּ זוּטָא רֵישׁ פֶּרֶק ט"ז, וּבְאָבוֹת דְּרַבִּי נָתָן, אָמַר רַבִּי שִׁמְעוֹן בֶּן יוֹחַאי, כָּל הַנּוֹתֵן דִּבְרֵי תוֹרָה עַל לִבּוֹ, מַעֲבִירִין מִמֶּנּוּ עֲשָׂרָה דְבָרִים קָשִׁים, הִרְהוּרֵי עֲבֵרָה, הִרְהוּרֵי חֶרֶב, הִרְהוּרֵי מַלְכוּת, הִרְהוּרֵי שְׁטוּת, הִרְהוּרֵי יֵצֶר הָרַע, הִרְהוּרֵי זְנוּת, הִרְהוּרֵי אִשָּׁה רָעָה, הִרְהוּרֵי עֲבוֹדָה זָרָה, הִרְהוּרֵי עַל בָּשָׂר וָדָם, הִרְהוּרֵי דְבָרִים בְּטֵלִים.

  - וּמַלְבִּשְׁתּוֹ עֲנָוָה וְיִרְאַת ה' עַל פָּנָיו וְכָל מִדָּה נְכוֹנָה

  - וְאֵינוֹ מִתְיָרֵא מִפִּתּוּיֵי יִצְרוֹ בְּעִנְיְנֵי הֲנָאוֹת הָעוֹלָם וְתַעֲנוּגוֹתָיו, כִּי יִצְרוֹ מָסוּר בְּיָדוֹ, לְכָל אֲשֶׁר יַחְפֹּץ יַטֶּנּוּ, וּבַעֲצָתָהּ תַּנְחֶהוּ, וְתַעֲמִידֵהוּ בְּקֶרֶן אוֹרָה, וְעַל כָּל דְּרָכָיו נָגַהּ אוֹר הַתּוֹרָה, עַד שֶׁגַּם כָּל עִנְיְנֵי זֶה הָעוֹלָם הֵם אֶצְלוֹ בְּעִנְיָן טוֹב, בְּמִדָּה וּבְמִשְׁקָל כָּרָאוּי.

  - כְּמַאֲמָרָם זִכְרוֹנָם לִבְרָכָה (קדושין ל, ב)

    - עַל הַכָּתוּב "וְשַׂמְתֶּם" (דברים יא) סַם תָּם, נִמְשְׁלָה תּוֹרָה כְּסַם חַיִּים

    - מָשָׁל לְאָדָם שֶׁהִכָּה אֶת בְּנוֹ מַכָּה גְדוֹלָה, וְהִנִּיחַ לוֹ רְטִיָּה עַל מַכָּתוֹ, וְאָמַר לוֹ, בְּנִי, כָּל זְמַן שֶׁרְטִיָּה זוֹ עַל מַכָּתְךָ, אֱכֹל מַה שֶּׁהֲנָאָתְךָ וּשְׁתֵה מַה שֶּׁהֲנָאָתְךָ, וְאֵין אַתָּה מִתְיָרֵא, וְאִם אַתָּה מַעֲבִירָהּ, הֲרֵי הִיא מַעֲלָה נוּמִי

    - כָּךְ אָמַר הַקָּדוֹשׁ בָּרוּךְ הוּא, בְּנִי, בָּרָאתִי יֵצֶר הָרַע בָּרָאתִי לוֹ תּוֹרָה תַּבְלִין,

---

592 Mishna Avot 6:1.
593 Mishlei 21:1.
594 An expression from a prayer formulated in Berachot 17a.
595 Kiddushin 30b.
596 Devarim 11:18.
597 **R. Chaim adds Note 52 here.** This note is brought at the end of this

Torah, you will not be under the control of [the Evil Inclination] as per "Surely if you improve yourself, you will be forgiven,"[598] but if you do not study Torah, then you will be in its control as this verse continues "but if you do not improve yourself, then sin rests at the door."[599]

- As Chazal explain[600] that "as you go forth it will guide you" means [the Torah will guide you] in this world, similarly:
  - Happy is a person who has acquired Torah. Why? As it protects him from bad ways, as per "as you go forth [it will guide you]."[601]
    - The Torah will guide and direct his heart to the point that 'his heart will be perfect with God'[602] and 'whose spirit is steadfast with God'[603] to serve Him with his entire heart and with both his [Good and Evil] Inclinations.[604]
  - "The words of the Sages are like goads." Why are words of Torah compared to a goad? Just as a goad guides a cow along the furrow to bring life to this world, so too words of Torah guide the hearts of those who study them away from the path of death and towards the path of life.[605]
- For there is no other remedy and rectification in this world at all [other than Torah] to save one from the net of his Evil Inclination, which is constantly spread out around his legs to trap him and bring him down to 'the lowest abyss,'[606] to kill him with an everlasting death, God forbid.
- However, with study of the Holy Torah one is then called "a live person," as through it he cleaves to his portion of true everlasting life, as per "For it is your life."[607]
  - As per Chazal:
    - What is the meaning of "You have made man like the fish of the sea?" Just as when fish die immediately on separation from the water, so too does man immediately die on separation from Torah.[608]

---

chapter and is entitled "Torah study is the only remedy for removing the Evil Inclination."
598 Bereishit 4:7.
599 Continuation of Bereishit 4:7.
600 Sotah 21a and Mishna Avot 6:9, quoting Mishlei 6:22.
601 Midrash Mishlei 6:22 and also in Vayikra Rabba Bechukotai 35:6.
602 1 Melachim 11:4.
603 Tehillim 78:8.

(הגהה נ"ב) אִם אַתֶּם עוֹסְקִין בַּתּוֹרָה אֵין אַתֶּם נִמְסָרִים בְּיָדוֹ, שֶׁנֶּאֱמַר (בראשית ד, ז) "הֲלֹא אִם תֵּיטִיב שְׂאֵת", וְאִם אֵין אַתֶּם עוֹסְקִין בַּתּוֹרָה אַתֶּם נִמְסָרִים בְּיָדוֹ, שֶׁנֶּאֱמַר "לַפֶּתַח חַטָּאת רֹבֵץ":

- וּכְמוֹ שֶׁפֵּרְשׁוּ זִכְרוֹנָם לִבְרָכָה (סוטה כא, א) "בְּהִתְהַלֶּכְךָ תַּנְחֶה אוֹתָךְ", בָּעוֹלָם הַזֶּה.
  ○ וּבְמִשְׁלֵי רַבְּתָא, אַשְׁרֵי אָדָם שֶׁקָּנָה לוֹ תוֹרָה, לָמָּה, שֶׁהִיא מְשַׁמְּרָה אוֹתוֹ מִדֶּרֶךְ רָעָה, דִּכְתִיב (משלי ו, כב) "בְּהִתְהַלֶּכְךָ" כו'. וְכֵן הוּא בְּוַיִּקְרָא רַבָּה פָּרָשָׁה ל"ה.
    □ כִּי הִיא מְיַשֶּׁרֶת וּמְכַוֶּנֶת אֶת לִבּוֹ, עַד אֲשֶׁר יְהֵא לְבָבוֹ שָׁלֵם עִם אֱלֹקָיו, וְנֶאֱמָנָה אֶת אֵל רוּחוֹ, לְעָבְדוֹ יִתְבָּרַךְ בְּכָל לְבָבוֹ בִּשְׁנֵי יְצָרָיו (ברכות נד.).
    □ כְּמוֹ שֶׁאָמְרוּ בְּפֶרֶק קַמָּא דַּחֲגִיגָה (ג' ב'), "דִּבְרֵי חֲכָמִים כַּדָּרְבוֹנוֹת" (קהלת יב, יא), לָמָּה נִמְשְׁלוּ דִבְרֵי תוֹרָה לְדָרְבָן, מַה דָּרְבָן זֶה מְכַוֵּן אֶת הַפָּרָה לִתְלָמֶיהָ לְהָבִיא חַיִּים לָעוֹלָם, אַף דִּבְרֵי תוֹרָה מְכַוְּנִין לֵב לוֹמְדֵיהֶן מִדַּרְכֵי מִיתָה לְדַרְכֵי חַיִּים. וְכֵן אָמְרוּ בְּבַמִּדְבַּר רַבָּה פָּרָשָׁה י"ה, וּבְתַּנְחוּמָא פָּרָשַׁת בְּהַעֲלֹתְךָ, וּבְרֵישׁ פָּרָשַׁת וַיֵּלֶךְ שָׁם:

- כִּי אֵין תְּרוּפָה וְתַקָּנָה אַחֶרֶת בָּעוֹלָם כְּלָל לְהִנָּצֵל מֵרֶשֶׁת יִצְרוֹ, אֲשֶׁר פּוֹרֵשׂ לְרַגְלָיו תָּמִיד לְלָכְדוֹ וּלְהַפִּילוֹ עַד שְׁאוֹל תַּחְתִּית, לַהֲמִיתוֹ מִיתַת עוֹלָם חַס וְשָׁלוֹם:

- אֶלָּא עַל יְדֵי הָעֵסֶק בַּתּוֹרָה הַקְּדוֹשָׁה, אֲשֶׁר אָז נִקְרָא "אִישׁ חַי", שֶׁהוּא דָבוּק עַל יָדָהּ בְּחֶלְקוֹ בְּחַיֵּי עוֹלָם הָאֲמִתִּיִּים, כְּמוֹ שֶׁכָּתוּב "כִּי הִיא חַיֶּיךָ" כו' (משלי ה, יג).
  ○ וְאָמְרוּ רַבּוֹתֵינוּ זִכְרוֹנָם לִבְרָכָה
    □ "מַאי דִּכְתִיב 'וַתַּעֲשֶׂה אָדָם כִּדְגֵי הַיָּם' כו' (חבקוק א, יד), מַה דָּגִים שֶׁבַּיָּם כֵּיוָן שֶׁפּוֹרְשִׁים מִן הַמַּיִם מִיָּד מֵתִים, אַף בְּנֵי אָדָם כֵּיוָן שֶׁפּוֹרְשִׁים מִן הַתּוֹרָה מִיָּד מֵתִים" (ע"ז ג, ב).

---

604 Berachot 54a.
605 Chagiga 3b quoting Kohelet 12:11; Bamidbar Rabba Naso 14:4; Midrash Tanchuma (Warsaw), Behaalotcha 15; Midrash Tanchuma (Warsaw), Vayelech 1.
606 Devarim 32:22.
607 Mishlei 4:13.
608 Avodah Zarah 3b quoting Chabakuk 1:14.

- Similarly, R. Akiva answers Papus ben Yehuda [with his analogy of fish]: and if in the environment where we can live [(i.e., the water) we are afraid, then how much more so should we be afraid in the environment where we would die (i.e., out of the water)].[609]
- Just as fish of the sea live in water, so too do Torah Sages, masters of the Mishna, live with the Torah, and if they are separated from the Torah, they immediately die.[610]
- "For they are life to all who find them." This is stated because anyone who finds words of Torah has found life.[611]
- Happy is the portion of Israel that the Torah teaches them the ways of God ... it is certain. It is written: "God's Torah is perfect ...." Happy is the portion of the one who studies Torah and does not separate from it, as anyone who separates from Torah for even one hour is as if he is separated from life in this world, as it is written: "For it is your life ..." and "for they add to you length of days and years of life and peace."[612]
- Happy is the portion of Israel that God wants them and that He gave them the true Torah, the Tree of Life, which a person grasps and inherits life in this world and in the World to Come. As anyone who exerts himself with Torah and grasps onto it has life and grasps onto life, and anyone who forsakes words of Torah and separates from the Torah is as if he is separated from life, because it is life and all of its words are life. This is as written "For they are life" and "and [Torah] will be health to your navel [and marrow to your bones]."[613]

Rabbi Chaim's Note:
Note 52 – Torah study is the only remedy for removing the Evil Inclination

- This can be explained homiletically, as per the verse "and the Tablets are the work of God, with the writing, the writing of God, *Charut*/hewn on the Tablets"[614] which Chazal explain: Do not read [it as "Charut" but rather as "Cherut"/freedom as the only free person is one who studies Torah].[615]
- This concept is explained by the Chasid, the Ramchal, as per this quotation above from Chazal that "I have created the Evil Inclination and I have created its antidote, the Torah":[616]

---

609 Berachot 61b.
610 Zohar III Shemini 42a.
611 Midrash Tanchuma Ekev 5.
612 Zohar I Lech Lecha 92a quoting Tehillim 19:8, Mishlei 4:13 and 3:2.

נפש　שער ד' - פרק ל"ב　החיים

- וְכֵן הֵשִׁיבוֹ רַבִּי עֲקִיבָא לְפַפּוּס "וּמָה בִּמְקוֹם חִיּוּתֵנוּ כָּךְ" כו' (ברכות ס"א ב').

- וּבְרַעְיָא מְהֵימְנָא סוֹף פָּרָשַׁת שְׁמִינִי, מַה נּוּנֵי יַמָּא — חִיּוּתָן בְּמַיָּא, אוֹף תַּלְמִידֵי חֲכָמִים, מָארֵי מַתְנִיתִין — חִיּוּתַיְהוּ בְּאוֹרַיְתָא, וְאִי אִתְפְּרָשָׁן מִנַּהּ מִיַּד מֵתִים.

- וּבְתַנְחוּמָא פָּרָשַׁת עֵקֶב "כִּי חַיִּים הֵם לְמוֹצְאֵיהֶם" (משלי ה, כב), כָּל מִי שֶׁמּוֹצֵא דִּבְרֵי תוֹרָה, חַיִּים הוּא מוֹצֵא כו', לָכֵן נֶאֱמַר "כִּי חַיִּים הֵם לְמוֹצְאֵיהֶם".

- וּבַזֹּהַר לֶךְ לְךָ צ"ב א', זַכָּאָה חוּלְקֵיהוֹן דְּיִשְׂרָאֵל, דְּאוֹרַיְתָא אוֹלִיף לְהוּ אוֹרְחוֹי דְּקוּדְשָׁא בְּרִיךְ הוּא כו', וַדַּאי, כְּתִיב (תהלים יט, ח) "תּוֹרַת ה' תְּמִימָה" וְגוֹ', זַכָּאָה חוּלְקֵיהּ מַאן דְּאִשְׁתַּדַּל בְּאוֹרַיְתָא וְלָא יִתְפְּרַשׁ מִנַּהּ, דְּכָל מַאן דְּיִתְפְּרַשׁ מֵאוֹרַיְתָא, אֲפִילוּ שַׁעֲתָא חֲדָא, כְּמָה דְּאִתְפְּרַשׁ מֵחַיֵּי דְעָלְמָא, דִּכְתִיב (משלי ה, יג) "כִּי הִיא חַיֶּיךָ" וְגוֹ', וּכְתִיב (משלי ג, ב) "אֹרֶךְ יָמִים וּשְׁנוֹת חַיִּים וְשָׁלוֹם יוֹסִיפוּ לָךְ".

- וּבְרֵישׁ פָּרָשַׁת בְּהַעֲלוֹתְךָ, זַכָּאָה חוּלְקֵיהוֹן דְּיִשְׂרָאֵל, דְּקוּדְשָׁא בְּרִיךְ הוּא אִתְרְעֵי בְּהוֹן, וִיהַב לְהוֹן אוֹרַיְתָא דִּקְשׁוֹט, אִילָנָא דְּחַיֵּי, דְּבֵיהּ אָחִיד בַּר נָשׁ, וְיָרִית חַיִּין לְהַאי עַלְמָא וְחַיִּין לְעַלְמָא דְּאָתֵי, דְּכָל מַאן דְּאִשְׁתַּדַּל בְּאוֹרַיְתָא וְאָחִיד בָּהּ, אִית לֵיהּ חַיִּין וְאָחִיד בְּחַיִּין, וְכָל מַאן דְּשָׁבִיק מִלֵּי דְּאוֹרַיְתָא וְאִתְפְּרַשׁ מֵאוֹרַיְתָא, כְּאִלּוּ מִתְפְּרַשׁ מֵחַיִּין, בְּגִין דְּהִיא חַיִּין, וְכָל מִלּוֹי חַיִּין, הֲדָא הוּא דִכְתִיב "כִּי חַיִּים הֵם" וְגוֹ' (שם ה, כב) וּכְתִיב (שם ג, ח) "רִפְאוּת תְּהִי לְשָׁרֶּךָ" וְגוֹ':

הַגָּהָה נ"ב

- וְיֵשׁ לוֹמַר עַל דֶּרֶךְ דְּרָשׁ, הַכָּתוּב "וְהַלֻּחֹת מַעֲשֵׂה אֱלֹהִים הֵמָּה וְהַמִּכְתָּב מִכְתַּב אֱלֹהִים הוּא חָרוּת" (שמות לב, טז) וכו', וְדָרְשׁוּ אַל תִּקְרָא וְכוּ':

- וְהָעִנְיָן, כְּעֵין שֶׁכָּתַב הֶחָסִיד הַלוּצַאטוֹ זצוק"ל, בְּסֵפֶר מְסִלַּת יְשָׁרִים (פרק ה) בְּמַאֲמָרָם זִכְרוֹנָם לִבְרָכָה הַנַּ"ל "בָּרָאתִי יֵצֶר הָרָע בָּרָאתִי לוֹ תוֹרָה תַּבְלִין"

---

613 Zohar III Behaalotcha 148b quoting Mishlei 4:22 and 3:8.
614 Shemot 32:16.
615 Mishna Avot 6:2.
616 Mesilat Yesharim 5.

- Just as it is with physical medication, that a doctor will prescribe a remedy for a sick person formulated from various potions and herbs by being tremendously precise with the weights and measures of each one, as per the requirements of the sickness of which the doctor is aware. Would it enter the head of the patient that he should make up a different antidote formulated with whatever he happens to have available? Who would be foolish and not understand? Surely the doctor is the one who understands the ailment and knows the nature of the remedy and how to formulate it correctly.
- Similarly, God says: "Don't imagine that you can escape the clutches of the Evil Inclination in ways which you consider to be appropriate. Did I not create the Evil Inclination and know its nature and I created the Torah as its antidote and elixir of life to heal from its sickness. Therefore, you should know that apart from Torah study alone there is no alternative way of successfully dealing with it."

• This is the meaning of "and the Tablets are the work of God" – these are the Luchot/Tablets of the heart which desires (as per "Inscribe them on the Luach/notice board of your heart");[617] God made them and He Knows the nature of the Evil Inclination which is implanted in your heart "with the writing, the writing of God," that to counter the effect of this, He has given you the concept of Torah study to indelibly write and inscribe them on the Tablets of your heart and use it to escape from the [trappings of] the Evil Inclination.
• Therefore, you should know that there is no other way whatsoever to free yourself from the Evil Inclination apart from involving yourself with Torah study.

33. ATTACH YOURSELF TO TORAH TO LIVE, OTHERWISE YOU ARE LITERALLY DEAD

• Therefore, we have been commanded by God with a dire warning that "This book of the Torah shall not move from your mouth and you shall review it day and night."[618] As per Chazal:
  - Come and see how strong is the power of the Torah and how superior it is over everything . . . and as a result of this a person must study it day and night and not turn away from it, as written: "and you shall review it day and night"; but if he does turn away or separate himself from it, it is as if he separates from the Tree of Life.[619]
  - A person should endeavor to engage himself with words of Torah, as words of Torah are analogous to bread and water . . . to teach you that just as it is impossible for a person to exist without bread and water, so

- שֶׁכְּמוֹ בְּעִנְיַן רְפוּאַת הַגּוּף, שֶׁהָרוֹפֵא נוֹתֵן לְהַחוֹלֶה תַּבְלִין מִמֶּזֶג מִכַּמָּה מִינֵי סַמָּנִים וַעֲשָׂבִים, וְהַכֹּל בְּמִדָּה וּמִשְׁקָל בְּדִקְדּוּק עָצוּם, כְּפִי הַנִּצְרָךְ לְעִנְיַן הַחֳלִי הַיָּדוּעַ לְהָרוֹפֵא, הַאִם יַעֲלֶה עַל דַּעַת הַחוֹלֶה שֶׁהוּא יַעֲשֶׂה לוֹ לִרְפָאוֹת חָלְיוֹ, תַּבְלִין אַחֵר, מִמֶּזֶג מְסַמָּנִים וַעֲשָׂבִים אֲחֵרִים כְּפִי שֶׁתַּעֲלֶה בְּיָדוֹ, מִי פֶתִי וְלֹא יָבִין, הֲלֹא הָרוֹפֵא הוּא הַיּוֹדֵעַ עִנְיַן חָלְיוֹ, וְיוֹדֵעַ טִבְעֵי הַסַּמָּנִים וְהָעֲשָׂבִים, הוּא הַיּוֹדֵעַ אֵיזֶה סַמָּנִים וַעֲשָׂבִים הַנִּצְרָכִים לְטֶבַע חָלְיוֹ, וְשִׁעוּר מִדָּתָם וּמִשְׁקָלָם.

- כֵּן אוֹמֵר הוּא יִתְבָּרַךְ שְׁמוֹ, אַל תְּדַמּוּ בְּנַפְשְׁכֶם לְהִמָּלֵט מִפְּתוּיֵי הַיֵּצֶר וְעִנְיָנָיו, בְּתַחְבּוּלוֹת וְעִנְיָנִים אֲשֶׁר תִּבְחֲרוּ לְעַצְמְכֶם כְּפִי דִמְיוֹנֵיכֶם, הֲלֹא אָנֹכִי שֶׁבָּרָאתִי הַיֵּצֶר הָרָע וְיוֹדֵעַ עִנְיָנוֹ, וְאָנֹכִי בָּרָאתִי נֶגֶד זֶה תּוֹרָה תַּבְלִין וְסַמָּא דְחַיֵּי, לִרְפָאוֹת חֶלְאַת עִנְיָנָיו, וְתֵדְעוּ שֶׁלְּבַד הָעֵסֶק בְּתַלְמוּד תּוֹרָה, אֵין שׁוּם תַּחְבּוּלָה אַחֶרֶת לָזֶה:

- זֶה שֶׁכָּתוּב "וְהַלֻּחוֹת מַעֲשֵׂה אֱלֹקִים הֵמָּה", הֵם לֻחוֹת הַלֵּב הַחוֹמֵר, (בְּעִנְיַן (מִשְׁלֵי ג, ג) "כָּתְבֵם עַל לוּחַ לִבֶּךָ") הוּא יִתְבָּרַךְ שְׁמוֹ עֲשָׂאָם, וְהוּא הַיּוֹדֵעַ עִנְיַן יֵצֶר הַנָּטוּעַ בְּלִבְּךָ. "וְהַמִּכְתָּב מִכְתַּב אֱלֹקִים הוּא", שֶׁנֶּגֶד זֶה, הוּא הַנּוֹתֵן לְךָ עִנְיַן עֵסֶק הַתּוֹרָה, לְכָתְבָם וּלְחָקְקָם עַל לֻחוֹת לִבְּךָ, לְהִמָּלֵט עַל יָדָהּ מֵעִנְיְנֵי הַיֵּצֶר:

- וְלָזֹאת תֵּדַע, שֶׁאֵין לְךָ בֶן חוֹרִין מֵעִנְיְנֵי הַיֵּצֶר, אֶלָּא מִי שֶׁעוֹסֵק בְּתַלְמוּד תּוֹרָה, וְלֹא שׁוּם תַּחְבּוּלָה אַחֶרֶת זוּלָתָהּ:

שער ד' - פרק ל"ג

- וְלָזֹאת נִצְטַוֵּינוּ בְּאַזְהָרָה נוֹרָאָה מִפִּיו יִתְבָּרַךְ, "לֹא יָמוּשׁ סֵפֶר הַתּוֹרָה הַזֶּה מִפִּיךָ וְהָגִיתָ בּוֹ יוֹמָם וָלַיְלָה" (יהושע א, ח). וּכְמוֹ שֶׁכָּתוּב

- בְּהַקְדָּמַת הַזֹּהַר (יא, א), תָּא חֲזֵי כַּמָּה הוּא חֵילָא תַּקִּיפָא דְאוֹרַיְתָא, וְכַמָּה הוּא עִלָּאָה עַל כֹּלָּא כוּ', וּבְגִין כָּךְ בָּעֵי לֵיהּ לְבַר נָשׁ לְאִשְׁתַּדְּלָא בְּאוֹרַיְתָא יְמָמָא וְלֵילְיָא, וְלָא יִתְעֲדֵי מִנָּהּ, הֲדָא הוּא דִכְתִיב "וְהָגִיתָ בּוֹ יוֹמָם וָלַיְלָה", וְאִי אִתְעֲדֵי אוֹ אִתְפָּרֵשׁ מִנָּהּ, כְּאִלּוּ אִתְפָּרֵשׁ מֵאִילָנָא דְחַיֵּי.

- וּבְתַנָּא דְּבֵי אֵלִיָּהוּ סֵדֶר אֵלִיָּהוּ זוּטָא פֶּרֶק י"ג אָמַר, וְיִשְׁתַּדֵּל אָדָם בְּעַצְמוֹ

---

617 Mishlei 3:3.
618 Yehoshua 1:8.
619 Zohar Introduction 11a.

too it is impossible for a person to exist without Torah, as per "This book of the Torah shall not move from your mouth."[620]

- The verse states: "It is a Tree of Life for those who grasp onto it"[621]
  - for a person must set it in his heart and awareness
  - that if he were drowning in a fast-flowing river and sees a strong tree in the river ahead of him, he will certainly exert himself to grasp onto it and attach himself to it with all of his strength without even momentarily weakening his grip, as his life is now entirely dependent on it; who would be foolish and not understand that if he would even be momentarily lazy, God forbid, and release his grip, he would immediately drown.
  - Similarly, the Holy Torah is called the "Tree of Life," that it is only at the time when a person grasps it with his love for it, and regularly studies and reviews it, that then he lives a true supernal life, attached and cleaving, so to speak, to God the very life of all the worlds,[622] as God and the Torah are One. If, God forbid, he neglects his studies and separates from his regular involvement with it by involving himself with the vain pursuits and enjoyments of the world, then he is separated and cut off from the supernal life, and drowns himself in the waters of sin, may the Merciful One save us.
  - As per the Zohar: Happy are Israel that God gave them the Torah of Truth to study it day and night, for one who studies Torah is free of all things, free from death, which does not have control over him . . . for one who studies Torah and grasps onto it, grasps the Tree of Life; if he weakens his attachment to the Tree of Life, then the Tree of Death rests upon him and grasps him, as per "If you weakened [on the day of affliction, your strength will be limited]."[623] Refer there.
- A person must greatly invest in immutably ingraining this awesome concept in the thoughts of his heart
  - that the entirety of a person and his life is only [relevant] when he is attached to the Holy Torah

---

620 Eliyahu Zuta Parsha 13. R. Chaim references other sources where a similar sentiment is expressed:
- Midrash Tanchuma (Warsaw), Ki Tavo 3, where Torah is compared to water.
- Midrash Tanchuma (Warsaw), Haazinu 3, where Torah is compared to rain.
- Midrash Tehillim 1:18, where Torah is compared to water.

621 Mishlei 3:18.

622 The reference here to God as "Chai Olamim" can be understood in two ways, which are really two aspects of the same sentiment. Its usual translation is *everlasting life* relating to time but it also literally means *the life of the worlds*

בְּדִבְרֵי תוֹרָה, שֶׁדִּבְרֵי תוֹרָה הֵן מְשׁוּלִים בְּלֶחֶם וּבְמַיִם כו', לְלַמֶּדְךָ, שֶׁכְּשֵׁם שֶׁאִי אֶפְשָׁר לוֹ לָאָדָם לַעֲמוֹד בְּלֹא לֶחֶם וּבְלֹא מַיִם, כָּךְ אִי אֶפְשָׁר לוֹ לָאָדָם לַעֲמוֹד בְּלֹא תוֹרָה, שֶׁנֶּאֱמַר "לֹא יָמוּשׁ סֵפֶר הַתּוֹרָה הַזֶּה מִפִּיךָ" וְגוֹ'. וְכֵן אָמְרוּ בְּתַנְחוּמָא פָּרָשַׁת תָּבֹא, בְּפָסוּק "וְהָיָה אִם שָׁמוֹעַ", וּבְפָרָשַׁת הַאֲזִינוּ, וּבְמִדְרָשׁ תְּהִלִּים מִזְמוֹר א':

- וְאָמַר הַכָּתוּב (משלי ג, יח) "עֵץ חַיִּים הִיא לַמַּחֲזִיקִים בָּהּ" וְגוֹ'
  - כִּי צָרִיךְ הָאָדָם לִקְבֹּעַ בְּלִבּוֹ, וִידַמֶּה בְּדַעְתּוֹ.
  - כִּי אִלּוּ הָיָה טוֹבֵעַ בְּנַחַל שׁוֹטֵף, וְרוֹאֶה לְפָנָיו בַּנָּהָר אִילָן חָזָק, וַדַּאי יְאַמֵּץ כֹּחַ לְהִתְאַחֵז וּלְהִתְדַּבֵּק עַצְמוֹ בּוֹ בְּכָל כֹּחוֹ, וְלֹא יַרְפֶּה יָדָיו הֵימֶנּוּ אֲפִלּוּ רֶגַע אֶחָד, אַחַר שֶׁרַק בָּזֶה תָּלוּי עַתָּה כָּל חִיּוּתוֹ, מִי פֶתִי וְלֹא יָבִין, שֶׁאִם יִתְעַצֵּל חַס וְשָׁלוֹם אַף רֶגַע אֶחָד, וְיַרְפֶּה יָדָיו מֵהִתְאַחֵז בּוֹ, יִטְבַּע תֵּכֶף.
  - כֵּן הַתּוֹרָה הַקְּדוֹשָׁה נִקְרֵאת "עֵץ חַיִּים", אִילָנָא דְחַיֵּי, שֶׁרַק אוֹתוֹ הָעֵת שֶׁהָאָדָם אָחוּז בְּאַהֲבָתָהּ, וְעוֹסֵק וּמֶהְגֶּה בָּהּ בִּקְבִיעוּת, אָז הוּא חַי הַחַיִּים הָאֲמִתִּים הָעֶלְיוֹנִים, קָשׁוּר וְדָבוּק כִּבְיָכוֹל בְּחֵי הָעוֹלָמִים יִתְבָּרַךְ שְׁמוֹ, דְּקוּדְשָׁא בְּרִיךְ הוּא וְאוֹרַיְתָא חַד. וְאִם חַס וְשָׁלוֹם יַנִּיחַ תַּלְמוּדוֹ, וּפוֹרֵשׁ מִקְּבִיעוּת הָעֵסֶק בָּהּ, לַעֲסוֹק בְּהַבְלֵי הָעוֹלָם וַהֲנָאוֹתָיו, הוּא נִפְסָק וְנִכְרָת מֵהַחַיִּים הָעֶלְיוֹנִים, וְטוֹבֵעַ עַצְמוֹ בְּמַיִם הַזֵּדוֹנִים, רַחֲמָנָא לִיצְּלָן.
  - וּבַזֹּהַר וַיֵּצֵא קנ"ב ב', זַכָּאִין אִנּוּן יִשְׂרָאֵל, דְּקוּדְשָׁא בְּרִיךְ הוּא יָהַב לוֹן אוֹרַיְתָא דִּקְשׁוֹט, לְאִשְׁתַּדְּלָא בָּהּ יְמָמָא וְלֵילְיָא. דְּהָא כָּל מַאן דְּאִשְׁתַּדַּל בְּאוֹרַיְתָא, אִית לֵיהּ חֵירוּ מִכֹּלָּא, חֵירוּ מִן מוֹתָא דְּלָא יָכְלָא לְשָׁלְטָאָה עֲלֵיהּ כו', בְּגִין דְּכָל מַאן דְּאִשְׁתַּדַּל בְּאוֹרַיְתָא, וְאִתְאֲחִיד בָּהּ, אִתְאֲחִיד בְּאִילָנָא דְחַיֵּי, וְאִי אַרְפֵּי גַּרְמֵיהּ מֵאִילָנָא דְחַיֵּי, הָא אִילָנָא דְמוֹתָא שַׁרְיָא עֲלוֹי, וְאִתְאֲחִיד בֵּיהּ, הֲדָא הוּא דִכְתִיב (משלי כד, י) "הִתְרַפִּיתָ" כו', עַיֵּן שָׁם:

- וְכַמָּה צָרִיךְ הָאָדָם, לִתְקֹעַ וְלִקְבֹּעַ זֶה הָעִנְיָן הַנּוֹרָא בְּמַחְשְׁבוֹת לִבּוֹ, בַּל תִּמּוֹט
  - שֶׁכָּל הָאָדָם וְחַיָּיו הוּא רַק אוֹתוֹ הָעֵת שֶׁהוּא דָּבוּק בַּתּוֹרָה הַקְּדוֹשָׁה

---

relating to space. It has been translated here as relating to space to follow the theme of Makom presented earlier but as expressed previously God provides life inseparably in both space and time so both translations are equally valid.

623 Zohar I Vayetze 152b quoting Mishlei 24:10.

- but when he removes and separates himself from it to involve himself in the attractions of this dark world
- he hands himself over to his Evil Inclination
- with his life having no purpose, as he will have already drowned in the waters of sin, may the Merciful One save us
- and entrenched himself in depths of evil
- and is literally considered to be dead even while still being in this world
- aimlessly stumbling 'a shadow of death without order'[624] 'unaware that his life is lost.'[625]

• Therefore, the Torah itself states: "One who sins against me damages his soul"[626] and "Guard yourself and be extremely careful with your soul – lest you forget the things . . . ."[627] As per Chazal:
  - An analogy is made to a master who gives a *free bird* to his servant saying: Don't think that if you lose it I will take a small payment for it, I will take your very life.[628]
  - God says to man: My candle, [the Torah,] is in your hand, and your candle, [your soul,] is in Mine; if you guard over my candle, I will guard yours, and if you extinguish mine, [I will extinguish yours].[629] Refer there.

34. TORAH STUDY CAUSES GOD TO DWELL IN THIS WORLD

• From the time of the destruction of our Temple when the children were exiled from their Father's table, the Shechina departed and is divorced, so to speak, and not tranquil, and there is no remnant except [within] this Torah. So when Israel, the Holy People, 'chirp and vocalize'[630] [the Torah] properly they become a small sanctuary for It [the Shechina], to prepare and maintain It, [allowing It] to dwell with them and spread Its wings over them, so to speak, and with that It rests a little, as per Chazal:
  - From the day the Temple was destroyed, God is only connected to this world through the four cubits of Halacha alone.[631]

---

624 Iyov 10:22.
625 Mishlei 7:23.
626 Mishlei 8:36.
627 Devarim 4:9.
628 Menachot 99b. The *free bird* relates to a bird that can live anywhere and is analogous to the Torah with the master (God) instructing his servant (us) that the Torah is priceless and one stands to forfeit one's life for losing it.

- וּכְשֶׁמְּסַלֵּק וּפוֹרֵשׁ עַצְמוֹ הֵימֶנָּה, לַעֲסֹק בְּנִוְיוֹ שֶׁל זֶה הָעוֹלָם הֶחָשׁוּךְ
- הֲרֵי הוּא מָסוּר בְּיַד יִצְרוֹ
- וְלָמָּה לוֹ חַיִּים, כִּי כְּבָר נִטְבַּע בַּמַּיִם הַזֵּדוֹנִים רַחֲמָנָא לִיצְלָן
- וְנִשְׁקַע בְּעָמְקֵי מְצוּלוֹת הָרָע
- וְנֶחְשָׁב כְּמֵת מַמָּשׁ גַּם בְּעוֹדוֹ בָּזֶה הָעוֹלָם
- הוֹלֵךְ מִדֵּחִי אֶל דֶּחִי, צַלְמָוֶת וְלֹא סְדָרִים, וְלֹא יֵדַע כִּי בְנַפְשׁוֹ הוּא:
- וְלָזֹאת, הַתּוֹרָה עַצְמָהּ אָמְרָה תֹּאמַר "וְחוֹטְאִי חוֹמֵס נַפְשׁוֹ" (משלי ח, לו) וּכְמוֹ שֶׁכָּתוּב (דברים ה, ט) "הִשָּׁמֶר לְךָ וּשְׁמֹר נַפְשְׁךָ מְאֹד פֶּן תִּשְׁכַּח אֶת הַדְּבָרִים" כו'. וּכְמַאֲמָרָם זִכְרוֹנָם לִבְרָכָה עַל זֶה
- "מָשָׁל לְאָדָם שֶׁמָּסַר צִפּוֹר דְּרוֹר לְעַבְדּוֹ, אָמַר לוֹ, כִּמְדֻמֶּה אַתָּה שֶׁאִם אַתָּה מְאַבְּדָהּ אִיסָר אֲנִי נוֹטֵל מִמְּךָ, נִשְׁמָתְךָ אֲנִי נוֹטֵל מִמְּךָ" (מנחות צ"ט ב').
- וְכַיָּדוּעַ מַאֲמָרָם זִכְרוֹנָם לִבְרָכָה עַל זֶה בִּדְבָרִים רַבָּה רֵישׁ פָּרָשָׁה ד', שֶׁאָמַר הַקָּדוֹשׁ בָּרוּךְ הוּא לָאָדָם, נֵרִי בְּיָדְךָ, וְנֵרְךָ בְּיָדִי, אִם שָׁמַרְתָּ אֶת נֵרִי, אֲנִי מְשַׁמֵּר אֶת נֵרְךָ, וְאִם לֹא שָׁמַרְתָּ אֶת נֵרִי כו', עַיֵּן שָׁם. וְכֵן הוּא בְּתַנְחוּמָא פָּרָשַׁת תִּשָּׂא, וּבְמִדְרַשׁ תְּהִלִּים מִזְמוֹר י"ז, עַיֵּן שָׁם:

שער ד' - פרק ל"ד

- וּמֵעֵת חָרְבַּן בֵּית קָדְשֵׁנוּ, וְגָלוּ הַבָּנִים מֵעַל שֻׁלְחַן אֲבִיהֶם, שְׁכִינַת כְּבוֹדוֹ יִתְבָּרַךְ אָזְלָא וּמִתְרַכָּא כִּבְיָכוֹל וְלֹא תַרְגִּיעַ, וְאֵין שִׁיּוּר רַק הַתּוֹרָה הַזֹּאת, כְּשֶׁיִּשְׂרָאֵל עַם הַקֹּדֶשׁ מְצַפְצְפִים וּמֶהְגִּים בָּהּ כָּרָאוּי, הֵן הֵמָּה לָהּ לְמִקְדָּשׁ מְעַט, לְהָכִין אוֹתָהּ וּלְסַעֲדָהּ, וְשׁוֹרָה עִמָּהֶם, וּפוֹרֶשֶׂת כְּנָפֶיהָ עֲלֵיהֶם כִּבְיָכוֹל, וּבֵין כָּךְ אִית לַהּ נַיְחָא מְעַט כו'. כְּמַאֲמָרָם זִכְרוֹנָם לִבְרָכָה
- בְּפֶרֶק קַמָּא דִּבְרָכוֹת (ח, א), "מִיּוֹם שֶׁחָרַב בֵּית הַמִּקְדָּשׁ אֵין לוֹ לְהַקָּדוֹשׁ בָּרוּךְ הוּא בְּעוֹלָמוֹ אֶלָּא אַרְבַּע אַמּוֹת שֶׁל הֲלָכָה בִּלְבַד":

---

629 Devarim Rabba Re'eh 4:4; Midrash Tanchuma (Warsaw), Ki Tisa 28; Midrash Tehillim 17:8.
630 Yishayahu 8:19.
631 Berachot 8a.

- From where do we know that the Shechina rests on even a single person who sits and studies Torah? From "In every place where My Name is mentioned [I will come to you and Bless you]."[632]
- "For one who has found Me has found life." God says: One who is found with words of Torah, I will be found with him wherever he is; therefore, it says: "For one who has found Me has found life."[633]
- He began and said:[634] "When you besiege a city . . . [do not destroy its trees . . . for you shall eat from it . . . for the man is the tree of the field]."
  - "Do not destroy its trees" – this refers to a Torah Sage who is the Tree of Life . . .
  - "You shall eat from it," will the destroyer be able to eat from it? No.
  - But "eat from it" means from that *hard rock*[635] from which all the strong holy winds emanate, for there is no benefit and longing for the Holy Spirit in this world apart from the Torah of that Tzaddik, who, so to speak, sustains [this world] more effectively than all of the sacrifices of the world . . .
  - and from the day of the destruction of the Temple and the cessation of the sacrifices, God only has the words of Torah, and the Torah is renewed [from the Torah Sage's] mouth.
  - Therefore, it says "you shall eat from it," as there is no sustenance in this world apart from this Torah Sage and those like him . . .
  - "For the man is the tree of the field" – a person known in the supernal and lower realms is referred to as a "tree of the field," a large and strong tree from that field which God Blessed which can be relied upon, he is the tree that is permanently known in that field.
- This is also the inner meaning of: What is the meaning of "you shall eat from it [and not cut it down] for the man is the tree of the field . . ."? . . . . If he is a respectable Torah Sage, you shall eat from him [and not cut him down], but if not [then you shall destroy him and cut him down].[636]
- How should a person control himself with God? By controlling himself with Torah, as one who controls himself with Torah, controls the Tree of Life and, so to speak, provides power to strengthen the Collective of Israel, but if he weakens [his commitment to Torah] the verse says "If you were weak [in your day of difficulty, your strength will be restricted]," if he weakens his commitment to Torah then at

---

632 Berachot 6a quoting Shemot 20:21.
633 Midrash Mishlei 8:35.
634 Zohar III Balak 202a quoting and expounding Devarim 20:19.

וְאָמְרוּ שָׁם (ברכות ו, א) עוֹד, מִנַּיִן שֶׁאֲפִלּוּ אֶחָד שֶׁיּוֹשֵׁב וְעוֹסֵק בַּתּוֹרָה, שֶׁשְּׁכִינָה שְׁרוּיָה עִמּוֹ, שֶׁנֶּאֱמַר (שמות כ, כא) "בְּכָל הַמָּקוֹם אֲשֶׁר אַזְכִּיר" וְכוּ'.

וּבְמִשְׁלֵי רַבְּתָא סוֹף פָּרָשָׁה ח' "כִּי מֹצְאִי מָצָא חַיִּים", אָמַר הַקָּדוֹשׁ בָּרוּךְ הוּא, כָּל מִי שֶׁהוּא מָצוּי בְּדִבְרֵי תוֹרָה, אַף אֲנִי מָצוּי לוֹ בְּכָל מָקוֹם, לְכָךְ נֶאֱמַר "כִּי מֹצְאִי מָצָא חַיִּים".

וּבַזֹּהַר בָּלָק רכ"ב א', פָּתַח וְאָמַר "כִּי תָצוּר אֶל עִיר כוּ'

לֹא תַשְׁחִית אֶת עֵצָהּ" (דברים כ, יט), דָּא תַּלְמִיד חָכָם, דְּאִיהוּ אִילָנָא דְחַיֵּי כוּ'

"כִּי מִמֶּנּוּ תֹאכֵל", וְכִי הַהוּא מְחַבְּלָא אָכִיל מִנֵּיהּ, לָא

אֶלָּא "כִּי מִמֶּנּוּ תֹאכֵל", הַהוּא טִנָּרָא תַּקִּיפָא, הַהִיא דְּכָל רוּחִין תַּקִּיפִין קַדִּישִׁין נַפְקִין מִנָּהּ, דְּלֵית הֲנָאָה וְתֵיאוּבְתָּא לְרוּחַ קוּדְשָׁא בְּהַאי עָלְמָא אֶלָּא אוֹרַיְתָא, דְּהַהוּא זַכָּאָה דִּכְבִיכוֹל אִיהוּ מְפַרְנֵם לָהּ, וְיָהִיב לָהּ מְזוֹנָא בְּהַאי עָלְמָא, יַתִּיר מִכָּל קָרְבָּנִין דְּעָלְמָא כוּ'

וּמִיּוֹמָא דְּאִתְחֲרִיב בֵּית מַקְדְּשָׁא, וּבָטְלוּ קָרְבָּנִין, לֵית לֵיהּ לְקוּדְשָׁא בְּרִיךְ הוּא אֶלָּא אִנּוּן מִלִּין דְּאוֹרַיְתָא, וְאוֹרַיְתָא דְּאִתְחַדְּשַׁת בְּפוּמֵיהּ.

בְּגִין כָּךְ "כִּי מִמֶּנּוּ תֹאכֵל", וְלֵית מְזוֹנָא בְּהַאי עָלְמָא אֶלָּא מִמֶּנּוּ, וְאִנּוּן דִּכְוָתֵיהּ כוּ'

"כִּי הָאָדָם עֵץ הַשָּׂדֶה", דָּא אִקְרֵי אָדָם דְּאִשְׁתְּמוֹדַע עֵילָּא וְתַתָּא, "עֵץ הַשָּׂדֶה", אִילָנָא רַבְרְבָא וְתַקִּיף, דְּהַהִיא שָׂדֶה אֲשֶׁר בֵּרְכוֹ ה', דְּסָמִיךְ עֲלֵיהּ, אִילָן דְּאִשְׁתְּמוֹדַע לְהַהוּא שָׂדֶה תָּדִיר.

וְזֶהוּ גַּם כֵּן הַמְכֻוָּן הַפְּנִימִי בְּמַאֲמָרָם זִכְרוֹנָם לִבְרָכָה בְּפֶרֶק קַמָּא דְתַעֲנִית (ז, א), מַאי דִכְתִיב "כִּי הָאָדָם עֵץ הַשָּׂדֶה כוּ', כִּי מִמֶּנּוּ תֹאכֵל כוּ', (שם) אִם תַּלְמִיד חָכָם הָגוּן הוּא "מִמֶּנּוּ תֹאכֵל" כוּ', וְאִם לָאו כוּ'.

וּבַזֹּהַר וַיִּשְׁלַח קע"ד ב', וְהֵיךְ יִתְתְּקַף בַּר נָשׁ בֵּיהּ בְּקוּדְשָׁא בְּרִיךְ הוּא, יִתְקַף

---

635 This *hard rock* is a reference to the source of the souls of the collective of Israel from which all souls are hewn (see references to the place from which souls are hewn in G1:14).

636 Taanit 7a. The basic meaning is that one should eat/learn from a respectable Torah Scholar, but if he does not have a proper character, you should shun him. The inner meaning is that the Torah Scholar's attachment to and dissemination of Torah literally provides life.

- the time when he will have difficulty he will, so to speak, reject the Shechina which is the strength of the world.[637]
- It is through Torah study that one, so to speak, makes a *dwelling place*[638] for God in this lowest world 'that His honor should dwell on Earth.'[639]
  - As per Chazal: Until the Torah was given to Israel, it says that "and Moshe ascended to God," but after the Torah was given, God says: "and they shall make Me a Sanctuary and I will dwell *in* them."[640]
- These words will suffice for a thinking person
  - and through them he will see and understand his [required] path in holiness, 'and righteousness will grasp its way'[641]
  - to preserve his study of the Holy Torah all the days of his life
  - 'to despise bad and choose good'[642]
  - for himself and for all the creations and all the worlds
  - to provide pleasure for his Maker and Creator.
- May it be God's Will
  - 'that He open up our hearts with His Torah and that He should place Love and Fear of Him in our hearts'[643]
  - and thereby complete His intention in creating His Universe
  - 'that the Universe will be rectified with His Sovereignty'[644] and 'each creation [will know its Creator]'[645]
  - 'and All will accept the yoke of His Majesty'[646]
  - according to The Blessed Supernal Will
  - 'and God will be One and His Name will be One.'[647]

Amen – May His Will be so!

---

637 Zohar I Vayishlach 174b quoting Mishlei 24:10.
638 This expression comes from Midrash Tanchuma (Warsaw), Bechukotai 3 and Naso 16 which identify that the ultimate desire of God is for a *dwelling place* in this world. See G1:13:N13 and G2:17:N38.
639 Tehillim 85:10.
640 Shemot Rabba Terumah 33:7 quoting Shemot 19:3 and 25:8. This comment is accentuated by the interpretation of the Shela of "and I will dwell in them" as meaning that God will dwell inside each and every individual who makes himself a personal sanctuary of God (e.g., Shela Shaar HaOtiyot Ot Kuf Kedushah 8).
641 Iyov 17:9.

בְּאוֹרַיְתָא, דְּכָל מַאן דְּאִתְתְּקַף בְּאוֹרַיְתָא אִתְתְּקַף בְּאִילָנָא דְּחַיֵּי, וְכִבְיָכוֹל יָהִיב תּוּקְפָּא לִכְנֶסֶת יִשְׂרָאֵל לְאִתְתַּקְּפָא, וְאִי הוּא יִתְרַפֵּי, מַה כְּתִיב (משלי כד, י) "הִתְרַפִּיתָ", אִי אִיהוּ אִתְרַפֵּי מִן אוֹרַיְתָא "בְּיוֹם צָרָה צַר כֹּחֶכָה", בְּיוֹמָא דְּיֵיתֵי לֵיהּ עָקוּ, כִּבְיָכוֹל דָּחִיק לָהּ לִשְׁכִינְתָּא, דְּאִיהִי חֵילָא דְּעָלְמָא:

- וּבְעֵסֶק הַתּוֹרָה הוּא עוֹשֶׂה כִּבְיָכוֹל דִּירָה לוֹ יִתְבָּרַךְ בַּתַּחְתּוֹנִים, לִשְׁכֹּן כְּבוֹד בָּאָרֶץ יִתְבָּרַךְ שְׁמוֹ.

כְּמַאֲמָרָם זִכְרוֹנָם לִבְרָכָה בִּשְׁמוֹת רַבָּה פָּרָשָׁה ל"ג, עַד שֶׁלֹּא נִתְּנָה תּוֹרָה לְיִשְׂרָאֵל, "וּמֹשֶׁה עָלָה אֶל הָאֱלֹקִים", מִשֶּׁנִּתְּנָה תּוֹרָה, אָמַר הַקָּדוֹשׁ בָּרוּךְ הוּא "וְעָשׂוּ לִי מִקְדָּשׁ וְשָׁכַנְתִּי בְּתוֹכָם":

- וְדַי בִּדְבָרֵינוּ אֵלֶּה לַמַּשְׂכִּיל
  ○ אֲשֶׁר מִתּוֹכָם יִרְאֶה וְיָבִין דַּרְכּוֹ בַּקֹּדֶשׁ, וְיֹאחַז צֶדֶק דַּרְכּוֹ
  ○ לַעֲמֹד עַל מִשְׁמֶרֶת הָעֵסֶק בַּתּוֹרָה הַקְּדוֹשָׁה, כָּל הַיָּמִים אֲשֶׁר הוּא חַי
  ○ וְלִהְיוֹת מָאוֹס בָּרָע וּבָחוֹר בַּטּוֹב
  ○ לוֹ וּלְכָל הַבְּרִיּוֹת וְהָעוֹלָמוֹת כֻּלָּם
  ○ לַעֲשׂוֹת נַחַת רוּחַ לְיוֹצְרוֹ וּבוֹרְאוֹ יִתְבָּרַךְ:

- וִיהִי רָצוֹן מִלְּפָנָיו יִתְבָּרַךְ שְׁמוֹ
  ○ שֶׁיִּפְתַּח לִבֵּנוּ בְּתוֹרָתוֹ, וְיָשֵׂם בְּלִבֵּנוּ אַהֲבָתוֹ וְיִרְאָתוֹ
  ○ וְיַשְׁלִים כַּוָּנָתוֹ בִּבְרִיאַת עוֹלָמוֹ
  ○ שֶׁיְּתַקֵּן עוֹלָם בְּמַלְכוּת שַׁדַּי, וְיֵדַע כָּל פָּעוּל כו'
  ○ וִיקַבְּלוּ כֻלָּם עַל מַלְכוּתוֹ יִתְבָּרַךְ
  ○ כְּפִי הָרָצוֹן הָעֶלְיוֹן יִתְבָּרַךְ
  ○ וְהָיָה ה' אֶחָד וּשְׁמוֹ אֶחָד:

אָמֵן כֵּן יְהִי רָצוֹן:

---

642 Yishayahu 7:15.
643 From the U'va LeZion prayer.
644 From the Aleynu prayer.
645 From the prayers of Yamim Noraim.
646 From the Aleynu prayer.
647 Zecharia 14:9 and the Aleynu prayer.

Finished and Completed

On "it is good",[648] Tuesday of the weekly Torah portion of
"and the person who God chooses,"[649] Twenty-sixth of Sivan,
[in the year] "my eyes are upon the faithful of the land"[650]
Blessed be He 'who gives strength to the weary'[651]
"Blessed are You God who has taught me His Statutes"[652]
"Open my eyes and I will see the wonders of Your Torah"[653]

---

648 A reference to Tuesday in relation to which "it is good" is mentioned twice in the account of the Creation (Bereishit 1:10 and 1:12).
649 Bamidbar 16:7, i.e., Parshat Korach.
650 Tehillim 101:6, with the numerical value of this quotation summing to 584, i.e., the Jewish year 5584 (1824), this date Tuesday 26 Sivan 5584 being the publication date of the first edition.
651 An expression borrowed from Yishayahu 40:29 commonly used when concluding a major work. An early reference to this practice is at the conclusion of Pesikta DeRav Kahana.
652 Tehillim 119:12.
653 Tehillim 119:18.

תַּם וְנִשְׁלַם

בכי טוב ג' לסדר והי' האיש אשר יבחר ה', כ"ו סיון
"עיני בנאמני ארץ" לפרט. (תקפ"ד)
ברוך נותן ליעף כח.
ברוך אתה ה' למדני חקיך.
גַּל עֵינַי וְאַבִּיטָה נִפְלָאוֹת מִתּוֹרָתֶךָ.

About the Author

AVINOAM FRAENKEL is an experienced Hi-Tech professional, currently working as a Product Manager for a global provider of business management software solutions.

Following high school graduation, Avinoam studied in Yeshivot in America (Chabad, Morristown, N.J.) and Israel (Kerem B'Yavneh). Recently, he completed a Halacha study program in a working man's Kollel, receiving Smicha from Rabbi Zalman Nechemia Goldberg and Rabbi Chaim Perlmutter.

Avinoam lives in Bet Shemesh, Israel, with his wife Tania and daughters, Miri and Gila.